The Gallup Poll

Public Opinion 2009

Other Gallup Publications Available from SR Books:

The Gallup Poll Cumulative Index: Public Opinion, 1935–1997
ISBN 0-8420-2587-1 (1999)

The Gallup Poll: Public Opinion Annual Series

2008 (ISBN 978-1-4422-0105-7)
2007 (ISBN 0-7425-6239-5)
2006 (ISBN 0-7425-5876-2)
2005 (ISBN 0-7425-5258-6)
2004 (ISBN 0-7425-5138-5)
2003 (ISBN 0-8420-5003-5)
2002 (ISBN 0-8420-5002-7)
2001 (ISBN 0-8420-5001-9)
2000 (ISBN 0-8420-5000-0)
1999 (ISBN 0-8420-2699-1)
1998 (ISBN 0-8420-2698-3)
1997 (ISBN 0-8420-2697-9)
1996 (ISBN 0-8420-2696-0)
1995 (ISBN 0-8420-2695-2)
1994 (ISBN 0-8420-2560-X)
1993 (ISBN 0-8420-2483-2)
1992 (ISBN 0-8420-2463-8)

1991 (ISBN 0-8420-2397-6)
1990 (ISBN 0-8420-2368-2)
1989 (ISBN 0-8420-2344-5)
1988 (ISBN 0-8420-2330-5)
1987 (ISBN 0-8420-2292-9)
1986 (ISBN 0-8420-2275-0)
1985 (ISBN 0-8420-2249-X)
1984 (ISBN 0-8420-2234-1)
1983 (ISBN 0-8420-2220-1)
1982 (ISBN 0-8420-2214-7)
1981 (ISBN 0-8420-2200-7)
1980 (ISBN 0-8420-2181-7)
1979 (ISBN 0-8420-2170-1)
1978 (ISBN 0-8420-2159-0)
1972–77 (ISBN 0-8420-2129-9, 2 vols.)
1935–71 (ISBN 0-394-47270-5, 3 vols.)

International Polls

The International Gallup Polls: Public Opinion, 1979
ISBN 0-8420-2180-9 (1981)

The International Gallup Polls: Public Opinion, 1978
ISBN 0-8420-2162-0-9 (1980)

The Gallup International Opinion Polls: France, 1939, 1944–1975
2 volumes ISBN 0-394-40998-1 (1976)

The Gallup International Opinion Polls: Great Britain, 1937–1975
2 volumes ISBN 0-394-40992-2 (1976)

The Gallup Poll

Public Opinion 2009

EDITED BY
FRANK NEWPORT

ROWMAN & LITTLEFIELD PUBLISHERS, INC.
Lanham • Boulder • New York • Toronto • Oxford

ACKNOWLEDGEMENTS

The Gallup Poll represents the efforts of a number of talented and dedicated individuals. I wish to express my gratitude to James Clifton, Chairman and CEO of Gallup, whose continuing vision and commitment to the value of social and economic analysis of poll data undergird all that is in this volume. I also acknowledge the central role of the Poll staff, including Jeffrey Jones, Managing Editor; Lydia Saad, Senior Editor; Lymari Morales, News Director for Gallup.com; and Tracey Sugar, who compiled the Chronology. Judith Keneman, Executive Assistant to the Editor in Chief, edited the text and the graphs and managed the assembly of materials and the publication process. Professor Fred Israel, City University of New York, and George Gallup Jr. deserve special credit for their contributions to the first twenty-six volumes in this series.

Alec Gallup, the coeditor of the *Gallup Poll* series for many years, passed away on June 22, 2009. Alec worked with the Gallup Poll for over fifty years, first with his father, Dr. George Gallup, who founded the Poll, and then with new associates after Dr. Gallup's death in 1984. Alec was one of the world's most knowledgeable pollsters, and he had a lifelong commitment to the value of measuring public opinion scientifically and releasing the results publicly for all to use. It is with sadness that we acknowledge Alec's passing, but with gladness that we remember Alec's central role in the history of the Gallup Poll.

ROWMAN & LITTLEFIELD PUBLISHERS, INC.

Published in the United States of America
by Rowman & Littlefield Publishers, Inc.
A wholly owned subsidiary of The Rowman & Littlefield Publishing Group, Inc.
4501 Forbes Boulevard, Suite 200, Lanham, Maryland 20706
www.rowmanlittlefield.com

PO Box 317
Oxford
OX2 9RU, UK

ISSN 0195-962X

Cloth ISBN-13: 978-1-4422-0519-2
eISBN: 978-1-4422-0520-8

Printed in the United States of America

♾ ™ The paper used in this publication meets the minimum requirements of American National Standard for Information Sciences—Permanence of Paper for Printed Library Materials, ANSI/NISO Z39.48-1992.

CONTENTS

INTRODUCTION

The Gallup Poll: Public Opinion 2009 contains the findings of the more than 500 Gallup Poll reports released to the American public during the year 2009. The latest volume reveals the attitudes and opinions of individuals and key groups within the American population concerning national and international issues and events of the year, and it reports on Americans' views of the economy, their personal financial situation and well-being, and the political arena.

The 2009 volume is the most recent addition to the thirty-six-volume Gallup collection, *Public Opinion, 1935-2009*, the largest compilation of public opinion findings ever published and one of the largest reference works produced on any subject. The Gallup collection documents the attitudes and opinions of Americans on national and international issues and events from Franklin D. Roosevelt's second term to the present. In 2007 a new index volume was published, so that with the previous index volumes, readers can search for topics all the way back to 1935.

Shown in detail are results of tens of thousands of questions that the Gallup Poll—the world's oldest and most respected public opinion poll—has asked of the public over the last seven decades. Results of the survey questions appear in the Gallup Poll reports reproduced in the thirty-six volumes. These reports, the first of which was released on October 20, 1935, have been provided on a continuous basis since that time, most recently as daily updates on Gallup's website, www.gallup.com.

The thirty-six-volume collection documents public opinion from 1935 to the present in the following five separate and distinct areas:

1. *Measuring the Strength of Support for the President, Political Candidates, and Political Parties.* For over seventy years, Gallup has measured, on a continuous basis, the strength of support for the president, for the congressional opposition, and for various political candidates and parties in national elections. This is the role most closely associated with Gallup in the public's mind.

2. *Monitoring the Economy.* An important Gallup Poll objective has been monitoring the U.S. economy in all of its permutations from the perspective of the American consumer. Gallup now assesses Americans' views on economic conditions, the job market, and personal financial concerns on a daily basis—providing a continuous record of this vital component of the U.S. economy.

3. *Gauging and Charting the Public's Mood.* From its earliest days the Gallup Poll has sought to determine, on an ongoing basis, Americans' satisfaction or dissatisfaction with the direction in which the nation appeared to be headed and with the way they thought that their personal lives were progressing. This process also has involved regular assessments of the people's mood regarding the state of the nation's economy as well as the status of their personal finances, their jobs, and other aspects of their lives.

4. *Recording the Public's Response to Major News Events.* Gallup has recorded the public's attitudes and opinions in response to every major news event of the last seven decades. Examples include Adolf Hitler's invasion of the Soviet Union, the bombing of Pearl Harbor, the dropping of the atomic bomb on Hiroshima, the assassination of President John F. Kennedy, the moon landing, the taking of U.S. hostages in Iran, the O. J. Simpson trial verdict, the impeachment proceedings of President Bill Clinton, the September 11 terrorist attacks, the Iraq War, Hurricane Katrina and its aftermath, and the election of the nation's first black president in 2008.

5. *Measuring Americans' Views on Key Policy Issues.* A primary ongoing Gallup polling activity has been to document the collective will of the American people in terms of major policy issues and initiatives under consideration by elected

representatives. Gallup routinely measures Americans' priorities, including monthly assessments of the most important problem facing the nation, interest in and awareness of issues and pending legislation, and overall sentiments on pressing national issues.

Two of the most frequently asked questions concerning the Gallup Poll are: Who pays for or provides financial support to the Poll? And who determines which topics are covered by the Poll or, more specifically, who decides which questions are asked on Gallup surveys? Since its founding in 1935 the Gallup Poll has been underwritten by Gallup itself, in the public interest, and by the nation's media. In recent years, funding has come from the national daily newspaper *USA Today*. The Gallup Poll also receives financial support from subscriptions to the Gallup Brain, sales of the monthly magazine, and this annual volume.

Suggestions for poll questions come from a wide variety of sources, including *USA Today* and other print and broadcast media, institutions as well as from individuals, and from broad editorial consideration of the key and pressing issues facing the nation. In addition, the public themselves are regularly questioned about the problems and issues facing the nation as they perceive them. Their answers establish priorities and provide an up-to-the-minute list of topic areas to explore through the Poll.

The Gallup Poll, as it is known today, began life on October 20, 1935, as a nationally syndicated newspaper feature titled "America Speaks—The National Weekly Column of Public Opinion." For brevity's sake, the media quickly came to refer to the column as The Gallup Poll, after its founder and editor in chief, Dr. George H. Gallup. Although Dr. Gallup had experimented during the 1932 presidential and 1934 congressional election campaigns to develop more accurate techniques for measuring public opinion, including scientific sampling, the first Gallup survey results to appear in print were those reported in the initial October 20, 1935, column.

Although the new scientific opinion polls enjoyed almost immediate popular success, their initial efforts were met with skepticism from many quarters. Critics questioned, for example, how it was possible to determine the opinions of the entire American populace based on only 1,000 interviews or less, or how one know whether people were telling the truth. The credibility of the polls as well as their commercial viability was enhanced significantly, however, when Gallup correctly predicted that Roosevelt would win the 1936 presidential election in a landslide, directly contradicting the forecast of the Literary Digest Poll, the poll of record at that time. The Digest Poll, which was not based on scientific sampling procedures, claimed that FDR's Republican challenger, Alfred M. Landon, would easily win the election.

Over the subsequent seven decades, scientifically based opinion polls have gained a level of acceptance to where they are used today to investigate virtually every aspect of human experience in most nations of the world. To a large extent, this acceptance is due to the record of accuracy achieved by the polls in pre-election surveys. For example, in the eighteen presidential elections since 1936, the average deviation between Gallup's final pre-election survey figures and the actual election results is 2.0 percentage points and, since 1960, only 1.5 points. Correspondingly, in the thirteen midterm congressional elections measured since 1950, the deviation between Gallup's final election survey figures and the actual election results is 1.4 percentage points. These tests of candidate strength or "trial heats," which were introduced by Gallup in the 1930s (along with the presidential "approval" ratings), demonstrate that scientific survey techniques can accurately quantify public sentiment.

In 2008 Gallup began an unprecedented program of daily tracking surveys, interviewing 1,000 national adults virtually each day of the year. Daily interviewing allows Gallup to track important health, well-being, political, and economic indicators on a continuous basis and also creates large databases used for detailed analysis of small demographic, political, and regional subgroups. The benefits of this major initiative in survey research procedures will be apparent to the reader as he or she reviews the content of this volume.

Frank Newport

THE SAMPLE

Most Gallup Poll findings are based on telephone surveys. The majority of the findings reported in Gallup Poll surveys are based on samples consisting of a minimum of 1,000 interviews.

Design of the Sample for Telephone Surveys

The findings from the telephone surveys are based on Gallup's standard national residential and cell telephone samples, consisting of directory-assisted random-digit telephone samples utilizing a proportionate, stratified sampling design. The random-digit aspect of the residential telephone sample is used to avoid "listing" bias. Numerous studies have shown that households with unlisted telephone numbers are different from listed households. "Unlistedness" is due to household mobility or to customer requests to prevent publication of the telephone number. To avoid this source of bias, a random-digit procedure designed to provide representation of both listed and unlisted (including not-yet-listed) numbers is used.

Beginning in 2008, Gallup began including cell phone telephone numbers in its national samples to account for the growing proportion of Americans who are "cell phone only." Cell phone samples are also based on random-digit dial procedures using lists of all cell phone exchanges in the United States.

Telephone numbers for the continental United States are stratified into four regions of the country. The sample of telephone numbers produced by the described method is representative of all telephone households within the continental United States.

Only working banks of telephone numbers are selected. Eliminating nonworking banks from the sample increases the likelihood that any sampled telephone number will be associated with a residence.

Within each household contacted on a residential landline, an interview is sought with the adult eighteen years of age or older living in the household who has had the most recent birthday (this is a method commonly employed to make a random selection within households without having to ask the respondent to provide a complete roster of adults living in the household). In the event that the sample becomes disproportionately female (due to higher cooperation rates typically observed for female respondents), the household selection criteria are adjusted to select only the male in the household who has had the most recent birthday (except in households where the adults are exclusively female). Calls made on cell phones do not use the same respondent selection procedure since cell phones are typically associated with a single individual rather than shared among several members of a household.

A minimum of three calls (and up to six calls) is attempted to each selected telephone number to complete an interview. Time of day and the day of the week for callbacks are varied to maximize the chances of reaching a respondent . All interviews are conducted on weekends or weekday evenings in order to contact potential respondents among the working population.

The final sample is weighted so that the distribution of the sample matches current estimates derived from the U.S. Census Bureau's Current Population Survey (CPS) for the adult population living in households with a landline or cellular telephone in the continental United States.

Weighting Procedures

After the survey data have been collected and processed, each respondent is assigned a weight so that the demographic characteristics of the total weighted sample of respondents match the latest estimates of the demographic characteristics of the adult population available from the U.S. Census Bureau. Gallup weights data to census estimates for gender, race, age, educational attainment, and region. Telephone surveys are weighted to match the characteristics of the adult population living in households with access to a telephone.

The procedures described above are designed to produce samples approximating the adult civilian population (eighteen and older) living in private households. Survey percentages may be applied to census estimates of the size of these populations to project percentages into numbers of people. The manner in which the sample is drawn also produces a sample that approximates the distribution of private households in the United States. Therefore, survey results also can be projected to numbers of households.

Sampling Tolerances

In interpreting survey results, it should be borne in mind that all sample surveys are subject to sampling error—that is, the extent to which the results may differ from what would be obtained if the whole population surveyed had been interviewed. The size of such sampling errors depends largely on the number of interviews. The design of the survey methodology, including weighting the sample to population estimates, should also be taken into account when figuring sample error.

The following tables may be used in estimating the maximum sampling error of any percentage. The computed allowances have taken into account the effect of the sample design and weighting upon sampling error for a typical Gallup poll. They may be interpreted as indicating the maximum range (plus or minus the figure shown) within which the results of repeated samplings in the same time period could be expected to vary, 95 percent of the time, assuming the same sampling procedure, the same interviewers, and the same questionnaire.

Table A shows how much allowance should be made for the sampling error of a percentage near 50% (which produces the largest uncertainty or sampling error; sampling error decreases as the percentages move further away from 50% in either direction).

Let us say a reported percentage is 49% for a group that includes 1,000 respondents. We go to the column for a sample size of 1,000 The number here is 4, which means that the 33 percent obtained in the sample is subject to a maximum sampling error of plus or minus 4 points. Another way of saying it is that very probably (95 chances out of 100) the average of repeated samplings would be somewhere between 29 and 37, with the most likely figure being the 33 obtained.

In comparing survey results in two samples, such as for men and women, the question arises as to how large must a difference between them be before one can be reasonably sure that it reflects a real difference. In Table B, the number of points that must be allowed for in such comparisons is indicated.

Here is an example of how the table would be used: Let us say that 50 percent of men respond a certain way and 40 percent of women also respond that way, for a difference of 10 percentage points between them. Can we say with any assurance that the 10-point difference reflects a real difference between men and women on the question? The sample contains approximately 500 men and 500 women.

Since the percentages are near 50, we consult Table B, and since the two samples are about 500 per-

TABLE A
Recommended Allowance for Sampling Error of a Percentage

	In Percentage Points (at 95 in 100 confidence level)* Sample Size				
	1,000	*750*	*500*	*250*	*100*
Percentages near 50	4 (3.6)	4	5	7	11

*The chances are 95 in 100 that the sampling error is not larger than the figures shown.

TABLE B
Recommended Allowance for Sampling Error of the Difference

	In Percentage Points (at 95 in 100 confidence level)* Percentages near 50		
	750	500	250
Size of sample			
750	6		
500	6	7	
250	8	8	10

*The chances are 95 in 100 that the sampling is not larger than the figures shown.

sons each, we look for the number in the column headed "500" that is also in the row designated "500." We find the number 7 here. This means that the allowance for error should be 7 points, and that in concluding that the percentage among men is somewhere between 3 and 17 points higher than the percentage among women, we should be wrong only about 5 percent of the time. In other words, we can conclude with considerable confidence that a difference exists in the direction observed and that it amounts to at least 3 percentage points.

DESCRIPTIONS OF GALLUP ECONOMIC MEASURES USED IN THIS VOLUME

Gallup's **Employment/Underemployment Index** provides continuous monitoring of U.S. employment and underemployment and serves as a key adjunct to the U.S. government's monthly tracking. This index—based on the combination of responses to a set of questions about employment status—is designed to measure U.S. employment accurately, in accordance with International Conference of Labour Statisticians standards. Based on an individual's responses to the question series (some of which are asked of only a subset of respondents), Gallup classifies respondents into one of six employment categories: employed full time for an employer; employed full time for self; employed part time, but do not want to work full time; employed part time, but want to work full time; unemployed; and out of the workforce. Using these categorizations, Gallup further divides the workforce into those who are employed and those who are underemployed. Employed respondents are those in the workforce who are either employed full time or working part time but do not want to work full time. Underemployed respondents are those in the workforce who are either unemployed or employed part time, but want to work full time. Gallup interviews 1,000 Americans daily—or about 30,000 per month. Because of its daily tracking of other political, business, and well-being measures, Gallup provides insights not available from any other source on the health, well-being, optimism, financial situations, and politics of those who are working or seeking work.

Gallup's **Economic Confidence Index** is based on the combined responses to two questions asking Americans, first, to rate economic conditions in this country today and, second, whether they think economic conditions in the country as a whole are getting better or getting worse. The resulting index correlates at a .96 level with the Reuters/University of Michigan Index of Consumer Sentiment and at a .84 level with the Conference Board's Consumer Confidence Index. Gallup's Economic Confidence Index is updated daily, based on interviews conducted the previous night, as well as weekly, providing a far more up-to-date assessment than the monthly reports from the two traditional indices, which are often weeks old when issued. Further, Gallup's monthly sample of about 15,000 consumers far exceeds the Reuters/Michigan sample of 500 and the Conference Board's undisclosed but widely assumed-to-be sample of about 3,500 mail-in surveys.

Gallup's **Job Creation Index** is based on employed Americans' estimates of their companies' hiring and firing practices. Gallup asks its sample of employed Americans each day whether their companies are hiring new people and expanding the size of their workforces, not changing the size of their workforces, or letting people go and reducing the size of their workforces. The resulting index—computed on a daily and a weekly basis by subtracting the percentage of employers letting people go from the percentage hiring—is a real-time indicator of the nation's employment picture across all industry and business sectors. Gallup analysis indicates that the Job Creation Index is an excellent predictor of weekly jobless claims that the U.S. Labor Department reports each Thursday. The index has about a 90% chance of predicting the direction of seasonally adjusted initial weekly jobless claims and a better-than-90% chance of predicting the direction of seasonally adjusted initial claims on a four-week average basis. It also has a better-than-80% probability of projecting the direction of the unemployment rate as reported by the Labor Department on the first Friday of every month. In some ways, Gallup's Job Creation Index is more meaningful than the government's weekly new jobless claims measure, given that not everyone who is laid off files for unemployment. The index may also pick up hiring trends days or weeks before they are manifested in the official unemployment rate or other lagging indicators. Finally, the index measures job creation (hiring) and job loss (letting go) on a continuous basis. This provides additional real-time insight not available from broadly aggregated indicators and unemployment data.

Gallup's **Consumer Spending** measure is calculated from responses to a basic question asking Americans each day to estimate the amount of money they spent "yesterday," excluding the purchase of a home or an automobile, or normal household bills. The result is a real-time indicator of discretionary retail spending, fluctuations in which are sensitive to shifts in the economic environment. Gallup's average monthly estimate of spending is correlated at the .65 level with the U.S. government's report of total U.S. retail sales (not seasonally adjusted) and exhibits similarly positive and substantial correlations to other government measures of retail sales. These positive correlations indicate that changes in Gallup's spending estimates are related to changes in both direction and magnitude of actual consumer spending as reported by the government. Further, Gallup's Consumer Spending measure provides estimates on a continuing basis, giving an early read on what the government eventually reports roughly two weeks after the close of each month. Gallup's continuous surveying allows for analysis of spending patterns on a daily and a weekly basis, which is particularly important to understanding seasonal variations in spending. The spending measure allows business and investment decisions to be based on essentially real-time information.

THE GALLUP-HEALTHWAYS WELL-BEING INDEX™

A number of stories within this volume reference the Gallup-Healthways Well-Being Index, a daily inventory of Americans' well-being based on the World Health Organization's definition of health as not only the absence of infirmity and disease but also a state of physical, mental, and social well-being. The Gallup-Healthways Well-Being Index is based on Gallup's daily interviews with 1,000 Americans and provides measures which help determine the correlation between the places where people work and the communities in which they live, and how that and other factors impact their well-being.

STATE OF THE STATES POLLS

A number of stories included in this volume are based on Gallup's "State of the States" series, analyses which examine state-by-state differences on the political, economic, and well-being measures that Gallup tracks each day. State of the States stories are based on aggregated data for six-month or full-year time periods, providing large enough samples for meaningful analyses of responses in each of the 50 states and the District of Columbia.

Gallup Poll Accuracy Record
Presidential Elections

	Candidates	*Final Gallup Survey*	*Election Result*	*Gallup Deviation*
2008	Obama	55	53	2
	McCain	44	46	-2
	Other	1	1	0
2004	Bush	49	51	-2
	Kerry	49	48	1
	Other	2	1	1
2000	Gore	46	48.4	-2.4
	Bush	48	47.9	0.1
	Nader	4	2.7	1.3
	Buchanan	1	0.4	0.6
	Other	1	0.6	0.4
1996	Clinton	52	49.2	2.8
	Dole	41	40.9	0.1
	Perot	7	8.5	-1.5
1992	Clinton	49	43	6
	Bush	37	37.5	-0.5
	Perot	14	18.9	-4.9
1988	Bush	56	53.4	2.6
	Dukakis	44	45.7	-1.7
1984	Reagan	59	58.8	0.2
	Mondale	41	40.6	0.4
1980	Reagan	47	50.8	-3.8
	Carter	44	41	3
	Anderson	8	6.6	1.4
	Other	1	1.6	-0.6
1976	Carter	48	50.1	-2.1
	Ford	49	48	1
	McCarthy	2	0.9	1.1
	Other	1	0.9	0.1
1972	Nixon	62	60.7	1.3
	McGovern	38	37.6	0.4
1968	Nixon	43	43.4	-0.4
	Humphrey	42	42.7	-0.7
	Wallace	15	13.5	1.5

2009 Chronology

December 2008

December 1 President-elect Barack Obama announces National Security Team and other Cabinet members. Most notably Obama introduces Hillary Clinton, his rival in the Democratic presidential primary, as his pick for Secretary of State.

December 9 Illinois Governor Rod Blagojevich is accused of selling now former Senator Barack Obama's Senate seat. Several phone conversations with advisers were recorded by the FBI since the Nov. 4, 2008, election in which they discovered that the Governor plotted ways to benefit financially from his duty to fill Chicago's Senate seat, which was vacated by Obama.

December 10 Congress votes in favor of a $14 billion rescue package that provides emergency loans to Chrysler and General Motors. This assistance is critical, considering that these two companies have said they cannot survive until the end of 2008.

December 11 Well-known investment manager Bernard Madoff is charged with defrauding hundreds of clients of as much $50 billion in a huge Ponzi scheme. This could be one of the largest swindles in Wall Street history.

December 14 A reporter for Al Baghdadia, a Cairo-based satellite television network, hurls his shoes at President Bush and calls him a "dog" at a news conference in Baghdad.

December 15 The Illinois state legislature begins impeachment proceedings against Governor Rod Blagojevich.

December 19 Out-going President George W. Bush hands the fate of the automakers to President-elect Barack Obama as he announces plans to lend GM and Chrysler $17.4 billion to survive the next three months.

December 30 Rod Blagojevich names Roland Burris as former Senator Barack Obama's successor. The move is criticized by state legislators.

January 2009

January 5 Leon Panetta is named CIA Director by President-elect Barack Obama. Panetta was the former U.S. representative from California and chief of staff to President Clinton. Both Republicans and Democrats question whether Panetta's experience has prepared him for the role.

January 13 Timothy Geithner, Treasury Secretary nominee, is questioned for failing to pay taxes from 2001 to 2004 on his salary from the International Monetary Fund. Although an embarrassment for someone who would be the head of the IRS, the matter was solved with Geithner paying back taxes, with interest.

January 14 Retailers confirm that dismal 2008 holiday sales are the result of the weak economy. Online sellers such as Amazon, however, reported much more positive results in late December.

January 15 US Airways Flight 1549 lands in New York's Hudson River after allegedly striking a flock of geese. All passengers and crew survived.

January 20 President Barack Obama and Vice President Joe Biden are sworn into office. The inauguration featured Pastor Rick Warren, singer Aretha Franklin, poet Elizabeth Alexander, and Reverand Anthony Lowrey.

January 21 Hillary Rodham Clinton, President Obama's former rival for the Democratic presidential nomination, is confirmed as Obama's pick for Secretary of State.

January 22 In an executive order signed by President Obama, all secret prisons and detention camps run by the CIA, including Guantanamo Bay in Cuba, are been ordered closed. Prisoners will be moved to new locations.

January 27 Timothy Geithner is confirmed as Secretary of Treasury.

February 2009

February 1 Tom Daschle, former senator from South Dakota, withdraws his name from contention as Secretary of Health and Human Services. Daschle failed to pay $128,000 in taxes for using a friend's car service and experienced intense media scrutiny for several days.

February 4 An announcement by President Barack Obama states that a $500,000 pay cap on salaries of executive will be imposed on companies receiving government bailouts. This comes after the revelation that many companies receiving bailout funding are rewarding their executives and employees with billions of dollars in bonus money.

February 10 In a vote mostly along party lines, the Senate approves an $838 billion stimu-

lus plan. This is the second of two similar stimulus packages.

February 12 Congress reaches a deal on the stimulus package at $787 billion.

February 15 Hugo Chavez, President of Venezuela, wins his bid to end presidential term limits in his country. This will allow him to run for reelection. Chavez has already been in power for a decade.

February 24 In his first congressional address, President Barack Obama speaks of the need for immediate action to resurrect the failing economy and outlines his plans to invest in energy, health care, and education. He also warns that the government bailouts are probably unfinished.

February 26 President Barack Obama reveals the 2010 fiscal budget, which totals over $3 trillion. The aim of the budget is to halve the federal deficit by the end of his term in office.

February 27 President Barack Obama announces a date to end the war in Iraq in front of a crowd of Marines in Camp Lejeune, NC. Obama's intention is to withdraw most American troops out of Iraq by August 31, 2010.

March 2009

March 4 An arrest warrant is issued for President Omar Hassan Ahmad al Bashir, President of Sudan, charging him with war crimes and crimes against humanity in the Darfur region of Africa.

March 10 Following a speech by Federal Reserve Chairman Ben Bernanke, calling for broad reforms of the financial regulatory system, the stock market sees its biggest day of 2009.

March 12 After pleading guilty to all criminal charges against him for operating a massive Ponzi scheme, Bernard Madoff is sent to jail to await sentencing. Sentencing will take place June 16, 2009. Madoff faces a maximum of 150 years in prison.

March 20   President Barack Obama lays out his plan for fighting al Qaeda and the Taliban in Afghanistan and Pakistan. The plan indicates sending additional troops to Afghanistan and increasing the amount of aid to Pakistan. Both Democrats and Republicans see this plan as favorable.

March 29   Chief executive of General Motors, Rick Waggoner, resigns at the request of the Obama administration. GM has lost $30.9 billion in 2008 and has requested billions in federal aid as part of the stimulus package.

April 2009

April 2   At the G-20 Summit, world leaders pledge $1.1 trillion to help stimulate economies in developing countries, encourage world trade, and more strictly regulate financial firms. Former Illinois Governor Rod Blagojevich is indicted on 16 felony counts of corruption for attempting to sell President Obama's vacated Senate seat.

April 8   An American cargo ship, the Maersk Alabama, is hijacked by Somali pirates off the Horn of Africa—the first time for an American ship at sea. Richard Phillips, the ship's captain, is taken hostage. US Navy Seals free Phillips after 5 days in captivity on his own ship.

April 9   The North Korean Parliament elects Kim Jong-il, the current leader, to another 5-year term. This represents his third term in office, despite failing health.

April 23   Chrylser, the third largest U.S. auto maker, is asked by the Treasury Department to file chapter 11 bankruptcy as soon as possible. Chrylser is work-

ing on an agreement with Italian automaker Fiat to secure more government financing.

April 26   The swine flu is declared a public health emergency in the U.S. after confirmation of 20 cases. None of the cases have resulted in death.

April 28   Arlen Specter, Senator from Pennsylvania, declares he will run as a Democrat in the 2010 election. Specter served as a Republican Senator for 29 years.

April 29   The U.S. loses its first victim to the swine flu, a Mexican-American child visiting Texas with family.

April 30   Justice David H. Souter announces his retirement from the U.S. Supreme Court after 19 years of service. He was appointed by President George H. W. Bush in 1990.

May 2008

May 11   Lt. Gen. Stanley McChrystal replaces fired top U.S. Commander Gen. David McKiernan. McKiernan was believed to be too conventional in his approach to the war, and the Defense Department and Pentagon wanted someone more innovative.

May 14   Chrysler announces its plans to shut down 25% of its dealerships nationwide in an attempt to reduce costs after filing for bankruptcy.

May 15   In its attempt to avoid bankruptcy like its fellow car manufacturer, General Motors announces it will not renew franchises with 1,100 of its dealers.

May 19   The Senate passes a bill that imposes stricter regulations on the credit card industry.

May 26   New York Federal Appeals Judge Sonia Sotomayor is nominated to the

Supreme Court. President Obama makes this nomination after Justice David Souter announced his resignation from the bench. Sotomayor would be the first Hispanic Supreme Court Justice.

May 31 Controversial late-term abortion doctor George Tiller is killed in his Kansas church while handing out bulletins.

June 2009

June 1 General Motors files for bankruptcy and announces that it will close 14 plants in the US.

June 4 President Barack Obama makes what is considered a risky speech during a visit to Cairo, Egypt, by calling for "a new beginning between the United States and Muslims around the world."

June 8 Two American journalists, Euna Lee and Laura Ling, are found guilty of "illegal entry" into North Korea and are sentence to 12 years in a labor prison. The two are employed by Current TV.

June 10 A shooting occurs at the entrance of the Holocust Museum in Washington, DC, killing a security guard. The alleged shooter, James W. von Brunn, an 88-year white supremacist, is also critically injured.

June 13 Iranian president Mahmoud Ahmadinejad wins his reelection campaign by a landslide. Accusations follow regarding ballot tampering and fraud, which leads to widespread protests.

June 25 "King of Pop" Michael Jackson is dead at the age of 50. He is found unconscious in his home and is pronounced dead at a Los Angeles hospital. Mark Sanford, governor of South Carolina, admits to lying about his recent disappearance to cover up his year-long extramarital affair.

June 29 Bernard Madoff is sentenced to 150 years in prison for a engineering a multiyear, multibillion-dollar Ponzi scheme.

June 30 The reelection of Iranian president Mahmoud Ahmadinejad is found to be valid by The Guardian Council of Iran. Ahmadinejad will serve his second four-year term. Al Franken wins the US senate seat for Minnesota, the Supreme Court rules, after an eight-month battle over a recount.

July 2009

July 3 Sarah Palin announces her resignation as Governor of Alaska. Palin was a first-term Republican governor and a former vice-presidential candidate. Her decision is predicated on her desire to spend more time with her family and her lack of interest in running for reelection in 2010.

July 13 Congressional hearings for the confirmation of Sonia Sotymayor begin.

July 14 Just months after repaying bailout money, Goldman Sachs posts significant profit for the 2nd quarter of the year.

July 16 Following in Goldman Sachs footsteps, JB Morgan Chase posts an increase profit of 36% over last year.

July 17 Bank of America and Citigroup both post profit increases.

July 28 Supreme Court nominee Sonia Sotomayor is endorsed by the Senate Judiciary Committee.

August 2009

August 4 American journalists Euna Lee and Laura Ling are pardoned by North Korea. This pardon comes after former President Bill Clinton visits the country and its president Kim Jong-il on a humanitarian mission.

August 5   Iranian President Mahmoud Ahmadinejad is inaugurated and begins his second term.

August 6   Supreme Court nominee Sonia Sotomayor is confirmed. She is the first Hispanic Supreme Court justice and the third woman to serve on the Court.

August 11   Sonia Sotomayor becomes the 111th Supreme Court justice and is sworn in by Chief Justice John Roberts.

August 25   Senator Edward "Ted" Kennedy dies of brain cancer at the age of 77. President Obama nominates Ben Bernanke for a second term as Federal Reserve Chairman.

September 2009

September 9   In a survey released by the Federal Reserve, the economy is showing signs of slow recovery.

September 15   US Admiral Mike Mullen suggests that the US will need to send in additional troops to Afghanistan. This suggestion is despite dissention from Democrats.

September 24   Paul Kirk, former Democratic National Committee chairman and friend of the late Ted Kennedy, is named temporary replacement to Kennedy's vacant Senate seat.

October 2009

October 1   General Motors announces it will shut down the Saturn line of cars. This is the result of broken takeover talks with the Penske Auto Group. Saturn will close 350 dealerships nationwide.

October 2   Rio de Janeiro, Brazil, wins the bid for the 2016 Olympics.

October 9   President Barack Obama wins the Nobel Peace Prize for his "extraordinary efforts to strengthen international diplomacy and cooperation between peoples."

October 15   A report by the Obama administration indicates that businesses who have received stimulus money from the federal government have created or saved over 30,000 jobs to date. It is the goal of the president to save or create 3.5 million jobs over two years.

October 19   The use or sale of medical marijuana will no longer be federally prosecuted as long as they are in compliance with state law.

October 21   Top-paid employees at firms that received stimulus money are ordered by the Obama administration to take pay cuts.

November 2009

November 4   Secretary of State Hillary Rodham Clinton calls for the release of three American hikers that are accused of espionage in Iran. The hikers were arrested while hiking in Iran over the summer and were accused of spying by Iranian officials. New York Yankees win the World Series against the Philadelphia Phillies. This represents their 27th World Series win.

November 5   A shooting at Fort Hood army base leaves 13 dead and 31 injured. Maj. Nidal Malik Hasan is identified as the alleged shooter. He is an army psychiatrist and his motives are unknown, though he was supposed to be deployed to Iraq or Afghanistan soon.

November 10   John Allen Muhammad is executed in a Virginia prison. Muhammad is the DC sniper who killed 10 people in a shooting spree in the nation's capital in 2002.

November 12   Maj. Nidal Malik Hasan, alleged Fort Hood shooter, is charged with 13 counts of premeditated murder and will be tried in military court. He could face the death penalty.

November 13 The Obama administration announces that Khalid Shaikh Mohammed will stand trial in criminal court in Manhattan. Mohammed is the self-professed organizer of the September 11 attacks on the US that killed 3,000 people.

November 16 A new study recommends that women wait until the age of 50 to begin breast cancer screenings with mammograms.

November 20 Afghanistani President Hamid Karzai is sworn in for his second five-year term. One of his campaign promises was to have Afghanistan's army have full control of the country's security within five years.

November 23 After making headlines in June 2009 after a brief disappearance from office, South Carolina Governor Mark Sanford is facing 37 counts of using his office for personal financial gain.

December 2009

December 1 American student Amanda Knox is convicted by an Italian jury of murdering her former roommate. The trial was widely followed around the world. President Obama announces that the US military will be deploying an additional 30,000 troops to Afghanistan to prevent Taliban insurgencies. This surge will begin in January 2010.

December 3 The General Electric Company sells NBC Universal to Comcast for $30 billion. Comcast is the nation's largest cable operator and will now own 51% of NBC, leaving GE with 49%.

December 6 All but $42 million of the $370 billion that was loaned to banks and other companies has been repaid. This is more than the Treasure Department expected.

December 15 The federal government takes over part of an Illinois prison for the transfer of prisoners from Guantanamo Bay. The closing of Guantanamo Bay was one of the president's campaign promises.

December 18 Five nations, including the US, reach an agreement on a deal to fight global warming. Leaders of the US, China, India, Brazil, and South Africa will form an accord that will create a system for monitoring pollution reduction, require wealthy nations to provide billions of dollars to poor nations that are affected by climate change, and set a goal of limiting the global temperature rise to 2 degrees celcius.

December 21 The federal government announces new regulations on airline travel, the "Passenger Bill of Rights," that will limit the amount of time that airlines can keep passengers waiting on the tarmac without giving them food or letting them off the plane.

December 25 A Nigerian man allegedly attempts to set off an explosive device hidden in his underwear on a flight from Amsterdam to Detroit. The explosive was a mixture of powder and liquid that did not alert airport security. The alleged bomber claims he was directed by Al Qaeda.

January 02, 2009

LIBERALS' CONFIDENCE IN OBAMA REMAINS HIGH

Conservatives' opinions of president-elect becoming more positive

by Jeffrey M. Jones, Gallup Poll Managing Editor

Gallup Poll Daily tracking finds support for Barack Obama among liberal Democrats holding steady at 93% despite news reports that his core supporters are disappointed with some of his cabinet appointments and other decisions. Meanwhile, in recent weeks, Obama's ratings have improved among conservative Republicans, up from 23% to 29%.

Confidence That Barack Obama Will Be a Good President, by Party Identification and Political Ideology

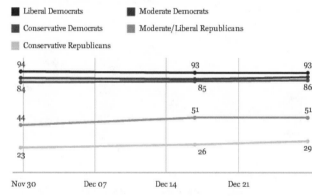

More than 9 in 10 liberal Democrats have expressed confidence that Obama will make a good president since Gallup began tracking these opinions after the election last November. Moderate and conservative Democrats show nearly as high levels of confidence.

Obama's recent decision to have conservative preacher Rick Warren deliver the invocation at the Jan. 20 presidential inauguration and his choices of Republicans Robert Gates and Ray LaHood for cabinet positions have been controversial among members of the political left. Additionally, women's groups have been reported as expressing disappointment that Obama has not selected more women for cabinet-level positions in his administration. But these decisions apparently have not shaken liberal Democrats' confidence in Obama to any perceptible degree, according to aggregated data of thousands of Gallup Poll daily interviews from the immediate post-election period (Nov. 5–30), early December (Dec. 1–17) after he announced many of his cabinet choices, and in recent days (Dec. 18–28) after announcing Warren's role in the inauguration, arguably his most controversial action to date.

Earlier, Gallup documented a slight drop in confidence in Obama among liberals (regardless of party affiliation) immediately after he announced his national security team, which included Gates but also former presidential rival Hillary Clinton. But that dip proved to be temporary, and liberals as a group now support Obama at the same levels seen right after his election. (Confidence among all liberals was 89% in the immediate post-election phase, and is 89% over the last two weeks.)

Perhaps because his choices may signal a more politically moderate approach to governing, conservative, moderate, and liberal Republicans have become more confident in Obama's potential in recent weeks.

Now, a slim majority of moderate and liberal Republicans, 51%, say they are confident Obama will be a good president, up from 44% in November. Conservative Republicans remain largely skeptical of Obama's abilities, but in recent weeks his stock has risen slightly among this group, from 23% to 29%.

Since confidence in Obama is steady among Democrats, and the changes among Republicans (though notable) have been fairly small, there has only been a slight increase in confidence in Obama among all Americans, from 65% in November to 67% over the last two weeks.

There have been greater changes in Obama's basic favorable ratings, which have increased from an already high 67% in the first few weeks after the election to 72% in the most recent data.

Here again, opinions of Obama are extremely positive and highly stable among Democrats, but have shown significant improvement among Republicans. Conservative Republicans' average favorable ratings have increased by 11 percentage points since November, and moderate and liberal Republicans show a 13-point increase.

Favorable Opinion of Barack Obama, by Party Identification and Political Ideology

	Liberal Democrats	Moderate Democrats	Conservative Democrats	Moderate/ Liberal Republicans	Conservative Republicans
Nov 5-30	95%	91%	87%	48%	26%
Dec 1-17	95%	90%	88%	61%	33%
Dec 18-28	96%	91%	90%	61%	37%
Change	+1	0	+3	+13	+11

Implications

While a few of Obama's recent actions may have been unpopular with some liberal opinion leaders and led to news reports of liberal discontent with him, Gallup finds that liberal Democrats nationwide continue to express strongly positive opinions of the president-elect. And while his high level of support among Democrats has remained steady since he was elected, Republicans' ratings of Obama have become more positive in recent weeks.

This does not rule out the possibility that liberal Democrats still rate Obama positively on balance but have become less enthusiastic about him in ways that would not be picked up by the basic confidence and favorability measures reported here. These measures only offer respondents a positive or negative response, so any drop in the degree of positive (or negative) feeling would not be apparent.

Survey Methods

Results are based on aggregated telephone interviews from Gallup Poll Daily tracking, from Nov. 5–Dec. 28, 2008. Gallup interviews no less than 1,000 national adults, aged 18 and older, each day. The Obama questions are asked of a random half of each day's sample. For results based on the total sample of 4,022 national adults interviewed between Dec. 18 and Dec. 28, one can say with 95% confidence that the maximum margin of sampling error is ±2 percentage points.

Margins of error for subgroups will be larger than for the overall sample.

Interviews are conducted with respondents on land-line telephones (for respondents with a land-line telephone) and cellular phones (for respondents who are cell-phone only).

In addition to sampling error, question wording and practical difficulties in conducting surveys can introduce error or bias into the findings of public opinion polls.

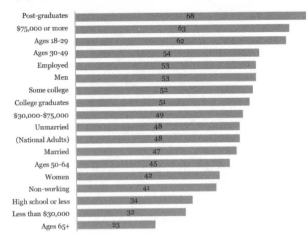

Frequent Internet Use by Demographic Groups
% Saying they use the Internet "more than an hour a day"

Gallup Poll, December 4-7, 2008

January 02, 2009

NEARLY HALF OF AMERICANS ARE FREQUENT INTERNET USERS

Less affluent, non-working, unmarried post big gains in usage since last year

by Lymari Morales, Gallup Poll Staff Writer

Americans' frequent use of the Internet has almost doubled over the last five years; 48% now report using the Internet more than one hour per day compared to 26% in 2003.

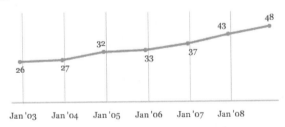

How much time, if at all, do you personally spend using the Internet -- more than an hour a day, up to one hour a day, a few times a week, a few times a month or less, or never?

% More than one hour

Large education, income, and age gaps continue to exist in terms of Internet usage. Post-graduates, those making more than $75,000 per year, and those under age 30 are the most frequent users of the Internet, with more than 6 out of 10 in each group saying they use the Internet more than one hour per day. At the same time, the least educated, least affluent, and oldest Americans are those who least often use the Internet, with about one-third or fewer in each group saying they use the Internet more than one hour per day. Smaller, though noteworthy, gaps also exist between men and women, and the employed versus the non-working.

Among these demographic groups, several posted gains in frequent Internet use in the past year (more than one hour per day) significantly greater than the five percentage point gain measured among adults nationwide. The five groups posting double-digit gains are those making less than $30,000 per year, those who are not working,

ing, those who are unmarried, those who are under age 30, and those with post-graduate educations.

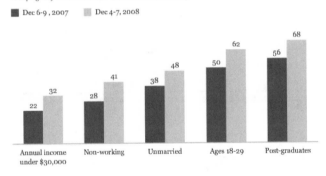

Demographic Groups Posting Double-Digit Gains in Frequent Internet Use
% Saying they use the Internet "more than an hour a day"

■ Dec 6-9 , 2007   ▨ Dec 4-7, 2008

Men, and those 65 and older, round out the groups posting gains greater than the national average. The gains among men are particularly interesting when compared to the negligible change among women. Further, it is worth noting that college graduates, those aged 30–49 years, and those making $75,000 or more per year were actually slightly less likely than one year ago to report using the Internet more than one hour per day.

Bottom Line

Americans are using the Internet more frequently than ever. While the most educated, most affluent, and youngest Americans are those more likely to say they use the Internet more than one hour per day, the less affluent, non-working, and unmarried are increasing their usage at noteworthy rates.

Overall, the shifts recorded over the past year suggest that some of the historical gaps in Internet use across demographic groups may be narrowing. If these changes continue, it would represent an important closing of the economic and educational Internet divides.

With the Internet still in its infancy according to most technology experts, it is reasonable to anticipate continued growth in use among all of these sectors in the years to come. At the same time, the

Changes in Frequent Internet Use from 2007-2008

% Saying they use the Internet "more than than hour a day"

	Dec 6-9, 2007	Dec 4-7, 2008	Change
National adults	43	48	5
By Gender			
Men	44	53	9
Women	41	42	1
By Age			
18-29	50	62	12
30-49	56	54	-2
50-64	45	45	0
65+	14	23	9
By Annual Income			
$75,000 or more	65	63	-2
$30,000-$75,000	41	49	8
Less than $30,000	22	32	10
By Education			
Post-graduates	56	68	12
College graduates	56	51	-5
Some college	48	52	4
High school or less	30	34	4
By Employment Status			
Employed	54	53	-1
Non-working	28	41	13
By Marital Status			
Married	46	47	1
Unmarried	38	48	10

fact that several groups show either stable or declining usage certainly gives rise to the question of whether some sort of plateau is possible. In either case, business leaders—and advertisers in particular—will be well-served to keep these burgeoning trends in mind. While targeting content toward the most educated, most affluent, and youngest Americans may be an effective strategy today, the growth evident among their counterparts at the other end of the spectrum suggests new strategies may be needed to cater to the frequent Internet users of tomorrow.

Survey Methods

Results are based on telephone interviews with 1,009 national adults, aged 18 and older, conducted Dec. 4–7, 2008. For results based on the total sample of national adults, one can say with 95% confidence that the maximum margin of sampling error is ±3 percentage points.

Interviews are conducted with respondents on land-line telephones (for respondents with a land-line telephone) and cellular phones (for respondents who are cell-phone only).

In addition to sampling error, question wording and practical difficulties in conducting surveys can introduce error or bias into the findings of public opinion polls.

January 05, 2009

DESPITE RECENT LOWS, BUSH APPROVAL AVERAGE IS MIDRANGE

Extreme high and low ratings characterize Bush presidency

by Jeffrey M. Jones, Gallup Poll Managing Editor

Extreme highs and lows have characterized George W. Bush's job approval ratings as president. His record 90% approval rating early in his presidency following the Sept. 11 terrorist attacks stands in stark contrast to his sub-30% approval ratings during most of his final year in office, which rank among the lowest ratings ever measured.

George W. Bush's Job Approval Ratings Trend

 % Approve

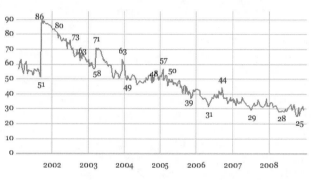

Because of these ups and downs, Bush's 49% approval average for his presidency will rank him in the middle of the pack (7th of 11) of post-World War II presidents. His average to-date of 49.4% is similar to Richard Nixon's 49.1% but slightly better than Harry Truman's and Jimmy Carter's historical lows below 46%.

John Kennedy's 70.1% average for his brief two-and-a-half year term rates as the highest. Bush's father averaged 60.1% during his one-term presidency.

Gallup Approval Averages for Presidents During Entire Presidency, 1945-present

President	Average
Kennedy	70.1%
Eisenhower	65.0%
G.H.W. Bush	60.1%
Clinton	55.1%
Johnson	55.1%
Reagan	52.8%
G.W. Bush	49.4%*
Nixon	49.1%
Ford	47.2%
Carter	45.5%
Truman	45.4%

*To date

Bush's Solid First Term

Bush's first term may be remembered most for the several "rallies" in public support for him in response to international crises.

The 35-percentage-point increase in Bush's approval rating following the Sept. 11 terrorist attacks is the largest "rally" in public support for a president in polling history. Just before the attacks occurred, 51% of Americans approved of the job he was doing as the president. By the end of that week, 86% did. In subsequent days, his rating inched up further to 90%, the highest Gallup has ever measured for a president.

That rally in support showed remarkable staying power, and Bush's approval rating remained above 80% for nearly 6 months and above 70% for 10 months. He remained popular with a 63% approval rating at the time of the 2002 elections, helping Republicans to achieve rare Congressional seat gains in a midterm election year.

In late 2002 and early 2003, the United States and its allies were contemplating military action in Iraq to remove Saddam Hussein from power. During this time, Bush's approval rating held in the low 60s and high 50s. But in response to the March 19 invasion, Bush received a second major rally in public support, seeing his rating jump from 58% to 71%. That 13-point increase is among the five highest rallies Gallup has measured for a president since World War II.

The 71% rating would be as high as Bush's approval rating would get after that, though he received a third significant rally in support (from 56% to 63%) in December 2003 after the United States captured Saddam Hussein.

Bush began his re-election year of 2004 with a strong 60% approval rating, but that quickly dipped to 49% as the Democratic presidential nomination campaign focused media attention on the opposition's criticism of the incumbent president. Bush spent most of his re-election year around the 50% mark—a significant number since it has generally been an indicator of re-election success. Ultimately, Bush won re-election in a closely fought contest with an approval rating of 48%.

During his first term, Bush had an average 62.2% approval rating. That ranks as the fourth best first term average approval rating among post-World War II presidents, behind Lyndon Johnson, Kennedy, and Dwight Eisenhower, and just ahead of his father, the elder George Bush.

Gallup Approval Averages for Presidents During First Term, 1945-present

President	Average
Johnson	74.2%
Kennedy	70.1%
Eisenhower	69.6%
G.W. Bush	62.2%
G.H.W. Bush	60.9%
Nixon	55.8%
Truman	55.6%
Reagan	50.3%
Clinton	49.6%
Ford	47.2%
Carter	45.5%

Second-Term Blues

Following his re-election, Bush's support went back above the majority level, reaching 57% in early February 2005 after Iraq held successful elections. That turned out to be the high point for Bush's second term, as the Bush administration had difficulty responding to mounting difficulties in Iraq and the devastating effects of Hurricane Katrina. By September 2005, his approval rating dipped to 40%, and fell below that mark after his ill-fated attempt to nominate White House counsel Harriet Miers to the Supreme Court.

Bush's troubles continued to mount in 2006, as the Iraq war dragged on, gas prices climbed, and the government was unable to agree on legislation to address illegal immigration. In May 2006, just 31% of Americans approved of the job Bush was doing, a new low for his presidency.

Bush's popularity recovered somewhat in subsequent months as gas prices stabilized, and reached 44% as Americans recognized the fifth anniversary of the Sept. 11 terrorist attacks. That would be the last time Bush's approval rating exceeded 40%. His greater than two-year string of sub-40% approval ratings is the longest for any president since the advent of polling. Bush's growing unpopularity surely helped Democrats gain control of Congress in the 2006 midterm elections for the first time since 1994.

Bush's approval rating fell below 30% in July 2007 as gas prices once again reached high levels. Bush's final year in office was marked by ratings around 30%, including a new low of 25% in the days after Congress passed controversial legislation to bail out major financial institutions. Bush matched that term low of 25% approval in the final 2008 pre-election poll, as Barack Obama was elected his successor and Democrats made further gains in the House and Senate.

Toward the end of his presidency, the bulk of Bush's limited public support came from Republicans, in particular conservative Republicans.

With just a couple weeks left in his second term, Bush has averaged only 36.5% approval since the term began in January 2005. Bush's weak second term is tied with Truman's, and only slightly better than what Nixon got leading up to his resignation from office. Bill Clinton and Eisenhower had the highest second term averages.

Gallup Approval Averages for Presidents During Second Term, 1945-present

President	Average
Clinton	60.6%
Eisenhower	60.5%
Reagan	55.3%
Johnson	50.3%
Truman	36.5%
G.W. Bush	36.5%
Nixon	34.4%

The Bush Presidency

Some of the highest high and lowest low approval ratings for a president have characterized Bush's presidency. In many ways, it is similar to Truman's presidency. Truman entered office with very high approval ratings following Franklin Roosevelt's death and U.S. victory in World War II. That popularity faded by the time Truman was up for re-election in 1948, but he managed an unexpected victory. The ongoing war in Korea and a poor economy made Truman very unpopular for much of his second term, including an all-time low approval rating of 22% in 1952. Truman and Bush were replaced by popular presidents from the opposition party.

President Bush, first lady Laura Bush, and others have tried to downplay the president's low approval ratings by arguing that history may judge his presidency more favorably. Only time will tell whether that will in fact happen, but it is true that average approval ratings do not necessarily correlate with how people judge presidents in retrospect. For example, the public generally regard Nixon as one of the worst presidents, even though other presidents have had lower approval rating averages while in office. And people generally view

Ronald Reagan as one of the better recent presidents despite a rather mediocre 53% average approval rating during his presidency.

Survey Methods

Results are based on telephone interviews with approximately 1,000 national adults, aged 18 and older, conducted at various times in 2001–2008. For results based on each separate sample of national adults, one can say with 95% confidence that the maximum margin of sampling error is ±3 percentage points.

In addition to sampling error, question wording and practical difficulties in conducting surveys can introduce error or bias into the findings of public opinion polls.

January 06, 2009
111TH CONGRESS BEGINS IN VERY DISAPPROVING ENVIRONMENT
Only 19% approved of Congress on average in 2008

by Frank Newport, Gallup Poll Editor in Chief

Newly elected members of Congress are being sworn in on Tuesday in Washington at a time when Americans are very negative in their views of Congress. In Gallup's most recent reading—based on interviewing in December, the final month of the previous Congress—only 20% of Americans said they approved of the way Congress is handling its job, and for all of 2008, congressional approval averaged only 19%.

Do you approve or disapprove of the way Congress is handling its job?

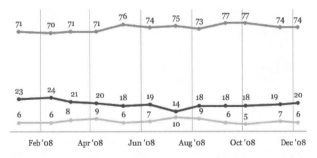

The congressional job approval average for 2008 included the all-time Gallup low point of 14% in July. The general pattern for last year included slightly higher ratings as 2008 began, a bottoming out in the summer, and a slight improvement as the year ended.

The current low ratings of Congress are down from the already-low averages of 27% in 2007 and 25% in 2006. Ratings for Congress were higher in the earlier years of the decade, including a 56% average in 2001 and a 54% average in 2002, both of which reflect at least in part the generally positive way in which Americans rated governmental institutions after the 9/11 terrorist attacks.

Despite the fact that Democrats control both houses of Congress, rank-and-file Americans who identify themselves as Democrats are only slightly more positive about Congress than are independents or Republicans.

Yearly Averages of Congressional Job Approval

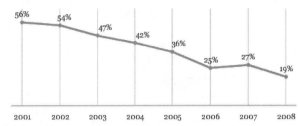

Congressional Approval and Disapproval, by Political Party
Dec. 4-7, 2008

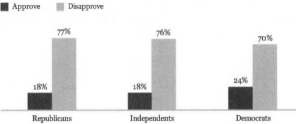

Twenty-four percent of Democrats in Gallup's December update approved of the job Congress is doing, compared to 18% of both independents and Republicans.

A separate *USA Today*/Gallup poll in December showed that Americans' approval of both "the Republicans in Congress" and "the Democrats in Congress" is at least somewhat higher than the overall generic approval of Congress. This is in part because the Americans who identify with each party give their party relatively high ratings (52% of Republicans approve of the Republicans in Congress, and 60% of Democrats approve of the Democrats in Congress), causing the overall average to go up.

Approval of Parties in Congress
% Approving

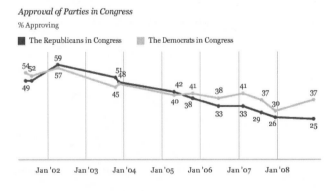

Still, even though higher than the overall approval of Congress, approval of the Democrats in Congress is not high on an absolute basis, with a majority of Americans disapproving of the way Democrats are handling their jobs. Approval of the Republicans in Congress is just slightly above the generic approval.

Bottom Line

It may be clichéd to say so, but it is clear that returning and newly elected members of the U.S. Congress have their work cut out for them as they gather in the nation's capital to open the 111th Congress.

Three-quarters of the American public, deeply dissatisfied with the way things are going in the country and deeply dissatisfied with the economy, disapprove of the way Congress is handling its job. The only good news may be that virtually the only direction for the new Congress to go is up.

Survey Methods

Results are based on telephone interviews with 1,009 national adults, aged 18 and older, conducted Dec. 4–7, 2008. For results based on the total sample of national adults, one can say with 95% confidence that the maximum margin of sampling error is ±3 percentage points.

Interviews are conducted with respondents on land-line telephones (for respondents with a land-line telephone) and cellular phones (for respondents who are cell-phone only).

In addition to sampling error, question wording and practical difficulties in conducting surveys can introduce error or bias into the findings of public opinion polls.

January 07, 2009

AS INAUGURATION NEARS, AMERICANS STILL CONFIDENT IN OBAMA

Sixty-five percent confident in Obama's ability to be a good president

by Frank Newport, Gallup Poll Editor in Chief

Gallup Poll Daily tracking shows that 65% of Americans continue to say they are confident in Barack Obama's ability to be a good president. Although down slightly over the last several days after peaking at 70% on Jan. 2–4, Obama's confidence rating remains high and within the general range he has enjoyed since being elected on Nov. 4.

Confidence in Obama's Ability to Be a Good President

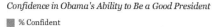

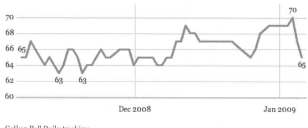

Gallup Poll Daily tracking

Obama's confidence rating has ranged from a low of 63% at two points in November to the recent high of 70%.

The slight decline in his confidence rating in recent days perhaps reflects the fact that Obama, who moved to Washington this week (although not yet into the White House, of course), is more visible and has been much in the news concerning his cabinet picks, his high-ticket economic stimulus proposal, and perhaps his reaction (or lack of one) to the situation in the Middle East.

Still, the 65% rating is well within the span of Obama's confidence ratings since his election, as noted, and it will take several

more days to see whether the public's ratings of the president-elect begin to trend downward as Obama enters the daily political grind full-time. Gallup will continue to track confidence in Obama until Inauguration Day, Jan. 20, and will then switch to the standard job approval rating used to measure public reaction to presidents since Harry Truman.

There is the predictable variation in confidence in Obama's ability to be a good president by party.

Confidence in Obama's Ability to Be a Good President
Gallup Poll Daily tracking, Jan. 2-6, 2009

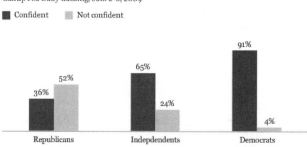

Although Republicans are certainly much less confident in Obama than either independents or, particularly, Democrats, their current 36% confidence rating is relatively high. By way of comparison, the accompanying graph shows the partisan breakout in President Bush's job approval rating for the first few days of this month.

George W. Bush Job Approval
Gallup Poll Daily tracking, Jan. 2-5, 2009

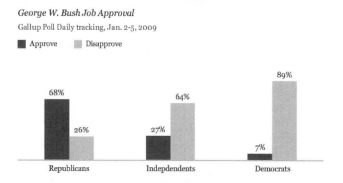

The dramatic contrast between Obama and Bush is evident. Although the two measures are somewhat different, and Obama is clearly still enjoying a pre-inauguration honeymoon of public support that passed long ago for Bush, the 7% of Democrats who approve of the job Bush is doing can be contrasted with the 36% of Republicans who are confident that Obama will be a good president. Obama also receives much greater partisan loyalty from Democrats (91% of whom are confident) than Bush receives from Republicans (68% approve of the job he is doing).

Survey Methods

Results are based on aggregated telephone interviews from Gallup Poll Daily tracking, from Nov. 5, 2008–Jan. 6, 2009. Gallup interviews no less than 1,000 national adults, aged 18 and older, each day. The Obama questions are asked of a random half of each day's sample. For results based on an average three-day rolling average of approximately 1,500 interviews, one can say with 95% confidence that the maximum margin of sampling error is ±3 percentage points.

Interviews are conducted with respondents on land-line telephones (for respondents with a land-line telephone) and cellular phones (for respondents who are cell-phone only).

In addition to sampling error, question wording and practical difficulties in conducting surveys can introduce error or bias into the findings of public opinion polls.

January 07, 2009
GAINS UNDER BUSH SEEN ON AIDS, RACE RELATIONS, LITTLE ELSE
Economy, U.S. position in world seen as suffering the most

by Jeffrey M. Jones, Gallup Poll Managing Editor and Lydia Saad, Senior Editor

George W. Bush's legacy may change in perhaps unforeseen ways as it seasons over time, but at the close of his administration, the American public perceives that more ground has been lost than gained in the United States over the past eight years on a whole range of issues. Bush leaves office with his efforts to combat AIDS being the achievement that Americans are most likely to give him credit for improving.

U.S. Made Progress, Lost Ground, or Stood Still in This Area Since George W. Bush Took Office

Jan. 2-4, 2009

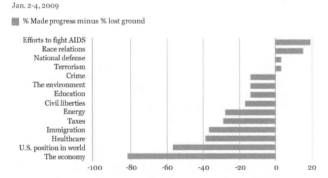

Americans are more positive than negative about the fight against AIDS, with 38% saying the country has made progress over the last eight years and 19% saying it has lost ground, resulting in a net 19-point positive score for that issue.

The public also generally perceives that race relations have improved on Bush's watch—40% say the country has gained ground in this area versus 25% who say it has lost ground. But that could largely be ascribed to Barack Obama's election as the nation's first black president, something that doesn't reflect directly on Bush's leadership in this area.

While Bush argues that the country has been made safer by his anti-terrorism policies—the proof being that no major terrorist incident has occurred on U.S. soil since 9/11—Americans are only marginally positive about the nation's progress on terrorism. Roughly 4 in 10 say the United States has made progress on terrorism and national defense—two of the highest such marks for any issue in the poll. However, nearly as many say the country has lost ground in

these areas, leaving net scores just slightly above 0 (+3 for both issues).

Americans are overwhelmingly negative about the paths the U.S. economy and the U.S. position in the world have taken under Bush, and in general are more negative than positive about how conditions have changed in 10 of 14 major areas since Bush took office.

Bush entered office hoping to make a positive mark on U.S. education with policies ultimately contained in the No Child Left Behind Act. He also pushed major tax cuts through Congress in 2001 and 2003 as core elements of his economic strategy. Nevertheless, more Americans perceive that education and taxes have lost ground than say they have gained ground in the past eight years.

Americans are largely negative in their reviews of conditions in healthcare, immigration, and energy, in addition to taxes. They are moderately negative about civil liberties, crime, and the environment, as well as about education.

Bottom Line

Given that Bush is one of the least popular exiting presidents, it is not surprising that Americans find few areas in which they think the country has improved on his watch. The administration's recent attempts to tout Bush's efforts to combat AIDS seem to square with public perceptions, as he receives his most positive scores on this issue. While substantial percentages of Americans see gains in the areas of terrorism and national defense, there are about as many critics as supporters in these areas, so the net scores are not all that strong.

During much of Bush's presidency, it seemed clear that foreign policy would dominate his legacy, for better or for worse. Americans' general sense that the U.S. position in the world has suffered under Bush is certainly a negative critique, but their more divided assessments of progress on national defense and fighting terrorism could temper their overall assessments of his foreign policy record over time. However, recent events have put more focus on the economy as a defining issue for Bush—though whether that's the case in the coming years remains to be seen—and on this, the public's overwhelming criticism of the Bush era is quite clear.

Survey Methods

Results are based on telephone interviews with 3,037 national adults, aged 18 and older, conducted Jan. 2–4, 2009. For results based on the total sample of national adults, one can say with 95% confidence that the maximum margin of sampling error is ±2 percentage points.

Interviews are conducted with respondents on land-line telephones (for respondents with a land-line telephone) and cellular phones (for respondents who are cell-phone only).

In addition to sampling error, question wording and practical difficulties in conducting surveys can introduce error or bias into the findings of public opinion polls.

January 08, 2009

CONSUMER EXPECTATIONS IMPROVING WITH NEW YEAR

But will they continue to do so in the weeks ahead?

by Dennis Jacobe, Gallup Chief Economist

Consumer expectations are getting a little better as the new year gets underway. The percentage of consumers saying the economy is "getting better" minus the percentage saying it is "getting worse" improved to -58 points during the week ending Jan. 4, 2009, after having hit -70 in mid-December as a reflection of deteriorating consumer expectations.

Net Economic Outlook Among U.S. Consumers, August 2008-January 2009 Trend

Percentage saying economic conditions are "getting better" minus percentage saying they are "getting worse," in percentage points

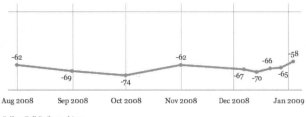

Gallup Poll Daily tracking

Both Upper- and Lower-Income Consumer Expectations Improving

Lower-income Americans (those with monthly household incomes of less than $2,000) continue to be less pessimistic than their upper-income counterparts (those with monthly incomes of $7,500 or more) about the future direction of the U.S. economy. The reverse was the case back in August and September of last year. The two income groups' outlooks became roughly equal in October, and since November, greater pessimism has been evident among upper-income Americans.

The net percentage "getting better" among lower-income Americans was -51 points last week, compared to -58 among upper-income households. Still, consumer expectations have improved among both income groups during the past week and particularly compared to mid-December.

Net Economic Outlook Among Upper- and Lower-Income U.S. Consumers, August 2008-January 2009 Trend

Percentage saying economic conditions are "getting better" minus percentage saying they are "getting worse," in percentage points

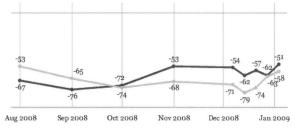

Gallup Poll Daily tracking

Commentary

It seems rather ironic that consumer expectations for the future of the U.S. economy have improved somewhat even as President-elect Obama describes the economic situation as "dire," the president of the Federal Reserve Bank of Kansas City suggests the outlook for the first half of 2009 is "grim," and recent economic reports show economic activity plummeted during the fourth quarter of last year. Of course, the uptick in consumer expectations could simply reflect more positive spirits associated with the Christmas/New Year's period. Lower gas prices may also be helping encourage consumers. However, it seems more likely that many consumers, like many on Wall Street, are encouraged by talk of an enormous government stimulus plan and the soon-to-arrive Obama inauguration.

Whether consumers are encouraged by holiday cheer, talk of a new stimulus plan, or something else, it will be interesting to see how they respond to the economic headlines over the days and weeks ahead. On the one hand, they will hear about an increasingly depressing jobs situation. They are also likely to see numerous references to the potential for economic disaster as political leaders make the case for the economic stimulus legislation. Worst of all, they may end up seeing a rash of bankruptcies as the fallout of dismal holiday sales is realized.

On the other hand, there is likely to be at least a temporary euphoria as the nation celebrates the historic inauguration of the new president-elect. This optimistic atmosphere could gain momentum as the planned dramatic action by the federal government is outlined in more detail and the unprecedented actions of the Fed begin to be felt on Main Street.

Gallup will continue to monitor consumer perceptions and report on them daily as the new year unfolds.

Survey Methods

Gallup is interviewing no fewer than 1,000 U.S. adults nationwide each day during 2008 and 2009. The economic questions analyzed in this report are asked of a random half-sample of respondents each day. The results reported here are based on combined data of more than 8,000 interviews in August, September, October, and November. For results based on this sample, the maximum margin of sampling error is ±1 percentage point.

The questions for December are based on combined data of more than 3,000 interviews conducted weekly. For results based on these samples, the maximum margin of sampling error is ±2 percentage points.

Interviews are conducted with respondents on land-line telephones (for respondents with a land-line telephone) and cellular phones (for respondents who are cell-phone only).

In addition to sampling error, question wording and practical difficulties in conducting surveys can introduce error or bias into the findings of public opinion polls.

January 08, 2009

MAJORITY OF AMERICANS FAVOR $775 BILLION ECONOMIC STIMULUS

Support particularly high for infrastructure investment and tax cuts

by Frank Newport, Gallup Poll Editor in Chief

New Gallup polling shows that 53% of Americans favor and 36% oppose Congress' passing a new $775 billion stimulus package of the type President-elect Barack Obama described in his Thursday speech on the economy. There is even higher support for specific elements it could include, such as major new government spending for infrastructure, income tax cuts, and tax incentives for businesses.

Do you favor or oppose Congress passing a new $775 billion economic stimulus program as soon as possible after Barack Obama takes office?

Jan. 6-7, 2009

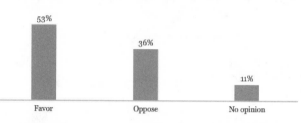

Questions asking Americans about a new stimulus plan were included in Gallup Poll Daily tracking Tuesday and Wednesday nights, just before Obama's Thursday speech in which he more formally proposed such a plan. The question wording included specific references to the cost of a new program ($775 billion), and the fact that it would be passed as soon as possible after Obama takes office. These explicit references to Obama may have had the effect of lowering overall support. Indeed, the breakout of support by partisanship shows that Republicans are much less likely than independents or Democrats to support the plan, perhaps foreshadowing the challenge Obama will have in convincing Republican lawmakers to go along with his proposal.

Do you favor or oppose Congress passing a new $775 billion economic stimulus program as soon as possible after Barack Obama takes office?

Jan. 6-7, 2009

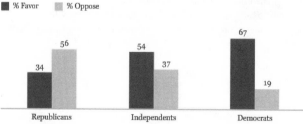

Most likely, this tepid response from Republicans represents both a typical conservative reluctance to increase government spending by such a large amount, as well as a negative reaction to the fact that the plan is being pushed by the Democratic president-elect.

Still, given that 11% of Americans interviewed don't have an opinion on the issue of the stimulus package, the results show that

the measure "passes" by a 17-point margin (53% to 36%) when those in favor are compared to those opposed.

When Americans are asked about four different elements that are widely being discussed as part of the new stimulus bill (Obama has not yet put forth a highly specific proposal), support for three of the four is significantly higher than the overall level of support for the bill itself.

Do you favor or oppose each of the following as part of a new economic stimulus package -- [RANDOM ORDER]?

Jan. 6-7, 2009

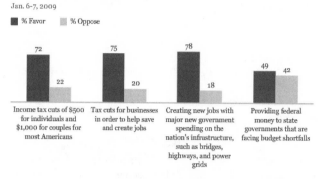

It is important to note that the wording of these specifics did not mention costs directly, perhaps making it easier for respondents to say they favored them. Also, the questions asking about spending more on infrastructure and providing tax incentives for businesses included references to the benefit from each in creating jobs, reminding respondents of potential positive outcomes.

As can be seen in the accompanying graph, support is highest for the idea of creating new jobs with "major new government spending on the nation's infrastructure," with slightly lower, but still very high, support for tax cuts for businesses ("to help save and create jobs") and income tax cuts for individuals and couples. Support is significantly lower for the idea of providing federal money to state governments that are facing budget shortfalls.

Implications

These data suggest first and foremost that Obama has the support of a majority of the American people in his attempt to prod Congress to pass a huge economic stimulus plan in the weeks after he takes office. Obama raised the stakes on passage of his plan on Thursday by warning that the economy could become "dramatically worse" if it doesn't pass.

The data also suggest—from a marketing perspective—that Obama and his team might be better off talking about the elements of his plan one by one rather than by focusing solely on the overall idea of spending huge amounts of money for a broad bill. In addition, Obama might note that the concept of giving federal money to state governments, if included in the final plan, appears to be the least popular. (Support could be higher if the benefits were more clearly defined in terms of either saving certain programs or keeping state taxes from rising.)

Obama does face resistance to his proposal from rank-and-file Republicans across the country, suggesting that it may not be smooth sailing for his bill when those who are pushing it come up against GOP members of the House and Senate.

Survey Methods

Results are based on telephone interviews with 972 national adults, aged 18 and older, conducted Jan. 6–7, 2009. For results based on

the total sample of national adults, one can say with 95% confidence that the maximum margin of sampling error is ±3 percentage points.

Interviews are conducted with respondents on land-line telephones (for respondents with a land-line telephone) and cellular phones (for respondents who are cell-phone only).

In addition to sampling error, question wording and practical difficulties in conducting surveys can introduce error or bias into the findings of public opinion polls.

January 09, 2009
AMERICANS NOT PRESSING FOR BIGGER ROLE IN GAZA CONFLICT
Few believe Obama should announce his views before he's president

by Lydia Saad, Gallup Poll Senior Editor

Israel's military action in the Gaza Strip after recent Hamas rocket fire into southern Israel has put international pressure on the United States to advocate an immediate cease-fire; but only 33% of Americans, according to a Jan. 6–7 Gallup Poll, say the Bush administration should be doing more to end the conflict than it already is doing.

Thinking about the current fighting between the Israelis and Palestinians in Gaza, do you think the Bush administration should be doing more, is doing the right amount, or should be doing less to help resolve the conflict?
Asked of Form B half-sample

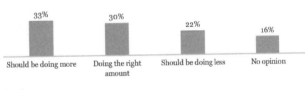

Jan. 6-7, 2009

In polling conducted the first two days after Israeli mortar fire killed more than 40 Palestinians sheltered in a United Nations-run school, Americans are more likely to believe the Bush administration should expand its role in ending the Gaza conflict than pull back, 33% vs. 22%. However nearly a third—30%—say that the administration is already doing the right amount to resolve it. Thus, a combined 52% do not push for more involvement.

Secretary of State Condoleezza Rice has been leading the administration's response to the Gaza crisis by trying to promote the idea of a cease-fire that is "durable, sustainable, and indefinite." That differs from the "immediate" cease-fire that many other world leaders have called for, and it reflects the administration's support for Israel's goal of neutralizing Hamas' ability to conduct further attacks on Israel. As Israeli Prime Minister Ehud Olmert said recently, his objective is that "quiet will reign supreme" in southern Israel.

Half of self-described "liberals" (50%) in the latest survey want the Bush administration to do more to resolve the conflict. That compares with only 32% of "moderates" and 24% of "conservatives."

Previous Gallup polling has shown liberals to be much less sympathetic than conservatives to the Israelis in the Israeli-Palestinian dispute. Thus, it is likely that liberals favor an immediate cessation

of the Gaza hostilities, even if that doesn't serve Israel's security interests.

Preference for Bush Administration Action in Resolving Gaza Conflict by Political Ideology
Asked of Form B half-sample

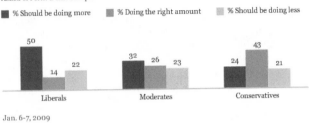

Jan. 6-7, 2009

Similarly, Democrats are more likely than Republicans to favor greater action by the Bush administration to resolve the conflict.

Preference for Bush Administration Action in Resolving Gaza Conflict by Political Party
Asked of Form B half-sample

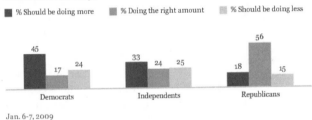

Jan. 6-7, 2009

Public opinion is less slanted in favor of stepping up U.S. efforts to resolve the Gaza conflict when the same question is asked in terms of what the *United States* should do, rather than what the *Bush administration* should do.

According to the split-sample experiment, in which survey respondents were randomly assigned to the two different forms of the question, 29% of Americans believe the United States should do more to resolve the Gaza conflict, versus 25% saying it should do less; 33% say it is doing the right amount. This contrasts with the 11 percentage-point gap in views about the Bush administration, with 33% saying it should do more and only 22% saying it should do less.

This difference is largely because Democrats and independents are significantly more likely to favor greater action when the question is framed in terms of the Bush administration rather than the country, generally.

Percentage Favoring More Action by Bush Administration/United States on Gaza Conflict
Split sample results by Party ID

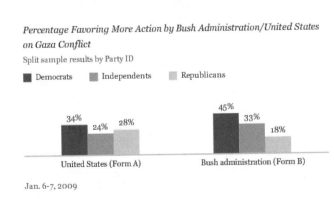

Jan. 6-7, 2009

Bottom Line

Public opinion about U.S. involvement in resolving the Gaza conflict is reminiscent of how Americans reacted to the hostilities between Israel and Hezbollah in Lebanon in 2006. A Gallup Poll conducted in July 2006 found only a third of Americans saying the United States should press for an immediate cease-fire between Israel and Hezbollah, 20% saying it should wait before calling for a cease-fire, and 43% saying it should not get involved at any point.

Contemporaneous polling showed Americans weren't necessarily strongly pro-Israel in the matter—only half approved of Israel's military actions in Lebanon, while 38% disapproved. Americans simply did not favor heavy U.S. involvement in the region. Given several options for the role the United States should play in bringing about peace between Israel and Hezbollah, only 14% of Americans said the United States should take the leading role. More than half (56%) said the United States should be involved but that the United Nations should take the leading role, and another 29% said the United States should not be involved at all.

That sentiment may very well apply to how Americans perceive the Gaza conflict today. While the public may believe the United States should have a place at the diplomatic table, it may not want to see the United States leading the Palestinian-Israeli peace effort, or expending time and other resources on it that may be needed closer to home.

Survey Methods

Results are based on telephone interviews with 2,049 national adults, aged 18 and older, conducted Jan. 6–7, 2009. For results based on the total sample of national adults, one can say with 95% confidence that the maximum margin of sampling error is ±3 percentage points.

For results based on the 1,077 national adults in the Form A half-sample and 972 national adults in the Form B half-sample, the maximum margins of sampling error are ±3 percentage points.

Interviews are conducted with respondents on land-line telephones (for respondents with a land-line telephone) and cellular phones (for respondents who are cell-phone only).

In addition to sampling error, question wording and practical difficulties in conducting surveys can introduce error or bias into the findings of public opinion polls.

January 12, 2009

CONSUMER SPENDING CONTINUES SLIDE IN FIRST DAYS OF JANUARY
Spending lower than last year at this time

by Frank Newport, Gallup Poll Editor in Chief

Gallup's consumer spending measure has continued to slide as the new year has begun, with Americans spending a daily average of $58 across the three-day period of Jan. 6–8, one of the lowest amounts of the past year.

The trend of the Gallup Poll spending measure from Nov. 1 (roughly the beginning of the Christmas shopping season) through this past week reflects the various ups and downs one would expect. Average daily spending was at $97 for the first three days of November, followed by an increase about a week and a half into the month,

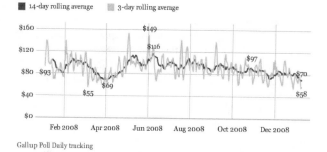

Gallup Daily: U.S. Consumer Spending
Results reported in both a 3-day and a 14-day rolling average
■ 14-day rolling average   ■ 3-day rolling average

Gallup Poll Daily tracking

a second increase in the days around Thanksgiving, and a final increase in December, about 10 days before Christmas. Since that time, the trends have been down, dropping to a not-unexpected low point of $55 between Dec. 22 and Dec. 27 (encompassing Christmas Day), with just a limited recovery in the days since. The $58 average for the three-day period of Jan. 6–8 is within a few dollars of the Christmas low point, which in turn matched the all-time low last March.

The daily average for the last 14 days is $70, the lowest such average since last April.

Gallup began measuring self-reported consumer spending at the beginning of last year. Spending was relatively robust as 2008 began, with three-day spending averages of at least $100 for a number of the days in the first half of the month.

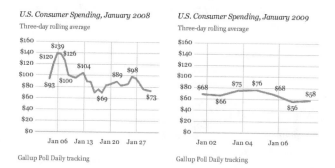

U.S. Consumer Spending, January 2008
Three-day rolling average

Gallup Poll Daily tracking

U.S. Consumer Spending, January 2009
Three-day rolling average

Gallup Poll Daily tracking

Spending then settled back down, but the lowest three-day average of January 2008 was $69, still well above the current average of $58. Thus, the data from the first week of January this year suggest—to no great surprise—a continuation of the drop in consumer spending seen for most of 2008, and certainly a lower level of spending than was the case a year ago at roughly this same period of time.

Implications

Consumer spending is in many ways the core of the U.S. economy, and as consumers pull back on their spending, many sectors of the economy concomitantly falter. Gallup Poll Daily tracking data on the economy document the drop in spending that has occurred since the beginning of the summer, and the bad news is that the first indications of spending in the new year look equally if not more dismal.

Survey Methods

For the Gallup Poll Daily tracking survey, Gallup is interviewing no fewer than 1,000 U.S. adults nationwide each day during 2008. The consumer spending question is asked of a random half sample of each day's interviews, and for any given three-day rolling average of results, consisting of approximately 1,500 interviews, the maximum margin of sampling error is ±3 percentage points.

Results for the Jan. 6–8, 2009, rolling average are based on telephone interviews with 1,438 national adults, aged 18 and older. For results based on the total sample of national adults, one can say with 95% confidence that the maximum margin of sampling error is ±3 percentage points.

Interviews are conducted with respondents on land-line telephones (for respondents with a land-line telephone) and cellular phones (for respondents who are cell-phone only).

In addition to sampling error, question wording and practical difficulties in conducting surveys can introduce error or bias into the findings of public opinion polls.

The average "Iraq mistake" percentage for 2008 was 59%. Thus, although Bush responded to the question about Iraq mainly in terms of the wisdom of the surge, current Gallup data show that regardless of the success of that specific decision, a majority of Americans still believe that the initial rationale and decision to send troops to Iraq was a mistake.

In view of the developments since we first sent our troops to Iraq, do you think the United States made a mistake in sending troops to Iraq, or not?

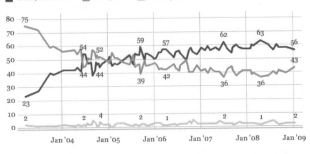

January 12, 2009
FACT-CHECKING PRESIDENT BUSH'S FINAL PRESS CONFERENCE
On Iraq and U.S. global standing, Bush paints different picture than constituents do

by Frank Newport, Gallup Poll Editor in Chief

President George W. Bush held the last official press conference of his administration Monday and, in the course of the 47-minute event, responded to several questions that dealt at least to a degree with public opinion. Bush's responses to two issues in particular—Iraq and the United States' position in the world—can be looked at in the light of Gallup Poll data on the topics under consideration.

1. Iraq

Press Question: In the past, when you've been asked to address bad poll numbers or your own popularity, you've said that history will judge that you did the right thing, that you thought you did the right thing. But without getting into your motives or your goals, I think a lot of people, including Republicans, including some members of your own administration, have been disappointed at the execution of some of your ideals, whether Iraq or Katrina or the economy. What would your closing message be to the American people about the execution of these goals?

THE PRESIDENT: Well, first of all, hard things don't happen overnight, Jake. And when the history of Iraq is written, historians will analyze, for example, the decision on the surge. The situation was—looked like it was going fine and then violence for a period of time began to throw—throw the progress of Iraq into doubt. And rather than accepting the status quo and saying, oh, it's not worth it or the politics makes it difficult or, you know, the party may end up being—you know, not doing well in the elections because of the violence in Iraq, I decided to do something about it—and sent 30,000 troops in as opposed to withdrawing.

Regardless of the advisability and impact of the surge of troops in Iraq, Gallup Polls continue to show that a majority of Americans believe it was a mistake for the United States to be involved there—despite the fact that about half of Americans agree with the president that the situation there appears to have improved as a result of the surge.

2. Standing of the United States in the World

PRESS QUESTION: One of the major objectives that the incoming administration has talked frequently about is restoring America's moral standing in the world. And many of the allies of the new president—I believe that the president-elect himself has talked about the damage that Gitmo, that harsh interrogation tactics that they consider torture, how going to war in Iraq without a U.N. mandate have damaged America's moral standing in the world. I'm wondering basically what is your reaction to that? Do you think that is that something that the next president needs to worry about?

THE PRESIDENT: I strongly disagree with the assessment that our moral standing has been damaged. It may be damaged amongst some of the elite, but people still understand America stands for freedom, that America is a country that provides such great hope.

Gallup doesn't track Americans' views of the *moral* standing of the United States as perceived around the world, but does track a question asking more generally about how the United States rates in the world's eyes. Americans' views in response to this "standing in the world" question have clearly diminished during the Bush years despite the president's strong assertion that the country's standing has not been damaged.

In the months following the Sept. 11, 2001, terrorist attacks, as many as 79% of Americans felt that the United States rated favorably in the eyes of the world. That dropped to 40% in June 2007 and 43% in February 2008. Overall, since February 2005, a majority of Americans have felt that the United States rates unfavorably in the eyes of the world.

Earlier this month, Gallup asked Americans if the United States had made progress, stood still, or lost ground in terms of a variety of issues in the eight years since Bush took office. One of these issues was the "U.S. position in the world." On this retrospective measure, 69% of Americans say the United States lost ground during the Bush years, 12% say the country gained ground, and 17% say the United States' position in the world stayed about the same.

This was the most negative response to any of the 14 issues tested except for the economy.

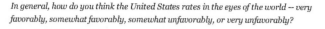

In general, how do you think the United States rates in the eyes of the world -- very favorably, somewhat favorably, somewhat unfavorably, or very unfavorably?

■ % Very/Somewhat favorably   ▨ % Very/Somewhat unfavorably

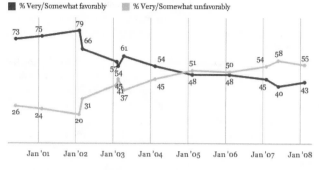

Now I'm going to mention some issues facing the country and ask whether you believe the United States has made progress, stood still, or lost ground in each during the last eight years, since George W. Bush became president. How about in terms of -- The United States' position in the world?

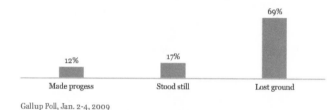

Gallup Poll, Jan. 2-4, 2009

Bottom Line

President Bush is understandably interested in putting the best possible light on his administration in the final days of his time in office. And it is true that—as Bush and Vice President Dick Cheney often opine—the true verdict on his administration may not be rendered until its historical impact is measured decades from now. But in terms of contemporary American public opinion on the two issues reviewed in this article—Iraq and the image of the United States in the world—it is clear that Americans still view the former as a mistake (despite the success of the surge), and that the significant majority of Americans perceive the latter as having deteriorated during Bush's tenure in office.

Survey Methods

Results discussed in this article are based on Gallup Polls, which are in turn based on telephone interviews with national adults, aged 18 and older. For results based on a typical sample of approximately 1,000 national adults, one can say with 95% confidence that the maximum margin of sampling error is ±3 percentage points.

Interviews are conducted with respondents on land-line telephones (for respondents with a land-line telephone) and cellular phones (for respondents who are cell-phone only).

In addition to sampling error, question wording and practical difficulties in conducting surveys can introduce error or bias into the findings of public opinion polls.

January 13, 2009

AS SENATE HEARINGS BEGIN, HILLARY CLINTON'S IMAGE SOARS

by Jeffrey M. Jones, Gallup Poll Managing Editor

A new Gallup Poll finds 65% of Americans saying they have a favorable opinion of Hillary Clinton, the highest rating for her in almost 10 years.

Hillary Clinton Favorable Ratings

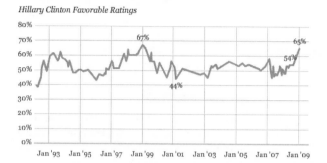

Clinton had not had a favorable rating above 60% since 1999, after having been consistently above that level during the Monica Lewinsky scandal that led to the impeachment but ultimate acquittal of husband Bill Clinton. That included Hillary Clinton's all-time high 67% favorable rating immediately after the House of Representatives voted to impeach the president in December 1998.

Since late 1999, Hillary Clinton's favorable ratings have been around 50%, ranging from a low of 44% in March 2001 to a high of 58% in February 2007.

The last measure in 2008, taken just before the Democratic National Convention last August and following months of a hotly contested Democratic nomination campaign with Barack Obama, was 54%. Since that time, her image has improved among most key demographic and political subgroups, but much more among women than men.

Change in Hillary Clinton's Favorable Rating, by Gender

■ August 2008   ▨ January 2009

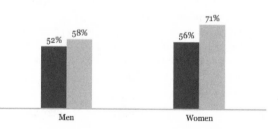

Now President-elect Obama has tapped Clinton to be his secretary of state. Clinton's confirmation begins Tuesday, and she is widely expected to be confirmed.

Americans generally have a positive view of the kind of job she would do if confirmed—a majority say she will be an outstanding (26%) or above-average (30%) secretary of state. Only 14% give her a negative evaluation.

Implications

Hillary Clinton has been a national public figure for over 16 years, and her public image has waxed and waned during this time. She—

Assuming she is confirmed by the Senate, what kind of secretary of state do you think Hillary Clinton will be?

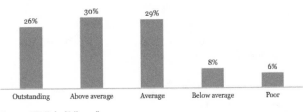

Jan. 9-11 USA Today/Gallup poll

ratings for each of the previous two quarters. Individual Gallup approval readings on Bush exceeded that figure several times in the past year, including a 33% reading in September. However, the current 34% approval score is Bush's highest since January 2008, and a sharp improvement from the 25% recorded right before the November elections.

Bush mainly has members of his own party to thank for the fact that he is ending his presidency with an approval rating above 30%. Republicans' approval of him rose from 67% in mid-December to 75% in the current poll—their highest rating of Bush in nearly a year. By contrast, approval of Bush remains extremely scarce among Democrats, and continues to fall under 30% among independents.

along with Obama— is currently enjoying a wave of positive feeling as she prepares to become the next U.S. secretary of state.

George W. Bush Job Approval, by Party ID -- Recent Trend

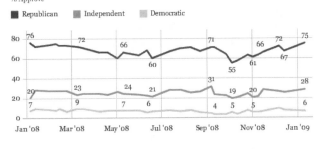

Survey Methods

Results are based on telephone interviews with 1,031 national adults, aged 18 and older, conducted Jan. 9–11, 2009. For results based on the total sample of national adults, one can say with 95% confidence that the maximum margin of sampling error is ±3 percentage points.

Interviews are conducted with respondents on land-line telephones (for respondents with a land-line telephone) and cellular phones (for respondents who are cell-phone only).

In addition to sampling error, question wording and practical difficulties in conducting surveys can introduce error or bias into the findings of public opinion polls.

Historical Exit Ratings

Bush joins Jimmy Carter and Harry Truman as presidents since the end of World War II whose final job approval ratings in office registered in the low 30s.

Final Job Approval Rating for Recent Presidents
Ranked by % "Approve"

		Approve	Disapprove	Net approve
		%	%	Pct. pts.
Bill Clinton:	Jan 10-14, 2001	66	29	+37
Ronald Reagan:	Dec 27-29, 1988	63	29	+34
Dwight Eisenhower:	Dec 8-13, 1960	59	28	+31
George H.W. Bush:	Jan 8-11, 1993	56	37	+19
Gerald Ford:	Dec 10-13, 1976	53	32	+21
Lyndon Johnson:	Jan 1-6, 1969	49	37	+12
Jimmy Carter:	Dec 5-8, 1980	34	55	-21
George W. Bush:	Jan 9-11, 2009	34	61	-27
Harry Truman:	Dec 11-16, 1952	32	56	-24
Richard Nixon:	Aug 2-5, 1974	24	66	-42

Note: Presidents who died in office (Franklin Roosevelt and John Kennedy) not shown.

January 14, 2009
BUSH PRESIDENCY CLOSES WITH 34% APPROVAL, 61% DISAPPROVAL
Three-quarters of Republicans approve of Bush, up slightly from recent months

by Lydia Saad, Gallup Poll Senior Editor

A new *USA Today*/Gallup poll, conducted Jan. 9–11, finds 34% of Americans approving of the overall job George W. Bush is doing as president and 61% disapproving. Those ratings are a shade better than what Bush has received for most of the past year, and may represent the kind of lame-duck approval bounce Gallup has seen for other presidents.

In one sense, Bush's final rating is worse than either Carter's or Truman's, because his disapproval score is significantly higher. Whereas Bush and Carter share identical 34% final job approval ratings, 61% of Americans disapprove of the job Bush is doing, compared with 55% who said they disapproved of Carter in December 1980. Similarly, whereas Bush's final approval rating is slightly higher than Truman's 32% in 1952, his disapproval rating is also higher (61% vs. 56%), resulting in a lower net approval rating for Bush.

Only Richard Nixon was explicitly less popular at the time of his exit than Bush is today. Gallup's final approval polling on Nixon, in which 24% of Americans said they approved of the job he was doing, was conducted Aug. 2–5, 1974, less than a week before Nixon resigned from office over the Watergate break-in political scandal.

Do you approve or disapprove of the way George W. Bush is handling his job as president?

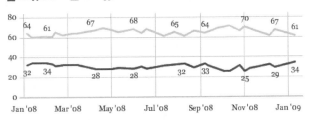

Bush had been averaging a 29% approval rating for the last quarter of his presidency up to now—identical to his average approval

Those with the highest job approval at the conclusion of their presidencies were all two-term presidents: Bill Clinton, with 66% approval; Ronald Reagan, with 63%; and Dwight Eisenhower, with 59%. However, even two presidents who were rebuffed by voters in their efforts to seek a second term—George H.W. Bush and Gerald Ford—received majority approval in their final days. Close to half of Americans also approved of the job Lyndon Johnson was doing in the final days of his administration.

Lame-Duck Advantage

One benefit of leaving office is that presidents often enjoy a small bounce in their job approval scores. As Gallup Poll Managing Editor Jeff Jones described last month, "It is common for presidents who are about to leave the White House to receive a bump in their job approval ratings between Election Day and Inauguration Day."

For Bush, this bump amounts to nine points, from his 25% approval rating in a Gallup Poll conducted Oct. 31–Nov. 2, 2008, to the 34% recorded today. The largest such shift Gallup has recorded was for George H. W. Bush, whose approval score rose 22 points after the 1992 election. However, Reagan, Clinton, Ford, and Johnson also benefited from the softening of public opinion that seems to occur during this period.

Bottom Line

Bush has what most would consider the unwanted distinction of registering one of the lowest final job approval ratings of any modern president leaving office at the natural end of his term, and the highest disapproval. While his approval rating has improved since Election Day, the vast majority of Democrats and even most independents still disapprove of how he is handling the job. Only Republicans generally approve of the job Bush is doing, but that may, in fact, be just fine with a president who says his goal has been to do what he believed is right, not what would make him popular.

Survey Methods

Results are based on telephone interviews with 1,031 national adults, aged 18 and older, conducted Jan. 9–11, 2009. For results based on the total sample of national adults, one can say with 95% confidence that the maximum margin of sampling error is ±3 percentage points.

Interviews are conducted with respondents on land-line telephones (for respondents with a land-line telephone) and cellular phones (for respondents who are cell-phone only).

In addition to sampling error, question wording and practical difficulties in conducting surveys can introduce error or bias into the findings of public opinion polls.

January 14, 2009
LAURA BUSH LEAVES WHITE HOUSE AS POPULAR FIGURE

by Jeffrey M. Jones, Gallup Poll Managing Editor

The latest *USA Today*/Gallup poll finds 76% of Americans saying they have a favorable opinion of first lady Laura Bush. The public has viewed her very positively during George W. Bush's entire

term as president, with her favorable ratings ranging between 63% and 80%.

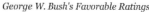

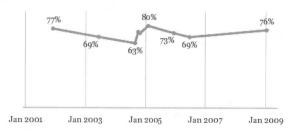

Laura Bush's favorable rating is nearly twice as high as her husband's current 40% (his job approval rating is slightly lower at 34%). The president began his tenure in office with high favorable ratings himself—never falling below 60% until his fourth year in office. His favorables began to decline in his re-election year of 2004, and have declined further since then, following the general trajectory of his job approval rating. His current favorable rating actually represents an improvement from last year's term-low 32%.

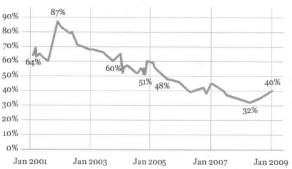

George W. Bush's Favorable Ratings

Laura Bush is rated more positively by Republicans (89%) than by independents (76%) or Democrats (66%). But all three groups have a very positive impression of her.

In contrast, only Republicans (77%) have an overall favorable view of the president, given that just 37% of independents and 11% of Democrats have a positive opinion of him.

Comparison to Other First Ladies

In general, the president's job makes him more susceptible to criticism than the first lady, so it is not surprising for the president to have lower favorable ratings than the first lady. But can Laura Bush be meaningfully compared to other first ladies?

Gallup has asked the favorability question in the current format only since 1993, beginning with the end of Barbara Bush's tenure as first lady and spanning the entire Hillary Clinton and Laura Bush years. From 1993 to early 2001, Clinton's favorable rating averaged 56%, compared with 73% for Laura Bush from 2001 to 2009. Clinton's personal high favorable rating of 67% is just slightly better than Bush's lowest favorable rating of 63%.

The fact that Laura Bush has a higher average favorable rating as first lady than Clinton likely reflects Clinton's more active role as first lady, including her involvement in controversial policy matters such as the attempt to reform the national healthcare system. It also reflects Republicans' generally negative opinions of her throughout the Clinton administration years.

But while Laura Bush has generally been viewed more positively as first lady than Hillary Clinton was, she may not be quite as popular a first lady as her mother-in-law, Barbara Bush, at least based on a comparison of how both were viewed at the end of their husbands' presidencies. Just before the elder George Bush left the White House in January 1993, 85% of Americans had a favorable opinion of Barbara Bush, significantly better than the current 76% rating for Laura Bush.

Survey Methods

Results are based on telephone interviews with 1,031 national adults, aged 18 and older, conducted Jan. 9–11, 2009. For results based on the total sample of national adults, one can say with 95% confidence that the maximum margin of sampling error is ±3 percentage points.

Interviews are conducted with respondents on land-line telephones (for respondents with a land-line telephone) and cellular phones (for respondents who are cell-phone only).

In addition to sampling error, question wording and practical difficulties in conducting surveys can introduce error or bias into the findings of public opinion polls.

January 15, 2009

AMERICANS WANT DETAILS BEFORE RELEASE OF MORE TARP FUNDS
Both Democrats and Republicans favor blocking funds until there are more details

by Frank Newport, Gallup Poll Editor in Chief

A majority of Americans (62%) say Congress should block President-elect Obama's request to release the remaining $350 billion in Troubled Asset Relief Program (TARP) funds until more details are provided about how the funds will be spent. The rest of Americans are split between saying the funds should be released immediately and saying they should not be released at all.

As you may know, about half of the money from last year's $700 billion financial rescue plan has been used, and President-elect Obama has now asked Congress for the other half to be released. Which would you rather see happen – for Congress to allow the remaining $350 billion to be released, for Congress to block the release unless more details are provided about how the funds will be used, or for Congress to block the release of the $350 billion entirely?

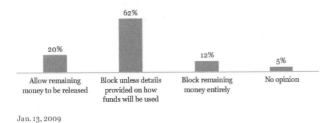

Jan. 13, 2009

President Bush, accommodating a request from Obama, formally asked for the release of the remaining half of the TARP funds ear-

lier this week. The funds will automatically be released after 15 days unless Congress passes a law blocking their release. A number of congressional leaders, including some Democrats and Republicans, have threatened to do just that—citing concerns that the Obama administration must be much more explicit about what is going to be done with the second half of the appropriated TARP money. These concerns in part reflect criticism that spending of the first half of the TARP funds was badly mismanaged.

Obama made a personal trip to Capitol Hill on Tuesday, lobbying for release of the funds and providing more details about how the money will be spent. The Senate could vote on the issue as early as Thursday.

In general, the threat of blocking the release of the TARP funds appears to be one with which the average American is sympathetic. Given three choices of what to do with the remaining funds, 62% say Congress should block the release "unless more details are provided about how the funds will be used," and another 12% say Congress should block the funds entirely. Only 20% favor Congress' simply allowing the funds to be released.

The differences by political orientation in response to this question are not as large as one might expect or as large as is typical in such situations, particularly given that the survey question explicitly referred to Obama in connection with allowing the release of the funds.

Which would you rather see happen?
By political party

■ % For Congress to allow remaining $350 billion to be released
■ % For Congress to block release unless details are provided about how funds will be used
■ % For Congress to block release of $350 billion entirely

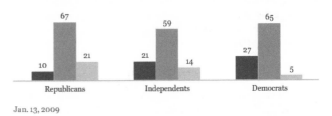

Jan. 13, 2009

A majority of all three political groups favor blocking the funds until details are provided about how they are to be used. Democrats are somewhat more likely to say they favor just allowing the funds to be released, and Republicans are more likely to say they favor blocking the funds entirely, but both of these percentages are below 30%.

Implications

A clear majority of more than 6 out of 10 Americans are willing to have Congress block the release of the second half of the TARP funds unless more detailed explanations of how the money is to be spent are put forward. President-elect Obama has perhaps already begun to meet these requirements by going to Capitol Hill Tuesday and explaining in more detailing how the money will be spent. The Obama team also put forth a letter to Congress from Dr. Larry Summers, the new head of National Economic Council in the Obama White House, detailed how the TARP money will be spent. All of these efforts, at least as far as the American public is concerned, would appear to be justified if the $350 billion is to be released.

Survey Methods

Results are based on telephone interviews with 1,011 national adults, aged 18 and older, conducted Jan. 13, 2009. For results based on the total sample of national adults, one can say with 95% confidence that the maximum margin of sampling error is ±3 percentage points.

Polls conducted entirely in one day, such as this one, are subject to additional error or bias not found in polls conducted over several days.

Interviews are conducted with respondents on land-line telephones (for respondents with a land-line telephone) and cellular phones (for respondents who are cell-phone only).

In addition to sampling error, question wording and practical difficulties in conducting surveys can introduce error or bias into the findings of public opinion polls.

January 16, 2009

AMERICANS EXPECT HISTORY TO JUDGE BUSH WORSE THAN NIXON

Majority say he will be remembered as a below-average or poor president

by Lydia Saad, Gallup Poll Senior Editor

A mere 17% of Americans believe George W. Bush will go down in history as an outstanding or above-average president—out of sync with Bush's own confidence that his presidency will be appreciated with time. Another 23% of Americans predict he will be remembered as "average" while 59% say "below average" or "poor."

Perceptions of How George W. Bush Will Go Down in History

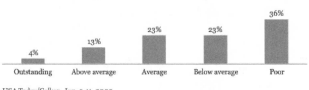

USA Today/Gallup, Jan. 9-11, 2009

The bleakness of Americans' current forecast for Bush's historical stature is highlighted by the contrast between their ratings of Bush and those of several former U.S. presidents.

According to the Jan. 9–11 *USA Today*/Gallup poll, Americans think four of the last seven presidents are more likely to be remembered in positive than in negative terms. This includes highly praiseworthy ratings for Ronald Reagan and Bill Clinton. Only Bush, Jimmy Carter, and Richard Nixon—the only U.S. president ever to have resigned from office—receive more subpar than stellar reviews.

Although Bush is about tied with Nixon in perceptions that history will remember him as an outstanding or above-average president, he fares worse than Nixon on the basis of his "below average" and "poor" ratings: 59% for Bush vs. 48% for Nixon. As a result, Bush's net positive score (total percent outstanding or above average minus total percent below average or poor) is worse than Nixon's: -42 for Bush versus -33 for Nixon.

How do you think each of the following presidents will go down in history -- as an outstanding president, above average, average, below average, or poor?

Listed in order of Net positive score (% outstanding/above average minus % below average/poor)

	Outstanding/ Above average	Average	Below average/ Poor	Net positive
	%	%	%	Pct. pts.
Ronald Reagan	64	26	9	55
Bill Clinton	50	29	20	30
Gerald Ford	23	58	11	12
George H.W. Bush	28	49	21	7
Jimmy Carter	26	39	29	-3
Richard Nixon	15	32	48	-33
George W. Bush	17	23	59	-42

USA Today/Gallup, Jan. 9-11, 2009

There is also a bit of irony embedded in the presidential rankings. President Bush falls well below his father, George H.W. Bush, whose defeat in 1992 was reportedly one of Bush's motivations for running for governor of Texas in 1994 and, later, for president.

Poor Stature Ratings Tethered to Low Job Approval

Public perceptions about Bush's standing in history were nearly as negative when last measured about two years ago. At that time, Bush's overall job approval rating was also anemic: 38% approved of Bush's job performance in December 2006 compared with 34% today.

By contrast, in June 2004, five months before Bush's re-election and at a time when his approval rating stood at 49%, nearly as many Americans believed history would remember his presidency as outstanding or above average as below average or poor (31% vs. 38%).

Trend in Perceptions of How George W. Bush Will Go Down in History

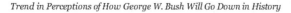
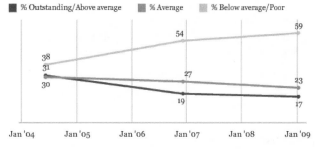

Bush's image could certainly improve over time, not unlike the changes seen in Americans' retrospective approval ratings of John F. Kennedy, Reagan, Carter, and Gerald Ford. All of these presidents had higher "retrospective approval" ratings in a June 2006 Gallup Poll compared with their final approval ratings upon leaving office. However, the 2006 approval scores for Clinton, George H.W. Bush, and Nixon were about the same as their final presidential approval ratings, and Lyndon Johnson's score was slightly worse. Thus, the nostalgia effect is not a sure bet.

Bottom Line

While Bush, Vice President Cheney, and other members of the outgoing administration foresee vindication for the decisions and policies that have made Bush broadly unpopular in his time, many historians have already declared Bush "the worst president ever."

If Bush's reputation is to improve, it will most likely depend on a positive outcome for Iraq in the coming years, but also on how well his successors manage the same global and economic challenges he has faced. While it is impossible to predict how those factors will play out, there is much more room for his reputation to improve than to worsen. As of today, a solid majority of Americans perceive that Bush's long-term reputation will be subpar. That is the worst forecast for any recent president, including Nixon.

Survey Methods

Results are based on telephone interviews with 1,031 national adults, aged 18 and older, conducted Jan. 9–11, 2009. For results based on the total sample of national adults, one can say with 95% confidence that the maximum margin of sampling error is ±3 percentage points.

Interviews are conducted with respondents on land-line telephones (for respondents with a land-line telephone) and cellular phones (for respondents who are cell-phone only).

In addition to sampling error, question wording and practical difficulties in conducting surveys can introduce error or bias into the findings of public opinion polls.

January 16, 2009
OBAMA WINS 83% APPROVAL RATING FOR TRANSITION
Forty-five percent rate Obama's appointments as above average or outstanding

by Frank Newport, Gallup Poll Editor in Chief

President-elect Barack Obama receives a remarkably high 83% approval rating for the way in which he has handled the presidential transition, significantly higher than the approval level for either of his immediate predecessors just before they first took office.

Do you approve or disapprove of the way Barack Obama is handling his presidential transition?

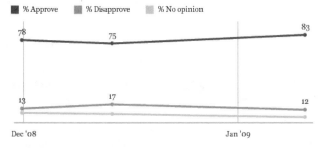

Obama's transition approval rating has actually increased slightly over the last month, despite the fact that he has encountered a few "speed bumps" in terms of his Cabinet appointments, including the withdrawal of his appointee for commerce secretary, New Mexico Gov. Bill Richardson, who was forced to drop out owing to investigations into possible improper business dealings in his home state.

Gallup asked Americans in January 1993 and January 2001 the same transition approval question concerning Bill Clinton and George W. Bush, respectively. In both instances, Americans were quite positive, although at a level well below their approval of Obama today.

Do you approve or disapprove of the way ... is handling his presidential transition?

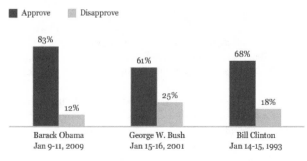

Rating Obama's Appointments

Obama doesn't fare quite as well on a comparative basis when Americans are asked to rate the appointments he has made to Cabinet-level positions.

How would you rate the appointments President-elect Barack Obama has made so far to Cabinet-level positions? Would you say his choices have been -- outstanding, above average, average, below average, or poor?
Numbers in percentages

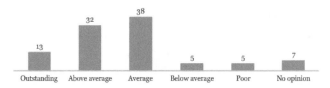

Forty-five percent of Americans say Obama's appointments have been above average or outstanding, with 38% saying they have been average and 10% below average. That is only slightly higher than the 38% who rated Bush's Cabinet-level appointments positively in January 2001. At the same time, both Obama and Bush received significantly higher marks for their Cabinet-level appointments than Clinton, who received only 27% and 32% positive ratings in two polls conducted in January 1993.

Confidence in Obama to Be a Good President

Gallup's continuing tracking (since the Nov. 4 election) of the public's confidence in Obama to be a good president provides additional evidence of the positive way he has handled the potential pitfalls of the transition period.

Are you confident or not confident in Barack Obama's ability to be a good president?

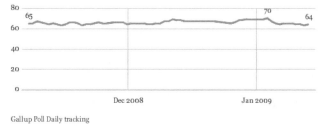

Gallup Poll Daily tracking

Obama had a 65% confidence rating in the first few days after his Nov. 4 election victory, has averaged 66% over the two and a half months between then and now, and has a 64% rating through Wednesday night of this week—evidence of his steady hand at the transition tiller.

Implications

A review of Gallup Poll data reinforces the conclusion that President-elect Obama has come through his transition period in very positive fashion, significantly more so than either of his immediate past predecessors, Bush or Clinton. Not only does the public give Obama very high approval ratings for the way in which he has handled the transition, but Americans' confidence in him to be a good president has remained positive and steady, and since his election, his favorable rating has climbed by 10 points to its highest point since Gallup first began to measure it in December 2006.

Survey Methods

Results are based on telephone interviews with 1,031 national adults, aged 18 and older, conducted Jan. 9–11, 2009. For results based on the total sample of national adults, one can say with 95% confidence that the maximum margin of sampling error is ±3 percentage points.

Interviews are conducted with respondents on land-line telephones (for respondents with a land-line telephone) and cellular phones (for respondents who are cell-phone only).

In addition to sampling error, question wording and practical difficulties in conducting surveys can introduce error or bias into the findings of public opinion polls.

January 19, 2009
DOMESTIC PRIORITIES TOP AMERICANS' TO-DO LIST FOR OBAMA
Public would like Obama to keep promises in areas of healthcare, energy, and economy

by Jeffrey M. Jones, Gallup Poll Managing Editor

Americans think it is very important that Barack Obama follow through on his promises to address problems in healthcare, energy, and the economy. They are less likely to view his pledges to withdraw U.S. troops from Iraq or expand U.S. military power in Afghanistan as critical priorities.

At least 7 in 10 say it is very important for Obama to follow through on his pledges to ensure all children have health insurance coverage, double the production of alternative energy, and reduce healthcare costs for the typical family by up to $2,500 per year.

Two major planks of his economic stimulus program—a major spending program on the nation's infrastructure to help create jobs, and cutting income taxes—are viewed as very important promises by roughly 6 in 10 Americans.

Only a slim majority of 51% say it is very important that Obama withdraw most U.S. combat troops from Iraq within 16 months, one of his most prominent campaign promises. And fewer, 43%, assign a high degree of importance to his pledge to increase U.S. military strength in Afghanistan.

Importance of Obama's Keeping His Promises

	% Very important
Ensure all children have health insurance	73
Double production of alternative energy	70
Reduce healthcare costs for families	70
Enact major spending program on infrastructure	60
Cut taxes for 95% of working families	57
Withdraw most troops from Iraq within 16 months	51
Increase military strength in Afghanistan	43
Lift restrictions on gov't. funding of embryonic stem-cell research	42
Close Guantanamo prison	32
Make it easier for unions to organize	28

USA Today/Gallup poll, Jan. 9-11, 2009

There are three promises—two domestic and one international—that are lower priorities for Americans: lifting restrictions on government funding of embryonic stem-cell research (42%), closing the Guantanamo Bay prison for terrorist suspects (32%), and making it easier for labor unions to organize (28%). News reports suggest that Obama may in fact follow through with the first two of these and issue executive orders concerning them within the first several days of his administration.

For nearly every one of these potential actions, Democrats are more likely than Republicans to identify them as very important to do. The sole exception comes in regard to increasing U.S. military strength in Afghanistan, which ranks at the top of the Republican priority list (with 55% saying it is very important for Obama to do) but at the bottom of Democratic list.

Ratings of Obama Promises as Very Important, by Party Affiliation

	Democrats	Independents	Republicans
Ensure all children have health insurance	91%	69%	54%
Double production of alternative energy	83%	68%	53%
Reduce healthcare costs for families	86%	68%	53%
Enact major spending program on infrastructure	73%	58%	44%
Cut taxes for 95% of working families	67%	51%	50%
Withdraw most troops from Iraq within 16 months	74%	50%	25%
Increase military strength in Afghanistan	35%	39%	55%
Lift restrictions on gov't. funding of embryonic stem-cell research	55%	41%	28%
Close Guantanamo prison	45%	30%	20%
Make it easier for unions to organize	42%	25%	13%

USA Today/Gallup poll, Jan. 9-11, 2009

What Will Obama Be Able to Accomplish?

A separate question in the poll asked Americans, for each of the items, whether they think Obama will accomplish it as president. At least a majority of Americans say he will accomplish each one, ranging from a low of 53% for cutting income taxes for American families to a high of 80% for enacting a major spending program on infrastructure.

No fewer than 65% of Democrats think Obama will be able to accomplish each of the goals. Republicans are more skeptical, however, with at least a majority thinking he can accomplish only 5 of the 10 goals tested in the survey. Republicans are least confident he can withdraw most U.S. troops from Iraq in the near future.

Economy Dominant as Most Important Problem

The economy remains the runaway leader when Americans are asked to name the most important problem facing the country. Nearly 8 in

Just your best guess, do you think Barack Obama will or will not accomplish each of the following as president?

	% Yes, will accomplish
Enact major spending program on infrastructure	80
Increase military strength in Afghanistan	68
Ensure all children have health insurance	62
Lift restrictions on gov't. funding of embryonic stem-cell research	61
Double production of alternative energy	59
Close Guantanamo prison	59
Make it easier for unions to organize	59
Reduce healthcare costs for families	56
Withdraw most troops from Iraq within 16 months	54
Cut taxes for 95% of working families	53

USA Today/Gallup poll, Jan. 9-11, 2009

Think Obama Will Accomplish Goals, by Party Affiliation

	Democrats	Independents	Republicans
	%	%	%
Enact major spending program on infrastructure	87	80	72
Increase military strength in Afghanistan	68	70	65
Ensure all children have health insurance	80	60	44
Lift restrictions on gov't. funding of embryonic stem-cell research	67	59	55
Double production of alternative energy	74	56	44
Close Guantanamo prison	65	58	55
Make it easier for unions to organize	68	55	54
Reduce healthcare costs for families	72	52	42
Withdraw most troops from Iraq within 16 months	70	50	38
Cut taxes for 95% of working families	67	50	41

USA Today/Gallup poll, Jan. 9-11, 2009

10 Americans mentions some economic concern, with the most common being general mentions of the economy (57%). But unemployment (11%) and a lack of money (8%) are also significant concerns.

The Iraq war is the top non-economic problem, mentioned by 13% of respondents, followed by dissatisfaction with government (5%), healthcare (4%), moral and ethical decline (3%), and national security (3%).

Survey Methods

Results are based on telephone interviews with 1,009 national adults, aged 18 and older, conducted Jan. 9–11, 2009. For results based on the total sample of national adults, one can say with 95% confidence that the maximum margin of sampling error is ±3 percentage points.

Interviews are conducted with respondents on land-line telephones (for respondents with a land-line telephone) and cellular phones (for respondents who are cell-phone only).

In addition to sampling error, question wording and practical difficulties in conducting surveys can introduce error or bias into the findings of public opinion polls.

January 19, 2009
POLL: LITTLE OBJECTION TO RICK WARREN GIVING INAUGURAL PRAYER
Only 9% object to Obama's selection of Warren to give prayer on Tuesday

by Frank Newport, Gallup Poll Editor in Chief

Despite media reports of controversy over Barack Obama's selection of mega-church pastor Rick Warren to give the prayer at Tuesday's inauguration, the average American seems to be either unaware of the selection or to approve. Fifty-two percent of Americans say they don't know enough about the decision to have an opinion either way. Among Americans who do have an opinion, those who approve outweigh those who disapprove 39% to 9%.

Do you appove or disapprove of Obama's decision to have Rick Warren give the Inaugural prayer?

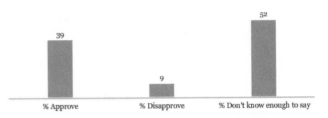

The news media have been regularly reporting on controversy aroused by Obama's decision to choose Rick Warren for the inaugural prayer. The objection to Warren—the pastor of the huge Saddleback Church in Orange County, Calif., and author of the best-selling "The Purpose Driven Life"—appears to be based on Warren's recent support for California's Proposition 8 that defined marriage as only between and man and a woman, and for other conservative statements Warren has made about gay rights.

But the results of a Gallup Poll tracking question asked Friday and Saturday show that any controversy over the selection is apparently contained to a small segment of American society.

Overall, less than 10% of Americans end up saying that they disapprove of Warren's giving the prayer.

Bottom Line

News media accounts of negative reactions to president-elect Barack Obama's decision to select Rick Warren to deliver the Inaugural prayer appear to reflect more of the vocal positions of interest groups than an opinion that is shared by the majority of the American public.

Survey Methods

Results are based on telephone interviews with 1,046 national adults, aged 18 and older, conducted Jan. 16–17, 2009. For results based on the total sample of national adults, one can say with 95% confidence that the maximum margin of sampling error is ±3 percentage points.

Interviews are conducted with respondents on land-line telephones (for respondents with a land-line telephone) and cellular phones (for respondents who are cell-phone only).

In addition to sampling error, question wording and practical difficulties in conducting surveys can introduce error or bias into the findings of public opinion polls.

January 20, 2009

OPTIMISM ABOUNDS AS POWER CHANGES HANDS IN WASHINGTON

Public predicts brighter future for the country and success for Obama

by Lydia Saad, Gallup Poll Senior Editor

Americans' high hopes for the country under the Obama presidency are perhaps best represented by the new *USA Today*/Gallup poll finding that 72% of Americans think the country will be better off four years from now. Only 20% believe it will be worse off.

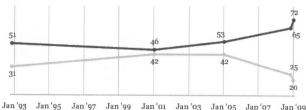

Do you think the country will be better off or worse off four years from now?

■ % Better off   % Worse off

Public optimism about where the country will stand after Barack Obama's first term as president is substantially higher in the Jan. 9–11 survey than was seen in advance of recent inaugural ceremonies. That includes George W. Bush's second turn at the presidential Bible in January 2005, when 53% of Americans said the country would be better off; 46% on the eve of Bush's first inauguration in 2001; and 51% immediately after Bill Clinton's election in 1992.

Optimism about the country's future has even expanded somewhat in the short time since Obama's election victory—72% of Americans currently say the country will be better off in four years vs. 65% just after the election—reinforcing the success Obama has had in maintaining public support during his presidential transition period.

Majority Expect Obama to Be Above Average

Today's relatively high level of optimism about the country may spring from sheer hopefulness on the part of Americans that the serious economic problems facing the country can't last. Indeed, while 92% of Democrats and 67% of independents foresee better times, 52% of Republicans do as well. However, there is also much evidence that it is tied directly to their faith in Obama.

Six in 10 Americans (62%) expect Obama to be an outstanding or above-average president while only 11% think he will be below average or poor. The worst most people say about him is that he will be "average," a view held by 25% of Americans.

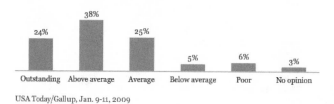

What kind of president do you think Barack Obama will be -- outstanding, above average, average, below average, or poor?

USA Today/Gallup, Jan. 9-11, 2009

Most Democrats and a solid majority of independents, compared with only 34% of Republicans, predict Obama will be above average or outstanding as president. However, most of the remaining Republicans expect Obama to be average rather than subpar.

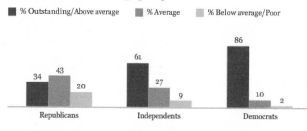

Forecast for Obama Presidency, by Party ID

■ % Outstanding/Above average   ■ % Average   ■ % Below average/Poor

USA Today/Gallup, Jan. 9-11, 2009

Not only are Americans' expectations for Obama high in an absolute sense, but they are higher than Gallup found for George W. Bush in January 2001, and for George H.W. Bush in January 1989—just before each became president. (Gallup did not ask the same question in reference to Clinton before his first inauguration in1993.)

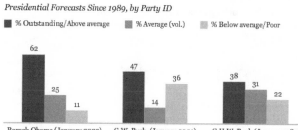

Presidential Forecasts Since 1989, by Party ID

■ % Outstanding/Above average   ■ % Average (vol.)   ■ % Below average/Poor

Additionally, the overwhelming majority of Americans, 80%, perceive Obama to be a "uniter" by nature (rather than a "divider"). This contrasts with 58% calling George W. Bush a "uniter" in 2001. Also, 66% expect the Obama administration to "create a new spirit of idealism" in the country, higher than the 57% saying this of the Clinton administration in 1993.

Presidential Qualities

Beyond these general views about Obama's presidency, most Americans express confidence that he can handle several specific aspects of the job of president.

Confidence in Obama to "work effectively with Congress to get things done" is particularly high. Nearly 9 in 10 Americans say they are confident he will do this, including 44% saying they are very confident. While 74% of Americans in January 2001 were confident in George W. Bush on this matter, only 27% were "very confident."

Obama also generates somewhat higher confidence than did Bush in his ability to "manage the executive branch effectively" (84% vs. 77%) and to "fulfill the proper role of the United States in world affairs" (80% vs. 72%).

Confidence levels in Obama to handle an international crisis and to prevent major scandals in his administration are similar to those initially seen for Bush. Obama lags Bush on only one dimension: using military force wisely.

Confidence in Obama's/Bush's Ability to Handle Various Issues as President

	Obama (January 2009)	Bush (January 2001)	Obama (January 2009)	Bush (January 2001)
	Total confident	Total confident	Very confident	Very confident
	%	%	%	%
Work effectively with Congress to get things done	89	74	44	27
Manage the executive branch effectively	84	77	44	33
Fulfill the proper role of the United States in world affairs	80	72	42	31
Defend U.S. interests abroad	75	--	37	--
Prevent major scandals in his administration	74	77	34	39
Handle an international crisis	73	71	34	32
Use military force wisely	71	78	34	41

Bottom Line

Americans' broad confidence that Obama will be a successful president only adds to the large body of polling evidence that Americans are investing an extraordinary degree of hope in his coming leadership. Since the election, Gallup has seen this in Obama's consistently high favorability and confidence ratings. It is also evident in Obama's top positioning on Gallup's Most Admired Man list in December—the first time since Dwight Eisenhower that a president-elect has won this distinction.

In its totality, Obama's extraordinary popularity seems proportionate to the challenges he faces entering office, and may in fact be essential to stirring public support to his side when he needs it in the days ahead.

Survey Methods

Results are based on telephone interviews with 1,013 national adults, aged 18 and older, conducted Jan. 9–11, 2009. For results based on the total sample of national adults, one can say with 95% confidence that the maximum margin of sampling error is ±3 percentage points.

Interviews are conducted with respondents on land-line telephones (for respondents with a land-line telephone) and cellular phones (for respondents who are cell-phone only).

In addition to sampling error, question wording and practical difficulties in conducting surveys can introduce error or bias into the findings of public opinion polls.

January 21, 2009

AMERICANS SEND NO CLEAR MANDATE ON GUANTANAMO BAY
Slightly more prefer keeping the prison open than prefer closing it, but 20% unsure

by Lymari Morales, Gallup Poll Staff Writer

With President Barack Obama already taking action relating to the U.S. prison Guantanamo Bay on his first full day in office, Americans are sending no clear mandate on the issue. Slightly more think the United States should not close the prison than say it should, 45% to 35%.

These views are similar to those expressed in 2007, at which time 33% favored closing the prison but 53% were opposed and 13%

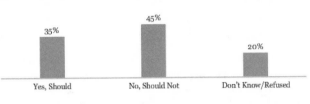

Do you think the United States should -- or should not -- close the prison at the Guantanamo Bay military base in Cuba?

■ Jan 16-17 2009

had no opinion. The major difference since that time is that slightly fewer now favor keeping the prison open (from 53% to 45%), and slightly more do not express an opinion (from 13% to 20%).

About 245 prisoners remain at the U.S. prison in Guantanamo Bay, Cuba, where at least 800 detainees have spent time since the Bush Administration began holding terrorist suspects there after 9/11. The Bush Administration contends the remaining prisoners are "the worst of the worst," but the long-term detentions there have become a symbol, in the United States and abroad, of U.S. mismanagement of the war on terrorism. The incoming Obama Administration has signaled it will swiftly make good on its campaign promise to close the prison, but Obama himself has said "it is more difficult than people realize." A recent Gallup Poll finds that closing Guantanamo is, in fact, not a top priority for Americans, only 32% of whom consider it "very important" that Obama fulfill his promise to do so, far fewer than say the same about other issues regarding healthcare, energy, and tax cuts. Now this additional question shows that a slight plurality favors keeping the prison open, although one out of five have no opinion on the issue. The poll also sheds light on the extent to which views on Guantanamo Bay break decisively down party lines. More than two-thirds of Republicans (69%) think the U.S. should keep the prison open, while more than half of Democrats (51%) think the prison should be closed.

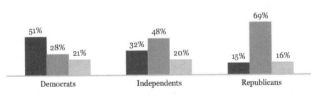

Do you think the United States should -- or should not -- close the prison at the Guantanamo Bay military base in Cuba?

■ Yes, Should ■ No, Should Not ■ Don't Know/Refused

A similar divide is evident by ideology. More than two-thirds of self-described liberals (68%) want to close the prison, while 61% of conservatives want to keep it open.

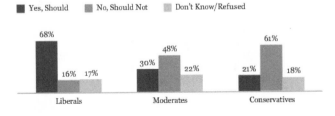

Do you think the United States should -- or should not -- close the prison at the Guantanamo Bay military base in Cuba?

■ Yes, Should ■ No, Should Not ■ Don't Know/Refused

Taken together, two conclusions can be made in terms of Americans' views on Guantanamo Bay. President Obama's most loyal supporters—Democrats and liberals—do lean decisively toward closing the U.S. prison there. But Americans overall do not express such a clear preference, and in fact are more likely to prefer keeping the prison open. While swift action to close the prison at Guantanamo Bay will draw a clear dividing line between the policies of the Bush Administration versus the Obama Administration, it is more likely to be well-received by Obama's most loyal base of support than by the broader cross-section of Americans who have generally given high marks to Obama's presidential decisions so far. If Obama does choose to close the prison, which these data suggest would go against public opinion, at least to an extent, it could provide an early test of how much Americans' high ratings of Obama to date will reflect the more controversial decisions Obama, as president, will now be forced to make.

Survey Methods

Results are based on telephone interviews with 1,046 national adults, aged 18 and older, conducted Jan. 16–17, 2009. For results based on the total sample of national adults, one can say with 95% confidence that the maximum margin of sampling error is ±3 percentage points.

Interviews are conducted with respondents on land-line telephones (for respondents with a land-line telephone) and cellular phones (for respondents who are cell-phone only).

In addition to sampling error, question wording and practical difficulties in conducting surveys can introduce error or bias into the findings of public opinion polls.

January 21, 2009

IN U.S., 60% TUNED IN TO INAUGURATION AS IT HAPPENED

Nearly half (46%) rate Obama's speech as excellent

by Lydia Saad, Gallup Poll Senior Editor

Six in 10 Americans tuned in live to the presidential inauguration ceremonies on Tuesday. Another 20% heard or read news reports of the event while 20% caught none of it.

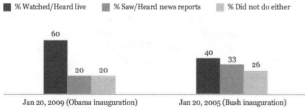

Which of the following applies to you -- you watched or listened to the inauguration ceremonies as they happened, you watched, listened to, or read news reports about the inauguration ceremonies, or you did not do either?

The live audience included 70% of nonworking Americans, but also 53% of those currently employed—suggesting that many workers either took the day off or had the opportunity to watch or hear the ceremonies at work.

Americans were clearly more interested in the inauguration of Barack Obama than they were in George W. Bush's second inauguration four years ago. In 2005, only 40% of Americans said they watched or heard the inaugural ceremonies live.

The greater attention paid to Obama's inaugural likely stems from the combination of his taking office for the first time, his being the first Democrat in eight years to assume the presidency, and the historic significance of the nation's installing its first African-American president.

High Praise for the Speech

There was considerable pressure on President Obama, known for his oratory skills, to deliver an impressive inauguration speech, and from Americans' perspective, he succeeded. Among those who saw or otherwise followed the inauguration on Tuesday, close to half—46%—say Obama's speech was "excellent." That compares with a 25% excellent rating for Bush's 2005 inauguration speech. Another 35% say Obama's speech was good, while only 15% consider it "just okay" or worse.

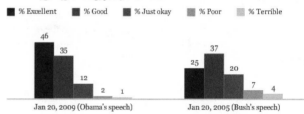

Based on what you have heard or read, how would you rate [Barack Obama's/George W. Bush's] inauguration speech? Would you rate it as -- excellent, good, just okay, poor, or terrible?

More broadly, 62% of Americans say the inauguration makes them feel more hopeful about the next four years. Only 11% say it makes them feel less hopeful.

Bush's inauguration was associated with far less optimism, as just 43% felt more hopeful about the country over his upcoming term while 25% felt less hopeful.

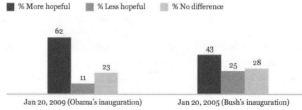

Based on what you have heard or read about today's inauguration, does it make you feel more hopeful about the next four years, less hopeful, or does it not make any difference?

Democratic Enthusiasm

Democrats show an extraordinarily high degree of enthusiasm around this year's inauguration, with 74% saying they watched or heard it live, 71% rating Obama's speech "excellent," and 91% reporting that the day's events made them feel more hopeful about the next four years.

While one might expect such positive reactions from the supporters of a president's own party, four years ago, only 48% of

Republicans watched Bush's inauguration live, 46% rated Bush's speech "excellent," and 77% felt more hopeful about the next four years as a result of the inauguration.

Partisan Groups' Reaction to Inauguration of President From Same Political Party, 2005 vs. 2009

■ Democrats' reaction to Obama's 2009 inauguration

▨ Republicans' reaction to Bush's 2005 inauguration

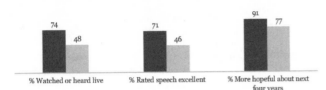

Today, while Republicans are decidedly less positive than are Democrats about the 2009 inauguration, few Republicans are negative in their reactions. Half of Republicans watched or heard the inauguration live. And while just 14% of Republicans who heard or saw Obama's speech rate it "excellent," another 41% consider it "good." Also, slightly more Republicans say they are more hopeful than less hopeful about the next four years, 31% vs. 27%.

By contrast, in 2005 just 33% of Democrats tuned in to the inauguration ceremonies, only 11% felt more hopeful about the next four years while 53% felt less hopeful, and a mere 3% rated Bush's speech "excellent."

Partisan Groups' Reaction to Inauguration of President From Opposing Political Party, 2005 vs. 2009

■ Republicans' reaction to Obama's 2009 inauguration

▨ Democrats' reaction to Bush's 2005 inauguration

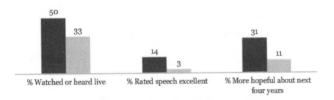

Independents generally fall between the two partisan groups in their reactions to this year's inauguration, although they are no more likely than Republicans to report having tuned in live. Fifty-two percent of independents say they watched or heard the inauguration ceremony as it happened, 36% rate Obama's speech "excellent," and 57% are more hopeful about the future.

Bottom Line

Bush won re-election in 2004 with nearly 51% of the national popular vote, not much lower than the nearly 53% for Obama in 2008. Nevertheless, public reaction to Obama's swearing-in ceremony is altogether different than it was to Bush's in 2005, with Obama's ceremony garnering heavy viewership/listenership, highly positive reviews for Obama's speech, and broad optimism among Americans about the next four years.

The reason may be twofold. Obama enters office as an empty vessel, someone who has not yet had to make the kind of big policy

Reaction to Obama Inauguration, by Party ID

■ Democrats ▨ Independents ▨ Republicans

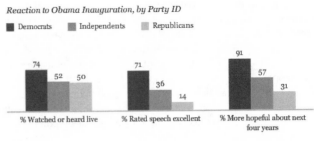

Jan. 20, 2009

decisions that inevitably bring public criticism. This may explain the difference between Republicans' relatively positive reviews of Obama today compared with Democrats' negative reviews of Bush four years ago. At the same time, the degree of enthusiasm Obama engenders from Democrats nationwide is remarkable even by partisan standards. Although the vast majority of Republicans approved of the job Bush was doing as president in January 2005, they showed nowhere near the level of enthusiasm for his second inaugural as Democrats show today for Obama's inaugural. Obama enjoys a special relationship with his Democratic base, and it will be interesting to see how long it endures.

Survey Methods

Results are based on telephone interviews with 1,012 national adults, aged 18 and older, conducted Jan. 20, 2009. For results based on the total sample of national adults, one can say with 95% confidence that the maximum margin of sampling error is ±3 percentage points.

Interviews are conducted with respondents on land-line telephones (for respondents with a land-line telephone) and cellular phones (for respondents who are cell-phone only).

In addition to sampling error, question wording and practical difficulties in conducting surveys can introduce error or bias into the findings of public opinion polls.

January 23, 2009
DEMOCRATS' 2008 ADVANTAGE IN PARTY ID LARGEST SINCE '83
An average of 36% of Americans identified as Democrats last year

by Jeffrey M. Jones, Gallup Poll Managing Editor

An average of 36% of Americans identified themselves as Democrats and 28% as Republicans in 2008. That eight-point advantage is the largest for the Democratic Party since Gallup began regularly conducting its polls by telephone in 1988.

Those data are based on the average party identification in Gallup's 2008 stand-alone polls, consisting of more than 30,000 interviews.

The year-by-year trend shows that Democrats have gained ground against Republicans in each of the last five years, going from a deficit of two points in 2003 to the most recent eight-point advantage.

Additionally, the 36% of Americans who identified as Democrats last year matches the high point in Democratic identification

Democratic Advantage in Party Identification, 1988-2008
Percentage of self-described Democrats minus percentage of self-described Republicans, in percentage points

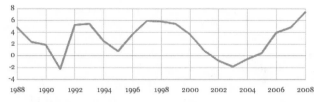

since 1988, when it was also 36%. But since fewer Americans identified as Republicans last year (28%) than in 1988 (31%), the Democratic advantage was larger in 2008.

Party Identification Yearly Averages, Gallup Polls, 1988-2008
■ % Republican ▦ % Democrat

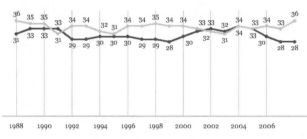

One would have to go back to 1983, when Democrats held a decisive 19-point advantage in party identification (43% to 24%), to find a significantly better showing for the Democratic Party in any Gallup polling. In 1984, the year Ronald Reagan was re-elected, the Democratic-Republican gap narrowed considerably. Since then, neither party has enjoyed a double-digit advantage in any year, though Democrats have held an advantage in almost all of these years.

Democratic Support Above Majority Level

A second measure of party support—which adds independents who say they "lean" toward one party or the other into that party's total—also shows 2008 to have been a banner year for the Democratic Party. Last year, 52% of Americans identified as Democrats or said they leaned to the Democratic Party, compared with 40% who identified with or leaned to the Republican Party. That is the best showing for the Democrats—in terms of both the percentage of Democratic supporters and their advantage over Republicans—since Gallup began regularly tracking this measure of party support in 1991.

"Leaned" Party Identification Yearly Averages, Gallup Polls, 1991-2008
■ % Republican/Lean Republican ▦ % Democrat/Lean Democrat

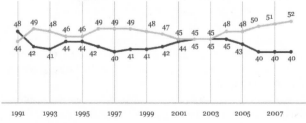

This marks the third successive year that a majority of Americans either identified as Democrats or leaned to that party, something neither party accomplished from 1991 through 2005.

Implications

The Democratic Party is currently riding a winning streak in party affiliation, which has manifested itself in the party's decisive victories in the 2006 and 2008 elections. Barack Obama's election and popularity will surely help to advance the Democratic policy agenda—something the party had difficulty doing the last two years with a narrow Senate majority and George W. Bush in the White House.

It is not clear at this point whether the Democratic Party can return to the days when it enjoyed consistent double-digit advantages in party identification from the late 1950s through the early 1980s. The challenge for the party is to keep the positive momentum going while governing with total control of the legislative and executive branches of government. Clearly, much of the Democratic momentum in recent years has been the result of dissatisfaction with the way the Republicans were governing the nation. The Republicans, in turn, will attempt to regroup as the minority party and win back some of the support they have lost in recent years.

Survey Methods

Results are based on averages from all 2008 Gallup stand-alone polls in 2008, consisting of more than 30,000 interviews with national adults, aged 18 and older. For this total number of interviews, one can say with 95% confidence that the maximum margin of sampling error is ±1 percentage point.

Interviews are conducted with respondents on land-line telephones (for respondents with a land-line telephone) and cellular phones (for respondents who are cell-phone only).

In addition to sampling error, question wording and practical difficulties in conducting surveys can introduce error or bias into the findings of public opinion polls.

January 24, 2009
OBAMA STARTS WITH 68% JOB APPROVAL
One of the better initial ratings of post-World War II presidents

by Lydia Saad, Gallup Poll Senior Editor

In the first Gallup Poll job approval rating of his administration, President Barack Obama receives a 68% approval rating from Americans.

Do you approve or disapprove of the way Barack Obama is handling his job as president?

Jan. 21-23, 2009
Gallup Poll Daily tracking

The survey was conducted from Wednesday through Friday, Jan. 21–23, spanning Obama's first three full days on the job. Only 12% of Americans disapprove of how he has performed thus far, while 21% have no opinion.

Obama's 68% approval score is on the high end of the range of initial job approval ratings Gallup has recorded for the previous eight presidents who were elected to their first term. The low percentage of Americans disapproving of his performance is fairly typical for new presidents—although Bill Clinton and George W. Bush both started with much higher public disapproval.

A more thorough discussion of Obama's initial job approval ratings and the historical context for them will be published on gallup.com on Monday, Jan. 26.

Gallup is tracking Obama's job approval rating daily, and will be reporting it daily on gallup.com on the basis of three-day rolling averages.

Survey Methods

Results are based on telephone interviews with 1,591 national adults, aged 18 and older, conducted Jan. 21–23, 2009. For results based on the total sample of national adults, one can say with 95% confidence that the maximum margin of sampling error is ±3 percentage points.

Interviews are conducted with respondents on land-line telephones (for respondents with a land-line telephone) and cellular phones (for respondents who are cell-phone only).

In addition to sampling error, question wording and practical difficulties in conducting surveys can introduce error or bias into the findings of public opinion polls.

January 26, 2009
OBAMA'S INITIAL APPROVAL RATINGS IN HISTORICAL CONTEXT
Rank among the best for a newly elected president since World War II

by Jeffrey M. Jones, Gallup Poll Managing Editor

With a 69% job approval rating in the latest Gallup Poll Daily update, Barack Obama continues a strong start to his presidency. That rating follows his initial approval rating of 68%—based on Jan. 21–23 polling and reported Saturday—and ranks him near the top of the list of presidents elected after World War II.

Presidents' Initial Job Approval Ratings in Gallup Polls

President	Dates of first poll	% Approval	% Disapproval	% No opinion
Eisenhower	53 Feb 1-5	68	7	25
Kennedy	61 Feb 10-15	72	6	22
Nixon	69 Jan 23-28	59	5	36
Carter	77 Feb 4-7	66	8	26
Reagan	81 Jan 30-Feb 2	51	13	36
Bush	89 Jan 24-26	51	6	43
Clinton	93 Jan 24-26	58	20	22
Bush	01 Feb 1-4	57	25	18
Obama	09 Jan 21-23	68	12	21

Includes presidents elected to first term in office

In fact, only John Kennedy had a higher initial approval rating—72% in 1961—though Dwight Eisenhower and Jimmy Carter also had ratings in the mid- to high 60s. But Gallup did not measure those three presidents' initial ratings until early February, and new presidents' approval ratings typically increase in the first few months of their presidencies. Thus, Obama's initial approval rating of 68% looks more impressive compared to the average 55% approval rating for the four presidents whose first ratings were measured in January after their inaugurations.

In general, the American public rates all new presidents positively—all have received majority approval in their debut ratings—though Obama is clearly near the top of the list. The three presidents who took office after the death or resignation of their predecessors tended to start out with even greater public support, as the nation rallied around the new chief executive in times of crisis. These include Harry Truman in 1945 with an 87% approval rating, Lyndon Johnson with 78% in 1963, and Gerald Ford with 71% in 1974.

Obama's 12% disapproval in Jan. 21–23 polling is low on an absolute basis, but does fall on the high end of what Gallup has measured historically, as the majority of post-World War II presidents have begun their terms with disapproval ratings below 10%. But Obama's higher-than-average first disapproval rating may simply reflect the passing of a bygone political era, as four of the last five presidents (including Obama) have had disapproval ratings above 10% in Gallup's first measurement. The only exception is the elder George Bush in 1989.

However, Obama fares significantly better on this count than his two immediate predecessors—Bill Clinton (20% disapproval) and George W. Bush (25%). Both started with relatively high opposition from supporters of the other political party—41% of Republicans disapproved of the job Clinton was doing in early 1993, and, in early February 2001, 46% of Democrats disapproved of the job George W. Bush was doing as president. By comparison, a relatively low 30% of Republicans disapprove of Obama.

In fact, Republicans are more likely to approve than disapprove of Obama's performance thus far, according to an average of the first four days of Gallup tracking on Obama job approval. More than 6 in 10 independents, and nearly 9 in 10 Democrats, approve.

Barack Obama's Job Approval Ratings, by Party Affiliation

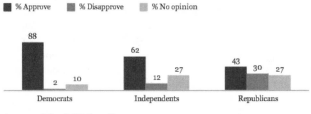

Jan. 21-24 Gallup Poll Daily tracking

At the outset of his presidency, Obama has majority approval from all ideological groups, including 83% of self-identified liberals, 75% of moderates, and 52% of conservatives.

In addition to liberals and Democrats, two of the key groups from Obama's winning electoral coalition—young adults (79% of 18- to 29-year-olds) and nonwhites (78%)—give him especially positive initial evaluations.

And, consistent with the pattern of last year's election campaign, women (71%) are more positive toward Obama than are men (64%).

Survey Methods

Results are based on telephone interviews with 1,614 national adults, aged 18 and older, conducted Jan. 22–24, 2009, and 1,591 national adults, aged 18 and older, conducted Jan. 21–23, 2009. For results based on these total samples of national adults, one can say with 95% confidence that the maximum margin of sampling error is ±3 percentage points.

Interviews are conducted with respondents on land-line telephones (for respondents with a land-line telephone) and cellular phones (for respondents who are cell-phone only).

In addition to sampling error, question wording and practical difficulties in conducting surveys can introduce error or bias into the findings of public opinion polls.

January 26, 2009
JANUARY UPTICK IN U.S. INVESTORS' OPTIMISM

Change of administrations and stimulus efforts making investors slightly less pessimistic

by Dennis Jacobe, Gallup Chief Economist

American investors remain highly pessimistic about the overall U.S. investment climate in January, with the Gallup Index of Investor Optimism now at -40. But just as Gallup has found among consumers, investors are slightly less pessimistic this month than they were in December (-49).

Gallup Index of Investor Optimism, December 2007-January 2009

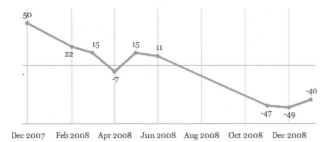

Slight Improvement Along Both Dimensions

Gallup's Index of Investor Optimism—based on a survey of those having $10,000 or more of investable assets—is designed to reflect American investors' views of the investment climate. Econometric analysis has shown that Gallup's Index is a somewhat better predictor of the future direction of the U.S. economy than traditional consumer confidence measures. The Index peaked in January 2000 at 178—prior to the bursting of the dot-com bubble. Before last year, the low for the Index was 5 in March 2003, reflecting investor concerns at the outset of the Iraq war. The new low of -49, as noted, was registered in December 2008.

January's results show investors to be slightly less pessimistic than they were late last year along both dimensions of the Index.

Investors remain highly negative about the economic outlook for the next 12 months, with the Economic Dimension of the Index at -59—although this is slightly better than December's -64. At the same time, investors remain somewhat positive about their personal portfolios, with the Personal Dimension at +19—up from +15 in December.

Economic Dimension, Gallup Index of Investor Optimism

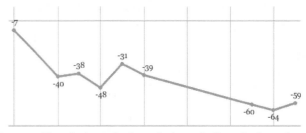

Personal Dimension, Gallup Index of Investor Optimism

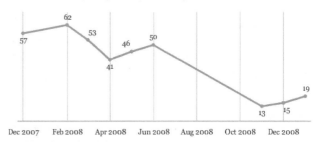

Slight Obama Bounce in Investor Perceptions

The big money on Wall Street seems less than enthusiastic about the change in power in Washington, D.C., and the new Obama economic team, with the Dow down about 8% so far this year. In sharp contrast, Gallup's Index of Investor Optimism suggests that U.S. investors as a group are a little *less* pessimistic this January than they were during the last couple of months of 2008. In this regard, investors seem to share the modest bounce in confidence among all Americans reflected by Gallup's other attitudinal economic measures.

Given the country's dreadful economic performance during the last year of the Bush economic team, it is not hard to see how a change in teams—or, for that matter, the historic inauguration of last week—could inspire at least a marginal improvement in investor and consumer confidence. In fact, it seems likely that the Conference Board will report a slight improvement in its Consumer Confidence Index on Tuesday morning.

Still, the fact that both investors and consumers remain highly pessimistic about the future course of the U.S. economy illustrates the major confidence problem that exists at this time. Consumers are worried about the overall economy, fearful about their jobs, and pulling back from spending, particularly as far as big-ticket items are concerned. The resulting downward economic spiral characterized by increasing unemployment and increasing fear has just begun to unfold.

The Federal Reserve is making unprecedented efforts to get credit flowing but the credit crunch persists. Congress is debating an unprecedented fiscal stimulus plan, but old-time politics seems to dominate this legislative effort, with Democrats arguing that all spending is "stimulative" and Republicans countering that only tax cuts will work.

The real economic challenge facing the new Obama administration is not just to pass a new fiscal stimulus plan, but to adopt a plan that will begin restoring investor and consumer confidence in the U.S. economy in the months ahead. And this requires something of a consensus among the nation's business and political leaders.

It seems like this should be possible when the legislation involved is expected to total somewhere between $800 billion and $1 trillion. Still, political calculus sometimes conflicts with both good economic policy and economic consensus building. Regardless, Gallup's daily economic measures will let Americans know quickly whether the president's and Congress' efforts are succeeding in building investor and consumer confidence.

Survey Methods

Gallup Poll Daily interviewing includes no fewer than 1,000 U.S. adults nationwide each day during 2008. The Index of Investor Optimism results are based on questions asked of 1,000 or more investors over a three-day period each month Jan. 16–18, 2009, and Dec. 16–18, Nov. 24–26, June 3–6, April 25–28, March 28–31, and Feb. 28–March 2, 2008. For results based on these samples, the maximum margin of sampling error is ±3 percentage points.

Results for May are based on the Gallup Panel study and are based on telephone interviews with 576 national adults, aged 18 and older, conducted May 19–21, 2008. Gallup Panel members are recruited through random selection methods. The panel is weighted so that it is demographically representative of the U.S. adult population. For results based on this sample, one can say with 95% confidence that the maximum margin of sampling error is ±5 percentage points.

For investor results prior to 2008, telephone interviews were conducted with at least 800 investors, aged 18 and older, and having at least $10,000 of investable assets. For the total sample of investors in these surveys, one can say with 95% confidence that the maximum margin of sampling error is ± 4 percentage points.

In addition to sampling error, question wording and practical difficulties in conducting surveys can introduce error or bias into the findings of public opinion polls.

January 27, 2009
THURSDAY'S JOBLESS CLAIMS LIKELY DOWN SLIGHTLY
Gallup's hiring measure suggests weekly jobless claims will be below last week's 589,000

by Dennis Jacobe, Gallup Chief Economist

U.S. employees' perceptions of the job situation at their companies remain negative, though a little less so last week than the week before, with Gallup's hiring measure at -4 for the week ending Jan. 24—slightly better than the prior week's -6. In turn, this suggests that the Labor Department will likely report Thursday that seasonally adjusted weekly jobless claims were down from last week's 589,000, but still far exceeded the 527,000 reported just two weeks ago.

Jobless Claims Likely to Be Down, but Still High

Even as major U.S. companies continue to announce major layoffs, a number of variables make it hard to predict the exact number of

Net New Hiring Activity, Weekly Average
% of companies hiring minus % letting people go, in percentage points

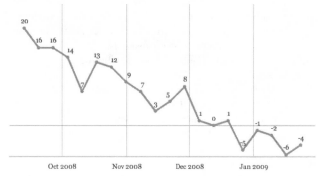

weekly jobless claims the Labor Department will report each Thursday. There is often a lag between layoff announcements and their realization. Further, the surge in claims last week may have reflected a balancing of the understated numbers reported during the holidays. Regardless, Gallup's new hiring measure suggests the job market continues to weaken even if Thursday's jobless claims are not as bad as last week's report.

In addition to the weekly net hiring estimate, Gallup also reports a four-week average. Gallup's four-week average jobless claims measure is not only more stable but is a better predictor of actual unemployment levels in the marketplace. The roll off of the artificially low weekly jobless claims numbers of the holiday period continues to distort the government's seasonally adjusted four-week average jobless claims reports a bit. As a result, Thursday's government report of the seasonally adjusted four-week average jobless claims is likely to show a substantial increase even as Gallup's weekly average of new hiring would indicate a small decline.

Net New Hiring Activity, Four-Week Rolling Trend
% of companies hiring minus % letting people go, in percentage points

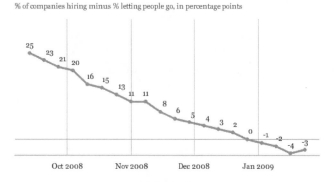

Jobs Losses as a Leading Indicator

Normally, jobs are seen as essentially a trailing indicator of economic performance. As the economy slows and after some lag, people lose their jobs, confirming the economic downturn. However, in the unfolding recession, job losses may be something of a leading indicator—at least, in the job-driven phase of the current recession.

As job losses continue to mount, Americans' confidence in their own future employment will continue to decline, and the pullback in spending—particularly on big-ticket items—will continue. When jobs begin to stabilize and increase, consumer confidence and spending are likely to improve. This is why it is essential that the stimulus plan create jobs—not just expand the social safety net.

In this regard, the jobs situation seems likely to continue deteriorating during the weeks ahead. The poor holiday sales mean that many retailers and small businesses are likely to need more financing than usual to get through the normally slow sales period at the beginning of the year. However, this essential financing may not be available, given the current financial crisis and associated credit crunch.

A lack of retail and small-business financing at this critical time could lead to numerous additional business closings. In turn, this would add to the already serious jobs crisis. It will be important to see whether the Federal Reserve has plans to support these financing needs when the Federal Open Market Committee reports on the results of its current meeting Wednesday afternoon. This is also an area where the banking bailout (TARP) funds could help preserve jobs.

Over the weeks and months ahead, jobs are likely to become an even bigger issue. As policy-makers respond, it is essential that they keep in mind that the private sector and particularly small business create "real" jobs. The federal government needs to facilitate that private-sector job creation—not try to replace it.

Survey Methods

Using weekly results for 2008, Gallup's analysis suggests that its hiring measure has a better than 7-in-10 probability of correctly projecting the direction of weekly jobless claims and a better than 8-in-10 probability of predicting the direction of the four-week average of jobless claims.

Gallup's hiring measure is based on aggregated interviews with a nationally representative sample of more than 2,000 U.S. workers each week. Gallup asks current full- and part-time employees whether their employers are hiring new people and expanding the size of their workforces, not changing the size of their workforces, or letting people go and reducing the size of their workforces. Gallup's hiring measure is computed by subtracting the "letting go and reducing" percentage from the "hiring and expanding" percentage. The assumption is that employees across the country have a good feel for what's happening in their companies, and that these insider perceptions can yield a meaningful indication of the nation's job situation.

Gallup's Net New Hiring Activity measure was initiated in January 2008. It is an effort to assess U.S. job creation or elimination based on the self-reports of more than 2,000 individual employees aggregated each week about hiring and firing activity at their workplaces. For results based on these samples, the maximum margin of sampling error is ±3 percentage points.

Interviews are conducted with respondents on land-line telephones (for respondents with a land-line telephone) and cellular phones (for respondents who are cell-phone only).

In addition to sampling error, question wording and practical difficulties in conducting surveys can introduce error or bias into the findings of public opinion polls.

January 28, 2009

STATE OF THE STATES: POLITICAL PARTY AFFILIATION

Rhode Island, Massachusetts, Hawaii, and District of Columbia are most Democratic

by Jeffrey M. Jones, Gallup Poll Managing Editor

This is the first in a four-part series on the "State of the States" to be released this week on Gallup.com. The series examines state-by-state differences in party affiliation, religiosity, consumer confidence, and employer hiring and letting go, based on Gallup Poll Daily tracking data collected throughout 2008.

An analysis of Gallup Poll Daily tracking data from 2008 finds Rhode Island, Massachusetts, and Hawaii to be the most Democratic states in the nation, along with the District of Columbia. Utah and Wyoming are the most Republican states.

Top 10 Democratic States		Top 10 Republican States	
State	Democratic advantage	State	Democratic advantage
	Pct. pts.		
District of Columbia	75		Pct. pts.
Rhode Island	37	Utah	-23
Massachusetts	34	Wyoming	-20
Hawaii	34	Idaho	-15
Vermont	33	Alaska	-11
New York	27	Nebraska	-7
Connecticut	26	Kansas	-2
Maryland	26	Alabama	-1
Illinois	24	Arizona	0
Delaware	23	South Carolina	0
		Three tied at	1

Gallup Poll Daily tracking

Gallup Poll Daily tracking

In 2008, Gallup interviewed more than 350,000 U.S. adults as part of Gallup Poll Daily tracking. That includes interviews with 1,000 or more residents of every U.S. state except Wyoming (885) and North Dakota (953), as well as the District of Columbia (689). There were more than 15,000 interviews conducted with residents of California, New York, Pennsylvania, Texas, and Florida.

This large data set provides the unique ability to give reliable estimates of state-level characteristics for 2008. Each sample of state residents was weighted by demographic characteristics to ensure it is representative of the state's population.

In order to rank the states on partisanship, Gallup analyzes "leaned" party identification by state. This measure adds partisan-leaning independents to the percentage who identify with either of the parties. Thus, the Republican total includes Republican identifiers and independents who lean Republican, and the Democratic total likewise includes Democratic identifiers and independents who lean Democratic.

This helps makes the state data more comparable because the percentage who identify as political independents varies greatly by state, from a low of 25% in the District of Columbia to a high of 53% in Rhode Island.

The accompanying map shows party strength by state for 2008, ranging from states that can be considered solidly Democratic (a Democratic advantage in party identification of 10 percentage points or more) to those that can be considered solidly Republican (a Republican advantage in party identification of 10 percentage points or more). States in which the partisan advantage is less than 5 points in either direction are considered "competitive."

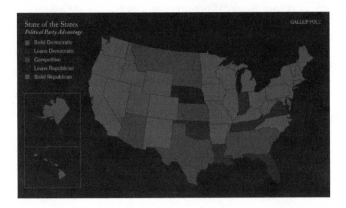

What is immediately clear from the map is that residents of the United States were very Democratic in their political orientation last year. In fact, Gallup has earlier reported that a majority of Americans nationwide said they identified with or leaned to the Democratic Party in 2008.

All told, 29 states and the District of Columbia had Democratic party affiliation advantages of 10 points or greater last year. This includes all of the states in the Northeast, and all but Indiana in the Great Lakes region. There are even several Southern states in this grouping, including Arkansas, North Carolina, and Kentucky.

An additional six states had Democratic advantages ranging between 5 and 9 points.

In contrast, only five states had solid or leaning Republican orientations in 2008, with Utah, Wyoming, Idaho, and Alaska in the former group, and Nebraska in the latter.

The most balanced political states in 2008 were Texas (+2 Democratic), South Dakota (+1), Mississippi (+1), North Dakota (+1), South Carolina (even), Arizona (even), Alabama (+1 Republican), and Kansas (+2 Republican).

Relation to 2008 Election Outcome

Given that most states had a Democratic advantage in party affiliation last year, to some degree it can be argued that Barack Obama could have won many more electoral votes than he did. In fact, Obama won 28 states (plus the District of Columbia) to John McCain's 22 in the 2008 election.

There are several reasons for possible disparities between the party affiliation data and the voting outcomes in a given state. First, turnout has typically been an equalizer in U.S. electoral politics because Democrats almost always have an advantage in identification, but Republicans have been competitive in national and state elections over the last three decades because Republicans are usually more likely than Democrats to vote. Second, one's partisan leaning is not a perfect predictor of voting in a presidential election, in which candidate-specific characteristics can influence a voter's choice. Third, the party affiliation data reported here cover all of 2008, while presidential election voting was limited to Nov. 4 or the weeks leading up to it.

But the rank-ordering of the states on the Democratic-to-Republican continuum generally follows the election results quite closely— Obama won 22 of the 23 most Democratic states (West Virginia being the only exception), and McCain won the 17 most Republican states.

Virginia, Florida, and Indiana (all with +9 Democratic partisanship advantages) are arguably the most impressive wins for Obama, since they were the least Democratic states he won. McCain managed to win West Virginia, which had a 19-point Democratic advantage, as well as three other solidly Democratic states—Kentucky (+13), Arkansas (+12), and Missouri (+11). McCain also swept the states that had narrow Democratic advantages of less than five points.

2008 Partisanship and Presidential Election Winner, by State

	Dem-Rep gap	2008 winner
	Pct. pts.	
District of Columbia	75	Obama
Rhode Island	37	Obama
Massachusetts	34	Obama
Hawaii	34	Obama
Vermont	33	Obama
New York	27	Obama
Connecticut	26	Obama
Maryland	26	Obama
Illinois	24	Obama
Delaware	23	Obama
Maine	19	Obama
California	19	Obama
New Jersey	19	Obama
West Virginia	19	McCain
Iowa	18	Obama
Wisconsin	18	Obama
Ohio	18	Obama
Michigan	17	Obama
Oregon	17	Obama
Washington	17	Obama
Pennsylvania	16	Obama
Minnesota	15	Obama
New Mexico	14	Obama
Kentucky	13	McCain
New Hampshire	13	Obama
Arkansas	12	McCain
Nevada	11	Obama
Missouri	11	McCain
Colorado	11	Obama
North Carolina	11	Obama
Louisiana	9	McCain
Indiana	9	Obama
Florida	9	Obama
Virginia	9	Obama
Oklahoma	6	McCain
Tennessee	5	McCain
Montana	4	McCain
Georgia	4	McCain
Texas	2	McCain
South Dakota	1	McCain
Mississippi	1	McCain
North Dakota	1	McCain
South Carolina	0	McCain
Arizona	0	McCain
Alabama	-1	McCain
Kansas	-2	McCain
Nebraska	-7	McCain
Alaska	-11	McCain
Idaho	-15	McCain
Wyoming	-20	McCain
Utah	-23	McCain

Implications

The political landscape of the United States has clearly shifted in the Democratic direction, and in most states, a greater proportion of state residents identified as Democrats or said they leaned to the Democratic Party in 2008 than identified as Republicans or leaned Republican.

As recently as 2002, a majority of states were Republican in orientation. By 2005, movement in the Democratic direction was becoming apparent, and this continued in 2006. That dramatic turn-around is clearly an outgrowth of Americans' dissatisfaction with the way the Republicans (in particular, President George W. Bush) governed the country.

With Democratic support at the national level the highest in more than two decades and growing each of the last five years, Republican prospects for significant gains in power in the near term do not appear great. But the recent data do show that party support can change rather dramatically in a relatively short period of time.

Survey Methods

Results are based on telephone interviews with 355,334 national adults, aged 18 and older, conducted in 2008 as part of Gallup Poll Daily tracking. For results based on the total sample of national adults, one can say with 95% confidence that the maximum margin of sampling error is ±1 percentage point.

The margin of sampling error for most states is ±1 percentage point, but is as high as ±4 percentage points for the District of Columbia, Wyoming, and North Dakota.

Interviews are conducted with respondents on land-line telephones (for respondents with a land-line telephone) and cellular phones (for respondents who are cell-phone only).

In addition to sampling error, question wording and practical difficulties in conducting surveys can introduce error or bias into the findings of public opinion polls.

Party Identification by State, 2008
Gallup Poll Daily tracking

	% Democrat/ Lean Democrat	% Republican/ Lean Republican	Dem-Rep gap (pct. pts.)	Number of interviews
District of Columbia	84.1	8.7	75	689
Rhode Island	60.4	23.8	37	1,526
Massachusetts	60.3	26.3	34	8,750
Hawaii	60	26.2	34	1,146
Vermont	58.9	26.2	33	1,446
New York	57.2	30.2	27	21,398
Connecticut	56.7	30.4	26	4,901
Maryland	58.2	31.9	26	6,397
Illinois	55.9	31.6	24	12,583
Delaware	56	32.8	23	1,019
Maine	53.1	33.7	19	2,938
California	52.2	32.8	19	37,098
New Jersey	53.2	34.1	19	10,138
West Virginia	53.8	35	19	2,618
Iowa	52.5	34.4	18	4,091
Wisconsin	52.3	34.5	18	7,827
Ohio	52.7	35	18	13,850
Michigan	51.1	34	17	10,662
Oregon	52	35.2	17	6,077
Washington	50.9	34.1	17	9,546
Pennsylvania	52.9	37.1	16	21,457
Minnesota	50.8	35.7	15	7,075
New Mexico	49.9	36.1	14	2,532
Kentucky	51.6	38.1	13	5,441
New Hampshire	49.3	36.1	13	2,096
Arkansas	49.1	36.6	12	3,577
Nevada	49.1	37.8	11	2,690
Missouri	48.8	37.9	11	7,904
Colorado	48.8	38.2	11	6,611
North Carolina	49.2	38.5	11	11,092
Louisiana	48.5	39.1	9	4,109
Indiana	47.2	37.9	9	8,135
Florida	48.2	39	9	18,543
Virginia	47.5	38.5	9	9,386
Oklahoma	47.5	41.9	6	5,027
Tennessee	45.7	40.7	5	7,732
Montana	44.4	40.5	4	1,778
Georgia	45.4	41.8	4	9,269
Texas	43.4	41	2	19,415
South Dakota	45.3	44	1	1,076
Mississippi	45.1	44	1	2,968
North Dakota	41.7	41.1	1	953
South Carolina	43.5	43.4	0	4,792
Arizona	42.8	43.2	0	7,660
Alabama	43.9	44.7	-1	5,499
Kansas	41.4	43.4	-2	3,628
Nebraska	40.7	47.3	-7	2,434
Alaska	36.6	47.2	-11	1,262
Idaho	34.6	49.9	-15	2,252
Wyoming	34.5	54.5	-20	885
Utah	32.4	55.1	-23	3,356

January 28, 2009
IN U.S., SLIM MAJORITY SUPPORTS ECONOMIC STIMULUS PLAN
Issue is highly charged along partisan lines

by Lydia Saad, Gallup Poll Senior Editor

As President Barack Obama tries to win over reluctant Republicans on his economic stimulus plan, a slim majority of the American public wants to see Congress pass the roughly $800 billion package of new government spending and tax breaks. According to Gallup Poll Daily tracking on Tuesday, 52% of the nation's adults are in favor of Congress passing the plan and 37% are opposed, while 11% have no opinion.

Lobbying for and against the bill has intensified in recent weeks, led by Obama, himself, appearing on Capitol Hill to argue for it, as conservative media personalities offer up blistering critiques. Republican leaders in Congress have mostly stayed on the sidelines.

Despite all the focus on the plan, public opinion on the subject is virtually identical to where it stood three weeks ago. A Gallup Poll conducted Jan. 6–7 found 53% of Americans in favor of Congress passing a major economic stimulus program (then estimated at $775 billion) while 36% were opposed.

Current attitudes about the plan remain strongly partisan. Nearly three in four Democrats (73%) favor its passage while 59% of Republicans are opposed. Political independents are closely split, with 46% in favor and 40% opposed—not an extraordinary level of support for the plan among the political center.

Implications

Although the stimulus package is expected to pass the U.S. House of Representatives with little difficulty, Obama continues to seek

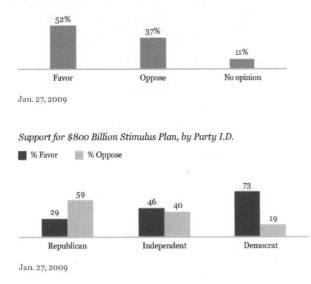

As you may know, Congress is considering a new economic stimulus package of at least 800 billion dollars. Do you favor or oppose Congress passing this legislation?

Favor 52%
Oppose 37%
No opinion 11%

Jan. 27, 2009

Support for $800 Billion Stimulus Plan, by Party I.D.

■ % Favor   ■ % Oppose

Republican: 29 / 59
Independent: 46 / 40
Democrat: 73 / 19

Jan. 27, 2009

Republican support as it moves to the Senate. Without that bipartisan buy in—not just in Congress, but from American citizens—Obama could pay a heavier price, long term, if the stimulus spending is not ultimately perceived as successful.

Although former President George W. Bush enjoyed high overall job approval ratings at the time he first sent U.S. troops to Iraq in 2003 (and had majority support for the decision to begin the war), that decision provoked a significant partisan breach that ultimately led to the downfall of his popularity. While Obama doesn't need Republicans' support to pass this plan, he clearly sees the benefit in attempting to maintain GOP goodwill toward his presidency.

Survey Methods

Results are based on telephone interviews with 1,053 national adults, aged 18 and older, conducted Jan. 27, 2009. For results based on the total sample of national adults, one can say with 95% confidence that the maximum margin of sampling error is ±3 percentage points.

Interviews are conducted with respondents on land-line telephones (for respondents with a land-line telephone) and cellular phones (for respondents who are cell-phone only).

In addition to sampling error, question wording and practical difficulties in conducting surveys can introduce error or bias into the findings of public opinion polls.

January 28, 2009
STATE OF THE STATES: IMPORTANCE OF RELIGION
Overall, 65% of Americans say religion is an important part of their daily lives

by Frank Newport, Gallup Poll Editor in Chief

This is the second in a four-part series on the "State of the States" being released this week on Gallup.com. The series examines state-

by-state differences in party affiliation, religiosity, consumer confidence, and employer hiring and letting go, based on Gallup Poll Daily tracking data collected throughout 2008.

An analysis of more than 350,000 interviews conducted by Gallup in 2008 finds Mississippi, Alabama, South Carolina, Tennessee, Louisiana, and Arkansas to be the most religious states in the nation. Vermont, New Hampshire, Maine, and Massachusetts are the least religious states.

Top 10 Most Religious States	
Is religion an important part of your daily life?	
State	**% Yes**
Mississippi	85
Alabama	82
South Carolina	80
Tennessee	79
Louisiana	78
Arkansas	78
Georgia	76
North Carolina	76
Oklahoma	75
Kentucky (tie)	74
Texas (tie)	74

Gallup Poll Daily tracking

Top 10 Least Religious States	
Is religion an important part of your daily life?	
State	**% Yes**
Vermont	42
New Hampshire	46
Maine	48
Massachusetts	48
Alaska	51
Washington	52
Oregon	53
Rhode Island	53
Nevada	54
Connecticut	55

Gallup Poll Daily tracking

The large data set of interviews conducted as part of the Gallup Poll Daily tracking program in 2008 provides uniquely reliable estimates of state-level characteristics. Each sample of state residents was weighted by demographic characteristics to ensure it is representative of the state's population.

There are a number of ways to measure the relative religiosity of population segments. For the current ranking, Gallup uses the responses to a straightforward question that asks: "Is religion an important part of your daily life?" The rankings are based on the percentage of each state's adult (18 and older) population that answers in the affirmative.

The United States is generally a religious nation, although the degree of this religiosity varies across states and regions of the country. A robust 65% of all Americans (across the entire U.S. population) reported in 2008 that religion was important in their daily lives.

Is religion an important part of your daily life?

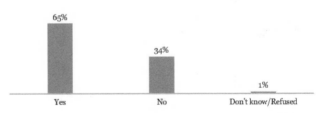

Yes 65%
No 34%
Don't know/Refused 1%

Gallup Poll Daily tracking, U.S. adults 18 and older, 2008 aggregate of 355,334 interviews

Additionally, at least half of the residents of all but four states (Vermont, New Hampshire, Maine, and Massachusetts) say religion is important in their daily lives.

And, although there is a wide range in the self-reported importance of religion, from a high of 85% for residents of Mississippi to a low of 42% for residents of Vermont, the distribution of religiosity by state takes the shape of a bell-shaped curve, clustered around the overall nationwide mean of 65%. Twenty-three of the 50 states and District of Columbia are in the range of 60% to 70% saying religion is important.

The accompanying map shows religiosity by state for 2008, ranging from states that can be considered the most religious to those that are the least religious on a relative basis. (The full data for all states appear at the end of the article.)

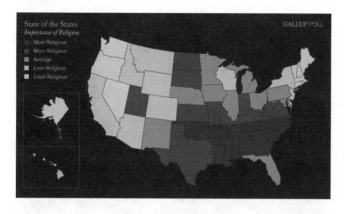

The map demonstrates that the relative importance of religion in Americans' lives has interesting geographical differentiation. Clearly, Southern states are populated by residents with relatively high religiosity, as are several other states in the middle of the country, stretching from Texas through Oklahoma to Kansas and the two Dakotas.

At the same time, states whose residents are least likely to report that religion is important tend to be concentrated in New England and the far West (with the exception of Utah). Additionally, levels of religiosity are lower in several Mid-Atlantic states.

Implications

The question of why residents of some states (e.g., Mississippi and other Southern states) are highly likely to report that religion is an important part of their lives, while residents of other states (e.g., Vermont and other New England states) are much less likely to report the same is fascinating, but difficult to answer simply.

Differing religious traditions and denominations tend to dominate historically in specific states, and religious groups have significantly different patterns of religious intensity among their adherents. The states have differing racial and ethnic compositions, which in turn are associated with differing degrees of religiosity. Certain states may attract in-migrants with specific types of religious intensity. In addition, there may be differing "state cultures" that are themselves associated with life approaches that give varying degrees of credence to religion as a guiding force.

Survey Methods

Results are based on telephone interviews with 355,334 national adults, aged 18 and older, conducted in 2008 as part of Gallup Poll Daily tracking. For results based on the total sample of national adults, one can say with 95% confidence that the maximum margin of sampling error is ±1 percentage point.

The margin of sampling error for most states is ±1 percentage point, but is as high as ±4 percentage points for the District of Columbia, Wyoming, and North Dakota.

Interviews are conducted with respondents on land-line telephones (for respondents with a land-line telephone) and cellular phones (for respondents who are cell-phone only).

IMPORTANCE OF RELIGION

Is religion an important part of your daily life?

State	% Yes
Mississippi	85
Alabama	82
South Carolina	80
Tennessee	79
Louisiana	78
Arkansas	78
Georgia	76
North Carolina	76
Oklahoma	75
Kentucky	74
Texas	74
West Virginia	71
Kansas	70
Utah	69
Missouri	68
Virginia	68
South Dakota	68
North Dakota	68
Indiana	68
Nebraska	67
New Mexico	66
Pennsylvania	65
Florida	65
Maryland	65
Ohio	65
Iowa	64
Minnesota	64
Illinois	64
Michigan	64
Delaware	61
Wisconsin	61
District of Columbia	61
Idaho	61
Arizona	61
New Jersey	60
Wyoming	58
Colorado	57
Hawaii	57
California	57
Montana	56
New York	56
Connecticut	55
Nevada	54
Rhode Island	53
Oregon	53
Washington	52
Alaska	51
Massachusetts	48
Maine	48
New Hampshire	46
Vermont	42

Gallup Poll Daily tracking

In addition to sampling error, question wording and practical difficulties in conducting surveys can introduce error or bias into the findings of public opinion polls.

January 29, 2009
STATE OF THE STATES: CONSUMER CONFIDENCE
No economic oasis, little relief to be found across the country

by Lydia Saad, Gallup Poll Senior Editor

This is the third in a four-part series on the "State of the States" being released this week on Gallup.com. The series examines state-by-state differences in party affiliation, religiosity, consumer confidence, and employer hiring and letting go, based on Gallup Poll Daily tracking data collected throughout 2008.

According to combined Gallup Poll Daily tracking for all of 2008, residents of Rhode Island had the lowest level of confidence in the U.S. economy of any state in the union last year, followed by Michigan, Maine, and Massachusetts. Residents of North Dakota, Utah, and Texas were the least economically discouraged, although regardless of relative differences, Americans living in every state have been significantly more negative than positive about the nation's economy over the past year.

Gallup Poll Economic Perceptions, 10 Least Negative States

State	Index
North Dakota	-69
Utah	-70
Texas	-73
Mississippi	-75
Louisiana	-75
Nebraska	-77
Kansas	-82
Oklahoma	-82
Montana	-82
South Dakota	-83

Gallup Poll Daily tracking

Gallup Poll Economic Perceptions, 10 Most Negative States

State	Index
Rhode Island	-125
Michigan	-119
Maine	-117
Massachusetts	-112
Vermont	-109
Connecticut	-109
West Virginia	-109
Nevada	-108
New York	-107
New Jersey	-106

Gallup Poll Daily tracking

The top 10 states in economic confidence—led by North Dakota, Utah, and Texas—are all oil-producing states whose economies, to varying degrees, benefited from surging oil prices in 2008. However, a strong farm industry may have been the bigger positive factor for some of these states, such as Nebraska.

The bottom 10 states—including Rhode Island, Michigan, Maine, and Massachusetts—are mostly clustered in the East, where the crisis in the financial services industry only adds to the labor market problems created by a withering manufacturing base and a construction slowdown.

The source of economic pessimism in Michigan is no mystery given the woes besetting the U.S. auto industry. Rhode Island has been competing with Michigan in recent months for the highest unemployment rate of any state in the country.

The Bad, the Worse, and the Ugly

Gallup's Economic Perceptions Index is based on two questions—one asking Americans to rate current U.S. economic conditions and the other asking them whether those conditions are getting better or getting worse. The Index score is the sum of net positive ratings of the current economy ([% excellent plus % good] minus % poor) and the net positive outlook for the economy (% getting better minus % getting worse). The maximum values of the Index are +200 for the most positive possible responses and -200 for the most negative.

In 2008, the average state scores ranged from -69 on the high end (North Dakota) to -125 on the low end (Rhode Island). Dividing these scores into equal thirds creates three categories of states as shown on the accompanying map: those simply Negative in their economic perceptions (scoring -69 to -88 on the Index), those More Negative in their perceptions (-89 to -107), and those Most Negative (-108 to -125). (The full data for all states appear at the end of the article.)

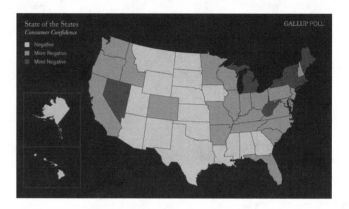

As is clear from the map, a broad swath of the center of the country descending straight down from Montana and North Dakota to the Southern border has the least negative perceptions of the economy, while most states on the West Coast and in the Eastern half of the country are more negative.

These findings are drawn from Gallup's 2008 daily tracking program, including interviews with more than 185,000 national adults from Jan. 2, 2008, through the end of the year. The overall Gallup Economic Perceptions Index score is thus an average of consumer attitudes across a period of declining confidence (the Index fell from -46 at the start of 2008 to -113 at the end of the year), with a particularly sharp drop occurring after the start of the financial collapse in mid-September. Current consumer attitudes are therefore more negative than what is indicated by the 2008 Index values, but in all likelihood the 2008 rank order of the states continues to hold in early 2009.

Bottom Line

Gallup's Economic Confidence Index measures public perceptions about the U.S. economy, but it's clear that those perceptions are colored by the economic picture closer to home. Residents of Rhode Island, Michigan, and other states hit hard by unemployment, falling housing prices, and other recessionary trends have a much more severe assessment of national conditions than do those in better-performing states. But no state is blind to the broader economic picture, as negative perceptions heavily outweigh positive ones, even in places where jobs can, mercifully, still be found.

Survey Methods

Results are based on telephone interviews with 186,718 national adults, aged 18 and older, conducted in 2008 as part of Gallup Poll Daily tracking. (Economic questions were asked of a random half-sample of survey respondents.) For results based on the total sample of national adults, one can say with 95% confidence that the maximum margin of sampling error is ±1 percentage point.

Gallup Poll Economic Perceptions Index by State, 2008

Ranked by index value, from least negative to most negative

	Economic Perceptions Index Value	Number of interviews
North Dakota	-69	484
Utah	-70	1,738
Texas	-73	10,204
Mississippi	-75	1,558
Louisiana	-75	2,186
Nebraska	-77	1,283
Kansas	-82	1,941
Oklahoma	-82	2,629
Montana	-82	911
South Dakota	-83	569
Alabama	-84	2,846
Alaska	-85	676
Wyoming	-85	464
Georgia	-86	4,901
Iowa	-86	2,164
Arizona	-87	4,008
New Mexico	-87	1,333
Hawaii	-87	558
Virginia	-90	4,942
South Carolina	-91	2,556
Washington	-91	4,996
Idaho	-91	1,202
Minnesota	-92	3,774
Colorado	-92	3,439
North Carolina	-93	5,897
Arkansas	-96	1,878
Tennessee	-97	4,100
Oregon	-98	3,117
Indiana	-98	4,379
Wisconsin	-98	4,117
Missouri	-99	4,194
Illinois	-100	6,594
New Hampshire	-100	1,102
District of Columbia	-100	363
Kentucky	-101	2,914
Delaware	-103	546
Maryland	-103	3,403
Florida	-103	9,841
California	-104	19,475
Pennsylvania	-105	11,209
Ohio	-105	7,247
New Jersey	-106	5,274
New York	-107	11,236
Nevada	-108	1,395
West Virginia	-109	1,384
Connecticut	-109	2,537
Vermont	-109	752
Massachusetts	-112	4,521
Maine	-117	1,558
Michigan	-119	5,543
Rhode Island	-125	780

Gallup Poll Daily tracking

The margin of sampling error for most states is ±2 percentage points, but is as high as ±6 points for the District of Columbia, Wyoming, and North Dakota.

Interviews were conducted with respondents on land-line telephones (for respondents with a land-line telephone) and cellular phones (for respondents who are cell-phone only).

In addition to sampling error, question wording and practical difficulties in conducting surveys can introduce error or bias into the findings of public opinion polls.

January 29, 2009
STATE OF THE STATES: JOB-MARKET CONDITIONS
Employee reporting provides insight into job-market conditions across the country

by Dennis Jacobe, Gallup Chief Economist

This is the fourth in a four-part series on the "State of the States" being released this week on Gallup.com. The series examines state-by-state differences in party affiliation, religiosity, consumer confidence, and employer hiring and letting go, based on Gallup Poll Daily tracking data collected throughout 2008.

According to combined Gallup Poll Daily tracking for all of 2008, oil-producing states Wyoming, Louisiana, Oklahoma, and Texas took four of the top five spots as the "best state job markets." By way of contrast, long economically depressed Michigan and housing disaster states Florida and Nevada took three of the four "worst state job market" spots.

Top 10 Best Job Markets

State	Index
Wyoming	40
Louisiana	35
South Dakota	33
Oklahoma	32
Texas	31
North Dakota	30
West Virginia	28
Utah	28
Nebraska	26
Mississippi	26

Gallup Poll Daily tracking

Top 10 Worst Job Markets

State	Index
Michigan	3
Rhode Island	5
Florida	8
Nevada	9
Delaware	10
Vermont	10
New Jersey	11
California	11
Connecticut	12
District of Columbia	13

Gallup Poll Daily tracking

These results are based on aggregated data from more than 100,000 interviews with employed adults in 2008. Gallup asked those who were employed whether their companies were hiring workers and expanding the size of their labor forces, not changing the size of their workforces, or laying off workers and reducing the number of employees they had. The figures reported here represent the net difference between the percentage reporting an expansion and the percentage reporting a reduction in their workforces.

Over the course of 2008, nationwide and in each state, this net score was positive. However, over the last several weeks it has been near zero or negative as job losses have mounted.

In addition to South Dakota and the four oil-producing states mentioned above, other "best job market" states include oil states like North Dakota, those benefiting from coal like West Virginia, and farm states with comparatively good economies from ethanol and a strong commodities market like Nebraska. Financial-crisis states in the Northeast, including Rhode Island, Delaware, Vermont, New Jersey, Connecticut, and Maine are some of the "worst job market" states, as is the housing crash state of California.

The second quintile of "better job market" states includes those with comparatively better economies because they are also energy-related, like Alaska, and farm-related, like Kansas. Similarly, the second-worst quintile of "poor job market" states have economies damaged by the financial debacle, like New York; the manufacturing depression, like Ohio; and the housing disaster, like Arizona.

Not surprisingly, there is a great deal of overlap between state job-market conditions and state consumer confidence. Eight of the best job-market states are in the top 10 in terms of consumer confidence and 6 of the worst job-market states are in the bottom 10 in consumer confidence. (The full data for all states appear at the end of the article.)

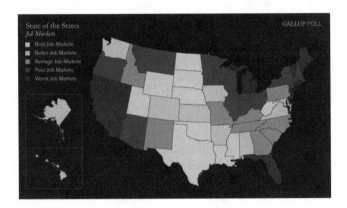

Bubble Economics

The state job-market results for 2008 tend to reflect the "bubble" economics of recent years. For example, the fallout from the housing-bubble collapse has cratered the job market in many states, as has the crash of the financial services bubble. For the year as a whole, the energy and commodities bubbles created some comparatively good job-market conditions, but now that those bubbles have burst, many of those states that had the best job markets in 2008 are beginning to experience bubble-bursting fallout in their job markets.

The reality is that all of the recent business-sector and geographic bubbles have produced tremendous economic uncertainty and instability. In turn, Gallup's net new hiring measure shows that these economic conditions have produced a crashing job market throughout 2008. While the net new hiring numbers were positive for 2008 as a whole, they were negative as the year came to a close, indicating that job losses continue to accelerate—surging past the 100,000-a-week rate.

Right now, everyone seems to be counting on the Federal Reserve and the federal government to stop the bleeding. The question is whether this proposed "solution" will stimulate the real private-sector economy, increasing the demand for new employees and creating new jobs, or will simply end up creating another unsustainable government spending bubble.

Survey Methods

Results are based on telephone interviews with 112,276 employed adults, aged 18 and older, conducted in 2008 as part of Gallup Poll Daily tracking. For results based on the total sample of national adults, one can say with 95% confidence that the maximum margin of sampling error is ±1 percentage point.

The maximum margin of sampling error for the states ranges from ±1 percentage point for large states such as California to as high as ±8 percentage points for the District of Columbia.

Gallup's Net New Hiring Index by State, 2008

% of employees saying their companies are hiring people minus % saying their companies are letting people go

	Net New Hiring Index	Number of interviews
Wyoming	40	314
Louisiana	35	1,286
South Dakota	33	377
Oklahoma	32	1,518
Texas	31	6,268
North Dakota	30	322
West Virginia	28	718
Utah	28	1,150
Nebraska	26	817
Mississippi	26	889
Kansas	25	1,230
Alabama	25	1,590
Arkansas	24	1,000
Virginia	24	3,259
Iowa	24	1,374
Alaska	24	489
Maryland	23	2,272
Hawaii	22	350
Colorado	22	2,267
Washington	22	3,013
New Mexico	21	783
Tennessee	21	2,358
South Carolina	20	1,437
Georgia	20	3,031
Kentucky	20	1,650
Pennsylvania	20	6,588
Idaho	20	692
North Carolina	20	3,515
Missouri	19	2,476
Montana	18	572
New York	18	6,752
Indiana	18	2,650
Massachusetts	18	2,865
Arizona	18	2,229
Wisconsin	17	2,614
New Hampshire	17	690
Minnesota	17	2,407
Illinois	17	4,106
Ohio	15	4,248
Oregon	15	1,750
Maine	14	904
District of Columbia	13	249
Connecticut	12	1,677
California	11	11,774
New Jersey	11	3,322
Vermont	10	510
Delaware	10	326
Nevada	9	812
Florida	8	5,235
Rhode Island	5	474
Michigan	3	3,077

Gallup Poll Daily tracking

Interviews are conducted with respondents on land-line telephones (for respondents with a land-line telephone) and cellular phones (for respondents who are cell-phone only).

In addition to sampling error, question wording and practical difficulties in conducting surveys can introduce error or bias into the findings of public opinion polls.

Gallup instituted routine economic measurements in 1992. Satisfaction tended to run higher than positive economic ratings in the post-9/11 period from late 2001 through 2004, but since then, these attitudes have been more closely linked.

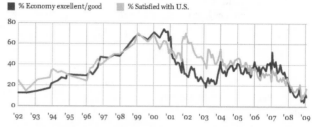

U.S. Satisfaction vs. Rating of Current Economic Conditions, 1992-2009

■ % Economy excellent/good   ■ % Satisfied with U.S.

Obama Boosts Democrats' Satisfaction; Dampens Republicans'

Both the election of Obama on Nov. 4 and his inauguration on Jan. 20 appear to have improved Democrats' and independents' perceptions of the country, but they have had the opposite effect on Republicans. As a result, all three party groups now report similar levels of satisfaction: 15% for Republicans, 16% for independents, and 18% for Democrats. That contrasts with Gallup's pre-election polling, in which Republicans were significantly more positive than independents and Democrats.

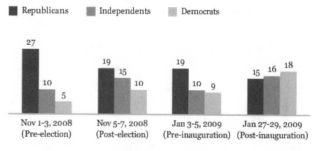

Percentage Satisfied With United States -- Recent Trend, by Party ID

■ Republicans   ■ Independents   ■ Democrats

The partisan shift in satisfaction seen around the transfer of the presidency from one political party to the other in 2008 and 2009 is quite modest relative to the last such political change, when George W. Bush succeeded Bill Clinton as president in 2001. At that time, Gallup documented a switch from a strong Democratic lead over Republicans in satisfaction in October 2000 (78% of Democrats were satisfied versus 50% of Republicans) to a strong Republican lead over the Democrats by February 2001 (67% versus 44%).

Similar reversals in partisan satisfaction ratings were seen around the previous two party shifts in the White House: the transitions from Jimmy Carter to Ronald Reagan in 1981 and from George H.W. Bush to Bill Clinton in 1993. However, U.S. satisfaction was measured less frequently in those eras, so those assessments are made on the basis of polling conducted several months into each administration. Gallup will return to this analysis in the coming months to see how partisan satisfaction with the country under Obama compares with that under Reagan and Clinton during their first years in office.

February 02, 2009
U.S. SATISFACTION REMAINS LOW UNDER OBAMA
Seventeen percent of Americans are satisfied, versus 13% before the election

by Lydia Saad, Gallup Poll Senior Editor

Public satisfaction with the state of the nation remains in short supply just over a week after President Barack Obama was sworn in. Only 17% of Americans are satisfied with the way things are going in the country in Gallup Poll Daily tracking from Jan. 27–29; 80% are dissatisfied.

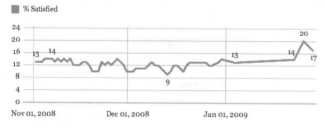

U.S. Public Satisfaction With the Country, Since November 2008

■ % Satisfied

This 17% U.S. satisfaction rating is slightly better than the 13% rating seen at the start of January, as well as the 13% right before the presidential election in November, and reflects an uptick in satisfaction that occurred right after the inauguration. Still, satisfaction remains extraordinarily low relative to more prosperous times in the nation's recent history—such as 1999 and 2002, when over 60% of Americans were satisfied.

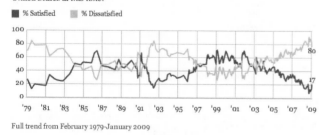

In general, are you satisfied or dissatisfied with the way things are going in the United States at this time?

■ % Satisfied   ■ % Dissatisfied

Full trend from February 1979-January 2009

The connection between low public satisfaction with the country and consumer anxiety about the economy is clear in Gallup's trends for both measures; the two have been quite parallel since

Bottom Line

Negative feelings about the economy remain the primary driver of public attitudes about the country, and that is dampening the satisfaction scores of all Americans—Republican and Democratic alike. Nevertheless, the arrival of a new Democratic administration has changed attitudes at the margins, making Democrats and independents somewhat more upbeat than they had been prior to the election, and Republicans less satisfied. The net result is a slight overall increase in satisfaction.

Survey Methods

Results are based on telephone interviews with 1,560 national adults, aged 18 and older, conducted Jan. 27–29, 2009. For results based on the total sample of national adults, one can say with 95% confidence that the maximum margin of sampling error is ±3 percentage points.

Interviews are conducted with respondents on land-line telephones (for respondents with a land-line telephone) and cellular phones (for respondents who are cell-phone only).

In addition to sampling error, question wording and practical difficulties in conducting surveys can introduce error or bias into the findings of public opinion polls.

February 02, 2009

AMERICANS APPROVE OF MOST OBAMA ACTIONS TO DATE

Widespread support for decisions on ethics reform, interrogations, fuel standards

by Jeffrey M. Jones, Gallup Poll Managing Editor

Of seven actions Barack Obama has taken during the early days of his presidency, five are supported by large majorities of Americans.

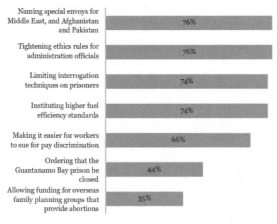

Approval of Barack Obama's Actions as President

Naming special envoys for Middle East, and Afghanistan and Pakistan	76%
Tightening ethics rules for administration officials	76%
Limiting interrogation techniques on prisoners	74%
Instituting higher fuel efficiency standards	74%
Making it easier for workers to sue for pay discrimination	66%
Ordering that the Guantanamo Bay prison be closed	44%
Allowing funding for overseas family planning groups that provide abortions	35%

Jan. 30-Feb. 1 USA Today/Gallup poll

The Jan. 30–Feb. 1 *USA Today*/Gallup poll asked Americans to say whether they approve or disapprove of seven specific actions Obama has taken as president. Americans' general support for most of these is in line with Obama's initial overall job approval ratings.

The public is most supportive of his decisions to name special envoys to oversee the administration's efforts in the Middle East, and Pakistan and Afghanistan, and to tighten rules on people working as lobbyists either before or after serving in his administration. Both of these moves are favored by 76% of Americans.

Americans are nearly as supportive of Obama's actions to limit the interrogation methods that can be used on military prisoners—actions designed to ensure the United States does not resort to torture to find out information from prisoners. Seventy-four percent of Americans favor that decision, the same percentage who favor his executive order to institute higher fuel efficiency standards.

Two in three Americans approve of his signing a bill to make it easier for workers to sue for pay discrimination, the first legislation he has signed into law as president.

The public does not agree with everything Obama has done, however. For example, more Americans say they disapprove (50%) than approve (44%) of his decision to order the closing of the Guantanamo Bay prison for terrorist suspects in Cuba within a year.

Further, Obama's decision to reverse the prohibition on funding for overseas family-planning providers may be the least popular thing he has done so far. This was an executive order that forbade federal government money from going to overseas family-planning groups that provide abortions or offer abortion counseling. Fifty-eight percent of Americans disapprove of Obama's decision to lift this ban, while only 35% approve of it. The ban on federal funds to these groups was put in place by Ronald Reagan, but lifted by Bill Clinton. George W. Bush re-instituted the ban after taking office in 2001, but Obama has once again lifted it.

The abortion and Guantanamo Bay prison decisions are especially unpopular among Republicans; only 8% approve of the former and 11% of the latter. But these are also the least popular decisions among independents and Democrats as well, though a majority of Democrats still approve of both.

Republicans are in general less supportive of all of Obama's important early actions than are Democrats and independents, as would be expected. But a majority of Republicans do approve of four of the seven decisions, including 58% who approve of limitations on certain interrogation techniques, something the Bush administration resisted.

Approval of Barack Obama's Actions as President, by Political Party

	Democrats	Independents	Republicans
Naming special envoys for Middle East, and Afghanistan and Pakistan	87%	76%	61%
Tightening ethics rules for administration officials	86%	73%	69%
Limiting interrogation techniques on prisoners	88%	73%	58%
Instituting higher fuel efficiency standards	89%	73%	56%
Making it easier for workers to sue for pay discrimination	85%	66%	41%
Ordering that the Guantanamo Bay prison be closed	68%	46%	11%
Allowing funding for overseas family planning groups that provide abortions	59%	33%	8%

Jan. 30-Feb. 1 USA Today/Gallup poll

Implications

While the public has not supported everything Obama has done in his presidency thus far, he continues to receive strong overall job approval ratings around 66%. It appears that Americans believe the good outweighs the bad to this point in the Obama presidency.

Admittedly, many of Obama's early actions have been noncontroversial, and ones that did not receive a great deal of continuing news coverage. His work in passing an economic stimulus plan is a departure from that, and may provide a stiffer test of how strong his public support is. The U.S. House version of his plan met with opposition from the entire Republican caucus, and the Senate will work this week to craft a different version of the plan that enjoys broader partisan support.

Still, like prior presidents, Obama appears to be enjoying solid public support during this early stage or "honeymoon" phase of his administration.

Survey Methods

Results are based on telephone interviews with 1,027 national adults, aged 18 and older, conducted Jan. 30–Feb. 1, 2009. For results based on the total sample of national adults, one can say with 95% confidence that the maximum margin of sampling error is ±3 percentage points.

Interviews are conducted with respondents on land-line telephones (for respondents with a land-line telephone) and cellular phones (for respondents who are cell-phone only).

In addition to sampling error, question wording and practical difficulties in conducting surveys can introduce error or bias into the findings of public opinion polls.

February 03, 2009

GALLUP'S MEASURE SUGGESTS MORE JOBLESS CLAIMS

Four-week average likely to surge past 565,000

by Dennis Jacobe, Gallup Chief Economist

Gallup's hiring measure for the four weeks ending Jan. 31 fell to -4 from -3 the previous week, suggesting that on Thursday, the Labor Department is likely to report a surge past 565,000 in the seasonally adjusted four-week moving average of jobless claims—up from 542,500 the previous week.

Net New Hiring Activity, Four-Week Rolling Trend
% of companies hiring minus % letting people go, in percentage points

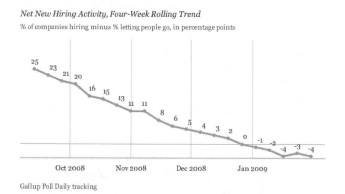

Gallup Poll Daily tracking

The surge in the four-week moving average is due in part to the roll-off of some low numbers reported early this year and in part to the continued high level of jobless claims in recent weeks.

Gallup's New Hiring Measure Remains Negative

Gallup's weekly new hiring measure, like its rolling four-week measure, shows that U.S. employees' perceptions of the job situation at their companies remain negative—at -4 for the week ending Jan. 31. In turn, this suggests the job market continues to weaken, with this Thursday's government report of weekly jobless claims likely to remain near or even move slightly higher than last week's 588,000. Still, predicting small changes in weekly claims tends to be difficult given their volatility, particularly when seasonal adjustments are applied to them at this time of year. In this regard, Gallup's four-week moving average of jobless claims is not only a more stable but also a better predictor of actual conditions in the job market.

Net New Hiring Activity, Weekly Average

% of companies hiring minus % letting people go, in percentage points

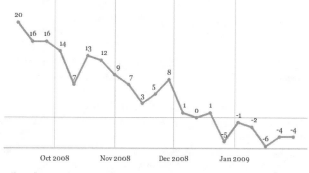

Gallup Poll Daily tracking

Jobs Continue to Disappear

Gallup's new hiring measure suggests that the U.S. economy is continuing to lose more than 125,000 jobs each week. Given this context, it might be assumed that the new and unprecedented fiscal stimulus plan moving through Congress would be focused on ways to "slow the bleeding" in the job market and recapture consumer confidence. Unfortunately, most Americans don't seem to think this will be the case, with 78% concerned that the plan will not stimulate the economy quickly enough and only 10% believing it will improve the economy this year.

Congress needs to remember as it works its legislative will that this new stimulus effort needs to be almost as much psychological as economic. Right now, consumers are afraid to spend because they see the economy in a virtual free-fall, and their most reasonable course of action is to hunker down. While substituting government spending for private spending may provide some short-term benefits, behavioral economics suggests that success will be achieved only if this effort can instill in consumers new confidence that the overall economy will soon improve.

In turn, the only way the stimulus plan can really change the current consumer psychology is for the nation's leaders, both on Main Street and on Wall Street, to come to a consensus that the effort will succeed—creating new jobs and bringing the downward spiral of the economy to a halt. Right now, Americans don't seem to believe the current plan will achieve these goals. If that continues to be the case, then the majority of Americans are likely to be right in their assessment that this unprecedented spending plan will do too little, too late in the face of the current jobs crisis.

Using weekly results for 2008, Gallup's analysis suggests that its hiring measure has a better than 7-in-10 probability of correctly projecting the direction of weekly jobless claims and a better than 8-in-10 probability of predicting the direction of the four-week average of jobless claims.

Gallup's hiring measure is based on aggregated interviews with a nationally representative sample of more than 2,000 U.S. workers each week. Gallup asks current full- and part-time employees whether their employers are hiring new people and expanding the size of their workforces, not changing the size of their workforces, or letting people go and reducing the size of their workforces. Gallup's hiring measure is computed by subtracting the "letting go and reducing" percentage from the "hiring and expanding" percentage. The assumption is that employees across the country have a good feel for what's happening in their companies, and that these insider perceptions can yield a meaningful indication of the nation's job situation.

Gallup's Net New Hiring Activity measure was initiated in January 2008. It is an effort to assess U.S. job creation or elimination based on the self-reports of more than 2,000 individual employees aggregated each week about hiring and firing activity at their workplaces. For results based on these samples, the maximum margin of sampling error is ±3 percentage points.

Interviews are conducted with respondents on land-line telephones (for respondents with a land-line telephone) and cellular phones (for respondents who are cell-phone only).

In addition to sampling error, question wording and practical difficulties in conducting surveys can introduce error or bias into the findings of public opinion polls.

February 04, 2009

FEW AMERICANS PERCEIVE A MORE CIVIL TONE IN D.C.

by Lydia Saad, Gallup Poll Senior Editor

President Barack Obama came to office making the time-honored promise to raise the level of political discourse in Washington, but thus far, most Americans don't see that his promise is panning out. According to a new *USA Today*/Gallup poll, as many Americans think the "overall tone and level of civility" between Republicans and Democrats in Washington has gotten worse since the election as say it has improved: 23% vs. 21%. Half say it has stayed the same.

Last week's negotiations over the economic stimulus package in the U.S. House of Representatives, ending in a nearly straight party-line vote, offered Americans their first good look at Republicans and Democrats interacting during the Obama administration. In its aftermath, the majority of all three party groups think the political tone in Washington has remained about the same since Obama's election.

Beyond that, by nearly 2 to 1, Democrats are more likely to say the tone has improved, rather than gotten worse: 28% vs. 15%. However, by an even wider margin, 36% vs. 10%, Republicans are more likely to believe the tone has gotten worse. Independents are about evenly split in their perceptions.

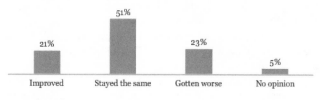

Since Barack Obama was elected, do you think the overall tone and level of civility in Washington between Republicans and Democrats has -- [improved, stayed the same, or gotten worse]?

USA Today/Gallup, Jan. 30-Feb. 1, 2009

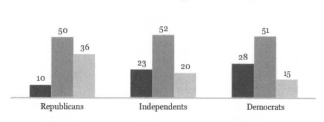

Perceptions of Change in Tone in Washington, by Party ID

USA Today/Gallup, Jan. 30-Feb. 1, 2009

"Staying the same" isn't necessarily a negative assessment of civility in Washington, particularly because public attitudes about politics can be highly jaded. Nevertheless, given that the political climate has had such bad press through much of the last two administrations, from Bill Clinton's through George W. Bush's, and that Obama has made a point of trying to improve it, it would be difficult to argue that the status quo is positive.

The Jan. 30–Feb. 1 poll included a follow-up question for those who say the political climate is staying the same or getting worse, asking them which party in Washington is more to blame for the lack of improvement. Overall, 41% of this group blames the Republicans, 30% blame the Democrats, and another 30% fault both parties equally or blame neither party.

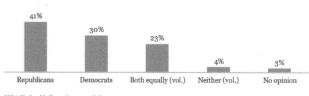

Who do you blame more for the lack of improvement in the overall tone in Washington -- [the Republicans in Washington (or) the Democrats in Washington]?
Based on those who say the tone in Washington has not improved

USA Today/Gallup, Jan. 30-Feb. 1, 2009
(vol.) = Volunteered response

Among Americans who say the tone and level of civility in Washington has stayed the same under Obama, 45% blame the Republicans in Washington while only 22% blame the Democrats. However, among those who believe the tone has gotten worse (disproportionately Republican in party affiliation), nearly half (49%) blame the Democrats while 32% blame the Republicans.

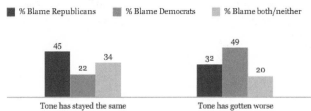

Party Blamed for Lack of Improved Tone in Washington, by Perceptions of How Tone Has Changed

USA Today/Gallup, Jan. 30-Feb. 1, 2009

Bottom Line

In the category of small favors, Obama can feel gratified that a slight majority of Americans believe the political tone in Washington hasn't grown any worse under his presidency. But given his efforts at bipartisanship, including traveling to Capitol Hill to meet with Republican leaders and even hosting a bipartisan Super Bowl party at the White House, he could well be disappointed in the finding that as many Americans say the political climate has gotten worse since his election as say it has improved.

All in all, the acrimony between Republicans and Democrats within the House last week—perhaps amplified across talk radio—seems to be carrying the moment. As a result, the new poll finds a higher percentage of Republicans saying the political tone is worsening (36%) than of Democrats saying it's improving (28%). With the Democrats controlling both houses of Congress and the White House, it is unlikely that rank-and-file Republicans will sense a positive change in the political climate unless more rank-and-file Democrats come to that conclusion.

Survey Methods

Results are based on telephone interviews with 1,027 national adults, aged 18 and older, conducted Jan. 30–Feb. 1, 2009. For results based on the total sample of national adults, one can say with 95% confidence that the maximum margin of sampling error is ±3 percentage points.

For results based on 740 national adults who say the tone in Washington has not improved, the maximum margin of sampling error is ±4 percentage points.

Interviews are conducted with respondents on land-line telephones (for respondents with a land-line telephone) and cellular phones (for respondents who are cell-phone only).

In addition to sampling error, question wording and practical difficulties in conducting surveys can introduce error or bias into the findings of public opinion polls.

February 04, 2009

IN U.S., WORRY ABOUT MAKING MONTHLY PAYMENTS ADDING UP

Those who are very worried are much more likely to be stressed or angry

by Elizabeth Mendes and Brett Pelham, Gallup Poll Staff Writers

Five separate Gallup Polls conducted in 2008 found the percentage of Americans who report they are somewhat or very worried about keeping up with their monthly payments rose dramatically in December to 30%, up from 21% in February. Monthly payments include the amount of money they owe on a mortgage, credit card, car loan, or other personal loan or line of credit.

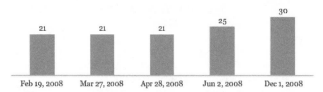

How confident or worried do you feel about keeping up with your monthly payments these days?
% "Somewhat" or "Very" worried

FULL QUESTION WORDING: Thinking for a moment about the total amount of debt you have, that is, the amount of money you owe a bank or any other lender for a mortgage, credit card, car loan, or any other personal loan or credit line. How confident or worried do you feel about keeping up with your monthly payments these days?

The loss of over 2.5 million jobs in 2008 will certainly continue to hinder the ability of many Americans to meet the demands of their monthly financial obligations. According to the most recent data released by the Federal Reserve the delinquency rate on residential real estate loans rose to 5.08% in the third quarter of 2008, up from 2.72% at the same time in 2007. Likewise, the delinquency rate on credit cards rose to 4.79% in the third quarter of 2008, up from the 4.35% reported during the same quarter in 2007.

Income and Education Make a Difference

Combining all five survey points to examine demographic differences reveals that those Americans with the lowest incomes, and those with less than a high school education, are the most worried about keeping up with their monthly payments, at 40% and 36%, respectively. Worry about monthly debt is lowest among those making $90,000 or more a year, at 14%.

The Emotional Toll of Unmanageable Debt

Gallup also finds a clear relationship between worry about paying off debt and negative emotions, consistent with previous findings revealing the financial crisis' damaging effect on well-being. Americans who are very worried that they can't keep up with their bills are four times more likely to be angry and nearly three times more likely to be stressed than those who are very confident that they can keep up with their bills.

While these data are the result of a combined sample across all five survey points in order to provide more accurate estimates of the relationships, separate analyses of these relationships for each of the five time periods show that the same patterns were evident both before and after worry levels increased in June and December of 2008.

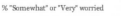

How confident or worried do you feel about keeping up with your monthly payments these days?

% "Somewhat" or "Very" worried

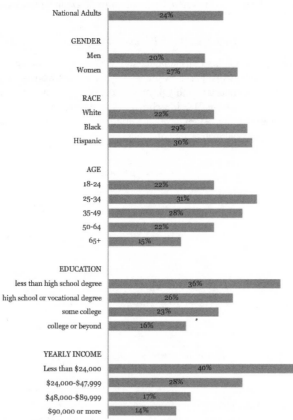

National Adults	24%
GENDER	
Men	20%
Women	27%
RACE	
White	22%
Black	29%
Hispanic	30%
AGE	
18-24	22%
25-34	31%
35-49	28%
50-64	22%
65+	15%
EDUCATION	
less than high school degree	36%
high school or vocational degree	26%
some college	23%
college or beyond	16%
YEARLY INCOME	
Less than $24,000	40%
$24,000-$47,999	28%
$48,000-$89,999	17%
$90,000 or more	14%

Aggregate of interviews conducted on Feb 19, Mar 27, Apr 28, Jun 2, and Dec 1, 2008

How confident or worried do you feel about keeping up with you monthly payments these days?

■ % Saying they experienced ANGER a lot of the day yesterday

░ % Saying they experienced STRESS a lot of the day yesterday

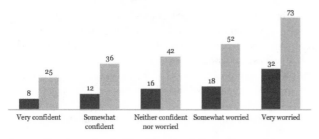

Aggregate of interviews conducted on Feb 19, Mar 27, Apr 28, Jun 2, and Dec 1, 2008

With an astounding 200,000 job cuts made in January 2009 alone, and as unemployment checks begin to run out for the millions who lost jobs in 2008, meeting monthly debt payments is likely to become an increasing problem for many Americans.

Survey Methods

Results are based on telephone interviews with 4,996 adults in the U.S., aged 18 and older, conducted Feb. 19, March 27, April 28, June 2, and Dec. 1, 2008. For results based on the total sample of national adults, one can say with 95% confidence that the maximum margin of sampling error is ±1 percentage point. In addition to sampling error, question wording and practical difficulties in conducting surveys can introduce error or bias into the findings of public opinion polls.

February 05, 2009

MEDIA COVERAGE OF OBAMA GETS MIXED AND PARTISAN REVIEWS

Nearly half see coverage as about right, but views diverge by party, job approval

by Lymari Morales, Gallup Poll Staff Writer

As President Barack Obama led a media blitz Tuesday to push for his economic stimulus plan and mitigate the damage caused by the fresh exit of two high-level nominees, a sizable minority of Americans may have been watching with skeptical eyes. More than one-third (38%) do not think the media have been tough enough in their coverage of Obama, while nearly half (48%) say media coverage has been about right.

In its coverage of Barack Obama and his administration so far, do you think the news media has been too tough, about right, or not tough enough?

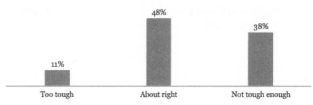

USA Today/Gallup, Jan. 30-Feb. 1, 2009

Rather than giving a speech or holding a press conference, Obama turned to the nation's networks to push for the passage of his economic stimulus package. Sharing the spotlight, however, were the tax-related departures of nominees Tom Daschle and Nancy Killefer, and a growing chorus of voices questioning the media's ability to objectively cover Obama, including a Monday *New York Times* article identifying former journalists who now work for the Obama administration.

A *USA Today/*Gallup poll conducted last weekend, before this round of interviews and the events cited above, reveals that views about media coverage of Obama break decisively down party lines. Two-thirds of Democrats see the coverage as "about right" while two-thirds of Republicans see it as "not tough enough." Independents are about evenly split between the two options. Fewer than one in five of any partisan group says coverage has been too tough.

Not surprisingly, Americans' underlying views of Obama's job performance are also highly related to their views on this issue. Of the minority of Americans who disapprove of Obama's job performance, 84% say the media has not been tough enough on him. Of those who approve, 65% see the coverage as about right.

Gallup asked a follow-up question of the 38% of Americans who say the media have not been tough enough on Obama, gauging their

In its coverage of Barack Obama and his administration so far, do you think the news media has been too tough, about right, or not tough enough?

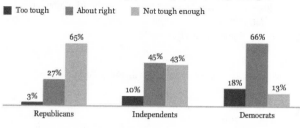

USA Today/Gallup, Jan. 30-Feb. 1, 2009

Views of Media Coverage of Obama, by Obama Job Approval

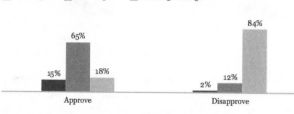

USA Today/Gallup, Jan. 30-Feb. 1, 2009

level of concern that the media will not be able to fulfill their duties of providing oversight of the administration's actions. Among this group, 85% are at least somewhat concerned about this, including 61% who are very concerned.

How concerned are you that the news media will not fulfill its duties of providing oversight to the public about what the administration is doing?
(Asked of those who think news media are not being tough enough)

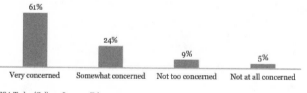

USA Today/Gallup, Jan. 30-Feb. 1, 2009

Bottom Line

Just two weeks into his presidency, Obama is facing both legislative and personnel challenges for which Americans will want answers. As both Obama and the media go about their work, they will do so under the watchful eye of the American public. To date, Americans have been relatively forgiving of both, but it remains to be seen how long either honeymoon will last.

Survey Methods

Results are based on telephone interviews with 1,027 national adults, aged 18 and older, conducted Jan. 30–Feb. 1, 2009. For results based on the total sample of national adults, one can say with 95% confidence that the maximum margin of sampling error is ±3 percentage points.

Interviews are conducted with respondents on land-line telephones (for respondents with a land-line telephone) and cellular phones (for respondents who are cell-phone only).

In addition to sampling error, question wording and practical difficulties in conducting surveys can introduce error or bias into the findings of public opinion polls.

February 05, 2009

LIMBAUGH WELL-LIKED BY MANY, BUT NOT ALL, REPUBLICANS

Strong majority of Democrats have negative opinions of the conservative talk-show host

by Frank Newport, Gallup Poll Editor in Chief

Conservative talk-show host Rush Limbaugh is viewed favorably by 60% of Republicans nationwide, while 23% have an unfavorable opinion of him. In sharp contrast, only 6% of Democrats view Limbaugh favorably, while 63% view him unfavorably.

Do you have a favorable or unfavorable opinion of Rush Limbaugh, or have you never heard of him?

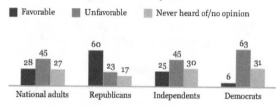

Jan. 30- Feb. 1, 2009

Limbaugh has been much in the news recently as media outlets have played up his highly vocal opposition to President Obama in general and to Obama's economic stimulus plan in particular. The president himself was provoked enough by Limbaugh to bring up his name in his public comments about the stimulus plan, saying, "You can't just listen to Rush Limbaugh and get things done." Since then, Limbaugh's role in influencing Republican positions on public policy issues, including in particular the stimulus package, has been a topic of discussion.

Given the deliberately partisan and ideological nature of Limbaugh's radio program, the sharp divide in views of the talk-show host by partisanship are not surprising. Still, the data from Gallup's Jan. 30–Feb. 1 poll show that Republican support for Limbaugh is not monolithic. Although a clear majority of 60% of Republicans have a favorable opinion of Limbaugh, a not-insignificant 23% have an unfavorable opinion. Seventeen percent of Republicans say they have no opinion of Limbaugh either way (either because they haven't heard of him or don't know enough about him to say).

Almost a third of Democrats say they have no opinion of Limbaugh, but negative views of him among Democrats outweigh positive opinions by more than a 10-to-1 ratio. Among independents, negatives outweigh positives by a 45% to 25% margin.

Gallup asked a similar question about Limbaugh in a slightly different context six years ago, with generally similar results.

Implications

Limbaugh is a radio personality whose continuing viability depends on maintaining high levels of listenership, which in turn depend at

Next, we'd like to get your overall opinion of some talk show hosts, political commentators, and authors. As I read each name, please say if you have a favorable or unfavorable opinion of these people -- or if you have never heard of them. How about... Rush Limbaugh?

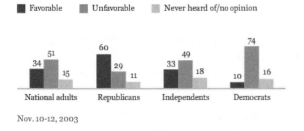

Nov. 10-12, 2003

least in part on his ability to generate "buzz" and controversy. So it is no surprise that Limbaugh has taken on President Obama in a provocative manner. It's a little more surprising, perhaps, that Obama acknowledged Limbaugh in his public remarks, thus elevating the opinions of the talk-show host to national news status.

The data from the recent Gallup Poll confirm what has been found previously and what follows from common sense, given the target audience for Limbaugh's radio show. He enjoys a positive image among the majority of Republicans (although about one in four Republicans view him negatively), while having a much more negative image among independents and particularly among Democrats.

Survey Methods

Results are based on telephone interviews with 1,027 national adults, aged 18 and older, conducted Jan. 30–Feb. 1, 2009. For results based on the total sample of national adults, one can say with 95% confidence that the margin of sampling error is ±3 percentage points.

For results based on the sample of 289 Republicans, the maximum margin of sampling error is ±6 percentage points.

For results based on the sample of 346 independents, the maximum margin of sampling error is ±6 percentage points.

For results based on the sample of 376 Democrats, the maximum margin of sampling error is ±6 percentage points.

Interviews are conducted with respondents on land-line telephones (for respondents with a land-line telephone) and cellular phones (for respondents who are cell-phone only).

In addition to sampling error, question wording and practical difficulties in conducting surveys can introduce error or bias into the findings of public opinion polls.

February 06, 2009
CONFIDENCE IN OBAMA REMAINS HIGH AFTER CABINET TROUBLES
Public believes controversy a normal part of filling high government positions

by Jeffrey M. Jones, Gallup Poll Managing Editor

President Barack Obama had to face tough questioning from the media this week over his process for choosing his top advisers after Tom Daschle and Nancy Killefer withdrew their nominations for fail-

ing to pay back taxes. But Americans' support for Obama is hardly shaken, with fewer than one in five saying they are less confident now in Obama's ethical standards and his ability to manage the government than they were before he took office. A majority say they are "more confident" in both regards.

Confidence in Aspects of the Obama Administration Now Compared to Before the Inauguration

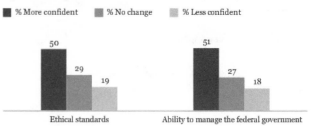

USA Today/Gallup, Feb. 4, 2009

Most of those who say they now have less confidence in Obama are Republican identifiers. Thus, a great number of those who claim to be affected in a negative way probably did not have a great deal of confidence in Obama to begin with.

Additionally, the president's 65% job approval rating in Feb. 2–4 Gallup Poll Daily tracking is essentially the same as it has been throughout his brief time in office.

Do you approve or disapprove of the job Barack Obama is doing as president?
2009 trend

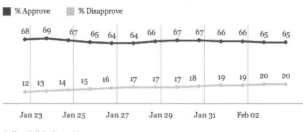

Gallup Poll Daily tracking

The public may be largely taking these Cabinet controversies in stride because it tends to view them as nothing out of the ordinary, according to the Feb. 4 *USA Today/*Gallup poll that probed reaction to the controversies.

Specifically, the poll finds 58% of Americans describing the controversies as "a normal part of the process of filling high-level government positions in any new administration." Only half that number—29%—think they reflect poorly on the Obama administration, saying the administration "appears to be having more problems filling high government positions than is typical for new administrations." The remaining 12% have no opinion.

In addition to concerns about his nominees' ethics given their tax woes, Obama has also faced criticism for making exceptions to his pledge to not appoint former lobbyists to positions in his administration. This may have also applied to Daschle, who drew considerable income from healthcare consulting after finishing his Senate career, and was to be tasked with overhauling the nation's healthcare system.

Nevertheless, at least half of Americans think Obama has made progress so far on his promises to change the way Washington

works (50%) and to limit the influence lobbyists have in his administration (53%).

Has Barack Obama Made Progress in Keeping This Promise So Far?

USA Today/Gallup, Feb. 4, 2009

A majority of 56% of Americans say they agree with Daschle's decision to withdraw his nomination, while just 10% say he should have continued his efforts to be confirmed. Thirty-four percent do not have an opinion on the matter.

The public is slightly more likely to believe that the Daschle situation is just another example of a culture of corruption in Washington (39%) than an isolated case of wrongdoing or a mistake on one individual's part (24%). Thirty-seven percent do not know enough about the controversy to offer an opinion.

Survey Methods

Results are based on telephone interviews with 1,012 national adults, aged 18 and older, conducted Feb. 4, 2009. For results based on the total sample of national adults, one can say with 95% confidence that the maximum margin of sampling error is ±3 percentage points.

Interviews are conducted with respondents on land-line telephones (for respondents with a land-line telephone) and cellular phones (for respondents who are cell-phone only).

In addition to sampling error, question wording and practical difficulties in conducting surveys can introduce error or bias into the findings of public opinion polls.

Polls conducted entirely in one day, such as this one, are subject to additional error or bias not found in polls conducted over several days.

February 09, 2009
OBAMA HAS UPPER HAND IN STIMULUS FIGHT
Obama's 67% approval rating on the stimulus is more than twice that of Republicans

by Frank Newport, Gallup Poll Editor in Chief

The American public gives President Barack Obama a strong 67% approval rating for the way in which he is handling the government's efforts to pass an economic stimulus bill, while the Democrats and, in particular, the Republicans in Congress receive much lower approval ratings of 48% and 31%, respectively.

These findings, based on Gallup Poll interviews conducted Feb. 6–7, underscore the degree to which Obama appears to be maintaining the upper hand over his opponents from a public opinion perspective as he and congressional leaders wrangle over the precise

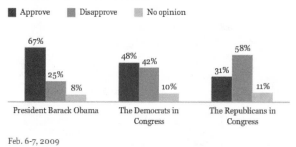

Do you approve or disapprove of the way each of the following has handled the government's efforts to pass an economic stimulus bill? How about -- [RANDOM ORDER]?

Feb. 6-7, 2009

form and substance of a new economic stimulus plan. (Recent Gallup polling also shows that a slight majority of Americans in general favor the idea of passing a stimulus plan of around $800 billion, a sentiment that has stayed constant over the last several weeks.)

Obama will address the stimulus issue before a nationwide audience on Monday night with his first prime-time news conference. He will also conduct town-hall meetings this week in Elkhart, Ind., and Fort Myers, Fla., as part of his efforts to help sell his view of the urgency of passing a stimulus package. The new Gallup data certainly suggest that these public relations efforts will find a generally receptive audience.

The data in particular show the sharp divide between the public's views of how Obama has handled efforts to pass a stimulus bill and its views of how the Republicans have handled this—a divide that quantitatively produces a 36-point approval gap.

Some of this difference may be attributable to pre-existing views of the entities involved in the stimulus plan wrangling. President Obama's overall job approval rating (64% as of Sunday, Feb. 8) is very close to his approval rating on the stimulus, while Gallup's last measure of favorable ratings for the Republicans in Congress (in December 2008) was 25%.

These relatively positive sentiments toward Obama were reflected in recent Gallup polling that asked Americans whether their confidence in Obama's ability to improve the economy and manage the government had gotten better or had gotten worse since his inauguration. At least half of Americans said their confidence had increased, while only 17% to 18% said they had less confidence.

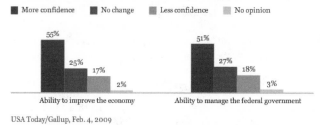

Thinking back to the way you felt before Barack Obama took office, would you say you now have -- [ROTATED: more confidence, has there been no change, (or do you now have) less confidence] -- in the Obama administration's [RANDOM ORDER]?

USA Today/Gallup, Feb. 4, 2009

Critically Important?

Obama's recent efforts to create a sense of urgency that a new bill be passed would appear to resonate with at least half of the American public. The new Gallup Poll shows that a majority of Americans (51%) say passing a new economic stimulus plan is "critically important" for improving the nation's economy, while another 29% say it is important. Only 16% say it is "not that important."

In terms of improving the economy, how important do you think it is that the government pass an economic stimulus plan -- critically important, important, but not critical, or not that important?

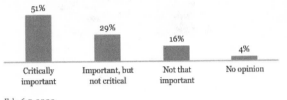

Feb. 6-7, 2009

Previous research has suggested that there is a sharp partisan divide concerning almost everything involved with the massive economic stimulus plan. The sense of urgency that it be passed is no exception.

In terms of improving the economy, how important do you think it is that the government pass an economic stimulus plan -- critically important, important, but not critical, or not that important?

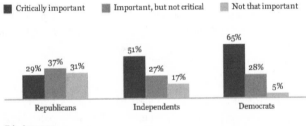

Feb. 6-7, 2009

Only 29% of Republicans are willing to say that passing a new stimulus bill is critically important, contrasted with the nearly two-thirds of Democrats who hold this view.

Still, a clear majority of Republicans say it's at least important to pass the bill.

Bottom Line

President Obama would appear to have the upper hand in the current focus on Congress' efforts to pass a major economic stimulus bill. Not only does Obama get much higher approval ratings for the way in which he is handling the stimulus issue than do either the Democrats or, in particular, the Republicans in Congress, but a majority of Americans agree with him that passing such a bill is critically important for improving the nation's economy.

Survey Methods

Results are based on telephone interviews with 1,018 national adults, aged 18 and older, conducted Feb. 6–7, 2009, as part of Gallup Poll Daily tracking. For results based on the total sample of national adults, one can say with 95% confidence that the maximum margin of sampling error is ±3 percentage points.

Other results are based on telephone interviews with 1,012 national adults, aged 18 and older, conducted Feb. 4, 2009. For results based on the total sample of national adults, one can say with

95% confidence that the maximum margin of sampling error is ±3 percentage points.

Interviews are conducted with respondents on land-line telephones (for respondents with a land-line telephone) and cellular phones (for respondents who are cell-phone only).

In addition to sampling error, question wording and practical difficulties in conducting surveys can introduce error or bias into the findings of public opinion polls.

Polls conducted entirely in one day, such as the one on Feb. 4, are subject to additional error or bias not found in polls conducted over several days.

February 09, 2009
GOV'T. PROJECTS SEEN AS BETTER FOR JOB CREATION THAN TAX CUTS
Public thinks government funding better approach by 50% to 42%

by Jeffrey M. Jones, Gallup Poll Managing Editor

When it comes to creating jobs, Americans are slightly more likely to say that government funding of infrastructure improvements and other projects is a better approach than relying on tax cuts for individuals and businesses, according to a new Gallup Poll.

Generally speaking, which do you think is the better approach to creating jobs -- [ROTATED: tax cuts for individuals and businesses (or) increased government funding of infrastructure improvements and other projects]?

Feb. 6-7, 2009

The Feb. 6–7 Gallup Poll was conducted as the U.S. Senate neared a vote on a more than $800 billion economic stimulus package compromise, and after the federal government reported the highest unemployment rate in 16 years.

The stimulus package agreement hammered out in the Senate late last week contains much more government spending than tax cuts. Most (if not all) Senate Democrats and a few Republicans are likely to vote for that bill this week. Republicans have argued that economic stimulus legislation should place a greater emphasis on tax cuts than on spending, but Senate Republicans failed in an attempt to pass a much smaller stimulus bill that took that approach last week. However, the current Senate proposal does contain more tax cuts than the stimulus bill passed by the House of Representatives.

Differences among rank-and-file partisans on this issue follow those reflected in the congressional debate. Americans who identify themselves as Republicans are much more likely to view tax cuts as the better approach to creating jobs, while Democrats take the opposing view by nearly the same wide margin. Independents favor increased funding over tax cuts by 50% to 36%.

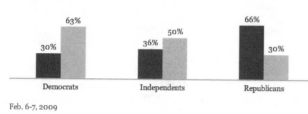

Views of Better Approach to Job Creation, by Party Affiliation

■ Tax cuts for individuals/businesses   ■ Increased government funding of projects

Feb. 6-7, 2009

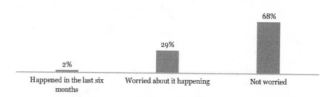

For each of the following, please indicate whether it has happened to you in the last six months, whether you are worried it might happen to you in the near future, or if you are not worried about it happening to you in the foreseeable future.

Based on adults employed full- or part-time

USA Today/Gallup, Jan. 30-Feb. 1, 2009

Implications

To the extent that job creation is a key goal if not the most important goal of the economic stimulus package, the mix of spending and tax cuts in the current economic stimulus bill appears to fit with the preferred approach of the American public. Given a choice, Americans opt for increased funding of government projects over tax cuts by a slim margin.

More broadly, public support for an economic stimulus bill of $800 billion or more has been just above the majority level among Americans, according to recent Gallup polling. While that level of support is hardly overwhelming, 80% of Americans do say it is important to pass an economic stimulus plan, including 51% who say it is very important to do so.

Barack Obama will attempt to bolster public and congressional support for the plan over the next few days by holding public events in Indiana and Florida, and a nationally televised prime-time news conference Monday evening.

Survey Methods

Results are based on telephone interviews with 1,018 national adults, aged 18 and older, conducted Feb. 6–7, 2009, as part of Gallup Poll Daily tracking. For results based on the total sample of national adults, one can say with 95% confidence that the maximum margin of sampling error is ±3 percentage points.

Interviews are conducted with respondents on land-line telephones (for respondents with a land-line telephone) and cellular phones (for respondents who are cell-phone only).

In addition to sampling error, question wording and practical difficulties in conducting surveys can introduce error or bias into the findings of public opinion polls.

February 10, 2009
MAJORITY OF WORKERS NOT WORRIED ABOUT BEING LAID OFF
Still, 41% have close friends or relatives who have lost jobs

by Frank Newport, Gallup Poll Editor in Chief

Despite the overwhelming tsunami of bad economic news sweeping over Americans in recent months, 68% of workers say they have not been laid off in the last six months and are not worried about being laid off in the near future.

This question was part of a series included in the Jan. 30–Feb. 1 *USA Today*/Gallup poll, which asked employed Americans about five different job-related consequences of the bad economy.

A small 2% of current full- or part-time workers say they have been laid off in the last six months. (This number is very low because workers who had been laid off and had not found a new job would not be included in the base of currently employed workers to whom this question was addressed.) Another 29% of workers say they are worried that they will be laid off, leaving a clear majority of 68% of workers who are apparently unworried (or at least not concerned enough to tell a survey interviewer they are worried).

This is a classic case of interpretation. Is the glass half-empty or half-full? Almost all economic news Gallup measures on a continuing basis has been very negative for months now. That includes the current 80% of those interviewed in Gallup Poll Daily tracking who say the economy is getting worse rather than getting better, and a Gallup update in January showing that 86% of Americans say it's a bad time to find a quality job. From this perspective, it might seem surprising that two-thirds of workers seemingly remain optimistic and claim not to be worried about being laid off despite the current economic environment. And, more broadly, the data provide another example of Americans' tendency to be much more robustly positive about their own personal situations than they are about the situation "out there," across the country.

But these numbers can also be viewed from a more negative perspective. Past Gallup Poll questions have found lower percentages of workers claiming they were worried about being laid off, suggesting that the current percentage reflects a deterioration in the jobs situation. Between 2003 and 2008, only between 14% and 20% of workers said they were worried about being laid off in the near future. (The most recent such survey, conducted last August, found 15% worried that they would be laid off.) Given the differences between these surveys and the current survey in terms of context and question wording, these older trends cannot be precisely compared to the current data. Still, even if the older data are used as only a rough baseline, it would appear that the current 29% worried (and 2% who have been laid off) is high on a relative basis.

Other Concerns

The current poll included questions about four other work-related situations in addition to losing one's job.

Notably, 12% of workers say their hours have already been cut back within the last six months, 9% say their benefits have been reduced, 8% have had their wages reduced, and 2% say their companies have outsourced jobs overseas. Adding these numbers to the percentage who are worried about these events occurring in the near future yields net "worried"/"already happened" percentages between 10% and 40%. Still, as is the case for the data on job layoffs, from a more positive perspective, these data also show that the clear majority of American workers are not worried about these events transpiring.

For each of the following, please indicate whether it has happened to you in the last six months, whether you are worried it might happen to you in the near future, or if you are not worried about it happening to you in the foreseeable future.

Based on adults employed full- or part-time

	Happened in last six months	Worried about it happening	Not worried	No opinion
	%	%	%	%
Having your hours at work cut back, including being furloughed	12	24	64	*
Having your benefits reduced	9	31	59	2
Having your wages reduced	8	24	68	*
Being laid off	2	29	68	*
Your company moving jobs to countries overseas	2	8	88	2

* Less than 0.5%

USA Today/Gallup, Jan. 30-Feb. 1, 2009

Friends and Relatives

At the same time, separate questions in the Jan. 30–Feb. 1 poll reinforce the degree to which the public has at least been personally confronted with the jobs problem in American society (even if many of those working do not appear to be highly concerned about their own situations). Forty-one percent of Americans say that they themselves, another person living in their household, or a close friend or immediate family member has lost a job within the last six months. When the question is expanded to include distant relatives or friends, a larger total of 63% know someone who has lost a job.

Please tell me whether any of the following have been laid off or lost a job in the last six months.

Relationship	Yes, lost a job	No, did not	No opinion
	%	%	%
A more distant relative or friend	52	47	1
A close friend or immediate family member such as a parent, child, brother, or sister	36	64	*
You or another person living in your household	19	81	*
COMBINED RESULTS			
You/Close friend/Family member laid off in last six months	41		
Total who know anyone laid off in the last six months	63		

* Less than 0.5%

USA Today/Gallup, Jan. 30-Feb. 1, 2009

One note of interest is the difference by partisanship in the responses to the question asking whether respondents or some member of their households has been laid off or lost a job in the last six months. Democrats are more than twice as likely as Republicans to respond in the affirmative, no doubt reflecting in part that Democrats have significantly lower incomes on average than do Republicans.

Implications

Many of today's economic statistics can be looked at from two different perspectives. While January's 7.6% unemployment rate is very high by historical standards, it still indicates that well over 90% of Americans who want work have a job. Similarly, although the 29% of Americans who say they are worried about losing their jobs (and the 2% who say they have lost a job within the last six months) is very high, the fact that 68% of Americans are not worried about los-

Please tell me whether you or another person living in your household have been laid off or lost a job in the last six months.

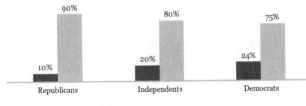

USA Today/Gallup, Jan. 30-Feb. 1, 2009

ing their jobs could be seen as a sign of psychological worker resilience.

Survey Methods

Results are based on telephone interviews with 1,027 national adults, aged 18 and older, conducted Jan. 30–Feb. 1, 2009. For results based on the total sample of national adults, one can say with 95% confidence that the maximum margin of sampling error is ±3 percentage points.

For results based on the sample of 541 adults employed full- or part-time, the maximum margin of sampling error is ±5 percentage points.

Interviews are conducted with respondents on land-line telephones (for respondents with a land-line telephone) and cellular phones (for respondents who are cell-phone only).

In addition to sampling error, question wording and practical difficulties in conducting surveys can introduce error or bias into the findings of public opinion polls.

February 11, 2009

BEST PRESIDENT? LINCOLN ON PAR WITH REAGAN, KENNEDY

However, Lincoln has unique bipartisan appeal

by Lydia Saad, Gallup Poll Senior Editor

Less than a month into Barack Obama's presidency, Obama's desire to emulate Abraham Lincoln can be found in his speeches, his bipartisan gestures, and his "team of rivals" approach to picking a cabinet. But Lincoln is not matchless as Americans' pick for the nation's greatest president. Given a list of five presidents to choose from, Americans are as likely to name John Kennedy as Lincoln (22% each), while 24% choose Ronald Reagan.

If you had to choose, which one of these U.S. presidents would you regard as the greatest -- [ROTATED: George Washington, Abraham Lincoln, Franklin Roosevelt, John Kennedy, (or) Ronald Reagan]?

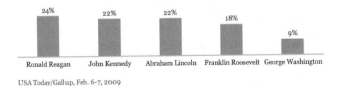

USA Today/Gallup, Feb. 6-7, 2009

These findings are from a *USA Today*/Gallup poll conducted Feb. 6–7. The question gave respondents the choice of five presidents often lauded for their leadership: two Democrats (Kennedy and Franklin Roosevelt), two Republicans (Reagan and Lincoln), and the symbolic father of the country and Lincoln's co-honoree on Presidents Day, George Washington.

These five presidents have consistently ranked among the most revered presidents when Gallup has asked Americans to say, in an open-ended format, whom they consider the greatest president.

Republicans and Democrats Agree on Lincoln

According to the new poll, while Lincoln isn't the top choice for greatest president among either Republicans or Democrats, he enjoys a bipartisan appeal that is unique among the highest-ranking presidents. He places second among Democrats (behind Kennedy), second among Republicans (behind Reagan), and first among independents—although the four most recent presidents are nearly tied among independents.

By contrast, Reagan's strong showing is mainly owing to his extraordinary popularity among Republicans, 52% of whom name Reagan as the greatest. Reagan is also one of the top-rated presidents among independents, but places fourth among Democrats. Similarly, Kennedy ranks first among Democrats and does well among independents, but places last among Republicans.

Which U.S. President Is Greatest, by Party ID

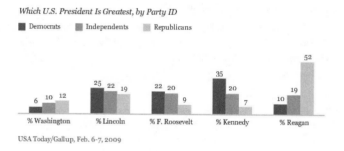

USA Today/Gallup, Feb. 6-7, 2009

Bottom Line

Lincoln has dominated the initial comparisons of Obama to his Oval Office predecessors—it's an appealing linkage given the thread connecting Lincoln's transcendent role in the emancipation of blacks to Obama's milestone achievement in black history.

Strong biographical, oratorical, and leadership connections have also been drawn between Obama and Reagan, Roosevelt, and Kennedy. However, Obama's personal admiration for Lincoln seems to ensure that the Lincoln comparisons will prevail.

While Reagan and Kennedy are just as likely as Lincoln to be well-regarded by Americans on the whole, Lincoln's unique bipartisan appeal makes him the safer choice for Obama to pattern himself after. Indeed, 200 years after his birth, Lincoln may be one of the nation's most powerful forces for political harmony.

Survey Methods

Results are based on telephone interviews with 1,018 national adults, aged 18 and older, conducted Feb. 6–7, 2009, as part of Gallup Poll Daily tracking. For results based on the total sample of national adults, one can say with 95% confidence that the maximum margin of sampling error is ±3 percentage points.

Interviews are conducted with respondents on land-line telephones (for respondents with a land-line telephone) and cellular phones (for respondents who are cell-phone only).

In addition to sampling error, question wording and practical difficulties in conducting surveys can introduce error or bias into the findings of public opinion polls.

February 11, 2009
ON DARWIN'S BIRTHDAY, ONLY 4 IN 10 BELIEVE IN EVOLUTION
Belief drops to 24% among frequent church attenders

by Frank Newport, Gallup Poll Editor in Chief

PRINCETON, NJ—On the eve of the 200th anniversary of Charles Darwin's birth, a new Gallup Poll shows that only 39% of Americans say they "believe in the theory of evolution," while a quarter say they do not believe in the theory, and another 36% don't have an opinion either way. These attitudes are strongly related to education and, to an even greater degree, religiosity.

Do you, personally, believe in the theory of evolution, do you not believe in evolution, or don't you have an opinion either way?

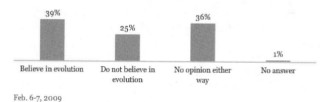

Feb. 6-7, 2009

There is a strong relationship between education and belief in Darwin's theory, as might be expected, ranging from 21% of those with high-school educations or less to 74% of those with postgraduate degrees.

Belief in Evolution, by Education Level

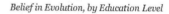

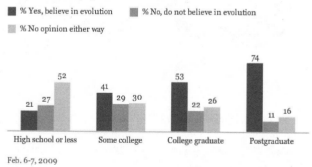

Feb. 6-7, 2009

Those with high-school educations or less are much more likely to have no opinion than are those who have more formal education. Still, among those with high-school educations or less who have an opinion on Darwin's theory, more say they do not believe in evolution than say they believe in it. For all other groups, and in particular those who have at least a college degree, belief is significantly higher than non-belief.

Darwin's theory has been at the forefront of religious debate since he published *On the Origin of Species* 150 years ago. Even to this day, highly religious individuals claim that the theory of evolution contradicts the story of creation as outlined in the book of Genesis in the Bible.

Thus, it comes as no surprise to find that there is a strong relationship between church attendance and belief in evolution in the current data. Those who attend church most often are the least likely to say they believe in evolution.

Belief in Theory of Evolution, by Church Attendance

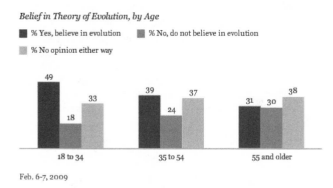

Feb. 6-7, 2009

Previous Gallup research shows that the rate of church attendance is fairly constant across educational groups, suggesting that this relationship is not owing to an underlying educational difference but instead reflects a direct influence of religious beliefs on belief in evolution.

Younger Americans, who are less likely to be religious than those who are older, are also more likely to believe in evolution. Still, just about half of those aged 18 to 34 say they believe in evolution.

Belief in Theory of Evolution, by Age

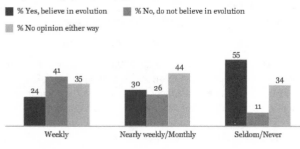

Feb. 6-7, 2009

Implications

As Darwin is being lauded as one of the most important scientists in history on the 200th anniversary of his birth (on Feb. 12, 1809), it is perhaps dismaying to scientists who study and respect his work to see that well less than half of Americans today say they believe in the theory of evolution, and that just 55% can associate the man with his theory.

Naturally, some of this is because of educational differences. Americans who have lower levels of formal education are significantly less likely than others to be able to identify Darwin with his theory, and to have an opinion on it either way. Still, the evidence is clear that even to this day, Americans' religious beliefs are a significant predictor of their attitudes toward Darwin's theory. Those who

attend church most often are the least likely to believe in evolution, and most likely to say they do not believe in it.

Survey Methods

Results are based on telephone interviews with 1,018 national adults, aged 18 and older, conducted Feb. 6–7, 2009, as part of Gallup Poll Daily tracking. For results based on the total sample of national adults, one can say with 95% confidence that the maximum margin of sampling error is ±3 percentage points.

Interviews are conducted with respondents on land-line telephones (for respondents with a land-line telephone) and cellular phones (for respondents who are cell-phone only).

In addition to sampling error, question wording and practical difficulties in conducting surveys can introduce error or bias into the findings of public opinion polls.

February 11, 2009
STIMULUS SUPPORT EDGES HIGHER, NOW 59%
Support up mainly among Democrats; flat among independents

by Lydia Saad, Gallup Poll Senior Editor

Public support for an $800 billion economic stimulus package has increased to 59% in a *USA Today*/Gallup poll conducted Tuesday night, up from 52% in Gallup polling a week ago, as well as in late January.

As you may know, Congress is considering a new economic stimulus package of at least $800 billion. Do you favor or oppose Congress passing this legislation?*

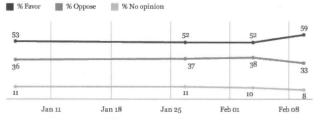

* Jan. 6-7, 2009 wording: Do you favor or oppose Congress passing a new $775 billion economic stimulus program as soon as possible after Barack Obama takes office?

Most of the newfound support comes from rank-and-file Democrats, suggesting President Barack Obama's efforts to sell the plan over the past week—including in his first televised news conference on Monday—have shored up support within his own party. Last week, Gallup found 70% of Democrats in favor of Congress passing the economic stimulus package, but today that figure is 82%.

Over the same period, support for the stimulus package held steady among independents, with a slight majority in favor of it. The percentage of Republicans favoring the package rose slightly from 24% to 28%, but remains below the 34% support received in early January, before Congress began its formal consideration of the package.

Economic Views Not Related to Stimulus Views

According to Gallup Poll Daily tracking from Feb. 8–10, only 11% of Americans consider U.S. economic conditions to be "excellent"

Support for $800 Billion Economic Stimulus Package, by Party I.D. *
% in favor

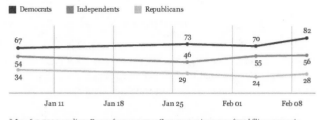

■ Democrats   ■ Independents   ■ Republicans

67 ... 73 ... 70 ... 82
54 ... 46 ... 55 ... 56
34 ... 29 ... 24 ... 28

Jan 11   Jan 18   Jan 25   Feb 01   Feb 08

* Jan. 6-7, 2009 wording: Do you favor or oppose Congress passing a new $775 billion economic stimulus program as soon as possible after Barack Obama takes office?

or "good", while 29% call them "only fair", and 59% "poor." However, there is very little difference in support for the stimulus package among these groups of differing economic perceptions. The majority of all three groups favor Congress approving upward of $800 billion in economic stimulus programs.

Support for $800 Billion Economic Stimulus Package, by Rating of Current Economic Conditions

■ % Favor stimulus plan   ■ % Oppose it

54   42   59   37   61   30

Economy is "excellent" or "good"   Economy is "only fair"   Economy is "poor"

USA Today/Gallup, Feb. 10, 2009

Similarly, there is little difference in support for the plan according to Americans' personal financial situation. About a third of Americans tell Gallup they worried about money "yesterday"—suggesting they are in a certain amount of financial distress. Accordingly, 63% of this attitudinal group favors passage of the plan. However, 58% of those who did not worry about money "yesterday" support the plan as well.

Support for $800 Billion Economic Stimulus Package, by Reported Worry About Money "Yesterday"

■ % Favor stimulus plan   ■ % Oppose it

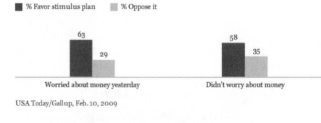

63   29   58   35

Worried about money yesterday   Didn't worry about money

USA Today/Gallup, Feb. 10, 2009

Bottom Line

Obama's salesmanship appears to have been effective in recent days, helping to build public support for the economic stimulus package, and thus push Congress to pass a final version by his desired Presidents Day deadline. At the least, he has stemmed any erosion of support in the face of some spirited conservative opposition. While most of the increase in support is among Democrats, the plan retains solid support from independents and has not lost any ground recently among Republicans.

Although the stimulus plan is purportedly being passed to address the nation's economic problems, Americans' perceptions of

the economy—and of their own personal financial situations—have little bearing on their support for it. Political orientation is the over-riding factor.

Survey Methods

Results are based on telephone interviews with 1,021 national adults, aged 18 and older, conducted Feb. 10, 2009, as part of Gallup Poll Daily tracking. For results based on the total sample of national adults, one can say with 95% confidence that the maximum margin of sampling error is ±3 percentage points.

Interviews are conducted with respondents on land-line telephones (for respondents with a land-line telephone) and cellular phones (for respondents who are cell-phone only).

In addition to sampling error, question wording and practical difficulties in conducting surveys can introduce error or bias into the findings of public opinion polls.

Polls conducted entirely in one day, such as this one, are subject to additional error or bias not found in polls conducted over several days.

February 12, 2009

NO MANDATE FOR CRIMINAL PROBES OF BUSH ADMINISTRATION

Most favor investigations into controversial terror techniques, possible abuse of Justice Dept.

by Jeffrey M. Jones, Gallup Poll Managing Editor

Earlier this week, Sen. Patrick Leahy called for a special commission to investigate possible government wrongdoing by the Bush administration in its anti-terror policies, as well as possible attempts to politicize the Justice Department through the firing of U.S. attorneys who were viewed as potentially disloyal to the administration. While Americans appear to support some kind of investigation into these matters, no more than 41% favor criminal probes.

Preferred Action on Bush Administration Policies/Actions

■ Criminal investigation   ■ Investigation by independent panel   ■ Neither

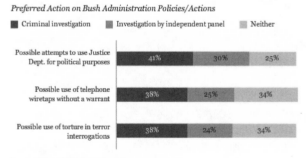

	Criminal investigation	Investigation by independent panel	Neither
Possible attempts to use Justice Dept. for political purposes	41%	30%	25%
Possible use of telephone wiretaps without a warrant	38%	25%	34%
Possible use of torture in terror interrogations	38%	24%	34%

Jan. 30-Feb. 1 USA Today/Gallup poll

These results are based on a Jan. 30–Feb. 1 *USA Today*/Gallup poll. In addition to Leahy's recent call for a "truth commission" that would investigate but not prosecute Bush administration officials, a House committee led by Rep. John Conyers is awaiting responses to subpoenas of former Bush administration officials regarding Bush-era policies and actions.

For each of three controversial actions or policies of the Bush administration, survey respondents were asked whether there should be a criminal investigation by the Justice Department or an investigation by an independent panel that would issue a report of findings but not seek any criminal charges, or whether neither should be done.

While no more than 41% of Americans favor a criminal investigation into any of the matters, at least 6 in 10 say there should be either a criminal investigation or an independent probe into all three. This includes 62% who favor some type of investigation into the possible use of torture when interrogating terrorism suspects, 63% who do so with respect to the possible use of telephone wiretaps without obtaining a warrant, and 71% who support investigating possible attempts to use the Justice Department for political purposes.

So far, President Obama has been reluctant to pursue such investigations, but Leahy and Conyers in particular are calling for an accounting of what happened on Bush's watch.

Perhaps not unexpectedly, a majority of Democratic identifiers favor a criminal probe into all three matters—including 54% who do so with respect to warrantless wiretaps, 51% for the possible use of torture, and 52% for the firing of U.S. attorneys.

In contrast, Republicans are most likely to oppose any type of investigation, including a majority who say so in regard to the possible use of torture (54%) and warrantless wiretaps (56%). Republicans are more receptive to an investigation into possible efforts to politicize the Justice Department, with 24% favoring a criminal probe and 28% in favor of an independent panel report. Still, the greatest number (43%) of Republicans think there should be no investigation into the Justice Department matter.

Independents' views on all three matters fall in between those of Republicans and Democrats, with a majority favoring some type of investigation but (unlike Democrats) not a criminal probe.

Preferred Action on Bush Administration Policies/Actions, by Political Party Affiliation

	Favor criminal investigation	Favor special panel	Favor neither
	%	%	%
Use of torture			
Democrats	51	29	16
Independents	39	20	38
Republicans	20	24	54
Warrantless wiretaps			
Democrats	54	23	18
Independents	39	26	34
Republicans	15	26	56
Firing U.S. attorneys			
Democrats	52	33	11
Independents	41	30	25
Republicans	24	28	43

Jan. 30-Feb. 1 USA Today/Gallup poll

Implications

At this point, it is unclear whether investigations into possible Bush-era wrongdoing will in fact take place. Though Congress has the power to conduct investigations on its own, it may follow Obama's stated intention of concentrating House and Senate efforts on attempting to improve the economy and rescue troubled financial institutions over backward-looking probes into whether Bush administration officials violated the law or otherwise acted unethically in certain situations.

Survey Methods

Results are based on telephone interviews with 1,027 national adults, aged 18 and older, conducted Jan. 30–Feb. 1, 2009. For results based on the total sample of national adults, one can say with 95% confidence that the maximum margin of sampling error is ±3 percentage points.

Interviews are conducted with respondents on land-line telephones (for respondents with a land-line telephone) and cellular phones (for respondents who are cell-phone only).

In addition to sampling error, question wording and practical difficulties in conducting surveys can introduce error or bias into the findings of public opinion polls.

February 12, 2009
IN U.S., HEALTH HABITS IMPROVING, BUT UPHILL CLIMB REMAINS
Younger, lowest-income, and single Americans the least healthy

by Elizabeth Mendes, Gallup Poll Staff Writer

According to the Gallup-Healthways Well-Being Index (WBI), the health habits of many Americans are improving during this new year, but there's still a long way to go. The WBI's Healthy Behavior subindex, an in-depth measure of Americans' exercise, eating, and smoking habits, rose to 61.2 in January; a slight reversal of the sharp decline that occurred at the end of 2008. Even with this uptick, the healthy behavior score is still considerably lower than the 63.3 recorded last January.

Healthy Behavior Index (HBI)

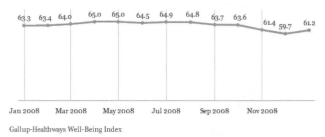

Gallup-Healthways Well-Being Index

The Healthy Behavior sub-index score includes four questions that look individually at smoking, healthy eating, weekly consumption of fruits and vegetables, and weekly exercise frequency. In reviewing the trend for each individual item, Dr. Jim Harter, Gallup Chief Scientist for Workplace Management and Well-Being, reports that the movement in the overall Healthy Behavior Index score "is pretty clearly reflected in the eating healthy and exercise items," and that "the smoking rate has not changed much." There may also be a seasonal effect related to the holidays and New Year's resolutions. At the same time, the year to year decline from January 2008 to January 2009 suggests the stress and financial strain of the recession may also be taking a toll on Americans' health.

Health Report Cards Vary

Assessing the current state of affairs in January 2009 finds older Americans to be much more likely than any other group to report healthy behaviors. Americans 65 years of age and older have a score of 71 on the Healthy Behavior sub-index, almost 10 points above the national average. Women, people who are married, and those in the highest income bracket also have Healthy Behavior scores that are better than the national average. Younger Americans, those in the lowest income bracket, and single individuals are the least likely to report healthy behaviors.

Healthy Behavior Index – January 2009

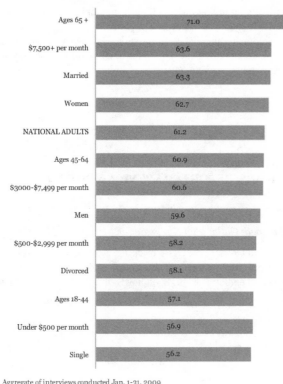

Aggregate of interviews conducted Jan. 1-31, 2009
Gallup-Healthways Well-Being Index

A Steep Climb to Better Health

Looking specifically at each of the questions that compose the Healthy Behavior sub-index reveals large percentages of Americans are not eating healthily and getting appropriate amounts of exercise. In the first month of 2009 less than half of Americans (46%) said that in the last seven days they had exercised on two or more of those days for at least 30 minutes.

While two-thirds of respondents (66%) said they ate healthily all day "yesterday," a smaller number, 54%, reported that in the last seven days they had eaten at least five servings of fruits and vegetables on three or more of those days. This disconnect may mean that for many Americans the definition of what eating healthily is could be unclear and that they are unaware of the U.S. Centers for Disease Control and Prevention's recommended servings of fruits and vegetables.

As Americans continue to struggle under the weight of the economic crisis, Amy Neftzger, Healthways Lead Researcher, points to the importance of raising awareness about healthy eating habits

Individual Healthy Behavior Index Questions

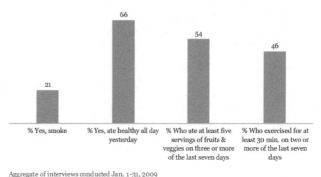

Aggregate of interviews conducted Jan. 1-31, 2009
FULL QUESTION WORDING: 1.) Do you smoke? 2.) Did you eat healthy all day yesterday? 3.) In the last seven days, on how many days did you: Have five or more servings of fruits and vegetables? 4.) In the last seven days, on how many days did you: Exercise for 30 or more minutes?

during times of undue stress. Neftzger says that in stressful situations "some individuals are prone to 'stress eating' and either overeat or resort to comfort foods, and these comfort foods tend to be higher in fat and caloric content than healthier choices, such as a salad."

Another important component of the Healthy Behavior sub-index is the smoking rate. In this analysis of January 2009 data, 21% of Americans say that they smoke. The smoking rate is currently highest among very low income Americans (34%) and lowest for those aged 65 and older (11%).

Bottom Line

The increase in the Healthy Behavior sub-index in January, though small, is a positive sign that, even amid one of the worst economic downturns in the nation's history, Americans are continuing to place importance on their health. Eating healthily and exercising more may, in fact, play a vital role in raising an individual's well-being and helping to deal with stress. With just 46% of the population saying they exercise relatively frequently and slightly more than half reporting eating the weekly recommended servings of fruits and vegetables, it is clear that millions of Americans are in need of continued education and encouragement around critical healthy behaviors. Neftzger notes, "Healthy behaviors have been linked to disease prevention and increased quality of life. With the prevalence rates of conditions such as diabetes on the increase, we should strive to improve the national HBI score each year so that we can improve the health of the nation."

Survey Methods

For the Gallup-Healthways Well-Being Index, Gallup is interviewing no fewer than 1,000 U.S. adults nationwide each day. Monthly results comprise roughly 30,000 interviews. For results based on these samples, the maximum margin of sampling error is ±2 percentage points.

Interviews are conducted with respondents on land-line telephones (for respondents with a land-line telephone) and cellular phones (for respondents who are cell-phone only).

In addition to sampling error, question wording and practical difficulties in conducting surveys can introduce error or bias into the findings of public opinion polls

February 12, 2009

INAUGURATION BOUNCE IN CONSUMER CONFIDENCE DISAPPEARS

Consumers' economic assessments and future expectations turning more negative

by Dennis Jacobe, Gallup Chief Economist

With President Obama warning about dire consequences if Congress did not pass a fiscal stimulus bill and with January's dismal jobs report marking the highest unemployment rate in 16 years, there has been a quick end to the bounce in consumer mood that occurred around January's presidential inauguration.

Consumer Confidence Index, August 2008-February 2009 Trend

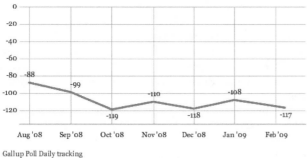

Gallup Poll Daily tracking

Gallup's Consumer Confidence Index Worsens

Consumer perceptions of the economy deteriorated during the first half of 2008, with Gallup's Consumer Confidence Index becoming increasingly negative as gas prices rose and ultimately surpassed $4 a gallon. Consumers began to feel somewhat better in the summer as gas prices moderated, but consumers turned even more negative as the financial crisis erupted during the fall. The presidential election and the subsequent inauguration both seemed to help improve the consumer mood somewhat, as did the inauguration. However, in both cases, the improvement in consumer confidence was short-lived.

Commentary

New Gallup polling suggests President Obama may be making progress in selling the unprecedented fiscal stimulus plan, with 59% of Americans now supporting the legislation, which he may sign this week after the House and Senate reconciled their versions of the bill on Wednesday.

While efforts to sell the plan may have the unintended consequence of worsening consumer confidence in the immediate term, as reflected by the early February Gallup Consumer Confidence Index, final passage of the stimulus bill may make at least some Americans a little more optimistic.

However, it may be that the Treasury's financial rescue program will be even more important as far as improving consumer and investor confidence is concerned. It is essential that the U.S. financial system return to something approximating normal functioning as soon as possible. And, this could end up being extremely difficult. It may be that the reason Treasury Secretary Timothy Geithner has yet to produce the details of the new financial rescue program has to do with the need to get the fiscal stimulus bill passed by the Congress before those details are revealed.

Survey Methods

Gallup has been interviewing no fewer than 1,000 U.S. adults nationwide each day during 2008 and 2009. The economic questions analyzed in this report are asked of a random half-sample of respondents each day. The results reported here are based on combined data of more than 8,000 interviews in August, September, October, November, and December 2008, and in January 2009. For results based on these samples, the maximum margin of sampling error is ±1 percentage point.

The questions for Feb. 2–8, 2009, are based on combined data of 3,404 interviews. For results based on these samples, the maximum margin of sampling error is ±3 percentage points.

Interviews are conducted with respondents on land-line telephones (for respondents with a land-line telephone) and cellular phones (for respondents who are cell-phone only).

In addition to sampling error, question wording and practical difficulties in conducting surveys can introduce error or bias into the findings of public opinion polls.

February 13, 2009

AMERICANS' REPORTED SPENDING DOWN 40% FROM LAST YEAR

Three-quarters say they are cutting back

by Lydia Saad, Gallup Poll Senior Editor

According to Gallup Poll Daily tracking, Americans, on average, spent $61 per day in stores, restaurants, gas stations, or online in the 14-day period ending Feb. 11. Spending is down 40% from the $102 average for the same two-week period a year ago.

Americans' Self-Reported Daily Retail Spending

Fourteen-day rolling average

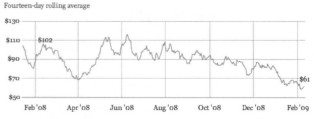

These figures are based on Americans' self-reports of the total amount they spent the prior day on purchases other than a home, motor vehicle, or their normal monthly bills.

The current average spending figure is nearly the lowest Gallup has recorded since the measure was established in January 2008. Although reported spending has been going down fairly steadily since late September, the 14-day average spending figure fell below $60 last week for the first time, to $58, and has since held close to that level.

Year-to-year spending has dropped sharply at every major income level.

Separately, a Jan. 30–Feb. 1 *USA Today*/Gallup poll found three-quarters of Americans (74%) saying they have cut back on their spending in the last six months because of concerns about their household income. Thirty-eight percent of Americans say they have cut back "a lot" and 36% have cut back "a little."

Average Daily Spending, by Monthly Household Income
Based on 14-day average

■ Jan 29-Feb 11, 2008   ▨ Jan 29-Feb 11, 2009

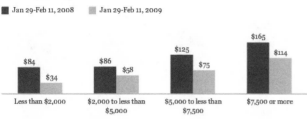

Less than $2,000	$2,000 to less than $5,000	$5,000 to less than $7,500	$7,500 or more
$84 / $34	$86 / $58	$125 / $75	$165 / $114

In the last six months, have you cut back on spending because you were concerned about your household income, or not? (If "yes":) Have you cut back a lot, or only a little?

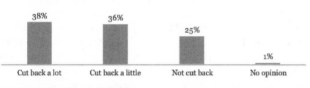

Cut back a lot	Cut back a little	Not cut back	No opinion
38%	36%	25%	1%

USA Today/Gallup, Jan. 30-Feb. 1, 2009

Upper-income Americans (those earning $75,000 or more per year) are less likely than those living in middle- and lower-income households to say they have cut back a lot, but they are more likely to have cut back a little. As a result, the percentage saying they have not cut back at all is close to 25% at every income level.

Spending Changes in Last Six Months
Based on annual household income

■ Cut back a lot   ▨ Cut back a little   ▨ Not cut back

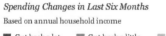

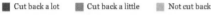

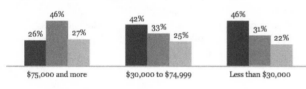

$75,000 and more	$30,000 to $74,999	Less than $30,000
26% / 46% / 27%	42% / 33% / 25%	46% / 31% / 22%

USA Today/Gallup, Jan. 30-Feb. 1, 2009

Bottom Line

Consumer confidence was in decline for much of 2008, and plummeted after the banking crisis started in September. Since then, confidence has remained low, and Gallup has found mounting negative perceptions among U.S. workers about the hiring conditions at their places of employment. From January through November 2008, Gallup's hiring measure consistently found more workers saying their companies were hiring than saying their companies were letting people go. However, by December, more said their companies were cutting staff. The measure has remained negative on balance in 2009.

Sharply falling gas prices from late September through much of December could account for some of the decline in household spending late last year. However, since January, gas prices have increased, while spending has continued to trend downward. It seems clear that, compounding the already-weak state of consumer confidence in place last year, the deteriorating jobs climate has been affecting Americans' confidence in their future income stream, if not causing

them real financial distress, and this has caused Americans to pull back on their spending.

Survey Methods

Results are based on telephone interviews with 1,027 national adults, aged 18 and older, conducted Jan. 30–Feb. 1, 2009. For results based on the total sample of national adults, one can say with 95% confidence that the maximum margin of sampling error is ±3 percentage points.

Interviews are conducted with respondents on land-line telephones (for respondents with a land-line telephone) and cellular phones (for respondents who are cell-phone only).

The latest consumer spending results are based on telephone interviews with roughly 500 national adults, aged 18 and older, conducted each day from Jan. 29–Feb. 11, 2009 as part of Gallup Poll Daily tracking. For the $61 average daily spending estimate based on the total sample of approximately 7,000 national adults, one can say with 95% confidence that the maximum margin of sampling error is ±$6.

In addition to sampling error, question wording and practical difficulties in conducting surveys can introduce error or bias into the findings of public opinion polls.

February 13, 2009
MAJORITY OF AMERICANS SUPPORT DIRECT DIPLOMACY WITH IRAN
Despite continuing to be highly unfavorable toward the country overall

by Lymari Morales, Gallup Poll Staff Writer

Americans appear to support the Obama administration's push for "face-to-face" dialogue with Iran: 56% say the United States should engage in direct diplomacy with Iran, while 38% say it should not.

Do you think the United States should or should not engage in direct diplomacy with Iran?

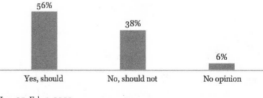

Yes, should	No, should not	No opinion
56%	38%	6%

Jan. 30-Feb. 1, 2009

In his first press conference since taking office, President Barack Obama reiterated his commitment to seeking a new, more diplomatic approach to dealing with Iran, focused on "constructive dialogue, where we can directly engage with them." At the same time, President Obama was clear to detail the United States' dissatisfaction with Iran on several fronts—namely its financing of terrorism, its hostility toward Israel, and its pursuit or development of a nuclear weapon. Iran's president Mahmoud Ahmadinejad quickly responded, saying that Iran is "ready to hold up talks, but talks in a fair atmosphere with mutual respect."

Gallup Polls conducted this year and in the past reveal that Americans' opinions about Iran tend to fall in line with the new president's approach. Last year, 73% said they prefer that the United States employ economic and diplomatic strategies to compel Iran to end its nuclear weapons program, and 67% said they support the U.S. president meeting with leaders of foreign countries considered enemies of the United States. Americans last year also named Iran as the country that poses the single greatest threat to stability in the world.

A new Gallup Poll completed this week finds that currently, 80% of Americans say they hold an unfavorable opinion of Iran—more than say the same about any other country.

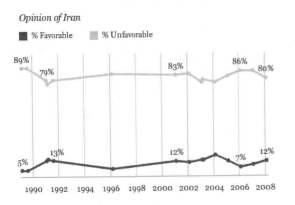

Opinion of Iran

The Diplomacy-Ready Demographics

Certain subgroups of the U.S. population are more ready than others to support forging ahead with direct diplomacy with Iran. At 74%, those with post-graduate educations are the most likely to favor this approach. Moderates, Democrats, liberals, college graduates, and middle-aged Americans also express solid support at or just below two-thirds.

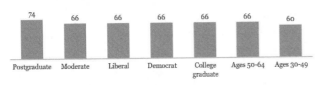

Subgroups Most Likely to Support Direct Diplomacy With Iran
% Yes, should

Jan. 30-Feb. 1, 2009

More Cautious Constituencies

Interestingly, younger Americans are the most resistant to direct diplomacy with Iran, with 38% in favor and 56% opposed. Keeping them company among the most cautious constituencies are conservatives, Republicans, and the less educated, though it is worth noting that levels of support among these groups still hover at or near 50%.

Sandwiched between these groups with levels of support near the national average are Americans aged 65 and older (56%), independents (54%), and those with some college education (51%).

Implications

Americans' support for direct diplomacy with Iran should be encouraging for the Obama administration as it pursues that approach, reit-

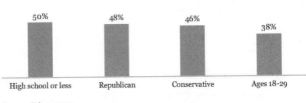

Subgroups Least Likely to Support Direct Diplomacy With Iran
% Yes, should

Jan. 30-Feb. 1, 2009

erated at this week's news conference. Although there are the expected differences in support for the idea among partisan and ideological groups, few demographic groups show decided opposition to direct diplomacy. At the same time, it is interesting to note that younger Americans—a group that overwhelmingly supported Obama's candidacy for president—are the most resistant. This may be due to having lived all or most their adult years in a post 9/11-era in which former President Bush constantly reiterated the threats posed by the "axis of evil." With such low ratings for Iran overall, there remains much room for improvement in Americans' views of the country—and a new way forward appears to be exactly what many would embrace.

Survey Methods

Results are based on telephone interviews with 1,027 national adults, aged 18 and older, conducted Jan. 30–Feb. 1, 2009 and with 1,022 national adults, aged 18 and older, conducted Feb. 9–12, 2009. For results based on the total sample of national adults, one can say with 95% confidence that the maximum margin of sampling error is ±3 percentage points.

Interviews are conducted with respondents on landline telephones (for respondents with a landline telephone) and cellular phones (for respondents who are cell phone only).

In addition to sampling error, question wording and practical difficulties in conducting surveys can introduce error or bias into the findings of public opinion polls.

February 16, 2009
AMERICANS ADVOCATE REDUCED SERVICES TO HELP POSTAL SERVICE
Preferred to higher stamp prices or government assistance

by Jeffrey M. Jones, Gallup Poll Managing Editor

When given a choice of three options for helping the U.S. Postal Service out of its financial difficulties, a majority of Americans prefer cutbacks in services—such as ending Saturday mail delivery and closing post office branches—to either government assistance or higher stamp prices.

The Postal Service has lost nearly $8 billion over the last two years, and, with sharp declines in the amount of mail being sent, it is facing similar or larger losses in the future. It has asked Congress for permission to cut back to five-day-a-week delivery, and recently received permission to raise postage prices; this will take effect in May.

What Would You Most Like to See Done to Help the Postal Service Out of Its Financial Difficulties?

USA Today/Gallup, Jan. 30-Feb. 1, 2009

What Would You Most Like to See Done to Help the Postal Service Out of Its Financial Difficulties, by Race

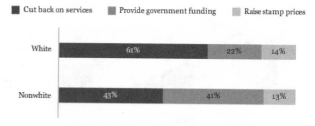

USA Today/Gallup, Jan. 30-Feb. 1, 2009

What Would You Most Like to See Done to Help the Postal Service Out of Its Financial Difficulties, by Political Party Affiliation

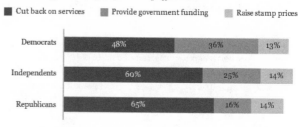

USA Today/Gallup, Jan. 30-Feb. 1, 2009

With only 27% preferring government assistance—something the post office has not received since 1982—and 14% preferring significantly higher stamp prices, Americans appear more than willing to give up some of the conveniences the Postal Service has long offered, including six-day-a-week delivery and thousands of local post office branches.

It is possible the limited support for government funding of the Postal Service may reflect concern over the vast amounts of money Washington is spending in an attempt to revive the economy and help out struggling industries. The poll provides some support for this idea, as those who said they were "very closely" following news about the economic stimulus plan Congress was debating favored cuts in postal services over government funding by a 43-point margin (64% to 21%). That compares to a smaller 25-point margin (54% to 29%) among those who were less attentive to the stimulus debate.

Nearly every key demographic subgroup is willing to accept reduced postal services rather than higher prices or government assistance. The notable exception is young adults—among those aged 18 to 29, just 35% favor cuts in services, while 43% would like to see the government provide funds to keep the Postal Service running as now.

What Would You Most Like to See Done to Help the Postal Service Out of Its Financial Difficulties, by Respondent Age

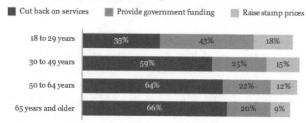

USA Today/Gallup, Jan. 30-Feb. 1, 2009

Also, nonwhites (41%) are nearly twice as likely as whites (22%) to favor government assistance, and significantly less likely than whites to advocate cuts in services.

There are modest political party differences. While the greatest number of Republicans, independents, and Democrats all favor cuts in services, Republicans (65%) are more likely than Democrats (48%) to do so. In turn, Democrats (36%) are more likely than Republicans (16%) to favor government assistance.

Implications

Americans seem willing to forgo some of the Postal Service conveniences they have become accustomed to, as opposed to paying to keep those services directly (through higher stamp prices) or indirectly (through taxpayer funds). This is an attitude shared widely by Americans of nearly every demographic or attitudinal characteristic.

Survey Methods

Results are based on telephone interviews with 1,027 national adults, aged 18 and older, conducted Jan. 30–Feb. 1, 2009. For results based on the total sample of national adults, one can say with 95% confidence that the maximum margin of sampling error is ±3 percentage points.

Interviews are conducted with respondents on land-line telephones (for respondents with a land-line telephone) and cellular phones (for respondents who are cell-phone only).

In addition to sampling error, question wording and practical difficulties in conducting surveys can introduce error or bias into the findings of public opinion polls.

February 16, 2009
U.S. SURPASSES CHINA IN FORECAST FOR ECONOMIC POWERHOUSE
Economic confidence in United States surges among Democrats

by Lydia Saad, Gallup Poll Senior Editor

In spite of the United States' current economic troubles, Americans have a brighter view than they did a year ago about the country's global economic competitiveness. In February 2008, Americans were more likely to name China than the United States as the "leading economic power in the world today." Today the United States and China are about tied.

Which one of the following do you think is the leading economic power in the world today -- [The United States, The European Union, Russia, China, Japan, India]?

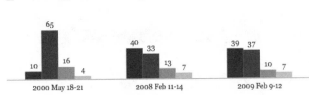

■ % China   ■ % United States   ■ % Japan   ■ % European Union

No other country named by more than 2% of respondents in any year

Furthermore, by 45% to 34%, Americans now believe the United States, not China, will be the world's top economic power in 20 years. This is a sharp reversal from February 2008, when Americans named China over the United States by about the same margin.

Looking ahead 20 years, which one of the following countries do you expect to be the world's leading economic power at that time -- [The United States, The European Union, Russia, China, Japan, India]?

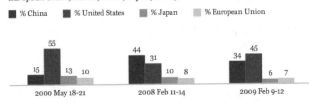

■ % China   ■ % United States   ■ % Japan   ■ % European Union

No other country named by more than 4% of respondents in any year

The 2009 data come from Gallup's annual World Affairs survey, updated Feb. 9–12. For both questions, Gallup offered respondents the choice of five countries plus the European Union.

Gallup first asked the pair of questions in May 2000, when the United States was unrivaled as the perceived economic powerhouse. In 2000, more Americans thought Japan, rather than China, was the current leading economic power (16% vs. 10%), and Japan and the European Union were not far behind China in perceptions of which country would be the leading power in 2020.

Perceptions changed dramatically in 2008, with the U.S. economy flagging and China's rapid economic growth gaining visibility. China emerged at the top of both rankings that year.

Democrats Show Renewed Confidence in United States

Recent news that the worldwide financial crisis is impinging on China's rapid economic growth could be influencing Americans' perspectives on the United States' global competitiveness. However, politics appears to be the major factor in changes in these views.

Democrats—who, unlike Republicans, are widely supportive of President Barack Obama's economic stimulus package—are much more likely to predict the United States will be the leading economic power in 20 years than they were a year ago: 51% today versus 28% in 2008. Independents are a bit more likely to name the United States (37%, up from 23%), while there has been no change among Republicans.

Current Perceptions of Top Economic Power

The current finding that only 37% of Americans believe the United States is the world's greatest economic power may not be surprising given the attention paid to China's remarkable economic growth in recent years.

Japan, which actually exceeds China in total economic output, falls well below both the United States and China in mentions of the dominant economic power today. Russia and India, neither of which rank among the world's top 10 economies (in terms of overall gross domestic product), are disregarded by most Americans as the leading economic power.

College graduates have only a slightly different sense of the global economic rank order than do those with less formal education. A year ago, however, the views of college graduates on this question were no different than the views of those with no college education.

Prediction of World's Leading Economic Power in 20 Years, by Party ID

Mentions of China and the United States

	Republicans	Independents	Democrats
	%	%	%
2009			
China	35	36	31
United States	47	37	51
2008			
China	39	44	48
United States	46	23	28

World's Current Leading Economic Power, by Education

Mentions of China and the United States

	College graduate	Some college	No college
	%	%	%
2009			
China	35	44	37
United States	44	30	37
2008			
China	40	45	37
United States	37	28	34

Since 2008, most of the shift in mentions by age from China to the United States in terms of which is the current economic leader has come from young adults. In 2008, 50% of those 18 to 34 years of age named China and only 23% named the United States. Today, young adults are about evenly divided, with 38% naming the United States and 36% naming China. The views of middle-aged and older adults have not changed much.

World's Current Leading Economic Power, by Age

Mentions of China and the United States

	18 to 34 years	35 to 54 years	55 and older
	%	%	%
2009			
China	36	41	39
United States	38	34	39
2008			
China	50	38	36
United States	23	32	41

Outlook for Economic Power

The question of which country will be the leading economic power in 20 years is more subjective. Carrying current rates of growth forward, China could conceivably become the world's largest national economy in terms of GDP in that time frame; however, the unfolding financial crisis now adds considerable uncertainty to the equation.

Gallup finds no generational differences this year in perceptions about which country will be the leading economic power in 20 years: all three major age groups are more likely to name the United States than China. A year ago, all three groups were more likely to name China; however, this tendency was particularly strong among young adults.

Predictions of World's Leading Economic Power in 20 Years, by Age
Mentions of China and the United States

	18 to 34 years	35 to 54 years	55 and older
	%	%	%
2009			
China	37	28	38
United States	43	47	42
2008			
China	50	40	45
United States	20	35	33

College graduates were in 2008, and remain in 2009, the most likely of all educational categories to believe China will be the future economic leader.

Predictions of World's Leading Economic Power in 20 Years, by Education
Mentions of China and the United States

	College graduate	Some college	No college
	%	%	%
2009			
China	40	34	29
United States	37	47	49
2008			
China	51	45	39
United States	27	27	38

Bottom Line

Only 37% of Americans today recognize the United States as the world's dominant economic power, while a similar percentage believe that distinction goes to China. As far off the mark as this may be when looking at current GDP figures by country, it is quite different from perceptions a year ago, when only 33% named the United States and 40% selected China.

Americans' predictions for which nation will be No. 1 economically in 20 years have changed even more over the past year. The increased optimism about the United States' future economic standing is striking because it runs counter to Americans' highly negative current assessments of the nation's economy. The fact that China's economy has stumbled along with everyone else's over the past year may be a factor in cracking the perception that China is unstoppable in attaining economic superiority. However, Democrats' (and, to a lesser extent, independents') confidence in Obama and the economic stimulus package appears to be a major factor.

Survey Methods

Results are based on telephone interviews with 1,022 national adults, aged 18 and older, conducted Feb. 9–12, 2009. For results based on the total sample of national adults, one can say with 95% confidence that the maximum margin of sampling error is ±3 percentage points.

Interviews are conducted with respondents on land-line telephones (for respondents with a land-line telephone) and cellular phones (for respondents who are cell-phone only).

In addition to sampling error, question wording and practical difficulties in conducting surveys can introduce error or bias into the findings of public opinion polls.

February 17, 2009
CONGRESS' APPROVAL RATING JUMPS TO 31%
More positive ratings from Democrats largely responsible for increase

by Jeffrey M. Jones, Gallup Poll Managing Editor

Gallup's latest congressional job approval rating, from a Feb. 9–12 poll, shows a sharp 12 percentage-point increase from last month, rising from 19% to 31%. While still quite negative on an absolute basis, this is the best rating for Congress in nearly two years.

Congressional Job Approval Ratings, 2006-2009

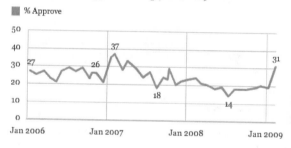

Congress' approval ratings have been below 30% pretty consistently since October 2005. There have been a few exceptions to this, with ratings as high as 37% in early 2007 after the Democrats took party control of Congress after their victories in the November 2006 midterm elections, but those quickly disappeared. More recently, approval ratings of Congress had been about 20% or lower, including an all-time low rating of 14% in July 2008.

This month's sharp increase largely reflects a more positive Democratic review of Congress. Since the previous measure from early January, Barack Obama has been inaugurated as president, and now Democrats have party control of both the legislative and the executive branches of the federal government.

Democrats' average approval ratings of Congress more than doubled from January (18%) to February (43%). Independents show a smaller increase, from 17% to 29%, while Republicans are now less likely to approve of Congress than they were in January.

The more positive ratings for Congress among Democrats may also reflect an implicit endorsement of the work Congress has been doing to pass the economic stimulus plan, which had considerable support among rank-and-file Democrats, according to recent Gallup Polls.

Congressional Job Approval Ratings, January and February 2009, by Political Party

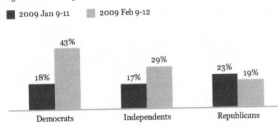

■ 2009 Jan 9-11   ▨ 2009 Feb 9-12

43%

18%   29%   23%
      17%   19%

Democrats   Independents   Republicans

Surge in Congress Job Approval in Historical Perspective

Gallup has been measuring public approval of Congress on a monthly basis since January 2001. During that time, there have been only two month-to-month increases larger than the 12-point jump observed this month.

The largest single-month increase was a 42-point rally in congressional support after the Sept. 11 terrorist attacks, from 42% in a Sept. 7–10, 2001, poll to 84% in mid-October 2001. Gallup found similar increases in ratings of other government institutions around that time.

The next-largest jump of 14 points occurred after Democrats took party control of both the U.S. House and the U.S. Senate in early 2007. There was also a 10-point increase from March to April 2003, which spanned the time of the beginning of the U.S. war with Iraq.

Largest Month-to-Month Increases in Congressional Approval Ratings, 2001-2009

	First month rating	Second month rating	Increase
September-October 2001	42%	84%	+42 pts.
December 2006-January 2007	21%	35%	+14 pts.
January-February 2009	19%	31%	+12 pts.
March-April 2003	48%	58%	+10 pts.

In general, Congress' approval ratings tend to be low. In fact, the current 31% score is very near the historical average of 35% in Gallup Polls since 1974. That compares with an average 55% approval rating for presidents historically.

Survey Methods

Results are based on telephone interviews with 1,022 national adults, aged 18 and older, conducted Feb. 9–12, 2009. For results based on the total sample of national adults, one can say with 95% confidence that the maximum margin of sampling error is ±3 percentage points.

Interviews are conducted with respondents on land-line telephones (for respondents with a land-line telephone) and cellular phones (for respondents who are cell-phone only).

In addition to sampling error, question wording and practical difficulties in conducting surveys can introduce error or bias into the findings of public opinion polls.

February 17, 2009
OBAMA SIGNS STIMULUS INTO LAW WITH MAJORITY SUPPORT
Support for bill among American public is highly partisan

by Frank Newport, Gallup Poll Editor in Chief

President Barack Obama signed the new $787 billion stimulus bill into law today in Denver with the general support of a majority of the American public, albeit a public sharply divided along party lines—just as was the case in Congress where the bill was deliberated and voted on over the last several weeks. The bill becomes law at a time when almost 8 in 10 Americans believe the U.S. economy is getting worse, and fewer than 1 in 10 say it's a good time to find a quality job.

*As you may know, Congress is considering a new economic stimulus package of at least $800 billion. Do you favor or oppose Congress passing this legislation?**

■ % Favor   ■ % Oppose   ▨ % No opinion

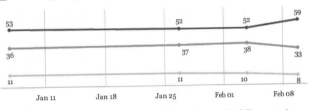

53		52	52		59
36		37	38		33
11		11	10		8

Jan 11   Jan 18   Jan 25   Feb 01   Feb 08

* Jan. 6-7, 2009 wording: Do you favor or oppose Congress passing a new $775 billion economic stimulus program as soon as possible after Barack Obama takes office?

Gallup's Feb. 11 update on the public's view of the stimulus bill showed 59% in favor of "a new stimulus package of at least $800 billion". This demonstrates a marginal increase in the level of support found in an earlier February poll, as well as one in late January (52% in both cases). Opposition over the last month has been running between 37% in late January to 33% in Feb. 10 polling.

Polling from Feb. 4 shows that a stimulus bill described as "reduced by up to $200 billion" received increased support from those who do not approve of the initial bill, described as "at least $800 billion". In fact, the final bill, which passed in both houses of Congress and was signed into law by Obama today, came in slightly below the $800 billion figure used in Gallup's survey question. It is not clear if the small reduction in cost of the final bill to $785 billion would change the level of public support from what Gallup measured when the bill was described as "at least $800 billion".

It has been well documented that public support for a stimulus bill is highly partisan, echoing what occurred in Congress. In Gallup's Feb. 11 update, 82% of Democrats supported the bill compared to just 28% of Republicans.

*Support for $800 Billion Economic Stimulus Package, by Party I.D.**

% in favor

■ Democrats   ■ Independents   ▨ Republicans

67		73	70		82
54		46	55		56
34		29	24		28

Jan 11   Jan 18   Jan 25   Feb 01   Feb 08

* Jan. 6-7, 2009 wording: Do you favor or oppose Congress passing a new $775 billion economic stimulus program as soon as possible after Barack Obama takes office?

The final bill includes a long list of ways in which the government money is to be spent in the months and years to come. Gallup's recent polling of a short list of things that could be included in the bill showed public support was highest for money to be spent on education (the final bill includes up to $100 billion for education) and for tax cuts for individuals and families. Americans considered the least important aspects of the bill to be money for state and local governments and tax cuts for businesses.

How do you think Obama's economic stimulus plan would affect the nation's economy -- would it -- [ROTATED: make it a lot better, make it a little better, not affect it, (or) make it worse]?

(Asked of those who think stimulus plan will make economy better) Do you think Obama's economic stimulus plan would improve the nation's economy this year, or would it take longer than that?

COMBINED RESULTS

	%
Make economy better	64
(Economy would improve this year)	10
(Would take longer)	54
Not affect economy	15
Make economy worse	17
No opinion	4

USA Today/Gallup, Jan. 30-Feb. 1, 2009

The bill becomes law at a time when Gallup's measures of the public's opinions on the economy and their financial situations are at or near the lowest seen since Gallup began tracking these indicators:

- 79% of Americans say the U.S. economy is getting worse
- Only 10% rate the current U.S. economy as excellent or good
- Just 9% say now is a good time to find a quality job, the lowest in Gallup's history of asking this question since 2001

By a six percentage point margin, employed Americans are more likely to say that their companies are letting people go and reducing the size of their work force, rather than hiring employees and expanding their work force

The economy is overwhelmingly seen as the most important problem facing the nation.

Implications

A review of Gallup polling suggests a majority of Americans supported President Obama when he signed the massive economic stimulus bill into law today, but this support is far from universal. About a third of Americans, mostly Republicans, oppose the bill. Americans believe that some aspects of the spending bill—including education and tax cuts—are very important, but are much less likely to believe that other items, such as money for state and local governments, are important.

The bill was signed into law at a time when Americans are reporting extremely negative views of the economy and the job market, and it is clear that this bill is expected to address what is overwhelmingly considered by the public to be the number one problem facing the country.

February 18, 2009
NO PERCEIVED GAINS IN U.S. WORLD STANDING POST-BUSH
Just 32% are satisfied with the United States' position in the world

by Jeffrey M. Jones, Gallup Poll Managing Editor

It is apparently going to take more than having a new president for Americans to perceive increased international prestige for the United States. Even though a new Gallup Poll finds Americans widely perceiving that other world leaders respect President Obama, just 32% are satisfied with the position of the United States in the world today, and 45% believe other countries perceive the United States favorably—both little changed from last year, when George W. Bush was still president.

Changes in Perceptions of U.S. Standing in the World, 2008 vs. 2009

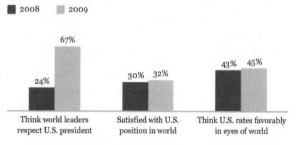

These results are based on Gallup's annual World Affairs poll, conducted each February since 2001, including Feb. 9–12 of this year.

President Obama will attempt to improve the United States' international image, beginning with his visit to Canada on Thursday, his first international trip as president. Obama seems better positioned to handle this than his immediate predecessor. The 2009 poll finds 67% of Americans saying world leaders respect Obama, compared with just 24% who said this about Bush a year ago.

Obama's score on this measure rivals that of Bush shortly after the Sept. 11 terrorist attacks (75%), when he enjoyed wide public support.

Despite this, Obama has much work to do to improve Americans' views of their nation's international standing. Since the early part of the Bush presidency, Gallup has documented a significant decline in Americans' satisfaction with the United States' position in the world. This measure barely increased from 30% in 2008 to 32% after Obama's inauguration.

On the whole, would you say that you are satisfied or dissatisfied with the position of the United States in the world today?

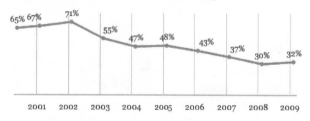

Gallup's annual polling on World Affairs also shows a decline since 2002 in the percentage of Americans who think the United States rates favorably in the eyes of the world. Again, there is little sign of improvement in these views since Bush departed from the White House.

In general, how do you think the United States rates in the eyes of the world -- very favorably, somewhat favorably, somewhat unfavorably, or very unfavorably?

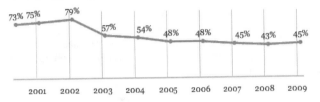

The downward paths of both trends likely reflect Americans' recognition that many Bush-era foreign policies were not supported by leaders of other countries. The most notable of these was the war in Iraq, but there were others such as the Kyoto global warming agreement and the controversial treatment of war prisoners.

Obama has pledged a new and arguably more cooperative approach to foreign policy, and has named special envoys to the Middle East and the Pakistan-Afghanistan region, as well as signaling the possibility of direct diplomacy with Iran. Vice President Joe Biden and Secretary of State Hillary Clinton have also taken extended foreign trips.

This new leadership and new approach to foreign policy may help explain the slight increase in the percentage of Americans who believe the United States should take "the leading role" in world affairs. Currently, 23% of Americans say this, the highest Gallup has measured since February 2003, when 26% did. As has typically been the case, a majority (52%) say the United States should play "a major role, but not the leading role" in world affairs. Only about one in four Americans say the United States should play a minor role (17%) or no role at all (6%).

Obama's Initial Foreign Affairs Approval Rating

Since much of Obama's work as president to date has focused on domestic concerns like the economy, it is not surprising that a substantial proportion of Americans (24%) do not yet have an opinion on how the new president has handled foreign affairs. But so far, many more approve (54%) than disapprove (22%) of his actions in this area.

That compares with a 59% approval rating and a 30% disapproval rating for his handling of the economy.

Do you approve or disapprove of the way Barack Obama is handling -- [RANDOM ORDER]?

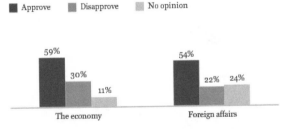

Feb. 9-12, 2009

Both of these are somewhat lower than his overall approval rating, which has averaged 65% to date in Gallup Poll Daily tracking.

Implications

Thus far, Americans perceive no immediate benefit to the United States' world standing from the recent transition of power from the Bush to the Obama administration. But Americans do think the potential is there, given the widely held view that other world leaders respect Obama.

Obama's trip to Canada on Thursday will begin to shine a brighter light on his foreign policy, and on his ability to make progress for the United States in international affairs.

Survey Methods

Results are based on telephone interviews with 1,022 national adults, aged 18 and older, conducted Feb. 9–12, 2009. For results based on the total sample of national adults, one can say with 95% confidence that the maximum margin of sampling error is ±3 percentage points.

Interviews are conducted with respondents on land-line telephones (for respondents with a land-line telephone) and cellular phones (for respondents who are cell-phone only).

In addition to sampling error, question wording and practical difficulties in conducting surveys can introduce error or bias into the findings of public opinion polls.

February 18, 2009
AMERICANS MORE NEGATIVE THAN POSITIVE ABOUT FOREIGN TRADE
Have held more negative views since 2005

by Jeffrey M. Jones, Gallup Poll Managing Editor

Gallup's annual World Affairs poll shows Americans holding a slightly more negative than positive view of foreign trade, with more perceiving it as a "threat to the economy from foreign imports" (47%) than as "an opportunity for economic growth through increased U.S. exports" (44%). Americans' opinions on trade have been more negative than positive in recent years.

What do you think foreign trade means for America? Do you see foreign trade more as -- an opportunity for economic growth through increased U.S. exports or a threat to the economy from foreign imports?

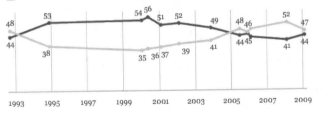

Increased trade with Asian nations is one of several items on Secretary of State Hillary Clinton's agenda on her tour of Asia this week, along with the global economic crisis, climate change, and North Korean nuclear disarmament. President Obama will discuss trade on his first international trip (to Canada) on Thursday.

Gallup has documented a shift in Americans' perceptions on foreign trade in recent years. From 1994 (the year NAFTA went into effect) through 2003, the public was much more likely to perceive trade as an opportunity for economic growth, with a high of 56% taking this view in a May 2000 survey.

But in recent years, as the economy has had its ups and downs and Americans have wrestled with the economic implications of job outsourcing, illegal immigration, and the safety of many food and toy imports, those views have changed. Since 2005, Americans have become more likely to perceive foreign trade as a threat to the U.S. economy. That reached a high of 52% last February—the only time a majority has held this perception—before decreasing slightly this year.

One of the largest differences by subgroup in views of foreign trade is by household income. Wealthier Americans hold a much more positive view than do Americans with more limited financial resources.

Views of Foreign Trade, by Annual Household Income

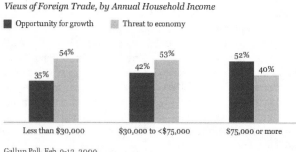

Gallup Poll, Feb. 9-12, 2009

There are only minor differences by party, as Republicans, Democrats, and independents are all slightly more likely to see foreign trade as a threat to U.S. imports than as an opportunity to promote U.S. exports.

Views of Foreign Trade, by Political Party Affiliation

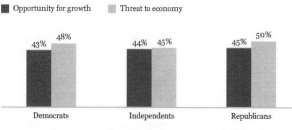

Gallup Poll, Feb. 9-12, 2009

Since 2000, when Gallup recorded the most positive evaluations of foreign trade, all key demographic and political subgroups have increasingly come to view foreign trade as a threat to the U.S. economy. This shift is particularly strong among middle-income Americans (from 32% to 53%), whose finances are probably more likely to be affected by trade developments than those of upper-income Americans. Also, many subgroups who held particularly positive views of foreign trade in 2000—including Republicans, upper-income Americans, and those with postgraduate educations—have moved more toward an anti-trade position.

Implications

As with many policies, there are pluses and minuses to foreign trade. And while many economists and political leaders may hold

Percentage Viewing Foreign Trade as a Threat to U.S. Economy, by Subgroup, 2000 vs. 2009

	2000	2009	Change
	%	%	Pct. pts.
Gender			
Men	34	44	10
Women	37	51	14
Race			
White	37	49	12
Nonwhite	28	43	15
Age			
18 to 29 years	29	41	12
30 to 49 years	36	48	12
50 to 64 years	38	50	12
65+ years	41	46	5
Region			
East	41	52	11
Midwest	39	50	11
South	35	46	11
West	28	42	14
Education			
High school or less	46	54	8
Some college	34	51	17
College grad only	32	39	7
Postgraduate	11	29	18
Household income			
Less than $30,000	42	54	12
$30,000 to $74,999	32	53	21
$75,000 or more	22	40	18
Party affiliation			
Democrat	35	48	13
Independent	39	45	6
Republican	33	50	17
Ideology			
Liberal	32	40	8
Moderate	36	52	16
Conservative	38	49	11

a more pro- than anti-trade position, the public does not necessarily share that position. In fact, as the Obama administration seeks to preserve or expand current trade relationships, the public is slightly more likely to take a negative than a positive view of foreign trade.

Survey Methods

Results are based on telephone interviews with 1,022 national adults, aged 18 and older, conducted Feb. 9–12, 2009. For results based on the total sample of national adults, one can say with 95% confidence that the maximum margin of sampling error is ±3 percentage points.

Interviews are conducted with respondents on land-line telephones (for respondents with a land-line telephone) and cellular phones (for respondents who are cell-phone only).

In addition to sampling error, question wording and practical difficulties in conducting surveys can introduce error or bias into the findings of public opinion polls.

February 19, 2009

CANADA REMAINS AMERICANS' MOST FAVORED NATION

Great Britain nearly ties Canada for top spot

by Lydia Saad, Gallup Poll Senior Editor

Barack Obama's first foreign visit as president on Thursday will be to a country, Canada, that enjoys the highest favorable rating of 19 nations rated in Gallup's Feb. 9–12 World Affairs survey. Nine in 10 Americans view the United States' neighbor to the north favorably, while only 6% view it unfavorably.

Next, I'd like your overall opinion of some foreign countries. What is your overall opinion of ... ? Is it very favorable, mostly favorable, mostly unfavorable, or very unfavorable?

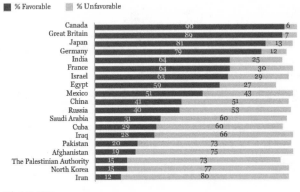

Feb. 9-12, 2009

Great Britain, another English-speaking ally of the United States, nearly matches Canada in its U.S. popularity, with an 89% favorable rating. Japan and Germany fall a notch lower, viewed favorably by about 8 in 10 Americans, followed by France, India, and Israel, all with positive ratings around 64%.

Iran ranks last on the list, with a 12% favorable rating and an 80% unfavorable rating, followed by North Korea and the Palestinian Authority, both with 15% favorable scores. Afghanistan and Pakistan are viewed as only slightly better, with 19% and 20% favorable ratings, respectively.

This is the fourth straight year that Canada has topped the country rankings, including with a 92% favorable rating in 2008.

Favorability Trends

All of the 19 countries rated this year were included in Gallup's 2008 World Affairs survey as well as in most of Gallup's annual measurements since the World Affairs survey was launched in 2001. Earlier Gallup Poll trends, from as far back as 1979, exist for many of the countries.

According to the long-term trends, the 2009 favorability ratings for both Russia and Mexico are the lowest Gallup has seen in many years.

Favorability toward Mexico peaked at 74% in 2003 and 2005, but has fallen each year since 2005. Today's 51% favorable rating of Mexico is significantly lower than the 58% found last year, and is the lowest Gallup has recorded since 1993. Heightened attention to illegal immigration from Mexico, as well as to intensifying violence in the Mexican drug war, could explain the deterioration of Mexico's U.S. image in recent years.

Americans' Overall Opinion of Mexico

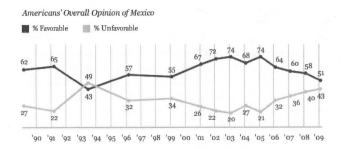

Americans' favorability toward Russia has also been sinking since 2005, when 61% of U.S. adults felt favorably toward the nation's former Cold War nemesis. More generally, public attitudes toward Russia have been somewhat volatile over the years, and seemingly sensitive to shifts in U.S.-Russian diplomatic relations.

Positive feelings toward Russia registered 66% in February 2002, matching the historical high point first reached in 1991. Favorability toward Russia plummeted to 40% in March 2003, likely capturing U.S. resentment against Russia for its opposition to the Iraq war. However, by February 2004, Russia's favorable rating had bounced back to 59%. The current 40% favorable rating of Russia is down from 48% a year ago, which could reflect U.S. public reaction to Russia's recent military crackdown on Russian separatists and the resulting conflict with Georgia, the former Soviet republic.

Americans' Overall Opinion of Russia*

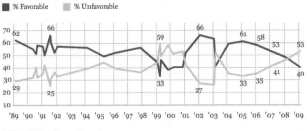

* "Soviet Union" from 1989-1992

The only country to gain more than a few percentage points in popularity over the past year is Iraq. While ratings of Iraq remain much more negative than positive, the latest 28% favorable rating is up from 20% a year ago, and from 15% in 2007. The high point in favorability of Iraq was 29% in 2005, but attitudes were more negative in 2006, 2007, and 2008, as the Iraq war dragged on and U.S. casualties mounted, with little hope for a successful conclusion to the conflict.

With Iraq assuming a greater degree of responsibility for its own governance and internal security over the past year, and after the orderly provincial elections in late January, Americans seem to be feeling more positive about Iraq.

Summary Ratings

In addition to reviewing the favorable ratings of the individual countries, Gallup categorizes countries according to their political relationship with the United States, as either allies, non-allies, or adversaries. The average favorable ratings of the countries in each group allow Gallup to track broad patterns in Americans' perceptions of the world, as well as discern whether the distance between atti-

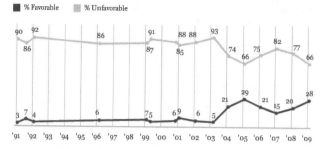

Americans' Overall Opinion of Iraq

■ % Favorable   ■ % Unfavorable

90 92   86   91   88 88 93
86   87   85   74 75   82 77
                              66   66

3 7 4   6   7 5 6 9 6 5   21 29 21 15 20 28

'91 '92 '93 '94 '95 '96 '97 '98 '99 '00 '01 '02 '03 '04 '05 '06 '07 '08 '09

tudes toward the United States' friends and attitudes toward its foes is widening or narrowing.

Allies

The 2009 World Affairs survey includes eight U.S. allies as defined by membership in NATO or by official U.S. designation as a major non-NATO ally. These are Canada, France, Germany, Great Britain, Egypt, Israel, Japan, and Pakistan. The average favorable rating of all eight countries in 2009 is 68%.

Adversaries

The survey includes three countries with which the United States has no formal diplomatic relations: Cuba, Iran, and North Korea. In line with the U.S. government's position toward these countries, the three receive an average favorable rating from Americans of just 19%. (From 2001 through 2004, the category also included Iraq.)

Non-Allies

The survey includes another eight countries that currently fall into neither category: Afghanistan, China, India, Iraq, Mexico, Russia, Saudi Arabia, and the Palestinian Authority. While the United States has strong diplomatic relations with each of these and, in the case of India, has signed an important civil nuclear agreement, none of them is linked with the United States in a formal defense or diplomatic pact. The average U.S. favorability rating toward these eight countries is 36%.

While the 2009 composite rating of the eight non-ally nations is fairly low, ratings of the individual non-ally countries are quite varied, ranging from 15% for the Palestinian Authority to 64% for India. In fact, U.S. public opinion of India is more consistent with ratings of U.S. allies than with those of non-allies.

2009 Country Favorable Ratings Summarized by Category

■ Average favorable rating

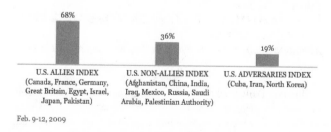

U.S. ALLIES INDEX (Canada, France, Germany, Great Britain, Egypt, Israel, Japan, Pakistan)	U.S. NON-ALLIES INDEX (Afghanistan, China, India, Iraq, Mexico, Russia, Saudi Arabia, Palestinian Authority)	U.S. ADVERSARIES INDEX (Cuba, Iran, North Korea)
68%	36%	19%

Feb. 9-12, 2009

Americans' average ratings of the United States' allies and adversaries included in this year's poll were highest in February

2001, but by 2004 had fallen 11 percentage points, from 75% to 64%. Attitudes have since leveled off close to a 70% average favorability rating.

Average ratings of U.S. adversaries declined sharply between 2001 and 2003—largely because of decreased favorability toward North Korea and, to a lesser extent, Iraq. This followed former President George W. Bush's declaration that Iran, Iraq, and North Korea constituted an "axis of evil" that must be fought. The composite rating has since fluctuated between 13% and 20%.

Perhaps most interesting is the downward trend in average favorability toward the middle group of countries, falling from 49% in 2001 and 44% in 2002 to 40% by 2006 and 36% today. The drop is owing to the aforementioned declines in favorability toward Russia and Mexico, as well as in perceptions of Afghanistan (from 26% favorability in 2002 to 19% today). The only country in this group to see real improvement in its image since 2001 is India.

Summary Country Favorable Ratings -- 2001-2009

% Average favorable rating

■ U.S. Allies Index   ■ U.S. Non-Allies Index   ■ U.S. Adversaries Index

75 71 66 64 70 68 69 71 68
49 44 42 43 49 40 40 38 36
20 18 15 20 18 13 15 16 19

'01 '02 '03 '04 '05 '06 '07 '08 '09

* Iraq categorized as U.S. adversary from 2001-2004

Survey Methods

Results are based on telephone interviews with 1,022 national adults, aged 18 and older, conducted Feb. 9–12, 2009. For results based on the total sample of national adults, one can say with 95% confidence that the maximum margin of sampling error is ±3 percentage points.

Interviews are conducted with respondents on land-line telephones (for respondents with a land-line telephone) and cellular phones (for respondents who are cell-phone only).

In addition to sampling error, question wording and practical difficulties in conducting surveys can introduce error or bias into the findings of public opinion polls.

February 19, 2009
AMERICANS SEE AFGHANISTAN WAR AS STILL WORTH FIGHTING
Though many would like faster withdrawal of troops than is likely

by Lymari Morales, Gallup Poll Staff Writer

Americans likely view President Barack Obama's decision to send more troops to Afghanistan as unfortunate but necessary. Since mid-2008, a majority of Americans have perceived things in Afghanistan to be going very or moderately badly for the United States, and 70% currently think the Taliban will retake control if U.S. forces are withdrawn.

In general, how would you say things are going for the U.S. in Afghanistan -- [ROTATED: very well, moderately well, moderately badly, (or) very badly]?

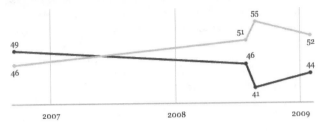

Thinking now about U.S. military action in Afghanistan that began in October 2001, do you think the United States made a mistake in sending military forces to Afghanistan, or not?

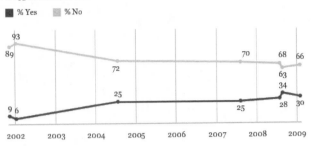

President Obama's decision, announced on Tuesday, to send 17,000 additional troops to Afghanistan was accompanied by a White House statement stressing that urgent action was needed because "the Taliban is resurgent in Afghanistan." This assertion would appear to reflect the opinions of a majority of Americans. When surveyed about Afghanistan earlier this month, Americans overwhelmingly said they would expect Afghanistan to fall under the Taliban's control if the United States and its allies withdrew their forces. Only 21% said they did not expect the Taliban to retake control, and 9% had no opinion.

The harsh realities of the United States' continued involvement in both Afghanistan and Iraq amid a precarious economic situation at home likely weigh on many Americans. In fact, Americans are almost evenly divided about whether the United States should keep a significant number of troops in Afghanistan until the situation improves (48%) or whether it should set a timetable for withdrawal (47%). Those who support a timetable mostly favor getting troops out sooner rather than later. But at least 6 in 10 Americans either favor keeping troops in Afghanistan with no timetable, or favor a long-range timetable of more than two years.

Views on Keeping Troops in Afghanistan vs. Setting a Timetable for Withdrawal

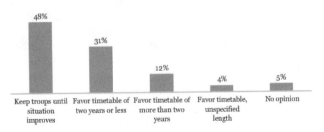

The top U.S. commander in Afghanistan predicted this week that the United States would likely need to stay heavily committed in Afghanistan for the next three to five years. While a sizable minority of Americans would prefer a timetable for withdrawal sooner than that, the data suggest many would support a decision to stay longer.

Americans for the most part support the underlying rationale for the U.S. presence in Afghanistan. Only 30% say it was a mistake to send troops to Afghanistan, compared with 66% who disagree—though those numbers have tightened slightly in recent years.

By comparison, since October 2006, a majority of Americans have consistently said the United States made a mistake in sending troops to Iraq.

Americans have a clear opinion as to what should be the primary goal of U.S. involvement in Afghanistan. Given a choice, a majority (54%) say it should be to weaken terrorists' ability to stage attacks against the United States rather than building a stable democratic government in that country (30%).

Bottom Line

In a Gallup Poll conducted last month, 68% of Americans said they expected Obama to increase military strength in Afghanistan, and 43% considered this very important. Thus, Americans are likely not surprised by the decision to increase U.S. troop strength in that country, something Obama promised to do throughout the 2008 presidential campaign. Importantly, Americans still support the basic decision to send U.S. troops there, something that has not been the case for the Iraq war for quite some time, and fear rather severe consequences (re-established Taliban control) if the United States abandons its mission.

Survey Methods

Results are based on telephone interviews with 1,027 national adults, aged 18 and older, conducted Jan. 30–Feb. 1, 2009. For results based on the total sample of national adults, one can say with 95% confidence that the maximum margin of sampling error is ±3 percentage points.

Interviews are conducted with respondents on land-line telephones (for respondents with a land-line telephone) and cellular phones (for respondents who are cell-phone only).

In addition to sampling error, question wording and practical difficulties in conducting surveys can introduce error or bias into the findings of public opinion polls.

February 20, 2009
DESPITE STIMULUS BILL, NO SIGN OF UPTICK IN CONSUMER MOOD
Attitudes remain as negative now as they were in early February

by Frank Newport, Gallup Poll Editor in Chief

Gallup Poll Daily tracking shows no sign yet that the new $787 billion stimulus plan passed by Congress and signed into law this week by President Obama has made any change in the way Americans view the U.S. economy; 79% continue to say the economy is getting worse, almost exactly the same percentage as that seen in the first days of the month and as the average for February so far.

Right now, do you think that economic conditions in the country as a whole are getting better or getting worse?
Gallup Poll Daily tracking

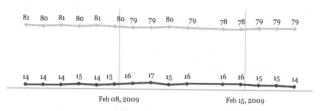

How would you rate economic conditions in this country today -- as excellent, good, only fair, or poor?
February 2009 Trend

	Excellent	Good	Only fair	Poor
	%	%	%	%
Feb 16-18, 2009	1	7	30	62
Feb 15-17, 2009	1	9	31	59
Feb 14-16, 2009	1	9	31	59
Feb 12-15, 2009	1	8	32	59
Feb 11-14, 2009	1	6	31	61
Feb 10-12, 2009	1	8	28	62
Feb 9-11, 2009	1	9	27	62
Feb 8-10, 2009	1	10	29	59
Feb 7-9, 2009	*	9	31	59
Feb 6-8, 2009	1	7	32	60
Feb 5-7, 2009	1	6	31	62
Feb 4-6, 2009	1	6	33	60
Feb 3-5, 2009	1	7	32	59
Feb 2-4, 2009	1	8	31	59
Feb 1-3, 2009	1	7	30	60

Gallup Poll Daily tracking
* Less than 0.5%

The impact of the stimulus bill on the "real" economy—in terms of jobs and increased consumer spending—won't be known for some time. Indeed, critics of the bill say it may be years before the massive increase in government spending begins to be reflected in such hard indicators. Still, it is a reasonable hypothesis that the stimulus bill could have a more immediate impact on consumer psychology, with Americans' views of the economy in theory perking up in anticipation of the bill's effects.

Current Gallup tracking data, however, do not support this hypothesis. Americans appear to be just as negative about the economy now as they were earlier in February, before the bill's passage became a certainty. The average values for Gallup's direction-of-the-economy question between Feb. 1 and Feb. 18 are 15% getting better and 80% getting worse. The values for the first three days of February were 14% better and 81% worse, and the values for Feb. 16–18 are 14% getting better and 79% getting worse. All of these figures represent a very stable pattern throughout the month.

An analysis of trends in the "getting better"/"getting worse" indicator by party show a slight tendency for Democrats to have become more positive about the economy since the beginning of the month, while Republicans have become more negative. These changes are not great, however, and essentially balance themselves out, producing the result of little change in the overall numbers between the two time periods.

Right now, do you think that economic conditions in the country as a whole are getting better or getting worse?
By party ID

	Getting better Feb 1-3, 2009	Getting worse Feb 1-3, 2009	Getting better Feb 16-18, 2009	Getting worse Feb 16-18, 2009
	%	%	%	%
Republicans	11	84	6	90
Independents	14	80	13	79
Democrats	19	76	22	72

Gallup Poll Daily tracking

Perhaps not unexpectedly, there has been little change in the last few weeks in the way Americans rate the current economy.

Although there have been some fluctuations, the basic distribution of attitudes across these categories appears to be very similar in early February to what it is today, with roughly 10% describing current conditions as "excellent" or "good" and about 60% rating conditions "poor."

Bottom Line

The fact that Congress was going to agree on and pass a stimulus bill has been evident for a number of days, and Obama's signing of that bill made it official this week. So far, however, there is no sign in

Gallup's continuous tracking of Americans' views of the economy that the bill has made any difference. Attitudes now are no different from what they were at the beginning of the month.

It may take more time for consumers to adjust to the potentially positive impact of the bill, of course, and Gallup's daily monitoring of consumer confidence may reflect this in the days to come. For the moment, however, it's business as usual as far as the public's economic mood is concerned, and that business remains very negative.

Survey Methods

Results are based on telephone interviews with 1,501 national adults, aged 18 and older, conducted Feb. 16–18, 2009, as part of Gallup Poll Daily tracking. For results based on the total sample of national adults, one can say with 95% confidence that the maximum margin of sampling error is ±3 percentage points.

Interviews are conducted with respondents on land-line telephones (for respondents with a land-line telephone) and cellular phones (for respondents who are cell-phone only).

In addition to sampling error, question wording and practical difficulties in conducting surveys can introduce error or bias into the findings of public opinion polls.

February 20, 2009
JOB-MARKET PESSIMISM REACHES NEW HIGH
Ninety percent say now is a bad time to find a quality job

by Dennis Jacobe, Gallup Chief Economist

The percentage of Americans saying now is a "bad time" to find a quality job reached 90% in February—up 30 percentage points from January 2008, and the highest level since Gallup began asking this question in October 2001.

Thinking about the job situation in America today, would you say that it is now a good time or a bad time to find a quality job?

% Saying "bad time," January 2008-February 2009 trend

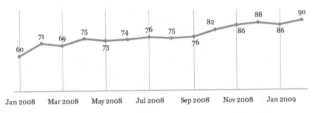

The prior high point in pessimism on this measure was 88% in December 2008. Before the recent economic downturn, the high point was 81% in both March and August 2003, around the beginning of the Iraq war.

And while the Gallup trend line has never found more than 49% of Americans saying now is a good time to find a quality job, several polls conducted by the University of Connecticut and Rutgers University in the late 1990s and 2000 found 69% or more of Americans in the labor force optimistic about the job market.

Most Important Problem

Surely the surging of the U.S. unemployment rate from 4.9% in January 2008 to 7.6% in January 2009 has contributed to the record-high pessimism about finding a "quality" job. Another indication of the country's growing jobs problem is the sharp increase in the percentage volunteering that unemployment is the nation's most important problem. In January 2008, only 5% of respondents suggested this as the country's most important problem. By January 2009, this had jumped to 11%, before it essentially doubled to 20% in February. This is the highest degree of concern about jobs expressed by Americans since the 20% measured in February 2004.

Percentage of Americans Mentioning Unemployment as the Nation's Most Important Problem

January 2008-February 2009 Trend

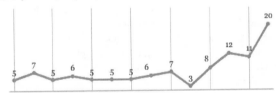

Gallup Poll Daily tracking

The current high level of worry about unemployment is more consistent with sentiment during the recession of the early 1990s (when Gallup found as many as 27% mentioning jobs as the nation's most important problem) than it is with the 40% to 50% range recorded during the early 1980s recession, with its double-digit unemployment rates. Still, if expectations of continued economic decline in the months ahead are correct, February's near-doubling of "jobs" on the "most important problem" measure may be only the start of a sharp deterioration in this trend.

Survey Methods

Results are based on telephone interviews with 1,022 national adults, aged 18 and older, conducted Feb. 9–12, 2009. For results based on

the total sample of national adults, one can say with 95% confidence that the maximum margin of sampling error is ±3 percentage points.

Interviews are conducted with respondents on land-line telephones (for respondents with a land-line telephone) and cellular phones (for respondents who are cell-phone only).

In addition to sampling error, question wording and practical difficulties in conducting surveys can introduce error or bias into the findings of public opinion polls.

February 23, 2009
ASSESSING OBAMA'S JOB APPROVAL AT THE ONE-MONTH MARK
Receives solid approval, but not extraordinary in historical terms

by Lydia Saad, Gallup Poll Senior Editor

President Barack Obama remains highly popular among the U.S. public at the end of his first month in office. However, the 63% of Americans currently approving of his job performance is down slightly from his initial 68% rating in January. The percentage disapproving has doubled, from 12% to 24%.

Do you approve or disapprove of the job Barack Obama is doing as president?

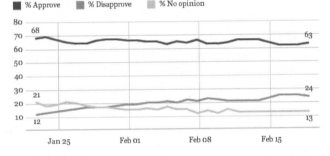

Increased public disapproval of Obama over the past month is mainly offset by a decrease in the percentage of Americans saying they have no opinion of his job performance. The latest figures are based on Gallup Poll Daily tracking from Feb. 19–21.

These shifts result in a slightly different profile for Obama relative to past presidents than what he enjoyed in the immediate afterglow of his inauguration. While Obama's initial 68% job approval rating was one of the highest in Gallup polling history (from Dwight Eisenhower through George W. Bush), his current 63% job approval rating is typical of how the last several presidents have fared at the one-month mark.

According to Gallup polling on all elected presidents from Richard Nixon through George W. Bush (this excludes Gerald Ford, who assumed office after Nixon resigned), the range of job approval for new presidents after about a month in office extends from 55% for Ronald Reagan to 71% for Jimmy Carter. The average one-month approval rating for all six past presidents is 62%—nearly identical to Obama's current 63%.

The average first-month disapproval rating for these same past presidents was 16%. However, Obama's slightly higher 24% disapproval score is similar to those seen for the most recent two presidents—Bush and Bill Clinton—perhaps owing to heightened partisanship or media scrutiny in recent years.

Presidents' Job Approval Ratings at One Month Mark*

Elected presidents since Richard Nixon, in chronological order

President (survey date)	Approve	Disapprove	No opinion
	%	%	%
Richard Nixon (Feb. 20-25, 1969)	60	6	34
Jimmy Carter (Feb. 18-21, 1977)	71	9	20
Ronald Reagan (Feb. 13-16, 1981)	55	18	27
George Bush (Feb. 28-Mar. 2, 1989)	63	13	24
Bill Clinton (Feb. 26-28, 1993)	59	29	12
George W. Bush (Feb. 19-21, 2001)	62	21	17
Average for Nixon through G.W. Bush	62	16	22
Barack Obama (Feb. 19-21, 2009)	63	24	13

* Based on surveys with field period starting closest to Feb. 20 for each year

Republican Support Slipping Away

Obama has not retained his initial level of job approval mainly because rank-and-file Republicans—who already lagged well behind Democrats in their approval of Obama in January—have quickly become even more critical.

According to weekly aggregates of Gallup Poll Daily tracking interviews, Obama has lost no support from Democrats and independents since taking office, but his approval rating from Republicans has dropped steadily week by week, from 41% at the start of his term to just 30% today.

President Obama Job Approval -- Weekly Average by Party ID
% Approve

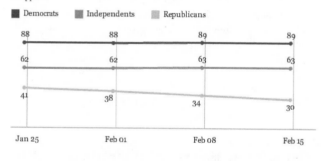

More precisely, the steepest drop in approval of Obama has come from conservative Republicans, whose support descended from 36% in his first, partial week on the job (Jan. 21–25) to 22% by his fourth week (Feb. 9–15). Approval among liberal and moderate Republicans fell only slightly over the same period, from 53% to 47%.

President Obama Job Approval -- Weekly Average by Party ID/Ideology
% Approve

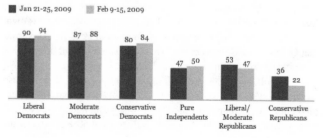

The only other substantial change seen in approval of Obama among demographic subgroups is an 11-point drop among upper-middle-income Americans (those making from $5,000 to $7,499 per month), from 69% approval in Obama's first week as president to 58% in his fourth. This could reflect variations by household income in Americans' reactions to the economic stimulus bill (Gallup's Feb. 10 survey on the stimulus bill found the least support for it by income among this group). Nevertheless, overall, support for Obama remains quite high among all income groups.

President Obama Job Approval -- Weekly Average by Monthly Household Income
% Approve

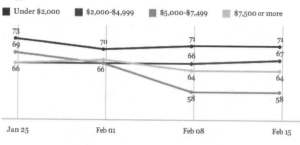

Bottom Line

All newly elected presidents start off with a relatively high approval score, as well as a high percentage of Americans expressing "no opinion" about their job performance. As they start to make decisions, deliver speeches, and work with Congress, fewer Americans have "no opinion" about their performance, and most presidents see an initial rise in their approval rating. Historically, that rise has been evident after a month, and continues at least through the first 100 days.

The traditional presidential honeymoon period seems to be following a different pattern so far in the Obama presidency—previously seen only for Bill Clinton's—in which the balance of opinion about him has become more negative rather than more positive as more people have been able to judge his job performance. The fact that the decline is seen exclusively among Republicans, however, could mean that the bottom has been reached, or at least that Obama's approval won't fall much further, as long as Democrats and independents continue to support the economic recovery policies now largely defining Obama and his administration.

Survey Methods

The latest results are based on telephone interviews with 1,614 national adults, aged 18 and older, conducted Feb. 19–21, 2009, as part of Gallup Poll Daily tracking. For results based on the total sample of national adults, one can say with 95% confidence that the maximum margin of sampling error is ±3 percentage points.

Results based on weekly aggregates of Gallup Poll Daily tracking are based on interviews with approximately 3,000 national adults.

Interviews are conducted with respondents on land-line telephones (for respondents with a land-line telephone) and cellular phones (for respondents who are cell-phone only).

In addition to sampling error, question wording and practical difficulties in conducting surveys can introduce error or bias into the findings of public opinion polls.

February 23, 2009

U.S. INVESTOR OPTIMISM HITS NEW LOW

In addition to Wall Street, average investor confidence plunged last week

by Dennis Jacobe, Gallup Chief Economist

American investor optimism plunged in February, as the Gallup Index of Investor Optimism—a broad measure of investor perceptions—fell 24 points to -64, a new low.

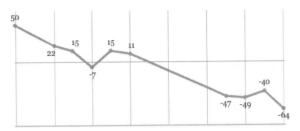

Gallup Index of Investor Optimism, December 2007-February 2009

New Low in Investor Optimism

Neither the president's signing of the new fiscal stimulus bill last Tuesday nor his announcement of a new housing rescue plan on Wednesday was able to keep Gallup's Index of Investor Optimism—a survey of those having $10,000 or more of investable assets—from plunging to its lowest level since its inception in October 1996.

The Index peaked at 178 in January 2000, just prior to the bursting of the dot-com bubble. Last year, the Index turned negative for the first time in its history, reaching its previous low of -49 in December. Before last year, the low for the Index was 5 in March 2003, reflecting investor concerns at the outset of the Iraq war.

Optimism deteriorated along both dimensions of the Index in February. Investor expectations for the U.S. economy over the next 12 months became even more negative, as the Economic Dimension of the Index worsened by 11 points to -70—worse than December's -64 and a new low. At the same time, investors' expectations for their personal portfolios worsened by 13 points to 6—a new low for the Personal Dimension.

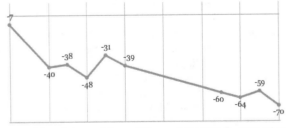

Economic Dimension, Gallup Index of Investor Optimism

Survey Methods

Gallup Poll Daily interviewing includes no fewer than 1,000 U.S. adults nationwide each day during 2008. The Index of Investor Optimism results are based on questions asked of 1,000 or more investors

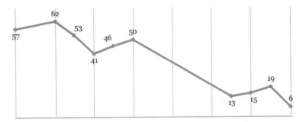

Personal Dimension, Gallup Index of Investor Optimism

over a three-day period each month, conducted Feb. 17–19 and Jan. 16–18, 2009, and Dec. 16–18, Nov. 24–26, June 3–6, April 25–28, March 28–31, and Feb. 28–March 2, 2008. For results based on these samples, the maximum margin of sampling error is ±3 percentage points.

Results for May are based on a Gallup Panel study and are based on telephone interviews with 576 national adults, aged 18 and older, conducted May 19–21, 2008. Gallup Panel members are recruited through random selection methods. The panel is weighted so that it is demographically representative of the U.S. adult population. For results based on this sample, one can say with 95% confidence that the maximum margin of sampling error is ±5 percentage points.

For investor results prior to 2008, telephone interviews were conducted with at least 800 investors, aged 18 and older, and having at least $10,000 of investable assets. For the total sample of investors in these surveys, one can say with 95% confidence that the maximum margin of sampling error is ±4 percentage points.

Interviews are conducted with respondents on land-line telephones (for respondents with a land-line telephone) and cellular phones (for respondents who are cell-phone only).

In addition to sampling error, question wording and practical difficulties in conducting surveys can introduce error or bias into the findings of public opinion polls.

February 23, 2009

STRONG BIPARTISAN SUPPORT FOR OBAMA'S MOVE ON AFGHANISTAN

Republicans more likely than Democrats to support sending in more troops

by Frank Newport, Gallup Poll Editor in Chief

President Obama's decision to send an additional 17,000 troops to Afghanistan is supported by 65% of the American public, including not only majority support from Democrats, but even larger support from Republicans—marking one of the few instances in which a president receives more support for a policy decision from those who identify with the opposing political party than he does from his own.

A new *USA Today*/Gallup poll, conducted Feb. 20–22, shows that Obama's decision receives 75% support from Republicans, 57% from independents, and 65% from Democrats.

The poll, conducted Feb. 20–22, also shows that 77% of those Americans who approve sending 17,000 troops would go further and also approve if Obama decided later to send an additional 13,000 troops. Taken as a whole, the results indicate that 50% of Americans

Do you approve or disapprove of Obama's decision to send 17,000 more troops to Afghanistan?

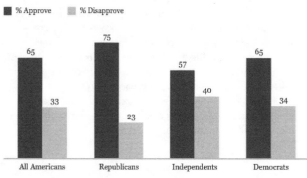

approve of sending both 17,000 troops to Afghanistan now and an additional 13,000 later, while 15% approve only of the initial 17,000 increment.

Do you approve or disapprove of Obama's decision to send 17,000 more troops to Afghanistan?

	%
Approve of sending 17,000 more troops	65
Would approve of sending 13,000 more troops later	50
Would not approve of sending more troops later	15
Disapprove of sending 17,000 more troops	33
Should maintain current number of troops	6
Should reduce number of troops	9
Should withdraw all troops	17
Should send more than 17,000 troops now	1
No opinion	2

The majority of those who oppose sending 17,000 more troops say that the level of U.S. troops should be reduced or withdrawn altogether, while a small percentage of those who oppose sending more say that keeping troop levels as they are now is appropriate. All in all, 17% of Americans both disapprove of sending more troops and say that all U.S. troops should be withdrawn from Afghanistan, while 9% disapprove and want troops reduced, but not withdrawn altogether. Just 6% disapprove of sending more but feel troops should be kept at their current levels.

Survey Methods

Results are based on telephone interviews with 1,013 national adults, aged 18 and older, conducted Feb. 20–22, 2009. For results based on the total sample of national adults, one can say with 95% confidence that the maximum margin of sampling error is ±3 percentage points.

Interviews are conducted with respondents on land-line telephones (for respondents with a land-line telephone) and cellular phones (for respondents who are cell-phone only).

In addition to sampling error, question wording and practical difficulties in conducting surveys can introduce error or bias into the findings of public opinion polls.

February 24, 2009
AMERICANS TELL OBAMA WHAT THEY WANT TO HEAR IN SPEECH
Economy is dominant issue, with jobs the top specific economic concern

by Lydia Saad, Gallup Poll Senior Editor

As President Barack Obama addresses a joint session of Congress Tuesday night, three in four Americans—74%—say they are most eager to hear what he has to say about the nation's economic challenges. That includes 18% who specifically want to hear his ideas about the jobs situation.

As you may know, Barack Obama will address a joint session of Congress Tuesday night. What issue or issues would you most like to see Obama talk about in his speech?

Rank order of economic issues

NET: Mention any economic issue	74%
Jobs/Unemployment/Job creation	18%
Banking situation/Bailout/Financial crisis	15%
Economic stimulus package/How money will be spent	14%
Housing crisis/Home foreclosures/Plans for solving	11%
Healthcare	10%
Help for the middle class	3%
Taxes/Tax cuts	3%
Social Security/Medicare/Help for seniors	3%
Government spending (general)	2%
Corporate greed/Corruption	2%
Other economic	2%
Economy (nonspecific)	15%

USA Today/Gallup, Feb. 20-22, 2009

A new *USA Today*/Gallup poll, conducted Feb. 20–22, asked Americans to name the issues they most want to hear Obama address in his speech Tuesday night. The U.S. economy is referenced in various ways by 74% of Americans. More specifically, 18% of Americans say they would most like to see Obama talk about jobs, job creation, or unemployment in his speech. Nearly as many, 15%, mention the banking crisis or banking bailouts. Fourteen percent mention the recently adopted $787 billion economic stimulus package, including some who specifically say they want Obama to explain how the money will be spent.

Another 11% specifically want to hear Obama's plans for addressing the nation's housing and mortgage crisis, and an additional 10% want him to discuss healthcare.

While the economic downturn is clearly Issue No. 1 for the president and Congress to deal with right now, a third of Americans remain interested in what Obama has to say on at least one non-economic issue. Chief among these is the United States' military involvement in Iraq (4%), Afghanistan (3%), or both (5%). Another 3% want Obama to discuss U.S. foreign policy, 2% say national defense, and 1% cite the Israeli-Palestinian conflict or the Middle East. A net 17% of Americans name at least one of these military or foreign policy issues.

A smattering of other issues are each mentioned by fewer than 5% of Americans, including education (4%), government corruption (2%), illegal immigration (2%), and energy (1%).

As you may know, Barack Obama will address a joint session of Congress Tuesday night. What issue or issues would you most like to see Obama talk about in his speech?

Rank order of non-economic issues

NET: Mention any non-economic issue	34%
The wars (nonspecific)	5%
Education	4%
War in Iraq	4%
War in Afghanistan	3%
Foreign policy (general)	3%
National security/National defense	2%
Government corruption	2%
Illegal immigration/Border control	2%
Energy	1%
Abortion	1%
Middle East/Israel	1%
Environment/Climate change	1%

USA Today/Gallup, Feb. 20-22, 2009

Given Obama's high job approval ratings among fellow Democrats, anything he says Tuesday night will most likely be well-received by that part of the television audience. To the extent he wants to make greater inroads with Republicans, the new poll suggests Obama should spend some time discussing the banking crisis, as well as the stimulus package and how it will be spent. Republicans show more interest than Democrats in what Obama has to say on both topics.

Democrats are more interested than Republicans in hearing about jobs and unemployment, as well as the housing crisis, healthcare, and education.

Issue Most Like to See President Obama Address -- by Party ID

Selected issues shown

	Republicans	Independents	Democrats
	%	%	%
Stimulus package/how spent	19	12	13
Banking crisis/Bailout	19	15	13
Jobs/Unemployment	12	20	22
Housing crisis/Foreclosures	8	10	14
The wars (nonspecific)	6	3	7
National security/defense	6	2	*
Healthcare	5	9	14
Education/Schools	2	2	8

* Less than 0.5%
USA Today/Gallup, Feb. 20-22, 2009

Bottom Line

Americans are deeply concerned about the U.S. economy, evidenced by the 78% now holding a negative view of economic conditions, and the growing percentage of U.S. workers reporting that hiring conditions where they work are getting worse. Gallup also recently reported that the rate of Americans' retail spending is down sharply from a year ago. While Obama and the 111th Congress have been hard at work trying to address the many serious economic problems contributing to consumer worry, Americans are hardly weary of hearing about the issue: They want Obama to focus on it when he speaks before Congress on Tuesday.

Survey Methods

Results are based on telephone interviews with 1,013 national adults, aged 18 and older, conducted Feb. 20–22, 2009. For results based on the total sample of national adults, one can say with 95% confidence that the maximum margin of sampling error is ±3 percentage points.

Interviews are conducted with respondents on land-line telephones (for respondents with a land-line telephone) and cellular phones (for respondents who are cell-phone only).

In addition to sampling error, question wording and practical difficulties in conducting surveys can introduce error or bias into the findings of public opinion polls.

February 24, 2009
OBAMA JOB APPROVAL DIPS BELOW 60% FOR FIRST TIME
Fifty-nine percent now approve as more express no opinion on his performance

by Jeffrey M. Jones, Gallup Poll Managing Editor

For the first time since Gallup began tracking Barack Obama's presidential job approval rating on Jan. 21, fewer than 60% of Americans approve of the job he is doing as president. In Feb. 21–23 polling, 59% of Americans give Obama a positive review, while 25% say they disapprove, and 16% have no opinion.

Barack Obama Presidential Job Approval Ratings

Gallup Poll Daily tracking (Jan. 21-Feb. 23, 2009)

To date, Obama has averaged 64% approval, but, as the graph shows, there has been a slight but perceptible decline in his approval rating since he took office. This decline has largely occurred among Republicans.

The drop below 60% approval within the past week—from 63% in Feb. 18–20 polling to 59% in Feb. 21–23 polling—has mostly come among independents. Late last week, 62% of independents approved of Obama, compared with 54% in the last three days. His approval rating among Democrats has dipped slightly (but not to a statistically significant degree), while approval among Republicans has not changed.

While Obama's overall approval rating has fallen by four percentage points in recent days (from 63% in Feb. 18–20 polling to the current 59%), his disapproval rating has been steady (24% in Feb. 18–20 polling to the current 25%). Rather, the percentage of Americans without an opinion of his job performance has increased, from 13% to 16%. In essence, Americans in recent days are becoming increasingly unsure about how Obama is doing, rather than becoming more critical.

Barack Obama Presidential Job Approval Ratings
Feb. 18-20 and Feb. 21-23, by Political Party

	Approve	Disapprove	No opinion
Democrats (Feb 18-20)	89%	3%	8%
Democrats (Feb 21-23)	86%	6%	9%
Change	-3	+3	+1
Independents (Feb 18-20)	62%	20%	18%
Independents (Feb 21-23)	54%	23%	23%
Change	-8	+3	+5
Republicans (Feb 18-20)	27%	61%	12%
Republicans (Feb 21-23)	27%	56%	18%
Change	0	-5	+6

As the table suggests, most of the movement among independents in recent days has been from the approval to the no opinion category. And his disapproval rating has dropped among Republicans, with a concomitant increase in no opinion. Thus, Americans' assessments of Obama are in a period of flux.

Given that Obama is addressing the nation tonight, he has a tremendous opportunity to convert Americans who are now on the fence—in addition to those who now disapprove of him—into supporters. The latest *USA Today*/Gallup poll shows Americans are most interested in hearing about economic matters, particularly how Obama will address unemployment, the mortgage crisis, and how the economic stimulus package will be administered.

Survey Methods

Results are based on telephone interviews with 1,553 national adults, aged 18 and older, conducted Feb. 21–23, 2009, as part of Gallup Poll Daily tracking. For results based on the total sample of national adults, one can say with 95% confidence that the maximum margin of sampling error is ±3 percentage points.

Interviews are conducted with respondents on land-line telephones (for respondents with a land-line telephone) and cellular phones (for respondents who are cell-phone only).

In addition to sampling error, question wording and practical difficulties in conducting surveys can introduce error or bias into the findings of public opinion polls.

February 24, 2009

AMERICANS' VIEWS ON BANK TAKEOVERS APPEAR FLUID

Support varies significantly, depending on how the process is worded

by Frank Newport, Gallup Poll Editor in Chief

With all eyes on the possibility of increased U.S. government ownership of embattled bank Citibank, and with increased discussion of the need for a government takeover of other major banks, a new *USA Today*/Gallup poll indicates that Americans' reactions to these prospects vary significantly, depending on how the process is described to them. A majority of Americans (54%) favor a tempo-

rary government "takeover" of major U.S. banks, but a much lower minority (37%) favor a temporary "nationalization" of the banks.

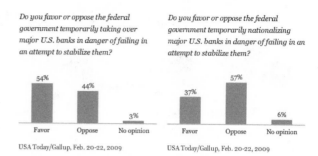

USA Today/Gallup, Feb. 20-22, 2009   USA Today/Gallup, Feb. 20-22, 2009

The new poll, conducted Feb. 20–22, used a split-sample technique to gauge the impact of different descriptions of the bank takeover situation. A random half of the sample was asked whether they favored or opposed "the federal government temporarily *taking over* major U.S. banks in danger of failing in an attempt to stabilize them," while the other half was asked whether they favored or opposed "the federal government temporarily *nationalizing* major U.S. banks in danger of failing in an attempt to stabilize them."

(Separate Gallup questioning shows only 39% favoring "giving aid to U.S. banks and financial companies in danger of failing," when this idea is included in a list of possible steps the government could take to deal with problems in the economy. Fifty-nine percent oppose it. These results are almost identical to those seen regarding possible "nationalizing" of banks.)

Taken together, these results reflect the power of language when it comes to describing government policies: the words "taking over" are significantly more palatable to the average American than "nationalizing."

The data thus suggest that a great deal of fluidity exists in Americans' attitudes toward the ways the federal government could relate to the current banking crisis. A majority of Americans object to "nationalizing" the banks temporarily (and an equally large majority object to "giving aid" to banks in danger of failing). At the same time, it is possible that a majority of Americans could be persuaded to support the government's "taking control" of major U.S. banks, at least temporarily.

It appears the final determination of whether a majority of the public ends up supporting government actions regarding bank ownership will depend on exactly how the whole process plays out.

Not surprisingly, there are significant partisan differences in response to the two ways of asking about the government's taking

Do you favor or oppose the federal government temporarily taking over major U.S. banks in danger of failing in an attempt to stabilize them?

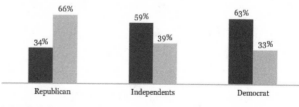

USA Today/Gallup, Feb. 20-22, 2009

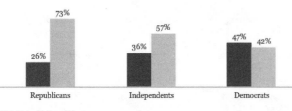

Do you favor or oppose the federal government temporarily nationalizing major U.S. banks in danger of failing in an attempt to stabilize them?

USA Today/Gallup, Feb. 20-22, 2009

control of banks.

Democrats are more likely than independents and, in particular, Republicans to favor the government's taking over or nationalizing major U.S. banks, regardless of the question wording; Republicans are the least likely to respond affirmatively to either wording.

Implications

It is likely that, on average, the American public has not thought much about the prospect of the government having to take majority ownership of ailing major banks in order to keep them from failing. Thus, when confronted with a survey question asking about just such a possibility, the public appears to be particularly susceptible to the way the idea is described. It seems clear that the word "nationalizing" does not have a great deal of appeal; a majority opposes government involvement when it is described in this way. In contrast, "taking over" appears to have a more benign connotation, and a majority favors the process when it is so described.

These results may indicate the potential range of public opinion if and when this issue becomes a prominent one and a realistic possibility. The range is fairly large, stretching from 37% to 54% approval, suggesting that in many ways, either side could win the battle for public support for this type of policy—and the side that prevails may do so on the basis of how the issue of government involvement is framed.

Survey Methods

Results are based on telephone interviews with 1,013 national adults, aged 18 and older, conducted Feb. 20–22, 2009. For results based on the total sample of national adults, one can say with 95% confidence that the maximum margin of sampling error is ±3 percentage points.

Interviews are conducted with respondents on land-line telephones (for respondents with a land-line telephone) and cellular phones (for respondents who are cell-phone only).

In addition to sampling error, question wording and practical difficulties in conducting surveys can introduce error or bias into the findings of public opinion polls.

February 24, 2009
VIEWS ON GOVERNMENT AID DEPEND ON THE PROGRAM
Majorities support foreclosure aid, oppose bank and auto bailouts

by Frank Newport, Gallup Poll Editor in Chief

The new administration of President Barack Obama has proposed a number of major government stimulus or aid packages aimed at jump-starting the flagging economy, assisting homeowners who face foreclosure, and providing help for the shaky economic situations of the banking and auto manufacturing sectors of the economy.

As you may know, the federal government has taken many steps to deal with problems in the economy in recent months. Please tell me whether, in general, you favor or oppose the government doing each of the following. How about -- [RANDOM ORDER]?

	Favor	Oppose	No opinion
	%	%	%
Funding new government programs to help create jobs	83	17	1
Giving aid to state governments in serious financial trouble	67	30	3
Giving aid to homeowners who are in danger of losing their homes to foreclosure	64	33	3
Giving aid to U.S. automakers who are in danger of going bankrupt	41	58	1
Giving aid to U.S. banks and financial companies in danger of failing	39	59	2

USA Today/Gallup, Feb. 20-22, 2009

Each of these plans has generated controversy. The Obama administration and other advocates have argued that the massive government spending on these programs is necessary to keep a bad economic situation from getting far worse. Critics have found fault with the amounts of money involved and the long-term impact or the lack thereof.

And the American public? A review and analysis of recent polling assessing the various government initiatives makes it possible to summarize American public opinion as follows: 1) Americans are generally behind the $787 billion stimulus plan (officially known as the "American Recovery and Reinvestment Act"), signed into law on Feb. 17, although with significant reservations; 2) Americans are solidly in favor of aid to homeowners facing foreclosure; 3) Americans are solidly against giving further aid to the auto companies; and 4) Americans are generally against the idea of providing further aid to ailing banks (although support for an actual government takeover of failing banks is fluid and depends on how such a process is described).

1. The American Recovery and Reinvestment Act

A majority of Americans support the broad stimulus plan that President Obama signed into law on Feb. 17. However, there is no majority consensus that it will make things better, and there are concerns about various aspects of the plan.

A Feb. 10 Gallup Poll showed 59% support for the new stimulus law just prior to its passage by Congress. A Feb. 19–22 *Washington Post*/ABC News poll conducted after the plan became law found a similar 64% support for the plan, described in that poll as the government spending "about $800 billion on tax cuts, construction projects, and aid to states and individuals to try to stimulate the economy."

Despite this overall majority support, there is no consensus on Americans' part that the plan will greatly improve economic conditions. Only 47% of Americans in a Feb. 20–22 *USA Today*/Gallup poll say the economy will be better off than if no stimulus had been passed, and a quarter say the economy will be worse off. While 53% of Americans in a Feb. 18–22 *New York Times*/CBS News poll say the stimulus package will make the current economic crisis better, only 32% say it will create "a substantial number" of new jobs and just 19% say it will shorten the recession significantly.

The Gallup Poll shows that 41% of Americans say it would have been better to spend less on the stimulus package, while the *New York Times*/CBS News poll shows that almost 7 out of 10 say even more money will be needed to stimulate the economy in the months ahead.

The Gallup Poll also asked Americans to assess the greater risk between 1) spending government money to improve the economy but adding too much to the federal debt, and 2) spending too little to stimulate the economy. A majority of Americans said the first risk (adding too much to the federal debt) is the greater of the two.

2. Housing Foreclosure Relief Program

All current polling shows that a majority of better than 6 in 10 Americans support a government program to provide relief to homeowners facing foreclosure. This is a robust finding, evident across different question wordings in four separate recent polls.

Gallup found 64% support for homeowner relief worded as "giving aid to homeowners who are in danger of losing their homes to foreclosure." The *New York Times*/CBS News poll showed 61% support for "a plan to help homeowners refinance their mortgages, avoid foreclosure and make more credit available for mortgages." The *Washington Post*/ABC News poll found 64% support for "the federal government using $75 billion to provide refinancing assistance to homeowners to help them avoid foreclosure on their mortgages." A CNN/Opinion Research poll found 63% support for "the federal government providing assistance to homeowners who cannot pay their mortgages."

Even with solid support for the idea, Gallup polling shows that slightly over half of Americans do not think this program is necessarily a fair one.

3. Federal Aid to Banking

Current polling shows majority opposition to the idea of providing further government aid to ailing or failing banks in the United States. This is again a robust finding, evident across different question wordings in several recent polls.

Gallup's Feb. 20–22 poll shows that a majority of 59% of Americans are opposed to "giving aid to U.S. banks and financial companies in danger of failing."

The *New York Times*/CBS News poll shows, in somewhat similar fashion, 39% approval/50% disapproval for the idea of "the federal government providing money to banks and other financial institutions to try to help fix the country's economic problems." The CNN/Opinion Research Poll finds that 62% of Americans oppose the idea of providing the "remaining money"—after having been told as part of the question wording that "last fall Congress and President Bush approved a government program that would spend up to $700 billion to provide assistance to banks and other large financial institutions. About half that money has already been spent."

At the same time, Gallup polling shows that support for the separate idea of the federal government taking control of ailing banks is fluid, and depends on the words used to describe such a process. A majority of Americans favor the idea of a temporary government *takeover* of failing banks in order to stabilize them, but a majority is in opposition when such action is described as *nationalizing* the banks.

4. Auto bailout

All current polling shows that a majority of Americans oppose the federal government spending more money to help bail out the auto companies, beyond what it has already provided.

Gallup finds 58% opposition to "giving aid to U.S. automakers who are in danger of going bankrupt." The *New York Times*/CBS News poll finds 68% saying no more assistance should be provided to major U.S. auto companies after respondents had been told that the federal government has "given some of the major U.S. auto companies more than $13 billion dollars in loans to prevent them from going into bankruptcy." The *Washington Post*/ABC News poll shows 68% opposition to providing an additional $14 billion in government loans to the U.S. automakers given that "the federal government has provided $25 billion in loans to two of the big U.S. automakers and put in place a government board to oversee their restructuring." The CNN/Opinion Research poll finds that 61% of Americans oppose a program to provide two of the major U.S. auto companies with "several billion dollars in assistance."

Implications

American public opinion concerning new government spending to address various problems plaguing the U.S. economy can be fairly well summarized—at least for the moment. There is majority support for the stimulus bill President Obama signed into law last week, albeit with significant trepidations about its impact. There is majority support for the concept of helping homeowners who face foreclosure. On the other hand, there is clear majority opposition to government spending to help bail out failing banks and failing U.S. auto companies.

February 25, 2009
AMERICANS ENDORSE OBAMA'S APPROACH, BUT WARY OF DEBT
Give green light to stimulus package, but indicate spending can go too far

by Lydia Saad, Gallup Poll Senior Editor

Even before he addressed Congress and the nation on Tuesday about his plans for leading the country out of economic peril, President Barack Obama was enjoying solid public support for his work to date. For instance, 59% of those surveyed in a Feb. 20–22 *USA Today*/Gallup poll said Obama is going at about the right speed in addressing the nation's problems. This was little different from a month ago.

Also, more Americans say the economic stimulus package supported by Obama contains either the right amount of government spending or too little spending, rather than too much: 54% to 41%.

The Debt Caveat

At the same time, Obama's options on the economy going forward could be constrained by the public's fears about burdening the country with too much debt.

Do you think Barack Obama is -- [moving too fast, doing about right, or not moving fast enough] -- in addressing the major problems facing the country today?

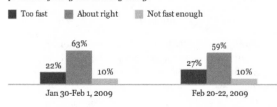

USA Today/Gallup

Regardless of whether you favor or oppose the economic stimulus bill that Congress passed, do you think it would have been better for the government to spend more money to stimulate the economy, better for the government to spend less money, or is the amount of spending in the bill about right?

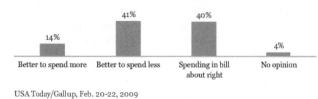

USA Today/Gallup, Feb. 20-22, 2009

Of four major criticisms that have been leveled at Obama's economic policies, mainly from the political right, the possibility of expanding the federal debt sparks the most public concern. More than four in five Americans say they are worried about the amount of money being added to the federal debt, including 54% who are "very worried."

By contrast, fewer than half of Americans are very worried that the government's recent steps to address the economy will essentially fail to work, or that the increased borrowing needed to pay for them will spur inflation. Even fewer, just 34%, are very worried about the expanded role the government is playing in the nation's economy. (While large majorities of Americans are at least "somewhat worried" about each of these things, the greatest political impact would seem to result from Americans feeling "very worried.")

Regardless of whether you favor or oppose the steps the government has taken in recent months to address economic problems, how worried are you about each of the following -- very worried, somewhat worried, not too worried, or not worried at all?

Very worried

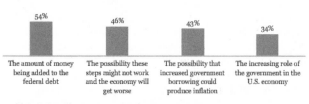

USA Today/Gallup, Feb. 20-22, 2009

In contrast to Democrats, Republicans are highly unified in their deep concern about the federal debt: 71% say they are very worried about it. Only 36% of Democrats, but a majority of independents (60%), are highly worried.

This potentially critical point about the federal debt—and the partisan nature of responses—is reinforced in a separate question ask-

Economic Concerns, by Party ID

% Very worried

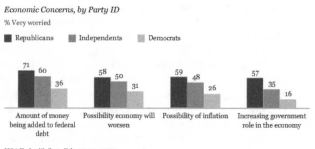

USA Today/Gallup, Feb. 20-22, 2009

ing Americans whether they think the greater economic risk is spending too little money to improve the economy, or adding considerable amounts of money to the federal debt. Overall, 59% of Americans say adding too much to the federal debt is the greater danger, while only 37% choose spending too little on the economy.

Most Republicans (81%) say adding too much money to the federal debt poses the greater danger. Democrats fall on the other side, but with a less persuasive majority: 54% say spending too little to improve the economy is the greater risk. Again, independents generally share Republicans' sentiments on this issue.

Perception of Which Economic Risk Is Greater, by Party ID

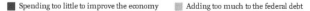

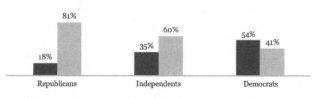

USA Today/Gallup, Feb. 20-22, 2009

Public Seems Comfortable for Now

Obama's recent announcement that he will cut the federal budget deficit in half by 2013 suggests he is aware of Americans' aversion to expanding the debt and may be trying to pre-empt Republican efforts to use that against his economic plans. However, Americans' support thus far for the economic stimulus package indicates they don't believe government spending is high enough at this point to pose a danger.

In addition to Gallup's recent finding that 59% of Americans supported passage of the economic stimulus bill in Congress, fewer than half of Americans—41%—now say it would have been better to spend less money than what was contained in that bill. About the same number (40%) say the spending is about right, while 14% say it would have been better to spend more. Thus, by a 54% to 41% margin, Americans largely endorse the scope of spending in the stimulus package—despite their debt concerns.

Of course, there are sharp differences in these views by party, with most Democrats in favor of spending at least as high as that contained in the stimulus package, and most Republicans in favor of less spending.

Democrats See a Quicker Recovery

Americans still see a long road to recovery for the economy. The vast majority (71%) believe it will be two or more years before the econ-

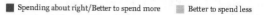

Perception of Economic Stimulus Spending, by Party ID

■ Spending about right/Better to spend more   Better to spend less

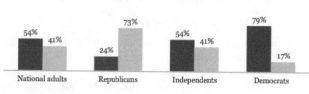

	National adults	Republicans	Independents	Democrats
Spending about right/Better to spend more	54%	24%	54%	79%
Better to spend less	41%	73%	41%	17%

USA Today/Gallup, Feb. 20-22, 2009

omy starts to recover, with an average prediction of 4.1 years. However, this is slightly more optimistic than was seen in December, when 81% thought it would take two or more years, and the average predicted time was 5.2 years.

Republicans' outlook for economic recovery has hardly changed over the past two months, hovering around 5 years, while that of Democrats' has brightened somewhat, shrinking from 5.1 to 3.2 years.

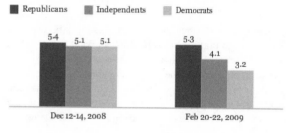

Mean Number of Years Before Economy Starts to Recover

■ Republicans   ■ Independents   ■ Democrats

	Republicans	Independents	Democrats
Dec 12-14, 2008	5.4	5.1	5.1
Feb 20-22, 2009	5.3	4.1	3.2

Bottom Line

Obama has the upper hand in leading the nation on the economy right now. Americans are comfortable with the pace of his actions and the scope of his economic spending, and they have become a bit more optimistic than before he took office about how long it will take for the economy to turn around. All of these attitudes could have become even more favorable to Obama after his address to Congress on Tuesday.

Still, the partisan breach beneath the surface of these attitudes is striking. Democrats express strong confidence in the economic measures Obama has taken in the past month. Republicans are highly wary of the amount of government spending involved, and what that means for the federal debt.

For now, independents are falling squarely on the Democrats' side in their reactions to Obama's economic leadership; but their latent concern about the federal debt is something Republican leaders can potentially work with, and something Obama and his advisers will have to monitor.

Survey Methods

Results are based on telephone interviews with 1,013 national adults, aged 18 and older, conducted Feb. 20–22, 2009. For results based on the total sample of national adults, one can say with 95% confidence that the maximum margin of sampling error is ±3 percentage points.

Interviews are conducted with respondents on land-line telephones (for respondents with a land-line telephone) and cellular phones (for respondents who are cell-phone only).

In addition to sampling error, question wording and practical difficulties in conducting surveys can introduce error or bias into the findings of public opinion polls.

February 25, 2009
AMERICANS ON HOUSING AID: UNFAIR BUT NECESSARY
Fifty-one percent say helping homeowners pay their mortgages is "unfair"

by Dennis Jacobe, Gallup Chief Economist

By 51% to 46%, Americans are more likely to say that government aid to help certain homeowners who cannot pay their mortgages is "unfair" rather than "fair." At the same time, 59% of Americans say such government aid is necessary to stabilize the U.S. housing market.

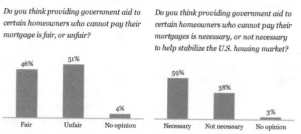

Do you think providing government aid to certain homeowners who cannot pay their mortgage is fair, or unfair?

Fair	Unfair	No opinion
46%	51%	4%

Do you think providing government aid to certain homeowners who cannot pay their mortgages is necessary, or not necessary to help stabilize the U.S. housing market?

Necessary	Not necessary	No opinion
59%	38%	3%

USA Today/Gallup, Feb. 20-22, 2009   USA Today/Gallup, Feb. 20-22, 2009

Mortgage Aid

The S&P/Case-Shiller Index released Tuesday shows housing prices in 20 U.S. metropolitan areas were down 18.5% in December from the prior year. RealtyTrac reports that home foreclosures were up 17.8% in January from a year earlier. Given this context, it seems reasonable that the federal government should consider aid to distressed homeowners to prevent even further deterioration in these numbers.

While many Americans see the government's mortgage plan as "unfair"—perhaps feeling that making mortgage payments is an individual's responsibility, and tax dollars shouldn't be used to help those who cannot make their payments—a solid majority see such mortgage assistance as necessary. Additionally, most see President Obama's proposals as not doing any harm to the housing market—60% believe these efforts to reduce home foreclosures will make the housing market a little (54%) or a lot (6%) better, 21% say it will make no difference, and only 15% think it will make things worse.

At the same time, Americans are evenly split on whether the home mortgage plan will help stabilize housing prices in their communities—the essential rationale for government intervention—with 46% saying it will and 48% saying it will not.

Housing Aid: Mortgage Aid vs. Foreclosure Relief

Given the general level of economic distress and the unprecedented intervention of the federal government in the U.S. economy, utilizing the behavioral economics concept of "framing"—that is, positioning these initiatives as being helpful to everyone and to the

Impact on the Housing Market of Obama Administration's Proposals to Reduce Foreclosures

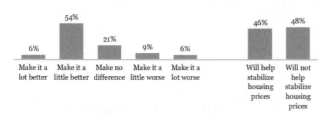

USA Today/Gallup, Feb. 20–22, 2009

economy as a whole, as opposed to individual groups—is taking on increasing importance. This is the case with the idea of "nationalization" of banks as well as with housing aid.

Although Americans feel that the provision of government aid for some distressed homeowners is unfair, a separate question in the poll found, at a general level, that 64% of Americans favor "giving aid to homeowners who are in danger of losing their homes to foreclosure." While both ways of framing the issue may help keep people in their homes, mortgage aid seems a lot less "fair" than aid to help people avoid foreclosure.

In this regard, it seems that many Americans may not recognize the inability of the modern housing finance system to deal with the current foreclosure debacle, as was possible in the past. Before securitization—the combination and sale of a package of mortgage loans or other investments—began to dominate the mortgage market, lenders holding mortgages in their portfolios had strong incentives to work with borrowers during times of economic stress. Lenders wanted borrowers to continue paying on their loans so they could keep the mortgage loans out of the "problem" category, and they would find a way to provide borrowers with forbearance during difficult economic times.

Securitization not only separates the mortgage loan holder from the lender who made the loan but may actually have divided it up among many investors across the globe. As a result, finding a way for the mortgage loan investor, the lender, and the borrower to work out a forbearance arrangement, even when it is advantageous to everyone involved, has become an incredible challenge. And all of the alternative solutions may also appear unfair, although they have not been tested in recent survey research. In this regard, addressing these problems using a new round of securitization—possibly by making and packaging new, specially underwritten and priced mortgage loans—may not only be "unfair" but may also compound the existing mortgage finance debacle.

Survey Methods

Results are based on telephone interviews with 1,013 national adults, aged 18 and older, conducted Feb. 20–22, 2009. For results based on the total sample of national adults, one can say with 95% confidence that the maximum margin of sampling error is ±3 percentage points.

Interviews are conducted with respondents on land-line telephones (for respondents with a land-line telephone) and cellular phones (for respondents who are cell-phone only).

In addition to sampling error, question wording and practical difficulties in conducting surveys can introduce error or bias into the findings of public opinion polls.

February 26, 2009
AMERICANS REJECT SEQUEL TO AUTO BAILOUT
More than 7 in 10 say Congress should not approve more loans

by Lydia Saad, Gallup Poll Senior Editor

Supplying Detroit automakers with more taxpayer dollars to ward off bankruptcy doesn't fly with most Americans, 72% of whom say Congress should not authorize the additional $21 billion in emergency loans that General Motors and Chrysler are now requesting. Only 25% say Congress should provide the money.

As you may know, in December the federal government gave $17 billion in loans to General Motors and Chrysler to keep those auto manufacturers from going bankrupt. Earlier this week, General Motors and Chrysler asked the government for $21 billion in additional loans as part of restructuring plans they submitted to the Treasury Department. Do you think Congress should or should not approve these additional loans?

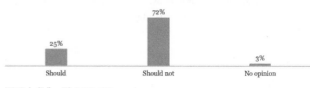

USA Today/Gallup, Feb. 20–22, 2009

President Barack Obama intimated in his speech before Congress Tuesday night that he, himself, does not want to reward the auto companies for their past poor performance. However, it is hard to find a constituency within the American public that might agree with his simultaneous commitment to help them anyway. The highest levels of support for granting the auto industry a second round of loans are found among self-described liberals (35%) and Democrats (33%).

Even in the Midwest—the geographic hub of the U.S. auto industry—only 28% of Americans think the federal government should make the loans.

Subgroup Support for Additional $21 Billion in Loans to U.S. Auto Companies
% Government should approve the loans

	Feb 20–22, 2009
	%
Men	27
Women	23
East	22
Midwest	28
South	24
West	26
18 to 34 years	18
35 to 54 years	27
55 years and older	28
Republicans	15
Independents	25
Democrats	33
Conservatives	18
Moderates	26
Liberals	35

USA Today/Gallup

Support for government aid to U.S. automakers is a bit higher when Americans are asked about it more generally, and in the context of four other economic rescue-oriented proposals. But even on this basis, only 41% of Americans favor "giving aid to U.S. automakers who are in danger of going bankrupt"; 58% are opposed.

Bailing out the auto industry ranks low on the list of economic measures tested in the Feb. 20–22 *USA Today*/Gallup poll—about tied for last with giving aid to failing U.S. banks and other financial companies (39%). By comparison, Americans are much more amenable to government aid for homeowners in danger of losing their homes (64% in favor), and to aid to strapped state governments (67%).

As you may know, the federal government has taken many steps to deal with problems in the economy in recent months. Please tell me whether, in general, you favor or oppose the government doing each of the following.

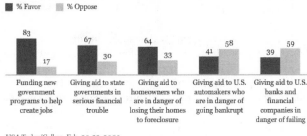

USA Today/Gallup, Feb. 20-22, 2009

Public Split Over U.S. Auto Survival

The Feb. 20–22 poll also asked Americans about the likelihood the U.S. car companies will remain in business. Currently, a bare majority of Americans—51%—believe all of the Big Three U.S. auto companies will find a way to survive, while 47% predict one or more of them will go out of business.

This prognosis is worse than in mid-December, when 57% of Americans thought all three companies would survive.

Just your best guess, do you think one or more of the Big Three U.S. auto companies will go out of business, or will all three find a way to survive?

USA Today/Gallup

How important these perceptions are to public support for the auto industry is at best unclear. Seven in 10 Americans who think all three companies will survive oppose a second round of emergency loans, as do 74% of those who predict one or more of them will likely go out of business.

Bottom Line

Whether it's because of their badly reviewed testimony before Congress last year, their perceived mismanagement of their companies, or because of bailout fatigue, more generally, the U.S. auto executives' latest plea for taxpayer help is being met with little sympathy.

Views on Loans to Auto Companies, Based on Perceptions of Whether the Companies Will Survive

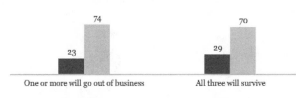

USA Today/Gallup, Feb. 20-22, 2009

Only 41% of Americans are generally in favor of providing aid to the auto industry to keep it out of bankruptcy. And that support drops to 25% when Americans are asked specifically whether the companies should now receive $21 billion in loans—in addition to the billions already provided last year.

Survey Methods

Results are based on telephone interviews with 1,013 national adults, aged 18 and older, conducted Feb. 20–22, 2009. For results based on the total sample of national adults, one can say with 95% confidence that the maximum margin of sampling error is ±3 percentage points.

Interviews are conducted with respondents on land-line telephones (for respondents with a land-line telephone) and cellular phones (for respondents who are cell-phone only).

In addition to sampling error, question wording and practical difficulties in conducting surveys can introduce error or bias into the findings of public opinion polls.

February 26, 2009
OBAMA SPEECH BOLSTERS CONFIDENCE FOR MANY AMERICANS
Of those who watched, 57% are now more confident about his plans to fix the economy

by Lymari Morales, Gallup Poll Staff Writer

President Barack Obama's address to Congress Tuesday night appears to have bolstered confidence among many Americans. Four in 10 (41%) say they are now more confident in his plans to improve the economy, including 57% of those who watched or listened to the speech live.

In a one-night Gallup Poll conducted Wednesday night, Americans overall were about evenly split between saying Obama's speech made them more confident and saying it had no effect on their opinion. But those who reported watching or listening to the speech live were far more likely to say it made them more confident, outnumbering by a 2-to-1 margin those who said it had no effect. Fewer than 2 in 10 Americans in either group said the speech made them less confident.

While not technically a State of the Union address, Obama's speech was significant in that it was his first address to a joint session of Congress since he took office, set against the backdrop of continuing economic distress, mounting job losses, and the recent passage of the American Recovery and Reinvestment Act.

Based on what you have heard or read about last night's speech, are you now more confident or less confident in President Obama's plans to improve the economy, or did the speech not affect your opinion either way?

■ More confident   ■ No effect   ▓ Less confident

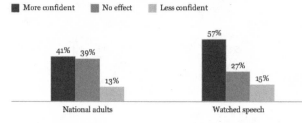

Gallup Poll, Feb. 25, 2009

All in all, 45% of Americans told Gallup they watched or listened to the speech live versus 26% who said they did not watch the speech live but read, heard, or watched news reports about it, and 29% who did not do either. While one might expect a partisan tilt in the viewership, Democrats were only slightly more likely than independents or Republicans to say they watched the speech live.

Which of the following applies to you -- you watched or listened to Barack Obama's speech last night live as he gave it, you saw, heard, or read news coverage of the speech, or you did not do either?

■ % Watched live   ■ % Watched news reports   ▓ % Did not do either

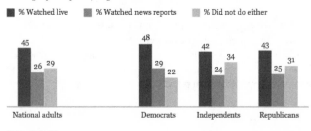

Gallup Poll, Feb. 25, 2009

While Americans of all political stripes devoted similar levels of attention to the speech, their reactions were decidedly partisan. Nearly two-thirds of Democrats (62%) said the speech made them more confident in Obama's economic plans, compared to only 16% of Republicans. More than half of Republicans (51%) said the speech had no effect and 28% said it made them less confident.

Based on what you have heard or read about last night's speech, are you now more confident or less confident in President Obama's plans to improve the economy, or did the speech not affect your opinion either way?

■ More confident   ■ No effect   ▓ Less confident

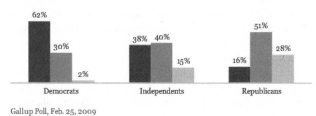

Gallup Poll, Feb. 25, 2009

News coverage of Obama's speech has been largely positive, with editorials calling it "confident" and "reassuring." It appears to have come at just the right time for Obama, whose job approval rating in Gallup Poll Daily tracking dipped below 60% for the first time

in the reporting period leading up to the speech. He has been gaining in the days since then, and Gallup plans a new report this Friday to more fully examine Obama's job approval after the speech. Overall, Americans' positive reactions to the speech are a good sign for the new president as he leads the nation through this unprecedented economic crisis. Now, Obama's test will be to see if he can translate confidence in his economic plans to improved confidence in the economy itself in the weeks and months ahead.

Survey Methods

Results are based on telephone interviews with 1,025 national adults, aged 18 and older, conducted Feb. 25, 2009. For results based on the total sample of national adults, one can say with 95% confidence that the maximum margin of sampling error is ±3 percentage points.

For results based on the 519 national adults who reported watching the speech live, the maximum margin of sampling error is ±5 percentage points.

Interviews are conducted with respondents on land-line telephones (for respondents with a land-line telephone) and cellular phones (for respondents who are cell-phone only).

In addition to sampling error, question wording and practical difficulties in conducting surveys can introduce error or bias into the findings of public opinion polls. Polls conducted entirely in one day, such as this one, are subject to additional error or bias not found in polls conducted over several days.

February 27, 2009
WORRY ABOUT MONEY PEAKS WITH FORTY-SOMETHINGS
Drops off significantly for older Americans

by Frank Newport, Gallup Poll Editor in Chief

Despite news accounts of the financial plight of older Americans who find themselves on declining retirement incomes in the current recession, analysis of February Gallup Poll Daily tracking data shows that worry about money "yesterday" peaks at 46% in the 40 to 49 age group, and then drops off significantly past that point to only 17% among those aged 70 to 89.

Did you worry about money yesterday?
% Worried about money, by respondent age

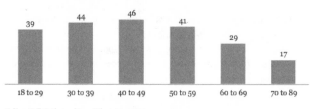

Gallup Poll Daily tracking, Feb. 1-24, 2009

Each day, Gallup Poll Daily tracking asks Americans if they worried about money "yesterday." On average, well under half say they did. (Worry is higher during the week and lower on weekends.)

Gallup's personal finance measure averaged just 32% worried in January 2008, when Gallup began tracking it. The percentage who worried grew gradually through August, jumped in September, and by October was at 43%, 11 points above its early 2008 average. Worry dropped slightly in November. In January and so far in February of this year, worry is down slightly more, to 37%. This is still higher than its level in January and February of last year, but is certainly below last fall's peak.

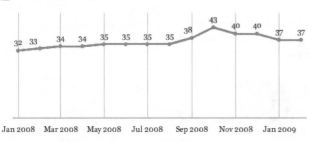

Did you worry about money yesterday?
2008-2009 trend

■ % Worried about money

Gallup Poll Daily tracking

One might think that worry would be higher among older Americans, given recent publicity about the plight of older Americans who are forced to make do in situations in which their retirement incomes (and overall wealth) may be dropping. One recent *New York Times* article, for example, quoted Alicia Munnell, director of the Center for Retirement Research at Boston College, as saying: "There's a terrified older population out there."

But Gallup's analysis of Feb. 1–24 tracking data, involving more than 11,000 interviews, shows conclusively that this is not the case. Worry about money begins to drop off at age 50 and continues to drop thereafter. (Analysis shows that the current February findings reflect the same patterns evident during 2008.)

Specifically, worry about money in these February data advances slightly from the 18- to 29-year-old age group—39% of whom worried about money "yesterday"—through the 40 to 49 age group, where it peaks at 46%. From age 50 on, however, worry decreases steadily, reaching a low of only 17% among those 70 to 89.

Employment Status

Older Americans are less likely to be employed than those who are younger and, therefore, on average, have lower incomes. Being employed and having a higher income are both associated with lower levels of worry. Thus, the finding that older Americans worry less about money occurs *despite* the fact that this older population group has lower average incomes and lower employment levels.

The accompanying graph shows that the financial concerns of those not working are particularly high in the middle-aged years relative to those who *are* employed. By ages 60 to 69, the difference by employment is negligible. But in general, the decline in worry among older Americans occurs regardless of employment status.

Income

The general relationship between income and worry is in the expected direction. Regardless of age group, those who make at least $60,000 a year are less likely to worry about money than are those

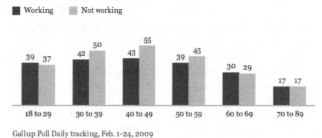

Did you worry about money yesterday?
% Worried about money, by employment status and age

■ Working   ■ Not working

Gallup Poll Daily tracking, Feb. 1-24, 2009

making less than $60,000 a year. This gap by income persists even among those in the 70-and-older age category. (The worry gap by income is largest among those 40 to 59.)

All in all, the data show that age appears to have an independent effect on financial worry regardless of financial status.

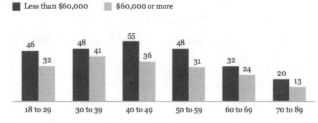

Did you worry about money yesterday?
% Worried about money, by annual household income and age

■ Less than $60,000   ■ $60,000 or more

Gallup Poll Daily tracking, Feb. 1-24, 2009

Gender

Women are generally at least slightly more likely than men to say they worried about money, with the exception of the 30 to 39 age group, in which men and women are about equally likely to say this. The gender gap is largest among those 40 to 49. Diminished financial worry among older Americans occurs across both genders; yet even among the oldest Americans in the sample, women are slightly more likely than men to be worried.

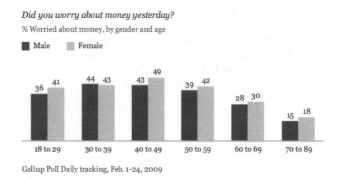

Did you worry about money yesterday?
% Worried about money, by gender and age

■ Male   ■ Female

Gallup Poll Daily tracking, Feb. 1-24, 2009

Bottom Line

Americans' daily worry about money declines steadily after age 50, and this relationship between worry and age occurs regardless of work status, income, or gender.

Results are based on telephone interviews with 11,361 national adults, aged 18 and older, conducted Feb. 1–24, 2009, as part of Gallup Poll Daily tracking. For results based on the total sample of national adults, one can say with 95% confidence that the maximum margin of sampling error is ±2 percentage points.

Interviews are conducted with respondents on land-line telephones (for respondents with a land-line telephone) and cellular phones (for respondents who are cell-phone only).

In addition to sampling error, question wording and practical difficulties in conducting surveys can introduce error or bias into the findings of public opinion polls.

February 27, 2009
OBAMA APPROVAL RATING INCREASES TO 67%
Had dropped to 59% prior to his Tuesday congressional address

by Jeffrey M. Jones, Gallup Poll Managing Editor

In the days immediately after Barack Obama's nationally televised address to Congress on Tuesday night, his public support has increased significantly to 67% in Feb. 24–26 Gallup Daily polling, and is now just two points below his term high. This comes on the heels of a term-low 59% reported by Gallup on Tuesday.

Barack Obama's Presidential Job Approval Rating

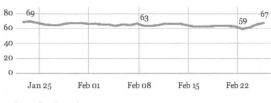

Gallup Poll Daily tracking

Obama's speech was well-received, and appears to have won him back support he had been losing in prior days, and then some.

The speech certainly came at an opportune time for Obama, but a recovery was easily achievable because the decline in his approval rating was accompanied by an increase in the percentage of Americans expressing no opinion, rather than an increase in the proportion disapproving of his performance in office.

Since the speech, the percentage having no opinion of Obama has fallen back to 11% from 16%, while his approval rating has increased eight points. There has been a slight drop in his disapproval rating as well, from 25% to 21%.

Obama's approval rebound is due to increased support from all political groups, but especially from independents and Republicans, whose support had been waning. Over the past week, independents' approval of Obama dropped from 62% to 54%, but is now back to 62%. There has been a sharp increase in support among Republicans, from 27% to 42%. Democrats' support for Obama was already extremely high at 86%, but even this has climbed slightly, to 90% in the latest polling.

Barack Obama's Presidential Job Approval Rating

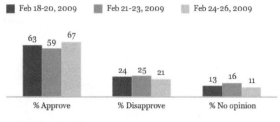

Gallup Poll Daily tracking

Barack Obama's Presidential Job Approval Rating, by Political Party

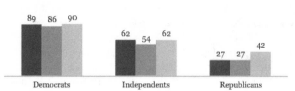

Gallup Poll Daily tracking

Survey Methods

Results are based on telephone interviews with 1,551 national adults, aged 18 and older, conducted Feb. 24–26, 2009, as part of Gallup Poll Daily tracking. For results based on the total sample of national adults, one can say with 95% confidence that the maximum margin of sampling error is ±3 percentage points.

Interviews are conducted with respondents on land-line telephones (for respondents with a land-line telephone) and cellular phones (for respondents who are cell-phone only).

In addition to sampling error, question wording and practical difficulties in conducting surveys can introduce error or bias into the findings of public opinion polls.

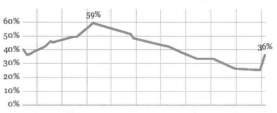
Approval Ratings of Republicans in Congress, 1999-2009

IMAGE BOOST FOR BOTH DEMOCRATS, REPUBLICANS IN CONGRESS

Both parties in Congress show significant increases in job approval

by Jeffrey M. Jones, Gallup Poll Managing Editor

Both the Republicans and the Democrats in Congress are more popular now than they were last December. While still quite low at 36%, the approval rating for Republicans is up significantly from December. There has been a similar increase in the rating of Democrats over this time.

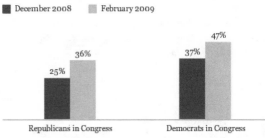
Approval Ratings of Republicans and Democrats in Congress

■ December 2008   ▓ February 2009

These results are based on a *USA Today*/Gallup poll conducted Feb. 20–22. Gallup recently reported a similar rise in Congress' overall approval rating. These increases suggest that both parties have benefited perceptually from the change in government from the Bush administration to the Obama administration. And even though Republicans have largely opposed the popular new president's proposals since he took office Jan. 20, they still are viewed significantly more positively now than they were at the end of last year.

In fact, the current approval rating is the best Gallup has measured for the Republicans in Congress since October 2005, when 38% approved. The high since 1999, when Gallup began asking about approval for the parties in Congress, was 59% in April 2002. That reading came as government institutions continued to receive enhanced public support in the wake of the 9/11 terrorist attacks.

Interestingly, Americans of all political affiliations show similar increases of about 10 percentage points in their ratings of the Republicans in Congress compared with last December. But only Republicans have an overall positive view of the Republicans in Congress, at 61% approval.

Meanwhile, the Democrats in Congress are also enjoying a boost in their popularity, with their 47% approval rating their best since November 2003 and also significantly better than the current rating for Republicans.

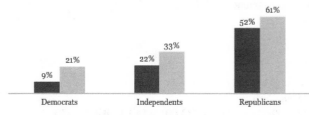
Changes in Approval Ratings of Republicans in Congress, by Political Party

■ December 2008   ▓ February 2009

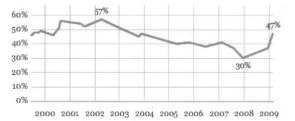
Approval Ratings of Democrats in Congress, 1999-2009

But the changes in congressional Democrats' ratings are not as broad-based as those observed for the Republicans in Congress. There have been 20- and 12-point increases in the ratings of the Democrats in Congress among Democrats and independents, respectively, but a 5-point *decrease* among Republicans.

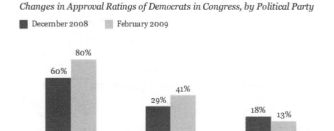
Changes in Approval Ratings of Democrats in Congress, by Political Party

■ December 2008   ▓ February 2009

Implications

While Congress is usually the least popular of the three major branches of the federal government, it has enjoyed a boost in popularity in recent weeks, which is evident not only in the way Americans view the institution overall but also in how they view both of the congressional parties.

But both parties' ratings are up from historical lows or near-lows, so the recent gains still leave them—especially the lower-rated Republicans—with a lot of room for improvement.

Survey Methods

Results are based on telephone interviews with 1,013 national adults, aged 18 and older, conducted Feb. 20–22, 2009. For results based on the total sample of national adults, one can say with 95% confidence that the maximum margin of sampling error is ±3 percentage points.

Interviews are conducted with respondents on land-line telephones (for respondents with a land-line telephone) and cellular phones (for respondents who are cell-phone only).

In addition to sampling error, question wording and practical difficulties in conducting surveys can introduce error or bias into the findings of public opinion polls.

March 02, 2009

INITIAL REACTION TO OBAMA BUDGET TILTS POSITIVE

About a third of Americans have yet to form an opinion

by Frank Newport, Gallup Poll Editor in Chief

Americans' first reactions to President Barack Obama's new 10-year budget plan are more positive than negative, although a sizable group of Americans say they haven't been following news about the plan and have not yet formed an opinion. The weekend Gallup Poll finds 44% of Americans saying their reaction to the new plan is positive and 26% saying it's negative, with the rest having no opinion.

From what you know or have heard about Barack Obama's budget plan, is your first impression of it generally positive or generally negative, or don't you know enough to say?

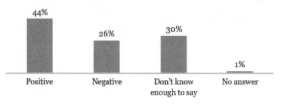

Feb. 27-28, 2009

The poll data clearly show that Americans are sharply divided along party lines in their initial reactions to the budget plan, which includes $3.6 trillion in spending in 2010 and a wide variety of spending plans and tax adjustments in the years thereafter. More than 6 in 10 Republicans say their first reaction is negative and nearly 7 in 10 Democrats say their reaction is positive. Reaction to the plan is more evenly divided among independents, but is generally more positive than negative.

Americans who identify themselves as liberals (about 20% of this sample) are strongly positive, while moderates (39% of the sample) are more positive than negative, and conservatives (37% of the sample) are more negative than positive. Conservatives are not as strongly negative about the plan as are Republicans, reflecting at least

in part the fact that conservatives in America today are not monolithically Republican.

From what you know or have heard about Barack Obama's budget plan, is your first impression of it generally positive or generally negative, or don't you know enough to say?

By party ID and ideology

	Generally positive	Generally negative	Do not know enough to say	Refused
	%	%	%	%
Republicans	14	63	24	--
Independents	37	25	38	*
Democrats	69	5	25	1
Conservatives	27	46	27	--
Moderates	46	17	37	1
Liberals	73	6	21	1

* Less than 0.5%
Feb. 27-28, 2009

The Gallup Poll was conducted Feb. 27–28, just a day or two after Obama's unveiling of his massive budget plan on Thursday. At the time of the interviewing, a quarter of Americans said they were following news about the plan very closely, with another 42% following the news somewhat closely, leaving about a third who were following news about the plan not too closely or not at all.

How closely have you been following the news about the 10-year federal budget plan announced by President Barack Obama on Thursday — very closely, somewhat closely, not too closely, or not at all?

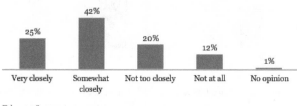

Feb. 27-28, 2009

The data show that those who are following the plan very closely are somewhat more likely to have a negative reaction to it than are those who are playing less close attention. Among the most attentive group, positive reactions exceed negative ones by only about six percentage points. Among the less attentive groups, the spread between positive and negative is much larger.

From what you know or have heard about Barack Obama's budget plan, is your first impression of it generally positive or generally negative, or don't you know enough to say?

By how closely respondents are following news about Obama's 10-year budget plan

■ Generally positive   ■ Generally negative   ■ Don't know enough to say

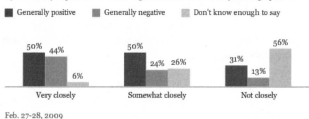

Feb. 27-28, 2009

This could, of course, indicate that paying close attention to the plan generates a more negative reaction, suggesting in turn that as more Americans hear and read about the plan, reactions will become less supportive. However, an examination of the data shows that Republicans and conservatives at this early juncture are more likely to be paying very close attention to the plan than are Democrats and liberals. Thus, the overall finding that those paying attention are most negative could be simply a reflection of the pre-existing ideologies and/or orientations of the types of people who follow the news closely, rather than a reflection of the plan's content per se.

How closely have you been following the news about the 10-year federal budget plan announced by President Barack Obama on Thursday -- very closely, somewhat closely, not too closely, or not at all?

By party ID and ideology

	Very closely	Somewhat closely	Not too closely	Not at all
	%	%	%	%
Republicans	32	46	15	7
Independents	23	41	20	15
Democrats	25	42	22	10
Conservatives	34	39	16	11
Moderates	20	42	24	13
Liberals	21	50	20	9

Feb. 27-28, 2009

Bottom Line

The initial public reactions to President Obama's new 10-year budget proposal are highly partisan, with Democrats and liberals (and, to a lesser degree, independents) evincing a positive reaction, while Republicans and conservatives respond in a much more negative fashion. These public opinion differences reflect the sharp divergence in the comments and reactions of politicians and commentators over the weekend, with Democrats and Obama staffers defending the budget, while Republicans and conservatives generally were highly critical.

At this juncture in history, more Americans identify as Democrats than Republicans. That fact, coupled with the finding that independents are more positive than negative about the budget, yields the situation in which the public's overall reaction to the budget plan in this nascent phase of the debate is more positive than negative.

About a third of Americans have not yet formed even an initial reaction to President Obama's new 10-year budget proposal, and, separately, a third say they have paid little attention to the news about the budget. Most of the rest say they have followed news about the plan "somewhat closely" rather than "very closely." There will be intensive news coverage of the debate over the plan in the coming weeks, and it is possible that public opinion will shift as the process unfolds.

Survey Methods

Results are based on telephone interviews with 1,023 national adults, aged 18 and older, conducted Feb. 27–28, 2009. For results based on the total sample of national adults, one can say with 95% confidence that the margin of sampling error is ±3 percentage points.

Interviews are conducted with respondents on land-line telephones (for respondents with a land-line telephone) and cellular phones (for respondents who are cell-phone only).

In addition to sampling error, question wording and practical difficulties in conducting surveys can introduce error or bias into the findings of public opinion polls.

March 03, 2009
AS BRITISH P.M. VISITS, BRITAIN REIGNS AS TOP U.S. ALLY
British Prime Minister Gordon Brown unknown to most Americans

by Jeffrey M. Jones, Gallup Poll Managing Editor

When asked to choose which of five nations is the United States' most valuable ally, Americans are slightly more likely to choose Great Britain than Canada. Far fewer give this distinction to Japan, Israel, or Germany.

If you had to choose, which of the following countries do you think is the most valuable ally for the United States -- [ROTATED: Canada, Great Britain, Israel, Japan, (or) Germany]?

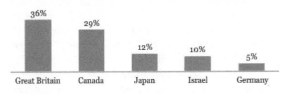

Feb. 27-28, 2009

The new Gallup Poll was conducted Feb. 27–28 in anticipation of British Prime Minister Gordon Brown's March 3 White House visit, his first since Barack Obama became president. Gallup asked Americans to choose which of five highly rated countries from Gallup's Feb. 9–12 World Affairs survey they consider to be the United States' "most valuable ally."

Two in three Americans choose one of the United States' primary English-speaking allies—Great Britain or Canada—which are also the two countries that received the highest favorable ratings.

There are variations in the extent to which Americans name Canada or Great Britain as the United States' top ally. For example, Republicans are significantly more likely to choose Great Britain than Canada, while Democrats are slightly more likely to choose Canada than Great Britain.

Views of Most Valuable U.S. Ally, by Political Party Affiliation

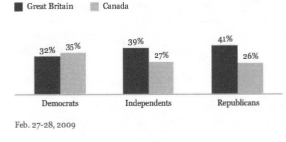

Feb. 27-28, 2009

Residents of the Midwest, many of whose home states border Canada, are more likely to consider Canada than Great Britain as the United States' top ally, but Great Britain is the leader in the East, South, and West.

Views of Most Valuable U.S. Ally, by Region

■ Great Britain ▨ Canada

	East	Midwest	South	West
Great Britain	44%	31%	32%	38%
Canada	29%	39%	24%	28%

Feb. 27-28, 2009

Non-Hispanic whites (40%) are more likely than nonwhites (26%) to name Great Britain as the most valuable U.S. ally, but Britain is the most frequently chosen country for both groups. Non-whites are about as likely to name Japan (22%) and Canada (22%) as to name Great Britain.

Favorable Ratings

Great Britain has consistently ranked at or near the top of the country favorable list each time Gallup has measured Americans' views of countries over the last decade. This year, 89% of Americans said they had a favorable opinion of Great Britain, including 36% who had a very favorable opinion. Only Canada—with a 90% favorable rating, including 39% very favorable—had a similarly high reading.

Since 1989, when Gallup first asked Americans to rate Great Britain, an average of 87% of Americans have rated it favorably. Over this time, favorable ratings of Great Britain have narrowly ranged between 81% and 91%, and have been at the higher end of that range the last several years.

What is your overall opinion of Great Britain? Is it very favorable, mostly favorable, mostly unfavorable, or very unfavorable?

■ % Favorable

[line graph showing % Favorable from 1990 to 2008, ranging between roughly 80 and 90]

On the other hand, British Prime Minister Brown, who has been in office since June 2007, remains largely unknown to Americans. The Feb. 27–28 poll finds 69% of Americans saying either that they have never heard of him (40%) or that they are not familiar enough with him to have an opinion (29%). To the extent Americans are familiar with Brown, they view him much more positively (25%) than negatively (6%).

The U.S. visit is likely to attract quite a bit of media attention, and could help raise Brown's profile in the eyes of Americans.

Former British Prime Minister Tony Blair was much better known—and extremely well-liked—by Americans. The last time

Gallup asked Americans to rate Blair—in March 2007, shortly before Brown succeeded him—65% rated Blair favorably and only 20% unfavorably.

Implications

Americans view Great Britain very positively—as favorably as any other nation in the world. But among some of the most highly rated countries in Americans' eyes, Great Britain is most likely to be regarded as the United States' most valuable ally.

The close U.S.-British relationship has served the United States well in terms of finding support for its foreign and military policies, including the Iraq war, and should continue to do so as a new generation of American and British leaders meets to discuss solutions to the global financial crisis and other matters of international importance.

Survey Methods

Results are based on telephone interviews with 1,023 national adults, aged 18 and older, conducted Feb. 27–28, 2009, as part of Gallup Poll Daily tracking. For results based on the total sample of national adults, one can say with 95% confidence that the maximum margin of sampling error is ±3 percentage points.

Interviews are conducted with respondents on land-line telephones (for respondents with a land-line telephone) and cellular phones (for respondents who are cell-phone only).

In addition to sampling error, question wording and practical difficulties in conducting surveys can introduce error or bias into the findings of public opinion polls.

March 03, 2009
AMERICANS' SUPPORT FOR ISRAEL UNCHANGED SINCE GAZA CONFLICT
Most Americans sympathize with Israel, view it favorably

by Lydia Saad, Gallup Poll Senior Editor

The Obama administration has signaled it will be more energetic than its predecessor in brokering a Mideast peace, with the appointment of a special envoy and with Secretary of State Hillary Clinton's visit to the region this week. While their government may be steering a new course, Americans' views toward the Israeli-Palestinian conflict haven't changed: nearly 6 in 10 (59%) say their sympathies in the conflict lie more with the Israelis; just 18% side with the Palestinians.

In the Middle East situation, are your sympathies more with the Israelis or more with the Palestinians?

■ % Israelis ▨ % Palestinians ▨ % Both/Neither/No opinion

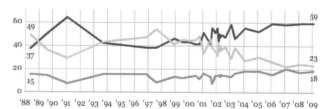

'88 '89 '90 '91 '92 '93 '94 '95 '96 '97 '98 '99 '00 '01 '02 '03 '04 '05 '06 '07 '08 '09

According to Gallup's annual World Affairs survey, updated Feb. 9–12, 2009, about a quarter of Americans are partial to neither the Israelis nor the Palestinians. This includes 9% saying they favor neither side, 4% saying they favor both equally, and 10% with no opinion. The 59% favoring Israel this year is identical to what Gallup found in February 2008, and similar to the annual reading each year since 2006.

Additionally, the new poll finds 63% of Americans holding a favorable view of Israel, including 21% holding a very favorable view of that country. Only 29% have an unfavorable view of Israel, including just 8% "very unfavorable."

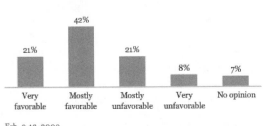

Overall Opinion of Israel

Feb. 9-12, 2009

Favorability toward Israel was slightly higher a year ago at this time, when 71% viewed it favorably. Israel's military incursion into Gaza in December and January that killed more than 1,000 civilians and resulted in a major humanitarian crisis may have dampened American favorability toward that country slightly. However, today's rating of Israel is identical to the average favorability score for Israel since January 2000.

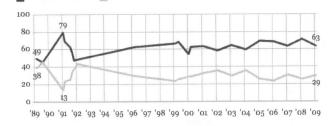

Overall Opinion of Israel -- Full Trend, 1989-2009

By contrast, the Palestinian Authority is seen in a mostly negative light, with only 15% viewing it positively and 73% negatively. And, among those holding strong views, the balance of opinion is even more negative: just 1% have a very favorable view vs. 30% very unfavorable.

Favorability toward the Palestinian Authority has varied some since 2000, ranging from 11% to 27%, but has registered close to 15% for each of the past three years.

Aid for Gaza

The issue at hand this week in the Middle East is international funding for humanitarian and economic aid to the war-torn Gaza Strip.

Attending a Gaza aid conference in Egypt on Monday, Secretary of State Hillary Clinton said the United States will provide $900 million in aid to the Palestinians, but specified that only $300 mil-

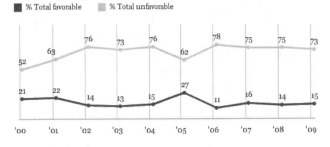

Overall Opinion of the Palestinian Authority -- Full Trend, 2000-2009

lion would be directed toward Gaza and that all of it would be channeled through the U.S.-backed Palestinian Authority led by President Abbas in the West Bank, not the Hamas-led government in Gaza.

This isolation of Hamas in U.S. aid to the Palestinians would seem to be consistent with the American public's general opposition to providing the Hamas government with any financial assistance, even if it were to formally recognize Israel. According to a Gallup Poll conducted shortly after the Hamas party won the January 2006 Palestinian elections, only 35% favored providing aid to the Palestinian Authority under Hamas leadership under any conditions (5% unconditionally and 30% if Hamas were to recognize Israel), while 57% said the United States should not provide that government with any aid.

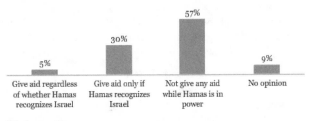

Preferred Policy for U.S. Aid to the Palestinian Authority

Feb. 6-9, 2006

Two of the more prominent participants in the Gaza aid conference are Egypt, the host country, and Saudi Arabia, which has pledged $1 billion of the $5 billion raised. Egypt is nearly as highly ranked as Israel, according to the two countries' overall favorable ratings among Americans (59% for Egypt vs. 63% for Israel), although far fewer have a "very favorable" view of Egypt than of Israel (8% vs. 21%, respectively).

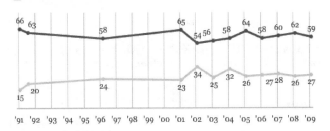

Overall Opinion of Egypt -- Full Trend, 1991-2009

Americans view Saudi Arabia far less well, with only 31% favorable and 60% unfavorable. Opinion of Saudi Arabia fell sharply between February 2001 and February 2002—spanning the terrorist attacks on Sept. 11, 2001, which involved several Saudi-born hijackers—and has yet to recover.

Overall Opinion of Saudi Arabia -- Full Trend, 1991-2009

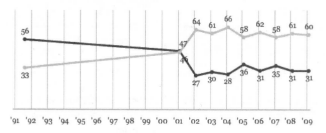

Bottom Line

President Barack Obama's desire to achieve a two-state solution to the Israeli-Palestinian conflict on his watch—something Clinton reiterated this week—may put him at odds with the newly elected leadership of Israel, but not necessarily with the American public. In 2002, Gallup found 48% of Americans in favor of an independent Palestinian state on the West Bank and Gaza Strip, and only 27% opposed. Support rose to 74% under the provision that the Palestinian government demonstrated it could stop suicide bombings in Israel.

At the same time, Clinton's recent assurance that U.S. support for Israel is "unshakable, durable, [and] fundamental" is consistent with Israel's broadly positive image in the United States, as well as with Israel's solid advantage over the Palestinians in American "sympathies."

Survey Methods

Results are based on telephone interviews with 1,022 national adults, aged 18 and older, conducted Feb. 9–12, 2009. For results based on the total sample of national adults, one can say with 95% confidence that the maximum margin of sampling error is ±3 percentage points.

Interviews are conducted with respondents on land-line telephones (for respondents with a land-line telephone) and cellular phones (for respondents who are cell-phone only).

In addition to sampling error, question wording and practical difficulties in conducting surveys can introduce error or bias into the findings of public opinion polls.

March 04, 2009
NET NEW HIRING SUGGESTS MORE JOB LOSSES
Gallup's model suggests February's unemployment rate may hit or exceed 7.8%

by Dennis Jacobe, Gallup Chief Economist

Gallup's unemployment-rate model predicts that the government will report a worsening of the U.S. unemployment rate on Friday. Gallup conducts more than 8,000 interviews each month with U.S. employees, to ascertain their perceptions of the job situation at their com-

panies. Monthly net new hiring (the percentage of employees who said their companies were hiring minus the percentage saying their companies were letting people go) was -6 in February, worse than the -4 of January. Both are substantially worse than the 28 score of January 2008.

Net New Hiring Activity, Monthly Trend, January 2008-February 2009
% of companies hiring minus % letting people go, in percentage points

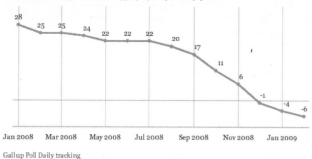

Gallup Poll Daily tracking

Unemployment Continues to Worsen

In February 2008, the U.S. unemployment rate was 4.8%. By January 2009, it had reached 7.6%—its highest level since September 1992. Gallup's projection, based on its Net New Hiring survey results, suggests the February 2009 unemployment rate is likely to reach at least 7.8% when the Labor Department reports it on Friday. A 7.8% unemployment rate would be the worst such rate for the United States since June 1992; anything higher would be the worst since at least January 1984.

U.S. Unemployment Rate
Gallup projection for February 2009 includes statistical range from 7.8% to 8.2%

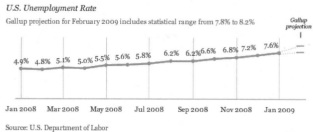

Source: U.S. Department of Labor

The monthly trend in Gallup's Net New Hiring measure is inversely related to the U.S. unemployment rate and, based on its 13-month history, the measure provides Gallup with a better than 8-in-10 chance of accurately estimating the unemployment rate's future direction. Of course, many factors make such projections difficult, with probably the most important of these being the potential for job seekers to get discouraged and stop looking for work (and thus not be included in the government's official unemployment rate). As the job situation worsens, the size of the labor force often shrinks, reducing the percentage reported as unemployed.

Survey Methods

Gallup's hiring measure is based on aggregated interviews with a nationally representative sample of more than 8,000 U.S. workers each month. Gallup asks current full- and part-time employees whether their employers are hiring new people and expanding the size of their workforces, not changing the size of their workforces, or letting people go and reducing the size of their workforces.

Gallup's hiring measure is computed by subtracting the "letting go and reducing" percentage from the "hiring and expanding" percentage. The assumption is that employees across the country have a good feel for what's happening in their companies, and that these insider perceptions can yield a meaningful indication of the nation's job situation. For results based on these samples, the maximum margin of sampling error is ±3 percentage points.

Interviews are conducted with respondents on land-line telephones (for respondents with a land-line telephone) and cellular phones (for respondents who are cell-phone only).

In addition to sampling error, question wording and practical difficulties in conducting surveys can introduce error or bias into the findings of public opinion polls.

March 04, 2009
"BUY AMERICAN" FEELING GROWS AS AUTOMAKERS STRUGGLE
U.S. cars most favored by older and lower-income Americans

by Lydia Saad, Gallup Poll Senior Editor

On the heels of the bleak news that U.S. automakers sold 41% fewer cars in February than they did a year ago, Gallup polling offers some reassurance that Detroit brands are still in demand. In fact, the percentage of Americans saying they would only consider cars from American companies when making a new-car purchase has increased slightly in recent months, from 30% in mid-December to 37% today.

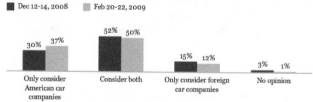

Apart from the current financial difficulties the U.S. auto companies are facing, in general, when making a decision about getting a new car, would you -- [only consider cars from an American company, consider cars by both American and foreign companies, (or) only consider cars from foreign companies]?

According to the Feb. 20–22 *USA Today*/Gallup poll, a mere 12% of Americans now say they would only consider buying a foreign car, thus giving American automakers some advantage over foreign car companies. However, the largest group, 50%, says it would consider cars from both U.S. and foreign companies—highlighting just how competitive the domestic market is for U.S. automakers.

Relatively few Americans of any group say they would only consider buying cars from foreign companies. By contrast, there is significant variation in support for buying only American cars among different subsets of the population.

Perhaps most troubling for Detroit in terms of the long-term outlook for its product is the finding that adults from 18 to 34 years of age are far less likely than older generations to limit themselves to American cars. Just 27% of respondents in this age bracket tell Gallup they would only consider buying American cars, compared with 37% of those 35 to 54 years of age, and 45% of those 55 and older.

Car Buying Preferences, by Age

USA Today/Gallup, Feb. 20-22, 2009

The buy-American mentality is less prevalent as household income goes up, falling from 49% of those earning less than $30,000 per year to 37% among middle-income earners to just 26% among those earning $75,000 or more.

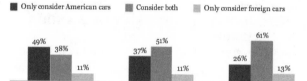

Car Buying Preferences, by Annual Household Income

USA Today/Gallup, Feb. 20-22, 2009

There is strong regional support for the Big Three automakers in the American Midwest—the traditional home of the U.S. auto industry—where 52% of adults say they would only consider cars from American companies. Elsewhere, the rate is a consistent 31% to 34%.

Car Buying Preferences, by Region

USA Today/Gallup, Feb. 20-22, 2009

There are only slight differences along partisan lines in car-buying preferences, with 39% of Democrats, 37% of Republicans, and 33% of independents favoring American cars. The distinctions are a bit stronger along ideological lines, with conservatives more inclined than liberals to buy American: 40% vs. 30%. Moderates fall squarely in between, at 35%.

Bottom Line

Whether it's because of patriotism, taxpayer self-interest, or sympathy for U.S. automakers, slightly more Americans are in a buy-American mood when it comes to cars than was true a few months ago.

While that's good news for Chrysler and General Motors, both of which stand on the brink of bankruptcy, the increase in such sentiment from 30% in December to 37% today may be too little, too late to offset the larger contraction in the car market altogether as a result of the economic slump.

Survey Methods

Results are based on telephone interviews with 1,013 national adults, aged 18 and older, conducted Feb. 20–22, 2009. For results based on the total sample of national adults, one can say with 95% confidence that the maximum margin of sampling error is ±3 percentage points.

Interviews are conducted with respondents on land-line telephones (for respondents with a land-line telephone) and cellular phones (for respondents who are cell-phone only).

In addition to sampling error, question wording and practical difficulties in conducting surveys can introduce error or bias into the findings of public opinion polls.

What are you planning to do with your current investments in the stock market over the next month or so?

Based on stock owners

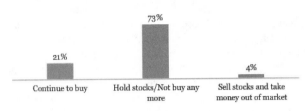

Gallup Poll, March 4, 2009

March 05, 2009

IN U.S., MAJORITY STILL SEE STOCKS AS A GOOD LONG-TERM BUY

But few stock owners plan to invest more over the next month

by Lymari Morales, Gallup Poll Staff Writer

As the Dow Jones Industrial Average plunged below 7,000 this week, President Barack Obama reacted by saying, "buying stocks is a potentially good deal if you've got a long-term perspective on it." A new Gallup Poll conducted Wednesday night—after the first gains in six days—found that 53% of Americans and 67% of stock owners agree that stocks remain a good long-term investment.

Do you think stocks remain a good long-term investment, or not?

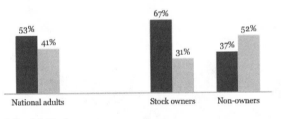

Gallup Poll, March 4, 2009

Although majorities of both groups endorse investing in the market in theory, views on actually buying stocks in the current economic environment are an entirely different story. When respondents who identified themselves as stock owners (about 6 in 10 Americans) were asked what actions they plan to take "over the next month or so" in regard to their investments, just 21% said they plan to buy more stocks. An overwhelming 73% said they plan to hold their stocks but not buy any more in the near term. Just 4% said they plan to sell stocks and take money out of the market in the next month.

The distinction between short-term decision-making and longer-term prospects likely hinges on how long Americans think it will take for the stock market to recover. When Americans are asked in an open-ended fashion how long they think it will be before the stock market shows "a sustained recovery," 43% suggest it will happen before the end of 2010, while another 27% suggest it will take two to three years. That leaves more than one in five Americans predicting that it won't recover for at least four years. In this case, stock owners do not differ much from national adults overall in their views.

Just your best guess, how long do you think it will be before the stock market shows a sustained recovery? [OPEN-ENDED]

	% National adults	% Stock owners	% Non-owners
By the end of this year/In 2009	18	20	16
In one year/By the end of next year/In 2010	25	26	25
Two to three years	27	29	24
Four to five years	13	15	12
Longer than five years	6	5	8
Will never recover	2	2	2
Don't know	8	4	13

Gallup Poll, March 4, 2009

Bottom Line

Despite a tumbling market that concerns even the likes of Warren Buffett, a majority of Americans have faith in the long-term viability of the stock market. More than half believe stocks remain a good long-term investment, including more than two-thirds of stock owners. But risking near-term cash for long-term gains is something few are actually willing to do in the current environment. The fact that the vast majority of stock owners do not plan to buy more stocks over the next month or so suggests that it will take more than what some would consider bargain-basement prices to lure investors back into the market.

Survey Methods

Results are based on telephone interviews with 1,003 national adults, aged 18 and older, conducted March 4, 2009. For results based on the total sample of national adults, one can say with 95% confidence that the maximum margin of sampling error is ±3 percentage points.

For results based on the 617 stock owners, the maximum margin of sampling error is ±4 percentage points.

Interviews are conducted with respondents on land-line telephones (for respondents with a land-line telephone) and cellular phones (for respondents who are cell-phone only).

In addition to sampling error, question wording and practical difficulties in conducting surveys can introduce error or bias into the findings of public opinion polls.

Polls conducted entirely in one day, such as this one, are subject to additional error or bias not found in polls conducted over several days.

March 05, 2009

U.S. SATISFACTION IMPROVES SLIGHTLY BUT STEADILY

Increase appears to be political in nature

by Jeffrey M. Jones, Gallup Poll Managing Editor

Americans' satisfaction with the state of the nation remains low—at an average of 21% for the past week, including 20% in the most recent data, from March 1–3. But this measure has shown a slight but steady improvement from 14% in early February.

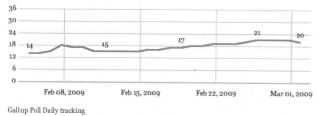

Percentage of Americans Satisfied With Way Things Are Going in the United States

Gallup Poll Daily tracking

Gallup has measured national satisfaction daily since Barack Obama took office, and also did so in late October through December 2008. In the latter part of 2008, satisfaction ratings ranged from a low of 9% in Dec. 12–14 polling to a high of just 14% in the first few days after the election and after Thanksgiving.

Little seemed to change when Obama first took office—in Jan. 21–23 polling, 14% of Americans said they were satisfied. After showing a brief improvement in late January, the percentage who reported being satisfied with the state of the nation settled back to 14% by early February. But since that time, satisfaction has shown a slight but steady improvement, and has been 20% or higher each of the last seven days.

These increases have occurred even as Gallup finds little or no improvement in key economic measures, such as consumer confidence, job-market perceptions, and consumer spending.

Rather, the increase appears to be largely political in nature, likely reflecting a slightly more positive outlook on national affairs after the change in presidential administration and the Obama government's recent attempts to address the problems facing the country.

The higher satisfaction ratings in recent weeks are mainly apparent among Democrats and, to a lesser degree, independents. Democrats' satisfaction with the country has increased from an average of 20% for the first week of February to 27% last week. Independents have shown a smaller, five percentage-point increase, while Republican satisfaction has essentially stayed the same, aside from a slight decline in the middle of the month.

Satisfaction Ratings by Party, Weekly Averages in February 2009

Numbers in percentages

■ Democrats   ■ Independents   ■ Republicans

Gallup Poll Daily tracking

Notably, since late 2008, Republicans and Democrats have flipped as to which party is reporting higher average satisfaction levels. This is a common phenomenon Gallup has observed when previous presidential administrations have changed from one party to the other.

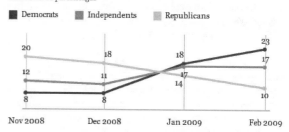

Satisfaction Ratings by Party, Monthly Averages

Numbers in percentages

■ Democrats   ■ Independents   ■ Republicans

* Results for January 2009 are based on polling conducted Jan. 21-31
Gallup Poll Daily tracking

Since November, Democrats' average satisfaction level has jumped from 8% to 23%, while Republicans' numbers have declined from 20% to 10%. Independents show a slight improvement, from 12% to 17%.

Looking at this slightly differently, it can be seen that both Americans identifying with the party of the incumbent president and those aligned with the opposition party have shown at least slightly higher levels of satisfaction in February than at the tail end of last year, even as those parties have traded places. Specifically, satisfaction among those identifying with the party of the president is higher now (23% among Democrats) than it was in November (20% among Republicans). Likewise, the opposition party's supporters have also shown a slight increase (from 8% among Democrats in November to 10% among Republicans now).

Implications

American voters chose to change the course of the nation last November by electing the Democrat Obama to replace the Republican George W. Bush as president. To date, the change in government has apparently had a modest positive effect on Americans' perceptions of how things are going in the United States. But Americans are still well aware that the economy is in poor shape, and see little immediate prospects for improvement.

When satisfaction levels have bottomed out in the past, as in 1979 and 1992, it has taken roughly two years before returning to pre-decline levels.

Survey Methods

Results are based on telephone interviews with 1,574 national adults, aged 18 and older, conducted March 1–3, 2009, as part of Gallup Poll Daily tracking. For results based on the total sample of national adults, one can say with 95% confidence that the maximum margin of sampling error is ±3 percentage points.

Interviews are conducted with respondents on land-line telephones (for respondents with a land-line telephone) and cellular phones (for respondents who are cell-phone only).

In addition to sampling error, question wording and practical difficulties in conducting surveys can introduce error or bias into the findings of public opinion polls.

March 09, 2009

LAYOFFS' SECOND-HAND EFFECTS ON THOSE STILL WORKING

Employees at companies laying off workers are much more worried

by Frank Newport, Gallup Poll Editor in Chief

A new Gallup analysis finds that worry about money is far greater among U.S. workers whose companies are reducing the size of their workforces (50%) compared to those whose companies are either keeping their workforces steady (35%) or hiring (30%).

Now think more generally about the company or organization you work for, including all of its employees. Based on what you know or have seen, would you say that, in general, your company or employer is hiring new people and expanding the size of its workforce, not changing the size of its workforce, (or) letting people go and reducing the size of its workforce?

Did you worry about money yesterday?

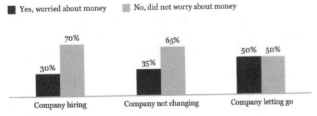

Gallup Poll Daily tracking, January-February 2009

These data are based on a Gallup analysis of more than 14,000 interviews conducted in January and February of this year, and demonstrate a progression of worry among employees, based on whether their companies are hiring, staying steady, or letting people go.

These findings reinforce the idea that in today's economy, everything is tied to everything else. The ability of many companies to prosper and avoid layoffs depends in part on the willingness of American consumers to continue buying their goods and services. But if these consumers are employed in companies that are laying people off, their financial worries may restrict their willingness to spend, thus forming a difficult-to-break cycle.

Financial Worry

The data used in this analysis come from two questions included in Gallup Poll Daily interviewing. The first asks Americans whether they worried about money "yesterday." The second asks employed Americans whether their company is hiring, maintaining its current workforce, or laying people off.

On average, 38% of employees Gallup interviewed in January and February of this year worried about money the day before they were interviewed, while 62% said they did not. Overall, 23% of employees said their companies were hiring, 47% said the size of their companies' workforces was remaining steady, and 27% said their companies were reducing the size of their workforces and letting people go.

As noted above, the key finding of the current analysis is the significantly higher level of financial worry among employees in companies that are currently laying people off, compared to those who work in companies in which layoffs are not happening. It's impor-

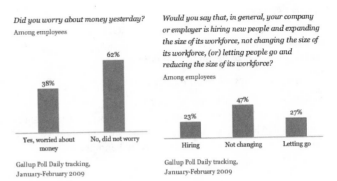

Did you worry about money yesterday?
Among employees

Would you say that, in general, your company or employer is hiring new people and expanding the size of its workforce, not changing the size of its workforce, (or) letting people go and reducing the size of its workforce?
Among employees

Gallup Poll Daily tracking, January-February 2009

Gallup Poll Daily tracking, January-February 2009

tant to keep in mind that all respondents included in this analysis were employed at the time of the interview. But current employment status apparently does not shelter workers from the psychological impact of what's happening at their places of employment.

Is it possible that other, secondary factors might explain this relationship? Previous analysis has shown that income is related to worry about money: Americans with higher household incomes tend to have lower levels of financial worry. Thus, one hypothesis could be that workers with lower incomes are more likely to work in firms susceptible to layoffs and, thus, that these workers would worry regardless of what's happening in their particular places of employment.

The data do not support this hypothesis. Across four levels of annual income, ranging from less than $24,000 to $90,000 or more, employees of firms that are letting people go are the most likely to report worrying about money.

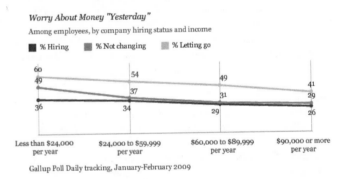

Worry About Money "Yesterday"
Among employees, by company hiring status and income

■ % Hiring ■ % Not changing ■ % Letting go

Gallup Poll Daily tracking, January-February 2009

What about age? Again, as is seen in the accompanying graph, it does not appear that age explains the relationship. Older workers in general tend to worry less, but across the age spectrum, workers appear to be affected by whether their firms are laying people off.

Worry About Money "Yesterday"
Among employees, by company hiring status and age

■ % Hiring ■ % Not changing ■ % Letting go

Gallup Poll Daily tracking, January-February 2009

A similar analysis shows that the hiring/firing status of one's firm has a significant impact on worry among both male and female employees. Women in general are more likely than men to worry, but the impact of their employer's hiring status is present for both genders.

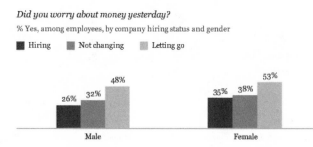

Did you worry about money yesterday?

% Yes, among employees, by company hiring status and gender

■ Hiring ■ Not changing □ Letting go

Gallup Poll Daily tracking, January-February 2009

And the relationship persists across the four major regions of the country. Employees in the Midwest and South are in general somewhat less likely to worry about money than are those on the two coasts, but regardless of region, working for a company that is laying people off is strongly associated with increased worry about personal finances.

Did you worry about money yesterday?

% Yes, among employees, by company hiring status and region

■ Hiring ■ Not changing □ Letting go

Gallup Poll Daily tracking, January-February 2009

Bottom Line

Employed Americans' tendency to worry about money is significantly higher if they work in a firm that is laying people off and reducing its workforce as opposed to a firm that is not. This relationship between worry and company hiring status occurs regardless of the employee's income level, gender, region, or age.

Previous Gallup analysis has established that worry about money is related to demographic and geographic variables. Those with lower incomes, women, middle-aged Americans, and those living on the East or West Coasts are more likely than others to worry about money. The current analysis indicates that one's workplace environment also has an apparently independent impact on financial worry: Being in a work situation in which others are being laid off appears in and of itself to be associated with worry about money.

The data highlight some of the difficulties policy-makers face in attempting to fix the U.S. economy. Stanching job losses would appear to be one way to increase consumer positivity and confidence, which in turn can be assumed to be necessary if an increase in consumer spending is to occur. However, many companies will not begin hiring again until consumer spending increases, raising the age-old question of which comes first, the chicken or the egg. Whether the recently passed economic stimulus package and other efforts will manage to break this cycle remains to be seen.

Survey Methods

Results are based on telephone interviews with 14,097 employed adults, aged 18 and older, conducted Jan. 2–Feb. 28, 2009, as part of Gallup Poll Daily tracking. For results based on the total sample of national adults, one can say with 95% confidence that the maximum margin of sampling error is ±1 percentage point.

Interviews are conducted with respondents on land-line telephones (for respondents with a land-line telephone) and cellular phones (for respondents who are cell-phone only).

In addition to sampling error, question wording and practical difficulties in conducting surveys can introduce error or bias into the findings of public opinion polls.

March 09, 2009
MAJORITY OF AMERICANS LIKELY SUPPORT STEM CELL DECISION
Fifty-two percent support easing Bush-era restrictions or lifting restrictions entirely

by Lymari Morales, Gallup Poll Staff Writer

A majority of Americans likely support President Barack Obama's executive order Monday doing away with the rules on federal funding of embryonic stem cell research that were in place under the Bush administration. In a Gallup Poll conducted last month, 38% of Americans said they support easing those restrictions and another 14% said they favor no restrictions at all. About 4 in 10 Americans favor keeping the Bush restrictions or eliminating federal funding altogether.

As you may know, the federal government currently provides very limited funding for medical research that uses stem cells obtained from human embryos. Which would you prefer the government do ... ?

Gallup Poll, Feb. 20-22, 2009

President Obama's executive order overturns George W. Bush's 2001 decision to restrict government funding to stem cell lines created before Aug. 9, 2001. Bush's order left scientists to rely on private donations to work with the hundreds of lines created since then. Obama's order doesn't specify which lines can now be used, and instead gives the National Institutes of Health 120 days to develop new rules.

Because stem cells harvested from embryos can morph into other types of cells in the body, scientists want to use them for research that might help them better treat, and possibly cure, serious conditions from diabetes to paralysis. Opponents of embryonic stem cell research say any medical advances are not worth what they see as the destruction of human life.

Americans' views on government funding for stem cell research have remained fairly stable since 2004, with the majority consistently supporting fewer restrictions on funding, rather than maintaining or strengthening the current restrictions.

As you may know, the federal government currently provides very limited funding for medical research that uses stem cells obtained from human embryos. Which would you prefer the government do ... ?

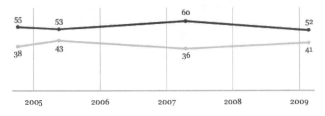

Views on government funding of embryonic stem cell research are, of course, highly political. While a strong majority of Democrats support fewer or no restrictions (64%), a majority of Republicans support keeping the Bush administration restrictions or not funding the research at all (57%). Notably, relatively few Americans of any political background favor the more extreme positions: no restrictions on government funding or not funding stem cell research at all.

As you may know, the federal government currently provides very limited funding for medical research that uses stem cells obtained from human embryos. Which would you prefer the government do ... ?

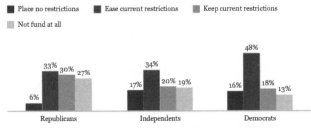

Gallup Poll, Feb. 20-22, 2009

Self-identified conservatives are the most likely to say the government should not fund embryonic stem cell research at all (32%) while self-identified liberals are the most likely to favor no restrictions whatsoever (28%).

Americans' inclination to support some sort of government funding for embryonic stem cell research is underscored by findings from Gallup's May 2008 update on values and beliefs, which found 6 in 10 Americans (62%) saying medical research using stem cells obtained from human embryos is morally acceptable while 30% said it is morally wrong.

Overall, a majority of Americans are likely to support Obama's decision to overturn existing restrictions on federal funding for embryonic stem cell research, including many Democrats and liberals in particular. While Republicans and conservatives lean more toward keeping the Bush administration's restrictions or eliminating federal funding altogether, it is important to note that most Americans—

As you may know, the federal government currently provides very limited funding for medical research that uses stem cells obtained from human embryos. Which would you prefer the government do ... ?

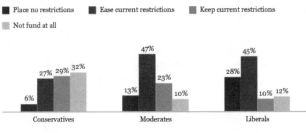

Gallup Poll, Feb. 20-22, 2009

Next, I'm going to read you a list of issues. Regardless of whether or not you think it should be legal, for each one, please tell me whether you personally believe that in general it is morally acceptable or morally wrong. How about medical research using stem cells obtained from human embryos?

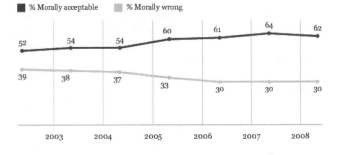

regardless of political or ideological orientation—want some sort of restrictions in place. Thus, lawmakers and those entrusted with overseeing the new policy should proceed with caution as they ponder actions that could take Obama's decision Monday even further—be it by passing legislation in Congress to make the move irreversible or by overturning the existing ban on experiments on such embryos.

Survey Methods

Results are based on telephone interviews with 1,013 national adults, aged 18 and older, conducted Feb. 20–22, 2009. For results based on the total sample of national adults, one can say with 95% confidence that the maximum margin of sampling error is ±3 percentage points.

Interviews are conducted with respondents on land-line telephones (for respondents with a land-line telephone) and cellular phones (for respondents who are cell-phone only).

In addition to sampling error, question wording and practical difficulties in conducting surveys can introduce error or bias into the findings of public opinion polls.

March 10, 2009
WELL-BEING RANKINGS REVEAL STATE STRENGTHS AND WEAKNESSES
Utah, Hawaii, Wyoming take top three spots in national well-being rankings

by Elizabeth Mendes, Gallup Poll Staff Writer

Utah, Hawaii, and Wyoming top the nation in well-being in an analysis of more than 350,000 interviews conducted in 2008. West Virginia, Kentucky, and Mississippi have the lowest well-being ratings.

State & Congressional District Resource for Well-Being
A product of the Gallup-Healthways Well-being Index

Content and Design. AHIP-All Rights Reserved. © AHIP 2009
Data. Copyright © 2008 Gallup. All rights reserved. Used with permission.

10 Highest Well-Being States

Rank	State	Well-Being Index
1	Utah	69.2
2	Hawaii	68.2
3	Wyoming	68
4	Colorado	67.3
5	Minn.	67.3
6	Maryland	67.1
7	Wash.	67.1
8	Mass.	67
9	California	67
10	Arizona	66.8

AHIP State & Congressional District Resource for Well-Being – A product of the Gallup-Healthways Well-Being Index

10 Lowest Well-Being States

Rank	State	Well-Being Index
50	W. Va.	61.2
49	Kentucky	61.4
48	Mississippi	61.9
47	Ohio	62.8
46	Arkansas	62.9
45	Indiana	63.3
44	Missouri	63.8
43	Oklahoma	64
42	Tennessee	64
41	Michigan	64

AHIP State & Congressional District Resource for Well-Being – A product of the Gallup-Healthways Well-Being Index

Top and Bottom Ranking States in Each of the Well-Being Sub-Indices

Sub-Index	Rank #1	Rank #50
Life Evaluation	Hawaii	West Virginia
Emotional Health	Hawaii	West Virginia
Physical Health	Minnesota	West Virginia
Healthy Behavior	New Mexico	Kentucky
Work Environment	Utah	Hawaii
Basic Access	Mass.	Mississippi

These new, state-level data are the results from The AHIP State and Congressional District Resource for Well-Being. The Well-Being Index score for the nation and for each state is an average of six sub-indexes, which individually examine life evaluation, healthy behaviors, work environment, physical health, emotional health, and access to basic necessities. The questions in each sub-index are asked nightly of 1,000 national adults, aged 18 and older.

The Well-Being Index national average for 2008 is 65.9, with each point (1.0) representing approximately 2.2 million people nationally. In terms of the total population in the United States, this means that approximately 145 million people aged 18 and older have favorable well-being. Across all the states, well-being varies by a range of eight points, thus even in the lowest-ranked states, there are a majority of citizens who have favorable well-being.

Mapping well-being scores across the country, a clear pattern emerges with higher well-being states located primarily in the West and lower well-being states clustered in the Midwest and the South. Standing out among its high-ranking western counterparts is Nevada, with a slightly below average well-being score and a rank of 38th. Also defying the overarching geographic pattern of well-being are Maryland and Massachusetts, the only two states in the Northeast to rank in the top 10.

In addition to the overall well-being score, the states are also ranked on each of the six sub-indexes. Hawaii takes the top spot in both emotional health and in life evaluation. Minnesotans report the best physical health in the nation, while New Mexico is first in healthy behaviors. Utah has the number one work environment in the country and Massachusetts comes out on top in terms of access to basic necessities.

On the other side of the ledger, West Virginia has the lowest score on three of the six sub-indexes: life evaluation, emotional health, and physical health. Kentucky ranks last on healthy behav-iors, and Mississippi is at the very bottom in terms of access to basic necessities.

States in the top tier in overall well-being are not necessarily the highest ranking states in each of the six sub-indexes. Hawaii, for instance, does rank high on five of the six sub-indexes, but reports the lowest quality work environments out of all 50 states. On the flipside, certain bottom ranked states in overall well-being shine in select sub-indexes. Oklahoma is eighth to last in overall well-being, but reports the third best score for work environment in the country. All told, in order for the Well-Being Index national average to increase in 2009, every state will need to make significant improvements in at least one sub-index area.

Survey Methods

Results are based on telephone interviews with more than 350,000 national adults, aged 18 and older, conducted in 2008 as part of Gallup Poll Daily tracking. For results based on the total sample of national adults, one can say with 95% confidence that the maximum margin of sampling error is ±1 percentage point.

Interviews are conducted with respondents on land-line telephones (for respondents with a land-line telephone) and cellular phones (for respondents who are cell-phone only).

In addition to sampling error, question wording and practical difficulties in conducting surveys can introduce error or bias into the findings of public opinion polls.

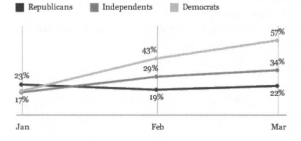

March 11, 2009
APPROVAL OF CONGRESS HITS FOUR-YEAR HIGH, FUELED BY DEMS

by Jeffrey M. Jones, Gallup Poll Managing Editor

Americans' job approval rating of Congress is up an additional 8 points this month, after a 12-point increase last month, and now stands at 39%—the most positive assessment of Congress since February 2005.

Do you approve or disapprove of the way Congress is handling its job?
2004-2009 trend

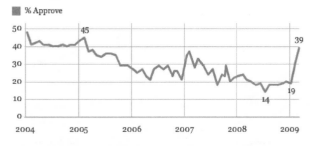

Americans who identify themselves as Democrats are mostly responsible for the improved ratings of Congress measured in the March 5–8 Gallup Poll. After showing a 25-point increase in their approval of Congress from January to February and a further 14-point increase in March, a majority of Democrats (57%) now approve of the job the Democratic-controlled Congress is doing. Independents also show improved ratings of Congress, but not nearly to the extent that Democrats do. Republicans' evaluations of Congress have changed very little this year.

Quick Turnaround

Even though Congress' job approval rating is still low on an absolute basis, the recent ratings represent a quick turnaround from the historically low ratings of 2008. Last year, on average, only 19% of Americans approved of the job Congress was doing—one of the three lowest yearly congressional approval averages in Gallup records dating back to 1974, along with 1979 (19%) and 1992 (18%).

In January of this year, Congress' job approval rating remained low at 19%, before jumping to 31% in February after the change in presidential administrations from Republican George W. Bush to Democrat Barack Obama. But this month brings an even more positive evaluation of Congress, with 39% of Americans now approving.

The latest increase suggests the reason for the improved ratings of Congress in 2009 may go beyond simply the change from split

control to one-party control of the federal government, to include an assessment of the work Congress has been doing with the new president on the economy and other issues.

Such an explanation seems plausible given that a majority of Democrats now approve of the job Congress is doing, and that the gap between Democratic and Republican approval of Congress is growing, as Congress passes and President Obama signs laws to deal with the economy and other issues that largely follow a Democratic philosophy of governing.

Even though the Democratic Party had majority control of both houses of Congress in 2007–2008, it was able to achieve little of its legislative agenda while Republican Bush remained in the White House. This lack of results may have soured Democrats' opinions of Congress. During this time, rank-and-file Democrats' approval ratings of Congress sank to as low as 11% in July 2008, after starting out near 40% shortly after the party took control of Congress in early 2007.

Congressional Job Approval Among Democrats, 2007-2009

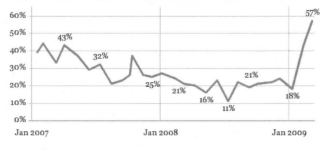

Now that the strengthened Democratic-controlled Congress is able to pass most of what it wants with little or no help from Republicans, and can count on the president to sign it into law, rank-and-file Democrats hold Congress in much greater esteem. The 57% approval rating for Congress among Democrats is the best the party has given the institution since March 2002, when Congress' job approval scores were at historical highs in the aftermath of the Sept. 11 terrorist attacks.

Survey Methods

Results are based on telephone interviews with 1,012 national adults, aged 18 and older, conducted March 5–8, 2009. For results based on the total sample of national adults, one can say with 95% confidence that the maximum margin of sampling error is ±3 percentage points.

Interviews are conducted with respondents on land-line telephones (for respondents with a land-line telephone) and cellular phones (for respondents who are cell-phone only).

In addition to sampling error, question wording and practical difficulties in conducting surveys can introduce error or bias into the findings of public opinion polls.

March 11, 2009

INCREASED NUMBER THINK GLOBAL WARMING IS "EXAGGERATED"

Most believe global warming is happening, but urgency has stalled

by Lydia Saad, Gallup Poll Senior Editor

Although a majority of Americans believe the seriousness of global warming is either correctly portrayed in the news or underestimated, a record-high 41% now say it is exaggerated. This represents the highest level of public skepticism about mainstream reporting on global warming seen in more than a decade of Gallup polling on the subject.

Thinking about what is said in the news, in your view is the seriousness of global warming -- [generally exaggerated, generally correct, or is it generally underestimated]?

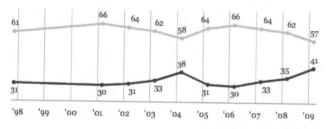

As recently as 2006, significantly more Americans thought the news underestimated the seriousness of global warming than said it exaggerated it, 38% vs. 30%. Now, according to Gallup's 2009 Environment survey, more Americans say the problem is exaggerated rather than underestimated, 41% vs. 28%.

The trend in the "exaggerated" response has been somewhat volatile since 2001, and the previous high point, 38%, came in 2004. Over the next two years, "exaggerated" sentiment fell to 31% and 30%. Still, as noted, the current 41% is the highest since Gallup's trend on this measure began in 1997.

Since 1997, Republicans have grown increasingly likely to believe media coverage of global warming is exaggerated, and that trend continues in the 2009 survey; however, this year marks a relatively sharp increase among independents as well. In just the past year, Republican doubters grew from 59% to 66%, and independents from 33% to 44%, while the rate among Democrats remained close to 20%.

Notably, all of the past year's uptick in cynicism about the seriousness of global warming coverage occurred among Americans 30 and older. The views of 18- to 29-year-olds, the age group generally

most concerned about global warming and most likely to say the problem is underestimated, didn't change.

Percentage Saying News of Global Warming Is Exaggerated, by Party ID

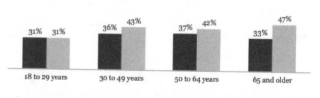

Percentage Saying News of Global Warming Is Exaggerated, by Age
Recent trend

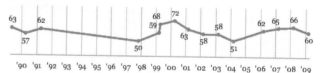

Dampened Concern

Apart from these findings about news coverage of global warming, the March 5–8 poll shows in a similar vein that Americans are a bit less concerned about the seriousness of global warming per se than they have been in recent years.

Six in 10 Americans indicate that they are highly worried about global warming, including 34% who are worried "a great deal" and 26% "a fair amount." Overall worry is similar to points at the start of the decade, but is down from 66% a year ago and from 65% in 2007.

I'm going to read you a list of environmental problems. As I read each one, please tell me if you personally worry about this problem a great deal, a fair amount, only a little, or not at all.

The "greenhouse effect" or global warming

■ % Great deal/Fair amount

63 62   68 72   62 65 66
57   59   58   60
                    50   63 58   51

'90 '91 '92 '93 '94 '95 '96 '97 '98 '99 '00 '01 '02 '03 '04 '05 '06 '07 '08 '09

The 2009 Gallup Environment survey measured public concern about eight specific environmental issues. Not only does global warming rank last on the basis of the total percentage concerned either a great deal or a fair amount, but it is the only issue for which public concern dropped significantly in the past year.

Also, compared with last year, fewer Americans believe the effects of global warming have begun to occur. The figure is now 53%, down from 61% in March 2008. At the same time, a record-high 16% say the effects will never occur. (Prior to now, Gallup polling found no more than 11% of Americans saying the effects of global warming would never happen.)

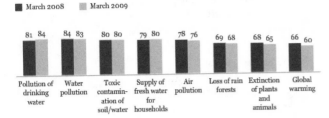

Percentage Worried Great Deal or Fair Amount About Each Problem

■ March 2008   ▨ March 2009

| | 81 84 | 84 83 | 80 80 | 79 80 | 78 76 | 69 68 | 68 65 | 66 60 |

Pollution of drinking water / Water pollution / Toxic contamination of soil/water / Supply of fresh water for households / Air pollution / Loss of rain forests / Extinction of plants and animals / Global warming

Which of the following statements reflects your view of when the effects of global warming will begin to happen -- [they have already begun to happen, they will start happening within a few years, they will start happening within your lifetime, they will not happen within your lifetime, but they will affect future generations, (or) they will never happen]?

■ % Already begun

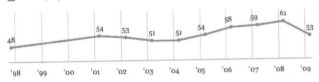

48   54   53   51   51   54   58   59   61   53
'98 '99 '00 '01 '02 '03 '04 '05 '06 '07 '08 '09

Most Doubt Warming Is a "Serious Threat"

Altogether, 68% of U.S. adults believe the effects of global warming will be manifest at some point in their lifetimes, indicating the public largely believes the problem is real. However, only 38% of Americans, similar to the 40% found in 2008, believe it will pose "a serious threat" to themselves or their own way of life.

This fear that global warming will pose a serious threat in one's lifetime steadily expanded from 25% in 1997 to 40% in 2008. The drop this year to 38% is not statistically significant; however, it is the first time since 1997 that the rate of concern has not increased.

Do you think that global warming will pose a serious threat to you or your way of life in your lifetime?

■ % Yes   ▨ % No

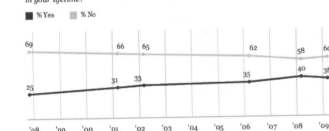

69   66   65   62   58   60
25   31   33   35   40   38
'98 '99 '00 '01 '02 '03 '04 '05 '06 '07 '08 '09

Bottom Line

Americans generally believe global warming is real. That sets the U.S. public apart from the global-warming skeptics who assembled this week in New York City to try to debunk the science behind climate change. At the same time, with only 34% of Americans saying they worry "a great deal" about the problem, most Americans do not view the issue in the same dire terms as the many prominent leaders advancing global warming as an issue.

Importantly, Gallup's annual March update on the environment shows a drop in public concern about global warming across several different measures, suggesting that the global warming message may have lost some footing with Americans over the past year. Gallup has documented declines in public concern about the environment at times when other issues, such as a major economic downturn or a national crisis like 9/11, absorbed Americans' attention. To some extent that may be true today, given the troubling state of the U.S. economy. However, the solitary drop in concern this year about global warming, among the eight specific environmental issues Gallup tested, suggests that something unique may be happening with the issue.

Certainly global warming has received tremendous attention this decade, including with Al Gore's Academy Award-winning documentary "An Inconvenient Truth." It is not clear whether the troubled economy has drawn attention away from the global warming message or whether other factors are at work. It will be important to see whether the 2009 findings hold up in next year's update of the annual environmental survey.

Survey Methods

Results are based on telephone interviews with 1,012 national adults, aged 18 and older, conducted March 5–8, 2009. For results based on the total sample of national adults, one can say with 95% confidence that the maximum margin of sampling error is ±3 percentage points.

Interviews are conducted with respondents on land-line telephones (for respondents with a land-line telephone) and cellular phones (for respondents who are cell-phone only).

In addition to sampling error, question wording and practical difficulties in conducting surveys can introduce error or bias into the findings of public opinion polls.

March 12, 2009

ON ECONOMY, REPUBLICANS TRUST BUSINESS; DEMS TRUST GOV'T.

Americans overall not increasingly worried about government power

by Frank Newport, Gallup Poll Editor in Chief

While 64% of Republicans say they place more trust in businesses to solve the nation's economic problems, 72% of Democrats say they trust the government more, underscoring the enormous philosophical divide in the way Republicans and Democrats view the government's role in solving the country's economic problems.

The findings from the March 5–8 Gallup Poll show that the sharply differing opinions of Republican versus Democratic elected representatives in Washington reflect the same type of partisan divide among rank-and-file Americans.

The Democratic president and the Democratic-controlled Congress have taken extraordinary actions to fix the economy over the last month or two, presumably under the assumption that government intervention is the only way to pull the country out of the current economic slump. These actions include passing an almost $800 billion stimulus bill and promulgating budget proposals that envision heavy government involvement in tackling a wide variety of economic (and other) problems.

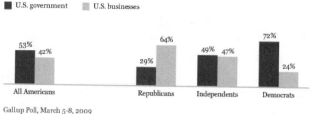

Who do you trust more to solve the United States' economic problems -- the U.S. government or U.S. businesses?

■ U.S. government   ▨ U.S. businesses

All Americans 53% 42% — Republicans 29% 64% — Independents 49% 47% — Democrats 72% 24%

Gallup Poll, March 5-8, 2009
Based on 500 national adults in Form B

Republicans have protested the massive government actions, and many Republican leaders, along with conservative commentators such as Rush Limbaugh, have not hesitated to argue that the United States is heading down the road to socialism and essentially a government-controlled economy.

Despite the differences by party, the data show that overall, Americans tilt toward the Democratic position—with a majority saying they trust the government more than businesses to solve the nation's economic problems.

This overall average is driven largely by the fact that there are more Democrats than Republicans in the United States at this point. Because independents are evenly split in their trust in government versus business to solve economic problems, the government approach wins out when the entire U.S. population is aggregated. If there were a national referendum on the desirability of the government taking the lead in solving the nation's economic problems as opposed to letting the capitalist system sort the problems out on its own, it appears that the government option would win.

Two other Gallup questions measuring Americans' views of the role and power of government show roughly the same patterns.

One long-standing Gallup trend question asks whether government is doing too much that should be left to individuals and businesses, or whether the government should do more to solve the country's problems. Democrats are highly likely to say government should do more, while Republicans are even more likely to choose the alternative that government is trying to do too much.

Some people think the government is trying to do too many things that should be left to individuals and businesses. Others think that government should do more to solve our country's problems. Which comes closer to your own view?

■ Government doing too much   ▨ Government should do more

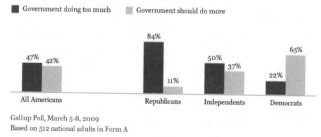

All Americans 47% 42% — Republicans 84% 11% — Independents 50% 37% — Democrats 22% 65%

Gallup Poll, March 5-8, 2009
Based on 512 national adults in Form A

Overall, the sentiment that government is doing too much wins out, but by a narrower margin than was the case in the late summer of 2008. The huge government stimulus bills and other government plans do not appear to have caused any increase in concern that the government is doing too much—at least not yet.

Some people think the government is trying to do too many things that should be left to individuals and businesses. Others think that government should do more to solve our country's problems. Which comes closer to your own view?

■ % Government doing too much   ■ % Government should do more
▨ % Mixed/Depends (vol.)

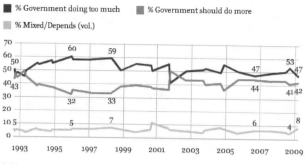

(vol.) = Volunteered response

The Democratic-Republican split in response to this question is quite similar to what was found in Gallup's Sept. 8–11, 2008, poll—conducted just before Gallup's economic mood indices and other indicators of the public's frame of mind dropped into deeply negative territory. This similarity suggests that whatever has happened in recent months has not in and of itself had a dramatic effect on underlying sentiments among partisan groups.

Is the Government Doing Too Much, or Should It Do More?

■ % Government doing too much   ▨ % Government should do more

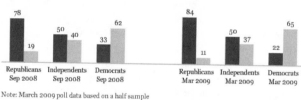

Republicans Sep 2008 78 19 — Independents Sep 2008 50 40 — Democrats Sep 2008 33 62 — Republicans Mar 2009 84 11 — Independents Mar 2009 50 37 — Democrats Mar 2009 22 65

Note: March 2009 poll data based on a half sample

In similar fashion, the update of a different Gallup trend question in the March 5–8 poll also shows that, compared with last September, there has been no jump in concern that the government has too much power. Republicans and Democrats again have sharply differing views on this issue.

Do you think the federal government today -- has too much power, has about the right amount of power, or has too little power?

■ % Too much   ■ % About the right amount   ▨ % Too little

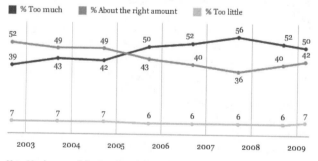

Note: March 2009 poll data based on a half sample

Almost 7 out of 10 Republicans say the federal government has too much power, while just about the same percentage of Democrats say government has either the right amount of power or too little power. Independents tilt toward saying government has too much power.

Do you think the federal government today – has too much power, has about the right amount of power, or has too little power?

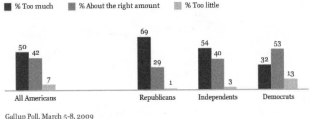

Gallup Poll, March 5-8, 2009
Based on 500 national adults in Form B

Bottom Line

These data clearly show an enormous partisan divide in the way Americans look at the role of government in society. Republicans are strongly likely to say that they trust business, rather than government, to solve the nation's economic problems; that government is attempting to do too much that should be left to individuals and businesses; and that government has too much power. Democrats hold just the opposite views, while independents are somewhere in the middle.

There is no evidence of any trend toward Americans saying either that government is doing too much that should be left to individuals and businesses, or that government has too much power. If anything, there has been a slight movement in the opposite direction. In short, there is no sign to this point that Americans overall have become more worried that government is gaining too much power or attempting to do too much.

Still, despite the trends, slight pluralities of Americans say that government is trying to do too much and that government has too much power.

Americans appear at this moment to trust government more than business when it comes to the economy specifically, no doubt reflecting the dire straits in which the economy finds itself. But when the economy recovers in the months or years ahead, the data suggest the potential for some sort of backlash or increased objection to an increased governmental role in U.S. society.

Survey Methods

Results are based on telephone interviews with 1,012 national adults, aged 18 and older, conducted March 5–8, 2009. For results based on the total sample of national adults, one can say with 95% confidence that the maximum margin of sampling error is ±3 percentage points.

For results based on the 512 national adults in the Form A half-sample and 500 national adults in the Form B half-sample, the maximum margins of sampling error are ±5 percentage points.

Interviews are conducted with respondents on land-line telephones (for respondents with a land-line telephone) and cellular phones (for respondents who are cell-phone only).

In addition to sampling error, question wording and practical difficulties in conducting surveys can introduce error or bias into the findings of public opinion polls.

March 13, 2009
AMERICANS ON ENERGY: PROMOTE BOTH NEW SOURCES AND OLD
Solid majority want increased efforts to encourage alternative energy production

by Jeffrey M. Jones, Gallup Poll Managing Editor

Americans endorse increased government efforts to encourage energy production from alternative sources of energy, but at the same time do not believe the government should reduce its financial support for the production of energy from traditional sources. Only 30% think the government should decrease the monetary support and incentives it provides to producers of energy from oil and gas.

Would you prefer the government to increase, decrease, or not change the financial support and incentives it gives for producing energy from these sources?

Gallup Poll, March 5-8, 2009

These findings are based on Gallup's annual Environment Survey, conducted March 5–8.

The Obama administration has prioritized investment in renewable energy, and a significant proportion of the recently passed economic stimulus bill is aimed at doing that. The administration also promises to cut carbon emissions and sees the use of clean-energy sources such as wind, solar, and nuclear as key to achieving that goal. Additionally, the administration has indicated it would reduce subsidies and add excise taxes on production of oil and gas in areas like the Gulf of Mexico.

More than three-quarters of Americans say they support increased government financial support and incentives to produce energy from alternative sources, while just 8% say the government should do less in this regard and 13% say it should continue what it is doing.

And while Americans are far less likely to favor increased government aid to produce energy from traditional sources—only 39% hold this view—another 28% want these efforts maintained. Thus, two in three Americans think government should continue to support energy production from oil and gas at either current or heightened levels. Just 30% call for a reduction in these efforts.

It appears the public clearly recognizes the need to develop alternative energy sources and the benefits of doing so, but may also think it is too soon to do away with the current way of doing things. In general, Americans are concerned about the energy situation—42% describe it as "very serious," which is down slightly from last year's 46%, but at the higher end of what Gallup has measured in the last decade. Also, Americans are somewhat more willing to live with environmental degradation in the pursuit of energy sources than they have been in the past—47% say the government should put a greater emphasis on environmental protection over energy exploration versus 46% who say the development of energy supplies should be the greater priority. This parity is a departure from the past, as Americans have typically come down on the side of environmental protection by a significant margin in prior Gallup Polls.

Higher Priority -- Protection of the Environment or Development of U.S. Energy Supplies?

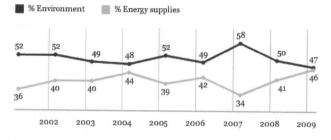

Alternative and Traditional Energy Preferences

Combining respondents' answers to the traditional and alternative energy-policy questions provides a better sense of what Americans would ideally like to see done. This analysis shows that the greatest number of Americans (33%) favor increasing government support or incentives to produce energy from both sources. Eighteen percent favor increased efforts to encourage alternative energy production while not changing current government efforts aimed at traditional energy production.

Preferences for Government Incentives for Producing Energy From Alternative and Traditional Sources

	Increase traditional	Not change traditional	Decrease traditional
Increase alternative	33%	18%	24%
Not change alternative	3%	8%	2%
Decrease alternative	3%	2%	3%

Gallup Poll, March 5-8, 2009

Note: Miscellaneous categories (e.g., No opinion) not shown

All told, 62% of Americans say they favor increased government assistance for development from both types of energy sources (33%), increased efforts on one while efforts on the other are maintained (21%—mostly those who want to see alternative energy efforts expanded), or maintaining current government activity on both (8%).

About one in four Americans think the government should increase its support for alternative energy but decrease support for traditional energy. Three percent think the government should cut back its financial assistance in both areas.

Implications

Americans largely endorse government efforts to increase alternative energy production through the use of financial support or incentives, directly in line with the Obama administration's stated objectives. And though Americans are not as enthusiastic about increasing the government's support for traditional energy production, they also don't want to see a reduction in government support of those efforts.

It is unclear whether the poor state of the economy has made Americans less willing to do away with traditional energy approaches, but Gallup has found over the years that sentiments in favor of environmental protection wax and wane in response to the health of the economy.

Survey Methods

Results are based on telephone interviews with 1,012 national adults, aged 18 and older, conducted March 5–8, 2009. For results based on the total sample of national adults, one can say with 95% confidence that the maximum margin of sampling error is ±3 percentage points.

Interviews are conducted with respondents on land-line telephones (for respondents with a land-line telephone) and cellular phones (for respondents who are cell-phone only).

In addition to sampling error, question wording and practical difficulties in conducting surveys can introduce error or bias into the findings of public opinion polls.

March 13, 2009

AMERICANS REMAIN CRITICAL OF THE UNITED NATIONS

Nevertheless, most want the organization to have a meaningful function

by Lydia Saad, Gallup Poll Senior Editor

For the seventh straight year, about 6 in 10 Americans—now 65%—say the United Nations is doing a poor job of solving the problems under its care. Only 26% believe it is doing a good job.

Do you think the United Nations is doing a good job or a poor job in trying to solve the problems it has had to face?

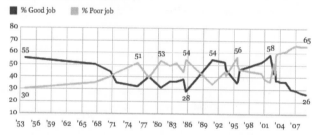

Republicans are more critical of the United Nations than are Democrats; older Americans are more critical than younger adults; and college graduates more so than those with no college education. However, the majority of these groups say the organization is doing a poor job.

Gallup measures the American public's attitudes about the United Nations each year as part of its February World Affairs survey. This year's update was conducted Feb. 9–12.

Though this year's 26% positive score is just one percentage point lower than last year's 27%, it is technically the worst job rating for the United Nations since Gallup began polling on the subject in 1953. It is also well below the U.N.'s peak ratings of 50% or more, obtained at various points over the years, including a 58% rating in 2002.

Americans have viewed the United Nations critically in the past. Gallup found just over half believing the organization was doing a poor job in August 1995, August 1985, October 1983, September 1980, and November 1975. And there was a particularly long spell, from 1971 through at least 1985, when Americans' U.N. ratings were typically more negative than positive. There is a gap in Gallup trends

Perceptions of Job United Nations is Doing

	Good job	Poor job
	%	%
Men	22	72
Women	29	59
18 to 34 years	37	54
35 to 54 years	24	67
55 and older	19	72
College graduate	21	71
Some college	24	66
No college	30	61
Republicans	20	72
Independents	22	67
Democrats	34	58

Feb. 9-12, 2009

from 1985 to 1990, but in 1990, public approval of the United Nations finally improved during the run-up to the 1991 Gulf War.

More recently, from May 2000 to February 2002—both before and after the 9/11 terrorist attacks—the United Nations received some of its best performance ratings. However, U.S. public perceptions of the United Nations turned sharply negative in 2003, when the organization rebuffed the United States' request for authorization to use military force in Iraq. Its "good job" rating fell from 50% in January 2003 to 37% in March 2003, and—with several subsequent years of bad publicity surrounding U.N. mismanagement of the Iraqi Oil for Food program, sexual abuse charges against U.N. peacekeepers in Africa and other places, and various financial corruption scandals—the U.N.'s image has yet to recover.

Down, but Not Out

Despite the seven-year stretch of negative evaluations of the United Nations, Americans continue to believe the organization should have an important role in world affairs.

Given three options for what kind of function it should have, nearly two-thirds of Americans either say the United Nations should have a leading role in world affairs, in which all countries are required to follow its policies (26%), or say it should have a major role whereby it establishes policies but nations can still act separately when they disagree with it (38%).

Only 31% would narrow the U.N.'s role to nothing more than a forum for communication among countries. This includes 30% saying the United Nations should have a minor role of this kind, and 1% volunteering that the organization should not exist.

From 2001 through 2008, the total percentage of Americans favoring a leading or major role for the United Nations varied mainly between 68% and 69%, with a slightly higher 75% recorded in 2007. Today's 64% is thus a notch lower than the recent norm.

Although Republicans are less likely than Democrats to advocate a significant role for the United Nations, a majority of Republicans nevertheless think it should play a leading or major role—resulting in broad partisan agreement on this issue.

Bottom Line

U.S. public perceptions of the United Nations became quite negative in 2003, when the international body failed to back the

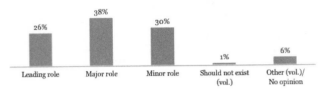

Now thinking more specifically, which of the following roles would you like to see the United Nations play in world affairs today -- should it play -- [a leading role where all countries are required to follow U.N. policies, a major role, where the U.N. establishes policies, but where individual countries still act separately when they disagree with the U.N., (or should it play) a minor role, with the U.N. serving mostly as a forum for communication between nations, but with no policy-making role]?

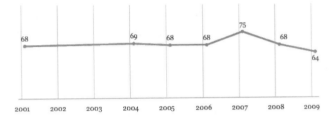

Feb. 9-12, 2009
(vol.) = Volunteered response

Trend in Support for the United Nations Playing a Leading or Major Role in World Affairs

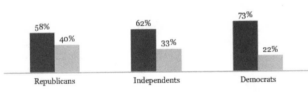

Preference for Role United Nations Should Play in World Affairs, by Party ID

Feb. 9-12, 2009

United States' intervention in Iraq, and that has turned into a seven-year slump. Not only has the United Nations had no major achievement to tout since then to restore its image among Americans, but it has been weighed down by bad publicity over financial and other problems. If the history of public opinion toward the United Nations is any guide, attitudes could rebound, but that would most likely result from an international military event of some kind in which the United Nations is seen as a partner to the United States.

Notwithstanding the low esteem in which Americans now hold the United Nations, the international organization maintains its general appeal as an instrument for bringing nations together and even establishing policies for individual countries to follow.

Survey Methods

Results are based on telephone interviews with 1,022 national adults, aged 18 and older, conducted Feb. 9–12, 2009. For results based on the total sample of national adults, one can say with 95% confidence that the maximum margin of sampling error is ±3 percentage points.

Interviews are conducted with respondents on land-line telephones (for respondents with a land-line telephone) and cellular phones (for respondents who are cell-phone only).

In addition to sampling error, question wording and practical difficulties in conducting surveys can introduce error or bias into the findings of public opinion polls.

March 16, 2009
SELF-REPORTED CONSUMER SPENDING DECLINES IN EARLY MARCH
Gallup's Consumer Spending Index shows upper-income Americans spending less

by Dennis Jacobe, Gallup Chief Economist

Americans' self-reported spending in stores, restaurants, gas stations, and online averaged $57 per day during the first 14 days of March—down from $64 during both January and February.

Gallup Consumer Spending Index

Next, we'd like you to think about your spending yesterday, not counting the purchase of a home, motor vehicle, or your normal household bills. How much money did you spend or charge yesterday on all other types of purchases you may have made, such as at a store, restaurant, gas station, online, or elsewhere?

Gallup Poll Daily tracking
Note: March data are from March 1-14

The March 1–14 average is down 31% from the $83 of the same 14-day period a year ago. During March 12–14, consumer spending fell further to $51—up from $45 for the prior three days, which was the low for any three-day period since daily monitoring began in January 2008.

Upper-Income Spending Declining

While February's retail sales were down slightly less than expected, Gallup's self-reported consumer spending measure finds Americans spending less in March than in February. Not only are lower- and middle-income consumers continuing to pull back on their spending, but upper-income Americans are doing so as well.

Pullback in Consumer Spending Continuing

Gallup's self-reported consumer spending measure tends to corroborate the impression that there was a dramatic pullback in Americans' spending starting in September of last year—particularly among upper-income consumers. Spending by consumers earning $90,000 or more a year rose from $136 per day in January 2008 to $162 in

Gallup Consumer Spending Index, by Income

Next, we'd like you to think about your spending yesterday, not counting the purchase of a home, motor vehicle, or your normal household bills. How much money did you spend or charge yesterday on all other types of purchases you may have made, such as at a store, restaurant, gas station, online, or elsewhere?

Gallup Poll Daily tracking
Note: March data are from March 1-14

Change in Gallup Consumer Spending Index, by Income

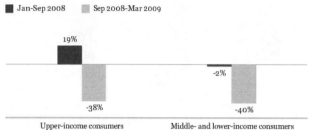

Gallup Poll Daily tracking

September 2008—an increase of 19%. In sharp contrast, spending by lower- and middle-income consumers was essentially unchanged, going from $87 in January to $85 in September. Since September 2008, upper-income spending has fallen by 38% to an average of $101 per day during the first half of March 2009, while consumer spending among the rest of Americans has fallen by 40% to $51.

Survey Methods

Gallup's Consumer Spending Index is based on aggregated interviews with a nationally representative sample of more than 12,000 adults aged 18 or older each month. For results based on these samples, the maximum margin of sampling error is ±1 percentage point.

Interviews are conducted with respondents on land-line telephones (for respondents with a land-line telephone) and cellular phones (for respondents who are cell-phone only).

In addition to sampling error, question wording and practical difficulties in conducting surveys can introduce error or bias into the findings of public opinion polls.

March 16, 2009
OBAMA'S APPROVAL EQUAL TO OR BETTER THAN BUSH'S, CLINTON'S

Biggest change since inauguration has been decline among Republicans

by Frank Newport, Gallup Poll Editor in Chief

President Barack Obama's job approval rating, at 61% in the latest three-day average of Gallup Poll Daily tracking, is slightly above where George W. Bush's and in particular Bill Clinton's were at this point in mid-March of the first years of their administrations.

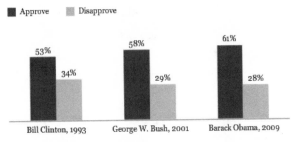

Presidential Job Approval, Mid-March of First Year of Presidencies, Obama vs. Bush vs. Clinton

Gallup's mid-March job approval rating for Bush, measured March 9–11, 2001, was 58%, with 29% disapproval. Gallup's March 12–14, 1993, approval rating for Clinton was 53%, with 34% disapproval. Both of these approval ratings are lower than Obama's current 61%. Bush's disapproval rating in mid-March 2001 was about the same as Obama's is now (28%), while Clinton's disapproval rating was significantly higher.

These comparisons suggest that President Obama is holding his own compared to the two presidents who came before him, despite some decline in his approval rating since his inauguration on Jan. 20.

Obama's first Gallup job approval rating, based on a three-day rolling average of interviewing conducted Jan. 21–23, was 68%, with 12% disapproval and 21% with no opinion. As the percentage of Americans with no opinion of his presidency has decreased over the last seven weeks, his approval has been trending down, and his disapproval moving up.

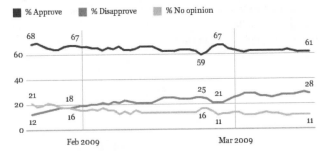

Do you approve or disapprove of the way Barack Obama is handling his job as president?

Obama's job approval rating is now lower than it was when he first took office, but this broad trend masks several short-term ups and downs over the weeks of his still-young presidency so far. But, for the month of March to date, the president's approval ratings

appear to have stabilized. Obama's approval rating between March 1 and March 15—based on the three-day rolling averages reported by Gallup—has been in a narrow band between 61% and 63%, while his disapproval rating has been in a similarly narrow range between 25% and 29%.

As is the case for most presidents, there are sharp partisan differences in Obama's job approval rating. Among Republicans, Obama's average approval for the past week (March 9–15) is 26%, among independents it is 59%, and among his fellow Democrats, 91%.

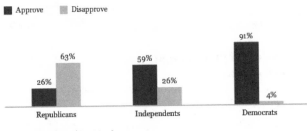

Barack Obama Job Approval, by Party ID

Gallup Poll Daily tracking, March 9-15, 2009

The analysis of weekly trends in Obama's approval ratings by party make it clear what's behind the changes observed since his inauguration: the major shift has been a significant decline in approval among Republicans. His approval rating among Democrats and independents has stayed roughly the same.

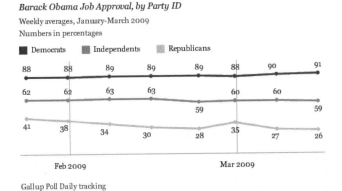

Barack Obama Job Approval, by Party ID

Weekly averages, January-March 2009
Numbers in percentages

Gallup Poll Daily tracking

Bottom Line

Although Obama's job approval ratings have become more negative in the weeks since his inauguration, they remain at or above the ratings of his two immediate predecessors at similar points in their nascent presidencies. The major reason Obama's ratings have declined has been a drop in approval among Republicans, from 41% to 26%. Obama's approval ratings among independents and Democrats remain high, and have not changed significantly.

Survey Methods

Results are based on telephone interviews with 1,547 national adults, aged 18 and older, conducted March 13–15, 2009, as part of Gallup Poll Daily tracking. For results based on the total sample of national adults, one can say with 95% confidence that the maximum margin of sampling error is ±2 percentage points.

Interviews are conducted with respondents on land-line telephones (for respondents with a land-line telephone) and cellular phones (for respondents who are cell-phone only).

In addition to sampling error, question wording and practical difficulties in conducting surveys can introduce error or bias into the findings of public opinion polls.

March 17, 2009
MAJORITY RECEPTIVE TO LAW MAKING UNION ORGANIZING EASIER

But most Americans not closely following news about union bill in Congress

by Lydia Saad, Gallup Poll Senior Editor

A new Gallup Poll finds just over half of Americans, 53%, favoring a new law that would make it easier for labor unions to organize workers; 39% oppose it. This is a key issue at stake with the Employee Free Choice Act now being considered in Congress.

Generally speaking, would you favor or oppose a new law that would make it easier for labor unions to organize workers?

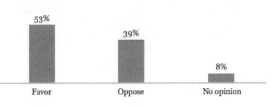

March 14-15, 2009

The poll reveals sharply differing reactions to the issue within the general public according to political orientation. Most Democrats (70%) say they would favor a law that facilitates union organizing, while a majority of Republicans (60%) say they would oppose it. Independents lean in favor of such a law, 52% vs. 41%.

Opinion on a Law That Would Make It Easier for Labor Unions to Organize Workers, by Party ID

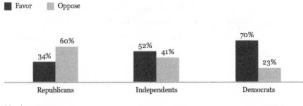

March 14-15, 2009

As originally proposed, the 2009 Employee Free Choice Act (in its House and Senate versions) strengthens the "majority signature" or "card check" basis for union organizing by automatically unionizing any workplace in which a majority of workers have signed a union authorization card. The act would eliminate employers' ability to call for secret-ballot elections (although employees can still call for one), and would make changes to enforcement of labor pro-

tections and contract-settlement procedures. Thus far, the proposal has not been a prominent item in the mainstream national news; however, it has sparked fierce union-versus-business debate in Washington and appears headed toward a close vote in the U.S. Senate.

By their own admission, most Americans are not paying very close attention to the congressional debate on this issue. According to the March 14–15 survey, only 12% of U.S. adults say they are following news about the union-organizing bill "very closely" and another 22% say they are following it "somewhat closely." Nearly two-thirds of Americans say they are following it less closely than that (26%), or not at all (39%).

How closely have you been following news about a bill in Congress that would change the rules governing how unions can organize workers?

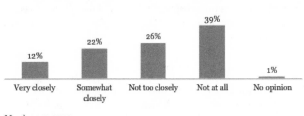

March 14-15, 2009

Those most closely following news about the union-organizing bill are the most opposed to the general concept of a law making it easier for unions to organize: just 40% are in favor; 58% are opposed. The bill enjoys its highest support—58%—among those not following the bill at all.

Opinion on a New Law Making It Easier for Unions to Organize Workers
By how closely respondents are following news about a bill that would change union-organizing rules

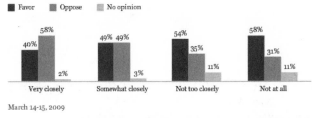

March 14-15, 2009

Bottom Line

Previous Gallup polling has shown that Americans are fundamentally sympathetic to labor unions, and these underlying attitudes are no doubt reflected in their general support for legislation characterized as making it easier for workers to unionize. For example, Gallup's annual polling on workplace issues, conducted each August, has found consistently high approval of labor unions in recent years, including a 59% approval rating last summer. The current level of support for a new law facilitating more union membership—53% in favor—is only slightly less favorable to unions.

The current findings could bode well for the pro-union side of the issue as it ramps up the public-information component of its lobbying efforts, particularly at a time when corporate America has serious image problems. Americans appear to be a sympathetic audience for a basic argument behind the law if it is described simply as making it easier for unions to organize.

At the same time, Americans have barely begun to pay attention to the issue. The 12% who are following it "very closely" is exceptionally low relative to public attention to other news issues Gallup has measured over the last two decades. And, while Americans are broadly supportive of labor unions, Gallup's August 2008 Workplace survey found only 35% in favor of unions having greater influence. In this context, with the arguments against card check yet to be fully aired and debated, it could be a troubling sign for unions that no more than 53% of Americans immediately support this fundamental aspect of the card-check bill.

The Employee Free Choice Act is a complex piece of legislation with numerous components, making it difficult to assess overall support for the bill among a population that is largely unaware of it. General support for the idea of "making it easier for unions to organize" as measured in the current poll is telling, but not necessarily indicative of public reaction to the bill if and when the political debate spills over into news headlines. Future Gallup polling will explore public reaction to specific aspects of the bill's provisions, and will continue to monitor overall support for the concept of making it easier for workers to unionize.

Survey Methods

Results are based on telephone interviews with 1,024 national adults, aged 18 and older, conducted March 14–15, 2009, as part of Gallup Poll Daily tracking. For results based on the total sample of national adults, one can say with 95% confidence that the maximum margin of sampling error is ±3 percentage points.

Interviews are conducted with respondents on land-line telephones (for respondents with a land-line telephone) and cellular phones (for respondents who are cell-phone only).

In addition to sampling error, question wording and practical difficulties in conducting surveys can introduce error or bias into the findings of public opinion polls.

March 18, 2009
IN U.S., MORE OPTIMISM ABOUT IRAQ, LESS ABOUT AFGHANISTAN
New high of 42% say war in Afghanistan a mistake

by Jeffrey M. Jones, Gallup Poll Managing Editor

A new *USA Today*/Gallup poll finds growing concern about the war in Afghanistan at the same time that Americans' optimism about Iraq is growing or holding steady.

Forty-two percent of Americans now say the United States made a mistake in sending troops to Afghanistan, up from 30% earlier this year and establishing a new high. Meanwhile, the 53% who say the Iraq war is a mistake is down slightly from 56% in January, and 60% last summer.

These results are based on a March 14–15 *USA Today*/Gallup poll, conducted just before the six-year anniversary of the U.S. invasion of Iraq. As the United States is reducing the size of its military force in Iraq and increasing its troop strength in Afghanistan, the public's opinions about the two wars seem to be adjusting accordingly.

Now, just 38% of Americans say things are going well for the United States in Afghanistan. That is down from 44% in January and is the lowest Gallup has found since it first asked this question in September 2006.

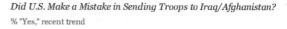

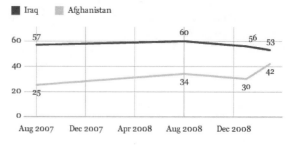

Did U.S. Make a Mistake in Sending Troops to Iraq/Afghanistan?
% "Yes," recent trend

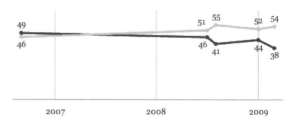

How would you say things are going for the U.S. in Afghanistan?

Still, the new low in assessments of U.S. progress in Afghanistan compares favorably to the low point for the Iraq war from January 2007, when only 28% thought things were going well for the United States in Iraq. But perceptions have shifted rather dramatically since then, and now 51% of Americans give a positive assessment of the Iraq war.

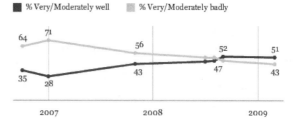

How would you say things are going for the U.S. in Iraq?
Recent trend

That increasingly optimistic view about Iraq extends to Americans' perceptions of the United States' chances for ultimate success in that war. Sixty-four percent now believe the United States can win the war, and 42% believe it will do so. Both are the best assessments Gallup has measured since June 2006.

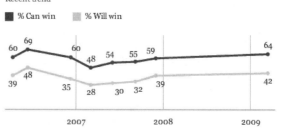

Think the U.S. Can/Will Win War in Iraq
Recent trend

Politicized and Non-Politicized Wars

It is important to point out that even as American support for the Afghanistan war is declining, and even as Americans perceive greater progress in Iraq than in Afghanistan, public support for the war in Afghanistan is still higher than for the Iraq war.

Americans have been supportive of U.S. military operations in Afghanistan since they were launched in October 2001 in response to the Sept. 11 terrorist attacks. In contrast, the Iraq war began with limited international backing and with most Democratic members of Congress—including many who authorized military action in Iraq—quickly coming to oppose the war.

The political nature of the Iraq war and the significantly less political nature of the Afghanistan war are evident in support for the two wars by political party, particularly with regard to Democrats' opinions. Even as opposition to the Iraq war has declined slightly, the overwhelming majority of Democrats (83%) still say it was a mistake to send troops there. Only 53% of Democrats say this about the war in Afghanistan. Meanwhile, independents' and Republicans' views on each of the wars are similar.

Views of Iraq and Afghanistan Wars as a Mistake, by Political Party

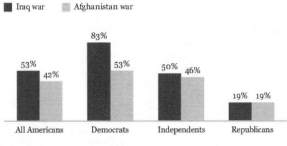

USA Today/Gallup, March 14-15, 2009

Since the Afghanistan war has not been politicized to the extent the Iraq war has been, majority support for it continues more than seven years after the Afghanistan conflict began. In the case of Iraq, support dipped below the majority level a little over a year into the war (June 2004), and has consistently remained below that level since August 2005.

Implications

With reports of increased difficulty in achieving U.S. objectives in Afghanistan, and with the Obama administration's committing greater resources to the mission, it is unclear whether majority support for the war will continue without tangible signs of progress. But signs of progress can quickly turn around Americans' perceptions of the conflict (if not their basic support), as has occurred with regard to the Iraq war in recent years, essentially since the "surge" of troops in Iraq was implemented.

It is possible that Republicans may seek to pin a continued lack of progress in Afghanistan on President Obama, and thus their generally high level of support for the effort could dwindle. But that is far from a sure bet given Republicans' generally greater concern about terrorism and typical support for government steps designed to prevent it.

Survey Methods

Results are based on telephone interviews with 2,021 national adults, aged 18 and older, conducted March 14–15, 2009, as part of Gallup

Poll Daily tracking. The Iraq and Afghanistan questions were asked of random halves of the total sample.

Results for the Iraq questions are based on telephone interviews with 1,024 national adults in Form A. Results for the Afghanistan questions are based on telephone interviews with 997 national adults in Form B. For each set of results, one can say with 95% confidence that the maximum margin of sampling error is ±3 percentage points.

Interviews are conducted with respondents on land-line telephones (for respondents with a land-line telephone) and cellular phones (for respondents who are cell-phone only).

In addition to sampling error, question wording and practical difficulties in conducting surveys can introduce error or bias into the findings of public opinion polls.

March 18, 2009
OUTRAGED AMERICANS WANT AIG BONUS MONEY RECOVERED
Views persist across party lines

by Lymari Morales, Gallup Poll Staff Writer

Three in four Americans (76%) want the government to take actions to block or recover the bonuses insurance giant AIG paid its executives after receiving federal bailout funds.

Which comes closer to your thinking about this matter -- [ROTATED: the government should not intervene because the AIG bonuses were part of existing contracts in place before the bailout money was given to AIG, (or) the government should take actions to try to block or recover any bonuses paid to AIG executives because the company was given government bailout money]?

Gallup Poll, March 17, 2009

The results are based on a one-night Gallup Poll conducted March 17, 2009, after reports that AIG, the recipient of about $170 billion in federal aid, recently paid its executives $165 million in bonuses. AIG contends it had to pay the money because of existing contracts that were in place before the company received bailout funds. On Capitol Hill Wednesday, members of the House Financial Services committee said they were determined to get the money back, demanding from Chairman and CEO Edward Liddy the names of the bonus recipients.

Answering questions from lawmakers, Liddy acknowledged that doling out the bonus money was "distasteful." Reports about the AIG bonuses have dominated the news cycle this week, with lawmakers and journalists chiming in about taxpayer "outrage." In the Tuesday night Gallup Poll, 59% of Americans said they were personally "outraged" by the bonuses. One in four (26%) said they were "bothered" and just 1 in 10 (11%) said they were not that bothered.

All in all, when the responses to the two questions are combined, the results show that a majority of 55% of Americans are outraged

How do you, personally, feel about these bonuses -- outraged, bothered, or not particularly bothered?

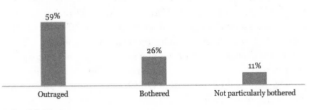

Gallup Poll, March 17, 2009

and want the bonuses blocked or recovered, while another 21% are not outraged but still want the bonuses blocked.

Views Cut Clear Across Party Lines

Americans' frustration with AIG and their desire for government action are apparent across party lines. Majorities of Democrats, independents, and Republicans say they are outraged and, separately, say they want the government to take action. These views are most prevalent among Democrats, but the differences across partisan groups are much smaller than is the case on many policy and social issues.

Views on AIG Bonuses, by Party Affiliation

■ % Who say government should try to block/recover bonuses   ▨ % Outraged

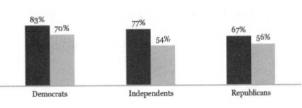

Gallup Poll, March 17, 2009

Implications

The fact that a majority of Americans, including Republicans and Democrats, are "outraged" about the AIG bonuses and want the government to take action to get the money back provides a strong mandate for lawmakers trying to resolve the issue. While Congress weighs the legal options available, including a bill that would impose a 70% tax on "excessive" compensation paid to employees of bailed-out companies, they can do so knowing the American people are eager for them to do something. While the episode no doubt puts a stain on Bush and Obama administration efforts to stabilize the economy by propping up struggling companies, the Gallup Poll shows that in this situation, Americans would likely welcome bipartisan action to help remedy the frustration many of them currently feel.

Survey Methods

Results are based on telephone interviews with 1,012 national adults, aged 18 and older, conducted March 17, 2009. For results based on the total sample of national adults, one can say with 95% confidence that the maximum margin of sampling error is ±3 percentage points.

Interviews are conducted with respondents on land-line telephones (for respondents with a land-line telephone) and cellular phones (for respondents who are cell-phone only).

In addition to sampling error, question wording and practical difficulties in conducting surveys can introduce error or bias into the findings of public opinion polls.

Polls conducted entirely in one day, such as this one, are subject to additional error or bias not found in polls conducted over several days.

March 19, 2009
AMERICANS: ECONOMY TAKES PRECEDENCE OVER ENVIRONMENT
First time majority has supported economy in 25 years of asking question

by Frank Newport , Gallup Poll Editor in Chief

For the first time in Gallup's 25-year history of asking Americans about the trade-off between environmental protection and economic growth, a majority of Americans say economic growth should be given the priority, even if the environment suffers to some extent.

With which one of these statements about the environment and the economy do you most agree -- [ROTATED: protection of the environment should be given priority, even at the risk of curbing economic growth (or) economic growth should be given priority, even if the environment suffers to some extent]?

■ % Environment   ▨ % Economic growth   ▨ % Equal priority (vol.)

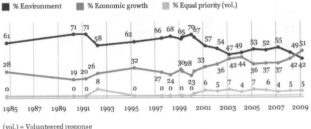

(vol.) = Volunteered response

Gallup first asked Americans about this trade-off in 1984, at which time over 60% chose the environmental option. Support for the environment was particularly high in 1990–1991, and in the late 1990s and 2000, when the dot-com boom perhaps made economic growth more of a foregone conclusion.

The percentage of Americans choosing the environment slipped below 50% in 2003 and 2004, but was still higher than the percentage choosing the economy. Sentiments have moved up and down over the last several years, but this year, the percentage of Americans choosing the environment fell all the way to 42%, while the percentage choosing the economy jumped to 51%.

The reason for this shift in priorities almost certainly has to do with the current economic recession. The findings reflect many recent Gallup results showing how primary the economy is in Americans' minds, and help document the fact of life that in times of economic stress, the public can be persuaded to put off or ignore environmental concerns if need be in order to rejuvenate the economy.

The Economy Versus Energy

Although the importance of energy as a policy concern in Americans' minds has moderated since last summer's high gas prices, a different trade-off question shows that Americans are more inclined now than in past years to favor giving the priority to energy production over the environment.

The question, which Gallup has used in this format since 2001, asks Americans whether they favor protection of the environment at the risk of limiting energy supplies, or favor the development of U.S. energy supplies at the risk of harming the environment. Respondents this year are essentially equally likely to choose the environmental option as they are to choose the energy production option, marking—albeit by just one or two percentage points—the highest percentage choosing energy and the lowest percentage choosing the environment in the nine years of asking the question.

With which one of these statements about the environment and energy production do you most agree -- [ROTATED: protection of the environment should be given priority, even at the risk of limiting the amount of energy supplies -- such as oil, gas and coal -- which the United States produces (or) development of U.S. energy supplies -- such as oil, gas and coal -- should be given priority, even if the environment suffers to some extent]?

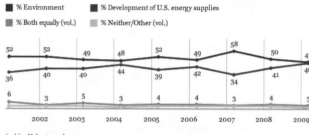

(vol.) = Volunteered response

Bottom Line

There is little question that the current economic crisis poses a significant challenge for the environmental movement in this country. Previous Gallup research has shown that concern about global warming has diminished this year, and the research reviewed here shows clearly that Americans are more willing than ever to forgo protection of the environment if needed in order to ensure economic growth or the production of energy. With the economy as bad as it has been in recent memory, Americans' preferences have swung even more strongly in the direction of the economy over the environment.

Survey Methods

Results are based on telephone interviews with 1,012 national adults, aged 18 and older, conducted March 5–8, 2009. For results based on the total sample of national adults, one can say with 95% confidence that the maximum margin of sampling error is ±3 percentage points.

Interviews are conducted with respondents on land-line telephones (for respondents with a land-line telephone) and cellular phones (for respondents who are cell-phone only).

In addition to sampling error, question wording and practical difficulties in conducting surveys can introduce error or bias into the findings of public opinion polls.

March 20, 2009
ECONOMIC OPTIMISM REACHES 20-MONTH HIGH
Though still dismally low, 27% now say the economy is improving

by Lydia Saad, Gallup Poll Senior Editor

Public optimism about the U.S. economy—although still scarce, with only 27% of Americans saying the economy is getting better and 67% saying it is getting worse—is now broader than at any point in Gallup's 15 months of daily consumer polling.

Right now, do you think that economic conditions in the country as a whole are getting better or getting worse?

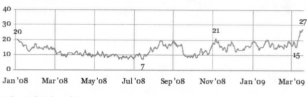

Gallup Poll Daily tracking

The 27% "getting better" figure, from March 17–19 Gallup Poll Daily tracking, is up from 15% recorded March 7–9. It is the highest economic optimism reading Gallup has recorded since daily tracking began in January 2008, and, according to Gallup's monthly economic readings prior to that, the highest since July 2007.

Gallup began to see significant improvement in Americans' evaluation of the economic direction last week, coinciding with the start of a sustained rebound in the Dow Jones Industrial Average since that index sank to a 12-year low on March 9. With the Dow closing up on six of the last eight trading days, Americans have clearly had a basis for feeling encouraged about the economy.

As reported on gallup.com Thursday, Gallup finds no recent increase in consumers' self-reported retail spending, or in worker perceptions about hiring conditions at their companies, suggesting any real impact from the improved optimism on the economy is yet to be felt.

Along the same lines, Gallup tracking finds little improvement in consumer perceptions of the economy's current state. Polling from the same March 17–19 period finds 57% of Americans calling economic conditions "poor," only slightly better than the 63% from March 7–9.

How would you rate economic conditions in this country today -- as excellent, good, only fair, or poor?

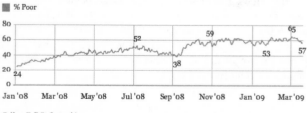

Gallup Poll Daily tracking

Among different income groups, the most dramatic increase in economic optimism in March has been among those earning $90,000 or more—not surprising, given upper-income Americans' greater investment in the stock market. In this group, optimism has grown from 10% saying the economy is "getting better" in early March to 27% this week. This top-earning group was initially the least likely to say the economy is getting better, but is now on par with middle-income earners, and closely trails low-income Americans in its outlook.

Economic Outlook, by Annual Household Income -- % "Getting Better"
Weekly averages since early March*

Note: Week of March 16 is partial

Improved economic optimism is seen among all partisan groups, but, in accordance with the shifts seen by income, the increase is particularly sharp among Republicans. (Republicans' household income skews higher than that of independents and Democrats.) The percentage of Republicans saying the economy is getting better has advanced from an average of 8% for the week spanning March 2–8 to 20% thus far in the week that began on March 16. This 12-point gain compares with a 9-point gain among Democrats and a 7-point gain among independents.

Economic Outlook, by Party ID -- % "Getting Better"
Weekly averages since early March*

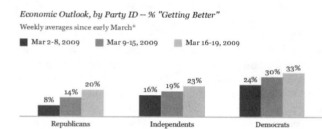

Note: Week of March 16 is partial

Survey Methods

Results are based on telephone interviews with 1,464 national adults, aged 18 and older, conducted March 17–19, 2009, as part of Gallup Poll Daily tracking. For results based on the total sample of national adults, one can say with 95% confidence that the maximum margin of sampling error is ±3 percentage points.

Interviews are conducted with respondents on land-line telephones (for respondents with a land-line telephone) and cellular phones (for respondents who are cell-phone only).

In addition to sampling error, question wording and practical difficulties in conducting surveys can introduce error or bias into the findings of public opinion polls.

March 20, 2009
SUPPORT FOR NUCLEAR ENERGY INCHES UP TO NEW HIGH
Majority believes nuclear power plants are safe

by Jeffrey M. Jones, Gallup Poll Managing Editor

A majority of Americans have been supportive of the use of nuclear energy in the United States in recent years, but this year's Gallup Environment Poll finds new high levels of support, with 59% favoring its use, including 27% who strongly favor it.

Favor the Use of Nuclear Energy as One of the Ways to Provide Electricity for the U.S.?

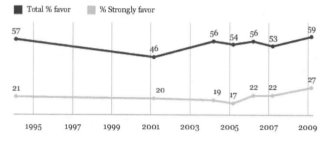

Support for nuclear energy had been fairly steady in the mid-50% range since Gallup first asked about it in 1994, apart from a 46% reading in 2001. The percentage who say they *strongly* favor nuclear energy had also been fairly stable at around 20%, before increasing to 27% this year.

Gallup has always found consistent and large gender differences in Americans' views of nuclear power, and the same applies this year—71% of men favor the use of nuclear energy, compared with only 47% of women. Both groups show their highest level of support for nuclear power to date.

Favor Use of Nuclear Energy, by Gender

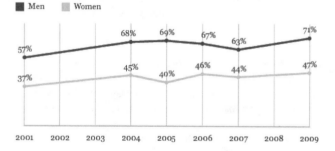

Additionally, upper-income Americans have consistently favored nuclear energy at much higher levels than lower-income respondents. This year, 75% of Americans whose total annual household incomes are at least $75,000 favor using nuclear power to produce electricity in the United States, compared with just 41% of those in households with annual incomes of less than $30,000. Only once in the last eight years has support reached 50% among the low-income group.

This year, both Republicans and Democrats show their highest level of support for using nuclear energy since 2001. However, Republicans continue to be much more in favor of it than Democrats are, 71% to 52%.

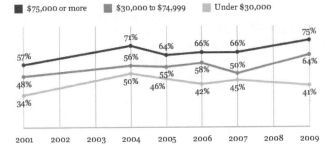

Favor Use of Nuclear Energy, by Household Income

■ $75,000 or more   ■ $30,000 to $74,999   ▢ Under $30,000

71%   75%
57%   56%   64%   66%   66%
          55%   58%   50%   64%
48%   50%   46%   42%   45%
34%   41%

2001   2002   2003   2004   2005   2006   2007   2008   2009

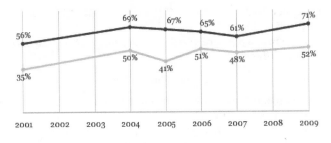

Favor Use of Nuclear Energy, by Political Party Affiliation

■ Republicans/Republican leaners   ▢ Democrats/Democratic leaners

          69%   67%   65%   61%   71%
56%
          50%   41%   51%   48%   52%
35%

2001   2002   2003   2004   2005   2006   2007   2008   2009

Safety of Nuclear Power

Americans may have not fully embraced the use of nuclear energy because of concerns about potential health risks from a nuclear meltdown or the nuclear waste that power plants produce. The poll finds that a majority of Americans, 56%, believe nuclear power plants are safe, but a substantial minority of 42% disagree.

Generally speaking, do you think nuclear power plants are safe or not safe?

56%   42%

Safe   Not safe

Gallup Poll, March 5-8, 2009

Opinions about the safety of nuclear power vary by subgroup in much the same way they do on the basic favor/oppose question.

For example, 72% of men but only 41% of women believe nuclear power plants are safe.

Upper-income respondents (75%) are more than twice as likely as lower-income respondents (36%) to say nuclear power plants are safe.

And while 73% of Republicans are confident in the safety of nuclear power plants, only 46% of Democrats agree.

Implications

There are clearly challenges to expanding nuclear energy use in the United States. Although most Americans support the use of nuclear energy, the level is hardly an overwhelming majority. And there remain concerns among a substantial minority of Americans about

the safety of nuclear power plants. Indeed, in prior years, Gallup has found Americans reluctant to support the construction of nuclear power plants in their local communities.

President Obama has said that nuclear power is part of his overall plan to expand the use of alternative energy in the United States, and if public support for it continues to grow, it would seem likely that more Americans would come to rely on nuclear energy.

Survey Methods

Results are based on telephone interviews with 1,012 national adults, aged 18 and older, conducted March 5–8, 2009. For results based on the total sample of national adults, one can say with 95% confidence that the maximum margin of sampling error is ±3 percentage points.

Each question reported here was asked of a random half-sample of approximately 500 adults, and the margin of sampling error for each is ±5 percentage points.

Interviews are conducted with respondents on land-line telephones (for respondents with a land-line telephone) and cellular phones (for respondents who are cell-phone only).

In addition to sampling error, question wording and practical difficulties in conducting surveys can introduce error or bias into the findings of public opinion polls.

March 23, 2009
U.S. INVESTOR OPTIMISM SHOWS SHARP IMPROVEMENT
March reading is up from all-time low

by Dennis Jacobe, Gallup Chief Economist

The Gallup Index of Investor Optimism, a broad measure of investor perceptions, showed a sharp improvement in March, increasing 41 points to -23—up from -64 in February, which was its lowest level since the Index's inception in 1996.

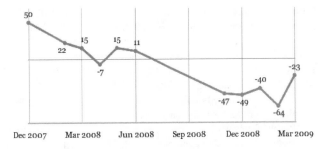

Gallup Index of Investor Optimism, December 2007-March 2009

50
22   15   15   11
     -7   -23
                              -40
               -47   -49
                    -64

Dec 2007   Mar 2008   Jun 2008   Sep 2008   Dec 2008   Mar 2009

Economic Optimism Shows Sharp Improvement

While the Index—a survey of those with $10,000 or more in investable assets—reflects continued pessimism among investors as a group, it more than reversed its February plunge. The Index peaked at 178 in January 2000, just prior to the bursting of the dot-com bubble. Last year, it turned negative for the first time in its history. Before last year, its low was 5 in March 2003, reflecting investor concerns at the outset of the Iraq war.

Investor optimism about the direction of the U.S. economy over the next 12 months improved significantly in March, as the Economic Dimension of the Index increased 30 points to -40. This is basically the same level of optimism about the economy that investors held in June 2008 (when this dimension was at -39) and a year ago (-38).

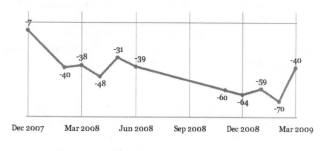

Economic Dimension, Gallup Index of Investor Optimism, December 2007-March 2009

Portfolio Optimism Also Improves

Investors' optimism expectations for their personal portfolios over the next 12 months also improved in March, as the Personal Dimension of the Index increased 11 points to 17—up from 6 in February and essentially the same as January's 19.

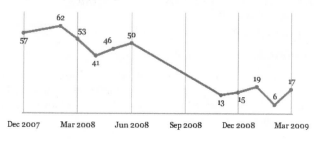

Personal Dimension, Gallup Index of Investor Optimism, December 2007-March 2009

Survey Methods

Gallup Poll Daily interviewing includes no fewer than 1,000 U.S. adults nationwide each day during 2008 and 2009. The Index of Investor Optimism results are based on questions asked of 1,000 or more investors over a three-day period each month, conducted March 16–18, Feb. 17–19, and Jan. 16–18, 2009; and Dec. 16–18, Nov. 24–26, June 3–6, April 25–28, March 28–31, and Feb. 28–March 2, 2008. For results based on these samples, the maximum margin of sampling error is ±3 percentage points.

Results for May of last year are based on the Gallup Panel study and are based on telephone interviews with 576 national adults, aged 18 and older, conducted May 19–21, 2008. Gallup Panel members are recruited through random selection methods. The panel is weighted so that it is demographically representative of the U.S. adult population. For results based on this sample, one can say with 95% confidence that the maximum margin of sampling error is ±5 percentage points.

For investor results prior to 2008, telephone interviews were conducted with at least 800 investors, aged 18 and older, and having at least $10,000 of investable assets. For the total sample of investors in these surveys, one can say with 95% confidence that the maximum margin of sampling error is ±4 percentage points.

Interviews are conducted with respondents on land-line telephones (for respondents with a land-line telephone) and cellular phones (for respondents who are cell-phone only).

In addition to sampling error, question wording and practical difficulties in conducting surveys can introduce error or bias into the findings of public opinion polls.

March 23, 2009
DESPITE RECESSION, NO UPTICK IN AMERICANS' RELIGIOSITY
Self-reported importance of religion and church attendance have remained steady

by Frank Newport, Gallup Poll Editor in Chief

Despite suggestions that the economic recession might cause religiosity among Americans to increase, there has been no evident change over the past 15 months in either Americans' self-reported church attendance or the importance of religion in their daily lives. Forty-two percent on average have reported attending church every week or nearly every week during that time, and 65% have reported that religion is important in their daily lives. These results are based on an analysis of more than 425,000 interviews Gallup has conducted since January 2008.

Is religion an important part of your daily life?
Weekly trend, January 2008-March 2009

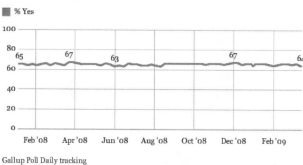

Gallup Poll Daily tracking

How often do you attend church, synagogue, or mosque — at least once a week, almost every week, about once a month, seldom, or never?
Weekly trend, February 2008-March 2009

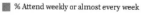

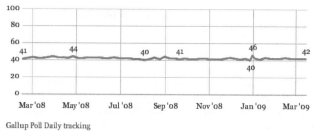

Gallup Poll Daily tracking

It is not an unreasonable conjecture that the current recession would cause Americans to increasingly turn to religion as a surcease from their economic or personal sorrow. But that does not appear to be the case. Even as the percentage of Americans who are negative about the economy has increased, particularly from September through December of last year, there have been no significant changes in the percentages of Americans who say religion is important in their daily lives, or who report attending church weekly or almost every week.

No Change Among Partisan Groups

Although there have been week-to-week fluctuations on these measures among Democrats, independents, and Republicans, there has also been no systematic change in religious adherence evident among any of these partisan groups over the last 15 months.

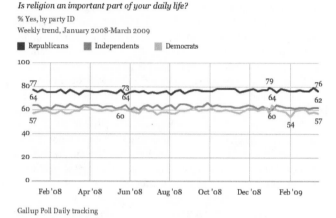

Is religion an important part of your daily life?
% Yes, by party ID
Weekly trend, January 2008-March 2009

Gallup Poll Daily tracking

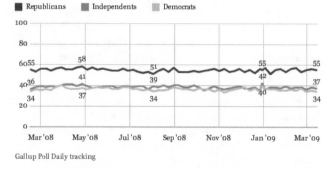

How often do you attend church, synagogue, or mosque -- at least once a week, almost every week, about once a month, seldom, or never?
% Attend weekly or almost every week, by party ID
Weekly trend, February 2008-March 2009

Gallup Poll Daily tracking

In general, as is seen in the accompanying charts, Republicans are the most religious of the three partisan groups, and have remained so over the past year. Independents are slightly more religious than Democrats, but the same relative patterns of religiosity among these groups have continued since January of last year.

Implications

The two questions reviewed in this analysis represent fairly general measures of religiosity. Still, it would be expected that if there were an overall turn toward religion in these deeply troubled times, it

would be reflected as an uptick in the average percentage of Americans saying religion is important and/or in self-reported church attendance. Neither has happened. These appear to be very steady indicators that have not been affected by the abrupt changes in the economic climate.

This is not to rule out the possibility that the recession has caused changes in the religiosity of Americans in ways that would not be captured in these measures. For example, Americans could be praying more often. Or those who are already religious (as measured by these questions) could be more intense in their religious commitment now. But at least as far as self-reports of church attendance and religious importance go, Gallup finds no evidence of a recession-driven turn to religion.

Survey Methods

Results are based on telephone interviews with 428,516 national adults, aged 18 and older, conducted January 2008 through March 15, 2009, as part of Gallup Poll Daily tracking. For results based on the total sample of national adults, one can say with 95% confidence that the maximum margin of sampling error is ±1 percentage point.

Interviews are conducted with respondents on land-line telephones (for respondents with a land-line telephone) and cellular phones (for respondents who are cell-phone only).

In addition to sampling error, question wording and practical difficulties in conducting surveys can introduce error or bias into the findings of public opinion polls.

March 24, 2009
AIG, CONGRESS, GEITHNER TARGET OF BONUS BACKLASH
No consensus on best way to recover bonus money

by Jeffrey M. Jones, Gallup Poll Managing Editor

For the most part, the central players in the AIG bonus controversy have come out looking badly—with one notable exception. A majority of Americans are dissatisfied with the way AIG management, Congress, and Treasury Secretary Geithner have handled the matter. Only President Obama gets a more positive than negative evaluation.

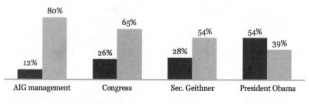

Satisfaction With Way Each of the Following Has Handled AIG Bonus Matter

March 21-22 USA Today/Gallup poll

This is based on a new *USA Today*/Gallup poll, conducted March 21–22, after a week when the AIG bonuses dominated the news headlines.

While the AIG executives' role in the controversy is obvious, a provision inserted into the $787 billion economic stimulus bill passed by Congress paved the way for the bonuses to be paid. Also, it was reported that both Geithner and Obama knew the bonuses were being paid before the story became public. Geithner will likely face questions about his role in the matter when he testifies before Congress Tuesday.

Still, Americans believe the AIG executives shoulder the greatest blame. Given a choice of four major players in the drama, 46% of Americans say AIG executives are most to blame for the payouts, far more than say this about Congress, Geithner, or Obama.

In your view, which of the following is most to blame for the fact that these bonuses were paid -- [ROTATED: President Barack Obama, Treasury Secretary Tim Geithner, Congress, AIG management]?

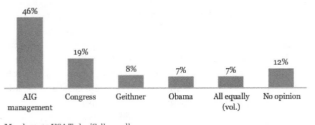

March 21-22 USA Today/Gallup poll
(vol.) = Volunteered response

Recovering the Money

An instant Gallup reaction poll to the AIG bonus controversy conducted early last week showed that a majority of Americans described themselves as "outraged" by the bonuses, and three in four said the government should recover the money.

While testifying before Congress last week, AIG CEO Edward Liddy indicated that he had asked the recipients of the larger bonus amounts to voluntarily return at least half the money. The U.S. House of Representatives responded by passing a bill to impose heavy taxes on any bonuses paid to higher-income employees by companies receiving significant amounts of federal bailout money, which would essentially chew up the total amount of the bonus.

Sixty-nine percent of Americans believe that "all" of the bonus money should be recovered, while 13% say "half" of it should be, and 12% believe none of it should be.

Although Americans are in wide agreement that the money should be returned, they show a decided lack of consensus on how that should be accomplished. Only 25% would seem to agree with the House approach of passing a new law to heavily tax the money. Roughly the same proportion (27%) would favor asking the employees to voluntarily return the money. Also, a similar percentage (26%) would prefer that the government try to recover it through legal proceedings based on existing laws or by making the return a condition for the company's receiving additional government bailout money. The remaining 23% of Americans do not have an opinion or do not believe the money should be recovered.

Notably, only 29% of self-identified Democrats favor a new law to tax the bonuses, along the lines of what the Democratically controlled House passed last week. Democrats are as likely to favor voluntary return of the bonuses (28%) or trying to recover the bonus through other government means (28%).

Republicans, too, show little consensus on the best way to recover the bonuses: 26% favor voluntary returns of the money, 24%

What Is the Best Way to Recover the AIG Bonus Money?

	Mar 21-22, 2009
Ask the AIG executives to voluntarily return the money	27%
Not pass a new law but try to recover the money through legal actions or as a condition of payment of additional bailout money	26%
Have Congress pass a new law imposing heavy taxes on bonuses paid to executives at companies that receive bailout money	25%
Money should not be recovered	12%
No opinion	11%

support heavy taxes on it, and 21% prefer that the government recover it by means other than new legislation.

Nineteen percent of Republicans say the bonus money should not be returned, compared with 11% of independents and only 7% of Democrats.

Implications

Outrage over the AIG bonuses is widespread among American citizens as well as U.S. government officials. Americans believe both AIG and the federal government—aside from President Obama—handled the matter poorly. And the public overwhelmingly believes the money should be recovered in part or in its entirety.

What is less clear is exactly how that money should be recovered. The House took a step by passing the tax measures last week, but it is unclear whether the Senate will take a similar approach or whether Obama would sign such legislation into law. And while there are other options besides the tax approach—including AIG executives' returning the money on their own, as some reportedly have done, or a lawsuit to recover the money—so far the public has not coalesced behind one approach or the other.

That could change in the coming days as the Senate and President Obama develop other approaches to recovering the money and try to round up the necessary support to move forward.

Survey Methods

Results are based on telephone interviews with 2,019 national adults, aged 18 and older, conducted March 21–22, 2009. All questions were asked of randomly selected half-samples of respondents. Sample sizes for the random half-samples vary between 1,003 and 1,012 national adults. For results based on these samples of national adults, one can say with 95% confidence that the maximum margin of sampling error is ±3 percentage points.

Interviews are conducted with respondents on land-line telephones (for respondents with a land-line telephone) and cellular phones (for respondents who are cell-phone only).

In addition to sampling error, question wording and practical difficulties in conducting surveys can introduce error or bias into the findings of public opinion polls.

March 25, 2009

IN U.S., JOB-MARKET PERCEPTIONS REMAIN BLEAK

Fewer than 1 in 10 say it is a good time to find a quality job

by Jeffrey M. Jones, Gallup Poll Managing Editor

Perceptions of the U.S. job market have not improved in March, with only 9% of Americans saying it is "a good time to find a quality job"—matching the record low set in February.

Thinking about the job situation in America today, would you say that it is now a good time or a bad time to find a quality job?

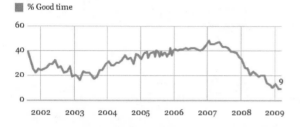

Gallup has asked the public to assess the job market each month since October 2001. Americans have never been overly positive in their assessments during this time, with a high of just 48% saying it was a good time to find a quality job in January 2007; however, perceptions have not previously descended as low as the February and March 2009 readings of 9%. Prior to the current economic crisis, the worst reading had been in March 2003—just before the Iraq war began—when 16% said it was a good time to find a quality job.

Ratings of the job market are almost universally bleak: no major segments of the population—based on demographic, regional, or political groupings—are substantially more positive than the national average about the job situation at this time.

Gallup's other key measure of the job market relies on employees' reports of what is occurring at their workplaces, as opposed to more general perceptions about the broader job market. As part of its daily polling, Gallup asks working Americans whether their employers are hiring people and expanding the size of their workforces, laying off people and reducing the size of their workforces, or not making any changes.

For much of 2008, even as the economy began to deteriorate, the value of the Gallup Net New Hiring Index was positive—that is, employees were more likely to report that their companies' workforces were expanding rather than contracting. But that changed at the end of 2008, and to this day, employees are more likely to say their companies are letting workers go rather than adding more. For the week of March 16–22, 26% of U.S. workers said their companies were reducing the number of workers they have while 22% said their workplaces were adding workers.

The net score of -4 for the past week is just shy of the 2008–2009 low of -6 achieved several times in recent weeks.

Implications

Just as both Gallup job-market measures were not tanking in the early months of 2008 even as the economy was in recession and consumer confidence was declining, so these measures are not yet responding to the recent uptick in consumer optimism about the direction of the U.S. economy.

It appears that it may take more than a slight bump up in consumer confidence in the overall economy (which remains on balance negative) for Americans to perceive an improving jobs situation.

Employee Self-Reports of Company Hiring/Layoffs

Based on weekly averages from Gallup Poll Daily tracking

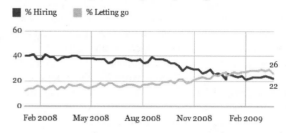

Survey Methods

Results are based on telephone interviews with 1,012 national adults, aged 18 and older, conducted March 5–8, 2009. For results based on the total sample of national adults, one can say with 95% confidence that the maximum margin of sampling error is ±3 percentage points.

Interviews are conducted with respondents on land-line telephones (for respondents with a land-line telephone) and cellular phones (for respondents who are cell-phone only).

In addition to sampling error, question wording and practical difficulties in conducting surveys can introduce error or bias into the findings of public opinion polls.

March 25, 2009

WATER POLLUTION AMERICANS' TOP GREEN CONCERN

Worry about environmental problems has edged up since 2004

by Lydia Saad, Gallup Poll Senior Editor

The folks behind World Water Day—a largely U.N.-sponsored effort to focus attention on freshwater resource management, observed this past Sunday—may be on to something. Pollution of drinking water is Americans' No. 1 environmental concern, with 59% saying they worry "a great deal" about the issue. That exceeds the 45% worried about air pollution, the 42% worried about the loss of tropical rain forests, and lower levels worried about extinction of species and global warming.

I'm going to read you a list of environmental problems. As I read each one, please tell me if you personally worry about this problem a great deal, a fair amount, only a little, or not at all. First, how much do you personally worry about ... ?

	Great deal	Fair amount	Only a little/Not at all
	%	%	%
Pollution of drinking water	59	25	16
Pollution of rivers, lakes, and reservoirs	52	31	17
Contamination of soil and water by toxic waste	52	28	19
Maintenance of the nation's supply of fresh water for household needs	49	31	19
Air pollution	45	31	24
The loss of tropical rain forests	42	26	32
Extinction of plant and animal species	37	28	34
The "greenhouse effect" or global warming/ Global warming	34	26	40

March 5-8, 2009

All eight issues tested in the 2009 Gallup Environment survey, conducted March 5–8, appear to be important to Americans, evidenced by the finding that a majority of Americans say they worry at least a fair amount about each one. However, on the basis of substantial concern—that is, the percentage worrying "a great deal" about each—there are important distinctions among them.

The four water-related issues on the poll fill the top four spots in this year's ranking. In addition to worrying about pollution of drinking water, roughly half of Americans also express a high degree of worry about pollution of rivers, lakes, and reservoirs (52% worry a great deal about this), and water and soil contamination from toxic waste (52%). About half worry about the maintenance of the nation's supply of fresh water for household needs (49%).

Air pollution places fifth among the environmental problems rated this year; 45% are worried a great deal about it. That issue is closely followed by the loss of tropical rain forests, with 42%—although significantly more Americans say they worry little or not at all about rain forests than say this about air pollution (32% vs. 24%).

Extinction of plant and animal species and global warming are of great concern to just over a third of Americans. However, since more Americans express little to no worry about global warming than say this about extinction, global warming is clearly the environmental issue of least concern to them. In fact, global warming is the only issue for which more Americans say they have little to no concern than say they have a great deal of concern.

Net Worried About Environmental Issues
Percentage worried a great deal minus percentage worried only a little or not at all
In percentage points

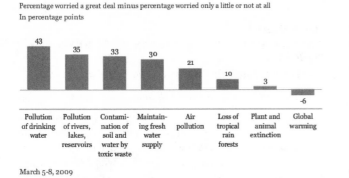

March 5-8, 2009

Trends

Gallup has maintained annual trends on public concern for these eight environmental issues since 2000. The long-term picture since 2000—based on substantial concern about the issues—is one of declining concern except for the maintenance of household water, which has increased slightly.

However, as exemplified by the trends in concern about pollution of rivers, lakes, and reservoirs, as well as concern about air pollution, the declines were most evident between 2000 and 2004, with the 2004 levels dipping to a record low for most issues.

Since 2004, public concern about the eight environmental matters rated this year has either been stable, or risen. The largest increase in concern is seen with global warming. Despite remaining at the bottom of the list of expressed concerns, the issue has nevertheless seen an eight-point increase in the last five years. There has been a similar seven-point increase in concern about the loss of tropical rain forests over that time.

*U.S. Public Concern About Pollution of Rivers, Lakes, and Reservoirs**
Percentage worried "a great deal"

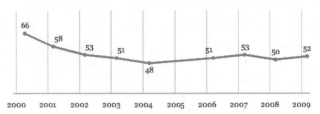

*U.S. Public Concern About Air Pollution**
Percentage worried "a great deal"

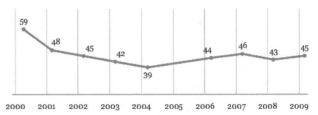

Percentage Worried "a Great Deal" About Each Environmental Issue
Selected years*

	April 2000	March 2004	March 2009
	%	%	%
Pollution of rivers, lakes, and reservoirs	66	48	52
Air pollution	59	39	45
The loss of tropical rain forests	51	35	42
The "greenhouse effect" or global warming	40	26	34
Contamination of soil and water by toxic waste	64	48	52
Pollution of drinking water	72	53	59
Extinction of plant and animal species	45	36	37
Supply of fresh water for household needs	42	47	49

Bottom Line

The era of water pollution as a hot political issue in the United States ended sometime after the Environmental Protection Agency received powerful regulatory tools with the 1972 Clean Water Act and the follow-up 1987 Water Quality Act. Still, given the essential nature of water to sustaining human and other life, it is not surprising to find that some form of water pollution has been the top-ranking environmental issue of concern to Americans in each Gallup reading since 1989. Mention water in the context of environmental problems, and more than half of Americans still say it's something that greatly concerns them.

Beyond water pollution, air pollution is the next-highest-ranking environmental issue. However, three issues register less public concern—notable because they nevertheless are widely discussed in the media and public affairs: loss of tropical rain forests, extinction of plant and animal species, and global warming.

Survey Methods

Results are based on telephone interviews with 1,012 national adults, aged 18 and older, conducted March 5–8, 2009. For results based on the total sample of national adults, one can say with 95%

confidence that the maximum margin of sampling error is ±3 percentage points.

Interviews are conducted with respondents on land-line telephones (for respondents with a land-line telephone) and cellular phones (for respondents who are cell-phone only).

For results based on the 512 national adults in the Form A half-sample and 500 national adults in the Form B half-sample, the maximum margins of sampling error are ±5 percentage points.

In addition to sampling error, question wording and practical difficulties in conducting surveys can introduce error or bias into the findings of public opinion polls.

March 26, 2009
AMERICANS MORE UPBEAT ABOUT U.S. DEFENSE READINESS
Shift mainly due to confidence surge among Democrats

by Lydia Saad, Gallup Poll Senior Editor

After four years of declining public confidence in the nation's military preparedness, Gallup's annual World Affairs survey documents a sharp reversal. Currently, 54% of Americans say the country's national defense is about right, up from 41% a year ago.

Do you, yourself, feel that our national defense is stronger now than it needs to be, not strong enough, or about right at the present time?

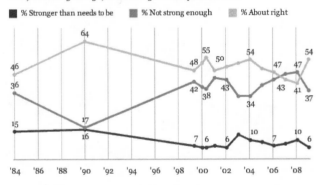

As a corollary to the recent increase in public contentment with the nation's defense, the percentage of Americans saying national defense is not strong enough has dropped from 47% to 37%.

An additional 6% of Americans now say the nation's defense is stronger than it needs to be. Thus, combined with the 54% saying national defense is about right, 6 in 10 Americans believe the nation's defense is at least adequate, if not too great.

The primary reason for the positive turnaround in public perceptions about national defense since last year is that Democratic confidence on the issue has surged. A year ago at this time, with former President George W. Bush still in office, only 37% of Democrats thought U.S. defenses were about right. Today, with President Barack Obama at the helm, that figure is 64%.

At the same time, there has been no change in the percentage of Republicans who say national defense is about right, and a smaller, 10-point increase among independents.

Evaluating Defense Spending

A separate question in the Feb. 9–12 poll asked Americans whether they believe the government is spending too much, about the right amount, or too little for national defense and military purposes.

While the majority of Americans still fall into the dove or hawk category when it comes to defense spending (saying spending is either too high or too low), more are satisfied with spending compared to a year ago: now 41%, up from 30%.

Percentage Saying National Defense Is "About Right"

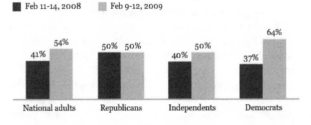

The poll was conducted prior to Obama's Feb. 24 address to Congress, in which he promised to crack down on waste in the defense budget and to end the war in Iraq.

In this case, Democrats are almost entirely responsible for the uptick in public support for the current level of government defense spending. The percentage of Democrats saying defense spending is about right grew from 16% in 2008 to 40% today, compared with a four-point increase among independents and a one-point decline among Republicans.

There is much discussion as to the amount of money the government in Washington should spend for national defense and military purposes. How do you feel about this? Do you think we are spending too little, about the right amount, or too much?

Despite Democrats' movement toward the center on this question, they remain much more likely than Republicans to believe the government is spending too much on defense: 43% vs. 11%. By contrast, while nearly half of Republicans think defense spending is about right, a substantial minority (39%) say it is too little.

Percentage Saying Defense Spending Is "About Right"

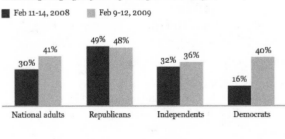

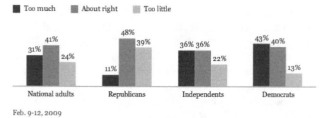

Government Spending on Defense

■ Too much ■ About right ■ Too little

National adults: 31%, 41%, 24%
Republicans: 11%, 48%, 39%
Independents: 36%, 36%, 22%
Democrats: 43%, 40%, 13%

Feb. 9-12, 2009

Bottom Line

Public confidence in the nation's defense is higher today than it was a year ago, largely because Democrats have become more positive on the question. Now, a majority of all three partisan groups say the U.S. national defense is either about right or too strong: 72% of Democrats, 58% of independents, and 52% of Republicans.

Americans are a mixed lot when it comes to the scope of defense spending. However, in contrast to a year ago, when the largest segment said the government was spending too much on defense (44%), today the plurality say the government is spending the right amount (41%). Again, Democrats are mainly responsible for the shift because of their increased support for the current level of defense spending.

Democrats' heightened satisfaction with the status quo on these issues may be a direct reflection of their confidence in Obama to curb defense spending and rebalance national defense policy in ways they agree with. Alternatively, it may simply reflect a "natural" tendency for members of a new president's party to feel more positively about the actions of government when someone of their own party is in the White House. However, Gallup polling on the same defense issues in 2000 and 2001 found no comparable changes in the views of Republicans, spanning the presidential transition from Democrat Bill Clinton to Republican George W. Bush.

Survey Methods

Results are based on telephone interviews with 1,022 national adults, aged 18 and older, conducted Feb. 9–12, 2009. For results based on the total sample of national adults, one can say with 95% confidence that the maximum margin of sampling error is ±3 percentage points.

Interviews are conducted with respondents on land-line telephones (for respondents with a land-line telephone) and cellular phones (for respondents who are cell-phone only).

In addition to sampling error, question wording and practical difficulties in conducting surveys can introduce error or bias into the findings of public opinion polls.

March 27, 2009
UNEMPLOYMENT FAR MORE WORRISOME FOR BLACKS THAN WHITES
Blacks nearly twice as likely to cite it as the nation's most important problem

by Jeffrey M. Jones, Gallup Poll Managing Editor

While the vast majority of both blacks and whites name at least one economic issue as the most important problem facing the country, they differ in the extent to which they specifically mention unem-

ployment, with jobs a much greater concern among blacks (29%) than among whites (16%).

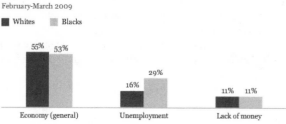

Mentions of Economic Issues as Most Important Problem Facing the Country, by Race

February-March 2009

■ Whites ■ Blacks

Economy (general): 55%, 53%
Unemployment: 16%, 29%
Lack of money: 11%, 11%

This is based on aggregated data from Gallup's "most important problem" question from February and March. Economic issues have dominated the responses to this question for much of the past year, and over the two months, an average of 83% of Americans named some economic concern as the United States' biggest problem.

The black-white differences on unemployment concerns are consistent with government reports that historically have found a much higher unemployment rate among blacks than among whites.

In addition to blacks, Americans with less formal education also show a heightened concern about the job market. Over the last two months, an average of 26% of Americans with a high school education or less have named unemployment as the nation's most important problem, compared with 17% of those who have attended college but not completed it and only 10% of college graduates.

By comparison, those with more formal education tend to focus their concerns on the broader economy.

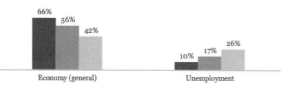

Mentions of Economic Issues as Most Important Problem Facing the Country, by Education

February-March 2009

■ College graduate ■ Some college ■ High school or less

Economy (general): 66%, 56%, 42%
Unemployment: 10%, 17%, 26%

Democrats (20%) and independents (20%) differ somewhat from Republicans (14%) in the extent to which they name unemployment as the most important problem.

There are modest party differences on other issues—mostly between Republicans and Democrats—such as healthcare (11% Democratic, 5% Republican), the federal budget deficit (7% Republican, 2% Democratic), and moral and ethical decline (7% Republican, 1% Democratic).

March Update

In the March monthly update, from a March 5–8 Gallup Poll, 80% of all Americans name at least one economic issue as the nation's top problem, with the most common being the economy in general (51%), unemployment (16%), and a lack of money (11%). In addition, 12% name healthcare, 6% the war in Iraq, and 6% dissatisfaction with government.

What do you think is the most important problem facing this country today? [OPEN-ENDED]

March 5-8, 2009

	% Mentioning
Economy (general)	51
Unemployment	16
Healthcare	12
Lack of money	11
Iraq war	6
Dissatisfaction with government	6
Federal budget deficit	5
Ethical/Moral decline	4
Inflation	3
Education	3

The percentage naming the Iraq war is the lowest since August 2003, when 5% did so. It was the most commonly mentioned issue each month from April 2004 through January 2008.

The 12% who mention healthcare is up from 6% the prior month, aided by President Obama's healthcare initiative, announced as the poll was being conducted.

Survey Methods

Results are based on telephone interviews with 1,012 national adults, aged 18 and older, conducted March 5–8, 2009. For results based on the total sample of national adults, one can say with 95% confidence that the maximum margin of sampling error is ±3 percentage points.

Results for the subgroups are based on aggregated data from the Feb. 9–12 and March 5–8 polls, consisting of interviews with 2,034 total national adults.

Interviews are conducted with respondents on land-line telephones (for respondents with a land-line telephone) and cellular phones (for respondents who are cell-phone only).

In addition to sampling error, question wording and practical difficulties in conducting surveys can introduce error or bias into the findings of public opinion polls.

March 27, 2009
ONE IN FOUR AMERICANS WORRY ABOUT MONTHLY PAYMENTS
Half of Americans plan to decrease their debt; nearly as many say it is a bad time to borrow

by Dennis Jacobe, Gallup Chief Economist

The percentage of Americans saying they are worried about keeping up with their monthly payments over the next six months reached 23% this month—up from 19% a year ago and 15% in March 2007.

Americans Reducing Their Debt

Even as Gallup's Consumer Mood Index shows Americans to be less pessimistic about the U.S. economy than they have been at any time since the financial crisis took hold in mid-September 2008, a new Gallup Personal Credit Index poll shows that 23% of consumers are either very (6%) or somewhat (17%) worried that they will not be able to continue making their monthly payments over the next six months.

The increase since last March in consumer worry about meeting monthly expenses (from 19% to 23%) contrasts with a slight

Looking to six months from now, how confident or worried do you expect to feel about keeping up with your monthly payments these days? Do you expect you will be very confident, somewhat confident, neither confident nor worried, somewhat worried, or very worried?

% Very worried + somewhat worried

March trend, 2005-2009

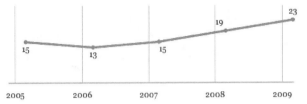

improvement in Gallup's Consumer Mood Index over the same period (from -91 to -83). This would seem to signify that the year-long economic struggle has taken a toll on consumers' sense of financial security that won't be immediately rectified by an upturn in confidence about the economy.

Further reflecting consumers' continuing financial fears, 34% of Americans say they have reduced their total amount of debt over the past six months. Even more importantly for the future course of the economy, 50% say they intend to reduce their total debt over the next six months.

Americans' Views Regarding Their Total Debt Over the Past Six Months

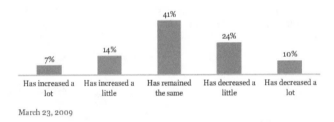

March 23, 2009

Americans' Intentions Regarding Their Total Debt Over the Next Six Months

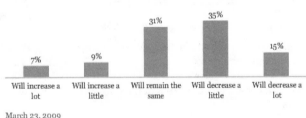

March 23, 2009

Many Americans Say Now a Bad Time to Borrow

Forty-six percent of Americans say now is a bad time to borrow, up slightly from 42% a year ago and almost twice as high as the 27% of March 2005. At the same time, the percentage of consumers saying it is a good time to borrow has fallen from 26% in March 2005 to 19% in March 2009.

Survey Methods

Gallup Poll Daily interviewing includes no fewer than 1,000 U.S. adults nationwide each day during 2008 and 2009. Gallup Personal Credit Index results are based on questions asked of 1,000 or more

Given interest rates and your overall amount of debt, do you think NOW is a good time or a bad time to borrow more money, or is it neither a good nor a bad time?

March trend, 2005-2009

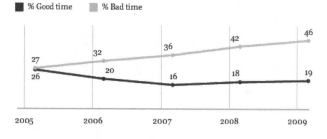

■ % Good time   ■ % Bad time

adults, aged 18 and older, conducted March 27, 2008, and March 23, 2009. For results based on these samples, the maximum margin of sampling error is ±3 percentage points.

For results prior to 2008, telephone interviews were conducted with 1,000 or more adults, aged 18 and older. For the total sample in each of these surveys, one can say with 95% confidence that the maximum margin of sampling error is ±3 percentage points.

Interviews are conducted with respondents on land-line telephones (for respondents with a land-line telephone) and cellular phones (for respondents who are cell-phone only).

In addition to sampling error, question wording and practical difficulties in conducting surveys can introduce error or bias into the findings of public opinion polls.

Polls conducted entirely in one day, such as this one, are subject to additional error or bias not found in polls conducted over several days.

March 30, 2009

CATHOLICS SIMILAR TO MAINSTREAM ON ABORTION, STEM CELLS

Catholics actually more liberal on some issues

by Frank Newport, Gallup Poll Editor in Chief

Despite the Roman Catholic Church's official opposition to abortion and embryonic stem-cell research, a Gallup analysis finds almost no difference between rank-and-file American Catholics and American non-Catholics in terms of finding the two issues morally acceptable.

Moral Acceptability of Abortion and Embryonic Stem-Cell Research, Among Catholics and Non-Catholics

% Morally acceptable

■ Catholics   ■ Non-Catholics

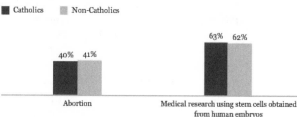

2006-2008 Gallup Values and Beliefs polls

The stance of the Catholic church on moral issues has come into the spotlight in recent days with the announcement that President Barack Obama will be giving the commencement address and receiving an honorary degree at the University of Notre Dame in May. Notre Dame is one of the largest Catholic universities in the United States, and some Catholic officials, students, alumni, and others have objected publicly to Obama's appearance, pointing to the fact that Obama's positions on embryonic stem-cell research and abortion are at odds with the church's. Some of those objecting have argued further, for example, that there is "great concern among Catholics nationwide about President Obama's future impact on American society, the family, and the Catholic church."

The argument of those who protest the extension of the invitation to Obama is that Catholics have a distinctly conservative position on these moral issues. That is certainly the case as far as official church doctrine is concerned, but not when it comes to average American Catholics. The new Gallup analysis, based on aggregated data from Gallup's 2006–2008 Values and Beliefs surveys, indicates that Catholics in the United States today are actually more liberal than the non-Catholic population on a number of moral issues, and on others, Catholics have generally the same attitudes.

The accompanying chart shows the percentage of Catholics and non-Catholics who find each of nine moral issues morally acceptable. Catholics are at least slightly more liberal than non-Catholics on the issues of gambling (an issue to which the Catholic church is not totally opposed), sex between an unmarried man and woman, homosexual relations, and having a baby out of wedlock. Catholics are essentially tied with non-Catholics on the moral acceptability of abortion, divorce, and stem-cell research using human embryos. Only on the death penalty are Catholics slightly less likely than non-Catholics to find the issue morally acceptable.

Moral Acceptability of Issues, Among Catholics and Non-Catholics

% Morally acceptable

	Catholics	Non-Catholics
	%	%
Abortion	40	41
The death penalty	61	68
Sex between an unmarried man and woman	67	57
Divorce	71	66
Medical research using stem cells obtained from human embryos	63	62
Having a baby outside of marriage	61	52
Gambling	72	59
Homosexual relations	54	45

2006-2008 Gallup Values and Beliefs polls

Committed Catholics

In general, Americans who are the most religious also tend to be the most conservative on moral issues. Catholics are no exception. Regular churchgoing Catholics (defined as those who attend church weekly or almost every week) are significantly *less* likely to find most issues measured in this research morally acceptable than are Catholics who do not attend church regularly. These committed Catholics' views on all these issues are much more in line with the church's teachings than are the views of non-practicing Catholics. However, even among committed Catholics, a slim majority seem to be at odds with the church's positions on premarital sex, embryonic stem-cell research, divorce, and the death penalty.

Moral Acceptability of Issues, by Church Affiliation and Attendance
% Morally acceptable

	Catholics	Catholics	Non-Catholics	Non-Catholics
	Regular church attendance	Nonregular church attendance	Regular church attendance	Nonregular church attendance
	%	%	%	%
Abortion	24	52	19	56
The death penalty	52	67	66	69
Sex between an unmarried man and woman	53	77	30	75
Divorce	63	77	46	79
Medical research using stem cells obtained from human embryos	53	70	45	73
Having a baby outside of marriage	48	70	29	67
Gambling	67	75	40	72
Homosexual relations	44	61	21	61

2006-2008 Gallup Values and Beliefs polls

The data show that regular churchgoing non-Catholics also have very conservative positions on moral issues. In fact, on most of the issues tested, regular churchgoers who are not Catholic are *more* conservative (i.e., less likely to find a given practice morally acceptable) than Catholic churchgoers.

The accompanying table shows that regular churchgoers who are Catholic are significantly more liberal than churchgoing non-Catholics on gambling, sex before marriage, homosexual relations, having a baby out of wedlock, and divorce. Committed Catholics are at least slightly more likely than devout non-Catholics to say that abortion and embryonic stem-cell research—the two key issues highlighted by those protesting Obama's appearance at Notre Dame—are morally acceptable. Only on the death penalty are committed Catholics more conservative than regular churchgoers who are not Catholic.

Religious non-Catholics are certainly not adopting these positions because of official Catholic doctrine. It appears that the underlying dimension of religiosity—as measured in this analysis by church attendance—is most predictive of conservative positions on moral issues, not whether an individual is Catholic.

Implications

It is no doubt heartening to the Catholic hierarchy that devout Catholics, defined as those who attend church very frequently, are more likely than non-devout Catholics to adhere to the church's position on moral issues. But the data make it less clear whether practicing Catholics have adopted their positions as a result of adherence to church doctrine, or as a more natural function of their basic religiousness.

More generally, the data do not suggest that there is a uniquely conservative component to attitudes on moral issues based on the simple fact of being Catholic.

These data on the attitudes of rank-and-file Catholics in and of themselves do not speak directly to the issue of Notre Dame's invitation to President Obama. It is possible that Catholics who themselves do not adhere to Catholic church positions on moral issues could still object to Obama's being honored by Notre Dame. And Catholic leaders' objections to the Obama situation could themselves be at least partly a reflection of the leaders' awareness of and concern over the fact that in today's contemporary American culture, there is little differentiation between Catholics and non-Catholics in

terms of adherence to conservative Catholic church positions on moral issues.

Survey Methods

Results are based on telephone interviews with an aggregated sample of 3,022 national adults, aged 18 and older, interviewed in polls conducted in May 2006, May 2007, and May 2008. For results based on the total sample of national adults, one can say with 95% confidence that the maximum margin of sampling error is ±2 percentage points.

Interviews are conducted with respondents on land-line telephones (for respondents with a land-line telephone) and cellular phones (for respondents who are cell-phone only).

In addition to sampling error, question wording and practical difficulties in conducting surveys can introduce error or bias into the findings of public opinion polls.

March 30, 2009
AMERICANS DIVIDED ON TREASURY SECRETARY GEITHNER
Democrats approve; Republicans disapprove

by Frank Newport , Gallup Poll Editor in Chief

Americans are split essentially down the middle when asked to assess the job Tim Geithner is doing as Treasury secretary: 42% say they approve, 40% disapprove, and 18% have no opinion.

Do you approve or disapprove of the way Treasury Secretary Tim Geithner is handling his job?

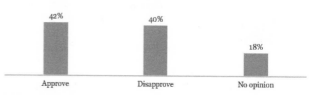

Gallup Poll, March 27-29, 2009

Geithner has become one of the most visible Treasury secretaries in decades. This reflects the extreme importance of government economic policy in the current recession, the expanded power given to the secretary of the Treasury in last year's economic bailout legislation, and the fact that Geithner has been one of the primary public faces on the Obama administration's extraordinary and massive intervention in the nation's economic and business life.

Some critics have assailed the way in which Geithner has handled his responsibilities, especially relative to the AIG bonus controversy, and there have been calls for his resignation. Republican Rep. Connie Mack, one of those calling for his resignation, was quoted as saying "[Geithner] has lost the confidence of the American people." Nevertheless, Obama has continued to stand publicly behind his Treasury secretary.

The new data are from a Gallup Poll conducted March 27–29. If the American public has "lost confidence" in Geithner, it might be expected that a majority would now disapprove of the job he is doing as Treasury secretary. That is not the case. At the same time, a majority does not approve of the job he is doing, either. The public remains divided, with no tilt in sentiments in either direction.

It is not a good sign for Geithner, perhaps, that he receives significantly lower approval ratings than does his boss. In the same poll in which Geithner receives 42% approval, Obama receives a 64% approval rating (and a 30% disapproval rating). This is not the first time this differential between Obama and his Treasury secretary has surfaced. A Gallup Poll conducted last week showed that Americans are much more satisfied with the way Obama has handled the crisis concerning bonuses paid to AIG executives than they are with Geithner's role in that situation.

For whatever reason, Obama's approval rating has been quite stable throughout his brief presidency, suggesting that events or the news have had little impact on the public's views of him. Geithner to this point does not appear to get the same benefit of the doubt.

Predictably, there are large partisan differences in Geithner's job approval rating.

Do you approve or disapprove of the way Treasury Secretary Tim Geithner is handling his job?

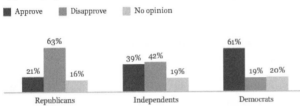

Gallup Poll, March 27-29, 2009

Republicans' and Democrats' views on the Treasury secretary are virtual mirror images of each other. Sixty-three percent of the former disapprove, while 61% of the latter approve. Independents are about evenly split.

Survey Methods

Results are based on telephone interviews with 1,007 national adults, aged 18 and older, conducted March 27–29, 2009. For results based on the total sample of national adults, one can say with 95% confidence that the maximum margin of sampling error is ±3 percentage points.

Interviews are conducted with respondents on land-line telephones (for respondents with a land-line telephone) and cellular phones (for respondents who are cell-phone only).

In addition to sampling error, question wording and practical difficulties in conducting surveys can introduce error or bias into the findings of public opinion polls.

AMERICANS CONTINUE TO OPPOSE GM, CHRYSLER LOANS
Fifty-nine percent disapprove of the loans the government has made

by Jeffrey M. Jones, Gallup Poll Managing Editor

A new *USA Today*/Gallup poll finds that a majority of Americans disapprove of the loans made to General Motors and Chrysler late last year to help them avoid bankruptcy.

Do you approve or disapprove of the federal loans given to General Motors and Chrysler last year to help them avoid bankruptcy?

USA Today/Gallup, March 27-29, 2009

On Monday, the government rejected the automakers' own restructuring plans and imposed new deadlines and conditions for each to receive further government loans. That includes Chrysler's working out a partnership with Italian automaker Fiat, and General Motors' replacing its CEO and getting concessions from its unions and bondholders as part of more aggressive restructuring plans.

The new poll results, from a March 27–29 poll, are in line with what Gallup has found in earlier polling about government aid to two of the Big Three U.S. automakers.

In February, when asked about government aid to U.S. automakers in a general sense, just 41% of Americans favored the concept while 58% were opposed.

Gallup found even less public support when it asked about the specific GM and Chrysler requests for additional federal loans after they had submitted their restructuring plans to the government last month. At the time, only 25% of Americans believed Congress should approve these additional loans to GM and Chrysler, while 72% thought it should not do so.

In November 2008, when the automakers' plight was first gaining widespread national attention, Americans were somewhat more likely to favor government aid, but were still slightly more likely to oppose (49%) than to favor (47%) it.

Democrats One of Few Groups That Supports Loans

The new poll finds most key demographic or attitudinal subgroups within the U.S. population disapproving of the government loans made to GM and Chrysler last December to help them avoid bankruptcy. Democrats are a notable exception, as 57% approve, more than twice the level of Republicans, whose support is among the lowest. Independents' views are closer to those of Republicans.

Even though the Midwest is the traditional home to the U.S. auto industry, residents of that area of the country are no more likely to approve of the GM and Chrysler loans than are those living in other parts of the United States. Only 40% of Midwesterners approve, compared with 42% of those living in the East, 38% of Southern residents, and 39% of those residing in the West.

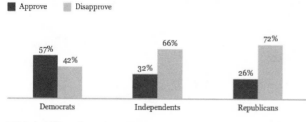

Approve/Disapprove of Federal Loans to GM and Chrysler, by Political Party

■ Approve ▦ Disapprove

USA Today/Gallup poll, March 27-29, 2009

Implications

It is pretty well-established at this point that Americans oppose the idea of government assistance to the U.S. automakers. Over the next two months, Chrysler's and General Motors' fates will become clearer as they work to meet the government's guidelines for restructuring to receive further assistance. Without that assistance, there is a high probability that one or both will enter bankruptcy. Either outcome—bankruptcy or successful restructuring—does have the potential to shift Americans' views on federal aid for U.S. auto manufacturers.

Survey Methods

Results are based on telephone interviews with 1,007 national adults, aged 18 and older, conducted March 27–29, 2009. For results based on the total sample of national adults, one can say with 95% confidence that the maximum margin of sampling error is ±3 percentage points.

Interviews are conducted with respondents on land-line telephones (for respondents with a land-line telephone) and cellular phones (for respondents who are cell-phone only).

In addition to sampling error, question wording and practical difficulties in conducting surveys can introduce error or bias into the findings of public opinion polls.

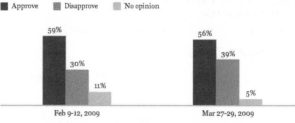

Do you approve or disapprove of the way Barack Obama is handling the economy?

■ Approve ■ Disapprove ■ No opinion

59% 30% 11% Feb 9-12, 2009

56% 39% 5% Mar 27-29, 2009

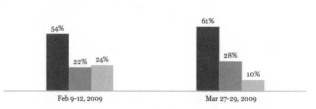

Do you approve or disapprove of the way Barack Obama is handling foreign affairs?

■ Approve ■ Disapprove ■ No opinion

54% 22% 24% Feb 9-12, 2009

61% 28% 10% Mar 27-29, 2009

April 01, 2009
OBAMA WORKING WITH 61% APPROVAL ON FOREIGN AFFAIRS
President does less well on the economy and the deficit

by Frank Newport, Gallup Poll Editor in Chief

President Barack Obama—currently on his first multi-stop trip abroad since he took office—is enjoying a 61% job approval rating at home for handling foreign affairs, up seven points since February. His job approval rating for handling the economy—56%—is down by the slight margin of three points, but is higher than his rating for handling the federal budget deficit.

Do you approve of the way Barack Obama is handling ... ?

■ 2009 Feb 9-12 ■ 2009 Mar 27-29

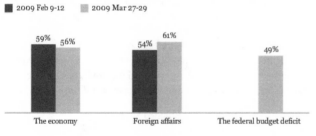

59% 56% The economy
54% 61% Foreign affairs
49% The federal budget deficit

Obama's major focus in his first months in office has been the economy. Still, he has found time to make significant announcements regarding troop levels in Iraq and Afghanistan, and his administration has been dealing with tense situations involving China's interception of U.S. naval vessels in the Pacific and a pending rocket launch by North Korea. Obama's secretary of state, Hillary Clinton, has made several diplomatic trips overseas, and Obama himself has now embarked on a high-profile trip to Great Britain, France, Germany, the Czech Republic, and Turkey.

Throughout all this, as more Americans have formed an opinion of Obama's handling of foreign policy, his approval and disapproval ratings on this dimension have each increased. Contrasted with a Feb. 9–12 Gallup Poll, the current March 27–29 *USA Today*/Gallup poll shows that Obama's approval on foreign affairs has gone from 54% to 61%, while his disapproval has risen from 22% to 28%.

The shift in Obama's job approval rating on handling the economy has been more negative than positive. His economic approval rating has slipped slightly, from 59% in February to 56% today, while his disapproval rating has jumped from 30% to 39% over that time.

The current poll also includes the first measurement of Obama's handling of the federal budget deficit, an issue on which Obama has received some criticism given that his multi-trillion-dollar budget proposal relies to a significant degree on borrowing to pay for it.

Therefore, this is perhaps predictably the most negative of the three dimensions tested in the poll—although, by a slight margin, Americans are still more positive than negative about Obama's handling of the issue (49% approve and 44% disapprove).

Democrats give Obama high marks on all three measures. Independents are significantly more positive than negative on the economy and foreign affairs, but essentially break even on their rating of how Obama is handling the deficit. Finally, Republicans are quite negative on his handling of the economy and the deficit, but somewhat less so when it comes to foreign affairs.

Do you approve of the way Barack Obama is handling ... ?
By political party

■ The economy ■ Foreign affairs ■ The federal budget deficit

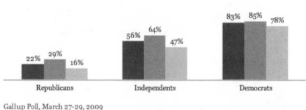

22% 29% 16% Republicans
56% 64% 47% Independents
83% 85% 78% Democrats

Gallup Poll, March 27-29, 2009

Survey Methods

Results are based on telephone interviews with 1,007 national adults, aged 18 and older, conducted March 27–29, 2009. For results based on the total sample of national adults, one can say with 95% confidence that the maximum margin of sampling error is ±3 percentage points.

Interviews are conducted with respondents on land-line telephones (for respondents with a land-line telephone) and cellular phones (for respondents who are cell-phone only).

In addition to sampling error, question wording and practical difficulties in conducting surveys can introduce error or bias into the findings of public opinion polls.

April 01, 2009

CIGARETTE TAX WILL AFFECT LOW-INCOME AMERICANS MOST

More than half of smokers earn less than $36,000 per year

by Lydia Saad, Gallup Poll Senior Editor

The 62-cent increase in federal cigarette taxes going into effect Wednesday is nearly three times as likely to affect low-income Americans as it is to affect high-income Americans. That's because 34% of the lowest-income Americans smoke, compared with only 13% of those earning $90,000 or more per year.

Percentage Who Smoke, by Annual Household Income

Gallup-Healthways Well-Being Index
Jan. 2-Dec. 29, 2008

The rate of adult smoking in the United States is, in fact, directly related to household income, dropping in linear fashion as income rises. Overall, 21% of American adults smoke.

These findings are based on more than 350,000 interviews with U.S. adults aged 18 and older in 2008, conducted as part of the Gallup-Healthways Well-Being Index.

A different way to look at this smoking-by-income data is that slightly more than half of today's smokers (53%) earn less than $36,000 per year—making cigarette taxes highly regressive. Another 35% of smokers earn between $36,000 and $89,999 per year, while only 12% of all smokers make at least $90,000 annually.

The Income Profile of Smokers

Percentage of adult U.S. smokers falling into each yearly income category

Gallup-Healthways Well-Being Index
Jan. 2-Dec. 29, 2008

Will the Financial Burden Lead to Cessation?

While the explicit purpose of the latest federal cigarette tax increase is to fund reauthorization and expansion of the federal Children's Health Insurance Program, anti-smoking advocates hope it will encourage many smokers to give up cigarettes. In addition to the public health benefits, this would ultimately save smokers money by sparing them the entire expense of cigarettes—currently averaging about $5 per pack, though this varies widely across the country.

As Dr. Timothy Gardner, president of the American Heart Association, was recently quoted as saying, "Every time that the tax on tobacco goes up, the use of cigarettes goes down."

How much will the new 62-cent federal surtax on cigarettes add to the financial pressure that lower-income smokers already feel? It's unclear; however, more than 6 in 10 smokers at the lowest income level tell Gallup they worried about money "yesterday." The rate of financial worry remains fairly high through those making $59,999 per year, but then falls to just over a third among those making $60,000 or more.

In other words, low-income smokers are already highly anxious about money; it's conceivable that the additional cost for a pack of cigarettes could push them into quitting.

Percentage of Smokers Who Worried About Money "Yesterday," by Annual Household Income

Gallup-Healthways Well-Being Index
Jan. 2-Dec. 29, 2008

Still, for most smokers, the annual cost of this tax increase isn't enormous. According to Gallup's 2008 Consumption Survey, most smokers (61%) smoke less than a pack of cigarettes per day. Another 30% smoke about one pack, while only 6% admit to smoking more than a pack a day.

On this basis, for 9 in 10 smokers, the total added expense of the new cigarette tax will be no more than 62 cents per day, or about $225 per year. Heavy smokers will find the tax increase more onerous, but they may also be the most resistant to quitting at any price.

Bottom Line

From the Gallup-Healthways smoking data reviewed here, it's clear the new 62-cent federal tax increase on a pack of cigarettes will have a disproportionately heavy financial impact on lower-income Americans. However, lower-income Americans are also highly worried about money right now, suggesting some might quit smoking over the rising cost. That would result in both financial and health benefits for those who quit.

Although President Obama signed the new cigarette tax increase into law in February, many Americans are probably becoming aware of it only this week, just as the tax goes into effect. Even if the new tax does come as a surprise, the general public may not be highly upset by it. Most Americans don't smoke, and the last time Gallup asked Americans explicitly about cigarette taxes, in 2005, only a third thought they were too high. Another third said they were about right, while 25% said they were too low. At the same time, about half said cigarette taxes should be raised to help discourage smoking.

Survey Methods

Results are based on telephone interviews with 354,800 national adults, aged 18 and older, conducted between Jan. 2, 2008 and Dec. 29, 2008, as part of the Gallup-Healthways Well-Being Index. For results based on the total sample of national adults, one can say with 95% confidence that the maximum margin of sampling error is less than ±1 percentage point.

Interviews are conducted with respondents on land-line telephones (for respondents with a land-line telephone) and cellular phones (for respondents who are cell-phone only).

In addition to sampling error, question wording and practical difficulties in conducting surveys can introduce error or bias into the findings of public opinion polls.

April 02, 2009
MICHELLE OBAMA'S FAVORABLE RATING ECLIPSES HER HUSBAND'S
Both president and first lady are quite popular

by Jeffrey M. Jones, Gallup Poll Managing Editor

Americans have very positive impressions of both President Barack Obama and first lady Michelle Obama. But in the latest Gallup Poll, Mrs. Obama receives a slightly better favorable rating, 72% to 69%.

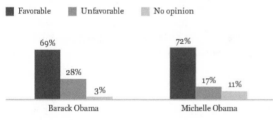

Favorable Ratings of Barack and Michelle Obama

■ Favorable   ■ Unfavorable   ■ No opinion

Gallup Poll, March 27-29, 2009

While the three percentage-point difference between the two favorable ratings is not statistically significant, Michelle Obama's much lower unfavorable ratings compared with the president's (17% vs. 28%) give her the clear edge in public favorability.

These results are based on a March 27–29 Gallup Poll. Compared to the last time Gallup asked Americans for their basic views of the Obamas—in January, just before Inauguration Day—Mrs. Obama's rating has improved, while her husband's has gone down. But the president's 78% favorable rating in January—perhaps inflated by the excitement about his pending inauguration—ranks among the highest Gallup has recorded since it began measuring popularity using this format in 1992. So even as his rating has settled down to 69%, he remains very popular.

Favorable Ratings of Barack and Michelle Obama

■ % Favorable, Barack Obama   ■ % Favorable, Michelle Obama

It is not uncommon for first ladies to be more popular than their husbands, in terms of either their favorable ratings or their job approval ratings. To illustrate, Laura Bush averaged a 71% favorable rating from 2001–2009, compared to George W. Bush's 56% average. The greater popularity of first ladies likely reflects that their role is far less controversial than that of the president, which often results in less partisan ratings of the first lady.

That pattern is evident in the current data. While Democrats and independents rate the president and first lady similarly, Republicans have a more positive view of Michelle Obama than of Barack Obama. Of course, Republicans are not as positive toward either of the Obamas as are Democrats or independents.

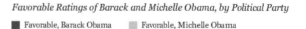

Favorable Ratings of Barack and Michelle Obama, by Political Party

■ Favorable, Barack Obama   ■ Favorable, Michelle Obama

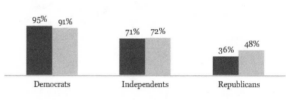

Gallup Poll, March 27-29, 2009

Presidential Favorability vs. Job Approval

The president's 69% favorable rating also exceeds his job approval rating, which has mostly been in the low 60% range since he took office. Again, that is also typical—presidents usually receive higher favorable ratings (which assess their likability) than job approval ratings (which ask for a job-performance evaluation). There is a notable exception to this general pattern, however. After the Monica Lewinsky scandal broke, Americans had much more positive feelings about the job Bill Clinton was doing as president than about him as a person. Prior to the scandal, the opposite was true.

Survey Methods

Results are based on telephone interviews with 1,007 national adults, aged 18 and older, conducted March 27–29, 2009. For results based on the total sample of national adults, one can say with 95% confidence that the maximum margin of sampling error is ±3 percentage points.

Interviews are conducted with respondents on land-line telephones (for respondents with a land-line telephone) and cellular phones (for respondents who are cell-phone only).

In addition to sampling error, question wording and practical difficulties in conducting surveys can introduce error or bias into the findings of public opinion polls.

April 02, 2009

U.S. UNEMPLOYMENT LIKELY HEADING HIGHER

Gallup's model suggests March unemployment rate may hit or exceed 8.3%

by Dennis Jacobe, Gallup Chief Economist

Gallup's projection, based on its Net New Hiring Index, suggests the March 2009 unemployment rate is likely to reach at least 8.3%—and could go as high as 8.7%—when the Labor Department reports it on Friday. This would further augment the remarkable two percentage-point increase seen between September 2008 and February 2009, including nearly a full point between December and February.

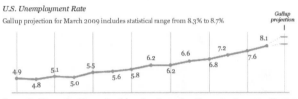

U.S. Unemployment Rate

Gallup projection for March 2009 includes statistical range from 8.3% to 8.7%

Source: U.S. Department of Labor

Unemployment Continues to Worsen

Gallup's unemployment-rate model—based on its four-week average Net New Hiring measure (the percentage of employees saying their companies are hiring minus the percentage saying their companies are letting people go)—was -5 in March, which is essentially unchanged from the -6 of February and the -4 of January. All three are substantially worse than the +25 score of March 2008.

The unemployment rate has been increasing recently, while Gallup's Net New Hiring measure has been negative but also stable. Statistical models based on the relationship between these two indicators show that no change in the Net New Hiring measure predicts continued increases in the unemployment rate. This is also consistent with the government's report on Thursday that seasonally adjusted four-week average jobless claims hit a 26-year high of 656,750 in the week ending March 28 and continuing claims hit 5.73 million.

The monthly trend in Gallup's Net New Hiring measure is inversely related to the U.S. unemployment rate and, based on its 15-month history, the measure provides Gallup with a better than 8-in-10 chance of accurately estimating the unemployment rate's future direction.

Each month, Gallup conducts more than 8,000 interviews with U.S. employees, to ascertain their perceptions of the job situation at their companies. Of course, many factors make such unemployment-rate projections difficult, with probably the most important of these being the potential for job seekers to get discouraged and stop looking for work (and thus not be included in the government's official unemployment rate). As the job situation worsens, the size of the labor force often shrinks, reducing the percentage reported as unemployed.

Job Market: Leading or Lagging Indicator?

The unemployment rate has traditionally been regarded as a lagging economic indicator. Essentially, it simply measures the fallout of the U.S. economy's overall direction, whether positive or negative. As a result, the continuing plunge in the jobs market is both expected and discounted as a predictor of future economic activity.

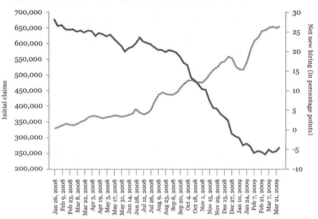

Relationship Between Seasonally Adjusted 4-Week Initial Unemployment Claims and 4-Week Gallup Net New Hiring Measure

■ Initial unemployment claims ■ Net new hiring (% hiring minus % firing)

However, this recession is not like the others of the post-World War II period. Right now, in this consumer-driven downturn, one of the major factors keeping consumers from borrowing and spending is the fear of job losses. The auto company promotions promising continuation of monthly payments for consumers who buy a new car and then lose their jobs are emblematic of this fear on the part of the potential car-buying consumer.

As a result, the worsening jobs situation is likely to reinforce consumer tendencies to pull back on spending. It could also lead lenders to raise their lending standards even more as they try to avoid increased consumer credit losses. Further, businesses currently in survival mode might see the persistent deterioration of the jobs market as a sign that consumer spending will continue to worsen. In turn, they may continue to reduce inventories, cut capital spending, and let even more people go, continuing a vicious downward spiral. In this sense, the jobs market may now serve as a leading indicator of when consumers' fear of losing their jobs will begin to moderate. And, signs of such a moderation could be a huge plus for the U.S. economy.

Whether the unemployment situation is a leading, lagging, or coincident economic indicator, Gallup's Net New Hiring Index will continue to provide daily and weekly monitoring of the important and changing conditions in today's jobs market.

Survey Methods

Gallup's hiring measure is based on aggregated interviews with a nationally representative sample of more than 8,000 U.S. workers each month. Gallup asks current full- and part-time employees whether their employers are hiring new people and expanding the size of their workforces, not changing the size of their workforces, or letting people go and reducing the size of their workforces. Gallup's hiring measure is computed by subtracting the "letting go and reducing" percentage from the "hiring and expanding" percentage. The assumption is that employees across the country have a good feel for what's happening in their companies, and that these insider perceptions can yield a meaningful indication of the nation's job situation. For results based on these samples, the maximum margin of sampling error is ±3 percentage points.

Interviews are conducted with respondents on land-line telephones (for respondents with a land-line telephone) and cellular phones (for respondents who are cell-phone only).

In addition to sampling error, question wording and practical difficulties in conducting surveys can introduce error or bias into the findings of public opinion polls.

April 03, 2009

LITTLE CHANGE IN NEGATIVE IMAGES OF BUSH AND CHENEY

Favorable ratings for both are at or near their all-time lows

by Lydia Saad, Gallup Poll Senior Editor

Neither George W. Bush's deliberate silence about the Obama administration nor Dick Cheney's ready criticism of it appear to have altered U.S. public perceptions about either man. The former president and former vice president are each viewed unfavorably by 63% of Americans, very similar to where they stood with the public in their final White House years.

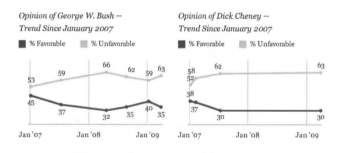

The last reading on Bush's favorability that Gallup recorded during his presidency came in a Jan. 9–11, 2009, survey. At that time, 40% of Americans viewed him favorably and 59% unfavorably. However, this represented an unusual spurt in positive feelings toward Bush, possibly due to changes in media coverage of the embattled president as his term ended, or because of Americans' generally buoyant mood leading up to Inauguration Day. (Barack Obama's favorable reading in the same survey was also higher than in previous and subsequent polling.)

The 35% of Americans viewing Bush favorably today is close to his all-time low of 32% in April 2008, and matches a favorable rating from August of that year. Bush's ratings have consistently been in negative territory since July 2005, a sharp contrast to his generally positive image throughout his first term.

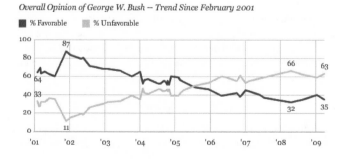

Partisan Differences Hold Firm

In delivering his first post-White House speech last month in Canada, Bush ruled out second-guessing the sitting president. In reference to Barack Obama, Bush was quoted by the Associated Press as stating, "There are plenty of critics in the arena. He deserves my silence." Bush went further, saying "I think it is essential that he be helped in office."

Despite Bush's seemingly "post-partisan" stance toward the new president, Democrats' reactions to Bush remain overwhelmingly negative. Only 10% have a favorable view of him and 89% an unfavorable view, little different from their views of him in August of last year—at the height of the rancorous election season.

Bush continues to be viewed favorably by about 3 in 10 independents and roughly 3 in 4 Republicans.

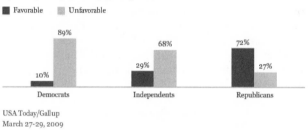

USA Today/Gallup
March 27-29, 2009

Cheney's Ratings

The 30% of Americans viewing Dick Cheney favorably today matches Gallup's previous favorable reading on him, obtained in July 2007, which was his all-time low. Cheney's image was somewhat better in the first half of 2007, but the last time he was viewed more favorably than unfavorably was in June 2005.

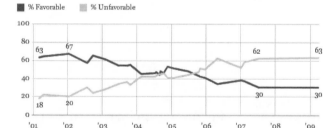

In the same week that Bush demurred when provided with an opening to critique Obama, Cheney readily took issue with the new administration on several counts during a television interview, responding "I do" when the host asked him whether he believes Obama's policies make the country "less safe."

Democrats today feel nearly as negative about Cheney as they do about Bush: only 12% view him favorably while 82% view him unfavorably. This is statistically unchanged from July 2007—however, with favorable ratings near the 10% level, Democratic opinion of Cheney could not go much lower.

Most independents also view Cheney negatively, while a majority of Republicans view him favorably.

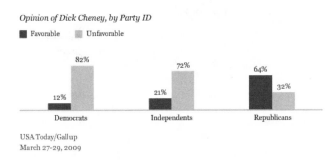

Opinion of Dick Cheney, by Party ID

■ Favorable ☐ Unfavorable

USA Today/Gallup
March 27-29, 2009

Bottom Line

Bush and Cheney have only begun to emerge publicly after departing Washington, D.C., in January. Thus far, Bush has promised to stay out of the political fray while Cheney has stepped squarely back into it. If this distinction holds over time, it could conceivably contribute to a divergence in how Americans perceive the two—with Bush's personal image among Democrats softening while views toward Cheney become even more polarized. Of course, other factors will come into play as Bush and Cheney establish their post-presidential roles in public affairs, and as the Bush presidency continues to be assessed. At this early juncture, however, public attitudes about the two former leaders have not yet changed.

Survey Methods

Results are based on telephone interviews with 1,007 national adults, aged 18 and older, conducted March 27–29, 2009. For results based on the total sample of national adults, one can say with 95% confidence that the maximum margin of sampling error is ±3 percentage points.

Interviews are conducted with respondents on land-line telephones (for respondents with a land-line telephone) and cellular phones (for respondents who are cell-phone only).

In addition to sampling error, question wording and practical difficulties in conducting surveys can introduce error or bias into the findings of public opinion polls.

April 03, 2009
MOST AMERICANS CONCERNED ABOUT MEXICO'S DRUG VIOLENCE
Fifty-one percent are very concerned

by Jeffrey M. Jones, Gallup Poll Managing Editor

A new Gallup Poll finds 79% of Americans saying they are concerned about "drug violence in Mexico," including 51% who are "very concerned."

These results are based on an April 1–2 Gallup Poll that asked Americans to indicate how concerned they are with Mexican drug violence, as well as a number of other potential international threats to the United States.

Violence from Mexican drug cartels is an emerging issue. Already, Secretary of State Hillary Clinton, Secretary of Homeland Security Janet Napolitano, and Attorney General Eric Holder have met with Mexican officials to discuss the issue. Earlier, the U.S. government issued a travel warning for U.S. citizens living or vacationing in Mexico. There are concerns that the violence is spilling across the border into the United States.

That may explain why residents of the South and West—which include the states located closest to Mexico—express greater concern about the issue than Eastern and Midwestern residents.

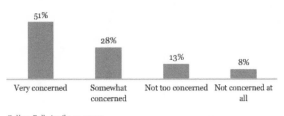

How concerned are you about drug violence in Mexico?

Gallup Poll, April 1-2, 2009

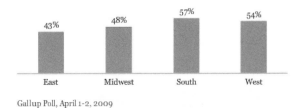

Concern About Drug Violence in Mexico, by Region

■ Very concerned

Gallup Poll, April 1-2, 2009

Additionally, concern varies rather dramatically by age, with older Americans much more worried than younger Americans. This pattern is evident in regard to most other international issues tested in the survey, but is especially pronounced with regard to Mexican drug violence.

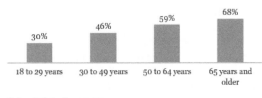

Concern About Drug Violence in Mexico, by Age

■ Very concerned

Gallup Poll, April 1-2, 2009

At this point, there are not meaningful party differences—50% of Democrats say they are very concerned about the issue, compared with 47% of independents and 56% of Republicans. But the issue could take on partisan overtones in the future as the government attempts to design policies to address the issue.

Implications

Relative to other issues, Mexican drug violence has not received a great deal of attention in the national news media—economic issues have generally dwarfed any international concerns thus far in Barack Obama's presidency. But even with the rather limited attention it has received, Americans are aware enough about the issue to express concern about it. The fact that it is occurring in a neighboring country and has the potential to spill over into the United States (and is reportedly already doing so in cities like Phoenix) may help explain the relatively high level of concern.

Survey Methods

Results are based on telephone interviews with 988 national adults, aged 18 and older, conducted April 1–2, 2009, as part of Gallup Poll Daily tracking. For results based on the total sample of national adults, one can say with 95% confidence that the maximum margin of sampling error is ±3 percentage points.

Interviews are conducted with respondents on land-line telephones (for respondents with a land-line telephone) and cellular phones (for respondents who are cell-phone only).

In addition to sampling error, question wording and practical difficulties in conducting surveys can introduce error or bias into the findings of public opinion polls.

April 06, 2009
AMERICANS SEE NEWER THREATS ON PAR WITH ONGOING CONFLICTS
Concerns about Iran and North Korea similar to those about Afghanistan and Iraq

by Lymari Morales, Gallup Poll Staff Writer

In a sign of the times, Americans are now about as concerned about Iran's and North Korea's nuclear capabilities and drug violence in Mexico as they are about the conflicts in Afghanistan and Iraq, and international terrorism in general. At least 8 in 10 Americans express some level of concern about each.

How concerned you are about each of the following international matters -- are you very concerned, moderately concerned, not too concerned, or not concerned at all? How about -- [RANDOM ORDER]?

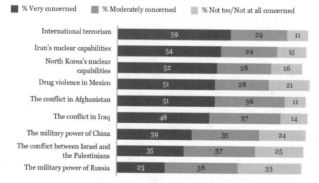

Gallup Poll, April 1-2, 2009

These are the findings of a Gallup Poll conducted April 1–2, 2009, before North Korea's weekend rocket launch, in which Americans were asked to state their levels of concern about a variety of

international matters. While the long-standing issues of international terrorism, Afghanistan, and Iraq rank highest in terms of overall concern, it is noteworthy that Americans express similar levels of concern about the emerging threats posed by Iran, North Korea, and Mexico.

Key Findings

- International terrorism concerns Americans most—88% say they are concerned, including 59% who are very concerned.
- Americans are next-most likely to be "very concerned" about Iran's nuclear capabilities (54%) and North Korea's nuclear capabilities (52%). In terms of overall concern, the rankings of both are nearly as high as those of Afghanistan and Iraq.
- Americans are slightly more likely to be "very concerned" about the conflict in Afghanistan (51%) than about the conflict in Iraq (48%). These ongoing conflicts rank second and third, respectively, in terms of overall concern.
- The emerging issue of drug violence in Mexico is rated almost on par with concerns about Afghanistan, Iraq, Iran, and North Korea—79% of Americans are concerned, including 51% who are very concerned.
- The military threat posed by China concerns Americans more than the military threat posed by Russia—39% are very concerned about China, while 25% are very concerned about Russia. While these threats are less worrisome to Americans than the others discussed thus far, more than 6 in 10 Americans do express some concern about them.
- The conflict between Israel and the Palestinians concerns 72% of Americans—ranking it toward the bottom of the overall list. Only 35% are very concerned.

While Americans overall deliver a pretty solid consensus on the threats they deem very troubling, the results by partisan group do diverge somewhat. Republicans are in most cases more likely than Democrats to be "very concerned" about these international matters—especially in regard to international terrorism, Iran, and North Korea, where the gap in reported concern is at least 20 percentage points in each case. Republicans and Democrats are most aligned on Iraq, Afghanistan, the Israeli-Palestinian conflict, and Mexico.

How concerned you are about each of the following international matters -- are you very concerned, moderately concerned, not too concerned, or not concerned at all? How about -- [RANDOM ORDER]?

% Very concerned

	Republicans	Independents	Democrats	Difference, Republicans minus Democrats
	%	%	%	Pct. pts.
International terrorism	76	51	55	21
Iran's nuclear capabilities	70	46	50	20
North Korea's nuclear capabilities	67	47	46	21
The conflict in Afghanistan	56	47	52	4
Drug violence in Mexico	56	47	50	6
The military power of China	53	33	35	18
The conflict in Iraq	51	46	48	3
The conflict between Israel and the Palestinians	41	27	37	4
The military power of Russia	33	21	22	11

Gallup Poll, April 1-2, 2009

Taken together, these findings underscore the difficult road ahead for the Obama administration in terms of international security and foreign affairs. Prior to President Obama's trip abroad over the past week, 61% of Americans said they approved of the way he was handling foreign affairs. During his trip, Obama reacted strongly against North Korea's rocket launch, urged allies to take a firm stand against Iran, and accepted invitations to visit both China and Russia. It remains to be seen how such actions might affect Americans' relatively high level of worry about the many and diverse international threats facing the United States at this time.

Survey Methods

Results are based on telephone interviews with 988 national adults, aged 18 and older, conducted April 1–2, 2009. For results based on the total sample of national adults, one can say with 95% confidence that the maximum margin of sampling error is ±3 percentage points.

These questions were asked of random half-samples for two nights of Gallup Daily polling, which interviews 1,000 U.S. adults each night.

Interviews are conducted with respondents on land-line telephones (for respondents with a land-line telephone) and cellular phones (for respondents who are cell-phone only).

In addition to sampling error, question wording and practical difficulties in conducting surveys can introduce error or bias into the findings of public opinion polls.

April 07, 2009
OBAMA APPROVAL RATING STABLE, POLARIZED
Averaging 62% approval thus far

by Jeffrey M. Jones, Gallup Poll Managing Editor

President Barack Obama's overall job approval rating has been highly stable since mid-February, averaging 62% since Feb. 16, as well as in the most recent week, from March 30 through April 5.

Weekly Presidential Approval Averages for Barack Obama
Based on Gallup Poll Daily tracking

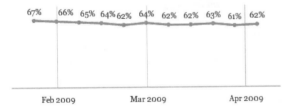

Still enjoying a honeymoon period, Obama's approval rating has fallen only slightly from its 67% starting point even as he has outlined an ambitious agenda that has been controversial to some with regard to the costs to taxpayers and the proposed expansion of the federal government's role in the economy.

So far, Obama's actions have served to turn off only a rather limited number of Republicans. He began his term with a 41% approval rating among Republicans—not outstanding but certainly healthy when juxtaposed against the largely single-digit approval rat-

ings for George W. Bush among Democrats in the last year and a half of his presidency.

Obama's approval rating among Republicans declined rather quickly in the weeks after his inauguration and was 27% this past week. So even though he still claims a substantial minority of Republicans as supporters, this group is about one-third smaller than at the outset of his presidency.

Meanwhile, Obama's approval ratings among Democrats and independents have been highly stable. Last week's averages of 90% approval from Democrats and 60% from independents nearly match the averages for his presidency to date.

Weekly Presidential Approval Averages for Barack Obama, by Political Party
Based on Gallup Poll Daily tracking

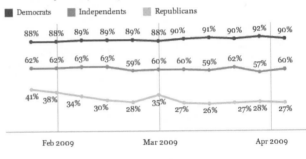

The drop in Republican support, coupled with the high and stable approval ratings from Democrats, has led to a widening partisan gap in evaluations of Obama. After beginning at 47 points between Democrats (88%) and Republicans (41%), the gap in approval stood at 63 points in last week's data (90% versus 27%).

Democratic-Republican Gap in Barack Obama's Presidential Job Approval Ratings, by Week
Based on Gallup Poll Daily tracking

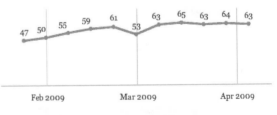

Partisan Gaps in Historical Context

Partisan gaps in presidential job approval are nothing new—Gallup has consistently observed Democratic-Republican differences in ratings of the president since it began measuring job approval ratings in the 1940s. But for many recent presidents, the gap has far exceeded the historical norm.

For the seven presidents from Harry Truman to Jimmy Carter, the median or typical partisan gap in presidential approval rating was 35 points. That began to change during Ronald Reagan's presidency, as he ushered in a new era of conservative policies that did not sit well with most Democrats. Consequently, during his tenure in office, the median party gap in approval ratings was 53 points.

George H.W. Bush succeeded Reagan, promising a "kinder, gentler" approach to governing, and his ratings were less polarized and more in line with the historical data, with a median 37-point party gap.

But Bush's record was a bit of an anomaly in recent history. Bill Clinton's policies and—perhaps more importantly—his personal behavior were problematic for most Republicans, and during his presidency, the typical party gap in approval ratings was 55 points.

George W. Bush succeeded Clinton and set new standards for political polarization, with a median 64-point difference between Republicans' and Democrats' ratings of him, including record 83-point party divides in the fall of 2004.

To this point, the typical party gap for Barack Obama has been 61 points. This puts him much more in line with the recent Bush record than with earlier presidents.

To the extent Republicans are evaluating Obama on the substance of his policies and proposals (particularly his domestic policies) there may be little for them to like, since Obama's policies have largely followed usual Democratic doctrine. Thus, a wide partisan gap is understandable—even for a president trying to avoid one. But Obama's best efforts at creating a post-partisan presidency are complicated by the ideological hegemony within the congressional party caucuses and the partisan pundits filling the airwaves, print pages, and blogosphere, seeking to convince those who watch, listen, or read of the correctness of their views and the incorrectness of their opponents' views. In such an environment, it is not surprising that George W. Bush's later approval ratings were in single digits among Democrats while he maintained rather healthy ratings among Republicans.

These forces may help to explain the stability in Obama's approval rating among all Americans, as well as the large partisan divide in his public evaluations.

Survey Methods

Results are based on telephone interviews with 3,559 national adults, aged 18 and older, conducted March 30–April 5, 2009, as part of Gallup Poll Daily tracking. For results based on the total sample of national adults, one can say with 95% confidence that the maximum margin of sampling error is ±2 percentage points.

Interviews are conducted with respondents on land-line telephones (for respondents with a land-line telephone) and cellular phones (for respondents who are cell-phone only).

In addition to sampling error, question wording and practical difficulties in conducting surveys can introduce error or bias into the findings of public opinion polls.

April 08, 2009
SATISFACTION RATINGS CONTINUE SLOW, STEADY CLIMB
Percentage satisfied with conditions in U.S. is double pre-Obama reading

by Jeffrey M. Jones, Gallup Poll Managing Editor

Americans' reported satisfaction with the way things are going in the country remains decidedly negative, but has slowly and steadily improved in recent weeks. In March 30–April 5 Gallup Daily polling, 26% of Americans were satisfied, up from 15% in mid-February.

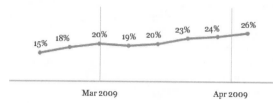

In general, are you satisfied or dissatisfied with the way things are going in the United States at this time?

Gallup asks Americans whether they are satisfied or dissatisfied with the way things are going each day as part of Gallup Poll Daily tracking.

As of now, satisfaction is double what it was in Gallup's last Bush-era measurement, 13% in late December 2008 and early January 2009. After Barack Obama took office, satisfaction improved slightly, to 17% in the first week of his presidency, before dipping to 15% in mid-February, about the time the stimulus bill was passed.

In six of the seven weeks since, there has been at least a marginal increase in satisfaction from the prior week.

The rebound in satisfaction has mainly been the result of greater optimism among Democrats. Now, 40% are satisfied, up from 21% in mid-February. There has been a smaller increase among independents over this time, from 14% to 23%. Even Republicans' reported satisfaction has improved, though it is still quite low at 13%, after bottoming out at 7% in mid-February.

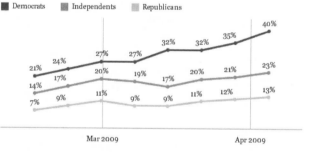

Satisfied With the Way Things Are Going in the United States, by Party Affiliation

Gallup has asked this version of the satisfaction question in polling since 1979. The 26% of Americans now satisfied is higher than in any Gallup measurement in 2008, which included the historical low reading of 7% in October.

The last time Gallup found satisfaction running significantly higher than the current figure was April 2007, when 33% reported being satisfied.

Implications

Americans are still generally discouraged about the state of the country, but there are signs of optimism. In addition to the recent rise in satisfaction, Gallup has noted a steady increase in the percentage of Americans who say the economy is getting better. Most of the increase in satisfaction is the result of increased positivity among Democrats, who have greater confidence in the approach the new administration is taking to address the economy and other major problems facing the country.

April 09, 2009

CHURCH-GOING AMONG U.S. CATHOLICS SLIDES TO TIE PROTESTANTS

However, long-term decline may have leveled off in past decade

by Lydia Saad, Gallup Poll Senior Editor

According to Gallup Poll trends on church attendance among American Christians, weekly attendance among Protestants has been fairly steady over the past six decades, averaging 42% in 1955 versus 45% in the middle of the current decade. However, attendance among Roman Catholics dropped from 75% to 45% over the same period.

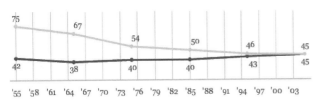

Percentage Saying They Attended Church in Past Seven Days
Based on aggregated data in Gallup religion surveys from the middle of each decade

Most of the decline in church attendance among American Catholics occurred in the earlier decades, between 1955 and 1975; however, it continued at a rate of four percentage points a decade through the mid-1990s, and church attendance has since leveled off at 45%.

The Gallup Poll's rich archives of religious preference and church attendance data have been mined in time to provide a detailed picture of church attendance trends among U.S. Christians heading into Easter Sunday. Multiple surveys were combined for each decade starting with the 1950s, using Gallup religion surveys conducted closest to the middle of the decade. This provides ample sample size to examine the church attendance patterns of Protestants and Catholics, and of various age categories within those religious groups.

On the basis of these 10-year snapshots of church attendance, the percentage of Catholics saying they went to church in the past week is essentially unchanged between 1995 and today. That's an extremely important finding given the upheaval in the U.S. Roman Catholic

Church caused by the sexual abuse scandals that erupted earlier this decade. Gallup polling in 2002 and 2003 found a decline in the percentages of Catholics saying they had attended church in the past week; however, attendance rebounded by the end of 2003 and has since remained on par with its pre-scandal level of about 45%.

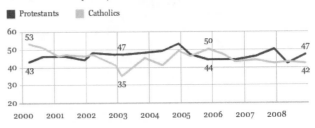

Church Attendance Among Protestants and Catholics, 2000-2008
% Attended church in last seven days
Trend based on Gallup surveys conducted between 2000 and 2008

Young Catholics Drop Out of Church by the 1970s

Beyond the divergent attendance trends of Protestants and Catholics, the historical data reveal distinct generational patterns in church attendance within each Christian faith.

In 1955, adult Catholics of all ages attended church at similar rates, with between 73% and 77% saying they attended in the past week. By the mid-1960s, weekly attendance of young Catholics (those 21 to 29 years of age) started to wane, falling to 56%, while attendance among other age groups dropped only slightly, to around 70%. By the mid-1970s, only 35% of Catholics in their 20s said they had attended in the past week, but attendance was also starting to fall among those in their 30s, 40s, and 50s.

Attendance for most of the groups continued to fall from the 1970s to the 1990s. However, over the past decade it has generally stabilized, particularly among Catholics in their 20s and 30s.

Across this entire period, attendance among Catholics aged 60 and older has dropped from 73% to 58%.

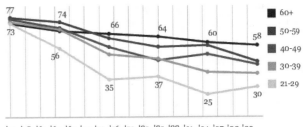

Church Attendance Among Catholics, by Age
% Attended church in last seven days

Protestant Attendance Steady Among Most Age Groups

The picture in attendance by age is entirely different among Protestants. Apart from a temporary dip in weekly church attendance among 21- to 29-year-old Protestants in the 1960s and 1970s, attendance has stayed the same or increased among all the age groups. It even rebounded among young Protestants in the 1980s, and is now close to 1950s levels.

Of course, the "Protestant" moniker encompasses many distinct religious denominations, some of which have reportedly experienced

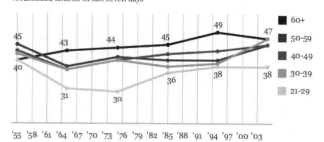

Church Attendance Among Protestants, by Age
% Attended church in last seven days

60+
50-59
40-49
30-39
21-29

'55 '58 '61 '64 '67 '70 '73 '76 '79 '82 '85 '88 '91 '94 '97 '00 '03

high growth in membership over the past few decades, while others have been in decline. The figures reported here represent averages for all Protestant faiths.

Bottom Line

The increasingly spare attendance at regular mass has been of considerable concern to the Catholic Church in the United States for some time. Theologians and other observers have variously offered the cultural upheaval of the 1960s, changes to the church brought about in the 1960s by the Second Vatican Council, and national publicity in 2002 over sexual abuse lawsuits against Catholic priests as possible contributors to the trend.

Whatever the causes, it is clear that U.S. Catholics' once-nearly uniform obedience to their church's requirement of weekly mass attendance has faded, and Catholics are now no different from Protestants in their likelihood to attend church. This has occurred among Catholics of all age categories, but is most pronounced among those under 60. The good news for the Catholic Church is that the drop in attendance seems to have slowed or abated altogether in the last decade, spanning a most difficult period for the church around 2002, when attendance did suffer temporarily.

U.S. Protestant church attendance has also been steady over the past decade, but is actually higher now than it was in the 1970s and 1980s, in part the result of a resurgence of regular attendance among young adults.

Survey Methods

These results are based on aggregates of Gallup Poll surveys for the following periods: 1955, 1965–1966, 1975, 1983–1986, 1995–1996, 2005–2008.

April 10, 2009
THIS EASTER, SMALLER PERCENTAGE OF AMERICANS ARE CHRISTIAN

Americans more likely now than in previous decades to say they have no religious identity

by Frank Newport, Gallup Poll Editor in Chief

The percentage of Americans who identify with some form of a Christian religion has been dropping in recent decades, and now stands at 77%, according to an aggregate of Gallup Polls conducted in 2008. In 1948, when Gallup began tracking religious identification, the percentage who were Christian was 91%.

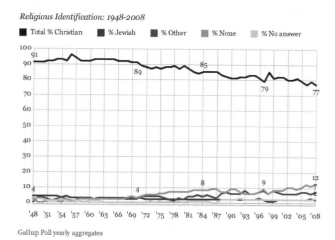

Religious Identification: 1948-2008

Total % Christian   % Jewish   % Other   % None   % No answer

Gallup Poll yearly aggregates

Christian America comprises those who in response to a basic religious identity question say they are Roman Catholic or some form of a non-Catholic Christian religion. The latter group consists of those who identify themselves as Protestant or as Christian in some other way. An analysis shows that it is this group of non-Catholic Christians that has, on a percentage basis, dropped the most over the decades.

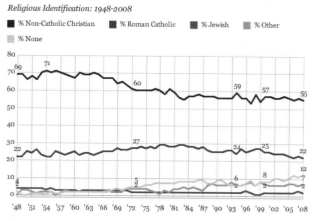

Religious Identification: 1948-2008

% Non-Catholic Christian   % Roman Catholic   % Jewish   % Other
% None

Gallup Poll yearly aggregates

As seen in the accompanying graph, the percentage of Americans identifying as Protestant or another non-Catholic Christian religion has been declining since the mid-1960s. When Gallup began tracking religious identification, the percentage of U.S. adults identifying with some non-Catholic Christian religion was routinely in the high 60%-low 70% range. The percentage fell below 60% for the first time in 1979, and since 2000 has been between 55% and 57%.

The percentage of Americans identifying as Roman Catholic has stayed within a range between 20% and 30% over the last 60 years. Catholics were 22% of the U.S. adult population in 1948, according to Gallup's estimates. That percentage rose over the years and reached its high point in the 1970s and 1980s, when the U.S. population was nearly 30% Catholic. In the last several years, Gallup's estimate of the percentage Catholic has been 22% to 23%.

The relative shrinkage of the Christian percentage of the U.S. population in recent years means that other groups by definition have expanded. The Gallup trend data show that the most significant expansion has come among the group that does not identify with any religion, followed by a more modest expansion of those who identify with another, non-Christian, religion.

The accompanying graph shows Gallup trends since 1948 in the percentage of Americans saying they have no religious identity.

Percentage of Americans With No Religious Identification: 1948-2008

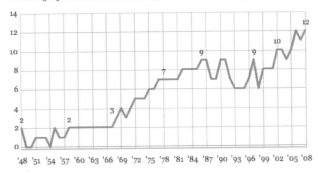

Gallup Poll yearly aggregates

In 1948, 2% of Americans interviewed by Gallup volunteered that they had "no religion." The number stayed in that range until about 1970. By 1972, Gallup had measured 5% with "no religion." Gallup trends show the percentage gradually increasing since that time, with a very modest decline from an average of 8% in the early 1990s to 6% from 1993–1995, and then some fluctuation in the late 1990s, with the percentage settling in the 9% to 12% range since 2002. (Additionally, in 2008, an average of 3% of Americans did not answer the question on religious identity. Whether these people truly do not have a religious identity, or were confused or had several religious identities, is unknown.)

The group of Americans who are classified as "Other" includes the less than 1% who are estimated to be Muslim, and small percentages who are Buddhist, Hindu, or other non-Christian religions. The percentage of Americans classified in this Other category was near 0% in 1948, but was at 3% in 1949 and was generally in the 2% to 3% range through the 1950s and 1960s. It has risen in recent decades to as high as 8% in 1997, and is 7% today.

Implications

The United States remains a dominantly Christian nation. More than three-quarters of all Americans identify as Christian. And the vast majority of those who identify with any religion say they are Christian in some form or another.

Yet, the percentage of Americans who in theory could celebrate Easter this weekend as part of their religion is down significantly from where it was 50 or 60 years ago.

There are many theoretical explanations for the increase in those with no religious identity at the expense of those identifying with a Christian religion. Two social scientists at the National Opinion Research Corporation, Tom W. Smith and Seokho Kim, contemplating similar data from the General Social Survey in 2004, concluded: "In sum, an array of social forces from cohort turnover, to immigration, to reduced retention rates, indicate that the Protestant share of the population will continue to shrink and they will soon lose their majority position in American society."

The share of the population held by any religious group is based on a complex set of factors relating to internal reproduction (births), in-migration (from converts and from people moving into the country who have a particular religious identity), and out-migration (people who leave the religion and people with a particular religious identity who leave the country). In-migration from other countries in recent years may have helped boost the percentage of non-Christians in the population. In-migration from Catholic Mexico and Catholic Central American countries has also, at the same time, helped keep the percentage of Catholics as high as it is. The big shift has apparently been the out-migration of those whose parents may have identified with a specific Christian religion, but who upon growing up have become more likely to tell a survey interviewer that they have no specific religious identity.

Gallup (and other survey researchers) measure religious identity by asking Americans to name their religion. It is possible that Americans who previously would have identified themselves with the religion of their upbringing now feel freer to tell a survey interviewer that they have no religious identity.

It is important to note that basic religious identification says little about the relevance of that identity to the person's life. Identifying with a religion doesn't indicate how actively the individual practices the religion. It doesn't indicate whether the person rigorously adheres to that religion's beliefs. It simply states that the person has some connection to and some identity with a specific type of religion. Data from measures of religious intensity or commitment are needed to flesh out the portrait of the ways in which Americans' religiosity may have changed over the years.

Gallup survey data on religious identification extend back only to 1948, about a quarter of the life of the country. Obviously, this evidence speaks only to the *recent* history of religious identity in the United States. There is no real scientific way of putting recent survey history of religious identity into a longer time frame going back much before World War II. (Some scholars argue that, in fact, Americans were not very religious by some measures at the time of the Revolution in Colonial America.) It is thus important to keep in mind that the trends reviewed in this analysis are only part of the portrait of the ebb and flow of religion in the United States since the nation's founding well over two centuries ago.

Survey Methods

These results are based on aggregates of Gallup Poll surveys for each year from 1948 through 2008.

April 13, 2009

VIEWS OF INCOME TAXES AMONG MOST POSITIVE SINCE 1956

by Jeffrey M. Jones, Gallup Poll Managing Editor

A new Gallup Poll finds 48% of Americans saying the amount of federal income taxes they pay is "about right," with 46% saying "too high"—one of the most positive assessments Gallup has measured since 1956. Typically, a majority of Americans say their taxes are too high, and relatively few say their taxes are too low.

These results are based on the Gallup Economy and Personal Finance poll, conducted each April, including April 6–9 of this year.

Do you consider the amount of federal income tax you have to pay as too high, about right, or too low?

■ % Too high ■ % About right ■ % Too low

Since 1956, there has been only one other time when a higher percentage of Americans said their taxes were about right—in 2003, when 50% did so after two rounds of tax cuts under the Bush administration.

The slightly more positive view this year may reflect a public response to President Barack Obama's economic stimulus and budget plans. He has promised not to raise taxes on Americans making less than $250,000, while cutting taxes for lower- and middle-income Americans. The latter has already begun, as the government has reduced the withholding amount for federal income taxes from middle- and lower-income American workers' paychecks.

In this year's poll, slim majorities of both lower- and middle-income Americans say they pay about the right amount of taxes, while upper-income Americans tend to think they pay too much. The views of upper-income Americans have not changed in the past year, while both middle- and lower-income Americans are more likely to say they pay the right amount of tax.

Perceptions of Taxes Paid, by Household Income, 2008 and 2009 Gallup Polls

Annual household income	Too high	About right	Too low
2009			
Less than $30,000	39%	51%	6%
$30,000 to $74,999	45%	52%	1%
$75,000 and above	53%	44%	3%
2008			
Less than $30,000	46%	41%	2%
$30,000 to $74,999	53%	44%	1%
$75,000 and above	52%	44%	3%

As is usually the case, there are partisan differences in views of taxes—most Democrats think the taxes they pay are about right, while most Republicans say their taxes are too high. Independents are about evenly divided. Compared with last year, each group is slightly more likely to say its taxes are about right.

Six in 10 Continue to Say Taxes are Fair

The poll also finds 61% of Americans saying they regard the income taxes they have to pay this year as fair. There has been very little change on this measure in the last six years.

Generally speaking, Americans seem to take a more positive view of their taxes when the country is at war. From 1997 through 2001, the percentage saying their taxes were fair ranged from 45% to 51%. In early 2002, after the United States had begun military operations in Afghanistan in response to the 9/11 terrorist attacks,

Perceptions of Taxes Paid, by Party Affiliation, 2008 and 2009 Gallup Polls

Party affiliation	Too high	About right	Too low
2009			
Democrat	40%	55%	3%
Independent	48%	46%	3%
Republican	53%	43%	1%
2008			
Democrat	45%	47%	3%
Independent	54%	40%	2%
Republican	58%	39%	1%

Do you regard the income tax which you will have to pay this year as fair?
Recent trend

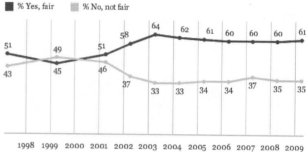

■ % Yes, fair ■ % No, not fair

58% said their taxes were fair. After the Iraq war began in 2003, the percentage increased to 64%, and it has been above 60% ever since.

Going back even further, Gallup asked the same question in the 1940s. While the country was still fighting World War II, 85% or more of Americans said the taxes they paid were fair. The first post-war measurement, in 1946, saw this percentage tumble to 62%.

Implications

As the remaining U.S. tax filers prepare to send their income-tax returns before the April 15 deadline, Gallup finds Americans' views of their federal income taxes about as positive as at any point in the last 60 years. This may reflect the income-tax cut that was part of the $787 billion economic stimulus plan, as well as a continuing sense of patriotism with the country fighting two wars.

Obama has promised not to raise taxes on all but the wealthiest Americans. There are concerns that his proposed budget relies too much on borrowed money, and the president may be forced to raise taxes on a greater percentage of Americans, or to scale back his plans to reform the healthcare system and invest in education and alternative energy.

Survey Methods

Results are based on telephone interviews with 1,027 national adults, aged 18 and older, conducted April 6–9, 2009. For results based on the total sample of national adults, one can say with 95% confidence that the maximum margin of sampling error is ±3 percentage points.

Interviews are conducted with respondents on land-line telephones (for respondents with a land-line telephone) and cellular phones (for respondents who are cell-phone only).

In addition to sampling error, question wording and practical difficulties in conducting surveys can introduce error or bias into the findings of public opinion polls.

April 13, 2009
AMERICANS MOST CONFIDENT IN OBAMA ON ECONOMY
Democratic leaders in Congress fare better than Republican leaders

by Frank Newport , Gallup Poll Editor in Chief

Over two-thirds of Americans—71%—have a great deal or a fair amount of confidence in President Obama to do or recommend the right thing for the economy, a much higher level of confidence than is given to Federal Reserve Chairman Ben Bernanke, Treasury Secretary Tim Geithner, or the Democratic or Republican leaders in Congress.

Please tell me how much confidence you have in each to do or to recommend the right thing for the economy -- a great deal, a fair amount, only a little, or almost none. How about -- [ROTATED]?

■ % Great deal/Fair amount

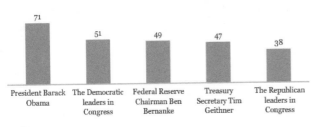

April 6-9, 2009

These results, from a new April 6–9 Gallup Poll, show that President Obama continues to be the individual upon whom Americans are most willing to bestow their confidence when it comes to the economy.

Americans' confidence in Obama on the economy is roughly similar to the confidence rating the public gave to President George W. Bush in April 2001, then in his initial quarter of governing, as is the case now for Obama. Obama gets slightly higher "a great deal of confidence" ratings than did Bush, while Bush received a slightly higher "fair amount" rating. In 2002 and 2003, Bush's ratings were similar to Obama's now. By April of 2008, his last year in office, Bush's overall confidence ratings on the economy had dropped to just 34%. (At that time, however, his overall job approval ratings had also dropped below 30%.)

As previous Gallup research has shown, Obama inspires significantly higher confidence than does Geithner, his Treasury secretary. Federal Reserve Chairman Bernanke has been instrumental in pushing through dramatic economic policies and changes in an effort to stimulate the economy, and Americans accord him about the same level of confidence as they give to Geithner—but again, lower than the public's confidence in Obama.

Bernanke was sworn in as chairman of the Federal Reserve in early 2006, under the Republican administration of George W. Bush. Bernanke's current confidence ratings are quite similar to where they have been over the last three years, despite the upheaval in the nation's economy in the last year.

It is unlikely that many Americans have a highly sophisticated understanding of the complex economic policies enacted in the last several months by either Bernanke or Geithner. Yet only 17% and 14% of Americans, respectively, are not able or willing to give an opinion on confidence in these two men's actions on the economy.

Please tell me how much confidence you have in each to do or to recommend the right thing for the economy -- a great deal, a fair amount, only a little, or almost none. How about -- [ROTATED]?

	Great deal	Fair amount	Only a little/ Almost none	No opinion
	%	%	%	%
President Barack Obama	38	33	29	*
The Democratic leaders in Congress	10	41	45	3
Treasury Secretary Tim Geithner	9	38	39	14
Federal Reserve Chairman Ben Bernanke	7	42	35	17
The Republican leaders in Congress	5	33	58	4

* Less than 0.5%
April 6-9, 2009

Americans are not overwhelmingly positive about either the Democratic or the Republican leaders in Congress. Still, the Democrats fare better on a comparative basis. Fifty-one percent of Americans have a great deal or a fair amount of confidence in the Democratic leaders, compared to 38% in the Republican leaders.

There are interesting differences in confidence levels in these individuals and leaders by partisan orientation.

Please tell me how much confidence you have in each to do or to recommend the right thing for the economy -- a great deal, a fair amount, only a little, or almost none. How about -- [ROTATED]?

% Great Deal/Fair amount, by political party

	Democrats	Independents	Republicans
President Barack Obama	97	68	38
Federal Reserve Chairman Ben Bernanke	64	44	36
Treasury Secretary Tim Geithner	70	43	24
Democratic leaders in Congress	79	46	19
Republican leaders in Congress	27	36	57

April 6-9, 2009

- Obama gets almost universal confidence from Democrats, two-thirds support from independents, and just over one-third confidence from Republicans.
- Geithner appears to be somewhat more politicized than Bernanke. Geithner's confidence rating ranges from 70% among Democrats to just 24% among Republicans. Bernanke, on the other hand, has a more modest 28-point partisan gap, with a 64% confidence rating among Democrats vs. 36% among Republicans.
- The partisan ratings of Bernanke have shifted from last year, when he was serving under a Republican president. At that time, the Fed chairman received a 61% confidence rating from Republicans, 43% from independents, and just a 40% rating from Democrats. Apparently, Americans associate the Fed chairman with the particular president he happens to be serving under.
- Democrats have more faith in their leaders than Republicans do in theirs. Seventy-nine percent of Democrats say they have confidence in the Democratic leaders in Congress on the economy. Although this is lower than the confidence Democrats have in Obama, it is higher than the 57% confidence rating Republicans give the Republican leaders in Congress.

Survey Methods

Results are based on telephone interviews with 1,027 national adults, aged 18 and older, conducted April 6–9, 2009. For results based on the total sample of national adults, one can say with 95% confidence that the maximum margin of sampling error is ±3 percentage points.

Interviews are conducted with respondents on land-line telephones (for respondents with a land-line telephone) and cellular phones (for respondents who are cell-phone only).

In addition to sampling error, question wording and practical difficulties in conducting surveys can introduce error or bias into the findings of public opinion polls.

April 15, 2009
MORE SAY LOW-INCOME AMERICANS PAYING FAIR SHARE OF TAXES
No change in perceptions of taxes paid by middle-income Americans

by Jeffrey M. Jones, Gallup Poll Managing Editor

Americans' perceptions of the taxes paid by those with lower incomes have shifted in the past year. Now, 41% say lower-income people are paying their "fair share" of federal taxes, up from 32% last year. At the same time, the percentage who believe lower-income Americans are paying "too much" in taxes has dropped from 51% to 39%.

Please tell me if you think lower-income people are paying their fair share in federal taxes, paying too much, or paying too little?

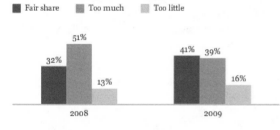

This marks a new low in perceptions that lower-income people are paying too much in taxes going back to 1992, when Gallup first asked the question. The percentage saying lower-income people pay their fair share is the highest since 1994.

Please tell me if you think lower-income people are paying their fair share in federal taxes, paying too much, or paying too little?

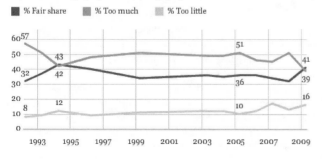

The changes may reflect a response to Barack Obama's plans for federal income taxes. Obama has promised to cut taxes for low- and middle-income Americans, while raising taxes only on the wealthiest

Americans. Most working Americans have already begun to receive a tax cut through lower withholding amounts in their paychecks—a provision in the recently passed economic stimulus package.

Americans are still most likely to say that middle-income people pay their fair share of taxes, as they have in six of the last seven years. Now, 50% hold this view. Meanwhile, just 23% say upper-income taxpayers pay their fair share, while 60% say they pay too little.

Please tell me if you think each of the following are paying their fair share in federal taxes, paying too much, or paying too little?

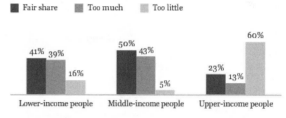

April 6-9, 2009

There has been virtually no change in Americans' perceptions of middle-income taxpayers' contributions over the past year. But the 50% who say they are paying their fair share remains on the high end of what Gallup has found historically. Prior to 2003 and the income-tax cuts enacted under George W. Bush, Americans were more likely to say middle-income Americans paid too much in taxes.

Please tell me if you think middle-income people are paying their fair share in federal taxes, paying too much, or paying too little?

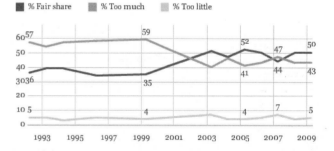

Americans have consistently said that upper-income people pay too little in taxes. But with Obama promising to increase taxes on those earning $250,000 or more per year to help pay for his domestic policy agenda, the percentage of Americans who hold this view has dipped slightly to 60%, the lowest percentage Gallup has found to date. There has been a slight bump up in the percentage who now say upper-income people pay too much, to a new high of 13%.

Implications

Obama promised to take an economic approach different from Bush's, in hopes of reviving the economy. And while Obama has only begun to fulfill his promises of cutting taxes for the middle class and raising taxes on those earning $250,000 or more, Americans' views about the taxes different income groups pay have already shifted.

By this time next year, Obama's first budget will be in effect and he will have begun to implement his tax policy, and Americans'

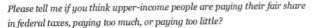

Please tell me if you think upper-income people are paying their fair share in federal taxes, paying too much, or paying too little?

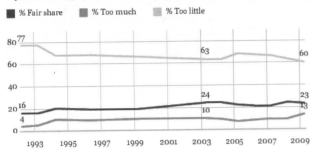

opinions on the fairness of taxes that different income groups pay may change further.

Survey Methods

Results are based on telephone interviews with 1,027 national adults, aged 18 and older, conducted April 6–9, 2009. For results based on the total sample of national adults, one can say with 95% confidence that the maximum margin of sampling error is ±3 percentage points.

Interviews are conducted with respondents on land-line telephones (for respondents with a land-line telephone) and cellular phones (for respondents who are cell-phone only).

In addition to sampling error, question wording and practical difficulties in conducting surveys can introduce error or bias into the findings of public opinion polls.

April 15, 2009

AMERICANS OK WITH SHORT-TERM GOVERNMENT GROWTH

Americans more worried about government spending than government power

by Frank Newport, Gallup Poll Editor in Chief

Although a majority of 53% of Americans approve of the expansion of the U.S. government to help fix the current economic crisis, most of that group would like to see the government's role reduced once the crisis is over. Additionally, a majority of Americans say President Obama's proposals for government action to fix the economy involve too much government spending.

Thinking about the way the federal government has responded to the financial crisis in recent months, generally speaking, do you approve or disapprove of the expansion of the government's role in the economy?

USA Today/Gallup, March 27-29, 2009

A recent *USA Today*/Gallup poll, conducted March 27–29, probed Americans' views of the government's role in addressing the nation's financial crisis. The responses underscore the conclusion that Americans have conflicting attitudes about the whole process.

After having been asked about their views of the government's expanded role in the economy, those who said they approved were asked if they wanted it to be a permanent expansion, or if the role of government should be reduced once the crisis is over.

Views of Expanded Role of Government in Economy

	%
Approve of expanded role, but want it reduced when crisis is over	39
Approve of expanded role, would like to see it permanent	13
Disapprove of expanded role	44
Unsure/Don't know	3

USA Today/Gallup, March 27-29, 2009

Only 13% of Americans both approve of the government's expansion to address the crisis and want that expansion to be permanent. On the other end of the spectrum, 44% of Americans disagree with the expansion to begin with. That leaves another group of about 4 out of 10 Americans who favor the expansion but want it to be cut back once the crisis is resolved.

There also appears to be a difference in the way in which Americans view an expansion of government "power" and government "spending": the former appears to be more palatable than the latter.

A random half-sample of those interviewed in the poll were asked "Do you think President Obama's proposals to address the economic problems in the country call for too big an expansion of government power, the right amount, or not a big enough expansion of government power?"

(Asked of a half sample) Do you think President Obama's proposals to address the economic problems in the country call for too big an expansion of government power, the right amount, or not a big enough expansion of government power?

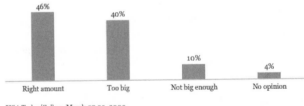

USA Today/Gallup, March 27-29, 2009

Just 40% say it is too big an expansion. (That's similar to the 44% who say they disapprove of the overall expansion of the government in the question reviewed above.) In contrast, 46% of Americans say the expansion of government power is the right amount, while another 10% say it is not big enough.

On the other hand, when a different half-sample was asked virtually the same question but with the word "spending" substituted for "power" ("Do you think President Obama's proposals to address the economic problems in the country call for too much government spending, the right amount, or not enough spending?"), the responses were considerably more negative. Fifty-five percent say Obama's proposals involve too much government spending.

The differences in responses to these questions are predictably partisan. Democrats generally are much more likely to approve of

(Asked of a half sample) Do you think President Obama's proposals to address the economic problems in the country call for too much government spending, the right amount, or not enough spending?

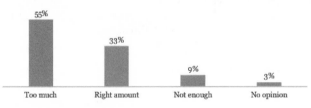

USA Today/Gallup, March 27-29, 2009

the expansion of government, and to say that the increase in government power and government spending is needed or is not enough. Republicans generally are opposed to government expansion.

Issues Relating to the Expansion of Government

	Republicans/ Republican-leaning independents	Democrats/ Democratic-leaning independents
	%	%
Expansion of government's role in the economy in response to the financial crisis		
Approve	26	78
Disapprove	72	20
Obama's proposals to address economic problems		
Right amount of/Not a big enough expansion of government power	24	86
Too big an expansion of government power	73	11
Obama's proposals to address economic problems		
Right amount of/Not enough spending	13	67
Too much spending	86	31

USA Today/Gallup, March 27-29, 2009

Implications

Americans traditionally have been worried about too much government power, and in recent years—including 2009—have been consistently more likely to say government is trying to do too many things that should be left to individuals and businesses than to say government should do more to solve the country's problems.

Still, as the questions reviewed here show, a majority of Americans are apparently willing to sanction the sharp expansion of government involvement in the nation's economy as necessary to fix the major financial problems facing the country. But most of these approve of only a short-term expansion. The overwhelming majority of Americans either don't approve of the government expansion to begin with or want it curtailed once the crisis passes. Americans also are worried about the increase in government spending. (And other Gallup questions have shown that there is concern about the impact of the current policies on the nation's federal deficit.)

All of this could have significant political implications. Once the financial crisis begins to pass and the economy is on a better footing, there appears to be the potential for a backlash against the increased size, power, and spending of the government that has occurred since President Obama took office. Republican leaders are already criticizing the expanded government role in the economy.

There is little doubt that this will become a significant thrust of the GOP's efforts to increase its share of House and Senate seats in

the 2010 elections. The data suggest that Americans have a latent distrust of a permanent expansion of the federal government's role, meaning that Republican candidates may have fertile soil in which to plant their seeds of opposition in the coming years if the larger role of government stays in place once the economy improves.

Survey Methods

Results are based on telephone interviews with 1,007 national adults, aged 18 and older, conducted March 27–29, 2009. For results based on the total sample of national adults, one can say with 95% confidence that the maximum margin of sampling error is ±3 percentage points.

For results based on the 532 national adults in the Form A half-sample and 475 national adults in the Form B half-sample, the maximum margins of sampling error are ±5 percentage points.

Interviews are conducted with respondents on land-line telephones (for respondents with a land-line telephone) and cellular phones (for respondents who are cell-phone only).

In addition to sampling error, question wording and practical difficulties in conducting surveys can introduce error or bias into the findings of public opinion polls.

April 16, 2009
AMERICANS SEE BUYERS' MARKET IN HOUSING
Seventy-one percent think now is a good time to buy a house

by Dennis Jacobe, Gallup Chief Economist

Plunging housing prices combined with historically low interest rates have persuaded 71% of Americans that now is a "good time" to buy a house—up 18 percentage points from a year ago and the highest level of housing-purchase optimism in four years.

For people in general, do you think that now is a GOOD time or a BAD time to buy a house?

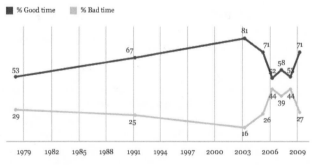

Housing Prices: Expectations Slightly More Pessimistic

The S&P/Case-Shiller Home Price Index shows that housing prices in 20 U.S. metropolitan areas were down 19% in January 2009 compared to a year ago. Accordingly, in an April 6–9 survey, Gallup finds that Americans' outlook for home prices in their areas is slightly more pessimistic than it was a year ago. Fewer Americans now expect housing prices to increase over the next 12 months (22%) than did so in April 2008 (29%), and more expect them to stay the same or decrease (76% vs. 69%).

Consumers' housing-price expectations in 2008 and 2009 stand in sharp contrast to those of the three previous years, when at least half of Americans expected housing prices to increase and fewer than one in five expected them to decrease.

Housing-Price Expectations Over Next 12 Months

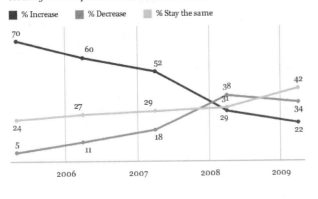

■ % Increase   ■ % Decrease   ▒ % Stay the same

Survey Methods

Results are based on telephone interviews with 1,027 national adults, aged 18 and older, conducted April 6–9, 2009. For results based on the total sample of national adults, one can say with 95% confidence that the maximum margin of sampling error is ±3 percentage points.

Interviews are conducted with respondents on land-line telephones (for respondents with a land-line telephone) and cellular phones (for respondents who are cell-phone only).

In addition to sampling error, question wording and practical difficulties in conducting surveys can introduce error or bias into the findings of public opinion polls.

April 17, 2009

OBAMA AVERAGES 63% APPROVAL IN HIS FIRST QUARTER
Highest first-quarter average since 1977

by Jeffrey M. Jones, Gallup Poll Managing Editor

Barack Obama's first quarter in office concludes on Sunday, and during this early stage of his presidency he has averaged a solid 63% job approval, reaching as high as 69% in the initial days of his presidency and falling as low as 59% on a few occasions.

Barack Obama's Job Approval Ratings During His First Quarter in Office

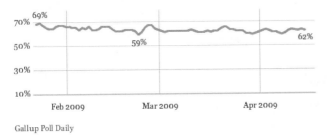

Gallup Poll Daily

Obama's 63% first-quarter average matches the historical average of 63% for elected presidents' first quarters since 1953. However, it is the fourth highest for a newly elected president since that time, and the highest since Jimmy Carter's 69% in 1977. The historical first-quarter average includes two presidents whose scores exceeded 70% (John Kennedy's 74% and Dwight Eisenhower's 71%).

Presidents' First-Quarter Approval Averages
Presidents elected to their first terms

President	Dates	Average	Number of measurements
Eisenhower	Jan 20-Apr 19, 1953	71%	4
Kennedy	Jan 20-Apr 19, 1961	74%	3
Nixon	Jan 20-Apr 19, 1969	62%	5
Carter	Jan 20-Apr 19, 1977	69%	7
Reagan	Jan 20-Apr 19, 1981	60%	5
G.H.W. Bush	Jan 20-Apr 19, 1989	57%	4
Clinton	Jan 20-Apr 19, 1993	55%	6
G.W. Bush	Jan 20-Apr 19, 2001	58%	7
Obama	Jan 20-Apr 19, 2009	63%	81

The average for all presidents' first quarters since World War II—both presidents who were elected and those who took office after the death or resignation of their predecessors—is slightly higher, at 66%. Harry Truman (87%) and Lyndon Johnson (76%) are two presidents who came into office mid-term and had very high initial approval ratings.

From a broader historical perspective, Obama's 63% quarterly average is well above the historical norm for all approval ratings, regardless of presidential quarter. It ranks in the 74th percentile of all presidential quarters since 1945, and is significantly better than the 54% average rating for all presidential quarters.

Looking Ahead

Obama's job approval rating has not shown much variation to date, generally holding steady in the low 60% range. While such presidential "honeymoons" do not last forever, to the extent history is a guide, Obama's healthy ratings can be expected to persist for at least another quarter.

Six of the last 11 presidents saw essentially no change in their approval ratings from the first to the second quarter in office. The ones who did see significant movement tended to start out with ratings that were higher (Truman and Carter) or lower (George H.W. Bush) than the norm.

Gerald Ford and Bill Clinton both saw rather abrupt ends to their honeymoons. Ford's controversial pardon of Nixon sent his approval ratings plummeting. An early September 1974 poll (conducted mostly before Ford pardoned Nixon on Sept. 8) measured a 66% approval rating for Ford. By the next poll, Ford's approval rating was down to 50%, and continued declining thereafter.

Clinton's 55% first-quarter average is the lowest for a recent president, and, after a number of controversial actions, his approval rating sank to 44% in his second quarter in office.

Changes in Presidential Job Approval Averages From First to Second Quarter

President	First-quarter average	Second-quarter average	Change (in percentage points)
Truman	87%	82%	-5
Eisenhower	71%	72%	+1
Kennedy	74%	76%	+2
Johnson	76%	76%	0
Nixon	62%	62%	0
Ford	59%	44%	-15
Carter	69%	64%	-5
Reagan	60%	61%	+1
G.H.W. Bush	57%	64%	+7
Clinton	55%	44%	-11
G.W. Bush	58%	56%	-2

There is not a typical pattern as to when honeymoons end. Several presidents who did not show declining approval ratings in their second quarter in office did so by their third quarter, but others' ratings held steady for the better part of their first year. Still others, including both Bushes, saw increases in their approval ratings after international crises.

Implications

President Obama is off to a solid start as president, as far as his job approval ratings are concerned. His 63% first-quarter average is better than the averages of each of his four predecessors, and the fourth best since 1953. Perhaps the biggest legislative accomplishment of his first quarter has been the passage of the economic stimulus bill. In the second quarter, Congress will likely begin work in earnest on his proposed budget. How that process plays out, whether the economy shows definite signs of improvement, and how well Obama deals with ongoing international challenges, will determine whether his ratings stay strong or begin to show decline.

Survey Methods

Results are based on aggregated telephone interviews with approximately 500 national adults, aged 18 and older, conducted each day from Jan. 21–April 15, 2009, as part of Gallup Poll Daily tracking. For results based on the total sample of national adults, one can say with 95% confidence that the maximum margin of sampling error is ±3 percentage points.

Interviews are conducted with respondents on land-line telephones (for respondents with a land-line telephone) and cellular phones (for respondents who are cell-phone only).

In addition to sampling error, question wording and practical difficulties in conducting surveys can introduce error or bias into the findings of public opinion polls.

April 17, 2009

REPUBLICANS AND DEMOCRATS SWAP VIEWS ON BERNANKE

Democrats' confidence in Fed chairman has surged, while Republicans' has faded

by Lydia Saad, Gallup Poll Senior Editor

Despite Federal Reserve Chairman Ben Bernanke's solid roots in the Bush administration, new Gallup polling finds 64% of Democrats nationwide feeling confident in Bernanke's input on the economy, compared with only 36% of Republicans. This is a complete reversal of the Fed chairman's image among partisans a year ago, under President Bush, when Republicans had the greater confidence in Bernanke, 61% vs. 40%.

Confidence in Ben Bernanke on the Economy -- by Party ID

Please tell me how much confidence you have in each [person or group] to do or to recommend the right thing for the economy -- a great deal, a fair amount, only a little, or almost none. How about Federal Reserve Chairman Ben Bernanke?

% Great deal/Fair amount of confidence

Bernanke's image among independents has been much more stable. Just under half of independents in both 2008 and 2009 have said they have a great deal or fair amount of confidence in Bernanke "to do or to recommend the right thing for the economy."

The latest results are based on Gallup's annual Economy and Personal Finance survey, conducted April 6–9.

Though appointed by the president, the Federal Reserve chairman heads an independent agency that is not part of a presidential administration. Indeed, the last three chairmen—Bernanke, Alan Greenspan, and Paul Volcker—worked with both Republican and Democratic presidents. Nevertheless, the Gallup Poll trends suggest that Americans view the Fed chairman as another member of the president's economic team. Bernanke was appointed by President George W. Bush in early 2006, and received solid support from rank-and-file Republicans as long as Bush was president. However, now that Barack Obama is president, Democrats widely applaud Bernanke's performance, while Republican support for him has dropped substantially.

The net effect of the stability in views among independents, combined with the switch in confidence ratings among Republicans and Democrats, is that Bernanke's overall economic confidence rating is about the same now (49%) as it was in 2008. In fact, each year since 2007, Gallup has found about half of Americans saying they have a great deal or fair amount of confidence in Bernanke on the economy.

As reported on Gallup.com Monday, Americans' confidence in Bernanke on the economy is similar to their confidence in Treasury Secretary Tim Geithner, as well as in the Democratic leaders in Congress; it exceeds confidence in the Republican leaders in Congress, but lags well behind confidence in Obama.

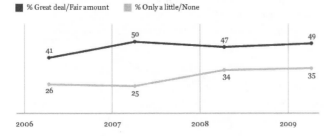

Confidence in Ben Bernanke on the Economy

■ % Great deal/Fair amount ▨ % Only a little/None

Please tell me how much confidence you have in each to do or to recommend the right thing for the economy -- a great deal, a fair amount, only a little, or almost none. How about -- [ROTATED]?

	Great deal	Fair amount	Only a little/ Almost none	No opinion
	%	%	%	%
President Barack Obama	38	33	29	*
The Democratic leaders in Congress	10	41	45	3
Treasury Secretary Tim Geithner	9	38	39	14
Federal Reserve Chairman Ben Bernanke	7	42	35	17
The Republican leaders in Congress	5	33	58	4

* Less than 0.5%

April 6-9, 2009

Bottom Line

Bernanke was tapped to head the Federal Reserve for a four-year term by Republican President George W. Bush in 2006, and prior to that he was chairman of Bush's Council of Economic Advisers. Not surprisingly, in his first three years as Fed chairman, from 2006 through 2008, Republicans had much more confidence in Bernanke than did Democrats.

Now, with a Democrat in the Oval Office, the pattern has switched. Either Americans are under the mistaken impression that Bernanke is a member of the Obama administration, or they simply perceive that he is supportive of Obama's economic recovery agenda, and therefore Republicans and Democrats view his work on the economy accordingly.

Survey Methods

Results are based on telephone interviews with 1,027 national adults, aged 18 and older, conducted April 6–9, 2009. For results based on the total sample of national adults, one can say with 95% confidence that the maximum margin of sampling error is ±3 percentage points.

Interviews are conducted with respondents on land-line telephones (for respondents with a land-line telephone) and cellular phones (for respondents who are cell-phone only).

In addition to sampling error, question wording and practical difficulties in conducting surveys can introduce error or bias into the findings of public opinion polls.

April 20, 2009
BIG GOV'T. STILL VIEWED AS GREATER THREAT THAN BIG BUSINESS
Democrats' views have changed, now view big business as greater threat

by Jeffrey M. Jones, Gallup Poll Managing Editor

Gallup's recent update of its long-standing trend question on whether big business, big labor, or big government will be the biggest threat to the country in the future finds Americans still viewing big government as the most serious threat. However, compared to Gallup's last pre-financial-crisis measurement in December 2006, more now see big business and fewer see big government as the greater threat.

In your opinion, which of the following will be the biggest threat to the country in the future -- big business, big labor, or big government?

■ 2006 Dec 11-14 ▨ 2009 Mar 27-29

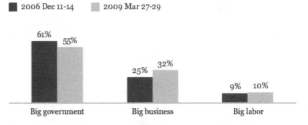

These shifts in attitudes have occurred even as the government has taken on an expanded role in regulating U.S. financial institutions in response to the financial crisis, under the Bush and Obama administrations.

Americans' responses to these developments vary according to their partisan affiliation.

Now, 80% of Republicans view big government as the biggest threat to the country, up from 68% in December 2006. At the same time, Democrats' perceptions of the greater threat are completely reversed. In December 2006, 55% of Democrats said big government posed the greater threat, while 32% said big business did. In the latest poll, a majority of Democrats now view big business as the greater threat (52%) while only about one in three think big government is.

Independents' views did not change much over this period, with solid majorities in both polls saying big government is the greater threat.

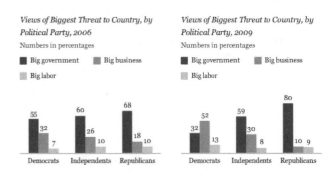

Views of Biggest Threat to Country, by Political Party, 2006
Numbers in percentages
■ Big government ■ Big business
▨ Big labor

Views of Biggest Threat to Country, by Political Party, 2009
Numbers in percentages
■ Big government ■ Big business
▨ Big labor

Longer-Term Trend

Gallup's history of asking this question dates back to 1965. Since that time, Americans have always viewed big government as posing the greatest threat of the three institutions tested, although the percentage naming it has varied over time.

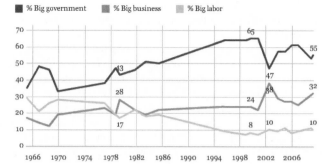

In your opinion, which of the following will be the biggest threat to the country in the future -- big business, big labor, or big government?

■ % Big government   ■ % Big business   ■ % Big labor

Survey Methods

Results are based on telephone interviews with 1,007 national adults, aged 18 and older, conducted March 27–29, 2009. For results based on the total sample of national adults, one can say with 95% confidence that the maximum margin of sampling error is ±3 percentage points.

Interviews are conducted with respondents on land-line telephones (for respondents with a land-line telephone) and cellular phones (for respondents who are cell-phone only).

In addition to sampling error, question wording and practical difficulties in conducting surveys can introduce error or bias into the findings of public opinion polls.

From the 1960s through the early 1980s, half or less of Americans named big government as the greatest threat. That view expanded greatly in the 1990s—reaching a high of 65% in 1999 and 2000—as concerns about the power of big labor greatly subsided.

In 2002, after the wave of accounting scandals at companies like Enron and WorldCom, opinions shifted, and the percentage mentioning big business as the greatest threat peaked at 38%, while concern about big government dipped below the majority level for the first time since 1981.

As the accounting crisis faded in people's memories, Americans again became more concerned with the reach of government (reaching 61% in 2005 and 2006), until the recent financial crisis caused more to fear the power of big business.

Implications

A primary thrust of the American political tradition is a fear of centralized government with too much power. And the U.S. capitalist economic system has given businesses wide latitude to operate with minimal government interference. But those values were put to the test last year as the imminent collapse of several major U.S. corporations threatened to drive the country into an economic depression. The government responded by infusing some of these failing companies with cash and in some cases taking on significant ownership in the companies.

Gallup has now conducted two post-crisis updates of this question (Dec. 4–7, 2008, and March 27–29, 2009) and has found similar results each time, both overall (In December, 53% said big government was the greater threat and 31% said big business was) and by party (there have been some minor changes since December as Republicans have become slightly more likely to identify big government and Democrats slightly more likely to identify big business as the greater threat).

Thus, the change in administrations from Republican to Democratic and the government's additional actions to stabilize failing companies or address other economic problems since early December has not caused fear of big government to escalate any further beyond what was the case late last year.

Given the timing of the December poll, it is not clear whether the initial shift came in response to the financial bailout from last fall or perhaps was a more basic partisan reaction to the election of a Democratic president in November. Whatever the cause, Republicans have grown somewhat more concerned about the threat of big government and Democrats have grown more concerned about the threat of big business, but Americans as a whole still rate big government as the greater threat.

April 20, 2009
AMERICANS INCREASINGLY CONCERNED ABOUT RETIREMENT INCOME
Expected reliance on 401(k) plans shows major drop from last year

by Frank Newport, Gallup Poll Editor in Chief

For the first time this decade, a majority of non-retired Americans, 52%, doubt they will have enough money to live comfortably once they retire; only 41% say they will. In 2002, by contrast, 59% of non-retirees were confident that they would have enough retirement income to live comfortably.

When you retire, do you think you will have enough money to live comfortably, or not?

Based on non-retirees

■ % Yes, enough   ■ % No, not enough   ■ % No opinion

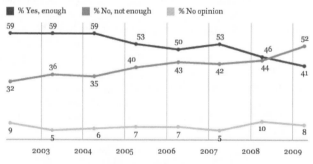

This year's update, included as part of Gallup's annual Economy and Personal Finance survey conducted April 6–9, also shows an 18-point drop in this measure among non-retirees compared to just five years ago. This marks the first time since Gallup has been tracking the measure that a majority of those not retired say they will *not* have enough money to live comfortably in retirement.

The reasons for this rising concern about retirement income become clearer when one examines trends in how much non-retirees expect to rely on each of 10 income sources in retirement.

One of the biggest changes concerns non-retirees' views of their **401(k) and other tax-exempt plans such as IRAs and Keogh plans**. In Gallup's first reading of this measure in 2001, almost 6 out

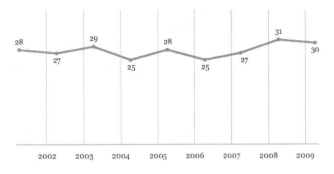

How much do you expect to rely on Social Security when you retire?
% Major source of income

28   27   29   25   28   25   27   31   30

2002   2003   2004   2005   2006   2007   2008   2009

of 10 non-retirees said these would be a major source of income when they retired. That percentage has fluctuated since then, but this year's 42% reading is the lowest Gallup has measured. It also represents a drop of 12 points since last year. There is little doubt that this reflects the major drop in the stock market over the last year, and the resulting "statement shock" that has confronted many workers when they open up their 401(k) statements and see the major decline in their overall value.

There has been a more modest decline since 2001 in perceived reliance on **individual stock or stock mutual fund investments**. Never high to begin with (in 2001, 24% said these would be a major source of retirement income), this year's percentage is the same as last year's (17%)—which is the low reading for the decade.

Perceived reliance on a **work-sponsored pension plan** is also the lowest Gallup has measured. Just 24% of non-retirees say this will be a major source of retirement income. That can be compared to 34% in 2001, and 31% as recently as two years ago.

Given the decline in the value of other investments, one might expect that more Americans would say they are going to rely on **Social Security** as a major source of retirement income. But that has not occurred. The 30% of Americans who say Social Security will be a major source of income is actually down one percentage point from last year, and not substantially different from what has been measured across the previous years of this decade.

Of interest is the slow but steady increase in the percentage of non-retired Americans who say they will rely on **part-time work** in their retirement. Only 10% said part-time work would be a major source of retirement income in 2001, but that number has more than doubled to 22% today.

Implications

It is probably not surprising that Americans have a more pessimistic attitude about funding their retirement now than they did a few years ago. Americans have been told repeatedly in recent years that Social Security alone will not provide enough to live on—and even that the Social Security system will eventually run out of money. Fewer Americans today enjoy the potential benefit of a traditional pension plan. Thus, Americans have come to realize that more of their retirement income will need to come from their own resources.

And those resources, to the extent that they have been invested in stocks, are way down in value this year compared to years past. This is reflected in the finding that Americans' expected reliance on their 401(k) plans as a major income source has dropped signifi-

cantly. Since there has been no concomitant increase in expected reliance on other income sources (other than perhaps part-time work), it is almost inevitable that there would be increased concern on the part of non-retirees that they will not have enough money to live comfortably in retirement.

It's worth noting that despite the sharp decline in expected reliance on 401(k) and other retirement savings plans, these remain at the top of the list when Americans are asked how much of a source each of the 10 different income streams will be in their retirement years. This signals that expected comfort in retirement could increase if the stock market continues to pull out of its current slump in the months ahead. Still, given the maxim "once burned, twice shy," many Americans may never again believe that their personal savings plans are going to grow inevitably and steadily in the years before they retire, leaving open the possibility that their worries will continue regardless of external circumstances.

Survey Methods

Results are based on telephone interviews with 676 non-retirees, aged 18 and older, conducted April 6–9, 2009. For results based on this sample, one can say with 95% confidence that the maximum margin of sampling error is ±4 percentage points.

Interviews are conducted with respondents on land-line telephones (for respondents with a land-line telephone) and cellular phones (for respondents who are cell-phone only).

In addition to sampling error, question wording and practical difficulties in conducting surveys can introduce error or bias into the findings of public opinion polls.

April 21, 2009
IN U.S., OUTLOOK FOR ENVIRONMENTAL QUALITY IMPROVING
Forty-one percent say it is getting better, up from 26% last year

by Jeffrey M. Jones, Gallup Poll Managing Editor

With Earth Day approaching, Americans still on balance believe the quality of the environment in the U.S. is getting worse rather than better; however, their outlook is significantly brighter now than a year ago.

Right now, do you think the quality of the environment in the country as a whole is getting better or getting worse?

■ % Getting better   ▨ % Getting worse

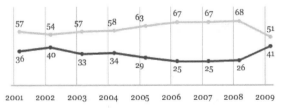

57   54   57   58   63   67   67   68   51

36   40   33   34   29   25   25   26   41

2001   2002   2003   2004   2005   2006   2007   2008   2009

These results are based on Gallup's annual Environment poll, conducted March 5–8. This year's poll marks a new high in the percentage of Americans saying the environment is getting better, one percentage point above the 40% recorded in 2002.

The increased optimism about the quality of the environment is likely an outgrowth of the change in presidential administrations from George W. Bush's to Barack Obama's. Obama has promised to increase U.S. efforts to protect the environment, and as recently as last week (but after the poll was conducted), the Environmental Protection Agency ruled that greenhouse gases endanger public health. This ruling allows the EPA to increase regulations to limit greenhouse gas emissions. Congress is also considering major environmental legislation.

Both Democrats and independents have shown significant increases since last year in the percentage who believe the environment is getting better. There has been only a slight improvement in Republicans' outlook.

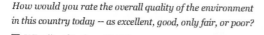

Environment Getting Better or Worse, by Party Affiliation, 2008

Environment Getting Better or Worse, by Party Affiliation, 2009

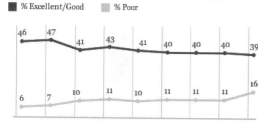

At the same time that Americans' optimism about the future of environmental quality is improving, their views of present conditions are little changed from recent years. If anything, they are slightly worse, as 16% now describe conditions as poor, up from 11% last year and the highest in the nine-year history of the Environment poll. The 39% who say conditions are excellent or good is essentially the same as what Gallup has found the last five years.

How would you rate the overall quality of the environment in this country today -- as excellent, good, only fair, or poor?

Consistent with prior years' surveys, Republicans and Democrats have diverging views of the overall health of the environment—55% of Republicans say it is excellent or good, more than twice the number of Democrats (26%) who say the same. Independents' views are almost precisely midway between the other two party groups' views.

Implications

Americans show increased optimism about the future quality of the environment, but it will take more than just the election of an environmentally friendly president for the public to begin to perceive that

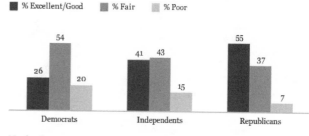

Ratings of Environmental Quality in the United States, by Party Affiliation

March 5-8, 2009

the current condition of the environment is actually improving. The government is likely to take significant steps toward protecting the environment in the coming months, and in future years, Americans will judge whether those efforts have had their intended effect on environmental quality.

Survey Methods

Results are based on telephone interviews with 1,012 national adults, aged 18 and older, conducted March 5–8, 2009. For results based on the total sample of national adults, one can say with 95% confidence that the maximum margin of sampling error is ±3 percentage points.

Interviews are conducted with respondents on land-line telephones (for respondents with a land-line telephone) and cellular phones (for respondents who are cell-phone only).

In addition to sampling error, question wording and practical difficulties in conducting surveys can introduce error or bias into the findings of public opinion polls.

April 22, 2009
AMERICANS HAVE WIDESPREAD PERSONAL FINANCIAL CONCERNS
No single problem dominates when they are asked about their personal financial situations

by Frank Newport , Gallup Poll Editor in Chief

Americans today are worried about a wide variety of personal financial problems, rather than—as has been the case within the past year—indicating high levels of worry about one or two specific problems. The top problems Americans name when asked about the most important financial problem facing their families include "lack of money" (15%), the cost of owning or renting a home (12%), healthcare (11%), jobs (10%), and too much debt (10%).

The biggest change over the last year in Americans' views of their personal financial problems has come in the ebb and flow of concerns about energy prices and inflation.

Last July, with gas prices hovering at $4 a gallon or more in most places across the country, 29% of Americans said their biggest financial problem was the cost of gas, followed by another 18% who said it was the high cost of living. Now, with gas prices having settled back down to around $2 a gallon, only 3% of Americans name gas prices as their No. 1 financial problem, and just 6% mention inflation.

What is the most important financial problem facing your family today?

	Apr 6-9, 2009
	%
Lack of money/Low wages	15
Cost of owning/renting a home	12
Healthcare costs	11
Unemployment/Loss of job	10
Too much debt/Not enough money to pay debts	10
College expenses	6
High cost of living/Inflation	6
Retirement savings	4
Stock market/Investments	4
Taxes	3
Lack of savings	3
Energy costs/Oil and gas prices	3
State of the economy	2
Transportation/Commuting costs	2
Interest rates	1
Controlling spending	1
Social Security	*
Other	2
None	15
No opinion	3

* Less than 0.5%
Note: Percentages add to more than 100% due to multiple responses.

Percentage of Americans Mentioning Energy Costs/Oil and Gas Prices as Their Most Important Personal Financial Problem
February 2008-April 2009 trend

No single specific financial problem has come forward to take the place of gas prices in the current economic climate. Rather, Americans appear to have a diffuse set of issues—the most prevalent of which revolve around the simple lack of money.

Implications

The Obama administration and Congress continue to face the daunting challenge of fixing the nation's financial problems—and in so doing, to help jump-start consumers' willingness to increase their spending and other economic activity. The data from Gallup's annual Economy and Personal Finance poll reviewed here show there is no single silver bullet that is likely to bolster Americans' personal financial optimism. When asked to name the most important personal financial problem facing their families, Americans offer up a wide variety of concerns—most of which stem from the obvious and simple fact that they do not have enough money.

The percentage of Americans who specifically tell Gallup interviewers that jobs are the most important problem is relatively small (10%). Likewise, just 12% of Americans mention the burden of housing costs, and 11% mention healthcare costs. Each of these has been or will be the focus of specific programs aimed at alleviating

Americans' financial concerns. Fixing each of these may in fact ultimately have a salutary effect on Americans' overall economic angst, yet none of them appears to be a cure-all.

Survey Methods

Results are based on telephone interviews with 1,027 national adults, aged 18 and older, conducted April 6–9, 2009. For results based on the total sample of national adults, one can say with 95% confidence that the maximum margin of sampling error is ±3 percentage points.

Interviews are conducted with respondents on land-line telephones (for respondents with a land-line telephone) and cellular phones (for respondents who are cell-phone only).

In addition to sampling error, question wording and practical difficulties in conducting surveys can introduce error or bias into the findings of public opinion polls.

April 22, 2009
HIGH EXPECTATIONS FOR OBAMA ON THE ENVIRONMENT
Almost 8 in 10 Americans believe he will do good job of protecting environment

by Frank Newport, Gallup Poll Editor in Chief

President Barack Obama has entered the presidency with much higher public expectations for him on the environment than met George W. Bush eight years ago. Seventy-nine percent of Americans currently say Obama will do a good job of protecting the environment, compared to just 51% who felt that way about Bush in March 2001.

Do you think George W. Bush/Barack Obama will do a good job or a poor job in handling each of the following issues as president? How about -- protecting the nation's environment?

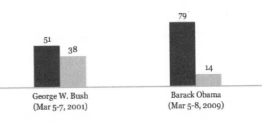

It's important to note that Bush in March 2001 and Obama in March 2009 had nearly identical overall job approval ratings, Obama at 65% and Bush at 63%. This suggests that the difference in public perceptions of the two presidents' potential to protect the environment is not just an artifact of their overall standing in the public's mind, but rather represents independent (and divergent) evaluations on the environmental issue.

Obama's positive image on the environment is so high in part because he gets unusually positive ratings from Republicans on the issue.

A remarkable 65% of Republicans in the March 2009 poll said Obama would do a good job of handling the environment, along with

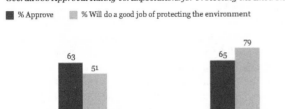

Overall Job Approval Rating vs. Expectations for Protecting the Environment

■ % Approve   ▨ % Will do a good job of protecting the environment

George W. Bush (March 2001)   Barack Obama (March 2009)

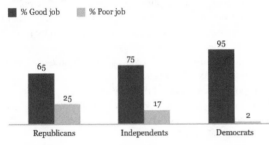

Do you think Barack Obama will do a good job or a poor job in ...
protecting the nation's environment?

By political party

■ % Good job   ▨ % Poor job

Republicans   Independents   Democrats

March 5-8, 2009

75% of independents and 95% of Democrats. By contrast, only 36% of Democrats back in 2001 felt that Bush would do a good job of protecting the environment, along with 45% of independents and 72% of Republicans.

The unusual nature of Republicans' positive perceptions of Obama on the environment is highlighted when those perceptions are contrasted with Republicans' positive ratings of his overall job performance. Only 32% of Republicans in the Environmental poll approved of the job Obama is doing as president, less than half the percentage of Republicans who (in the same poll) said Obama would do a good job of protecting the environment.

It is also worth noting that there was very little difference in the overall salience of the environment to Americans between March 2001 and March 2009, as measured by their top-of-mind mentions of the environment as the nation's top problem. In both 2001 and 2009, an identical 2% named the environment or pollution as the most important problem facing the country.

Bottom Line

The American public has high expectations for President Obama's ability to deal with the environment. Almost 8 out of 10 say Obama will do a good job of protecting the environment, much higher than the percentage who felt this way about Bush shortly after he took office in 2001. Obama's ability to follow through on these expectations, however, could be hampered by the fact that Americans' priorities at this point are more focused on the economy than on the environment.

Survey Methods

Results are based on telephone interviews with 1,012 national adults, aged 18 and older, conducted March 5–8, 2009. For results based on the total sample of national adults, one can say with 95% confidence that the maximum margin of sampling error is ±3 percentage points.

Interviews are conducted with respondents on land-line telephones (for respondents with a land-line telephone) and cellular phones (for respondents who are cell-phone only).

In addition to sampling error, question wording and practical difficulties in conducting surveys can introduce error or bias into the findings of public opinion polls.

April 23, 2009
AMERICANS STEADY IN BACKING FRIENDLIER U.S.-CUBA RELATIONS
Majority support for diplomatic relations, fewer trade and travel restrictions

by Lymari Morales, Gallup Poll Staff Writer

As President Barack Obama weighs the future of U.S.-Cuba relations, Americans continue to express support for closer ties. Since 1999, a majority of Americans have consistently said they favor re-establishing U.S. diplomatic relations with Cuba—including 60% in a new Gallup Poll conducted after Obama's decision last week to relax some restrictions.

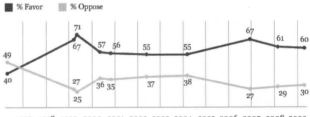

Do you favor or oppose re-establishing U.S. diplomatic relations with Cuba?
Gallup trend since 1996

■ % Favor   ▨ % Oppose

1997 1998 1999 2000 2001 2002 2003 2004 2005 2006 2007 2008 2009

While Obama's move did not go as far as re-establishing full diplomatic relations with Cuba, his decision to grant Cuban-Americans rights to travel freely to Cuba and to send remittances there, and to give U.S. telecommunications companies the right to pursue business there represent a first step. On Sunday at the Summit of the Americas in Trinidad and Tobago, Obama said that America's existing policy toward Cuba isn't working and that he would welcome reciprocal moves by Cuba to put the two nations on a path toward better relations.

Over the past decade, Gallup has found Americans remarkably steadfast in their views about U.S. relations with Cuba—particularly in regard to the U.S. trade embargo. Since 1999, Americans have been more likely to support than oppose the U.S. government's ending its trade embargo against Cuba—with support narrowly ranging between 48% and 51%, including 51% in the new poll.

Americans more widely support ending restrictions on travel to Cuba—with 64% in favor.

Americans' views toward U.S.-Cuba policy remain divergent across political and ideological lines. Majorities of Democrats and liberals support re-establishing diplomatic relations and ending the trade embargo, while Republicans and conservatives tend to be far less supportive. There is more agreement on ending travel restrictions, something that a majority of each group supports.

Apart from their diplomatic relations, do you favor or oppose the United States government ending its trade embargo against Cuba?

Asked of a half sample

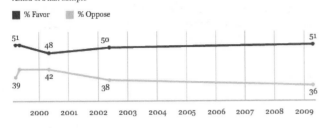

Apart from their diplomatic relations, do you favor or oppose the United States government ending its restrictions on Americans traveling to Cuba?

Asked of a half sample

Gallup Poll, April 20-21, 2009

Americans' Views on Easing Restrictions on Cuba

By party and ideology

	% Favor	% Oppose
Re-establishing diplomatic relations		
Republicans	42	50
Independents	62	28
Democrats	72	17
Conservatives	43	47
Moderates	69	22
Liberals	75	18
Ending the trade embargo		
Republicans	44	47
Independents	56	35
Democrats	54	29
Conservatives	37	50
Moderates	55	33
Liberals	73	18
Ending travel restrictions		
Republicans	57	36
Independents	60	29
Democrats	74	19
Conservatives	54	38
Moderates	74	19
Liberals	70	27

Gallup Poll, April 20-21, 2009

Overall, Gallup Polls regarding U.S. relations with Cuba find Americans generally accepting of the U.S. taking a friendlier stance toward the island nation, as has been true over the past decade. However, Americans do distinguish between different specific policies toward Cuba. The fact that a solid majority support re-establishing U.S. diplomatic relations with Cuba—and have consistently done so

for the past decade—suggests that Obama's first step in this direction was likely well-received by the American public. Moves toward making it easier for all Americans to travel to Cuba will likely find majority support among the American public as well. Ending the trade embargo will be a tougher sell and likely a partisan battle.

Editorial note: While readers may be interested in Cuban-Americans' views on U.S.-Cuba relations, they represent a percentage of the overall U.S. population too small to be separated out in a standard nationwide poll such as this one.

Survey Methods

Results are based on telephone interviews with 1,051 national adults, aged 18 and older, conducted April 20–21, 2009. For results based on the total sample of national adults, one can say with 95% confidence that the maximum margin of sampling error is ±3 percentage points.

For results based on the half-samples of 524 national adults in Form A and 527 national adults in Form B, the maximum margin of sampling error is ±4 percentage points.

Interviews are conducted with respondents on land-line telephones (for respondents with a land-line telephone) and cellular phones (for respondents who are cell-phone only).

In addition to sampling error, question wording and practical difficulties in conducting surveys can introduce error or bias into the findings of public opinion polls.

April 23, 2009

AMERICANS' CONFIDENCE IN BANKS HITS NEW LOW

However, 58% express "a great deal" or "quite a lot" of confidence in their primary bank

by Dennis Jacobe, Gallup Chief Economist

As the Treasury and banking regulators prepare to provide a description of their banking "stress" tests on Friday and the results on May 4, the percentage of Americans saying they have a "great deal" or "quite a lot" of confidence in U.S. banks has fallen to 18%—down 14 percentage points from a June 2008 Gallup Poll and 23 points from a June 2007 poll.

Sharp Drop in Banking Confidence

Percentage saying they have "a great deal"/"quite a lot" of confidence in U.S. banks

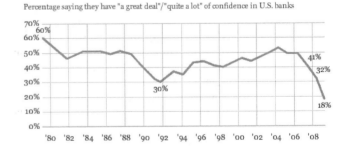

Confidence in U.S. Banking Takes a Plunge

New data from Gallup Poll Daily tracking, measured from April 6–19, show that one of the casualties of the ongoing financial crisis is the amount of confidence Americans have in U.S. banks. With only 5% expressing "a great deal" of confidence and 13% "quite a lot" of confidence, Americans' confidence in banking has now fallen to its lowest level since Gallup began asking about the subject in April 1979. The previous low of 30% confident was recorded during the 1990–91 recession and reflected the fallout associated with the S&L debacle of the late 1980s. More than one in three Americans currently say they have "very little" confidence in U.S. financial institutions.

Confidence in U.S. Financial Institutions or Banks, 2009

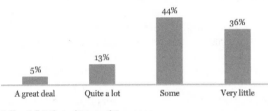

Gallup Poll Daily tracking, April 6-19, 2009

Most Still Have Confidence in Their Main Bank

Despite the precipitous nature of this general decline in banking confidence, many Americans continue to express confidence in the main or primary bank where they do most of their banking business. In fact, 25% say they have "a great deal" and 33% "quite a lot" of confidence in their main bank. Only about 1 in 10 Americans express "very little" confidence in the bank where they do most of their banking.

Confidence in Your Primary/Main Bank, 2009

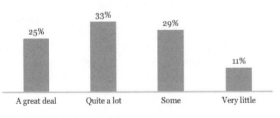

Gallup Poll Daily tracking, April 6-19, 2009

Such a finding is consistent with what Gallup has found in ratings of other areas such as education, healthcare, and crime. Americans generally rate their own local providers and institutions as much better than those in the broader United States.

Given the much higher confidence in Americans' own banks and the current trend toward re-intermediation resulting from savers "shifting to safety," it follows that more Americans intend to increase their money with their primary bank than to decrease it. In this regard, the poll shows that over the next three months, 29% of Americans say they plan to increase the money they have with their main bank while 9% say they intend to decrease their balances. And while 72% say they are "not at all likely" to switch their main bank in the next three months, 7% say they are likely to do so.

Commentary

The sharp drop in banking confidence over the past few years—and during the past year in particular—illustrates the enormous task fac-

Americans' Intentions Toward Their Primary Bank, 2009
Increase/Decrease money you have, Likelihood to switch

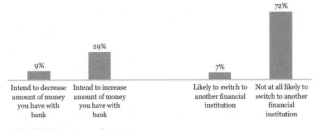

Gallup Poll Daily tracking, April 6-19, 2009

ing the Treasury, the Federal Reserve, and banking regulators in their efforts to restore trust in the U.S. banking system. Given this context, it may be good news that only 9% of Americans say they intend to decrease the money they have with their primary bank and only 7% say they are likely to switch to another primary bank. On the other hand, the transaction costs associated with switching banks remain high and consumers tend to be less likely to switch their primary bank than other banks they deal with, so these results could also be seen as not so good.

Needless to say, however, the way the banking "stress" tests are framed and interpreted over the next couple of weeks could be important to the confidence Americans have in individual banks and in U.S. banking as a whole. Increased federal deposit insurance and the willingness of the Fed and the Treasury to act to keep a major financial services firm from collapsing have created a strong safety net for today's depositors. Still, uninsured depositors and stockholders could flee banking institutions that are perceived as not having done well in the government's stress tests.

In a sense, these kinds of evaluations almost invite a rush to safety and soundness in the form of quality banks. On the other hand, this whole stress-test effort could, at least over time, have the salutary effect of starting to rebuild Americans' confidence in U.S. banking institutions as a whole—an essential first step in bringing the current financial crisis and associated credit crunch to an end.

Whatever happens, Gallup will continue to monitor and report on Americans' confidence in their banks and their intentions to change their deposits or switch banks in the weeks ahead.

Survey Methods

Results are based on telephone interviews with 1,730 national adults, aged 18 and older, conducted April 6–19, 2009, as part of Gallup Poll Daily tracking. For results based on the total sample of national adults, one can say with 95% confidence that the maximum margin of sampling error is ±3 percentage points.

Interviews are conducted with respondents on land-line telephones (for respondents with a land-line telephone) and cellular phones (for respondents who are cell-phone only).

In addition to sampling error, question wording and practical difficulties in conducting surveys can introduce error or bias into the findings of public opinion polls.

April 27, 2009

SLIM MAJORITY WANTS BUSH-ERA INTERROGATIONS INVESTIGATED

Majority says use of harsh techniques on terrorism suspects was justified

by Jeffrey M. Jones, Gallup Poll Managing Editor

A new Gallup Poll finds 51% of Americans in favor and 42% opposed to an investigation into the use of harsh interrogation techniques on terrorism suspects during the Bush administration. At the same time, 55% of Americans believe in retrospect that the use of the interrogation techniques was justified, while only 36% say it was not. Notably, a majority of those following the news about this matter "very closely" oppose an investigation and think the methods were justified.

Would you favor or oppose a government investigation into the use of harsh interrogation techniques of terrorism suspects?

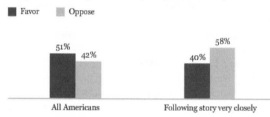

Gallup Poll Daily tracking, April 24-25, 2009

Based on what you know or have read, do you think the use of harsh interrogation techniques for terrorism suspects was justified or not justified?

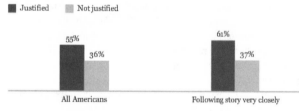

Gallup Poll Daily tracking, April 24-25, 2009

These results are based on an April 24–25 Gallup Poll. The Obama administration recently released documents that revealed the Bush administration's legal justification for using so-called "enhanced interrogation techniques" such as waterboarding and sleep deprivation that many consider to be torture. Congress followed that release by issuing a report saying Bush administration officials in fact authorized the use of such techniques.

The release of the documents was controversial, and now momentum is growing in Congress for an investigation into the Bush policy on interrogating terrorism suspects.

Sixty-one percent of Americans say they are following news about this issue closely, including 26% who are following it very closely. Republicans and Democrats are about equally likely to be paying close attention to this matter.

While a slim majority favors an investigation, on a relative basis the percentage is quite low because Americans are generally quite supportive of government probes into potential misconduct by public officials. In recent years, for example, Americans were far more likely to favor investigations into the firing of eight U.S. attorneys

(72%), government databases of telephone numbers dialed by Americans (62%), oil company profits (82%), and the government's response to Hurricane Katrina (70%).

Support for an inquiry into the Bush-era interrogation policy may be relatively limited because a majority of Americans believe the use of the techniques for questioning terrorism suspects was justified. Former Vice President Dick Cheney has probably been the most prominent person to argue that the information that may have been obtained from such practices kept Americans safe from further terrorist attacks. Cheney, not surprisingly, opposes an investigation.

To gain a better understanding of how Americans feel about the matter, Gallup combined the results of the questions on whether the techniques were justified and whether the government should investigate. All told, the greatest number of Americans, 30%, seem to agree with Cheney's position that the ends justified the means and that no investigation is necessary. Nearly as many (25%), though, would appear to side with many congressional Democrats who say the techniques should not have been used and an investigation is warranted. Twenty-three percent think the techniques were warranted yet still favor an investigation, while 10% think the methods should not have been used but nevertheless oppose an official inquiry.

Views on Harsh Interrogation of Terrorism Suspects

	Think use was justified	Think use was not justified
Favor an investigation	23%	25%
Oppose an investigation	30%	10%

Gallup Poll Daily tracking, April 24-25, 2009
Percentages show the percentage of all Americans who hold both views; 12% of Americans cannot be classified because they do not have an opinion on one or both questions.

If (as seems likely) the government does undertake an investigation, Gallup asked Americans which institution they would prefer conduct it. Given a choice among Congress, a bipartisan commission, or the Justice Department, 43% say they have no preference. Those who do have a preference are slightly more likely to prefer a bipartisan commission to the Justice Department, while relatively few say Congress.

Those who favor a probe are no different from the broader public in their preferences for who should conduct it.

Suppose there is an investigation into the use of harsh interrogation techniques of terrorism suspects. Which of the following would you most like to see conduct it, or don't you have a preference?

■ Bipartisan commission ■ Justice Department ■ Congress ■ No preference

All Americans: 25% 22% 8% 43%
Favor an investigation: 22% 25% 10% 42%

Gallup Poll Daily tracking, April 24-25, 2009

Implications

One of the key findings of this Gallup Poll is that a majority of Americans in retrospect believe the use of harsh interrogation techniques by the Bush administration was justified. Some of those who believe the techniques were justified still believe that an investigation into what transpired would be appropriate, but when all is said and done, just a bare majority of 51% of Americans support an investigation, while 42% oppose it.

President Obama did not call for an investigation when releasing the details of the Bush team's legal opinions on the use of harsh terrorism techniques, but seemed to leave open the possibility last week.

Survey Methods

Results are based on telephone interviews with 1,044 national adults, aged 18 and older, conducted April 24–25, 2009, as part of Gallup Poll Daily tracking. For results based on the total sample of national adults, one can say with 95% confidence that the maximum margin of sampling error is ±3 percentage points.

Interviews are conducted with respondents on land-line telephones (for respondents with a land-line telephone) and cellular phones (for respondents who are cell-phone only).

In addition to sampling error, question wording and practical difficulties in conducting surveys can introduce error or bias into the findings of public opinion polls.

April 27, 2009

IN U.S., 32% SAY SPENDING LESS IS THEIR "NEW NORMAL"

Six in 10 say they enjoy saving more than spending

by Frank Newport , Gallup Poll Editor in Chief

A new Gallup Poll finds that about a third of Americans, 32%, say they have been spending less in recent months, and that they intend to solidify this behavior as their "new, normal" pattern in the years ahead. Twenty-seven percent say they are saving more now and intend to make this their new, normal pattern in the years ahead.

Self-Reports in Spending and Saving

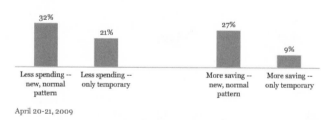

April 20-21, 2009

These findings help shed light on a key question relating to the long-term impact of the current recession. In the short term, consumer behavior has certainly changed, but to what degree will the spending and saving patterns of the average American be modified even after the recession is over?

It is difficult to project behavior with precision. Humans are not always able to predict accurately what they will do in the future, given the realities that many factors may change in ways not yet anticipated.

Still, the measure of consumer intentions provides a good starting point in the process of attempting to forecast consumer behavior

after the current recession fades away. To that end, Gallup's April 20–21 poll included questions asking Americans to indicate how they have modified their spending and saving behaviors in recent months, and to project how likely it is that these changed behaviors will become permanent. The results show that a slight majority of Americans believe—at least at this point—that they will normalize new spending or saving behavior into a fixed pattern in future years.

Spending

Fifty-three percent of Americans say they have been spending less in recent months compared to what they used to. This will come as no surprise given the widely documented downturn in retail sales since the recession began, and trends evident in Gallup's Daily Consumer spending measure. Thirty percent of Americans say they have been spending about the same in recent months. A perhaps-surprising 17% report spending *more* now than they used to. (Gallup did not probe for reasons why Americans' spending or saving habits may have changed.)

In general, would you say you have been spending -- [ROTATED: more money, the same amount, (or) less money] -- in recent months than you used to?

(If spending more money or less money) Just your best guess, do you think this change in your spending habits -- [ROTATED: will become your new, normal pattern for years ahead (or) is just a temporary change in your spending patterns]?

COMBINED RESULTS	Apr 20-21, 2009
Spending more money	17%
-- Will become new, normal pattern	6%
-- Temporary change in spending patterns	11%
Spending same amount of money	30%
Spending less money	53%
-- Will become new, normal pattern	32%
-- Temporary change in spending patterns	21%
No opinion	*

* Less than 0.5%

The majority of those spending less say this will become their new, normal pattern for years to come. This yields the aforementioned 32% of all Americans for whom, at least based on current projections, spending less will become a new way of life. This is offset to a small degree by the 6% of Americans who say they have been spending more in recent months and that they will make this their new, normal pattern in the years ahead.

Saving

Overall, results are mixed when Americans are asked about their recent changes in saving. Thirty-six percent say they have been saving more in recent months. But almost as many, 32%, say they are saving less. Although there has been much speculation that Americans have become more saving-oriented, these results show that many Americans apparently have not had the luxury of being able to increase their saving rate in the current recessionary environment.

Would you say you have been saving -- [ROTATED: more money, the same amount, (or) less money] -- in recent months than you used to?

(If saving more money or less money) Just your best guess, do you think this change in your saving habits -- [ROTATED: will become your new, normal pattern for years ahead (or) is just a temporary change in your saving patterns]?

COMBINED RESULTS	Apr 20-21, 2009
Saving more money	36%
-- Will become new, normal pattern	27%
-- Temporary change in saving patterns	9%
Saving same amount of money	31%
Saving less money	32%
-- Will become new, normal pattern	10%
-- Temporary change in saving patterns	22%
No opinion	1%

By a 3-to-1 ratio, those who are now saving more say this will become a new, normal pattern. This constitutes 27% of the total population. This in turn is counterbalanced by the much smaller 10% of Americans who say they are saving *less* now and that this will become a new normal.

Putting it Together

All in all, 51% of Americans project that they are going to settle into a new, normal pattern relating to *either* spending or saving. Within this universe, a group of significant interest is those who say they are going to be not only spending less in the years ahead but also saving more—behaviors that would mark them as true exemplars of the "new frugality."

The current survey results suggest that this group is actually a fairly small minority, constituting just 15% of the adult population. Translated into millions of people, this is not an insignificant number—but certainly not a dominant end result of the recession.

Another 16% of Americans say spending less will settle in as their new, normal behavior—but they do not think they will at the same time manage to save more. Eleven percent say they will be saving more—but not managing to spend less.

Spending and Saving Patterns
All numbers in this chart represent % of national adults

	New, normal behavior: spending more	New, normal behavior: spending less	No new, normal behavior relating to spending
New, normal behavior: saving more	1%	15%	10%
New, normal behavior: saving less	1%	4%	5%
No new, normal behavior relating to saving	3%	12%	46%

April 20-21, 2009

Are You the Spending or the Saving Kind?

From time to time in recent years, Gallup has asked Americans whether they are the type of person who more enjoys spending or more enjoys saving.

The results prior to this year have been fairly consistent, with a slight edge in the direction of those who say they enjoy saving money more.

This year, the "saving money" edge has increased, so that there is now a 22-point gap between those who say they enjoy saving money more (59%) and those who say they enjoy spending money more (37%).

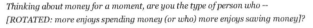

Thinking about money for a moment, are you the type of person who -- [ROTATED: more enjoys spending money (or who) more enjoys saving money]?

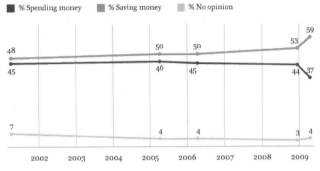

This question focuses on a mindset rather than self-reports of behavior. As the question reviewed above indicates, a majority of Americans overall say they have been spending less in recent months. Together, these data would suggest that people may be not only behaving in this fashion, but adopting a new, frugal mindset or mental orientation toward money.

There is little relationship between an individual's annual income and his or her responses to this question. Those with high incomes appear to be only slightly more likely to be the types of people who enjoy spending, compared to those with low incomes.

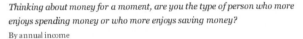

Thinking about money for a moment, are you the type of person who more enjoys spending money or who more enjoys saving money?
By annual income

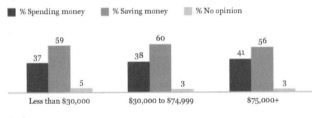

April 20-21, 2009

Implications

The fact that about a third of Americans say they intend to continue spending less in the years ahead is presumably not good news to the nation's retailers—although it may play more positively in the minds of commentators who argue that America has become too consumerist in its cultural ethos.

It is important to note the obvious in regard to these projective sentiments—that, as has been said, while intentions are nice, actual behavior is what counts. Americans' plans to cut back on spending as a "new, normal" part of their lifestyles may well change once the economy gets back on its feet and things overall appear more financially rosy. Additionally, it is worth re-emphasizing that these findings do not project to an overwhelmingly or totally pervasive consumer upheaval. The "spending less as a new, normal pattern" viewpoint is held by much less than a majority of Americans, and this group is at least slightly countered by the 6% who say they will spend more in the years ahead.

Still, the fact that almost 6 out of 10 Americans say they are the types of people who enjoy saving more than spending should give pause for thought. This finding suggests that the "new frugality" that has been so talked about may indeed have a chance of settling in as a new cultural norm. If so, then retailers may need to plan on more measured consumer expenditures as they project years into the future.

Survey Methods

Results are based on telephone interviews with 1,051 national adults, aged 18 and older, conducted April 20–21, 2009. For results based on the total sample of national adults, one can say with 95% confidence that the maximum margin of sampling error is ±3 percentage points.

Interviews are conducted with respondents on land-line telephones (for respondents with a land-line telephone) and cellular phones (for respondents who are cell-phone only).

In addition to sampling error, question wording and practical difficulties in conducting surveys can introduce error or bias into the findings of public opinion polls.

April 29, 2009
IN U.S., WORRIES ABOUT SWINE FLU NOT YET AFFECTING BEHAVIOR
Twenty-two percent worried "yesterday" about getting swine flu

by Frank Newport, Gallup Poll Editor in Chief

Although 22% of Americans report worrying about getting swine flu, there appears to be only minimal impact on the public's daily behavior so far, despite extensive news coverage about the virus and its potential spread. A Gallup Poll conducted Tuesday night shows that just 1% to 3% of Americans say they decided not to go shopping or go out to a restaurant, canceled an airline trip, decided not to use mass transit, stayed home from work, or kept a child home from school because of concerns about swine flu.

Did you, personally, do any of the following yesterday because of a concern about swine flu, or not? How about -- [RANDOM ORDER]?

	% Yes	% No
Worried about getting swine flu	22	78
Canceled or postponed a scheduled airplane trip	1	99
Decided not to use mass transit, such as bus, subway, or train	3	96
Decided not to go out shopping or to a restaurant	3	96
Kept a child home from school*	2	97
Stayed home from work**	1	99
Shopped online or by phone for something you would normally purchase at a store	3	97

Gallup Poll, April 28, 2009
* Those with children under 18 only
**Employees only

The Gallup Poll was conducted Tuesday night, April 28. While 22% of those interviewed reported they personally worried about getting swine flu "yesterday," the incidence of worry varies among demographic and regional subgroups of the population:

Americans 55 years of age and older are slightly less likely to worry than those who are younger, reinforcing Gallup-Healthways data showing that the incidence of flu in general is lower among older Americans.

Those with children under 18 in the home are slightly more likely to be worried than those who don't have children in the home.

Worry is slightly less prevalent in the Midwest than elsewhere.

Did you, personally, worry yesterday about getting swine flu, or not?

By age, region, and presence of children under 18 in home

	% Yes	% No
Total	22	78
18 to 34	27	73
35 to 54	24	76
55+	16	84
Have children under 18 in home	26	74
No children under 18 in home	19	81
East	25	74
Midwest	18	81
South	21	79
West	23	77

Gallup Poll, April 28, 2009

Although the sample size of Hispanics in the poll is too small to provide reliable estimates, the data suggest that Hispanics are considerably more likely than non-Hispanics to worry about getting swine flu. Given that the swine flu epidemic apparently originated in Mexico, and that most of the reported deaths have occurred there, this connection is understandable.

The Gallup data indicate that the swine flu situation has not caused major shifts in Americans' behavior so far, at least based on self-reports. The poll asked Americans whether they had—as a result of concerns about swine flu—changed their behavior "yesterday" in several different ways. Very small percentages of Americans replied in the affirmative for each behavior measured.

Certainly even 1% of the population can be a significant group of people if extrapolated to the overall adult population of roughly 220 million. But very low percentages such as these, as recorded in random-sample surveys, must be interpreted with caution. The survey in which these data were obtained involved interviews with 1,021 individuals and, as is true with any survey, the results of each question are an estimate of the underlying population that carries with it a margin of sampling error. Experience also indicates that there will be a small percentage who respond in the affirmative to almost any survey question, regardless of the question.

It is thus a reasonable interpretation to say that the survey results point to an estimate of behavioral change among the adult population that is quite minimal as a result of swine flu concern. (At the same time, it is important to realize that the scope of these questions was limited to changes in behavior "yesterday," and the percentages may be higher if Americans are asked to report on their behavior over a longer time span.)

These data provide an important baseline measure of public reaction to the swine flu outbreak, and Gallup will update the estimates of changes in these behaviors in the coming days.

There are minor variations by region in response to these behavioral indicators. Those living in the West are somewhat more likely than those living elsewhere to say they decided not to go out shopping or to a restaurant as a result of concern over swine flu. Future surveys will show whether behavioral change as a result of swine flu continues to appear higher in the Western region of the country.

Survey Methods

Results are based on telephone interviews with 1,021 national adults, aged 18 and older, conducted April 28, 2009, as part of Gallup Poll Daily tracking. For results based on the total sample of national adults, one can say with 95% confidence that the maximum margin of sampling error is ±3 percentage points.

Interviews are conducted with respondents on land-line telephones (for respondents with a land-line telephone) and cellular phones (for respondents who are cell-phone only).

In addition to sampling error, question wording and practical difficulties in conducting surveys can introduce error or bias into the findings of public opinion polls.

Polls conducted entirely in one day, such as this one, are subject to additional error or bias not found in polls conducted over several days.

April 30, 2009
DEMOCRATS MAINTAIN SEVEN-POINT ADVANTAGE IN PARTY ID
Have held significant edge since 2006

by Jeffrey M. Jones, Gallup Poll Managing Editor

Gallup Polls conducted in the first quarter of 2009, from January through March, find an average of 35% of Americans identifying themselves as Democrats and 28% as Republicans. The seven-point gap is similar to what Gallup has found since 2006, when the political tide turned in the Democrats' favor.

Party Identification, Average by Quarter, 1988-2009 Gallup Polls

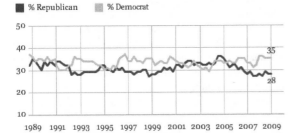

In fact, there has been no change in national partisanship since the last quarter of 2008, when 35% of Americans identified as Democrats, 28% as Republicans, and 35% as independents. That

means the Democratic Party's advantage has neither expanded nor contracted since Barack Obama took office and began to pursue a largely Democratic legislative agenda.

Democrats enjoyed similar advantages over Republicans in terms of party identification in 1992–1993 and again in the late 1990s.

Since the fourth quarter of 2006, the percentage of Americans identifying as Republicans has consistently been below 30%. During this time, Democrats won big victories in the 2006 midterm elections, which gave them party control of Congress, and won back the White House while expanding their majorities in both houses in the 2008 elections.

The Democrats are now poised to enjoy a working Senate majority of 60 seats after Pennsylvania Sen. Arlen Specter's switch from Republican to Democrat and the probable victory of Democrat Al Franken in the disputed Senate election in Minnesota. A majority of 60 seats is enough to overcome the use of a filibuster to defeat or delay a vote on legislation, and means Democrats could essentially pass any legislation they want as long as their coalition votes together.

The Democratic advantage in partisanship expands to double digits once the political leanings of independents are taken into account. Aggregated data from the first quarter of 2009 show that 52% of Americans identified as Democrats or said they were independent but leaned to the Democratic Party, while 39% identified as Republicans or leaned Republican.

That 13-point Democratic advantage is among the highest Gallup has found since 1991, when it began regularly measuring leaned party identification.

Leaned Party Identification, Average by Quarter, 1991-2009 Gallup Polls

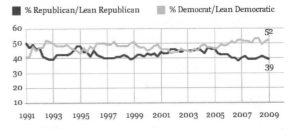

In the final quarter of 2008, leaned party identification was 51% Democrat and 40% Republican, so the Democratic advantage on this measure has increased slightly since Obama took office.

Bottom Line

The immediate outlook for the Republican Party is certainly bleak, with the Democratic Party maintaining significant advantages over it by almost any measure, perhaps most importantly in national party identification. Americans clearly have not reacted in a negative way to Obama's approach to governing, as he enjoys approval ratings above 60%—better than those of most recent presidents.

It could be a while before Republicans are able to regain a majority in Congress, but they may be able to begin chipping away at the Democratic majority as soon as the 2010 midterm elections, especially considering that the president's party usually loses seats at midterm.

While it is probably not likely that history will repeat itself, it is notable that Democrats held the same seven-point advantage in party identification that they enjoy now in the first quarter of 1993, when Bill Clinton took office. By the time of the 1994 midterm elections, the parties were back to even on national partisanship and Republicans won enough seats to take control of both houses of Congress.

Survey Methods

Results are based on aggregated data from several polls, each consisting of interviews with approximately 1,000 national adults, aged 18 and older, conducted between January and March 2009. For each poll, one can say with 95% confidence that the maximum margin of sampling error is ±3 percentage points.

Interviews are conducted with respondents on land-line telephones (for respondents with a land-line telephone) and cellular phones (for respondents who are cell-phone only).

In addition to sampling error, question wording and practical difficulties in conducting surveys can introduce error or bias into the findings of public opinion polls.

April 30, 2009
U.S. INVESTOR OPTIMISM LEVELS OFF IN APRIL
Remains up significantly compared to February

by Dennis Jacobe, Gallup Chief Economist

After its sharp improvement of 41 points in March, American investor optimism stabilized in April, as the Gallup Index of Investor Optimism—a broad measure of investor perceptions—improved 3 points to -20. This is not much different from the -23 of March and essentially consolidates the sharp improvement since February's -64 reading, which is the lowest for the Index since its 1996 inception.

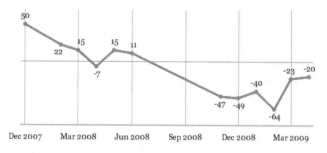

Gallup Index of Investor Optimism, December 2007-April 2009

Portfolio Optimism Improves Slightly

Despite April's being a surprisingly good month for U.S. equity markets, investors' expectations for their personal portfolios over the next 12 months improved only slightly, as the Personal Dimension of the Index increased by four points to 21. This is essentially the same as the 19 of January, and suggests that investors remain cautiously optimistic about the performance of their personal portfolios this year.

Economic Optimism Levels Off

Investor optimism about the U.S. economy's direction over the next 12 months leveled off in April, as the Economic Dimension was

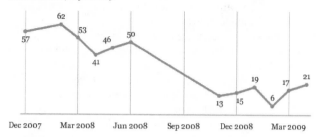

Personal Dimension, Gallup Index of Investor Optimism, December 2007-April 2009

essentially unchanged at -41, compared to -40 in March. Investors as a group thus remain pessimistic about the economic outlook, but much less so than they were in February, when this dimension was at -70, or even in January, when it was at -59. Current investor optimism about the economy's direction is essentially the same as it was in June 2008, when this dimension was at -39.

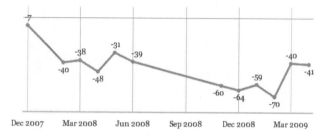

Economic Dimension, Gallup Index of Investor Optimism, December 2007-April 2009

Commentary

The sharp improvement in investor confidence in March and its leveling off in April is consistent with Gallup's monitoring of consumer confidence as reflected by its Consumer Mood Index. However, it also suggests that many average investors may not yet share the Wall Street speculation that the worst is over for the U.S. economy—an assumption that appears to have sent the S&P 500 surging to a three-month high.

Actually, the stabilizing of investor optimism overall and the continued investor pessimism about the economy's direction over the next year seems more consistent with current economic conditions than with Wall Street's recent performance. Just Wednesday, it was reported that the U.S. economy contracted by 6.1% in the first quarter, and Thursday, the Commerce Department reported that consumer spending fell 0.2% in March while incomes declined for the fifth time in the last six months.

Looking ahead, it seems likely that the impending Chrysler bankruptcy and the continued struggles of General Motors could negatively affect the economy in terms of both jobs and consumer confidence. Further, although Gallup's polling shows that concerns about the swine flu virus have yet to affect consumer behaviors, the finding that 22% of Americans are worried about getting it suggests the potential for economic damage if current trends continue. And next week, the Federal Reserve Board and the Treasury Department will release the findings of the so-called banking "stress tests."

On the positive side, it is noteworthy that Gallup's net new hiring measure for the week ending April 26 suggests some stabilization of the jobs market, as does the Labor Department's announcement of a small decline in jobless claims to 631,000 for the week ended April 25. Still, the number of people on the jobless benefit rolls hit 6.27 million—another new record.

At this point, it seems the economy may be stabilizing, just like investor optimism and consumer mood. However, it still seems premature to declare whether this means the real economy has reached bottom or whether another drop from here will eventuate.

Author's note: Gallup's Index of Investor Optimism—a survey of those having $10,000 or more of investable assets—peaked at 178 in January 2000, just prior to the bursting of the dot-com bubble. Last year, the Index turned negative for the first time in its history. Before last year, the low for the Index was 5 in March 2003, reflecting investor concerns at the outset of the Iraq war.

Survey Methods

Gallup Poll Daily interviewing includes no fewer than 1,000 U.S. adults nationwide each day during 2008. The Index of Investor Optimism results are based on questions asked of 1,000 or more investors over a three-day period each month, conducted April 21–23, March 16–18, Feb. 17–19, and Jan. 16–18, 2009; and Dec. 16–18, Nov. 24–26, June 3–6, April 25–28, March 28–31, and Feb. 28–March 2, 2008. For results based on these samples, the maximum margin of sampling error is ±3 percentage points.

Results for May are based on the Gallup Panel study and are based on telephone interviews with 576 national adults, aged 18 and older, conducted May 19–21, 2008. Gallup Panel members are recruited through random selection methods. The panel is weighted so that it is demographically representative of the U.S. adult population. For results based on this sample, one can say with 95% confidence that the maximum margin of sampling error is ±5 percentage points.

For investor results prior to 2008, telephone interviews were conducted with at least 800 investors, aged 18 and older, and having at least $10,000 of investable assets. For the total sample of investors in these surveys, one can say with 95% confidence that the maximum margin of sampling error is ± 4 percentage points.

Interviews are conducted with respondents on land-line telephones (for respondents with a land-line telephone) and cellular phones (for respondents who are cell-phone only).

In addition to sampling error, question wording and practical difficulties in conducting surveys can introduce error or bias into the findings of public opinion polls.

May 01, 2009

OBAMA APPROVAL HIGH AMONG MUSLIMS, JEWS, AND CATHOLICS

Catholics give Obama higher approval score than Protestants

by Lydia Saad, Gallup Poll Senior Editor

Gallup Poll Daily tracking during President Obama's first 100 days in office finds broad support for him among Americans affiliated with most major U.S. religions. U.S. Muslims and Jews give Obama his highest job approval ratings, at 85% and 79%, respectively. He also receives solid majority support from Roman Catholics (67%) and Protestants (58%), and more approval than disapproval from Mormons.

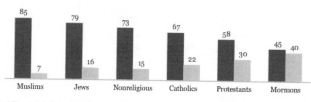

Job Approval of President Barack Obama, by Religious Preference

Gallup Poll Daily tracking, Jan. 21-April 29, 2009

Obama also enjoys broad support—73% approval—from the sizable group of Americans with no religious affiliation, including those calling themselves atheists or agnostics.

These findings are based on large sample sizes for each religious group contained in the combined Gallup Poll Daily tracking results from Jan. 21–April 29, 2009. This includes interviews with approximately 55,000 Protestants (defined in this study as those who identify themselves either as Protestant or with another non-Catholic Christian religion), 24,000 Catholics, 2,500 Jews, 1,600 Mormons, and 350 Muslims.

Catholics Broadly Supportive of Obama

The University of Notre Dame's recent invitation to Obama to deliver its 2009 commencement address—and the associated decision to confer an honorary doctorate degree on him—has sparked outrage, protests, and boycotts against the university among some Catholics and Catholic bishops. The critics of that invitation say the university's acts implicitly condone Obama's more liberal positions on abortion and embryonic stem-cell research—issues of significant disagreement between the Roman Catholic Church and the new president. However, the controversy would seem not to resonate with

rank-and-file Catholics, most of whom approve of Obama's job performance to date (and who don't necessarily concur with the church on the relevant policy issues).

Obama's job approval ratings among Catholics and Protestants have varied slightly from week to week since his inauguration, dipping a bit in February and March, but are about the same today as they were in January.

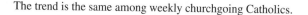

President Obama Job Approval by Religious Preference, Weekly Averages

% Approve; numbers in percentages

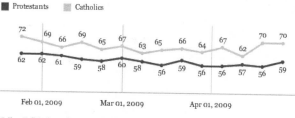

Gallup Poll Daily tracking, Jan. 21-April 26, 2009

The trend is the same among weekly churchgoing Catholics.

President Obama Job Approval Among Catholics, by Weekly Church Attendance, Weekly Averages

% Approve; numbers in percentages

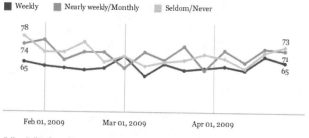

Gallup Poll Daily tracking, Jan. 21-April 26, 2009

Even Catholics who consider themselves "conservative" politically are more likely to approve than disapprove of Obama's job performance. This distinguishes Catholics from Protestants, as conservative Protestants are more likely to disapprove. More generally, liberals and moderates among both Christian groups express far more widespread approval of Obama than do conservatives.

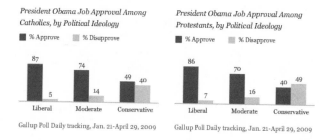

President Obama Job Approval Among Catholics, by Political Ideology

Gallup Poll Daily tracking, Jan. 21-April 29, 2009

President Obama Job Approval Among Protestants, by Political Ideology

Gallup Poll Daily tracking, Jan. 21-April 29, 2009

In fact, 53% of Catholics voted for Obama for president in November, almost identical to the 52.9% of the popular vote Obama won in the 2008 election. Catholics' 67% approval of Obama in his first 100 days is slightly higher than his overall 63% average approval rating for the same period. Thus, relative to the population,

Catholics have become a bit more supportive of Obama as president than they were in the election.

Protestants' 58% average approval rating of Obama for the first 100 days lags behind the 63% national average, just as their 47% support in the election lagged behind Obama's overall support.

Both in the election and now, Jewish and nonreligious Americans' support for Obama has registered way above average. No Gallup or exit-poll data on Muslims or Mormons is available to make the same comparison.

2008 General Election Vote for Obama vs. 2009 Obama Job Approval
% Approve, by religious preference

	2008 general election vote for Obama^	2009 Obama job approval*
	%	%
National	53	63
Catholics	53	67
Protestants	47	58
Jews	78	79
Nonreligious	75	73

^ 2008 Obama vote among Catholics and Protestants based on Gallup Poll; 2008 Obama vote among Jews and nonreligious Americans based on National Election Pool exit poll.
* 2009 Obama job approval based on Gallup Poll Daily tracking, Jan. 21-April 29, 2009

Muslims and Jews United for Obama

The commonality between U.S. Jews and Muslims in their broad approval of Obama is notable given the global friction between Jews and Muslims with respect to Mideast politics.

High U.S. Jewish support for Obama is not surprising given that Jews are traditionally heavily Democratic in their political orientation. Democratic Jews supported Hillary Clinton by a slight margin over Obama in the battle for the Democratic nomination last year, but they gradually came around to supporting him in large numbers for the general election.

Obama signaled he will be aggressive in seeking an end to the Israeli-Palestinian conflict by appointing a special envoy for Middle East peace, and by directing Secretary of State Hillary Clinton to actively pursue a two-state solution to the conflict. It is not clear whether U.S. Jews endorse Obama's approach, but the fact that four in five approve of the job he is doing—consistent with their vote for him in the election—suggests they at least tolerate it.

Obama is rated far less well by Jewish conservatives than he is by moderate and liberal Jews—similar to the pattern seen with Catholics and Protestants. However, a much smaller proportion of Jews are conservative (20%) than is true for either Catholics (38%) or Protestants (45%).

President Obama Job Approval Among Jews, by Political Ideology

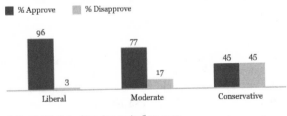

Gallup Poll Daily tracking, Jan. 21-April 29, 2009

Bottom Line

Obama's first 100 days have been successful by just about every public-opinion gauge. More than 6 in 10 Americans say he has met or exceeded their expectations, and a majority of every demographic subgroup of the population—aside from Republicans and conservatives—approves of the job he is doing.

Although Obama has dusted up some controversy among conservative Catholics and has stepped into the always-thorny Mideast political fray, his image thus far among Catholics seems untarnished, and his image among Jews, Muslims, and nonreligious Americans is extraordinarily positive. Protestants and Mormons are more conservative in their politics than members of other religions, and thus more moderate in their approval of Obama. But even among these groups, more approve of his job performance than disapprove.

Survey Methods

Results are based on telephone interviews with 99,494 national adults, aged 18 and older, conducted Jan. 21–April 29, 2009, as part of Gallup Poll Daily tracking. For results based on the total sample of national adults, one can say with 95% confidence that the maximum margin of sampling error is ±0.5 percentage points.

For results based on religious subgroups, the sample sizes and associated margins of error are shown in the accompanying table.

What is your religious preference -- are you Protestant, Roman Catholic, Mormon, Jewish, Muslim, another religion, or no religion? (If "another religion" ask: Would that be a Christian religion or is it not a Christian religion?)

	% of sample	Sample size	Margin of error
	%	-n-	±
Protestant/Other Christian	55	54,626	0.5
Catholic	25	24,377	1
None/Atheist/Agnostic	12	11,848	1
Jewish	2	2,478	2
Mormon	2	1,628	3
Muslim	0.4	356	6
Other non-Christian religion	2	2,106	2
No response given	2	2,075	2
Total	100	99,494	0.3

Gallup Poll Daily tracking, Jan. 21-April 29, 2009

Interviews are conducted with respondents on land-line telephones (for respondents with a land-line telephone) and cellular phones (for respondents who are cell-phone only).

In addition to sampling error, question wording and practical difficulties in conducting surveys can introduce error or bias into the findings of public opinion polls.

May 01, 2009

SWINE FLU WORRIES 25% IN U.S., SLIGHT IMPACT ON BEHAVIORS

Now 6% say they skipped shopping or eating out because of flu concerns

by Frank Newport, Gallup Poll Editor in Chief

One out of four adult Americans interviewed by Gallup Thursday said they worried about getting swine flu "yesterday," a slight increase over the 22% who said they worried in Gallup's initial poll on April 28. There have been similarly slight, but not statistically significant, increases in Gallup's tracking measures of the impact of the flu situation on behavior, including small rises in the percentage who have canceled or postponed shopping or eating out (from 3% to 6%) or airplane travel (from 1% to 3%). The percentage of parents who kept children home from school has moved from 2% on Tuesday to 5% on Thursday.

Did you, personally, do any of the following yesterday because of a concern about swine flu, or not? How about -- [RANDOM ORDER]?
% Yes, did

	Apr 28, 2009	Apr 30, 2009
Worried about getting swine flu	22	25
Canceled or postponed a scheduled airplane trip	1	3
Decided not to use mass transit, such as bus, subway, or train	3	4
Decided not to go out shopping or to a restaurant	3	6
Kept a child home from school*	2	5
Stayed home from work**	1	1
Shopped online or by phone for something you would normally purchase at a store	3	2

* Those with children under 18 only
**Employees only

The latest Gallup Poll update on the impact of swine flu, or H1N1 virus, on the attitudes and behavior of the average American was conducted Thursday night, April 30. The percentage of those interviewed who reported that they personally worried about getting swine flu "yesterday" (25%) is up three points from Tuesday night's data. A change of this size is not statistically significant.

The lack of a major jump in worry is notable given the increased news coverage of the swine flu situation over the last several days, including publicity about the death of at least one person in the United States, the World Health Organization's labeling of the situation as an imminent pandemic, the closing of schools across the country—including the entire Fort Worth, Texas, public school system—and reports that Mexico is virtually shutting down as a result of the flu.

Perhaps reflecting the news coverage of swine flu outbreaks in schools, the trends show slightly larger growth in concern among Americans aged 18 to 34 and among those with children in the home than among other groups. The increase in worry was also slightly larger in the Midwest and South than on either the East or West coasts.

Gallup's tracking of the impact of the flu situation on reported behavior shows results that are in a general sense similar to the impact on overall worry. The slight increases in self-reported behavioral changes that have occurred are not statistically significant.

- The percentage of Americans who say they have decided not to go shopping or out to a restaurant because of concern about swine flu is up from 3% to 6%—not a statistically significant change, but a movement in the direction that, if continued, could begin to have an effect on consumer spending.

Did you, personally, worry yesterday about getting swine flu, or not?
% Yes, did
By age, region, and presence of children under 18 in home

	Apr 28, 2009	Apr 30, 2009
Total	22	25
18 to 34	27	35
35 to 54	24	25
55+	16	19
Have children under 18 in home	26	32
No children under 18 in home	19	21
East	25	25
Midwest	18	23
South	21	26
West	23	26

- Despite widespread news coverage of Vice President Biden's comment that Americans should avoid mass transit, there has been only a one-point increase in the percentage who in fact say they decided not to take a trip on mass transit.
- There was a two-point increase in the percentage of Americans who canceled an airplane trip, but the percentage is still very low, at 3%.
- The percentage of Americans with children under 18 at home who report having kept at least one of those children home from school has moved from 2% to 5%.
- There was no increase in working Americans' reports that they stayed home from work (1% both Tuesday and Thursday), and a decrease of one point in the percentage who say they shopped online or by phone as a result of concerns about swine flu.

As noted, none of the changes in these reports over the last two days is statistically significant. Still, if these trends continue, the impact of the flu will almost certainly begin to be felt in America's retail sector, something that is not an optimal occurrence given the currently parlous economic times.

Gallup will continue to update the estimates of changes in these behaviors in the coming days.

Survey Methods

Results are based on telephone interviews with 1,010 national adults, aged 18 and older, conducted April 30, 2009. For results based on the total sample of national adults, one can say with 95% confidence that the maximum margin of sampling error is ±3 percentage points.

Trend results are based on telephone interviews with 1,021 national adults, aged 18 and older, conducted April 28, 2009. For results based on the total sample of national adults, one can say with 95% confidence that the maximum margin of sampling error is ±3 percentage points.

Interviews are conducted with respondents on land-line telephones (for respondents with a land-line telephone) and cellular phones (for respondents who are cell-phone only).

In addition to sampling error, question wording and practical difficulties in conducting surveys can introduce error or bias into the findings of public opinion polls.

Polls conducted entirely in one day, such as this one, are subject to additional error or bias not found in polls conducted over several days.

May 04, 2009

MAJOR GAINS IN BLACKS' RATINGS OF THEIR STANDARD OF LIVING

Increases first observed in January; ratings have recovered to early 2008 levels

by Jeffrey M. Jones, Gallup Poll Managing Editor

Gallup Poll Daily tracking of Americans' assessments of their standard of living finds continued improvement among blacks after a dramatic 31-point spike in January. Blacks' score on Gallup's Standard of Living Index dropped to as low as -1 during the height of the financial crisis last October, remaining low in November and December, but it now stands at +62.

Gallup Standard of Living Index Score Among Blacks

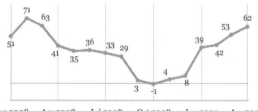

The Standard of Living Index is based on respondents' reported satisfaction with their current standard of living and their assessments of whether it is getting better or getting worse. Positive scores indicate that more Americans have a positive view of their standard of living, and negative scores mean more Americans have a negative view. In general, Americans tend to be more positive than negative when asked about their living standard.

Gallup monitors Americans' reported standard of living as part of its daily polling, which began in January 2008. The results reported here are based on monthly aggregates of roughly 30,000 interviews per month.

On the first of the two Index questions—measuring overall satisfaction or dissatisfaction with one's current standard of living—blacks (as well as the broader population of all U.S. adults) have been consistently more likely to say they are satisfied than dissatisfied. However, the gap between the percentage satisfied and the percentage dissatisfied shrank to single digits last fall, with 52% of blacks satisfied and 47% dissatisfied in the November data. Those assessments were essentially unchanged in December, but in January they improved significantly, with nearly 6 in 10 blacks satisfied, and have continued to increase since then to the current 64%.

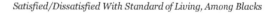

Satisfied/Dissatisfied With Standard of Living, Among Blacks

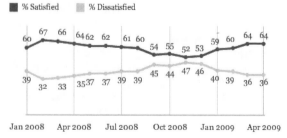

There has been a similar—though perhaps more dramatic—shift in blacks' reports of whether their standard of living is "getting better" or "getting worse," the second of the two Index questions. In October, significantly more blacks said their standard of living was getting worse (49%) rather than better (37%). But by January, those numbers had switched places, with 52% of blacks saying their standard of living was getting better and only 32% saying worse. Now, 59% of blacks report their standard of living as improving.

Standard of Living Getting Better/Worse, Among Blacks

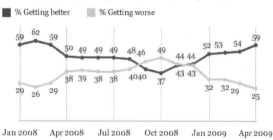

The continued improvement on both Index components has pushed blacks' Standard of Living Index score to +62 in April.

Notably, blacks' score on this index has exceeded that for whites in each of the last three months. Prior to that, whites' score had always been higher than blacks' score.

Gallup Standard of Living Index Score Among Blacks and Whites

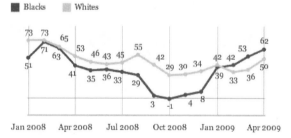

It is important to note that the data reported here are based on *self-reports* of standard of living. It is not clear that blacks' objective standard of living has improved greatly in the last few months. Therefore, much of the decline and subsequent improvement during the last year may have been largely perceptual in nature, as opposed to reflecting concrete change.

Given the timing of the recent increase in January, it is hard not to believe it reflects enthusiasm among the black community about Barack Obama's presidency. Blacks may perceive their standard of living to be improving under a Democratic administration—headed by an African-American president—which promises to be more in tune with their needs than the prior Republican administration.

Gallup has documented overwhelming support for Obama among the black community, with more than 9 in 10 saying they approve of the job he is doing as president.

There has not been a similar pattern of change in whites' perceptions of their standard of living. After a slight improvement from a +34 Index score in December to +42 in January, the Index score for whites fell back into the 30s. To the extent that whites were hopeful about the prospects of a new administration, it apparently was on a much smaller level and was shorter lived than was the case among blacks.

However, even if the recent improvement is driven to a degree by enthusiasm for changes in the political guard, it is important to point out that blacks' current ratings of their standard of living are similar to what they were in the first quarter of 2008, before the economy started to deteriorate rapidly. Thus, the recent improvement may simply represent a restoration of earlier levels, rather than an improvement above and beyond what had existed before.

Bottom Line

It is unlikely that the election of a new president would have much of an immediate effect on most individuals' actual standard of living. Most Americans would continue to work in the same jobs that they had before the election, with the same income and the same expenses. But having a president that one believes in may just lead people to have a much sunnier outlook, not only on the government but on other aspects of life, and may cause them to rate conditions in a variety of areas more positively. In prior research, Gallup has in fact demonstrated that Americans who identify with the president's party usually give higher ratings to conditions on a national level (such as the economy, national defense, and education, to name a few)—and even on a personal level (their own finances)—than do Americans who support the opposition party.

Obama's domestic policies may have the effect of raising blacks' actual standard of living in the future, but given that he has been in office only a short while and the most tangible benefit blacks may have seen thus far is a small income-tax cut, it is probably more likely that the recent improvement in blacks' reported standard of living reflects their confidence in the political leadership and is more perceptual in nature than a real improvement in their living standard.

Survey Methods

Results are based on telephone interviews with 29,379 national adults, aged 18 and older, conducted April 1–30, 2009, as part of Gallup Poll Daily tracking. For results based on the total sample of national adults, one can say with 95% confidence that the maximum margin of sampling error is ±1 percentage point.

For results based on the sample of 1,765 blacks, the maximum margin of sampling error is ±3 percentage points.

For results based on the sample of 23,988 non-Hispanic whites, the maximum margin of sampling error is ±1 percentage point.

Interviews are conducted with respondents on land-line telephones (for respondents with a land-line telephone) and cellular phones (for respondents who are cell-phone only).

In addition to sampling error, question wording and practical difficulties in conducting surveys can introduce error or bias into the findings of public opinion polls.

Gallup's Standard of Living Index is computed as follows: (% Satisfied with standard of living minus % Dissatisfied) + (% Saying standard of living getting better minus % Saying standard of living getting worse).

May 05, 2009
AMERICANS' SATISFACTION WITH U.S. DOUBLES SINCE JANUARY
At 34%, however, satisfaction is still low on an absolute basis

by Frank Newport, Gallup Poll Editor in Chief

Although still low on an absolute basis, the percentage of Americans who are satisfied with the way things are going in the United States has doubled since Barack Obama took office, moving from 17% in mid-January to 34% for the week ending May 3. All of the increase has come from Democrats (among whom a majority are now satisfied) and, to a lesser degree, independents; Republicans' satisfaction is no different now than it was in mid-January, and remains very low.

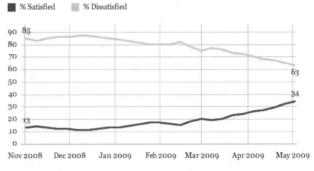

Satisfaction With the Way Things Are Going in the United States

Gallup Poll, Oct. 27, 2008-May 3, 2009

Gallup's satisfaction measure was at 17% when measured Jan. 19–25, the week Obama was inaugurated. After remaining low for much of February, satisfaction began to climb in March and through April to its current 34% level.

A situation in which only a third of Americans are satisfied with the way things are going is, of course, not high on an absolute basis, but still represents the highest level of satisfaction Gallup has measured since early 2007. The all-time high on this measure in Gallup's 30-year history of asking the question is 71% in February 1999, at the end of the Bill Clinton impeachment situation. The all-time low is 7% from a poll last October, conducted shortly after Congress rejected but then ultimately passed financial rescue legislation designed to prop up failing financial institutions, and after the collapse of Lehman Brothers and the government bailout of AIG in September.

Obama took office this January with satisfaction levels lower than they were at the start of his immediate two predecessors' terms. In January 2001, the month in which George W. Bush was inaugurated, U.S. satisfaction was higher, at 56% (and slipped slightly, to 50%, by April of that year). In January 1993, when Bill Clinton took office, satisfaction was at 29% (and fell slightly to 25% by February, the only time Gallup measured satisfaction in Clinton's first four months in office).

Major Partisan Differences

The data represented in the accompanying graph make it clear how much partisanship has driven the recent changes in overall levels of satisfaction with the way things are going in the U.S.

Although all partisan groups had low satisfaction levels in the waning months of the Bush administration, Republicans' satisfaction was still higher than that of either independents or Democrats, as

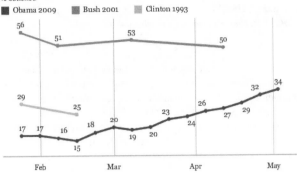

Satisfaction With the Way Things Are Going in the United States
% Satisfied
■ Obama 2009   ■ Bush 2001   □ Clinton 1993

Satisfaction With the Way Things Are Going in the United States
% Satisfied, by political party

■ Democrats   ■ Independents   □ Republicans

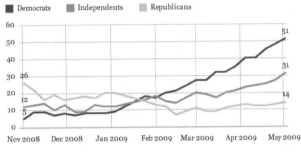

Gallup Poll, Oct. 27, 2008-May 3, 2009

long as Bush remained president. By the week of Obama's inauguration, however, there was an about-face, with Democrats and independents showing increased levels of satisfaction, while Republicans' satisfaction dropped. Since then, Republicans have maintained their dour look on the way things are going in the country, with satisfaction levels fluctuating week by week between 7% and the current 14%. Democrats' satisfaction, meanwhile, has gained steadily, going from 18% to the current 51%. Satisfaction among independents has almost doubled, from 16% to 31%.

Comparison to "Right Track/Wrong Track" Measures

Gallup's satisfaction measure is different in some ways from the "right track, wrong track" measure used by other polling organizations, although all of these general measures tend to trend in the same direction. Asking the public whether things are on the "right track or the wrong track" most likely captures attitudes that are more about direction, momentum, or expectations. Asking Americans whether they are satisfied with the way things are going most likely captures more of an assessment of the current situation. This helps explain why Gallup's satisfaction measure, at 34%, remains at least somewhat lower than some current "right track/wrong track" measures that are as high as 50% in an ABC News/*Washington Post* poll (April 21–24), 43% in an NBC News/*Wall Street Journal* poll (April 23–26), and 41% in a CBS News/*New York Times* poll (April 22–26). All of these measures, like Gallup's, have shown significant movement in the positive direction since January.

Survey Methods

Weekly results presented in this analysis are based on telephone interviews with approximately 3,500 national adults, aged 18 and

older, each week, as part of Gallup Poll Daily tracking. For results based on each week's total sample of national adults, one can say with 95% confidence that the maximum margin of sampling error is ±2 percentage points.

Interviews are conducted with respondents on land-line telephones (for respondents with a land-line telephone) and cellular phones (for respondents who are cell-phone only).

In addition to sampling error, question wording and practical difficulties in conducting surveys can introduce error or bias into the findings of public opinion polls.

May 06, 2009
REPUBLICANS FACE STEEP UPHILL CLIMB AMONG WOMEN
Men increasingly identifying as independents, drifting away from GOP

by Jeffrey M. Jones, Gallup Poll Managing Editor

Among women, Democrats maintain a solid double-digit advantage in party identification over Republicans, 41% to 27%. In contrast, men are equally divided in their party loyalty between Republicans (28%) and Democrats (30%), and are currently most likely to say they are politically independent (40%).

Party Identification by Gender, Gallup Polls, First Quarter 2009

■ Democrat   ■ Independent   □ Republican

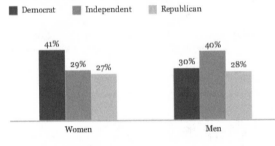

These results are based on aggregated data from Gallup Polls conducted in the first quarter of 2009.

The current results for women are typical of what Gallup has found over the past year, with roughly 4 in 10 identifying themselves as Democrats. The Democratic Party has held an advantage among women in Gallup polling throughout this decade, with support usually in the high 30% range. The current 41% female Democratic identification matches the high achieved several times since 2000.

Party Identification Among Women, Quarterly Averages, 2000-2009
Gallup Polls

■ % Democrat   ■ % Independent   □ % Republican

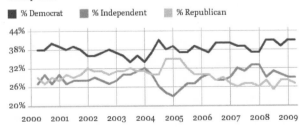

At various times over the past decade, the plurality of male partisans have shifted between Republican and independent identification, with no more than 31% of men identifying as Democrats in any quarter. Since late 2006, however, the gap between the percentage of men identifying as independents and the percentage identifying as Republicans has grown, and independent men have outnumbered Republican men for the last two years running. Over this time, Republican identification among men has largely been on par with Democratic support, a clear negative sign for the GOP given the solid support the Democratic Party has among women.

Party Identification Among Men, Quarterly Averages, 2000-2009 Gallup Polls

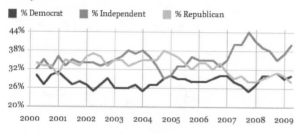

Party Support Including Leaning Independents

Women's affinity for the Democratic Party looks even stronger when independents' partisan leanings are taken into account. By this measure of party identification, Democrats currently enjoy a 22-point advantage over Republicans, with 57% of women identifying as Democrats or saying they are independent but leaning Democratic, compared with 35% who identify with or lean to the Republican Party. This gap is one of the largest Gallup has measured in any quarter this decade.

Party Identification (Including Leaning Independents) Among Women, Quarterly Averages, 2000-2009 Gallup Polls

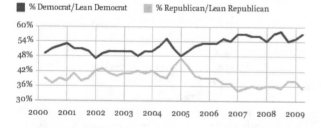

Among men, the Democratic and Republican Parties have been more closely matched on this measure of party identification throughout this decade. However, the trend is clear—the advantage Republicans held for much of the 2000s disappeared in 2006, and Democrats have maintained at least a small edge since then. In the most recent quarter, 47% of men identified as Democrats or leaned Democratic, compared with 42% who identified as Republicans or leaned Republican.

Implications

The last three years have brought little in the way of good news for the Republican Party, including two decisive national election defeats. During this time, Democrats have expanded their advantage in party identification nationally and have solidified their support

Party Identification (Including Leaning Independents) Among Men, Quarterly Averages, 2000-2009 Gallup Polls

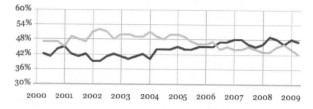

among women. Republicans' former advantage over Democrats in leaned party identification among men has disappeared, though the parties remain competitive.

If there is any silver lining for the Republican Party, it is that while men have become less likely to identify as Republicans, they have not necessarily moved in great numbers to the Democratic Party, but instead have shifted more toward an independent political orientation. That would seem to indicate at least a possibility that men who formerly identified as Republicans could someday return to the Republican fold.

Survey Methods

Results are based on aggregated data from several polls, each consisting of interviews with approximately 1,000 national adults, aged 18 and older, conducted between January and March 2009. For each poll, one can say with 95% confidence that the maximum margin of sampling error is ±3 percentage points.

Interviews are conducted with respondents on land-line telephones (for respondents with a land-line telephone) and cellular phones (for respondents who are cell-phone only).

In addition to sampling error, question wording and practical difficulties in conducting surveys can introduce error or bias into the findings of public opinion polls.

May 06, 2009
AHEAD OF STRESS TESTS, CONFIDENCE IN U.S. BANKS REMAINS LOW
While 35% have "very little" confidence in banks, only 20% have "a great deal" or "quite a lot"

by Dennis Jacobe, Gallup Chief Economist

As Thursday's official release of the so-called bank "stress tests" approaches, Americans' confidence in U.S. banks remains at low levels. Between 18% and 20% of Americans have expressed "a great deal" or "quite a lot" of confidence over the past four weeks, while between 35% and 39% have said they have "very little" confidence.

Confidence in U.S. Banking

Gallup began asking Americans about their confidence in banking in April 1979. Prior to this year, the combined "great deal" and "quite a lot of confidence" numbers had not fallen below the 30% of the 1990–91 recession—a percentage that also reflected the fallout of the S&L debacle of the late 1980s. Thus, the early April 2009 reading

Please tell me how much confidence you, yourself, have in today's U.S. financial institutions or banks.

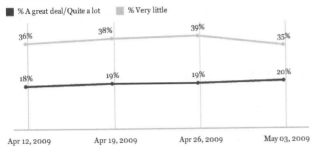

Gallup Poll Daily tracking

of 18% who have a great deal/quite a lot of confidence in U.S. banks represents a new low.

Even as confidence in U.S. banks in general has plunged, many Americans continue to express confidence in the main or primary bank where they do most of their banking business. Over the last four weeks, 60% have said they have a great deal (27%) or quite a lot (33%) of confidence in their main bank. Only 12% have expressed very little confidence in that bank. This higher level of confidence in one's primary bank is consistent with Gallup Poll findings more generally showing that Americans typically rate their own local providers and institutions much better than those in the broader United States.

Please tell me how much confidence you, yourself, have in your primary or main bank, that is, the bank or financial institution where you do most of your banking.

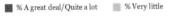
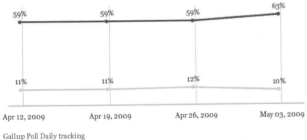

Gallup Poll Daily tracking

Survey Methods

Results are based on telephone interviews with 805 national adults, aged 18 and older, conducted April 6–12; 924 adults, conducted April 13–19; 3,995 adults, conducted April 20–26; and 975 adults, conducted April 27–May 3, 2009, as part of the Gallup Poll Daily tracking. For results based on these samples, one can say with 95% confidence that the maximum margin of sampling error is between ±2 and ±4 percentage points.

Interviews are conducted with respondents on land-line telephones (for respondents with a land-line telephone) and cellular phones (for respondents who are cell-phone only).

In addition to sampling error, question wording and practical difficulties in conducting surveys can introduce error or bias into the findings of public opinion polls.

May 08, 2009

DEMOCRATS DO BEST AMONG GENERATION Y AND BABY BOOMERS
Republicans do better among Generation X

by Frank Newport, Gallup Poll Editor in Chief

Although Democrats currently enjoy a party identification advantage over Republicans among Americans at every age between 18 to 85, the Democrats' greatest advantages come among those in their 20s and baby boomers in their late 40s and 50s. Republicans, on the other hand, come closest to parity with Democrats among Generation Xers in their late 30s and early 40s and among seniors in their late 60s.

Party Identification by Age

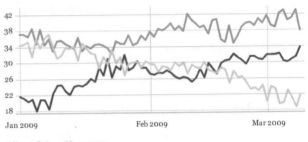

Gallup Poll, Jan 2-May 5, 2009

These conclusions are based on an analysis of more than 123,000 interviews conducted by Gallup between Jan. 2 and May 5 of this year. This extremely large group of interviews allows for the analysis of party identification for each of the 67 distinct ages between 18 and 85. Gallup conducted interviews with at least 650 respondents at each age, with the average sample size of 1,756 per age year.

As shown in the graph above, there is significant variation in political party identification across the age spectrum in the United States today.

- The percentage of Americans who identify as **independents** is directly and inversely related to age. More than one-third of the youngest Americans identify as independents, a percentage that drops steadily as the population ages, reaching a low of around 20% among those 80 years of age and older.
- The percentage of Americans who identify as **Republicans** follows roughly the opposite pattern. Only around 20% of young Americans below the age of 25 identify as Republicans. The percent Republican grows slightly from that point as age increases, up until roughly Americans' mid-40s, and then settles back among baby boomers in their late 40s and 50s. As Americans age into their 60s, the Republican percentage climbs, reaching levels of about 30% and above on average after age 67.
- The percentage of Americans who identify as **Democrats** follows still a different path. Democrats are quite strong among the youngest Americans, particularly those under age 24, among whom more identify as Democrats than independents. The percent Democrat stays at about the one-third mark until about age 45, when it climbs slightly and remains higher through the 50s and early 60s. From that point on, the percent Democrat hovers around the 40% point, although there is quite a bit of fluctuation from age to age for Americans in their late 60s, 70s, and early 80s.

From a broad perspective, Republicans face a deficit among Americans of all ages. At no single age does the percent Republican exceed the percent Democrat. Still, the range of this Democratic advantage (% Democrat minus % Republican) is quite large, extending from an 18 percentage point Democratic advantage among those 21, 23, and 25, down to just a 3-point edge among those 39, 43, and 69.

Partisan Gap by Age
% Democrat minus % Republican

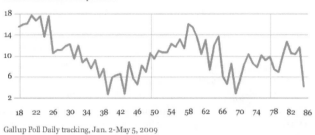

Gallup Poll Daily tracking, Jan. 2-May 5, 2009

Demographers and social observers have made attempts over the years to classify Americans into generational groups based on the social, political, economic, and cultural environment of the years in which they grew up and "came of age." The most clearly delineated such group is the **baby boomers**, generally agreed to be those born between 1946 and 1964—or roughly ages 45 to 63 today. **Generation X** follows the baby boom and is generally considered to be those born between 1965 and 1979—or roughly between ages 30 and 44. Those younger than Generation X have been labeled **Generation Y** or the "Millennials," who are 18 to 29 today. There are various ways of grouping those who preceded the baby boom generation, including the famous sobriquet "The Greatest Generation" used by Tom Brokaw in his book of the same name, but it is convenient to label those who today are 64 and older as **seniors** (even though some in this group would no doubt resist that label).

The current data suggest that political party identification in the United States today follows these generational patterns to a perhaps surprising degree.

Partisan Gap by Generational Group
% Democrat minus % Republican

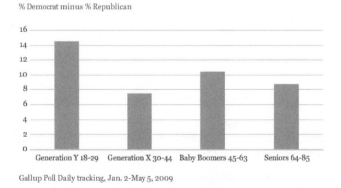

Gallup Poll Daily tracking, Jan. 2-May 5, 2009

Generation Y (18 to 29) clearly is skewed fairly strongly in the direction of being either independent or Democratic in political orientation. This group constitutes a significant weakness for the Republican Party.

Generation X (30 to 44) includes some of the strongest support for Republicans. For whatever reasons, the Democratic over Republican gap among Generation Xers, particularly those ages 37 to 43 at the heart of this generation, is on a relative basis much closer to parity than for any other age group with the exception of those in their late 60s.

Baby Boomers (45 to 63) skew Democratic in their political orientation, with the Democratic advantage reaching a peak at ages 58 and 59.

Seniors have a more mixed pattern of party identification, with Republicans gaining on a relative basis among those in their late 60s, but with Democrats doing better as Americans age into their 70s and early 80s.

Bottom Line

Democrats have a significant advantage over Republicans today in terms of overall party identification, and the data reviewed here show that this advantage holds at every age between 18 and 85.

At the same time, there are clear ebbs and flows in the degree of this Democratic advantage across the age spectrum. Democrats have the greatest advantage vis-á-vis Republicans among Americans at the very youngest voting age and also among members of the fabled baby boom, particularly those in their late 50s. Republicans do relatively better among those who are in Generation X, including in particular those in their late 30s and early 40s. Republicans also show greater support among older Americans in their late 60s.

Certainly some of these patterns are typical generational differences. Younger Americans have in the past been more likely to be independents and Democrats regardless of the particular cohort involved.

There is also the hypothesis that the differences are explained by the unique circumstances that surrounded the coming of age of the generations. Baby boomers, as is well known, grew up in the tumultuous age of civil rights, Vietnam, Woodstock, and Watergate. It is certainly possible that these events have marked this generation in a more Democratic or liberal direction for life. Many Generation Xers came of age during the Reagan-Bush years (1980 to 1992) or the "Republican Revolution" marked by the 1994 midterm elections. Today's Generation Y has reached maturity in a time period largely marked by the administration of George W. Bush, and certainly for many the nascent Obama administration is a major formative factor in their political orientation.

Survey Methods

Results are based on telephone interviews with 123,890 national adults, aged 18 and older, conducted Jan. 2 to May 5, 2009, as part of Gallup Poll Daily tracking. For results based on the total sample of national adults, one can say with 95% confidence that the maximum margin of sampling error is less than ±1 percentage point. The maximum margin of sampling error for each individual age varies depending on sample size, ranging from +/- 2% to 4% for any individual age.

Interviews are conducted with respondents on land-line telephones (for respondents with a land-line telephone) and cellular phones (for respondents who are cell-phone only).

In addition to sampling error, question wording and practical difficulties in conducting surveys can introduce error or bias into the findings of public opinion polls.

May 08, 2009

SAVINGS ACCOUNTS, REAL ESTATE SEEN AS BEST INVESTMENTS

Stocks, bonds less likely to be viewed as the best long-term investment

by Jeffrey M. Jones, Gallup Poll Managing Editor

When asked which of four common investments is best for the long term, Americans divide equally between savings accounts and real estate, with fewer choosing stocks or mutual funds as well as bonds.

Which of the following do you think is the best long-term investment -- [ROTATED: bonds, real estate, savings accounts or CDs, (or) stocks or mutual funds]?

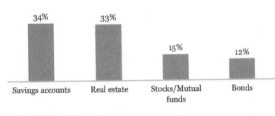

Gallup Poll, April 6-9, 2009

These results are based on Gallup's annual Economy and Personal Finance poll, conducted April 6–9, and reflect the reality of the U.S. investment climate. Stocks have lost much value over the past year and real estate prices have continued to fall. While savings accounts usually offer little return on the invested money, the fact that they return anything has probably made them a better investment in recent years than either stocks or real estate.

Savings accounts have ranked first or tied for first the last three times Gallup has asked this question, including last September, during the height of the financial crisis, and in last year's Economy and Personal Finance poll. Prior to that, savings accounts ranked no better than third among the four options.

Trend in Views of the Best Long-Term Investment

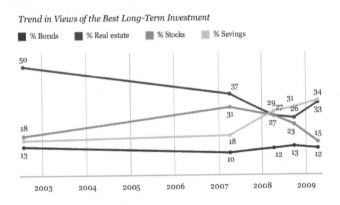

There has been some recovery in perceptions of real estate as the best long-term investment—it dipped to a low of 26% last September but now is at 33%. Americans may believe that the housing market is beginning to pick back up. A separate question in the poll found 71% saying now is a good time to buy a house, up 18 points from a year ago and the highest since 2005.

But even with the improvement this year, housing still ranks well below where it did during the real-estate boom years—in 2002,

50% of Americans said housing was the best long-term investment.

Similarly, stocks have lost some of their luster in recent years. In the 2007 Economy and Finance survey, 31% of Americans chose stocks as the best long-term investment. But that percentage has declined in each of the three polls since then, and has hit a new low of just 15%. Since the poll was conducted, stocks have recovered some of their lost value, but this remains much lower than before the financial crisis took hold.

Bonds—like savings accounts—tended to perform better than most other investments in the past year, but Americans' perceptions of bonds as the best long-term investment have varied little in response to economic conditions, ranging between 10% and 13% since 2002.

Implications

Americans' perceptions of the best long-term investment have shifted in line with changes in the real-world performance of the most common investments. Earlier this decade during the housing boom, real estate was the runaway winner as the best investment in Americans' minds, but as housing prices dropped, so did faith in real estate. It has recovered somewhat this year as Americans perceive an improving housing market.

The huge losses in stock investments over the past year have caused Americans to downgrade stocks, and as of the early April date of these results, the percentage of Americans viewing stocks or mutual funds as having the greatest long-term potential has hit a new low.

These changes have allowed savings accounts to gain in popularity, and thus a low-risk, low-reward investment now ranks at the head of the pack in terms of being viewed as the best long-term investment.

Survey Methods

Results are based on telephone interviews with 1,027 national adults, aged 18 and older, conducted April 6–9, 2009. For results based on the total sample of national adults, one can say with 95% confidence that the maximum margin of sampling error is ±3 percentage points.

Interviews are conducted with respondents on land-line telephones (for respondents with a land-line telephone) and cellular phones (for respondents who are cell-phone only).

In addition to sampling error, question wording and practical difficulties in conducting surveys can introduce error or bias into the findings of public opinion polls.

May 11, 2009

APPROVAL OF CONGRESS REMAINS STEADY AT 37%

Last three months mark a substantial uptick compared to 2008

by Frank Newport, Gallup Poll Editor in Chief

Americans give Congress a job approval rating of 37% in Gallup's latest update, conducted May 7–10—not statistically different from the previous two readings in March and April. However, all three of these ratings are significantly higher than the average job approval rating of 19% recorded for all of 2008.

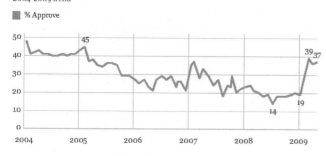

Do you approve or disapprove of the way Congress is handling its job?
2004-2009 trend

■ % Approve

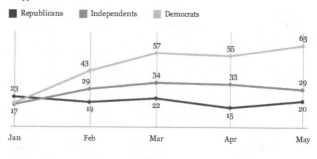

Congressional Job Approval, by Party ID, January-May 2009
% Approve

■ Republicans   ■ Independents   ■ Democrats

Congressional job approval reached an all-time low of 14% last July (with 75% disapproval). Approval moved up slightly through the fall of 2008 and into January of this year, and then jumped by 12 points in February, after both President Obama and the new House and Senate had begun work. Approval edged up slightly more in March, and—as noted—has remained fairly constant since.

From a long-term perspective, it is interesting to note that job approval of Congress has averaged 35% since 1974, when Gallup began measuring it in the current format (this overall average is based on the average of yearly averages since that time; Gallup did not ask about congressional job approval in 1984, 1985, and 1989). Thus, the current 37% job approval rating is fairly typical of what has been measured over the last 35 years.

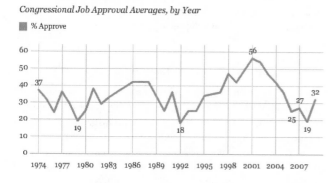

Congressional Job Approval Averages, by Year

■ % Approve

The lowest yearly congressional job approval in Gallup's history was 18% in 1992. Last year, 2008, was one of two years (along with 1979) in which congressional job approval was almost as low, at 19%.

The highest years for congressional job approval in Gallup's history were 2001 (56%) and 2002 (54%), reflecting the classic "rally effect" that resulted in Americans' evincing high ratings for their government in the aftermath of the Sept. 11, 2001, terrorist attacks. After 2002, congressional job approval fell each year through 2006, with a slight increase in 2007, and then the fall to 19% last year.

In terms of partisan differences, the current May reading reflects the same pattern as evidenced in March and April—with Democrats' approval of Congress well above the 50% level, while independents and Republicans remain much less positive.

Survey Methods

Results are based on telephone interviews with 1,015 national adults, aged 18 and older, conducted May 7–10, 2009. For results based on the total sample of national adults, one can say with 95% confidence that the maximum margin of sampling error is ±3 percentage points.

Interviews are conducted with respondents on land-line telephones (for respondents with a land-line telephone) and cellular phones (for respondents who are cell-phone only).

In addition to sampling error, question wording and practical difficulties in conducting surveys can introduce error or bias into the findings of public opinion polls.

May 13, 2009

NO CLAMOR FOR HIGH COURT APPOINTEE TO BE WOMAN, MINORITY

As in 2005, majority of Americans say gender, race, and ethnicity of appointee don't matter

by Frank Newport, Gallup Poll Editor in Chief

Despite the widely reported expectation that President Barack Obama will be looking for a qualified woman—perhaps from a minority racial or ethnic group—to fill the seat to be vacated by the retiring Justice David Souter, 64% of Americans say it doesn't matter to them whether Obama appoints a woman, with slightly higher percentages saying the same about the appointment of a black or Hispanic.

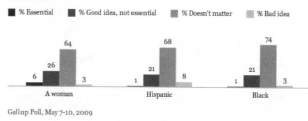

Do you think it is essential that the next Supreme Court justice be (a woman/Hispanic/black), is it a good idea, but not essential, does it not matter to you, or do you think it is a bad idea?

■ % Essential   ■ % Good idea, not essential   ■ % Doesn't matter   ■ % Bad idea

Gallup Poll, May 7-10, 2009

Justice Sandra Day O'Connor announced her resignation from the Court in 2005 and was replaced by a man (Samuel Alito), meaning that the Court today includes only one female justice, Ruth Bader Ginsburg, who herself has been battling cancer. As a result, there has been much speculation that President Obama will almost certainly nominate a female justice to avoid the possibility that within the next several years, the Court would have nine male justices. Still, as was the case four years ago, when there were two vacancies on the court (after Chief Justice William Rehnquist passed away and before

O'Connor's seat was filled), there is very little demand from the American public that Obama replace Souter with a woman.

Just 6% of Americans say it is "essential" that Obama appoint a woman, while another 26% say it would be "a good idea, but not essential." This combined percentage of 32% is smaller than the 43% and 47%, respectively, who responded in similar fashion in the Gallup Polls conducted in September and October 2005 about O'Connor's prospective replacement.

Views on Whether the Next Supreme Court Justice Should Be a Woman
Numbers in percentages

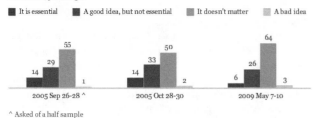

^ Asked of a half sample

These 2005 polls, as noted, were conducted at a time of significant turnover on the Supreme Court—with O'Connor announcing her retirement in the summer of that year, and the death of Rehnquist on Sept. 3. The Senate ultimately confirmed John Roberts as the new chief justice in late September, and after Bush's nomination of Harriet Miers was withdrawn in late October, the Senate took up confirmation hearings on Bush's nomination of Alito, who was ultimately confirmed on Jan. 31, 2006.

In the current poll, women are more likely than men to feel it is important that a woman be the next Supreme Court justice, but not by as large a margin as might be expected. Thirty-eight percent of women say it is essential or a good idea for the next Supreme Court justice to be a woman, compared with 24% of men. However, even with this gender difference, a majority of women (as well as a larger majority of men) say it doesn't matter to them.

Views on Whether the Next Supreme Court Justice Should Be a Woman
By gender

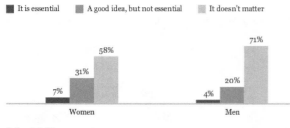

Gallup Poll, May 7-10, 2009

There are also partisan differences on this issue, with 26% of Republicans, 28% of independents, and 41% of Democrats saying it is essential or a good idea that the next justice be a woman. But again, a majority of all three groups say it does not matter to them.

There has been very little change over the last four years in the public's feelings about the next justice's being Hispanic or black, demographic characteristics that have also come up in news reports about Obama's contemplations of his choice of justice to replace Souter.

Sixty-eight percent of Americans say it doesn't matter to them whether a Hispanic is appointed, and 74% say it doesn't matter

Views on Whether the Next Supreme Court Justice Should Be Hispanic/Black

	It is essential	A good idea, but not essential	It doesn't matter	A bad idea	No opinion
	%	%	%	%	%
Hispanic					
2009 May 7-10	1	21	68	8	1
2005 Sep 26-28	3	23	69	4	1
Black					
2009 May 7-10	1	21	74	3	1
2005 Sep 26-28	5	21	71	2	1

Gallup Poll, May 7-10, 2009

whether a black is appointed. Both of these percentages are roughly the same as Gallup measured in 2005. The Supreme Court currently has one black justice (Clarence Thomas) and has never had a justice of Hispanic ethnicity.

Implications

It is unclear how much the average American knows about the current demographic composition of the Supreme Court. Still, as was the case four years ago, the current results suggest that—for whatever reason—there is simply no large groundswell of demand from the American public for the appointment of a new justice who possesses particular demographic characteristics.

By all accounts, there is a high probability that Obama will in fact appoint a woman, and perhaps one who is either black or Hispanic, no doubt in response to his own beliefs and/or pressure from certain interest groups or constituencies. It does not appear, however, that he would need to do so in response to the feelings of the broad constituency of average Americans.

Survey Methods

Results are based on telephone interviews with 1,015 national adults, aged 18 and older, conducted May 7–10, 2009. For results based on the total sample of national adults, one can say with 95% confidence that the maximum margin of sampling error is ±3 percentage points.

Interviews are conducted with respondents on land-line telephones (for respondents with a land-line telephone) and cellular phones (for respondents who are cell-phone only).

In addition to sampling error, question wording and practical difficulties in conducting surveys can introduce error or bias into the findings of public opinion polls.

May 14, 2009
AMERICANS MORE LIKELY TO SAY MORAL VALUES "GETTING BETTER"
Still overwhelmingly believe values are getting worse

by Jeffrey M. Jones, Gallup Poll Managing Editor

Though Americans still widely perceive moral values to be deteriorating rather than improving in the United States, there has been a significant increase since last year in the percentage who say moral values are getting better.

These results are based on the latest Gallup Values and Beliefs Poll, conducted annually each May, including May 7–10 this year.

Right now, do you think the state of moral values in the country as a whole is getting better or getting worse?

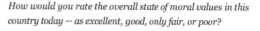

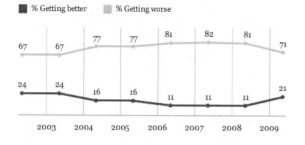

The current results are the least negative Gallup has found in the May Values polls since 2003, when 24% said U.S. moral values were getting better. Outside of the May Values series, Gallup found a slightly better reading of 27% shortly after George W. Bush won re-election in 2004—a year in which voters ranked moral values as the No. 1 issue to their vote in the National Exit Poll.

The improved optimism about moral values evident in the current data is generally the result of higher ratings from Democrats. Democrats (including independents who lean Democratic) are almost three times as likely to say moral values are getting better as they were in May 2008. Essentially the same proportion of Republicans say moral values are improving this year as last year.

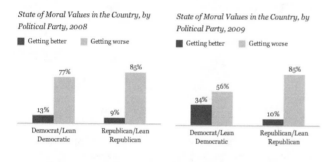

This is the latest example of a likely "Obama effect" that has caused Americans to perceive improving national conditions in a variety of areas, thanks largely to greater optimism among Democrats. Gallup has measured sharp increases since last year in the percentage of Americans rating the economy, the environment, and now, moral values as getting better.

Increases in Perceptions That National Conditions Are Getting Better, Gallup Polls, 2009 vs. 2008

In percentage points

Area	Change in % getting better, all Americans	Change among Democrats/ Democratic leaners	Change among Republicans/ Republican leaners
U.S. economy (May 2009 vs. May 2008)	+29	+46	+9
Environment (March 2009 vs. March 2008)	+15	+25	+5
Moral values (May 2009 vs. May 2008)	+10	+21	+1

Even as Americans perceive some positive momentum in U.S. moral values, their ratings of the current state of moral values are essentially unchanged from last year and years prior. Currently, 17% of Americans rate the state of moral values in the U.S. today as

"excellent" or "good," compared with 15% last year and an average of 18% in Values Polls from 2002–2008.

At the other end of the spectrum, 45% say the state of moral values in the United States is poor, which is similar to last year's 44% but technically the highest Gallup has found to date.

How would you rate the overall state of moral values in this country today — as excellent, good, only fair, or poor?

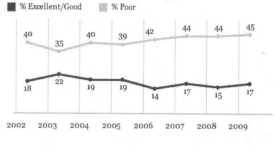

Ideological Differences

Americans who identify their political philosophy as "liberal" are the most optimistic about U.S. moral values, in terms of their assessments of both current conditions and whether values are improving. More liberals rate current U.S. moral values as excellent or good (32%) than as poor (27%), the only major demographic or attitudinal subgroup to do so. That is a far cry from the 11% excellent/good and 53% poor ratings from conservatives.

Ratings of State of Moral Values in This Country Today, by Political Ideology

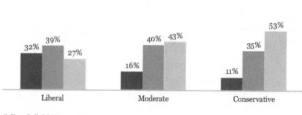

Gallup Poll, May 7-10, 2009

Similarly, liberals are more likely to say moral values are getting better (45%) than getting worse (42%). This is the first time in the eight-year history of this question that a major subgroup has had a net-positive rating on this measure.

Ratings of Moral Values as Getting Better or Getting Worse, by Political Ideology

Gallup Poll, May 7-10, 2009

Implications

Americans are not rating the current state of moral values in the country any more positively this year than last, but there is the sense by a small but growing proportion of the American public (mostly on the left side of the political spectrum) that things are getting better in this area. But this sense of improving conditions may merely reflect increased enthusiasm for a new presidential administration—chiefly among Democrats, who largely share Obama's political outlook—as opposed to real, observed improvement in Americans' moral values.

Survey Methods

Results are based on telephone interviews with 1,015 national adults, aged 18 and older, conducted May 7–10, 2009. For results based on the total sample of national adults, one can say with 95% confidence that the maximum margin of sampling error is ±3 percentage points.

Interviews are conducted with respondents on land-line telephones (for respondents with a land-line telephone) and cellular phones (for respondents who are cell-phone only).

In addition to sampling error, question wording and practical difficulties in conducting surveys can introduce error or bias into the findings of public opinion polls.

May 14, 2009
"THRIVING" ECLIPSES "STRUGGLING" FOR FIRST TIME SINCE EARLY '08
Improvement in "thriving" in line with improving standard-of-living perceptions

by Elizabeth Mendes, Gallup Poll Staff Writer

More Americans were "thriving" than "struggling" in April—a first since February 2008.

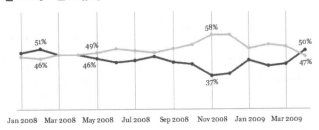

Gallup-Healthways Well-Being Index: Life Evaluation Trend
Based on the Cantril Self-Anchoring Striving Scale

Monthly aggregates since January 2008

In an aggregate of interviews conducted in April 2009, the Gallup-Healthways Well-Being Index finds 50% of Americans to be thriving and 47% struggling. This is a positive reversal of a trend that started last spring and worsened as the effects of the financial crisis permeated many Americans' lives. In April, the Index also recorded an overall national composite index score of 65.8—up from 64.3 in March, but still below the 66.7 in April of last year.

Gallup and Healthways began tracking life evaluation last year, with the monthly average percentage of thriving Americans peaking at 51% in February 2008, declining substantially as the economic crisis escalated in the fall of 2008, and hitting a low of 37% last

November. From January to March 2009, the monthly thriving percentages remained low compared to last year.

Based on the Cantril Self-Anchoring Striving Scale, the Gallup-Healthways Well-Being Index asks at least 1,000 Americans each day to evaluate their current lives as well as their expectations of where they will be in five years, using a ladder with steps numbered from 0 to 10, where "0" indicates the worst possible life and "10" the best possible life. Americans classified as "thriving" say they *presently stand on step 7 or higher of the ladder* and *expect to stand on step 8 or higher five years from now.* "Suffering" Americans are those who say they *presently stand on steps 0 to 4 of the ladder* and *expect to stand on steps 0 to 4 five years from now.* Americans whom Gallup does not classify as thriving or suffering are considered to be "struggling."

Gallup tracks several other measures daily and finds a clear relationship between the Life Evaluation measure and the Gallup Standard of Living Index. Specifically, the percentage who are thriving appears to increase and decrease in tandem with the percentage who say their standard of living is getting better.

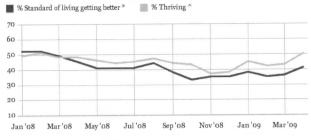

Standard of Living Getting Better vs. "Thriving" Americans
Monthly aggregates since January 2008

^ Gallup-Healthways Well-Being Index
* Gallup Poll Daily tracking

Similar to the pattern seen with life evaluation, April marks the first month since August 2008 in which the percentage of people who perceive their standard of living as getting better exceeds the percentage who perceive it as getting worse. James K. Harter, Ph.D., Gallup's chief scientist for workplace management and well-being, adds that "the ladder has historically been very income- and status-sensitive, and the standard-of-living and life evaluation items correlate very highly with each other."

In May so far, Gallup continues to find the Standard of Living Index on the rise, hitting its highest level in more than a year in the week leading up to Mother's Day, and the percentage of thriving Americans continuing to outnumber those who are struggling. Along with these improving perceptions of Americans' personal lives, Gallup also reports positive momentum in its Consumer Mood Index, which measures views on current economic conditions and economic outlook. If these attitudinal measures stabilize or recover further in the weeks and months ahead, they could be a tentative leading indicator that Americans are mentally bouncing back from the shock of the recession and could lead to a turnaround in consumer spending, which is yet to be seen.

Survey Methods

Results are based on telephone interviews with approximately 30,000 adults per month in the United States, aged 18 and older, conducted January 2008 to April 2009 as part of Gallup Poll Daily tracking. For results based on each monthly sample of national adults, one can say with 95% confidence that the maximum margin of sampling error is ±0.2 percentage points.

Interviews are conducted with respondents on land-line telephones (for respondents with a land-line telephone) and cellular phones (for respondents who are cell-phone only).

In addition to sampling error, question wording and practical difficulties in conducting surveys can introduce error or bias into the findings of public opinion polls.

About the Gallup-Healthways Well-Being Index™

The Gallup-Healthways Well-Being Index™ measures the daily pulse of U.S. well-being and provides best-in-class solutions for a healthier world. To learn more, please visit www.well-beingindex .com.

May 15, 2009
MORE AMERICANS "PRO-LIFE" THAN "PRO-CHOICE" FOR FIRST TIME
Also, fewer think abortion should be legal "under any circumstances"

by Lydia Saad, Gallup Poll Senior Editor

A new Gallup Poll, conducted May 7–10, finds 51% of Americans calling themselves "pro-life" on the issue of abortion and 42% "pro-choice." This is the first time a majority of U.S. adults have identified themselves as pro-life since Gallup began asking this question in 1995.

With respect to the abortion issue, would you consider yourself to be pro-choice or pro-life?

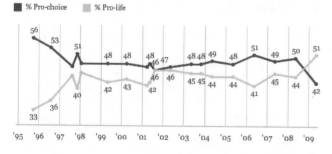

The new results, obtained from Gallup's annual Values and Beliefs survey, represent a significant shift from a year ago, when 50% were pro-choice and 44% pro-life. Prior to now, the highest percentage identifying as pro-life was 46%, in both August 2001 and May 2002.

The May 2009 survey documents comparable changes in public views about the legality of abortion. In answer to a question providing three options for the extent to which abortion should be legal, about as many Americans now say the procedure should be illegal in all circumstances (23%) as say it should be legal under any circumstances (22%). This contrasts with the last four years, when Gallup found a strong tilt of public attitudes in favor of unrestricted abortion.

Do you think abortions should be legal under any circumstances, legal only under certain circumstances, or illegal in all circumstances?

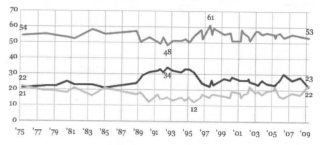

Gallup also found public preferences for the extreme views on abortion about even—as they are today—in 2005 and 2002, as well as during much of the first decade of polling on this question from 1975 to 1985. Still, the dominant position on this question remains the middle option, as it has continuously since 1975: 53% currently say abortion should be legal only under certain circumstances.

When the views of this middle group are probed further—asking these respondents whether they believe abortion should be legal in most or only a few circumstances—Gallup finds the following breakdown in opinion.

Combined Position on Legality of Abortion

Americans' recent shift toward the pro-life position is confirmed in two other surveys. The same three abortion questions asked on the Gallup Values and Beliefs survey were included in Gallup Poll Daily tracking from May 12–13, with nearly identical results, including a 50% to 43% pro-life versus pro-choice split on the self-identification question.

With respect to the abortion issue, would you consider yourself to be pro-choice or pro-life?

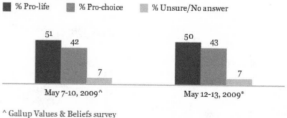

^ Gallup Values & Beliefs survey
* Gallup Poll Daily tracking

Additionally, a recent national survey by the Pew Research Center recorded an eight percentage-point decline since last August in those saying abortion should be legal in all or most cases, from 54% to 46%. The percentage saying abortion should be legal in only a few or no cases increased from 41% to 44% over the same period. As a result, support for the two broad positions is now about even, sharply different from most polling on this question since 1995, when the majority has typically favored legality.

Republicans Move to the Right

The source of the shift in abortion views is clear in the Gallup Values and Beliefs survey. The percentage of Republicans (including independents who lean Republican) calling themselves "pro-life" rose by 10 points over the past year, from 60% to 70%, while there has been essentially no change in the views of Democrats and Democratic leaners.

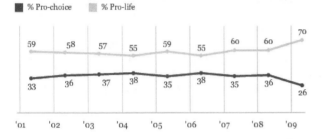

Recent Trend in Self-Identified Position on Abortion
Based on Republicans/Republican leaners

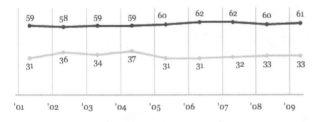

Recent Trend in Self-Identified Position on Abortion
Based on Democrats/Democratic leaners

Similarly, by ideology, all of the increase in pro-life sentiment is seen among self-identified conservatives and moderates; the abortion views of political liberals have not changed.

Recent Trend in Percentage "Pro-Life," Based on Political Ideology

"Pro-Life" Up Among Catholics and Protestants

One of the more prominent news stories touching on the abortion issue in recent months involves President Barack Obama's commencement speech and the bestowal of an honorary doctorate degree

on him at the University of Notre Dame—a Roman Catholic institution—on Sunday. The invitation has drawn criticism from conservative Catholics and the church hierarchy because of Obama's policies in favor of legalizing and funding abortion, and the controversy might have been expected to strengthen the pro-life leanings of rank-and-file Catholics.

Nevertheless, the swelling of the pro-life position since last year is seen across Christian religious affiliations, including an eight-point gain among Protestants and a seven-point gain among Catholics.

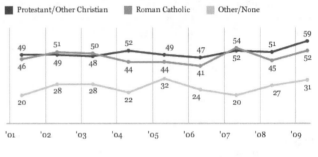

Recent Trend in Percentage "Pro-Life," Based on Religious Preference

Gender Agreement

A year ago, Gallup found more women calling themselves pro-choice than pro-life, by 50% to 43%, while men were more closely divided: 49% pro-choice, 46% pro-life. Now, because of heightened pro-life sentiment among both groups, women as well as men are more likely to be pro-life.

Men and women have been evenly divided on the issue in previous years; however, this is the first time in nine years of Gallup Values surveys that significantly more men and women are pro-life than pro-choice.

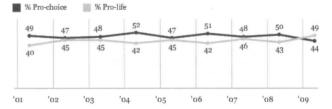

Recent Trend Abortion Position, Based on Women

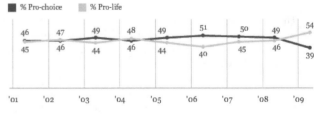

Recent Trend Abortion Position, Based on Men

Bottom Line

With the first pro-choice president in eight years already making changes to the nation's policies on funding abortion overseas, expressing his support for the Freedom of Choice Act, and moving toward rescinding federal job protections for medical workers who refuse to participate in abortion procedures, Americans—and, in particular, Republicans—seem to be taking a step back from the pro-choice position. However, the retreat is evident among political moderates as well as conservatives.

It is possible that, through his abortion policies, Obama has pushed the public's understanding of what it means to be "pro-choice" slightly to the left, politically. While Democrats may support that, as they generally support everything Obama is doing as president, it may be driving others in the opposite direction.

Survey Methods

Results are based on telephone interviews with 1,015 national adults, aged 18 and older, conducted May 7–10, 2009. For results based on the total sample of national adults, one can say with 95% confidence that the maximum margin of sampling error is ±3 percentage points.

Gallup Poll Daily results are based on telephone interviews with 971 national adults, aged 18 and older, conducted May 12–13, 2009, as part of Gallup Poll Daily tracking. For results based on the total sample of national adults, one can say with 95% confidence that the maximum margin of sampling error is ±3 percentage points.

Interviews are conducted with respondents on land-line telephones (for respondents with a land-line telephone) and cellular phones (for respondents who are cell-phone only).

In addition to sampling error, question wording and practical difficulties in conducting surveys can introduce error or bias into the findings of public opinion polls.

May 18, 2009

GOP LOSSES SPAN NEARLY ALL DEMOGRAPHIC GROUPS

Only frequent churchgoers show no decline in support since 2001

by Jeffrey M. Jones, Gallup Poll Managing Editor

The decline in Republican Party affiliation among Americans in recent years is well documented, but a Gallup analysis now shows that this movement away from the GOP has occurred among nearly every major demographic subgroup. Since the first year of George W. Bush's presidency in 2001, the Republican Party has maintained its support only among frequent churchgoers, with conservatives and senior citizens showing minimal decline.

So far in 2009, aggregated Gallup Poll data show the divide on leaned party identification is 53% Democratic and 39% Republican—a marked change from 2001, when the parties were evenly matched, according to an average of all of that year's Gallup Polls. That represents a loss of five points for the Republicans and a gain of eight points for the Democrats.

The parties were also evenly matched on basic party identification in 2001 (which does not take into account the partisan leanings of independents), with 32% identifying themselves as Republicans, 33% as Democrats, and 34% as independents. The 2009 data show the GOP losing five points since then, with identification increasing three points among both Democrats and independents.

As was shown earlier, the GOP's loss in leaned support over this time is evident among nearly every subgroup. The losses are sub-

Change in Republican Party Identification and Leaning, 2001 vs. 2009

Change in Republican Party Identification and Leaning, 2001 vs. 2009 (continued)

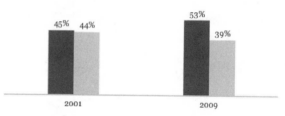

Leaned Party Identification, All Americans, 2001 vs. 2009

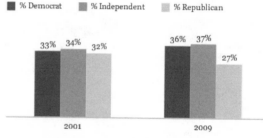

Basic Party Identification, All Americans, 2001 vs. 2009

stantial among college graduates, which have shown a decline in GOP support of 10 points. (The losses are even greater—13 points—among the subset of college graduates with postgraduate educations.) This may reflect in part Barack Obama's strong appeal to educated voters, a major component of his winning coalitions in both the Democratic primaries and the general election.

Aside from education, for which the parties were basically at even strength in 2001, the Republicans' losses tend to be greater among groups that were not strong GOP supporters to begin with. These include self-identified liberals and moderates, church non-attenders, and lower-income and young adults. Thus, a big factor in the GOP's overall decline is the Democratic Party's consolidating its support among normally Democratically leaning groups.

In turn, the GOP has generally avoided significant losses among only its most loyal groups, including frequent churchgoers and self-identified conservatives. The Republican Party maintains majority support among these two groups.

Changes in Leaned Party Identification, College Graduates, 2001 vs. 2009

Two exceptions to this general pattern are senior citizens, and racial and ethnic minorities. Republican support among blacks and the larger group of nonwhites has not changed much in the past eight years, but these groups have shown only very limited support for the Republican Party. And while Obama's candidacy seemed to attract young voters to the Democratic Party during the 2008 presidential campaign, it did not have the same effect on older voters. As a result, the share of older voters aligned with the Republican Party has generally held steady.

Changes in Leaned Republican Party Identification, by Subgroup, 2001 vs. 2009

	2001	2009	Republican loss
	%	%	Pct. pts.
College graduate	47	37	-10
18 to 29 yrs old	41	32	-9
Midwest	46	37	-9
Less than $30,000 annual income	37	28	-9
$30,000 to <$75,000 annual income	48	39	-9
Moderate ideology	37	28	-9
Seldom/Never attend church	38	29	-9
Liberal ideology	17	9	-8
Not married	37	29	-8
Male	49	42	-7
$75,000+ annual income	54	47	-7
White	50	44	-6
50 to 64 yrs old	44	38	-6
East	39	33	-6
Attend church nearly weekly/monthly	46	40	-6
Female	40	35	-5
West	45	40	-5
Married	51	46	-5
30 to 49 yrs old	46	42	-4
South	47	43	-4
College nongraduate	43	40	-3
Black	12	10	-2
Nonwhite	23	22	-1
65+ yrs old	42	41	-1
Conservative ideology	66	65	-1
Attend church weekly	52	52	0

Implications

The Republican Party clearly has lost a lot of support since 2001, the first year of George W. Bush's administration. Most of the loss in support actually occurred beginning in 2005, after Hurricane Katrina and Bush's nomination of Harriet Miers to the Supreme Court—both of which created major public relations problems for the administration—and amid declining support for the Iraq war. By the end of

2008, the party had its worst positioning against the Democrats in nearly two decades.

The GOP may have stemmed those losses for now, as it does not appear to have lost any more support since Obama took office. But as the analysis presented here shows, the losses the GOP has suffered have come among nearly all demographic groups apart from some of the most ardent Republican subgroups.

Survey Methods

Results are based on telephone interviews with 7,139 national adults, aged 18 and older, in Gallup polls conducted January-April 2009. For results based on the total sample of national adults, one can say with 95% confidence that the maximum margin of sampling error is ±1 percentage point.

Margins of error for subgroups will be larger.

Interviews are conducted with respondents on land-line telephones (for respondents with a land-line telephone) and cellular phones (for respondents who are cell-phone only).

In addition to sampling error, question wording and practical difficulties in conducting surveys can introduce error or bias into the findings of public opinion polls.

May 18, 2009
AMERICANS CONSIDER CROSSING BORDERS FOR MEDICAL CARE
Competition for high-quality, affordable medical care no longer local

by Christopher Khoury, Gallup Poll Staff Writer

While domestic healthcare costs are expected to increase to an estimated 21% of GDP by 2010, some Americans may be interested in taking their healthcare spending elsewhere. A recent Gallup Poll finds that up to 29% of Americans would consider traveling abroad for medical procedures such as heart bypass surgery, hip or knee replacement, plastic surgery, cancer diagnosis and treatment, or alternative medical care, even though all are routinely done in the United States.

Would you, or would you not, personally consider traveling outside the United States for treatment in a foreign country for each of the following medical procedures?

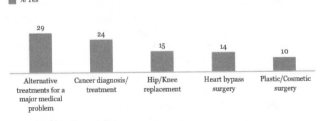

Gallup Poll Daily tracking, April 16-20, 2009

Have Ailments, Will Travel

Medical travel, categorized as *inbound* (from other countries to the U.S.) and *outbound* (to other countries from the U.S.), was originally a luxury afforded to the rich—particularly those inbound to the

United States and European countries for treatment at world-class facilities. Yet the increasing cost of medical care in the United States and large numbers of uninsured (at least 48 million people, according to the Kaiser Commission on Medicaid and the Uninsured) may be making outbound travel an option worth considering.

Gallup finds that sizable proportions of Americans would "consider traveling outside the United States for treatment in a foreign country" for a variety of procedures and medical treatments. Twenty-nine percent of respondents would consider traveling out of the U.S. for alternative medical treatments for a major medical problem, and 24% would seek cancer diagnosis and treatment abroad. Americans are less likely to say they would consider traveling abroad for orthopedic procedures (15%), heart treatment (14%), or elective cosmetic surgery (10%).

Can't Pass Up a Good Bargain

The poll of 5,050 U.S. adults involved a split-sample experiment, in which one random half-sample was asked the "direct" question, reported above, on whether they would consider treatment abroad. The second half was asked whether they would consider treatment abroad, assuming "the quality was the same and the costs significantly cheaper." Given this additional phrasing, the percentage saying they would consider medical treatment outside U.S. borders increased by 12 percentage points, on average.

Willingness to Travel Abroad for Medical Procedures, by Assumptions Made About Treatment

% Who would consider traveling abroad

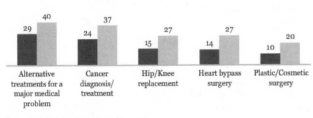

Gallup Poll Daily tracking, April 16-20, 2009

Across regions, respondents in the Midwest are consistently the least willing to consider obtaining treatments outside the country, whereas respondents in the West are consistently the most willing. Southerners are also below average in their willingness to obtain treatments outside the country, with the exception of hip or knee replacement.

Healthcare coverage is an important factor in the likelihood that Americans would consider getting health treatment abroad. Those who report that they don't have health insurance are more likely to consider going abroad for medical treatment. For example, 37% of respondents without health insurance would seek cancer care abroad as compared to 22% with health insurance.

Those without health insurance were on average 11 points more likely to say they would consider treatment abroad if the cost and quality provisions were included in the question than if they were not included.

Bottom Line

A sizable minority of Americans view the healthcare diagnosis and treatment available beyond national borders as something they would

Willingness to Travel Abroad for Medical Procedures, by Respondent Health Insurance Status

% Who would consider traveling abroad (no assumptions made about treatment)

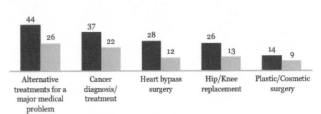

Gallup Poll Daily tracking, April 16-20, 2009

Willingness to Travel Abroad for Medical Procedures, Among Those Without Health Insurance

By assumptions made about treatment

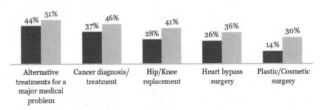

Gallup Poll Daily tracking, April 16-20, 2009

consider using. If strides in insurance reimbursements, overseas hospital quality, and affordability continue, it will be an increasingly attractive option for Americans. The data suggest the estimated population of 48 million Americans without health insurance are motivated by costs and would be more likely than those with health insurance coverage to consider seeking medical care from alternative sources.

Survey Methods

Results are based on telephone interviews with 5,050 national adults aged 18 and older, split into samples of 2,524 and 2,572, conducted April 16–20, 2009, as part of Gallup Poll Daily tracking. For results based on these samples of national adults, one can say with 95% confidence that the maximum margin of sampling error is ±2 percentage points.

Interviews are conducted with respondents on land-line telephones (for respondents with a land-line telephone) and cellular phones (for respondents who are cell-phone only).

In addition to sampling error, question wording and practical difficulties in conducting surveys can introduce error or bias into the findings of public opinion polls.

May 19, 2009

AMERICANS GREEN-LIGHT HIGHER FUEL EFFICIENCY STANDARDS

Majority support spans political parties and demographics

by Lymari Morales, Gallup Poll Staff Writer

A recent Gallup Poll reveals solid majority support for higher fuel efficiency standards such as those President Obama announced Tuesday. In March, 80% of Americans said they favored higher fuel efficiency standards for automobiles.

Support for Setting Higher Fuel Efficiency Standards for Automobiles

Gallup Poll, March 5-8, 2009

Flanked by executives from the auto industry, Obama announced standards that will require that all new vehicles average 35.5 miles per gallon by 2016. The president's plan will also require new greenhouse emissions standards, which, in 2007, 79% of Americans told Gallup they supported. The Obama administration puts the total additional cost per vehicle at $1,300, with an environmental benefit equivalent to taking 177 million cars off the road. Obama estimated that the additional cost to car buyers would be offset within three years by costs saved on gasoline.

Obama announced his proposal along with state governors from both sides of the aisle. While Democrats show more widespread support for higher fuel efficiency standards, 72% of Republicans also say they are in favor—highlighting the opportunity for bipartisan collaboration on this issue.

Support for Setting Higher Fuel Efficiency Standards for Automobiles
% Favor, by party ID

Gallup Poll, March 5-8, 2009

An examination of support among demographic subcategories also finds strong majority support for higher fuel efficiency standards—generally above 70%—across the board. Support varies slightly by region: 77% in the West, 79% in the South, 82% in the Midwest, and 83% in the East.

Not surprisingly, Americans who feel more strongly about the environment and the need to protect it are more likely to support higher fuel efficiency standards. However, even Americans who are not particularly worried about the environment or global warming also favor higher fuel standards: three-quarters of each group is in favor.

Support for Setting Higher Fuel Efficiency Standards for Automobiles
% Favor, by views on environment

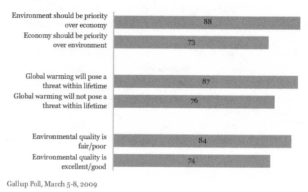

Gallup Poll, March 5-8, 2009

Underscoring Obama's likely confidence in moving forward with his decision, 68% of Americans last July said they would be more rather than less likely to vote for a candidate who supported raising fuel mileage standards on vehicles.

Would you be more likely or less likely to vote for a candidate who supported raising fuel mileage standards on vehicles?

Gallup Poll, July 25-28, 2008

Implications

Gallup finds strong and consistent majority support for higher fuel efficiency standards, as it typically does for proposals designed to help the environment. It has also recorded similar support in the last few years for higher emissions standards. However, it important to note that Americans' support for specific environmental policies or actions is often somewhat lower (but still usually above the majority level) when respondents are reminded of the costs they may have to bear personally.

In the past, Gallup has found somewhat fewer Americans willing to buy a hybrid car when the higher costs of hybrids are mentioned than when they are not mentioned, and lower support for steps to curb air pollution, depending on how much the costs of the products they buy would increase. To this end, Obama was smart to describe how an additional higher upfront cost is likely to be offset by spending less on gas in the future. To maintain the high levels of support with which the government begins this endeavor, both the administration and the auto industry would be well-served to ensure that the benefits to consumers ultimately do outweigh the costs.

Survey Methods

Results are based on telephone interviews with 1,012 national adults, aged 18 and older, conducted March 5–8, 2009. For results based on the total sample of national adults, one can say with 95% confidence that the maximum margin of sampling error is ±3 percentage points.

Interviews are conducted with respondents on land-line telephones (for respondents with a land-line telephone) and cellular phones (for respondents who are cell-phone only).

In addition to sampling error, question wording and practical difficulties in conducting surveys can introduce error or bias into the findings of public opinion polls.

May 20, 2009
REPUBLICANS MOVE TO THE RIGHT ON SEVERAL MORAL ISSUES
No change in Democrats' attitudes about what is morally acceptable

by Lydia Saad, Gallup Poll Senior Editor

According to Gallup's annual "moral acceptability" measure, updated in May, Americans have inched to the right on a handful of the 15 issues rated, including divorce, use of animal fur in clothing, gambling, and embryonic stem-cell research. Public opinion about the moral acceptability of the other items is essentially unchanged, with no significant increases in support for traditionally liberal positions.

Recent Trend in Acceptance of Social Matters and Policies

% Morally acceptable

	May 8-11, 2008	May 7-10, 2009	Change
	%	%	Pct. pts.
Buying and wearing clothing made of animal fur	54	61	7
Medical testing on animals	56	57	1
Gay or lesbian relations	48	49	1
Cloning animals	33	34	1
Death penalty	62	62	0
Suicide	15	15	0
Polygamy, when one husband has more than one wife at the same time	8	7	-1
Married men and women having an affair	7	6	-1
Cloning humans	11	9	-2
Sex between an unmarried man and woman	61	57	-4
Having a baby outside of marriage	55	51	-4
Abortion	40	36	-4
Gambling	63	58	-5
Medical research using stem cells obtained from human embryos	62	57	-5
Divorce	70	62	-8

Despite these slight changes, a majority of Americans continue to view divorce, gambling, and embryonic stem-cell research as morally acceptable, and acceptance of using animal fur for clothing has only strengthened. The death penalty, premarital sex, and medical testing on animals also meet with Americans' approval, ethically.

Only about half of Americans consider having a baby outside of marriage, as well as gay or lesbian relations, to be morally acceptable. Nearly as many say these actions are morally wrong, making them the social issues tested on which there is the greatest disagreement.

Abortion, cloning (whether of animals or humans), suicide, polygamy, and extramarital affairs are all viewed as morally wrong by solid majorities of Americans.

Republicans Adopt More Conservative Stances

As Gallup recently reported with respect to Americans' shift toward the "pro-life" position on abortion, most of the uptick in support for

Next, I'm going to read you a list of issues. Regardless of whether or not you think it should be legal, for each one, please tell me whether you personally believe that in general it is morally acceptable or morally wrong.

May 7-10, 2009

	Morally acceptable	Morally wrong
	%	%
Divorce	62	30
The death penalty	62	30
Buying and wearing clothing made of animal fur	61	35
Gambling	58	36
Medical research using stem cells obtained from human embryos	57	36
Sex between an unmarried man and woman	57	40
Medical testing on animals	57	36
Having a baby outside of marriage	51	45
Gay or lesbian relations	49	47
Abortion	36	56
Cloning animals	34	63
Suicide	15	80
Cloning humans	9	88
Polygamy, when one husband has more than one wife at the same time	7	91
Married men and women having an affair	6	92

conservative positions over the past year is the result of Republicans (including independents who lean Republican) moving to the political right in their views. There have been no significant increases in conservative views among Democrats (including Democratic-leaning independents).

Over the past year, the percentage of Republicans saying embryonic stem-cell research is morally acceptable fell by nine points, from 50% to 41%—a new low for Republicans on this issue since Gallup began measuring it in 2002. At the same time, acceptance among Democrats has held steady at 74%.

The last time Gallup found any substantial change among Republicans or Democrats in attitudes about stem-cell research using human embryos was in May 2005; at that time, Democrats' support increased by 14 points compared to the previous year. This may have reflected the enhanced partisan debate over the issue during the 2004 presidential campaign, with the Democratic presidential candidate, John Kerry, strongly supporting the research.

Trend in Moral Acceptability of Stem-Cell Research Using Human Embryos

% Morally acceptable

■ Republicans/Lean Republican   ▨ Democrats/Lean Democratic

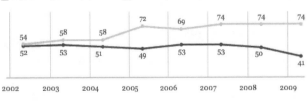

As for gambling, divorce, and use of clothing made of animal fur, the Republican rightward shifts since 2008 merely put Republican views back to where they were at other points in recent years.

While only 52% of Republicans today say divorce is morally acceptable, down from 64% a year ago, it is similar to their 55% approval in 2007, as well as 53% at the start of the trend in 2001.

The 10-point increase among Republicans since last year in the moral acceptability of using animal fur for clothing, from 63% to 73%, restores their attitudes to where they were three years ago.

Trend in Moral Acceptability of Divorce

% Morally acceptable

■ Republicans/Lean Republican   ■ Democrats/Lean Democratic

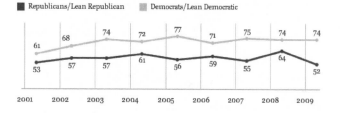

Trend in Moral Acceptability of Buying and Wearing Clothing Made of Animal Fur

% Morally acceptable

■ Republicans/Lean Republican   ■ Democrats/Lean Democratic

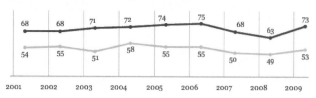

Similarly, while Republican support for gambling has dropped by six points since May 2008, the 55% support for gambling today is consistent with Republican attitudes only two years ago.

Trend in Moral Acceptability of Gambling

% Morally acceptable

■ Republicans/Lean Republican   ■ Democrats/Lean Democratic

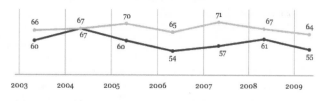

Although in the May 7–10 Values and Beliefs survey, Gallup found a 10-point increase over last year (from 60% to 70%) in the percentage of Republicans calling themselves "pro-life," the same poll shows only a 5-point—and not statistically significant—decrease in the percentage of Republicans calling abortion "morally acceptable."

Trend in Moral Acceptability of Abortion

% Morally acceptable

■ Republicans/Lean Republican   ■ Democrats/Lean Democratic

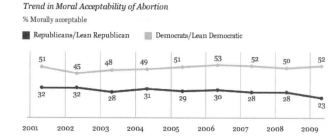

Expanded Democratic Tolerance for Gay/Lesbian Relations

Since May 2008, Democrats' views have shifted on only 1 of the 15 issues. Gallup trends document a seven-point increase in the percentage viewing gay and lesbian relations as morally acceptable, from 59% to 66%. While the 2009 reading is technically the highest

percentage of Democrats taking this position in the nine years of Gallup polling on the subject, it is similar to the 63% in 2007.

This year's change among Democrats is offset by a slight (though not statistically significant) decline in the percentage of Republicans viewing gay and lesbian relations as morally acceptable, as well as a larger drop in tolerance among the relatively small number of Americans who consider themselves politically independent with no leaning toward either party. As a result, there has been little change in the overall views of Americans on the issue.

Trend in Moral Acceptability of Gay/Lesbian Relations*

% Morally acceptable

■ Republicans/Lean Republican   ■ Democrats/Lean Democratic

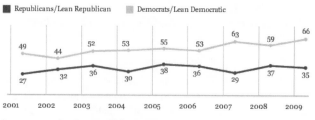

* 2001-2004 wording: Homosexual behavior; 2005-2008 wording: Homosexual relations

Bottom Line

Americans' views about what is and isn't morally acceptable in today's culture have not changed dramatically over the past year. To the extent they have changed, they have moved slightly to the right on a handful of issues, almost entirely because of more pronounced conservative shifts among Republicans and Republican-leaning independents. This is particularly evident with respect to lower Republican support for divorce and embryonic stem-cell research, and increased Republican support for the use of animal fur in clothing.

Survey Methods

Results are based on telephone interviews with 1,015 national adults, aged 18 and older, conducted May 7–10, 2009. For results based on the total sample of national adults, one can say with 95% confidence that the maximum margin of sampling error is ±3 percentage points.

Interviews are conducted with respondents on land-line telephones (for respondents with a land-line telephone) and cellular phones (for respondents who are cell-phone only).

In addition to sampling error, question wording and practical difficulties in conducting surveys can introduce error or bias into the findings of public opinion polls.

May 21, 2009

PELOSI GETS POOR MARKS FOR HANDLING INTERROGATION MATTER

More disapprove than approve of speaker's response

by Jeffrey M. Jones, Gallup Poll Managing Editor

More Americans disapprove than approve of House Speaker Nancy Pelosi's handling of the matter concerning the government's use of harsh interrogation techniques on terrorism suspects. Majorities approve of President Barack Obama's and the CIA's handling of the matter.

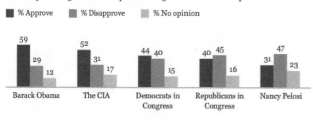

Do you approve or disapprove of how each of the following has handled the matter of interrogation techniques used against terrorism suspects?

■ % Approve   ■ % Disapprove   ▨ % No opinion

May 19 Gallup Poll

Even though Obama has pledged that the United States will no longer use harsh interrogation techniques (like waterboarding) that many consider to be torture, the issue has remained in the news, with some in Congress—including Pelosi—calling for an investigation into the use of such techniques during the Bush administration.

Last week, Pelosi attempted to respond to allegations that she learned of the use of waterboarding in September 2002 during a CIA briefing of congressional leaders. In her press conference, she asserted that the CIA misled her by denying that waterboarding was being used, even though government reports indicate it had been used on an al Qaeda terror suspect in the month prior to that briefing. The CIA responded and disputed her assertions that the agency misled her. Republican leaders have roundly criticized her remarks.

Sixty percent of Americans say they are following the news about the government's use of harsh interrogation techniques closely, including 22% who say they are following it "very closely." Republicans (66%) are slightly more likely than independents or Democrats (each 59%) to be following the matter closely.

The May 19 poll finds Pelosi largely losing the public relations game, as she gets a significantly more negative review for her handling of the matter than do the other major players in the controversy, including the CIA. Also, notably, Americans are much more critical of Pelosi's handling of the matter than they are of the broader group of the Democrats in Congress she leads as speaker of the House.

Those who are paying the closest attention to the matter are especially critical of Pelosi, with 63% of this group disapproving of her, compared with just 30% who approve. This highly attentive group is generally somewhat more critical than the general public is of each of the actors—aside from the CIA, which is rated much more positively by those who are following the matter closely (63% approve) than by the broader population (52% approve).

Approve/Disapprove of How Each Is Handling Terror Interrogation Matter
Based on those following news about the matter very closely

■ % Approve   ▨ % Disapprove

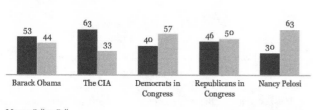

May 19 Gallup Poll

As might be expected, Republicans and Democrats have very different opinions on how each of the actors has handled the matter. Democrats generally approve of the way Obama, congressional

Democrats, and Pelosi have reacted, while Republicans evaluate the Congressional Republicans' and the CIA's actions positively. Democrats are about evenly divided in their evaluations of the CIA—with 42% approving and 41% disapproving. By comparison, Pelosi's rating among Democrats is more positive than negative, 45% to 31%.

Approve of How Each Is Handling Terror Interrogation Matter, by Political Party

	Democrats	Independents	Republicans
Barack Obama	82%	55%	35%
The CIA	42%	50%	72%
Democrats in Congress	65%	39%	22%
Republicans in Congress	19%	45%	65%
Nancy Pelosi	45%	26%	17%

May 19 Gallup Poll

Implications

Although there are no trend data on this particular question, it appears that Pelosi's attempt last week at damage control did not do a great deal to bolster her image on the interrogation situation. More Americans disapprove than approve of her handling of the interrogation matter, particularly those paying a high level of attention to the controversy. Also, Americans make a clear distinction between Pelosi and her fellow Democrats in Congress and in the White House. So far, the Democratic caucus is standing firmly behind its leader. But the controversy is certainly an unwelcome distraction to the Democrats as they seek to pass an ambitious agenda this summer.

Survey Methods

Results are based on telephone interviews with 997 national adults, aged 18 and older, conducted May 19, 2009. For results based on the total sample of national adults, one can say with 95% confidence that the maximum margin of sampling error is ±3 percentage points.

Interviews are conducted with respondents on land-line telephones (for respondents with a land-line telephone) and cellular phones (for respondents who are cell-phone only).

In addition to sampling error, question wording and practical difficulties in conducting surveys can introduce error or bias into the findings of public opinion polls.

Polls conducted entirely in one day, such as this one, are subject to additional error or bias not found in polls conducted over several days.

May 21, 2009
UPPER-INCOME SPENDING DECLINING IN EARLY MAY
Gallup's self-reported Monitor of Consumer Spending provides new insights

by Dennis Jacobe, Gallup Chief Economist

Upper-income Americans' self-reported spending in stores, restaurants, gas stations, and online averaged $94 per day during the first 15 days of May—down 15% from April and down 48% from the same period a year ago. Unless this turns around quickly, the economy is likely to see "dead shoots" replacing the "green shoots" of economic recovery—particularly for upscale retailers and big-ticket-item sales.

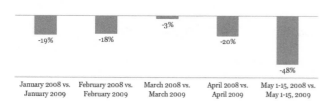

January 2008 vs. January 2009	February 2008 vs. February 2009	March 2008 vs. March 2009	April 2008 vs. April 2009	May 1-15, 2008 vs. May 1-15, 2009

Upper-Income Spending Worsening

Gallup's self-reported consumer spending measure finds that upper-income Americans (those earning $90,000 or more a year) spent 15% less during the first half of May (an average of $94 per day) than they did in April ($111)—giving May the lowest average daily spending rate of the year. In terms of seasonally comparable spending, upper-income spending is off 48% from the first half of May 2008—also representing the sharpest year-to-year decline seen thus far in 2009. It should be noted that year-ago comparables are artificially high as a result of last year's relatively large tax rebates and their positive, if temporary, impact on consumer spending. Of course, this effect is mitigated somewhat in this instance because the rebates were phased out for many upper-income consumers.

Upper-Income Consumer Spending

Average spending per day

■ 2008   ▨ 2009

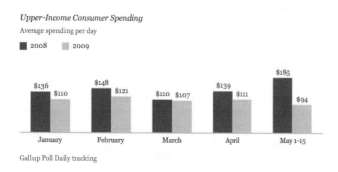

January	February	March	April	May 1-15

Gallup Poll Daily tracking

Middle- and Lower-Income Spending

During the first half of May, Gallup's self-reported consumer spending measure among middle- and lower-income Americans showed a month-to-month increase of 12%, with average May spending increasing to $58 per day from $52 per day during April. However, when compared to a year ago, May 1–15 spending by these consumers is actually down 48%. This is worse than the 30% decline in year-to-year spending that has taken place in each of the past two months among middle- and lower-income consumers. This larger May decline could also reflect in part the impact of the 2008 tax rebates on May spending.

Survey Methods

Gallup's Monitor of Consumer Spending is based on aggregated interviews with a nationally representative random sample of approximately 500 adults aged 18 or older each day. For monthly results that are based on samples of approximately 14,000, the maximum margin

Middle- and Lower-Income Consumer Spending

Average spending per day

■ 2008   ▨ 2009

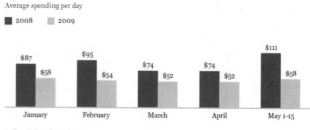

January	February	March	April	May 1-15

Gallup Poll Daily tracking

of sampling error is ±1 percentage point. Results for May 1–15, 2008, are based on a sample of 5,788 national adults and for May 1–15, 2009, on a sample of 5,490 national adults. For these samples, the maximum margin of sampling error is ±2 percentage points.

Interviews are conducted with respondents on land-line telephones (for respondents with a land-line telephone) and cellular phones (for respondents who are cell-phone only).

In addition to sampling error, question wording and practical difficulties in conducting surveys can introduce error or bias into the findings of public opinion polls.

May 22, 2009
RECESSION ALTERING PLANS FOR HALF OF SUMMER TRAVELERS
Higher percentage of Americans than in past summers not planning to travel at all

by Jeffrey M. Jones, Gallup Poll Managing Editor

A new *USA Today*/Gallup poll finds that only half of Americans plan to travel this summer, and of those with plans, 52% (or 25% of all Americans) say they are altering those plans in response to the current economic recession.

Effect of Economic Recession on Summer Recreation/Travel Plans

■ Changing plans   ■ Going ahead with plans
▨ Did not have travel plans

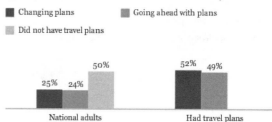

National adults	Had travel plans

USA Today/Gallup poll, May 18-19, 2009

The poll was conducted May 18–19 in advance of the summer travel season, which is traditionally kicked off by the Memorial Day holiday weekend.

It is possible that the impact of the recession may be even greater than the poll results discussed above suggest. The 50% of Americans who indicated they do not have travel plans this summer is significantly higher than what Gallup found in both 2006 (38%) and 2008 (41%), when it sought to assess the impact of high gas prices on summer travel plans. Thus, it's possible that the recession is causing a significant proportion of Americans who traveled in previous summers to rule out taking a vacation this year.

Percentage of Americans With No Plans to Travel During the Summer, 2006-2009 Gallup Polls

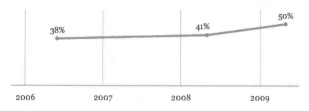

As might be expected, the poor economy is having its greatest impact on lower-income Americans. There seems to be a tipping point at $60,000 annual household income, with those at or above that limit more likely to say they will go ahead with their plans unaltered than change them, and the reverse true for those below that income level.

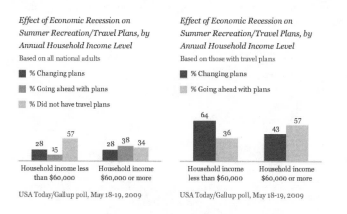

Effect of Economic Recession on Summer Recreation/Travel Plans, by Annual Household Income Level

Based on all national adults

■ % Changing plans
▦ % Going ahead with plans
▨ % Did not have travel plans

USA Today/Gallup poll, May 18-19, 2009

Effect of Economic Recession on Summer Recreation/Travel Plans, by Annual Household Income Level

Based on those with travel plans

■ % Changing plans
▨ % Going ahead with plans

USA Today/Gallup poll, May 18-19, 2009

Those who are changing their summer recreation plans to meet the challenges of the economic recession are relying on a variety of techniques to do so. When those in this group are asked to say whether each of five different actions is a way in which they have changed their plans, the most commonly cited change is cutting back on the total cost of a vacation by spending less on food, lodging, and entertainment. Eighty-nine percent say they have changed their plans in this manner. Seventy-three percent say they will vacation somewhere closer to home than they originally planned to.

Additionally, 63% of those who are revising their plans are taking the most drastic step of canceling outright one or more trips they planned to take. That translates to 32% of those who had summer travel plans, and 16% of all Americans.

The seriousness of the economic situation is underscored by the finding that most of those who have had to change their plans this year do not expect these remedies to be temporary. The poll finds fully 75% of those who are changing their plans this year saying they expect the economy to force them to do so again next year (42%) or even beyond the next two years (33%).

Implications

Gas prices have been rising in recent weeks, but remain well below where they were last year at this time. That may not matter as much

How Summer Recreation Plans Are Changing in Response to Recession

	Percentage of those who have changed their plans	Percentage of all those who had travel plans	Percentage of all U.S. adults
	%	%	%
Cutting back on costs by spending less on food, lodging, or entertainment while on trips	89	46	22
Going somewhere closer than you had planned to go for vacation	73	38	18
Shortening the number of days for a trip or trips you were planning to make	65	34	16
Using a cheaper means of transportation, such as a car instead of an airline flight	64	33	16
Canceling a trip or trips you were planning to make	63	32	16

USA Today/Gallup poll, May 18-19, 2009

Just your best guess, how long do you think the economic recession will cause you to have to cut back on summer recreation plans -- just this year, for the next two years, or for longer than that?

Based on those who are changing their summer recreation plans

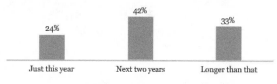

USA Today/Gallup poll, May 18-19, 2009

to Americans as the effects of the broader economic recession, which is causing about half of Americans who planned to travel this summer (about one-fourth of the total population) to revise those plans. But the effects of the recession may go beyond those figures, given the apparent increase this year in the percentage of Americans who do not have travel plans, and the fact that many who were forced to adjust this year expect to have to do so again next year and possibly beyond.

That certainly is not welcome news for the travel industry. And with Americans cutting back on spending in general, the summer of 2009 may end up producing a lot fewer vacation memories than prior summers.

Survey Methods

Results are based on telephone interviews with 984 national adults, aged 18 and older, conducted May 18–19, 2009, as part of Gallup Poll Daily tracking. For results based on the total sample of national adults, one can say with 95% confidence that the maximum margin of sampling error is ±3 percentage points.

Interviews are conducted with respondents on land-line telephones (for respondents with a land-line telephone) and cellular phones (for respondents who are cell-phone only).

In addition to sampling error, question wording and practical difficulties in conducting surveys can introduce error or bias into the findings of public opinion polls.

MILITARY VETERANS OF ALL AGES TEND TO BE MORE REPUBLICAN

Political difference highest among younger veterans

by Frank Newport, Gallup Poll Editor in Chief

Veterans are more likely to be Republican than are those of comparable ages who are not veterans. This Republican skew is at least minimally evident across all age groups, ranging from a 15-point difference in the percentage Republican between veterans and nonveterans in the 25–29 age group, to a 2-point difference in the 85+ group.

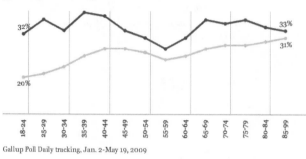

Percentage Identifying With the Republican Party, by Veteran Status and Age

Gallup Poll Daily tracking, Jan. 2-May 19, 2009

These results are based on an analysis of more than 138,000 interviews conducted as part of the Gallup Poll Daily tracking program since January of this year. Respondents were classified as veterans/active military based on an affirmative response to this question: "In the past or at the present time, are you or have you been a member of the United States military?" Fourteen percent of Americans indicate that they have served in the military in the past or are currently on active duty. (It should be noted that normal survey procedures would not include active-duty military serving overseas or on ships at sea.)

Ninety-one percent of those who have served in the military at some point in their lives are men. Looked at differently, over one-quarter—27%—of men aged 18 and older say they are veterans or currently serving in the military, compared to just 2% of adult women.

The basic distribution of current or past military service among men in this country is remarkably differentiated by age. Veteran status is just slightly above 10% for men under age 35, rises slightly among men between 35 and 54, and then begins to rise sharply among men 55 years of age or older. Veteran status levels off at about the 50% mark among men in their 60s, and rises again after that age point, peaking at the 70%+ level among men now aged 80 or older.

These trends correspond directly to the status of the draft and wartime environment in which men came of age.

The military draft officially ended in 1973. This means that men who today are roughly aged 55 and younger were for the most part not subject to the draft. For men currently 56 and older, on the other hand, the draft was very much a reality as they reached age 18. So, too, was a series of international conflicts that required a large military, including the Vietnam War, the Cold War, the Korean War, and, for the oldest group, World War II. The high incidence of military service among these older men documents the

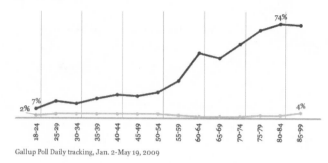

Percentage Who Report Being Military Veteran or on Active Duty, by Gender and Age

Gallup Poll Daily tracking, Jan. 2-May 19, 2009

degree to which military service in those eras was much more universal than it is today.

Political Differences

For the entire adult population, 34% of veterans and those currently on active military service are Republican, compared to 26% of those who are not veterans, while 29% of veterans identify themselves as Democrats, compared to 38% of those who are not veterans. (Thirty-three percent of veterans are independents, compared to 29% of nonveterans.)

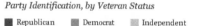

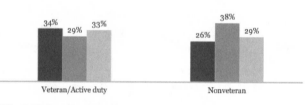

Party Identification, by Veteran Status

Gallup Poll Daily tracking, Jan. 2-May 19, 2009

It has been well documented that there are major generational differences in the political orientation of Americans across age groups today. Still, the current analysis shows that regardless of the underlying patterns of political identification that pertain at each age group, veterans (or those currently in the military) of all ages are more Republican and less Democratic than those who are not veterans.

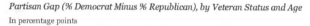

Partisan Gap (% Democrat Minus % Republican), by Veteran Status and Age
In percentage points

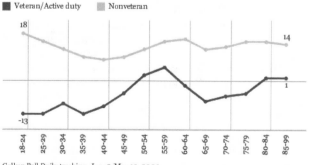

Gallup Poll Daily tracking, Jan. 2-May 19, 2009

The accompanying graph displays the "net partisan gap" (% Democratic identity minus % Republican identity) of veterans and nonveterans at each age group. This gap value is lower among veterans than nonveterans at all age groups—meaning that veterans are less Democratic and more Republican in orientation. The difference in these "net partisan gap" values ranges from a high of 31 points among those 18–24 to a low of 10 points among those 50–54.

Since more than 9 out of 10 veterans are men, and since men as a group skew more Republican and less Democratic than women, it is possible that some of the differences are the result of the comparison of a largely male population of veterans with a mixed-gender population of nonveterans. But an analysis of the differences in partisan gap among men only (that is, comparing male veterans to male nonveterans at each age group) shows that the partisan differences persist.

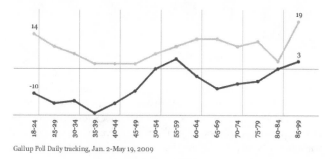

Partisan Gap (% Democrat Minus % Republican), by Veteran Status and Age -- Men Only

■ Veteran/Active duty   ▨ Nonveteran

Gallup Poll Daily tracking, Jan. 2-May 19, 2009

Different Patterns at Work?

It is difficult to establish the precise causal relationship between military service and Republican orientation. It may be that service in the military per se socializes an individual in certain ways that in turn lead to a more Republican viewpoint—either at the time or in later years. On the other hand, there may be a selection factor at work, such that individuals already disproportionately Republican in orientation are more likely to join the military, meaning that the causal factor predates actual military service.

The latter explanation seems more reasonable for the younger age cohorts considered in this research. For the most part, Americans who are now aged 55 and under, as noted, volunteered to serve rather than having been drafted. Under these conditions, a reasonable hypothesis seems to be that more conservative/more Republican persons would be disproportionately represented in the ranks of volunteers, suggesting that the major reason for the observed veteran/nonveteran political difference lies in the backgrounds of those who choose to serve.

On the other hand, those who are now 56 and older were generally subject to the draft and presumably had a lot less choice in whether they served. That would be particularly true for Americans now 70 and older, among whom the majority are veterans. Here a more reasonable hypothesis may be that the socialization process that took place as part of military training and service, coupled with the impact such service has on an individual's reflection on politics and policy later in life, had a greater impact on the observed more Republican orientation among these veterans.

No doubt both processes are at work to at least some degree across the age spectrum. Whatever the cause, the data are clear: having served in the military is associated with a more Republican and less Democratic political identity.

Survey Methods

Results are based on telephone interviews with 138,049 national adults, aged 18 and older, conducted Jan. 2–May 19, 2009, as part of Gallup Poll Daily tracking. For results based on the total sample of national adults, one can say with 95% confidence that the maximum margin of sampling error is ±1 percentage point.

Interviews are conducted with respondents on land-line telephones (for respondents with a land-line telephone) and cellular phones (for respondents who are cell-phone only).

In addition to sampling error, question wording and practical difficulties in conducting surveys can introduce error or bias into the findings of public opinion polls.

May 26, 2009

IN U.S., NEARLY HALF EXERCISE LESS THAN THREE DAYS A WEEK
Americans who are exercising experience more happiness and less stress

by Elizabeth Mendes, Gallup Poll Satff Writer

The Gallup-Healthways Well-Being Index finds that only about one in four Americans (27%) are getting 30 minutes of exercise five or more days per week. Another 24% report exercising for at least 30 minutes on three or four of the last seven days, while nearly half (49%) report exercising for at least 30 minutes less than three days per week.

In the last seven days, on how many days did you:
Exercise for 30 or more minutes?
Adults aged 18 and older

Less than 3 days per week (less than 90 minutes)	49%
3-4 days per week (90-120 minutes)	24%
5 days or more per week (150 minutes or more)	27%

Aggregate of interviews conducted May 1, 2008-April 30, 2009
Gallup-Healthways Well-Being Index

Gallup analyzed the results of more than 400,000 interviews, conducted from May 2008 to April 2009, during National Physical Fitness and Sports Month, observed every May since 1983. During the month of May the government works to promote the Department of Health and Human Services Physical Activity Guidelines. The guidelines state that in order to garner substantial health benefits, adults need a minimum of 30 minutes of *moderate-intensity* physical activity at least five days a week or at least 75 minutes of *vigorous-intensity* physical activity each week.

The DHHS Physical Activity Guidelines are the result of an extensive review of the scientific research on exercise and promote a level of physical activity proven to provide health benefits.

Amy Neftzger, Lead Researcher at Healthways, states that these health benefits are well-documented and include "a healthy weight, the slowing and prevention of the onset of diseases such as heart disease and type 2 diabetes, and helping to build bone strength."

Americans at a normal weight, according to Body Mass Index classifications, are more likely to report exercising 30 minutes five or more days per week than those who are overweight or obese. Of the respondents whose BMI falls within the normal weight range, 32% report exercising on five days or more in the last seven, compared to 28% of those who are overweight and 20% of those who are obese.

Percentage of Adults Exercising at least 30 minutes per day, 5 days or more per week
By BMI

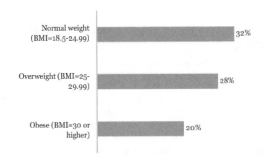

Aggregate of interviews conducted May 1, 2008-April 30, 2009
Gallup-Healthways Well-Being Index

Aside from the differences in reported amount of exercise by BMI, there is little demographic variation. Older Americans are slightly more likely to say they are exercising at least 30 minutes at least five days per week than those who are younger. Men are also more likely than women, by a small margin, to report exercising on five or more days in a week.

Percentage of Adults Exercising at least 30 minutes per day, 5 days or more per week
By gender and age

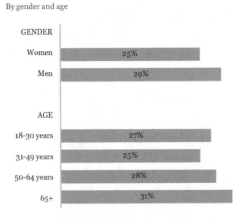

Aggregate of interviews conducted May 1, 2008-April 30, 2009
Gallup-Healthways Well-Being Index

Emotional Benefits

In addition to the well-known physical health benefits of exercise, the Gallup-Healthways Well-Being Index reveals a compelling emotional benefit to frequent exercise. Those who exercise at least two days per week report experiencing more happiness and less stress than those who do not. Further, the benefits tend to increase slightly with more frequent exercise, save for those who exercise seven days per week.

Number of Days Americans Report Exercising for at Least 30 Minutes and Stress, Happiness

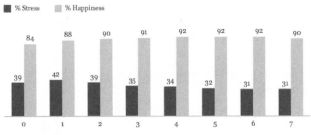

Aggregate of interviews conducted Jan 2008 - May 2009
Gallup-Healthways Well-Being Index

Exercising more frequently also appears to increase a person's likelihood to say they feel well-rested and have enough energy. Again, the Gallup-Healthways Well-Being Index reveals increasing benefits for each additional day of exercise, save for the seventh day, when benefits subside slightly. Both of these measures peak when a person reports getting 30 minutes of exercise six days per week.

Number of Days Americans Report Exercising for at Least 30 Minutes and Energy, Rest

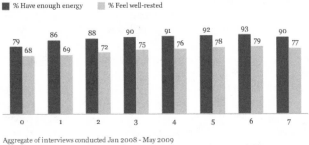

Aggregate of interviews conducted Jan 2008 - May 2009
Gallup-Healthways Well-Being Index

Given the documented benefits of frequent exercise for an individual's physical and emotional health, it is concerning to find that just under 50% of Americans report exercising less than three days a week. Neftzger notes that "the benefits of exercise are not in question and most individuals know that they should exercise, but what seems to be lacking is the motivation." Something that can assist motivation, she adds, is "finding a friend to exercise with you, which would also serve to boost social time, another proven key to higher well-being."

Survey Methods

Results are based on telephone interviews with over 400,000 adults in the United States, aged 18 and older, conducted January 2008 to April 2009 as part of Gallup Poll Daily tracking. For results based on the total sample of national adults, one can say with 95% confidence that the maximum margin of sampling error is ± 1 percentage point. In addition to sampling error, question wording and practical difficulties in conducting surveys can introduce error or bias into the findings of public opinion polls.

About the Gallup-Healthways Well-Being Index™

The Gallup-Healthways Well-Being Index™ measures the daily pulse of U.S. well-being and provides best-in-class solutions for a healthier world. To learn more, please visit well-beingindex.com.

May 27, 2009
MAJORITY OF AMERICANS CONTINUE TO OPPOSE GAY MARRIAGE
No change in support from last year

by Jeffrey M. Jones, Gallup Poll Managing Editor

Americans' views on same-sex marriage have essentially stayed the same in the past year, with a majority of 57% opposed to granting such marriages legal status and 40% in favor of doing so. Though support for legal same-sex marriage is significantly higher now than when Gallup first asked about it in 1996, in recent years support has appeared to stall, peaking at 46% in 2007.

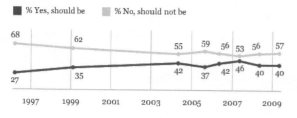

Do you think marriages between same-sex couples should or should not be recognized by the law as valid, with the same rights as traditional marriages?

The lack of change in public opinion on same-sex marriage seen in the new *USA Today*/Gallup poll occurs in an environment in which an increasing number of states have taken steps to legalize such unions. Same-sex marriages are now legal in Massachusetts, Connecticut, Maine, and Iowa, and will be legal in Vermont in September.

On Tuesday, California's Supreme Court refused to add that state to the list, by upholding the Proposition 8 referendum, approved by voters, that banned same-sex marriage in the state. The referendum was put on the November 2008 ballot in response to an earlier court decision that allowed same-sex couples to legally marry in California.

Among major demographic or attitudinal subgroups, self-identified liberals show the greatest support for legal gay marriage at 75% in the May 7–10 poll. By contrast, only 19% of conservatives think same-sex marriages should be legally valid.

Just a slim majority (55%) of Democrats approve of gay marriage, but they are more likely to do so than independents (45%) and Republicans (20%).

Younger Americans have typically been much more supportive of same-sex marriage than older Americans, and that is the case in

Should Same-Sex Marriages Be Recognized by the Law as Valid, by Political Ideology

USA Today/Gallup poll, May 7-10, 2009

the current poll. A majority of 18- to 29-year-olds think gay or lesbian couples should be allowed to legally marry, while support reaches only as high as 40% among the three older age groups.

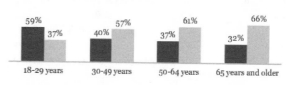

Should Same-Sex Marriages Be Recognized by the Law as Valid, by Age

USA Today/Gallup poll, May 7-10, 2009

A separate question in the poll found close to half of Americans, 48%, saying that allowing legal same-sex marriages would change society for the worse. That is more than three times the 13% who believe legal gay marriage would change society for the better. The remaining 38% say it would have no effect on society or do not have an opinion on the matter.

These results are essentially unchanged from a Gallup Poll conducted six years ago.

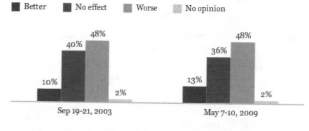

Just your best guess, do you think that allowing two people of the same sex to legally marry will change our society for -- [ROTATED: the better, will it have no effect, or will it change our society for the worse]?

Support Higher for Gay Rights Not Involving Marriage

Though Americans seem reluctant to endorse gay marriage, the poll finds most Americans supporting gay rights in a variety of other areas.

In an update of a question Gallup has asked since 1977, a majority of 56% of Americans say gay or lesbian relations between consenting adults should be legal. A plurality (if not a majority) of the public has taken this view all but one time Gallup has asked the question this decade.

Do you think gay or lesbian relations between consenting adults should or should not be legal?

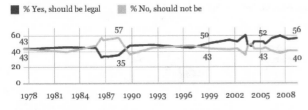

Note: 1977-2008 wording: Do you think homosexual relations between consenting adults should or should not be legal?

Americans' views about allowing gay men and lesbians to serve in the military have undergone a major shift since Bill Clinton attempted to change military policy early in his administration. No more than 43% of Americans favored military service by openly gay soldiers in 1993, according to several NBC News/*Wall Street Journal* polls conducted that year. Clinton and the military eventually compromised on the so-called "Don't Ask, Don't Tell" policy that allowed gays to serve as long as they did not disclose their sexual orientation.

Today, the latest *USA Today*/Gallup poll finds 69% of Americans in favor of military service by openly gay men and lesbians. While the Clinton-era policy remains in place, President Obama promised during the campaign to change it.

Americans also show broad support for gay rights in the following areas:

- Sixty-seven percent say gay and lesbian domestic partners should have access to health insurance and other employee benefits.
- Nearly three in four Americans, 73%, believe gay and lesbian domestic partners should have inheritance rights.
- Sixty-seven percent favor a proposal to expand hate-crime laws to cover crimes committed against gays or lesbians.
- Only 28% of Americans believe that gays or lesbians should not be hired as elementary school teachers. Sixty-nine percent believe they should be allowed to teach children.

Americans are somewhat less supportive of adoption rights for gay couples, though a majority (54%) still support this. The current level of support does represent an increase from *Newsweek* polls conducted in 2002 (46%) and 2004 (45%).

Implications

While Americans have become increasingly likely to believe that the law should not discriminate against gay individuals and gay couples, the public still seems reluctant at this point to extend those protections to the institution of marriage. Public support for gay marriage appears to have stalled in the last two years, even as the gay marriage movement has scored a number of legal and legislative victories at the state level in the past year.

In addition to the states that have recently legalized gay marriage, New Hampshire and New York are currently considering legislation to make gay marriage legal in their states. The California Supreme Court ruling announced Tuesday is a significant setback for the gay rights movement; however, it is possible for voters to undo Proposition 8 by passing a new referendum.

Clearly, much of the action on gay marriage policy is taking place at the state level. President Obama personally does not support gay marriage, but believes that states should decide the matter for themselves. Thus, he seems unlikely to seek a national standard.

State courts have obviously played an important part in deciding gay marriage laws; at this point it is not known whether the issue will make its way to the U.S. Supreme Court in the future.

Survey Methods

Results are based on telephone interviews with 1,015 national adults, aged 18 and older, conducted May 7–10, 2009. For results based on the total sample of national adults, one can say with 95% confidence that the maximum margin of sampling error is ±3 percentage points.

Interviews are conducted with respondents on land-line telephones (for respondents with a land-line telephone) and cellular phones (for respondents who are cell-phone only).

In addition to sampling error, question wording and practical difficulties in conducting surveys can introduce error or bias into the findings of public opinion polls.

May 28, 2009
POSITIVE INITIAL REACTION TO SOTOMAYOR NOMINATION
Americans believe intellect, experience most important in Obama's choice

by Frank Newport, Gallup Poll Editor in Chief

Americans' first reactions to the news of President Obama's nomination of Judge Sonia Sotomayor to serve on the U.S. Supreme Court are decidedly more positive than negative, with 47% rating the nomination as "excellent" or "good," 20% rating it "only fair," and 13% rating it "poor."

As you may know, President Obama has nominated Judge Sonia Sotomayor to serve on the U.S. Supreme Court. Generally speaking, how would you rate Obama's choice of Sonia Sotomayor as a nominee to the U.S. Supreme Court -- as excellent, good, only fair, or poor?

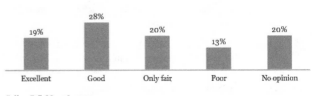

Gallup Poll, May 26, 2009

These results are based on a one-night poll conducted Tuesday, the same day Obama officially announced Sotomayor as his choice to replace the retiring Justice David Souter on the Supreme Court.

Gallup conducted similar reaction polls immediately after former President George W. Bush's nominations of John Roberts, Samuel Alito, and Harriet Miers for the Supreme Court in 2005. Although in all instances, the reactions were more positive than negative, the net positive rating (the percentage *excellent* or *good* minus the percentage *only fair* or *poor*) was highest for Roberts and Sotomayor, and lowest for Alito and Miers.

Given that Sotomayor's nomination was made by a Democratic president, it is not surprising to find reactions to her selection that are much more positive among Democrats than among Republicans.

Immediate Reactions to Recent Supreme Court Nominations

	Excellent	Good	Only fair	Poor	No opinion	Net positive
	%	%	%	%	%	(% Exc./Good minus % Only fair/Poor, in pct. pts.)
Sonia Sotomayor (May 26, 2009)	19	28	20	13	20	+14
Samuel Alito (Nov 1, 2005)	17	26	22	17	18	+4
Harriet Miers (Oct 3-4, 2005)	11	33	25	16	15	+3
John Roberts (Jul 20, 2005)	25	26	20	14	15	+17

Ratings of Obama's Choice of Sonia Sotomayor as Supreme Court Nominee
By party ID

	Excellent	Good	Only fair	Poor	No opinion
	%	%	%	%	%
Republican	9	20	24	28	19
Independent	15	25	22	14	22
Democrat	33	39	16	1	11

Gallup Poll, May 26, 2009

Ratings of Obama's Choice of Sonia Sotomayor as Supreme Court Nominee
By gender

	Excellent	Good	Only fair	Poor	Don't know
	%	%	%	%	%
Male	18	24	22	19	15
Female	21	33	18	7	19

Gallup Poll, May 26, 2009

Immediate Reactions to Recent Supreme Court Nominations, by Gender
% Excellent/Good

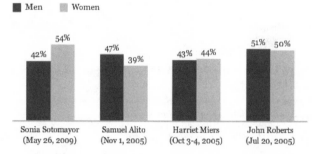

Comparing ratings of Sotomayor to those of the three previous nominees (all chosen by the Republican President Bush) suggests that the current partisan reaction to Sotomayor follows a fairly standard pattern. Between 72% and 79% of those identifying with the party of the president making the nomination react positively to the candidates. There is a slightly larger range in positive ratings among those identifying with the party *not* controlling the White House at the time of the nomination: from a high of 31% of Democrats who supported Roberts and 29% of Republicans who support Sotomayor, to a low of 18% of Democrats who supported Alito.

Immediate Reactions to Recent Supreme Court Nominations, by Party ID
% Excellent/Good

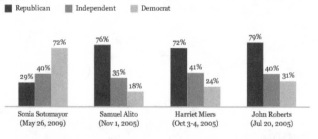

There are two primary reasons why Sotomayor's nomination could in theory appeal to women:

1. She would become the second female justice on the Court.
2. She has been nominated by a Democratic president at a time when women are significantly more likely to identify with his party than with the Republican Party.

Indeed, the data show a significant gender skew in reaction to Sotomayor's appointment.

Interestingly, the gender gap in positive reactions to Sotomayor is the largest such gap for the four most recent Supreme Court nominations—in either direction. Alito had higher approval among men than among women (by eight points), but both Miers and Roberts had essentially the same level of positive reactions across genders.

Much of the discussion about Obama's nomination decision has focused on his clear intent to appoint a woman, given the fact that there is currently only one female justice on the Court. Additionally, it has been widely noted that Sotomayor would be the first Hispanic on the Court if she is confirmed by the Senate.

Still, it appears Americans believe that Sotomayor's intellectual credentials and experience were more important to Obama in his decision to nominate her than were her demographic characteristics.

The May 26 Gallup Poll asked Americans for their perceptions of the importance of five of Sotomayor's characteristics in Obama's thinking when he decided to nominate her. The public downgrades the perceived importance to Obama of Sotomayor's gender and ethnicity; only 39% and 34%, respectively, call these very important to him. Instead, majorities believe that he heavily valued her experience as a federal judge (61%), her intellect (59%), and her views and judicial record (52%).

How important do you think each of the following considerations was to Barack Obama when he chose Sonia Sotomayor as his nominee for the U.S. Supreme Court?
Sorted by "very important"

	Very important	Somewhat important	Not too important	Not important at all	No opinion
	%	%	%	%	%
Her 17 years of experience as a federal judge	61	28	4	3	4
Her intellect	59	24	4	4	8
Her views on major issues and past judicial decisions	52	30	4	4	11
She is a woman	39	27	12	18	4
She is Hispanic	34	27	13	21	5

Gallup Poll, May 26, 2009

Survey Methods

Results are based on telephone interviews with 1,015 national adults, aged 18 and older, conducted May 26, 2009. For results based on the total sample of national adults, one can say with 95% confidence that the maximum margin of sampling error is ±3 percentage points.

Interviews are conducted with respondents on land-line telephones (for respondents with a land-line telephone) and cellular phones (for respondents who are cell-phone only).

In addition to sampling error, question wording and practical difficulties in conducting surveys can introduce error or bias into the findings of public opinion polls.

Polls conducted entirely in one day, such as this one, are subject to additional error or bias not found in polls conducted over several days.

May 29, 2009
KNOWING SOMEONE GAY/LESBIAN AFFECTS VIEWS OF GAY ISSUES
Opposition to gay marriage higher among those who do not know someone who is gay/lesbian

by Lymari Morales, Gallup Poll Staff Writer

While 57% of Americans oppose legalizing gay marriage, Americans who personally know someone who is gay or lesbian are almost evenly divided on the matter, with 49% in favor and 47% opposed. Among those who do not personally know anyone who is gay, 72% oppose legalized gay marriage while just 27% favor it.

Views on Gay Marriage, by Personally Knowing Someone Who Is Gay or Lesbian

USA Today/Gallup poll, May 7-10, 2009

The results are from a May 7–10, 2009, *USA Today/*Gallup poll, which asked Americans their views on a number of issues relating to gays and lesbians. Overall, a majority of Americans (58%) say they have a friend, relative, or coworker who is gay or lesbian—basically unchanged since Gallup first asked this question in 2003.

Do you have any friends or relatives or coworkers who have told you, personally, that they are gay or lesbian?

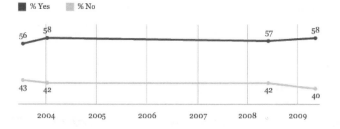

Examining personal experience by ideology, 71% of self-identified liberals say they personally know someone who is gay

or lesbian—far more than is true among moderates and conservatives, who align more closely with the national average.

Personally Knowing Someone Who Is Gay or Lesbian, Within Ideological Groups

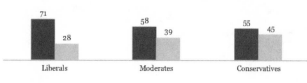

USA Today/Gallup poll, May 7-10, 2009

Views of gay marriage are strongly related to ideology. But the increase in support among those who personally know someone who is gay or lesbian is not merely a reflection of the fact that liberals are more likely to know someone of same-sex orientation. Further analysis reveals that, when controlling for ideology, those who know someone who is gay or lesbian are significantly more supportive of gay marriage than are those of the same political persuasion who do not personally know someone who is gay or lesbian.

Americans who know someone who is gay or lesbian are about evenly split between saying legalizing gay marriage will change society for the worse (39%) and that it will have no effect on society (40%). Nearly two-thirds of Americans (63%) who do not personally know a gay or lesbian person believe that legalized gay marriage will change society for the worse—far greater than the 48% of national adults who say the same. Only a small minority of Americans believe legal gay marriage will change society for the better, but those who personally know someone who is gay or lesbian are three times more likely to say this than are those who do not know anyone who is gay or lesbian.

Views of the Effect of Legalizing Gay Marriage on Society, by Personally Knowing Someone Who Is Gay or Lesbian

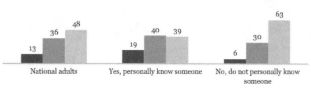

USA Today/Gallup poll, May 7-10, 2009

Experience and Acceptance

In addition to the findings on gay marriage, Gallup similarly finds those with personal experience with gay or lesbian individuals more accepting of same-sex relations in general. While a majority of Americans overall (56%) think same-sex relations should be legal, two-thirds (67%) of those who personally know a gay or lesbian individual say this. A majority (57%) of those who do not personally know anyone who is gay say gay or lesbian relations should not be legal.

Of those who say they personally know someone who is gay or lesbian, 88% say they are comfortable around these individuals, compared to 64% of those who do not personally know someone who is

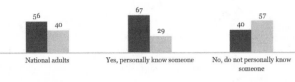

Views of Gay/Lesbian Relations, by Personally Knowing Someone Who Is Gay or Lesbian

■ % Gay/Lesbian relations should be legal   ░ % Gay/Lesbian relations should not be legal

	National adults	Yes, personally know someone	No, do not personally know someone
Legal	56	67	40
Not legal	40	29	57

USA Today/Gallup poll, May 7-10, 2009

gay or lesbian. Among adults overall, fewer than 2 in 10 say they are uncomfortable around someone who is gay or lesbian, but that number increases to 3 in 10 among those who do not personally know anyone who is gay or lesbian.

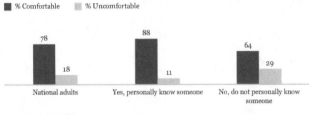

Comfort Level Around Gays and Lesbians, by Personally Knowing Someone Who Is Gay or Lesbian

■ % Comfortable   ░ % Uncomfortable

	National adults	Yes, personally know someone	No, do not personally know someone
Comfortable	78	88	64
Uncomfortable	18	11	29

USA Today/Gallup poll, May 7-10, 2009

Bottom Line

The Gallup Poll data reviewed above show conclusively that many views toward gay and lesbian issues are related—in some instances, strongly so—to personal experience with individuals who are gay or lesbian. There are two plausible explanations for this relationship. One is that exposure to gays and lesbians leads to greater acceptance, regardless of one's ideological leanings. The second is that people who are more accepting of gays and lesbians are more likely to put themselves into situations in which they are exposed to gays and lesbians—in terms of cities and regions of residence, as well as workplace and social choices. Both of these processes are at work, though it is difficult to say which is more important.

Whatever the direction of causality, the data do make a strong case that knowing someone who is gay or lesbian fosters more accepting attitudes on many of the issues surrounding gay and lesbian relations today.

Survey Methods

Results are based on telephone interviews with 1,015 national adults, aged 18 and older, conducted May 7–10, 2009. For results based on the total sample of national adults, one can say with 95% confidence that the maximum margin of sampling error is ±3 percentage points.

Interviews are conducted with respondents on land-line telephones (for respondents with a land-line telephone) and cellular phones (for respondents who are cell-phone only).

In addition to sampling error, question wording and practical difficulties in conducting surveys can introduce error or bias into the findings of public opinion polls.

May 29, 2009
OBAMA APPROVAL COMPARES FAVORABLY TO PRIOR PRESIDENTS
Only three presidents since Eisenhower have had higher May ratings

by Jeffrey M. Jones, Gallup Poll Managing Editor

So far in May, Barack Obama has averaged 65% job approval. Since World War II, only three of the previous eight presidents elected to their first terms—Dwight Eisenhower, John Kennedy, and Ronald Reagan—have had a higher average approval rating in May of their first year. Obama's average exceeds those of the three most recent presidents—George H.W. Bush, Bill Clinton, and George W. Bush.

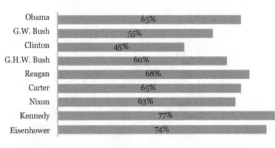

Presidential Job Approval Averages in May of First Year in Office

Obama	65%
G.W. Bush	55%
Clinton	45%
G.H.W. Bush	60%
Reagan	68%
Carter	65%
Nixon	63%
Kennedy	77%
Eisenhower	74%

Since he became president, the trend line on Obama's job approval rating in Gallup Poll Daily tracking has been fairly flat. However, his May average to date of 65% does represent a slight improvement over his ratings from the prior three months, which ranged from 62% to 64%.

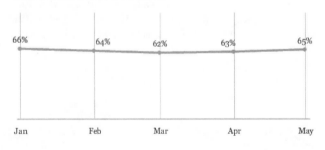

Barack Obama Job Approval, by Month

Jan	Feb	Mar	Apr	May
66%	64%	62%	63%	65%

Historically, there has been no clear pattern in the trends for presidential approval ratings through May of a president's first year in office—four of the previous eight post-World War II presidents showed increases in their approval ratings from February (Gallup does not have January readings for all presidents) to May, and four showed decreases.

The four presidents whose approval ratings increased were Eisenhower (+6 points), Kennedy (+5), Richard Nixon (+3), and Reagan (+15). Reagan's sharp increase was the product of a fairly low initial average of 53% combined with a spike in his approval rating associated with a rally in support after John Hinckley's attempted assassination of him in late March 1981.

Obama would fall into the group of presidents who have increased their approval averages from February to May, though his rating has improved by just a single percentage point during this time, from 64% to 65%.

Presidents Whose Approval Averages Increased, February to May of First Year in Office

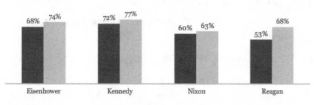

Declining approval ratings in the first four months of a president's term have been the norm recently. Of the last five presidents before Obama, only Reagan enjoyed an increase in his approval rating during this time. Jimmy Carter (-4 points), George H.W. Bush (-3), Clinton (-10), and George W. Bush (-4) all saw drops in public support.

Presidents Whose Approval Averages Decreased, February to May of First Year in Office

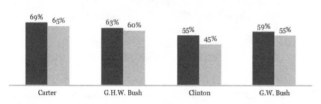

A number of factors probably contributed to Clinton's rather large decline in support. In terms of policy, he faced a backlash from the military and the public over his attempts to change policy to allow openly gay men and women to serve in the military, and he was unable to pass his proposed economic stimulus plan. Clinton had problems filling the attorney general position, and there was controversy over the siege of the Branch Davidians' Waco, Texas, compound. Also not to be dismissed was the public relations disaster created when Los Angeles International Airport runways were closed to allow the president to get a high-priced haircut.

Honeymoon Still Going On for Obama

Obama's consistent monthly averages above 60% clearly indicate he is still enjoying the honeymoon phase of his presidency. That level of support has been typical for presidents at this point in their terms; even though many presidents experienced declines in their approval ratings by May of their first year in office, all managed to stay at or above the 60% level except George W. Bush and Clinton.

Obama has had a few individual ratings of 59% in Gallup Poll Daily tracking, but not enough to push his average for any given week or month below 60%.

His popular support will certainly be tested in the coming months, though, as Congress begins work on some of his more ambitious initiatives, including his 2010 budget and healthcare reform. In addition to the ongoing wars in Iraq and Afghanistan, he is also attempting to advance the Middle East peace process and deal with the increasingly serious situation in North Korea.

However, to date, according to the American public, he seems to be performing better than most of his immediate predecessors, and not worse than most post–World War II presidents.

Survey Methods

Results are based on telephone interviews with 13,310 national adults, aged 18 and older, conducted May 1–27, 2009, as part of Gallup Poll Daily tracking. For results based on the total sample of national adults, one can say with 95% confidence that the maximum margin of sampling error is ±1 percentage point.

Interviews are conducted with respondents on land-line telephones (for respondents with a land-line telephone) and cellular phones (for respondents who are cell-phone only).

In addition to sampling error, question wording and practical difficulties in conducting surveys can introduce error or bias into the findings of public opinion polls.

June 01, 2009

REPUBLICAN BASE HEAVILY WHITE, CONSERVATIVE, RELIGIOUS

Democrats are more likely to be moderate or liberal, Hispanic, or black or other races

by Frank Newport, Gallup Poll Editor in Chief

More than 6 in 10 Republicans today are white conservatives, while most of the rest are whites with other ideological leanings; only 11% of Republicans are Hispanics, or are blacks or members of other races. By contrast, only 12% of Democrats are white conservatives, while about half are white moderates or liberals and a third are non-white.

Composition of Political Parties by Racial, Ethnic, and Ideological Groups

	Republican	Independent	Democrat
	%	%	%
Hispanic	5	14	11
Black	2	6	19
Other race	4	7	6
Non-Hispanic white, conservative	63	25	12
Non-Hispanic white, not conservative	26	48	53

Gallup Poll Daily tracking, May 1–27, 2009

These data reinforce the basic challenge facing the Republican Party today as it ponders how best to remedy a situation that finds Democrats in control of the White House and both houses of Congress. Republicans have a clear monopoly on the allegiance of white conservative Americans, but the GOP's challenge is figuring out whether this is enough of a base on which to build for the future. The alternative is for the GOP to broaden its base to include more minorities and/or more whites who are moderate or liberal in their ideological outlook—groups now predominantly loyal to the Democratic Party.

The current analysis is based on a sample of more than 26,000 interviews Gallup conducted May 1–27, 2009. Each of the three major political groupings—those who identify themselves as Republicans, as Democrats, and as independents—was decomposed into five mutually exclusive and exhaustive categories:

1. Hispanics
2. Non-Hispanic blacks
3. Non-Hispanics who identify their race as something other than white or black
4. Non-Hispanic whites who identify themselves as conservative
5. Non-Hispanic whites who identify their ideology as something other than conservative—including moderates, liberals, and those who don't express an ideological preference

The results show clearly that the Republican Party today is first and foremost a political entity dominated by white Americans. Eighty-nine percent of rank-and-file Republicans are non-Hispanic whites, leaving just 5% who are Hispanic (of any race), 2% who are black, and 4% of other races.

Further, by well over a 2-to-1 ratio, whites who identify as Republicans claim a conservative, rather than a moderate or liberal, ideology (or have no opinion when asked about their ideology).

Democrats have a significantly more diverse party composition. Well over a third (36%) of Democrats are nonwhite (Hispanic, or black or some other race) and the 64% of Democrats who are white are strongly skewed—by more than a 4-to-1 ratio—toward an ideological position that is moderate or liberal rather than conservative.

Independents, as would be expected, are somewhere between Republicans and Democrats in terms of their racial, ethnic, and ideological composition. Twenty-seven percent of independents are Hispanic, or are black or identify with another race, and, by about a 2-to-1 ratio, white independents split toward the non-conservative ideological position.

Religiosity

A similar pattern is found when the three partisan groups are broken down into segments based on race, ethnicity, and religious intensity (among whites, as measured by church attendance).

Composition of Political Parties by Racial, Ethnic, and Religious Groups

	Republican	Independent	Democrat
	%	%	%
Hispanic	5	14	11
Black	2	6	19
Other race	4	7	6
Non-Hispanic white, religious	49	25	20
Non-Hispanic white, not religious	40	48	44

Gallup Poll Daily tracking, May 1–27, 2009

About half of Republicans are non-Hispanic whites who are strongly religious, defined as those who attend church about once a week or more frequently. Forty percent of Republicans are whites who attend less frequently.

Democrats, on the other hand, comprise only 20% highly religious whites, with more than twice as many whites who attend church less frequently. The pattern of church attendance among independents is similar to that among Democrats, but independents have higher percentages of whites in both the religious and the nonreligious categories.

Implications

A great deal of attention has been paid to the plight of Republicans who at this juncture in history find themselves not controlling the presidency, the House, or the Senate. Plus, numerous surveys conducted by Gallup and other firms have shown that the GOP appears to be suffering on a number of perceptual dimensions compared to the Democrats (as measured by Gallup and by other recent surveys).

The data reviewed here highlight an essential dilemma the Republicans face as they ponder their future. The Republican Party's constituency is overwhelmingly white—and the significant majority of those whites are ideologically conservative, while a majority are highly religious, as defined by church attendance. The Democratic

Party, on the other hand, has more than three times the percentage of nonwhites among its identifiers as does the GOP. And white Democrats are much more likely to be moderate or liberal than conservative, and are much more likely to be infrequent church attenders rather than frequent church attenders.

Does the Republican Party in essence "stick to the knitting" and cling to its core conservative principles? Or should the Republicans make an effort to expand their base—among whites who are moderate or less religious, and/or the various nonwhite groups who to this point are largely ignoring the Republican Party in favor of the Democrats? The decision the party makes in response to this question could be pivotal in helping determine its future.

Survey Methods

Results are based on telephone interviews with 26,314 national adults, aged 18 and older, conducted May 1–27, 2009, as part of Gallup Poll Daily tracking. For results based on the total sample of national adults, one can say with 95% confidence that the maximum margin of sampling error is ±1 percentage points.

Interviews are conducted with respondents on land-line telephones (for respondents with a land-line telephone) and cellular phones (for respondents who are cell-phone only).

In addition to sampling error, question wording and practical difficulties in conducting surveys can introduce error or bias into the findings of public opinion polls.

June 01, 2009

AMONG WORKERS, SERVICE EMPLOYEES RATE OBAMA HIGHEST

Professionals give Obama higher approval than business owners

by Lydia Saad, Gallup Poll Senior Editor

President Barack Obama's job approval rating averaged 65% in Gallup Poll Daily tracking in May, and was nearly identical among employed as well as unemployed Americans. However, workers in some occupational categories gave him broader support than others.

On the high end, 71% of service workers, such as police officers, waiters and waitresses, barbers, and nurses' aides, approved in May of how Obama handled his job.

Obama received his lowest average rating—52%—from workers in farming, fishing, and forestry. Obama's ratings were only a bit higher among workers employed in transportation (54%) and in installation/repair (57%), as well as among self-employed business owners (55%).

Each of the remaining major categories of workers identified in Gallup's Daily tracking gave the president a job approval rating close to his 65% overall average. This includes manufacturing employees, professionals (such as lawyers, doctors, and teachers), clerical workers, sales employees, business and government managers or officials, and those working in construction, mining, and the trades.

Business Owners Come Around

Obama's overall job approval rating was a bit higher in May than in the prior two months (62% in March and 63% in April). Since March, the sharpest increases in support for him among occupational

Average Job Approval Rating for President Obama in May 2009, by Occupation
Based on adults employed full- or part-time

	Approve
	%
Service industry	71
Manufacturing/Production	68
Professional	65
Clerical/Office	65
Sales	64
Manager/Executive, Government official	60
Construction/Mining	60
Installation/Repair	57
Business owner (self-employed)	55
Transportation	54
Farming/Fishing/Forestry	52

Gallup Poll Daily tracking, May 1-31, 2009

groups have come from business owners—a group epitomized late in the 2008 presidential campaign by "Joe the Plumber," whose question to Obama about small-business taxes heightened media attention to that issue. Business owners' approval rose from 44% in March to 51% in April and 55% in May.

The 44% March figure for business owners is the only occupation-based, sub-50% job approval rating of Obama in the past three months. Thus, the increase to 55% is particularly notable. However, because only 3% of employed Americans identified themselves as business owners in Gallup's May polling, this change had little effect on Obama's overall job rating.

Change in Approval of Obama Between March and May 2009, by Occupation
Based on adults employed full- or part-time

	March	May	Change ^
	%	%	Pct. pts.
Business owner (self-employed)	44	55	+11
Sales	56	64	+8
Service industry	63	71	+8
Manufacturing/Production	62	68	+6
Clerical/Office	61	65	+4
Professional	62	65	+3
Farming/Fishing/Forestry	50	52	+2
Transportation	53	54	+1
Manager/Executive, Government official	60	60	0
Installation/Repair	60	57	-3
Construction/Mining	63	60	-3

^ Changes of less than 6 percentage points are not statistically significant
Gallup Poll Daily tracking

Approval of the president also rose among sales workers (from 56% in March to 64% in May), among service workers (from 63% to 71%), and among manufacturing and production workers (from 62% to 68%).

None of the remaining occupational groups show a statistically significant change in support for Obama in May compared with March.

More generally, workers who are members of labor unions are a bit more likely to have approved of Obama's job performance than are nonunion employees. In May, the figures were 71% and 64%, respectively. However, the rank order of occupations according to Obama approval does not correspond directly to the rate of union membership in each occupational group. For instance, only 12% of service employees tell Gallup they belong to a union, compared with 20% of installation and repair workers—but the latter group's support for Obama is much lower.

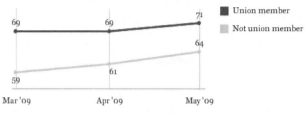

Approval of Obama by Union Membership -- Trend Since March

Based on adults employed full- or part-time

Numbers in percentages

Gallup Poll Daily tracking

One of the more notable distinctions in assessments of Obama by occupation is between professionals and business owners. In May, there was a 10-point difference between the two, with 65% of professionals compared with 55% of business owners approving. Nearly one in five professionals are union members, including teachers; however, even excluding these workers, 64% of nonunion professionals approved of Obama in May.

The distinction highlights the consistently strong support Obama has enjoyed from highly educated Americans since he become the Democratic Party's nominee for president last year. More generally, Americans with postgraduate educational backgrounds, as well as professional workers, tend to be more Democratic in their political orientation than the public at large: 41% of professional workers are Democratic, versus 27% Republican and 30% independent. By contrast, just 29% of business owners are Democratic, while 31% are Republican and 34% independent.

Bottom Line

Various occupations are hardly homogenous in their demographic or political makeup; their members have a variety of educational backgrounds, reside in all parts of the country, and some are more financially well off than others. However, there appears to be some commonality within some occupational groups that distinguishes their views toward Obama from those of other occupations. This is seen most clearly with service workers, who give Obama higher approval, on average, than any other category of workers. Workers in farming, fishing, and forestry, along with installation/repair workers, transportation workers, and business owners, are markedly lower in their approval of the president—but even among these groups, majorities approve of Obama's performance in office.

Survey Methods

Results are based on aggregated data from Gallup Poll Daily tracking for the months of March 2009, April 2009, and May 2009. Each month's aggregated data consist of interviews with more than 30,000 national adults, aged 18 and older, including more than 17,000 adults employed full- or part-time. Results based on specific occupational categories have smaller sample sizes; the May 2009 sample sizes are shown below.

Interviews are conducted with respondents on land-line telephones (for respondents with a land-line telephone) and cellular phones (for respondents who are cell-phone only).

In addition to sampling error, question wording and practical difficulties in conducting surveys can introduce error or bias into the findings of public opinion polls.

June 02, 2009
MAJORITY OF AMERICANS FAVOR SOTOMAYOR CONFIRMATION
Many more say her views are "mainstream" rather than "extreme"

by Jeffrey M. Jones, Gallup Poll Managing Editor

Americans are generally supportive of President Barack Obama's nomination of Judge Sonia Sotomayor to the U.S. Supreme Court. A majority of Americans, 54%, say they would like to see the Senate confirm her to the Court, according to a May 29–31 *USA Today*/Gallup poll. Currently, 28% are against her confirmation and 19% have not yet formed an opinion.

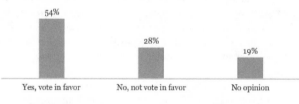

As you may know, Sonia Sotomayor is the federal judge nominated to serve on the Supreme Court. Would you like to see the Senate vote in favor of Sotomayor serving on the Supreme Court, or not?

USA Today/Gallup, May 29-31, 2009

The level of support for Sotomayor is similar to what Gallup initially found for past nominees who were confirmed by the Senate, including Clarence Thomas, Ruth Bader Ginsburg, and Samuel Alito. Americans were slightly more positive toward John Roberts' nomination.

Notably, two nominees who did not make it to the Supreme Court—Robert Bork (who was rejected in the Senate vote) and Harriet Miers (who withdrew)—received significantly lower initial support.

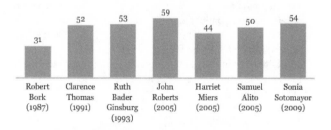

Initial Support for Recent U.S. Supreme Court Nominees

% Yes, would like to see Senate vote in favor

Initial public support has been a good barometer of the public's eventual judgment of the nominees. The percentage favoring a nominee's confirmation generally has not varied much in either direction from the time of nomination to the time of confirmation. Even the high-profile confirmation hearings for Thomas did not move support for his nomination below the majority level, though opposition did increase from 17% to 30% from July to October 1991.

At this early stage, a majority of Republicans, 57%, already oppose Sotomayor's nomination. Meanwhile, a slim majority of independents and a solid majority of Democrats favor it.

Would You Like to See Senate Vote in Favor of Sotomayor Nomination, by Political Party

USA Today/Gallup, May 29-31, 2009

Implications

Public opinion about Sotomayor's nomination to the Supreme Court is right in line with what Gallup has found for other nominees who now serve on the nation's highest court. Past polling would indicate that, in the coming weeks and months, the initial level of support for Sotomayor is not likely to change much. Such polling shows that the main effect of the confirmation process appears to have been to move more Americans from an undecided position to a position in opposition to the nomination, but rarely has support moved dramatically up or down.

This suggests that, to a large degree, first impressions of Supreme Court nominees are lasting. Presumably, this would especially be the case among Americans who are predisposed to support the president on almost any decision he makes—namely, his party's supporters. Already, three-quarters of Democrats favor the Sotomayor nomination.

The historical data also suggest that Americans' first impressions generally predict the ultimate Senate vote—the two nominees who did not garner majority support from Americans on their initial reading did not wind up as Supreme Court justices. All those who were favored by a majority were confirmed, regardless of the specifics of their confirmation processes.

Survey Methods

Results are based on telephone interviews with 1,015 national adults, aged 18 and older, conducted May 29–31, 2009. For results based on the total sample of national adults, one can say with 95% confidence that the maximum margin of sampling error is ±3 percentage points.

Interviews are conducted with respondents on land-line telephones (for respondents with a land-line telephone) and cellular phones (for respondents who are cell-phone only).

In addition to sampling error, question wording and practical difficulties in conducting surveys can introduce error or bias into the findings of public opinion polls.

June 03, 2009

AMERICANS OPPOSE CLOSING GITMO AND MOVING PRISONERS TO U.S.

Public does not believe prison has weakened U.S. national security

by Jeffrey M. Jones, Gallup Poll Managing Editor

By a better than 2-to-1 margin, Americans are opposed to closing the Guantanamo Bay prison that houses terror suspects and moving some of those prisoners to the United States. Americans express even more widespread opposition to the idea of moving the prisoners to prisons in their own states if Guantanamo is closed.

As you may know, since 2001, the United States has held people from other countries who are suspected of being terrorists in a prison at Guantanamo Bay in Cuba. Do you think the United States should -- or should not -- close this prison and move some of the prisoners to U.S. prisons?

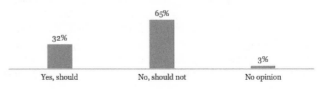

USA Today/Gallup poll, May 29-31, 2009

Suppose the prison at Guantanamo Bay is closed. Would you favor or oppose moving some of those prisoners to a prison in your state?

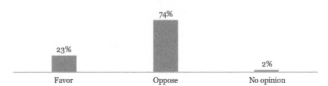

USA Today/Gallup poll, May 29-31, 2009

These results are based on a May 29–31 *USA Today/*Gallup poll. Early in his administration, President Obama announced that he would close the controversial prison within a year. However, his policy received a bit of a rebuke last month when the U.S. Senate rejected funding for the closure until the president outlines a plan for what to do with the terror suspects still being held there. Even some prominent Democratic senators rejected the idea of moving Guantanamo detainees to U.S. prisons.

Americans are especially resistant to closing the prison and transferring the terrorism suspects to prisons in their own states—only 23% favor this, while 74% are opposed. That represents a nine-point falloff from the 32% who support moving prisoners to the United States (with no specific location mentioned). Thus, even a segment of Americans who in general support closing Guantanamo are opposed to moving its terrorism suspects to prisons in their own "backyard."

The poll indicates that Americans tend to be emotionally invested in the outcome of the policy—7 in 10 say they would be "upset" if Obama does not follow their preferred course of action on the issue.

However, most of the highly charged sentiment comes from those who oppose closing the prison. Fifty-four percent of Americans not only say they oppose closing Guantanamo and moving prisoners to the United States, but say they would be "upset" if the government does this. By contrast, only 18% of Americans support closing the prison and would be upset if the government does not do so.

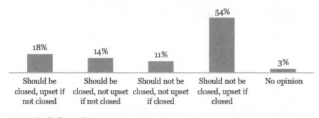
Polling by other firms has found greater support for closing Guantanamo, using different question wordings. Most of these differ from the Gallup question in that they associate the policy with President Obama and do not mention what would be done with the terror suspects who are currently housed at Guantanamo.

For example, a May 28–June 1 AP/GfK poll finds Americans evenly divided, with 47% approving of President Obama's "decision to close the U.S. military prison in Guantanamo Bay within a year," and 47% disapproving.

Most of the other recent polling is structured similarly to the AP wording, and finds similar results. The only other recent poll that addresses the handling of the prisoners is an April 22–26 CBS News/*New York Times* poll, which found 47% saying the U.S. should "continue to operate the prison" and 44% saying it should "close the prison and transfer the prisoners somewhere else."

That poll was conducted before the Senate vote. Much of the discussion after that vote concerned the possibility that some of the prisoners would be sent to U.S. prisons. Thus, it is possible the poll's results would differ if asked today because it may now be clearer to Americans that transferring prisoners "somewhere else" might include the United States.

Republicans are almost united in opposition to closing Guantanamo and moving some prisoners to U.S. prisons—91% are opposed. Independents also show solid opposition. Democrats—who have typically favored closing the prison in previous Gallup polling—also do so in the current poll, but by only a slim 53% to 42% margin.

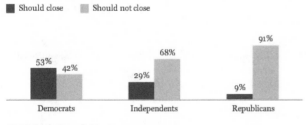
Implications

The Guantanamo Bay prison closure could end up being one of the more difficult policies for the Obama administration to carry out, par-

ticularly because Congress has made it clear that it will not fund the closure without details about how it will be done.

The fact that the significant majority of Americans oppose closing Guantanamo when they are told that some of the prisoners would be sent to the U.S. highlights the difficulties Obama will face in deciding what to do with the prisoners whom no other country will take. Obama still has time to sort through the possibilities, as his executive order calling for the closure of Guantanamo includes a 12-month period in which to do so.

Survey Methods

Results are based on telephone interviews with 1,015 national adults, aged 18 and older, conducted May 29–31, 2009. For results based on the total sample of national adults, one can say with 95% confidence that the maximum margin of sampling error is ±3 percentage points.

Interviews are conducted with respondents on land-line telephones (for respondents with a land-line telephone) and cellular phones (for respondents who are cell-phone only).

In addition to sampling error, question wording and practical difficulties in conducting surveys can introduce error or bias into the findings of public opinion polls.

June 04, 2009
AMERICANS REMAIN SKEPTICAL ABOUT MIDDLE EAST PEACE
Just 32% think Israel and Arabs will ever live in peace

by Lydia Saad, Gallup Poll Senior Editor

With President Barack Obama seeking to engage the Arab world with his speech in Cairo, Americans' confidence that there will ever be peace in the Middle East is at near-record lows. Only 32% of U.S. adults surveyed by *USA Today* and Gallup in late May believe "there will come a time when Israel and the Arab nations will be able to settle their differences and live in peace"; 66% disagree.

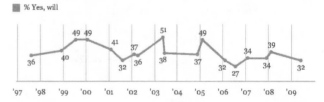
Current attitudes about the chances for Mideast peace are nearly the most negative that Gallup has found in more than a decade of polling on this question. The only time fewer Americans were optimistic about Arab-Israeli peace was in July 2006, when only 27% believed it could be achieved. This coincided with the Israeli-Hezbollah war in southern Lebanon, and followed the election victory of Hamas in the Palestinian Territories in January.

Americans' outlook for Mideast peace has since remained quite downbeat. However, as the long-term trend shows, public optimism about the conflict has varied, and has a history of rebounding from pessimistic lows—particularly after U.S.-brokered peace talks in 1999, 2003, and 2005.

One thing that does not appear to be a factor, at least in terms of the recent trend, is politics. There has been little change over the past year—spanning the change in presidential administrations from that of Republican George W. Bush to that of Democrat Obama—in the outlook for peace among rank-and-file Republicans and among rank-and-file Democrats.

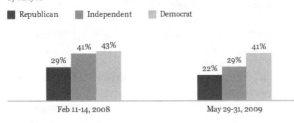

Percentage Saying Israel and Arab Nations Will One Day Live in Peace
by Party ID

General Support for Palestinian Statehood

After the Cairo speech, the hard work for the Obama administration will be advancing its goal of a two-state solution to the Israeli-Palestinian conflict. While the establishment of an independent Palestinian state formed the basis for the "road map" to peace outlined in the 2003 peace accords, the newly elected prime minister of Israel, Benjamin Netanyahu, appears to be backing off from that goal, and Palestinian President Mahmoud Abbas recently indicated that he is not prepared to resume peace talks without a greater commitment to statehood from Israel.

Americans favor the establishment of an independent Palestinian state on the West Bank and Gaza Strip. Fifty-one percent in the new poll say they favor this; only 29% are opposed. An additional 20% have no views on the matter.

While support for Palestinian statehood is slightly lower today than what Gallup found in May 2003 (58%), it is higher than at any other time historically since Gallup first asked the question in 1994. Each time Gallup has asked it, more Americans have been in favor of a Palestinian state than opposed to it.

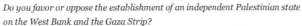

Do you favor or oppose the establishment of an independent Palestinian state on the West Bank and the Gaza Strip?

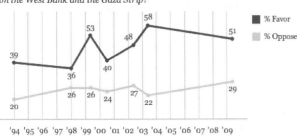

"No opinion" response not shown

Politically, Democrats and political independents are much more supportive of Palestinian statehood than are Republicans. Republicans have typically more closely aligned themselves with the Israeli side of the conflict than have Democrats.

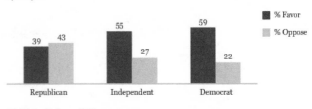

Support for an Independent Palestinian State
By Party ID

USA Today/Gallup poll, May 29-31, 2009

Bottom Line

President Obama's speech in Cairo comes at a time when many Americans may think he has set some impossible foreign policy goals for his administration. Most Americans believe the Muslim world views the United States unfavorably, and thus, Americans may be skeptical that he can transform those attitudes. They have also seen enough failures and setbacks in negotiations between Israel and the Palestinians over the past decade that they are, perhaps, jaded about the chances peace will ever come about. However, Americans generally support the two-state solution Obama will be advancing over the coming months, and they may feel encouraged by the image of an American president being welcomed in the heart of the Arab world, and in one of the few Arab or Muslim countries Americans largely admire.

More generally, a majority of Americans just prior to the speech said they approved of the job Obama is doing of handling the situation in the Middle East. This rating was taken after his recent White House meetings with Netanyahu and Abbas, in which he called on Israel to halt the construction of new settlements on the West Bank. The challenge for Obama will be maintaining public support for his efforts if Arab-Israeli peace proves elusive, or if he is perceived as being too tough on Israel—a country Americans are generally sympathetic to in the Mideast conflict.

Do you approve or disapprove of the way Barack Obama is handling the situation in the Middle East?

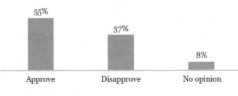

USA Today/Gallup poll, May 29-31, 2009

Survey Methods

The latest results are based on telephone interviews with 1,015 national adults, aged 18 and older, conducted May 29–31, 2009. For results based on the total sample of national adults, one can say with 95% confidence that the maximum margin of sampling error is ±3 percentage points.

Interviews are conducted with respondents on land-line telephones (for respondents with a land-line telephone) and cellular phones (for respondents who are cell-phone only).

In addition to sampling error, question wording and practical difficulties in conducting surveys can introduce error or bias into the findings of public opinion polls.

June 05, 2009

CONSERVATIVES SHIFT IN FAVOR OF OPENLY GAY SERVICE MEMBERS

Weekly churchgoers also show double-digit increase in support from 2004

by Lymari Morales, Gallup Poll Staff Writer

Americans are six percentage points more likely than they were four years ago to favor allowing openly gay men and lesbian women to serve in the military, 69% to 63%. While liberals and Democrats remain the most supportive, the biggest increase in support has been among conservatives and weekly churchgoers—up 12 and 11 percentage points, respectively.

Do you favor or oppose allowing openly gay men and lesbian women to serve in the military?
% Favor

	November 2004	May 2009	Change
	%	%	Pct. pts.
National adults	63	69	6
Conservatives	46	58	12
Moderates	72	77	5
Liberals	83	86	3
Republicans	52	58	6
Independents	63	67	4
Democrats	78	82	4
Attend church weekly	49	60	11
Attend church nearly weekly/monthly	66	70	4
Attend church seldom/never	73	76	3

Most recent results from USA Today/Gallup poll conducted May 7-10, 2009

The finding that majorities of weekly churchgoers (60%), conservatives (58%), and Republicans (58%) now favor what essentially equates to repealing the "Don't Ask, Don't Tell" policy implemented under President Clinton in 1993 is noteworthy for several reasons. First, the data show that these traditionally conservative groups are shifting on this issue, supporting it to a far greater extent than they support legalized gay marriage. Second, it suggests the political playing field may be softer on this issue, and President Barack Obama will be well-positioned to forge ahead with his campaign promise to end the military ban on openly gay service members with some support from more conservative segments of the population. To date, it is estimated that more than 12,500 servicemen and servicewomen have been discharged under the policy, including more than 200 since Obama took office.

Overall, the groups most in favor of allowing openly gay service members to serve in the military continue to be liberals (86%) and Democrats (82%), followed by Americans 18 to 29 (78%)—whose support registered a nine-point jump in support from 2004.

While men (64%) and Americans 65 and older (60%) have levels of support more in line with right-leaning groups than with left-leaning groups on this issue, they join virtually all other demographic segments of the population in registering an increase in support since 2004.

The only exception to the trend in favor of openly gay service members is seen among those with a high school education or less, who showed 57% support in both surveys.

Do you favor or oppose allowing openly gay men and lesbian women to serve in the military?
% Favor

	November 2004	May 2009	Change
	%	%	Pct. pts.
Men	57	64	7
Women	69	73	4
18-29 years	69	78	9
30-49 years	65	69	4
50-64 years	67	69	2
65+ years	52	60	8
East	70	77	7
Midwest	70	76	6
South	50	57	7
West	68	71	3

Most recent results from USA Today/Gallup poll conducted May 7-10, 2009

Bottom Line

Gallup Poll data from 2009 reveal that majority support among Americans for repealing "Don't Ask, Don't Tell" has only strengthened in recent years. Repealing the policy is a promise Obama made on the campaign trail and is one that gay rights groups have recently been more vocal in urging him to fulfill. While the administration to date has not taken action on the issue, the Gallup Poll data indicate that the public-opinion environment favors such a move.

In particular, the more conservative segments of the population who could be expected to be most resistant to such a policy change have shifted in favor of repealing the existing ban, to the extent that majority support now spans all segments of the population. At the same time, it is important to note that the Gallup Poll data do not break out the attitudes of current members of the military or provide a read on the views of current military leadership, whose reactions may be a major factor in the Obama administration's decisions on a change in policy.

As the Obama administration weighs the political and military consequences of a policy change on this issue, it can do so knowing Americans are for the most part strongly in favor of change toward allowing gay men and lesbian women to serve openly alongside their fellow service members.

Survey Methods

Results are based on telephone interviews with 1,015 national adults, aged 18 and older, conducted May 7–10, 2009, and with 1,015 national adults, aged 18 and older, conducted Nov. 19–21, 2004. For results based on these total samples of national adults, one can say with 95% confidence that the maximum margin of sampling error is ±3 percentage points.

Interviews are conducted with respondents on land-line telephones (for respondents with a land-line telephone) and cellular phones (for respondents who are cell-phone only).

In addition to sampling error, question wording and practical difficulties in conducting surveys can introduce error or bias into the findings of public opinion polls.

June 08, 2009

OBAMA RATED HIGHEST AS PERSON, LOWEST ON DEFICIT, SPENDING

Obama doing better than Bush and Clinton at similar points in their first year in office

by Frank Newport, Gallup Poll Editor in Chief

While 67% of Americans view President Barack Obama favorably, his overall job approval rating and his ratings on specific areas are less positive. At the low end of the spectrum, only 45% of Americans approve of Obama's handling of federal spending, and 46% of his handling of the federal budget deficit.

Opinion of Barack Obama and His Handling of Various Issues

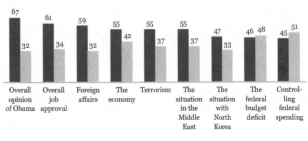

USA Today/Gallup poll, May 29-31, 2009

These conclusions are based on data collected in a May 29–31 *USA Today*/Gallup poll.

Obama's favorable and unfavorable ratings have trended upward since December 2006, when Gallup first measured opinion of him, as the percentage of Americans saying they have no opinion of Obama has steadily dropped. At all times during the last two and a half years, however, Obama's favorable ratings have exceeded his unfavorable ratings by a significant amount. His highest favorable rating to date came in a Jan. 9–11, 2009, poll—shortly before his inauguration—when 78% of Americans said they had a favorable opinion, with only 18% unfavorable. Since then, Obama's favorable rating has dropped, but his positive still outweighs his negative rating by better than a 2-to-1 ratio.

Next, we'd like to get your overall opinion of some people in the news. As I read each name, please say if you have a favorable or unfavorable opinion of these people -- or if you have never heard of them. How about -- Barack Obama?

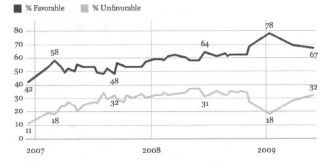

Obama's favorable rating is now slightly higher than that of his immediate predecessor, George W. Bush, at the same point in his first year. Bush had a 65% favorable rating in April 2001 and a 62%

favorable rating in June of that year. By June of Bill Clinton's first year in office (1993), his favorable rating had fallen to 48%.

Favorability Ratings of Barack Obama, George W. Bush, and Bill Clinton in Their First Year in Office

% Favorable

	January	February	March	April	May	June
	%	%	%	%	%	%
Barack Obama (2009)	78		69		67	
George W. Bush (2001)	62	66	66	65		62
Bill Clinton (1993)	66			63		48

As noted, Americans are more positive in their opinions of Obama as a person than they are when asked to rate his job performance, as well as how he has handled a series of specific issues or policy areas. Because there are different levels of "don't knows" in response to the list, the accompanying table displays an **approval-to-disapproval ratio** for each dimension.

Opinion of Barack Obama's Job Performance and His Handling of Various Issues

	% Approve	% Disapprove	Approval ratio
Foreign affairs	59	32	1.844
Overall job approval	61	34	1.794
Terrorism	55	37	1.486
The situation in the Middle East	55	37	1.486
The situation with North Korea	47	33	1.424
The economy	55	42	1.310
The federal budget deficit ^	46	48	0.958
Controlling federal spending ^	45	51	0.882

USA Today/Gallup poll, May 29-31, 2009
^ Asked of a half sample

Obama's highest issue-specific approval-to-disapproval ratios come in terms of international issues, including overall foreign policy, terrorism, the Middle East, and North Korea. Obama's ratio for his handling of the economy is lower. He receives his lowest ratings—with an approval-to-disapproval ratio below 1.0—for his handling of the federal budget deficit and controlling federal spending.

Implications

This latest Gallup Poll shows that the U.S. public has significantly differentiated views on various dimensions relating to Obama. Americans are most positive when asked about their basic opinions of Obama as a person. They also are positive when asked to assess his overall job performance, and on aspects of his performance relating to foreign and international issues. Americans have become increasingly less positive about Obama's handling of the economy in recent months, and are most negative when asked to say whether they approve of his handling of the federal deficit and federal spending.

The good news for Obama is that the public continues to be quite positive when asked to rate him as a person and to rate his overall job performance—both of which are presumably summaries of Americans' views of their president across all of the ways in which he could be evaluated. Obama's favorable rating is higher than were those of Bush or Clinton at this point in the first months of their presidencies, and his approval rating is also higher than those for Bush, Clinton, or Bush the elder in May of their first year in office.

Survey Methods

Results are based on telephone interviews with 1,015 national adults, aged 18 and older, conducted May 29–31, 2009. For results based on the total sample of national adults, one can say with 95% confidence that the maximum margin of sampling error is ±3 percentage points.

Interviews are conducted with respondents on land-line telephones (for respondents with a land-line telephone) and cellular phones (for respondents who are cell-phone only).

In addition to sampling error, question wording and practical difficulties in conducting surveys can introduce error or bias into the findings of public opinion polls.

June 09, 2009
AMERICANS' SATISFACTION PLATEAUS OVER THE PAST MONTH
One-third are satisfied, on par with a month ago

by Lymari Morales, Gallup Poll Staff Writer

Americans' satisfaction with the way things are going in the country has ebbed and flowed slightly over the past month, only to return to month-ago levels. Gallup Poll Daily tracking from June 6–8 finds 33% of Americans satisfied and 64% dissatisfied—roughly the same as the 35% satisfied and 62% dissatisfied in surveys conducted May 6–8—but much improved from the start of the year.

Gallup Daily: State of the Nation

In general, are you satisfied or dissatisfied with the way things are going in the United States at this time?

■ % Satisfied   ▨ % Dissatisfied

Though Americans' satisfaction is still more than double what it was when President Obama took office, it is noteworthy that satisfaction has leveled off over the past month, rather than continuing the trend of positive improvement recorded from March through early May. It remains low on an absolute basis. The all-time high on this measure in Gallup's 30-year history of asking the question is 71% in February 1999 and the all-time low is 7% last October.

The past month has no doubt seen a mixed bag of news, including President Obama's trip to the Middle East and Europe, a jump in the U.S. unemployment rate to 9.4%, the government-backed bankruptcies of General Motors and Chrysler, Obama's nomination of Sonia Sotomayor to the U.S. Supreme Court, Obama's commencement speech at the University of Notre Dame, and the murder of abortion doctor George Tiller.

Throughout all of this action, Republicans, independents, and Democrats showed measurable swings in their satisfaction levels, but

Gallup now finds satisfaction almost identical to one month ago among each of these three groups. About half of Democrats (48%) are satisfied, as are 31% of independents and 15% of Republicans.

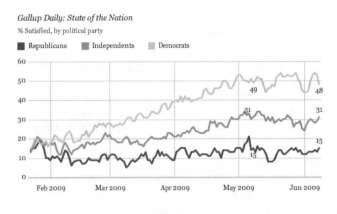

Gallup Daily: State of the Nation
% Satisfied, by political party

■ Republicans   ▨ Independents   ▨ Democrats

Bottom Line

The initial, steady improvement in Americans' satisfaction recorded from January to May has more recently been replaced with fluctuation in the same range as recorded a month ago. One-third of Americans (33%) are satisfied with how things are going in the country, including 48% of Democrats but just 15% of Republicans. The leveling off seen over the past month suggests Americans may be moving beyond their initial positive reactions to the new administration and now more objectively assessing life in the "new normal"—which, simply stated, finds a new president juggling a whole host of issues, including a still-struggling economy and an uncertain world scene. Whatever the causes, Gallup Poll Daily tracking finds the American public's mood—at least temporarily—at a plateau at which only about one-third appear willing to say they are satisfied with the way things are going in the U.S.

Gallup tracks Americans' satisfaction daily and posts updated data each day at 1 p.m. Eastern.

Survey Methods

Results are based on telephone interviews conducted since Jan. 21, 2009, with rolling three-day averages of approximately 1,500 national adults, aged 18 and older, as part of Gallup Poll Daily tracking. For results based on these total samples of national adults, one can say with 95% confidence that the maximum margin of sampling error is ±3 percentage points.

Interviews are conducted with respondents on land-line telephones (for respondents with a land-line telephone) and cellular phones (for respondents who are cell-phone only).

In addition to sampling error, question wording and practical difficulties in conducting surveys can introduce error or bias into the findings of public opinion polls.

June 10, 2009

LIMBAUGH, GINGRICH, CHENEY SEEN AS SPEAKING FOR GOP

Obama overwhelmingly seen as main person who speaks for Democrats

by Frank Newport, Gallup Poll Editor in Chief

Asked to name the "main person who speaks for the Republican Party today," Republicans across the country are most likely to name three men: Rush Limbaugh, Newt Gingrich, and Dick Cheney. Democrats are most likely to say Limbaugh speaks for the GOP, followed by Cheney. Both Republicans and Democrats overwhelmingly say Barack Obama is the main person who speaks for the Democratic Party, although Republicans are significantly more likely than Democrats to mention Speaker of the House Nancy Pelosi.

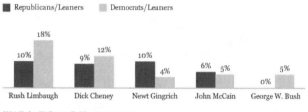

Who is the main person who speaks for the Republican Party today?

■ Republicans/Leaners ■ Democrats/Leaners

USA Today/Gallup poll, May 29-31, 2009

These results are based on an open-ended question included in a May 29–31 *USA Today*/Gallup poll. It comes as the Republican Party is attempting to regroup after losing last November's presidential election, and is looking for ways to reorganize and strengthen in time for the 2010 midterm elections.

The responses to the Republican leadership question provide hard evidence that there is in fact a significant leadership vacuum confronting the GOP today. Forty-seven percent of Republicans and Republican-leaning independents could not come up with a single name in response to the party spokesperson question. In contrast, a much lower 17% of Democrats could not name an individual as the person who speaks for their party.

Who do you think is the main person who speaks for the Republican Party today?

	National adults	Republicans/Leaners	Democrats/Leaners
	%	%	%
Rush Limbaugh	13	10	18
Dick Cheney	10	9	12
John McCain	6	6	5
Newt Gingrich	6	10	4
George W. Bush	3	*	5
Michael Steele	1	2	1
John Boehner	1	*	1
Mitt Romney	1	2	-
Other	9	14	5
No one	14	17	10
Everyone	1	1	1
No opinion	37	29	39

* Less than 0.5 %
USA Today/Gallup poll, May 29-31, 2009

Additionally, no one person dominates even among Republicans who are able to name someone who speaks for their party. Radio talk-show host Limbaugh, former Speaker Gingrich, and former Vice President Cheney—although at the top of the list—are all mentioned by only 9% or 10% of Republicans. The only other individuals named by more than 1% of Republicans are Sen. John McCain at 6%, Republican National Committee Chairman Michael Steele at 2%, and former Massachusetts Gov. and presidential candidate Mitt Romney, also at 2%. Of notable interest is the fact that less than 1% of Republicans name George W. Bush in response to the question. This reflects at least in part that Cheney has been highly visible and outspoken since leaving office, while Bush has largely remained silent, publicly.

Democrats are most likely to name Limbaugh as the person who speaks for the Republican Party (18%). Since Limbaugh is not a popular person with Democrats, the frequency with which Democrats name him is no doubt a negative characterization of the GOP from those who identify with the rival party. The talk-show host is followed on Democrats' list by Cheney at 12%, then McCain and Bush at 5% each. Gingrich is apparently not on the Democrats' radar as much as he is on Republicans'; the former speaker receives 4% mentions from Democrats, compared to the 10% mentions he receives from those who identify with his own party. (This past Monday, Republicans gathered for a House and Senate campaign committee fund-raiser in Washington, and Gingrich gave the keynote address.)

Democrats have little difficulty in naming the individual who is the main person who speaks for their party—Obama, mentioned by 67% of Democrats. Six percent of Democrats name Pelosi, and 3% Hillary Clinton.

Who do you think is the main person who speaks for the Democratic Party today?

	National adults	Republicans/Leaners	Democrats/Leaners
	%	%	%
Barack Obama	58	54	67
Nancy Pelosi	11	20	6
Hillary Clinton	3	3	3
Joe Biden	1	*	1
Harry Reid	1		*
Other	6	5	6
No one	3	3	1
Everyone	1	*	1
No opinion	17	13	15

* Less than 0.5%
USA Today/Gallup poll, May 29-31, 2009

Republicans are also most likely to name Obama as the main spokesperson for the Democrats. But 20% of Republicans name Nancy Pelosi. Recent Gallup polling shows that Pelosi is highly unpopular with Republicans, suggesting that, just as a number of Democrats are happy to characterize the GOP (presumably in a negative way) as being led by Limbaugh, a number of Republicans are just as happy to characterize the Democrats as being led by Pelosi.

Discussion

While being associated with the party of the sitting president gives the Democrats a natural advantage over the Republicans in having a well-defined person representing them, these data clearly underscore the leadership vacuum that confronts the Republican Party today. Almost half of those who identify with or lean toward the GOP cannot think of a single political or other figure when asked to name the main person who speaks for their party. And none of the three individuals whom Republicans name—Limbaugh, Cheney, and Gingrich—would likely be characterized as new visionaries or individuals bringing a fresh or new face to the Republican political scene. None of the three hold elective office at this time, all are older white males (the youngest of the three is Limbaugh, who is 58), and only one has a realistic chance of running for the presidency in the future (Gingrich).

Perhaps most importantly, none of these is mentioned by more than 10% of Republicans, a telling indication that rank-and-file Republicans today simply have no single consensus leader around whom they can gather their forces.

Most pundits and political observers already have a list of possible candidates who could end up battling for the 2012 Republican presidential nomination—including (in addition to Gingrich) Sarah Palin, Romney, Mike Huckabee, Charlie Crist, and Jeb Bush. Gingrich is the only one on this list who is mentioned by more than 2% of Republicans as the person who—at this point in time—speaks for their party.

Survey Methods

Results are based on telephone interviews with 1,015 national adults, aged 18 and older, conducted May 29–31, 2009. For results based on the total sample of national adults, one can say with 95% confidence that the maximum margin of sampling error is ±3 percentage points.

Interviews are conducted with respondents on land-line telephones (for respondents with a land-line telephone) and cellular phones (for respondents who are cell-phone only).

In addition to sampling error, question wording and practical difficulties in conducting surveys can introduce error or bias into the findings of public opinion polls.

June 11, 2009

REPUBLICANS DOWN ON THEIR OWN PARTY
Almost 4 out of 10 Republicans have unfavorable image of their party

by Frank Newport, Gallup Poll Editor in Chief

Almost 4 out of 10 (38%) Republicans and Republican-leaning independents have an unfavorable opinion of their own party, while just 7% of Democrats and Democratic-leaning independents have an unfavorable opinion of the Democratic Party. Additionally, a May 29–31 *USA Today*/Gallup poll shows that the top-of-mind images of the Republican Party among Republicans are considerably more negative than are the images of the Democratic Party among Democrats.

Although it is generally well known that the Republican Party has an image problem today (after all, the Democrats have control of the White House and both houses of Congress), these findings reinforce the depth of that problem by pointing out the degree to which Republicans themselves have a lower opinion of their party than Democrats do of their party, as noted above. The only saving grace, perhaps, is the finding that Democrats are slightly more positive in their opinions of the Republican Party than is the case the other way around.

Among all Americans, the poll shows a 19-point advantage for the Democratic Party over the Republican Party when it comes to the two parties' respective favorable images—a finding little changed

Opinion of Republican and Democratic Parties, by Party ID

Next, we'd like to get your overall opinion of some people in the news. As I read each name, please say if you have a favorable or unfavorable opinion of these people -- or if you have never heard of them. How about . . .

	Republicans/ Republican leaners	Democrats/ Democratic leaners
	%	%
The Republican Party		
Favorable	58	17
Unfavorable	38	78
The Democratic Party		
Favorable	12	89
Unfavorable	85	7

USA Today/Gallup poll, May 29-31, 2009

from last November, when Gallup last updated the parties' images. Fifty-three percent of Americans today have a favorable opinion of the Democratic Party, compared to just 34% who have a favorable opinion of the Republican Party.

Opinion of Democratic Party

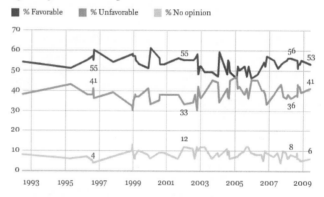

The Republican Party's image deficit is further evidenced by the examination of responses given to open-ended questions asking Americans what comes to mind when they think about the Republican Party and, separately, the Democratic Party. (Answers were recorded verbatim and coded into categories.)

The data make it clear that Republicans are more likely to have negative images of their own party than are Democrats of their party. Among Republicans, two of the top five categories of responses about the GOP's image are categorized by Gallup coders

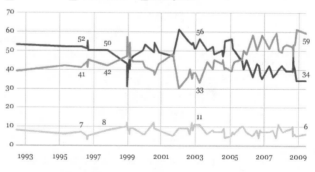

Opinion of Republican Party

as a general "unfavorable" response (given by 19% of Republicans) and that the GOP has lost its direction (9%).

None of the top five categories of responses about the image of the Democratic Party among Democrats is negative. In fact, one of the starkest contrasts is between the percentage of Democrats whose responses are broadly "unfavorable" (2%) compared to the percentage of Republicans who say the same about their party (19%).

Not surprisingly, both Republicans and Democrats have negative things to say about the *other* party. For Republicans, the top images associated with the Democratic Party are "liberal," "big spending," "unfavorable," "self-centered/out for themselves," and (tied) "big government" and "socially conscious/progressive." For Democrats, the top images associated with the Republican party are "unfavorable," "conservative," "cater to the rich," "George Bush," and "lost their direction."

Top-of-Mind Image of the Republican Party

Now, we'd like to ask you about your impressions of the two major political parties. First of all, what comes to mind when you think of -- the Republican Party?

	Republicans/ Republican leaners	Democrats/ Democratic leaners
	%	%
Unfavorable	19	31
Conservative	21	15
Favorable	14	2
Lost their way/No direction	9	5
Caters to rich	1	10
George W. Bush	1	6
Closed-minded/Not open to new ideas	3	4
Caters to big business	1	4
Poor economic conditions	1	4

USA Today/Gallup poll, May 29-31, 2009

Top-of-Mind Image of Democratic Party

Now, we'd like to ask you about your impressions of the two major political parties. First of all, what comes to mind when you think of -- the Democratic Party?

	Republicans/ Republican leaners	Democrats/ Democratic leaners
	%	%
Liberal	19	15
Favorable	1	18
For the people/working, middle, lower class	1	17
Socially conscious/Progressive	7	13
Big spending/Spend a lot of money	15	2
Unfavorable	12	2
Self-centered/Out for themselves	8	1
Big government	7	1
Barack Obama	2	4

USA Today/Gallup poll, May 29-31, 2009

Implications

All of these data taken together underscore the challenges facing the Republican Party today. Not only are Americans' basic opinions of the GOP significantly more negative than are their opinions of the Democratic Party, but the top-of-mind images of the Republican Party also include more negative categories than is the case for the Democrats.

Perhaps most worrisome to the Republicans is the fact that a substantial minority of Americans who identify with or lean toward the Republican Party also have negative views of the party. Almost 4 out of 10 Republicans say their opinions of the party are unfavorable, and a number of Republicans volunteer that the first thing that comes

to mind when they think about the GOP is "unfavorable" or "lost its direction."

Taken together with Gallup Poll evidence showing that almost half of Republicans cannot name an individual who speaks for the party, the results reinforce what Republican leaders already know—that there are significant challenges ahead as the party gears up for the important 2010 midterm elections and the 2012 presidential election that follows.

Survey Methods

Results are based on telephone interviews with 1,015 national adults, aged 18 and older, conducted May 29–31, 2009. For results based on the total sample of national adults, one can say with 95% confidence that the maximum margin of sampling error is ±3 percentage points.

Interviews are conducted with respondents on land-line telephones (for respondents with a land-line telephone) and cellular phones (for respondents who are cell-phone only).

In addition to sampling error, question wording and practical difficulties in conducting surveys can introduce error or bias into the findings of public opinion polls.

June 11, 2009
MOST DISAPPROVE OF MAJORITY GOVERNMENT OWNERSHIP OF GM
Close to half say they would be less likely to buy a car from a bankrupt automaker

by Jeffrey M. Jones, Gallup Poll Managing Editor

A new Gallup Poll, conducted June 9–10, finds 55% of Americans saying they disapprove of the government's investing $50 billion in General Motors to make the government the majority owner of that automaker.

As you may know, the U.S. government is investing $50 billion in General Motors and will own 60% of that company when General Motors emerges from bankruptcy. All in all, do you approve or disapprove of these government actions?

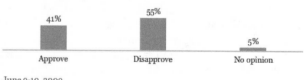

June 9-10, 2009

Americans are remarkably well-informed about the financial status of the Big Three U.S. automakers—80% correctly identify General Motors as having declared bankruptcy and 74% also know Chrysler has done the same. Additionally, 85% of Americans correctly say that the third major U.S. automaker, Ford, has not declared bankruptcy.

Since the Big Three's woes became widely known late last year, Americans have generally not been supportive of the government bailing them out.

Next, I'm going to mention three car companies. As I name each one, please tell me, from what you know or have read, if that company has declared bankruptcy or not.

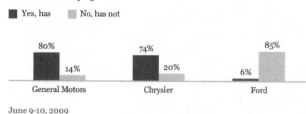

June 9-10, 2009

In the latest poll, opposition to the government's GM rescue efforts is greatest with Republicans, among whom 78% disapprove. A majority of independents, 58%, also disapprove. In contrast, Democrats are nearly twice as likely to approve (62%) as to disapprove (34%).

Residents of the Midwest—the traditional home of the U.S. auto industry—show greater support for the government's action to aid GM than Americans residing in other parts of the country. But even among Midwest residents, more disapprove than approve of the government's actions in this matter.

View of Government Assistance to GM, by Region

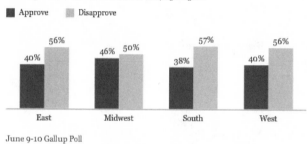

June 9-10 Gallup Poll

How Might Bankruptcy Affect Auto Sales?

It is well-documented that U.S. auto sales have slowed dramatically in the past year, and it's not clear when or if auto sales will pick up. The new Gallup Poll finds Americans are, for the most part, not currently shopping for new cars. Only 20% say they are "extremely," "very," or "somewhat likely" to "buy a new car from a dealer within the next 12 months," including just 7% who are extremely or very likely to do so.

Generally speaking, Americans are somewhat reluctant to buy a new car from a bankrupt automaker—49% say the fact that a car company has declared bankruptcy makes them less likely to buy a car from that manufacturer. Most of the rest, 44%, say it makes no difference to their decision, while 4% say they would be more likely to buy from a bankrupt automaker.

These attitudes are essentially the same among the one in five Americans who are at least somewhat likely to buy a car in the next 12 months.

Implications

The Bush and Obama administrations decided that General Motors and Chrysler were too big to fail and have, in recent months, invested large sums of public money in helping these carmakers stay alive.

Effect of Auto Company Bankruptcy on Decision to Buy New Car From That Company

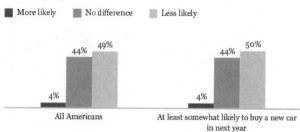

Thus far, the American public does not endorse the government's efforts to save GM, and close to half of Americans claim to be less likely to consider buying a car from a bankrupt automaker.

There may be some comfort for GM and Chrysler in the finding that about half of potential car buyers would be no less likely to buy cars from a bankrupt automaker. But given a rather limited car buyer pool, any factor that might discourage a potential buyer from purchasing their vehicles could potentially make recovery for GM and Chrysler even more difficult.

Survey Methods

Results are based on telephone interviews with 1,007 national adults, aged 18 and older, conducted June 9–10, 2009, as part of Gallup Poll Daily tracking. For results based on the total sample of national adults, one can say with 95% confidence that the maximum margin of sampling error is ±3 percentage points.

Interviews are conducted with respondents on land-line telephones (for respondents with a land-line telephone) and cellular phones (for respondents who are cell-phone only).

In addition to sampling error, question wording and practical difficulties in conducting surveys can introduce error or bias into the findings of public opinion polls.

June 12, 2009
WOMEN MORE LIKELY TO BE DEMOCRATS, REGARDLESS OF AGE
Women from 18 to 85 are more Democratic than men of the same age

by Frank Newport, Gallup Poll Editor in Chief

A new Gallup analysis of almost 150,000 interviews conducted from January through May of this year sheds new light on the substantial gender gap that exists in American politics today. Not only are women significantly more likely than men to identify as Democrats, and less likely to identify as independents, but—with only slight variation—this gap is evident across all ages, from 18 to 85, and within all major racial, ethnic, and marital-status segments of society.

A recent Gallup analysis confirmed the existence of a fundamental gender gap in American political party identification today, although the exact nature of that gap has varied over recent years. The major distinction in political party identification today seems to revolve around the percentage of each gender who identify as

Partisan Gap, by Age and Gender

Partisan gap: % Democratic minus % Republican

■ Women   ■ Men

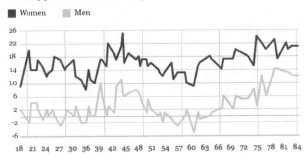

Gallup Poll, January-May 2009

Democrats versus independents; men and women have been similar in terms of identification with the Republican Party this year.

In the current analysis of 149,192 Gallup Poll Daily tracking interviews conducted in January through May of this year, 41% of women identify as Democrats, some nine points higher than the 32% of men who identify as Democrats. The 34% of men in this sample who are independents can be contrasted with the smaller 26% of women who are independents. There is little difference by gender in terms of identification as Republicans—28% of men are Republicans, compared to 25% of women.

Identification With Political Party, by Gender

■ Republican   ■ Democrat   ■ Independent

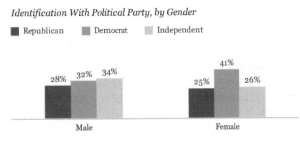

Gallup Poll Daily tracking, January-May 2009

Overall, the data confirm that men currently have a much more even distribution of party identification than do women. The range across the three partisan groups for men is just 6 points, from a low of 28% identifying as Republicans to a high of 34% identifying as independents. On the other hand, the range for women is a much larger 16 points, from 25% Republican to 41% Democratic.

The Age Factor

Previous Gallup research has shown significant variations in party identification across age groups in the American population. Baby boomers (aged 45–63) are more likely than average to identify as Democrats, as are younger Americans in Generation Y (aged 18–29), while Generation X (aged 30–44) as well as older Americans are somewhat more Republican in orientation. The new Gallup analysis, importantly, shows the persistence of a gender gap not only within each of these broad age groups, but at every age, from 18 to 85, even as the overall party identification patterns shift across the age spectrum.

The accompanying chart displays the "partisan gap" for men and for women at each age. The broad trends certainly document the fact that the Democratic over Republican advantage varies across age

groups. Democrats have their greatest advantage among baby boomers and the very young, and are weakest, relatively speaking, among those in their late 30s and in their mid- to late 60s. *The key point for the current analysis, however, is that these variations occur among **both** men and women.* There is, as noted, a gender gap in this partisan orientation measure at every age point, from 18 to 85.

Three additional charts display the gender differences in the percentages identifying as Republicans, independents, and Democrats across all age groups. The gender gap is largest in terms of Democratic and independent identification, and smallest for the percentage identifying as Republicans, but for the most part, a gender gap exists for every age in terms for each of these three partisan groups.

Democratic Identification, by Age and Gender

% Democrat

■ Women   ■ Men

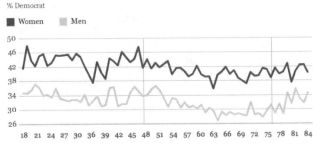

Gallup Poll, January-May 2009

Republican Identification, by Age and Gender

% Republican

■ Women   ■ Men

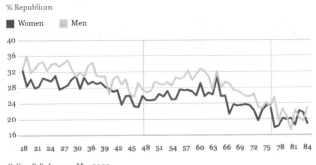

Gallup Poll, January-May 2009

Independent Identification, by Age and Gender

% Independent

■ Women   ■ Men

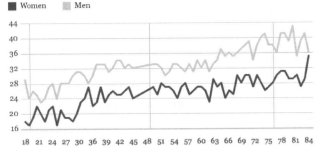

Gallup Poll, January-May 2009

Implications

Although the existence of a gender gap in American politics has been well established, the very large sample sizes available with

Gallup Poll Daily tracking allow for a more-detailed-than-normal examination of the nature of gender differences. The remarkable finding is that women of all ages are more Democratic in orientation than are men of the same ages, and that women of all ages are also less likely than men of the same ages to be independent. (The differences by age in the percentage identifying as Republican are much smaller.)

This means that whatever forces are at work that determine party identification in America today—socialization, cultural patterns, social position, social status, and life orientation—are already in place by the time young men and women reach the age of 18. And, these same patterns seem to have affected or are currently affecting men and women in their 80s in a similar fashion. The fact that the gender gap persists not only across age groups, but within major racial, ethnic, and marital-status groups reinforces the conclusion that a gender difference in political orientation is a fundamental part of today's American political and social scene.

Survey Methods

Results are based on telephone interviews with 149,192 national adults, aged 18 and older, conducted Jan. 2–May 31, 2009, as part of Gallup Poll Daily tracking. For results based on the total sample of national adults, one can say with 95% confidence that the maximum margin of sampling error is ±1 percentage point.

Interviews are conducted with respondents on land-line telephones (for respondents with a land-line telephone) and cellular phones (for respondents who are cell-phone only).

In addition to sampling error, question wording and practical difficulties in conducting surveys can introduce error or bias into the findings of public opinion polls.

June 12, 2009
U.S. INVESTOR OPTIMISM SURGES IN MAY
Investors, pessimistic since late 2008, are now neutral on the future investment environment

by Dennis Jacobe, Gallup Chief Economist

The Gallup Index of Investor Optimism—a broad measure of investor perceptions—surged 19 points in May to -1, indicating that investors are now essentially neutral on the future direction of the economy. The Index has improved 63 points from February's -64 reading, which is the lowest for the Index since its 1996 inception.

Gallup Index of Investor Optimism, December 2007-May 2009

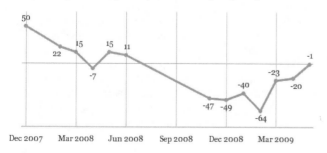

Portfolio Optimism Improves

Investors' expectations for their personal portfolios over the next 12 months improved in May, as the Personal Dimension of the Index increased by six points to 27. This is the highest level of personal optimism for investors this year, and suggests that after the sharp improvement in the equities markets, investors remain cautiously optimistic about the performance of their personal portfolios over the next 12 months.

Personal Dimension, Gallup Index of Investor Optimism, December 2007-May 2009

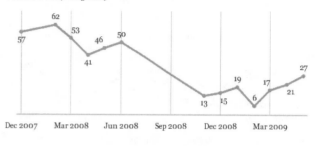

Economic Optimism Improves

Investor optimism about the U.S. economy's direction over the next 12 months also improved in May, as the Economic Dimension surged 13 points to -28. While investors as a group remain pessimistic about the economic outlook, they are much less so than they were in February, when this dimension was at -70. In fact, investor optimism about the economic outlook is at its best level since December 2007—essentially when the current recession began.

Economic Dimension, Gallup Index of Investor Optimism, December 2007-May 2009

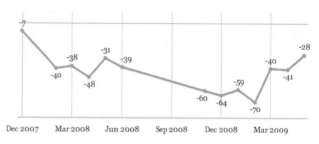

Survey Methods

Gallup Poll Daily tracking includes no fewer than 1,000 U.S. adults interviewed nationwide each day during 2008. The Index of Investor Optimism results are based on questions asked of 1,000 or more investors over a three-day period each month, conducted May 26–28, April 21–23, March 16–18, Feb. 17–19, and Jan. 16–18, 2009; and Dec. 16–18, Nov. 24–26, June 3–6, April 25–28, March 28–31, and Feb. 28–March 2, 2008. For results based on these samples, the maximum margin of sampling error is ±3 percentage points.

Results for May 2008 are from a Gallup Panel study and are based on telephone interviews with 576 national adults, aged 18 and older, conducted May 19–21, 2008. Gallup Panel members are recruited through random selection methods. The panel is weighted so that it is demographically representative of the U.S. adult population. For results based on this sample, one can say with 95% confidence that the maximum margin of sampling error is ±5 percentage points.

For investor results prior to 2008, telephone interviews were conducted with at least 800 investors, aged 18 and older, and having at least $10,000 of investable assets. For the total sample of investors in these surveys, one can say with 95% confidence that the maximum margin of sampling error is ±4 percentage points.

Interviews are conducted with respondents on land-line telephones (for respondents with a land-line telephone) and cellular phones (for respondents who are cell-phone only).

In addition to sampling error, question wording and practical difficulties in conducting surveys can introduce error or bias into the findings of public opinion polls.

June 15, 2009

"CONSERVATIVES" ARE SINGLE-LARGEST IDEOLOGICAL GROUP
Percentage of "liberals" higher this decade than in early '90s

by Lydia Saad, Gallup Poll Senior Editor

Thus far in 2009, 40% of Americans interviewed in national Gallup Poll surveys describe their political views as conservative, 35% as moderate, and 21% as liberal. This represents a slight increase for conservatism in the U.S. since 2008, returning it to a level last seen in 2004. The 21% calling themselves liberal is in line with findings throughout this decade, but is up from the 1990s.

How would you describe your political views -- [very conservative, conservative, (or) moderate, liberal, (or) very liberal]?

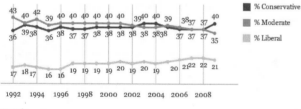

Annual averages
1992-2009; 2009 data based on January-May surveys

These annual figures are based on multiple national Gallup surveys conducted each year, in some cases encompassing more than 40,000 interviews. The 2009 data are based on 10 separate surveys conducted from January through May. Thus, the margins of error around each year's figures are quite small, and changes of only two percentage points are statistically significant.

To measure political ideology, Gallup asks Americans to say whether their political views are very conservative, conservative, moderate, liberal, or very liberal. As has been the case each year since 1992, very few Americans define themselves at the extremes of the political spectrum. Just 9% call themselves "very conservative" and 5% "very liberal." The vast majority of self-described liberals and conservatives identify with the unmodified form of their chosen label.

Party-Based Ideology

There is an important distinction in the respective ideological compositions of the Republican and Democratic Parties. While a solid

2009 Detailed Political Ideology

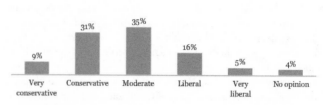

2009 data based on January-May surveys

majority of Republicans are on the same page—73% call themselves conservative—Democrats are more of a mixture. The major division among Democrats is between self-defined moderates (40%) and liberals (38%). However, an additional 22% of Democrats consider themselves conservative, much higher than the 3% of Republicans identifying as liberal.

True to their nonpartisan tendencies, close to half of political independents—45%—describe their political views as "moderate." Among the rest, the balance of views is tilted more heavily to the right than to the left: 34% are conservative, while 20% are liberal.

Gallup trends show a slight increase since 2008 in the percentages of all three party groups calling themselves "conservative," which accounts for the three percentage-point increase among the public at large.

2009 Political Ideology, by Party ID

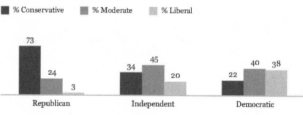

2009 data based on January-May surveys

Thus far in 2009, Gallup has found an average of 36% of Americans considering themselves Democratic, 28% Republican, and 37% independent. When independents are pressed to say which party they lean toward, 51% of Americans identify as Democrats, 39% as Republicans, and only 9% as pure independents.

Ideological tendencies by leaned party affiliation are very similar to those of straight partisan groups. However, it is worth noting the views of pure independents—a group usually too small to analyze in individual surveys but potentially important in deciding elections. Exactly half of pure independents describe their views as moderate, 30% say they are conservative, and 17% liberal.

As reported last week on Gallup.com, women are more likely than men to be Democratic in their political orientation. Along the same lines, women are more likely than men to be ideologically "moderate" and "liberal," and less likely to be "conservative."

Still, conservatism outweighs liberalism among both genders.

The pattern is strikingly different on the basis of age, and this could have important political implications in the years ahead. Whereas middle-aged and older Americans lean conservative (vs. liberal) in their politics by at least 2 to 1, adults aged 18 to 29 are just as likely to say their political views are liberal (31%) as to say they are conservative (30%).

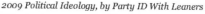

2009 Political Ideology, by Party ID With Leaners

■ % Conservative   ■ % Moderate   ▨ % Liberal

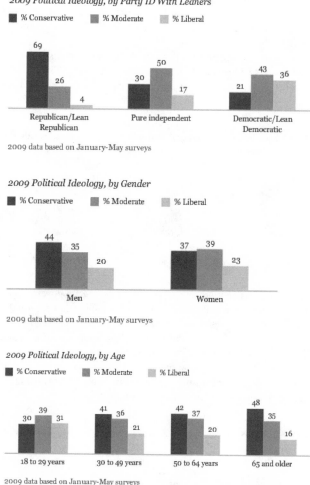

2009 data based on January-May surveys

2009 Political Ideology, by Gender

■ % Conservative   ■ % Moderate   ▨ % Liberal

2009 data based on January-May surveys

2009 Political Ideology, by Age

■ % Conservative   ■ % Moderate   ▨ % Liberal

2009 data based on January-May surveys

Future Gallup analysis will look at the changes in the political ideology of different age cohorts over time, to see whether young adults in the past have started out more liberal than they wound up in their later years.

Bottom Line

Although the terms may mean different things to different people, Americans readily peg themselves, politically, into one of five categories along the conservative-to-liberal spectrum. At present, large minorities describe their views as either moderate or conservative—with conservatives the larger group—whereas only about one in five consider themselves liberal.

While these figures have shown little change over the past decade, the nation appears to be slightly more polarized than it was in the early 1990s. Compared with the 1992–1994 period, the percentage of moderates has declined from 42% to 35%, while the percentages of conservatives and liberals are up slightly—from 38% to 40% for conservatives and a larger 17% to 21% movement for liberals.

Survey Methods

Results are based on aggregated Gallup Poll surveys of approximately 1,000 national adults, aged 18 and older, interviewed by telephone. Sample sizes for the annual compilations range from approximately 10,000 to approximately 40,000. For these results, one

can say with 95% confidence that the maximum margin of sampling error is ±1 percentage point.

In addition to sampling error, question wording and practical difficulties in conducting surveys can introduce error or bias into the findings of public opinion polls.

June 15, 2009
DESPITE "PANDEMIC," SWINE FLU WORRY DWINDLES
Few in any region are worried; gender gap gone

by Lydia Saad, Gallup Senior Editor

A new Gallup Poll—conducted in the first few days after the World Health Organization declared the H1N1 flu a pandemic—finds only 8% of Americans saying they worried "yesterday" about getting the so-called swine flu. This is down from 13% in mid-May and from the high of 25% in the early days of the outbreak, in late April.

Did you, personally, worry yesterday about getting swine flu, or not?
April 28-June 14, 2009, trend

■ % Yes, worried

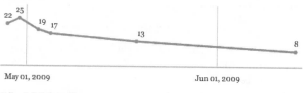

Gallup Poll Daily tracking

As of Friday, June 12, the Centers for Disease Control and Prevention reported nearly 18,000 confirmed or probable cases of H1N1 flu in the United States, and 45 deaths. The fact that cases have now been reported in all 50 states and the District of Columbia is reflected in the fairly uniform level of public concern across the four major regions of the country.

Worry About Getting Swine Flu, by Region
■ % Who worried "yesterday"

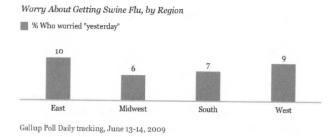

Gallup Poll Daily tracking, June 13-14, 2009

Bottom Line

In some scenarios, the word "pandemic" might be expected to cause widespread panic among the American public; however, in the case of the H1N1 flu, it appears to have had no effect. Americans are less concerned about personally getting the illness than at any previous point in the outbreak. Now that they have had two full months to assess the severity of the swine flu in the United States since the first

U.S. case was reported on April 15, they may be better able to put its associated risks into perspective with other illnesses—such as the "normal" seasonal flu.

Survey Methods

Results are based on telephone interviews with 998 national adults, aged 18 and older, conducted June 13–14, 2009, as part of Gallup Poll Daily tracking. For results based on the total sample of national adults, one can say with 95% confidence that the maximum margin of sampling error is ±3 percentage points.

Interviews are conducted with respondents on land-line telephones (for respondents with a land-line telephone) and cellular phones (for respondents who are cell-phone only).

In addition to sampling error, question wording and practical difficulties in conducting surveys can introduce error or bias into the findings of public opinion polls.

June 16, 2009

MOST AMERICANS FAVOR GOV'T. ACTION TO LIMIT EXECUTIVE PAY

A majority of Democrats favor such an approach, while most Republicans are opposed

by Jeffrey M. Jones, Gallup Poll Managing Editor

Just days after the Obama administration announced a series of proposals seeking more oversight of the salaries and bonus structures for executives at publicly traded companies, a new Gallup Poll finds that most Americans (59%) endorse government action to limit executive pay.

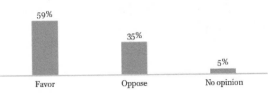

Do you favor or oppose the federal government taking steps to limit the pay of executives at major companies?

Gallup Poll, June 13-14, 2009

There has been a great deal of public anger over executives who have received large paydays while their companies teetered on the brink of collapse and needed government money to survive. The most prominent example came earlier this year, when it was revealed that many top executives at insurance company AIG—one of the biggest recipients of government bailout money—were paid bonuses.

In conjunction with the economic stimulus legislation passed by Congress earlier this year, the Treasury Department has put limits on the pay of executives at companies receiving federal bailout money; their pay plans must now be approved by a federal "pay czar" and their bonuses may be no greater than one-third of their total compensation.

The latest proposals seek to go further and attempt to change the rules governing how executive pay is determined at publicly traded companies (including those that did not receive bailout money), shifting the power from company management to independent corporate compensation commissions and giving shareholders a voice in the process.

Seventy-seven percent of self-identified Democrats favor the government's taking steps to limit executive pay, as do 56% of independents. More Republicans oppose (56%) than favor (42%) the idea.

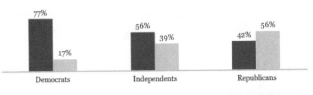

Favor/Oppose Federal Government Taking Steps to Limit the Pay of Executives, by Party Affiliation

Gallup Poll, June 13-14, 2009

Older Americans are less supportive of the federal government's trying to encourage limits on executive pay. Those aged 65 or older divide about evenly, with 46% in favor of and 44% opposed to government intervention in executive pay. That compares with a solid majority of 63% support among Americans younger than age 65.

Additionally, only a slim majority of upper-income Americans, 51%, favor government limits on executive pay. Support is higher among Americans at lower income levels.

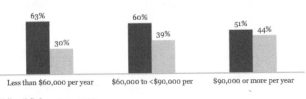

Favor/Oppose Federal Government Taking Steps to Limit the Pay of Executives, by Household Income

Gallup Poll, June 13-14, 2009

Implications

While some Republican elected officials see these latest proposals as another example of harmful government intervention in the private sector, Americans in general favor the idea of the federal government's getting involved to try to limit the amount of money corporate executives make.

It is unclear whether this results from a general notion among the public that executives are paid too much, or whether it is tied to a sense that executives at poorly performing companies do not deserve high salaries, particularly companies that received federal bailout money.

The Obama administration is trying to take an indirect approach by relying on shareholders and independent compensation commissions to reject exorbitant pay plans, rather than trying to set absolute limits on how much executives can make.

Survey Methods

Results are based on telephone interviews with 998 national adults, aged 18 and older, conducted June 13–14, 2009. For results based on

the total sample of national adults, one can say with 95% confidence that the maximum margin of sampling error is ±3 percentage points.

Interviews are conducted with respondents on land-line telephones (for respondents with a land-line telephone) and cellular phones (for respondents who are cell-phone only).

In addition to sampling error, question wording and practical difficulties in conducting surveys can introduce error or bias into the findings of public opinion polls.

June 17, 2009
ON HEALTHCARE, AMERICANS TRUST PHYSICIANS OVER POLITICIANS
Fifty-eight percent of Americans confident in Obama to recommend the right approach

by Lydia Saad, Gallup Poll Senior Editor

Nearly three-quarters of Americans (73%) say they are confident in doctors to recommend the right thing for reforming the U.S. healthcare system. That is significantly higher than the public confidence extended to President Barack Obama, as well as to six other entities that will be weighing in during the emerging healthcare reform debate.

Next, we have a question about healthcare policy in the United States. As I read some names and groups, please say whether you are confident or not confident in each to recommend the right thing for reforming the U.S. healthcare system.

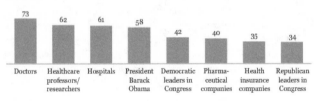

Gallup Poll Daily tracking, June 13-14, 2009

While the public trusts the views of doctors the most, more than 6 in 10 Americans are also confident in university professors or researchers who study healthcare policy (62%) and in hospitals (61%).

At 58%, Obama fares better than congressional leaders on both sides of the aisle; however, the Democratic leaders in Congress have more credibility on healthcare reform than do the Republican leaders: 42% vs. 34%.

In terms of the major private-sector healthcare debate participants, confidence in what the pharmaceutical companies might advocate as the solution is only slightly higher than what health insurance companies might propose, 40% vs. 35%.

Medical Professionals Have Bipartisan Reach

Doctors, hospitals, and university researchers may not generally be viewed as political powerhouses. But when it comes to healthcare reform, all three entities have a potentially important advantage over government leaders. As the Gallup Poll results suggest, they are well-positioned to have bipartisan clout with the public.

Obama and the leaders of the two parties in Congress are trusted on healthcare by most of their own party's members, but are distrusted by most of the opposing party's. By contrast, large majorities of Republicans, independents, and Democrats say they have confidence in what doctors, hospitals, and university professors and researchers recommend on healthcare.

Percentage Confident in Each on Healthcare Reform, by Party ID

	Democrats	Independents	Republicans	Democratic/ Republican gap
	%	%	%	Pct. pts.
MEDICAL/RESEARCH PROFESSIONALS				
Hospitals	60	57	68	8
Doctors	69	71	80	11
University healthcare policy professors/researchers	70	59	56	14
POLITICIANS				
President Obama	85	53	28	57
Democratic leaders	70	36	15	55
Republican leaders	19	27	65	46
PRIVATE INDUSTRY				
Pharmaceutical companies	35	35	52	17
Health insurance companies	33	32	42	9

Gallup Poll Daily tracking, June 13-14, 2009

Obama stands out among elected officials on this issue because he not only enjoys the confidence of his own party members (Democrats), but he receives majority support from independents. The 53% of independents saying they are confident in Obama to recommend the right thing on healthcare contrasts with only 36% of independents confident in congressional Democratic leaders, and 27% confident in congressional Republican leaders.

Bottom Line

President Obama received a lukewarm response at his speech before the annual meeting of the American Medical Association on Monday in which he outlined his case for enacting comprehensive healthcare reform this year. While the members present reportedly welcomed some of his remarks, some also booed him for failing to endorse limits on medical malpractice awards.

Obama has yet to unveil a comprehensive plan for reforming healthcare; the administration is still sponsoring healthcare forums at the White House and around the country to gather information and ideas. However, given Americans' high regard for doctors' opinions on healthcare reform, Obama may find it important to keep trying to bring the AMA, and other professional doctors' groups, on board with his approach. Of course, public confidence in hospitals and academic experts on the issue is nothing to sneeze at, either; their support for any plan Obama submits could help him counter possible opposition from the medical profession.

Survey Methods

Results are based on telephone interviews with 1,009 national adults, aged 18 and older, conducted June 13–14, 2009, as part of Gallup Poll Daily tracking. For results based on the total sample of national adults, one can say with 95% confidence that the maximum margin of sampling error is ±3 percentage points.

Note: These questions were asked of random half-samples for two nights of Gallup Poll Daily tracking, which interviews 1,000 U.S. adults each night.

Interviews are conducted with respondents on land-line telephones (for respondents with a land-line telephone) and cellular phones (for respondents who are cell-phone only).

In addition to sampling error, question wording and practical difficulties in conducting surveys can introduce error or bias into the findings of public opinion polls.

June 18, 2009
AMERICANS VIEW NORTH KOREA AS GREATER THREAT THAN IRAN
Both easily beat out Iraq and Afghanistan as perceived direct threats to U.S. security

by Jeffrey M. Jones, Gallup Poll Managing Editor

A new Gallup Poll finds 51% of Americans saying North Korea currently poses a direct threat to U.S. security. That is the highest percentage seen for eight countries or territories tested in the poll whose political climates or ongoing conflicts present a threat to U.S. interests in the world.

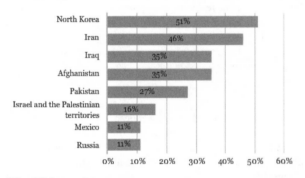

Percentage of Americans Who Believe Countries Pose a Direct Threat to U.S. Security

Gallup Poll, June 15-16, 2009

The June 15–16 poll was conducted amid continuing concern about North Korea's nuclear weapons program, but before North Korea on Wednesday pledged to launch a large-scale attack against any country that infringed on its sovereignty. President Obama said Wednesday that North Korea's nuclear program was a "grave threat" to the world.

In addition to the 51% who believe North Korea represents a direct threat to U.S. security, 34% say it is a serious threat to U.S. interests in the world, though not a direct threat to the U.S. itself. Only 10% believe North Korea does not represent a threat to the United States in either regard.

Iran is the only country of the eight tested that rivals North Korea in terms of being perceived as a direct threat to U.S. security. Iranian citizens have been rallying after last week's presidential election in that country, with many protesting alleged fraud in the balloting. Current president Mahmoud Ahmadinejad was declared the winner of the vote, but since the protests began, the Iranian government has agreed to a limited recount of ballots.

As is the case with North Korea, the vast majority of Americans view Iran as either a direct threat to U.S. security or a serious threat to U.S. interests in the world; only 9% say it is not a threat.

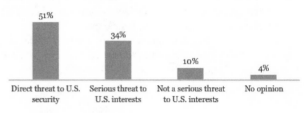

Americans' Views of North Korea as a Threat to the United States or Its Interests in the World

Gallup Poll, June 15-16, 2009

Iraq, which, along with North Korea and Iran, formed what former President George W. Bush termed an "axis of evil," is viewed as a direct threat to U.S. security by 35% of Americans.

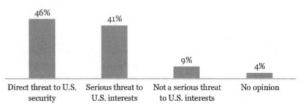

Americans' Views of Iran as a Threat to the United States or Its Interests in the World

Gallup Poll, June 15-16, 2009

Americans' views of Iraq have improved in recent years as U.S. military action has made increasing progress in bringing stability to that country. But the fact that the U.S. military is still actively engaged in Iraq helps explain why a substantial proportion of Americans still perceive it as a direct threat to the United States.

Americans' perceptions of Afghanistan—the other country in which the U.S. is conducting a large-scale military operation—are similar to those for Iraq. Americans are somewhat less concerned about Pakistan, though both Pakistan and Afghanistan are major fronts in the war on terror.

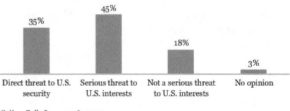

Americans' Views of Iraq as a Threat to the United States or Its Interests in the World

Gallup Poll, June 15-16, 2009

While relatively few Americans regard the conflict between Israel and the Palestinian territories as a direct threat to U.S. security, about half say it is a serious threat to U.S. interests in the world.

Political Differences in Perceived Threat

For the most part, Republicans and Democrats differ only slightly in terms of how threatening they think the various countries are, with

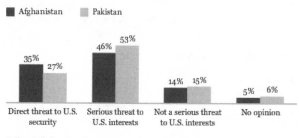

Americans' Views of Afghanistan and Pakistan as Threats to the
United States or Its Interests in the World

■ Afghanistan　■ Pakistan

Gallup Poll, June 15-16, 2009

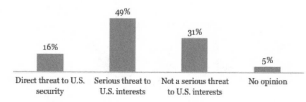

Americans' Views of Israeli/Palestinian Conflict as a Threat to the
United States or Its Interests in the World

Gallup Poll, June 15-16, 2009

Republicans are more likely to regard each of the countries as a greater threat. However, there are much greater party differences in views of Iran and North Korea—roughly two-thirds of Republicans view each of these countries as a direct threat to U.S. security, but fewer than half of Democrats do.

Percentage of Americans Who Believe Countries Pose a Direct Threat to
U.S. Security, by Political Party

	% Democrats	% Independents	% Republicans
North Korea	45	51	66
Iran	38	44	64
Afghanistan	33	37	40
Iraq	33	31	44
Pakistan	25	30	31
Israel and the Palestinian territories	13	16	22
Russia	10	10	14
Mexico	8	11	15

Gallup Poll, June 15-16, 2009

Implications

Americans' perceptions of other countries have proven responsive to developments in the international arena.

Americans appear to be taking North Korea's increasingly combative rhetoric and actions seriously—51% believe North Korea represents a direct threat to U.S. security. That is a greater proportion of Americans than say the same about nations that are larger or wealthier than North Korea, or in which the U.S. has ongoing military operations. If North Korea defies the latest round of U.N. sanctions and continues to expand its nuclear weapons program, Americans' concerns about the threat North Korea poses to the United States may grow.

Meanwhile, the final outcome of the Iranian election could also affect Americans' perceptions of that country as a threat—in terms

of whether Iran stays the course it has taken under Ahmadinejad (which could increase the perceived threat to the U.S.) or goes in a slightly more moderate direction under his challenger (which could reduce it).

Survey Methods

Results are based on telephone interviews with 1,031 national adults, aged 18 and older, conducted June 15–16, 2009. For results based on the total sample of national adults, one can say with 95% confidence that the maximum margin of sampling error is ±3 percentage points.

Interviews are conducted with respondents on land-line telephones (for respondents with a land-line telephone) and cellular phones (for respondents who are cell-phone only).

In addition to sampling error, question wording and practical difficulties in conducting surveys can introduce error or bias into the findings of public opinion polls.

June 19, 2009
OBAMA JOB APPROVAL SLIPS TO 58% FOR FIRST TIME
Lowest reading for Obama thus far in Gallup Poll Daily tracking

by Lydia Saad, Gallup Poll Senior Editor

President Barack Obama's job approval rating fell to 58% in Gallup Poll Daily tracking from June 16–18—a new low for Obama in Gallup tracking, although not dissimilar to the 59% he has received on four other occasions.

Do you approve or disapprove of the job Barack Obama is doing as president?

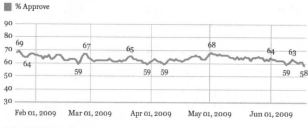

Gallup Poll Daily tracking

Thirty-three percent of Americans now disapprove of the job Obama is doing as president, just one point shy of his record-high 34% disapproval score from early June.

Since Obama took office in January, his approval rating in Gallup tracking has averaged 63%, and most of his three-day ratings have registered above 60%. Approval of Obama did fall to 59% in individual readings in February, March, April, and early June; however, in each case, the rating lasted only a day before rebounding to at least 60%.

The latest decline in Obama's approval score, to 58%, results from a drop in approval among political independents as well as among Republicans. Democrats remain as highly supportive of the president as ever.

Obama's approval rating was 60% from June 13–15, at which time 88% of Democrats, 60% of independents, and 25% of Republicans approved of the job he was doing. In the June 16–18 polling, Democrats' approval of him stands at 92%—up slightly—whereas approval is down among both independents (by seven points) and Republicans (by four points).

President Obama Job Approval, by Party ID -- Recent Trend

Discreet three-day tracking poll surveys since June 1-3, 2009

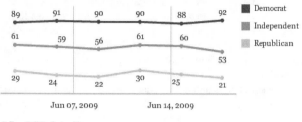

Gallup Poll Daily tracking

Bottom Line

Since February, Obama's weekly approval ratings from Republicans have consistently averaged close to 30% and from independents, close to 60%. With Republican approval now down to 21% and independent approval down to 53%, Obama's overall job approval has dipped to a new low for his presidency.

It is not clear what's behind the decline, but two issues have received considerable play in the news this week, and could be contributing factors. On Monday, the president received bad news on healthcare reform from the Congressional Budget Office, whose estimate of the cost of one reform plan caused sticker shock on Capitol Hill. This may be feeding into public concerns about the administration's deficit spending. At the same time, the disputed Iranian presidential election has been front-page news. Obama's cautious response has sparked sharp criticism from Republican Sen. John McCain and many on the political right who are eager for him to declare the election a "fraud," and to show more solidarity with the Iranian protestors.

Survey Methods

Results are based on telephone interviews with 1,504 national adults, aged 18 and older, conducted June 16–18, 2009, as part of Gallup Poll Daily tracking. For results based on the total sample of national adults, one can say with 95% confidence that the maximum margin of sampling error is ±3 percentage points.

Interviews are conducted with respondents on land-line telephones (for respondents with a land-line telephone) and cellular phones (for respondents who are cell-phone only).

In addition to sampling error, question wording and practical difficulties in conducting surveys can introduce error or bias into the findings of public opinion polls.

June 19, 2009
MOST AMERICANS DON'T FORESEE $4 GAS PRICES THIS YEAR
Fifty-six percent say prices causing them hardship, but just 12% report severe hardship

by Lydia Saad, Gallup Poll Senior Editor

After seven successive weeks of rising gas prices in the United States, Americans, on average, predict gas will go up to $3.39 a gallon this year. That forecast is 70 cents higher than the average $2.69 Americans say they currently pay for a gallon of regular gas, but is still significantly lower than the record-high $4.11 pump price the government reported last July.

How high do you think the price of a gallon of gasoline will go in the area where you live this year?

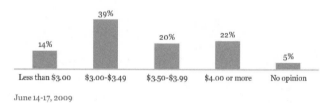

June 14-17, 2009

The slight majority of Americans (53%) in the June 14–17 Gallup Poll believe gas prices will top out at no more than $3.49 per gallon in 2009. Forty-two percent believe they will go higher than that, including only 22% who predict they will hit $4 or more.

Implications

Rising gas prices are beginning to affect Americans—a majority say the higher prices are causing them financial hardship. Still, Americans do not expect gas prices to climb as high as they did last year.

But even a more modest increase in gas prices is unwelcome news for consumers and the broader U.S. economy. U.S. consumers have pulled back significantly on their spending this year, even as gas prices were at low levels for much of the early part of 2009. Higher gas prices would leave Americans with even less disposable income to spend to help get the economy moving again.

Survey Methods

Results are based on telephone interviews with 1,011 national adults, aged 18 and older, conducted June 14–17, 2009. For results based on the total sample of national adults, one can say with 95% confidence that the maximum margin of sampling error is ±3 percentage points.

Interviews are conducted with respondents on land-line telephones (for respondents with a land-line telephone) and cellular phones (for respondents who are cell-phone only).

In addition to sampling error, question wording and practical difficulties in conducting surveys can introduce error or bias into the findings of public opinion polls.

June 22, 2009

RATING OF SUPREME COURT IMPROVES AS PARTISANS SWITCH SIDES

In a shift from last fall, most Democrats now approve; most Republicans disapprove

by Jeffrey M. Jones, Gallup Poll Managing Editor

The latest Gallup Poll finds 59% of Americans approving of the job the U.S. Supreme Court is doing, a significant improvement from ratings near 50% for the past two years, and just below the high of 62% measured in September 2000 and June 2001.

Do you approve or disapprove of the way the Supreme Court is handling its job?

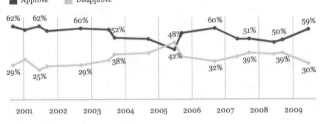

The overall number, though higher, masks considerable change in views of the Supreme Court by party since last fall. The new June 14–17 poll finds 70% of Democrats approving of the job the Supreme Court is doing, much higher than the 57% of independents and 49% of Republicans who approve. Last fall—during the final months of the Bush administration—the party ratings were nearly the reverse, with Republicans giving the court much higher marks than Democrats.

Supreme Court Approval Ratings by Party Affiliation, September 2008 vs. June 2009

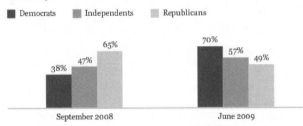

Given the timing of the September 2008 and June 2009 polls, it is unclear what impact President Obama's nomination of Judge Sonia Sotomayor to the Supreme Court has had on Republicans' and Democrats' views of the court. The dramatic party shift may simply reflect a phenomenon Gallup has observed in the past coinciding with changes in presidential administrations, with supporters of the new president's party turning much more positive about government institutions and conditions in the country more generally, and supporters of the outgoing president taking a dimmer view of both.

Gallup found a change in party ratings of the Supreme Court during the Clinton-Bush transition between 2000 and 2001. That change was greatly aided, however, by the court's decision in Bush v. Gore, which effectively awarded the disputed 2000 presidential election to Bush.

To cite a more recent example, Democrats' and Republicans' views of Federal Reserve Chairman Ben Bernanke (a Bush

Supreme Court Approval Ratings by Party Affiliation, September 2000 vs. January 2001

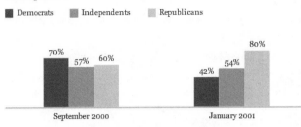

appointee) flipped this year, now that Bernanke is serving under a Democratic president.

But the improved overall ratings of the Supreme Court probably also reflect a more positive view of government in general, given the change in administrations from George W. Bush's to Barack Obama's—particularly because none of the Supreme Court's rulings thus far in the 2008–2009 term has been particularly controversial. Gallup has documented a similar increase in ratings of Congress, and Obama has enjoyed relatively high approval ratings throughout his term.

Even taking into account the party switch in ratings of the Supreme Court, all major party groups show higher ratings than those of the comparable groups last fall. Specifically, approval ratings of the court among supporters of the president's party (Republicans last fall; Democrats currently) are higher now (70%) than in September (65%). Supreme Court approval by the party out of the White House (Democrats last fall; Republicans currently) has also improved—from 38% to 49%. And independents have shown a 10 percentage-point increase in approval over the last nine months.

The latest poll comes just before the close of the Supreme Court's 2008–2009 term, and would not reflect the impact of any yet-to-be-announced high-profile decisions. One highly anticipated decision involves the affirmative action case brought by New Haven, Conn., firefighters. In this ruling, the high court could potentially reverse an appeals court decision made in part by Sotomayor.

Survey Methods

Results are based on telephone interviews with 1,011 national adults, aged 18 and older, conducted June 14–17, 2009. For results based on the total sample of national adults, one can say with 95% confidence that the maximum margin of sampling error is ±3 percentage points.

Interviews are conducted with respondents on land-line telephones (for respondents with a land-line telephone) and cellular phones (for respondents who are cell-phone only).

In addition to sampling error, question wording and practical difficulties in conducting surveys can introduce error or bias into the findings of public opinion polls.

June 22, 2009

MAJORITY DISAPPROVES OF NEW LAW REGULATING TOBACCO

Only a small minority believes smoking should be made illegal in the United States

by Jeffrey M. Jones, Gallup Poll Managing Editor

By 52% to 46%, more Americans disapprove than approve of the new law expanding the federal government's power to regulate the manufacturing and marketing of tobacco products. Opposition is especially strong among smokers.

Do you approve or disapprove of a new law that gives the federal government power to regulate the manufacturing and marketing of cigarettes and other tobacco products?

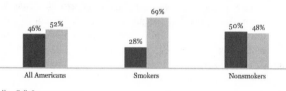

Gallup Poll, June 14-17, 2009

These results are based on a new Gallup Poll, conducted June 14–17. Earlier this month, the U.S. House of Representatives and the U.S. Senate passed bills by overwhelming majorities to increase the federal government's ability to regulate tobacco. But apparently the public does not share the same enthusiasm for government regulation of tobacco as did Congress.

In addition to the smoker-nonsmoker difference, attitudes vary significantly according to education and political party affiliation. Whereas 62% of postgraduates approve of the new legislation, only 36% of those with a high school education or less share this view. Part of this difference may stem from the fact that those with lower levels of formal education are more likely to smoke than those with higher levels.

Opinion of New Government Power to Regulate Tobacco, by Education

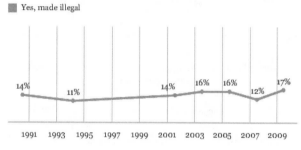

Gallup Poll, June 14-17, 2009

The differences by party affiliation are not quite as large as the educational differences, but show that a majority of Democrats approve of the new governmental powers, while most Republicans disapprove.

Few Favor Smoking Ban

Given Americans' apparent reluctance to endorse increased government regulation of tobacco, it probably comes as no surprise that only a very small minority favor an outright ban on smoking in the United

Opinion of New Government Power to Regulate Tobacco, by Party ID

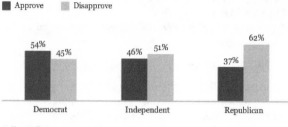

Gallup Poll, June 14-17, 2009

States. The poll finds just 17% of Americans saying smoking should be made "totally illegal" in this country. Gallup has never found widespread support for a universal smoking ban, ranging from 11% to the current 17%, since 1990.

Should smoking in this country be made totally illegal, or not?

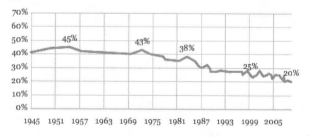

Smoking Prevalence at Historical Low

According to the poll, 20% of national adults 18 and older say they have smoked cigarettes in the past week—tying a November 2007 reading for the lowest since Gallup first asked the question in 1944. The high point is 45% in 1954.

Have you, yourself, smoked any cigarettes in the past week?

Just as the proportion of smokers is declining over time, so is the amount of smoking. Among smokers, 56% say they smoke less than a pack of cigarettes each day, while 42% smoke a pack or more. Since 1999, a majority of smokers have reported smoking less than one pack of cigarettes per day. Prior to that, most smokers reported smoking more than a pack per day.

Implications

Even as fewer Americans are smoking today than in the past, and as those who do smoke report smoking fewer cigarettes, the public

About how many cigarettes do you smoke each day?

Based on smokers

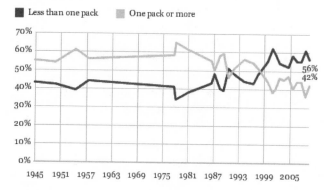

■ Less than one pack   One pack or more

Do you approve or disapprove of the way Congress is handling its job?

■ % Approve

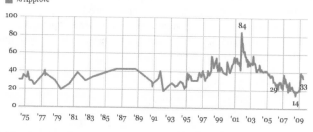

appears somewhat reluctant to back policies aimed at further reducing the prevalence of smoking. A slight majority disapproves of recent legislation that gives the federal government more power to regulate tobacco, and the vast majority opposes the most extreme anti-smoking policy of a total ban on smoking in the United States.

The precise reasons for Americans' lack of support for anti-smoking policies are unclear. However, it may be that Americans place a higher value on allowing people the freedom to choose to smoke over the public health benefits that would come from reducing smoking even further.

Survey Methods

Results are based on telephone interviews with 1,011 national adults, aged 18 and older, conducted June 14–17, 2009. For results based on the total sample of national adults, one can say with 95% confidence that the maximum margin of sampling error is ±3 percentage points.

Interviews are conducted with respondents on land-line telephones (for respondents with a land-line telephone) and cellular phones (for respondents who are cell-phone only).

In addition to sampling error, question wording and practical difficulties in conducting surveys can introduce error or bias into the findings of public opinion polls.

June 23, 2009

CONGRESS' APPROVAL RATING DROPS TO 33%

Lowest since February, but still up from last year

by Frank Newport, Gallup Poll Editor in Chief

Americans' approval of the job Congress is doing has slipped to 33% this month, down from the recent high of 39% in March, but still significantly higher than job approval ratings of Congress over the last several years.

Although there was no change in the control of either the House of Representatives or the Senate as a result of the 2008 elections, Americans' approval of Congress shot up concurrently with the inauguration of the new president in January—going from 19% in early January to 31% in February to 39% in March. Congress' approval rating then dropped slightly in April and May, and this month is down further, as noted.

Job approval of Congress reached its all-time high of 84% in October 2001, part of the general "rally effect" that followed the terrorist attacks of Sept. 11 of that year. From that time until January of this year, congressional approval has generally been on a downward slope, dropping below 30% in October 2005, surfacing above 30% three times in the early months of 2007, and then deteriorating to an all-time low of 14% last July.

The slip in job approval to 33% this month appears to have been caused in part by a significant drop in approval among Democrats, whose 50% rating this month is the lowest since February. Republicans' rating is at 17% while independents' rating is at 31%, neither of which is sharply different from where each has been in the previous four months.

Do you approve or disapprove of the way Congress is handling its job?

% Approve

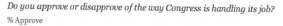

■ Republican   ■ Independent   ■ Democrat

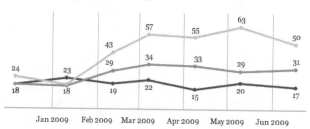

It is interesting to note, more broadly, that Republicans' approval of Congress did not change much as a result of the change of presidents. Republicans' ratings were low before Obama took office and are low now. On the other hand, there has been a significant shift in approval of Congress among Democrats. The current 50% approval rating of Congress among Democrats, although down from previous months this year, is still higher than it was last year or in early January of this year, when George W. Bush was in the White House. Although party control of Congress did not change with the 2008 elections, it is apparent that the election of a Democratic president shifted Democrats' overall view of the job the legislative branch is doing—perhaps because hopes have been increased that the Congress would be more effective with the new administration.

Survey Methods

Results are based on telephone interviews with 1,011 national adults, aged 18 and older, conducted June 14–17, 2009. For results based on the total sample of national adults, one can say with 95% confidence that the maximum margin of sampling error is ±3 percentage points.

Interviews are conducted with respondents on land-line telephones (for respondents with a land-line telephone) and cellular phones (for respondents who are cell-phone only).

In addition to sampling error, question wording and practical difficulties in conducting surveys can introduce error or bias into the findings of public opinion polls.

June 24, 2009

AMERICANS' CONFIDENCE IN MILITARY UP, BANKS DOWN

Surge in confidence around presidency reflects new administration

by Lydia Saad, Gallup Poll Senior Editor

At 82%, the percentage of Americans expressing high confidence in the U.S. military has returned to where it was at the beginning of the Iraq war in 2003. Public confidence in the military is up 11 percentage points from a year ago, and nearly matches the record-high 85% found during the 1991 Gulf War.

Percentage Great Deal/Quite a Lot of Confidence in the Military

1975-2009 trend

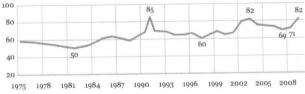

Even with the military's relatively low confidence ratings from 2004 through 2007—a period of broad public doubt about U.S. success in Iraq—the organization has ranked No. 1 or No. 2 in Gallup's annual Confidence in Institutions list almost every year since the measure was instituted in 1973, and has been No. 1 continuously since 1998.

According to the June 14–17 survey, small business ranks second among the 16 institutions tested this year, with a 67% confidence rating. The next-most-highly regarded U.S. institutions are the police, the church or organized religion, and the presidency. All of these entities elicit high confidence from a majority of Americans.

Public confidence in the presidency has risen by 25 points over the past year, exceeding the 11-point increase in confidence in the military. The percentage of Americans saying they have a great deal or quite a lot of confidence in the presidency has in fact doubled since June 2008, from 26% to 51%. This is directly correlated with President George W. Bush's 30% approval rating at this time a year ago, and Barack Obama's 58% rating in the mid-June survey. Historically, Gallup has found that confidence ratings for the presidency are closely linked with the job approval ratings of the sitting president.

At the same time, confidence in banks fell by 10 points, from 32% in June 2008 to a record-low 22% today. The previous low point for banks was 30% in October 1991.

Only the top five rated U.S. institutions this year inspire high confidence from a majority of Americans. The sixth-ranked institution is the Supreme Court, with a 39% rating, and the scores descend from there.

I am going to read you a list of institutions in American society. Please tell me how much confidence you, yourself, have in each one -- a great deal, quite a lot, some, or very little?

% Great deal/Quite a lot

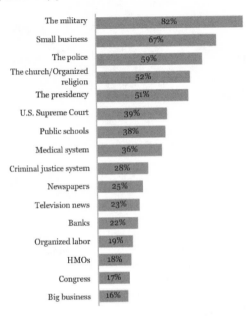

June 14-17, 2009

Percentage Great Deal/Quite a Lot of Confidence in the Presidency

1991-2009 trend

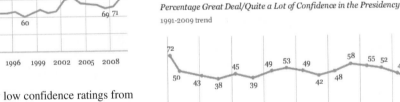

Percentage Great Deal/Quite a Lot of Confidence in Banks

1979-2009 trend

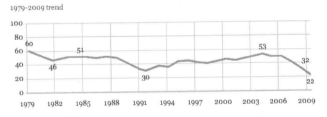

The lowest-ranking institutions in 2009 are big business and Congress. The 16% confidence rating for big business is the record worst for that institution, falling below the previous 18% low found in 2006 and 2007. By contrast, confidence in small business is up seven points, from 60% to 67%. As a result, there is now a 51-point difference in the confidence ratings of big business and small business, the largest gap seen between them in the five occasions both groups were included in the Confidence in Institutions list.

While still low at 17%, confidence in Congress is up slightly from the 12% recorded last year (consistent with the improvement seen in congressional job approval). That figure was not only the

Confidence in Big Business vs. Small Business
% Great deal/Quite a lot

Confidence in Big Business vs. Small Business
% Great deal/Quite a lot

■ Big business   ■ Small business

	July 1997	June 1998	June 2007	June 2008	June 2009
Big business	28	30	18	20	16
Small business	63	57	59	60	67

Confidence in Institutions, 2008 vs. 2009

Percentage with "a great deal" or "quite a lot" of confidence

	June 2008	June 2009	Change (pct. pts.)
The presidency	26	51	+25
The military	71	82	+11
The criminal justice system	20	28	+8
The U.S. Supreme Court	32	39	+7
Small business	60	67	+7
The public schools	33	38	+5
Congress	12	17	+5
Health Maintenance Organizations (HMOs)	13	18	+5
The church or organized religion	48	52	+4
Newspapers	24	25	+1
The police	58	59	+1
The medical system	35	36	+1
Television news	24	23	-1
Organized labor	20	19	-1
Big business	20	16	-4
Banks	32	22	-10

record low for Congress, but the lowest for any institution in the three decades of Gallup polling on this question.

Thus, of the three branches of government, the presidency currently engenders the most confidence from Americans, followed by the Supreme Court and then Congress.

Percentage Great Deal/Quite a Lot of Confidence in Congress
1973-2009 trend

In addition to sampling error, question wording and practical difficulties in conducting surveys can introduce error or bias into the findings of public opinion polls.

Summing Up Changes

The transition from the generally unpopular presidency of George W. Bush to the broadly popular presidency of Barack Obama has had a clear impact on Americans' willingness to express high levels of confidence in the presidency, and most likely also explains the smaller confidence boosts seen for other aspects of government, including Congress, the Supreme Court, the criminal justice system, and the public schools.

The increase in the already-high confidence levels in the military could be the result of several factors, including the improved political and military situation in Iraq and the setting of target dates for the withdrawal of most U.S. troops from that country.

The near-collapse of U.S. financial markets last fall and recent bankruptcies within the auto industry are obviously key contributors to reduced confidence in big business and banks. The increased confidence Americans show toward small business may simply be the natural result of contrasting small business with big business.

The only other significant change is a five-point increase in confidence in Health Maintenance Organizations, from 13% to 18%. Confidence in television news, newspapers, organized labor, the police, the medical system, and the church is unchanged.

Survey Methods

Results are based on telephone interviews with 1,011 national adults, aged 18 and older, conducted June 14–17, 2009. For results based on the total sample of national adults, one can say with 95% confidence that the maximum margin of sampling error is ±3 percentage points.

Interviews are conducted with respondents on land-line telephones (for respondents with a land-line telephone) and cellular phones (for respondents who are cell-phone only).

June 24, 2009

ECONOMY STILL TRUMPS, BUT DECLINES FURTHER AS TOP PROBLEM
Mentions of healthcare increase slightly amid legislative debate

by Lymari Morales, Gallup Poll Staff Writer

Mentions of the economy in Gallup's June update on this question match the net total mentions from June of last year, prior to the global economic collapse. The "net percent mentioning economic problems" reflects the total percentage of respondents who cite some aspect of the economy as the nation's most important problem. The single most frequently mentioned concern more broadly—a general reference to the economy—is down from 47% in May to 41% now. Specific mentions of unemployment are steady at 14%.

What do you think is the most important problem facing this country today?
2008-2009 trend

■ Net % mentioning economic problems

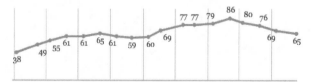

Despite the increase in gas prices since May, only 1% name fuel/oil prices as the most important problem facing the country. This pales in comparison to the 25% who mentioned fuel and oil prices in

United States' Most Important Problem -- Economic Mentions
Recent trend

	Mar 5-8, 2009	Apr 6-9, 2009	May 7-10, 2009	June 14-17, 2009
	%	%	%	%
NET ECONOMIC MENTIONS^	80	76	69	65
Economy in general	51	48	47	41
Unemployment/Jobs	16	17	14	14
Lack of money	11	9	7	6
Federal budget deficit/Federal debt	5	4	5	5
Recession	2	1	1	2
Fuel/Oil prices	1	*	*	1
High cost of living/Inflation	3	1	1	1

^ "Net economic mentions" is percentage of Americans naming at least one economic issue
* Less than 0.5%

June of last year, when gas prices reached $4 or more per gallon in many parts of the country.

What do you think is the most important problem facing this country today?
Recent trend

% Mentioning fuel/oil prices

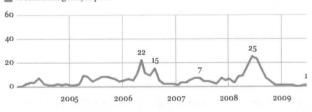

Among non-economic issues, mentions of healthcare increased slightly this month to 14%, from 9% in May, tying the aforementioned level of concern about unemployment. The increase is coincident with escalating news coverage of the debate over healthcare reform on Capitol Hill, though 12% did mention healthcare in March. Gallup's complete trend on this question reveals that mentions of healthcare increased significantly in 1993 and 1994, when Hillary Clinton made her attempt at healthcare reform during her husband's administration. If healthcare continues to dominate the news agenda in the months ahead, the percentage of Americans who mention it as the nation's most important problem can be expected to rise further.

What do you think is the most important problem facing this country today?
Recent trend

% mentioning healthcare

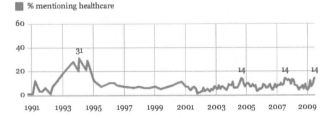

With the most recent increase, healthcare tops all other non-economic items mentioned, easily beating out the situation in Iraq and broader international and domestic issues.

United States' Most Important Problem -- Non-Economic Mentions
Recent trend

	Mar 5-8, 2009	Apr 6-9, 2009	May 7-10, 2009	June 14-17, 2009
	%	%	%	%
NET NON-ECONOMIC MENTIONS ^	38	38	48	48
Poor healthcare/hospitals; high cost of healthcare	12	7	9	14
Situation in Iraq/War	6	6	9	7
Dissatisfaction with government/Congress/politicians; poor leadership; corruption; abuse of power	6	5	8	6
Ethics/Moral/Religious/Family decline; dishonesty	4	4	7	4
International issues/problems	1	1	1	2
National security	2	2	3	2
Lack of respect for each other	1	2	1	2
Immigration/Illegal aliens	2	2	2	2
National security	2	3	3	2
Election year/Presidential choices/Election reform	--	1	*	2
Foreign aid/Focus overseas	1	1	1	2

^ "Net non-economic mentions" is percentage of Americans naming at least one non-economic issue
* Less than 0.5%

Bottom Line

While still high at 65%, Americans' level of concern about the economy has declined steadily over the past few months. This decline coincides with an increase in the number of Americans in Gallup Poll Daily tracking saying the economy is getting better, suggesting that Americans may in fact be feeling less negative about the country's economic situation. At the same time, it is possible that Americans have adjusted their expectations to a "new normal" and have thus become less likely than they were earlier this year to perceive the poor economy as the nation's most pressing problem.

Americans' level of concern over healthcare is up, though only slightly compared to March. It will be interesting to monitor whether this number will continue to increase amid the ongoing legislative debate over healthcare reform. It has a long way to go to match the level of concern recorded in the early '90s, though this was before 9/11 brought a whole host of additional international and national security concerns to the forefront.

Compared to a year ago, Americans are far less worried about fuel/oil prices, though again this may be a readjusting of expectations relative to all of the economic turmoil the country has experienced over the past calendar year. Additionally, concern about gas prices as the nation's top problem may be low for the simple reason that gas prices have not reached nearly as high a level as they did last summer.

Survey Methods

Results are based on telephone interviews with 1,011 national adults, aged 18 and older, conducted June 14–17, 2009. For results based on the total sample of national adults, one can say with 95% confidence that the maximum margin of sampling error is ±3 percentage points.

Interviews are conducted with respondents on land-line telephones (for respondents with a land-line telephone) and cellular phones (for respondents who are cell-phone only).

In addition to sampling error, question wording and practical difficulties in conducting surveys can introduce error or bias into the findings of public opinion polls.

June 25, 2009

EXTRAMARITAL AFFAIRS, LIKE SANFORD'S, MORALLY TABOO

Recent confessions of affairs by elected officials fly in face of Americans' normative standards

by Frank Newport, Gallup Poll Editor in Chief

Gov. Mark Sanford of South Carolina and Sen. John Ensign of Nevada—the latest elected officials to admit publicly to having extramarital affairs—are flying in the face of public opinion if they expect to find Americans condoning their dalliances. Gallup's latest Values and Beliefs update, conducted last month, shows that 92% of Americans say married men and women having an affair is morally wrong, garnering more opprobrium than any other moral issue tested in the poll.

Next, I'm going to read you a list of issues. Regardless of whether or not you think it should be legal, for each one, please tell me whether you personally believe that in general it is morally acceptable or morally wrong. How about -- [RANDOM ORDER]?

Sorted by "morally acceptable"

	Morally acceptable	Morally wrong
	%	%
Divorce	62	30
The death penalty	62	30
Buying and wearing clothing made of animal fur	61	35
Gambling	58	36
Medical research using stem cells obtained from human embryos	57	36
Sex between an unmarried man and woman	57	40
Medical testing on animals	57	36
Having a baby outside of marriage	51	45
Gay or lesbian relations	49	47
Doctor-assisted suicide	39	56
Abortion	36	56
Cloning animals	34	63
Suicide	15	80
Cloning humans	9	88
Polygamy, when one husband has more than one wife at the same time	7	91
Married men and women having an affair	6	92

Gallup Poll, May 7-10, 2009

Both Gov. Sanford and Sen. Ensign evinced deep regrets when they publicly announced their transgressions, and both apologized profusely for the distress their affairs had caused those around them. The overt acknowledgement that their actions were wrong may help these politicians gain at least some sympathy from their constituents and others around the country, given the stark fact that the American public overwhelmingly sticks by the position that affairs are morally wrong.

By way of contrast, almost 6 out of 10 Americans say unmarried men and women having sexual relations is morally acceptable. A little over half say having a baby out of wedlock is morally OK. But casting negative moral aspersions on having an extramarital affair is nearly universal, and even exceeds (by one point) the percentage who say polygamy is morally wrong.

There has been little change over the last eight years in Americans' views about married men and women having an affair.

Both Sanford and Ensign are Republicans, although there have certainly been Democratic elected officials who have admitted to

Married Men and Women Having an Affair: Morally Acceptable or Morally Wrong?
2001-2009 trend

	Morally acceptable	Morally wrong	Depends on situation (vol.)	Not a moral issue (vol.)	No opinion
	%	%	%	%	%
2009 May 7-10	6	92	1	1	1
2008 May 8-11	7	91	1	*	1
2007 May 10-13	6	91	2	*	1
2006 May 8-11	4	93	2	*	1
2005 May 2-5	5	93	1	*	1
2004 May 2-4	7	91	1	*	1
2003 May 5-7	6	93	*	*	1
2002 May 6-9	9	87	1	1	2
2001 May 10-14	7	89	3	*	1

* Less than 0.5%
(vol.) = Volunteered response

straying from the marital bed in recent years, including former North Carolina Sen. John Edwards and former President Bill Clinton. But with such a high percentage of Americans agreeing on the moral unacceptability of having an affair, there is, not surprisingly, only slight variation across party lines. Two percent of Republicans, 5% of independents, and 10% of Democrats say having an affair is morally acceptable.

Married Men and Women Having an Affair: Morally Acceptable or Morally Wrong?
By party ID

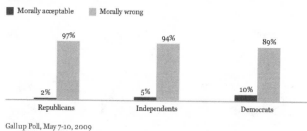

Gallup Poll, May 7-10, 2009

There is also a slight difference between men's views and women's views on extramarital affairs; 8% of men say they are acceptable, compared to 3% of women. And despite the conventional wisdom that young Americans may be more morally libertine than those who are older, 18- to 29-year-olds in the Gallup survey are little different in their views on the moral acceptability of extramarital affairs than are those 30 years of age and up.

Implications

Despite the fact that Americans overwhelmingly find the recent actions of Sanford and Ensign to have been morally wrong, it is unclear at this point how much of an impact their affairs will have on their careers. Neither has resigned from his office. Both had been mentioned as possible presidential contenders in 2012. A Gallup Poll from November 2007 showed that while 54% of Americans said it would bother them at least moderately if a presidential candidate has had an extramarital affair, another 46% said it would bother them either "not much" or "not at all."

Survey Methods

Results are based on telephone interviews with 1,015 national adults, aged 18 and older, conducted May 7–10, 2009. For results based on

the total sample of national adults, one can say with 95% confidence that the maximum margin of sampling error is ±3 percentage points.

Interviews are conducted with respondents on land-line telephones (for respondents with a land-line telephone) and cellular phones (for respondents who are cell-phone only).

In addition to sampling error, question wording and practical difficulties in conducting surveys can introduce error or bias into the findings of public opinion polls.

June 26, 2009
SHARP DIFFERENCES IN PARTISAN VIEWS OF ECONOMIC PROBLEMS
Republicans much more worried about regulation, taxes, and the deficit than are Democrats

by Frank Newport, Gallup Poll Editor in Chief

Republicans and Democrats view economic issues facing the country today from substantially different perspectives. Republicans are most likely to be worried about the increasing federal deficit, increasing federal income taxes, and problems state governments have in funding their budgets, while Democrats are most worried about the rising unemployment rate, Americans without healthcare insurance, and the increasing cost of healthcare.

Top Economic Worries, by Party ID

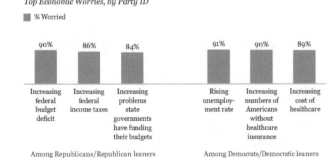

Gallup Poll, June 23-24, 2009

These results underscore the political tensions that have arisen as the Obama administration and Congress wrestle with how to fix the country's economic problems, while at the same time dealing with the longer-term impact of those efforts. Taken as a whole, Republicans are more concerned than Democrats about the impact of increased federal and state spending, and government regulation of business, while Democrats are more concerned about the societal problems that the increased spending and regulation are designed to address.

The findings are based on a June 23–24 Gallup Poll, which asked Americans whether they personally are worried about each of 12 economic issues. The list contains a number of the nation's currently pressing economic problems—including decreasing pay and wages and rising gas prices, in addition to unemployment and healthcare. It also includes efforts related to curing the problems—for example, increasing state and federal income taxes and the federal government's expanding ownership and regulation of private business and industry, along with the federal deficit.

The poll shows that there is no shortage of worry about economic issues for the average American today. At least half of those interviewed said they were worried about each of the 12 issues tested.

But the results among all Americans mask fundamental differences by partisanship in the worry expressed about many of these issues.

• Republicans are much more likely than Democrats to express worry about the five items included in the poll that represent *consequences* of attempting to fix economic problems: the federal government's expanding ownership and regulation of private business and industry, increasing federal and state taxes, and the increasing federal budget deficit.

• Democrats, on the other hand, are much more likely to be worried about the increasing numbers of Americans without health insurance, and, to a lesser degree, about the rising unemployment rate, the increasing cost of healthcare, and decreasing pay and wages for the average worker.

Please tell me whether you, personally, are worried or not worried about each of the following:
% Worried

	Republicans/ Leaners	Democrats/ Leaners	Democrats minus Republicans
	%	%	Pct. pts.
Increasing numbers of Americans without healthcare insurance	65	90	25
The rising unemployment rate	82	91	9
The increasing cost of healthcare	82	89	7
Decreasing pay and wages for the average worker	74	81	7
Increasing problems Americans have with personal debt and credit cards	75	74	-1
The increasing price of gas	79	76	-3
Increasing problems state governments have funding their budgets	84	79	-5
The increasing federal budget deficit	90	75	-15
Increasing state income taxes	78	59	-19
Increasing federal income taxes	86	62	-24
The federal government's increasing regulation of business and industry	78	40	-38
The federal government's expanding ownership of private corporations	82	42	-40

Gallup Poll, June 23-24, 2009

The partisan differences in worry about federal government's increasing ownership of corporations and increasing regulation of business and industry are the largest of any of the 12 issues: 82% of Republicans say they worry about the federal government's expanding ownership of private corporations, compared to only 42% of Democrats. And 78% of Republicans worry about the federal government's increasing regulation of business and industry, compared to just 40% of Democrats. In fact, only these two items generate less than a 50% "worry" percentage among either partisan group.

While there are sharp differences in expressed worry about many of the issues tested, there is general agreement between Republicans and Democrats on 3 of the 12 issues: problems with personal debt/credit cards, the increasing price of gas, and problems state governments have in funding their budgets.

All Americans

There are more Democrats than Republicans in today's political environment (in the sample used for these data, 48% were Democrats or leaned Democratic, while 38% were Republicans or leaned Republican), meaning that altogether, at least half of all Americans are worried about each problem.

Please tell me whether you, personally, are worried or not worried about each of the following:

	Worried	Not worried
	%	%
The rising unemployment rate	87	13
The increasing cost of healthcare	85	15
The increasing federal budget deficit	81	17
Increasing problems state governments have funding their budgets	81	18
Increasing numbers of Americans without healthcare insurance	79	21
Decreasing pay and wages for the average worker	78	22
The increasing price of gas	78	22
Increasing federal income taxes	74	25
Increasing problems Americans have with personal debt and credit cards	74	26
Increasing state income taxes	69	30
The federal government's expanding ownership of private corporations	60	37
The federal government's increasing regulation of business and industry	58	40

Gallup Poll, June 23-24, 2009

And, taken as a whole, Americans appear to be almost as worried about the increasing federal budget deficit as they are about rising unemployment and rising healthcare costs. Overall, the poll finds 87% saying they worry personally about unemployment and 85% about healthcare costs, while 81% worry about the increasing federal budget deficit. Across the entire sample, the lowest levels of worry are about the federal government's increasing ownership of, and regulation of, business.

Implications

These results highlight three important points about the ways Americans view government efforts to fix the nation's economic problems. First, it is clear that the deficit is a looming issue for Americans; it generates almost as much worry as do underlying problems such as unemployment and the cost of healthcare. Second, the data suggest that concern about federal ownership and regulation of business is on a relative basis less of a concern to Americans than other economic issues facing the country. And third, the data demonstrate the degree to which views on a number of economic issues are sharply different between Republicans and Democrats. Republicans in particular are much more concerned about government's increasing regulation and ownership of business, rising taxes, and the deficit than are Democrats.

All in all, the results show that the rationale for the Obama administration's efforts to deal with today's major economic problems is well-founded; large percentages of Americans of every political persuasion say they worry about such things as the rising unemployment rate and the increasing cost of healthcare. At the same time, the results also show there is public-opinion support for several potential arguments *against* the Obama administration's efforts, including first and foremost Americans' concerns that such efforts will unacceptably increase the federal budget deficit. Beyond the deficit, the results indicate that concern about increasing taxes, particularly at the federal level, may be a more potent argument among Americans than concern about too much control over private corporations.

Survey Methods

Results are based on telephone interviews with 989 national adults, aged 18 and older, conducted June 23–24, 2009. For results based on the total sample of national adults, one can say with 95% confidence that the maximum margin of sampling error is ±3 percentage points.

Interviews are conducted with respondents on land-line telephones (for respondents with a land-line telephone) and cellular phones (for respondents who are cell-phone only).

In addition to sampling error, question wording and practical difficulties in conducting surveys can introduce error or bias into the findings of public opinion polls.

June 26, 2009

AMERICANS OK WITH FEWER MAIL DAYS TO FIX POSTAL BUDGET

Most oppose raising stamp prices and cutting postal services to solve budget woes

by Lydia Saad, Gallup Poll Senior Editor

U.S. Postmaster General John E. Potter recently asked Congress for permission to cut the number of postal delivery days from six to five as a way to save his cash-strapped agency up to $3.5 billion annually—a proposal that seems acceptable to most Americans. Sixty-six percent of Americans whom Gallup polled June 17–18 are in favor of that fiscal remedy.

As you may know, the U.S. Postal Service recently announced that it is anticipating billions of dollars in losses this year. Please tell me whether you would strongly favor, favor, oppose, or strongly oppose each of the following as a way to help the Postal Service solve its financial problems.

▪ Reduce the number of mail delivery days from six days a week to five

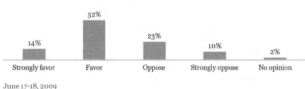

Strongly favor	Favor	Oppose	Strongly oppose	No opinion
14%	52%	23%	10%	2%

June 17-18, 2009

The United States Postal Service is being squeezed by the economic slowdown on one side, and competition from the Internet and private carriers on the other. The resulting decline in mail volume is the main reason the Postal Service is projected to lose more than $6 billion this fiscal year, but rising gas prices threaten to make matters even worse.

Still, three in four Americans say it is "very important" to them that the U.S. Postal Service remain in business. The traditional post office is more important to women than to men, and to older than to younger Americans, but the large majority of every demographic group calls it very important.

As for how to maintain the Postal Service, Gallup asked Americans about nine possible remedies that have been floated. Public support is highest for reducing mail delivery from six days a week to five, as well as for reducing to five the number of days that local post offices are open. Both measures are favored by 66% of Americans.

The only other solution backed by a majority of Americans is renting out post office buildings on nights and weekends for other uses—however, just a bare majority favors this (51%), while 46% are opposed.

How important is it to you, personally, that the U.S. Postal Service continues to stay in business -- very important, somewhat important, not too important, or not important at all?

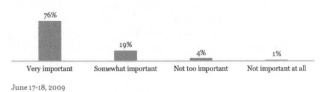

| Very important | Somewhat important | Not too important | Not important at all |
| 76% | 19% | 4% | 1% |

June 17-18, 2009

Ways to Help U.S. Postal Service Solve Its Financial Problems

■ Total % favor   ▨ Total % oppose

	Favor	Oppose
Reduce delivery days to five	66	33
Reduce days post office is open to five	66	32
Rent post office buildings after hours	51	46
Provide federal funding	48	48
Close some post office branches	44	54
Raise stamp prices	38	60
Reduce services offered at post offices	31	66
Lay off more USPS employees	17	80
Close your local post office	11	88

June 17-18, 2009

Americans are evenly divided at 48% over providing federal funding for the Postal Service, which until now has been self-supporting—reliant solely on income from stamps and other postal products and services. Even fewer Americans, 38%, are in favor of raising stamp prices; 60% oppose that remedy. This may reflect public displeasure with the steady pace of recent price hikes for stamps—rising by one or two cents in each of the last four years. Alternatively, it could indicate a more general desire to see the Postal Service tighten its belt even as many Americans are doing the same.

Just over half of Americans (54%) are opposed to closing some Postal Service offices, while 44% support that idea. At the same time, 88% are opposed to closing their own post office—indicating that the customary "not in my back yard" mindset could very well limit the political feasibility of broad-based branch closures.

Last month, the Postal Service announced it had cut staff by 25,000, reducing its overall workforce to below 635,000. Eight in 10 Americans currently say they are opposed to laying off more postal service employees. Americans also object to reducing the services offered at post offices. Only 31% favor this option while 66% are opposed.

Strong Opposition to Closing Local Branches

Americans' detailed responses to each proposal provide another way to assess the political viability of the various ways of keeping the Postal Service solvent. In fact, few Americans feel strongly about most of the proposals—saying they either strongly support or strongly oppose them.

The highest level of strong support is seen for reducing the number of mail delivery days and days that branches are open to the public. Slightly more Americans strongly favor these proposals than strongly oppose them.

With only 2% of Americans strongly in favor of having their local post office branch closed versus 37% strongly opposed, public opinion speaks loudest against this proposal. Attitudes are also substantially more negative than positive when it comes to laying off more postal employees and raising stamp prices.

Ways to Help U.S. Postal Service Solve Its Financial Problems

	Strongly favor	Favor	Oppose	Strongly oppose
	%	%	%	%
Reduce delivery days to five	14	52	23	10
Reduce days post office is open to five	12	54	22	10
Provide federal funding	9	39	35	13
Close some post office branches	7	37	45	9
Rent out post office buildings after hours	7	44	34	12
Raise stamp prices	4	34	40	20
Reduce services offered at post offices	3	28	51	15
Lay off more USPS employees	2	15	55	25
Close your local post office branch	2	9	51	37

June 17-18, 2009

Bottom Line

Americans want to continue receiving the postal services they are accustomed to, and they don't want to see their local post office branches boarded up, but they are willing to live with a shorter postal week if that's what it takes to keep the U.S. Postal Service in business. Congress and direct-mail marketers have reportedly been cool to the idea of reducing mail delivery days, but it sounds like the best solution to taxpayers.

Survey Methods

Results are based on telephone interviews with 992 national adults, aged 18 and older, conducted June 17–18, 2009, as part of Gallup Poll Daily tracking. For results based on the total sample of national adults, one can say with 95% confidence that the maximum margin of sampling error is ±3 percentage points.

Note: These questions were asked of random half-samples for two nights of Gallup Daily polling, which interviews 1,000 U.S. adults each night.

Interviews are conducted with respondents on land-line telephones (for respondents with a land-line telephone) and cellular phones (for respondents who are cell-phone only).

In addition to sampling error, question wording and practical difficulties in conducting surveys can introduce error or bias into the findings of public opinion polls.

June 29, 2009
DRINKING HABITS STEADY AMID RECESSION
Sixty-four percent drink, unchanged; beer is still the preferred beverage

by Lydia Saad, Gallup Poll Senior Editor

Despite some anecdotal reports of a surge in drinking accompanying the economic recession, Gallup's annual update on alcohol consumption finds little change in Americans' drinking habits. The percentage of U.S. adults who consume alcohol is fairly steady at 64%, and there has been little change in self-reported drinking volume.

Do you have occasion to use alcoholic beverages such as liquor, wine, or beer, or are you a total abstainer?

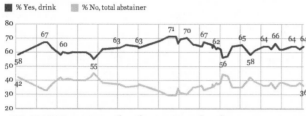

According to the June 14–17 Gallup Poll, the prevalence of drinking in the U.S. adult population is essentially unchanged compared with a year ago. Sixty-four percent of Americans tell Gallup they "have occasion to use alcoholic beverages." This falls within the narrow 62% to 66% range seen over the past decade.

In fact, the percentage of Americans saying they drink alcohol has been in the low to mid-60s fairly consistently since about 1947. The major exception was between 1974 and 1981, when slightly more Americans (from 68% to 71% for most of this period) said they drank alcohol. Since the advent of the question in 1939, the figure has dipped below 60% on only a few occasions.

About two-thirds of drinkers in the new survey—65%—say they have had at least one drink within the past seven days. This is identical to a year ago, and similar to the finding each year since 2001. The percentage of heavier drinkers—those consuming eight or more drinks in the past week—is currently 14%, also quite typical for the decade.

Number of Drinks Consumed in Past Week by Those Who Drink Alcohol

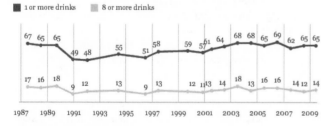

The average number of drinks consumed per drinker in the past week is 4.8. That is up slightly from 2008, but is similar to the figures for several years prior to that.

Stability, Also, in Preferred Drink

Nor does it appear that Americans' preferred beverage has changed with the economic times. Beer continues to beat out wine and liquor as the beverage consumers of alcohol say they drink most often. Four in 10 drinkers say they prefer beer, compared with 34% naming wine and 21% liquor.

Beer has been the top-ranking alcoholic beverage for each of the past four years, and every year since 1992 except 2005, when wine edged slightly ahead of it. Liquor has consistently ranked third, named by between 18% and 24% of drinkers.

When Gallup first asked Americans about their drinking preferences in 1992, beer was the runaway leader, named by 47%; just

Do you most often drink liquor, wine, or beer?
Based on those who drink alcohol

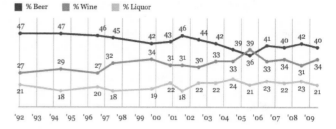

27% named wine. Since then, the prevalence of beer drinkers has contracted somewhat, while the percentage of wine fans has grown.

On Mars, They Drink Beer; on Venus, Wine

The sizable gender gap evident for many years in alcoholic-beverage preferences continues today. The majority of men say they most often drink beer; half of women choose wine. There is also a significant generational difference in preferences, with younger adults favoring beer and older adults favoring wine. As a result, there is a particularly wide gulf between younger men and older women, in terms of drink preferences.

Geographically, beer enjoys its greatest popularity in the Midwest. On the basis of education, wine is far more popular among people with at least some college background than it is among those who have not attended college.

Preferred Drink by Demographic Subgroup
Based on those who drink alcohol

	Beer	Wine	Liquor
	%	%	%
Men	58	19	18
Women	21	50	24
18 to 34 years	50	20	24
35 to 54 years	44	32	19
55 and older	26	50	21
Men 18 to 49	66	14	15
Men 50 and older	46	28	22
Women 18 to 49	25	41	26
Women 50 and older	15	60	21
East	37	36	21
Midwest	48	29	19
South	38	36	20
West	36	36	23
College graduate	36	44	17
Some college	37	36	22
No college	47	20	24

June 14-17, 2009

Bottom Line

The impact of the economic recession on alcohol sales is difficult to discern. Consumer spending on alcohol doesn't tell the full story because, according to some reports, Americans may be opting for cheaper wines, liquors, and beers. Thus, flat sales could actually mean higher volume. Also, changes in restaurant and bar sales have to be analyzed in comparison with changes in liquor purchases for home use.

The theory, at least, is that the recession may give people more reasons to drink, but less money to do it with. To the extent this is true, the effect seems to be a wash. Gallup finds no major changes in the percentage of Americans who drink alcohol (now 64%), in how much drinkers consume, or in their preferred drink—which, by a modest margin, continues to be beer.

Survey Methods

Results are based on telephone interviews with 1,011 national adults, aged 18 and older, conducted June 14–17, 2009. For results based on the total sample of national adults, one can say with 95% confidence that the maximum margin of sampling error is ±3 percentage points.

For results based on the sample of 677 adults who drink alcoholic beverages, the maximum margin of sampling error is ±4 percentage points.

Interviews are conducted with respondents on land-line telephones (for respondents with a land-line telephone) and cellular phones (for respondents who are cell-phone only).

In addition to sampling error, question wording and practical difficulties in conducting surveys can introduce error or bias into the findings of public opinion polls.

June 29, 2009
SPENDING CUTBACKS COMMON; DAILY MONEY WORRIES LESS SO
New normal seems to be less spending

by Frank Newport, Gallup Poll Editor in Chief

New Gallup polling shows that Americans are closely monitoring their daily family expenditures, with 71% saying they are cutting back on their spending and 88% saying they are watching their spending very closely. This is despite the fact that 78% of Americans say they have enough money to satisfy their basic needs, and a much smaller 21% say they worried "yesterday" that they spent too much money.

American Attitudes Toward Spending

Question	% Agree/Yes	% Disagree/No
Do you agree or disagree with the following statement? "You are watching your spending very closely."	88	10
At this time, are you cutting back on how much money you spend each week, or not?	71	28
Are you feeling pretty good these days about the amount of money you have to spend, or not?	56	44
Did you worry yesterday that you spent too much money, or not?	21	79
Do you have enough money to buy the things you need, or not?	78	22

Gallup Poll Daily tracking, June 8-27, 2009

These conclusions, based on samples of more than 2,300 respondents from Gallup Poll Daily tracking interviews conducted June 8–27, suggest that Americans may have reached a "new normal" of lessened expectations.

Overall, the results show that Americans have complex attitudes and emotions about their spending patterns in today's economic environment. There is clear evidence that Americans are concerned about their spending, and report adjusting the amount they spend downward. These self-reports confirm the finding from Gallup's Daily tracking of consumer spending, which shows that average daily expenditures are down significantly from where they were a year ago. Still, it appears that even with this lower level of spending, or perhaps because of it, most Americans do not appear to be anxiety ridden as they go about their daily lives. Most apparently don't worry about spending too much money, and most say they have enough money to buy the things they need.

Indicative of the generally positive state of affairs, a majority of 56% of Americans indicate that they are "feeling pretty good these days about the amount of money [they] have to spend."

These data don't allow for firm conclusions about the future. It is possible that this new normal behavior will continue in the years ahead regardless of changes in the economy, or it is possible that Americans will recalibrate their spending upward once the economy improves. Previous Gallup polling has shown that a majority of those who say they are spending less in the current economy claim that they will continue this new frugality even when the current economic climate improves.

A Minority Still Worries

The above analysis highlights the fact that—despite lowering spending—the majority of Americans are not worrying about their spending on a daily basis and have enough money to get by. In other words, the United States is apparently not facing a situation in which the majority of the population is fighting for its existence without enough money to survive on a daily basis.

At the same time, the good news that a high percentage of Americans give positive responses to several of these spending questions still leaves a minority of Americans—translating into millions of people—who do in fact worry daily about their spending and don't have enough money to buy the things they need. It is likely that there have always been at least some Americans who struggle daily on a financial basis; however, since these Gallup tracking questions are new, there is no track record to calibrate this level of response against previous periods of time prior to the current recession.

Differences by Income Level

There are perhaps not as many differences by income in responses to these questions about spending as might be imagined.

Those with the highest incomes are somewhat, but not dramatically, less likely to say they are cutting back on their spending and are watching their spending very closely. But those with the highest incomes are just slightly less likely to say they worried about spending too much money the day before the survey. There is a more substantial difference by income in response to the question about having enough money "to buy the things you need"; 95% of the highest income group agrees, but even among those making less than $24,000 a year, a slight majority also agree.

American Attitudes Toward Spending

% Agree/Yes, by monthly income

Question	Less than $2,000	$2,000-<$5,000	$5,000-<$7,500	$7,500 or more
Do you agree or disagree with the following statement? "You are watching your spending very closely."	93	91	89	81
At this time, are you cutting back on how much money you spend each week, or not?	74	74	70	60
Are you feeling pretty good these days about the amount of money you have to spend, or not?	43	55	64	64
Did you worry yesterday that you spent too much money, or not?	24	25	17	19
Do you have enough money to buy the things you need, or not?	51	79	89	95

Gallup Poll Daily tracking, June 8-27, 2009

Survey Methods

Results for each question reviewed in this article are based on telephone interviews with between 2,331 and 2,380 national adults, aged 18 and older, conducted June 8–27, 2009, as part of Gallup Poll Daily tracking. For results based on the total sample of national adults, one can say with 95% confidence that the maximum margin of sampling error is ±2 percentage points.

Interviews are conducted with respondents on land-line telephones (for respondents with a land-line telephone) and cellular phones (for respondents who are cell-phone only).

In addition to sampling error, question wording and practical difficulties in conducting surveys can introduce error or bias into the findings of public opinion polls.

June 30, 2009

MORE AMERICANS SEE DEMOCRATIC PARTY AS "TOO LIBERAL"

More believe Democratic Party's, rather than Republican Party's, views are about right

by Jeffrey M. Jones, Gallup Poll Managing Editor

A Gallup Poll finds a statistically significant increase since last year in the percentage of Americans who describe the Democratic Party's views as being "too liberal," from 39% to 46%. This is the largest percentage saying so since November 1994, after the party's losses in that year's midterm elections.

In general, do you think the political views of the Democratic Party are too conservative, too liberal, or about right?

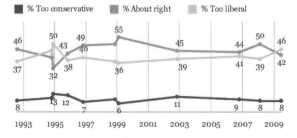

Most major demographic and attitudinal subgroups show at least a slight uptick since 2008 in perceptions that the Democratic Party is too liberal. The increasing perception of the Democrats as too far left comes as President Obama and the Democrats in Congress have expanded the government's role in the economy to address the economic problems facing the country. Additionally, the government is working toward major healthcare reform legislation and strengthening environmental regulations.

Notably, there has been no change over the past year in the percentage of Americans who say the Republican Party is "too conservative," though the 43% who say the party leans too far to the right matches the historical high mark set last year.

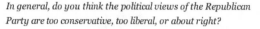
In general, do you think the political views of the Republican Party are too conservative, too liberal, or about right?

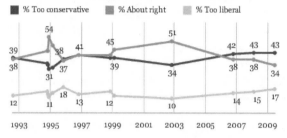

As a result, now slightly more Americans perceive the Democratic Party as being too liberal (46%) than view the GOP as being too conservative (43%).

But the Democratic Party still compares favorably to the Republican Party from the standpoint that more Americans say the Democrats' ideology is "about right" (42%) than say this about the Republicans' ideology (34%).

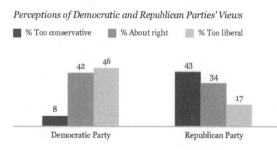
Perceptions of Democratic and Republican Parties' Views

Gallup Poll, June 14-17, 2009

In fact, the 34% who say the GOP is about right is a new low since the question was first asked in 1992, and a far cry from November 1994 and November 2002, when majorities thought the Republicans' views were appropriately balanced.

Independents' Views of the Parties

Political independents' perceptions of the two major parties' ideological orientation are important since both parties need to appeal to the political center in order to win elections. (The vast majority of partisan identifiers predictably view their chosen party's views as being about right and the other party's as being too extreme.)

Currently, independents are more likely to view both parties as being too extreme in either direction than to believe they are about right. But more independents say the Democratic Party (38%) than the Republican Party (25%) is about right.

Independents are a little more likely to say the Republican Party is too conservative than to say the Democratic Party is too liberal, in a slight departure from the results among all Americans.

Perceptions of Democratic and Republican Parties' Views, Among Political Independents

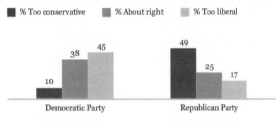

Gallup Poll, June 14-17, 2009

Since last year, there have been declining perceptions among independents that each party is about right in its ideological orientation—from 31% to 25% for the Republican Party and from 43% to 38% for the Democratic Party. Most of the decline in regard to the Democratic Party has been associated with an increase in seeing the party as "too liberal."

Implications

The Democratic Party continues to hold the upper hand over the Republican Party in the current U.S. political environment by a variety of measures, including party identification and party favorable ratings. However, compared to last year, Americans are significantly more likely to see the Democratic Party as too liberal, and as a result, they are somewhat more likely to view the party as being too far left than to perceive the Republican Party as too far right. That may expose a bit of a vulnerability for the Democratic Party, and if perceptions of the Democratic Party as being too liberal continue to grow, the GOP may be able to win back some of the support it has lost in recent years. But that may be possible only if the Republicans are at the same time able to convince the public that they are not too far to the political right.

Survey Methods

Results are based on telephone interviews with 1,011 national adults, aged 18 and older, conducted June 14–17, 2009. For results based on the total sample of national adults, one can say with 95% confidence that the maximum margin of sampling error is ±3 percentage points.

Interviews are conducted with respondents on land-line telephones (for respondents with a land-line telephone) and cellular phones (for respondents who are cell-phone only).

In addition to sampling error, question wording and practical difficulties in conducting surveys can introduce error or bias into the findings of public opinion polls.

Investor optimism about the direction of the U.S. economy over the next 12 months plunged 14 points in June, as the Economic Dimension of the Index fell to -42. Investors are now as pessimistic about the economic outlook as they were in April. Still, they remain much less pessimistic than they were in February, when this dimension was at -70.

Economic Dimension, Gallup Index of Investor Optimism, December 2007-June 2009

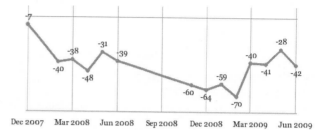

July 01, 2009
U.S. INVESTOR OPTIMISM TUMBLES IN JUNE
Investors are optimistic about their portfolios, pessimistic about the economic outlook

by Dennis Jacobe, Gallup Chief Economist

The Gallup Index of Investor Optimism—a broad measure of investor perceptions—tumbled 20 points to -21 in June, giving up May's gain and essentially returning to where it was in April. Still, the Index has improved by 43 points from February's -64 reading—its lowest level since its inception in October 1996.

Gallup Index of Investor Optimism, December 2007-June 2009

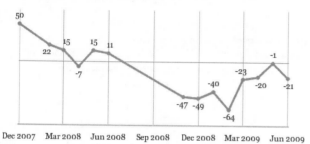

Portfolio Optimism Remains

Investors remain optimistic about the prospects for their personal portfolios over the next 12 months, with the Personal Dimension of the Index at 21 in June. This drops investor portfolio optimism back to April levels—wiping out the six-point increase that took place in May—and suggesting that, despite their concerns about the economy's direction, investors remain cautiously optimistic about the performance of their personal portfolios over the next 12 months.

Personal Dimension, Gallup Index of Investor Optimism, December 2007-June 2009

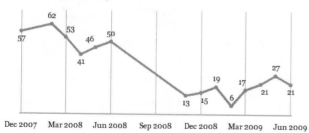

Commentary

The sharp decline in Gallup's Index of Investor Optimism in June—particularly the plunge in expectations for the economy—suggests that investors may be losing some of their hopes for an immediate improvement in the U.S. economy later this year. This is consistent with the leveling off of consumers' mood over the past few weeks and the drop in the consumer sentiment index on Tuesday.

Gallup's job-market and consumer spending measures suggest that the reality on Main Street has not improved substantially over the past couple of months. Perhaps the average investor and the American consumer see the fragile nature of the current U.S. economy more clearly than do those on Wall Street.

Author's Note: Gallup's Index of Investor Optimism—a survey of those having $10,000 or more of investable assets—peaked at 178 in January 2000, just prior to the bursting of the dot-com bubble. Last year, the Index turned negative for the first time in its history. Before last year, the low for the Index was 5 in March 2003, reflecting investor concerns at the outset of the Iraq war.

Survey Methods

Gallup Poll Daily interviewing includes no fewer than 1,000 U.S. adults nationwide each day during 2008. The Index of Investor Optimism results are based on questions asked of 1,000 or more investors over a three-day period each month, conducted June 25–27, May 26–28, April 21–23, March 16–18, Feb. 17–19, and Jan. 16–18, 2009; and Dec. 16–18, Nov. 24–26, June 3–6, April 25–28, March 28–31, and Feb. 28–March 2, 2008. For results based on these samples, the maximum margin of sampling error is ±3 percentage points.

Results for May 2008 are based on the Gallup Panel study and are based on telephone interviews with 576 national adults, aged 18 and older, conducted May 19–21, 2008. Gallup Panel members are recruited through random selection methods. The panel is weighted so that it is demographically representative of the U.S. adult population. For results based on this sample, one can say with 95% confidence that the maximum margin of sampling error is ±5 percentage points.

For investor results prior to 2008, telephone interviews were conducted with at least 800 investors, aged 18 and older, and having at least $10,000 of investable assets. For the total sample of investors in these surveys, one can say with 95% confidence that the maximum margin of sampling error is ± 4 percentage points.

Interviews are conducted with respondents on land-line telephones (for respondents with a land-line telephone) and cellular phones (for respondents who are cell-phone only).

In addition to sampling error, question wording and practical difficulties in conducting surveys can introduce error or bias into the findings of public opinion polls.

July 02, 2009
AMERICANS EXPECT SECURITY IN IRAQ TO WORSEN AFTER PULLOUT
While 58% say security will worsen, only 27% expect it to get "a lot" worse

by Lydia Saad, Gallup Poll Senior Editor

Gallup polling conducted on June 30, the deadline for U.S. forces to withdraw from urban areas of Iraq, finds Americans largely pessimistic about the likely impact of this change. Overall, 58% of Americans believe the security situation in Iraq will worsen now that much of it is in the hands of Iraqi security forces; only 36% believe security will stay the same or improve.

What do you think will happen to the security situation in Iraq now that responsibility for providing security in Iraq's major cities and towns has been transferred from U.S. forces to Iraqi security forces? Do you think the security situation in Iraq will -- [get a lot worse, get a little worse, stay the same, get a little better, (or) get a lot better]?

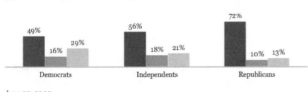

June 30, 2009

Republicans—who, among partisan groups, have long been the most supportive of U.S. military intervention in Iraq—are the most likely to believe security in Iraq will worsen, but even close to half of Democrats feel this way.

Outlook for Iraqi Security After Responsibility Is Transferred to Iraqi Security Forces

June 30, 2009

According to the detailed responses, Americans who believe deterioration in Iraqi security will follow the recent U.S. pullout are closely divided in their perceptions of how severe it will be. About 3 in 10

Americans say security will get a little worse while 27% say it will get a lot worse. Very few—only 4%—believe it will get a lot better.

Outlook for Iraqi Security After Responsibility Is Transferred to Iraqi Security Forces -- Detailed Responses

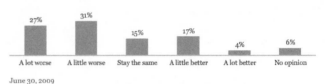

June 30, 2009

Late last year, the Iraqi parliament voted to approve the Status of Forces Agreement reached between President George W. Bush and Iraqi Prime Minister Nouri al-Maliki that established a time frame for the gradual reduction of U.S. military involvement in that country. The June 30 deadline for withdrawal of U.S. forces from major cities and towns represents the first phase of that build-down. The agreement calls for the removal of all U.S. troops from all areas of Iraq by December 31, 2011.

Despite the timely implementation of Phase 1, only 27% of Americans believe the complete withdrawal will happen by the 2011 deadline. Democrats (35% of whom expect that deadline to be met) are only slightly more confident about this withdrawal than are Republicans and independents (22% each).

As you may know, the security agreement signed last year between the United States and Iraq calls for the withdrawal of all U.S. forces from Iraq by the end of 2011. Just your best guess, do you think all U.S. forces will or will not be out of Iraq by that time?

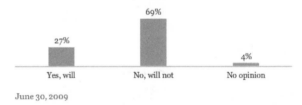

June 30, 2009

Americans who believe security in Iraq will improve are only slightly more likely to be confident the U.S. will be out on time in 2011 than are those who think security will worsen.

Prediction for Full U.S. Withdrawal From Iraq in 2011, According to Outlook for Iraqi Security

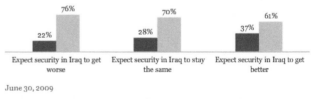

June 30, 2009

Bottom Line

Americans have been waiting a long time for the United States to pull out of Iraq. Gallup polling as far back as June 2005 found a majority of U.S. adults (51%) saying they favored a timetable for removing U.S. troops from Iraq, rather than maintaining forces there indefinitely. By September 2007, that figure was 60%, and it remained 60% in Gallup's last measure in February 2008.

Gallup polling that month also found 65% of Americans saying the U.S. has an obligation to establish a "reasonable level of stability and security" in Iraq before leaving. With violence in Iraq generally trending downward and the January elections there having gone smoothly, Americans no doubt welcome this week's milestone. However, even though the United States has thus far lived up to its part of the security pact with Iraq by withdrawing forces from urban areas and turning security there over to the Iraqis, most Americans are skeptical that the full withdrawal will occur on time.

Survey Methods

Results are based on telephone interviews with 1,011 national adults, aged 18 and older, conducted June 30, 2009, as part of Gallup Poll Daily tracking. For results based on the total sample of national adults, one can say with 95% confidence that the maximum margin of sampling error is ±3 percentage points.

Interviews are conducted with respondents on land-line telephones (for respondents with a land-line telephone) and cellular phones (for respondents who are cell-phone only).

In addition to sampling error, question wording and practical difficulties in conducting surveys can introduce error or bias into the findings of public opinion polls.

Polls conducted entirely in one day, such as this one, are subject to additional error or bias not found in polls conducted over several days.

July 02, 2009

AMERICANS' WORRY ABOUT TERRORISM NEARS 5-YEAR LOW

But most think security measures put in place after 9/11 should remain

by Lymari Morales, Gallup Poll Staff Writer

U.S. Homeland Security Secretary Janet Napolitano this week said the issue of terrorism "is always with us" and that "we have to be ever vigilant." Americans, however, are less worried about terrorism than at any point since August 2004—with 36% saying they are very or somewhat worried that they or a family member will become a victim.

Americans' collective level of worry about terrorism measured in the *USA Today*/Gallup poll, conducted June 8–9, is the lowest recorded since August 2004 (34%) and down sharply from the all-time high of 59% recorded in October 2001, just after the Sept. 11 attacks. The latest poll finds 30% who say they are not too worried about being a victim of terrorism and 34% who say they are not at all worried.

In a separate Gallup Poll, conducted June 14–17, only 1% mentioned terrorism as the most important problem facing the United States, consistent with Americans' perceptions of this issue over the past year, and tied for the lowest percentage giving this answer since 9/11. Mentions have been in the single-digit range since November 2006, and are down from a peak of 46% in October 2001.

Now, thinking for a moment about terrorism, how worried are you that you or someone in your family will become a victim of terrorism -- very worried, somewhat worried, not too worried, or not worried at all?

Gallup trend since 2000

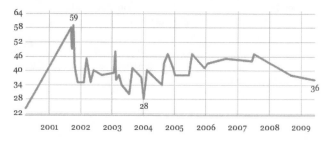

Currently, 73% of Americans say they have a great deal or fair amount of confidence in the U.S. government to protect its citizens from future acts of terrorism—unchanged from 2006, but down from 81% in 2004.

How much confidence do you have in the U.S. government to protect its citizens from future acts of terrorism -- a great deal, a fair amount, not very much, or none at all?

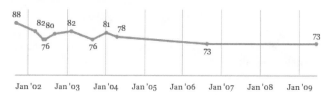

While most Americans are not personally worried that they or a family member will become a victim of terrorism, they do see a continued need for the post-Sept. 11 security measures aimed at preventing terrorist attacks. Most (83%) think those measures are still needed, while 14% think they could be dropped.

Now we'd like you to think more generally about the security measures put in place after September 11 that were aimed at preventing terrorist attacks. Which comes closer to your view -- [in general, these security measures are still needed (or) many of these security measures could now be dropped]?

USA Today/Gallup poll, June 8-9, 2009

Bottom Line

Americans are for the most part not personally worried that they or a family member will become a victim of terrorism, and they have a fairly high level of confidence in the U.S. government to protect them. While most agree that security measures implemented after 9/11 are still necessary, calls for continued vigilance like the one articulated by Napolitano this week are likely a good tactic to keep Americans ever aware of the ongoing threat.

Results are based on telephone interviews with 995 national adults, aged 18 and older, conducted June 8–9, 2009. For results based on the total sample of national adults, one can say with 95% confidence that the maximum margin of sampling error is ±3 percentage points.

Interviews are conducted with respondents on land-line telephones (for respondents with a land-line telephone) and cellular phones (for respondents who are cell-phone only).

In addition to sampling error, question wording and practical difficulties in conducting surveys can introduce error or bias into the findings of public opinion polls.

July 06, 2009

SPECIAL REPORT: IDEOLOGICALLY, WHERE IS THE U.S. MOVING?

Nearly 4 in 10 Americans say their views have grown more conservative

by Lydia Saad, Gallup Poll Senior Editor

Despite the results of the 2008 presidential election, Americans, by a 2-to-1 margin, say their political views in recent years have become more conservative rather than more liberal, 39% to 18%, with 42% saying they have not changed. While independents and Democrats most often say their views haven't changed, more members of all three major partisan groups indicate that their views have shifted to the right rather than to the left.

Thinking about your views on political issues and how they have changed in recent years, would you say you are now -- [more conservative than you were a few years ago, have your views not changed, (or are you) more liberal than you were a few years ago]?

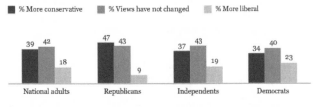

June 14-17, 2009

These findings, from a June 14–17 Gallup Poll, somewhat conform to Gallup's annual trends on Americans' self-defined political ideology. Thus far in 2009 (from January through May), 40% of Americans call themselves conservative, up from 37% in 2007 and 2008, and the highest level since 2004.

However, the results are conspicuously incongruous with the results of the 2008 elections, in which the Democratic Party won the White House for the first time in eight years, and increased its majority control in the U.S. House and Senate. Rather than suggesting an upturn in conservatism, the elections, the tattered image of the GOP, depressed identification with the Republican Party, and President Obama's broad popularity have many in and outside of the Republican Party wondering whether the country has outgrown the GOP's largely conservative platform.

Conservatives currently outnumber liberals in the population, and thus, conservatism has a natural advantage on any question ask-ing the public to choose between these standard ideological labels. So that's part of the explanation for the incongruity.

Indeed, in the latest survey, 38% of Americans describe their political views as conservative, and among this group 58% say their views have grown more conservative in recent years. Although a large segment of liberals (42%) say they have become more liberal, far fewer Americans in the poll (18%) describe themselves as liberal—thus providing little counterweight to the rightward movement of conservatives. At the same time, political moderates are twice as likely to say they have grown more conservative as opposed to more liberal (33% vs. 18%), thus further tipping the scales in favor of conservatism.

Self-Reported Change in Political Views in Recent Years

Based on current political ideology

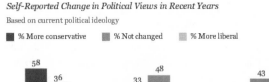

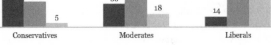

Americans' Views, Now vs. 2004

While it is valuable to know how Americans perceive their own ideological development, another means for evaluating such change is to assess how public opinion may have shifted on specific issues over the years.

Given the stark differences between the current political scene and the one surrounding the 2004 elections, 2004 represents a good comparison point for this analysis. Not only was there a five-point drop between 2004 and 2008 (from 51% to 46%) in the popular vote for the Republican presidential candidate, but there has been a similar drop (from 45% in 2004 to 40% in 2008 and 39% in 2009) in the percentage affiliating themselves with the Republican Party.

Have Americans' positions on major cultural, social, and policy issues shifted left accordingly? A broad review of the available trends suggests not. However, they have not shifted solidly right either, countering Americans' claims in the new poll that they have grown more conservative.

Major Domestic Issues

Americans' views about major domestic issues facing the country did change spanning the two most recent presidential elections, but not all of the attitudes have moved in the same direction.

Gallup polling shows Americans becoming more conservative on gun control between 2004 and 2008, with opposition to banning handguns growing from 63% to 69%. And disagreement with making gun laws "more strict" grew, from 45% to 49%.

Americans also became more likely to say the economy should be given priority over the environment when the two interests conflict—although that may reflect the difficult economic times, rather than an ideological shift away from environmentalism.

Gallup trends show Americans growing less conservative on immigration. According to a question asking whether the level of immigration into the United States should be increased, be decreased, or stay the same, the percentage favoring decreased immigration (a traditionally more Republican/conservative stance) fell from 49% in 2004 to 39% in 2008.

Changes in public attitudes on healthcare reform have been mixed. The percentage of Americans in favor of maintaining the current healthcare system based on private insurance was 63% in 2004 but 56% in March 2009—a drop of seven points for the traditionally conservative healthcare position. (Support for the alternative position—replacing the current healthcare system with a government-run system—grew from 32% to 39%.) At the same time, Gallup saw a seven-point increase, from 34% to 41%, in views that it is *not* the government's responsibility to provide all Americans with healthcare coverage.

Public opinion on several other domestic policy issues did not change appreciably—including on the death penalty and labor unions.

U.S. Domestic Issues -- Trend in Percentage Holding Conservative Position

Issue: Position	2004	2008/ 2009^	Change
	%	%	Pct. pts.
Environment: Protect economy over environment	44	51	7
Healthcare coverage: Not government reponsibility	34	41	7
Guns: Do not favor a ban on handguns	63	69	6
Guns: Want gun laws kept same/less strict	45	49	4
Death penalty: Favor	64	64	0
Labor unions: Want unions to have less influence	32	32	0
Healthcare: Favor maintaining current system	63	56	-7
Immigration: Want level to decrease	49	39	-10

^ Most recent result from 2008 or 2009

Although 32% of Americans in 2008 said they personally want unions to have less influence in the country, 35% said they want unions to have more influence—thus, the two opposing sides on the issue now battling it out over union-organizing legislation in Congress are about equally matched.

Values-Based Issues

Of seven values issues measured in 2004 and again in 2008 or 2009, Gallup found significant movement on just two, and only one on which Americans became more liberal (the government's role in promoting traditional values).

Views on gay rights and embryonic stem-cell research are similar now to where they were at the time of the 2004 elections, despite significant policy developments on each since then. Americans seem to be moving in a slightly more conservative direction on abortion this year, with a greater percentage calling themselves pro-life than pro-choice.

Frequent churchgoers have been a bedrock Republican constituency for at least the past three presidential elections, with the majority supporting the GOP candidate in each case. Thus, a significant decline in religiosity among Americans would almost certainly be detrimental to Republican candidates. However, Gallup finds no decline since 2004 in either regular church attendance or in the percentage calling themselves "born again."

Government Power and Spending

The issues surrounding government power and spending arguably changed late in the 2008 campaign, when the banking industry crisis erupted and Wall Street arrived in Washington, D.C., asking for a major bailout. However, Gallup polling just before the financial tsunami found Americans' views about the proper role of government similar to where they stood four years previously.

Values-Based Issues/Beliefs -- Trend in Percentage Holding Conservative Position

Issue: Position	2004	2008/ 2009^	Change
	%	%	Pct. pts.
Abortion: "Pro-life"	44	51	+7
Gay marriage: Should not be valid	55	57	+2
Religion: "Born again"	41	40	-1
Embryonic stem-cell research: Morally wrong	37	36	-1
Religion: Attend church weekly/nearly weekly	44	42	-2
Homosexuality: Not acceptable lifestyle	42	40	-2
"Traditional values": Government should promote	55	48	-7

^ Most recent result from 2008 or 2009

The percentage of Americans saying the government "is trying to do too many things that should be left to individuals and businesses" has fluctuated in a fairly narrow range since 2004, between 47% and 55%, thus not indicating any significant shift in Americans' outlook on the role of government over this period.

The percentage saying there is "too much" government regulation of business and industry was 37% in September 2004 and 38% in September 2008—also essentially unchanged.

Americans' belief that taxes are too high registered 50% in April 2004 and 52% in April 2008. This dropped to 46% in April 2009, most likely a reflection of widespread approval of the overall job Obama is doing as president.

Those saying the federal government has too much power rose from 42% in September 2004 to 52% in September 2008—on its face a sentiment more in tune with Republican than Democratic tenets. However, much of this change occurred shortly after the 2004 elections, and was the result of increased concern about government power among Democrats.

Power and Role of Government -- Trend in Percentage Holding Conservative Position

Issue: Position	2004	2008/ 2009^	Change
	%	%	Pct. pts.
Government: Has too much power	42	52	10
Government regulation of business/industry: Too much	37	38	1
Government role: Should leave more to individuals	49	47	-2
Taxes: Too high	50	46	-4

^ Most recent result from 2008 or 2009

Iraq and National Defense

Gallup trends document a clear drop between 2004 and 2008 in Americans' agreement with some core elements of the Republican Party's recent national security stance. The percentage saying that sending troops to Iraq was "not a mistake"—thus supporting President George W. Bush's original decision to launch the invasion of Iraq in 2003—fell from 52% in October 2004 to 39% in October 2008; however, it expanded somewhat to 43% in January 2009. And although Americans' support for U.S. involvement in Afghanistan remained high, their agreement with the decision to send troops to that country fell from 72% to 63% between July 2004 and August 2008, before recovering to 66% in January 2009.

More generally, public support for maintaining or increasing U.S. defense spending—positions much more in tune with Bush and the Republican Party than the Democrats—fell from 67% in February 2004 to 52% in February 2008. However, in February 2009—after the adoption in late 2008 of a timetable for withdrawal of U.S. troops from Iraq and with a new U.S. administration in office—support for maintaining or increasing U.S. defense spending rebounded to 65%.

Thus on defense issues, Americans moved to the left between 2004 and 2008, reflecting public dissatisfaction with the Iraq war, but have since reverted to levels near those of 2004.

Defense Issues -- Trend in Percentage Holding Conservative Position

Issue: Position	2004	2008	2009
	%	%	%
Defense spending: About right/Too little	67	52	65
Afghanistan: Not a mistake	72	63	66
Iraq: Not a mistake	52	39	43

Bottom Line

Given the 2008 election returns, many are asking whether the GOP has become too conservative on the issues or whether Americans have grown more liberal. At the same time, upon the end of the 2008–2009 Supreme Court term, court watchers are noting the divergence between the liberal direction in which Obama seems to be taking the country and the conservative direction being paved by Supreme Court Chief Justice John Roberts.

Which way do Americans want to be led? While the new Gallup Poll finds the public reporting a heightened sense of conservatism in its political outlook, Americans' specific policy positions have not changed much since 2004. To the extent they have, about as many of these positions have become more liberal as more conservative.

Aside from the trends, Gallup's recent polling from 2008–2009 indicates that a majority of Americans concur with the Republican Party's general philosophy on the death penalty, defense spending, gay marriage, the role of government, environmental protection, and handgun legislation. Americans are about as likely to agree with the Republican Party's general philosophy as they are to agree with the Democratic Party's in terms of abortion, government activism, government promotion of "traditional" values, taxes, changing the power of labor unions, and certain aspects of the need for healthcare reform. They are more likely to agree with the Democratic Party's philosophy on other aspects of healthcare reform, embryonic stem-cell research, government regulation of business, the Iraq war, and immigration.

With such a mix of political leanings, then, it is understandable that Americans can approve of the job Obama is doing as president (his approval ratings remain near his term average of 63%), and simultaneously approve of the job the Supreme Court is doing (59% now approve, up from 48% a year ago).

And for those seeking to understand why the Republican Party suffered such major election losses, they may find that political ideology has very little to do with it.

Survey Methods

The most recent results are based on telephone interviews with 1,011 national adults, aged 18 and older, conducted June 14–17, 2009. For results based on the total sample of national adults, one can say with 95% confidence that the maximum margin of sampling error is ±3 percentage points.

Except as noted, results to Gallup trend questions are based on telephone surveys including interviews with approximately 1,000 national adults, aged 18 and older, and have an associated margin of sampling error of ±3 percentage points.

In addition to sampling error, question wording and practical difficulties in conducting surveys can introduce error or bias into the findings of public opinion polls.

July 07, 2009
MANY AMERICANS STILL SEE POLITICAL FUTURE FOR PALIN
Most Americans' opinions of her not affected by resignation

by Jeffrey M. Jones, Gallup Poll Managing Editor

Alaska Gov. Sarah Palin's resignation—announced last Friday—fueled speculation that she may be setting up a run for president in 2012. A new *USA Today*/Gallup poll conducted Monday night finds a core of 19% of U.S. voters who say they are "very likely" to vote for her should she run, and an additional 24% who are somewhat likely to do so, giving her a decent reservoir of potential support to build upon. However, nearly as many voters (41%) currently say they would be not at all likely to vote for her.

If Sarah Palin were to run for president in 2012, how likely would you be to vote her for -- very likely, somewhat likely, not very likely, or not at all likely?
Based on registered voters

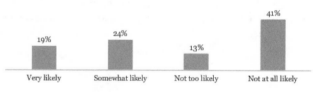

USA Today/Gallup poll, July 6, 2009

By way of comparison, when Gallup in 2005 asked a similar question about Hillary Clinton running for president in 2008, 52% of registered voters said they were at least somewhat likely to vote for her, including 28% who said they were very likely to do so.

Predictably, most Democratic registered voters (70%) say they are not at all likely to vote for Palin. While most Republican registered voters (72%) say they are likely to vote for Palin, only about half of these (35% of all Republican voters) can be considered solid supporters who say they are very likely to support Palin at this time.

Likelihood of Voting for Sarah Palin for President, by Political Party
Based on registered voters

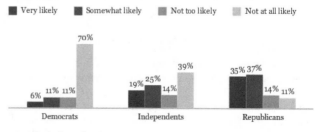

USA Today/Gallup poll, July 6, 2009

Even if Palin ultimately decides against a run for the White House, her high profile may allow her to take on a role as a major national political figure. When asked about her possibly having such a role, 39% of Americans say they would like to see her do this, including 67% of Republicans, 34% of independents, and 18% of Democrats.

Palin's announcement last Friday may have taken many political observers by surprise, but the data show her decision to resign the governorship did not affect most Americans' opinions of her. The poll finds 70% saying their opinion of Palin has not changed as a result of her resignation. Though this is clearly the minority of Americans, more say their opinion of her has gotten worse (17%) than improved (9%).

Does Governor Palin's decision to resign make you feel more favorably toward her, less favorably toward her, or does it not affect your opinion of her either way?

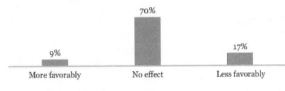

USA Today/Gallup poll, July 6, 2009

Majority Believes Media Unfair to Palin

Palin was a relatively unknown political figure when tapped to be John McCain's running mate, but she quickly energized the GOP ticket, drawing large crowds to their rallies during the presidential campaign. But news coverage of her quickly took a negative turn and many in the political world came to view her as a drag on the McCain campaign.

Palin herself has argued that she has been unjustly attacked by the news media, and most Americans seem to agree. The new poll finds 53% describing the news media's coverage of Palin as "unfairly negative," while just 9% say it has been "unfairly positive" and 28% say it has been "about right."

When Gallup asked a similar question about news coverage of Palin shortly after the Republican National Convention last September, Americans were more evenly divided in their views, with 33% saying the coverage was unfairly negative and the plurality of 36% saying it was about right. At that time, 21% thought the media were being unfairly positive toward Palin.

Implications

Palin's abrupt resignation with 18 months left in her first term as governor has probably raised more questions than answers about her political future. But the move has apparently not affected Americans' basic opinions of her to a large degree. As political observers eagerly await her next career move, roughly 19% of U.S. voters say they would be very likely to vote for her should she run for president in 2012, and another 24% say they would be somewhat likely to do so. While still the minority of all voters, it is perhaps not a bad start for an election still three years away, and arguably could put Palin in a better starting position than some of the lesser-known GOP candidates who may also seek the party's presidential nomination.

July 09, 2009

AMERICANS' WELL-BEING CONTINUES TO EDGE UPWARD

Plus: Key findings from 2008 set stage for new well-being rankings

by Elizabeth Mendes, Gallup Poll Staff Writer

Americans' collective well-being was slightly higher this June than it was throughout the summer of 2008—prior to the economic collapse—and significantly higher than in late 2008 and early 2009. The Gallup-Healthways Well-Being Index composite score of 66.8 for June represents year-over-year improvement from June 2008 and also comes close to the Index's all-time high of 67, recorded in February of last year.

Gallup-Healthways Well-Being Index
National adults, aged 18 and older

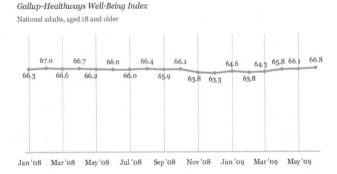

With June's 66.8 reading, the Well-Being Index has recorded four straight months of improvement. The Index is composed of six sub-indexes, covering life evaluation, emotional health, physical health, healthy behavior, work environment, and access to basic necessities. After it dropped significantly following the onset of the financial crisis last fall, the Well-Being Index score remained relatively low for several months before approaching pre-crisis levels again in April 2009.

The uptick in the Well-Being Index's national composite score in April and May of this year was propelled primarily by a sizable rebound in the Life Evaluation sub-index. The continued increase in the overall Index in June reflects not only sustained improvement in

Life Evaluation, but also positive change across each of the other five sub-indexes.

Gallup-Healthways Well-Being Index Composite Score and Sub-Index Scores
March-June 2009

	March 2009	April 2009	May 2009	June 2009
WELL-BEING INDEX	64.3	65.8	66.1	66.8
Life Evaluation	37.6	45.9	47.5	47.8
Emotional Health	78.0	78.6	78.6	79.2
Physical Health	76.0	76.5	76.1	77.0
Healthy Behavior	62.7	62.6	63.1	64.2
Work Environment	49.8	49.1	49.2	50.2
Basic Access	81.5	82.0	82.2	82.6

Gallup-Healthways Well-Being Index

While the June improvements in some of the sub-indexes may be due in part to the effects of seasonality, they likely also point to a more comprehensive recovery in the nation's level of well-being.

Key Findings From 2008 Set Stage for New Well-Being Rankings

As the monthly Well-Being Index score continues to inch its way up, the Gallup-Healthways Well-Being Index is getting set to release midyear 2009 State Well-Being Rankings in August. The following is a review of the top- and bottom-scoring states and congressional districts from the inaugural 2008 rankings.

- The 2008 national average for the Well-Being Index was 65.5.
- With a score of 69.2, Utah was the top-ranking state on overall Well-Being.
- West Virginia's Well-Being Index score of 61.2 put the state in last place.
- Two of the three states at the bottom of the Well-Being rankings are in the South: Mississippi and Kentucky.
- Hawaii ranked first on two of the six sub-indexes—Life Evaluation and Emotional Health—but ranked last on Work Environment.
- West Virginia ranked last on three of the six sub-indexes—Life Evaluation, Emotional Health, and Physical Health.
- Massachusetts ranked No. 1 on Basic Access, the sub-index that looks at 13 items, including access to affordable fruits and vegetables, shelter, and clean water, as well as whether respondents have a doctor and have health insurance.
- Mississippi, the state with the lowest per-capita median income, ranked last on Basic Access.
- Connecticut, the state with the highest per-capita median income, ranked third on Basic Access.
- Six of the congressional districts that ranked in the top 10 for overall Well-Being are in California.
- Ohio had the highest number of congressional districts (3) in the bottom 10 on Well-Being.
- Michigan's 13th District ranked last for Work Environment and California's 14th District came in first.
- Seven of the congressional districts that ranked in the top 10 for Healthy Behavior are in California.
- New Mexico was the top-ranking state for Healthy Behavior.
- Kentucky's 5th District ranks 435th (last) on three of the six sub-indexes—Physical Health, Life Evaluation, and Emotional Health, and ranks 433rd out of 435 on Healthy Behavior.
- Eight of the top-10-ranking states for Work Environment are located in the West.

These findings are just a sampling of those available at the AHIP State and Congressional District Resource for Well-Being, an interactive database and mapping tool that enables users to research and analyze the Gallup-Healthways Well-Being Index data along with the most up-to-date statistics from the Census Bureau.

Survey Methods

Results are based on telephone interviews with approximately 30,000 adults per month in the United States, aged 18 and older, conducted January 2008 to June 2009 as part of Gallup Poll Daily tracking. For results based on each monthly sample of national adults, one can say with 95% confidence that the maximum margin of sampling error is ±0.2 percentage points.

For the State and Congressional District Well-Being Rankings results are based on telephone interviews with more than 350,000 national adults, aged 18 and older, conducted in 2008 as part of Gallup Poll Daily tracking. For results based on the total sample of national adults, one can say with 95% confidence that the maximum margin of sampling error is ±1 percentage point.

Sample sizes vary for States and Congressional Districts. For results based on a sample size of 5,000, one can say with 95% confidence that the maximum margin of sampling error is ±1.4 percentage points; for results based on a sample size of 1,000, ±3.1 percentage points; for results based on 500, ±4.4 percentage points; for results based on 300, ±5.7 percentage points.

Interviews are conducted with respondents on land-line telephones (for respondents with a land-line telephone) and cellular phones (for respondents who are cell-phone only).

In addition to sampling error, question wording and practical difficulties in conducting surveys can introduce error or bias into the findings of public opinion polls.

July 10, 2009
DEMOCRATS MAINTAIN EDGE IN PARTY SUPPORT, BUT GAP SHRINKS
Advantage over Republicans is now 49% to 40%

by Jeffrey M. Jones, Gallup Poll Managing Editor

The Democratic Party continues to hold a solid advantage in party support over the Republican Party, as 49% of Americans interviewed in the second quarter of this year identified with or leaned to the Democratic Party, compared with 40% who did so for the Republican Party. However, that nine-point Democratic advantage is smaller than the 13-point edge Gallup measured in the first quarter of the year.

The latest results are based on an average of the Gallup Poll stand-alone polls conducted in the second quarter of 2009, consisting of more than 5,000 interviews with U.S. adults. Gallup Poll Daily tracking shows a similar pattern of change from the first quarter to the second quarter.

The declining Democratic advantage is due more to a drop in Democratic support (from 52% to 49%) than to an increase in Republican support (from 39% to 40%).

The lessening Democratic advantage may to some degree reflect a return to more typical party support levels, because the 13-point

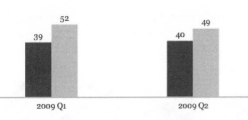

Leaned Party Identification, Quarterly Averages, 2009 Gallup Polls

■ % Republican/Lean Republican ▨ % Democrat/Lean Democratic

Democratic edge from the first quarter is on the high end of what Gallup has found since it began tracking this measure of party identification in 1991.

Even with the decline, Democrats continue to hold a solid advantage in leaned party identification, something they have enjoyed since the second quarter of 2005. Democrats have led the Republicans on this measure by at least 10 points for 11 of the last 13 quarters.

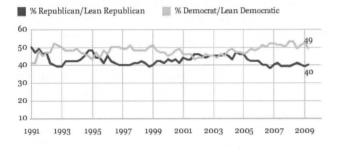

Leaned Party Identification, Average by Quarter, 1991-2009 Gallup Polls

■ % Republican/Lean Republican ▨ % Democrat/Lean Democratic

Party Identification

Gallup's basic measure of party identification—which does not take into account the partisan leanings of independents—shows a slight decline in Democratic Party identification in the first quarter of 2009 (from 35% to 34%) and a slight increase in independent identification (from 35% to 37%). There has been no change in Republican identification, which at 28% remains on the low end of what Gallup has measured for the past two decades.

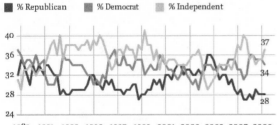

Party Identification, Average by Quarter, 1988-2009 Gallup Polls

■ % Republican ▨ % Democrat ▨ % Independent

As a result, the Democrats now hold a six-point advantage in party identification on this basic measure. The Democratic Party has held at least a four-point lead since the second quarter of 2006, a stretch of 13 consecutive quarters, including a recent high of nine points in the second quarter of 2008.

The fact that Democrats hold a six-point advantage on initial party identification compared with a larger nine-point lead on leaned party identification indicates that independents are currently a little more likely to lean to the Democratic Party than to the Republican Party.

Implications

Gallup polling shows a slight dip in Democratic support in the most recent quarter. However, the Democrats had such a large cushion that even with the drop, they maintain a sizable advantage over the Republican Party.

The data indicate also that, although the party gap may be shrinking, the Republicans have not made any significant gains of their own in recent months. Their support levels remain on the low end of what Gallup has measured for the past two decades.

Survey Methods

Results are based on averages from five Gallup surveys conducted between April and June 2009, each consisting of approximately 1,000 interviews with national adults, aged 18 and older. For results based on the total sample of national adults, one can say with 95% confidence that the maximum margin of sampling error is ±1 percentage point.

Interviews are conducted with respondents on land-line telephones (for respondents with a land-line telephone) and cellular phones (for respondents who are cell-phone only).

In addition to sampling error, question wording and practical difficulties in conducting surveys can introduce error or bias into the findings of public opinion polls.

July 13, 2009
MARRIAGE REMAINS KEY PREDICTOR OF PARTY IDENTIFICATION
Married Americans tilt Republican; unmarried Americans, Democratic

by Frank Newport, Gallup Poll Editor in Chief

A Gallup analysis of more than 29,000 interviews conducted in June highlights a continuing and significant marriage gap in party identification. The percentage of all Americans who identified as Republican in June was 28%, but is higher at 33% among those who are married, and a lower 21% among unmarried Americans. On the other hand, Democratic identification in June was at 35% overall, but 31% among married Americans, and 41% among those who are not married. This marriage gap in party identification is evident across races as well as age groups.

This marriage gap in American politics today is not new, but the current analysis underscores the fact that marital status remains one of the most reliable predictors of party identification among major demographic variables in the U.S. in 2009.

Being "unmarried" in America today encompasses a number of different life situations—including those who are single and have never married as well as those who are separated, divorced, widowed,

Party Identification, by Marital Status

■ Republican   ■ Independent   ■ Democrat

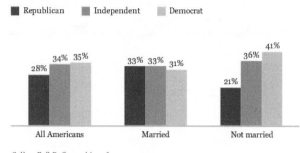

Gallup Poll Daily tracking, June 1-30, 2009

and those living in a domestic partnership. The large sample size for this data set allows for a detailed subdivision of unmarried Americans into each of these specific categories.

As can be seen in the accompanying graph, the particular circumstances of being unmarried do not appear to make a great deal of difference in terms of party identification. Democrats have a significant identification advantage over Republicans across each of these segments.

Party Identification, by Detailed Marital Status

■ % Republican   ■ % Independent   ■ % Democrat

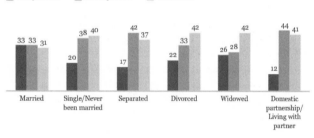

Gallup Poll Daily tracking, June 1-30. 2009

Noteworthy Findings

The largest Democratic-over-Republican identification advantage is among Americans living with a domestic partner (Gallup's data do not distinguish between those with partners of the same sex and those with partners of the opposite sex). Among those in a domestic partnership, 41% identify as Democrats and just 12% as Republicans.

Those who are single/never married, separated, and divorced all evidence the same 20-point Democratic advantage.

The Democratic advantage is a slightly smaller 16 points among those who are widowed.

There are also variations across these segments of unmarried Americans in terms of the percentage who identify as independents. Of note are the quite high 44% of those who live with a domestic partner and 42% of those who are separated who don't claim allegiance to either party.

Race and Age

Marital status is correlated with race, which in turn is associated with party identification. More specifically, nonwhites in America today are less likely than whites to be married, and nonwhites are more likely to identify as Democrats. Thus, it is possible to hypothesize that some of the relationship between marital status and party identification is based on these differences by race. The data, however,

show that the relationship between marriage and party identification persists among *both* whites and nonwhites.

Party Identification, by Race and Marital Status

■ % Republican   ■ % Independent   ■ % Democrat

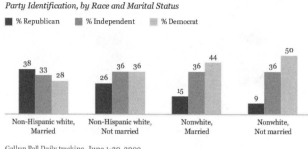

Gallup Poll Daily tracking, June 1-30, 2009

Republicans have a 10-point advantage over Democrats among married whites, and Democrats have a mirror-image 10-point advantage among unmarried whites.

Regardless of their marital status, Democrats do very well among nonwhite Americans. Still, marriage makes a difference. The Democratic advantage over Republicans is 29 points among married nonwhites and a larger 41 points among unmarried nonwhites.

What about age? Younger Americans are less likely than older Americans to be married, and are more likely to identify as Democrats. This leads to the hypothesis that these underlying age patterns could be a significant part of the explanation for the relationship between marriage and party identification. But, as is the case for differences by race, the data show that the marital status-party ID relationship persists across all age groups.

Party Identification, by Age and Marital Status

■ % Republican   ■ % Independent   ■ % Democrat

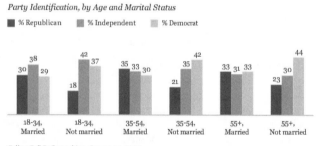

Gallup Poll Daily tracking, June 1-30, 2009

Republicans have a one-point advantage among 18- to 34-year-olds who are married, while Democrats have a large 19-point advantage among those 18–34 who are not married. Similar striking differences are found among those 35–54, and 55+. In each of these age groups, those who are not married are consistently and significantly more likely to be Democrats than those of the same age who are married.

Implications

It is difficult to tease out the precise reasons why those who are married in America today are disproportionally likely to identify with the Republican Party, and why those who are unmarried tilt toward the Democratic Party. Race and age factors may play somewhat of a role in explaining the relationship. But the relationship persists even after controlling for these two demographic variables.

The association between marital status and party identification is part of a broader constellation of values and political variables in

American society today that are inter-correlated with one another—including positions on issues and levels of religiosity. Marriage is a predictor of conservative ideology and conservative positions on social issues, which in turn predict high levels of Republican identification. Being unmarried is a predictor of more liberal ideology and more liberal positions on social issues, which predict higher levels of Democratic identification. Marriage is also associated with religious intensity, including church attendance and importance of religion in one's life. These measures of religion, in turn, are important predictors of party identification. But it is uncertain whether religion, ideology, and party lead to choice of marital status, or whether marital status leads Americans to different ideological, religious, and partisan choices.

Regardless of the precise causal paths involved, however, the data conclusively show that in America today, being married is significantly associated with increased Republican and decreased Democratic identification, while unmarried Americans tilt in the opposite direction.

Survey Methods

Results are based on telephone interviews with 29,351 national adults, aged 18 and older, conducted June 1–30, 2009, as part of Gallup Poll Daily tracking. For results based on the total sample of national adults, one can say with 95% confidence that the maximum margin of sampling error is ±1 percentage point.

Interviews are conducted with respondents on land-line telephones (for respondents with a land-line telephone) and cellular phones (for respondents who are cell-phone only).

In addition to sampling error, question wording and practical difficulties in conducting surveys can introduce error or bias into the findings of public opinion polls.

July 13, 2009
SUPPORT FOR SOTOMAYOR CONFIRMATION HOLDS STEADY AT 53%
Slight increase in unfavorable rating since late May

by Jeffrey M. Jones, Gallup Poll Managing Editor

As the Senate begins its confirmation hearings of U.S. Supreme Court nominee Sonia Sotomayor Monday, a new Gallup Poll finds Americans in favor of her winning Senate approval, by 53% to 33%. Since late May, shortly after her nomination was announced, the percentage in favor of her confirmation has changed little, but the percentage opposed has increased as the percentage with no opinion has gone down.

These results are based on a July 10–12 Gallup Poll, conducted in the final days before the hearings began. The 53% in favor of Sotomayor's confirmation is in line with those for recent nominees who won confirmation, including Samuel Alito, John Roberts, Ruth Bader Ginsburg, and Clarence Thomas, all of whose pre-hearing ratings were near 50%. It is higher than those of two nominees—Robert Bork and Harriet Miers—whose nominations were withdrawn or were defeated by the Senate.

There is not much evidence to suggest that Senate hearings change public support for Supreme Court nominees to a large degree.

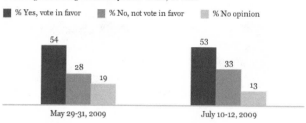

As you may know, Sonia Sotomayor is the federal judge nominated to serve on the Supreme Court. Would you like to see the Senate vote in favor of Sotomayor serving on the Supreme Court, or not?

Gallup took readings for Alito and Roberts immediately before, and upon completion of, their Senate hearings. Support for Alito's confirmation rose only slightly, from 49% to 54% in January 2006. Likewise, the needle barely moved (from 58% to 60%) after Roberts' confirmation hearings in September 2005.

This lack of movement was true even in the case of Thomas, whose hearings attracted national attention after accusations that he had sexually harassed a former colleague. From the initial measurement in July 1991, shortly after his nomination was announced, until immediately before the Senate vote that made him a Supreme Court justice in October 1991, the percentage of Americans in favor of confirming Thomas to the Court did not vary much, ranging only between 52% and 58%. During this time, opposition to Thomas did increase, but only to as high as 30%.

The new poll finds a majority of Americans saying they are following news about Sotomayor's Supreme Court nomination very (14%) or somewhat (39%) closely, down slightly from what Gallup measured in May (60%).

Among those following the nomination closely, 56% favor the Senate's voting in favor of her confirmation and 42% oppose it.

Politically, more than 7 in 10 Democrats are in favor of Senate confirmation for Sotomayor, as are 53% of independents. Republicans are about twice as likely to oppose as to favor confirmation. These party figures are little changed since late May.

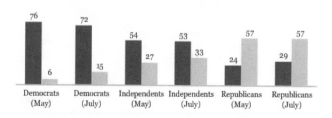

Favor/Oppose Sotomayor Confirmation, by Political Party, 2009

Sotomayor would be the third female justice in the Supreme Court's history. Men (54%) and women (53%) are about equally likely to support Sotomayor's confirmation. However, men are more likely to say they oppose her being confirmed to the Court while women are more likely to say they do not have an opinion.

Sotomayor Still Unknown to Many

More than a month after Sotomayor's nomination to the Supreme Court by U.S. President Barack Obama, a substantial percentage of Americans still do not have an opinion of her. When asked whether

Favor Sotomayor Confirmation, by Gender

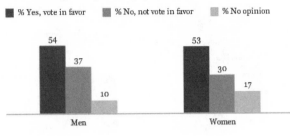

July 10-12, 2009

they have a favorable or unfavorable opinion of Sotomayor in general, 36% say they do not have an opinion either way, the same percentage Gallup found in May.

In general, Americans' basic evaluations of Sotomayor are significantly more positive (38%) than negative (26%). Her favorable rating of 38% is down slightly from 43% in May, and her unfavorable rating has increased from 21% to 26%.

Overall Opinion of Sonia Sotomayor

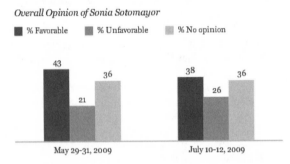

Implications

It is not clear that this week's Senate hearings will do much to change public sentiment about Sotomayor's Supreme Court nomination. Typically, Gallup has found little in the way of increased public support for Supreme Court nominees throughout the nomination process. Given that support for Sotomayor's confirmation is right in line with that for prior successful nominees, it is probably not critical for her to raise that support between now and the final Senate vote.

Survey Methods

Results are based on telephone interviews with 1,018 national adults, aged 18 and older, conducted July 10–12, 2009. For results based on the total sample of national adults, one can say with 95% confidence that the maximum margin of sampling error is ±3 percentage points.

Interviews are conducted with respondents on land-line telephones (for respondents with a land-line telephone) and cellular phones (for respondents who are cell-phone only).

In addition to sampling error, question wording and practical difficulties in conducting surveys can introduce error or bias into the findings of public opinion polls.

July 14, 2009

MAJORITY IN U.S. FAVORS HEALTHCARE REFORM THIS YEAR

Controlling costs a higher priority than expanding coverage

by Jeffrey M. Jones, Gallup Poll Managing Editor

As U.S. House leaders unveil a plan to reform the U.S. healthcare system, a *USA Today*/Gallup poll finds 56% of Americans in favor and 33% opposed to Congress' passing major healthcare reform legislation this year. Support for healthcare reform before the end of the year is sharply split along party lines, with 79% of Democrats in favor, compared with only 23% of Republicans.

Do you favor or oppose Congress passing a major healthcare reform bill this year?

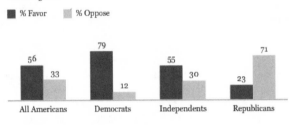

USA Today/Gallup poll, July 10-12, 2009

On Tuesday, House Democrats held a press conference in which they introduced their version of healthcare legislation. The Senate is still working on its version. With the specific outlines of healthcare reform still far from settled, the July 10–12 survey explored a number of other issues that Congress is considering as it works toward drafting legislation.

1. Goals of Reform

Any healthcare reform legislation will likely address the twin problems of covering a large number of uninsured Americans and keeping a lid on quickly rising costs for those who do have insurance. When asked which of the two is the more important goal, the public says, by 52% to 42%, that controlling costs is more crucial than expanding coverage.

Self-interest may partially explain people's conceptions of which goal is more important. Those without health insurance believe expanding coverage to nearly all Americans is the more important goal, while those who have insurance believe controlling costs is more imperative.

If you had to choose, which goal of healthcare reform would you say is more important -- [ROTATED: expanding healthcare coverage to include nearly all Americans (or) controlling rising healthcare costs in the U.S. today]?

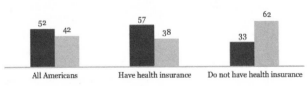

USA Today/Gallup poll, July 10-12, 2009

2. Preserving Choice and Reining in Costs

The poll tested five healthcare provisions that deal with choice, access, and cost control, and though there is some variation, at least three-quarters of Americans say each is extremely or very important to them.

At the upper end of the range, 93% of Americans say it is either extremely or very important for their health plan to cover any medical test or treatment they and their doctor think is necessary. Just under 9 in 10 ascribe this level of importance to being able to get health insurance regardless of job status or medical situation, and being able to choose any doctor or hospital they like.

Additionally, 83% say it is important that their health insurance be made more affordable, and 77% say it is important to have the option to keep the health insurance plan they have now.

Importance of Each to You in Light of Possible Changes to U.S. Healthcare System

	% Extremely important	% Very important	% Extremely/ Very important
Having your healthcare plan cover any medical test or treatment you and your doctor think you need	45	48	93
Being able to choose any doctor or hospital you like	41	47	88
Being able to get health insurance regardless of your job status or medical situation	43	43	86
Making your health insurance more affordable	40	43	83
Having the option to keep the health insurance plan you have now	34	43	77

USA Today/Gallup poll, July 10-12, 2009

One issue still to be ironed out is whether the government will require Americans to have health insurance. This is something the recently adopted Massachusetts healthcare reform plan does (with some exceptions), and it was a point of disagreement between Barack Obama and Democratic presidential nomination rival Hillary Clinton during the 2008 campaign (Obama did not support mandatory insurance).

When asked for its views, the public tilts in the direction of favoring this requirement, with 56% saying all Americans should be required to have health insurance; 42% disagree. Politically, 72% of Democrats favor mandatory health insurance, compared with 34% of Republicans.

Do you think all Americans should be required to have health insurance, or not?

■ % Should be required   ▨ % Should not

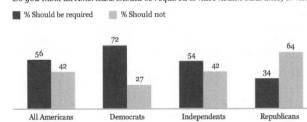

USA Today/Gallup poll, July 10-12, 2009

3. Paying for Reform

Perhaps the biggest obstacle to healthcare reform will be its high price tag, which some have estimated to be $1 trillion over 10 years.

When asked about six proposals being considered as possible ways to pay for the plan, Americans are most likely to favor a fine on employers who do not offer health insurance to their employees, and increasing income taxes on upper-income Americans.

The public shows more support than opposition for a new tax on soft drinks high in sugar, and reductions in the income-tax deductions upper-income Americans can take for home mortgages and charitable contributions.

Americans oppose taxing employees if their health plan's benefits rise above a certain level, as well as cutting back on Medicare costs. Opposition to the latter may reflect a fear that Medicare services may be cut rather than just being part of a cost-saving effort.

Please tell me whether you strongly favor, somewhat favor, somewhat oppose, or strongly oppose each as a way to pay for healthcare reform.

	Total % favor	Total % oppose
Requiring employers to pay a fee if they do not provide health insurance for their employees	62	35
Increasing income taxes on upper-income Americans	58	39
Instituting a new tax on soft drinks that are high in sugar	52	46
Lowering the amount of money upper-income Americans can deduct for home mortgage interest and charitable contributions on their tax returns	50	43
Requiring employees to pay taxes on their healthcare benefits if they are above a certain level	43	53
Saving money by cutting back on Medicare costs	38	58

USA Today/Gallup poll, July 10-12, 2009

4. The Political Situation

Those, including President Obama, who want to see healthcare reform passed this year have the backing of most Americans, though at 56%, it is hardly an overwhelming majority. And that support could drop, depending on the final details of the plan.

When asked separately how important it is for Congress to pass major legislation this year, half of Americans say it is extremely (26%) or very important (24%) to them, but 47% do not assign a high degree of importance to it.

Thus, it is not clear how strong the public mandate is for healthcare reform this year.

Obama and congressional Democrats are clearly taking the lead in getting healthcare reform done, but when asked which of four groups they trust most on the issue, nearly half of Americans say doctors and hospitals while a third name Obama and the Democrats in Congress. Only small minorities say they trust the Republicans in Congress or insurance companies. These findings largely echo what Gallup found earlier.

When it comes to possible changes in the healthcare system, which of the following do you trust most -- [ROTATED: President Obama and the Democrats in Congress, the Republicans in Congress, doctors and hospitals, (or) insurance companies]?

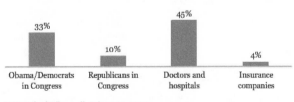

USA Today/Gallup poll, July 10-12, 2009

Implications

The Obama administration seems more likely to achieve major healthcare reform than did Bill Clinton, in part because some of the major interest groups that opposed reform in the 1990s are on board this time. However, Congress still has much work to do to pass reform, and it is not clear whether the final bill will have enough support to become law after the details are ironed out.

The poll finds that Americans think it is very important to have a wide choice of doctors, treatment options, and health plans, but also want to keep insurance affordable and guarantee access to it regardless of job or medical status. They favor many of the proposals being offered to help pay for reform, but not necessarily by very large majorities.

Survey Methods

Results are based on telephone interviews with 3,026 national adults, aged 18 and older, conducted July 10–12, 2009. For results based on the total sample of national adults, one can say with 95% confidence that the maximum margin of sampling error is ±2 percentage points.

Most questions were asked of a randomly selected half sample of 1,518 national adults, and have a maximum margin of sampling error of ±3 percentage points.

Interviews are conducted with respondents on land-line telephones (for respondents with a land-line telephone) and cellular phones (for respondents who are cell-phone only).

In addition to sampling error, question wording and practical difficulties in conducting surveys can introduce error or bias into the findings of public opinion polls.

July 15, 2009
UNEMPLOYMENT REMAINS PRESSING ISSUE FOR AMERICANS
More see it as the country's "most important problem"; healthcare also edges higher

by Lymari Morales, Gallup Poll Staff Writer

U.S. President Barack Obama may have sensed Americans' growing anxiety about unemployment in warning Tuesday that he expects the jobless rate to continue to increase over the next several months. Two in 10 Americans (19%) this month name unemployment/jobs as the country's most important problem—up from 14% last month and nearing the recent high point of 20% recorded in February.

What do you think is the most important problem facing this country today?
2008-2009 trend

% Mentioning unemployment/jobs

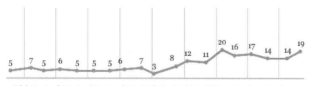

Mentions of unemployment/jobs as the country's most important problem edged lower in the months after Obama in February signed the $787 billion economic stimulus package into law, but this month's finding erases those gains. The U.S. government recently

reported a June unemployment rate of 9.5%, and Obama says he expects to see that number soon climb to the double-digit threshold of 10%. A different Gallup Poll conducted in late June found 87% of Americans saying they were worried about the rising unemployment rate, more than were worried about any other issue tested.

Americans' mentions of unemployment/jobs as the country's most important problem have yet to reach the levels found in the aftermath of recent recessions. In the early '90s, 27% of Americans at one point named unemployment/jobs as the most important problem, and that number hit 53% during a period of double-digit unemployment in 1983. Also, once in 2004, a statistically similar 20% named unemployment/jobs as the most important problem facing the country.

What do you think is the most important problem facing this country today?
1979-2009 trend

% Mentioning unemployment/jobs

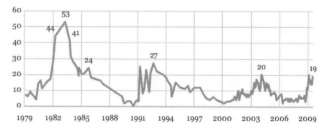

Currently, 69% of Americans volunteer something about the economy when asked, in an open-ended fashion, to name the most important problem facing the country. This is up from 65% a month ago and 61% last July. During the same period, the percentage naming unemployment/jobs as the most important problem has quadrupled, from 5% in July 2008 to 19% now.

United States' Most Important Problem -- Economic Mentions

		One month ago	One year ago
	Jul 10-12, 2009	Jun 14-17, 2009	Jul 10-13, 2008
	%	%	%
NET ECONOMIC MENTIONS^	69	65	61
Economy in general	38	41	35
Unemployment/Jobs	19	14	5
Lack of money	7	6	--
Federal budget deficit/Federal debt	4	5	2
Recession	3	2	1

^ "Net economic mentions" is percentage of Americans naming at least one economic issue

Job loss is hitting close to home for the 26% of working Americans who last week reported in Gallup Poll Daily tracking that their own employers were letting employees go, compared to 25% who said their employers were hiring, and 42% who said the size of their workforces were neither growing nor contracting. Underscoring the extent to which Americans are not personally seeing much improvement in the jobs situation, the monthly figures for June 2009 and January 2009 on this question are identical—with 26% of working Americans saying their employers were letting employees go, versus 23% who said their employers were hiring.

The July Gallup Poll also finds that the vast majority of Americans (87%) say now is a bad time to find a quality job, versus 11%

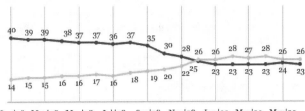

Employees' Reports of Their Own Companies Hiring/Letting Go

Based on monthly averages from Gallup Poll Daily tracking

■ % Hiring   ▨ % Letting people go

40 39 39 38 37 37 36 37 35 30 28 26 26 28 27 28 26 26

14 15 15 16 16 17 16 18 19 20 22 25 23 23 23 23 24 23

Jan '08 Mar '08 May '08 Jul '08 Sep '08 Nov '08 Jan '09 Mar '09 May '09

United States' Most Important Problem -- Non-Economic Mentions

| | One month ago | One year ago |
	July 10-12, 2009	June 14-17, 2009	July 10-13, 2008
	%	%	
NET NON-ECONOMIC MENTIONS ^	45	48	55
Poor healthcare/hospitals; high cost of healthcare	16	14	6
Dissatisfaction with government/ Congress/politicians; poor leadership; corruption; abuse of power	8	6	9
Situation in Iraq/War	5	7	18
Ethics/Moral/Religious/Family decline; dishonesty	2	4	6
National security	2	2	1
Education/Poor education/Access to education	2	1	3
Terrorism	2	1	2
Environment/Pollution	2	*	2

^ "Net non-economic mentions" is percentage of Americans naming at least one non-economic issue
* Less than 0.5%

who say it is a good time. This is in the middle of the narrow range Gallup has recorded since last October (82% to 90% bad time; 9% to 14% good time). The 90% who in February and March said it was a bad time to find a quality job are the highs for this measure since Gallup began asking the question in 2001, but are just a few points higher than the current reading.

Healthcare Edges Up Amid Legislative Debate

After the economy in general and unemployment/jobs, Americans today most often name healthcare as the most important problem facing the country—16% mention this, up from 14% in June and 6% a year ago. This is the most concern Americans have expressed about healthcare since 1993 and 1994—when the Clinton administration made its attempt at healthcare reform, just as the Obama administration is doing now. It is likely that the extensive coverage of the healthcare issue is playing a role in increasing its top-of-mind salience for Americans as a top problem facing the country.

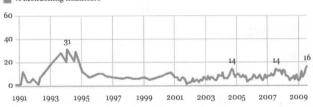

What do you think is the most important problem facing this country today?
Recent trend

■ % Mentioning healthcare

31

14 14 16

1991 1993 1995 1997 1999 2001 2003 2005 2007 2009

Healthcare now easily surpasses all non-economic issues mentioned, even tripling the situation in Iraq—which was considered the country's most important problem from April 2004 until the economy surpassed it in February 2008.

Implications

The steady climb in the nation's unemployment rate in the months after the February passage of a $787 billion economic stimulus package is clearly registering with Americans. Americans are now nearly as likely as they were before the passage of that bill to name unemployment/jobs as the most important problem facing the country. They are also almost as likely as they were before the bill's passage to say now is a bad time to find a quality job.

The slight easing in worry about unemployment from February until June suggests that Americans initially had some confidence in the Obama administration's claim that the stimulus would create enough jobs to keep the unemployment rate below 8%. But the increase in mentions of unemployment/jobs this month suggests more Americans may be beginning to doubt that claim. While President Obama and his economic advisers say the stimulus is on track and that an additional package isn't necessary at this point, unemployment clearly remains a pressing issue for Americans, and a further rise in the unemployment rate could trigger views even more negative than those recorded prior to the stimulus bill's passage. Without measurable improvement in economic attitudes, it is difficult to expect consumer behavior to change for the better, and thus the jobs situation continues to create a significant obstacle to true economic recovery.

Survey Methods

Results are based on telephone interviews with 1,018 national adults, aged 18 and older, conducted June 10–12, 2009. For results based on the total sample of national adults, one can say with 95% confidence that the maximum margin of sampling error is ±3 percentage points.

Interviews are conducted with respondents on land-line telephones (for respondents with a land-line telephone) and cellular phones (for respondents who are cell-phone only).

In addition to sampling error, question wording and practical difficulties in conducting surveys can introduce error or bias into the findings of public opinion polls.

July 15, 2009
OBAMA PRAISED FOR EFFORT, KNOCKED FOR SPENDING
Americans explain why they approve or disapprove of president's performance

by Lydia Saad, Gallup Poll Senior Editor

Americans who approve of the job President Barack Obama is doing largely cite his leadership in attempting to solve the nation's problems as the reason for conferring their approval. This accounts for 54% of his supporters. By contrast, nearly two-thirds of those who disapprove of Obama's job performance mention policy areas where they disagree with the president.

Reasons for Approving or Disapproving of Job Obama Is Doing as President

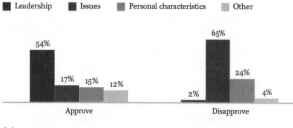

July 10-12, 2009

Reasons for Approval

In the Gallup Poll conducted this past weekend, July 10–12, 58% of Americans said they approve of the overall job Obama is doing, while 36% disapprove.

Thirty-one percent of Obama's approvers say they approve because he is doing a good job or "the best he can under difficult circumstances"; 15% say he is trying new things; and 8% credit him for taking on numerous issues. Thus, a combined 54% cite some aspect of the president's leadership in solving the nation's problems.

Beyond those giving the new president an A for effort, 17% credit him on specific issues. Seven percent of Obama's approvers cite improvements to the economy as the reason they applaud him, 6% say they agree with Obama's policy stances and programs, and 4% cite Obama's diplomacy and success in changing views of the United States around the world.

Most of the remaining praise Obama receives from his backers has to do with his personal characteristics or style: 5% say he is straightforward with people, 5% call him intelligent or smart, 3% say he keeps his promises, and 2% consider him honest. Another 5% are satisfied merely by their perception that Obama is "better than George W. Bush."

Why do you approve of the way Obama is handling his job as president?

Response category	%
Doing a good job/best he can under difficult circumstances	31
Trying new, different things/Changing things	15
Active/Taking on many issues	8
TOTAL LEADERSHIP	54
Economy is getting better/Fixing the economy	7
Agree with his policies/actions	6
More diplomatic/Changing views of U.S. around the world	4
TOTAL ISSUES	17
Transparent/Straightforward with the people	5
Intelligent/Smart	5
Keeping his promises	3
Honest/Has integrity	2
TOTAL PERSONAL CHARACTERISTICS	15
Hasn't messed up yet	5
Better than George W. Bush	5
Other	2
TOTAL OTHER	12
None	1
No opinion	5

July 10-12, 2009
Based on 556 national adults who approve; ±5 percentage points

Members of the smaller group of Americans who disapprove of Obama's job performance are most likely to attribute their views to the president's policies. Just over half of the combined 65% mentions in this category involve government spending: 24% say they disapprove because Obama is spending too much government money, 10% say it's because the economic stimulus plan is not working or wasteful and 4% say it's because Obama is borrowing too much.

Another major policy criticism of Obama—mentioned by 15% of those who disapprove of his job performance—is that the recent government bailouts and takeovers of private industry that Obama has sponsored are leading the nation toward socialism.

There are two significant knocks on Obama on a personal level. One, expressed by 14% of those disapproving of his job performance, is that he is inexperienced or "doesn't know what he is doing." Additionally, 10% say something along the lines that he is "all talk and no action," or "doesn't keep his promises." Only 2% of his detractors say he is doing too much.

Why do you disapprove of the way Obama is handling his job as president?

Response category	%
Spending too much	24
Leading nation toward socialism/Government takeovers/Bailouts	15
Economic stimulus plan not working, wasteful	10
Disagree with his policies	7
Borrowing too much	4
Military issues	2
Abortion issues	2
Plans for national healthcare	1
TOTAL ISSUES	65
Inexperienced/Doesn't know what he is doing	14
Doesn't keep his promises/Cannot trust/All talk and no action	10
TOTAL PERSONAL CHARACTERISTICS	24
Trying to do too much	2
TOTAL LEADERSHIP	2
Respondent is a Republican	3
Other	1
TOTAL OTHER	4
None	2
No opinion	3

July 10-12, 2009
Based on 403 national adults who disapprove; ±5 percentage points

Bottom Line

Praise for the job Obama is doing centers on his attentiveness to the country's problems, and includes a dose of admiration for his personal characteristics and style. Although positive, these assessments are relatively soft in contrast with the mainly policy-related criticisms of Obama from his detractors, largely centered on government spending and power.

Only six months into the job, it is natural that the president has little in the way of specific accomplishments driving his approval rating. Thus, at this early juncture, his supporters appear satisfied that Obama is on task. At the same time, the dramatic early steps Obama has taken to address the fragile economy—perhaps combined with the fact that these have yet to spark an economic recovery—have given his detractors a clear rallying point against him. The imbalance may be tenable for now, but a year from now, Obama may need more tangible economic or legislative achievements to sustain his majority approval ratings.

Survey Methods

Results are based on telephone interviews with 1,018 national adults, aged 18 and older, conducted July 10–12, 2009. For results based on the total sample of national adults, one can say with 95% confidence that the maximum margin of sampling error is ±3 percentage points.

Interviews are conducted with respondents on land-line telephones (for respondents with a land-line telephone) and cellular phones (for respondents who are cell-phone only).

In addition to sampling error, question wording and practical difficulties in conducting surveys can introduce error or bias into the findings of public opinion polls.

July 16, 2009

ROMNEY EDGES PALIN, HUCKABEE IN EARLY 2012 GOP TEST

Palin's favorable rating stable after announcement of her resignation

by Jeffrey M. Jones, Gallup Poll Managing Editor

About one in four Republicans and Republican-leaning independents make Mitt Romney their top choice for the 2012 Republican presidential nomination, giving him a slight edge over Sarah Palin and Mike Huckabee. Former House Speaker Newt Gingrich is the choice of 14% of Republicans, with much smaller numbers choosing current Govs. Tim Pawlenty of Minnesota and Haley Barbour of Mississippi.

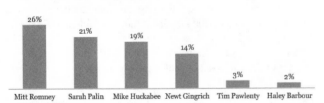

Candidate Most Likely to Support for the 2012 Republican Nomination for President
Based on Republicans and Republican-leaning independents

July 10-12, 2009

These results are based on a July 10–12 Gallup Poll, which asked Republicans to choose which of six possible candidates for the Republican presidential nomination they would be most likely to support in 2012.

As of this moment, Romney, one of John McCain's chief rivals for the 2008 Republican presidential nomination, holds a slight but not statistically significant 26% to 21% advantage over Palin, who was McCain's vice presidential running mate.

Palin's strong showing suggests she remains a contender for GOP front-runner status even after her surprising decision to resign as governor of Alaska, which she announced July 3. Some have speculated that she made that decision with an eye toward running for president in 2012.

Favorable Ratings of Leading Contenders

While Palin trails Romney in the current candidate preference test, she leads both him and Huckabee in terms of their respective favorable ratings among Republicans. Currently, 72% of Republicans and Republican-leaning independents have a favorable opinion of Palin, compared with 56% for Romney and 59% for Huckabee. But her lead on this measure largely reflects the fact that she is better known than the two former governors, given the substantially lower "no opinion" figures for her. Republicans rate each candidate more positively than negatively by better than 3-to-1 ratios.

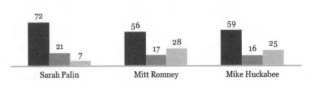

Favorable Ratings of Leading 2012 Republican Presidential Contenders
Based on Republicans and Republican-leaning independents

July 10-12, 2009

However, Huckabee's numbers among all Americans look better by comparison. Although each GOP contender receives a similar favorable rating from the American public—43% for Palin, 37% for Romney, and 42% for Huckabee—Huckabee's negatives are lower. As a result, his +19 net favorable score is much better than Romney's +8 and Palin's -2.

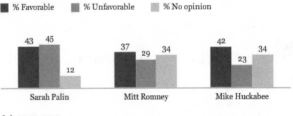

Favorable Ratings of Leading 2012 Republican Presidential Contenders
Based on all Americans

July 10-12, 2009

Palin's favorable rating is little changed from last November, immediately after the 2008 election. At that time, 48% viewed her favorably and 47% unfavorably. This suggests no widespread deterioration in her image after her surprising decision to resign her post as governor with more than a year left in her term.

Still, her image has suffered somewhat among Republicans during this time. In November, 81% of Republicans viewed her favorably and 14% unfavorably, compared with the current ratings of 72% favorable and 21% unfavorable after her announced resignation.

Implications

Presidential nomination preference polls conducted roughly three years before the party's nominating convention in general would not be expected to predict the eventual nominee. At this stage, these polls to a large degree reflect respondents' familiarity with the possible contenders. For example, Rudy Giuliani led most

GOP preference polls in 2007, but performed dismally in the actual primaries and caucuses.

However, these early polls do give an indication of who the likely front-runners will be heading into the campaign, which should kick off after the 2010 November midterm elections. They also provide insights into the implications of Palin's highly publicized decision to leave her job as governor of Alaska in the middle of her term. And, the Giuliani example notwithstanding, early front-runner status in Republican nomination contests is important, because historically, that person usually has won the nomination.

To the extent Palin, Romney, and Huckabee can capitalize on their higher name recognition than that of their possible challengers to raise money and build strong campaign organizations, they will be formidable contenders should they decide to pursue the 2012 Republican presidential nomination.

Survey Methods

Results are based on telephone interviews with 1,018 national adults, aged 18 and older, conducted July 10–12, 2009. For results based on the total sample of national adults, one can say with 95% confidence that the maximum margin of sampling error is ±3 percentage points.

For results based on the sample of 455 Republicans and Republican-leaning independents, the maximum margin of sampling error is ±5 percentage points.

Interviews are conducted with respondents on land-line telephones (for respondents with a land-line telephone) and cellular phones (for respondents who are cell-phone only).

In addition to sampling error, question wording and practical difficulties in conducting surveys can introduce error or bias into the findings of public opinion polls.

July 16, 2009
AMERICANS UPBEAT ON PROGRESS IN IRAQ, AFGHANISTAN
Majority (58%) say going into Iraq was a mistake; 36% say so about Afghanistan

by Frank Newport, Gallup Poll Editor in Chief

Americans remain much more likely to say U.S. involvement in Iraq was a mistake than to say the same about Afghanistan, despite the fact that Americans are more likely now than at any point since 2003 to say things are going well for the U.S. in Iraq.

Perceptions of U.S. Involvement in Iraq and Afghanistan, and How Things Are Going

	U.S. involvement in Iraq a mistake	U.S. involvement in Afghanistan a mistake	Things going well for U.S. in Iraq	Things going well for U.S. in Afghanistan
July 10-12, 2009	58%	36%	56%	54%

Fifty-eight percent of Americans say U.S. involvement in Iraq was a mistake, contrasted with 36% who say involvement in Afghanistan was a mistake. Americans' views of the way things are going in each war are roughly the same—56% say Iraq is going well for the U.S., while 54% say this about Afghanistan.

Since March 2003, Gallup has asked Americans on 79 different occasions whether the United States made a mistake in sending troops to Iraq, compared to having asked the same question about Afghanistan only nine times since November 2001. This relative emphasis on measuring public opinion about Iraq versus Afghanistan reflects the fact that Iraq dominated news coverage and political debate in the years after the initial invasion in March 2003, consigning Afghanistan until more recently to a status as the "other" or forgotten war.

The initial reaction to the Iraq war was very positive. Less than half of Americans said the war was a mistake for the first year and a quarter of U.S. involvement there. But by July 2004, perceptions had changed to the point where a majority said the war was a mistake. That percentage fell back under 50% in the months leading up to the 2004 presidential election and after President Bush was inaugurated for his second term. Beginning in late summer 2005, however, with only a few exceptions, a majority of Americans have said the Iraq war was a mistake in every survey until now. The high point for the perception that the war was a mistake, 63%, came in April 2008. The current 58% is roughly on par with measures over the last year.

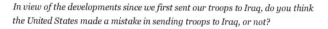
In view of the developments since we first sent our troops to Iraq, do you think the United States made a mistake in sending troops to Iraq, or not?

% Yes, a mistake

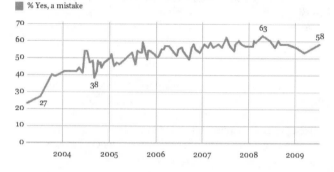

In Gallup's initial 2001 poll about Afghanistan, shortly after the U.S. invasion, and in the poll that followed in January 2002, a very small minority of 9% and 6% of Americans, respectively, said U.S. involvement in that country was a mistake. That number climbed to 25% in the summer of 2004 (at about the same time that a majority were saying the Iraq war was a mistake), and reached a high of 42% in March of this year. In the most recent poll, the "mistake" percentage for Afghanistan has settled back to 36%.

Thinking now about U.S. military action in Afghanistan that began in October 2001, do you think the United States made a mistake in sending military forces to Afghanistan, or not?

% Yes, a mistake

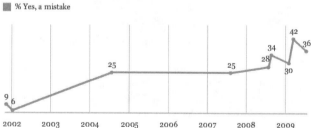

Perceptions of progress in Iraq have varied over the years.

Americans were initially very positive about the Iraq war. That optimism began to fade fast. By September 2003, less than half were willing to say things were going well in Iraq. The "going well" number popped back up to 55% in March 2004, and then was above 50% again in February and March 2005.

After that, however, perceptions that things were going well in Iraq fell back, reaching the all-time low of 28% in January 2007. More recently, in polls conducted last September and in March of this year, as well as in the current July 2009 poll, majorities have returned to the viewpoint that things are going well in Iraq. The current 56% "going well" percentage is as high as Gallup has measured vis-à-vis Iraq since July 2003, just months after the war began.

In general, how would you say things are going for the U.S. in Iraq -- very well, moderately well, moderately badly, (or) very badly?

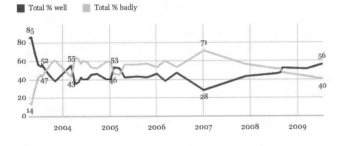

Gallup did not ask Americans about progress in Afghanistan using this question format in the first months of the involvement there, and has asked the question only sporadically since September 2006.

Almost half of Americans said things were going well for the U.S. in Afghanistan in that initial 2006 poll, but these positive perceptions began to slip, reaching a low of 38% in a survey conducted in March of this year. In the current poll, views of the situation in Afghanistan have rebounded to 54%, the highest in Gallup's limited record.

How would you say things are going for the U.S. in Afghanistan -- very well, moderately well, moderately badly, (or) very badly?

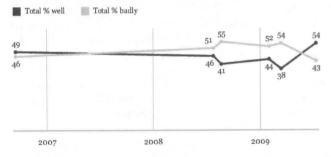

Views of the wars in Iraq and Afghanistan vary by partisan orientation, as would be expected for two wars begun in the Republican administration of George W. Bush.

Although all three partisan groups are less likely to view U.S. involvement in Afghanistan as a mistake than is the case for Iraq, major differences exist in the views of the three partisan groups for both wars. There is a 52-point gap between Republicans and Democrats in the mistake percentage for Iraq, and a 43-point gap between the same two groups in the mistake percentage for Afghanistan.

Implications

American public opinion about U.S. involvement in the two wars in Iraq and Afghanistan reveals important and lasting distinctions.

Views of Wars in Iraq and Afghanistan, by Party ID

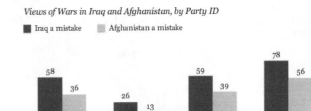

Gallup Poll, July 10-12, 2009

Americans have been more positive about the rationale for U.S. involvement in Afghanistan than for Iraq over the years, a distinction that persists to this day. A clear majority of Americans continue to say U.S. involvement in Iraq was a mistake, while a little more than a third say the same about Afghanistan.

These perceptual differences regarding the rationale for U.S. involvement in the two wars persist even though at this point, Americans are no more likely to say things are going well for the U.S. in Afghanistan than in Iraq. In fact, the 56% who say the war is going well in Iraq is the highest since July 2003, just a few months after Bush's famous "mission accomplished" speech. It is probable that this uptick in the public's views that things are going well in Iraq is related to the fact that the U.S. has withdrawn troops from major cities there and plans to withdraw most of its combat troops from the country by the end of 2011. Still, these more upbeat views have not materially altered Americans' negative views of the underlying rationale for the war.

At the same time, the U.S. has been ramping up its involvement in Afghanistan, and that has been accompanied by an increase in the percentage saying things are going well for the U.S. there. In the case of Afghanistan, in contrast to the situation in Iraq, the upbeat views of how things are going have been accompanied by a more upbeat view of the initial rationale for U.S. involvement.

All in all, the data suggest that in the long term, even after full U.S. withdrawal of combat troops from Iraq, there is a good chance that a majority of Americans will remain doubtful that involvement in that country was worth it. At the same time, it appears that even with continuing U.S. involvement in the Afghanistan situation, Americans may well remain much more positive about the rationale for the United States' going to war there.

Survey Methods

Results are based on telephone interviews with 1,018 national adults, aged 18 and older, conducted July 10–12, 2009. For results based on the total sample of national adults, one can say with 95% confidence that the maximum margin of sampling error is ±3 percentage points.

Interviews are conducted with respondents on land-line telephones (for respondents with a land-line telephone) and cellular phones (for respondents who are cell-phone only).

In addition to sampling error, question wording and practical difficulties in conducting surveys can introduce error or bias into the findings of public opinion polls.

July 17, 2009

PELOSI'S IMAGE STILL NEGATIVE, BOEHNER NOT WIDELY KNOWN

By 48% to 32%, more Americans view Pelosi unfavorably than favorably

by Lydia Saad, Gallup Poll Senior Editor

As the 111th Congress nears its August recess, Americans continue to view Democratic House Speaker Nancy Pelosi more unfavorably than favorably, 48% vs. 32%. House Republican Leader John Boehner's ratings are equally positive and negative; however, the majority of Americans have either not heard of him or don't know enough about the 10-term Republican congressman and two-term House GOP leader to rate him.

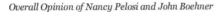

Overall Opinion of Nancy Pelosi and John Boehner

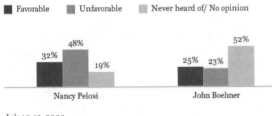

July 10-12, 2009

Pelosi's image in the latest Gallup Poll, conducted July 10–12, is little different from her image in May, when 34% of Americans viewed her favorably and 50% unfavorably. Pelosi's ratings turned more negative than positive between November 2008 and May 2009, spanning the controversy over what she knew and when she knew it regarding the CIA's use of water-boarding as a coercive interrogation technique. Even though that controversy has died down, her image has not recovered to date.

Overall Opinion of Speaker of the House, Nancy Pelosi

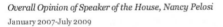
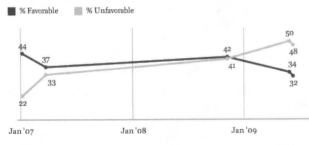

As seen in May, a bare majority of Democrats view Pelosi favorably, but Republicans as well as independents have mostly unfavorable views. In May, Gallup reported that the decline in Pelosi's ratings seen at that point was the result of lower favorability from Republicans and independents, with little change in Democrats' views. Since then, Republican favorability toward Pelosi has increased slightly, from 9% in May to 14% today, while the percentage of Democrats viewing her favorably has declined from 62% to 55%, its lowest point since she ascended to the speakership.

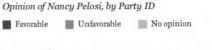

Opinion of Nancy Pelosi, by Party ID

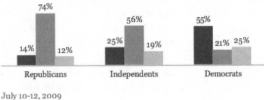

July 10-12, 2009

Views of Boehner

Boehner is not a familiar name to a majority of Democrats and independents, and he is largely unknown to nearly half of Republicans. Naturally, his image, among those who can rate him, is more favorable than unfavorable among Republicans and tilts negative among Democrats. In contrast to Pelosi's mostly negative ratings from independents, Boehner's ratings from this group are about equally balanced.

These ratings of Boehner are the first Gallup has obtained on the Ohio lawmaker.

Opinion of John Boehner, by Party ID

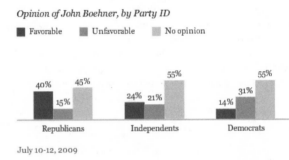

July 10-12, 2009

The high proportion of Americans who have no opinion of Boehner—52% overall—may reflect his mere two-plus years as the top-ranking Republican in the U.S. House, since his election to the leadership post after the 2006 elections. While Pelosi was chosen as House Speaker the same year—making her second in the line of succession to the president—she had previously served as House Democratic leader from 2003 through 2006, thus giving her a four-year advantage over Boehner on the national stage.

Bottom Line

At a time when Congress holds the power to pass landmark legislation in healthcare and energy and is considering additional economic stimulus spending that could affect the country for generations to come, Americans have less than full confidence in two of its leading power players. Pelosi's image is damaged to the point that just a third of Americans view her favorably and nearly half unfavorably. And while Americans are at least familiar with Pelosi, Boehner is an unknown commodity to nearly half the country, leaving only a quarter who view him favorably.

Survey Methods

Results are based on telephone interviews with 1,018 national adults, aged 18 and older, conducted July 10–12, 2009. For results based on

the total sample of national adults, one can say with 95% confidence that the maximum margin of sampling error is ±3 percentage points.

Interviews are conducted with respondents on land-line telephones (for respondents with a land-line telephone) and cellular phones (for respondents who are cell-phone only).

In addition to sampling error, question wording and practical difficulties in conducting surveys can introduce error or bias into the findings of public opinion polls.

July 17, 2009
MAJORITY OF AMERICANS SAY SPACE PROGRAM COSTS JUSTIFIED
Percentage has grown since 1979

by Jeffrey M. Jones, Gallup Poll Managing Editor

On the eve of the 40th anniversary of the U.S. moon landing, a majority of Americans say the space program has brought enough benefits to justify its costs. The percentage holding this view is now at 58% and has increased over time.

It is now 40 years since the United States first landed men on the moon. Do you think the space program has brought enough benefits to this country to justify its costs, or don't you think so?

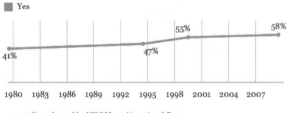

1979 poll conducted by NBC News/Associated Press

Notably, those old enough to remember the historic moon landing are actually somewhat less likely than those who are younger to think the space program's costs are justified. Among Americans aged 50 and older (who were at least 10 years old when the moon landing occurred), 54% think the space program's benefits justify its costs, compared with 63% of those aged 18–49.

It is now 40 years since the United States first landed men on the moon. Do you think the space program has brought enough benefits to this country to justify its costs, or don't you think so?
By age

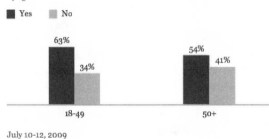

July 10-12, 2009

The July 10–12 Gallup Poll also finds that most Americans continue to express support for the current level of funding for NASA (46%) or an expansion of it (14%). But the 60% holding these views is on the low end of what Gallup has measured since 1984, when the question was first asked.

Do you think spending on the U.S. space program should be increased, kept at the present level, reduced, or ended altogether?

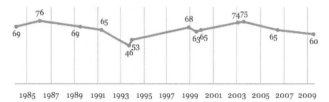

The two lowest readings of 46% and 53% were found in a pair of 1993 polls. In 1993, as now, Americans had highly negative evaluations of the economy, and the results suggest that when Americans have a negative outlook on the economy, they are apparently less willing to spend money for space exploration. In addition to a struggling economy, the lower 1993 NASA ratings are due to a number of problems that plagued the agency, including losing contact with the Mars Observer and several last-minute cancellations of planned space shuttle missions.

The high point in support for current or larger funding levels for NASA was 76% in January 1986, immediately after the space shuttle Challenger disaster.

NASA Gets Favorable Performance Review

Fifty-eight percent of Americans say NASA is doing an excellent (13%) or good (45%) job. The agency's ratings have been stable over the last several years. The high point was 76% in late 1998 after 1960s astronaut John Glenn made a return trip to space, and the low point was in September 1993.

How would you rate the job being done by NASA -- the U.S. space agency? Would you say it is doing an excellent, good, only fair, or poor job?

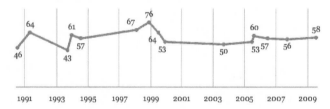

Ratings of NASA vary by education. Sixty-three percent of college graduates say NASA is doing an excellent or good job, compared with 55% of Americans without a college degree.

The educational differences are even greater in opinions on space program spending, with more than 7 in 10 college graduates saying the space program's benefits justify its costs and that NASA spending should be kept the same or increased. Only a slim majority of college non-graduates share these views.

Opinions on NASA/Space Program, by Educational Attainment

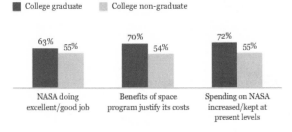

Self-Reports of Long-Term Changes in Spending

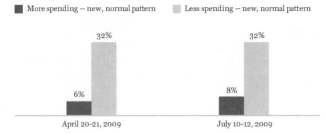

Bottom Line

Americans remain broadly supportive of space exploration and government funding of it. In fact, Americans are somewhat more likely to believe the benefits of the space program justify its costs at the 40th anniversary of the moon landing than they were at the 10th, 25th, and 30th anniversaries.

Although support for keeping NASA funding at its present level or increasing it is lower now than it has been in the past, the fact that 6 in 10 Americans hold this view in the midst of a recession suggests the public is firmly committed to the space program.

Survey Methods

Results are based on telephone interviews with 1,018 national adults, aged 18 and older, conducted July 10–12, 2009. For results based on the total sample of national adults, one can say with 95% confidence that the maximum margin of sampling error is ±3 percentage points.

Interviews are conducted with respondents on land-line telephones (for respondents with a land-line telephone) and cellular phones (for respondents who are cell-phone only).

In addition to sampling error, question wording and practical difficulties in conducting surveys can introduce error or bias into the findings of public opinion polls.

July 20, 2009
IN U.S., ONE-THIRD STILL SET ON SPENDING LESS AS NEW NORMAL
Americans' future spending trends show little significant change from April

by Frank Newport, Gallup Poll Editor in Chief

A new Gallup Poll shows 32% of Americans reporting that their recently depressed spending habits will become a "new normal" in the years ahead. These Americans say they have been spending less and plan on continuing that pattern in the future. Eight percent say their new normal will be spending more in the years ahead.

These results are little changed from April, when Gallup first asked these questions. This suggests there has been no further deterioration in Americans' projections of restrained future spending as the recession has worn on over the last two and a half months, but of course no major shift in the other direction, either. The impact of these results on the future of the U.S. consumer economy is a matter of interpretation. Clearly there will be at least some negative reper-

cussions on consumer spending going forward. But at the same time, two-thirds of Americans say that they have not changed their spending habits, that their spending changes in recent months will not be permanent in the years ahead, or that they will actually be spending more. The precise real-world impact of Americans' stated intentions to decrease their spending also depends on how much these individuals were going to spend in the first place. The economy would be affected more by a decrease in spending among previously high-rolling millionaires or affluent suburban families than it would be by a downward shift among the same number of low-income, low-spending senior citizens. There is no measure in the two Gallup surveys of the amount of money respondents typically spend or have spent in the past. There is also no indication of the exact dollar amount involved when survey respondents say they will spend "more" or spend "less." Still, a suggestion of the impact of changes in spending behavior is provided by analyzing the results within income groups. The accompanying table displays by income the percentage of those saying their new normal is to spend more or to spend less in the years ahead, based on a combined sample of those interviewed in Gallup's April and July surveys. While one might expect there to be differences in the impact of the recessionary economy across income groups, that is not the case. There is little substantive variation by income in the percentage saying their new normal is to spend less. Those with lower incomes are slightly more likely than higher-income Americans to say their new normal pattern is spending more, but not by much.

New Normal Spending Patterns, by Income

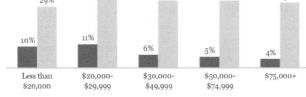

Aggregate of April 20-21 and July 10-12, 2009, polls

It can be assumed that those in the highest income groups on average spend the most money. Therefore it is perhaps good news that high-income Americans are not above the overall average in terms of saying their new normal is to spend less, assuming that such behavior would have a heightened impact on the economy as income increases. All in all, the results of the April and the July Gallup surveys are consistent in indicating that about a third of Americans, across the income spectrum, say they will spend less in the years ahead—presumably regardless of improvements in the economy. That "spend less" new normal is slightly counterbalanced by the 6% to 8% in the two surveys who say their new normal will be to spend more.

One in Four Americans Say Saving More Is New Normal

The July data on Americans' changes in saving patterns more or less reconfirm Gallup's April report, which concluded that the implications of these changes were "mixed."

Self-Reports of Long-Term Changes in Saving

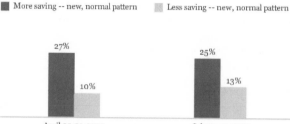

There has been little change between the April and July surveys. In both, about a quarter of Americans say they have recently been saving more, and that this will become their new, normal pattern in the years ahead. Between 10% and 13% say they have been saving less, and that this will be their new normal. This presumably suggests some harm, albeit modest, to consumer spending in the long run if these projections hold and Americans in fact do save more. (Of course, some observers conclude that saving more would be a positive for American families—despite the possible deleterious effect on retailers.)The data on saving across income groups show more variation than was the case for spending.

New Normal Saving Patterns, by Income

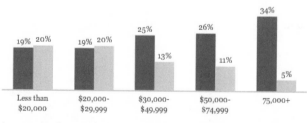

Aggregate of April 20-21 and July 10-12, 2009, polls

It is clear that higher-income Americans are most likely to say that their new, normal pattern is to save more in the years ahead. And, there is a comparative tendency for those with lower incomes to say their new, normal pattern is to save less in the years ahead. These patterns are not unexpected. Lower-income Americans have less discretionary income. They may not save much to begin with and/or don't have enough income to even consider the possibility of saving more in reaction to a recession. The fact that they are slightly more likely to say they will be saving less suggests a tendency to worry about being able to put money away in the future.

Implications

There have been no significant changes since April in the self-reported "new normal" spending and saving intentions of Americans when they are asked to look into their crystal balls and project into the future. About a third say they will spend less in the years ahead. About a quarter say they will save more. These self-reported intentions are counterbalanced to some degree by the finding that smaller percentages of Americans say they will actually spend more and, separately, will save less in the years ahead.As Gallup noted in April, when these self-assessments were first measured, it is difficult to know how firmly Americans will stick to their projections when the economy does pick up and unemployment drops. Good intentions to restrain spending and to save more could go out the window if the U.S. returns to flush and vibrant economic times. It is also difficult to measure the exact monetary implications of these future actions, given that an individual's claim that he or she is going to spend less could range from very modest cutbacks in the amount spent on lattes at Starbucks to wholesale cutbacks on purchases of new cars, major appliances, and vacation trips.Still, multiplied across tens of millions of American households, even a small reduction in spending, perhaps coupled with a small increase in saving, could have a major effect on the consumer economy in the years ahead. And these data suggest that if one takes Americans at their word, there will be at least some shift in the nation's economy to a "new normal" of more restrained consumer economic activity for some time to come.

Survey Methods

Results are based on telephone interviews with 1,018 national adults, aged 18 and older, conducted July 10–12, 2009. For results based on the total sample of national adults, one can say with 95% confidence that the maximum margin of sampling error is ±3 percentage points.

Interviews are conducted with respondents on land-line telephones (for respondents with a land-line telephone) and cellular phones (for respondents who are cell-phone only).

In addition to sampling error, question wording and practical difficulties in conducting surveys can introduce error or bias into the findings of public opinion polls.

July 20, 2009
OBAMA JOB APPROVAL TRENDS DOWNWARD IN SECOND QUARTER
Overall 62% second-quarter average compares favorably to immediate predecessors

by Jeffrey M. Jones, Gallup Poll Managing Editor

Barack Obama's second quarter as U.S. president, spanning April 20–July 19, began with some of the highest approval ratings of his presidency, but these slumped a bit near the end of the quarter, including a term-low 56% approval rating in July 5–7 polling. Overall, he averaged 62% approval for the quarter.

Obama's job approval rating generally exceeded the 62% quarterly average in April, May, and early June. This included 68% approval for April 30–May 2 polling, one point off Obama's 69% high. But since early June, with only a couple of exceptions, Obama's approval rating has been at or below 62%.

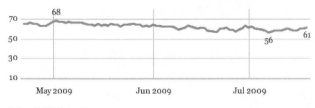

Gallup Daily: Barack Obama's Job Approval Ratings During His Second Quarter in Office

Gallup Poll Daily tracking

Specifically, from April 20 through June 8, Obama averaged 64% approval. Since then, his average is 59%. This recent decline probably reflects concern about increased government spending and involvement in the private sector, according to a recent Gallup survey that probed Americans for the reasons they approve or disapprove of Obama. Those who support him largely recognize his efforts toward addressing the problems facing the country.

Despite the ups and downs in Obama's second quarter, his overall average is little changed from the 63% average for his first quarter in office. And even though he has had numerous sub-60% individual ratings in June and July, all of these have still exceeded the historical average of 55% job approval for presidents from Truman through George W. Bush. On this basis, it can be argued that he is still in the honeymoon phase of his presidency.

Obama's 62% second-quarter average exceeds those for his immediate predecessors, George W. Bush (56%) and Bill Clinton (44%), but is similar to those for Presidents Nixon, Carter, Reagan, and the elder George Bush. Among presidents elected to their first terms since 1952, only Dwight Eisenhower (72%) and John Kennedy (76%) had second-quarter averages significantly better than Obama's.

Presidents' Second-Quarter Approval Averages

Presidents elected to their first terms

President	Second-quarter dates	Average	Number of measurements
Eisenhower	Apr 20-Jul 19, 1953	72%	2
Kennedy	Apr 20-Jul 19, 1961	76%	5
Nixon	Apr 20-Jul 19, 1969	62%	5
Carter	Apr 20-Jul 19, 1977	64%	6
Reagan	Apr 20-Jul 19, 1981	61%	5
G.H.W. Bush	Apr 20-Jul 19, 1989	64%	4
Clinton	Apr 20-Jul 19, 1993	44%	8
G.W. Bush	Apr 20-Jul 19, 2001	56%	9
Obama	Apr 20-Jul 19, 2009	62%	8

There has been no clear historical pattern as to whether presidents' approval ratings rise or fall in their third quarter in office. Eisenhower, Nixon, Carter, and Reagan saw their averages decline from the second to the third quarter. Kennedy's third-quarter average was essentially the same as his second-quarter average. But the elder and the younger Bush saw theirs increase. The elder Bush's apparently got an initial bounce after the Tiananmen Square incident in China in June 1989 but it remained high as Eastern European nations adopted political reforms and the U.S. economy remained strong during the third quarter. The younger Bush's soared after the Sept. 11, 2001, terrorist attacks. Clinton's average approval rating began to recover after bottoming out at 44% in his second quarter in office.

Obama's third quarter promises to be eventful, given his push for healthcare reform. While Congress has now drafted healthcare legislation, its passage is far from certain. Obama remains committed to reform, so its ultimate legislative success or failure could go a long way toward influencing how Americans evaluate him.

Survey Methods

Results are based on telephone interviews with 45,320 national adults, aged 18 and older, conducted April 20–July 19, 2009, as part of Gallup Poll Daily tracking. For results based on the total sample of national adults, one can say with 95% confidence that the maximum margin of sampling error is ±1 percentage point.

Interviews are conducted with respondents on land-line telephones (for respondents with a land-line telephone) and cellular phones (for respondents who are cell-phone only).

In addition to sampling error, question wording and practical difficulties in conducting surveys can introduce error or bias into the findings of public opinion polls.

July 21, 2009
MORE DISAPPROVE THAN APPROVE OF OBAMA ON HEALTHCARE
President is rated higher on international than on domestic issues

by Jeffrey M. Jones, Gallup Poll Senior Editor

As the debate over healthcare reform intensifies, the latest *USA Today*/Gallup poll finds that more Americans disapprove (50%) than approve (44%) of the way U.S. President Barack Obama is handling healthcare policy. There is a tremendous partisan gap in these views, with 74% of Democrats but only 11% of Republicans approving. Independents are more likely to disapprove than to approve of Obama's work on healthcare.

Do you approve or disapprove of the way Barack Obama is handling healthcare policy?

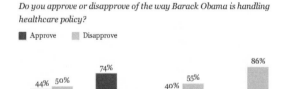

USA Today/Gallup poll, July 17-19, 2009

The president will attempt to regain the momentum in the healthcare reform debate, and perhaps to raise his standing on the issue, in a nationally televised press conference on Wednesday evening. He had set a deadline for Congress to pass reform legislation before its August recess, but that seems unlikely, and some in Congress are pushing for more time to consider legislation.

Obama's marks on healthcare are among the lowest of seven issues tested in the July 17–19 poll, better than only his rating for handling the federal budget deficit. He generally receives higher ratings on international issues than on domestic ones, with majority approval on all three matters relating to foreign policy. Americans are about equally divided on his handling of the economy, easily the top issue in the minds of the public.

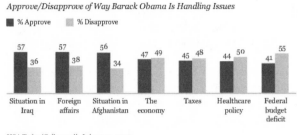

Approve/Disapprove of Way Barack Obama Is Handling Issues

USA Today/Gallup poll, July 17-19, 2009

Obama's ratings on the economy have declined over the course of the year, from 59% approval in February to 47% in the current poll. Most of this decline has occurred since late May, perhaps due to continued rising unemployment and some concern about the slow pace of spending from the economic stimulus package passed earlier this year.

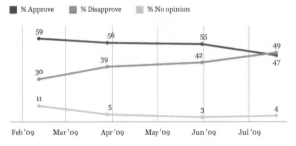

Approve/Disapprove of Way Barack Obama Is Handling the Economy

Obama's approval ratings for handling the federal budget deficit have also fallen in recent weeks, from 46% in late May to 41% in the current poll. Now, a majority of 55% of Americans disapprove of his handling of this issue.

Underscoring the deficit as an area of weakness for the president, a separate question in the poll finds 59% of Americans saying Obama's proposals to address the problems facing the country call for too much spending. Only 27% say he is spending the right amount to tackle the nation's problems.

While Obama's ratings for domestic issues are generally below the majority level and falling, his rating for handling foreign affairs (57%) is little changed since May, when 59% approved, and down only slightly from 61% in March. His disapproval rating on this issue has, however, climbed as the percentage having no opinion has dropped. But a majority of Americans continue to give him a favorable review for handling international matters.

Implications

Obama has decided to expend a significant amount of political capital to get healthcare reform passed, and its passage is far from certain. In a Monday television interview, he remarked that his lower approval ratings reflect that his administration is doing hard work. And while his ratings on healthcare and some other issues are generally weak, his overall approval ratings remain comfortably above the majority level—though they, too, are showing evidence of decline in recent weeks.

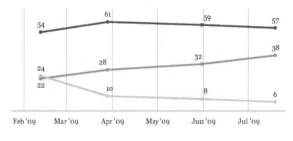

Approve/Disapprove of Way Barack Obama Is Handling Foreign Affairs

Survey Methods

Results are based on telephone interviews with 1,006 national adults, aged 18 and older, conducted July 17–19, 2009. For results based on the total sample of national adults, one can say with 95% confidence that the maximum margin of sampling error is ±4 percentage points.

Interviews are conducted with respondents on land-line telephones (for respondents with a land-line telephone) and cellular phones (for respondents who are cell-phone only).

In addition to sampling error, question wording and practical difficulties in conducting surveys can introduce error or bias into the findings of public opinion polls.

July 22, 2009
AMERICANS CONCERNED ABOUT GOVERNMENT SPENDING, EXPANSION
Large majorities of Republicans, independents say spending and expansion are "too much"

by Frank Newport, Gallup Poll Editor in Chief

Fueled by the sentiments of Republicans and independents, a new *USA Today*/Gallup poll shows that 59% of Americans say President Obama's proposals to address the major problems facing the country call for too much government spending, and 52% say Obama's proposals call for too much expansion of government power.

Impact of President Obama's Proposals to Address Major Problems

	Total sample	Republicans	Independents	Democrats
	%	%	%	%
Call for too much spending	59	90	66	28
Spending about right	27	5	21	50
Call for too little spending	11	4	10	17
Call for too much gov't expansion	52	83	60	17
About right	35	10	25	65
Call for too little gov't expansion	10	4	11	15

USA Today/Gallup poll, July 17-19, 2009

It is not surprising to find that Republicans are close to unanimity in their views on these issues, with 90% saying Obama's proposals involve too much spending and 83% saying they involve too much expansion of government power. Of more concern to the Obama administration, perhaps, is the finding that clear majorities of 66%

and 60% of independents, respectively, say Obama's proposals involve too much spending and too much government expansion.

Democrats are much more supportive of the administration, as would be expected. Still, a not-insignificant 28% believe that Obama's proposals call for too much spending, offset to a degree by the 17% who say Obama's proposals don't involve enough spending. By contrast, two-thirds of Democrats are satisfied that the expansion of government power that would result from Obama's proposals is about right.

One key point of discussion is whether the increases in government spending and the expansion of government power—even if distasteful to some—are necessary to meet today's recessionary economic environment. Germane to that discussion is the result of a separate question in the poll, which shows that two-thirds of Americans believe the challenges Obama faced when he became president are "more serious than the challenges other new presidents have faced."

Thinking now about the challenges Barack Obama faced when he became president, do you think these were -- [ROTATED: more serious, about the same, (or) less serious] -- than the challenges other new presidents have faced?

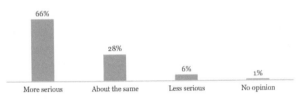

USA Today/Gallup poll, July 17-19, 2009

More than 8 out of 10 Democrats agree that Obama's challenges are more severe, along with two-thirds of independents. Republicans, as expected, are less likely to agree, but 44% say Obama's challenges are more serious, just about on par with the 45% of Republicans who say they are about the same as those of other recent presidents.

Gallup asked this same question in a more generic sense last October, in the midst of the presidential campaign between Obama and John McCain, and found a higher 84% of Americans saying the challenges facing the next president would be more serious than what other new presidents have faced.

For comparison (pre-election): Thinking now about the challenges facing the next president, do you think these will be -- [ROTATED: more serious, about the same, (or) less serious] -- than what other new presidents have faced?

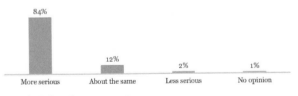

USA Today/Gallup poll, Oct 10-12, 2008

The comparison of the two results suggests that views of the severity of the problems facing Obama have softened, although this may be a reflection of the generic nature of the question last fall—asked about "the next president"—as opposed to the specific reference to Obama in the current version.

Implications

A good deal of Gallup data reinforce the idea that Americans are concerned about the long-term implications of increased levels of govern-

ment spending and the expansion of government's role in society that have become a part of the Obama administration's efforts to deal with the recession. Obama receives his lowest approval ratings (out of seven issues tested in the July 17–19 poll) on handling the federal budget deficit (41% approve; 55% disapprove). Thus, the finding that a majority of Americans are worried that Obama's proposals involve too much spending and too much big government are consistent with what would be expected—as are the very sharp partisan differences in these views.

The key for the Obama administration will be what happens as a result of the government spending and activity in the months ahead. If the economy picks up significantly within the next year and the unemployment rate drops, it will be easier for the administration to argue that its extreme measures have been worth it. If, however, the economy stays in the doldrums, then these data reinforce the conclusion that Obama's actions will provide potent fodder for critics to assail in forthcoming election campaigns.

Survey Methods

Results are based on telephone interviews with 1,006 national adults, aged 18 and older, conducted July 17–19, 2009. For results based on the total sample of national adults, one can say with 95% confidence that the maximum margin of sampling error is ±4 percentage points.

Interviews are conducted with respondents on land-line telephones (for respondents with a land-line telephone) and cellular phones (for respondents who are cell-phone only).

In addition to sampling error, question wording and practical difficulties in conducting surveys can introduce error or bias into the findings of public opinion polls.

July 22, 2009

ABOUT ONE IN SIX U.S. ADULTS ARE WITHOUT HEALTH INSURANCE

Highest uninsured rates among Hispanics, the young, and those with low incomes

by Frank Newport, Gallup Poll Editor in Chief and Elizabeth Mendes, Staff Writer

As congressional lawmakers debate healthcare reform legislation, partly aimed at expanding coverage to the uninsured, Gallup-Healthways Well-Being Index data for June reveal that 16.0% of American adults are currently without health insurance.

Do you have health insurance?
Among adults aged 18 and older

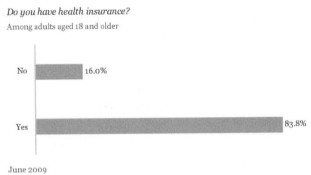

June 2009
Gallup-Healthways Well-Being Index

The June 2009 data encompass more than 29,000 daily tracking interviews of Americans aged 18 and older. Trend data show a small but measurable uptick in the percentage of uninsured adults over the last year and a half. The percentage uninsured averaged 14.8% among the approximately 350,000 adults interviewed in 2008, and rose to 16.2% among the 178,000 adults interviewed in the first six months of this year.

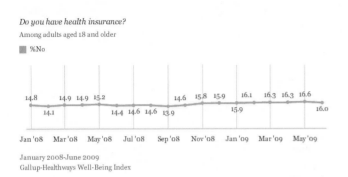

Do you have health insurance?
Among adults aged 18 and older

January 2008-June 2009
Gallup-Healthways Well-Being Index

In the months before November 2008, the percentage without health insurance ranged from a low of 13.9% to a high of 15.2%. From November 2008 through May 2009, Gallup found increases in the percentage of Americans reporting that they did not have coverage—with the percentage uninsured reaching a high of 16.6% in May, before dropping down to 16.0% in June.

The latest official estimate of healthcare coverage from the U.S. Census Bureau is for 2007, and reveals that 15.3% of all Americans (including children) are without insurance. This translates into the oft-cited figure of 46 million Americans without insurance. The Census figures show that those under 18 are more likely to be insured than those 18 and older, and extrapolations of the Census data suggest that the percentage of adults aged 18 and older without insurance in 2007 would be close to 17%. Given Gallup's estimate that the percentage uninsured has risen by about a percentage point in the first half of 2009 compared to 2008, it would not be surprising if the Census figures for 2009, when available, show an increase in the percentage who are uninsured compared to earlier years.

Demographics of the Uninsured

With an aggregated sample of more than 29,000 interviews in June, Gallup is able to report an up-to-date indication of segments of the adult population with the highest percentage uninsured. At 41.5%, Hispanic Americans are, by a significant margin, the demographic segment of the adult population most likely to be uninsured. Non-Hispanic black Americans are also significantly more likely than non-Hispanic white Americans to be uninsured, 19.9% vs. 11.6%. There is a strong relationship between age and income and health insurance coverage, with younger and low-income Americans significantly more likely to be uninsured than others. In fact, the two groups with the highest uninsured rates, other than Hispanics, are Americans who make less than $36,000 per year and those aged 18–29, with 28.6% and 27.6% uninsured, respectively.

Those aged 65 and older, and thus eligible for Medicare, are among the least likely to be uninsured, at 3.6%. High-income Americans, making $90,000 or more annually, also have high rates of health insurance coverage, with only 4.5% uninsured—far below the national average of 16.0%. In terms of region, those in the South and West are more likely than Americans in the East and Midwest to be uninsured.

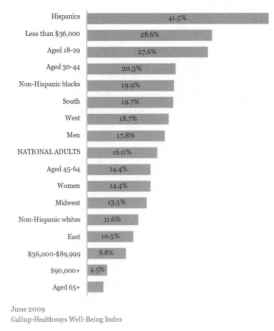

Percentage Uninsured Among Various Demographic Groups
Adults aged 18 and older

June 2009
Gallup-Healthways Well-Being Index

Bottom Line

The Gallup-Healthways Well-Being Index finds that while a large majority of Americans have health insurance, one in six in this country is without coverage. The current percentage of uninsured Americans (16.0%) represents a small, but measurable increase over last year. Hispanic Americans, at a rate approaching triple the national average, are the most likely subset of the population to be uninsured. Those making less than $36,000 per year are the second-most-likely group to be uninsured, with 18- to 29-year-olds following closely behind.

Survey Methods

For the Gallup-Healthways Well-Being Index, Gallup is interviewing no fewer than 1,000 U.S. adults nationwide each day. Monthly results comprise roughly 30,000 interviews. For results based on these samples, the maximum margin of sampling error is ±1 percentage point.

Interviews are conducted with respondents on land-line telephones (for respondents with a land-line telephone) and cellular phones (for respondents who are cell-phone only).

In addition to sampling error, question wording and practical difficulties in conducting surveys can introduce error or bias into the findings of public opinion polls.

July 23, 2009

AMERICANS TAKE LONGER-TERM VIEW ON STIMULUS, RECOVERY

Three in 10 now expect economic recovery to take five years or more

by Lymari Morales , Gallup Poll Staff Writer

Americans are more likely to say the Obama administration's economic stimulus plan has had no effect on the economy (49%) or their family's financial situation (64%) up to now than to say it has made either one better or worse.

Up until now, do you think Obama's economic stimulus plan has made _____ better, not had an effect, or made it worse?

■ Better ■ No effect ▨ Worse

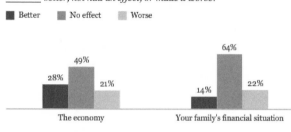

USA Today/Gallup poll, July 17-19, 2009

Nearly half of Americans (49%) say the stimulus plan passed earlier this year has had no effect on the economy thus far, while 28% say it has made the economy better and 21% say it has made the economy worse. Americans are even more likely, at 64%, to say the economic stimulus plan has had no effect on their family's financial situation, while 14% say it has made their family's financial situation better and 22% say it has made their financial situation worse.

Americans' long-term expectations of the economic stimulus plan are more positive. Nearly half (48%) say the stimulus will make the economy better in the long term, rather than having no effect (19%) or making it worse (31%). Americans express greater skepticism about the stimulus' long-term effect on their families, with responses about evenly split between "better" (35%) and "worse" (34%), and another 28% expecting the stimulus to have no effect.

In the long term, do you think Obama's economic stimulus plan will make _____ better, not have an effect, or make it worse?

■ Better ■ No effect ▨ Worse

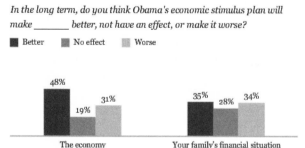

USA Today/Gallup poll, July 17-19, 2009

More Politics Than Pocketbook

An examination of the results to these questions by subgroup suggests Americans' views are likely driven more by politics than by economics. Republicans are far more likely than Democrats to say the stimulus has made and will make both the economy and their family's financial situation worse, and Democrats are far more likely

than Republicans to say the opposite. Independents are evenly divided about the economic stimulus' effect on the economy, for better or for worse, to date or in the future. They are slightly more negative than positive about its effect on their own families.

Views on Obama's Economic Stimulus, by Party ID

	Republicans	Independents	Democrats	Dem. minus Rep. gap
THE ECONOMY	%	%	%	Pct. pts.
Has made better	13	23	45	32
Had no effect	46	53	48	2
Has made worse	39	23	4	-35
Will make better	20	38	79	59
Will have no effect	21	22	14	-7
Will make worse	56	38	4	-52

	Republicans	Independents	Democrats	Dem. minus Rep. Gap
YOUR FAMILY'S FINANCIAL SITUATION	%	%	%	Pct. pts.
Has made better	7	10	23	16
Had no effect	58	67	67	9
Has made worse	35	23	9	-26
Will make better	13	27	62	49
Will have no effect	28	30	27	-1
Will make worse	58	39	8	-50

USA Today/Gallup poll, July 17-19, 2009

These views likely relate to Americans' highly partisan views on the amount of government spending and expansion of government power in President Obama's proposals to date.

Among income groups, Americans making $20,000 or less per year tend to be more positive about the effects of the economic stimulus than those in higher income categories, though the variation is not always steady or linear.

Views on Obama's Economic Stimulus, by Annual Income

	Less than $20,000	$20,000-$29,999	$30,000-$49,999	$50,000-$74,999	$75,000 or more	Gap between lowest and highest incomes
ECONOMY	%	%	%	%	%	Pct. pts.
Has made better	35	27	29	29	28	7
Had no effect	44	53	54	47	49	-5
Has made worse	19	17	16	23	23	-4
Will make better	64	47	48	49	41	23
Will have no effect	14	24	20	17	20	-6
Will make worse	18	27	31	32	37	-19
FAMILY FINANCIAL SITUATION	%	%	%	%	%	Pct. pts.
Has made better	28	13	13	14	9	19
Had no effect	54	68	64	69	66	-12
Has made worse	18	16	23	18	24	-6
Will make better	52	35	41	34	29	23
Will have no effect	23	32	28	26	32	-9
Will make worse	24	27	30	37	39	-15

USA Today/Gallup poll, July 17-19, 2009

Long-Term Time Horizon

When asked in an open-ended question how long they expect it to be before the economy starts to recover, 30% now say five years or more, up from 19% in February but similar to the 28% who said so in December. Overall, 68% of Americans now expect it to take two years or more before the economy starts to recover, little changed from 71% in February. One in four (27%) now expect it to take less than two years, about the same as the 24% in February who said this.

Just your best guess, how long do you think it will be before the economy starts to recover? [OPEN-ENDED]

	Dec 12-14, 2008	Feb 20-22, 2009	July 17-19, 2009
	%	%	%
Less than one year	6	8	9
One year	10	16	18
Two years	27	30	22
Three years	15	13	9
Four years	11	9	7
Five years or more	28	19	30

Bottom Line

Gallup data regarding the economic stimulus reveal that Americans for the most part are not yet seeing tangible effects of the plan, either in their own lives or in the economy more broadly. About half of Americans (48%) expect the stimulus to ultimately make the economy better, and 35% say so about their own family situations. But that leaves half or more who expect the plan either to have no effect or to make things worse. These views relate strongly to one's politics and to a lesser degree to one's economic status.

Overall, Americans are about as hopeful for a speedy economic turnaround as they were in February, but more inclined to say it could take five years or more.

Survey Methods

Results are based on telephone interviews with 1,006 national adults, aged 18 and older, conducted July 17–19, 2009. For results based on the total sample of national adults, one can say with 95% confidence that the maximum margin of sampling error is ±3 percentage points.

Interviews are conducted with respondents on land-line telephones (for respondents with a land-line telephone) and cellular phones (for respondents who are cell-phone only).

In addition to sampling error, question wording and practical difficulties in conducting surveys can introduce error or bias into the findings of public opinion polls.

July 23, 2009
BIDEN FAVORABILITY TRAILS OBAMA AND RECENT VPs
Favorable views of Biden have dropped from 59% to 48% since November

by Lydia Saad, Gallup Poll Senior Editor

In contrast to U.S. President Barack Obama, whose current favorable rating among Americans is similar to what it was just after the November election, Vice President Joe Biden has seen some erosion in his rating. As a result, Biden lags significantly behind Obama in popularity, and, at this stage of the new administration, has the lowest favorable rating of any of the most recent vice presidents.

Favorable Ratings for Recent Presidents and Vice Presidents
Ratings for each pair are those closest to mid-July of first year in office

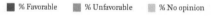
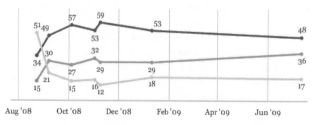

Forty-eight percent of Americans now view Biden favorably, down from 53% in January and 59% in the first few days after the election.

Being tapped as Obama's running mate last summer raised Biden's public profile tremendously—evidenced by increases in both his favorable and his unfavorable ratings after the Democratic National Convention. There was a corresponding decline (from 51% to 21%) in the percentage of Americans having no opinion of him. By October, Biden's "no opinion" rating had fallen to 15% and his favorable rating had increased to 57%. His favorable rating had remained above 50% in all subsequent Gallup measures, until now.

Overall Opinion of Vice President Joe Biden
September 2008-July 2009

President Obama's favorable rating jumped to an extraordinarily high 78% near the end of his presidential transition in January. However, apart from that single reading (driven by atypically high support from Republicans during that period), his favorable rating has consistently registered in the 60s since November, and is 66% in the latest reading from a July 10–12 Gallup Poll.

Bottom Line

Biden is not keeping up with Obama in popularity, and this distinguishes him from the previous two vice presidents, whose public

Favorable Ratings of Barack Obama
September 2008-July 2009

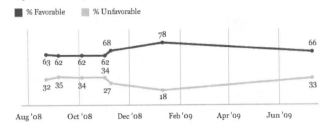

July 24, 2009

OBAMA GETS HIGH MARKS ON LEADERSHIP, EMPATHY

Even after slight decline, two in three say he exhibits these characteristics

by Jeffrey M. Jones, Gallup Poll Managing Editor

Solid majorities of Americans believe U.S. President Barack Obama is a strong and decisive leader and say he understands the problems Americans face in their daily lives. The president gets slightly lower marks on two other personal characteristics—being able to effectively manage the government and sharing Americans' values.

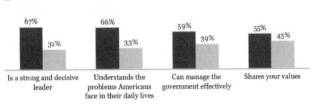

Thinking about the following characteristics and qualities, please say whether you think each applies or doesn't apply to Barack Obama.

USA Today/Gallup poll, July 17-19, 2009

images generally kept pace with those of their respective presidents. At this stage of the Bush and Clinton presidencies, both sitting vice presidents—Cheney and Gore, respectively—had favorable ratings very similar to those of the presidents with whom they served, and lower unfavorables.

Biden's image problem has been in evidence only since the inauguration, as his favorable ratings since January have been close to or greater than 20 points lower than Obama's; around election time, Biden trailed the president by fewer than 10 points.

Favorable Ratings of Barack Obama and Joe Biden
Numbers in percentages

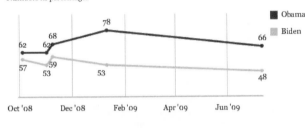

Survey Methods

Results are based on telephone interviews with 1,018 national adults, aged 18 and older, conducted July 10–12, 2009. For results based on the total sample of national adults, one can say with 95% confidence that the maximum margin of sampling error is ±4 percentage points.

Other results are based on telephone interviews with 1,006 national adults, aged 18 and older, conducted July 17–19, 2009. For these results, the maximum margin of error is ±4 percentage points.

Interviews are conducted with respondents on land-line telephones (for respondents with a land-line telephone) and cellular phones (for respondents who are cell-phone only).

In addition to sampling error, question wording and practical difficulties in conducting surveys can introduce error or bias into the findings of public opinion polls.

These results are based on the latest *USA Today*/Gallup poll, conducted July 17–19. The poll was conducted at a time when Obama's job approval ratings have fallen slightly, though his overall image remains positive. A Gallup Poll conducted earlier this month found 66% of Americans saying they have a favorable opinion of Obama. His favorables and his ratings on most personal characteristics exceed his job approval rating.

Coincident with the decline in Obama's job approval rating, each of the four personal dimensions tested in the July 17–19 poll is down from the prior readings in April, near the 100-day mark of Obama's presidency. Those April character readings were generally the most positive Gallup has found for Obama since it started measuring Americans' views of his personal qualities in March 2008.

Percentage of Americans Who Believe Characteristics and Qualities Apply to Barack Obama

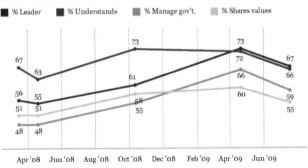

Even with the recent drop in the character ratings, Americans remain more likely to say Obama is a strong leader than they were during the 2008 presidential campaign. His current 59% rating for managing government also exceeds any of the measurements taken during the campaign. But his latest scores for understanding Americans' problems and sharing their values have dipped below where they were just before he was elected president.

The recent decline in Obama's character ratings are chiefly due to less positive evaluations from Republicans and, to a lesser extent, independents. The largest changes, both double-digit decreases, are seen in Republicans' views of Obama as a strong leader (down to 42% from 52% in April) and an effective government manager (down to 27% from 38% in April).

Ratings of Barack Obama's Personal Character, by Political Party, April-July 2009

	April 20-21, 2009	July 17-19, 2009	Change
Strong leader	%	%	Pct. pts.
Democrats	94	92	-2
Independents	67	63	-4
Republicans	52	42	-10
Understands problems			
Democrats	94	91	-3
Independents	67	61	-6
Republicans	50	41	-9
Can manage gov't.			
Democrats	90	88	-2
Independents	63	56	-7
Republicans	38	27	-11
Shares values			
Democrats	90	89	-1
Independents	56	50	-6
Republicans	28	21	-7

Now, roughly 9 in 10 Democrats believe Obama possesses each of the four characteristics. While a majority of independents say Obama is a strong leader (63%), understands Americans' problems (61%), and can manage government effectively (56%), half now say he shares their values. About one in five Republicans currently believe Obama shares their values.

Bottom Line

Americans' assessment of the job Obama is doing as president has become less positive over the last several weeks. But the public still has a positive opinion of him overall (based on his favorable rating) and still views him as having strong capabilities for leadership and empathy. He is currently trying to apply those skills to win passage of landmark healthcare reform legislation against growing resistance.

Survey Methods

Results are based on telephone interviews with 1,006 national adults, aged 18 and older, conducted July 17–19, 2009. For results based on the total sample of national adults, one can say with 95% confidence that the maximum margin of sampling error is ±4 percentage points.

Interviews are conducted with respondents on land-line telephones (for respondents with a land-line telephone) and cellular phones (for respondents who are cell-phone only).

In addition to sampling error, question wording and practical difficulties in conducting surveys can introduce error or bias into the findings of public opinion polls.

July 24, 2009

MOST IN U.S. WANT HEALTHCARE REFORM, BUT VARY ON URGENCY

Thirty percent favor new law, but not necessarily this year; a quarter oppose new law at any time

by Frank Newport, Gallup Poll Editor in Chief

Seven in 10 Americans favor the passage of new healthcare reform legislation, but less than half (41%) say a new law needs to be passed this year.

When it comes to healthcare reform legislation now being considered in Congress, what would you advise your representative in Congress to do?

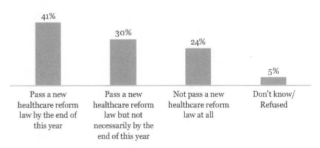

Gallup Poll Daily tracking, July 23, 2009

Results from a Gallup Poll conducted Thursday night, one day after President Obama's press conference at which he emphasized the importance of moving quickly on healthcare reform legislation, show that 41% of Americans would advise their representative in Congress to pass a new healthcare reform law by the end of this year; another 30% would say Congress should pass a new law, but not necessarily this year; and the remainder—24%—don't think Congress should pass a new healthcare reform law at all.

The urgency of the effort to pass new healthcare reform legislation has become a significant focus of President Obama's full-court press on the issue. Obama has argued that without a short-term deadline for passing such a law, momentum would be lost and inertia would rule—lowering the probability that such legislation would ever be passed.

The data show that about 4 out of 10 Americans generally agree with Obama—that a new healthcare law needs to be passed this year. But that leaves the majority of Americans who do not agree, either because they believe a delay is acceptable, or because they don't believe such a law is needed at all.

There are strong partisan differences in response to this question.

When it comes to healthcare reform legislation now being considered in Congress, what would you advise your representative in Congress to do?

By political party
■ Pass new healthcare reform law this year
■ Pass new healthcare reform law, but not necessarily this year
■ Do not pass healthcare reform law at all

Gallup Poll Daily tracking, July 23, 2009

Sixty-three percent of Democrats are behind the effort to pass a new healthcare law this year, with most of the rest choosing the alternative of passing a new law, but not necessarily this year. Almost half of Republicans, on the other hand, favor not passing a new healthcare reform law at all; the slight majority of the rest favor passing a new law, but not necessarily this year, leaving 22% of Republicans favoring a new law to be passed this year.

The crucial bloc of independents—at this point the largest of the three partisan groups—are much more mixed in their views, as would be expected. A little more than a third say pass a new law this year; a third say pass a new law, but not necessarily this year; and about a fourth say don't pass a new law at all.

Implications

The good news for the Obama administration: 7 in 10 Americans would advise their representative in Congress to pass a new healthcare reform law—one of President Obama's major domestic priorities. The not-so-good news for Obama is that less than half (41%) favor passing such a law this year, with 30% favoring a new law but saying it is not necessary to move that quickly. About a quarter of Americans, the majority of whom are Republicans, would advise their representative in Congress not to pass a new healthcare reform law at all.

Survey Methods

Results are based on telephone interviews with 1,030 national adults, aged 18 and older, conducted July 23, 2009, as part of Gallup Poll Daily tracking. For results based on the total sample of national adults, one can say with 95% confidence that the maximum margin of sampling error is ±3 percentage points.

Interviews are conducted with respondents on land-line telephones (for respondents with a land-line telephone) and cellular phones (for respondents who are cell-phone only).

In addition to sampling error, question wording and practical difficulties in conducting surveys can introduce error or bias into the findings of public opinion polls.

Polls conducted entirely in one day, such as this one, are subject to additional error or bias not found in polls conducted over several days.

July 27, 2009

CDC TOPS AGENCY RATINGS; FEDERAL RESERVE BOARD LOWEST

NASA ratings remain high, while Federal Reserve has lost ground

by Lydia Saad, Gallup Poll Senior Editor

At a time when Americans are discouraged about the direction of the country and hesitant about the scope of President Barack Obama's federal budget plans, the U.S. Centers for Disease Control and Prevention, NASA, and the FBI earn credit for a job well done from a majority of Americans. The 61% who say the CDC is doing an excellent or good job can be contrasted with the 30% who say this of the Federal Reserve Board, making the latter the worst reviewed of nine agencies and departments rated in the July 10–12 Gallup Poll.

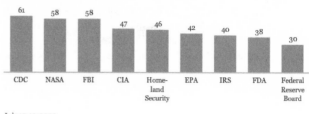

How would you rate the job being done by [agency/department]? Would you say it is doing an excellent, good, only fair, or poor job?

July 10-12, 2009

The two national security-oriented groups included in the recent poll—the CIA and the Department of Homeland Security—receive moderate performance ratings, with just under half of Americans saying each is doing an excellent or good job.

The Environmental Protection Agency, Internal Revenue Service, and Food and Drug Administration fall a notch lower in the rankings, as close to 40% of Americans give each of them credit for doing an excellent or good job. The relatively low ranking of the FDA is of particular note with regard to the scrutiny the agency has been under, given recent attention to U.S. food safety.

The new poll, conducted just prior to the 40th anniversary of the July 20, 1969, moon landing by Apollo 11—perhaps the most celebrated of all NASA achievements—finds NASA's rating about where it has been in recent years. While not nearly as high as it was in late 1998 (a month after John Glenn's successful return to space), NASA's current excellent/good score falls within the upper half of ratings it has received over the past two decades.

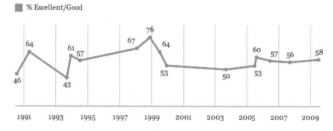

Job Ratings for NASA, the U.S. Space Agency

Today's rating of the FDA is the first measured by Gallup, but all other agencies on the list were previously rated in September 2003 (NASA, as shown, has been rated multiple times). The only significant changes since that time are a sharp deterioration in perceptions about the Federal Reserve, and a decline in highly positive views toward the CDC.

In 2003, the slight majority of Americans, 53%, said the Federal Reserve was doing an excellent or good job and 5% called it poor. Today, 30% of Americans praise the job the Fed is doing, while nearly as many, 22%, call it poor. While this ratings downturn coincides with a substantial drop in consumer confidence toward the U.S. economy over the same period, it is unclear how much of the Fed's image decline is due to the general decline in the country's economic climate, as opposed to specific perceptions about the agency's performance in carrying out its monetary responsibilities and possibly its role in the crisis surrounding U.S. financial markets. The Fed's low excellent/good rating may also reflect the higher-than-average percentage of Americans having "no opinion" about this arm of the government, relative to the other agencies rated.

Job Ratings for Federal Reserve Board

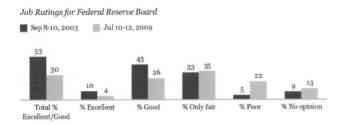

The CDC has had a particularly high public profile since April, when cases of the H1N1 virus, also known as swine flu, were first detected in the United States. Whether its role in tracking the disease and informing Americans about the illness has elevated or hurt the agency's image is not clear. However, compared with six years ago, fewer Americans believe the agency is doing an "excellent" job—now 11%, down from 18%. Overall, the percentage saying it is doing an excellent or good job is now 61%, down from 66%.

Job Ratings for the Centers for Disease Control and Prevention, or the CDC

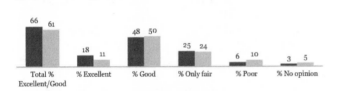

Bottom Line

Americans are broadly satisfied with the work the CDC, NASA, and the FBI are doing. The CIA and the Department of Homeland Security are also fairly well reviewed; however, the current job ratings of the EPA, IRS, FDA, and Federal Reserve Board all have significant room for improvement.

Survey Methods

Results are based on telephone interviews with 1,018 national adults, aged 18 and older, conducted July 10–12, 2009. For results based on the total sample of national adults, one can say with 95% confidence that the maximum margin of sampling error is ±3 percentage points.

Interviews are conducted with respondents on land-line telephones (for respondents with a land-line telephone) and cellular phones (for respondents who are cell-phone only).

In addition to sampling error, question wording and practical difficulties in conducting surveys can introduce error or bias into the findings of public opinion polls.

July 27, 2009
TWO IN THREE DOUBT CONGRESS' GRASP OF HEALTHCARE ISSUES
Americans perceive themselves as more knowledgeable than lawmakers

by Frank Newport, Gallup Poll Editor in Chief

Americans view themselves as more knowledgeable than members of Congress regarding the current debate over healthcare reform. Nearly half (48%) say they personally have a good understanding of the issues involved, while only 27% say so about members of Congress.

Would you say that you/members of Congress have a good understanding of the issues involved in the current debate over national healthcare reform, or not?

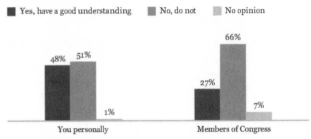

Gallup Poll Daily tracking, July 26, 2009

These Gallup findings are based on interviewing conducted Sunday, July 26, as the push toward new healthcare reform legislation continues to dominate the focus of Congress, the White House, and the national news media.

That less than 3 in 10 Americans believe that Congress has a good understanding of the issues involved in the healthcare debate underscores the basic lack of confidence that Americans have in the men and women they elect and send off to Washington to represent them. Gallup's recent update on confidence in institutions, for example, found that 17% of Americans have a great deal/quite a lot of confidence in Congress, near the bottom of the list of institutions tested.

The current data show that Americans are certainly not overly confident in their own understanding of healthcare reform. But the public's personal level of confidence—48% say they have a good understanding of healthcare reform—is substantially higher than the 27% who say members of Congress understand.

The American public can be split into four groups on the basis of their responses to these two questions.

Good Understanding of Issues Involved in Current Debate Over National Healthcare Reform

	%
Good understanding: personally and Congress	16
Congress has good understanding, but personally do not have a good understanding	11
Good understanding personally, but Congress does not have good understanding	30
Neither Congress nor personally have good understanding	35

Gallup Poll Daily tracking, July 26, 2009

It would be optimal in a democracy if the people of the country believed that they and their elected representatives in Congress had a good understanding of something as important as a major overhaul of the nation's healthcare system. But only about one in six Americans fit that description, leaving the vast majority of the public with doubts about the level of understanding of either themselves or Congress.

Indeed, the largest two groups of Americans are those who believe that Congress doesn't have a good understanding, but they personally do, and those pessimists (or realists) who simply say that healthcare reform is understood well by neither themselves nor Congress. The remaining group of 11% says that Congress understands but that they personally do not.

There are significant patterns of differences in response to these questions by partisan orientation:

- Republicans are above average in the belief that they personally understand the issues involved in healthcare reform, but below average in their belief that Congress understands. Given that the big push on healthcare reform is from a Democratic president, and that Congress is controlled by the Democrats, these findings are not surprising.

- Democrats are at about the average level in terms of believing that they personally understand, but slightly above average in their belief that Congress understands. Again, this is fitting given the Democratic control of Congress.

- Independents don't differ much from average in terms of their own beliefs that they understand healthcare reform, but are slightly below average in thinking that Congress has a good understanding.

Good Understanding of Issues Involved in Current Debate Over National Healthcare Reform, by Political Party

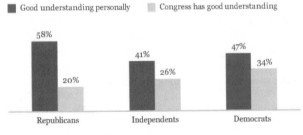

Gallup Poll Daily tracking, July 26, 2009

Implications

Americans have quite negative attitudes about Congress in general, making it less than surprising to find that the significant majority of the public believes that Congress does not have a good grasp on the issues involved in the current debate over healthcare reform. It is possible that if Gallup were to ask this "good understanding" question about any type of pending congressional legislation, we would find the same level of distrust that representatives fully understand the issues involved. Americans are certainly more confident in their own personal level of understanding of healthcare reform, but even with that, half don't believe that they personally have a good grasp of what's involved.

The overall finding that 16% of Americans believe that they and members of Congress have a good grasp of the issues in the healthcare reform debate could suggest that Americans would resist the idea of rushing healthcare legislation into law posthaste. Indeed, separate Gallup results from July 23 showed that less than half of Americans want healthcare reform legislation to be passed this year. The majority say Congress should pass healthcare reform legislation, but

not necessarily this year, or should not pass a new healthcare reform law at all.

Survey Methods

Results are based on telephone interviews with 526 national adults, aged 18 and older, conducted July 26, 2009. For results based on the total sample of national adults, one can say with 95% confidence that the maximum margin of sampling error is ±5 percentage points.

Interviews are conducted with respondents on landline telephones (for respondents with a landline telephone) and cellular phones (for respondents who are cell phone only).

In addition to sampling error, question wording and practical difficulties in conducting surveys can introduce error or bias into the findings of public opinion polls.

Polls conducted entirely in one day, such as this one, are subject to additional error or bias not found in polls conducted over several days.

July 29, 2009
BENEFITS OF HEALTHCARE REFORM A TOUGH SELL FOR AMERICANS
Americans least confident that reform will benefit them personally

by Frank Newport, Gallup Poll Editor in Chief

Forty-four percent of Americans believe a new healthcare reform law would improve medical care in the U.S., contrasted with 26% who say it would improve their personal medical care. Forty-seven percent of Americans believe reform will expand access to healthcare in the U.S., while 21% say it will expand their own access to healthcare.

Would a new healthcare reform law improve, not change, or worsen medical care in the U.S.?

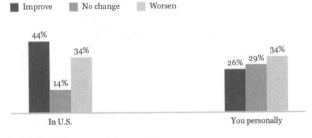

Gallup Poll Daily tracking, Jul 24-25, 2009

These results are important because much of the debate on healthcare reform rests on the assumption that it is imperative to fix what is assumed to be a broken healthcare system in the U.S. One aspect of the healthcare debate focuses on the benefits of healthcare reform to the country as a whole, while another addresses the benefits to the average American. Yet the majority of Americans are not sold on the notion that reform would have a positive effect on either.

The wariness with which the public approaches the possible effects of healthcare reform on their personal situations is evident from results showing that more Americans say healthcare would

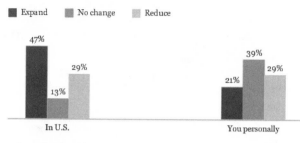

Would a new healthcare reform law expand, not change, or reduce access to healthcare in the U.S.?

Gallup Poll Daily tracking, Jul 24-25, 2009

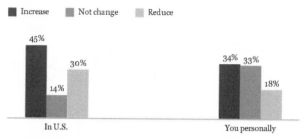

Would healthcare reform increase, not change, or reduce your own healthcare costs?

Gallup Poll Daily tracking, Jul 24-25, 2009

worsen their medical care and reduce their access to healthcare, than say it would have the contrasting, positive effects. These "net negative" results contrast with the net positive perceptions Americans have about the likely impact of healthcare reform on the U.S. more generally—albeit one that is quite muted.

Partisan Reactions

Healthcare reform is being pushed by a Democratic president and leaders in a Democrat-controlled House and Senate. Thus, it is not surprising to find that Democrats are much more likely to say that healthcare will have a positive effect, across all dimensions, than are independents or Republicans. This is particularly the case when it comes to the two questions asking about the effects of healthcare reform on U.S. medical care and access to healthcare nationally. While 70% and 65% of Democrats agree that reform will have a positive effect on these dimensions, respectively, only 18% and 22% of Republicans agree.

Impact of Healthcare Reform

% Positive responses

	Republicans	Independents	Democrats
	%	%	%
U.S medical care	18	43	70
U.S. access to healthcare	22	52	65
Own medical care	8	24	40
Own access to healthcare	8	25	29

Gallup Poll Daily tracking, Jul 24-25, 2009

Less than 1 out of 10 Republicans say that healthcare reform will have a positive effect on their personal medical care or access to healthcare, compared with a somewhat higher percentage of Democrats who hold these views. Independents' views on the impact of healthcare reform are in the middle between the Republican and Democrat extremes.

Costs

It appears to be a commonly held belief that healthcare reform will increase costs for the country as a whole and for the respondents personally, rather than decreasing these costs. Forty-five percent say that a new healthcare reform law would increase healthcare costs in the U.S., while 30% say it would reduce them. Thirty-four percent say a new healthcare reform law would increase their personal costs, while 18% say it would reduce them.

When Americans say that their personal healthcare costs will increase if a new reform law is passed, it could mean that these individuals perceive that they will pay doctors, hospitals, and providers more money, or that they will be paying more for all Americans' healthcare indirectly, through higher taxes. Whatever the case, the data show that a third of Americans believe their costs will go up in some way if healthcare reform is passed, almost twice as many as say their personal costs will go down.

Bottom Line

These results do not coalesce into a terribly optimistic picture of Americans' views of the perceived impact of healthcare reform:

- Whether the focus is access to healthcare or the quality of care, less than a majority of Americans are convinced that healthcare reform will be beneficial to either the country or to their own personal situations.
- Americans are less likely to believe healthcare reform will result in improvements to themselves personally than to the national healthcare situation.
- Americans believe that healthcare reform will increase costs rather than lower them, both nationally and for themselves.

Survey Methods

Results are based on telephone interviews with 2,017 national adults, aged 18 and older, conducted July 24–25, 2009. For results based on the total sample of national adults, one can say with 95% confidence that the maximum margin of sampling error is ±3 percentage points.

For results based on the sample of 485 national adults in the Form A/C half-sample, the maximum margin of sampling error is ±6 percentage points. For results based on the sample of 559 national adults in the Form A/D half-sample, the maximum margin of sampling error is ±5 percentage points.

Interviews are conducted with respondents on land-line telephones (for respondents with a land-line telephone) and cellular phones (for respondents who are cell-phone only).

In addition to sampling error, question wording and practical difficulties in conducting surveys can introduce error or bias into the findings of public opinion polls.

July 29, 2009

EARLY READ ON 2010 SUGGESTS MIDTERMS COULD BE COMPETITIVE

Democrats hold slight edge in 2010 vote among registered voters

by Jeffrey M. Jones, Gallup Poll Managing Editor

If the elections for Congress were held today, 50% of U.S. registered voters say they would vote for the Democratic candidate in their district and 44% for the Republican candidate.

Thinking for a moment about the elections for Congress next year, if the elections for Congress were being held today, which party's candidate would you vote for in your Congressional district -- [ROTATE: the Democratic Party's candidate or the Republican Party's candidate]?

Based on registered voters

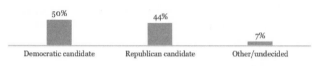

July 10-12

Gallup uses this "generic" ballot to measure support for the two parties in congressional elections. Historically, the final pre-election generic congressional ballot based on likely voters has proven to be an accurate predictor of the national two-party vote for the U.S. House in past midterm elections. The two-party vote closely corresponds to the share of seats each party wins in the U.S. House of Representatives.

Gallup's ability to predict the outcome using the generic ballot this far out from the election using registered voters is unclear given the limited historical data from years prior to the midterm elections.

However, past data do suggest that Democrats typically need a large lead on the generic ballot among all registered voters in midterm elections to maintain a lead once turnout is taken into account.

For example, the Democratic Party averaged an 11 percentage point lead among registered voters in all of Gallup's generic ballot polling leading up to the 2006 midterm elections, compared with an eight-point Democratic advantage in the actual 2006 House vote. In 2001–2002, the average Democratic lead among registered voters in the generic ballot was three points in an election the Republicans eventually won by four points. And in 1998, Democrats enjoyed an average six-point registered voter lead while the eventual House vote was about evenly split between Republican and Democratic candidates.

The six-point Democratic advantage among all registered voters in the current poll suggests the 2010 election could be quite close if it were held today given low turnout in midterm elections and the usual Republican advantages in turnout. (Gallup usually takes turnout into account late in the campaign by applying a likely voter model to the data, usually beginning in September or October in the year of the midterm elections.)

Thus, at this early stage, 2010 does not look like it is shaping up to be as strong a Democratic year as 2006 was, and that could make it difficult for the party to hold onto the gains it made in the 2006 midterm and 2008 presidential elections.

Party Loyalty High

The poll data suggest party loyalty in the 2010 congressional vote is likely to be high. Currently, Republicans say they would vote for the Republican candidate by 93% to 3%, while Democrats would vote for the Democratic candidate by an equally lopsided margin, 94% to 4%. Independents are currently evenly divided in their vote preference. Democrats maintain a lead on the overall ballot given the fact that more registered voters identify as Democrats than independents.

Vote Preference in 2010 Midterm Elections, by Political Party Affiliation

Based on registered voters

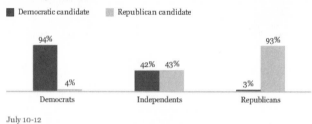

July 10-12

Party loyalty is typically quite high on the generic ballot, so, in large part, the outcome is determined by the voting preferences of independents and voter turnout by party. In 2006, Democrats had a substantial lead among independents, and Republicans held only a slight advantage in turnout compared to the Democrats. Thus, at this early stage, it appears as though Democrats may not be able to count on the same level of support among independents they enjoyed in the 2006 midterm elections, so offsetting any usual Republican advantage in turnout could be key to holding on to the gains made in the 2006 and 2008 elections.

Bottom Line

Gallup's initial read on 2010 midterm election voting preferences shows Democrats with a slight lead among registered voters, but one that is hardly large enough to suggest they are in a solid position with more than a year left before votes are cast.

Historically, the party whose president occupies the White House loses seats in a midterm election. Thus, the Democrats would probably expect to lose some of the seats they won in the House in 2006 and 2008. However, parties have been able to minimize their party's losses if not make gains in midterm elections when the president was popular, as in the 1998 and 2002 midterm elections. Although President Obama has been quite popular for much of his presidency, his approval ratings have declined in recent weeks.

Survey Methods

Results are based on telephone interviews with 916 registered voters, aged 18 and older, conducted July 10–12, 2009. For results based on the total sample of national adults, one can say with 95% confidence that the maximum margin of sampling error is ±4 percentage points.

Interviews are conducted with respondents on land-line telephones (for respondents with a land-line telephone) and cellular phones (for respondents who are cell-phone only).

In addition to sampling error, question wording and practical difficulties in conducting surveys can introduce error or bias into the findings of public opinion polls.

July 30, 2009

NEARLY 30% OF INSURED HAVE GOVERNMENT PLANS, UP FROM '08

Percentage with employer-provided care fell from 2008 to 2009

by Elizabeth Mendes, Gallup Poll Staff Writer

The Gallup-Healthways Well-Being Index reveals that currently 29.0% of adult Americans who have health insurance get their coverage through the government, a percentage which has increased since early 2008. More than half of insured Americans (56.5%) rely on an employer-based program and another 13.3% of the insured obtain their healthcare coverage through some other means, which includes purchasing it privately for themselves.

Is your primary health insurance coverage through an employer or union, through Medicare, Medicaid, military or veterans' coverage, or something else?

Among insured adults aged 18 and older

■ Employer-based

■ Government program (Medicaid, Medicare, or military/veterans' coverage)

■ Something else

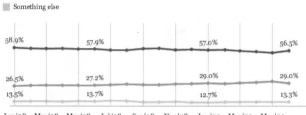

Monthly averages from January 2008-June 2009
Gallup-Healthways Well-Being Index

The percentage of insured American adults who report getting their insurance through a government program, including Medicaid, Medicare, or military/veterans' coverage, has increased over the last year and a half, to an average of 29.3% in 2009 from 27.5% in 2008. While still a majority, the percentage of insured Americans who have health coverage through an employer or union has decreased to an average of 56.2% in the first half of 2009 from the 2008 average of 57.9%.

In June 2009, 56.5% said they were covered through their employer or union versus 58.9% in January 2008. Currently, 29.0% of insured Americans have coverage through a government program, compared to 26.5% in January 2008. The 29.0% with government insurance in June is the sum total of the 20.4% of adults who have health insurance through Medicare, 4.7% through Medicaid, and 3.9% through military/veterans' coverage. The percent of insured who say their health insurance is through some other source has remained fairly steady—averaging 13.1% in 2009 and 13.5% in 2008.

These estimates are based on over 470,000 interviews, including approximately 26,000 per month with adults who have health insurance. While the changes are small in absolute terms, they are statistically meaningful based on the large sample sizes.

Older Americans vs. Working-Age Population

As would be expected, insured Americans who are between the ages of 18 and 64 are much more likely than those 65 and older (and thus eligible for Medicare) to be covered through employer-based insurance. In turn, older Americans are more likely than their younger counterparts to be covered through a government program. In June, 77.2% of those aged 65 and older report getting health insurance

coverage through a government plan versus 15.0% of those ages 18 to 64.

Insurance Type by Age

Among insured adults

■ Employer-based ■ Government program ■ Something else

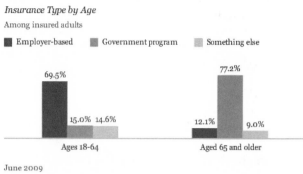

June 2009
Gallup-Healthways Well-Being Index

The trend over time in the percentage of insured Americans aged 65 and older reporting they have health coverage through the government shows some fluctuation month to month, but no significant increase from year to year. There has, however, been a measurable increase in the percentage of insured 18- to 64-year-olds who have health insurance through a government program, averaging 15.7% in the first six months of 2009 versus 14.5% in 2008.

Insurance Coverage by Age, 2008 vs. 2009

Among insured adults

	2008 (Jan-Dec Average)	2009 (Jan-Jun Average)	CHANGE
AGES 18-64			
Employer-based	69.7%	68.8%	-0.9
Government program	14.5%	15.7%	+1.2
Something else	14.8%	14.3%	-0.5
AGES 65 and Older			
Employer-based	12.9%	11.6%	-1.3
Government program	77.0%	77.7%	+0.7
Something else	8.7%	8.8%	+0.1

Gallup-Healthways Well-Being Index

Bottom Line

Previous Gallup research has shown that the overall percentage of adult Americans without health insurance has edged upward over the last year and a half to 16.0% in June 2009 from 14.8% in January 2008. The current data suggest that many of those who have dropped out of the ranks of the insured had employer-based insurance, leaving a larger percentage of the insured pool covered by a government program. Older Americans, as well as those between the ages of 18 and 64, have become less likely to have employer-based health insurance on average in 2009 compared with 2008. At the same time, government health coverage in both age groups has been increasing, pushing the current total percentage of Americans aged 18 and older with health insurance through a government program to 29.0% in June.

Survey Methods

For the Gallup-Healthways Well-Being Index, Gallup is interviewing no fewer than 1,000 U.S. adults nationwide each day. Monthly results comprise roughly 26,000 interviews. For results based on these samples, the maximum margin of sampling error is ±1 percentage point.

Interviews are conducted with respondents on land-line telephones (for respondents with a land-line telephone) and cellular phones (for respondents who are cell-phone only).

In addition to sampling error, question wording and practical difficulties in conducting surveys can introduce error or bias into the findings of public opinion polls.

July 31, 2009

SENIORS MOST SKEPTICAL OF HEALTHCARE REFORM

More seniors think reform law would be harmful, not beneficial, to them

by Lydia Saad, Gallup Poll Senior Editor

Seniors are the least likely of all age groups in the U.S. to say that healthcare reform will benefit their personal healthcare situation. By a margin of three to one, 36% to 12%, adults 65 and older are more likely to believe healthcare reform will reduce rather than expand their access to healthcare. And by 39% to 20%, they are more likely to say their own medical care will worsen rather than improve.

Would healthcare reform expand, not change, or reduce your own access to healthcare?

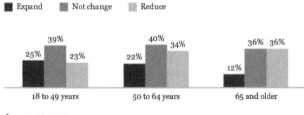

June 24-25, 2009

Would healthcare reform improve, not change, or worsen your own medical care?

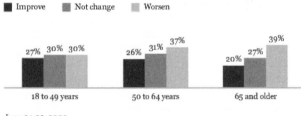

June 24-25, 2009

The responses of all Americans to these questions, part of July 24–25 Gallup Poll Daily tracking, were first reported on Gallup.com Wednesday.

In contrast to seniors, adults 18 to 49 are about evenly divided in their expectations for how healthcare reform will affect their own medical care and access. The middle age group, those ages 50 to 64, tend to be more dubious than younger adults that they will person-

ally benefit from either aspect of healthcare reform, but they are not as skeptical as seniors.

According to recent Gallup analysis, the overwhelming majority of seniors have health insurance coverage, and roughly three-quarters of those 65 and older are covered by a government-sponsored plan, such as Medicare or Medicaid. Thus it might be expected that seniors would be more negative about the potential impact of reform on their personal situations, but perhaps more positive about its impact on others. This is not the case.

In addition to being less likely to believe healthcare reform will improve their own medical care and access, seniors are far less likely than younger adults to believe the country as a whole will benefit. Only a quarter of seniors, versus about half of those 18 to 49 and 50 to 64 years, believe a reform law would expand access to healthcare nationally.

Would a new healthcare reform law expand, not change, or reduce access to healthcare in the U.S.?

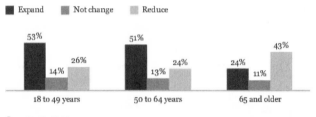

June 24-25, 2009

Similarly, only about a third of seniors, compared with close to half of younger adults, believe reform would improve medical care in the U.S.

Would a new healthcare reform law improve, not change, or worsen medical care in the U.S.?

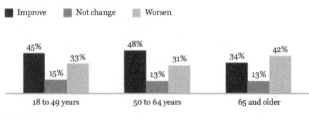

June 24-25, 2009

The three age groups have similar predictions for the cost implications of healthcare reform. About a third of adults in each age group predict their own healthcare costs would go up under healthcare reform, while less than one quarter believe costs would go down.

Also, seniors, as well as younger Americans, tend to believe healthcare reform would increase rather than decrease healthcare costs in the country as a whole.

Bottom Line

Gallup surveys suggest seniors are the most resistant of all age groups to Obama's healthcare reform initiative. While a fairly large subset of seniors think healthcare reform will have no effect on their medical care or access to healthcare, the remaining are much more negative than positive about the potential impact. And while seniors

Would healthcare reform increase, not change, or reduce your own healthcare costs?

■ Increase   ■ Not change   ■ Reduce

	18 to 49 years	50 to 64 years	65 and older
Increase	34%	35%	35%
Not change	31%	35%	34%
Reduce	16%	22%	13%

June 24-25, 2009

Would a new healthcare reform law increase, not change, or reduce healthcare costs in the U.S.?

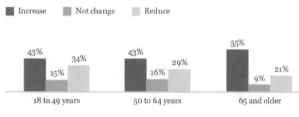

■ Increase   ■ Not change   ■ Reduce

	18 to 49 years	50 to 64 years	65 and older
Increase	43%	43%	55%
Not change	15%	16%	9%
Reduce	34%	29%	21%

June 24-25, 2009

have typically lagged behind younger Americans in their approval of the job Obama is doing as president, their support has now dropped below the symbolically important 50% mark.

Survey Methods

Results are based on telephone interviews with 2,017 national adults, aged 18 and older, conducted July 24–25, 2009. For results based on the total sample of national adults, one can say with 95% confidence that the maximum margin of sampling error is ±3 percentage points.

For results based on the sample of 485 national adults in the Form A/C half-sample, the maximum margin of sampling error is ±6 percentage points. For results based on the sample of 559 national adults in the Form A/D half-sample, the maximum margin of sampling error is ±5 percentage points.

Interviews are conducted with respondents on land-line telephones (for respondents with a land-line telephone) and cellular phones (for respondents who are cell-phone only).

In addition to sampling error, question wording and practical difficulties in conducting surveys can introduce error or bias into the findings of public opinion polls.

July 31, 2009
AMERICANS ON HEALTHCARE REFORM: TOP 10 TAKEAWAYS
Key findings from Gallup surveys

by Frank Newport, Gallup Poll Editor in Chief

A review of public opinion research on healthcare reform reveals that Americans may have hit the slowdown button. One primary cause for this appears to be public concerns about cost, but there are a number of additional elements involved. The bottom line is a sense that, while Americans apparently favor some type of healthcare reform in

the long term, they are in no hurry to see healthcare reform legislation passed in the short-term on a rushed schedule.

Herewith is a summary of 10 key elements of American public opinion on healthcare reform, based on a review of the latest survey research as of the week of July 27–31.

1. **Most Americans do not believe that the U.S. healthcare system is in a state of crisis. The economy outweighs healthcare as the most pressing problem facing the country and in Americans' personal lives.**

- Although the majority of Americans believe the U.S. healthcare system has major problems, less than 20% perceive that the U.S. healthcare system is in a state of crisis. This has not shifted significantly in 15 years.
- More Americans now mention healthcare as the nation's most important problem than was the case a few months ago. It is unlikely that the quality of healthcare deteriorated in four months, but rather that its salience has increased for the average American with the increased focus on the topic from politicians and the news media. This follows the pattern seen in 1993 and 1994; concern about healthcare shot up as the problem was being addressed in Washington, D.C., but dropped thereafter. The current percentage of Americans naming healthcare as the country's biggest problem is significantly lower than in 1994.
- At this point, almost 7 out of 10 Americans say economic-related issues are the nation's top problem; 16% say healthcare is the top problem.
- One in 10 Americans say healthcare is the most important financial problem facing their family.

2. **Americans are not convinced that healthcare reform will benefit them personally. This is, in part, because most Americans are satisfied with their current medical care and access to healthcare. Seniors in particular are not convinced that healthcare reform will benefit them.**

- Most Americans do not see a direct personal benefit for themselves if healthcare legislation is passed.
- Eighty-four percent of Americans are insured and most say they are satisfied with their insurance and healthcare.
- Americans are more likely to be convinced that new healthcare legislation will have a negative effect personally rather than a positive one, although a substantial minority falls in the middle, saying it will have no effect on them either way.
- Most Americans rate the quality of healthcare they receive and their healthcare coverage as excellent or good. These views have been stable in recent years.
- While younger adults (those 18 to 49) are as likely to believe reform could help them as say it could hurt them, older Americans, particularly those 65 years and older, are far less likely to perceive that their medical care or access to healthcare would improve under new healthcare legislation.

3. **Americans agree that healthcare costs are a major problem for the country. Americans do not, however, believe that healthcare reform would lessen costs—neither for the system as a whole nor for individuals.**

- An overwhelming 79% of Americans say that they are dissatisfied with the total cost of healthcare in this country.
- Forty-five percent say that healthcare costs would increase overall with a new healthcare reform law, compared to 30% who say they would decrease.
- Personally, 34% say their healthcare costs would increase under a new law; 18% say they would be reduced.

4. **The push for healthcare reform is occurring in an environment characterized by high levels of concern about fiscal responsibility, government spending, and the growing federal deficit. Americans are being asked to approve major new healthcare expenditures at a time when they are not yet convinced that the last massive outlay of government money—the stimulus—has made an impact.**

- Americans are worried about their country's budget deficit.
- President Obama gets his lowest marks on handling the federal deficit.
- Those who disapprove of Obama's job performance are most likely to say it is because of the high levels of spending introduced in his administration.
- A Pew Research poll released this week shows that those who are worried about new healthcare legislation are most likely to say it is because it involves too much spending and would increase the deficit.
- Less than a third of Americans perceive that the stimulus plan has made the U.S. economy better, although about half hold out hope that it will eventually.
- Americans, on balance, perceive that the stimulus plan has, thus far, had no effect or made their own financial situation worse (64% and 22%, respectively). Looking ahead, Americans are just as likely to say the stimulus' long-term effect will make their situation worse as make it better.

5. **Americans have relatively little confidence in Congress and thus, by inference, little confidence that Congress can effectively and efficiently reform the country's massive healthcare system.**

- Two-thirds of Americans say members of Congress do not have a good understanding of the issues involved in healthcare reform.
- Just 17% of Americans have a great deal or quite a lot of confidence in Congress, near the bottom of a list of institutions Gallup measures each year.

6. **Americans continue to have more confidence in President Obama on healthcare issues than in either the Democrats or Republicans in Congress. Obama's political capital, however, is waning. This leads to a circularity in which Obama's hard push for healthcare reform may hurt his approval ratings, and his falling approval ratings may hurt his credibility on healthcare reform. One inevitable byproduct of Obama's strong push on reform is the politicalization of healthcare. Most Democrats support it, Republicans oppose it, and independents are in the middle.**

- President Obama's job approval rating has fallen from an average of 66% in early May to 56% for the week of July 20–26.
- Given a list of sources for recommendations for healthcare guidance, Americans say they are more confident in Obama than in either Democratic or Republican leaders in Congress—although doctors, researchers, and hospitals are rated higher than Obama.
- Twenty-two percent of Republicans want a new healthcare law passed this year, compared to 63% of Democrats.

7. **Americans have mixed or ambivalent views of the role government should have in healthcare. They favor some government involvement, but not a government-run healthcare system.**

- Less than half of Americans favor replacing the current system with a government-run healthcare system.
- Americans responding to questions asked by various polling organizations in recent weeks indicate that they do favor a public option plan (run by the government) that would compete with private plans.
- Americans believe that it is the government's role to help see that all Americans have access to healthcare, although this sentiment was waning as of November 2008.

8. **On a case-by-case basis, Americans favor many specific proposals that have been put forth as ways of reforming healthcare.**

- Polls from several polling organizations released this week show that Americans favor a public option government plan to compete with employer plans, requiring insurance companies to cover everyone regardless of pre-existing conditions, tax credits to help some people pay for health insurance, and expansion of government plans to cover low-income Americans.
- Americans also appear to agree with a number of different ways of paying for healthcare reform, including taxes on the rich and requiring employers to pay a fee if they don't provide health insurance.

9. **Despite positive views of many specific reform proposals, Americans appear ambivalent at this juncture on the overall merits of passing a broad healthcare plan.**

- In mid-July a majority of Americans favored passing a major healthcare reform bill (described without reference to who is supporting it).
- By later in July, several organizations' surveys show a plurality of Americans opposed to passage of plans variously labeled as Obama's plan, the plan proposed by President Obama and the Congressional Democrats, healthcare proposals being discussed in Congress, or healthcare reform legislation being considered right now.
- Other recent poll questions, which describe the plan in great detail, continue to show plurality of majority support.
- A plurality, but not a majority, of Americans say that a new healthcare plan would improve the overall level of medical care and improve access to healthcare in the U.S.

10. **All in all, while the majority of Americans ultimately favor passage of healthcare reform, many are willing to wait until next year to see it happen.**

Bottom Line

Taken together, these findings underscore the conclusion that Americans' views on the push for healthcare reform are in a state of flux, perhaps mirroring the back and forth debate in Congress on this contentious issue. Two keys for the average American appear to be cost and urgency. The data suggest a continuing need to convince Americans of the return on investment of any proposed major investment in healthcare reform. Americans also appear dubious about the benefits of what they perceive to be less-than-fully-informed representatives in Washington rushing into a new healthcare reform law when the need for such legislation is not the highest on the public's agenda.

Presidential Job Approval Ratings

Late July-Early August of first year in office

President	Dates of Gallup polling	% Approve
Barack Obama	Jul 31-Aug 2, 2009	56
George W. Bush	Aug 3-5, 2001	55
Bill Clinton	Aug 8-10, 1993	44
George H.W. Bush	Aug 10-13, 1989	69
Ronald Reagan	Jul 31-Aug 3, 1981	60
Jimmy Carter	Aug 5-8, 1977	60

August 03, 2009

OBAMA JOB APPROVAL EDGES UP TO 56%

Rating up from administration low point of 52% early last week

by Frank Newport, Gallup Poll Editor in Chief

President Barack Obama's job approval rating, after hitting his administration low point of 52% in the middle of last week, has edged back up, and is 56% for the latest three-day period, July 31–Aug. 2.

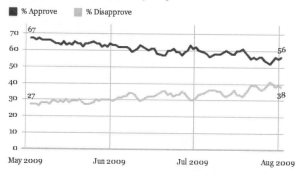

Gallup Daily: Obama Job Approval

Each result is based on a three-day rolling average

Gallup measures Obama's job approval rating on a daily basis, and reports three-day rolling averages consisting of approximately 1,500 interviews. Obama's three-day average was 61% as recently as July 17–19 but began to drop thereafter, reaching the aforementioned low point of 52% from July 27–29, Monday through Wednesday of last week. The high point for Obama was the 69% average that was measured in late January, just after he took office.

Obama's current 56% rating is about average for the job approval ratings of all presidents Gallup has measured since 1945, and is roughly equal to the approval rating of his immediate predecessor, George W. Bush, in early August 2001—Bush's first year in office. Comparisons of Obama's current standing to that of other recent presidents in the summer of their first year in office are mixed. Obama is well above where Bill Clinton was at about the same time in the summer of his first year, but he is at least a few points behind the positions of George H.W. Bush, Ronald Reagan, and Jimmy Carter at comparable times in their first year in the White House.

Obama has been prominent in news coverage of a number of different high-profile issues in recent days. Most visible has been Obama's full-court press on healthcare reform, in which he and his surrogates have taken every opportunity to make their case to the public—actions that of course have been countered by strong reaction from Republicans and others who are opposed to the proposed

massive changes in U.S. healthcare laws. Obama has also continued to address the nation's economic downturn and to tout the impact of his stimulus plan. He has been embroiled in controversy surrounding his public comments about the arrest of Harvard professor Henry Gates by the Cambridge, Mass., police. All of these are possible reasons for the decline in Obama's approval rating. Shifts in how these events are playing out to the public—including the fact that the House Energy and Commerce Committee approved healthcare reform legislation, some more positive economic news, and Obama's "beer summit" with Gates and Cambridge police Sgt. Crowley on the White House lawn—may help explain why his ratings have edged back up again.

The longer-term significance of the current uptick in Obama's ratings will not be known until it can be looked at in historical perspective. For those closely following day-to-day news cycles, however, the ups and downs in a president's job approval rating can be important indicators of the impact of various specific events on public support for the president. There has been a substantial amount of focus on Obama's job approval slide over the last week. The current data suggest that, at least for the moment, that slide has been arrested.

August will combine the usual downtime of a congressional recess and Obama's planned vacation (reportedly on Martha's Vineyard in Massachusetts) with continuing and active politicking on the healthcare reform issue on both sides of the debate. The impact—if any—of all of this on Obama's job approval rating remains to be seen.

Survey Methods

Results are based on telephone interviews with 1,591 national adults, aged 18 and older, conducted July 31–Aug. 2, 2009, as part of Gallup Poll Daily tracking. For results based on the total sample of national adults, one can say with 95% confidence that the maximum margin of sampling error is ±3 percentage points.

Interviews are conducted with respondents on land-line telephones (for respondents with a land-line telephone) and cellular phones (for respondents who are cell-phone only).

In addition to sampling error, question wording and practical difficulties in conducting surveys can introduce error or bias into the findings of public opinion polls.

POLITICAL PARTY AFFILIATION: 30 STATES BLUE, 4 RED IN '09 SO FAR

Utah and Wyoming are most Republican

by Jeffrey M. Jones, Gallup Poll Managing Editor

An analysis of Gallup Poll Daily tracking data from the first six months of 2009 finds Massachusetts to be the most Democratic state in the nation, along with the District of Columbia. Utah and Wyoming are the most Republican states, as they were in 2008. Only four states show a sizeable Republican advantage in party identification, the same number as in 2008. That compares to 29 states plus the District of Columbia with sizeable Democratic advantages, also unchanged from last year.

Top 10 Democratic States	
State	**Democratic advantage**
	Pct. pts.
District of Columbia	65
Massachusetts	34
Hawaii	29
Maryland	28
Vermont	28
Rhode Island	27
Illinois	26
New York	25
Connecticut	25
California	22

Jan.-June 2009 Gallup Poll Daily tracking

Top 10 Republican States	
State	**Democratic advantage**
	Pct. pts.
Utah	-23
Wyoming	-21
Idaho	-13
Alaska	-11
Alabama	-6
Mississippi	-1
North Dakota	0
Nebraska	0
Kansas	2
Arizona	2

Jan.-June 2009 Gallup Poll Daily tracking

These results are based on interviews with over 160,000 U.S. adults conducted between January and June 2009, including a minimum of 400 interviews for each state (305 in the District of Columbia). Each state's data are weighted to demographic characteristics for that state to ensure they are representative of the state's adult population.

Because the proportion of independents in each state varies considerably (from a low of 25% in Pennsylvania to a high of 50% in Rhode Island and New Hampshire), it is easiest to compare relative party strength using "leaned" party identification. Thus, the Democratic total represents the percentage of state residents who identify as Democratic, or who identify as independent but when asked a follow-up question say they lean to the Democratic Party. Likewise, the Republican total is the percentage of Republican identifiers and Republican-leaning independents in a state.

The accompanying map shows each state's relative party strength in the first half of 2009, which primarily covers the time since Barack Obama took office as president. States in which one of the parties enjoys a 10 or more percentage point advantage in leaned identification are considered *solid* supporters of that party. States with between a five- and nine-point advantage are considered *leaning* toward that party, and states with less than a five-point advantage for one of the parties are considered *competitive*.

As was the case in Gallup's analysis of 2008 yearly data, most states are currently Democratic in their party orientation, with the greatest number (30, including the District of Columbia) classified as solidly Democratic, with an additional 8 states leaning Democratic.

Meanwhile, only four states can be considered solidly Republican— Utah, Wyoming, Idaho, and Alaska, with Alabama falling into the leaning Republican category.

That leaves a total of eight states that are competitive in terms of party identification, with none showing a party advantage of greater than two points. These include Mississippi (+1 Republican), North Dakota and Nebraska (even), and Kansas, Arizona, Texas, South Carolina, and Montana (all +2 Democratic).

It is important to note that these categories only apply to a state population's party leanings and are not necessarily indicative of a party's electoral strength in that state. Election outcomes are decided on party support (which, as shown here, typically shows a Democratic advantage) but also turnout among party supporters (which typically works in the Republicans' favor).

The party strength totals for the first half of 2009 are similar to what Gallup reported earlier this year based on 2008 data. Compared to that report, there has been a net gain of two leaning Democratic states and a net loss of two competitive states, but no net change in the number of solidly Democratic, solidly Republican, or leaning Republican states.

Classification of states based on party identification, 2008 vs. first half of 2009

	2008	Jan-Jun 2009	Net change
Solidly Democratic	30	30	0
Leaning Democratic	6	8	+2
Competitive	10	8	-2
Leaning Republican	1	1	0
Solid Republican	4	4	0

Note: Solidly Democratic category includes 29 states plus the District of Columbia

However, despite the lack of *net* change, a total of nine states did shift from one category to another when comparing their classification based on 2008 data to their classification based on early 2009 data. Most of the movement was into or out of the competitive category, though two states (Colorado and Nevada) moved from a solid Democratic to leaning Democratic positioning.

Bottom Line

Since Obama was inaugurated, not much has changed in the political party landscape at the state level—the Democratic Party continues to hold a solid advantage in party identification in most states and in the nation as a whole. While the size of the Democratic advantage at the national level has shrunk in recent months, this has been due to an increase in independent identification rather than an increase in Republican support. That finding is echoed here given

States whose classification changed from 2008 data to Jan.-June 2009 data

State	2008	Jan-June 2009
Colorado	Solid Dem	Lean Dem
Nevada	Solid Dem	Lean Dem
Virginia	Competitive	Solid Dem
Indiana	Competitive	Solid Dem
Florida	Competitive	Lean Dem
Georgia	Competitive	Lean Dem
South Dakota	Competitive	Lean Dem
Alabama	Competitive	Lean Rep
Nebraska	Lean Rep	Competitive

that the total number of solid and leaning Republican states remains unchanged from last year. While the Republican Party is still able to compete in elections if they enjoy greater turnout from their supporters or greater support for its candidates from independent voters, the deck is clearly stacked in the Democratic Party's favor for now.

Survey Methods

Results are based on telephone interviews with 160,236 national adults, aged 18 and older, conducted Jan. 2 - June 30, 2009, as part of Gallup Poll Daily tracking. For results based on the total sample of national adults, one can say with 95% confidence that the maximum margin of sampling error is ±1 percentage point.

The margin of sampling error for most states is ±3 percentage points, but is as high as ±7 percentage points for the District of Columbia, and ±6 percentage points for Wyoming, North Dakota, South Dakota, Delaware and Hawaii.

Interviews are conducted with respondents on land-line telephones (for respondents with a land-line telephone) and cellular phones (for respondents who are cell-phone only).

In addition to sampling error, question wording and practical difficulties in conducting surveys can introduce error or bias into the findings of public opinion polls.

August 04, 2009
U.S. ABORTION ATTITUDES CLOSELY DIVIDED
Forty-seven percent of Americans identify as "pro-life," 46% as "pro-choice"

by Lydia Saad, Gallup Poll Senior Editor

A mid-July *USA Today*/Gallup survey finds 47% of Americans calling themselves "pro-life" and 46% "pro-choice." This is less positive for the "pro-life" position than was true in a Gallup survey in May. However, both 2009 readings show more Americans labeling themselves "pro-life" than has been the case in recent years.

The average figures for Americans' preferred abortion label across 18 Gallup surveys conducted from 1995 to 2008 are 49% for the "pro-choice" position and 42% for the "pro-life" position—a seven-point advantage for the "pro-choice" side. Both of Gallup's 2009 surveys show more Americans identifying as "pro-life" than as "pro-choice" (although the one-point advantage for "pro-life" in the July 2009 survey is not statistically significant.)

With respect to the abortion issue, would you consider yourself to be pro-choice or pro-life?

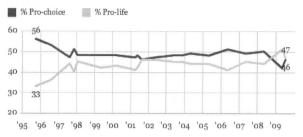

The May 7–10, 2009, Gallup survey found a significantly higher percentage of Americans identifying themselves as "pro-life" than "pro-choice," 51% vs. 42%. (A similar result was found in Gallup Poll Daily tracking from May 12–13.) Those surveys were conducted in the wake of considerable news coverage over the University of Notre Dame's decision to invite President Barack Obama to deliver the 2009 commencement address, an event that may have raised Americans' awareness of Obama's pro-choice views.

The current poll, conducted just over a month after abortion doctor George Tiller was killed by an anti-abortion activist, finds a nearly even split between the two sentiments. On a long-term basis, both 2009 measures, although differing slightly from one another, indicate a modest shift toward the "pro-life" position.

U.S. Adults' Self-Identified Position on Abortion

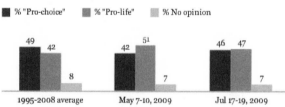

The current parity among the U.S. public between the "pro-choice" and "pro-life" camps is mirrored in a separate Gallup question asking Americans whether abortion should be legal in all circumstances, legal only under certain circumstances, or illegal in all circumstances. In Gallup's May and July 2009 surveys, the percentages favoring one of the two extreme positions are about equal. Currently, 21% say abortion should be legal without exceptions while 18% say it should be illegal.

Do you think abortions should be legal under any circumstances, legal only under certain circumstances, or illegal in all circumstances?

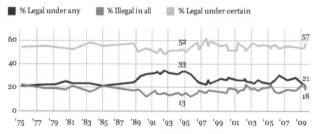

Apart from several readings between 2002 and 2005 when the two sides were closely matched, a significantly higher percentage of Americans has typically favored unfettered abortion rights than no legal access to abortion, peaking at a 20-point difference in September 1994, 33% vs. 13%. From 1988 through 2008, the average advantage for the "legal under any circumstances" position was 12 percentage points, 28% vs. 16%. That compares with a three-point advantage today.

U.S. Adults' Preference for Legality of Abortion

■ % Legal under any circumstances   ■ % Legal under certain circumstances
■ % Illegal in all circumstances   ■ % No opinion

^ Based on an average of the yearly averages in Gallup Polls from this period

Republicans Remain More "Pro-Life" Compared to Earlier in Decade

As was the case in May, the increase in "pro-life" sentiment in the current survey is the result of a higher percentage of Republicans (including independents who lean Republican) identifying themselves as such. Today, two-thirds of Republicans call themselves "pro-life," up roughly 10 points from earlier this decade.

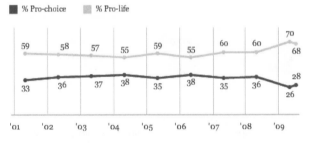

Recent Trend in Self-Identified Position on Abortion

Based on Republicans/Republican leaners

■ % Pro-choice   ■ % Pro-life

As seen in May, there has been no change in the outlook of Democrats on the issue, who generally favor the "pro-choice" position by 2 to 1.

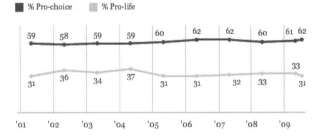

Recent Trend in Self-Identified Position on Abortion

Based on Democrats/Democratic leaners

■ % Pro-choice   ■ % Pro-life

Bottom Line

Americans' attitudes on abortion have varied over the past two decades, but the balance of opinion has consistently favored the abor-

tion rights side—ranging from a slight advantage to a significant advantage. Advocacy of abortion rights, as measured in Gallup polling, was particularly high from about 1989 to 1996, and continued to be the dominant position into 2001. It subsequently dwindled some through about 2005, then expanded again from 2006 through 2008. In 2009, the ratio of Americans identifying themselves as "pro-choice" versus "pro-life" and the percentage saying abortion should be legal "under any circumstances" are at or near the lowest levels seen in Gallup trends.

The source of the latest shift in abortion views—between 2008 and 2009—is clear. The percentage of Republicans (including independents who lean Republican) who call themselves "pro-life" has risen by nearly 10 points over the past year, from 60% to 68%—perhaps a reaction to the "pro-choice" presidency of Barack Obama—while there has been essentially no change in the views of Democrats and Democratic leaners.

Survey Methods

Results are based on telephone interviews with 1,006 national adults, aged 18 and older, conducted July 17–19, 2009. For results based on the total sample of national adults, one can say with 95% confidence that the maximum margin of sampling error is ±4 percentage points.

Interviews are conducted with respondents on land-line telephones (for respondents with a land-line telephone) and cellular phones (for respondents who are cell-phone only).

In addition to sampling error, question wording and practical difficulties in conducting surveys can introduce error or bias into the findings of public opinion polls.

August 05, 2009
CONSUMER CONFIDENCE: INCREASED OPTIMISM IN ALL STATES
Some of largest gains are in Northeastern states

by Jeffrey M. Jones, Gallup Poll Managing Editor

Though Americans remain cautious about the future course of the U.S. economy, they are much more optimistic in 2009 than they were in 2008. In the first half of 2009, 27% of Americans, on average, believed the economy was getting better, more than double the average for 2008 (13%). Following the District of Columbia at the top of the list, the states that currently are most optimistic about the economy are South Dakota, New Mexico, and North Dakota. Wyoming and West Virginia residents are the least optimistic.

The accompanying map shows the percentage saying the economy is getting better by state in the first half of 2009.

To underscore the improving optimism about the economy this year, Wyoming's state-low 18% "getting better" reading in 2009 matches the highest state scores from 2008.

Even though Americans' economic outlook remains more negative than positive on an absolute basis (from January through June, an average of 66% said the economy was getting worse), all states plus the District of Columbia express greater optimism about the economy this year than they did last year.

The greatest gains in optimism have come in the District of Columbia, South Dakota, Maine, and Massachusetts. Several other Northeastern states show increases near or exceeding 20 percentage points.

Top 10 States, Consumer Confidence

State	% Economy getting better
District of Columbia	39
South Dakota	37
New Mexico	34
North Dakota	34
Vermont	33
Massachusetts	33
Iowa	32
Maine	32
Maryland	31
Connecticut	31
Nevada	31

January-June 2009 Gallup Poll Daily tracking

Bottom 10 States, Consumer Confidence

State	% Economy getting better
Wyoming	18
West Virginia	19
Michigan	23
Ohio	25
Utah	25
Wisconsin	25
Idaho	25
Hawaii	25
Oklahoma	26
Kentucky	26

January-June 2009 Gallup Poll Daily tracking

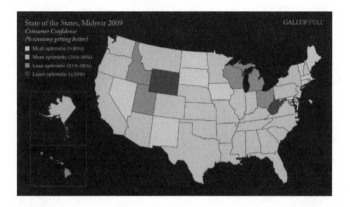

Top States, Consumer Confidence, 2008

State	% Economy getting better
Mississippi	18
Louisiana	18
Texas	17
Arizona	16
Utah	16
Nebraska	16
Montana	16
Georgia	16

2008 Gallup Poll Daily tracking

Consumer Confidence, by State, 2008 and 2009

% Economy getting better

	2008	January-June 2009	Change, 2008-2009
	%	%	Pct. pts.
District of Columbia	12	39	27
South Dakota	13	37	24
Maine	8	32	24
Massachusetts	9	33	24
Vermont	10	33	23
Rhode Island	7	28	21
Connecticut	10	31	21
Maryland	11	31	20
New Mexico	14	34	20
Iowa	13	32	19
New Jersey	11	30	19
New York	11	30	19
Nevada	12	31	19
North Dakota	15	34	19
Delaware	12	30	18
California	12	30	18
Illinois	12	30	18
New Hampshire	12	29	17
Colorado	12	29	17
Virginia	13	30	17
Pennsylvania	11	27	16
North Carolina	14	30	16
Washington	14	30	16
Florida	12	28	16
Oregon	12	28	16
Minnesota	13	28	15
Tennessee	13	28	15
Arkansas	14	29	15
Missouri	12	27	15
South Carolina	14	29	15
Alaska	14	29	15
Kansas	14	28	14
Kentucky	12	26	14
Indiana	13	27	14
Wisconsin	12	25	13
Alabama	15	28	13
Ohio	12	25	13
Texas	17	30	13
Arizona	16	29	13
Georgia	16	28	12
Nebraska	16	28	12
Michigan	11	23	12
Mississippi	18	30	12
Idaho	14	25	11
Oklahoma	15	26	11
Montana	16	27	11
Hawaii	15	25	10
Louisiana	18	28	10
Utah	16	25	9
West Virginia	11	19	8
Wyoming	15	18	3

Gallup Poll Daily tracking

On the other hand, Wyoming has shown the smallest increase—three points. West Virginia and Utah are the other two states to show less than a 10-point increase in economic optimism compared with last year.

To a large extent, the degree of change is related to a state's political orientation. Most of the states showing the greatest gains in economic optimism are solidly Democratic states, likely reflecting their enthusiasm about the new Democratic presidential administration. Likewise, many of the states showing the least improvement are Republican in orientation. Thus, there is a strong element of political partisanship in Americans' perceptions of where the economy is headed.

Rating of Current Economy

At the same time that Americans are more optimistic about the economy's *future direction*, the 2009 data show a less positive assessment of *current* economic conditions than was the case in 2008, on average.

In other words, Americans have higher hopes for the future this year compared to last, but do not believe those hopes have been realized as of yet. These data are corroborated by other Gallup economic data showing that Americans report spending less on a daily basis in 2009 than they did in 2008, and also that working Americans are less likely to report their employers are hiring new workers than was the case in 2008.

The percentage of state residents who rated the current economy "poor" in the first half of 2009 has increased in every state compared with last year, ranging from lows of one point in Vermont and two points in West Virginia to a 23-point increase in Wyoming.

Percentage Rating Current Economic Conditions as Poor, by State, 2008 and 2009

	2008	January-June, 2009	Change, 2008-2009
	%	%	Pct. pts.
Wyoming	38	61	23
Oregon	45	61	16
Colorado	41	57	16
Indiana	45	58	13
Oklahoma	38	51	13
Washington	42	54	12
Alaska	41	53	12
Nevada	51	62	11
Utah	32	43	11
South Carolina	43	53	10
Louisiana	38	48	10
Kansas	37	47	10
North Dakota	33	43	10
Ohio	48	58	10
Idaho	43	53	10
California	49	59	10
Arizona	43	53	10
Minnesota	40	49	9
North Carolina	43	52	9
Georgia	43	52	9
New Jersey	46	55	9
Alabama	41	50	9
Tennessee	46	55	9
Delaware	48	56	8
Texas	36	44	8
Iowa	38	46	8
Connecticut	48	56	8
Massachusetts	47	55	8
Hawaii	42	50	8
Virginia	41	49	8
Montana	40	48	8
Wisconsin	43	51	8
Michigan	56	63	7
New York	47	54	7
Kentucky	46	53	7
Arkansas	46	53	7
Missouri	46	53	7
District of Columbia	46	53	7
Pennsylvania	46	53	7
Florida	50	57	7
New Hampshire	45	51	6
Nebraska	36	42	6
Illinois	45	51	6
South Dakota	37	43	6
Maryland	45	51	6
Maine	50	56	6
New Mexico	41	46	5
Rhode Island	55	59	4
Mississippi	38	41	3
West Virginia	50	52	2
Vermont	48	49	1

Gallup Poll Daily tracking

For this measure, the relationship appears to be somewhat less strong between a state's political party leanings and the degree to which its ratings of the current economy have changed this year.

On an absolute basis, residents of Michigan had the most negative ratings of the economy in the first half of 2009, while residents of Mississippi were least likely to rate the economy as poor.

In addition to Michigan, Nevada, Oregon, and Wyoming residents had the most negative ratings of the economy in the first half of 2009, each with "poor" ratings exceeding 60%. Even the states

with the most positive evaluations of the economy on a relative basis, including Mississippi, Nebraska, the Dakotas, and Utah, had "poor" ratings above 40%.

Top 10 States, Current Economy Rating

State	% Poor
Mississippi	41
Nebraska	42
South Dakota	43
North Dakota	43
Utah	43
Texas	44
New Mexico	46
Iowa	46
Kansas	47
Montana	48
Louisiana	48

January-June 2009 Gallup Poll Daily tracking

Bottom 10 States, Current Economy Rating

State	% Poor
Michigan	63
Nevada	62
Oregon	61
Wyoming	61
Rhode Island	59
California	59
Ohio	58
Indiana	58
Florida	57
Colorado	57

January-June 2009 Gallup Poll Daily tracking

The accompanying map shows the percentage of each state's residents that rated the economy poor in the first half of 2009.

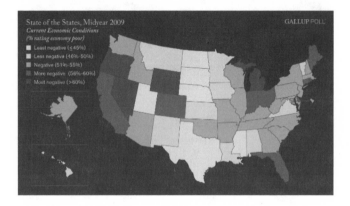

Bottom Line

Consumer attitudes in the United States have shifted over the past year, including more dour assessments of the current economy but also a sunnier outlook on where the economy is headed. These changes are evident in every state in the union as well as in the District of Columbia, though the magnitude of the change varies by state. To a large degree, particularly with regard to perceptions of the economy's future direction, these changes seem to be influenced by partisanship, as some of the more Democratic states tend to be most optimistic about where the economy is headed, now that President Obama is charged with turning the economy around.

Survey Methods

Results are based on telephone interviews with 78,688 national adults, aged 18 and older, conducted Jan. 2–June 30, 2009, as part of Gallup Poll Daily tracking. For results based on the total sample of national adults, one can say with 95% confidence that the maximum margin of sampling error is ±1 percentage point.

The margin of sampling error for most states is ±3 or ±4 percentage points, but is as high as ±10 points for the District of Columbia and ±9 points for Wyoming.

Interviews are conducted with respondents on land-line telephones (for respondents with a land-line telephone) and cellular phones (for respondents who are cell-phone only).

In addition to sampling error, question wording and practical difficulties in conducting surveys can introduce error or bias into the findings of public opinion polls.

August 05, 2009

AMERICANS RETURN TO TOUGHER IMMIGRATION STANCE

More want immigration decreased than kept the same or increased

by Lymari Morales, Gallup Poll Staff Writer

With some U.S. lawmakers and immigration rights activists stepping up calls for the Obama administration to pursue immigration reform, Gallup finds Americans less favorable toward immigration than they were a year ago. Half (50%) say immigration should be decreased, up from 39% last year. A third (32%) say immigration levels should be kept the same, down from 39%, and 14% say they should be increased, down from 18%.

In your view, should immigration be kept at its present level, increased, or decreased?

Gallup trend since 2000

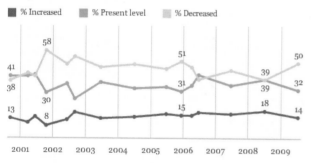

The most recent results, from a Gallup survey conducted July 10–12, 2009, mark a return to the attitudes that prevailed in the first few years after 9/11; attitudes softened from 2006 to last year. The shift toward a tougher stance this time around may reflect the country's economic situation, as Americans tend to become less pro-immigration during difficult economic times.

A similar shift is evident when Americans are asked more broadly whether immigration is a good thing or a bad thing for the country. Currently, 58% say it is a good thing—the lowest percentage saying so since 2003. The historical low for this measure, 52%, came in 2002, after the 9/11 attacks.

The latest Gallup findings preceded a letter that was circulated Monday by seven Illinois congressmen, aimed at urging the Obama administration to take up immigration reform this year. Immigrant activist groups have been eager for reform since a Bush administration bill was defeated in the Senate in 2007.

While these Gallup data do not specifically ask about proposals that might be included in comprehensive immigration reform, they

In your view, should immigration be kept at its present level, increased, or decreased?

By party ID

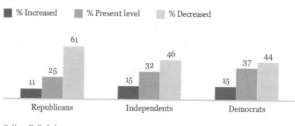

Gallup Poll, July 10-12, 2009

do suggest that Americans of all political persuasions are taking a tougher stance toward immigration than they did a year ago. Republicans are more likely than Democrats to want immigration decreased, as has typically been the case, but more than 4 in 10 independents and Democrats share this view.

In your view, should immigration be kept at its present level, increased, or decreased?

By region

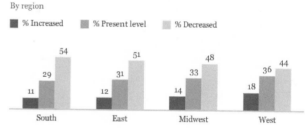

Gallup Poll, July 10-12, 2009

The 61% of Republicans who now say they would like to see immigration decreased is up from 46% in 2008. At the same time, the 44% of Democrats and 46% of independents who would like to see immigration decreased represent shifts in the same direction, up from the 39% and 37%, respectively, who said the same in 2008.

There are slight variations in views on immigration across the four major regions of the country. Americans in the South (54%) are the most likely to want immigration decreased, while those in the West (44%) are relatively less likely to say the same. Here again, each group has shifted toward a more anti-immigration stance.

On the whole, do you think immigration is a good thing or a bad thing for this country today?

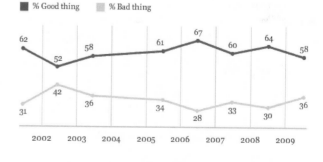

Americans have returned to a tougher stance on immigration than has been evident for the past few years. Republicans, in particular, have shifted most strongly toward decreasing immigration, with Democrats and independents moving in the same direction, but to a lesser degree. Thus, as lawmakers consider when and how to pursue immigration reform, they should do so mindful that Americans of all political persuasions are generally more resistant to immigration in broad measure than they were a year ago.

Author's note: While the views of Hispanics are important to debate and discussion about immigration, the sample size of Hispanics in the poll is not large enough to allow for meaningful interpretation.

Survey Methods

Results are based on telephone interviews with 1,018 national adults, aged 18 and older, conducted July 10–12, 2009. For results based on the total sample of national adults, one can say with 95% confidence that the maximum margin of sampling error is ±3 percentage points.

Interviews are conducted with respondents on land-line telephones (for respondents with a land-line telephone) and cellular phones (for respondents who are cell-phone only).

In addition to sampling error, question wording and practical difficulties in conducting surveys can introduce error or bias into the findings of public opinion polls.

August 06, 2009
VIEWS MIXED ON WHETHER OBAMA IS CHANGING WASHINGTON
Increase since April in view that civility between Democrats and Republicans is getting worse

by Jeffrey M. Jones, Gallup Poll Managing Editor

Since April, there has been a significant increase in the percentage of Americans who say the tone and level of civility between Republicans and Democrats in Washington have gotten worse since Barack Obama was elected president, from 24% to 35%. The plurality of Americans continue to perceive no change in this regard, but that is down from 52% to 42%. About one in five say things have improved in this area, a percentage that has been stable since Obama took office.

Since Barack Obama was elected, do you think the overall tone and level of civility in Washington between Republicans and Democrats has -- [ROTATED: improved, stayed the same, or gotten worse]?

These results are based on the most recent *USA Today*/Gallup poll, conducted July 17–19.

One of the central themes of the Obama candidacy was Obama's desire to bring a new style of governing to Washington, including fostering a greater sense of bipartisanship. In reality, that has not occurred, given nearly unanimous Republican opposition to most of Obama's and the congressional Democrats' policy initiatives—in particular, the economic stimulus plan and healthcare reform.

The public seems to have noticed, as more Americans perceive Democratic-Republican relations in Washington to be deteriorating than said so in the earlier months of the Obama presidency. The decline may also reflect a more general decline in confidence in Obama, as evidenced by the drop in his approval ratings from the mid-60s to the mid-50s in recent months.

Much of that change is due to the views of rank-and-file Republicans. Now, a majority of Republicans, 59%, see the level of civility between the parties as getting worse. In April, 32% of Republicans believed this.

Independents' and Democrats' views have not changed much since April. Independents are most inclined to believe that inter-party civility is staying the same, but are nearly twice as likely to say it is getting worse as to say it is getting better. Democrats are more likely to see conditions as improving than deteriorating, but close to half of Democrats perceive no change.

Views of Tone and Level of Civility in Washington Since Obama Elected, by Political Party

	Improved	Stayed the same	Gotten worse
April			
Democrats	33%	52%	12%
Independents	17%	50%	29%
Republicans	11%	55%	32%
July			
Democrats	34%	47%	16%
Independents	19%	43%	35%
Republicans	5%	34%	59%

USA Today/Gallup poll, July 17-19, 2009

Changing the Way Washington Works

During the campaign, Obama also promised to change the way things got done in Washington, positioning himself as an outsider with little experience in the capital, in contrast to his 2008 primary and general-election rivals, many of whom had served in Washington for decades.

When asked whether Obama has made progress in changing the way Washington works, Americans are evenly divided—49% say he has made progress; 48% say he has not. That's a slightly less positive evaluation than Americans gave him in April, near the 100-day mark of his presidency, when, by 53% to 45%, the public thought Obama was making progress.

Three in four Democrats believe Obama is making progress in changing Washington, but nearly as many Republicans take the opposing view. Independents are more likely to believe Obama has not made progress in changing Washington than to believe that he has.

Fostering a New Idealism

One of the stories of the 2008 campaign was the Obama candidacy's helping to bring many new voters into the political process, including

Barack Obama promised in his campaign to change the way Washington works. Based on what you have heard or read about his administration, do you think he has made progress or not made progress in doing this so far?

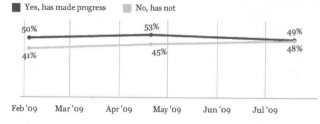

■ Yes, has made progress　　■ No, has not

Has Obama Made Progress in Changing the Way Washington Works, by Party Affiliation

■ Yes, has made progress　　■ No, has not

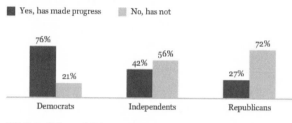

USA Today/Gallup poll, July 17-19, 2009

young adults and racial and ethnic minorities. Some speculated that the Obama presidency might create a new spirit of idealism in the United States, similar to what occurred during John Kennedy's administration.

The poll finds that most Americans, 58%, agree that the Obama administration is creating new idealism in the country; 39% do not believe this is happening. There has been a slight diminishing of this view compared to the days just before Obama took office, when 66% believed the Obama administration would foster idealism among Americans.

Members of Obama's key constituencies—young adults and minorities—are especially likely to believe his administration is making Americans more idealistic.

Specifically, 71% of 18- to 29-year-olds hold this view, compared to 46% of Americans aged 65 and older.

Think Obama Administration Is Creating a New Spirit of Idealism, by Age

■ Yes, is　　■ No, is not

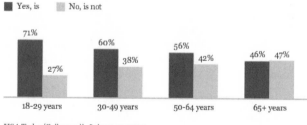

USA Today/Gallup poll, July 17-19, 2009

Similarly, 67% of nonwhites, compared with 55% of whites, sense a new spirit of idealism in the United States brought about by the Obama administration.

Bottom Line

The results on how much change the Obama administration has brought to the country thus far are mixed in the eyes of Americans.

Most Americans do not believe the level of civility between Democrats and Republicans in Washington is improving, and a growing percentage (mostly Republicans) believe it is actually getting worse. Americans are about evenly divided as to whether the Obama administration is making progress toward changing the way Washington works, but they are more inclined to believe his administration is creating a new sense of idealism in the United States.

Survey Methods

Results are based on telephone interviews with 1,006 national adults, aged 18 and older, conducted July 17–19, 2009. For results based on the total sample of national adults, one can say with 95% confidence that the maximum margin of sampling error is ±3 percentage points.

Interviews are conducted with respondents on land-line telephones (for respondents with a land-line telephone) and cellular phones (for respondents who are cell-phone only).

In addition to sampling error, question wording and practical difficulties in conducting surveys can introduce error or bias into the findings of public opinion polls.

August 07, 2009
RELIGIOUS IDENTITY: STATES DIFFER WIDELY
Catholics most prevalent in East, while other Christians are concentrated in the South

by Frank Newport, Gallup Poll Editor in Chief

The states of the union differ remarkably from one another in terms of their residents' religions. Non-Catholic Christians—the largest religious group in the country today—are heavily concentrated in the South and nearby states, while constituting only a minority of residents of Northeastern states, and of many Middle Atlantic and Western states.

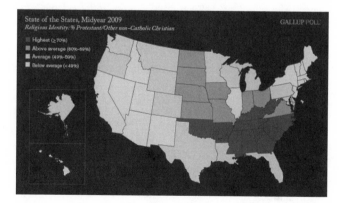

States that have lower percentages of non-Catholic Christians are proportionately much more heavily dominated by those of other religions, particularly Catholics, who are heavily represented in the Middle Atlantic and New England states.

Americans with no religious identity at all tend to be found most frequently in the Northeast and Northwest (plus Hawaii), while members of the Church of Jesus Christ of Latter-day Saints are most prevalent in Utah and surrounding states, and Jews in Mid-Atlantic states.

The accompanying maps give a portrait of this remarkable pattern of religious dispersion in the U.S. for these religious groups, based on a new analysis of more than 170,000 Gallup interviews conducted between January and June of this year. A good deal of the religious dispersion across the states is explainable by historical immigration patterns—particularly the impact of the large waves of European Catholics and Jews who came through ports of entry in the Middle Atlantic states in the 19th and early 20th centuries. (The analysis does not include Muslims or other non-Christian religions due to small sample sizes.)

The geographic concentration of Mormons in and around Utah reflects the cross-country migration of that group in the mid-1800s from Illinois and other Eastern states to their new home. The fact that certain states like Oregon and Vermont consist disproportionately of residents with no religious identity is more difficult to explain, with hypotheses focusing on the particular and idiosyncratic cultures of those states and/or the migration of certain types of Americans to those states over the decades.

The 10 states with the lowest percentages of Catholics are all in or close to the South, with the exception of Utah (with its high concentration of Mormons). Mississippi, with a 6% Catholic population, has the lowest proportion of Catholics of any state.

Protestants/Other Non-Catholic Christians

The largest religious group in America is the 54% of Americans who identify themselves as Protestants or who identify with a non-Catholic Christian religion. There are significant differences in the distribution of this group of non-Catholic Christians across the states of the union. In some states, the percentage of Protestants/other non-Catholic Christians rises to 80% or higher. In others, the percentage of those who are Catholic, some other religion, or no religion at all is so large that it drives down the percentage who are Protestant/other non-Catholic Christian to below one-third.

The proportion of non-Catholic Christians is clearly the highest in the traditional Bible Belt states of the South. In fact, all of the top 10 states in terms of proportion of non-Catholic Christians are Southern or on the fringes of the South; Mississippi and Alabama are at the top, with 81% and 80% Protestant/other Non-Catholic Christian, respectively.

The state with the lowest proportion of non-Catholic Christians is Utah. As will be seen below, the large percentage of Utah residents who are Mormon reduces all other religious categories to low representations. Other states that are low in terms of non-Catholic Christian representation are those with high percentages of Catholics, including Rhode Island, Massachusetts, Connecticut, New York, and New Jersey.

Jews

About 2% of American adults are Jewish, and the distribution of Jews across states is skewed toward Mid-Atlantic and New England states, as well as Florida and California.

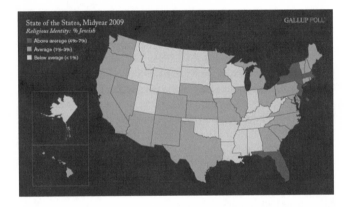

New York has the highest percentage of Jewish residents, at 7%. This figure is for the entire state of New York; the percentage Jewish in New York City is higher.

New York is followed by the District of Columbia and New Jersey, with 5% to 6% Jewish residents. Other states with a 3% or higher Jewish population are Massachusetts, Florida, Maryland, Rhode Island, California, and Connecticut.

A number of states have so few Jews that the estimate of the Jewish population rounds down to 0%. As one example, out of the 959 randomly selected adults Gallup interviewed in Montana from January to June of this year, none identified their religion as Jewish.

Catholics

About 24% of all American adults identified as Catholic between January and June of this year. The distribution of Catholics across the states is heavily skewed toward the New England and Mid-Atlantic states, the regions of the country through which the large waves of Catholic immigrants from Europe arrived in the 19th and 20th centuries.

The state with highest percentage Catholic is Rhode Island, at 53%, followed by Massachusetts, Connecticut, New Jersey, and New York. Two Midwestern states, Wisconsin and Illinois, are also in the top 10 states in terms of the percentage Catholic. States with higher percentages of Hispanic residents, including California and New Mexico, are above average in the proportion of their residents who are Catholic. Louisiana, home to immigrating French Canadians (Cajuns) several centuries ago, also has an above-average Catholic population.

Latter-day Saints (Mormons)

Mormons, who make up about 2% of the U.S population, have the most extremely differentiated geographic pattern of any of the religious groups used in this analysis, with the highest concentrations, as would be expected, in and around the state of Utah. Sixty-one percent of Utah residents interviewed by Gallup identified as Mormons.

Although this is by far the highest concentration of Mormons in any state, the fact that about 4 out of 10 Utah residents are *not* Mor-

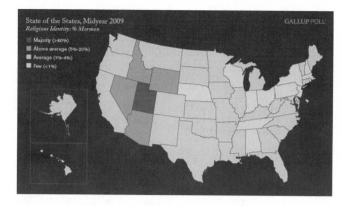

State of the States, Midyear 2009
Religious Identity: % Mormon

GALLUP POLL

- Majority (>60%)
- Above average (5%-20%)
- Average (1%-4%)
- Few (<1%)

national adults, one can say with 95% confidence that the maximum margin of sampling error is ±1 percentage point.

The margin of sampling error for most states is ±3 percentage points, but is as high as ±7 percentage points for the District of Columbia, and ±6 percentage points for Wyoming, North Dakota, South Dakota, Delaware, and Hawaii.

Interviews are conducted with respondents on land-line telephones (for respondents with a land-line telephone) and cellular phones (for respondents who are cell-phone only).

In addition to sampling error, question wording and practical difficulties in conducting surveys can introduce error or bias into the findings of public opinion polls.

mon underscores that Utah has a more diverse religious population than has been the case in previous decades, and certainly in the 19th century, when Brigham Young brought his band of religious followers across the country to settle in the territory that later became Utah.

Idaho and Wyoming—both contiguous to Utah—have 19% and 10% Mormon populations, respectively, while two other states contiguous to Utah also have above-average percentages of Mormons—Arizona at 6% and Nevada at 5%. A number of states, mostly in the Midwest and East, have less than a 1% Mormon population.

No Religious Identity

As was the case in a state-by-state analysis of the percentage of Americans saying religion is important in their daily lives, the states with the highest percentage of adult residents saying they have no religious identity are in the Northeast and the Northwest regions of the country.

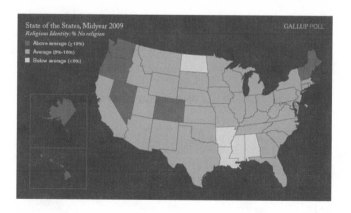

State of the States, Midyear 2009
Religious Identity: % No religion

GALLUP POLL

- Above average (≥19%)
- Average (8%-18%)
- Below average (<8%)

Oregon tops the list, with 25% of its residents claiming no particular religious identity, followed closely by Vermont at 24%. Other states with at least 20% "no religion" are Washington, Alaska, New Hampshire, Hawaii, and Maine.

At the other end of the spectrum, the most religious states in the union, based on the lowest percentages of those saying they have no religion, are Mississippi, where only 6% do not have a religion, followed by Alabama, Arkansas, North Dakota, and Louisiana.

Survey Methods

Results are based on telephone interviews with 178,543 national adults, aged 18 and older, conducted Jan. 2–June 30, 2009, as part of Gallup Poll Daily tracking. For results based on the total sample of

August 07, 2009
MEDICAL CAREERS SEEN AS BEST CHOICE FOR YOUNG MEN, WOMEN
No other field recommended in substantial numbers

by Lydia Saad, Gallup Poll Senior Editor

In today's highly challenging job market, Americans cite the medical field, more than any other profession, as the line of work they would recommend to both young men and young women looking for career advice. Thirty-seven percent would recommend medicine to young women, including 10% citing nursing specifically. Twenty-two percent would recommend medicine for young men, with less than one-half of one percent naming nursing.

Best Careers for a Young Man

	%
Medical field/Healthcare	22
Computers	7
Trades/Industrial/Blue collar	6
Technology/Electronics	5
Business/Self-employed/Sales	5
Engineering	5

July 10-12, 2009

Best Careers for a Young Woman

	%
Medical field/Healthcare	27
Nursing	10
Computers	7
Teaching	7
Business/Self-employed/Sales	5
Technology/Electronics	4

July 10-12, 2009

The majority of Americans who advocate the medical field as a career path for either gender mention medicine or healthcare generally; however—in addition to nursing—some specifically advise young people to become doctors, pharmacists, or veterinarians. Medicine is the only career to have increased on these measures since Gallup last updated them in 2005, and is now the overwhelming response on both questions.

Computers and business/sales are among the top professions named for both genders. Teaching appears in the top five only for young women, mentioned by 7% of Americans, but a not-insignificant 4% recommend it for young men.

Technology/electronics emerges in the top five recommended careers for young men, named by 5%; and, at 4%, it comes close among women. The trades and engineering both rank high for young men, mentioned by 6% and 5%, respectively, but fall low on the list for women.

Although the recent federal stimulus plans have helped make government a growth industry at a time when unemployment is hovering between 9% and 10%, only 3% of Americans mention government as a career for young men and only 2% for young women. Additionally, the military is recommended by 4% for men and by 2% for women.

No other career is mentioned by more than 2% of Americans.

Career Fads Come and Go

These findings are from a July 10–12 Gallup Poll, based on a question Gallup instituted in 1949. At that time, only career advice for young men was measured, but in 1950, the question about young women was added.

The data document several societal shifts over the past six decades. The trend for young men shows a surge in interest in engineering during the 1950s, a spike in teaching during the Vietnam War era (when students studying to become teachers could earn draft deferments), the emergence of computers and electronics technology in the 1980s, and the displacement of medicine as the top-rated field by computers in 1985, followed by a partial resurgence of medicine this decade.

Trend in Medical Field vs. Computers and Technology/Electronics as Recommended Careers for Young Men

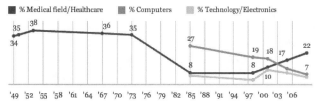

Trends in Engineering and Teaching as Recommended Careers for Young Men

The recommendations for women highlight the impact of the women's rights movement over the past half century, with career choices becoming less gender specific. In 1950, nursing was by far the lead recommendation for women, followed by teaching and then, to a lesser extent, secretarial work, home economics, and social work—all fields (with the exception of teaching) hardly mentioned at the time for men. By 1985, mentions of nursing and teaching had dropped considerably for women and the field of computers ranked No. 1 (as it did for men). Over the last two decades, more and more Americans have named medicine and healthcare for women, with nursing maintaining a relatively high degree of support.

Bottom Line

At a time when Americans widely recognize that a quality job is hard to come by, the healthcare industry—including medicine—is most widely considered the best career choice for young people. That may, in part, reflect assumptions about the social status of a medical career. However, the increase in the percentages recommending med-

Trends in Selected Occupations as Recommended Careers for Young Women

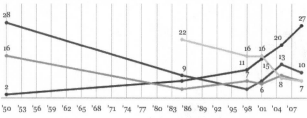

icine, nearly doubling for both men and women since 2001, no doubt reflects a growing perception that it's also a practical choice.

Survey Methods

Results are based on telephone interviews with 1,018 national adults, aged 18 and older, conducted July 10–12, 2009. For results based on the total sample of national adults, one can say with 95% confidence that the maximum margin of sampling error is ±4 percentage points.

Interviews are conducted with respondents on land-line telephones (for respondents with a land-line telephone) and cellular phones (for respondents who are cell-phone only).

In addition to sampling error, question wording and practical difficulties in conducting surveys can introduce error or bias into the findings of public opinion polls.

August 10, 2009
OBAMA JOB APPROVAL: HIGHEST IN D.C., HAWAII, VERMONT
Lowest rating in Wyoming

by Jeffrey M. Jones, Gallup Poll Managing Editor

From the time Barack Obama took office as president until the end of June, 63% of Americans, on average, approved of the job he was doing. The breakdown of his half-year approval ratings at the state level shows that Obama's approval rating was above 50% in all but two states, Wyoming and Alaska. His highest approval ratings were in the District of Columbia, Hawaii, Vermont, Maryland, and Massachusetts.

Top 10 States, Obama Job Approval		*Bottom 10 States, Obama Job Approval*	
State	**% Approve**	**State**	**% Approve**
District of Columbia	92	Wyoming	46
Hawaii	75	Alaska	49
Vermont	74	Idaho	50
Maryland	73	Utah	50
Massachusetts	73	West Virginia	51
Connecticut	71	Montana	52
New York	71	Oklahoma	53
Illinois	71	Colorado	55
Rhode Island	70	Kansas	55
New Jersey	69	Louisiana	55

January–June 2009 Gallup Poll Daily tracking   January–June 2009 Gallup Poll Daily tracking

Gallup tracks Obama's overall job approval ratings each day as part of Gallup Poll Daily tracking. The large number of interviews conducted nationally—more than 80,000 from Jan. 21 through June 30—allow Gallup to analyze the opinions of selected subgroups, including residents of each of the 50 U.S. states and the District of Columbia. Each state's data are weighted to Census-based demographic and regional parameters to be representative of the state's adult population. The accompanying map shows where Obama's support was higher and lower on a relative basis, by state.

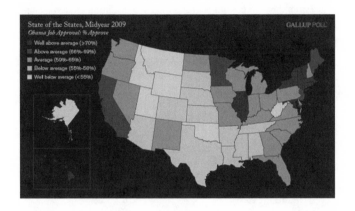

Since June, Obama's approval rating has descended into the 50s, sinking as low as 52% in late July before recovering somewhat and settling back in the mid- to upper 50s in recent days. An analysis of Gallup Poll Daily data collected in July and August suggests that Obama's approval rating has declined in most states compared with the January-June averages. While the recent state approval ratings are lower than those reported here, the relative rank ordering of states is largely similar.

In general, state patterns of support for Obama follow the political orientations of the states. For the most part, the states that Gallup classified as "solidly Democratic" (based on the party affiliation and leaning of its residents in the first half of the year) had approval ratings at or above the national average of 63%. The four states Gallup identified as being "solidly Republican"—Wyoming, Alaska, Utah, and Idaho—gave Obama his lowest average approval ratings. But even in these four states, his approval rating exceeded his disapproval rating.

Obama's poorest performance in a solidly Democratic state was in West Virginia, which had an average 51% approval rating. His worst showing in a competitive state was 52% in Montana, while his best showing in a competitive state was 63% in North Dakota.

North Dakota also gave Obama his highest approval rating of any state he did not carry in the 2008 presidential election. Obama's lowest approval rating in a state he won is Colorado's 55%.

Survey Methods

Results are based on telephone interviews with 81,022 national adults, aged 18 and older, conducted Jan. 21–June 30, 2009, as part of Gallup Poll Daily tracking. For results based on the total sample of national adults, one can say with 95% confidence that the maximum margin of sampling error is ±1 percentage point.

Margins of error for most states are ±3 or ±4 percentage points, but are as high as ±10 for the District of Columbia and ±8 for Wyoming.

Interviews are conducted with respondents on land-line telephones (for respondents with a land-line telephone) and cellular phones (for respondents who are cell-phone only).

In addition to sampling error, question wording and practical difficulties in conducting surveys can introduce error or bias into the findings of public opinion polls.

August 11, 2009
CONSTITUENTS DIVIDED, HIGHLY PARTISAN ON HEALTHCARE REFORM
Equally split in advising Congress to vote for (35%) or against (36%) a new law

by Frank Newport , Gallup Poll Editor in Chief

Americans at this point have mixed sentiments on the issue of a new healthcare reform bill. A new Gallup Poll finds that about the same percentage (35%) would tell their congressional representative to vote for a new healthcare reform bill when Congress reconvenes in September as say they would tell their representative to vote against such a bill (36%). The rest (29%) have no opinion either way at this time.

Would you advise your member of Congress to vote for or against a healthcare reform bill when they return to Washington in September, or do you not have an opinion?

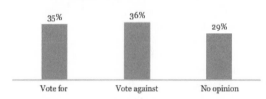

Gallup Poll, Aug. 6-9, 2009

Members of Congress are for the most part home in their districts this August, and are by all accounts facing highly opinionated constituencies on the issue of healthcare reform. News reports have highlighted often-contentious debates taking place at town hall meetings held by senators and representatives seeking input on the issue.

Previous Gallup Poll measures have shown majority support for the concept of healthcare reform but a July poll result indicated that when Americans are given choices about the timing for a new reform law, a majority say either that they support a bill but do not believe it needs to be passed this year, or that a new bill is not necessary at all. The current poll results, based on a different question wording, show that a sizable group of about 3 in 10 Americans are undecided on the issue, and those who have an opinion are evenly divided.

Highly Partisan Reactions

The new question on healthcare reform, included in Gallup's Aug. 6–9 poll, did not identify or connect the idea of a new healthcare reform law with any specific individual or party. Still, the responses are highly partisan. The majority of Republicans and Republican-leaning independents (66%) say they would tell their member of Congress to vote against a new healthcare reform bill. The majority of Democrats and Democratic-leaning independents (59%) say they would tell their member to vote for a reform bill. Only 10% of each party group has the contrary opinions, i.e., Republicans wanting their member to vote for a bill or Democrats wanting their member to vote against such a bill.

Would you advise your member of Congress to vote for or against a healthcare reform bill when they return to Washington in September, or do you not have an opinion?

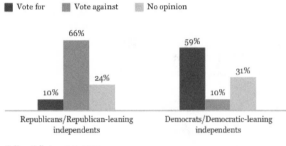

Gallup Poll, Aug. 6-9, 2009

A previous Gallup review of the healthcare reform issue showed that only about a fourth of Americans believe that members of Congress understand the issues involved in healthcare reform. Additionally, Americans see the economy rather than healthcare reform as the top problem facing the country at this point—although the percentage saying health issues are the top problem facing the country has been rising.

The latest measure reviewed here suggests that a sizable group of Americans are still open to persuasion on the issue. Both sides of the issue are working diligently to promote their side of the debate, including a new "Health Insurance Reform Reality Check" initiative by the White House. It is possible that the interaction between representatives and their constituents over the next several weeks—coupled with the intense media focus on healthcare reform—may further affect public opinion either for or against healthcare legislation as Congress returns to Washington in September.

Survey Methods

Results are based on telephone interviews with 1,010 national adults, aged 18 and older, conducted Aug. 6–9, 2009. For results based on the total sample of national adults, one can say with 95% confidence that the maximum margin of sampling error is ±4 percentage points.

Interviews are conducted with respondents on land-line telephones (for respondents with a land-line telephone) and cellular phones (for respondents who are cell-phone only).

In addition to sampling error, question wording and practical difficulties in conducting surveys can introduce error or bias into the findings of public opinion polls.

AMID DEBATE, OBAMA APPROVAL RATING ON HEALTHCARE STEADY
Americans disapprove of his handling of the issue, by 49% to 43%

by Jeffrey M. Jones, Gallup Poll Managing Editor

Americans rate President Barack Obama's handling of healthcare policy essentially the same as they did roughly three weeks ago, remaining slightly more likely to disapprove than approve. The update comes after several weeks of Congress' working to advance legislation through committees and the Obama administration's stepping up efforts to win public support.

Do you approve or disapprove of the way Barack Obama is handling healthcare policy?

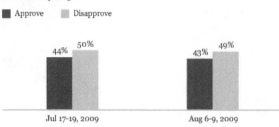

Healthcare reform has stirred spirited opposition in a series of town hall meetings between members of Congress and their constituents. Obama is trying to counter some of that opposition with his own healthcare push, as he vows to pass legislation before the end of the year.

Of four issues tested in the Aug. 6–9 Gallup Poll, Obama fares the worst on healthcare. His ratings on the economy are slightly better, with Americans evenly divided in their opinions of how he is handling this issue. The president gets better ratings for his handling of both foreign affairs and education.

Approval Rating of Obama on Issues

Aug. 6-9, 2009

All four issue ratings are lower than his overall job approval rating of 54%.

At least three-quarters of Democrats approve of Obama's handling of each of the four issues. Meanwhile, Obama gets no higher than a 24% approval rating from Republicans on any of the issues (education), including a low of 10% on healthcare.

Independents' ratings on each of the issues fall between those of the other two party groups, but closer to Republicans' than to Democrats' ratings, and do not reach the majority level on any issue.

Of the issues, Gallup has most frequently measured public opinions of Obama's handling of the economy and foreign affairs. Each

Approval Rating of Obama on Issues, by Party

	Democrats	**Independents**	**Republicans**
Education	81%	48%	24%
Foreign affairs	84%	45%	21%
The economy	84%	39%	13%
Healthcare policy	77%	35%	10%

Aug. 6-9, 2009

is now tied for the lowest of his presidency to date, and has declined from ratings near 60% earlier in his presidency, similar to the decline in his overall approval rating during this time.

Obama's rating on the economy declined the most between May and July, to the point where slightly more Americans gave him a negative than a positive evaluation. In the latest update, his ratings appear to have stabilized.

Approval Rating of President Obama on the Economy

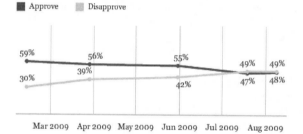

Obama's foreign affairs approval rating has declined less than his economy rating, but has dropped four points from the July reading.

Approval Rating of President Obama on Foreign Affairs

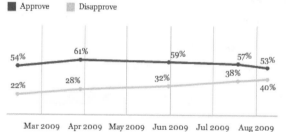

The Aug. 6–9 poll marks the first time Gallup has measured Obama's approval rating on education.

Survey Methods

Results are based on telephone interviews with 1,010 national adults, aged 18 and older, conducted Aug. 6–9, 2009. For results based on the total sample of national adults, one can say with 95% confidence that the maximum margin of sampling error is ±4 percentage points.

Interviews are conducted with respondents on land-line telephones (for respondents with a land-line telephone) and cellular phones (for respondents who are cell-phone only).

In addition to sampling error, question wording and practical difficulties in conducting surveys can introduce error or bias into the findings of public opinion polls.

August 12, 2009
TOWN HALL MEETINGS GENERATE INTEREST, SOME SYMPATHY
Americans overall more likely to be sympathetic to protestors' views than not

by Frank Newport, Gallup Poll Editor in Chief

More than two-thirds of Americans (69%) are closely following news accounts of town hall meetings on healthcare reform, and while 34% say the protests make them more sympathetic to the protestors' viewpoints and 21% say the protests make them less sympathetic, almost half either say the protests haven't affected their views either way or have no opinion.

From what you know or have read, have these town hall meeting protests against the proposed bills made you -- more sympathetic to the protestors' views, do the protests not make any difference to you either way, or have the protests made you less sympathetic to the protestors' views?

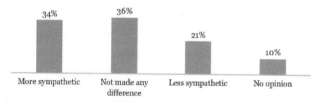

USA Today/Gallup poll, Aug. 11, 2009

Video clips of angry protestors speaking up at various town hall meetings held by members of Congress and senators on proposed healthcare reform legislation across the country have dominated news coverage of healthcare reform in recent days.

Survey Methods

Results are based on telephone interviews with 1,000 national adults, aged 18 and older, conducted Aug. 11, 2009, as part of Gallup Poll Daily tracking. For results based on the total sample of national adults, one can say with 95% confidence that the maximum margin of sampling error is ±4 percentage points.

Interviews are conducted with respondents on land-line telephones (for respondents with a land-line telephone) and cellular phones (for respondents who are cell-phone only).

In addition to sampling error, question wording and practical difficulties in conducting surveys can introduce error or bias into the findings of public opinion polls.

Polls conducted entirely in one day, such as this one, are subject to additional error or bias not found in polls conducted over several days.

August 12, 2009

WELL-BEING: HAWAII, UTAH STILL TOP THE NATION

Eight of 10 highest well-being states located in the West and Midwest

by Elizabeth Mendes, Gallup Poll Staff Writer

Americans in Hawaii and Utah continued to lead the nation in well-being in the first half of 2009, with the two states having switched places since 2008. West Virginia and Kentucky maintained their status as the states with the lowest well-being.

State of the States, Midyear 2009
AHIP State and Congressional District Resource for Well-Being
A product of the Gallup-Healthways Well-Being Index

Well-Being Index score
■ Higher range (66.0-69.4)
■ Mid-range (64.5-65.9)
□ Lower range (59.9-64.4)

GALLUP POLL

Top 10 States, Well-Being

State	Well-Being Index Score
Hawaii	69.4
Utah	68.7
Montana	67.5
Iowa	67.5
North Dakota	67.2
Vermont	67.0
Kansas	66.9
Maryland	66.9
Minnesota	66.9
Virginia	66.8
Idaho	66.8

January-June 2009
AHIP State and Congressional District Resource for Well-Being -- A product of the Gallup-Healthways Well-Being Index

Bottom 10 States, Well-Being

State	Well-Being Index Score
West Virginia	59.9
Kentucky	61.1
Arkansas	61.4
Mississippi	62.7
Ohio	63
Alabama	63.5
Indiana	63.5
Tennessee	63.6
Nevada	63.8
Rhode Island	63.8

January-June 2009
AHIP State and Congressional District Resource for Well-Being -- A product of the Gallup-Healthways Well-Being Index

These state-level data are from the Gallup-Healthways Well-Being Index and the AHIP State and Congressional District Resource for Well-Being, and are meant to provide a preliminary reading on the well-being of the states of the nation in anticipation of the complete 2009 rankings, which will encompass all 12 months of the year. The Well-Being Index score for the nation and for each state is an average of six sub-indexes, which individually examine life evaluation, emotional health, work environment, physical health, healthy behaviors, and access to basic necessities. The January through June 2009 aggregate includes more than 170,000 interviews conducted among national adults, aged 18 and older.

The midyear 2009 Well-Being Index score for the country so far in 2009 is 65.2, a moderate decline from 65.9 in 2008. The Well-Being Index is calculated on a scale of 0 to 100, where a score of 100 would represent ideal well-being. Well-Being Index scores among states vary by a range of 9.5 points.

Looking at change over time among states, Iowa's Well-Being Index composite score moved up the most, from 65.6 in 2008 to 67.5 in the first half of 2009. Well-being in Wyoming has trended down the most, dropping to 65.9 in 2009 from 68.0 last year, though it should be noted that Wyoming has a relatively small sample size at this point and thus a larger margin of error.

Four of the top 10 scoring states—Iowa, North Dakota, Kansas, and Minnesota—are in the Midwest. As in 2008, many of the states with lower Well-Being Index scores are located in the South. Nevada is the only Western state in the bottom 10.

The national scores for five of the six sub-indexes that make up the Well-Being Index trended down, though marginally, in the first six months of 2009 in comparison to 2008. Life Evaluation is the only sub-index to increase at the national level, with all but seven states moving in a positive direction in the first six months of 2009. Life evaluation improved the most in North Dakota and South Dakota, while Wyoming experienced the steepest decline.

At the other end of the spectrum, the January through June data show that nationally, Work Environment, which measures an individual worker's engagement with his or her job, is the sub-index that has moved the most in a negative direction. More than three-quarters of states have seen their Work Environment score move in a downward direction in 2009.

A look at the best and worst states on each of the sub-indexes at midyear 2009 reveals the extent to which the sub-indexes drive the overall rankings. In addition to having the best overall Well-Being Index score, Hawaii is also at the top in terms of Emotional Health. Utah does the best on Life Evaluation, Iowa tops the nation in Basic Access, North Dakota has the best Physical Health score, Vermont is first in terms of Healthy Behavior, and Idaho is the top scorer on Work Environment. On the flip side, West Virginia fares worst on three of the six sub-indexes—Life Evaluation, Emotional Health, and Physical Health—as it did in 2008. Kentucky performs worst on Healthy Behavior and Mississippi is at the bottom on Basic Access, also the same as in 2008. Delaware has the lowest Work Environment score.

Best and Worst States, Well-Being Sub-Indexes

Sub-Index	Best	Worst
Life Evaluation	Utah	West Virginia
Emotional Health	Hawaii	West Virginia
Work Environment	Idaho	Delaware
Physical Health	North Dakota	West Virginia
Healthy Behavior	Vermont	Kentucky
Basic Access	Iowa	Mississippi

January-June 2009
AHIP State and Congressional District Resource for Well-Being -- A product of the Gallup-Healthways Well-Being Index

Bottom Line

The overall well-being of the nation has thus far trended down 0.4 points in 2009, representing a modest decline from 2008 in Americans' collective well-being. At the midyear point, a number of Western and Midwestern states top the country on well-being, while Southern states are more prevalent toward the bottom of the list. The states at the very front and very back of the pack have remained unchanged from 2008, with Hawaii and Utah continuing to lead the nation on overall well-being, while West Virginia and Kentucky are trailing. While the data from the first six months of 2009 give a glimpse into where the well-being of states is headed, a more complete picture of state-level well-being will take shape after a full year of data collection.

Complete 2008 rankings are available at the AHIP State and Congressional District Resource for Well-Being, a one-of-a-kind interactive database that enables users to research and sort Gallup-Healthways Well-Being Index data alongside the most up-to-date statistics from the Census Bureau.

Editor's Note: Updates to the national Well-Being Index scores for 2008 and 2009 are reflected in this article.

Survey Methods

Results are based on telephone interviews with more than 178,545 national adults, aged 18 and older, conducted Jan. 2–June 30, 2009, as part of the Gallup-Healthways Well-Being Index. For results based on the total sample of national adults, one can say with 95% confidence that the maximum margin of sampling error is ±0.2 percentage points.

The margin of sampling error for most states is ±1–2 percentage points, but is as high as ±4 points for smaller states such as Wyoming, North Dakota, South Dakota, Delaware, and Hawaii.

The AHIP State and Congressional District Resource for Well-Being categorizes the District of Columbia as a congressional district.

Interviews are conducted with respondents on land-line telephones (for respondents with a land-line telephone) and cellular phones (for respondents who are cell-phone only).

In addition to sampling error, question wording and practical difficulties in conducting surveys can introduce error or bias into the findings of public opinion polls.

August 13, 2009
WORKER JOB SECURITY CONCERNS SPIKE TO NEW HIGHS
Close to half worried benefits will be reduced

by Jeffrey M. Jones, Gallup Poll Managing Editor

A new Gallup Poll finds a dramatic increase in the percentage of U.S. workers who are personally concerned about losing their job. Now, 31% say they are worried about being laid off, up from 15% last year and easily the highest Gallup has found since the question was first asked in 1997.

Historically, Gallup has not found a great deal of worry on the part of workers about being laid off, with typically about one in six workers expressing concern about this. But the economy has gone from bad to worse in the past year, including an unemployment rate above 9% for the first time since 1983, and up from 5.8% a year ago. And while the majority of workers continue to say they are not worried about losing their job, many more do so now than last year at this time.

The greater concern about layoffs is evident among workers from all demographic groups; however, the increase has been proportionately less among college graduates than among non-graduates.

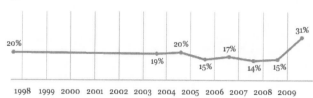

Next, please indicate whether you are worried or not worried about each of the following happening to you, personally, in the near future. How about that you will be laid off?

Based on employed Americans

■ Yes, worried

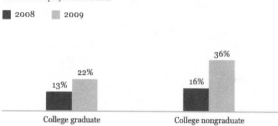

Worried About Being Laid Off, by Education, 2008 vs. 2009

Based on employed Americans

■ 2008   ▨ 2009

Greater worker anxiety stretches beyond basic worries about keeping one's job; Gallup also finds sharp increases from last year in the percentages of workers who are worried about their hours being cut back, their wages being reduced, and their benefits being reduced. On a relative basis, U.S. workers are most concerned about cuts in benefits (46%), followed by pay cuts (32%, and similar to the 31% worried about losing their jobs) and a reduction in hours (27%).

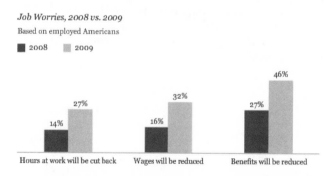

Job Worries, 2008 vs. 2009

Based on employed Americans

■ 2008   ▨ 2009

All of these items have surpassed their previous high measurements by more than 10 percentage points.

There is one exception to the general pattern of rising concern about one's job over the past year. There has been essentially no change in workers' expressed worry about their jobs being moved to a country overseas (10% in the latest poll, compared with 8% last year).

Bottom Line

The poor economy and high unemployment rate have helped to raise workers' anxiety about their jobs to levels not seen in the past decade, with concerns about being laid off, having hours cut, wages reduced, and benefits reduced all showing double-digit increases since last year.

Trend in Job Worries

% Worried

Based on employed Americans

■ Hours cut   ■ Wages reduced   ■ Benefits reduced

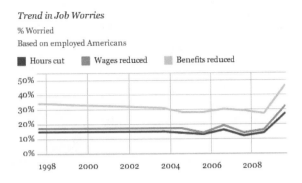

Top 10 Conservative States			Top 10 Liberal States	
	Total "conservative"			Total "liberal"
	%			%
Alabama	49		District of Columbia	37
Mississippi	48		Massachusetts	29
Utah	47		Vermont	28
Louisiana	47		Oregon	27
Oklahoma	47		Washington	26
South Carolina	46		New York	26
North Dakota	45		New Jersey	26
South Dakota	44		California	26
Idaho	44		Hawaii	24
Wyoming	44		Connecticut	24

January-June 2009 Gallup Daily tracking   January-June 2009 Gallup Daily tracking

For the most part, American workers have never expressed a large degree of worry about these types of job-related setbacks, so the sharp increases in worry—even though this still represents the minority of U.S. workers—is notable.

Worker anxiety will probably recede once the unemployment rate starts to dip and more workers who want jobs can find them. For several months running, only about 1 in 10 Americans in Gallup Polls have said it is a good time to find a quality job. So the concern about losing one's job or taking a forced cut in income or benefits is likely greater, given the added pessimism about being able to find a new job should it become necessary.

Survey Methods

Results are based on telephone interviews with 528 national adults, aged 18 and older, employed full- or part-time, conducted Aug. 6–9, 2009. For results based on the total sample of national adults, one can say with 95% confidence that the maximum margin of sampling error is ±5 percentage points.

Interviews are conducted with respondents on land-line telephones (for respondents with a land-line telephone) and cellular phones (for respondents who are cell-phone only).

In addition to sampling error, question wording and practical difficulties in conducting surveys can introduce error or bias into the findings of public opinion polls.

August 14, 2009

POLITICAL IDEOLOGY: "CONSERVATIVE" LABEL PREVAILS IN THE SOUTH

Conservatives outnumber liberals in nearly every state, but not in D.C.

by Lydia Saad, Gallup Poll Senior Editor

The strength of "conservative" over "liberal" in the realm of political labels is vividly apparent in Gallup's state-level data, where a significantly higher percentage of Americans in most states—even some solidly Democratic ones—call themselves conservative rather than liberal.

The most conservative states are found primarily in the South, led by Alabama and Mississippi. The figure approaches 50% in several Southern states, plus Utah. The most liberal states tend to be on the East and West coasts, led by Washington, D.C., and then Massachusetts, Vermont, and Oregon.

These findings are based on Americans' answers to a question asking whether their political views are very conservative, conservative, moderate, liberal, or very liberal. The data come from Gallup Daily tracking in the first half of 2009, encompassing interviews with more than 160,000 U.S. adults, with a minimum of 400 interviews for each state (and 300 in the District of Columbia).

The overall percentages of self-declared conservatives in each state range from a high of 49% in Alabama to a low of 23% in the nation's capital. The "liberal" label is embraced most widely in D.C., by 37%, followed by 29% in Massachusetts. At 14%, it is used least commonly in Louisiana.

Because the percentage of moderates varies by state—from 43% in Hawaii and Rhode Island down to 32% in Alabama—the percentage identifying themselves as "conservative" does not by itself provide a complete picture of the relative strength of conservatism across states. For this reason, the "net conservative" statistic—defined as the total percentage calling themselves conservative minus the total percentage defining themselves as liberal—is used in the accompanying map to identify the ideological makeup of each state.

States where the conservatives' advantage over liberals is greater than 25 percentage points are defined as Most Conservative. Net conservatism registering 20 to 25 points is defined as More Conservative; from 10 to 19 points, as Somewhat Conservative; and from 1 to 9 points, as Less Conservative. Only Washington, D.C., which has more liberals than conservatives, is defined as Liberal.

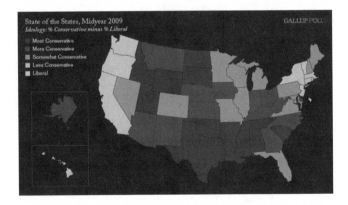

While Americans' party identification and political ideology are related, they are by no means one and the same. For instance, while residents of Alabama and Mississippi are the most likely to be conservative ideologically, they are not the most Republican in their party affiliation. According to Gallup's report on party identification by state earlier this month, that distinction goes to Utah, whose net conservative score is only slightly higher than that of South Dakota (a Democratic-leaning state).

In fact, while all 50 states are, to some degree, more conservative than liberal (with the conservative advantage ranging from 1 to 34 points), Gallup's 2009 party ID results indicate that Democrats have significant party ID advantages in 30 states and Republicans in only 4.

Bottom Line

Despite the Democratic Party's political strength—seen in its majority representation in Congress and in state houses across the country—more Americans consider themselves conservative than liberal. While Gallup polling has found this to be true at the national level over many years, and spanning recent Republican as well as Democratic presidential administrations, the present analysis confirms that the pattern also largely holds at the state level. Conservatives outnumber liberals by statistically significant margins in 47 of the 50 states, with the two groups statistically tied in Hawaii, Vermont, and Massachusetts.

When considered with party identification, these ideology findings highlight the role that political moderates currently play in joining with liberals to give the Democratic Party its numerical advantage.

Survey Methods

Results are based on telephone interviews with 160,236 national adults, aged 18 and older, conducted Jan. 2–June 30, 2009, as part of Gallup Daily tracking. For results based on the total sample of national adults, one can say with 95% confidence that the maximum margin of sampling error is ±1 percentage point.

The margin of sampling error for most states is ±3 percentage points, but is as high as ±7 percentage points for the District of Columbia, and ±6 percentage points for Wyoming, North Dakota, South Dakota, Delaware, and Hawaii.

Interviews are conducted with respondents on land-line telephones (for respondents with a land-line telephone) and cellular phones (for respondents who are cell-phone only).

In addition to sampling error, question wording and practical difficulties in conducting surveys can introduce error or bias into the findings of public opinion polls.

August 14, 2009
ECONOMY DECLINES FURTHER AS TOP PROBLEM; HEALTHCARE RISES
One in four now name healthcare, up from 16% a month ago

by Lymari Morales, Gallup Poll Staff Writer

At the same time that more Americans say the economy is getting better, the percentage who name an economic issue as the most important problem facing the country is down to 60% from 69% a month ago. Meantime, the healthcare debate is turning more attention to that issue, with 25% now calling it the country's most important problem—up from 16% a month ago.

What do you think is the most important problem facing this country today?
2008-2009 trend

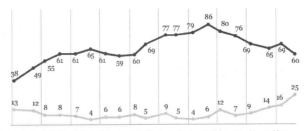

The percentage of Americans naming an economic issue as the most important problem facing the country remains high but has been decreasing steadily from a high of 86% in February. The current reading matches the 60% recorded Sept. 8–11, 2008, before economic bankruptcies and bailouts began in earnest in mid-September of last year. An even higher 65% named an economic issue in June 2008, driven in large part by high concern about fuel/oil prices at that time.

Looking at Americans' specific economic concerns now, the percentage who name the economy in general is down slightly, to 33% from 38% a month ago. Mentions of unemployment are also down, to 14% from 19%, while mentions of the federal budget or budget deficit are up slightly, to 7% from 4%—reflecting Americans' high level of concern about government spending.

United States' Most Important Problem -- Economic Mentions

		One month ago	One year ago
	Aug 6-9, 2009	Jul 10-12, 2009	Aug 7-10, 2008
	%	%	%
NET ECONOMIC MENTIONS^	60	69	59
Economy in general	33	38	38
Unemployment/Jobs	14	19	6
Federal budget deficit/Federal debt	7	4	2
Lack of money	6	7	--

^ "Net economic mentions" is percentage of Americans naming at least one economic issue

Healthcare Now Top of Mind

The healthcare reform debate raging in Washington, on television news, and in town hall meetings across America is clearly putting the spotlight on that issue, and may in part be the reason fewer Americans this month mention the economy as the nation's top problem. One in four (25%) now call healthcare the country's most important problem—up from 16% a month ago and 6% a year ago. The spike in the percentage of Americans mentioning healthcare is similar to what Gallup recorded when the Clinton administration made its attempt at healthcare reform in the early '90s—though mentions have not yet reached the high of 31% recorded in January 1994.

After healthcare, dissatisfaction with government/politicians continues to rank second on the list of non-economic issues.

Survey Methods

Results are based on telephone interviews with 1,010 national adults, aged 18 and older, conducted Aug. 6–9, 2009. For results based on the total sample of national adults, one can say with 95%

What do you think is the most important problem facing this country today?
Recent trend

■ % Mentioning healthcare

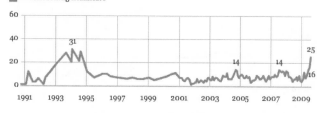

United States' Most Important Problem -- Non-Economic Mentions

	Aug 6-9, 2009	One month ago July 10-12, 2009	One year ago Aug 7-10, 2008
	%	%	%
NET NON-ECONOMIC MENTIONS ^	49	45	57
Poor healthcare/hospitals; high cost of healthcare	25	16	6
Dissatisfaction with government/ Congress/politicians; poor leadership; corruption; abuse of power	7	8	9
Situation in Iraq/War	5	5	19
Ethics/Moral/Religious/Family decline; dishonesty	2	2	4
Lack of respect for each other	2	1	*
Education/Poor education/Access to education	2	2	2
Immigration/Illegal aliens	2	1	3

^ "Net non-economic mentions" is percentage of Americans naming at least one non-economic issue
* Less than 0.5%

confidence that the maximum margin of sampling error is ±4 percentage points.

Interviews are conducted with respondents on land-line telephones (for respondents with a land-line telephone) and cellular phones (for respondents who are cell-phone only).

In addition to sampling error, question wording and practical difficulties in conducting surveys can introduce error or bias into the findings of public opinion polls.

August 17, 2009
AUTOMOBILE, BANKING INDUSTRY IMAGES SLIDE FURTHER
Most other major industries' images have improved this year

by Jeffrey M. Jones, Gallup Poll Managing Editor

Americans are more positive about most major businesses and industries this year, after being more negative nearly across the board in 2008. The banking and automobile industries are two notable exceptions, having seen their positive scores continue to drop this year. The biggest gainers since last year are the grocery industry, the airline industry, and the federal government.

In its annual Work and Education poll, Gallup asks Americans to rate each of 25 major businesses and industries as positive, negative, or neutral. This year's update, conducted Aug. 6–9, finds that many industries that took big image hits in last year's poll have recovered this year. For example, the grocery industry's 15-point gain in positive ratings nearly wipes out the 17-point decline it suffered in 2008, which was perhaps a response to rising food prices.

On another subject, for each of the following business sectors in the United States, please say whether your overall view of it is very positive, somewhat positive, neutral, somewhat negative or very negative.
Sorted by % positive, 2009

	% Positive, 2008	% Positive, 2009	Change Pct. pts.
Computer industry	60	62	2
Restaurant industry	51	57	6
Farming and agriculture	50	56	6
Internet industry	49	51	2
Grocery industry	36	51	15
Retail industry	39	44	5
Education	41	43	2
Travel industry	34	42	8
Telephone industry	39	41	2
Publishing industry	36	40	4
Television and radio industry	37	40	3
Sports industry	36	39	3
Movie industry	35	38	3
Healthcare industry	27	36	9
Accounting	36	34	-2
Airline industry	18	32	14
Advertising/Public relations industry	27	31	4
Electric and gas utilities	27	31	4
Pharmaceutical industry	31	31	0
The federal government	18	29	11
Banking	36	28	-8
The legal field	26	25	-1
Real estate industry	16	24	8
Automobile industry	29	24	-5
Oil and gas industry	15	21	6

The airline, travel, and oil and gas industries erased their 2008 losses—likely due to record-high fuel prices in 2008—while the real estate, restaurant, and retail industries also rebounded significantly from the steep drops they experienced last year.

But the banking industry lost an additional 8 points this year after a 14-point drop in 2008, and the automobile industry's positive ratings fell an additional 5 points after a 9-point drop in 2008.

The banking and automotive industries have been struggling financially but also raised the ire of the public when, for example, Wall Street executives continued to receive large bonuses while many of their companies suffered huge losses, and when members of Congress rebuked the Big Three auto executives for taking private jets to Washington to ask for government loans.

Only two years ago, more Americans viewed both industries more positively than negatively. As recently as 2006, a majority of Americans had positive ratings of the banking industry, and in 2003, most Americans viewed the automobile industry in positive terms.

Also notable in this year's data is an increase in ratings of the healthcare industry, which is up 9 points from last year to 36% positive, similar to its 2006 level. That could reflect its taking a much more positive view of healthcare reform this year than it did in 1993–1994, when its opposition helped defeat the Clinton administration's efforts. Still, the public does not hold the healthcare industry in very high regard, with its 36% positive and 48% negative rating.

Computer Industry Gets Highest Marks

On an absolute basis, the most positively rated industries are computers (62%), restaurants (57%), and farming and agriculture (56%). The least positive are oil and gas (21%), automobile (24%), real estate

Changes in Positive Ratings of Business and Industry Sectors, 2007-2008 and 2008-2009
In percentage points

	Change in positive ratings, 2007 to 2008	Change in positive ratings, 2008 to 2009
Accounting	-4	-2
Advertising and public relations industry	-8	4
Airline industry	-12	14
Automobile industry	-9	-5
Banking	-14	-8
Computer industry	-1	2
Education	-6	2
Electric and gas utilities	-4	4
Farming and agriculture	-1	6
Grocery industry	-17	15
Healthcare industry	-1	9
Internet industry	-5	2
Movie industry	-1	3
Oil and gas industry	-4	6
Pharmaceutical industry	-2	0
Publishing industry	-7	4
Real estate industry	-18	8
Restaurant industry	-12	6
Retail industry	-12	5
Sports industry	1	3
Telephone industry	-7	2
Television and radio industry	-4	3
The federal government	-3	11
The legal field	-5	-1
Travel industry	-8	8

Positive Ratings of Banking and Automobile Industries, 2001-2009

■ Automobile   ■ Banking

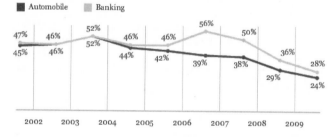

Highest Positive Ratings of Businesses and Industries, 2001-2009 Gallup Polls

Year	Business/Industry	% Positive ratings
2009	Computer	62
2008	Computer	60
2007	Restaurant	63
	Computer	61
2006	Restaurant	65
2005	Restaurant	58
	Grocery	58
	Farming	58
	Computer	57
2004	Computer	60
	Restaurant	58
2003	Computer	70
2002	Computer	62
	Restaurant	61
2001	Computer	67

Lowest Positive Ratings of Businesses and Industries, 2001-2009 Gallup Polls

Year	Business/Industry	% Positive ratings
2009	Oil and gas	21
2008	Oil and gas	15
	Real estate	16
2007	Oil and gas	19
	Federal government	21
2006	Oil and gas	15
2005	Oil and gas	20
2004	Oil and gas	21
2003	Oil and gas	35
	Legal	36
	Airline	37
2002	Legal	22
2001	Oil and gas	24

(24%), legal (25%), banking (28%), and—even after a significant increase likely due to the change in presidential administrations—the federal government (29%).

The computer industry has been the most positively rated (or tied for the highest from a statistical perspective) in all but one year since Gallup first asked this question in 2001. The exception was in 2006, when the restaurant industry ranked higher.

Similarly, the oil and gas industry has had the lowest or tied for the lowest positive ratings in all years except 2002, when the legal field was rated less positively.

Implications

2008 was a difficult year for U.S. business and industry, and the images of most industries declined as a result. While the full force of the financial crisis was not apparent when Gallup conducted its August 2008 update, gas prices were coming off record highs and Americans were decidedly pessimistic about the direction in which the economy was headed.

Now, in 2009, in part aided by a new presidential administration and some hope of better economic times, most industries' images have improved over last year, with the hard-hit banking and automobile industries standing as notable exceptions.

Survey Methods

Results are based on telephone interviews with 492 national adults, aged 18 and older, conducted Aug. 6–9, 2009. For results based on the total sample of national adults, one can say with 95% confidence that the maximum margin of sampling error is ±5 percentage points.

Interviews are conducted with respondents on land-line telephones (for respondents with a land-line telephone) and cellular phones (for respondents who are cell-phone only).

In addition to sampling error, question wording and practical difficulties in conducting surveys can introduce error or bias into the findings of public opinion polls.

August 17, 2009

HEALTHY BEHAVIOR: VERMONT BEST; KENTUCKY WORST

Western and Northeastern states fill out the top 10

by Elizabeth Mendes, Gallup Poll Staff Writer

The far-flung residents of snowy Vermont and the sun-soaked island of Hawaii in the first half of 2009 scored the highest in the nation for practicing healthful behaviors—including eating healthily, exercising, and not smoking. Americans living in the Southern states of Kentucky and Arkansas are the least likely to report practicing these healthy habits.

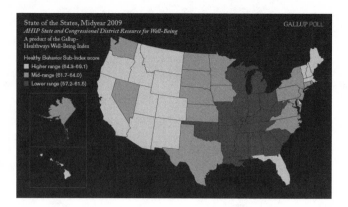

Top 10 States, Healthy Behavior

State	Healthy Behavior Index score
Vermont	69.1
Hawaii	67.8
Montana	66.7
California	65.6
New Mexico	65.4
New Hampshire	65.3
Maine	64.8
Delaware	64.7
Idaho	64.7
Wyoming	64.7
Oregon	64.7

January-June 2009
AHIP State and Congressional District Resource for Well-Being -- A product of the Gallup-Healthways Well-Being Index

Bottom 10 States, Healthy Behavior

State	Healthy Behavior Index score
Kentucky	57.2
Arkansas	57.3
West Virginia	58.3
Indiana	58.4
Ohio	58.8
Alabama	59.6
Tennessee	60.0
Oklahoma	60.1
Mississippi	60.1
Illinois	60.2
Louisiana	60.2

January-June 2009
AHIP State and Congressional District Resource for Well-Being -- A product of the Gallup-Healthways Well-Being Index

Best and Worst States on Items in Healthy Behavior Sub-Index

	Best score	Worst score
Smoking rate	Utah	West Virginia, Kentucky (tie)
Weekly exercise frequency	Vermont	Ohio
Eat healthy	New Mexico	Arkansas
Weekly consumption of fruits and vegetables	Vermont	North Dakota

January-June 2009
AHIP State and Congressional District Resource for Well-Being -- A product of the Gallup-Healthways Well-Being Index

The midyear results from the AHIP State and Congressional District Resource for Well-Being, a product of the Gallup-Healthways Well-Being Index, find the nation as a whole dropping substantively on the Healthy Behavior Sub-Index, from 63.7 in 2008 to 62.6 in the first half of 2009. The Healthy Behavior Sub-Index is one of six sub-indexes that make up the Gallup-Healthways Well-Being Index, and asks Americans four questions: do you smoke; did you eat healthy all day yesterday; in the last seven days, on how many days did you exercise for 30 minutes or more; and in the last seven days, on how many days did you have five or more servings of fruits and vegetables. The Healthy Behavior Sub-Index scores for the nation and for each state are calculated based on a scale from 0 to 100, where 100 would be a perfect score.

Healthy Behavior scores in most states are trending down in the first half of 2009 compared with 2008, though many have not decreased by a statistically significant degree. Mississippi, whose score ranks among the bottom 10, is the only state to record a statistically significant increase in its healthy behavior score thus far in 2009.

Clear patterns emerge when the results are mapped, with Western, Mountain, and Northeastern states—as well as Florida—performing the best, and states in the South and Midwest performing the worst.

Residents of Vermont, in addition to obtaining the highest score on the overall sub-index, are also the most likely to report frequent exercise and consumption of fruits and vegetables. Ohio residents are the least likely to report frequent exercise. Arkansas does the worst on the healthful diet dimension and North Dakota ranks last for weekly consumption of fruits and vegetables, specifically.

Americans living in Utah are the least likely of residents in all states to say they smoke, while residents of Kentucky and West Virginia are the most likely.

Complete 2008 rankings are available at the AHIP State and Congressional District Resource for Well-Being, a one-of-a-kind interactive database that enables users to research and sort Gallup-Healthways Well-Being Index data alongside the most up-to-date statistics from the Census Bureau.

Survey Methods

Results are based on telephone interviews with 178,545 national adults, aged 18 and older, conducted Jan. 2–June 30, 2009, as part of the Gallup-Healthways Well-Being Index. For results based on the total sample of national adults, one can say with 95% confidence that the maximum margin of sampling error is ±0.2 percentage points.

The margin of sampling error for most states is ±1–2 percentage points, but is as high as ±4 points for smaller states such as Wyoming, North Dakota, South Dakota, Delaware, and Hawaii.

References to "statistically significant" change relative to 2008 scores are always based on 95% (p<.05) confidence levels.

The AHIP State and Congressional District Resource for Well-Being categorizes the District of Columbia as a congressional district.

Interviews are conducted with respondents on land-line telephones (for respondents with a land-line telephone) and cellular phones (for respondents who are cell-phone only).

In addition to sampling error, question wording and practical difficulties in conducting surveys can introduce error or bias into the findings of public opinion polls.

August 18, 2009

MANY AMERICANS SEE STIMULUS' COSTS, NOT BENEFITS

Slim majority thinks it would be better to spend less on stimulus

by Jeffrey M. Jones, Gallup Poll Managing Editor

Several months after it was passed, Americans have their share of reservations about the economic stimulus plan. A slim majority of Americans, 51%, including most Republicans and independents, say it would have been better for the government to have spent less money to stimulate the economy. Three in 10 Americans—including nearly half of Democrats—say the government is spending the right amount, while 13% of the public believes the government should be spending more.

Regardless of whether you favor or oppose the economic stimulus bill that Congress passed, do you think it would have been better for the government to have spent more money, less, or was the amount of spending just right?

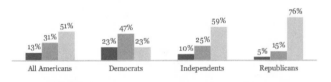

In addition to the amount being spent, a substantial proportion of Americans (46%) say they are "very worried" that money from the economic stimulus plan is being wasted. Only 20% say they are not worried about wasteful stimulus spending.

These results are based on the most recent *USA Today*/Gallup poll, conducted Aug. 6–9.

These concerns come on top of doubts about the effectiveness of the stimulus plan. While 41% of Americans think the stimulus plan is making the economy better than it would be if the plan had not been passed, 33% say it is not having an effect, and 24% believe it is making the economy worse.

That short-term assessment is actually more optimistic than what Americans project for the long-term: the percentage saying the stimulus plan will make the economy worse in the long run matches the percentage that believe it will ultimately make the economy better (38%).

Do you think the economic stimulus plan will make the economy better than if the plan had not passed, has it not had an effect, or has it made the economy worse than if the plan had not passed?

Short-term and long-term effects

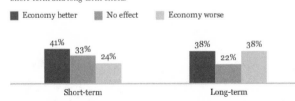

Two thirds of Democrats believe the stimulus plan is already improving the economy, a view shared by 35% of independents and 18% of Republicans. Republicans are about evenly divided over whether the economy is worse off (41%) or not any different (39%) than it would have been if no stimulus plan had passed.

In the short-term, do you think the economic stimulus plan will make the economy better than if the plan had not passed, has it not had an effect, or has it made the economy worse than if the plan had not passed?

By political party

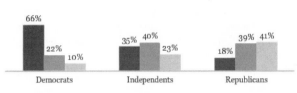

Republicans are even more likely to take a dim view of the stimulus plan in the long-term, as 62% believe the economy will be worse as a result. Democrats are about as likely to think it will benefit the economy over the long haul (69%). More independents expect the stimulus bill to hurt the economy in the long run (42%) rather than improve it (32%).

In the long-term, do you think the economic stimulus plan will make the economy better than if the plan had not passed, has it not had an effect, or has it made the economy worse than if the plan had not passed?

By political party

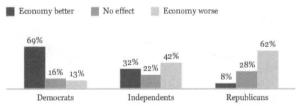

Some experts have argued that the amount included in the stimulus plan was actually less than was needed to pull the country out of the recession, and there has been some discussion that a second stimulus bill may be necessary. The public, not surprisingly given the reviews of the current stimulus plan, does not have much of an appetite for a second stimulus bill—65% are opposed, while 29% are in favor.

Republicans and independents widely oppose a second stimulus bill, while Democrats are somewhat more likely to favor than oppose it.

Would you favor or oppose Congress passing a second economic stimulus plan?

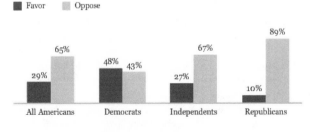

Bottom Line

It is still too early to judge whether the economic stimulus package will help the economy, as only a fraction of the money in the bill has been spent thus far. The American public, too, has yet to reach a consensus as to whether the economic stimulus bill is helping the economy, hurting it, or not making much difference. However, a substantial proportion of Americans are concerned about the amount of money that will be spent, and whether it will be wasted.

Since consumer confidence has perked up in recent weeks—perhaps due to better-than-expected unemployment numbers and GDP numbers released earlier this month—the public may see less of a need for additional stimulus legislation. But if Congress and the president decide one is necessary, they could encounter stiff public opposition to a second stimulus bill.

Survey Methods

Results are based on telephone interviews with 1,010 national adults, aged 18 and older, conducted Aug. 6–9, 2009. For results based on the total sample of national adults, one can say with 95% confidence that the maximum margin of sampling error is ±4 percentage points.

August 19, 2009

AMERICANS DOUBT EFFECTIVENESS OF "NO CHILD LEFT BEHIND"

Americans with an opinion are more negative than positive

by Frank Newport, Gallup Poll Editor in Chief

Americans provide a less-than-enthusiastic endorsement of the impact of the No Child Left Behind Act (NCLB), now in its eighth year. Of those familiar with the act, 21% say it has made the education received by public school students in the United States better, while almost half, 45%, say it has made no difference and 29% say it has made public school students' education worse.

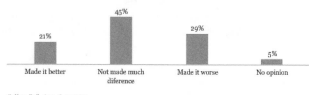

From what you have may have heard or read, do you think the No Child Left Behind Act has generally made the education received by public school students in the United States -- [ROTATED: better, has it not made much difference, (or has it made it) worse]?

Based on those who are familiar with No Child Left Behind Act

Gallup Poll, Aug. 6-9, 2009

The No Child Left Behind Act was signed into law on Jan. 8, 2002, as one of the first major pieces of domestic legislation of the George W. Bush administration. Although it is a complex law covering many different aspects of education, its primary purpose is to impose rigorous state-enacted testing standards on school systems across the country, with concomitant penalties for schools that do not show improvement. The legislation is up for reauthorization this year, and its goal is 100% proficiency for public school students in several subject areas, including math and reading, by the 2013–2014 school year.

At this point, 60% of Americans say they are either very or somewhat familiar with NCLB, with 14% saying they are not familiar at all with it.

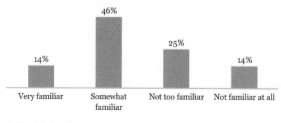

How familiar are you with the No Child Left Behind Act, the federal education law passed in 2002 -- very familiar, somewhat familiar, not too familiar, or not familiar at all?

Gallup Poll, Aug. 6-9, 2009

Although NCLB most directly affects parents with school-aged children, U.S. adults who have K-12 children are only slightly more familiar with the Act than are those with no K-12 children.

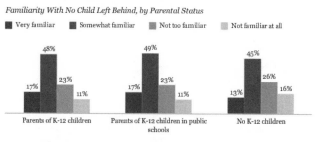

Familiarity With No Child Left Behind, by Parental Status

Gallup Poll, Aug. 6-9, 2009

The basic question about the effectiveness of NCLB was asked of those who said they were very, somewhat, or not too familiar with it, excluding those who said "not familiar at all." Within the larger group of those who have at least a passing familiarity with NCLB, there are significant differences in perceptions of its effectiveness by level of knowledge. Among those who are very familiar with NCLB, about 14% of the total adult population, views of NCLB skew very negative, with more than twice as many saying it has made things worse as saying it has made them better. Views are significantly less negative among those with lower levels of self-reported familiarity.

Opinion of No Child Left Behind, by Familiarity With NCLB

Asked of those very, somewhat, or not too familiar with No Child Left Behind

■ Has made public school education better ■ Has not made much difference
■ Has made public school education worse

Gallup Poll, Aug. 6-9, 2009

Parents of K-12 children, as well as the subset of parents of children in public schools, are somewhat more positive than those who have no children in school.

Opinion of No Child Left Behind, by Parental Status

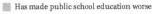

Asked of those very, somewhat, or not too familiar with No Child Left Behind

■ Has made public school education better   ■ Has not made much difference

▨ Has made public school education worse

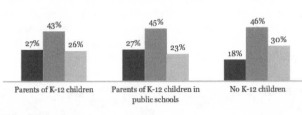

Parents of K-12 children | Parents of K-12 children in public schools | No K-12 children

Gallup Poll, Aug. 6-9, 2009

The NCLB Act has been heavily identified with President Bush, who pushed for the legislation as a national extension of policies enacted while he was governor of Texas. Yet the law passed with overwhelming bipartisan support and was actively supported by Democratic representatives and senators, including Democratic Sen. Edward Kennedy. At this point, Republicans have somewhat more positive views on the impact of NCLB than do independents or Democrats, although the differences are not large.

Opinion of No Child Left Behind, by Party ID

Asked of those very, somewhat, or not too familiar with No Child Left Behind

■ Has made public school education better   ■ Has not made much difference

▨ Has made public school education worse

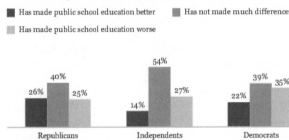

Republicans | Independents | Democrats

Gallup Poll, Aug. 6-9, 2009

There is no effusively positive attitude toward NCLB from any political group, as can be seen. Republicans are evenly divided in terms of those who say NCLB has so far made education for public school students better as opposed to worse. Independents and Democrats, on the other hand, tilt more in the "worse" direction.

Bottom Line

While NCLB is currently in limbo, awaiting congressional reauthorization, Gallup finds no consensus among either the entire American adult population or parents of school-aged children that the landmark education act has improved the quality of education received by public school children in the U.S. In fact, of those who are familiar with NCLB, a large majority say either it has had no effect on students' education or has made it worse. A bit of better news for supporters of NCLB is the finding that parents of school-aged children are a little more positive about the impact of the Act than are those who do not have children in school.

Of potential importance is the fact that those who claim to be very familiar with NCLB are most strongly convinced that it has had a negative impact. While this could indicate that more intimate exposure to NCLB and its implementation causes one to become more

negative, it could also be that critics of the law are much more engaged on the issue, and pay closer attention to it, than do those who support it.

Survey Methods

Results are based on telephone interviews with 1,010 national adults, aged 18 and older, conducted Aug. 6–9, 2009. For results based on the total sample of national adults, one can say with 95% confidence that the maximum margin of sampling error is ±4 percentage points.

For results based on the sample of 887 adults who are very, somewhat, or not too familiar with the No Child Left Behind Act, the maximum margin of sampling error is ±4 percentage points.

For results based on the sample of 233 parents with children in kindergarten through Grade 12, the maximum margin of sampling error is ±8 points.

Interviews are conducted with respondents on land-line telephones (for respondents with a land-line telephone) and cellular phones (for respondents who are cell-phone only).

In addition to sampling error, question wording and practical difficulties in conducting surveys can introduce error or bias into the findings of public opinion polls.

August 19, 2009
UNINSURED: HIGHEST PERCENTAGE IN TEXAS, LOWEST IN MASS.
Percentage of adults without health insurance is up in several states

by Elizabeth Mendes, Gallup Poll Staff Writer

Higher percentages of Texas, New Mexico, and Mississippi residents are without health insurance—roughly one in four—than is true for any other states in the U.S. In Massachusetts, where legislation requires all residents to carry health insurance coverage or face a tax penalty, 5.5% are without insurance—the lowest percentage in the country.

Ten States With the Lowest Percentages of Uninsured Residents

State	% Uninsured
Massachusetts	5.5%
Vermont	8.4%
Minnesota	8.7%
Hawaii	8.8%
Delaware	9.5%
Connecticut	9.7%
Pennsylvania	10.0%
New Jersey	11.8%
New York	11.9%
Rhode Island	12.2%

January-June 2009
Gallup-Healthways Well-Being Index

Ten States With the Highest Percentages of Uninsured Residents

State	% Uninsured
Texas	26.9%
New Mexico	25.6%
Mississippi	24.0%
Louisiana	22.4%
Nevada	22.2%
Oklahoma	22.2%
California	21.0%
Wyoming	20.7%
Florida	20.7%
Georgia	20.7%

January-June 2009
Gallup-Healthways Well-Being Index

These results are based on more than 178,000 interviews conducted from January-June 2009 as part of the Gallup-Healthways

Well-Being Index. In each daily survey of 1,000 Americans aged 18 and older, Gallup asks respondents whether they have health insurance. Based on these data, Gallup previously reported an increase in the number of uninsured adults nationwide from 14.8% in 2008 to 16.2% in 2009. Now, Gallup's examination of state-level data reveals that so far in 2009, the percentage of uninsured adults in every state has either increased or remained statistically unchanged from 2008. The greatest increases in the percentage of uninsured have been in Nebraska, New Mexico, and Utah.

Uninsured by State, 2008 and 2009

Sorted by January-June 2009 percentages

	2008	January-June 2009	Change, 2008-2009	Number of interviews in 2009
	%	%	Pct. pts.	
Texas	25.0%	26.9%	1.9	10179
New Mexico	21.3%	25.6%	4.3	1239
Mississippi	22.2%	24.0%	1.8	1497
Louisiana	19.7%	22.4%	2.7	2078
Nevada	21.4%	22.2%	0.8	1437
Oklahoma	20.6%	22.2%	1.6	2496
California	18.9%	21.0%	2.1	18794
Wyoming	18.4%	20.7%	2.3	454
Florida	18.7%	20.7%	2	9184
Georgia	18.6%	20.7%	2.1	4426
South Carolina	18.4%	20.4%	2	2595
Montana	19.4%	20.3%	0.9	959
Alaska	21.1%	20.2%	-0.9	654
Arkansas	21.2%	20.1%	-1.1	1844
Colorado	18.3%	20.0%	1.7	3214
Oregon	18.3%	19.4%	1.1	3038
West Virginia	19.6%	19.3%	-0.3	1371
North Carolina	18.1%	19.3%	1.2	5768
Idaho	17.8%	18.8%	1	1144
Utah	14.3%	18.1%	3.8	1554
Kentucky	16.1%	17.9%	1.8	2713
Tennessee	15.5%	17.8%	2.3	3776
Nebraska	12.6%	17.7%	5.1	1170
Alabama	16.1%	17.2%	1.1	2701
Missouri	15.9%	17.1%	1.2	4018
South Dakota	15.9%	16.8%	0.9	523
Indiana	14.7%	16.1%	1.4	4231
Washington	14.0%	15.5%	1.5	4939
Illinois	14.8%	15.0%	0.2	5958
Arizona	16.1%	14.9%	-1.2	3692
Kansas	13.0%	14.4%	1.4	1821
Michigan	13.4%	14.4%	1	5563
New Hampshire	10.9%	14.3%	3.4	1161
Ohio	13.9%	13.9%	0	6711
Iowa	11.4%	13.5%	2.1	2116
North Dakota	11.6%	12.9%	1.3	504
Maine	13.3%	12.9%	-0.4	1529
Maryland	10.6%	12.8%	2.2	3048
Wisconsin	10.9%	12.6%	1.7	3971
Virginia	12.3%	12.5%	0.2	4609
Rhode Island	9.2%	12.2%	3	789
New York	11.3%	11.9%	0.6	10744
New Jersey	10.6%	11.8%	1.2	5006
Pennsylvania	9.6%	10.0%	0.4	10947
Connecticut	9.6%	9.7%	0.1	2353
Delaware	10.2%	9.5%	-0.7	506
Hawaii	9.7%	8.8%	-0.9	577
Minnesota	8.6%	8.7%	0.1	3500
Vermont	10.5%	8.4%	-2.1	783
Massachusetts	4.2%	5.5%	1.3	4321

Gallup-Healthways Well-Being Index

The accompanying map depicts the geographical breakdown of the percentage of uninsured adults by state. States with comparatively lower uninsured populations are located primarily in the Northeast. Those with relatively higher percentages of uninsured are spread across the South and West. Given that Gallup has previously found that a disproportionate percentage of Hispanics are uninsured at the national level, it is worth noting that a number of states with the highest percentages of uninsured are also states with large percentages of Hispanic residents.

Bottom Line

President Obama and congressional leaders are working tirelessly to solidify a healthcare reform bill, with one key goal being the expansion of coverage to the uninsured. Gallup data showing that 5.5% of adults in Massachusetts are uninsured three years after the passage of healthcare reform legislation there underscore the difficulty of achieving universal coverage. Nationwide, the percentage of uninsured adults has increased or remained stable in the first six months of 2009 compared to 2008, suggesting that unless changes are made to the current system, whether or not those come from the federal government, a sizable proportion of the population would continue to go without coverage.

Survey Methods

Results are based on telephone interviews with 178,545 national adults, aged 18 and older, conducted Jan. 2–June 30, 2009, as part of the Gallup-Healthways Well-Being Index. For results based on the total sample of national adults, one can say with 95% confidence that the maximum margin of sampling error is ±0.2 percentage points.

The margin of sampling error for most states is ±1–2 percentage points, but is as high as ±4 percentage points for smaller states such as Wyoming, North Dakota, South Dakota, Delaware, and Hawaii.

Interviews are conducted with respondents on land-line telephones (for respondents with a land-line telephone) and cellular phones (for respondents who are cell-phone only).

In addition to sampling error, question wording and practical difficulties in conducting surveys can introduce error or bias into the findings of public opinion polls.

August 20, 2009

CONGRESS' JOB APPROVAL RATINGS GROW MORE POLARIZED

Democrats approve; Republicans and independents increasingly disapprove

by Lydia Saad, Gallup Poll Senior Editor

Gallup polling conducted in the first few days of Congress' August recess—a time when many members of Congress were preparing to meet their constituents in town hall meetings back in their districts—finds public approval of Congress on par with the lowest reading since February, a month after the 111th Congress convened. Thirty-one percent of Americans in Gallup's Aug. 6–9 survey approve of the job Congress is doing while 62% disapprove.

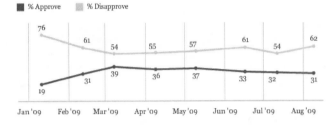

Do you approve or disapprove of the way Congress is handling its job?

Congress' latest job approval score is similar to where the reading stood in February, when 31% approved and 61% disapproved. The percentage approving climbed to 39% in March and remained within a few points of that number through May, but has since fallen back to the low 30s.

On a longer-term basis, the current rating of Congress is only slightly worse than the average rating Gallup has recorded over the prior two decades. From 1988 through 2008, approval of Congress averaged 36% and disapproval 55%. The average approval rating of Congress thus far in 2009 (32%) is somewhat better than those seen in the early '90s and is similar to those measured in the first few years of the Republican majority in Congress in 1995 and 1996. It is substantially worse than those recorded from 1998 through 2004, when (even before the 9/11 attacks in 2001) approval was consistently greater than 40%.

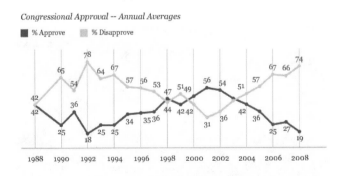

Congressional Approval -- Annual Averages

Partisan Breach

Sharp partisan differences are evident in Americans' ratings of Congress. A majority of Democrats approve of the job Congress is doing, but much larger majorities of Republicans and independents disapprove.

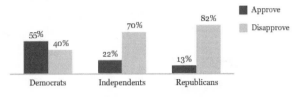

Congressional Approval, by Party ID
Aug. 6-9, 2009

In Gallup polling each month since March, at least half of Democrats have approved of the job the Democratic-led Congress is doing, including 55% in the latest survey. Approval among independents has typically been closer to 30%, although it dropped to 24% in July and to 22% in August. Positive evaluations of Congress by Republicans have been sparse, exceeding 20% only once; but the current 13% is the lowest yet.

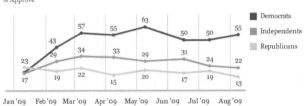

2009 Trend in Congressional Approval, by Party ID
% Approve

Such partisan differences may seem normal, but they are actually a sharp departure from 2007–2008 when, despite the presence of a Democratic majority in both the U.S. House and Senate, Democrats were not much more positive than Republicans about the job Congress was doing. This may have reflected Democratic frustration with the lack of congressional action on the Iraq war as well as on immigration and other issues of concern to Democrats.

By contrast, during most of the Republican-led Congress from 2000 to 2006, Republicans' approval of Congress was substantially higher than Democrats'.

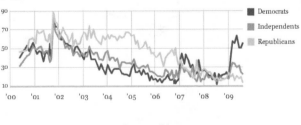

2000-2009 Trend in Congressional Approval, by Party ID
% Approve

Bottom Line

The 111th Congress, led by Speaker of the House Nancy Pelosi and Senate Majority Leader Harry Reid, appears to be meeting the expectations of most rank-and-file Democrats, earning a 55% job approval rating from Democrats nationwide in early August. In turn, Democratic support has kept Congress' overall rating above 30% thus far in 2009—a respectable level in the history of congressional approval ratings. No doubt the transition from a Republican presidential administration to a Democratic one has helped improve Democratic satisfaction with the job Congress is doing.

At the same time, the 22% approval rating of Congress from independents is little improved over last year, and not much better than the meager 13% rating from Republicans. And the descent in approval among independents and Republicans since March suggests that the same legislative activity in recent months that is satisfying to the Democratic base (including healthcare reform) may be draining support for Congress elsewhere.

Survey Methods

Results are based on telephone interviews with 1,010 national adults, aged 18 and older, conducted Aug. 6–9, 2009. For results based on the total sample of national adults, one can say with 95% confidence that the maximum margin of sampling error is ±4 percentage points.

Interviews are conducted with respondents on land-line telephones (for respondents with a land-line telephone) and cellular phones (for respondents who are cell-phone only).

In addition to sampling error, question wording and practical difficulties in conducting surveys can introduce error or bias into the findings of public opinion polls.

August 20, 2009
OBESITY AND DIABETES: ACROSS STATES, A CLEAR RELATIONSHIP
More states trending up than down on both health outcomes compared to 2008

by Dan Witters, Gallup Poll Staff Writer

Residents of Colorado, Hawaii, and Utah in the first half of 2009 were the least likely to be obese, while Mississippi, West Virginia, Alaska, and Arkansas residents were the most likely. The incidence of obese people runs nearly eight percentage points higher, on average, in the 10 most obese states compared with the 10 least obese states (30.5% vs. 22.7%, respectively).

10 Lowest Obesity States

State	Obesity rate
	%
Colorado	19.6
Hawaii	20.0
Utah	22.8
Montana	23.2
California	23.3
Nevada	23.3
Connecticut	23.6
New Hampshire	23.7
Vermont	23.8
Massachusetts	24.1

January-June 2009
Gallup-Healthways Well-Being Index

10 Highest Obesity States

State	Obesity rate
	%
Mississippi	33.1
West Virginia	31.6
Alaska	31.4
Arkansas	31.3
Louisiana	30.6
Tennessee	30.2
North Dakota	29.8
Texas	29.8
Indiana	29.4
Alabama	29.4
Kentucky	29.4

January-June 2009
Gallup-Healthways Well-Being Index

The midyear results for the Gallup-Healthways Well-Being Index (from January through June 2009) find obesity in the U.S. increasing to 26.6% in the first half of 2009 from 25.5% in all of 2008. (This is based on respondents' self-reports of their height and weight, which are then used to calculate standard Body Mass Index scores. Individual BMI values of 30 or above are classified as "obese.")

Following from the elevated rates of obesity, diabetes incidence has also shown a small but meaningful increase since 2008, with 11.0% of respondents nationwide thus far in 2009 acknowledging that they have been diagnosed with the disease, compared to 10.6% in all of last year.

The relationship between obesity and diabetes-related health outcomes is widely understood, and is confirmed by the Gallup-Healthways data, with an average diabetes rate of 9.1% in the 10 least obese states, compared to an average diabetes rate of 12.2% in the 10 most obese states (which includes an 11th state due to a three-way tie for 9th place). If the 10 most obese states had the same obesity rate as the 10 least obese, approximately 4.6 million fewer people would be obese and an estimated 1.8 million fewer would be diagnosed with diabetes in those 10 states alone. Underscoring the point, if all 50 states had the same average diabetes rate as the 10 *least obese* states, approximately 5 million fewer Americans would be diabetics.

West Virginia, Mississippi, Alabama, South Carolina, and Tennessee are the five states with the highest reported diabetes rates. Four of these five are also among the most obese in the nation. (Kentucky and Louisiana are also on both the 10 Most Obese and 10 Highest Diabetes lists.) North Dakota, Colorado, Utah, Montana, and Wyoming are the five states with the lowest incidence of diabetes. Again, substantial overlap exists between the low diabetes states and the low obesity states.

10 Lowest Diabetes States

State	Diabetes rate
	%
North Dakota	6.3
Colorado	7.6
Utah	7.7
Montana	8.4
Wyoming	8.6
Vermont	8.8
Minnesota	8.9
South Dakota	9.1
Nebraska	9.2
New Hampshire	9.2

January-June 2009
Gallup-Healthways Well-Being Index

10 Highest Diabetes States

State	Diabetes rate
	%
West Virginia	15.4
Mississippi	14.9
Alabama	14.0
South Carolina	13.7
Tennessee	13.6
Kentucky	12.9
Maine	12.6
Louisiana	12.2
North Carolina	11.9
Oklahoma	11.9

January-June 2009
Gallup-Healthways Well-Being Index

As seen in the accompanying maps, most states in the Mountain West, West, and Northeast (for obesity) tend to fare better in terms of diabetes and obesity than those in the South. The Midwest is more of a mixture, as is the Northeast for diabetes.

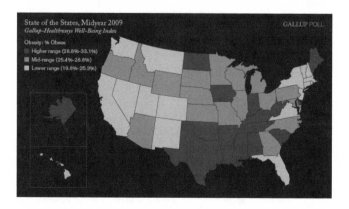

State of the States, Midyear 2009
Gallup-Healthways Well-Being Index
GALLUP POLL
Obesity: % Obese
Higher range (28.8%-33.1%)
Mid-range (25.4%-28.6%)
Lower range (19.6%-25.3%)

Thus far in 2009, Wyoming, Alaska, Minnesota, and Maine have had the greatest self-reported increases in obesity (via the Body Mass

Index) compared to last year, all representing substantive increases even when accompanying error ranges found in the samples are accounted for.

Diabetes, too, is up in a number of states so far in 2009. While an error range exists around each state's percentages, Maine, Rhode Island, Oregon, South Carolina, and Tennessee have all seen small but meaningful increases in the rate of diabetes since 2008.

In fact, when all 50 states are sorted into two groups according to change in obesity relative to 2008, the 25 states that have shown the greatest increases in obesity have had an average increase of 0.5 percentage points in diabetes, compared to a 0.2 percentage-point increase in diabetes among the 25 states with the lowest increases, or with slight decreases, in obesity.

The Gallup-Healthways Well-Being Index data on obesity and diabetes are subcomponents of the Physical Health Sub-Index, on which North Dakota and West Virginia, the best and worst states, respectively, in terms of diabetes, also rank best and worst respectively for overall physical health. The Physical Health Sub-Index is one of six domains used to calculate a state's overall well-being score.

Survey Methods

Results are based on telephone interviews with 178,545 national adults, aged 18 and older, conducted Jan. 2–June 30, 2009, as part of the Gallup-Healthways Well-Being Index. For results based on the total sample of national adults, one can say with 95% confidence that the maximum margin of sampling error is ±0.2 percentage points.

The margin of sampling error for most states is ±1–2 percentage points, but is as high as ±4 percentage points for smaller states such as Wyoming, North Dakota, South Dakota, Delaware and Hawaii.

Interviews are conducted with respondents on land-line telephones (for respondents with a land-line telephone) and cellular phones (for respondents who are cell-phone only).

In addition to sampling error, question wording and practical difficulties in conducting surveys can introduce error or bias into the findings of public opinion polls.

August 21, 2009
MOST AMERICANS EXPECT INCOME-TAX HIKE UNDER OBAMA
Even a majority of lower-income Americans expect an increase

by Jeffrey M. Jones, Gallup Poll Managing Editor

A new Gallup Poll finds that 68% of Americans believe their federal income taxes will be higher by the time Barack Obama's first term as president ends. This includes 35% who say their taxes will be "a lot higher."

By the year 2012, when President Obama's first term as president ends, do you think your federal income taxes will be -- [ROTATED: a lot higher, a little higher, the same, a little lower, (or) a lot lower] -- than they were when President Obama took office?

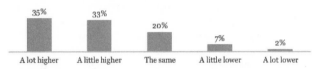

Gallup Poll, Aug. 6-9, 2009

Obama campaigned on the promise that he would raise income taxes on only the wealthiest Americans. While Americans were not necessarily convinced of that at the time—in Gallup's final 2008 pre-election poll, 49% thought their income taxes would be higher if Obama were elected—many more expect a tax hike now than did so during the campaign.

The rise in expectations that taxes will go up probably is a reflection on Obama's ambitious domestic agenda, which began with a $787 billion economic stimulus plan and is now focused on a roughly $1 trillion healthcare reform bill. Still, the Obama administration has made no definite plans to increase income taxes on any but the wealthiest Americans.

Despite this, even a majority of Americans in the lowest income group—whose annual household incomes are less than $30,000—believe their taxes will go up. Much larger majorities of middle- and upper-income Americans expect their taxes to be raised. Part of that relationship could be explained by the fact that upper-income Americans tend to be more Republican in their party orientation.

Expectations of Federal Income Taxes at End of Obama's First Term, by Annual Household Income

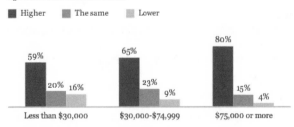

But even Obama's political base has doubts about his being able to hold the line on income taxes—48% of Democrats expect their taxes to rise during his first term. More than 7 in 10 independents and 9 in 10 Republicans agree.

Expectations of Federal Income Taxes at End of Obama's First Term, by Party ID

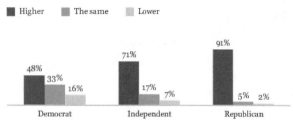

■ Higher ■ The same ■ Lower

Democrat: 48% 33% 16%
Independent: 71% 17% 7%
Republican: 91% 5% 2%

Ten Least Stressed States	
Did you experience the following feelings during A LOT OF THE DAY yesterday? How about stress?	
State	**% Yes**
Hawaii	31.4
North Dakota	31.8
Iowa	35.6
Wyoming	36.0
South Dakota	36.7
Kansas	36.9
Louisiana	37.0
Alaska	37.3
Montana	37.7
Maryland	37.8
Wisconsin	37.8
South Carolina	37.8

January-June 2009
Gallup-Healthways Well-Being Index

Ten Most Stressed States	
Did you experience the following feelings during A LOT OF THE DAY yesterday? How about stress?	
State	**% Yes**
Kentucky	44.9
West Virginia	43.7
Colorado	43.4
Connecticut	43.0
Rhode Island	42.8
Oregon	42.7
New Hampshire	42.5
New Jersey	42.4
Massachusetts	42.4
Indiana	42.4

January-June 2009
Gallup-Healthways Well-Being Index

Bottom Line

In a town hall meeting last week to discuss healthcare reform, a questioner asked President Obama how he would pay for his plan without raising Americans' taxes. Obama reiterated his pledge not to raise taxes on all but the wealthiest Americans—those making above $250,000 a year. But like that town hall questioner, most Americans remain skeptical that the administration can pay for healthcare reform and its other programs without raising their taxes.

Obama's pledge not to raise income taxes on average Americans evokes former president George H.W. Bush's "no new taxes" pledge during the 1988 presidential campaign. Bush's decision to break that pledge was politically damaging and likely contributed to his 1992 election defeat. That damage occurred even though, as in the case of Obama, most Americans expected during the early part of Bush's presidency that he would not be able to avoid raising taxes. Thus, Bush appears to have been harmed not by his decision to raise taxes as much as by his not being able to live up to his campaign pledge.

Survey Methods

Results are based on telephone interviews with 1,010 national adults, aged 18 and older, conducted Aug. 6–9, 2009. For results based on the total sample of national adults, one can say with 95% confidence that the maximum margin of sampling error is ±4 percentage points.

Interviews are conducted with respondents on land-line telephones (for respondents with a land-line telephone) and cellular phones (for respondents who are cell-phone only).

In addition to sampling error, question wording and practical difficulties in conducting surveys can introduce error or bias into the findings of public opinion polls.

August 21, 2009

STRESS AND HAPPINESS: OFTEN, BUT NOT ALWAYS, RELATED

Less stressed states usually, but not always, have more happy residents

by Brett W. Pelham, Gallup Poll Staff Writer

Residents of Hawaii and North Dakota had the lowest stress levels in the nation in the first half of 2009. Kentucky and West Virginia, two states that border each other, share the unhappy distinction of having residents with the highest stress levels.

These state-level data are from the Gallup-Healthways Well-Being Index. The stress score for each state is simply the percentage

of residents during the first six months of 2009 who report that they experienced stress "during a lot of the day yesterday." The January-June 2009 aggregate includes more than 170,000 interviews conducted among national adults, aged 18 and older.

It is easy to imagine why many Hawaiians might not feel stressed (think perpetual summer and beaches). The low percentage of stress among North Dakotans is likely explained by additional Gallup-Healthways data showing that North Dakota leads the nation in the Gallup-Healthways Physical Health Index. North Dakota's very low population density may also contribute to a less stressful lifestyle. Supporting the latter hypothesis is the fact that the 5 least densely populated states in the U.S. (Alaska, Wyoming, Montana, North Dakota, and South Dakota, in that order) all made the list of the 10 least stressed states. Densely populated Maryland is a noteworthy exception to this trend.

The states in which the highest percentage of people report being stressed have a mixture of population densities, with 5 of the 10 most stressed states being concentrated on the Eastern seaboard (Connecticut, Rhode Island, New Hampshire, New Jersey, and Massachusetts).

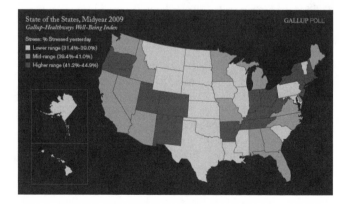

Happiness Not Quite the Opposite of Stress

The happiness score for each state is the percentage of residents during the first six months of 2009 who report that they experienced happiness "during a lot of the day yesterday." Because people rarely feel happy when they feel stressed, it seems reasonable to assume that the states with the lowest stress levels might also be the states in which the greatest percentage of people report being happy. This is generally the case. In fact, 6 of the 10 states with the lowest stress levels also made the list of the 10 happiest states. These states are Hawaii, North Dakota, Iowa, Wyoming, Kansas, and Montana. Seven of the 10 most stressed states also ranked in the bottom 10 in happiness. These are Kentucky, West Virginia, Connecticut, Rhode Island, New Jersey, Massachusetts, and Indiana. In general, there is not a lot of variation in reported happiness among the states, with just seven percentage points separating the top and bottom states.

Ten Happiest States

Did you experience the following feelings during A LOT OF THE DAY yesterday? How about happiness?

State	% Yes
Montana	91.3
North Dakota	90.5
Wyoming	90.0
Utah	89.8
Kansas	89.7
Vermont	89.5
Iowa	89.5
Nebraska	89.2
Minnesota	89.1
Hawaii	89.0
Colorado	89.0

January-June 2009
Gallup-Healthways Well-Being Index

Ten Least Happy States

Did you experience the following feelings during A LOT OF THE DAY yesterday? How about happiness?

State	% Yes
Rhode Island	84.0
West Virginia	84.4
New Jersey	84.7
Kentucky	85.1
New York	85.1
Florida	85.4
Mississippi	85.7
Massachusetts	85.7
Connecticut	85.8
Indiana	86.0
Ohio	86.0

January-June 2009
Gallup-Healthways Well-Being Index

There are some interesting exceptions to the rule that states in which more people are stressed usually have fewer people who are happy. The most striking of these is Colorado, which tied for 10th highest in happiness while ranking as the third highest in stress. Relative to the residents of other U.S. states, that is, residents of Colorado somehow managed to be relatively happy while also being very stressed.

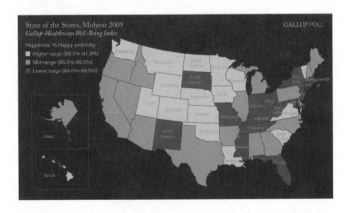

Change Over Time

In comparison with the total 2008 figures, the percentage of Americans so far this year who report having been happy has changed little, going down less than one point (from 87.9% to 87.2%). Likewise, the percentage who report having been stressed has increased only about one point in the same period (from 38.8% to 40.0%). Other Gallup-Healthways research documents that social time spent with friends and family is one of the strongest determinants of happiness, more so than outside factors such as financial worry. So in spite of the economic downturn, Americans' patterns and amount of time spent with friends and family may not have changed much from 2008 to 2009. Alternatively, happiness and stress may simply be highly stable measures that, in the absence of truly radical forces, do not show much change over time.

Bottom Line

Despite the tough economic times, the vast majority of Americans in all states report experiencing a lot of happiness, and that has been consistent from 2008 to 2009. Likewise, although a substantial percentage of Americans report feeling stressed, reports of stress remain below the majority level in all states and have not increased much despite the challenging economic times.

Survey Methods

Results are based on telephone interviews with 178,545 national adults, aged 18 and older, conducted Jan. 2–June 30, 2009, as part of the Gallup-Healthways Well-Being Index. For results based on the total sample of national adults, one can say with 95% confidence that the maximum margin of sampling error is ±0.2 percentage points.

The margin of sampling error for most states is ±1–2 percentage points, but is as high as ±4 percentage points for smaller states such as Wyoming, North Dakota, South Dakota, Delaware, and Hawaii.

Interviews are conducted with respondents on land-line telephones (for respondents with a land-line telephone) and cellular phones (for respondents who are cell-phone only).

In addition to sampling error, question wording and practical difficulties in conducting surveys can introduce error or bias into the findings of public opinion polls.

August 24, 2009

PARENTS RATE SCHOOLS MUCH HIGHER THAN DO AMERICANS OVERALL
Little change in recent years

by Frank Newport, Gallup Poll Editor in Chief

Three in four American parents (76%) are satisfied with the education their children receive in school, compared to 45% of the general public who are satisfied with the state of schools nationwide. These findings from Gallup's annual Work and Education survey are almost identical to what Gallup found last year, and have not changed materially since 2003.

Satisfaction With K-12 Education in the United States

■ % Satisfied with own child's education*   ▨ % Satisfied with U.S. education**

	2000	2001	2002	2003	2004	2005	2006	2007	2008	2009
Own child's	83	78	72	68	77	79	78	77	78	77	76
U.S.	47	36	48	47	48	53	46	45	46	44	45

*Based on parents of children attending K-12 this fall **Based on national adults

Gallup began asking about satisfaction with schools in this fashion in 1999, and since then, the percentage of Americans satisfied with the U.S. education system has ranged from a low of 36% in 2000 to a high of 53% in 2004. The average satisfaction level has been 46%—quite close to this year's reading of 45%. There has been little change in this measure over the last five years; it has ranged only between 44% and 46%.

It is not unusual to find that Americans rate aspects of society more negatively at the national level than they do at the local level. Education is a prime example of this phenomenon. The percentage of parents who say they are completely or somewhat satisfied with their own child's education has averaged 77% since 1999, 31 points higher than the average satisfaction rating all Americans give to U.S. K-12 education.

As has generally been the case over the last 10 years, the subset of parents who have children in public schools is little different from the overall sample of parents in terms of satisfaction with their children's education.

Satisfaction With Own Child's K-12 Education
Asked in reference to oldest child attending K-12

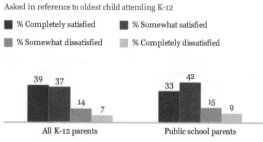

Gallup Poll, Aug. 6-9, 2009

The vast majority of K-12 children in America today attend public schools, although this has dipped slightly in recent years.

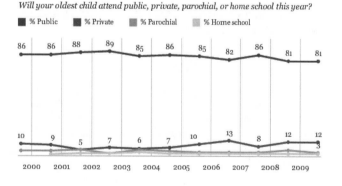
Will your oldest child attend public, private, parochial, or home school this year?

For the second year in a row, the proportion of schoolchildren who attend public schools, as measured by Gallup, is lower than the average for the years prior to 2008. In both 2008 and 2009, 81% of parents said their oldest child was in public school. The percentage was also low in 2006, but otherwise has consistently been at least 85% every year since 1999.

This year, 12% of parents say their child is going to private school, with another 3% saying their child is in parochial school.

The percentage of American parents who say their oldest K-12 child is being home-schooled has been very low since Gallup first measured home schooling in 1999. This year's 2% is exactly where

it has been since 2004. Less than 1% of parents indicated that their child was home-schooled when Gallup first measured home schooling in 1999.

Bottom Line

Gallup's trends on satisfaction with education—both nationally and among parents—have been fairly steady over the last decade. There had been a decline in parents' satisfaction with their children's education between 2000 and 2002, with a move back up after that point. The current level of parental satisfaction, however, remains slightly below the 83% recorded in 1999. There was a low point in 2000 for the general public's satisfaction with the education of children in the U.S.; this may have reflected the emphasis on problems with schools that was part of George W. Bush's campaign for the presidency that year. After a slight uptick in satisfaction in 2004, recent years have seen a very steady trend line on this measure. Still, as is the case for parents' satisfaction, overall satisfaction with schools in this country is no higher now than it was before the 2002 enactment of the sweeping No Child Left Behind legislation.

Survey Methods

Results are based on telephone interviews with 1,010 national adults, aged 18 and older, conducted Aug. 6–9, 2009. For results based on the total sample of national adults, one can say with 95% confidence that the margin of error is ±4 percentage points.

For results based on the sample of 233 parents with children in kindergarten through grade 12, the maximum margin of sampling error is ±8 percentage points.

Interviews are conducted with respondents on land-line telephones (for respondents with a land-line telephone) and cellular phones (for respondents who are cell-phone only).

In addition to sampling error, question wording and practical difficulties in conducting surveys can introduce error or bias into the findings of public opinion polls.

August 25, 2009
PUBLIC SAYS BETTER TEACHERS ARE KEY TO IMPROVED EDUCATION
Focus on basic curriculum also commonly mentioned

by Jeffrey M. Jones, Gallup Poll Managing Editor

Americans most commonly mention having higher-quality, better-educated, and more-involved teachers as the best way to improve kindergarten through grade 12 education in the United States. The next-most-common public prescription is to focus on a basic curriculum of reading, writing, and arithmetic. Improved funding, better teacher pay, and smaller class sizes also receive a significant number of mentions.

These findings are based on the results of an open-ended question in Gallup's annual Work and Education poll, conducted Aug. 6–9 of this year.

Notably, there is little mention of recent or ongoing federal government initiatives toward education, including the No Child Left Behind Act passed during the Bush administration. Most of the specific mentions of No Child Left Behind are negative in tone, and there

Just your opinion, what would be the best way to improve kindergarten through 12th grade education in the U.S. today? [OPEN-ENDED]

	% Mentioning
Quality teachers/better educated/more involvement/caring	17
Back to the basic curriculum (reading, writing, arithmetic)	10
Improve school funding	6
Reduce number of children in classroom	6
Better pay for the teachers	6
Teach more about real life/how to survive	5
More parental involvement	5
Improve standards for testing	4
Better discipline in schools	4
Hire more teachers	4
Get rid of/Abolish teachers' unions or the NEA	3
Stop the government from running schools/Get rid of No Child Left Behind	3
School vouchers	2
More resources in the schools for teaching	2
Spend more time/hours in school	2
Put God back in school	1
More schools/Improved schools	1
Year-round schooling	1
Better security/Safer schools	*
Other	2
None	4
No opinion	11

* Less than 0.5%
Gallup Poll, Aug. 6-9, 2009

are relatively few mentions (positive or negative) of its core elements, such as student testing. Two other common policy proposals—school vouchers and longer school years (including year-round schooling)—are barely mentioned. Thus, it appears Americans are focused on improving education at the local level rather than through federal government policy.

The views of parents with school-aged children are largely similar to those who do not have children in grades K-12, though there are some slight differences. Parents are a little more likely than nonparents to cite smaller class size and more parental involvement as keys to improving education.

Best way to improve kindergarten through 12th grade education
Among those who have school-aged children

	% Mentioning
Quality teachers	16
Basic curriculum	9
Smaller class size	9
More parental involvement	7
Teach about real life	6
Better teacher pay	5

Best way to improve kindergarten through 12th grade education
Among those who do not have school-aged children

	% Mentioning
Quality teachers	18
Basic curriculum	10
Improve school funding	7
Better teacher pay	6
Teach about real life	5
Smaller class size	5

In general, members of most political or demographic subgroups differ little in their ideas on how to improve education. However, self-identified political liberals (11%) are somewhat more likely than moderates (6%) or conservatives (4%) to advocate greater funding of schools, and somewhat less likely to suggest a greater focus on basic curriculum (5% of liberals say this, along with 11% of conservatives and 12% of moderates).

Americans' views on how to improve grade-school and high-school education have not changed much in the last half-decade, either. Gallup asked the same question in 2004, and teacher quality also topped the list at that time. The most significant change in the last five years is a decrease in the percentage of Americans who mention smaller class size, which tied with a focus on basic curriculum as the second-most-common response in 2004.

Best way to improve kindergarten through 12th grade education, 2004

	% Mentioning
Quality teachers	15
Smaller class size	11
Basic curriculum	10
Improve funding	7
More parental involvement	6
Better teacher pay	6
Better discipline in schools	5
Hire more teachers	5

Best way to improve kindergarten through 12th grade education, 2009

	% Mentioning
Quality teachers	17
Basic curriculum	10
Improve funding	6
Smaller class size	6
Better teacher pay	6
Teach about real life	5
More parental involvement	5

Bottom Line

As Gallup reported this week, less than half of Americans are satisfied with the quality of K-12 education in the United States. This satisfaction level has not changed much in recent years, nor have Americans' prescriptions for improving U.S. schools. The most common recommendation from average Americans—most of whose children have themselves been educated in the U.S. system—is for higher-quality teachers, those who are better educated, more involved, and more caring. More broadly, Americans seem to see many more solutions for improving education at the classroom level or local level rather than through new federal government initiatives.

Survey Methods

Results are based on telephone interviews with 1,010 national adults, aged 18 and older, conducted Aug. 6–9, 2009. For results based on the total sample of national adults, one can say with 95% confidence that the maximum margin of sampling error is ±4 percentage points.

Interviews are conducted with respondents on land-line telephones (for respondents with a land-line telephone) and cellular phones (for respondents who are cell-phone only).

In addition to sampling error, question wording and practical difficulties in conducting surveys can introduce error or bias into the findings of public opinion polls.

August 26, 2009
PRESIDENTIAL APPROVAL USUALLY FALLS BELOW 50%; TIMING VARIES
Obama at 51% approval in eighth month in office

by Jeffrey M. Jones, Gallup Poll Managing Editor

Barack Obama's latest job approval rating is 51%, according to Aug. 23–25 Gallup Daily tracking. [AUTHOR'S NOTE: Obama's job approval rating has fallen to 50% since this story was originally published.] Should his rating continue its downward trend and fall below

50%, he would—like most post-World War II presidents—have less-than-majority approval at some point in his presidency. However, Obama, in his eighth month in office, could hit this mark in a shorter time than has typically been the case. If his rating falls below 50% before November, it would represent the third-fastest drop to below majority approval since World War II, behind the declines for Gerald Ford (in his third month as president) and Bill Clinton (in his fourth month).

Length in Office Before Presidents' Job Approval Ratings Dropped Below 50%, Historical Gallup Polls

Note: Kennedy never had an approval rating below 50%

The time it has taken for presidents' approval ratings to drop below 50% has varied greatly.

- Dwight Eisenhower did not fall below the majority level until his fifth year in office, and his 48% approval rating in March and April 1958 was his only sub-50% approval rating.
- Both George Bushes were in office roughly three full years before their approval ratings slid below 50%. The younger Bush might have gotten there much faster if not for the post-Sept. 11 rally, as his approval rating just before the terror attacks was 51%, but it shot up to 86% days later.
- Lyndon Johnson and Richard Nixon both served more than two years in office before their approval ratings fell below 50%.
- Four presidents—Harry Truman (11 months into his term), as well as Ford, Reagan, and Clinton—dropped below majority approval in their first year in office.
- Jimmy Carter had relatively high early approval ratings and did not drop below 50% approval until February 1978, after a year in office.
- John Kennedy never had a sub-50% approval rating in his less-than-three-year term, though his ratings were on a downward trend at the time of his untimely death.

Excluding Kennedy's presidency, the average amount of time before a president lost majority approval is 23 months. The typical or median length is 13 months.

Ford's quick descent to below-majority approval was hastened by his unpopular decision to pardon Nixon in September 1974. Clinton also suffered from a series of missteps in attempting to change policy (gays in the military), fill positions within his administration (failed nominees Zoe Baird, Kimba Wood, and Lani Guinier), and controversy over a haircut he received aboard Air Force One at Los Angeles International Airport.

Obama began his term with one of the higher initial job approval ratings in recent history. His six-month honeymoon was slightly below average in length compared to those of other elected presidents in recent times. The recent further erosion in his public support—perhaps a result of the push for healthcare reform and concern over the growth in government spending—may result in one of the faster slides below majority approval for modern presidents.

However, falling below 50% would hardly mark a point of no return for Obama. All presidents went back above the 50% mark after their initial loss of majority public support. And Clinton and Reagan, who dropped below majority approval faster than most other presidents, easily won second terms in the subsequent election.

Survey Methods

Results are based on telephone interviews with 1,529 national adults, aged 18 and older, conducted Aug. 23–25, 2009, as part of Gallup Daily tracking. For results based on the total sample of national adults, one can say with 95% confidence that the maximum margin of sampling error is ±3 percentage points.

Interviews are conducted with respondents on land-line telephones (for respondents with a land-line telephone) and cellular phones (for respondents who are cell-phone only).

In addition to sampling error, question wording and practical difficulties in conducting surveys can introduce error or bias into the findings of public opinion polls.

August 26, 2009

SELF-EMPLOYED WORKERS CLOCK THE MOST HOURS EACH WEEK
Most government workers stay close to 40-hour work week

by Lymari Morales, Gallup Poll Staff Writer

Nearly half of self-employed Americans (49%) report working more than 44 hours in a typical work week, compared to 39% of American workers overall, 38% in government and in private business, and 30% in nonprofit organizations. More than half of government workers (55%) work a traditional 35- to 44-hour work week, making them the most likely to do so.

In a typical week, how many hours do you work?

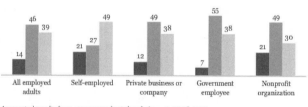

Aggregated results from surveys conducted each August, 2006-2009

Nonprofit and self-employed workers (21% of each group) are equally likely to say they work less than 35 hours per week, likely reflecting part-time work. However, a sizable percentage of self-employed workers—26%—say they work at least 60 hours per week, a much larger percentage than is found for workers of any other sector.

The findings are from aggregated results of 2006–2009 Gallup Work and Education surveys, which each August ask Americans how many hours they work in a typical work week.

Despite the current recession and resulting job losses, Gallup does not find any measurable change over the past few years in the number of hours Americans say they typically work. Essentially unchanged from 2006, 2007, and 2008, 45% of American full- and part-time workers this year said they typically work 35 to 44 hours, 25% said they work between 45 and 59 hours, 12% said they work 60 or more hours, and 17% said they work less than 35 hours per week.

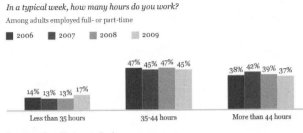

In a typical week, how many hours do you work?
Among adults employed full- or part-time

■ 2006 ■ 2007 ■ 2008 ■ 2009

Surveys conducted in August of each year

In addition to the results by job description, the aggregated analysis of the overall results across several years provides a large sample with which to more closely examine the results by demographic group. Workers with postgraduate education, those making at least $75,000 per year, and men are those most likely to work more than 44 hours per week. Those aged 65 and older, and those making less than $20,000 per year are the most likely to work less than 35 hours—again likely reflecting part-time work. Most other segments tend to skew toward the traditional work week.

In a typical week, how many hours do you work?
By gender, age, income, and education

■ % Less than 35 hours ■ % 35-44 hours ■ % More than 44 hours

	% Less than 35 hours	% 35-44 hours	% More than 44 hours
Postgraduate	11	36	53
$75,000 or more	10	37	53
Men	7	41	51
College graduate	13	43	43
30-49	13	44	43
50-64	13	47	40
$50,000-$74,999	12	48	38
Some college	15	50	34
H.S. or less	16	50	33
18-29	14	53	32
$30,000-$49,999	14	57	28
Women	22	51	26
$20,000-$29,999	18	59	23
65+	42	34	23
Less than $20,000	60	26	14

Aggregated results from surveys conducted each August, 2006-2009

Bottom Line

Despite the recession and higher unemployment, the American worker is clocking about the same number of hours as have been the standard for the past several years. Self-employed Americans stand out as those most likely to work atypically long hours, in many cases upwards of 60 hours per week. Government employees stand out as those most likely to work a typical 35- to 44-hour work week. By demographic group, it is clear that more education is related to more work hours, but, at the same time, that more work hours are related to more income.

Survey Methods

Results from the most recent survey are based on telephone interviews with 528 employed adults, aged 18 and older, conducted Aug. 6–9, 2009. For results based on the total sample of national adults,

one can say with 95% confidence that the maximum margin of sampling error is ±5 percentage points.

Aggregated results combine surveys conducted in Aug. 7–10, 2006; Aug. 13–16, 2007; Aug. 7–10, 2008; and Aug. 6–9, 2009. For results based on the aggregated sample of 2,163 employed adults, one can say with 95% confidence that the maximum margin of sampling error is ±3 percentage points.

Interviews are conducted with respondents on land-line telephones (for respondents with a land-line telephone) and cellular phones (for respondents who are cell-phone only).

In addition to sampling error, question wording and practical difficulties in conducting surveys can introduce error or bias into the findings of public opinion polls.

August 27, 2009
JOB SECURITY SLIPS IN U.S. WORKER SATISFACTION RANKINGS
Satisfaction with employer health benefits relatively high

by Lydia Saad, Gallup Poll Senior Editor

The disquieting nature of today's job market—rocked by the highest unemployment rates in over two decades—is reflected in workers' reduced satisfaction with their own job security. While 50% of Americans employed full- or part-time are completely satisfied with their job security today, this is the lowest level seen since 2003, and is down from a high of 56% in 2007.

Are you completely satisfied, somewhat satisfied, somewhat dissatisfied, or completely dissatisfied with ... your job security?

■ % Completely satisfied

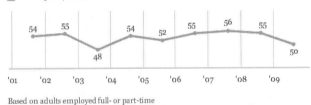

Based on adults employed full- or part-time
Surveys conducted in August of each year

Altogether, 80% of U.S. workers are either completely or somewhat satisfied with their job security, but most of the variation over time in this and other Gallup Poll job satisfaction ratings is seen in the percentage "completely satisfied."

This year's Gallup Poll Social Series Work and Education poll was conducted Aug. 6–9, at a time when Gallup Daily tracking showed as many American workers reporting that their workplaces were letting people go as said they were hiring (25% each for the week of Aug. 3–9). That stands in sharp contrast to the same week in 2008, when, by 2 to 1 (35% vs. 17%), more workers perceived that the sizes of the workforces at their places of employment were expanding.

At the same time, workers' satisfaction with nearly all other facets of their workplace experience has improved slightly or stayed the same since August 2008. The only area, in addition to job security, in which satisfaction declined (although not by a statistically significant amount) is pay.

Worker Satisfaction With 13 Aspects of Current Job -- 2008 vs. 2009 Results

% Completely satisfied

	August 2008	August 2009	Change
	%	%	%
The amount of vacation time you receive	51	56	+5
The recognition you receive at work for your work accomplishments	45	50	+5
Your chances for promotion	35	40	+5
The flexibility of your hours	61	65	+4
The amount of work that is required of you	50	54	+4
The physical safety conditions of your workplace	73	76	+3
Your boss or immediate supervisor	53	56	+3
The health insurance benefits your employer offers	40	43	+3
The retirement plan your employer offers	34	35	+1
The amount of on-the-job stress in your job	27	28	+1
Your relations with coworkers	69	69	0
The amount of money you earn	28	26	-2
Your job security	55	50	-5

Based on adults employed full- or part-time

Worker Satisfaction With 13 Aspects of Current Job

Ranked according to % completely satisfied

	Completely satisfied	Completely/ Somewhat satisfied	Total dissatisfied
	%	%	%
Physical safety conditions	76	95	5
Relations with coworkers	69	93	3
Flexibility of hours	65	86	12
Boss/Supervisor	56	81	10
Vacation time	56	76	19
Amount of work required	54	84	15
Job security	50	80	18
Recognition received	50	80	18
Health insurance benefits	43	67	23
Chances for promotion	40	66	22
Retirement plan offered	35	61	28
On-the-job stress	28	69	30
Amount of money you earn	26	71	28

Aug. 6-9, 2009

Based on workers employed full- or part-time

As a result of these shifts, some of which are quite small, workers are now registering the highest satisfaction levels Gallup has seen with respect to their vacation time (56% completely satisfied), health insurance benefits (43%), workload (54%), opportunities for promotion (40%), safety conditions (76%), and personal recognition (50%).

This year's survey marks only the second time that at least 40% of workers have been completely satisfied with the health insurance benefits offered by their employers. This is particularly noteworthy given the national healthcare reform debate, with some critics saying the public option could force workers out of their employers' plans and into the government's.

Are you completely satisfied, somewhat satisfied, somewhat dissatisfied, or completely dissatisfied with ... the health insurance benefits your employer offers?

■ % Completely satisfied

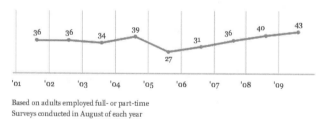

| '01 | '02 | '03 | '04 | '05 | '06 | '07 | '08 | '09 |

Based on adults employed full- or part-time
Surveys conducted in August of each year

Nevertheless, the overall ranking of workplace conditions according to employee satisfaction is very similar to last year's. The highest satisfaction levels, with 60% or more "completely satisfied," are seen for physical safety conditions, relations with coworkers, and flexibility of work hours. The lowest satisfaction, with fewer than 40% satisfied in 2009, is seen for pay, on-the-job stress, and employers' retirement plans. The biggest year-to-year change is the drop in placement of job security from 4th of 13 areas rated in 2008 to 7th place today.

Even with this year's slight increase in satisfaction, healthcare still ranks in the lower half of the job attributes. However, solid majorities of Americans are at least somewhat satisfied with their employers' healthcare benefits, as well as with all of the workplace dimensions rated.

Bottom Line

Amid all the economic uncertainty swirling around American workers today, Gallup finds an understandable softening of workers' sense of job security. At the same time, with satisfaction scores at or near record highs for many aspects of employment, workers are showing, perhaps, a bit greater appreciation for their jobs than in years past.

The implications of this could go well beyond workers' personal mood. Continued strong coworker and boss-worker relations in 2009—combined with expanded satisfaction around personal recognition, workload, and flex time—stand out as potentially beneficial to the U.S. economy at a time when greater worker innovation and productivity may be important catalysts for growth.

Survey Methods

Results are based on telephone interviews with 1,010 national adults, aged 18 and older, conducted Aug. 6–9, 2009. For results based on the total sample of national adults, one can say with 95% confidence that the maximum margin of sampling error is ±4 percentage points.

Interviews are conducted with respondents on land-line telephones (for respondents with a land-line telephone) and cellular phones (for respondents who are cell-phone only).

In addition to sampling error, question wording and practical difficulties in conducting surveys can introduce error or bias into the findings of public opinion polls.

August 27, 2009

BOOMERS' SPENDING, LIKE OTHER GENERATIONS', DOWN SHARPLY

Most generations' reported spending down $30 per day from last year

by Jeffrey M. Jones, Gallup Poll Managing Editor

Baby boomers' self-reported average daily spending of $64 in 2009 is down sharply from an average of $98 in 2008. But baby boomers— the largest generational group of Americans—are not alone in pulling back on their consumption, as all generations show significant declines from last year. Generation X has reported the greatest spending on average in both years, and is averaging $71 per day so far in 2009, down from $110 in 2008.

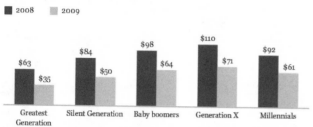

Self-Reported Spending "Yesterday," Gallup Daily Tracking
By generation

■ 2008　　□ 2009

According to Gallup's estimates, 36% of U.S. adults are part of the baby boom generation (born between 1946 and 1964), making it easily the largest of the five most commonly defined generations. At 24%, Generation X is the next largest.

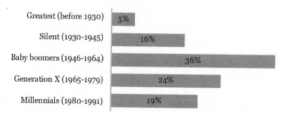

Estimated Share of the U.S. Adult Population, by Generation
Based on aggregate of 2009 Gallup Polls

With baby boomers constituting the largest bloc of U.S. consumers, their spending habits have a proportionately greater effect on the economy, given that consumer spending accounts for about two-thirds of the total gross domestic product.

Some experts attribute the sustained economic growth of the 1980s and 1990s to the fact that baby boomers reached their peak earning (and spending) years during this time. As they now near retirement age, the concern is that baby boomers will pull back on spending to make up for the losses suffered in their retirement savings over the past year, hindering an economic recovery.

Data from Gallup's Daily tracking survey—which asks U.S. consumers to report how much they spent "yesterday," excluding normal household bills and major purchases such as homes and cars—suggest boomers have already pulled back significantly this year from their reported average spending levels in 2008 (the Gallup Daily survey began in 2008, so data from prior years are not available).

But the fact that all American generations seem to be pulling back sharply on spending—even as optimism about the future of the U.S. economy has increased—does not bode well for a strong economic recovery in the near term.

While baby boomers' sheer numbers make their influence on the national economy greater than that of any other generation, their average reported spending is actually lower than that of Generation X. In 2009, average reported daily spending among Gen X'ers is $71, while it is $64 among baby boomers. Last year, the figures were $110 and $98, respectively. Higher spending among Generation X

is not a function of greater income, as the two groups have similar income distributions.

Self-Reported Annual Household Income, by Generation
Based on aggregate of 2009 Gallup Polls

■ Baby boomers　　□ Generation X

The most likely reason for the difference is that 71% of Gen X'ers have children under 18, according to Gallup estimates. Gallup has found the presence of young children in the household to be a major predictor of reported spending (in 2008 and 2009, the difference in reported average spending between parents with children under age 18 and non-parents was about $20). By comparison, only about one in four baby boomers have children under age 18.

Also notable in the data is the fact that reported spending by Millennials thus far in 2009 ($61) is roughly on par with that of baby boomers ($64). This is the case even though Millennials' reported income is quite a bit lower on average than baby boomers'.

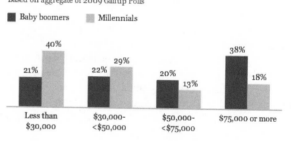

Self-Reported Annual Household Income, by Generation
Based on aggregate of 2009 Gallup Polls

■ Baby boomers　　□ Millennials

Bottom Line

Baby boomers have pulled back considerably on their spending this year, but they are not alone in doing so. Gallup finds significant declines among all generations in average reported daily spending in 2009 compared to 2008. Given that consumer spending is the primary engine of the U.S. economy, it's not clear how much the economy can grow unless spending increases from its current low levels. But spending may not necessarily be the best course of action for baby boomers as they approach retirement age and prepare to rely on Social Security and their retirement savings as primary sources of income. Indeed, the two generations consisting largely of retirement-age Americans consistently show the lowest levels of reported spending.

Survey Methods

Results are based on telephone interviews with more than 260,000 national adults, aged 18 and older, conducted January 2008–June 2009, as part of Gallup Daily tracking. For results based on the total sample of national adults, one can say with 95% confidence that the maximum margin of sampling error is ±1 percentage point.

For 2009 data, each generation consists of no fewer than 4,000 interviews. For 2008 data, each generation consists of no fewer than 10,000 interviews. The margin of error for each generation in 2008 and 2009 is ±1 percentage point.

Interviews are conducted with respondents on land-line telephones (for respondents with a land-line telephone) and cellular phones (for respondents who are cell-phone only).

In addition to sampling error, question wording and practical difficulties in conducting surveys can introduce error or bias into the findings of public opinion polls.

Generations were computed as follows: Gallup subtracted respondents' reported age in the survey from the year the survey was conducted (either 2008 or 2009). The resulting difference gives an estimated birth year (which could be off by one if the respondent's birthday came after the date of interview). Using this estimated birth year, respondents were assigned to generations as follows: Greatest Generation (born before 1930), Silent Generation (born 1930–1945), baby boomer (born 1946–1964), Generation X (born 1965–1979), and Millennials (born 1980–1991).

August 28, 2009

PRESIDENTIAL APPROVAL AND THE DOW: NO CLEAR RELATIONSHIP
History suggests no clear pattern

by Frank Newport, Jeffrey M. Jones, and Lydia Saad, Gallup Poll Editors

President Barack Obama's job approval rating has been steadily declining over the past several months at the same time that the Dow Jones Industrial Average has been steadily increasing. This inverse relationship between job approval and the stock market is not a common pattern with recent presidents. In fact, Gallup's analysis of job approval ratings and the Dow going back to 1977 finds few sustained periods where the Dow and presidential approval were strongly related (either positively or negatively).

Even for Obama, the current pattern is only recent. In the early months of his administration, Obama's job approval was positively related to the Dow, rather than negatively related, as is the case currently. (The accompanying graph, and all other graphs in this story, displays Dow closing values and presidential job approval ratings indexed to the respective averages for each presidential administration. The Dow figures represent the closing averages for the first day of each poll, or the most recent day before the poll began if the stock market was closed on the day the poll began.)

For the first several months of the Obama administration, through mid-June, Obama's approval rating and the Dow were not inversely related, as has been the case more recently. Although the Dow varied more than did Obama's job approval rating, the two were moving broadly in the same direction.

Things changed at roughly the end of June, when the Dow began a steady climb, while Obama's approval rating trended the other way. It is this recent inverse relationship that has caused commentators such as CNBC's Jim Cramer to speculate that the drop in Obama's job approval rating is causing investors to bid up stocks because of their belief that a less powerful Obama is good for business. However, if this is indeed what is happening, it should be noted that it has

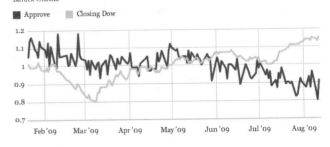

Presidential Approval and the Stock Market
Barack Obama

■ Approve   ▨ Closing Dow

occurred through a fairly small segment of the Obama administration's time in office so far.

Further, such relationships have a high probability of being coincidences, rather than indicators of a direct causal link, although the longer this relationship is maintained, the more likely it would seem that the two are directly related.

The current speculation that stock-market changes and Obama's job approval rating are somehow conjoined raises the question: Has this been seen before? A Gallup review of the five presidents prior to Obama shows that there is no clear or consistent relationship between job approval for these presidents (Democrat or Republican) and the Dow.

Jimmy Carter

There was no consistent relationship between public perceptions of Jimmy Carter's job performance and how the stock market performed. The Dow Jones average was essentially flat during Carter's presidency, while his approval rating generally waned during his four years as president, aside from a spike in late 1979 after U.S. hostages were seized in Iran. Carter's term was marked by some of the more challenging economic times of the post–World War II era—resulting in his generally low overall job approval ratings—but the Dow remained flat for most of his term, rather than declining. The patterns evident in the administration of this Democratic president, in other words, show little relationship to the pattern seen in the current Democratic administration.

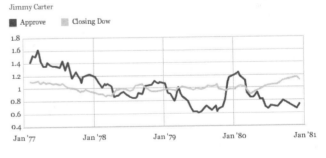

Presidential Approval and the Stock Market
Jimmy Carter

■ Approve   ▨ Closing Dow

Ronald Reagan

Reagan took office in a down economy, and in the early phases of his presidency the Dow stayed flat, while Reagan's high initial approval ratings declined as unemployment continued to rise. Beginning in mid-1982, the Dow began to rise slowly, as did Reagan's approval rating in early 1983—presumably as Americans sensed the economy turning around. In the latter part of Reagan's presidency, the Dow continued to rise but Reagan's approval rating sank as the Iran-Contra scandal erupted. Reagan's approval ratings were relatively unaffected by the Black Monday tanking of the stock market in October 1987. During 1988, both the stock market and Reagan's approval rating showed modest gains. In summary, during the Reagan administration as a whole, there was not a consistent pattern of correlation between the president's job approval ratings and the Dow.

Presidential Approval and the Stock Market
Ronald Reagan

■ Approval   ▨ Closing Dow

(chart)

George H.W. Bush

George H.W. Bush took office during generally good economic times, and in the early part of his presidency, both his approval rating and the stock market rose. The threat of war with Iraq and rising gas prices caused both to tumble in the latter part of 1990. Bush enjoyed a tremendous rally in support when war with Iraq commenced in early 1991. The stock market also rose, but much less sharply. Even though the country was in the midst of an economic recession in late 1990 and early 1991, the stock market did not show much negative momentum during this time. However, that recession clearly took its toll on public support for Bush, as his approval rating slid throughout 1992 and did not recover until after he was voted out of office that November.

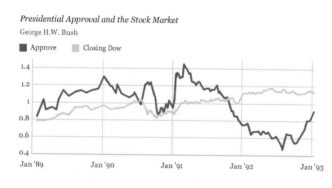

Presidential Approval and the Stock Market
George H.W. Bush

■ Approve   ▨ Closing Dow

(chart)

Bill Clinton

Public approval of Bill Clinton was fairly flat for the first three years of his presidency, averaging just under 50% from 1993 through 1995. At the same time, the Dow Jones Industrial stocks saw modest growth in 1993, no growth in 1994, and substantial growth in 1995. Hence, on its face, at this stage of Clinton's first term, there was no clear relationship between his approval ratings and the performance of the Dow.

The Dow began to rise at the very end of 1994 (timed, coincidentally or not, with the election of a Republican majority in both houses of Congress) and by 1995 was rising at an extremely fast clip.

The Dow continued to surge almost unabated through the middle of the dot-com boom in 1998.

Across this period, Clinton's approval rating saw gradual improvement, averaging 56% in 1996, 58% in 1997, and 64% in 1998—almost certainly helped by the strong economy. On Aug. 3, 1998, the Dow plunged 300 points in reaction to an escalating Asian financial crisis. Yet Gallup saw virtually no change in Clinton's approval ratings at this time, as they held in the mid- to low 60s. The stock market recovered and experienced another year of sharp growth in 1999. Yet, by this time, Clinton's approval rating had dipped slightly, averaging 61% for the year. Both the Dow Jones index and Clinton's approval ratings were flat in 2000—suggesting that the Dow was not dampened by a change in Clinton's ratings, nor were Clinton's ratings hurt by the sluggish Dow.

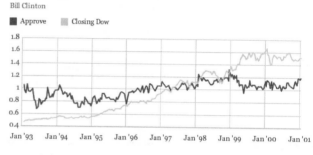

Presidential Approval and the Stock Market
Bill Clinton

■ Approve   ▨ Closing Dow

(chart)

George W. Bush

George W. Bush's presidency was marked by periods when his approval rating ran parallel to the Dow (the two rose or fell together), and periods when the two moved in different directions.

At the beginning of Bush's first term in 2001, both the Dow Jones Industrial Average and Bush's approval ratings were fairly flat—a generally acceptable condition for a president above 50% approval, but not the ideal trajectory for U.S. stocks. The Dow was dampened early on by the dot-com crash that was underway, and later by growing evidence that the U.S. was entering a recession. By early September, the weight of economic concerns seems to have helped push Bush's approval rating down to 51% at the same time that the market was sinking.

This link between Bush's approval rating and the economy/stock market may very well have continued and deepened had it not been for the events of Sept. 11. Bush's job approval score skyrocketed (to 90%) in the aftermath of the terrorist attacks, the Dow initially plummeted, and the two measures moved in opposing directions for most of the next six years.

Bush's approval rating gradually descended after his huge rally, and, dampened by mounting public opposition to the Iraq war, reached the low 30s by June 2007. Between mid-2007 and September 2008, Bush's job approval line largely flattened out in the low 30s (with occasional dips below 30%).

While Bush's stock was sinking, the Dow Jones Industrial Average was climbing. Between March 2003 and October 2007, the Dow nearly doubled, from about 7,700 to over 14,000. At this point, the Dow began to falter, and gave up more than 2,000 points over the next year (at the same time that Bush's approval rating held steady). The mostly downward path of the Dow continued until September 2008, when—in response to the failure of Lehman Brothers and AIG in mid-September—it lost more than 20% of its value in the span of one month, bottoming out below 8,500.

Bush's approval rating was pulled below 30% in late September 2008 and fell to a record-low 25% in October. These ratings could readily be attributed to the economic crisis befalling the country at that time, of which the tumbling stock market was the most dramatic symptom. Although the stock market fell further in November, it rebounded slightly after that, as did Bush's approval rating at the end of his term—finishing above 30%.

Presidential Approval and the Stock Market
George W. Bush

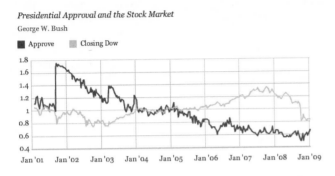

Implications

A wide variety of factors affect presidential job approval ratings, and a similarly wide array of variables are responsible for the rising and falling of the stock market. It is possible that awareness of a president's popularity could affect how people relate to the stock market, or that awareness of changes in the stock market could affect how people view the president. But clearly, many other factors could influence trends in both measures, including the very real possibility that what appears to be a relationship between the two is merely a coincidence.

At times, history makes it appear that the Dow could be a driving factor behind Americans' ratings of their president rather than the other way around. Thus, in Bill Clinton's later years, as noted above, it is certainly possible that the escalating Dow was in part responsible for the fact that his approval ratings stayed high throughout the Monica Lewinsky scandal and subsequent impeachment process.

Some observers have presumed the opposite in the current situation, however—that Obama's approval ratings *are* driving the Dow; i.e., that investors perceive the policies Obama is pushing as inimical to a healthy business environment for the healthcare industry, and that his falling approval ratings thus suggest a lower probability of his programs' passing and that, in turn, leads to bidding up the market. However, this does raise questions about why Obama's job approval and the Dow were positively correlated in the first few months of the year, when the administration was advancing other big government programs related to the stimulus package, banks, and auto companies.

In any case, Gallup trends suggest no systematic pattern by which Democratic presidents (who may be viewed on Wall Street as more anti-business than Republicans) find their job approval ratings inversely related to the stock market, nor a consistent pattern by which Republican presidents find a positive correlation.

More generally, from president to president, and from time period to time period within presidencies, the market and job approval ratings have moved in widely varying directions, displaying no systematic relationship.

August 28, 2009
U.S. INVESTOR OPTIMISM RISES TO HIGHEST LEVEL OF THE YEAR
Investors are more optimistic about their portfolios; less pessimistic about the economy

by Dennis Jacobe, Gallup Chief Economist

Consistent with Gallup's Consumer Confidence measure and the continued strong performance of the equity market, the Gallup Index of Investor Optimism—a broad measure of investor perceptions—in August hit a new 2009 high of 9. This represents a 12-point increase from July and is the first time the Index has been positive since June 2008. The Index has improved by 73 points from February's -64 reading—its lowest level since its inception in October 1996.

Gallup Index of Investor Optimism, November 2008-August 2009

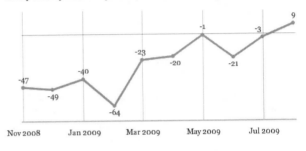

Portfolio Optimism at New High for the Year

For the second month in a row, average American investors have become more optimistic about the prospects for their personal portfolios. The Personal Dimension of the Index increased by 3 points to 31 in August and is up 10 points since June—suggesting that investors are more optimistic about the performance of their portfolios over the next 12 months than they have been all year. Personal portfolio optimism is up 25 points from its historical low of 6 in February.

Personal Dimension, Gallup Index of Investor Optimism, November 2008-August 2009

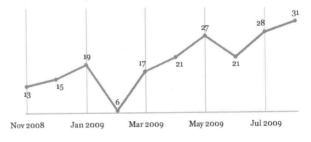

Economic Pessimism Diminishes

Investors are less pessimistic in August about the future direction of the U.S. economy, with the Economic Dimension of the Index improving another 9 points to -22 (a negative score means investors as a whole remain pessimistic along this dimension). This is a sharp 20-point improvement from June, when this dimension was at -42, and is much better than February's historical low of -70. Investors have not been positive about the economy's direction at any time measured since the recession began in December 2007.

Economic Dimension, Gallup Index of Investor Optimism, November 2008-August 2009

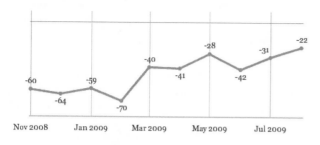

Americans' Spending Patterns, Summer 2009

■ % Saying they are cutting back on how much money they spend each week

■ % Saying they are watching their spending very closely

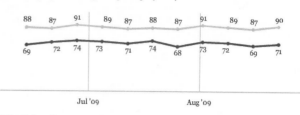

Gallup Daily tracking

Survey Methods

Gallup Poll Daily interviewing includes no fewer than 1,000 U.S. adults nationwide each day during 2008. The Index of Investor Optimism results are based on questions asked of 1,000 or more investors over a three-day period each month, conducted Aug. 18–21, July 24–26, June 25–27, May 26–28, April 21–23, March 16–18, Feb. 17–19, and Jan. 16–18, 2009; and Dec. 16–18, Nov. 24–26, June 3–6, April 25–28, March 28–31, and Feb. 28–March 2, 2008. For results based on these samples, the maximum margin of sampling error is ±3 percentage points.

Results for May 2008 are based on the Gallup Panel study and are based on telephone interviews with 576 national adults, aged 18 and older, conducted May 19–21, 2008. Gallup Panel members are recruited through random selection methods. The panel is weighted so that it is demographically representative of the U.S. adult population. For results based on this sample, one can say with 95% confidence that the maximum margin of sampling error is ±5 percentage points.

For investor results prior to 2008, telephone interviews were conducted with at least 800 investors, aged 18 and older, and having at least $10,000 of investable assets. For the total sample of investors in these surveys, one can say with 95% confidence that the maximum margin of sampling error is ±4 percentage points.

Interviews are conducted with respondents on land-line telephones (for respondents with a land-line telephone) and cellular phones (for respondents who are cell-phone only).

In addition to sampling error, question wording and practical difficulties in conducting surveys can introduce error or bias into the findings of public opinion polls.

August 31, 2009

CONSUMERS ADJUST ATTITUDES TOWARD SPENDING

Even Americans who have the ability to make major consumer purchases are cutting back

by Frank Newport, Gallup Editor in Chief and Dennis Jacobe, Chief Economist

Most Americans have consistently viewed themselves as financially cautious this summer, with about 9 out of 10 since early June saying they are watching their spending closely, and 7 in 10 saying they are cutting back on how much they spend each week. There has been little variation in these reported behaviors.

These data are part of a series of spending questions monitored as part of Gallup Daily tracking, and reported on an aggregated basis each week. Despite some evidence of positive change in overall consumer confidence this summer, the responses to these two spending questions echo the results of Gallup's monitor of actual consumer spending, which shows no sustained increase in self-reported spending throughout the summer months.

Solid majorities of Americans across all income categories report that they are watching their spending closely and are cutting back. Eight in 10 of those making $90,000 or more a year say they are watching their spending, and nearly two in three say they are cutting back on their spending—nearly as high as the percentage of middle- and lower-income Americans doing the same.

Spending Patterns by Annual Income, Summer 2009

■ Less than $24,000   ■ $24,000 to <$60,000
■ $60,000 to <$90,000   ■ $90,000 or more

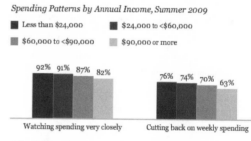

Gallup Daily tracking

Other Indicators

Several other Gallup Daily tracking indicators have shown little or no change throughout the summer in Americans' views of their personal financial situations or their attitudes about personal spending.

As one key example, about half of all Americans since early June have said they have enough money to make a major purchase or a significant home repair if necessary.

Would you be able right now to make a major purchase, such as a car, appliance, or furniture, or pay for a significant home repair if you needed to?

■ % Yes

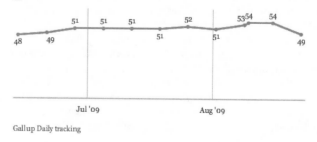

Gallup Daily tracking

Unlike views on reducing and monitoring spending, however, the ability to make a major purchase (such as buying a car, an appliance, or furniture) or to pay for a significant home repair if necessary does increase with income. Three in four Americans making $90,000 or more a year say they could handle such an expenditure, compared with one in five of those making less than $24,000 a year.

Would you be able right now to make a major purchase, such as a car, appliance or furniture, or pay for a significant home repair if you needed to?
By annual income

Gallup Daily tracking

Overall, these data suggest that simply having the financial wherewithal to make large purchases does not mean that one is going to spend with wild abandon.

Daily Worries

At the same time, Gallup's measures of attitudes toward spending continue to suggest that Americans may have adjusted—at least to some degree—to the idea of spending less and watching their spending closely.

Americans' Attitudes Toward Spending, Summer 2009

■ Did you worry yesterday that you spent too much money, or not? (% Yes)
■ Do you have enough money to buy the things you need, or not? (% Yes)

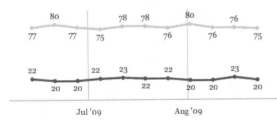

Gallup Daily tracking

About three-quarters of Americans say they have enough money to buy the things they need, and about 2 in 10 say they worried "yesterday" that they spent too much money. Thus, Americans seem to be adjusting well to what could be a period of "new normalcy"—adjusting in the sense that Americans tend to get through the day without worrying about spending money even though they have cut back and are closely monitoring their spending.

Of course, the ability to buy what one needs is limited by income, with 94% of those making $90,000 or more a year saying they can buy what they need, compared to 49% of those making less than $24,000 a year. On the other hand, worry about spending is more equally distributed across incomes, with 27% of those making less than $24,000 saying they worried about what they spent yesterday—not a great deal more than the 19% of those making $90,000 or more.

These data on worrying suggest that many of those feeling more "cash-strapped" tend to be able to get through a typical day without worrying about their situations.

Americans' Attitudes Toward Spending, Summer 2009
By annual income

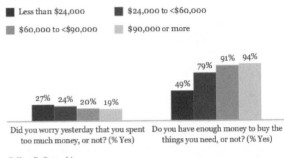

Gallup Daily tracking

The Summer Spending New Normal

Over the summer, consumer spending has been generally consistent at levels far below those of a year ago. Upon further investigation, Gallup's tracking of attitudes toward spending suggests that this stability in spending over the last several months may reflect a new normal—with Americans not only watching their spending closely and attempting to cut back, but at the same time appearing to have adjusted to this new behavior, with relatively few experiencing daily worry. This does not mean, of course, that Americans don't have pent-up desires to spend more when the economy recovers and/or when their incomes increase. It simply suggests that at the moment, Americans appear to be getting through their days with enough money to buy what they need, and also without constant worry.

Survey Methods

For Gallup Poll Daily tracking, Gallup interviews approximately 1,000 national adults, aged 18 and older, each day. The Gallup consumer perceptions of the economy and consumer spending results are based on random half-samples of approximately 500 national adults, aged 18 and older, each day. The Gallup job creation and job loss results are based on a random half sample of approximately 250 current full- and part-time employees each day. For the total samples of these surveys, one can say with 95% confidence that the maximum margin of sampling error is ±3 percentage points.

Interviews are conducted with respondents on land-line telephones (for respondents with a land-line telephone) and cellular phones (for respondents who are cell-phone only).

In addition to sampling error, question wording and practical difficulties in conducting surveys can introduce error or bias into the findings of public opinion polls.

August 31, 2009
MORE AMERICANS SEE SWINE FLU IN THEIR FUTURE
More than one-third now think it's likely they'll catch the virus

by Lydia Saad, Gallup Poll Senior Editor

The number of Americans who believe they are likely to contract the H1N1 virus this year has nearly doubled since early May, expanding from 20% to 36%. At the same time, substantially fewer Americans, 59%, down from 74%, are generally confident the U.S. government can handle a major outbreak of the so-called swine flu.

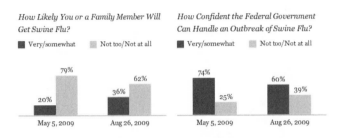

How Likely You or a Family Member Will Get Swine Flu?
■ Very/somewhat ▨ Not too/Not at all

How Confident the Federal Government Can Handle an Outbreak of Swine Flu?
■ Very/somewhat ▨ Not too/Not at all

Further evidence that the public is taking the illness more seriously than they did this spring comes from the finding that a slight majority of Americans, 55%, up from 46% in May, say they would get the swine flu vaccine later this year, assuming one is available.

Currently, 60% of those with no health insurance say they would seek a vaccination, as would 64% of those covered by Medicare or Medicaid and 51% who are covered by an employer or union plan.

Also, a slightly larger majority now believes the warnings the government issued about the dangers of swine flu are real rather than exaggerated—61% compared with 56% in May.

Suppose a vaccine for the swine flu virus is developed later this year. Do you think you, personally, would or would not get this vaccine?

■ Yes, would ▨ No, would not ▨ No opinion

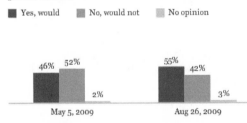

Apart from Americans' heightened belief that they or a family member are likely to contract the H1N1 virus, more also say they worried "yesterday" about the possibility. Currently 17% say they are worried, up from 8% in June, but the same as the 17% found in early May.

Americans 18 to 34 years of age express greater concern about contracting swine flu than those 55 and older, a consistent pattern in the Gallup trends this year. However, the younger age set is significantly less likely than older adults to believe themselves or a family member will contract the flu, and no more likely to say they will be vaccinated. Middle-aged adults show the least interest in obtaining the vaccine.

Adults with children under 18 at home are a bit more likely than those without children to say they personally worried yes-

Did you, personally, worry yesterday about getting swine flu, or not?
April 28-Aug. 26, 2009, trend

■ % Yes, worried

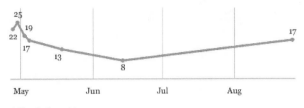

Gallup Daily tracking

Summary of Swine Flu Attitudes, by Age

	18 to 34 years	35 to 54 years	55 and older
	%	%	%
Worried about swine flu yesterday	21	18	14
Very/somewhat likely to get swine flu	24	38	41
Very/somewhat likely to receive vaccine	57	49	59

Aug. 26, 2009

terday about themselves contracting swine flu: 21% vs. 15%. At the same time, parents of minors are slightly less likely than nonparents to believe that someone in their family is likely to get the illness—33% vs. 38%—and are no more likely to plan on being vaccinated.

Even medicine can be political. While Gallup finds only minor differences by gender, age, and region in the country in confidence that the federal government is prepared to handle a major outbreak of swine flu, about half of Republicans (48%) and independents (54%) are confident compared with 77% of Democrats.

The overall decline in government confidence in handling an outbreak may be due in part to a loss of confidence in the Obama administration in general. When the May poll was conducted, two in three Americans approved of the job Obama was doing as president, compared with only about half today.

Bottom Line

Public anxiety about swine flu has ebbed and flowed since the first U.S. cases came to light in late April. The percentage saying they worried about the illness initially spiked to 25%, but has since not exceeded 17%, and in June fell to 8%. Although the figure is back up to 17%, Gallup finds relatively larger increases in the percentages of Americans believing they are at risk of being sickened by the virus and planning to be vaccinated.

Taken together, these findings suggest Americans may be comforted by news reports that the virus has thus far been no more deadly than the regular seasonal flu. Nevertheless, they appear mindful that the flu, already declared a pandemic, could mutate into something more severe this fall and spread rapidly, with no definitive date set for when a vaccine will become available.

Survey Methods

Results are based on telephone interviews with 1,007 national adults, aged 18 and older, conducted Aug 26, 2009, as part of Gallup Daily tracking. For results based on the total sample of national adults, one can say with 95% confidence that the maximum margin of sampling error is ±4 percentage points.

Interviews are conducted with respondents on land-line telephones (for respondents with a land-line telephone) and cellular phones (for respondents who are cell-phone only).

In addition to sampling error, question wording and practical difficulties in conducting surveys can introduce error or bias into the findings of public opinion polls.

Polls conducted entirely in one day, such as this one, are subject to additional error or bias not found in polls conducted over several days.

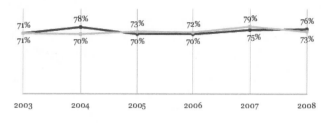

Rating of Healthcare Coverage, by Type of Insurance, 2003-2008 Gallup Polls

■ Medicare/Medicaid ■ Private

71% 78% 73% 72% 79% 76%
71% 70% 70% 70% 75% 73%

2003   2004   2005   2006   2007   2008

September 01, 2009

PRIVATE, PUBLIC HEALTH PLAN SUBSCRIBERS RATE PLANS SIMILARLY

More than 7 in 10 rate their coverage as excellent or good

by Jeffrey M. Jones, Gallup Poll Managing Editor

A Gallup analysis of historical data finds only a slight difference in how Americans with Medicaid or Medicare versus those with private insurance plans rate the quality of care they receive, and no difference in how the two groups rate their coverage.

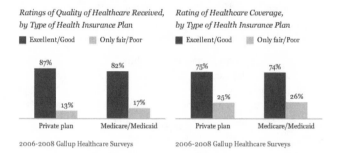

Ratings of Quality of Healthcare Received, by Type of Health Insurance Plan

■ Excellent/Good ■ Only fair/Poor

Private plan: 87% / 13%
Medicare/Medicaid: 82% / 17%

Rating of Healthcare Coverage, by Type of Health Insurance Plan

■ Excellent/Good ■ Only fair/Poor

Private plan: 75% / 25%
Medicare/Medicaid: 74% / 26%

2006-2008 Gallup Healthcare Surveys   2006-2008 Gallup Healthcare Surveys

These results are based on aggregated interviews with more than 3,000 U.S. adults, conducted in the 2006–2008 Gallup annual November Healthcare surveys. These include interviews with 1,753 Americans who have a private insurance plan and 1,049 who receive insurance through a government plan such as Medicare or Medicaid.

According to the data, more than 8 in 10 Americans rate the quality of care they receive as excellent or good, regardless of the type of plan they have. Although slightly more privately insured individuals (87%) than Medicare or Medicaid recipients (82%) rate their quality of care as excellent or good, the percentage giving their plan an excellent rating is the same for both groups (38%).

And roughly three in four Americans give a positive rating to their health coverage, whether it is privately or publicly funded, which includes a 31% excellent rating from those on Medicaid or Medicare plans and a 27% excellent rating from those on private plans.

In general, the overall results reinforce the notion that Americans are largely pleased with their own health insurance plans, be they publicly or privately funded. But the data do suggest that recipients of some government health plans, such as the well-established Medicaid and Medicare plans, are about as pleased with their healthcare as are those on private plans.

The pattern of largely similar ratings of coverage between Medicare/Medicaid recipients and privately insured Americans has persisted over time. Gallup has consistently found roughly 7 in 10 Americans with either a public or a private plan rating their coverage in positive terms.

Likewise, 8 in 10 insured Americans typically rate the quality of their care as excellent or good, regardless of the type of insurance plan they have.

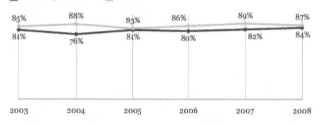

Rating of Healthcare Quality, by Type of Insurance, 2003-2008 Gallup Polls

■ Medicare/Medicaid ■ Private

85% 88% 83% 86% 89% 87%
81% 76% 81% 80% 82% 84%

2003   2004   2005   2006   2007   2008

The basic pattern of similar ratings of coverage and quality between those who have private and those who have government insurance generally holds when income is controlled for. That is especially the case in terms of the quality ratings, which are nearly identical for government-insured and privately insured individuals at all income levels.

However, an analysis of the data by age suggests that the private-government gap may be so small because senior citizens—the vast majority of whom are covered by Medicare—give very positive ratings to their healthcare coverage and quality. Among non-seniors, private plans tend to get better ratings than the traditional government plans on both coverage and quality.

Bottom Line

Perhaps the most contentious proposal for healthcare reform is the inclusion of a "public option" insurance plan that Americans could choose to take. The fate of a public option is very much in doubt at this time, and the details of such a plan are far from settled. But these data suggest that Americans who currently receive government-subsidized healthcare—those on Medicaid or Medicare—rate their healthcare similarly to the ratings of those who are privately insured.

It is not clear what the results discussed here might mean for satisfaction with a public healthcare option if it came to pass. The fact that Americans' ratings of their healthcare differ little, whether they have a private or a government plan, suggests that a properly constructed government health plan may not necessarily lead to perceptions of reduced quality or poor coverage from its beneficiaries. However, the fact that a public-private gap in quality ratings appears to exist for non-seniors (who presumably would be most likely to use a new public option) suggests that views about government-sponsored healthcare may differ by demographic group, possibly depending on one's likelihood of being affected.

Results are based on telephone interviews with 2,802 national adults, aged 18 and older, who have health insurance coverage, conducted in November 2006, November 2007, and November 2008. For results based on the total sample of national adults, one can say with 95% confidence that the maximum margin of sampling error is ±2 percentage points.

For results based on the sample of 1,753 adults with private insurance, the maximum margin of error is ±3 percentage points.

For results based on the 1,049 adults with public insurance, the maximum margin of error is ±3 percentage points.

Interviews are conducted with respondents on land-line telephones (for respondents with a land-line telephone) and cellular phones (for respondents who are cell-phone only).

In addition to sampling error, question wording and practical difficulties in conducting surveys can introduce error or bias into the findings of public opinion polls.

September 02, 2009
CONSERVATIVE DEMOCRATS, LIBERAL REPUBLICANS HARD TO FIND
About half of Americans follow conventional pairings of ideology and party

by Frank Newport, Gallup Poll Editor in Chief

Conservative white Democrats and moderate/liberal white Republicans are relatively rare creatures in the contemporary American political environment; 6% of Americans meet the former definition, and 11% the latter. Almost half of Americans, on the other hand, fit into the more conventional segments of moderate/liberal white Democrats or conservative white Republicans.

Segmenting the American Population

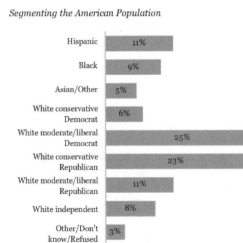

Gallup Daily tracking, July 1-Aug. 17, 2009
Note: Party groups include independents who lean toward each party

There has been a good deal of discussion recently about the polarization of American politics—the division of the body politic into battling camps of left-leaning Democrats and right-leaning Republicans, with few members of either party occupying the middle. In some observers' opinions, this contrasts with previous eras, during which there was more ideological diversity within the ranks of those who identified with each major party. Although some of this discussion focuses on the composition of the House and Senate, it is of parallel interest to look at the state of the overall American population along these same political and ideological lines.

The current Gallup analysis examines more than 47,000 interviews Gallup conducted from July to mid-August 2009, and focuses primarily on the combination of party and ideology among the 72% of American adults who are non-Hispanic whites. (The ideology and partisanship of blacks, Hispanics, and other ethnic and racial groups will be examined in future Gallup analyses.)

As seen above, white Americans indeed tend to group themselves into what can be called conventional political categories: Democrats (including independents who lean Democratic) who are moderate or liberal, and Republicans (including independents who lean Republican) who are conservative. Of all white Democrats, those who are moderate or liberal outnumber conservatives (sometimes called Blue Dog Democrats) by a 4-to-1 margin. On the other side of the political spectrum, by way of comparison, conservative Republicans outnumber moderate/liberal Republicans by a better-than 2-to-1 margin. A small segment of white Americans are "pure" independents who do not lean toward either political party.

Who Are the Conservative Democrats?

Generally, the ratio of conservative white Democrats to moderate/liberal white Democrats is highest in the following groups:
- Older Americans
- Less well-educated Americans

Democratic Groups by Demographic and Regional Segments

	White conservative Democrats	White moderate/ liberal Democrats	Ratio of conservative Democrats to moderate/ liberal Democrats
	%	%	
TOTAL POPULATION	5.6	24.8	0.23:1
Men	5.0	22.0	0.23:1
Women	6.2	27.3	0.23:1
High school education or less	8.6	20.5	0.42:1
Some college	5.2	23.5	0.22:1
College graduate	2.6	27.9	0.09:1
Postgraduate education	1.9	37.6	0.05:1
Under $24,000 per year	7.6	21.5	0.35:1
$24,000-<$60,000	6.6	26.9	0.25:1
$60,000-<$90,000	4.2	27.9	0.15:1
$90,000+	2.8	29.8	0.09:1
East	6.3	30.6	0.21:1
Midwest	7.6	28.9	0.26:1
South	5.4	18.2	0.30:1
West	3.5	24.3	0.14:1
18-29	3.2	24.1	0.13:1
30-49	4.1	22.9	0.18:1
50-64	6.3	27.5	0.23:1
65+	9.4	25.1	0.37:1
Religion important	6.1	17.9	0.34:1
Religion not important	4.8	38.3	0.13:1

Gallup Daily tracking, July 1-Aug. 17, 2009
Note: Includes independents who lean Democratic

- Lower-income Americans
- More religious Americans

In short, the universe of white Democrats in these population segments skews disproportionately toward conservative Democrats. There are no significant differences by gender, and only in the West are conservative Democrats somewhat less likely to be found on a proportionate basis than in other regions of the country.

Survey Methods

For Gallup Daily tracking, Gallup interviews approximately 1,000 national adults, aged 18 and older, each day. The data analyzed in this report are based on a sample of 47,413 national adults, aged 18 and older, interviewed between July 1 and Aug. 17, 2009. For this total sample, one can say with 95% confidence that the maximum margin of sampling error is ±1 percentage point.

Interviews are conducted with respondents on land-line telephones (for respondents with a land-line telephone) and cellular phones (for respondents who are cell-phone only).

In addition to sampling error, question wording and practical difficulties in conducting surveys can introduce error or bias into the findings of public opinion polls.

September 02, 2009
DEMOCRATIC ADVANTAGE IN PARTY AFFILIATION SHRINKS
Gap now 5 points, down from 17 in January

by Jeffrey M. Jones, Gallup Poll Managing Editor

In August, an average of 45% of Americans identified as Democrats or leaned to the Democratic Party, while 40% identified as Republicans or leaned to the Republican Party. This 5-point advantage represents a decided narrowing of the gap between the parties from the 17-point Democratic advantage in January.

Party Identification (Including Leaners), Monthly Averages, 2009

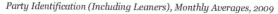
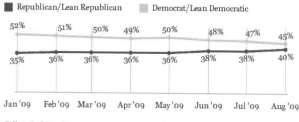

Gallup Daily tracking

These results are based on aggregated data from Gallup Daily tracking, consisting of roughly 30,000 interviews with U.S. adults each month. Gallup has observed a similar trend of a declining Democratic advantage in party identification in its 2009 cross-sectional surveys.

The total of 45% current Democratic support derives from 34% of Americans who identify as Democrats and 11% who identify as independents but say they lean to the Democratic Party. The Republican Party's 40% support total includes 28% Republican identifiers and 12% Republican-leaning independents.

The shrinking Democratic-Republican gap since January is due to a decline in Democratic identification (from 38% to 34%) and a shift in the leanings of independents, from largely Democratic to an essentially equal distribution. Importantly, there has been essentially no increase in Republican identification over this time.

Party Identification and Leaning, Monthly Averages, 2009

	% Democratic identifiers	% Democratic-leaning independents	% Republican-leaning independents	% Republican identifiers
January	38	14	8	27
February	37	14	9	27
March	36	14	9	27
April	36	13	9	27
May	37	13	10	26
June	35	13	10	28
July	34	13	11	27
August	34	11	12	28

Gallup Daily tracking

Why the Shift?

The narrowing of the gap may be merely a reflection of the difficulties a party has in governing. Democrats began to build up a party-identification advantage in 2005 as George W. Bush's job approval rating sank, which ultimately led to the Democrats' retaking party control of Congress in the 2006 elections and of the presidency in the 2008 election. Possible optimism about a new era of governing led Democrats in 2008 to rise to their greatest position of relative strength in more than two decades. A Gallup analysis found little evidence that the rise in Democratic fortunes was due to an embracing of the party's liberal-leaning issue positions.

Over the course of the year, President Barack Obama's approval rating has declined, particularly during the last two months. While Obama and the Democrats may be accurate in saying they inherited a lot of the problems with which they are currently dealing, Americans show concern about rising federal spending and exploding budget deficits as their political leaders attempt to fix the problems. The debate over healthcare reform is also putting party ideological differences into sharper focus, and Democratic Party leaders have been put on the defensive about some of the key elements for healthcare reform they favor, such as a public-option health insurance plan.

It is important to note, however, that while the Democratic advantage in party support is shrinking, it is not being accompanied by a notable increase in core Republican Party identification. Rather, the shrinking gap is due more to a loss of Democratic support and an increase in "soft" Republican support from a growing proportion of Republican-leaning independents.

Clearly, Republicans are in a better position vis-à-vis the Democrats than they were at the beginning of 2009, which is a positive sign as the 2010 midterm elections draw nearer, but the continued low share of Republican identifiers in the U.S. population is a sign that the GOP still has a way to go to recover its losses over the last few years.

Survey Methods

Results are based on telephone interviews with 31,174 national adults, aged 18 and older, conducted Aug. 1–31, 2009, as part of Gallup Daily tracking. For results based on the total sample of national adults, one can say with 95% confidence that the maximum margin of sampling error is ±1 percentage point.

Interviews are conducted with respondents on land-line telephones (for respondents with a land-line telephone) and cellular phones (for respondents who are cell-phone only).

In addition to sampling error, question wording and practical difficulties in conducting surveys can introduce error or bias into the findings of public opinion polls.

September 03, 2009
LABOR UNIONS SEE SHARP SLIDE IN U.S. PUBLIC SUPPORT
For first time, fewer than half of Americans approve of labor unions

by Lydia Saad, Gallup Poll Senior Editor

Gallup finds organized labor taking a significant image hit in the past year. While 66% of Americans continue to believe unions are beneficial to their own members, a slight majority now say unions hurt the nation's economy. More broadly, fewer than half of Americans—48%, an all-time low—approve of labor unions, down from 59% a year ago.

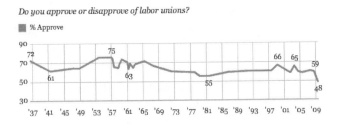

Do you approve or disapprove of labor unions?

These results are from the 2009 installment of Gallup's annual Work and Education survey, conducted Aug. 6–9. The 48% of Americans now approving of unions represents the first sub-50% approval since Gallup first asked the question in the 1930s. The previous low was 55%, found in both 1979 and 1981.

Public reaction to labor unions is one of the longest-running trends The Gallup Poll has maintained. Gallup first asked "Do you approve or disapprove of labor unions?" in 1936, a year after Congress passed the National Labor Relations Act establishing the right of most private-sector employees to join unions, to bargain collectively with their employers, and to strike. That first poll found 72% of Americans approving of unions and only 20% disapproving.

While approval of unions has declined since 2008 among most major demographic and political groups, the biggest drop has been among political independents.

Unions Help Own Workers, Hurt Other Workers and the Economy

Organized labor was put in the spotlight last December as Congress considered a major bailout package for the ailing U.S. auto industry. Gallup polling at that time found a substantial segment of Americans blaming the auto unions for the industry's problems, although more blamed auto executives.

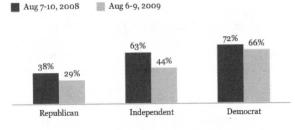

Approval of Labor Unions -- Recent Trend by Party ID

Perhaps accordingly, Gallup records significant increases in the August 2009 Work and Education survey compared with August 2006 in sentiment that unions have a negative effect on companies where workers are organized, and on the economy generally.

The percentage saying unions mostly hurt the companies where workers are organized has risen from 39% in 2006 to 46% in the latest poll. As a result, Americans are now evenly divided over whether unions mostly help or mostly hurt these companies, whereas in all previous measures the balance of opinion was positive.

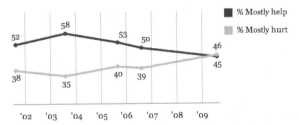

Overall, do you think labor unions mostly help or mostly hurt ... the companies where workers are unionized?

There has been an even larger jump in the percentage saying labor unions mostly hurt the U.S. economy, from 36% in 2006 to 51% today. This is the first time since the question was established in 1997 that more Americans have said unions hurt rather than help the economy. Americans' general concerns about the current state of the economy could certainly be a factor in these more negative views of unions, in addition to specific perceptions about unions.

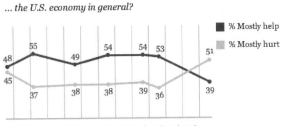

Overall, do you think labor unions mostly help or mostly hurt ... the U.S. economy in general?

Most Americans continue to believe unions are beneficial to their members: 66% in the 2009 poll say unions mostly help workers who are members of unions, while only 28% say unions mostly hurt them. However, this is a slightly less positive assessment than Gallup found in the previous measure in 2006, and is the lowest reading since the question was first asked in 1999.

Overall, do you think labor unions mostly help or mostly hurt ... workers who are members of unions?

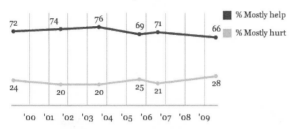

■ % Mostly help
□ % Mostly hurt

Americans' most negative assessments of unions—as has typically been the case—involve their impact on non-union workers. More than 6 in 10 Americans, up from about half in 2006, say unions mostly hurt non-union workers.

Overall, do you think labor unions mostly help or mostly hurt ... workers who are not members of unions?

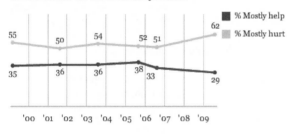

■ % Mostly help
□ % Mostly hurt

Americans living in union households and those in non-union households have sharply different assessments of unions' impact on each of the four dimensions mentioned above. However, the widest gap is in perceptions of unions' impact on the companies where workers are unionized. Of adults living in union households (representing 18% of all U.S. adults), 7 in 10 believe unions help the companies; only 39% of residents living in non-union households agree.

Perceived Impact of Unions on Workers, Companies, and the Economy
% Saying unions "mostly help" each, according to type of household

■ Union household　□ Non-union household

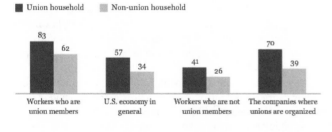

Unions on the Rise or Declining?

If unions are perceived as beneficial to their members and as hurting nonmembers, does this mean Americans would like unions' reach to be expanded or cut back?

The answer in this year's survey is relatively negative: 42% say they want unions to have less influence in the United States, compared with 25% favoring more influence. In August 2008, these figures were about even. However, factoring in the 28% of Americans who want unions to maintain their current influence results in a combined 53% backing the current power of unions—still the largest opinion segment.

Would you, personally, like to see labor unions in the United States have -- [more influence than they have today, the same amount as today, (or) less influence than they have today]?

■ Aug 7-10, 2008　□ Aug 6-9, 2009

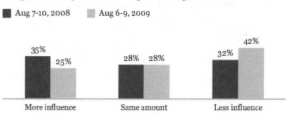

Americans' perceptions of unions' prospects for the future are slightly more negative. With the United States' manufacturing base in conspicuous decline and the auto industry's troubles headline news, 48% of Americans, up from 41% a year ago, predict that labor unions in the country will become weaker.

Thinking about the future, do you think labor unions in this country will become -- [stronger than they are today, the same as today, (or) weaker than they are today]?

■ Aug 7-10, 2008　□ Aug 6-9, 2009

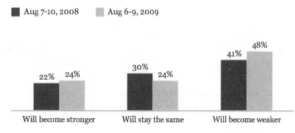

Bottom Line

This year's Gallup update on views toward unions comes in the midst of an economic recession and in the aftermath of major economic interventions by the U.S. government on behalf of two of the Big Three domestic auto companies.

The update also comes as the Employee Free Choice Act—a proposal to significantly change collective bargaining laws—is still under consideration by Congress. If passed as originally proposed, the bill would most likely make it easier for unions to organize. In fact, proponents of EFCA (who feel the current system is stacked against unions) say that's the intent. However, those changes may be going against the tide of public opinion, which currently is at historically low ebb for unions.

Survey Methods

Results are based on telephone interviews with 1,010 national adults, aged 18 and older, conducted Aug. 6–9, 2009. For results based on the total sample of national adults, one can say with 95% confidence that the maximum margin of sampling error is ±4 percentage points.

Interviews are conducted with respondents on land-line telephones (for respondents with a land-line telephone) and cellular phones (for respondents who are cell-phone only).

In addition to sampling error, question wording and practical difficulties in conducting surveys can introduce error or bias into the findings of public opinion polls

September 04, 2009

AMERICANS DIVIDED ON INVESTIGATING BUSH-ERA INTERROGATIONS

Forty-seven percent approve and 49% disapprove

by Jeffrey M. Jones, Gallup Poll Managing Editor

The American public is evenly divided on the Justice Department's appointment of a special prosecutor to investigate the Bush administration's use of harsh interrogation techniques on terrorism suspects. A new Gallup Poll finds that 47% of Americans approve and 49% disapprove.

As you may know, Attorney General Eric Holder has appointed a special prosecutor to investigate the U.S. government's use of harsh interrogation techniques against terrorism suspects during the Bush administration. From what you know or have read, do you approve or disapprove of this investigation?

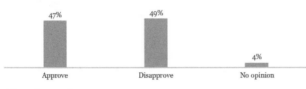

Gallup Poll, Aug. 31-Sept. 2, 2009

The Obama administration has grappled since it took office with whether to launch a probe into the Bush administration's use of controversial techniques such as waterboarding. Some members of Congress have long called for an investigation, but the president himself has seemed reluctant to back an investigation into the matter, saying he does not want to look backward on this issue. Nevertheless, Attorney General Eric Holder announced last week that his own review of a CIA report that detailed the government's interrogation program prompted him to begin a preliminary investigation into the matter.

The Aug. 31–Sept. 2 Gallup Poll finds that rank-and-file Democrats and Republicans have fairly uniform opposing views on this issue. Seventy-three percent of Democrats approve of the investigation, while 75% of Republicans oppose it. Republican Party leaders, most prominently former Vice President Dick Cheney, have publicly opposed a review of the government's former interrogation methods.

Independents are more likely to disapprove (55%) than to approve (40%) of the probe into Bush-era interrogation methods.

Approve/Disapprove of Investigation Into Use of Harsh Interrogation Techniques, by Party Affiliation

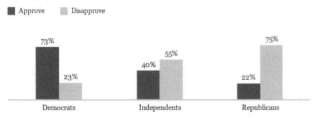

Gallup Poll, Aug. 31-Sept. 2, 2009

Notably, opposition to the investigation runs much higher among the attentive public—Americans who say they follow news about national politics "very closely." Among this group, 36% approve and 63% disapprove of the investigation. On the other hand, a majority

of Americans who follow national political news less closely approve of the investigation.

Approve/Disapprove of Investigation Into Use of Harsh Interrogation Techniques, by How Closely Follow National Political News

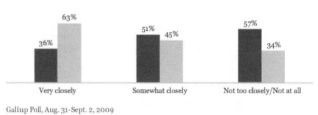

Gallup Poll, Aug. 31-Sept. 2, 2009

The relationship between following the news closely and being more likely to disapprove of the investigation is not merely a function of Republicans (who largely oppose the investigation) disproportionately paying close attention to national political news. The party affiliation of attentive Americans is in fact relatively balanced among Republicans (32%), Democrats (29%), and independents (37%).

Rather, the solid opposition to the investigation among more attentive Americans is due to the fact that Republicans (90% disapprove) and independents (71% disapprove) who follow the news closely are overwhelmingly opposed, much more so than the broader groups of Republicans and independents. Democrats who pay close attention to the news still favor the investigation by a wide margin (74% approve).

Bottom Line

When Attorney General Holder announced the appointment of a special prosecutor to investigate the use of harsh interrogation methods, he acknowledged it would be controversial. The new Gallup data underscore this assumption, finding a U.S. public that is evenly divided as to whether his decision to pursue an investigation is the right one.

Survey Methods

Results are based on telephone interviews with 1,026 national adults, aged 18 and older, conducted Aug. 31–Sept. 2, 2009. For results based on the total sample of national adults, one can say with 95% confidence that the maximum margin of sampling error is ±4 percentage points.

Interviews are conducted with respondents on land-line telephones (for respondents with a land-line telephone) and cellular phones (for respondents who are cell-phone only).

In addition to sampling error, question wording and practical difficulties in conducting surveys can introduce error or bias into the findings of public opinion polls.

September 04, 2009

AMERICANS SAY AFGHANISTAN GOING BADLY, BUT NOT A MISTAKE

Democrats remain more negative on the war than Republicans or independents

by Frank Newport, Gallup Poll Editor in Chief

At a time when Afghanistan commander Gen. Stanley McChrystal is almost certain to request an increase in U.S. troops in that country, a Gallup update finds less than half of Americans, 37%, saying that U.S. involvement there was a mistake, up slightly from a year ago. At the same time, a record high 61% of Americans say things are going badly for the U.S. in Afghanistan.

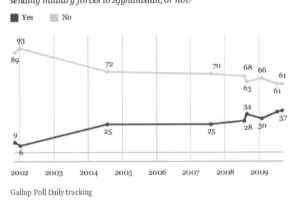

Thinking now about U.S. military action in Afghanistan that began in October 2001, do you think the United States made a mistake in sending military forces to Afghanistan, or not?

Gallup Poll Daily tracking

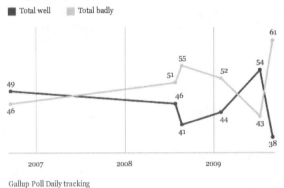

In general, how would you say things are going for the U.S. in Afghanistan—[ROTATED: very well, moderately well, moderately badly, (or) very badly]?

Gallup Poll Daily tracking

McChrystal's recent report to his bosses on the status of the war in Afghanistan has not been made public, but its arrival at the Pentagon has been accompanied by speculation that McChrystal will most likely request an increase in U.S. troops in Afghanistan in the weeks ahead. Several news stories near the end of last week indicated that Defense Secretary Robert Gates may be open to the idea of an increase in troops, although there are also reports that other advisers to President Barack Obama are against troop increases.

Gallup has asked the "mistake" question about Afghanistan nine times since President George W. Bush first deployed troops there in October 2001. Public sentiment that involvement in Afghanistan was

a mistake was 9% in November 2001, then fell to 6% in January 2002, but reached 25% in 2004. Since August 2008, Gallup has consistently found 30% or more of Americans saying it was a mistake to send troops to Afghanistan, with the current 37% reading just slightly above the 34% recorded a year ago and the 36% reading in July of this year. Sixty-one percent say that U.S. involvement was not a mistake.

This majority support for the concept of the Afghanistan war does not mean Americans are positive in their assessment of how things are going at the current time for the U.S. The 61% of Americans who say the war is going badly is the most negative assessment of the war over the six times Gallup has asked this question in its regular polling.

A year ago, 55% said the war was going badly. In July of this year this negative assessment had dropped to 43%.

The fact that the American public still believes the U.S. did the right thing in becoming militarily involved in Afghanistan, while acknowledging that things are going badly at the moment, contrasts with Americans' attitudes about Iraq, which form essentially the opposite pattern. In July, Gallup found a majority of Americans saying things are going well for the U.S. in Iraq, but that a majority also continues to believe that U.S. involvement in that country *was* a mistake.

The Obama administration inherited U.S. involvement in Afghanistan from the Bush administration, under whose watch the war was initiated and pursued for over seven years. Still, at this point Afghanistan is a war managed by a Democratic administration, and Obama may well make a decision to expand U.S. troop presence in Afghanistan in the weeks ahead. He would do so even as a slight majority of rank and file Democrats across the country says that the decision to be involved in Afghanistan was a mistake. A strong majority of Republicans, on the other hand, disagree. Independents do not think the war was a mistake by about a 2–1 margin.

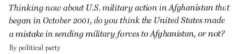

Thinking now about U.S. military action in Afghanistan that began in October 2001, do you think the United States made a mistake in sending military forces to Afghanistan, or not?

By political party

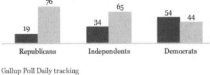

Gallup Poll Daily tracking

Democrats are also more likely than either Republicans or independents to say that things are going badly for the U.S. in Afghanistan, although less than half of all respondents in each of the three partisan groups say that things are going well.

Implications

The American public maintains a view of the war in Afghanistan that is distinctly different from its view of the situation in Iraq. Americans continue to believe that U.S. involvement in Iraq was a mistake, even as they acknowledge that things are going well there. By contrast, the majority of Americans in Gallup's most recent poll believe that the Afghanistan war was *not* a mistake, even though most agree that, at this juncture, things are going badly there for the U.S.

In general, how would you say things are going for the U.S. in Afghanistan—[ROTATED: very well, moderately well, moderately badly, (or) very badly]?

By political party

■ % Well   ▨ % Badly

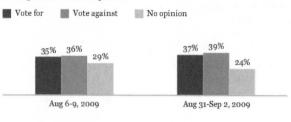

Gallup Poll Daily tracking

The next major step in Afghanistan could be a decision to send additional U.S. troops to that region of the world. Since most Americans accept that involvement there was the correct decision, it could be argued that Americans would be amenable to the idea of expanding troop presence there. Still, the reaction of the public to such a decision will need to be monitored.

On a more specific political level, Obama and his advisors may soon face a difficult situation given that rank and file Democrats are more likely to say that U.S. involvement in the war has been a mistake.

Survey Methods

Results are based on telephone interviews with 1,026 national adults, aged 18 and older, conducted Aug. 31–Sep. 2, 2009. For results based on the total sample of national adults, one can say with 95% confidence that the maximum margin of sampling error is ±4 percentage points.

Interviews are conducted with respondents on land-line telephones (for respondents with a land-line telephone) and cellular phones (for respondents who are cell-phone only).

In addition to sampling error, question wording and practical difficulties in conducting surveys can introduce error or bias into the findings of public opinion polls.

September 08, 2009
AMERICANS STILL SHARPLY DIVIDED ON HEALTHCARE REFORM
Opponents more likely than supporters to base their 2010 vote on the issue

by Lydia Saad, Gallup Poll Senior Editor

The American people are no less divided on healthcare reform today than they were a month ago. A new Gallup Poll finds 39% of Americans saying they would direct their member of Congress to vote against a healthcare reform bill this fall while 37% want their member to vote in favor.

One in four Americans (24%) say they have no opinion about which way their representative should vote on a healthcare reform bill, down only slightly from early August.

The new Gallup Poll, conducted Aug. 31–Sept. 2, suggests the issue could be politically potent in 2010. Sixty-four percent of Americans say their representative's position on healthcare reform will be a major factor in their vote in the next congressional election; just over a third say it will be no more than a minor factor.

Would you advise your member of Congress to vote for or against a healthcare reform bill when they return to Washington in September, or do you not have an opinion?

■ Vote for   ■ Vote against   ▨ No opinion

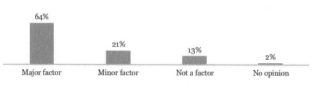

How much will your representative's position on healthcare reform affect your vote in the next congressional elections? Will it be a major factor, a minor factor, or not a factor in your vote?

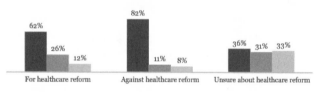

Aug. 31-Sept. 2, 2009

Opponents of reform have the edge in intensity here. Among Americans who want their member of Congress to vote *against* healthcare reform, 82% say the issue will be a major factor in their vote in next year's elections. Among those wanting their member to vote *for* reform, 62% say the issue will be a major factor for them.

Importance of Representative's Healthcare Reform Position to Vote for Congress
Based on respondents' preference for how own member of Congress should vote

■ Major factor   ■ Minor factor   ▨ Not a factor/No opinion

62% 26% 12%   82% 11% 8%   36% 31% 33%

For healthcare reform   Against healthcare reform   Unsure about healthcare reform

Aug. 31-Sept. 2, 2009

Demographic Breaks on Support for Healthcare Reform

Public attitudes about how members of Congress should vote on healthcare reform are highly partisan. Two-thirds of Democrats (68%) want their representative to support a healthcare reform bill while a comparably sized majority of Republicans (72%) want their member to vote against it. Independents lean against healthcare reform, 44% vs. 29%, although their opposition does not rise to the level of a majority (28% of independents offer no opinion).

Apart from Democrats, support for healthcare reform is highest among women, lower-income Americans, those with postgraduate education, and residents of the East.

Looking at support by gender and age, women under 50 are particularly supportive (47% in favor of passage vs. 27% against), whereas women 50 and older are about evenly split.

A slight majority of upper-income Americans want their representative to vote against healthcare reform. Middle-income Americans are divided on the question while lower-income Americans are more supportive than opposed.

Young and middle-aged Americans are closely divided in their views, while adults 55 and older lean against reform. These generational findings are consistent with other Gallup polling in recent months finding seniors to be the most hesitant of all age groups about healthcare reform.

Subgroup Preferences for How Member of Congress Should Vote on Healthcare Reform Bill

	Vote for	Vote against	Not sure	Net Vote for*
	%	%	%	
Men	32	47	21	-15
Women	42	33	26	9
18 to 34 years	34	34	31	0
35 to 54	41	37	22	4
55 and older	35	44	21	-9
Men 18 to 49	30	45	25	-15
Men 50 and older	35	48	16	-13
Women 18 to 49	47	27	26	20
Women 50 and older	37	36	26	1
$75,000 and over	36	52	13	-16
$30,000 to $74,999	40	38	22	2
Less than $30,000	38	25	37	13
Postgraduate	48	38	13	10
College grad	33	53	13	-20
Some college	39	44	18	-5
H.S. or less	31	30	39	1
East	45	33	22	12
Midwest	36	36	28	0
South	32	43	25	-11
West	37	44	19	-7
Republican	10	72	19	-62
Independent	29	44	28	-15
Democrat	68	9	23	59

Aug. 31–Sept. 2, 2009

* "Vote for" minus "vote against"

Bottom Line

A month of town-hall meetings across the country during Congress' August recess has hardly budged Americans' views about passing a healthcare reform bill, or helped many more Americans form an opinion. The public is as divided over healthcare reform today as at the beginning of August (37% in favor and 39% opposed), with a large segment still undecided.

Although the two sides on healthcare reform are about evenly matched numerically, opponents may have a political edge. The 82% of reform opponents saying the issue will be a major factor in their vote for Congress next year eclipses the 62% of reform advocates who say the same.

Survey Methods

Results are based on telephone interviews with 1,026 national adults, aged 18 and older, conducted Aug. 31–Sept. 2, 2009. For results based on the total sample of national adults, one can say with 95% confidence that the maximum margin of sampling error is ±4 percentage points.

Interviews are conducted with respondents on land-line telephones (for respondents with a land-line telephone) and cellular phones (for respondents who are cell-phone only).

In addition to sampling error, question wording and practical difficulties in conducting surveys can introduce error or bias into the findings of public opinion polls.

September 09, 2009
HIGH COURT TO START TERM WITH NEAR DECADE-HIGH APPROVAL
More consider the high court "about right" than "too liberal" or "too conservative"

by Lydia Saad, Gallup Poll Senior Editor

As the U.S. Supreme Court convenes Wednesday with recently sworn-in Justice Sonia Sotomayor on the bench, Gallup finds Americans broadly upbeat about the performance of the high court. Sixty-one percent of Americans approve and 28% disapprove of the job the Supreme Court is doing—among the most positive ratings the court has received in the past decade.

Do you approve or disapprove of the way the Supreme Court is handling its job?

■ % Approve   % Disapprove

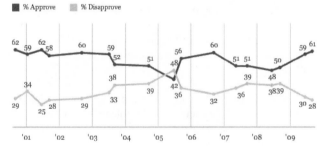

Overall views of the Supreme Court were nearly as positive as it concluded its last term in June. At that time, 59% of Americans approved of the court's job performance and 30% disapproved. However, approval was significantly lower in September 2008, when 50% approved and 39% disapproved.

As Gallup noted earlier this year, the improved ratings of the Supreme Court evident in 2009 are the result of surging approval from Democrats and slightly improved ratings from independents. Republicans' support for the court is lower than it was a year ago, but not by nearly as much as the increase seen among Democrats.

More Americans Content With Court's Ideological Tenor

The heightened public approval of the Supreme Court since last year is accompanied by a slight increase—from 43% to 50%—in the percentage of Americans saying the court is "about right" ideologically. That's a positive shift for the court, and represents an all-time high.

At the same time, Gallup finds a nearly complete reversal of the percentages saying the court is either "too liberal" or "too conservative."

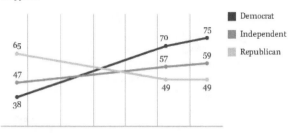

Approval of U.S. Supreme Court: 2008-2009 Trend, by Party ID

% Approve

- ■ Democrat
- ■ Independent
- ■ Republican

Today, 19% call the court too conservative, down from 30% in September 2008, while 28% call it too liberal, up from 21%.

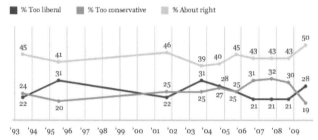

In general, do you think the current Supreme Court is too liberal, too conservative, or just about right?

- ■ % Too liberal
- ■ % Too conservative
- ■ % About right

In the past year, both Republicans and independents have become more likely to say the Supreme Court is too liberal. For Republicans, this is now the dominant view (held by 49%), while independents remain most likely to believe the court is about right (46%).

By contrast, Gallup documents a substantial increase in Democratic contentment with the court's leanings. The majority of Democrats (59%) now say the court is about right, up from 34% in 2008. Since last September, the percentage of Democrats saying the court is too conservative has fallen from 50% to 30%.

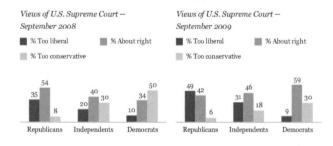

Views of U.S. Supreme Court -- September 2008

- ■ % Too liberal
- ■ % Too conservative
- ■ % About right

Views of U.S. Supreme Court -- September 2009

- ■ % Too liberal
- ■ % Too conservative
- ■ % About right

Bottom Line

Now that the political dust storm created by President Obama's nomination of Sotomayor is over, the Supreme Court heads into its 2009–2010 session with public support similar to its most positive ratings of the past decade. Americans who are inclined to perceive an ideological slant to the court are now more likely to consider the court too liberal than too conservative; however, fully half of Americans say the court is about right.

One reason public attitudes toward the court have improved over the past year could simply be that Americans are feeling more positive about government in general. In fact, Gallup approval ratings for the president, Congress, and the Supreme Court are all substantially higher today than they were a year ago, when President George W. Bush was still in office.

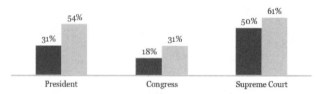

Approval Ratings of Three Branches of Government -- Year Ago vs. Today

- ■ Sep 8-11, 2008
- ■ Aug 31-Sep 2, 2009

An absence of highly controversial Supreme Court decisions during the last term—like those that created a backlash against the court in other years—may also be a factor.

Aside from the increased approval of the court since September 2008, Gallup finds major partisan shifts beneath the surface. Democrats' support for the court has surged, Republicans' support has slumped, and independents continue to fall in the middle, albeit with a solid majority still approving.

Survey Methods

Results are based on telephone interviews with 1,026 national adults, aged 18 and older, conducted Aug. 31–Sept. 2, 2009. For results based on the total sample of national adults, one can say with 95% confidence that the maximum margin of sampling error is ±4 percentage points.

Interviews are conducted with respondents on land-line telephones (for respondents with a land-line telephone) and cellular phones (for respondents who are cell-phone only).

In addition to sampling error, question wording and practical difficulties in conducting surveys can introduce error or bias into the findings of public opinion polls.

September 09, 2009
ECONOMY, HEALTHCARE TOP "MOST IMPORTANT PROBLEM" LIST
Mentions of healthcare approach all-time high

by Jeffrey M. Jones, Gallup Poll Managing Editor

A new Gallup Poll finds 26% of Americans mentioning "healthcare" when asked to name the most important problem facing the United States today. That is slightly lower than the 29% who mention the economy in general terms. Fifteen percent name unemployment specifically, while between 8% and 10% mention dissatisfaction with government, the federal budget deficit, and the Iraq war.

The Aug. 31–Sept. 2 poll was conducted prior to President Obama's nationally televised address to Congress Wednesday

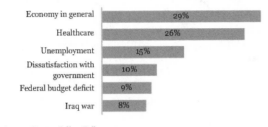

What do you think is the most important problem facing this country today? [OPEN-ENDED]

Aug. 31-Sept. 2 Gallup Poll

night laying out Obama's goals on healthcare reform. Momentum toward healthcare legislation appeared to stall during Congress' August recess, when many members heard strong opposition to some of the possible elements of a plan from constituents at town hall meetings.

Although healthcare reform stayed in the news throughout August, the percentage of Americans naming it as the most important problem has barely changed from the prior survey's 25%.

Longer term, the issue has become more top-of-mind for Americans over the course of the year as the president and Congress have focused on crafting legislation that would expand coverage to the uninsured and attempt to rein in exploding healthcare costs. As recently as April, 7% of Americans named healthcare as the most important problem, and 4% did so just prior to Obama's taking office in January. This trend suggests the public may be taking its cues from government leaders as to the importance of the issue, rather than government leaders' acting in response to widespread citizen demands to address healthcare.

The level of concern measured in this month's poll is historically high, but still below what Gallup measured in the early 1990s, during the last major push for healthcare reform under the Clinton administration. In January 1994, 31% of Americans mentioned healthcare as the most important problem facing the country. Once the Clinton reform effort failed, concern about the issue faded, with roughly 5%-10% continuing to cite it as the most important problem from 1995–2008.

Percentage Mentioning Healthcare as Most Important Problem, 1990-2009

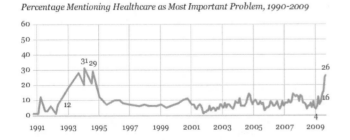

Economic Concern Fading

In recent months, Gallup has documented an uptick in consumer confidence. Coincident with that, Gallup finds a decline in the proportion of Americans mentioning "the economy" in general as the most important problem. In February, 57% of Americans did so, and the percentage has declined at least slightly each month since.

Also in February, 86% of Americans mentioned any economic issue—including the economy in general, but also unemployment, the deficit, and inflation—in response to this open-ended question. That combined percentage has also declined, and in September, just over half (57%) of Americans mention any economic issue.

Mentions of the Economy as the Most Important Problem, 2009

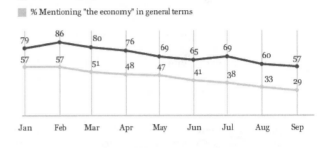

Domestic Issues Dominate

The current "most important problem" data clearly indicate that Americans' attention is focused on domestic rather than international issues. Eight percent mention the war in Iraq—which had been the top-rated issue for about four years, from 2004 to early 2008. Now, five domestic issues are more frequently mentioned. In addition to Iraq, 2% mention national security, and 1% each say terrorism, the military and national defense, the situation in the Middle East, and foreign aid.

What do you think is the most important problem facing this country today? [OPEN-ENDED]

Issue	% Mentioning
Economy in general	29
Healthcare	26
Unemployment	15
Dissatisfaction with government	10
Federal budget deficit	9
Iraq war	8
Moral decline	5
Lack of money	5
Education	3
Immigration	2
National security	2
Judicial system	1
Lack of respect for each other	1
Taxes	1
Inflation	1
Poverty	1
Terrorism	1
Environment	1
Race relations	1
Military/Defense	1
War in Middle East	1
Corporate corruption	1
Recession	1
Foreign aid	1
Abortion	1
Energy	1
Gay rights	1
Fuel prices	1
Social Security	1
Trade deficit	1

Issues mentioned by 1% or more of respondents

Bottom Line

President Obama's speech on healthcare could represent a pivotal moment in the drive for healthcare reform. The issue ranks near the top of Gallup's most important problem list, although it is unclear whether that status indicates a strong desire for reform among the American public, or merely reflects what Americans are hearing in the news.

As of early September, public opinion about passing a healthcare reform plan is sharply divided, with 37% in favor, 39% opposed, and 24% unsure.

It will be important to see how Americans respond once Obama and his working legislative coalition draft and promote a specific plan that they will try to pass through Congress.

Survey Methods

Results are based on telephone interviews with 1,026 national adults, aged 18 and older, conducted Aug. 31–Sept. 2, 2009. For results based on the total sample of national adults, one can say with 95% confidence that the maximum margin of sampling error is ±4 percentage points.

Interviews are conducted with respondents on land-line telephones (for respondents with a land-line telephone) and cellular phones (for respondents who are cell-phone only).

In addition to sampling error, question wording and practical difficulties in conducting surveys can introduce error or bias into the findings of public opinion polls.

September 10, 2009
AMERICANS' TRUST IN LEGISLATIVE BRANCH AT RECORD LOW
Public places much more trust in the judicial and executive branches

by Frank Newport, Gallup Poll Editor in Chief

At a time when President Obama is asking Congress to develop and pass far-reaching healthcare reform legislation, a record-low 45% of Americans say they have a great deal or fair amount of trust in the legislative branch of government, far fewer than trust the judicial (76%) or executive (61%) branches. Second only to the judicial branch are Americans themselves—73% trust "the American

people as a whole" to make judgments about the issues facing the country.

These results, from Gallup's Aug. 31–Sept. 2 Governance survey, update trust ratings extending back to the 1970s that Gallup has updated regularly every September since 2001.

The data make it clear that the president faces a situation in which the American people trust his branch of government significantly more than the branch to which he has essentially delegated the nuts and bolts of developing a new healthcare plan. Recognition of this fact was perhaps behind the president's decision to make a personal plea to the American people with his healthcare speech before Congress (and the nation) on Wednesday night.

The trends for trust in the three branches of government reveal that Americans since 1998 have consistently had a higher degree of trust in the judicial branch than in the other two branches.

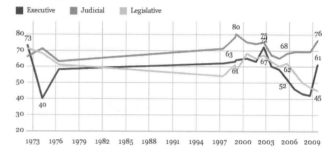

Trends in Trust and Confidence in Branches of Government
% "Great deal" plus "fair amount"

Trust in the executive branch approached an all-time high in 2002, about a year after the 9/11 terrorist attacks and as George W. Bush was still enjoying high job approval ratings. Trust in the legislative branch that year was also relatively high. From that point on, however, trust in both branches began to decrease, and in the latter years of the Bush administration, Americans placed greater trust in the legislative than in the executive branch. This year, coincident with a new presidential administration, trust in the executive branch has jumped, while trust in the legislative branch has continued to decrease, reaching its lowest level in Gallup history.

Trust in the three branches is extraordinarily differentiated by partisan identity.

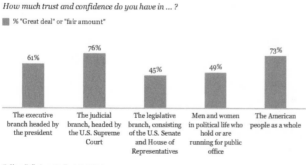

How much trust and confidence do you have in ... ?
■ % "Great deal" or "fair amount"

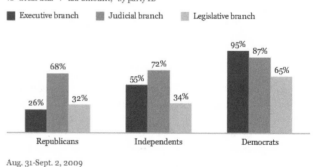

Trust in Three Branches of Government, 2009
% "Great deal" + "fair amount," by party ID

The largest difference in trust levels between Republicans and Democrats, not surprisingly, comes in terms of the executive branch. Almost all Democrats (95%) currently trust the executive branch, compared to just a quarter of Republicans. (Independents are in the middle, at 55%.) There is a smaller gap in terms of trust in the legislative branch; the gap is even smaller for the judicial branch. Still, across the board, Democrats trust all three branches of government most, while Republicans trust all three much less than Democrats do, and two out of three less than independents do.

There has been a diametric shift in trust in the executive branch this year when compared to last year's Gallup update. In September 2008, only 14% of Democrats trusted the executive branch (then headed, of course, by George W. Bush), compared to 83% of Republicans. The judicial branch has seen the same type of shift in trust—although not nearly as large—possibly reflecting the recent confirmation of Obama-appointed Justice Sonia Sotomayor to the U.S. Supreme Court.

Trust in Three Branches of Government, 2008
% "Great deal" + "fair amount," by party ID

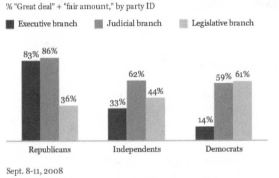

Sept. 8-11, 2008

Differences in partisan trust in the legislative branch are roughly the same this year as they were last year.

Higher Trust in People Than in Politicians

In addition to measuring public confidence in the three formal branches of the federal government, Gallup asks Americans to rate their trust in the primary actors in America's democratic system—the men and women who hold elected office, and the people who are charged with electing them to office under the United States' democratic system of government.

Trust in the "men and women in political life in this country who either hold or are running for public office" has dropped to an all-time low of 49% this year, after bumping up to 66% in the middle of the 2008 presidential election campaign. At points in the 1970s, about two-thirds of Americans reported having a great deal or fair amount of trust in the men and women in politics, and this had never been below the majority level until now.

By contrast, there has been a consistently high level of trust in "the American people as a whole when it comes to making judgments under our democratic system about the issues facing our country" over the last several decades, albeit it with a slight downward drift in recent years. The current trust level of 73% is up slightly from a few years ago, but remains below the all-time high of 86% in 1976.

Implications

President Obama has ceded to Congress the specific details of creating new healthcare reform legislation, forging a different path than

How much trust and confidence do you have in general in men and women in political life in this country who either hold or are running for public office?

■ % Great deal or fair amount

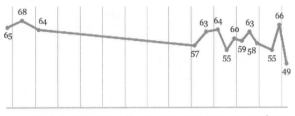

How much trust and confidence do you have in the American people as a whole when it comes to making judgments under our democratic system about the issues facing our country?

■ % Great deal or fair amount

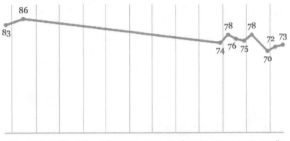

did President Bill Clinton, who in 1994 presented a plan that had been essentially developed by his administration's healthcare team. Obama's decision comes as Americans are according Congress and the men and women in political office record-low levels of political trust. By contrast, trust in the executive branch has jumped back to levels not seen in six years. This suggests that Obama's decision to take a more prominent position in pushing the healthcare reform legislation, including his speech to Congress on Wednesday night, may have been well-advised.

The current data also underscore the degree to which Americans believe in themselves—the people of the country. In a democracy, of course, the people have the ultimate power, with the ability to hire and fire the representatives they send to Washington and, through their representatives, to influence the course of legislation the federal government creates.

The noisy town hall meetings on healthcare held across the country this summer may not have been representative of general public opinion, but they did call attention again to the implications of major new policy initiatives coming out of Washington that may not be in sync with the wishes and views of the people. At this point, with trust in Congress at a historically low level, it would appear that elected representatives need to spend more time than ever monitoring the views and opinions of their constituents before passing new policies into law.

Survey Methods

Results are based on telephone interviews with 1,026 national adults, aged 18 and older, conducted Aug. 31–Sept. 2, 2009. For results based on the total sample of national adults, one can say with 95% confidence that the maximum margin of sampling error is ±4 percentage points.

Interviews are conducted with respondents on land-line telephones (for respondents with a land-line telephone) and cellular phones (for respondents who are cell-phone only).

In addition to sampling error, question wording and practical difficulties in conducting surveys can introduce error or bias into the findings of public opinion polls.

September 10, 2009
IN U.S., TRUST IN STATE GOVERNMENT SINKS TO NEW LOW
Trust in local government relatively stable

by Jeffrey M. Jones, Gallup Poll Managing Editor

Americans' trust in state government is down sharply this year, after showing remarkable stability over the prior four readings.

How much trust and confidence do you have in the government of the state where you live when it comes to handling state problems -- a great deal, a fair amount, not very much, or none at all?

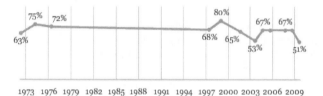

Gallup's annual Governance Poll, conducted Aug. 31–Sept. 2, finds 51% of Americans saying they have "a great deal" or "a fair amount" of trust in their state government to handle state problems, down from 67% from 2004 to 2008. The prior low occurred in 2003, when trust was 53%, due to an economic downturn but also possibly affected by the news about efforts to recall then-California Gov. Gray Davis.

The declining trust this year likely reflects the challenges many state governments have had in trying to pass state budgets while revenues are declining due to the economic recession. Forty-eight states faced budget shortfalls for fiscal year 2010, and the states were forced to raise taxes or make unpopular budget cuts to close the gaps. The most dramatic example is in California, which came close to bankruptcy this year as legislators struggled to find a way to fund its budget, before finally agreeing on a new budget in late July after several months of contentious negotiations.

California's home region of the West shows exceedingly low levels of trust in state government, at 38% (and 22% among the 98 California residents in the poll). Gallup found similarly low levels of trust in California as well as the nation as a whole in 2003, just before voters in the state successfully recalled Davis.

But the low levels of trust in the Golden State account for only a small part of the 2009 decline, as trust in state government is 54% among non-California residents.

In fact, trust in state government is down significantly from last year in all regions of the country, and is now above the majority level only in the South. The sharpest drop—27 percentage points—has occurred in the West, but there have been double-digit decreases in all four regions of the country.

Trust in State Government by Region, 2008 and 2009

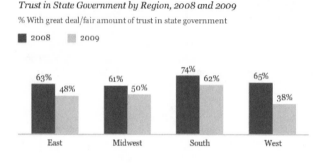

Americans' diminished trust in government does not apply to all levels of government, however. Gallup finds only a slight and not statistically meaningful drop since last year in public trust in local governments, from 72% to 69%.

And how much trust and confidence do you have in the local governments in the area where you live when it comes to handling local problems -- a great deal, a fair amount, not very much, or none at all?

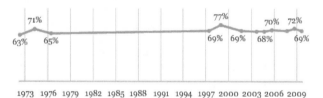

As reported earlier, Americans' trust in the executive and judicial branches of the federal government has increased, while their trust in the legislative branch and elected officials in general has fallen.

Bottom Line

The economic recession of 2008–2009 has had a negative financial impact on many industries in the United States, especially banking, housing, and the automobile industry. As a result, public perceptions of those industries' images have suffered this year. But the recession's effects may have also helped to spark a dramatic downturn in trust in state government, as governors and legislators across the country try to make up for lost revenue from declining tax receipts, at a time when demand for social programs is increasing. With the economy continuing to struggle, the coming year may not be much kinder to state government leaders, as the vast majority of states expect to see continued budget shortfalls.

Results are based on telephone interviews with 1,026 national adults, aged 18 and older, conducted Aug. 31–Sept. 2, 2009. For results based on the total sample of national adults, one can say with 95% confidence that the maximum margin of sampling error is ±4 percentage points.

Interviews are conducted with respondents on land-line telephones (for respondents with a land-line telephone) and cellular phones (for respondents who are cell-phone only).

In addition to sampling error, question wording and practical difficulties in conducting surveys can introduce error or bias into the findings of public opinion polls.

September 11, 2009
AMERICANS STILL PREFER REPUBLICANS FOR COMBATING TERRORISM
Majority of independents and most Republicans favor GOP on the issue

by Lydia Saad, Gallup Poll Senior Editor

Americans continue to give the Republican Party a slight edge over the Democratic Party—49% vs. 42%—in their perceptions of the party that will better protect the United States from international terrorism and military threats. The Republicans' edge on this issue is unchanged from last year but has diminished from earlier in the decade.

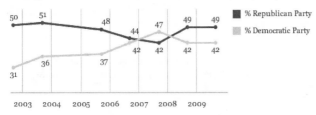

Party Better for Protecting the Country From International Terrorism and Military Threats

Gallup instituted this question in September 2002, a year after the 9/11 terrorist attacks against the United States. At that time, with President George W. Bush's approval rating approaching 70%, the Republicans had a substantial advantage over the Democrats as to which party would better protect the country from terrorism, 50% to 31%.

Since 9/11, the Republicans have led the Democrats in most yearly updates of the question on terrorism, with the exception of 2006–2007 (periods when Bush's approval rating was below 40%).

The Republicans rebounded to a 49% to 42% advantage on the issue in 2008—identical to today's margin. It is not entirely clear why the Republican Party resumed its lead over Democrats on the terrorism issue in 2008, with Bush's approval ratings still lagging. However, that survey was conducted just days after the Republican

National Convention, which advanced a major national security theme built around John McCain's military credentials.

Democrats Lead on Maintaining Prosperity

The new results are from an Aug. 31–Sept. 2 survey in which Gallup also asked Americans which party is better for keeping the country prosperous—a question instituted in 1951. Democrats currently lead on that measure by 50% to 39%, marking the fourth straight year in which the party has held a double-digit advantage.

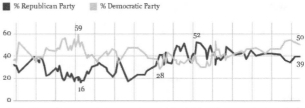

Party Better for Keeping the Country Prosperous

Republicans have not held a significant lead over Democrats on the prosperity measure since September 1994—and in November of that year, the Republican Party won majority control of Congress for the first time in 40 years. However, several times since then (including 2001–2003, 1999, and 1996–early 1998), the parties have been at about parity on the measure.

Partisans Line Up Accordingly

Naturally, the results for both party-preference questions are highly partisan. However, beyond the strong party loyalty of Republicans and Democrats, the variation in the extent of that loyalty, as well as in the attitudes of independents, is revealing.

Evenly balanced perceptions of the party that is better on a given issue would require the same percentage of Republicans and Democrats to name their own party as better, and independents to split evenly. However, that is not the case for either issue in this discussion, particularly with respect to terrorism.

Ninety-one percent of Republicans say the Republican Party will do a better job of protecting the country from terrorism. By contrast, a slightly smaller percentage of Democrats (84%) name their party as better on terrorism. Independents choose the Republicans by a wide margin, 52% vs. 31%.

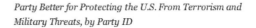

Party Better for Protecting the U.S. From Terrorism and Military Threats, by Party ID

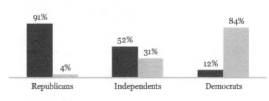

Aug. 31-Sept. 2, 2009

Conversely, regarding which party can do a better job of keeping the country prosperous, slightly more Democrats than Republicans choose their own party (94% vs. 83%, respectively). Independents in this case are evenly divided, with about 40% choosing each party.

Party Better for Keeping the U.S. Prosperous -- by Party ID

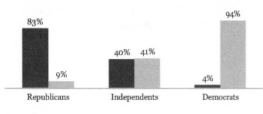

Aug. 31-Sept. 2, 2009

Bottom Line

Dwight Eisenhower ran for president in the 1950s on a platform of "Peace, Prosperity, and Progress." It's an elusive trio of goals that he, and every president since, has strived for with uneven success.

Half a century later, the threat of international terrorism is a pressing concern and the nation's economic climate is the worst it has been in decades. Americans would no doubt welcome a leader or political party that could provide the best solutions on both fronts. However, with more Americans naming the Republican Party as better on national security and more naming the Democratic Party as better for "prosperity," today there is clearly a split decision.

Survey Methods

Results are based on telephone interviews with 1,026 national adults, aged 18 and older, conducted Aug. 31–Sept. 2, 2009. For results based on the total sample of national adults, one can say with 95% confidence that the maximum margin of sampling error is ±4 percentage points.

Interviews are conducted with respondents on land-line telephones (for respondents with a land-line telephone) and cellular phones (for respondents who are cell-phone only).

In addition to sampling error, question wording and practical difficulties in conducting surveys can introduce error or bias into the findings of public opinion polls.

September 14, 2009

TWO IN THREE AMERICANS OPPOSE REP. JOE WILSON'S OUTBURST

Twenty-three percent are outraged, while 6% are thrilled

by Frank Newport, Gallup Poll Editor in Chief

Americans come down strongly in opposition to South Carolina Rep. Joe Wilson's "You lie!" outburst during President Obama's address to Congress on healthcare last Wednesday, though majorities on both

Do you support or oppose what [South Carolina Congressman] Joe Wilson did during the [Obama healthcare] speech?

(Asked of those who support Wilson's actions) Would you say you are thrilled by what Joe Wilson did, or you support it but are not thrilled?

(Asked of those who oppose Wilson's actions) Would you say you are outraged by what Joe Wilson did, or you oppose it but are not outraged?

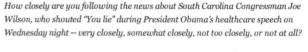

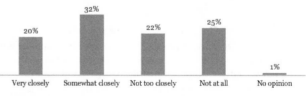

	%
Support Wilson's actions	21
--Thrilled by what he did	6
--Not thrilled	15
Oppose Wilson's actions	68
--Outraged by what he did	23
--Not outraged	45
No opinion	11

USA Today/Gallup, Sept. 11-13, 2009

sides of the issue do not seem passionate in their views. Sixty-eight percent of Americans interviewed in the Sept. 11–13 *USA Today*/Gallup poll say they oppose what Wilson did, while 21% say they support it.

Those who favor and those opposing Wilson's actions were asked if they were thrilled or outraged, respectively. Majorities on each side of the issue would not use these two words to describe their emotions, leaving 6% of Americans thrilled by the incident and 23% outraged.

President Obama has said he accepted the official apology Wilson issued on Wednesday night after the incident, although Democratic leaders want the House to pass an official reprimand this week if Wilson does not apologize to Congress directly. Wilson said over the weekend that he would not apologize again.

Americans were asked in the context of the survey how closely they had followed this news story.

How closely are you following the news about South Carolina Congressman Joe Wilson, who shouted "You lie" during President Obama's healthcare speech on Wednesday night -- very closely, somewhat closely, not too closely, or not at all?

Very closely	Somewhat closely	Not too closely	Not at all	No opinion
20%	32%	22%	25%	1%

USA Today/Gallup, Sept.11-13, 2009

A little more than half say they have followed it somewhat or very closely, leaving the rest who have not been following the news—including a quarter who say they haven't followed it at all. This puts the Wilson incident somewhat below the 60% "closely followed" average for news stories about which Gallup has asked the same question over the last several decades.

There is very little difference by party in attention paid to the incident, with slightly more than half of Republicans, independents, and Democrats saying they are following it very or somewhat closely.

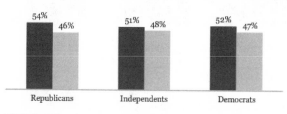

Majorities of all groups oppose Wilson's actions regardless of how closely they are following the news about those actions, with a higher "don't know" percentage among those who haven't followed the news.

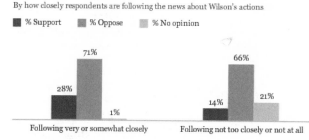

Implications

Americans by more than a 3-to-1 margin oppose rather than favor Rep. Wilson's shouting "You lie!" during President Obama's health-care speech last week. The fact that most Democrats oppose Wilson's actions is not surprising. The majority opposition among Republicans is perhaps a little more unexpected, particularly given the vocal support that conservative talk-show hosts have given to Wilson, and given reports that contributions to Wilson's re-election campaign have soared as a result of what he did. Republicans may be taking their cues on the incident from Republican leaders in the House and Senate, who have generally criticized Wilson's actions.

At the same time, the data show that Americans' reactions to the Wilson incident are somewhat muted, with little more than half saying they have followed the news about the actions closely—well below the average for stories Gallup has tracked over the decades. Additionally, the fact that a majority of both those who favor and those who oppose Wilson's actions opted *not* to say they were "thrilled" or "outraged," respectively, provides additional evidence that the emotional impact of those actions is perhaps less than some of the news coverage might lead one to expect.

Survey Methods

Results are based on telephone interviews with 1,030 national adults, aged 18 and older, conducted Sept. 11–13, 2009. For results based on the total sample of national adults, one can say with 95% confidence that the margin of sampling error is ±4 percentage points.

For results based on the 501 national adults in the Form A half-sample and 529 national adults in the Form B half-sample, the maximum margins of sampling error are ±5 percentage points.

Interviews are conducted with respondents on land-line telephones (for respondents with a land-line telephone) and cellular phones (for respondents who are cell-phone only).

In addition to sampling error, question wording and practical difficulties in conducting surveys can introduce error or bias into the findings of public opinion polls.

September 15, 2009
AMERICANS: UNCLE SAM WASTES 50 CENTS ON THE DOLLAR
Figures are 42 cents for state governments; 37 cents for local

by Lydia Saad, Gallup Poll Senior Editor

Americans are markedly cynical about the amount of waste in federal spending, more so than at several other times in recent history. On average, Americans believe 50 cents of every tax dollar that goes to the government in Washington, D.C., today are wasted. That's an increase from 46 cents per dollar in 2001.

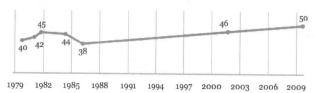

Perceptions of federal waste were significantly lower 30 years ago than they are today. In October 1979—Gallup's earliest reading—the estimate was 40 cents per dollar. The figure rose sharply by September 1981, perhaps influenced by President Ronald Reagan's sharp attacks on government spending that year as part of his supply-side approach to the federal budget. Americans' estimate for federal waste dipped to 38 cents (the lowest in Gallup records) during Reagan's second term, but rebounded into the mid-40s 15 years later. Now at 50 cents, the 2009 figure is the highest measured to date.

Looking at today's results more specifically, about a third of Americans (35%) believe more than half of every tax dollar is wasted, up from 26% in 2001. Another third mention a number between 26 and 50 cents while 21% say no more than 25 cents are wasted.

Americans are only a bit less critical of state government spending. The average amount they now say their own state wastes

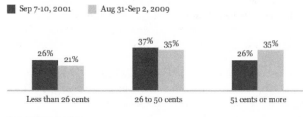

Recent Trend in Perceived Federal Tax Dollars Wasted

■ Sep 7-10, 2001   ▨ Aug 31-Sep 2, 2009

Less than 26 cents   26 to 50 cents   51 cents or more

Aug. 31-Sept. 2, 2009

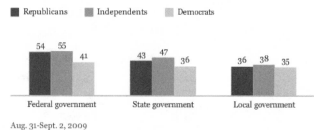

Mean Number of Cents Per Dollar Perceived Wasted by Each Level of Government, by Party ID

■ Republicans   ▨ Independents   ▨ Democrats

Federal government   State government   Local government

Aug. 31-Sept. 2, 2009

is 42 cents, again topping the previous high by a few cents. Slightly more Americans today, compared with eight years ago, believe more than 50 cents of each state tax dollar is wasted (23% today versus 16% in 2001).

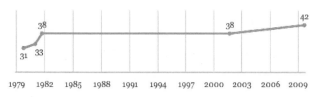

Perceived State Government Waste

How many cents of each tax dollar that goes to the government of this state would you say are wasted?

■ Mean cents wasted

1979 1982 1985 1988 1991 1994 1997 2000 2003 2006 2009

Local government fares best among the three levels of government, and has not seen much change in its reading since the last measurement. The average amount per dollar Americans believe their own local government wastes is 37 cents, similar to the 36 cents recorded in the Sept. 7–10, 2001, Gallup survey.

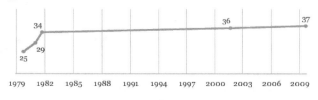

Perceived Local Government Waste

How many cents of each tax dollar that goes to your local government would you say are wasted?

■ Mean cents wasted

1979 1982 1985 1988 1991 1994 1997 2000 2003 2006 2009

Republicans and independents estimate higher levels of waste at the federal level than do Democrats. Additionally, Republicans are twice as likely today as they were in September 2001 (45% vs. 22%, respectively) to believe that the federal government wastes more than 50 cents per tax dollar. The percentage of independents estimating at least 51 cents of waste has risen by a smaller amount (from 33% to 40%), while the percentage of Democrats with this view has not changed.

With respect to waste at the state level, independents perceive greater waste in their own states than do either Republicans or Democrats. The three groups are about equal in their perceptions of waste at the local level.

Perceptions of waste in state government are the same among residents of the 28 states that currently have Democratic governors

as they are in the 22 states with Republican governors (averaging 42 cents per dollar for each). Perhaps surprisingly, even within Republican-led states, Republicans estimate a higher amount of waste than do Democrats.

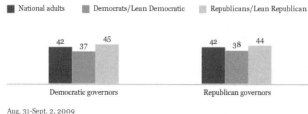

Perceived State Government Waste in Democratic- vs. Republican-Led States

Mean number of cents wasted, by party ID

■ National adults   ▨ Democrats/Lean Democratic   ▨ Republicans/Lean Republican

Democratic governors   Republican governors

Aug. 31-Sept. 2, 2009

Bottom Line

With President Obama promising to pay for healthcare reform through efficiencies in federal spending, Gallup finds Americans, on average, believing 50 cents of every tax dollar sent to Washington, D.C., are wasted. Perceptions of waste in state and local governments are a bit lower.

Across all time periods since Gallup first asked about government waste, Americans have believed the federal government is the most wasteful and local government the least, with state government falling somewhere in between. However, given the increases in perceived waste since the earliest readings, no level of government today can boast about its figures.

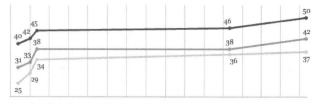

Summary of Perceived Waste

Mean number of cents wasted according to level of government

■ Federal government   ■ State government   ▨ Local government

1979 1981 1983 1985 1987 1989 1991 1993 1995 1997 1999 2001 2003 2005 2007 2009

Survey Methods

Results are based on telephone interviews with 1,026 national adults, aged 18 and older, conducted Aug. 31–Sept. 2, 2009. For results based on the total sample of national adults, one can say with 95%

confidence that the maximum margin of sampling error is ±4 percentage points.

Interviews are conducted with respondents on land-line telephones (for respondents with a land-line telephone) and cellular phones (for respondents who are cell-phone only).

In addition to sampling error, question wording and practical difficulties in conducting surveys can introduce error or bias into the findings of public opinion polls.

September 16, 2009
HEALTHCARE BILL SUPPORTERS CITE UNINSURED; FOES, BIG GOVERNMENT
Desire to cover uninsured largely behind support

by Jeffrey M. Jones, Gallup Poll Managing Editor

Americans are closely divided as to whether Congress should pass a healthcare bill this year. Thirty-eight percent say they would advise their member to vote for a bill, 40% would advise a "no" vote, and 22% do not have an opinion. When the leanings of those without an opinion are taken into account, 50% of Americans favor or lean toward favoring a bill, while 47% oppose it or lean toward opposition.

Would you advise your member of Congress to vote for or against a healthcare bill this year, or do you not have an opinion?

[IF NO OPINION: As of today, would you say you lean more toward advising your member of Congress to vote for a healthcare bill, or lean more toward advising your member of Congress to vote against a healthcare bill?]

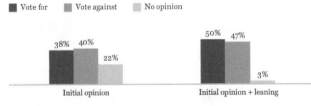

USA Today/Gallup, Sept. 11-13, 2009

These results are consistent with other Gallup research over the past month that finds Americans closely divided in their support for or opposition to a healthcare reform bill.

The new Sept. 11–13 *USA Today*/Gallup poll probed Americans' views on new healthcare legislation by asking why they favor or oppose such a bill.

Support for healthcare legislation seems primarily motivated by a desire to insure those who currently lack health insurance—36% say people need it and too many Americans lack it, 6% believe the country has a moral obligation to provide it, and 7% cite their own (or a family member's) lack of insurance. Cost is also a significant factor in support among healthcare bill proponents—as 11% believe legislation would make healthcare more affordable and 8% see it as a remedy for out-of-control costs. One in six supporters simply say the system is broken and needs fixing.

What is the main reason you favor a healthcare bill? [OPEN-ENDED]
Based on those who would advise their member to vote for a healthcare bill or lean to voting for a bill

	% Mentioning
People need health insurance/Too many uninsured	36
System is broken/Needs to be fixed	16
Would make healthcare more affordable	11
Costs are out of control/Would help control costs	8
Respondent or family member currently lacks coverage	7
Moral responsibility to provide/Obligation/Fair	6
To help the poor	4
Don't trust insurance companies	4
To help senior citizens	3
Other	1
No reason in particular	3
No opinion	2

USA Today/Gallup, Sept. 11-13, 2009

Americans who oppose healthcare legislation mainly do so because of concerns about big government, generally (17%) or government involvement in the healthcare system, specifically (11%). There are also concerns about how healthcare legislation will affect healthcare costs (9%) and about its cost to the government (8%), particularly in terms of its impact on the federal budget deficit. Many also express doubts that the proposals will work, either because they don't address the "real problems" in the system or because respondents believe that government-sponsored healthcare has not worked in other countries.

Notably, a rather substantial 14% cite a lack of specific information or details about the proposals as the reason for their opposition. It's possible that some of these Americans could switch sides and favor reform if the details were to their liking.

What is the main reason you oppose a healthcare bill? [OPEN-ENDED]
Based on those who wuold advise their member to vote against a healthcare bill or lean to voting against a bill

	% Mentioning
Against big government/Too much government involvement (general)	17
Need more information/clarity on how system would work	14
Government should not be involved in healthcare	11
Does not address real problems	10
Will raise costs of insurance/Make it less affordable	9
Would cost government too much/Too much spending/Increase the deficit	8
Will affect respondent's current health insurance	4
Oppose the "public option" proposal	4
Rushing it through process/Should take more time	4
Would hurt senior citizens/Medicare	4
Socialism/Socialized medicine	3
Illegal immigrants would benefit	2
People should not be required to buy health insurance	2
Has not worked in other countries	1
Would pay for abortions	1
Healthcare is a privilege, not an entitlement	1
Other	1
No reason in particular	1
No opinion	3

USA Today/Gallup, Sept. 11-13, 2009

Bottom Line

Americans—who were divided on healthcare reform legislation before President Obama addressed Congress last week—remain so after the speech. Part of this stems from deep partisan divisions, with the vast majority of Republicans opposed to reform and the vast majority of Democrats in favor.

The reasons Americans support or oppose new healthcare legislation are a mix of philosophical and practical concerns. Opponents of reform have philosophical concerns about the growing size and reach of the federal government, as well as practical concerns as to whether the plans being advanced would work to address the problems they see in the healthcare system. Supporters view too many Americans as lacking insurance in a practical sense, which aligns with a more philosophical belief that everyone should have health insurance.

It is unclear how much success the president and other healthcare reform proponents will have in changing Americans' philosophical views about healthcare, which are probably more fundamental to their worldviews and therefore resistant to change. However, the final details of the plan Congress may vote on—perhaps most importantly, how the government proposes to pay for it—could help to ease some of Americans' practical concerns, which could in turn increase support for healthcare reform.

Survey Methods

Results are based on telephone interviews with 1,030 national adults, aged 18 and older, conducted Sept. 11–13, 2009. For results based on the total sample of national adults, one can say with 95% confidence that the maximum margin of sampling error is ±4 percentage points.

For results based on the 498 national adults who favor a healthcare bill, the maximum margin of sampling error is ±5 percentage points.

For results based on the 499 national adults who oppose a healthcare bill, the maximum margin of sampling error is ±5 percentage points.

Interviews are conducted with respondents on land-line telephones (for respondents with a land-line telephone) and cellular phones (for respondents who are cell-phone only).

In addition to sampling error, question wording and practical difficulties in conducting surveys can introduce error or bias into the findings of public opinion polls.

September 16, 2009

MANY AMERICANS DOUBT COSTS, BENEFITS OF HEALTHCARE REFORM
Most center on how to pay for plan or hold down costs

by Jeffrey M. Jones, Gallup Poll Managing Editor

Americans are skeptical that President Obama's healthcare plan will be able to accomplish all he intends—to expand coverage to nearly all Americans without raising taxes on middle-class Americans or affecting the quality of care. Thirty-eight percent believe his plan will achieve all of these goals, while 60% do not think it will.

As you may know, President Obama is proposing a healthcare plan that is designed to expand coverage to nearly all Americans without raising taxes on the middle class or lowering the quality of healthcare. If Obama's plan is passed, do you think it would or would not be able to accomplish all of these goals?

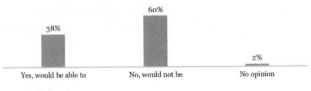

USA Today/Gallup, Sept. 11-13, 2009

Republicans are nearly united in thinking the plan will not accomplish these stated goals (90% believe it will not), and most independents (64%) agree. Two in three Democrats (66%), on the other hand, express optimism that the plan will achieve these aims.

These results are based on a Sept. 11–13 *USA Today*/Gallup poll, conducted in the days after Obama's prime-time address to Congress last Wednesday. The speech served as a renewed call to action for the American public and legislators to support healthcare reform. However, it does not appear to have materially increased support for the plan, and the poll reveals that Americans have doubts that the plan, as Obama described it, will work.

For example, less than a majority (43%) say they are confident that Obama's plan can be paid for mostly through cost savings in Medicare and other parts of the healthcare system, as Obama has proposed. Eleven percent are very confident of this.

How confident are you that most of the cost of President Obama's healthcare plan can be paid for through cost savings in Medicare and other parts of the existing healthcare system -- very confident, somewhat confident, not too confident, or not confident at all?

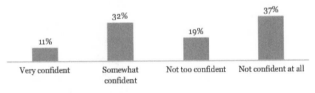

USA Today/Gallup, Sept. 11-13, 2009

On a more basic level, Americans do not expect healthcare legislation to improve the U.S. healthcare system in a number of areas—including quality, coverage, cost, and insurance-company requirements they would have to meet in order to get procedures covered. Although the public stops short of saying reform will make these things worse—given that about one in five expect the reforms not to make a difference either way—in three of the four areas, more predict healthcare legislation would make the situation worse rather than better.

These are key considerations given that support for a healthcare plan—currently 50%, including "soft" support—could drop considerably if Americans were convinced that reform would have a harmful effect on the middle class through higher taxes, higher costs for healthcare, or reduced coverage or quality of care.

Suppose a healthcare bill passes this year. Do you think -- [RANDOM ORDER] -- would get better, would not change, or would get worse than if no healthcare bill passes?

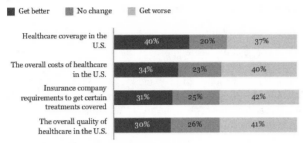

■ Get better   ■ No change   ☐ Get worse

	Get better	No change	Get worse
Healthcare coverage in the U.S.	40%	20%	37%
The overall costs of healthcare in the U.S.	34%	23%	40%
Insurance company requirements to get certain treatments covered	31%	25%	42%
The overall quality of healthcare in the U.S.	30%	26%	41%

USA Today/Gallup, Sept. 11-13, 2009

For example, the poll finds 26% of Americans saying they would support expanding health insurance coverage if it would result in higher taxes on the middle class; 13% would support expanded coverage if it would reduce the quality of care middle-class Americans receive.

Would you support or oppose a healthcare reform plan that would expand health insurance coverage to nearly all Americans if -- [RANDOM ORDER]?

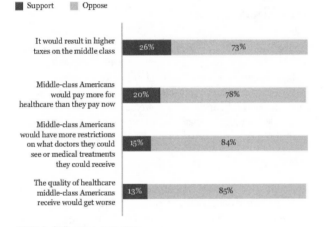

■ Support   ☐ Oppose

	Support	Oppose
It would result in higher taxes on the middle class	26%	73%
Middle-class Americans would pay more for healthcare than they pay now	20%	78%
Middle-class Americans would have more restrictions on what doctors they could see or medical treatments they could receive	15%	84%
The quality of healthcare middle-class Americans receive would get worse	13%	85%

USA Today/Gallup, Sept. 11-13, 2009

Bottom Line

Despite the fact that half of Americans support the idea of new healthcare legislation, many fewer are convinced that President Obama's healthcare reform plan can expand coverage and maintain quality while not increasing middle-class taxes, and that the plan can be paid for mostly through cost savings in the existing healthcare system.

The poll suggests that support could drop if Americans come to believe the middle class will be asked to bear an increased burden in terms of higher taxes, higher medical costs, or diminished quality in order to expand healthcare coverage to those who currently lack it.

With 50% of Americans backing healthcare reform in principle, it is unclear whether the president has enough of a public mandate at this point to convince reluctant members of Congress to vote for healthcare reform. Equally unclear is whether public support for healthcare reform will grow or decrease in the coming weeks as more details of the plan are hammered out in Congress. But as Congress continues to do its work, the president and other supporters of healthcare reform have an opportunity to continue making their case to Americans, and to allay some of the public's doubts about what their vision of reform would accomplish and at what cost.

Survey Methods

Results are based on telephone interviews with 1,030 national adults, aged 18 and older, conducted Sept. 11–13, 2009. For results based on the total sample of national adults, one can say with 95% confidence that the maximum margin of sampling error is ±4 percentage points.

Interviews are conducted with respondents on land-line telephones (for respondents with a land-line telephone) and cellular phones (for respondents who are cell-phone only).

In addition to sampling error, question wording and practical difficulties in conducting surveys can introduce error or bias into the findings of public opinion polls.

September 16, 2009
BUSINESS OWNERS RICHER IN WELL-BEING THAN OTHER JOB TYPES
Farming, fishing, and forestry workers rank high on many sub-indexes of well-being

by Brett W. Pelham, Gallup Poll Staff Writer

Business owners have the highest overall well-being of any occupational group according to Gallup-Healthways Well-Being Index data collected in the first eight months of 2009, followed closely by professionals and managers. Transportation and manufacturing workers have the lowest overall well-being.

Rankings by Occupation on the Gallup-Healthways Well-Being Index

Occupation	Overall Well-Being
Business Owner	72.5
Professional	71.5
Manager/Executive	70.9
Farming/Forestry	67.8
Sales	67.6
Clerical	66.1
Construction	65.0
Installation	64.4
Service	64.0
Transportation	62.6
Manufacturing	62.1

Gallup-Healthways Well-Being Index

The high well-being of self-employed business owners is particularly interesting in light of recent findings that business owners work longer hours than do people in any other occupational category. Their high well-being, despite working longer hours, supports Gallup research showing that working long hours is only highly detrimental to well-being for those who are less engaged in their work. In terms of income, business owners, on average, make slightly less than professionals and managers/executives, but still eclipse these groups in well-being. The three occupations highest in well-being are, in fact, those with the highest household income.

Perhaps the biggest surprise in these rankings is that those working in farming, forestry, and fishing, despite being tied for the lowest average income in these 11 groups, take the fourth spot in overall well-being. This is a group of jobs that often involve difficult working conditions. According to 2006 data from the Bureau of Labor Statistics, almost 90% of those who fall into this broad work category are farmers (including farm workers, ranchers, etc.). Farmers and farm workers, though their work is often very hard, may enjoy some of the same autonomous qualities in their work environment as business owners.

Bottom Line

Business owners do well both in overall well-being and in many of the six specific Well-Being Sub-Indexes. Professionals and managers do relatively well on most of the Well-Being Indexes, but they do not outperform other occupations to the extent that one might expect. Farm, fishing, and forestry workers fare better than most other groups, including many groups earning a comparable if not higher income. Transportation and manufacturing workers consistently scored at or near the bottom.

Together, the Gallup-Healthways Well-Being Index findings reveal that different labor often does result in different lives, especially when looking at six specific domains of well-being. Understanding the different components of well-being and which occupations thrive and suffer in each regard is an important step toward identifying areas of need where employers can make changes to improve the well-being of their workforce, in turn helping to improve the health of the national economy.

Survey Methods

Results are based on telephone interviews with 100,826 national adults, aged 18 and older, who are employed in one of the 11 job categories Gallup uses to assess occupation. Interviews were conducted Jan. 2–Aug. 19 2009, as part of the Gallup-Healthways Well-Being Index. However, because many Americans are not in the workforce, and because some Americans work in jobs that do not fit any of these job classifications, the final sample was 100,826.

Each occupational group has at least 1,900 respondents, which means that for most occupations and most indexes, the margin of sampling error is always less than ±3 percentage points. However, because farmers and small business owners often could not answer questions about their supervisors, sample sizes for these two groups on the Work Environment Index drop as low as 534. The margin of error for this smallest sample size (incorporating the design effect) is ±5 percentage points.

Interviews are conducted with respondents on land-line telephones (for respondents with a land-line telephone) and cellular phones (for respondents who are cell-phone only).

In addition to sampling error, question wording and practical difficulties in conducting surveys can introduce error or bias into the findings of public opinion polls.

September 17, 2009
OBAMA GETS HIGHEST APPROVAL ON IRAQ, LOWEST ON DEFICIT
Little change in Obama approval on economy, healthcare

by Frank Newport, Gallup Poll Editor in Chief

Of the seven specific issue approval ratings measured in a Sept. 11–13 *USA Today*/Gallup poll, President Obama gets his highest rating (56%) on his handling of Iraq, and his lowest (38%) on the federal deficit. Obama's approval ratings on handling the economy and healthcare, at 46% and 43%, respectively, are little changed over the past two months.

Do you approve or disapprove of the way Barack Obama is handling -- [RANDOM ORDER]?

Issue	Approve	Disapprove
	%	%
The situation in Iraq	56	38
The environment	54	33
Energy policy	50	37
The situation in Afghanistan	49	42
The economy	46	51
Healthcare policy	43	52
The federal budget deficit	38	58

USA Today/Gallup, Sept. 11-13, 2009

In the Sept. 11–13 survey, Obama's overall job approval rating is 54%. Of the seven issues tested, only for Iraq is Obama's approval rating higher than his overall approval rating. His ratings on five of the issues—energy policy, Afghanistan, the economy, healthcare policy, and the federal budget deficit—are below his overall approval rating, while his rating on handling the environment is identical to his overall rating.

The Economy

Obama's job approval ratings on handling the economy can be divided into two phases. In the most recent three measurements—taken over the last two months—his economic rating has held between 46% and 48%. Earlier in his administration—from February through May—Obama's economic ratings were higher, between 55% and 59%.

Gallup's consumer confidence measures have improved somewhat since mid-July, but Americans are apparently not yet giving credit to the president for their increased economic optimism.

Opinion of Barack Obama's Handling of the Economy

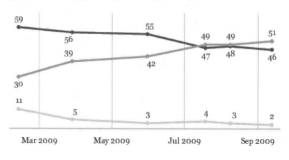

Healthcare

Despite the intensity with which the healthcare debate has been waged in recent months, and President Obama's ongoing involvement in that debate, there has been little change in the way Americans view Obama's handling of healthcare policy across Gallup surveys conducted in July and August, and in the current Sept. 11–13 survey. Obama's approval rating on healthcare has been 43% or 44% in all three surveys, and his disapproval rating has varied only slightly—between 49% and 52%.

Opinion of Barack Obama's Handling of Healthcare

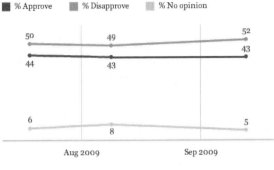

The Federal Budget Deficit

President Obama's approval rating on handling the federal budget deficit is down from 49% in March to 38% today, with at least a slight drop in each of the three surveys that followed the initial March reading. The president's current 38% approval on handling the deficit, and the accompanying 58% disapproval, is thus his worst rating to date on the issue, and the most negative reading on any of the seven issues tested in this survey.

Opinion of Barack Obama's Handling of the Federal Budget Deficit

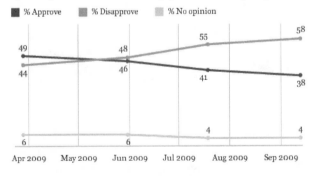

Iraq and Afghanistan

Gallup has measured public approval of Obama's handling of Iraq and Afghanistan only twice, in mid-July and in the current survey. In July, Obama's approval ratings for these two situations were virtually identical, at 57% for Iraq and 56% for Afghanistan. Approval on Iraq has stayed essentially the same in the current survey, but there has been a seven-point drop in Obama's approval rating for handling Afghanistan.

This current differentiation in perceived handling of the two wars occurs in contrast to recent Gallup findings showing that Amer-

Approval of Barack Obama's Handling of the Situations in Afghanistan and Iraq

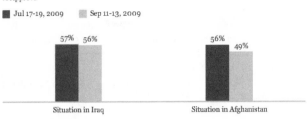

icans are much more likely to see the situation in Iraq as a mistake than they are to see Afghanistan this way.

Energy and the Environment

This survey marks the first time that Gallup has measured Obama's presidential approval ratings on energy policy and the environment. The president gets slightly higher marks for his handling of the environment than for energy policy (54% vs. 50%), although the difference is not large.

Opinion of Barack Obama's Handling of the Environment and Energy Policy

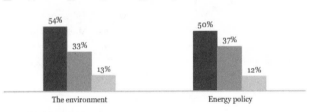

USA Today/Gallup, Sept. 11-13, 2009

Bottom Line

There is an 18-point spread between Obama's highest and lowest issue approval ratings in Gallup's Sept. 11–13 survey, from 56% on Iraq to 38% on the deficit. The fact that only one of the seven ratings exceeds Obama's overall job approval rating underscores that Americans are more positive about Obama in a general sense than in terms of most specific issues.

Obama's relative weaknesses at this time, as measured by public approval of the job he is doing handling various issues, would appear to be the deficit, healthcare, and the economy. The fact that there has been no change since July in Americans' ratings of how Obama is handling healthcare or the economy suggests that Americans' views on these issues may have become fairly entrenched—unless and until new administration or legislative actions are forthcoming to deal with either. It is also of note that Americans rate the president's handling of Afghanistan lower than his handling of Iraq—while two months ago, his approval ratings on the two wars were virtually identical.

Survey Methods

Results are based on telephone interviews with 1,030 national adults, aged 18 and older, conducted Sept. 11–13, 2009. For results based on the total sample of national adults, one can say with 95% confidence that the maximum margin of sampling error is ±4 percentage points.

For results based on the 501 national adults in the Form A half-sample and 529 national adults in the Form B half-sample, the maximum margins of sampling error are ±5 percentage points.

Interviews are conducted with respondents on land-line telephones (for respondents with a land-line telephone) and cellular phones (for respondents who are cell-phone only).

In addition to sampling error, question wording and practical difficulties in conducting surveys can introduce error or bias into the findings of public opinion polls.

September 17, 2009

BOTH PARTIES IN CONGRESS NEAR RECORD-LOW APPROVAL

Republicans unusually critical of the Republicans in Congress

by Lydia Saad, Gallup Poll Senior Editor

New *USA Today*/Gallup approval ratings of the two major parties in Congress show the Democrats faring slightly better than the Republicans, in line with the pattern in recent years. Thirty-six percent of Americans interviewed Sept. 11–13 approve of how the Democrats in Congress are doing their job; 27% approve of the Republicans. However, both parties' ratings are down significantly from earlier this year, returning them to the record-low levels seen in 2007 and 2008.

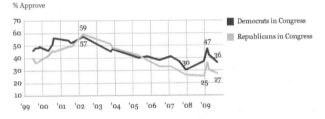

Approval of Congressional Republicans and Democrats, 1999-2009

Do you approve or disapprove of the way the [ROTATED: Democrats in Congress/Republicans in Congress] are handling their job?

The low point for the Democrats in Congress came in December 2007, when 30% approved; a low of 25% approved of the Republicans in December 2008 (with the Democrats' ratings marginally improved from 2007). The ratings surged in February of this year (to 47% for the Democrats and 36% for the Republicans) but declined in March and have now declined further.

Republicans Discouraged With Party's Performance

A key reason for congressional Republicans' depressed ratings in recent months is that rank-and-file Republicans' support for their own party in Congress has descended to unprecedented depths.

Although overall approval of the Republicans in Congress is about the same today as it was in December 2008, support among Republicans has dropped from 52% to 39%. At the same time, approval among Democrats has increased from 9% to 20%, helping

to keep the overall rating from setting a new low. Remarkably, an outright majority of Republicans today (58%) say they disapprove of the job the Republicans in Congress are doing.

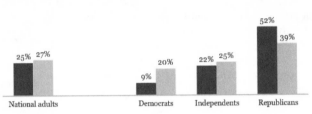

Approval of Republicans in Congress, December 2008 vs. September 2009

By contrast, since December there has been a slight increase in support for the Democrats in Congress from rank-and-file Democrats (from 60% to 67%) and a corresponding decline in support from Republicans (from 18% to 10%).

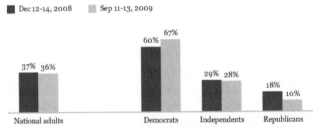

Approval of Democrats in Congress, December 2008 vs. September 2009

The 39% approval rating Republicans give to their own party in Congress is the lowest such reading in Gallup trends dating to 1999.

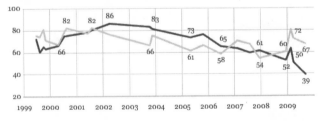

Partisans' Ratings of Own Party's Job Performance in Congress

Independents today give slightly higher approval ratings to the Democrats in Congress than to the Republicans, as is typically the case. However, independents' assessments of the Democrats have grown more negative between March and the Sept. 11–13 poll, falling from 36% to 28%. At the same time, independents' ratings of Republicans held steady. As a result, the gap in independents' views of the two parties is narrower now than it has been in recent polls.

Congress' Overall Job Rating Steady

Earlier this month, Gallup found 31% of Americans approving of the job Congress as a whole is doing, which is about the midpoint between the ratings Americans give the two parties individually (as

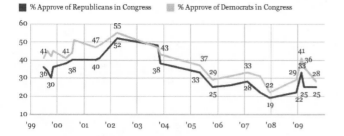

Independents' Views of Congressional Republicans and Democrats, 1999-2009

■ % Approve of Republicans in Congress   ▓ % Approve of Democrats in Congress

reviewed above). Congressional approval was also 31% in August, and has registered in the low 30s since June.

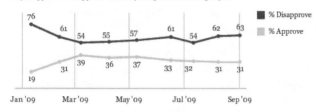

Congressional Approval -- 2009 Trend

Do you approve or disapprove of the way Congress is handling its job?

■ % Disapprove
▓ % Approve

At 31%, public approval of Congress is down from earlier this year, and certainly much lower than President Obama's recent job ratings. However, the average 32% approval of Congress seen thus far in 2009 is significantly better than the 19% recorded in 2008, and higher than the 25%-27% ratings seen in 2006 and 2007.

More importantly, approval of Congress today is only slightly below the average 36% rating found across the past two decades. Low public approval of Congress is the norm, and the 111th Congress is performing at just below par.

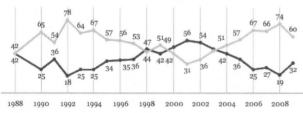

Congressional Approval -- Annual Averages, 1988-2009*

■ % Approve   ▓ % Disapprove

* 2009 figures are preliminary, through September

Bottom Line

Congress' overall job approval rating is slightly lower than average for the past two decades, but still exceeds the much lower ratings recorded from 2006 through 2008 (as well as in the early 1990s). By contrast, Americans' ratings of the two major parties in Congress are at or near their worst levels in a decade, in part because of heightened Republican discontent with both. Approval ratings of the Republicans and Democrats in Congress are also low among independents.

Positive ratings of both sides of the aisle in Congress surged earlier this year, most likely due to the burst in public optimism

around the new Obama presidency, but the surge in ratings has since subsided.

That Republicans in 2009 would be less approving of the Democrats in Congress, now that the Democrats have the backing of a Democratic president to help advance their legislative goals, is not surprising. Republicans' unparalleled criticism of the Republicans in Congress is less expected, but perhaps stems from frustration with their party's failure to stave off more of the Democratic agenda. Independents' low approval of both parties could be seen as a particularly troubling sign for the Democratic majority if it continues in 2010.

Survey Methods

Overall Congress approval results are based on telephone interviews with 1,026 national adults, aged 18 and older, conducted Aug. 31–Sept. 2, 2009. For results based on the total sample of national adults, one can say with 95% confidence that the maximum margin of sampling error is ±4 percentage points.

Congressional party approval ratings are based on telephone interviews with 1,030 national adults, aged 18 and older, conducted Sept. 11–13, 2009. For results based on the total sample of national adults, one can say with 95% confidence that the maximum margin of sampling error is ±4 percentage points.

Interviews are conducted with respondents on land-line telephones (for respondents with a land-line telephone) and cellular phones (for respondents who are cell-phone only).

In addition to sampling error, question wording and practical difficulties in conducting surveys can introduce error or bias into the findings of public opinion polls.

September 18, 2009

MOST AMERICANS STILL CREDIT OBAMA FOR BIPARTISAN EFFORTS

Six in 10 say he is making a sincere effort to work with Republicans

by Jeffrey M. Jones, Gallup Poll Managing Editor

President Barack Obama may have failed to achieve much bipartisan agreement on his major policies since he took office, but Americans give him credit for trying. Sixty percent say Obama has made a sincere effort to work with Republicans, down from prior measurements but still the majority view.

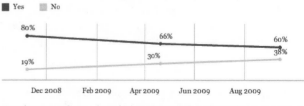

In dealing with the problems facing the country, do you think Barack Obama has or has not made a sincere effort to work with the Republicans in Congress to find solutions that are acceptable to both parties?

■ Yes   ▓ No

November 2008 wording: " ... do you think Barack Obama will or will not make a sincere effort ... "

Americans were much more optimistic about Obama's reaching across the aisle immediately after his election last fall, when 80% thought he would make a sincere effort to work with Republicans. After he took office, around the 100-day mark of his presidency, 66% thought he was making such an effort. Now, 60% believe he is acting in a bipartisan manner, according to the Sept. 11–13 *USA Today*/Gallup poll.

Democrats and Republicans diverge in their views of Obama's efforts. Ninety percent of Democrats believe Obama is attempting to work with congressional Republicans; 27% of rank-and-file Republicans agree. More than half of independents, 56%, view Obama as making a concerted effort toward bipartisanship.

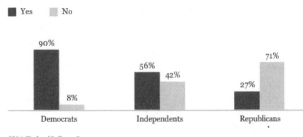

Do You Believe Obama Has Made Sincere Effort to Work With Republicans in Congress, by Party Affiliation

USA Today/Gallup, Sept. 11-13, 2009

Americans are much less likely to believe members of Congress in either party are trying to work with the other side than to believe Obama is. Thirty-three percent say the Republicans in Congress are making a sincere effort to work with Obama and the Democrats in Congress. Slightly more, 38%, believe the Democrats in Congress are trying to cooperate with the Republicans.

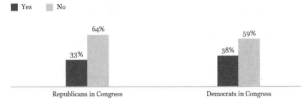

Do you think [the Republicans in Congress/the Democrats in Congress] have or have not made a sincere effort to work with [Barack Obama and the Democrats in Congress/the Republicans in Congress] to find solutions that are acceptable to both parties?

The trend lines in ratings of both congressional parties are similar, with a great deal of optimism about bipartisanship after last November's election—optimism that diminished greatly several months into the current session of Congress.

Less than half of Republicans (45%), Democrats (21%), and independents (33%) think the Republicans in Congress are trying hard to work with Obama and the Democrats in Congress, with rank-and-file Republicans most likely to believe this.

Most Democrats, 67%, think their party's congressional delegation is behaving in a bipartisan manner. But relatively small proportions of independents (29%) and Republicans (14%) agree.

Bottom Line

Earlier this year, Congress passed President Obama's economic stimulus plan with no House Republicans and only three Senate

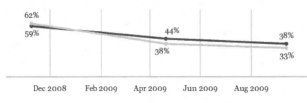

Trend in Rating of Republicans/Democrats in Congress as Making Sincere Effort to Find Solutions That Are Acceptable to Both Parties

November 2008 wording: " ... do you think the Democrats/Republicans in Congress will or will not make a sincere effort ... "

Republicans (one of whom later switched his party allegiance to the Democrats) voting for it. And it is unclear whether any Republicans in either chamber will support healthcare reform legislation that Obama backs and that is now working its way through Congress. Even so, most Americans give Obama credit for trying to be bipartisan even if the results of those efforts are not necessarily apparent.

That may stem from the public's recognizing some of the specific actions Obama has taken, such as meeting with Republican leaders about the stimulus bill and expressing a willingness to forgo elements of healthcare reform most distasteful to Republicans. It may also be due to a "halo effect" from positive feelings toward Obama in general—something that does not apply to members of Congress at this time.

Survey Methods

Results are based on telephone interviews with 1,030 national adults, aged 18 and older, conducted Sept. 11–13, 2009. For results based on the total sample of national adults, one can say with 95% confidence that the maximum margin of sampling error is ±4 percentage points.

Interviews are conducted with respondents on land-line telephones (for respondents with a land-line telephone) and cellular phones (for respondents who are cell-phone only).

In addition to sampling error, question wording and practical difficulties in conducting surveys can introduce error or bias into the findings of public opinion polls.

September 18, 2009

UPPER-INCOME CONSUMERS PULL BACK THEIR SPENDING

Decline of 37% from a year ago exceeds 28% decline among middle-, lower-income consumers

by Dennis Jacobe, Gallup Chief Economist

Despite a $2 trillion increase in U.S. household wealth last quarter, upper-income Americans' self-reported average daily spending in stores, restaurants, gas stations, and online is down 37% in the first half of September from September of a year ago. This decline—which is worse than the 28% decline in spending among middle- and

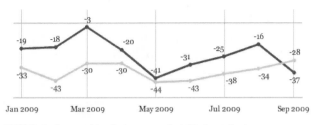

Year-to-Year Percent Change in Average Daily Consumer Spending

Gallup Daily tracking

■ Year-to-year % change, upper-income Americans

▨ Year-to-year % change, middle- and lower-income Americans

NOTE: September 2009 data reflect surveys conducted Sept. 1-15 of each year

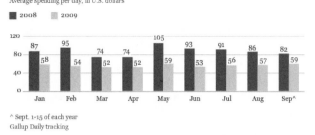

Middle- and Lower-Income Consumer Spending

Average spending per day, in U.S. dollars

■ 2008   ▨ 2009

^ Sept. 1-15 of each year
Gallup Daily tracking

lower-income Americans, and is worse than the August upper-income decline—is not good news, especially for upscale retailers and big-ticket-item sales.

Gallup finds Americans who earn $90,000 or more a year spending $3 less per day during the first half of September ($113) than they did in August ($116). This puts upper-income spending so far this month in the same $14 range ($107 to $121) that it has occupied throughout 2009, reinforcing the idea that there is a new normal in upper-income consumer spending. However, when year-ago spending over the same period ($180) is used as a seasonal adjustment, upper-income spending is off 37% from Sept. 1–15, 2008. That 37% year-to-year change represents the largest decline Gallup has seen in any month since May. It should be noted that year-ago comparables for May are artificially high due to last year's relatively large tax rebates and their positive, if temporary, impact on consumer spending. Of course, this effect was mitigated somewhat in this instance because the rebates were phased out for many upper-income consumers.

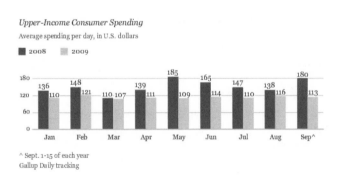

Upper-Income Consumer Spending

Average spending per day, in U.S. dollars

■ 2008   ▨ 2009

^ Sept. 1-15 of each year
Gallup Daily tracking

Middle- and Lower-Income Spending

During the first half of September, Gallup's consumer spending measure for middle- and lower-income consumers shows an increase to $59 per day, compared with $57 during August. Spending among these consumers remains in a tight $7 range ($52 to $59) and, as is the case with upper-income consumers, the spending pattern appears to be a new normal. Sept. 1–15 spending by these consumers is down 28% from a year ago—not as large as the early September decline in upper-income spending but consistent with the declines for middle- and lower-income consumers throughout 2009.

Implications

Early this week, Federal Reserve Board Chairman Ben Bernanke declared that the U.S. recession is probably over. On Wednesday, the Fed reported that industrial production increased for the second month in a row, and on Thursday, the Fed's Flow of Funds data revealed that Americans during the second quarter of this year gained wealth for the first time in seven quarters. All of this positive economic news seemed to reinforce the optimism on Wall Street, as the equity markets had another good week.

In contrast, Gallup's consumer spending data show the new normal for 2009 remains intact, with actual dollar spending staying in a tight range regardless of income, and overall spending down sharply from a year ago. More worrisome, upper-income spending in September seems to be trailing even further behind last year's comparables. In turn, this suggests that the $2 trillion increase in net worth that would presumably affect upper-income spending the most has instead had essentially no effect.

Of course, it may be that gains in wealth during the second quarter were distributed differently than the losses that preceded them. Further, it could be that for many consumers, this increase in wealth still left them with huge losses, compared with their peak net worth. Although it is not fashionable to discuss, the financial crisis had an enormous negative impact on upper-income Americans, as illustrated by the fact that U.S. household wealth remains more than $11 trillion below its third-quarter 2007 peak.

A meaningful economic recovery in the immediate term will require an upturn in spending—particularly among upper-income consumers—during the coming holiday season. At this point, the spending new normal suggests that even as household wealth is increasing, this needed upturn may not be materializing.

Survey Methods

For Gallup Daily tracking, Gallup interviews approximately 1,000 national adults, aged 18 and older, each day. The Gallup consumer spending results are based on random half-samples of approximately 500 national adults, aged 18 and older, each day. Results for Sept. 1–15, 2008, and Sept. 1–15, 2009, for middle- and lower-income consumers combined (those making less than $90,000 per year) are based on telephone interviews with 4,598 and 7,631 adults, respectively. For these results, one can say with 95% confidence that the maximum margin of sampling error is ±2 percentage points. Results for Sept. 1–15, 2008, and Sept. 1–15, 2009, for upper-income consumers (those making $90,000 or more per year) are based on telephone interviews with 1,242 and 2,402 adults, respectively, with a maximum margin of error of ±3 percentage points.

Interviews are conducted with respondents on land-line telephones (for respondents with a land-line telephone) and cellular phones (for respondents who are cell-phone only).

In addition to sampling error, question wording and practical difficulties in conducting surveys can introduce error or bias into the findings of public opinion polls.

September 21, 2009
AMERICANS MORE LIKELY TO SAY GOVERNMENT DOING TOO MUCH
Belief that government is over-regulating business is at high for decade

by Frank Newport, Gallup Poll Editor in Chief

Americans are more likely today than in the recent past to believe that government is taking on too much responsibility for solving the nation's problems and is over-regulating business. New Gallup data show that 57% of Americans say the government is trying to do too many things that should be left to businesses and individuals, and 45% say there is too much government regulation of business. Both reflect the highest such readings in more than a decade.

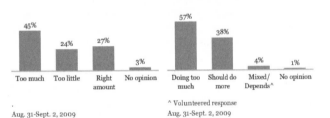

In general, do you think there is too much, too little, or about the right amount of government regulation of business and industry?

Some people think the government is trying to do too many things that should be left to individuals and businesses. Others think that government should do more to solve our country's problems. Which comes closer to your own view?

^ Volunteered response

Aug. 31-Sept. 2, 2009

Aug. 31-Sept. 2, 2009

These two measures are based on questions Gallup has asked each September since 2001, and intermittently before that. The 57% level of public concern about big government in this survey is, among other things, coincident with an extensively increased government involvement in the economy, and the extensive focus on a large-scale government effort to reform healthcare that was underway as this survey was being conducted.

Forty-five percent of Americans say there is too much regulation of business, while 27% say the amount of regulation is about right and 24% say there is too little regulation.

As seen in the accompanying graph, the 45% "too much" reading is the highest of the decade and is higher than the one Gallup reading prior to this decade, in March 1993. However, a March 1981 *Los Angeles Times* poll using this question wording recorded a 54% "too much" level. This was just after Ronald Reagan took office, and may have reflected Reagan's emphasis during the 1980 presidential campaign on the need to reduce government involvement in American society.

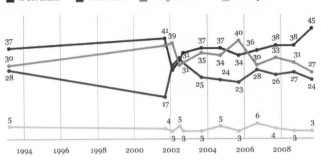

In general, do you think there is too much, too little, or about the right amount of government regulation of business and industry?

Aug. 31-Sept. 2, 2009

The accompanying table shows shifts in views of government regulation of business by partisan orientation between last year and this year.

In general, do you think there is too much, too little, or about the right amount of government regulation of business and industry?

By party ID

	% Too much, September 2008	% Too much, September 2009	Change (pct. pts.)
Total sample	38	45	7
Republicans	56	70	14
Independents	38	50	12
Democrats	23	21	-2

Gallup, Aug 31-Sep 2, 2009

All of the change in the "too much regulation" direction came among Republicans and independents. Democrats have remained roughly constant across the past year in their feelings on this issue. In both years, Republicans are the most likely to believe that there is too much regulation of business and industry, while Democrats are the least.

Government Trying to Do Too Much?

There has also been an uptick in the percentage of Americans who believe that the government is trying to do too much that should be left to business and individuals.

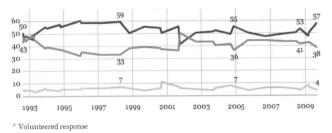

Some people think the government is trying to do too many things that should be left to individuals and businesses. Others think that government should do more to solve our country's problems. Which comes closer to your own view?

^ Volunteered response

Fifty-seven percent of Americans now believe that government is doing too much, slightly higher than the previous high points of the decade (55% in 2001 and 2004) and the highest since a 59% reading in 1998. Concern about too much government has thus returned to a level last measured in the Clinton administration.

Thirty-eight percent of Americans now say government should be doing more to solve the nation's problems.

A plurality of Americans, and often a majority, has tilted toward the "government is trying to do too much" position over the past 17 years. In fact, in Gallup's history of asking this question, only in 1992, 1993, and October 2001 (just weeks after the 9/11 terrorist attacks) did larger percentages of Americans say the "government should do more" than said the government was doing too much.

As was the case with the "government regulation of business" question, there are significant differences in attitudes toward this question by partisan orientation.

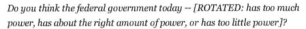

Is the Government Doing Too Much or Should It Do More to Solve Our Country's Problems?

By party ID

	% Doing too much	% Should do more
Republicans	80	17
Independents	63	33
Democrats	32	62

Aug. 31- Sept. 2, 2009

Republicans are largely united, tilting by more than 4 to 1 toward the position that the government is doing too much. Independents lean the same way, although not by as large a margin. Democrats, by contrast, say the government should be doing more to solve our country's problems, by about 2 to 1.

Too Much Government Power?

A third question included in Gallup's September survey does not show a change in attitudes toward government power—unlike the two questions reviewed above. This question asks directly: "Do you think the federal government today has too much power, has about the right amount of power, or has too little power?"

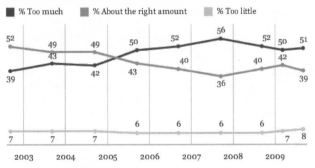

Do you think the federal government today -- [ROTATED: has too much power, has about the right amount of power, or has too little power]?

When Gallup first asked this question in September 2002—about a year after 9/11—a slight majority said the government had about the right amount of power. There was a shift in 2005, however, and from that point to the present, at least half of those interviewed have said the federal government has too much power.

Implications

The fact that Americans are more likely now than a year ago to say there is too much regulation of business is notable, given all that has happened over the last 12 months.

The White House has shifted from a Republican to a Democratic administration, and President Obama has pushed aggressive stimulus packages and government involvement in industry and healthcare. The government has spent huge amounts of money investing in two business sectors—the automobile and banking industries—under the assumption that large companies in these industries would have failed without government intervention. These actions, and the recognition that some failed businesses, particularly those in the investment banking sector, have previously operated without much government oversight, could in theory have caused an increased appreciation for governmental regulation. That has not occurred.

Instead, the current findings underscore that the average American is less appreciative of increased government control over business during the past year, rather than more so.

Survey Methods

Results are based on telephone interviews with 1,026 national adults, aged 18 and older, conducted Aug. 31–Sept. 2, 2009. For results based on the total sample of national adults, one can say with 95% confidence that the maximum margin of sampling error is ±4 percentage points.

Interviews are conducted with respondents on land-line telephones (for respondents with a land-line telephone) and cellular phones (for respondents who are cell-phone only).

In addition to sampling error, question wording and practical difficulties in conducting surveys can introduce error or bias into the findings of public opinion polls.

September 21, 2009

OBAMA'S LEADERSHIP QUALITIES STAND OUT TO AMERICANS

Seven in 10 say the president is willing to make hard decisions

by Jeffrey M. Jones, Gallup Poll Managing Editor

Of seven personal characteristics, Americans rate Barack Obama most highly for those that reflect on his leadership skills. Seventy-two percent say he "is willing to make hard decisions," and 66% describe him as "a strong and decisive leader." Sixty-four percent say he "can get things done."

The poll also shows that Obama gets high marks for empathy, as he has done since he rose to national prominence. Sixty-four percent say Obama understands the problems Americans face in their daily lives. No less than 63% of Americans have said this about Obama since the characteristic was first measured in March 2008.

His weakest traits, according to Americans, are those most closely tied to his politics—"shares your values" (52%) and "has mostly

Thinking about the following characteristics and qualities, please say whether you think each applies or doesn't apply to Barack Obama. How about -- [RANDOM ORDER]?

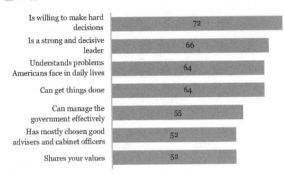

USA Today/Gallup, Sept. 11-13, 2009

Ratings of Barack Obama on Personal Characteristics

% "Applies"

- ■ Understands problems Americans face
- ■ Is a strong and decisive leader
- ■ Shares your values

73%
72%
60%
67%
66%
66%
55%
66%
64%
52%

May 2009   Jun 2009   Jul 2009   Aug 2009   Sep 2009

chosen good advisers and cabinet officers" (52%). Still, a majority of Americans attribute these positive characteristics to Obama.

As Obama's job approval rating has declined in recent months, so have his ratings on most personal characteristics. The biggest hit to Obama's image has come in perceptions that he can manage the government effectively. In April, near the 100-day mark of his presidency, 66% of Americans believed he was effectively managing the government. That declined to 59% in July, and now stands at 55%.

Ratings of Barack Obama as Being Able to Manage Government Effectively

■ Applies

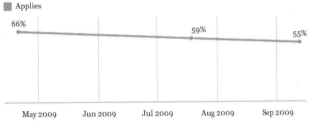

66%   59%   55%

May 2009   Jun 2009   Jul 2009   Aug 2009   Sep 2009

That decline is mostly due to changes in the way Republicans and independents view Obama's managerial competence. Democrats' views have barely changed (90% in April vs. 88% today), while Republicans' (38% vs. 21%) and independents' (63% vs. 50%) ratings are down more than 10 points each.

Obama's ratings among all Americans on the three other characteristics Gallup has tracked during Obama's presidency—shares your values, is a strong and decisive leader, and understands the problems Americans face in their daily lives—are also down from April. But most of those declines occurred between April and July, and all three readings appear to have leveled off and have not gotten appreciably worse in the September update.

Bottom Line

As Obama tries to address major challenges with the economy, the wars in Afghanistan and Iraq, and healthcare reform, Americans acknowledge his leadership qualities, including his willingness to make hard decisions and the strength and decisiveness of his leadership. At the same time, Americans are losing some confidence in his ability to manage the government effectively, perhaps in response to reports of mounting federal budget deficits.

Obama's job approval ratings in the low 50s are well above George W. Bush's ratings in the final years of his presidency, but in some ways, the trends in character ratings between the two are similar. As Bush's job approval rating declined in his second term in office, so did his ratings on the various personal characteristics. The decline in Bush's character ratings was especially evident in terms of his ability to manage the government, but he continued to receive his best ratings for his leadership qualities.

Survey Methods

Results are based on telephone interviews with 1,030 national adults, aged 18 and older, conducted Sept. 11–13, 2009. For results based on the total sample of national adults, one can say with 95% confidence that the maximum margin of sampling error is ±4 percentage points.

Interviews are conducted with respondents on land-line telephones (for respondents with a land-line telephone) and cellular phones (for respondents who are cell-phone only).

In addition to sampling error, question wording and practical difficulties in conducting surveys can introduce error or bias into the findings of public opinion polls.

September 22, 2009
HALF OF NEW LATINO IMMIGRANTS TO U.S. SEND MONEY ABROAD
U.S.-born Latinos are much less likely to send remittances, unless they report being religious

by Gerver Torres, Brett Pelham, and Steve Crabtree, Gallup Poll Staff Writers

About half (48% to 49%) of Latino immigrants who have come to the U.S. in the last 19 years say that in the last 12 months, they have sent money to someone living abroad—a number that holds remarkably steady whether they have lived in the U.S. less than 6 years or between 13 and 19 years. A Gallup survey of more than 1,000 U.S. Latinos finds that the percentage of Latino immigrants who send money (i.e., remittances) abroad is steady for those who have been living in the U.S. less than 20 years, and drops among those who have been in the country for at least 20 years. The rate of sending remittances drops off further among Latinos born in the U.S.—to 20%.

The findings are evidence of the close ties many Latinos retain with their home countries.

Percentage of Latino Immigrants Sending Remittances Abroad, by Years Living in the U.S.

In the past 12 months, did you or someone in this household provide help in the form of money or goods to another individual?

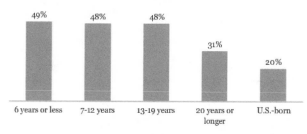

Answer options included "living inside the U.S.," "living outside the U.S.," "both," and "neither." Only remittances sent outside of the U.S. counted for this analysis.

March 27-May 6, 2009

Even among Latinos who immigrated to the U.S. at least 20 years ago, almost a third (31%) still report sending remittances. The consistency of these relationships is crucial to millions of Latin Americans who depend on remittances from the U.S. to cover basic living expenses—or to be able, for example, to take the financial risk of starting a new business. According to the World Bank, Mexico received more than $25 billion in remittances in 2007; a great deal of this money came from the U.S. No other Latin American country receives as much in remittances as Mexico does. However, many countries rely much more heavily on what they do receive. In both Honduras and Guyana, remittances accounted for more than 20% of GDP in 2007.

U.S.-born Latinos who say religion plays an important role in their daily lives are more than three times as likely to send remittances (26%) as are U.S.-born Latinos who say religion does *not* play such a role (7%).

Bottom Line

These findings demonstrate the power of social connections to drive important and enduring economic processes. The finding that so many Latinos report sending remittances is particularly impressive given the fact that Gallup surveyed these respondents in the spring of 2009, when the current economic crisis was in full bloom. People who continue to send remittances home after living abroad for many years are honoring a commitment that makes sense socially but seems to defy "rational" economic self-interest. Religion may play a role in reinforcing the perceived importance of those commitments and strengthening those ties over the long term. From an economic perspective, remittances cannot be understood without accounting for the "irrational" social influences of relationships and religion.

Survey Methods

Results are based on telephone interviews conducted with 1,003 U.S. Latinos, aged 18 and older, between March 27 and May 6, 2009. This includes 545 Latinos who report having been born abroad and 453 who report having been born in the U.S. For analyses of immigrant groups based on years living in the U.S., sample sizes range from 106 to 184. Sample sizes for the religiosity analyses according to nativity range from 115 to 366. The maximum 95% margin of error for the smallest single group, incorporating a design effect of 1.82,

is ±13 percentage points. Margins of error for the larger samples of 453 and 545 are both ±6 percentage points.

Interviews are conducted on land-line telephones (for respondents with a land-line telephone) and cellular phones (for respondents who are cell-phone only).

In addition to sampling error, question wording and practical difficulties in conducting surveys can introduce error or bias into the findings of public opinion polls.

September 23, 2009

COST IS FOREMOST HEALTHCARE ISSUE FOR AMERICANS
But public largely skeptical that healthcare reform will bring relief

by Lydia Saad, Gallup Poll Senior Editor

Americans are broadly satisfied with the quality of their own medical care and healthcare costs, but of the two, satisfaction with costs lags. Overall, 80% are satisfied with the quality of medical care available to them, including 39% who are very satisfied. Sixty-one percent are satisfied with the cost of their medical care, including 20% who are very satisfied.

How satisfied are you with -- very satisfied, satisfied, dissatisfied (or) very dissatisfied?

A. The quality of medical care available to you and your family
B. The cost of medical care for you and your family

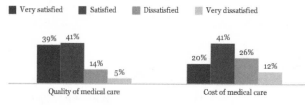

USA Today/Gallup, Sept. 11-13, 2009

There is a clear gulf in these perceptions between the health insurance haves and have-nots. According to a Sept. 11–13 *USA Today*/Gallup poll, the 85% of Americans with health insurance coverage are broadly satisfied with the quality of medical care they receive and with their healthcare costs. At 79%, satisfaction with costs among Medicare/Medicaid recipients is particularly high.

The 15% who are uninsured are far less satisfied with the quality of their medical care (50% are satisfied), and only 27% are satisfied with their healthcare costs. (Sixty-nine percent are dissatisfied with their costs.)

A question asking whether healthcare costs pose a major problem, a minor problem, or no problem personally for respondents provides another indication of the broad gap in concern about healthcare between the insured and the uninsured. Seventy-two percent of the uninsured say costs are a major problem. By contrast, 42% of adults with private insurance, and 40% of those with Medicare/Medicaid, say this.

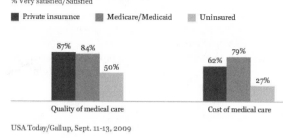

Satisfaction With Own Healthcare, Based on Insurance Coverage
% Very satisfied/Satisfied

■ Private insurance ■ Medicare/Medicaid ▢ Uninsured

USA Today/Gallup, Sept. 11-13, 2009

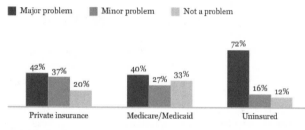

Perceived Seriousness of Rising Healthcare Costs to Personal Situation
Based on type of insurance coverage

■ Major problem ■ Minor problem ▢ Not a problem

USA Today/Gallup, Sept. 11-13, 2009

While healthcare costs do not appear to be a major impediment for the majority of insured Americans, on a relative basis, they are a much greater concern than two other leading healthcare system complaints: benefit reductions and insurance paperwork.

One in four insured Americans say reductions in what their insurance plan covers is a major problem for them; slightly fewer (18%) say insurance paperwork is a major problem. These figures compare with 42% of insured Americans who say rising healthcare costs pose a major problem.

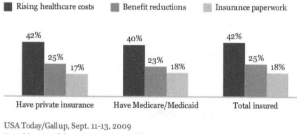

Percentage Calling Healthcare Issues a "Major Problem" for Themselves
Based on U.S. adults with health insurance

■ Rising healthcare costs ■ Benefit reductions ▢ Insurance paperwork

USA Today/Gallup, Sept. 11-13, 2009
See tables at end for exact question wording.

Another important indication of just how central the cost factor is to Americans' healthcare concerns comes from an open-ended measure of the major problems facing the healthcare system today. Close to 4 in 10 Americans (38%)—by far the largest percentage for any issue—explicitly cite the cost or affordability of healthcare as the nation's biggest healthcare problem. However, a large number of the less frequently cited issues have a cost component to them, including references to medical malpractice; overcharging; greed by insurance companies, drug companies, and hospitals; and waste and fraud.

After cost generally, the next-highest-ranked issues are the number of uninsured Americans (mentioned by 15%), followed by insurance companies and "insurance company greed" (13%).

Biggest Problem in U.S. Healthcare

What do you, personally, see as the biggest problem with healthcare in the United States today?

	%
Cost/Unaffordable	38
Too many uninsured	15
Insurance companies/Insurance company greed	13
Lack of availability/accessibility	8
Too many frivolous lawsuits/Medical malpractice	5
Too much bureaucracy/Government involvement	5
Overcharging/Excessive charges for medical procedures	3
Drug companies/Drug company greed	3
Problems with Medicaid/Medicare	3
Doctor/Hospital greed	3
Lack of portability of insurance	3
Illegal immigrants getting healthcare	2
Waste and fraud in the system	2
Cannot get insurance if have pre-existing condition	1
Other	2
Nothing	3
No opinion	5

USA Today/Gallup, Sept. 11-13, 2009
Results add to more than 100% due to multiple responses.

Cost is the top-ranked issue for the insured as well as the uninsured—mentioned by 43% of those with private insurance and 39% of the uninsured, compared with 26% of Medicare and Medicaid recipients.

All of this focus on healthcare costs could translate into substantial public support for healthcare reform if Americans believed it would help to contain their own costs. But according to the new poll, Americans are much more likely to believe their own costs would get worse rather than better—42% vs. 22%—if a healthcare bill passes this year.

The balance of opinion is also negative in perceptions of healthcare reform's impact on their own healthcare coverage, insurance company demands, and quality of care.

Predicted Impact of Healthcare Reform on Personal Healthcare Issues

■ % Would get better ■ % Would not change ▢ % Would get worse

USA Today/Gallup, Sept. 11-13, 2009

As reported last week, Gallup also finds Americans more pessimistic than optimistic about the impact of healthcare reform on the cost and quality of care in the country as a whole.

All of this could help explain why current support for passing a healthcare reform bill is at an anemic 38%—which stretches to 50% when undecided Americans are pressed to indicate a preference.

Bottom Line

Gallup finds that the biggest healthcare concern to Americans, in terms of both the nation and their own personal lives, is cost. The cost factor is deeply troubling on a personal level to the uninsured population, but also ranks as the top concern of the insured. At the same time, Americans are much more skeptical than optimistic about the likelihood that healthcare reform will reduce their own healthcare costs.

Survey Methods

Results are based on telephone interviews with 1,030 national adults, aged 18 and older, conducted Sept. 11–13, 2009. For results based on the total sample of national adults, one can say with 95% confidence that the maximum margin of sampling error is ±4 percentage points.

Interviews are conducted with respondents on land-line telephones (for respondents with a land-line telephone) and cellular phones (for respondents who are cell-phone only).

In addition to sampling error, question wording and practical difficulties in conducting surveys can introduce error or bias into the findings of public opinion polls.

September 23, 2009

REPUBLICAN PARTY'S IMAGE IMPROVES; STILL TRAILS DEMOCRATS'

Favorability gap between parties narrows

by Lydia Saad, Gallup Poll Senior Editor

The Republican Party's image—quite tattered in the first few months after the 2008 elections—has seen some recent improvement. Forty percent of Americans now hold a favorable view of the Republicans, up from 34% in May. The Republicans still trail the Democrats on this popularity measure, as 51% of Americans now view the Democrats favorably. With the Democrats' favorable rating dipping slightly since last November, their advantage has narrowed.

Party Favorable Ratings -- Trend Since January 2008

Please tell me whether you have a favorable or unfavorable opinion of each of the following parties.

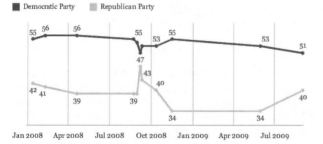

Notably, in contrast to the 80% of liberals who hold a favorable view of the Democrats, a much smaller 55% of conservatives have a favorable view of the Republicans.

After two consecutive polls—one in November 2008, and the other in May 2009—producing a near-record-low 34% favorable rat-

ing for the Republicans, today's finding restores the Republican Party's image to where it stood last October. Most of the recent increase is seen among rank-and-file Republicans. Republicans' favorable rating of their own party sank considerably this spring, to 63%, but is now back above 80%.

Recent Trend in Republican Party Favorability -- by Party ID

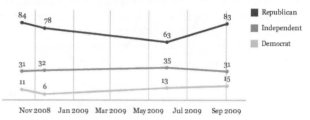

Across the same period, Democrats have enjoyed consistently high favorability ratings from rank-and-file Democrats. The percentage of independents viewing the party favorably has also been running higher than the percentage viewing the Republicans favorably. However, the 40% favorable rating from independents in the latest poll is down from 47% in the previous three measures.

Recent Trend in Democratic Party Favorability -- by Party ID

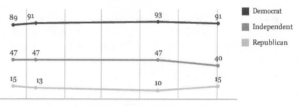

Bottom Line

The Republican Party is enjoying some improvement in its recently beleaguered favorability ratings from the American people. A major reason for this is that rank-and-file Republicans are feeling more positively toward the party today than they did in the first few months after the Democratic electoral victories last November. Still, the Republicans have a fair distance to go to reach parity with the Democrats on this measure—something they have not achieved since late 2005 (although they came close right after the Republican National Convention in September 2008). Restoring its image even more among Republicans, as well as among conservatives, could be a place for the Republican Party to start.

Survey Methods

Results are based on telephone interviews with 1,026 national adults, aged 18 and older, conducted Aug. 31–Sept. 2, 2009. For results based on the total sample of national adults, one can say with 95% confidence that the maximum margin of sampling error is ±4 percentage points.

Interviews are conducted with respondents on land-line telephones (for respondents with a land-line telephone) and cellular phones (for respondents who are cell-phone only).

In addition to sampling error, question wording and practical difficulties in conducting surveys can introduce error or bias into the findings of public opinion polls.

September 24, 2009
SENIORS LEAN AGAINST NEW HEALTHCARE LAW
Demographic analysis also reveals distinctions by race, income, and education

by Frank Newport, Gallup Poll Editor in Chief and Jeffrey M. Jones, Managing Editor

There are significant differences in views on a new healthcare law by age. The youngest Americans, aged 18–29, favor it by a 13-point margin, although more than 4 in 10 have no opinion on the issue. Support is more evenly divided among Americans 30–64, while those 65 and older are opposed by a 10-point margin.

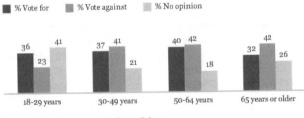

Advise Member of Congress to Vote for/Against Healthcare Bill, by Age

■ % Vote for   ■ % Vote against   ▨ % No opinion

August-September aggregated Gallup Poll data

Gallup has previously found older Americans most likely to oppose a new healthcare law, based on other measures of attitudes toward healthcare reform. Gallup research also shows that the vast majority of seniors are covered by the government's Medicare plan and therefore have lower concerns about coverage and cost.

This analysis is based on an aggregate of three Gallup Polls, conducted in August and September, in which a total of 3,066 Americans were asked whether they would advise their member of Congress to vote for or against a healthcare bill. Although the question wordings were not precisely the same (the first two polls asked about a "healthcare reform bill" while the third asked about a "healthcare bill"), the results were similar, with essentially equal proportions of Americans saying they would advise their member of Congress to vote for and to vote against a healthcare bill, and an average of 25% not having an opinion.

In general, the largest differences in support for new healthcare legislation by subgroup are based on the political variables of party and ideology. Democrats and liberals are highly likely to support it, while conservatives and Republicans are primarily against it.

The sections that follow analyze support by demographic groups, in order to provide more detailed information on the segments of the American population in which support for healthcare legislation is highest and those in which it is lowest, on a relative basis.

Gender

Men and women form almost an exact mirror image on the issue of a new healthcare law. Women favor it, while men are opposed.

Region

The only region of the country in which a new healthcare law receives a net positive reaction is the East, where residents are more

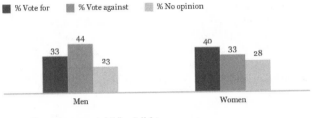

Advise Member of Congress to Vote for/Against Healthcare Bill, by Gender

■ % Vote for   ■ % Vote against   ▨ % No opinion

August-September aggregated Gallup Poll data

likely to say their representative in Congress should vote for it rather than against it, by a seven-point margin. Residents of the other three regions are at least slightly more opposed than in favor, by a two-point margin in the Midwest, a six-point margin in the South, and a four-point margin in the West.

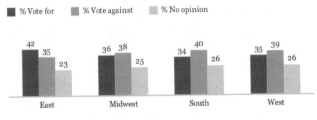

Advise Member of Congress to Vote for/Against Healthcare Bill, by Region

■ % Vote for   ■ % Vote against   ▨ % No opinion

August-September aggregated Gallup Poll data

Race

Support for healthcare reform is highly differentiated by race. Whites, who make up about 73% of the respondents in this sample, are strongly against a new healthcare law, by a 14-point margin. In contrast, nonwhites support healthcare legislation by a 30-point margin, including an overwhelming 65% to 9% support from blacks.

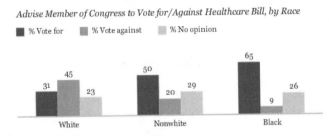

Advise Member of Congress to Vote for/Against Healthcare Bill, by Race

■ % Vote for   ■ % Vote against   ▨ % No opinion

August-September aggregated Gallup Poll data

Income

Support for a new healthcare law is directly related to income; it increases as income decreases. By a 13-point margin, Americans with $75,000 or more in annual household income would want their representative in Congress to vote against a new healthcare law. Those making between $30,000 and $75,000 are still opposed, but by a much smaller four-point margin. Support is significantly higher than opposition among those making less than $30,000 a year.

Education

The pattern of support by income is distinctly different from the pattern by education, even though these two measures of socioeco-

Advise Member of Congress to Vote for/Against Healthcare Bill, by Household Income

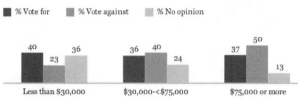

■ % Vote for   ■ % Vote against   ▨ % No opinion

August-September aggregated Gallup Poll data

one can say with 95% confidence that the maximum margin of sampling error is ±2 percentage points.

Margins of error for subgroups will be larger than the margin of error for the entire sample.

Interviews are conducted with respondents on land-line telephones (for respondents with a land-line telephone) and cellular phones (for respondents who are cell-phone only).

In addition to sampling error, question wording and practical difficulties in conducting surveys can introduce error or bias into the findings of public opinion polls.

nomic status are correlated. Americans with postgraduate education are in favor of a new healthcare law, by 48% to 39%. But there is a distinct shift against reform among those with four-year college degrees but no postgraduate education; this group opposes a new law by an even larger 17-point margin. Those with some college and those with high school education or less are much more evenly split in their attitudes, although the latter group has a large "don't know" component.

Advise Member of Congress to Vote for/Against Healthcare Bill, by Education

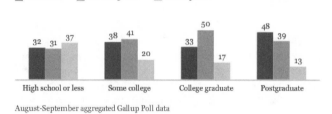

■ % Vote for   ■ % Vote against   ▨ % No opinion

August-September aggregated Gallup Poll data

September 24, 2009
OBAMA APPROVAL HOLDING STEADY IN LOW 50S
Averaging 52% approval in September

by Jeffrey M. Jones, Gallup Poll Managing Editor

Barack Obama's approval rating has been highly stable for much of September. Currently at 51% in Gallup Daily tracking, it has been 51%, 52%, or 53% in each three-day rolling average since Sept. 5.

Gallup Daily: Obama Job Approval Averages, September 2009

Each result is based on a three-day rolling average

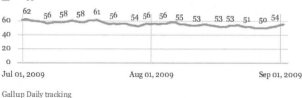

Gallup Daily tracking

Bottom Line

Senior citizens have always been a politically powerful group, and their current opposition to healthcare reform is a significant obstacle for Congress to overcome to pass legislation. Seniors' concerns about possible changes are understandable given that they currently are covered by Medicare for the most part, and are also the most likely to need healthcare. Gallup has also found that senior citizens are generally satisfied with their healthcare. It thus may be unclear to seniors just how the proposed changes to Medicare will affect the benefits and care they currently receive.

It is important to note, however, that seniors are not monolithically opposed to healthcare—partisanship remains a strong predictor of support for healthcare, even among older Americans. While it makes sense that older Republicans are overwhelmingly opposed to healthcare reform, older Democrats still on balance favor it, though not to the same extent that younger Democrats do.

The other differences by demographic groups generally mirror patterns of partisanship in the U.S. today. Women, minorities, those with low incomes, and those with either postgraduate degrees or low levels of education are most likely to identify as Democrats. All of these groups are also proportionately most likely to favor a new healthcare law.

This stability has persisted even as Obama has made a concerted push to increase support for his policies, particularly healthcare reform. On Sept. 9, he delivered a nationally televised address to Congress to outline his arguments for passing new healthcare legislation. And on Sept. 20, he made the unusual step of appearing on most of the major Sunday political talk shows, followed by an appearance on the David Letterman Show on Sept. 21.

While not able to gain positive momentum in his job approval scores, Obama has clearly halted the decline in support observed in his approval rating for much of July and August. That rating dipped as low as 50% in late August.

Gallup Daily: Obama Job Approval Averages, July-August 2009

Each result is based on a three-day rolling average

■ % Approve

Survey Methods

Results are based on telephone interviews with 3,066 national adults, aged 18 and older, conducted Aug. 6–9, Aug. 31–Sept. 2, and Sept. 11–13, 2009. For results based on the total sample of national adults,

Gallup Daily tracking

Since dropping to 50%, his approval rating recovered to as high as 55% in the first few days of September, but has been stuck in the low 50s since then. He has not had an approval rating of 60% or above since July 17–19.

During September, an average of 85% of Democrats, 47% of independents, and 17% of Republicans say they approve of the job Obama is doing as president. These party averages have also been stable throughout the month.

Obama's monthly average of 52% in September thus far (through Sept. 23) is among the lowest Gallup has measured for elected presidents since World War II in September of their first year in office. Only Bill Clinton had a lower average at this point in his presidency (50% in September 1993), while Ronald Reagan also averaged 52%, in September 1981. All three of these presidents entered office during difficult economic times.

John Kennedy had the highest "first September" average of 79%, while George W. Bush averaged 76% in September 2001, including a record-high 90% single-poll rating after the Sept. 11 terrorist attacks.

Elected Presidents' Job Approval Averages in September of First Year in Office

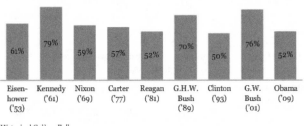

Historical Gallup Polls

Bottom Line

Just over half of Americans approve of the job Barack Obama is doing as president, a proportion that has been highly stable through most of September. Obama's attempts this month to sell healthcare reform to the public have not paid off in higher job approval ratings for him, but neither has his support dipped below the majority level even as it teetered on the brink of doing so late last month.

Survey Methods

Results for each three-day rolling average are based on telephone interviews with approximately 1,500 national adults, conducted in July, August, and September 2009, as part of Gallup Daily tracking. For results based on each three-day rolling average, one can say with 95% confidence that the maximum margin of sampling error is ±3 percentage points.

Interviews are conducted with respondents on land-line telephones and cellular phones.

In addition to sampling error, question wording and practical difficulties in conducting surveys can introduce error or bias into the findings of public opinion polls.

September 25, 2009

AMERICANS TILT AGAINST SENDING MORE TROOPS TO AFGHANISTAN

Most who oppose also advocate that the U.S. begin to withdraw troops

by Frank Newport, Gallup Poll Editor in Chief

Americans are more likely to say they would oppose (50%) rather than favor (41%) a possible decision by President Barack Obama to send more U.S. troops to Afghanistan.

Would you favor or oppose a decision by President Obama to send more U.S. troops to Afghanistan?

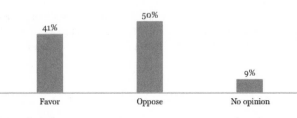

USA Today/Gallup, Sept. 22-23, 2009

The possibility that Obama will need to make a decision on U.S. troop strength in Afghanistan has increased in recent weeks, amid reports that the senior American military commander in Afghanistan—Gen. Stanley A. McChrystal—is preparing to deliver a formal request for additional troops in Afghanistan, perhaps by the end of this week.

This follows the recent news leak of McChrystal's assessment of the situation in Afghanistan, including his conclusion that more troops are needed in order to avoid failure in the war. Queried about the possibility of increasing U.S. forces in Afghanistan, President Obama said Sunday on NBC's "Meet the Press" that he will "have to ask some very hard questions anytime I send our troops in."

Questions on Afghanistan were included in Gallup's Sept. 22–23 Daily tracking, and were focused on the public's reaction if Obama does make a decision to send more troops to Afghanistan at some point in the near future.

The 50% of Americans who oppose a troop increase were asked whether they favored keeping troops at the current level, or whether they favored beginning a withdrawal of U.S. troops from Afghanistan. By an overwhelming 82% to 14% margin, those opposed to a troop increase say they favor withdrawal over keeping the status quo.

This leaves the overall disposition of Americans on the issue of troops in Afghanistan that is seen in the accompanying graph. Notably, as many Americans overall favor withdrawing troops from the country (41%) as favor increasing troop levels (41%).

The Afghanistan situation creates an unusual set of political cross-currents. A Republican president (George W. Bush) initiated the movement of U.S. troops to Afghanistan in 2001, and Republicans in general have been more supportive than Democrats of the Afghanistan war. If Obama does make a decision to send more troops, Republicans would be faced with the prospect of supporting a Democratic president's decision to initiate a policy they favor, while Democrats who oppose further escalation in Afghanistan

Americans' Views on Sending More U.S. Troops to Afghanistan

Would you favor or oppose a decision by President Obama to send more U.S. troops to Afghanistan?

(Asked of those who oppose sending more troops to Afghanistan) Which would you rather see President Obama do -- [ROTATED: keep the number of U.S. troops in Afghanistan about the same as now (or) begin to withdraw U.S. troops from Afghanistan]?

COMBINED RESPONSES

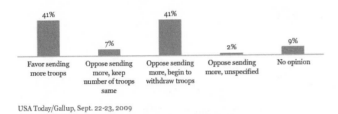

USA Today/Gallup, Sept. 22-23, 2009

would be faced with going against a president representing their own party.

The data indicate that Republicans do seem willing to support Obama should he make a decision to increase U.S. troop strength in Afghanistan. On the other hand, Democrats seem willing to oppose Obama in this case. Independents are also on the opposition side of the ledger.

Views on Sending More U.S. Troops to Afghanistan, by Party ID

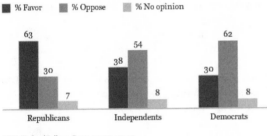

USA Today/Gallup, Sept. 22-23, 2009

Bottom Line

President Obama will by all accounts face a difficult choice regarding Afghanistan in the weeks ahead.

Gen. McChrystal—whom Obama's administration appointed to Afghanistan earlier this year—has already indicated that he is likely to request more troops for that country. Should Obama turn down such a request, he risks the ire of Republicans and others who will most likely argue that he is ignoring the wishes of his commanders on the ground, and making a mistake that could result in an increased risk of terrorism, among other things. Should he agree to order more troops, he will go against the wishes of the broad U.S. population—and, in particular, the rank-and-file of his own party, which at the moment is more opposed to than in favor of such an action.

Survey Methods

Results are based on telephone interviews with 1,053 national adults, aged 18 and older, conducted Sept. 22–23, 2009, as part of Gallup Daily tracking. For results based on the total sample of national adults, one can say with 95% confidence that the maximum margin of sampling error is ±4 percentage points.

Interviews are conducted with respondents on land-line telephones and cellular phones.

In addition to sampling error, question wording and practical difficulties in conducting surveys can introduce error or bias into the findings of public opinion polls.

September 28, 2009
IN U.S., CAUTIOUS OPTIMISM ABOUT ECONOMY IN YEAR AHEAD
Most expect economy to get better, but not be fully recovered

by Jeffrey M. Jones, Gallup Poll Managing Editor

Most Americans, 65%, expect the economy to improve over the next year—but only 2% think it will fully recover. Twenty-three percent expect the U.S. to still be in a recession, and 12% expect conditions to get worse than they are now.

Thinking about one year from now, do you think the U.S. economy will be -- fully recovered, better than it is now, but not fully recovered, still in a recession, or worse than it is now?

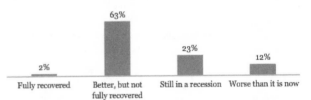

USA Today/Gallup, Sept. 11-13, 2009

The vast majority of Americans, 84%, believe the economy is currently in a recession, according to a Sept. 11–13 *USA Today*/Gallup poll. Gallup has updated this measure periodically since 1991. The 84% who now view the economy as in a recession ties the previous high Gallup measured in January 1992, and is much higher than what Gallup found in the last recession, in 2001.

Do you think the economy is now in a recession, or not?

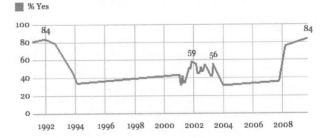

There is widespread consensus on this, and little difference by political party affiliation—85% of Republicans, 86% of independents, and 82% of Democrats believe the economy is in a recession.

Political differences are more apparent in predictions about where the economy is headed over the next 12 months, but at least half of all three major political party groups expect the economy to be better than it is now. There is much more agreement among Democrats (85%) than among independents (57%) or Republicans (50%) that the economy will improve.

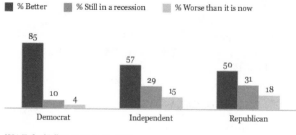

Views of U.S. Economy One Year From Now, by Party ID

USA Today/Gallup, Sept. 11-13, 2009

These differences likely reflect the fact that the Democratic Party is in charge of the federal government and is pursuing economic policies it favors. When asked what impact Barack Obama's policies have had on the economy, three in four Democrats say these have made the economy better, but the majority of Republicans, 54%, say his policies have made the economy worse.

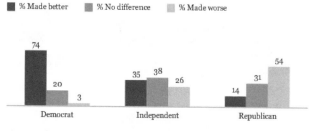

Views of Effect of Obama's Economic Policies on U.S. Economy, by Party ID

USA Today/Gallup, Sept. 11-13, 2009

Overall, Americans give Obama's policies a more favorable than unfavorable review—43% say his policies have made the economy better; 25% believe they have made it worse; and 30% believe they have not made a difference.

Not Completely out of the Woods?

A year ago, concerns about the financial crisis caused many political and economic leaders to predict that the economy could collapse without swift and significant government action. In early October, Congress finally agreed to a financial industry bailout bill, which President Bush signed.

Though the bailout legislation has been criticized, the economic collapse some feared never materialized. But given the economy's current fragile state, there is no guarantee that a collapse will not come. The poll finds that 61% of Americans are worried that an economic crash is still possible, including 20% who are very worried.

Whereas 69% of Republicans and 66% of independents are at least somewhat worried about a potential crash, only 49% of Democrats share this level of concern.

How worried are you that an economic crash is still possible in the U.S. in the next year -- very worried, somewhat worried, not too worried, or not worried at all?

USA Today/Gallup, Sept. 11-13, 2009

Bottom Line

Americans believe the economy is still in poor shape, but are cautiously optimistic about the next 12 months. Most think the economy will be better a year from now than it is currently, though few go as far as to say it will be fully recovered.

Though Americans do not express a high level of concern that the economy will go in the other direction toward a collapse, a majority are at least somewhat worried that this could occur.

Survey Methods

Results are based on telephone interviews with 1,030 national adults, aged 18 and older, conducted Sept. 11–13, 2009. For results based on the total sample of national adults, one can say with 95% confidence that the maximum margin of sampling error is ±4 percentage points.

Interviews are conducted with respondents on land-line telephones (for respondents with a land-line telephone) and cellular phones (for respondents who are cell-phone only).

In addition to sampling error, question wording and practical difficulties in conducting surveys can introduce error or bias into the findings of public opinion polls.

September 28, 2009
MORE AMERICANS PLUGGED INTO POLITICAL NEWS
Four in 10 Republicans, vs. 3 in 10 Democrats, follow it very closely

by Lydia Saad, Gallup Poll Senior Editor

Americans are paying closer attention to political news today than in any year without a presidential election since Gallup began regularly tracking this measure in 2001. The 36% of Americans who today say they follow news about national politics "very closely" is down from the record-high 43% Gallup found in September 2008, but matches the level found in September 2004—two polls conducted during presidential election years.

The previous high for a year without a presidential election was 31% in 2006—a midterm election year. The previous high for a year without a national election was 30%, in 2007.

Since 2001, Republicans have typically reported paying closer attention to political news than have Democrats, and that holds today.

Apart from the quadrennial spike in news attention around presidential elections, Americans' focus on political news has grad-

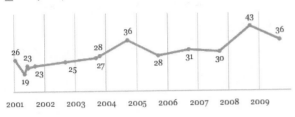

Attention to National Political News, 2001-2009

Overall, how closely do you follow news about national politics -- very closely, somewhat closely, not too closely, or not at all?

■ % Very closely

ually increased since 2001, when the percentage paying very close attention averaged 23%. (A Jan. 10–14, 2001, Gallup survey found 26% paying this level of attention, most likely because of the saturation news coverage of the 2000 presidential election and the concluding days of President Bill Clinton's administration. All other measures that year found no more than 23% closely following the news.)

The American public is generally an attentive group when it comes to national politics. In addition to the 36% who follow political news very closely, 42% say they follow it somewhat closely. Very few report paying no attention to political news, a finding consistent with Gallup's polling on this over the past decade, as well as in earlier measurements from 1995 and 1996.

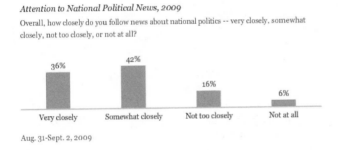

Attention to National Political News, 2009

Overall, how closely do you follow news about national politics -- very closely, somewhat closely, not too closely, or not at all?

Aug. 31-Sept. 2, 2009

Republicans and Independents More Plugged In Than Democrats

This year's survey, conducted Aug. 31–Sept. 2, finds Republicans and independents paying closer attention to the news than are Democrats. However, taking into account the higher level of little or no attention among independents, Republicans are the most attentive.

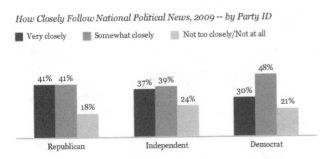

How Closely Follow National Political News, 2009 -- by Party ID

■ Very closely ■ Somewhat closely ▨ Not too closely/Not at all

Since 2001, Republicans have typically reported paying closer attention to political news than have Democrats, and that holds today.

Most often, Democrats and independents report similar levels of "very close" attention, except in the last two presidential election years, when Democrats' attention surged to roughly match Republicans'.

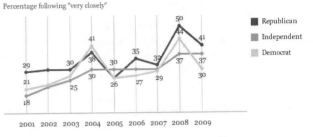

Attention to National Political News -- by Party ID

Percentage following "very closely"

■ Republican
■ Independent
▨ Democrat

Polls shown are from late August/September of each year.

The long-term increase in very close attention to national political news is seen among all three party groups. More Democrats (with an increase in very close attention from 21% in 2001 to 30% today) and Republicans (from 29% to 41%) are now following the news this closely than was the case eight years ago; independents show a slightly larger gain (from 18% to 37%).

In addition to differences by party affiliation, Gallup finds substantial variations by gender, age, education, and household income in the percentages following the news very closely. In that men are more news-conscious than women and older Americans more so than younger adults, one of the most attentive population subgroups is men aged 50 and older. One of the least attentive is younger women.

Bottom Line

Americans' consumption of political news has expanded over the past decade. The trend may reflect a greater politicization of the American public, regardless of political ideology, as attention is up among all three party groups. However, the increase since 2007 (from 30% to 36%) in the percentage following political news very closely may also stem from Barack Obama's busy legislative agenda in his first year as president.

Survey Methods

Results are based on telephone interviews with 1,026 national adults, aged 18 and older, conducted Aug. 31–Sept. 2, 2009. For results based on the total sample of national adults, one can say with 95% confidence that the maximum margin of sampling error is ±4 percentage points.

Interviews are conducted with respondents on land-line telephones (for respondents with a land-line telephone) and cellular phones (for respondents who are cell-phone only).

In addition to sampling error, question wording and practical difficulties in conducting surveys can introduce error or bias into the findings of public opinion polls.

September 29, 2009

RENEWED DESIRE FOR U.S. GOVERNMENT TO PROMOTE TRADITIONAL VALUES

Trend had been moving toward view that government should not favor any values

by Jeffrey M. Jones, Gallup Poll Managing Editor

Americans now show a clear preference for the government's promoting of "traditional values," a change from recent years, when the public's views were more divided, but a return to the prevailing view from 1993 through 2004.

Some people think the government should promote traditional values in our society. Others think the government should not favor any particular set of values. Which comes closer to your own view?

■ % Promote traditional values   ■ % Not favor any values

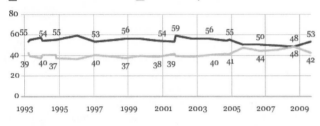

In this year's annual Gallup Governance poll, 53% of Americans say the government should promote traditional values, while 42% disagree and believe the government should not favor any particular set of values. Last year, Americans were divided right down the middle, with 48% taking each position. (The poll does not define what the term "traditional values" means; thus, respondents answer in light of their understanding of the term. The results by party and ideology discussed here suggest that respondents understand traditional values to be those generally favored by the Republican Party.)

The 2008 results marked the high point in the percentage opposed to a government role in promoting traditional morality since Gallup's initial measurement of this question in 1993. In contrast, the peak in favor of a government role in values (59%) came in October 2001, just after the Sept. 11 terrorist attacks, and at a time marked by heightened trust in government. (Gallup recorded a similar reading in January 1996.)

The shift in attitudes this year comes primarily from the political middle. Independents' views show a dramatic turnaround, from a 55%-37% split against government-promoted morality last year to a 54%-40% division in favor of it today. By contrast, Republicans' and Democrats' views have been relatively stable, with the former solidly in favor of the government's promoting traditional morality, and a majority of the latter opposed.

There has been a similar shift according to political ideology, with self-identified moderates moving toward favoring government involvement in promoting traditional morals; liberals' and conservatives' positions have been much more stable.

Bottom Line

Americans' views of the proper government role in promoting traditional values had moved in a more liberal direction since 2005, to the point that last year, as many said the government should not promote traditional values as said it should. If that trend had continued, 2009

Views on Government Role in Promoting Values, by Political Party, 2008 vs. 2009

	Promote traditional values	Not favor any values	Gap in favor of promoting traditional values (pct. pts.)
Democrats			
2008	37%	60%	-23
2009	42%	54%	-12
Independents			
2008	37%	55%	-18
2009	54%	40%	14
Republicans			
2008	71%	28%	43
2009	67%	31%	36

Views on Government Role in Promoting Values, by Political Ideology 2008 vs. 2009

	Promote traditional values	Not favor any values	Gap in favor of promoting traditional values (pct. pts.)
Liberal			
2008	26%	72%	-46
2009	28%	67%	-39
Moderate			
2008	39%	57%	-18
2009	51%	45%	6
Conservative			
2008	72%	25%	47
2009	68%	29%	39

would have marked the first time Gallup found more Americans preferring that the government refrain from actively promoting traditional values. Instead, Americans' attitudes reverted to a more conservative point of view on the matter. Now, Americans favor the government's promoting traditional values by an 11-point margin, similar to the double-digit margins favoring that view through much of the prior two decades.

Gallup has found several instances this year in which Americans' positions on policy issues—including moral issues such as abortion and stem cell research, but also global warming, defense, and taxes—have changed. On most of these issues, the changes have been toward a more conservative point of view. This could reflect an adjustment or moderation in the public's policy preferences in response to the change from a Republican to a Democratic presidential administration. That is, people with more moderate or loosely held issue positions may be perceiving that government policy is moving (too far) in one direction, and may be attempting to "balance" this by moving their own positions in the other direction. The fact that most of the movement on the "government role in promoting morality" question comes from independents and moderates is consistent with this possibility.

Survey Methods

Results are based on telephone interviews with 1,026 national adults, aged 18 and older, conducted Aug. 31–Sept. 2, 2009. For results based on the total sample of national adults, one can say with 95% confidence that the maximum margin of sampling error is ±4 percentage points.

Interviews are conducted with respondents on land-line telephones (for respondents with a land-line telephone) and cellular phones (for respondents who are cell-phone only).

In addition to sampling error, question wording and practical difficulties in conducting surveys can introduce error or bias into the findings of public opinion polls.

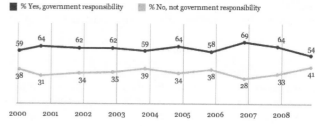

Do you think it is the responsibility of the federal government to make sure all Americans have healthcare coverage, or is that not the responsibility of the federal government?

■ % Yes, government responsibility   ▒ % No, not government responsibility

September 30, 2009
MANY IN U.S. SEE HEALTH INSURANCE AS PERSONAL RESPONSIBILITY
Majorities place responsibility on government when no alternative is presented

by Lydia Saad, Gallup Poll Senior Editor

In a recent Gallup survey, 89% of Republicans, 64% of independents, and 61% of Americans overall say Americans themselves—rather than the government—have the primary responsibility for ensuring that they have health insurance. Six in 10 Democrats say the government should be primarily responsible.

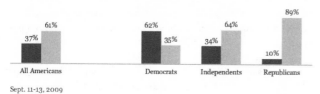

Health Insurance Views -- by Party ID

Which comes closer to your view about health insurance -- [the government should be primarily responsible for making sure all Americans have health insurance, (or) Americans themselves should be primarily responsible for making sure they and their families have health insurance]?

■ Government responsible   ▒ Americans responsible

Sept. 11-13, 2009

Other national polls on this topic have found a higher degree of public support for government involvement in guaranteeing healthcare coverage, but those question wordings do not provide a nongovernmental alternative.

For example, a Gallup question asks, "Do you think it is the responsibility of the federal government to make sure all Americans have healthcare coverage, or is that not the responsibility of the federal government?" The latest results, from November 2008, show 54% of Americans agreeing that it is the federal government's responsibility, and 41% disagreeing. While that 54% support is the lowest in Gallup trends—the peak being 69% in November 2006—it is still the majority view.

A question that the *New York Times*/CBS News poll has asked periodically since 1996 yields a similar result in its latest, mid-September update. In answer to "Do you think the federal government should guarantee health insurance for all Americans, or isn't this the responsibility of the federal government?" 51% of Americans say it is the government's responsibility; 40% disagree. (This reflects a decline in the "government responsibility" reading from earlier in

2009, and is the lowest such reading on this question in the poll's history of asking it.)

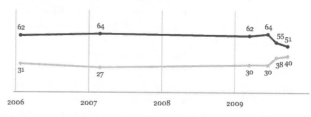

New York Times/CBS News Poll -- Recent Trend

Do you think the federal government should guarantee health insurance for all Americans, or isn't this the responsibility of the federal government?

■ % Government should guarantee   ▒ % Not government's responsibility

In July, a Fox News poll asked, "Do you think it is the responsibility of the federal government to make sure all Americans have healthcare, or is that not the responsibility of the federal government?" At that time, 51% of Americans said it was the government's responsibility and 46% disagreed—again, a significant drop from earlier this year.

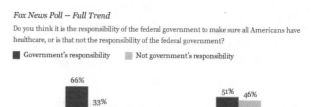

Fox News Poll -- Full Trend

Do you think it is the responsibility of the federal government to make sure all Americans have healthcare, or is that not the responsibility of the federal government?

■ Government's responsibility   ▒ Not government's responsibility

Given the declines in public support for government responsibility seen this year in both the *New York Times*/CBS News and the Fox News polls, it will be important to see if the Gallup variant of the same question—due to be updated in Gallup's November Health and Healthcare survey—shows a similar shift.

The differing results to questions asking about government responsibility for health insurance may not be contradictory. A reasonable hypothesis could be that Americans generally believe people should take responsibility for their own healthcare coverage, while at the same time believing the government should provide a safety net for those who need it.

A system in which Americans are "primarily responsible" for their families' health insurance—as the new Gallup question is phrased—would not preclude having a government-based insurance program for the poor, such as the Children's Health Insurance Program (CHIP) or Medicaid. By the same token, public support for the government's making sure "all Americans have healthcare coverage"—as other questions are phrased—isn't tantamount to support for mandated health insurance or a universal government-run system.

Bottom Line

An important principle behind the current push for healthcare reform is that healthcare is a basic right that the government ought to guarantee for all Americans. Not only are the details of achieving universal coverage proving to be highly controversial, but it is unclear how strongly Americans support the premise.

Americans tend to agree with the government's taking responsibility for guaranteeing healthcare coverage when asked in "yes or no" terms. However, they are more libertarian on the issue when asked whether the government or individual citizens should be primarily responsible for ensuring that coverage.

Survey Methods

Results are based on telephone interviews with 1,030 national adults, aged 18 and older, conducted Sept. 11–13, 2009. For results based on the total sample of national adults, one can say with 95% confidence that the maximum margin of sampling error is ±4 percentage points.

Interviews are conducted with respondents on land-line telephones (for respondents with a land-line telephone) and cellular phones (for respondents who are cell-phone only).

In addition to sampling error, question wording and practical difficulties in conducting surveys can introduce error or bias into the findings of public opinion polls.

September 30, 2009
MORE INDEPENDENTS LEAN GOP; PARTY GAP SMALLEST SINCE '05
Democratic advantage on leaned party ID is 48% to 42%

by Jeffrey M. Jones, Gallup Poll Managing Editor

In the third quarter of this year, 48% of Americans identified politically as Democrats or said they were independent but leaned to the Democratic Party. At the same time, 42% identified as Republicans or as independents who leaned Republican. That six-point spread in leaned party affiliation is the smallest Gallup has measured since 2005.

These results are based on an average of five Gallup and *USA Today*/Gallup polls conducted in the third quarter of 2009, encom-

passing interviews with more than 5,000 U.S. adults. Gallup's Daily tracking survey—established in 2008—has shown a similar narrowing of the party support gap in recent months.

Since Barack Obama took office as president in January, the Democratic advantage in leaned party identification has shrunk each quarter, from 13 points in the first quarter (52% to 39%) to 9 points in the second quarter (49% to 40%) and 6 points in the most recent quarter (48% to 42%).

Gallup measures party identification by first asking Americans whether they consider themselves Republicans, Democrats, or independents. Those who identify as independents or say they have no party preference are asked a follow-up question—whether they *lean* more to the Republican Party or to the Democratic Party. The figures reported here represent the combined total of identifiers and leaners for each party.

The last time Republicans were this close to Democrats in terms of total party support—during the second quarter of 2005—George W. Bush was in the early months of his second term as president. But the Bush administration suffered a series of setbacks that year, including ongoing difficulty in stabilizing Iraq, a slow response to Hurricane Katrina, and the ultimately withdrawn nomination of Harriet Miers to the Supreme Court, to name a few. Rising gas prices and a struggling economy only added to the problems plaguing the Bush administration during Bush's second term in office.

Bush's job approval rating sank over the course of 2005, from 52% at the start of the year to 43% by late December, including several sub-40% ratings in the fall. By the end of 2006, it had fallen to 35%, and it never again exceeded 38%.

During this time, an increasing number of Americans began to align themselves with the Democratic Party. The Democratic advantage in leaned party ID grew to as large as 14 percentage points in the fourth quarter of 2006 and again in the first quarter of 2008—the largest gap in favor of either party since Gallup began regularly measuring leaned party identification in 1991. Democrats maintained a double-digit lead for 11 of 12 quarters between the second quarter of 2006 and the first quarter of 2009. This solid edge in party support helped propel the Democratic Party to major victories in the 2006 and 2008 federal elections.

Since Barack Obama took office as president in January, the Democratic advantage in leaned party identification has shrunk each quarter, from 13 points in the first quarter (52% to 39%) to 9 points in the second quarter (49% to 40%) and 6 points in the most recent quarter (48% to 42%).

As the accompanying table indicates, the Democratic-Republican gap is narrowing because more independents now say they lean to the Republican Party—there has been no apparent increase in the percentage of Americans who identify as Republicans on the initial party-preference question. Likewise, the percentage of Americans identifying as Democrats has been fairly stable, but fewer independents now say they lean Democratic. Thus, the shifts in party support have come mainly among those with weak party attachments.

Bottom Line

Though Democrats maintain an edge in party support over Republicans, Americans' tendency to identify with or lean toward the Democratic Party is lessening, coming down from the heights it reached near the end of the Bush administration. The changes in party support have been mainly among those who do not have a firm party commitment—those who initially identify as independents but express a leaning toward either of the major parties.

Party Identification and Leaning, Quarterly Averages, 2005-2009

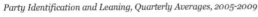

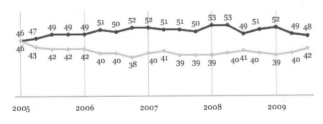

	% Democratic identifiers	% Democratic-leaning independents	% Republican-leaning independents	% Republican identifiers	Gap: total Dem minus total Rep (in pct. pts.)
2009-III	35	13	15	27	6
2009-II	34	15	12	28	9
2009-I	35	17	11	28	13
2008-IV	35	16	12	28	11
2008-III	35	14	12	29	8
2008-II	36	17	13	27	13
2008-I	36	17	11	28	14
2007-IV	32	18	12	27	11
2007-III	31	20	12	27	12
2007-II	33	18	12	29	10
2007-I	33	19	12	28	12
2006-IV	35	17	9	29	14
2006-III	35	15	9	31	10
2006-II	35	16	10	30	11
2006-I	33	16	10	32	7
2005-IV	33	16	10	32	7
2005-III	34	15	11	31	7
2005-II	33	14	10	33	4
2005-I	33	13	11	35	0

In fact, Gallup has found that independents are more likely to oppose than support healthcare reform, and to express concerns about increased government spending and the expansion of government power. Thus, the drop in Democratic support is partly a response to concerns about the policies Obama and the Democratic Congress are pursuing.

Whatever the causes, it is important to note that even as Republicans are closing the gap in party support, the percentage of Americans with a firm commitment to the Republican Party—those who identify themselves as Republicans—is not increasing.

Survey Methods

Results are based on telephone interviews with 5,090 national adults, aged 18 and older, in five polls conducted between July 1 and Sept. 30, 2009. For results based on the total sample of national adults, one can say with 95% confidence that the maximum margin of sampling error is ±1 percentage point.

Interviews are conducted with respondents on land-line telephones (for respondents with a land-line telephone) and cellular phones (for respondents who are cell-phone only).

In addition to sampling error, question wording and practical difficulties in conducting surveys can introduce error or bias into the findings of public opinion polls.

The average confidence reading for Sept. 1-15 was -25, compared to a more positive -22 for the second half of September (despite the more negative readings in the last three days of the month). The last half of September was also more positive than the August average of -25.

Consumer Confidence Index, Monthly/Half-Monthly Averages, August-September 2009

Period	Consumer Confidence Index	Period	Consumer Confidence Index
Aug 1-15	-23	Sep 1-15	-25
Aug 16-31	-25	Sep 16-30	-22
Aug 1-31	-25	Sep 1-30	-23

Gallup Daily tracking

The finding that September represented a slight increase in consumer confidence over August contrasts with reports from the Conference Board that consumer confidence for September was down slightly from the previous month (53.1 in September, compared to 54.5 in August).

On the other hand, the Reuters/University of Michigan Consumer Sentiment Index was more positive in September (73.5) than it was in August (65.7).

According to the Conference Board, its September numbers, released Sept. 29, were based on mail surveys received through Sept. 22, and it is likely that many of these were filled out in the first part of the month.

Therefore, the Conference Board figures tend to reflect attitudes as they existed in the first part of September, and Gallup's continuous tracking shows that consumer attitudes at that time were indeed more negative than they were later in the month.

As noted in Tuesday's weekly update on consumer confidence, the improved picture of consumer confidence has not yet translated into a sustained increase in consumer spending, nor does it reflect a sustained uptick in the jobs situation.

Survey Methods

Results are based on telephone interviews with 13,744 national adults, aged 18 and older, conducted Sept. 1-30, 2009, as part of Gallup Daily tracking. For results based on the total sample of national adults, one can say with 95% confidence that the maximum margin of sampling error is ±1 percentage point.

Interviews are conducted with respondents on land-line telephones and cellular phones.

In addition to sampling error, question wording and practical difficulties in conducting surveys can introduce error or bias into the findings of public opinion polls.

October 01, 2009

CONSUMER CONFIDENCE SLIGHTLY HIGHER IN SEPTEMBER

Confidence increased in second half of the month

by Frank Newport , Gallup Poll Editor in Chief

Consumer confidence for the month of September improved modestly over August, with most of the gains coming in the last half of the month. Overall, Gallup's Consumer Confidence Index for September was at -23, an improvement over August's -25 reading, and the most positive monthly average since Gallup Daily tracking began in January 2008.

Consumer Confidence Index

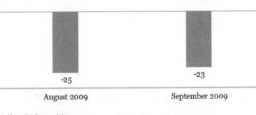

-25	-23
August 2009	September 2009

Gallup Daily tracking

Gallup's Consumer Confidence Index is based on interviews with 500 randomly selected Americans each day, for a total of approximately 15,000 interviews each month. The fact that the interviews are spread evenly over the month provides an accurate assessment of consumer attitudes for the entire monthly period, and allows for the analysis of trends as the month progresses.

A key finding in September is that consumer confidence gained for the most part in the second half of the month, although there was a drop-off in the last three days of the month, Sept. 28-30.

*Consumer Confidence Index, Weekly Averages, August-September 2009^*

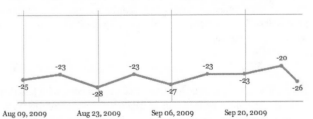

| Aug 09, 2009 | Aug 23, 2009 | Sep 06, 2009 | Sep 20, 2009 |

^ Note: Most recent reading (-26) reflects interviews conducted Sept. 28-30
Gallup Daily tracking

October 01, 2009

MANY AMERICANS REMAIN DISTRUSTING OF NEWS MEDIA

Less than half (45%) have great deal/fair amount of confidence; majority perceive bias

by Lymari Morales, Gallup Poll Staff Writer

Less than half of Americans (45%) say they have a great deal or fair amount of confidence in the media to report the news fully, accurately, and fairly—on par with last year's record-low 43%. About 2 in 10 Americans (18%) have no confidence in the media at all—which is also among the worst grades Gallup has recorded.

In general, how much trust and confidence do you have in the mass media -- such as newspapers, TV, and radio -- when it comes to reporting the news fully, accurately, and fairly -- a great deal, a fair amount, not very much, or none at all?

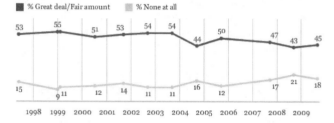

The findings are from the same Gallup survey, conducted Aug. 31-Sept. 2, 2009, that found more Americans following political news very closely than in any other recent year without a presidential election. Despite the relatively high level of interest in political news in particular, many Americans appear to be consuming their news skeptically. Ten percent say they have a great deal of confidence in the media's reporting and 35% have a fair amount, but 37% do not have very much confidence and 18% have none at all.

Americans' views about bias in the news are also fairly steady over the past few years. Currently, 45% say the media are too liberal, while 15% say too conservative and 35% say they are just about right. None of these percentages have budged more than three or four points since 2005.

In general, do you think the news media are -- [ROTATED: too liberal, just about right, or too conservative]?

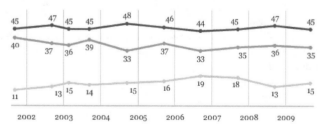

Taken together, the steady nature of Americans' views about media accuracy in general and bias in the news suggest fairly entrenched views about the news media, even amid turbulent changes in the industry. These include the economic challenges facing traditional news sources and the rise of less traditional sources, including blogs, citizen journalism, and open-to-anyone dissemination platforms such as Twitter. Gallup's question mentions newspapers, tele-

vision, and radio, and thus, any impact of the new media on these numbers, positive or negative, would be indirect.

Similarly well-established are the partisan nature of these views. Currently, 58% of Democrats say they have a great deal or fair amount of trust in media reporting and accuracy, compared to 39% of independents and 36% of Republicans. Republicans are slightly more likely than they were last year to say they have a great deal or fair amount of trust, though 27% say they have no trust at all, compared with 21% of independents and 6% of Democrats.

Trust in Media, by Party ID, 2008 vs. 2009

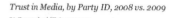

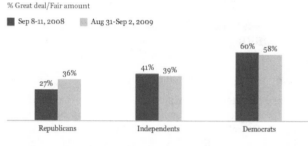

A full three-fourths of Republicans (74%) say the news media are too liberal, compared to 45% of independents and 21% of Democrats. In contrast, 2 in 10 Democrats (20%) and independents (19%), along with 4% of Republicans, say the news media are too conservative. Compared to 2008, Republicans are slightly less likely, and independents slightly more likely, to say the media are too liberal, while Democrats' views are essentially unchanged.

Views of Media Bias, by Party, 2008 vs. 2009

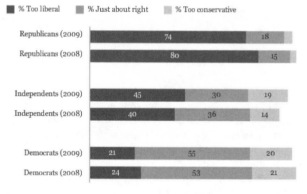

Who Does Trust the Media?

In addition to Democrats, nonwhites and those with a high school education or less place the most trust in the media, followed by liberals, women, and Americans 18 to 29. In all other demographic groups, less than a majority say they have a great deal or fair amount of trust in the media.

Bottom Line

Many Americans continue to distrust the news media, with less than half (45%) saying they have a great deal or fair amount of trust in the media to report the news fully, accurately, and fairly—a number in the range of what Gallup has found over the past three years. A majority perceive bias, though many more say the media are too liberal than say they are too conservative. Since 2008, Republicans have

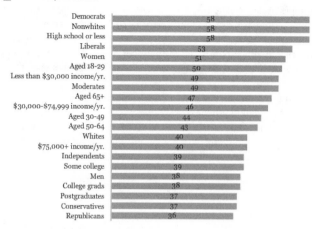

Trust in the Mass Media

By demographic group

■ % Great deal/Fair amount

Gallup, Aug. 31- Sept. 2, 2009

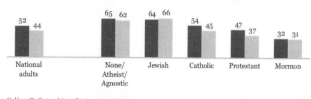

President Barack Obama Job Approval, by Religion -- September 2009

Numbers in percentages

■ All Americans ■ Non-Hispanic whites

Gallup Daily tracking, Sept. 1-30, 2009

shown some positive movement, albeit slight, on both of these measures, suggesting they may be finding more media outlets with which they do not have a complaint. Still, of all demographic groups, Republicans and conservatives remain the least trusting of the media, with independents showing only marginally more faith in the media's reporting. Taken together, the findings underscore the challenge facing the media as they struggle with economic difficulties and increasing competition from emerging platforms.

Survey Methods

Results are based on telephone interviews with 1,026 national adults, aged 18 and older, conducted Aug. 31- Sept. 1, 2009. For results based on the total sample of national adults, one can say with 95% confidence that the maximum margin of sampling error is ±4 percentage points.

Interviews are conducted with respondents on land-line telephones (for respondents with a land-line telephone) and cellular phones (for respondents who are cell-phone only).

In addition to sampling error, question wording and practical difficulties in conducting surveys can introduce error or bias into the findings of public opinion polls.

October 02, 2009

U.S. JEWS LEAD OTHER RELIGIOUS GROUPS IN SUPPORT OF OBAMA

Dip in approval among Jews similar to that among general public

by Lydia Saad, Gallup Poll Senior Editor

Gallup Daily tracking for the month of September found 64% of U.S. Jews approving of the job Barack Obama is doing as president, significantly higher than the 52% average among national adults in September, and also higher than was seen among Catholics, Protestants, and Mormons. Only nonreligious Americans equal Jews in their support for the president.

Obama receives broad approval from U.S. blacks and Hispanics, regardless of their religious affiliation; most of the variation in his support by religion is seen among non-Hispanic whites. Thus, it is instructive to look at the views of Obama by religion among the non-Hispanic white population.

On this basis, Obama's strength with U.S. Jews relative to other religious groups is even greater. Two-thirds of white Jews (66%) approve of the job Obama is doing, compared with 44% of whites nationwide, 45% of white Catholics, and 37% of white Protestants. (The "Protestant" category includes both those who identify themselves as Protestants, and those who identify themselves as Christians but not Catholics.)

The higher level of Jewish approval of Obama compared to approval from those of other religions conforms with the much greater Democratic orientation of Jews, politically. Two-thirds of Jews overall identify with or lean toward the Democratic Party, a much greater proportion than Gallup finds for any other religious group.

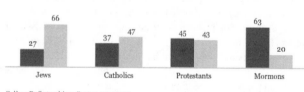

Party ID, by Religion -- September 2009

■ % Republican/Lean Republican ■ % Democratic/Lean Democratic

Gallup Daily tracking, Sept. 1-30, 2009

All of the religious groups covered in this analysis constitute at least 1% of the American public. Muslims are not included because, at less than 0.5% of Gallup's sample, there are too few cases to analyze in Gallup's September polling. However, previous Gallup analysis, based on aggregated samples across several months, has shown Muslims to be highly supportive of Obama.

Decline in Jews' Approval Conforms With National Average

Support for Obama among U.S. Jews has trended downward since January, when 83% approved. However, it remains positive by a 2-to-1 margin, 64% vs. 32%, in September.

Importantly, the decline in approval of Obama among Jews since January is no greater than that seen among the general public. This suggests that since Obama became president, his actions on Middle East policy issues—particularly relating to Iran and the Israeli-Palestinian dispute—have not had a disproportionately negative (or positive) impact on his image among U.S. Jews.

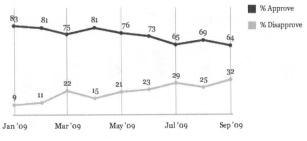

Trend in Obama Job Approval Among U.S. Jews -- Monthly Averages

■ % Approve
■ % Disapprove

Gallup Daily tracking

Between January and September, Obama's average monthly approval rating fell by 14 percentage points among all Americans and by 19 points among Jews. Both shifts represent about a 20% decline in approval from January.

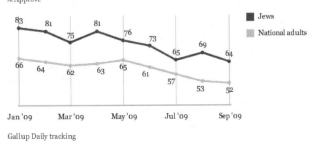

Trend in Obama Job Approval -- Monthly Averages

% Approve

■ Jews
■ National adults

Gallup Daily tracking

Bottom Line

President Obama enjoys staunch support from U.S. Jews—much higher than what he earns from Catholics and Protestants, particularly with regard to non-Hispanic whites. This confirms what Gallup found during the 2008 presidential election campaign, when Jews overwhelmingly indicated they were voting for Obama over John McCain. Jews' support for Obama as president has not remained at the lofty 83% level seen in January, but, at 64%, it is still high—and has descended merely on par with the decline seen among the public at large.

American Jews' solid backing of Obama stands in contrast to Jewish opinion in Israel, where many are still taking stock of the new American president and trying to determine his long-term policy intentions for the Mideast. A recent poll of Jews in Israel, sponsored by the *Jerusalem Post*, found only 4% believing Obama's policies are "pro-Israel" and 35% calling them evenly balanced, while 51% said they are "pro-Palestinian." By contrast, a previous survey found 88% of Israelis believing George W. Bush's policies were "pro-Israel."

For Israeli Jews, Obama's position toward their country is clearly of central importance to how they view Obama. Gallup has not polled American Jews since Obama's inauguration to measure whether they feel positively or negatively about his stance on Israel or on Mideast policies, more generally. Regardless, their net opinion of him is clearly positive. Much of this can probably be explained by U.S. Jews' heavy Democratic partisanship.

Survey Methods

The latest results are based on aggregated Gallup Daily tracking for the month of September, involving the half-sample of respondents

who were asked the President Obama approval question. This includes telephone interviews with 14,407 national adults, aged 18 and older, conducted Sept. 1-30, 2009. For results based on the total sample of national adults, one can say with 95% confidence that the maximum margin of sampling error is ±0.5 percentage points. For September results based on 379 Jews, the margin of sampling error is ±6 percentage points. The September results for other religious groups are based on larger sample sizes, with smaller associated margins of error.

Interviews are conducted with respondents on land-line telephones and cellular phones.

In addition to sampling error, question wording and practical difficulties in conducting surveys can introduce error or bias into the findings of public opinion polls.

October 05, 2009

IN U.S., OPPOSITION TO HEALTHCARE LEGISLATION DROPS MODESTLY
Support holds steady at 51%, while percentage unsure rises

by Jeffrey M. Jones, Gallup Poll Managing Editor

Americans' views on healthcare legislation have shifted modestly over the past three weeks, with a slight plurality (40%) now supporting the passage of a new healthcare bill, and with fewer (36%) saying they oppose a new bill. When the leanings of those without an opinion are taken into account, 51% of Americans favor or lean toward favoring a bill, while 41% oppose it or lean toward opposition—a more sizeable gap in favor than three weeks ago.

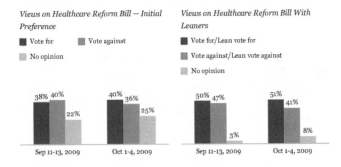

Views on Healthcare Reform Bill -- Initial Preference

■ Vote for   ■ Vote against
■ No opinion

Views on Healthcare Reform Bill With Leaners

■ Vote for/Lean vote for
■ Vote against/Lean vote against
■ No opinion

In terms of Americans' initial preference for passing healthcare legislation (that is prior to those without an opinion being asked which way they lean), their views since August have changed very little from one poll to the next. However, the cumulative effect has been a slight increase in support for the bill over the past two months (from 35% to 40%) and a corresponding decline in those holding no opinion.

That a quarter of Americans remain unsure may reflect the confusion created by the number of healthcare reform bills the House and Senate are still debating—with different provisions in each and still no clarity about whether the final bill will include a "public option."

The greater tilt in favor of a healthcare bill today is not because of increased support for it in recent weeks; rather, opposition has lessened, while a higher percentage of Americans express no opinion or leaning on healthcare reform.

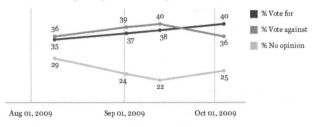

Trend in Initial Preference for Healthcare Reform Bill

% Vote for
% Vote against
% No opinion

36 39 40   40
35   37 38   36
29
    24 22   25

Aug 01, 2009   Sep 01, 2009   Oct 01, 2009

Aug. 6-9 and Aug. 31-Sep 2. wording: Would you advise your member of Congress to vote for or against a healthcare reform bill when they return to Washington in September, or do you not have an opinion?

Bottom Line

The gap between supporters and opponents of new healthcare reform legislation has increased modestly over the past three weeks. Still, Americans remain largely divided, with a significant proportion undecided, although the current poll marks the first time more Americans favor than oppose healthcare legislation this year. The 51% of Americans favoring or leaning in favor of a bill gives President Obama and his congressional allies a bare majority of support, but perhaps not the solid public backing needed to advance the bill in Congress.

Survey Methods

Results are based on telephone interviews with 1,013 national adults, aged 18 and older, conducted Oct 1-4, 2009. For results based on the total sample of national adults, one can say with 95% confidence that the maximum margin of sampling error is ±4 percentage points.

Interviews are conducted with respondents on land-line telephones (for respondents with a land-line telephone) and cellular phones (for respondents who are cell-phone only).

In addition to sampling error, question wording and practical difficulties in conducting surveys can introduce error or bias into the findings of public opinion polls.

October 05, 2009

AMERICANS LEAST HAPPY IN THEIR 50S AND LATE 80S

Differences by age and gender fit no simple pattern

by Frank Newport, Gallup Poll Editor in Chief and Brett Pelham, Staff Writer

A new analysis of more than 600,000 Gallup-Healthways Well-Being Index interviews conducted in 2008 and 2009 shows that happiness is highest among Americans who are in their early adulthood. Happiness drops among Americans in their 30s and 40s, and—in particular—among those in their 50s; it is higher among Americans in their 60s, drops among Americans in their late 70s and 80s, and then rises again among those older than 90. Men and women in most age groups have broadly equal happiness scores, with women scoring slightly higher than men in the middle-aged years, and notably higher after age 80.

This analysis is based on a definition of happiness developed from responses to two questions about mood and one about smiling

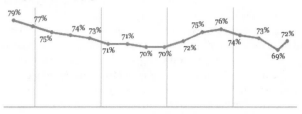

Percentage Who Say They Experienced Happiness, Enjoyment, and Smiling or Laughter During a Lot of the Day "Yesterday," January 2008-September 2009

Among national adults, by age

79% 77% 74% 73%   71%   75% 76%   73% 72%
     75%   71% 70% 70% 72% 74%   69%

18-20 21-25 26-30 31-35 36-40 41-45 46-50 51-55 56-60 61-65 66-70 71-75 76-80 81-85 86-90 91+

or laughing, all included in Gallup-Healthways Daily tracking. The questions are: (1) Did you experience happiness during a lot of the day yesterday? (2) Did you experience enjoyment during a lot of the day yesterday? and (3) Did you smile or laugh a lot yesterday? Survey respondents receive a positive happiness score if they respond affirmatively to all three questions. All other patterns of responses yield a score of zero.

The data reflect a cross-section of the American adult population at a particular point in time—January 2008-September 2009—and thus do not allow inferences to be made about the "normal" course of life events. The happiness of the respondents included in this analysis is a combination of the life circumstances into which they were born and through which they have lived, as well as generational circumstances that affect individuals at specific ages. Thus, it is not possible with these data to determine the degree to which happiness is a result of an individual's life history and experiences, as opposed to the individual's current circumstances (including health, family situation, and economic situation).

The Age Spectrum

On an absolute basis, a majority of all Americans of all ages are happy. Happiness reaches its very lowest point—69%—among Americans 86 to 90, meaning that even among this relatively less positive group, over two-thirds said they experienced happiness and enjoyment, and smiled or laughed a lot the day before they were interviewed. The happiest adult Americans are those aged 18-20, with a score of 79%.

The variations across age and gender show that at this time, Americans' happiness becomes progressively lower as one moves from groups of Americans in their 20s to those in their 30s and 40s, and—in particular—to American baby boomers who are now in their 50s. Thereafter, happiness is higher among the very oldest baby boomers and Silent Generation members in their 60s, but drops again among those 76 to 90. The data then show that the very oldest Americans, 91 years of age and older (of whom there are 9,654 in this sample), have a modestly more positive level of happiness in these latter years of their lives compared to youngsters only in their 80s. (Of course, this final "surge" in happiness may apply only to those of this very advanced age who enjoy enough independence to answer telephone calls and respond to the Gallup-Healthways survey.)

Given the cross-sectional nature of these data, it is not possible to determine whether these same happiness-by-age patterns will persist in the years ahead. It is possible, for example, that specific life circumstances of the core baby boomer group now in their 50s will stay with them throughout their lives, and that in the years ahead, they will not enjoy the increased happiness levels now apparent among those who are in their 60s.

Gender

Averaging across all age groups, there is only a very slight difference between women's and men's scores, with women, at 73.4, about one percentage point higher on average than men, at 72.5. Given the large sample sizes involved in this analysis (more than 300,000 men and more than 300,000 women), this gender difference is statistically significant, but substantively does not suggest a major gender effect.

The pattern of gender differences varies across age groups. The female skew in happiness is statistically significant (although still quite small) among Americans 36-65, and among those over 80. The gender gap in happiness is largest among the oldest Americans, aged 86 and older.

Percentage Who Say They Experienced Happiness, Enjoyment, and Smiling or Laughter During a Lot of the Day "Yesterday," January 2008-September 2009
By age and gender

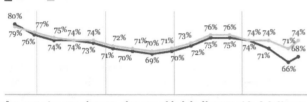

Gallup-Healthways Well-Being Index

Survey Methods

Results are based on telephone interviews with 608,221 national adults (306,167 women and 302,054 men), aged 18 and older, conducted Jan. 2, 2008-Sept. 21, 2009. For results based on the total sample of national adults, one can say with 95% confidence that the maximum margin of sampling error is less than ±1 percentage point. Margins of error for specific age/gender subgroups range from ±2 percentage points to less than ±1 point, depending on the size of the group.

Interviews are conducted with respondents on land-line telephones and cellular phones.

In addition to sampling error, question wording and practical difficulties in conducting surveys can introduce error or bias into the findings of public opinion polls.

October 06, 2009
APPROVAL OF U.S. CONGRESS FALLS TO 21%, DRIVEN BY DEMOCRATS
Lowest rating for Congress since January

by Frank Newport, Gallup Poll Editor in Chief

Americans' approval of the job Congress is doing is at 21% this month, down significantly from last month's 31% and from the recent high of 39% in March.

Congressional approval rose sharply in the months after President Obama's inauguration, from 19% in January to 31% in February and 39% in March. Approval then began to slip gradually,

Congressional Approval -- 2009 Trend
Do you approve or disapprove of the way Congress is handling its job?

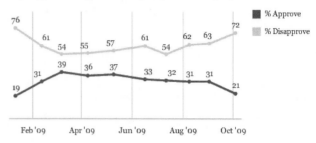

dipping to 31% by the end of the summer, before falling precipitously in October. Given the current 21% reading, it appears that any "honeymoon" period for the 111th Congress has eroded.

Approval of Congress today is significantly below the average 36% rating found across the past two decades.

Do you approve or disapprove of the way Congress is handling its job?

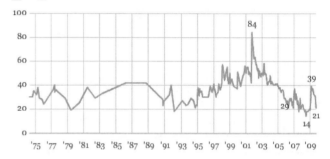

Congressional job approval reached its all-time high of 84% in October 2001, weeks after that year's Sept. 11 terrorist attacks, and at a time when presidential job approval also shot to all-time highs. Approval of Congress slowly declined from that point through the summer of 2008, reaching the all-time low of 14% in July of that year, as gas prices soared to record highs.

The current drop in overall job approval to 21% particularly reflects a substantial drop in approval among Democrats, whose 36% rating this month is 18 points lower than last month's 54%, and the lowest since January of this year.

Do you approve or disapprove of the way Congress is handling its job?
2009 trend, by party ID
% Approve

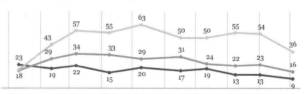

Republicans' already-low ratings of Congress have dropped marginally, to 9% from 13% last month. There is a similar pattern among independents, whose approval of Congress, now at 16%, is down from 23% last month.

Bottom Line

The reasons why Americans' ratings of Congress have fallen so significantly this month are not completely clear. The highly publicized and sometimes acrimonious debate over healthcare reform in recent weeks would seem a proximate and, therefore, possible explanation. It is also possible that Americans are frustrated with the lack of meaningful outcomes from Congress. A Gallup analysis of a drop in congressional job approval ratings in 2007 found that many who disapproved cited congressional inaction as the explanation.

Of note is the steep decline in approval among Democrats, who appear to be souring on the job that Congress is doing despite the fact that their party controls both the House and the Senate. For the first time since February, Democrats' approval of the job Congress is doing is below 50%—with only slightly more than a third of Democrats now approving. It is possible that after watching Democratic lawmakers defend healthcare reform in town hall meetings through the summer, rank-and-file Democrats may be disappointed that Congress hasn't followed through with more progress on that legislation this fall.

Congress remains the lowest rated of the three branches of government. Gallup Daily tracking puts President Obama's job approval ratings in the low 50% range in recent days, and Gallup's most recent assessment of the Supreme Court in late August/early September gave that institution a 61% job approval score.

Survey Methods

Results are based on telephone interviews with 1,013 national adults, aged 18 and older, conducted Oct. 1-4, 2009. For results based on the total sample of national adults, one can say with 95% confidence that the maximum margin of sampling error is ±4 percentage points.

Interviews are conducted with respondents on land-line telephones (for respondents with a land-line telephone) and cellular phones (for respondents who are cell-phone only).

In addition to sampling error, question wording and practical difficulties in conducting surveys can introduce error or bias into the findings of public opinion polls.

October 07, 2009
PARTIES NEARLY TIED FOR CONGRESS IN 2010
Voter preferences for Congress split 46% Democratic vs. 44% Republican

by Lydia Saad, Gallup Poll Senior Editor

Roughly a year before the 2010 midterm elections, Gallup finds the Republican and Democratic Parties nearly tied in the congressional ballot preferences of registered voters. Forty-six percent of registered voters say they would vote for the Democrat and 44% say the Republican when asked which party's candidate they would support for Congress, if the election were held today.

The Democratic Party held a slightly wider, six percentage-point lead on this important indicator of party strength in July, 50% to 44%. However, both 2009 results show a more competitive political environment than Gallup has generally seen since before the Democrats regained control of the U.S. House of Representatives in the 2006 midterm elections. Closer to elections, Gallup bases its results

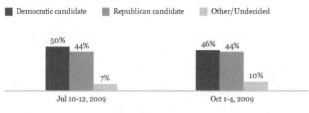

2009 Generic Congressional Ballot -- Preferences of Registered Voters

If the elections for Congress were being held today, which party's candidate would you vote for in your congressional district -- the Democratic Party's candidate (or) the Republican Party's candidate? (If unsure: As of today, do you lean more toward the Democratic Party's candidate (or) the Republican Party's candidate?)

on "likely voters." Doing so typically improves the Republicans' positioning by several points; thus, when Democrats lead slightly among registered voters, it is possible for Republicans to be ahead among likely voters.

As Gallup's "generic ballot" trend shows, the Democrats held a sizable lead among registered voters from about March 2006 through most of 2008. The Republicans nearly tied the Democrats immediately following the Republican National Convention in September 2008, but that proved short-lived. The gap widened to 7 points by mid-October, and to 15 points immediately prior to the 2008 elections—not only securing the Democrats' victory, but enabling them to greatly expand their majority position.

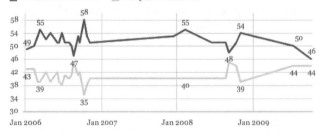

Generic Congressional Ballot, Recent Trend -- Preferences of Registered Voters

The closeness of the two parties in voter preferences today is similar to that found in most Gallup readings from 1994 through 2005 (spanning the period when Republicans won control of the U.S. House, and subsequently maintained it for more than a decade).

The Republican Party's relatively strong position on the generic ballot in the latest poll, conducted Oct. 1-4, stems from the support of political independents, who now favor Republican over Democratic candidates by 45% to 36%. In July, independents were evenly divided in their party voting preferences, whereas last fall they showed a clear preference for the Democrats.

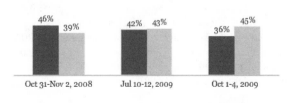

Generic Congressional Ballot -- Recent Trend, Based on Independent Registered Voters

Across these surveys, at least 90% each of Republicans and of Democrats have said they plan to vote for their own party's candidate. Today, that figure is 93% for the Democrats and 92% for the Republicans.

Bottom Line

For the second time this year, Gallup polling shows the Republicans within single digits of the Democrats in the congressional voting preferences of registered voters. That's a distinct shift away from the larger Democratic leads seen since the Democrats won back control of Congress in 2006, and a sign that if the 2010 elections were held today, Republicans would likely outperform Democrats, given usual turnout patterns.

The challenge for congressional Democrats is underscored by today's low approval of Congress. While it is far too early to say whether these indicators spell real trouble for the Democrats in 2010, they could provide some encouragement to the Republicans.

Survey Methods

Results are based on telephone interviews with 1,013 national adults, aged 18 and older, conducted Oct. 1-4, 2009. For results based on the total sample of national adults, one can say with 95% confidence that the maximum margin of sampling error is ±4 percentage points.

For results based on the sample of 906 registered voters, the maximum margin of sampling error is ±4 percentage points.

Interviews are conducted with respondents on land-line telephones (for respondents with a land-line telephone) and cellular phones (for respondents who are cell-phone only).

In addition to sampling error, question wording and practical difficulties in conducting surveys can introduce error or bias into the findings of public opinion polls.

October 07, 2009
AT 16.6%, NUMBER OF UNINSURED AMERICAN ADULTS TIES HIGH
Average percentage uninsured in 2009 significantly higher than in 2008

by Frank Newport, Gallup Poll Editor in Chief and Elizabeth Mendes, Staff Writer

As Congress continues to grapple with moving healthcare reform legislation forward, the Gallup-Healthways Well-Being Index finds that the percentage of uninsured American adults remains elevated in comparison to last year. That percentage was 16.6% last month, tying the high on this 21-month-old measure and up from the 13.9% who were without coverage in September 2008.

Gallup and Healthways started asking Americans aged 18 and older about their health insurance coverage on a daily basis in January 2008, with each monthly aggregate consisting of approximately 30,000 interviews. Throughout 2009, the percentage of uninsured Americans has been higher than in the comparable months of 2008, with some minor monthly fluctuations. At 16.2%, the average percentage of uninsured in the first nine months of 2009 is measurably higher than the 2008 average of 14.8%.

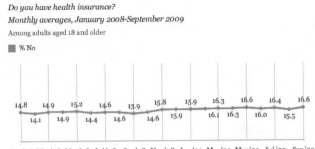

Do you have health insurance?
Monthly averages, January 2008-September 2009
Among adults aged 18 and older

■ % No

Gallup-Healthways Well-Being Index

A broader perspective reinforces the basic finding that the ranks of the uninsured have increased since January 2008. There have been seven quarters since then, and the estimated percentage uninsured in each quarter is based on approximately 90,000 interviews with adult Americans.

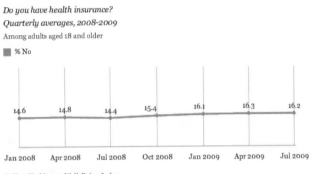

Do you have health insurance?
Quarterly averages, 2008-2009
Among adults aged 18 and older

■ % No

Gallup-Healthways Well-Being Index

The percentage uninsured jumped the most between the third and fourth quarters of 2008, coincident with the onset of the financial crisis. The first three quarters of this year have seen a further increase, with percentages holding fairly steady between 16.1% and 16.3%.

With a number of competing healthcare bills on the table, a primary point of contention continues to be how and to what extent the government should work to expand coverage to the millions of uninsured. While there has been some fluctuation in the estimated percentage of uninsured in 2009, the ranks of the uninsured have clearly remained higher compared to last year. Gallup continues to ask about health insurance on a daily basis as part of the Gallup-Healthways Well-Being Index, which provides the most up-to-date estimate available of the percentage uninsured, and will monitor it and report on changes in the months ahead.

To read about President Obama's use of Gallup's uninsured figure, check out Gallup Editor in Chief Frank Newport's blog Polling Matters.

Survey Methods

For the Gallup-Healthways Well-Being Index, Gallup is interviewing no fewer than 1,000 U.S. adults nationwide each day. Monthly results consist of roughly 30,000 interviews. For results based on these samples, the maximum margin of sampling error is ±1 percentage point.

Interviews are conducted with respondents on land-line telephones and cellular phones.

In addition to sampling error, question wording and practical difficulties in conducting surveys can introduce error or bias into the findings of public opinion polls.

October 08, 2009

AMERICANS DIVIDED ON SENDING MORE TROOPS TO AFGHANISTAN

Most believe generals should not make their preferred course of action public

by Jeffrey M. Jones, Gallup Poll Managing Editor

As the debate intensifies over the next steps for the United States in the war in Afghanistan, a new *USA Today*/Gallup poll finds Americans about evenly divided over whether the U.S. should increase its troop presence there. Forty-eight percent say they would favor a decision by President Obama to send more troops, while 45% would oppose it. Two weeks ago, the public leaned against a troop increase.

Would you favor or oppose a decision by President Obama to send more U.S. troops to Afghanistan?

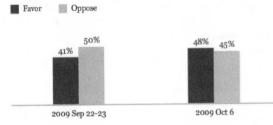

The Oct. 6 poll was conducted just before the eighth anniversary of U.S. military operations in Afghanistan. President Obama is now considering whether the U.S. should send more troops, something the commanding general in Afghanistan, Stanley McChrystal, recently called for. Other prominent U.S. military leaders support McChrystal's recommendations.

Those recommendations may have contributed to Americans' slightly more supportive position on increased troops. At the same time, the public pronouncements in favor of troop increases have created a bit of a public relations issue for the president, particularly if he ultimately decides to go against the commanders' recommendations.

The poll included a general question about this type of situation, asking Americans whether U.S. military commanders should make their positions publicly known when the U.S. is considering different courses of military action, or keep them private and reveal them only to the president and others in the military chain of command. The public—by a 2-to-1 margin—believes it is better for military commanders to keep their positions private.

Republicans (65%), Democrats (65%), and independents (60%) generally agree that commanders should keep their preferences private.

Public Support for U.S. Troops in Afghanistan

The poll indicates that the majority of Americans support a U.S. military presence in Afghanistan in general. In addition to the 48% who

When the United States is considering different courses of military action, should U.S. military commanders -- [ROTATED: make their positions publicly known (or should they) only state their positions privately to the president and others in the chain of command]?

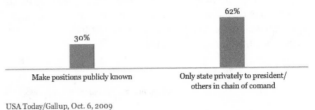

USA Today/Gallup, Oct. 6, 2009

favor an increase in the number of U.S. troops there, another 5% oppose it but believe the U.S. should maintain its current troop level. Thirty-eight percent of Americans—including half of Democrats—think the United States should begin to withdraw troops from Afghanistan. Republicans solidly back a troop increase, with 7 in 10 in favor.

Would you favor or oppose a decision by President Obama to send more U.S. troops to Afghanistan?

(Asked of those who oppose sending more troops to Afghanistan) Which would you rather see President Obama do -- [ROTATED: keep the number of U.S. troops in Afghanistan about the same as now (or) begin to withdraw U.S. troops from Afghanistan]?

Combined responses

	All Americans	Democrats	Independents	Republicans
Favor more U.S. troops in Afghanistan	48%	36%	41%	73%
Oppose more troops, prefer to keep current level	5%	5%	6%	4%
Oppose more troops, U.S. should begin to withdraw	38%	50%	44%	18%
Oppose more troops, unspecified	2%	4%	<0.5%	1%
No opinion	7%	5%	9%	5%

USA Today/Gallup, Oct. 6, 2009

In a broad sense, Americans agree that there are legitimate reasons to have troops in Afghanistan. For example, the poll finds 80% of Americans saying that weakening terrorists' ability to stage attacks against the United States is an important reason to keep U.S. troops stationed there. Somewhat fewer (69%), but still well above a majority, believe keeping the Taliban from taking control of Afghanistan is an important reason to have U.S. troops in that country. Americans are least likely to think that building a stable democratic government in the country is an important reason to keep U.S. troops in Afghanistan, but a majority (51%) still do.

Do you think that each of these is, or is not, an important reason to keep U.S. troops in Afghanistan? How about -- [RANDOM ORDER]?

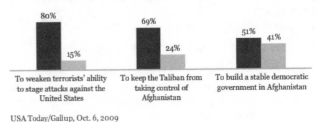

USA Today/Gallup, Oct. 6, 2009

Americans, however, are far from convinced that the United States is currently making progress toward these goals. Slim majorities think the U.S. is making progress toward weakening terrorist operations and keeping the Taliban from power. Less than one-third see progress toward building a stable democratic government. This might be understandable because nearly two months after the Afghan presidential election, an official winner has not been announced as allegations of fraud are investigated.

From what you know or have read, do you think the United States' military action in Afghanistan is or is not making progress toward achieving each of the following goals. How about -- [RANDOM ORDER]?

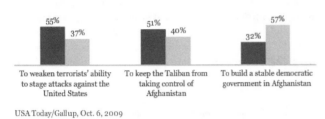

USA Today/Gallup, Oct. 6, 2009

Bottom Line

Though Americans are somewhat more supportive of increasing the number of U.S. troops in Afghanistan than they were a few weeks ago, they are still divided on the issue. Thus, the public does not appear to be providing President Obama with clear guidance on how it would like him to handle this difficult issue. Even so, Americans do see legitimate reasons for the United States to keep troops in Afghanistan, although significant proportions doubt that the United States is currently achieving those goals.

Survey Methods

Results are based on telephone interviews with 1,007 national adults, aged 18 and older, conducted Oct. 6, 2009. For results based on the total sample of national adults, one can say with 95% confidence that the maximum margin of sampling error is ±4 percentage points.

Interviews are conducted with respondents on land-line telephones and cellular phones.

In addition to sampling error, question wording and practical difficulties in conducting surveys can introduce error or bias into the findings of public opinion polls.

Polls conducted entirely in one day, such as this one, are subject to additional error or bias not found in polls conducted over several days.

October 09, 2009
IN U.S., RECORD-LOW SUPPORT FOR STRICTER GUN LAWS
Forty-four percent favor stricter laws on firearm sales

by Jeffrey M. Jones, Gallup Poll Managing Editor

Gallup finds a new low of 44% of Americans saying the laws covering firearm sales should be made more strict. That is down 5 points in the last year and 34 points from the high of 78% recorded the first time the question was asked, in 1990.

In general, do you feel that the laws covering the sale of firearms should be made more strict, less strict, or kept as they are now?

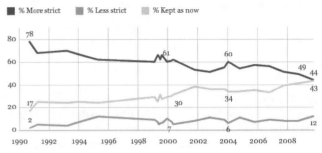

Today, Americans are as likely to say the laws governing gun sales should be kept as they are now (43%) as to say they should be made more strict. Until this year, Gallup had always found a significantly higher percentage advocating stricter laws. At the same time, 12% of Americans believe the laws should be less strict, which is low in an absolute sense but ties the highest Gallup has measured for this response.

These results are based on Gallup's annual Crime Poll, conducted Oct.1-4 this year.

The poll also shows a new low in the percentage of Americans favoring a ban on handgun possession except by the police and other authorized persons, a question that dates back to 1959. Only 28% now favor such a ban. The high point in support for a handgun-possession ban was 60% in the initial measurement in 1959. Since then, less than a majority has been in favor, and support has been below 40% since December 1993.

Do you think there should or should not be a law that would ban the possession of handguns, except by the police and other authorized persons?

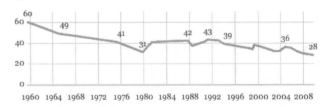

The trends on the questions about gun-sale laws and a handgun-possession ban indicate that Americans' attitudes have moved toward being more pro-gun rights. But this is not due to a growth in personal gun ownership, which has held steady around 30% this decade, or to an increase in household gun ownership, which has been steady in the low 40% range since 2000.

Gun Ownership in the United States

Nor are more pro-gun attitudes a specific reaction to the election of a Democratic president, Barack Obama, whose support for gun rights is questioned at times. Though the trends on both the gun-sales and the gun-possession measures have moved in a slightly more pro-gun direction this year compared to last, both trends had been moving in that direction during the latter part of the Bush administration, which strongly supported gun rights.

Rather, Americans as a whole may just be more accepting of gun rights now than in the past. Compared with views in 2000, each major demographic or attitudinal subgroup has shown a shift toward a more pro-gun stance on the question about whether gun laws should be more strict or less strict. (The results are similar on the question of a ban on handgun possession, with nearly every major demographic group less supportive of a ban now than at the start of the decade.)

Percentage Believing Gun Laws Should Be More Strict, by Subgroup, 2000 and 2009 Gallup Polls

	2000	2009	Change
All U.S. adults	62	44	-18
Men	52	33	-19
Women	72	55	-17
White	61	42	-19
Nonwhite	74	51	-23
18-29 years old	69	48	-21
30-49 years old	64	44	-20
50-64 years old	49	44	-5
65+ years old	64	45	-19
East	76	59	-17
Midwest	59	42	-17
South	59	42	-17
West	57	37	-20
Postgraduate education	68	55	-13
College graduate only	67	44	-23
Some college	59	44	-15
High school graduate or less	62	40	-22
Conservative	48	30	-18
Moderate	67	48	-19
Liberal	78	67	-11
Republican	44	28	-16
Independent	61	38	-23
Democrat	81	66	-15
Gun owner	40	20	-20
Gun non-owner	76	57	-19

Even with the change, there are some subgroups among whom a majority continues to favor stricter gun laws, including liberals (67%), Democrats (66%), Easterners (59%), gun non-owners (57%), postgraduates (55%), women (55%), and nonwhites (51%).

The groups least in favor of stricter gun laws are gun owners (20%), Republicans (28%), conservatives (30%), and men (33%).

Bottom Line

Americans continue to trend toward holding attitudes that are more in favor of gun rights, and Gallup today finds new low points in favor of gun control on two separate measures dating back at least two decades. While solidly against a ban on handgun possession, Americans are nonetheless about equally likely to say they favor stricter laws on firearm sales as to say these laws should not change. Still, the current poll marks the first time Gallup has not found a significantly higher proportion of Americans preferring tighter gun-sale regulations.

Survey Methods

Results are based on telephone interviews with 1,013 national adults, aged 18 and older, conducted Oct. 1-4, 2009. For results based on the total sample of national adults, one can say with 95% confidence that the maximum margin of sampling error is ±4 percentage points.

Interviews are conducted with respondents on land-line telephones (for respondents with a land-line telephone) and cellular phones (for respondents who are cell-phone only).

In addition to sampling error, question wording and practical difficulties in conducting surveys can introduce error or bias into the findings of public opinion polls.

October 12, 2009

OBAMA JOB APPROVAL AT 56% AFTER NOBEL WIN
Highest rating in more than two months

by Jeffrey M. Jones, Gallup Poll Managing Editor

Barack Obama appears to have gotten a slight bounce in support after he was announced as the Nobel Peace Prize winner on Friday. His 56% job approval rating for the last two Gallup Daily tracking updates is up from a term-low 50% as recently as last week, and 53% in the three days before the Nobel winner was announced.

Barack Obama's Presidential Job Approval Ratings During the Past Week
Gallup Daily tracking

■ % Approve

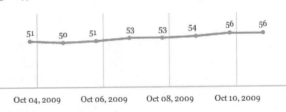

The positive momentum in Obama's approval rating is a departure from recent months, as his support has generally declined or been stagnant during this time. He has been below 60% since mid-July, and had been below 55% since early September. The current 56% approval rating is his best since a 58% reading in Aug. 5-7 polling.

It is unclear, however, whether Obama will be able to sustain the positive momentum of the past few days, especially after the president's and public's attention turns away from his surprise Nobel

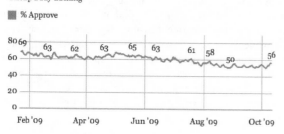

Barack Obama's Presidential Job Approval Ratings

Gallup Daily tracking

■ % Approve

Peace Prize win back to the legislative debate over health insurance reform and the administration's decision about what to do next in Afghanistan. Indeed, after Obama's approval ratings increased in Friday and Saturday interviewing, Obama's support in Sunday's polling was slightly lower.

In fact, odds are the bump will not last, since the improvement in his rating from his term-low 50% early last week has come exclusively among independents and Republicans, who are less likely to stay loyal to the president. Democratic support has not changed after Friday's Nobel announcement.

Change in Obama Job Approval Rating, Oct. 3-5 vs. Oct. 9-11

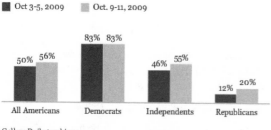

■ Oct 3-5, 2009   ■ Oct. 9-11, 2009

Gallup Daily tracking

Bottom Line

The public has taken a slightly more positive view of the president since he was announced as the Nobel Peace Prize winner last Friday, although his approval rating already seemed to be recovering somewhat even before the announcement (to 53%) from a 50% term-low early last week. But since Friday, his approval rating has gotten an additional boost and is now at levels not seen for Obama in over two months.

Survey Methods

Results are based on telephone interviews with 1,532 national adults, aged 18 and older, conducted Oct. 9-11, 2009, as part of Gallup Daily tracking. For results based on the total sample of national adults, one can say with 95% confidence that the maximum margin of sampling error is ±3 percentage points.

Interviews are conducted with respondents on land-line telephones and cellular phones.

In addition to sampling error, question wording and practical difficulties in conducting surveys can introduce error or bias into the findings of public opinion polls.

October 13, 2009

IN U.S., TWO-THIRDS CONTINUE TO SUPPORT DEATH PENALTY

Little change in recent years despite international opposition

by Frank Newport, Gallup Poll Editor in Chief

Gallup's annual Crime Survey finds that 65% of Americans continue to support the use of the death penalty for persons convicted of murder, while 31% oppose it—continuing a trend that has shown little change over the last six years.

Are you in favor of the death penalty for a person convicted of murder?

2001-2009 trends from Gallup Poll Crime Survey, conducted each October

■ % In favor   ■ % Not in favor

Opponents of the death penalty have pointed out that just five countries—China, Iran, Pakistan, Saudi Arabia, and the United States—carry out most of the known executions around the world, and that the number of countries that still allow the death penalty has been dwindling. Despite these worldwide trends, Gallup's annual October update on Americans' attitudes toward the death penalty shows no diminution in support for state-sanctioned executions in cases of murder. The current 65% support level is roughly equal with what has been measured for most of this decade.

Gallup's death-penalty data stretch back more than seven decades—making attitudes toward the death penalty one of Gallup's oldest trends. Gallup's earliest reading, in 1936, found that 59% of Americans supported the use of the death penalty in cases of murder, compared to 38% who opposed it. The all-time high level of 80% support came in September 1994, just before the midterm elections that swept Democrats out of power and at a time when Americans most often cited crime as the most important problem facing the nation. The low points came in the period of time from the mid-1950s through the early 1970s. During some of this time, the death penalty was illegal, and support dropped as low as 42% in 1966.

Are you in favor of the death penalty for a person convicted of murder?

■ % In favor   ■ % Not in favor

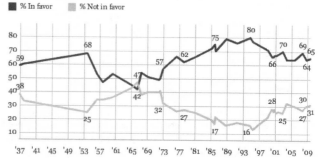

This year's update also shows that nearly half (49%) of Americans say the death penalty is not imposed often enough, roughly in

line with the trend on this measure since 2002. Twenty-four percent say it is imposed "about the right amount," while 20% say it is imposed too often—a percentage that has been only as high as 23% in recent years.

In your opinion, is the death penalty imposed -- [too often, about the right amount, or not often enough]?

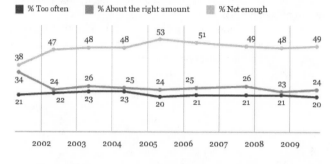

Opponents of the death penalty often argue that it is applied unfairly—that members of certain minority groups are more likely to receive the death penalty than others convicted of the same crimes, or that the arbitrary differences in trial procedures, judges, and jurisdictions can make a difference in who receives the death penalty and who doesn't. Still, a majority of Americans—57%—say they believe the death penalty is applied fairly in the country today, while 34% say it is applied unfairly. The "fairly" percentage is down slightly from the decade's high point of 61% in 2005.

Generally speaking, do you believe the death penalty is applied fairly or unfairly in this country today?

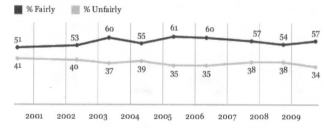

Another argument against the death penalty focuses on cases in which it has been shown that innocent people have been put to death. The finality of execution obviously precludes the possibility of redress if, at some later point, DNA or other evidence finds that the individual in question was wrongly convicted of his or her crime. The American public would appear to be somewhat sympathetic to this argument: this year's poll finds 59% of Americans agreeing that within the last five years, "a person has been executed under the death penalty who was, in fact, innocent of the crime he or she was charged with." A little less than a third disagree.

However, for many Americans, agreement with the assertion that innocent people have been put to death does not preclude simultaneous endorsement of the death penalty. A third of all Americans, 34%, believe an innocent person has been executed and at the same time support the death penalty. This is higher than the 23% who believe an innocent person has been executed and simultaneously oppose the death penalty.

Looked at differently, the data show that 57% of those who believe an innocent person has been executed also support the death

How often do you think that a person has been executed under the death penalty who was, in fact, innocent of the crime he or she was charged with -- do you think this has happened in the past five years, or not?

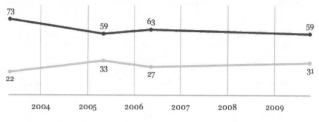

Relationship Between Support for Death Penalty and Belief That an Innocent Person Has Been Executed in the Last Five Years

Each number of a percentage of the total sample

	Believe that an innocent person has been executed in the last five years	Do not believe that an innocent person has been executed in the last five years
Support the death penalty in cases of murder	34%	23%
Opposed to the death penalty	25%	5%

penalty. This is significantly higher than the 39% who hold this belief and (perhaps more consistently) oppose the death penalty.

Partisan Differences

The death penalty is favored by most Republicans nationwide, but it also receives the general support of a solid majority of independents. Support for and opposition to the death penalty are roughly even among Democrats.

Support for the Death Penalty, by Party ID

Oct. 1-4, 2009

An Explicit Alternative to the Death Penalty?

Gallup research has found that support for the death penalty is lower if Americans are offered an explicit alternative—"life imprisonment, with absolutely no possibility of parole." In May 2006, for example, 65% of Americans supported the death penalty in general (matching the current figure), while, separately, 47% said they preferred the death penalty to life imprisonment as a penalty for murder when given that choice (48% favored life imprisonment).

Bottom Line

Despite a worldwide decline in the use of the death penalty, and the fact that it is outlawed in the majority of countries across the world, about two-thirds of Americans continue to support its use, similar to recent years' updates. Additionally, almost three-quarters of Americans believe that the death penalty is either used with about the right frequency today or not used often enough. Opponents of the death penalty often focus on the fact that individuals put to death have later been found to be innocent. But the data show that a campaign to increase belief that this situation occurs may not by itself increase opposition to the death penalty. A majority of Americans already agree that an innocent person has been executed within the last five years, but a majority of these simultaneously say they still support the use of the death penalty.

Survey Methods

Results are based on telephone interviews with 1,013 national adults, aged 18 and older, conducted Oct. 1-4, 2009. For results based on the total sample of national adults, one can say with 95% confidence that the maximum margin of sampling error is ±4 percentage points.

Interviews are conducted with respondents on land-line telephones (for respondents with a land-line telephone) and cellular phones (for respondents who are cell-phone only).

In addition to sampling error, question wording and practical difficulties in conducting surveys can introduce error or bias into the findings of public opinion polls.

October 14, 2009
AMERICANS PERCEIVE INCREASED CRIME IN U.S.

Nearly three in four, highest since early 1990s, believe there is more crime this year than last

by Jeffrey M. Jones, Gallup Poll Managing Editor

Gallup's annual Crime poll finds 74% of Americans saying there is more crime in the United States than there was a year ago, the highest measured since the early 1990s.

Is there more crime in the U.S. than there was a year ago, or less?

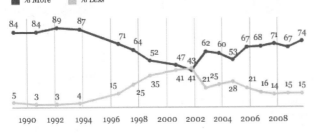

Gallup typically finds Americans perceiving increased crime in the United States, compared to the prior year. Only once—in October 2001—has this not been the case. Since 2005, however, the percentage saying there is more crime has been at or above the two-thirds level, something it had not been since 1996. In the late 1980s through the early 1990s, more than 8 in 10 Americans perceived crime to be increasing.

Whether there actually has been an increase in crime this year is hard to substantiate at this point, since official crime statistics for 2009 will not be released until next year. The most recent statistics, for the year 2008, show that crime in the U.S. decreased last year from 2007. Consistent with that change, Gallup's 2008 measurement

also showed a decline in the percentage of Americans perceiving more crime in the United States, from 71% in 2007 to 67% in 2008.

In addition to perceiving more crime this year in the United States as a whole, Americans also report an increase in local crime. The poll finds 51% of Americans saying there is more crime in their areas now than a year ago, up from 44% in 2008 but the same as the 2006-2007 results. The current data reflect the highest percentage Gallup has measured this decade and are just slightly lower than the record high of 54% in 1981 and 1992.

Since 2005, more Americans have indicated that there is increased rather than decreased crime in their local areas, but around the turn of the century, the opposite was true.

Is there more crime in your area than there was a year ago, or less?

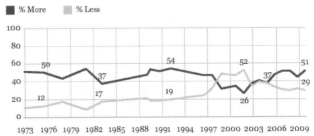

Residents of the South are most likely to perceive an increase in local crime (59%), compared with 50% of those living in the Midwest, 46% in the East, and 45% in the West.

Is there more crime in your area than there was a year ago, or less?
Results by region

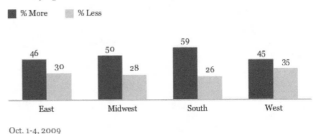

Oct. 1-4, 2009

Perceptions of greater local crime, however, have not led Americans to believe the crime problem is much more serious now than in the past. Twelve percent describe the problem of crime in their areas as either "extremely serious" or "very serious," essentially unchanged from last year (11%), and little different from what Gallup has measured since 2000. A majority of Americans have consistently described the crime problem in their local areas as "not too serious" or "not serious at all."

As has been the case, many more Americans view the crime problem in the United States as very serious, now 55% after dipping to 51% last year. Forty percent say the U.S. crime problem is "moderately serious" while 3% say it is not serious.

Bottom Line

Americans believe crime is on the rise both in the United States and in their local areas this year. The 2009 official government crime statistics reported next year will indicate whether that is in fact true. The perceived increase does not appear, however, to be a largely politi-

Overall, how would you describe the problem of crime in the area where you live -- is it extremely serious, very serious, moderately serious, not too serious, or not serious at all?

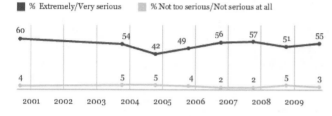

■ % Extremely/Very serious   ░ % Not too serious/Not serious at all

Overall, how would you describe the problem of crime in the United States -- is it extremely serious, very serious, moderately serious, not too serious, or not serious at all?

■ % Extremely/Very serious   ░ % Not too serious/Not serious at all

cal phenomenon, as at least 7 in 10 Democrats, Republicans, and independents all believe there is increased crime in the United States.

Even though the percentages seeing increases in crime at both local and national levels are the highest Gallup has seen in more than a decade, crime does not appear to be turning into a major issue at this point. The ratings of the seriousness of the crime problem are not much higher now than in the recent past, and crime continues to rank fairly low when Americans are asked to name the most important problem facing the country.

Survey Methods

Results are based on telephone interviews with 1,013 national adults, aged 18 and older, conducted Oct. 1-4, 2009. For results based on the total sample of national adults, one can say with 95% confidence that the maximum margin of sampling error is ±4 percentage points.

Interviews are conducted with respondents on land-line telephones (for respondents with a land-line telephone) and cellular phones (for respondents who are cell-phone only).

In addition to sampling error, question wording and practical difficulties in conducting surveys can introduce error or bias into the findings of public opinion polls.

October 14, 2009
U.S. SATISFACTION SINKS TO SIX-MONTH LOW
Economy remains nation's most important problem, but mentions of it are down

by Lydia Saad, Gallup Poll Senior Editor

Americans' satisfaction with the United States is no better today than a month ago; if anything, it may be a bit worse. Twenty-six percent of Americans interviewed Oct. 1-4 say they are satisfied with the way

things are going in the country, down slightly from 29% in early September. Currently, 71% are dissatisfied, the highest level since March.

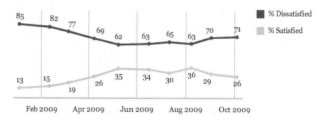

U.S. Satisfaction -- 2009 Trend
In general, are you satisfied or dissatisfied with the way things are going in the United States at this time?

■ % Dissatisfied   ░ % Satisfied

After starting the year at near-record-low levels, U.S. satisfaction increased, peaking at 36% in early August, but fell to 29% by late August/early September before edging down to today's 26%.

The reason for declining satisfaction since August is not clear from the issues Americans name as the nation's "most important problem"—a question Gallup asks each month. While the economy continues to be the top-ranked problem, the percentage citing it has been trending downward in recent months. At the same time, since early August there have been only minor increases in the percentages naming other highly ranked issues, including unemployment and dissatisfaction with government, and there has been no real change in mentions of healthcare, Iraq, or the federal budget deficit.

Most Important Problem -- Recent Trend in Top Mentions
What do you think is the most important problem facing this country today?

	Aug 6-9, 2009	Aug 31-Sep 2, 2009	Oct 1-4, 2009
	%	%	%
Economy in general	33	29	26
Healthcare/Healthcare costs	25	26	22
Unemployment/Jobs	14	15	17
Dissatisfaction with government	7	10	11
Federal budget deficit/Federal debt	7	9	5
Lack of money	6	5	4
Situation/War in Iraq	3	3	4
Ethics/Moral/Religious/Family decline	2	5	4
Situation/War in Afghanistan	1	1	3
Wars (nonspecific)	2	4	3

The 26% citing the economy in general this month is down from 33% in early August and well below the 48% seen in April. In fact, mentions of the economy have declined, at least slightly, each month since February and are now at their lowest level since January 2008. However, since last year, some of this concern has been redirected into unemployment; that issue shows a sharp increase in mentions this year compared with 2008.

The trend in satisfaction by party identification may offer some insights about the cause of the overall decline. Most of the decrease in U.S. satisfaction since August has occurred among independents (down 10 points) and Democrats (down 14 points), with little change seen among Republicans—whose satisfaction was already quite low.

A similar pattern is seen in Congress's job ratings this month, with approval dropping sharply since late August/early September

Most Important Problem -- 2008-2009 Trend in Top Economic Mentions

■ % Economy in general   ■ % Unemployment/Jobs   ■ % Federal budget deficit/Federal debt

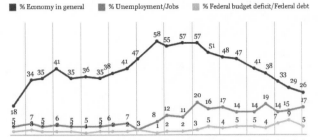

Feb '08 Apr '08 Jun '08 Aug '08 Oct '08 Dec '08 Feb '09 Apr '09 Jun '09 Aug '09 Oct '09

U.S. Satisfaction Since August -- Percent Satisfied, by Party ID

■ Aug 6-8, 2009   ■ Aug 31-Sep 2, 2009   ■ Oct 1-4, 2009

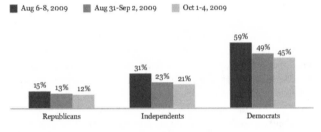

Republicans   Independents   Democrats

among Democrats and moderately among independents, but showing little change among Republicans.

Bottom Line

Americans' satisfaction with the country remains higher than at the start of the year; however, some of the increase seen on this measure in the first half of 2009 has been erased since August. Neither the economy, generally, nor unemployment specifically are obvious causes, as the percentages of Americans naming these as the nation's top problem have either not changed much or declined in recent months. Given that the decline in Americans' satisfaction is mainly concentrated among Democrats and independents, and that the pattern is mirrored in approval ratings of Congress, Congress' recent actions—or inaction—may be an important factor.

Survey Methods

Results are based on telephone interviews with 1,013 national adults, aged 18 and older, conducted Oct. 1-4, 2009. For results based on the total sample of national adults, one can say with 95% confidence that the maximum margin of sampling error is ±4 percentage points.

Interviews are conducted with respondents on land-line telephones (for respondents with a land-line telephone) and cellular phones (for respondents who are cell-phone only).

In addition to sampling error, question wording and practical difficulties in conducting surveys can introduce error or bias into the findings of public opinion polls.

October 15, 2009

AMERICANS SEE LITTLE HOPE OF FINDING A QUALITY JOB

Regional job conditions slightly better than earlier this year but remain far below a year ago

by Dennis Jacobe, Gallup Chief Economist

Gallup finds 10% of Americans feeling that now is a "good time" to find a quality job, reflecting no improvement since February, and less than the 33% who held similar views as the recession began in January 2008 and the 14% recorded as the financial crisis hit the economy in full force last October.

Finding a Quality Job Nationwide

Thinking about the job situation in America today, would you say that it is now a good time or a bad time to find a quality job?

■ % "Good time"

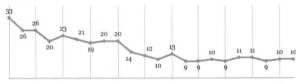

Jan '08 Mar '08 May '08 Jul '08 Sep '08 Nov '08 Jan '09 Mar '09 May '09 Jul '09 Sep '09

National job-creation trends, according to Gallup's Job Creation Index—a separate measure based on U.S. employees' self-reports of job conditions at their places of work—confirm Americans' perceptions that this is not a good time to be looking for work.

Job Creation Index, Nationwide, 2008-2009

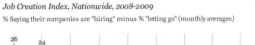
% Saying their companies are "hiring" minus % "letting go" (monthly averages)

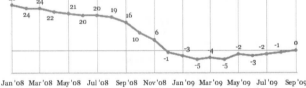

Jan '08 Mar '08 May '08 Jul '08 Sep '08 Nov '08 Jan '09 Mar '09 May '09 Jul '09 Sep '09

Gallup Daily tracking

Survey Methods

Results are based on telephone interviews with 1,013 national adults, aged 18 and older, conducted Oct. 1-4, 2009. For results based on the total sample of national adults, one can say with 95% confidence that the maximum margin of error is ±4 percentage points.

For Gallup Poll Daily tracking, Gallup interviews approximately 1,000 national adults, aged 18 and older, each day. The Gallup consumer spending results are based on random half-samples of approximately 500 national adults, aged 18 and older, each day. The Gallup Job Creation Index results are based on a random half sample of approximately 250 current full- and part-time employees each day.

Regional results for September are based on Gallup Poll Daily tracking interviews totaling more than 1,500 in all regions. For the total regional samples of these surveys, one can say with 95% confidence that the maximum margin of sampling error is ±3 percentage points.

Interviews are conducted with respondents on land-line telephones (for respondents with a land-line telephone) and cellular phones (for respondents who are cell-phone only).

In addition to sampling error, question wording and practical difficulties in conducting surveys can introduce error or bias into the findings of public opinion polls.

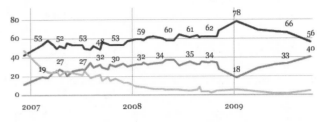

Favorable Ratings of Barack Obama

October 15, 2009
HILLARY CLINTON NOW MORE POPULAR THAN BARACK OBAMA
Secretary of state viewed favorably by 62% of Americans, president by 56%

by Jeffrey M. Jones, Gallup Poll Managing Editor

Hillary Clinton lost the 2008 Democratic presidential nomination to Barack Obama, but in one respect she now ranks ahead of Obama. The president's current favorable rating of 56% is down 22 percentage points since January. Over the same time span, Clinton's favorable rating has changed little, and now, at 62%, it exceeds Obama's.

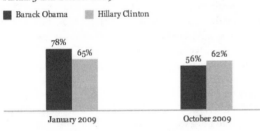

Favorable Ratings of Barack Obama and Hillary Clinton, January and October 2009

The results are based on an Oct. 1-4 Gallup survey. The poll was conducted before Obama was named the 2009 Nobel Peace Prize winner, which could have helped to improve his favorable rating over the 56% measured in the poll; however, it's not clear that any such shift would have lasted. In the first days after the prize's announcement, Obama's presidential job approval rating noticeably increased, but it has since retreated to its prior level.

The change in the relative popularity of Clinton and Obama since January may reflect the realities of their new roles. Obama came into office as president with a 78% favorable rating, among the highest Gallup has measured since it began tracking favorability in 1992. But after nearly nine months in office in which he has made or confronted difficult decisions—ranging from the economic stimulus package, to the auto industry bailout, to the wars in Iraq and Afghanistan, to health insurance reform, Obama's support has declined. His favorable rating now stands at 56%, and has fallen 10 points just since the last reading, in July. (Obama's job approval rating has followed a similar downward trajectory.)

The 56% favorable rating for Obama is his lowest since late 2007, when he had a 53% favorable rating, but at that time, 13% of Americans did not have an opinion of him. The current 40% unfavorable rating for Obama is his highest, and thus his most negative such rating to date.

Meanwhile, Clinton has helped advance Obama's foreign policy around the world, but in a far less prominent role than the president's. Now operating in a much less bright spotlight than Obama does, the former first lady's and U.S. senator's favorable rating remains strong at 62%, little changed since she became secretary of state.

Clinton's current favorable rating ranks among her best in the 17 years Gallup has polled Americans about her. Her highest favorable rating of 67% came in late December 1998, just after her husband, President Bill Clinton, was impeached by the U.S. House of Representatives.

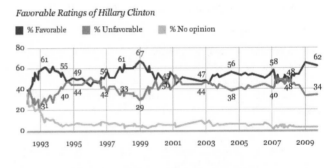

Favorable Ratings of Hillary Clinton

Partisan Views of Clinton and Obama

Clinton and Obama are about equally appreciated by Democrats—91% currently have favorable opinions of Clinton and 89% have favorable views of Obama. They fare about equally among independents, but Republicans have more positive views of Clinton (35%) than of Obama (19%).

Favorable Ratings of Hillary Clinton and Barack Obama, January and October 2009, by Political Party

	Democrats	Independents	Republicans
October			
Obama	89%	52%	19%
Clinton	91%	55%	35%
January			
Obama	95%	75%	60%
Clinton	93%	61%	35%

Republicans' more positive views of Clinton relative to Obama mark a reversal since January, when Republican ratings of Obama (60%) were much more positive than those of Clinton (35%). Thus, Obama's favorable rating has declined 41 points among Republicans since January, while Clinton's has not moved at all.

Independents' opinions of Obama have also soured, from 75% favorable to 52%. There have been only minor declines in Democrats' opinions of Obama.

Survey Methods

Results are based on telephone interviews with 1,013 national adults, aged 18 and older, conducted Oct. 1-4, 2009. For results based on the total sample of national adults, one can say with 95% confidence that the maximum margin of sampling error is ±4 percentage points.

Interviews are conducted with respondents on land-line telephones (for respondents with a land-line telephone) and cellular phones (for respondents who are cell-phone only).

In addition to sampling error, question wording and practical difficulties in conducting surveys can introduce error or bias into the findings of public opinion polls.

October 16, 2009
JOHN EDWARDS, SARAH PALIN BOTH SEE FAVORABLE RATINGS SLIDE
Edwards' popularity down 27 points since January 2008

by Jeffrey M. Jones, Gallup Poll Senior Editor

Former presidential and vice presidential candidate John Edwards, embroiled in personal scandal, is rated favorably by 21% of Americans and unfavorably by 59%. This is the first time more Americans have viewed Edwards negatively than positively, and reflects a 27-point drop in his favorable rating from Gallup's prior measurement in January 2008.

Favorable Ratings of John Edwards

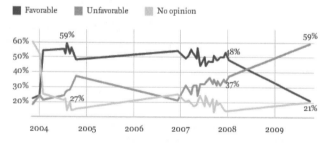

Edwards' favorable rating peaked at 59% in late July/early August 2004, after his nomination as John Kerry's vice presidential running mate at the Democratic National Convention that year. He averaged a 50% favorable rating from that point until he ended his subsequent 2008 presidential bid in January of that year.

Now, following his admission that he had an extramarital affair during his 2008 presidential campaign and allegations that Edwards' campaign made illegal payments to his mistress, Edwards' favorable rating has dropped 27 percentage points. Gallup has never before found as steep a decline in consecutive measurements of a prominent figure using the favorable/unfavorable format, which it began using in 1992.

The prior steepest declines were 24-point drops for the Rev. Jesse Jackson from 1999 to 2000 and baseball player Sammy Sosa

Largest Declines in Favorable Ratings Between Measurements, Gallup Polls, 1992-2009

	Decline (pct. pts.)	First measurement	Next measurement
John Edwards	27	48% (Jan '08)	21% (Oct '09)
Jesse Jackson	24	70% (May '99)	46% (Dec '00)
Sammy Sosa	24	83% (Dec '98)	59% (Jun '03)
Tom Cruise	23	58% (June '05)	35% (May '06)
Lamar Alexander	23	40% (Feb '96)	17% (Mar '99)
Mark McGwire	19	72% (Jun '00)	53% (Mar '05)
Ross Perot	18	38% (Jul '92)	20% (Sep '92)
Pope John Paul II	17	86% (Dec '98)	69% (Jan '99)
Arnold Schwarzenegger	16	72% (Feb '03)	56% (Aug '04)
Martha Stewart	16	46% (Jun '02)	30% (Jul '02)

from 1998 to 2003. Jackson's high 70% favorable rating in 1999 came after successful diplomatic missions to Yugoslavia and Sierra Leone in the spring of that year; his favorable score settled to a more typical 46% reading for him in late 2000. Thus, his 24-point drop was more due to the disappearance of his "bounce" than to an increasingly negative evaluation of him. However, that is not the case for Sosa, whose 83% rating in 1998 came after a season in which he and Mark McGwire battled to break Roger Maris' single-season home-run record, but who in 2003 was suspended for illegally doctoring his bat.

Gallup has seen larger declines in public figures' images in nonconsecutive polls. For example, George W. Bush's favorable rating fell from 87% shortly after the Sept. 11 terrorist attacks to 32% in his final year in office, a change of 55 points. Jackson's rating dropped to as low as 33% in March 2001 after Jackson admitted he fathered a child out of wedlock, a total drop of 37 points from his high. Rudy Giuliani experienced a 32-point decline spanning December 2006 to January 2008.

Edwards is far from the most reviled figure Gallup has polled about. His 57% unfavorable rating is well below those Gallup has measured for Osama bin Laden (97%), Saddam Hussein (96%), Mark Fuhrman (87%), Fidel Castro (83%), Monica Lewinsky (82%), and Yasser Arafat (80%). The highest unfavorable rating for a U.S. politician is 79% for David Duke.

While Edwards' national political career is most certainly finished, another former vice presidential candidate, Sarah Palin, may be just beginning hers. Palin became a bit of a sensation after John McCain tapped her as his running mate last August. But over the course of the campaign, her image suffered, going from a 53% favorable rating immediately after the 2008 Republican National Convention to 42% by the end of the campaign.

Palin's ratings have not recovered, and her current 40% favorable rating is the lowest for her since she became widely known after last year's Republican convention.

Favorable Ratings of Sarah Palin

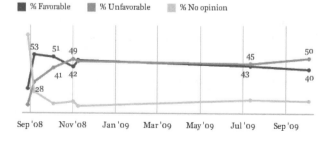

Despite the increasingly negative views of Palin overall, she is still seen as a possible contender for the 2012 Republican presidential nomination. Indeed, when Gallup tested a field of possible GOP candidates, Palin was competitive with Mitt Romney and Mike Huckabee for the lead.

Palin could compete for the 2012 nomination because she is still widely liked by Republicans—69% have a favorable opinion of her while only 25% view her unfavorably. But she may have difficulty succeeding in the general election, given that Democrats have overwhelmingly negative opinions of her, and independents view her more negatively than positively.

Favorable Ratings of Sarah Palin, by Political Party

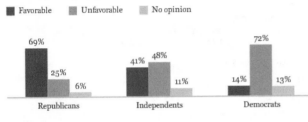

Gallup Poll, Oct. 1-4, 2009

Bottom Line

John Edwards in part used his 2004 vice presidential nomination as a springboard to a run for the presidency in 2008. After it became clear that the Democrats' choice would come down to Barack Obama or Hillary Clinton, he magnanimously suspended his campaign to let those two battle it out. Later that year, his scandal surfaced, and his image has suffered greatly as a result.

Palin may follow a similar path of moving from vice presidential candidate in one presidential election cycle to presidential candidate in the next. She has stayed in the news since the 2008 campaign ended, with her surprise decision to resign as governor earlier this year perhaps attracting the most attention. While Edwards was able to maintain a positive image between the 2004 and 2008 elections, Palin so far has not been able to do the same from the end of the 2008 campaign until now, with her favorable rating now down to 40%.

Survey Methods

Results are based on telephone interviews with 1,013 national adults, aged 18 and older, conducted Oct. 1-4, 2009. For results based on the total sample of national adults, one can say with 95% confidence that the maximum margin of sampling error is ±4 percentage points.

Interviews are conducted with respondents on land-line telephones (for respondents with a land-line telephone) and cellular phones (for respondents who are cell-phone only).

In addition to sampling error, question wording and practical difficulties in conducting surveys can introduce error or bias into the findings of public opinion polls.

October 16, 2009
TWO IN THREE AMERICANS WORRY ABOUT IDENTITY THEFT
Being a victim of car theft or home burglary when away rank a distant second

by Lydia Saad, Gallup Poll Senior Editor

Identity theft debuts on Gallup's Crime survey as Americans' top-ranked crime concern. Sixty-six percent of U.S. adults say they worry "frequently" or "occasionally" about being a victim of identity theft, higher than the reported anxiety about 11 other types of crime and the only crime that a majority worry about at least occasionally.

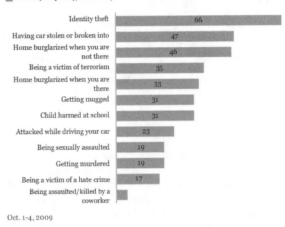

How often do you, yourself, worry about the following things -- frequently, occasionally, rarely, or never?

Oct. 1-4, 2009

Gallup trends measuring Americans' fear of being victims of specific crimes date back several decades, but for each of 10 crimes, the question has been updated annually on Gallup's Crime survey since 2000. Terrorism was added to the list in 2001, and 2009 marks the first year identity theft has been included.

Just under half of Americans worry frequently or occasionally about having their cars stolen or broken into (47%), as well as about having their homes burglarized when they are not there (46%). Roughly a third worry about being terrorism victims, having their homes burglarized when they are there, having their school-aged children physically harmed while attending school, and getting mugged.

Around 20% worry at least occasionally about being attacked while driving, being murdered, sexually assaulted, or being a hate-crime victim. Workplace violence places a distant last on the list, with 4% of all Americans saying this is something they worry about either frequently or occasionally. Even among employed Americans, the rate of worry on this item is a low 6%.

Gallup trends show little change over the past year in how much Americans worry about any of the different types of crime.

One example is the trend on fear of being a victim of terrorism. The 35% currently saying they frequently or occasionally worry about this is statistically similar to the levels recorded in 2007 and 2008.

Widespread Worry About Identity Theft

Among those who appear concerned about identity theft, 31% worry frequently—the highest level for any crime rated in 2009—and 35%

Trend in Worry About Being a Victim of Terrorism

■ % Worry frequently/occasionally

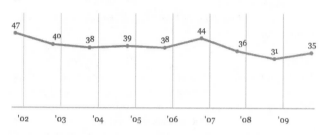

47	40	38	39	38	44	36	31	35
'02	'03	'04	'05	'06	'07	'08	'09

worry occasionally. Another 18% of Americans rarely worry about it, while 15%—the lowest for any crime—say they never worry.

Frequency of Worry About Being the Victim of Identity Theft

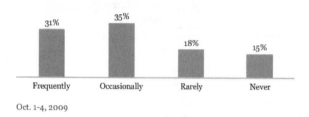

Frequently	Occasionally	Rarely	Never
31%	35%	18%	15%

Oct. 1-4, 2009

Men and women are about equally likely to say they worry about identity theft, but there are differences by income. Americans in households earning less than $30,000 per year are significantly less likely to say they worry frequently or occasionally about this crime than are those making higher amounts.

However, other data in the Oct. 1-4 survey suggest that identity theft is not related to income. According to respondents' self-reports of their crime victimization in the past year, 12% of low-income Americans—identical to the percentage in high-income households—say that they or another member of their household was the victim of identity theft in the past year.

Worry vs. Experience With Identity Theft -- by Household Income

■ Worry frequently/occasionally about identity theft

▨ Self or household member was the victim of identity theft in past year

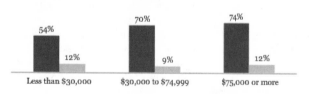

Less than $30,000	$30,000 to $74,999	$75,000 or more
54% / 12%	70% / 9%	74% / 12%

Americans report experiencing identity theft far less than they report worrying about it. Overall, 10% of all Americans say that they or another household member was the victim of identity theft in the past 12 months. This is slightly less than the 14% who say their household had a home, car, or other property vandalized, and the 16% who say money or property was stolen from their household. Fewer report that anyone in their household was the victim of a computer or an Internet crime (7%), had their apartment or home broken into (5%), or had a car stolen (3%). Even smaller percentages (1% to 2%) report having been victimized by various violent crimes.

Crime Victimization in Past Year

Please tell me which, if any, of these incidents have happened to you or your household within the last twelve months.

	% Yes, happened
Money or property stolen from you or another member of your household	16
A home, car, or property owned by you or another household member vandalized	14
You or another household member was the victim of identity theft	10
You or another household member was victim of computer-/Internet-based crime	7
Your house or apartment broken into	5
A car owned by you or another household member stolen	3
You or another household member mugged or physically assaulted	2
You or another household member sexually assaulted	1
Money or property taken by force, with gun, knife, weapon, or physical attack, or by threat of force	1

Oct. 1-4, 2009

Bottom Line

In 2009, identity theft is a top-of-mind crime for 66% of Americans, far more concerning to them than the typical violent crimes. One reason for the high level of worry about identity theft may be the spotlight that both lawmakers and identity-protection companies have turned on it. Although most victims can quickly undo the damage by canceling their credit cards, examples of people who have spent months or years trying to restore their credit or good name seem to have had an impact on Americans.

The high level of worry about identity theft is underscored by the much lower degrees of worry seen for other crimes—some of which may be more likely to happen.

Survey Methods

Results are based on telephone interviews with 1,013 national adults, aged 18 and older, conducted Oct. 1-4, 2009. For results based on the total sample of national adults, one can say with 95% confidence that the maximum margin of sampling error is ±4 percentage points.

Interviews are conducted with respondents on land-line telephones (for respondents with a land-line telephone) and cellular phones (for respondents who are cell-phone only).

In addition to sampling error, question wording and practical difficulties in conducting surveys can introduce error or bias into the findings of public opinion polls.

October 19, 2009

U.S. SUPPORT FOR LEGALIZING MARIJUANA REACHES NEW HIGH

Majority in the West favors taxing marijuana sales to boost state revenues

by Lydia Saad, Gallup Poll Senior Editor

Gallup's October Crime poll finds 44% of Americans in favor of making marijuana legal and 54% opposed. U.S. public support for legalizing marijuana was fixed in the 25% range from the late 1970s to the mid-1990s, but acceptance jumped to 31% in 2000 and has continued to grow throughout this decade.

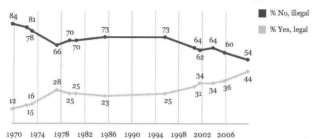

Support for Making Use of Marijuana Legal
Do you think the use of marijuana should be made legal, or not?

■ % No, illegal
▨ % Yes, legal

84 81 78 66 70 70 73 73 64 64 60 54
12 15 16 28 25 25 23 25 31 34 34 36 44 62

1970 1974 1978 1982 1986 1990 1994 1998 2002 2006

Public opinion is virtually the same on a question that relates to a public policy debate brewing in California—whether marijuana should be legalized and taxed as a way of raising revenue for state governments. Just over 4 in 10 Americans (42%) say they would favor this in their own state; 56% are opposed. Support is markedly higher among residents of the West—where an outright majority favor the proposal—than in the South and Midwest. The views of Eastern residents fall about in the middle.

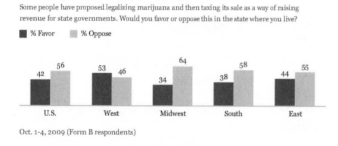

Views on Legalizing and Taxing Sale of Marijuana in Your State
Some people have proposed legalizing marijuana and then taxing its sale as a way of raising revenue for state governments. Would you favor or oppose this in the state where you live?

■ % Favor   ▨ % Oppose

	U.S.	West	Midwest	South	East
Favor	42	53	34	38	44
Oppose	56	46	64	58	55

Oct. 1-4, 2009 (Form B respondents)

The new findings come as the U.S. Justice Department has reportedly decided to loosen its enforcement of federal anti-marijuana laws by not pursuing individuals who buy or sell small amounts of the drug in conformity with their own states' medical marijuana laws. This seems likely to meet with U.S. public approval, as previous Gallup polling has found Americans generally sympathetic to legalizing marijuana for medical purposes. In 2003, 75% of Americans favored allowing doctors to legally prescribe marijuana to patients in order to reduce pain and suffering.

Bottom Line

Public mores on legalization of marijuana have been changing this decade, and are now at their most tolerant in at least 40 years. If public support were to continue growing at a rate of 1% to 2% per year, as it has since 2000, the majority of Americans could favor legalization of the drug in as little as four years.

Americans are no more—and no less—in favor of legalizing marijuana when the issue is framed as a revenue-enhancement tool for state governments. Regardless of how the question is asked, 53% of Americans living in the West—encompassing California, where the issue could be on the ballot in 2010—support legalization.

Survey Methods

Results are based on telephone interviews with 1,013 national adults, aged 18 and older, conducted Oct. 1-4, 2009. For results based on the total sample of national adults, one can say with 95% confidence that the maximum margin of sampling error is ±4 percentage points.

Interviews are conducted with respondents on land-line telephones (for respondents with a land-line telephone) and cellular phones (for respondents who are cell-phone only).

In addition to sampling error, question wording and practical difficulties in conducting surveys can introduce error or bias into the findings of public opinion polls.

October 20, 2009
MANY GUN OWNERS THINK OBAMA WILL TRY TO BAN GUN SALES
Fifty-five percent of this group, and 41% of all Americans, hold this belief

by Frank Newport, Gallup Poll Editor in Chief

A new Gallup poll may explain recent reports of increased gun and ammunition sales in the U.S. Majorities of those who personally own a gun (55%) and of those with a gun in the household (53%), as well as 41% of all Americans, believe that President Obama "will attempt to ban the sale of guns in the United States while he is president."

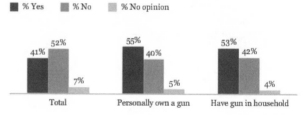

Just your best guess, do you think Barack Obama will attempt to ban the sale of guns in the United States while he is president, or not?

■ % Yes   ▨ % No   ▨ % No opinion

	Total	Personally own a gun	Have gun in household
Yes	41%	55%	53%
No	52%	40%	42%
No opinion	7%	5%	4%

Oct. 1-4, 2009

The issue of Obama's intentions relating to guns has particular relevance given the widespread news reports of sharply increased sales of guns and ammunition. Many of these reports suggest that the reason behind these increased sales is the belief—right or wrong—that the president intends to severely curtail the legal availability of guns and ammunition. A recent National Public Radio news story, for example, reported: "Gun dealers and bullet-makers are straining to keep up with record demand for ammunition. Some dealers think it's because of fear that President Obama might limit gun use. Although the president has made no specific proposal, bullets for sportsmen have been scarce for months."

And similar themes were struck in an Associated Press report: "American bullet-makers are working around the clock, seven days a week, and still cannot keep up with the nation's demand for ammunition. Shooting ranges, gun dealers, and bullet manufacturers say they have never seen such shortages. Bullets, especially for handguns, have been scarce for months because gun enthusiasts are stocking up, in part because they fear that President Obama and the Democratic-controlled Congress will pass antigun legislation—even though nothing specific has been proposed and the president [in May] signed a law allowing people to carry loaded guns in national parks."

Gallup's question documents that for a majority of gun owners, the belief that the president intends to try to ban the sale of guns is apparently quite real. One is reminded of the sociological principle that if people believe a situation to be real, the consequences are real—whether or not that belief is factually correct. Thus, although the survey did not ask directly whether those who hold the belief that Obama wants to ban gun sales have acted on that belief in terms of increased purchases of guns and ammunition, a connection between the belief and the behavior is a logical hypothesis.

Those who have guns in the home are demographically and politically distinct from those who do not, so it is not surprising to find that belief that Obama is going to try to prohibit gun sales follows these same patterns. For example, Republicans are significantly more likely than Democrats to have a gun in the home, and they are significantly more likely than Democrats to believe that Obama will attempt to ban the sale of guns. Additionally, the belief about Obama's intentions regarding guns is somewhat more prevalent in the Midwest and South than it is on either coast, and is higher among conservatives than among moderates or liberals.

Just your best guess, do you think Barack Obama will attempt to ban the sale of guns in the United States while he is president, or not?

% Yes, Obama will attempt to ban the sale of guns

	%
Republicans/Leaners	62
Democrats/Leaners	20
East	31
Midwest	46
South	47
West	36
Conservative	60
Moderate	28
Liberal	22

Oct. 1-4, 2009

Bottom Line

President Obama has never said, either on the campaign trail or after taking office, that he intends to push for a ban on the sale of all guns. Nevertheless, the reports of increased sales of guns and ammunition suggest that certain segments of society—in particular, gun owners—are acting as if this belief is true. The data reviewed here show that at least a majority of those who own guns or have guns in the household indeed do believe that Obama will attempt to ban the sale of all guns. It is not possible to establish that this belief has led directly to increased gun- or ammunition-purchasing behavior. But the possibility of such a connection appears quite real.

Survey Methods

Results are based on telephone interviews with 1,013 national adults, aged 18 and older, conducted Oct. 1-4, 2009. For results based on the total sample of national adults, one can say with 95% confidence that the maximum margin of sampling error is ±4 percentage points.

Interviews are conducted with respondents on land-line telephones (for respondents with a land-line telephone) and cellular phones (for respondents who are cell-phone only).

In addition to sampling error, question wording and practical difficulties in conducting surveys can introduce error or bias into the findings of public opinion polls.

October 21, 2009
IN U.S., 39% SAY VIEW ON HEALTHCARE "DEPENDS" ON DETAILS
Undecided group generally favors a "public option" component

by Lydia Saad, Gallup Poll Senior Editor

While the majority of Americans appear to have made up their minds on healthcare reform, 39% say their support for a final healthcare bill will depend on how the details still being worked out in Congress are resolved.

Prediction of Likely Support for Final Healthcare Reform Bill

As you may know, the White House and congressional Democrats are moving toward passing a healthcare bill, though the details of the final bill are still being worked out. Based on what you know or have read, do you think -- [you will support the final healthcare bill, does it depend on some of the decisions that have yet to be made about the bill, or (do you think) you will oppose the final healthcare bill]?

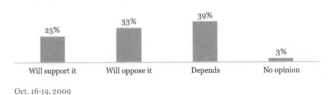

Oct. 16-19, 2009

The finding comes from a *USA Today*/Gallup poll conducted Oct. 16-19. In addition to the 39% of Americans still on the fence, 25% say they have already decided to support the final bill while a slightly larger number, 33%, say they will oppose it.

The percentage of Republicans saying they will *oppose* the final healthcare bill is higher than the percentage of Democrats who will *support* it, 62% vs. 47%, largely because more Democrats than Republicans are reserving their final judgment until the details of the legislation are worked out. Independents say they will oppose it by about 2 to 1, 36% vs. 19%, while the largest segment of this politically unanchored group (42%) says it depends.

Prediction of Likely Support for Final Healthcare Reform Bill — by Party ID

■ Support ■ Depends ■ Oppose

Oct. 16-19, 2009

The Prospect of a Public Option

With respect to one of the more contentious issues being debated—whether the plan should include a government-run insurance plan to compete with private providers (a so-called public option)—Americans are about evenly split, with 50% in favor and 46% opposed.

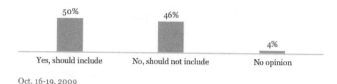

Public Support for a "Public Option" Component in Healthcare Reform Bill

If Congress passes a healthcare bill, do you think it should or should not include a public, government-run insurance plan to compete with plans offered by private insurance companies?

Oct. 16-19, 2009

Medicare Cuts Put Off Many

The new poll also asked Americans about three potential ways to pay for the healthcare bill. The public favors raising federal income taxes on high-income Americans; however, it broadly opposes reducing Medicare payments to doctors and hospitals, and taxing insurance plans that contain expensive benefits.

Support for Proposals to Help Pay for Healthcare Reform

Next, please tell me whether you favor or oppose each of the following as a way to pay for the healthcare bill.

	Favor	Oppose
	%	%
Imposing a surcharge on federal income taxes for individuals with annual incomes over $280,000 and families with incomes over $350,000	59	38
Reducing payments to Medicare providers, such as hospitals and doctors	36	61
Imposing a tax on insurance plans that have the most expensive benefit packages	34	61

Oct. 16-19, 2009

The views of the 39% who are undecided on healthcare may be of particular interest to the nation's lawmakers. The poll suggests these Americans would generally be receptive to a bill that includes a public option (56% are in favor), as well as one that raises income taxes on the wealthiest Americans to help pay for the plan (67% in favor). At the same time, they join the general public in opposing a reduction in Medicare payments to doctors and hospitals (62% opposed) and taxing insurance plans that contain expensive benefits (59% opposed).

Outright supporters of any healthcare reform bill widely back taxing the wealthy (82% are in favor) and including a public option (80%). A smaller majority favor taxing expensive benefit plans (58%), but supporters are split on reducing federal payments to Medicare providers: 48% are in favor and 49% opposed.

Outright opponents of any healthcare reform bill show broad opposition to all four provisions that might be included, but are particularly united against taxing healthcare plans that contain expensive benefits (82% are opposed).

In a follow-up question, Gallup pressed Americans who say their support for a healthcare reform bill "depends" to predict what

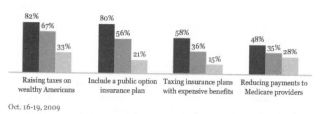

Support for Each Proposal Based on Current Position on Final Healthcare Bill

■ Support final bill   ■ Support will depend on details   ☐ Oppose final bill

Oct. 16-19, 2009

their position is likely to be once the details of the bill are worked out. Slightly more believe those decisions will cause them to support the final bill than to oppose it. When these "leaned" views are added into the equation, Americans overall appear closely split in their support of healthcare reform. Just under half—49%—are opposed to the final bill or think they will be opposed to it; 44% support it or lean that way.

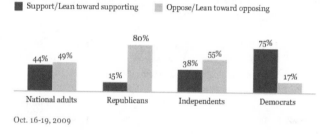

Combined Forecast for Support of Final Healthcare Reform Bill

■ Support/Lean toward supporting   ☐ Oppose/Lean toward opposing

Oct. 16-19, 2009

What's the Hurry?

By 58% to 38%, Americans would generally prefer to see Congress deal with healthcare reform "on a gradual basis over several years" rather than "try to pass a comprehensive healthcare reform plan this year." Advocates of the go-slow approach include 77% of Republicans and 63% of independents, compared with 39% of Democrats.

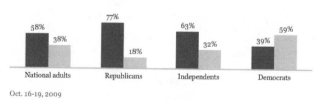

Preferred Pace of Healthcare Reform

If Congress is going to reform the healthcare system, should Congress deal with healthcare reform on a gradual basis over several years, or should Congress try to pass a comprehensive healthcare reform plan this year?

■ Reform on gradual basis   ☐ Pass comprehensive reform this year

Oct. 16-19, 2009

Notably, a slightly smaller majority of Americans today would rather see Congress take its time than said this toward the end of the healthcare reform debate in 1994 under President Bill Clinton. In August 1994—just as Congress was taking up a major healthcare reform compromise bill, and about a month before the bill was declared dead—68% of Americans said they preferred dealing with healthcare reform gradually while 28% wanted it passed that year.

Bottom Line

As the nation's elected representatives inch closer to fashioning a compromise healthcare reform bill to bring to the House and Senate floors for a final vote, Americans are still quite ambivalent on the issue. Roughly 4 in 10 are withholding final judgment until they see more specifics on the many unresolved details.

With more Democrats than Republicans falling into this "uncertain" category, it appears that the inclusion of a public option and other more liberal-oriented measures could be crucial to winning their backing. However, reducing payments to Medicare providers has the potential to deter support. Not only is this proposal broadly opposed by those who are uncertain about healthcare reform, but it divides even reform proponents.

Survey Methods

Results are based on telephone interviews with 1,521 national adults, aged 18 and older, conducted Oct. 16-19, 2009, including an oversample of 408 blacks, consisting of 102 interviews done as part of the random national sample and 306 interviews with blacks who had previously participated in national Gallup Polls and agreed to be re-interviewed at a later date. The data from the national sample and re-interviews are combined and weighted to be demographically representative of the national adult population in the United States and to reflect the proper proportion of blacks in the overall population. For results based on the total sample of national adults, one can say with 95% confidence that the maximum margin of sampling error is ±3 percentage points.

Interviews are conducted with respondents on land-line telephones (for respondents with a land-line telephone) and cellular phones (for respondents who are cell-phone only).

In addition to sampling error, question wording and practical difficulties in conducting surveys can introduce error or bias into the findings of public opinion polls.

October 21, 2009

OBAMA QUARTERLY APPROVAL AVERAGE SLIPS NINE POINTS TO 53%

Largest second- to third-quarter drop for an elected president

by Jeffrey M. Jones, Gallup Poll Managing Editor

In Gallup Daily tracking that spans Barack Obama's third quarter in office (July 20 through Oct. 19), the president averaged a 53% job approval rating. That is down sharply from his prior quarterly averages, which were both above 60%.

In fact, the 9-point drop in the most recent quarter is the largest Gallup has ever measured for an elected president between the second and third quarters of his term, dating back to 1953. One president who was not elected to his first term—Harry Truman—had a 13-point drop between his second and third quarters in office in 1945 and 1946.

The dominant political focus for Obama in the third quarter was the push for healthcare reform, including his nationally televised address to Congress in early September. Obama hoped that Congress would vote on healthcare legislation before its August recess, but that

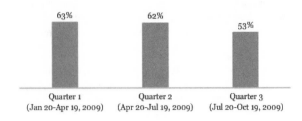

Barack Obama's Quarterly Job Approval Averages
Based on Gallup Daily tracking

Quarter 1 (Jan 20-Apr 19, 2009)	Quarter 2 (Apr 20-Jul 19, 2009)	Quarter 3 (Jul 20-Oct 19, 2009)
63%	62%	53%

Change in Presidential Job Approval Averages, Second to Third Quarter in Office, Elected Presidents

President	Second-quarter average %	Third-quarter average %	Change (pct. pts.)
Eisenhower	72	68	-4
Kennedy	76	77	+1
Nixon	62	60	-2
Carter	64	60	-4
Reagan	61	57	-4
G.H.W. Bush	64	69	+5
Clinton	44	48	+4
G.W. Bush	56	72	+16
Obama	62	53	-9

goal was missed, and some members of Congress faced angry constituents at town hall meetings to discuss healthcare reform. Meanwhile, unemployment continued to climb near 10%. The high point of Obama's third quarter may have been his winning of the Nobel Peace Prize during the quarter, which led to a noticeable but very brief bump in support.

More generally, Obama's 9-point slide between quarters ranks as one of the steepest for a president at any point in his first year in office. The highest is Truman's 19-point drop between his third and fourth quarters, followed by a 15-point drop for Gerald Ford between his first and second quarters. The largest for an elected president in his first year is Bill Clinton's 11-point slide between his first and second quarters.

Largest Declines in Average Job Approval Ratings Between Quarters During Presidents' First Year in Office

President	Change (pct. pts.)	Prior quarter	Subsequent quarter
Truman	-19	69% (3rd Qtr.)	50% (4th Qtr.)
Truman	-13	82% (2nd Qtr.)	69% (3rd Qtr.)
Ford	-15	59% (1st Qtr.)	44% (2nd Qtr.)
Clinton	-11	55% (1st Qtr.)	44% (2nd Qtr.)
Obama	-9	62% (2nd Qtr.)	53% (3rd Qtr.)
Reagan	-6	57% (3rd Qtr.)	51% (4th Qtr.)

In Obama's first quarter and second quarter, his job approval average compared favorably with those of prior presidents. But after the drop in his support during the last quarter, his average now ranks near the bottom for presidents at similar points in their presidencies. Only Clinton had a lower third-quarter average among elected presidents. (Gerald Ford averaged 39% during his third quarter in office, in 1975.)

Presidents' Third-Quarter Approval Averages

Presidents elected to their first terms

President	Third-quarter dates	Average	Number of measurements
Eisenhower	Jul 20–Oct 19, 1953	68%	4
Kennedy	Jul 20–Oct 19, 1961	77%	4
Nixon	Jul 20–Oct 19, 1969	60%	6
Carter	Jul 20–Oct 19, 1977	60%	6
Reagan	Jul 20–Oct 19, 1981	57%	5
G.H.W. Bush	Jul 20–Oct 19, 1989	69%	3
Clinton	Jul 20–Oct 19, 1993	48%	7
G.W. Bush	Jul 20–Oct 19, 2001	72%	10
Obama	Jul 20–Oct 19, 2009	53%	9

Obama's 53% third-quarter average is substandard from a broader historical perspective that encompasses all 255 presidential quarters for which Gallup has data going back to 1945. On this basis, Obama's most recent average ranks 144th, or in the 44th percentile, clearly below average not just for presidents' third quarters but for all presidents.

Survey Methods

Results are based on aggregated telephone interviews with 45,987 national adults, aged 18 and older, conducted July 20 through Oct. 19, 2009, as part of Gallup Daily tracking. For results based on the total sample of national adults, one can say with 95% confidence that the maximum margin of sampling error is ±1 percentage point.

Interviews are conducted with respondents on land-line telephones and cellular phones.

In addition to sampling error, question wording and practical difficulties in conducting surveys can introduce error or bias into the findings of public opinion polls.

October 22, 2009

IN U.S., HALF SEE OWN COSTS WORSENING UNDER HEALTHCARE BILL

More expect costs, quality, and coverage to get worse than did so in September

by Jeffrey M. Jones, Gallup Poll Managing Editor

Compared with last month, Americans have become more likely to say the costs their family pays for healthcare will get worse if a healthcare bill passes. Forty-nine percent of Americans say this, up from 42% in September. Meanwhile, the percentage who expect their costs to improve is unchanged.

In addition to costs, a greater percentage of Americans now compared with last month also expect their healthcare situation to get worse in terms of the quality of care they receive (from 33% in September to 39%), their healthcare coverage (from 33% to 37%), and the insurance company requirements they have to meet to get certain treatments covered (from 38% to 46%).

The Oct. 16-19 *USA Today*/Gallup poll was conducted as both houses of Congress move closer to a vote on healthcare reform legislation, including a key Senate Finance Committee vote in favor of a reform bill on Oct. 13.

Suppose a healthcare bill passes this year. Do you think the costs you and your family pay for healthcare would get better, would not change, or would get worse than if no healthcare bill passes?

But the poll finds no more than one-quarter of Americans believing their healthcare situation will improve in any of the four areas. And in each, substantially more expect the situation to get worse than expect it to get better if a healthcare bill passes.

Perceived Impact of Healthcare Bill on Your Own Healthcare in the Following Areas

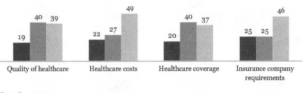

Oct. 16-19, 2009

Even so, Americans are still quite open to healthcare reform—25% say they will support the final bill and another 39% say their support or opposition depends on the details of the legislation yet to be worked out. The views of this undecided group could be crucial to healthcare reform legislation's ultimate fate. And in addition to their preferences for possible policy elements of the legislation, discussed Tuesday on Gallup.com, their judgments of the impact the legislation might have on their own care could influence their decisions on whether to support or oppose the final bill.

In general, Americans who are undecided on healthcare legislation predict it is more likely to make their own situations worse rather than better—especially in terms of cost (45% worse to 22% better), but in the three other areas as well. However, less than a majority in this group has negative expectations about any of the areas.

Perceived Impact of Healthcare Bill on Your Own Healthcare in the Following Areas

Based on those who are undecided about supporting or opposing healthcare legislation

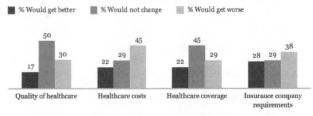

Oct. 16-19, 2009

As would be expected, those who are outright opposed to healthcare legislation expect it to make their situations worse in all four areas by wide margins. At least two in three opponents believe their own costs, quality, coverage, and insurance requirements will get worse if a healthcare bill passes; fewer than 1 in 10 expect any of these to improve.

Perceived Impact of Healthcare Bill on Your Own Healthcare in the Following Areas
Based on those who oppose healthcare legislation

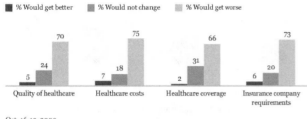

Oct. 16-19, 2009

Those who are committed supporters of healthcare legislation are much more likely to believe it will make their situations better rather than worse, although this does not reach the majority level in any area. One-fourth or less expect their healthcare to get worse in any respect if reform legislation becomes law.

Perceived Impact of Healthcare Bill on Your Own Healthcare in the Following Areas
Based on those who support healthcare legislation

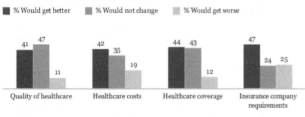

Oct. 16-19, 2009

Thus, one reason Americans as a whole expect healthcare reform to do more to reduce than to improve their current healthcare is because reform opponents are more widely convinced of its potential negative impact on their current healthcare than supporters are of its potential positive impact.

Bottom Line

Although Congress is making significant progress toward passing healthcare legislation, there is still much work to be done to finalize the bill and build public support for such a new law. Americans are not solidly behind new healthcare legislation at this point, with polls showing at best a closely divided public. That level of support persists despite the fact that most Americans doubt reform will improve their current healthcare in a number of respects.

It is unclear whether, in order to succeed in passing healthcare legislation, the president and his allies need to convince Americans that their own healthcare will improve after reform is passed—which is far from the prevailing view now—or whether it is sufficient just to convince them that their care will not suffer while addressing some of the existing problems in the U.S. healthcare system. Since September, Americans have become more likely to believe reform would have a detrimental effect on their own care in terms of cost, quality, and coverage, but as of now, these views still fall below the majority level.

Survey Methods

Results are based on telephone interviews with 1,521 national adults, aged 18 and older, conducted Oct. 16-19, 2009, including an over-

sample of 408 blacks, consisting of 102 interviews done as part of the random national sample and 306 interviews with blacks who had previously participated in national Gallup polls and agreed to be re-interviewed at a later date. The data from the national sample and re-interviews are combined and weighted to be demographically representative of the national adult population in the United States and to reflect the proper proportion of blacks in the overall population. For results based on the total sample of national adults, one can say with 95% confidence that the maximum margin of sampling error is ±3 percentage points.

Interviews are conducted with respondents on land-line telephones (for respondents with a land-line telephone) and cellular phones (for respondents who are cell-phone only).

In addition to sampling error, question wording and practical difficulties in conducting surveys can introduce error or bias into the findings of public opinion polls.

October 23, 2009
CONSUMERS SPEND MORE ON WEEKENDS, PAYDAY WEEKS

Average daily spending is lowest at beginning of work week

by Dennis Jacobe, Gallup Chief Economist and Jeffrey M. Jones, Managing Editor

Gallup's Daily monitoring of consumers' self-reported average daily spending in stores, restaurants, gas stations, and online finds that Americans spend the most on Saturdays, followed closely by Fridays; they spend the least on Mondays and Tuesdays.

Average Daily Spending, by Day of the Week
Jan. 2-Oct. 21, 2009

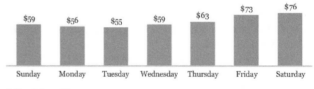

Gallup Daily tracking

As a result, weekend (Friday through Sunday) spending on an average daily basis far exceeds weekday spending. In part, this may result from current American lifestyles, with weekday demands leaving little time for shopping or entertainment outside the home. The findings are based on aggregated Gallup Daily tracking data from Jan. 2 to Oct. 21, 2009.

Paycheck Effect

Further, there appears to be a "paycheck effect," with spending during typical payday weeks (around the beginning and the middle of each month, for those who are paid once or twice a month) significantly higher than that during weeks without a payday. For the most part, this may reflect the fact that many Americans who are paid on a semi-monthly or monthly basis—like many who are paid weekly—

Average Daily Spending During Weekdays and Weekends
Jan. 2-Oct. 21, 2009

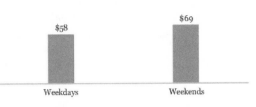

Weekdays $58
Weekends $69

Gallup Daily tracking

still live paycheck to paycheck. However, this situation may be intensified in the current economic climate as Americans make fewer shopping trips, buy relatively more when they do shop, and purchase more necessities and fewer impulse items.

Average Daily Spending, by Type of Week
Jan. 2-Oct. 21, 2009

Weeks with a payday^   Weeks without a payday
$69 $62

^ For employees who get paid once or twice a month
Gallup Daily tracking

This pattern has been especially evident in recent weeks. Average daily spending has changed by $10 or more from week to week during most weeks since early August, with increases generally occurring in the weeks containing the first and midpoint days of each month, and declines in the other weeks. Again, this may be the result of the factors noted earlier, or, alternatively, the possibility that many consumers simply feel more confident about spending when they have a greater amount of cash on hand and are less comfortable using credit.

Consumer Spending, Weeks Ending Aug. 9 Through Oct. 18, 2009
Self-reported average daily spending (weekly averages)

$79
$66 $62 $70 $72 $67 $76
        $56 $60 $60 $57

Sep 2009   Oct 2009

Gallup Daily tracking

Spending Differs by Gender and Age

Men report spending more on average than women do, which may be a reflection of the fact that men have higher average incomes than women (Gallup analysis shows income to be the greatest predictor of spending). Similarly, Americans aged 30 to 49—typically a time when people have growing families—tend to spend the most, while Americans 65 or older tend to spend the least. Indeed, those with

children under 18 spend significantly more on average than those without young children.

Average Daily Spending, by Gender and by Age, January to Mid-August 2009

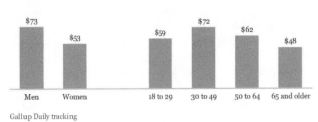

Men $73   Women $53   18 to 29 $59   30 to 49 $72   50 to 64 $62   65 and older $48

Gallup Daily tracking

Commentary

Over the past several months, consumer spending patterns appear to be changing. Gallup Daily results show that the "paycheck effect" seems to be intensifying as consumers spend more during the weeks when they are paid and less during other weeks.

At first, it seemed as though this might have been a sign that consumers were trying to break out of the "new normal." Perhaps consumer spending would follow economic confidence and begin to find an upward path. In turn, this would confirm that the end of the recession and the beginning of recovery was beginning to be felt on Main Street.

Instead, monthly averaging of today's consumer spending shows almost no change since January. The new normal level of spending is fully intact even as confidence improves and job layoffs seem to be easing compared to earlier in the year.

As noted earlier, this new intensified, paycheck-oriented spending pattern may be the result of a new shopping pattern, with consumers making fewer trips but buying more on each trip. Or it may be that consumers are just more comfortable shopping when they have cash. Or perhaps this is a reflection of the reduced willingness of consumers to use credit, their reduced desire to take on credit-card debt, or simply a lack of credit availability. Regardless, it appears that there may be a new "cash-based" consumer spending pattern developing.

This could have significant implications for how retailers price and time their sales; how they handle their merchandising; and how they evaluate their inventories. It could also be an interesting Christmas for everyone if it is more "cash-based" than "credit-based" this year.

Right now, Gallup's consumer spending data continue to show consumers spending roughly 30% less than they did during the same week a year ago across income groups—another possible sign of a more "cash-based" spending pattern. Unless this pattern changes, it is hard to see much cheer for retailers at Christmas or much improvement in jobs or the Main Street economy as the year ends.

Gallup's new behavioral economics-based Consumer Spending measure will be first to indicate whether this potential new consumer spending pattern persists in the weeks ahead.

Survey Methods

For Gallup Daily tracking, Gallup interviews approximately 1,000 national adults, aged 18 and older, each day. The Gallup consumer spending results are based on random half-samples of approximately 500 national adults, aged 18 and older, each day. For purposes of this analysis, a total of 140,114 interview results were compiled over the period of Jan. 2 to Oct. 21, 2009. Samples for individual days of the week totaled more than 19,000 completed interviews while those for weekdays totaled 80,230 and those for weekends totaled 59,884. For all of these samples, one can say with 95% confidence that the maximum margin of sampling error is ±1 percentage point.

Interviews are conducted with respondents on land-line telephones and cellular phones.

In addition to sampling error, question wording and practical difficulties in conducting surveys can introduce error or bias into the findings of public opinion polls.

October 23, 2009
AMERICANS' VIEWS ON OBAMA AND THE NOBEL PEACE PRIZE
Majority say it is not deserved, although about half are glad Obama received it

by Frank Newport, Gallup Poll Editor in Chief

The majority of Americans do not believe President Barack Obama deserved to win the Nobel Peace Prize (61%), but the public is split in its personal reaction to the announcement. Asked if they are "glad" Obama received the prize, 46% of Americans say yes and 47% say no.

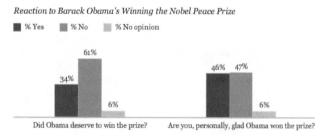

Reaction to Barack Obama's Winning the Nobel Peace Prize

Oct. 16-19, 2009

The Norwegian Nobel Committee's Oct. 9 announcement that President Obama had received the 2009 Nobel Peace Prize caught the world by surprise. One Associated Press report on the day of the announcement was headlined, "Gasps as Obama Awarded Peace Prize." Those startled by the announcement apparently included Obama himself, who said he was "surprised and deeply humbled" by the award. Obama appeared to recognize that the award was based more on the promise of his new administration than on its still-nascent record of accomplishments, saying, "Let me be clear: I do not view it as a recognition of my own accomplishments, but rather as an affirmation of American leadership on behalf of aspirations held by people in all nations." He went on to say, "To be honest, I do not feel that I deserve to be in the company of so many of the transformative figures who've been honored by this prize."

The *USA Today*/Gallup poll conducted about a week after the announcement did not ask Americans whether they believe that the award may ultimately be deserved, or whether it was appropriately given in anticipation of the potential of the Obama administration's peace efforts. The central question simply asked whether Obama "deserved" the award, and found Americans by roughly a 2-to-1 margin saying no rather than yes.

Not surprisingly, reaction to the awarding of the prize is partisan, although support for Obama's receiving the prize among Democrats is perhaps not as large as might be expected. Fifty-nine percent of Democrats say the award is deserved, which can be contrasted with the 84% of Democrats who in the same survey approve of Obama's job performance. Independents and, in particular, Republicans are highly likely to say Obama did not deserve to win the prize.

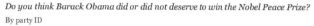

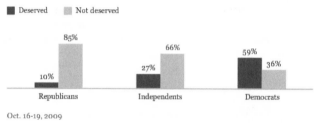

Do you think Barack Obama did or did not deserve to win the Nobel Peace Prize?
By party ID

Oct. 16-19, 2009

Emotional reactions to the award ("glad" versus "not glad") are somewhat more positive than perceptions of whether Obama deserved the award, across each of the three partisan groups. Seventy-six percent of Democrats are glad Obama received the award, as are 38% of independents and 21% of Republicans.

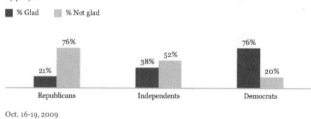

Are you, personally, glad that Barack Obama won the Nobel Peace Prize, or not?
By party ID

Oct. 16-19, 2009

There is a general and expected consistency between belief that Obama deserved the prize and being personally glad that he won. Three-quarters of Americans have either positive reactions to both of these questions or negative reactions to both.

Relationship Between Belief That Barack Obama Deserved the Nobel Peace Prize and Personal Reaction to the Award
Based on all national adults

	Deserved to win Nobel Peace Prize	Did not deserve
Glad Obama won Nobel Peace Prize	31%	14%
Not glad	2%	44%

Oct. 16-19, 2009

Among the two discordant groups, the larger consists of the 14% who say Obama did not deserve the award but at the same time are personally glad that he won. A very small 2% say he deserved the award but were not personally glad.

About a third of Americans who approve of the job Obama is doing as president in the Oct. 16-19 survey also say the Nobel award was not deserved. This suggests that some of the "undeserved" reaction to the award is based not on an overall negative opinion of Obama's job performance, but rather on a nuanced view that positive current performance is different than a body of work deserving of a Nobel Prize.

Belief That Barack Obama Deserved the Nobel Peace Prize, by Current Obama Job Approval

	Deserved to win Nobel Peace Prize	Did not deserve	No opinion
Approve of the job Obama is doing as president	60%	34%	6%
Do not approve	6%	90%	4%

Oct. 16-19, 2009

Bottom Line

Commentators in the U.S. and abroad have evinced widely varied reactions to the unusual choice of an American president in office for less than nine months as the recipient of this year's Nobel Peace Prize. The Nobel Peace Prize committee itself put more emphasis in its announcement on hope for the future than on Obama's actual accomplishments to date, lauding Obama's "vision," saying he has given the world "hope for a better future," and that he has created "a new climate in international politics." The current poll results, however, suggest that at least some rank-and-file Americans may be oriented more toward accomplishments rather than promise for the future.

Of note are the findings that a sizable group of those who approve of Obama's job performance and of Democrats say Obama did not deserve the Nobel Peace Prize. This suggests that the more negative responses to the awarding of the prize for some are not simply knee-jerk reactions to a disliked president, but rather more carefully thought-out reactions to the particular circumstances of the awarding of the prize.

Survey Methods

Results are based on telephone interviews with 1,521 national adults, aged 18 and older, conducted Oct. 16-19, 2009. For results based on the total sample of national adults, one can say with 95% confidence that the maximum margin of sampling error is ±3 percentage points.

Interviews are conducted with respondents on land-line telephones (for respondents with a land-line telephone) and cellular phones (for respondents who are cell-phone only).

In addition to sampling error, question wording and practical difficulties in conducting surveys can introduce error or bias into the findings of public opinion polls.

October 26, 2009
CONSERVATIVES MAINTAIN EDGE AS TOP IDEOLOGICAL GROUP
Compared with 2008, more Americans "conservative" in general, and on issues

by Lydia Saad, Gallup Poll Senior Editor

Conservatives continue to outnumber moderates and liberals in the American populace in 2009, confirming a finding that Gallup first noted in June. Forty percent of Americans describe their political views as conservative, 36% as moderate, and 20% as liberal. This marks a shift from 2005 through 2008, when moderates were tied with conservatives as the most prevalent group.

Political Ideology -- Annual Trends

How would you describe your political views -- [very conservative, conservative, (or) moderate, liberal, (or) very liberal]?

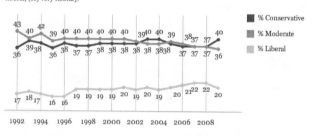

Annual averages, 1992-2009; 2009 data based on January-September surveys

The 2009 data are based on 16 separate Gallup surveys conducted from January through September, encompassing more than 5,000 national adults per quarter. Conservatives have been the dominant ideological group each quarter, with between 39% and 41% of Americans identifying themselves as either "very conservative" or "conservative." Between 35% and 37% of Americans call themselves "moderate," while the percentage calling themselves "very liberal" or "liberal" has consistently registered between 20% and 21%—making liberals the smallest of the three groups.

Political Ideology -- 2009, by Quarter

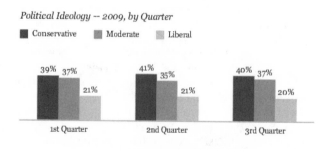

Independents Inch to the Right

Changes among political independents appear to be the main reason the percentage of conservatives has increased nationally over the past year: the 35% of independents describing their views as conservative in 2009 is up from 29% in 2008. By contrast, among Republicans and Democrats, the percentage who are "conservative" has increased by one point each.

As is typical in recent years, Republicans are far more unified in their political outlook than are either independents or Democrats. While 72% of Republicans in 2009 call their views conservative, independents are closely split between the moderate and conservative labels (43% and 35%, respectively). Democrats are about evenly divided between moderates (39%) and liberals (37%).

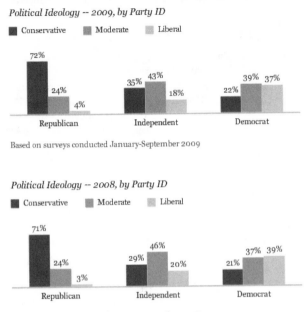

Political Ideology -- 2009, by Party ID

■ Conservative ■ Moderate ■ Liberal

Republican: 72%, 24%, 4%
Independent: 35%, 43%, 18%
Democrat: 22%, 39%, 37%

Based on surveys conducted January-September 2009

Political Ideology -- 2008, by Party ID

■ Conservative ■ Moderate ■ Liberal

Republican: 71%, 24%, 3%
Independent: 29%, 46%, 20%
Democrat: 21%, 37%, 39%

Based on surveys conducted January-December 2008

Americans Also Moving Right on Some Issues

In addition to the increase in conservatism on this general ideology measure, Gallup finds higher percentages of Americans expressing conservative views on several specific issues in 2009 than in 2008.

- Perceptions that there is too much government regulation of business and industry jumped from 38% in September 2008 to 45% in September 2009.
- The percentage of Americans saying they would like to see labor unions have less influence in the country rose from 32% in August 2008 to a record-high 42% in August 2009.
- Public support for keeping the laws governing the sale of firearms the same or making them less strict rose from 49% in October 2008 to 55% in October 2009, also a record high. (The percentage saying the laws should become *more* strict—the traditionally liberal position—fell from 49% to 44%.)
- The percentage of Americans favoring a decrease in immigration rose from 39% in June/July 2008 to 50% in July 2009.
- The propensity to want the government to "promote traditional values"—as opposed to "not favor any particular set of values"— rose from 48% in 2008 to 53% in 2009. Current support for promoting traditional values is the highest seen in five years.
- The percentage of Americans who consider themselves "prolife" on abortion rose from 44% in May 2008 to 51% in May 2009, and remained at a slightly elevated 47% in July 2009.
- Americans' belief that the global warming problem is "exaggerated" in the news rose from 35% in March 2008 to 41% in March 2009.

Gallup has not recorded heightened conservatism on all major social and political views held by Americans. For instance, attitudes on the death penalty, gay marriage, the Iraq war, and Afghanistan have stayed about the same since 2008. However, there are no major examples of U.S. public opinion becoming more liberal in the past

year. (Gallup's annual trends on healthcare will be updated in November, so those attitudes are not included in this review.)

The conservative shifts discussed here result as much from changes in political independents' views as from changes in Republicans' views. Democrats' views, by contrast, have generally changed only slightly—either to the conservative or liberal side—with two exceptions: Gallup finds greater movement in Democrats' views of abortion, which have become more liberal, and their views of labor unions, which have become more conservative.

Issue Positions and Changes in Those Positions, 2008 vs. 2009 -- by Party ID

Conservative position	Republicans	Independents	Democrats
Government regulation -- "too much"			
Change	+14	+12	-2
2009	70%	50%	21%
2008	56%	38%	23%
Labor union preference -- "have less influence"			
Change	+14	+10	+10
2009	63%	44%	26%
2008	49%	34%	16%
Sale of firearms -- "stay the same"/"make less strict"			
Change	+5	+10	+2
2009	71%	62%	34%
2008	66%	52%	32%
Immigration -- "decreased"			
Change	+15	+9	+5
2009	61%	46%	44%
2008	46%	37%	39%
Government role -- "promote traditional values"			
Change	-4	+17	+5
2009	67%	54%	42%
2008	71%	37%	37%
Abortion -- "pro-life"			
Change	+1	+12	-7
2009	67%	50%	28%
2008	66%	38%	35%
Global warming -- "exaggerated"			
Change	+7	+11	+4
2009	66%	44%	22%
2008	59%	33%	18%

Bottom Line

Americans are more likely to consider themselves conservative this year than they were in 2008, resulting in conservatives—now 40% of the American public—outnumbering moderates for the first time since 2004. While Gallup first documented this trend in June, the finding has been sustained through the third quarter.

Conservatism is most prevalent among Republicans. However, the overall increase in this ideological stance since 2008 comes largely from political independents, among whom 35% say they are conservatives thus far in 2009—compared with 29% last year. Independents have also become more conservative on a number of specific policy issues, including government and union power, the role of government relative to promoting values, gun laws, immigration, global warming, and abortion. Republicans, most of whom considered themselves ideologically conservative in 2008, have also grown more conservative on several of these issues this year, while less change is seen among Democrats.

All of this has potentially important implications at the ballot box, particularly for the 2010 midterm elections. The question is whether increased conservatism, particularly among independents, will translate into heightened support for Republican candidates. Right now, it appears it may. Although Gallup polling continues to show the Democratic Party leading the Republican Party in Americans' party identification, that lead has been narrowing since the beginning of the year and now stands at six points, the smallest since 2005. According to Gallup Managing Editor Jeff Jones, "the Democratic-Republican gap is narrowing because more independents now say they lean to the Republican Party." That trend aligns with the recent changes in how independents perceive their own ideology and where they stand on some key issues.

Survey Methods

The 2009 political ideology results reported here are based on 16 aggregated Gallup surveys conducted from January to September 2009. For results based on the total sample of 16,321 national adults, aged 18 and older, one can say with 95% confidence that the maximum margin of sampling error is ±1 percentage point.

Interviews are conducted with respondents on land-line telephones (for respondents with a land-line telephone) and cellular phones (for respondents who are cell-phone only).

In addition to sampling error, question wording and practical difficulties in conducting surveys can introduce error or bias into the findings of public opinion polls.

October 26, 2009

VICE PRESIDENT BIDEN'S FAVORABLE RATING CONTINUES TO DECLINE

Forty-two percent view vice president favorably, 40% unfavorably

by Jeffrey M. Jones, Gallup Poll Managing Editor

After peaking at 59% last November, Vice President Joe Biden's favorable rating continues to decline and now stands at 42%. That barely exceeds his 40% unfavorable rating, and is easily his worst evaluation since last year's Democratic National Convention.

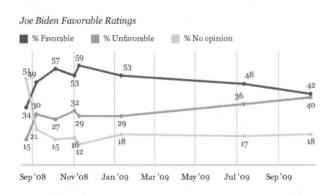

Joe Biden Favorable Ratings

These data are based on the latest *USA Today*/Gallup poll, conducted Oct. 16-19. Biden's favorable rating has dropped by five or six points each of the last three times Gallup has updated it—in Jan-

uary, before Barack Obama's inauguration; in July; and in the most recent poll.

The source of the decline—by party affiliation—has varied over time. During the post-election to pre-inauguration phase, Biden's favorable rating dropped significantly among Democrats, but it has been fairly steady since, and remains strong at 73%.

Republicans had relatively low opinions of Biden even at the peak of his popularity, with 33% holding a favorable opinion of him. Those views did not change appreciably until after he took office, but Republicans' views of Biden have declined in both post-inauguration readings, and now stand at 18% favorable.

Independents' opinions of Biden have declined more steadily since the post-election high mark, and now 32% of independents view the vice president favorably.

Trend in Joe Biden Favorable Ratings, by Party Affiliation

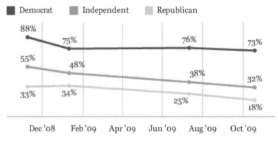

Biden's sagging popularity is not unique in the Obama administration. President Obama's favorable rating has declined as well, though it has taken a slightly different trajectory than Biden's. Obama's popularity soared to a pre-inauguration high of 78%, and has declined to 55% in the current poll, with about half of that decline occurring between January and March, and the other half between July and October.

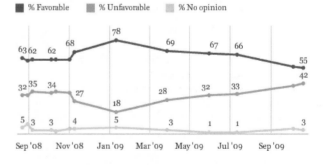

Barack Obama Favorable Ratings

Even first lady Michelle Obama's favorability rating has gone down, from 72% in March to 61% now.

Historical Comparison Not Kind to Biden

Gallup has measured public opinion of government leaders using the favorable/unfavorable question format since 1992, so it has comparable data only on Vice Presidents Al Gore and Dick Cheney.

Both Gore (63% in January 1993) and Cheney (61% in January 2001) had higher favorable ratings immediately before taking office than did Biden (53% in January 2009).

Though Gallup did not measure the vice presidents' favorable ratings often during the first year of each administration, the available data show both Gore (55% based on five measurements) and Cheney (65% based on three measurements) having higher average favorable ratings in their first year than Biden does (45% based on two measurements) thus far.

Biden also departs from his immediate predecessors in being significantly less popular than his boss. Gore's and Cheney's first-year averages were similar to Bill Clinton's and George W. Bush's, respectively.

Average Favorable Ratings for Presidents and Vice Presidents During Their First Year in Office

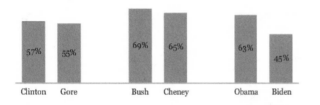

This may simply be a carryover from the presidential campaign. In the 1992 and 2000 elections, both members of the winning ticket were rated similarly just after the election and through much of their first year in office. The 2008 election was different in that Obama, one of the most popular presidential candidates in recent memory, chose a fairly well-established Washington senator who had run unsuccessfully for the top job, and Biden was never viewed as positively as his future boss. That gap in popularity persists, even as Obama's and Biden's favorable ratings have declined this year.

Republicans view Obama (17% favorable) and Biden (18%) about equally poorly, but Democrats (by 87% to 73%) and especially independents (by 55% to 32%) have significantly more positive opinions of Obama than of Biden.

Survey Methods

Results are based on telephone interviews with 1,521 national adults, aged 18 and older, conducted Oct. 16-19, 2009, including an oversample of 408 blacks, consisting of 102 interviews done as part of the random national sample and 306 interviews with blacks who had previously participated in national Gallup polls and agreed to be re-interviewed at a later date. The data from the national sample and re-interviews are combined and weighted to be demographically representative of the national adult population in the United States and to reflect the proper proportion of blacks in the overall population.

For results based on the total sample of national adults, one can say with 95% confidence that the maximum margin of sampling error is ±3 percentage points.

Interviews are conducted with respondents on land-line telephones (for respondents with a land-line telephone) and cellular phones (for respondents who are cell-phone only).

In addition to sampling error, question wording and practical difficulties in conducting surveys can introduce error or bias into the findings of public opinion polls.

October 28, 2009
AMERICANS SEE MORE PRIORITIES VYING FOR OBAMA'S ATTENTION
Economy still top issue, but Iraq and Afghanistan, healthcare, deficit up

by Jeffrey M. Jones, Gallup Poll Managing Editor

When given a choice of five issues, 4 in 10 Americans name the economy as the top priority for Barack Obama as president, easily the top percentage. However, that is down sharply from 64% in a poll conducted just after Obama was elected last November.

Which of the following should be Barack Obama's top priority as president -- [ROTATED: the economy, healthcare, the situations in Iraq and Afghanistan, energy, the federal budget deficit], or something else?

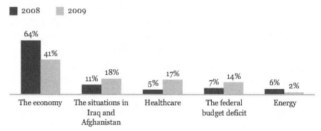

The drop in the percentage mentioning the economy as Obama's top priority coincides with Americans' more optimistic assessments about the nation's economic course now compared to last November, in part because the financial crisis has eased.

Gallup has seen a similar decline in concern about the economy over the course of 2009 in its monthly "most important problem" question.

With fewer Americans naming the economy as Obama's top priority, the Oct. 16-19 *USA Today*/Gallup poll finds increases in the percentage of Americans naming the situations in Iraq and Afghanistan, the federal budget deficit, and healthcare. Healthcare, which was barely on the public's radar last fall but has been the focus of the Obama domestic policy agenda in recent months, has shown the biggest increase, from 5% to 17%.

Equal percentages of Republicans and Democrats (40%) name the economy as the top priority for Obama. The two parties differ in the extent to which they assign importance to healthcare (more important among Democrats, 30% to 10%) and the federal budget deficit (more important among Republicans, 23% to 5%). Healthcare also ranks as a fairly low priority among independents, at 11%.

Top Priority for Obama, by Party Affiliation

USA Today/Gallup, Oct. 16-19, 2009
Note: Energy not shown

In last year's poll, at least 6 in 10 Republicans, Democrats, and independents named the economy as Obama's top priority; thus, all three groups show at least 20-point declines on this issue in the current poll. The most dramatic change in rated issue importance among party groups is the sharp increase in the percentage of Democrats who view healthcare as the top priority, from 6% to 30%. Also, the percentage of Republicans naming the deficit as the top Obama administration priority has doubled since last year, from 10% to 23%.

Top Priority for Obama, by Party Affiliation, 2008 vs. 2009

	The economy	The situations in Iraq and Afghanistan	Healthcare	The federal budget deficit
Democrat (2009)	40%	15%	30%	5%
Democrat (2008)	68%	13%	6%	4%
Independent (2009)	43%	21%	11%	15%
Independent (2008)	63%	10%	4%	6%
Republican (2009)	40%	18%	10%	23%
Republican (2008)	63%	12%	4%	10%

Note: Energy not shown

The current poll included a larger sample of blacks, and among this group, healthcare ranks a fairly close second to the economy as the top priority, 38% to 29%. Fewer whites (15%) than blacks mention healthcare as the top priority, while more name the federal budget deficit and situations in Iraq and Afghanistan.

Top Priority for Obama, by Race

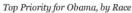

■ The economy   ■ The situations in Iraq and Afghanistan
■ Healthcare   ■ The federal budget deficit

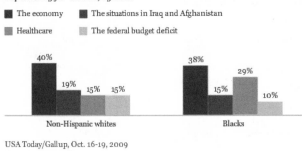

Non-Hispanic whites: 40%, 19%, 15%, 15%
Blacks: 38%, 15%, 29%, 10%

USA Today/Gallup, Oct. 16-19, 2009
Note: Energy not shown

Bottom Line

Americans continue to rank the economy as the Obama administration's top priority, but the percentage doing so has been cut by about one-third since last fall, perhaps because Americans' fears about the state of the economy have eased. Since Obama won the election, a greater proportion of Americans have come to view healthcare, the federal budget deficit, and the situations in Iraq and Afghanistan as greater priorities for the president. Healthcare and Afghanistan promise to take on even greater significance in the coming weeks as Congress hammers out a healthcare bill and Obama prepares to announce the next steps for United States' military policy in Afghanistan.

Survey Methods

Results are based on telephone interviews with 1,521 national adults, aged 18 and older, conducted Oct. 16-19, 2009, including an oversample of 408 blacks, consisting of 102 interviews done as part of the random national sample and 306 interviews with blacks who had pre-

viously participated in national Gallup Polls and agreed to be re-interviewed at a later date. The data from the national sample and re-interviews are combined and weighted to be demographically representative of the national adult population in the United States and to reflect the proper proportion of blacks in the overall population.

For results based on the sample of 408 blacks, the maximum margin of error is ±6 percentage points.

For results based on the sample of 933 non-Hispanic whites, the maximum margin of error is ±4 percentage points.

For results based on the total sample of national adults, one can say with 95% confidence that the maximum margin of sampling error is ±3 percentage points.

Interviews are conducted with respondents on land-line telephones (for respondents with a land-line telephone) and cellular phones (for respondents who are cell-phone only).

In addition to sampling error, question wording and practical difficulties in conducting surveys can introduce error or bias into the findings of public opinion polls.

October 28, 2009

ON HEALTHCARE, AMERICANS TRUST OBAMA MORE THAN CONGRESS

By 48% to 37%, more trust the Democrats than the Republicans in Congress

by Lydia Saad, Gallup Poll Senior Editor

As Senate Majority Leader Harry Reid tries to advance a healthcare reform bill onto the Senate floor, just under half of Americans, 48%, say they trust the Democrats in Congress to change the nation's healthcare system; 52% express little or no trust in them. Trust in President Obama on healthcare is a bit higher, at 55%, while trust in the Republicans in Congress—37%—is significantly lower.

Trust in Washington Leaders on Healthcare Reform

When it comes to making changes to the healthcare system, how much trust do you have in each of the following -- a great deal, a fair amount, not much, or none at all?

■ Great deal/Fair amount   ■ Not much/None

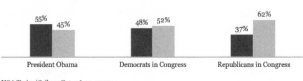

President Obama: 55%, 45%
Democrats in Congress: 48%, 52%
Republicans in Congress: 37%, 62%

USA Today/Gallup, Oct. 16-19, 2009

Notably, feelings of high trust toward Washington's leadership on healthcare are fairly scarce: 23% of Americans—predominantly Democrats—say they have a great deal of trust in Obama on the issue. However, the figure drops by more than half to 10% for the Democrats in Congress and halves again, falling to 4%, for the Republicans.

Republicans' Confidence in Own Party's Leadership Lags Democrats'

These views are predictably partisan in their general direction. Most Democrats express a great deal or fair amount of trust in Obama, as

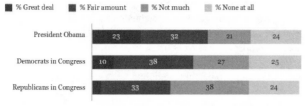

Trust in Washington Leaders on Healthcare Reform -- Detailed Ratings

■ % Great deal ■ % Fair amount ▨ % Not much ▨ % None at all

	% Great deal	% Fair amount	% Not much	% None at all
President Obama	23	32	21	24
Democrats in Congress	10	38	27	25
Republicans in Congress	33	38	24	

USA Today/Gallup, Oct. 16-19, 2009

well as in congressional Democrats; they have little to no trust in the Republicans. The reverse is true for Republicans. However, there is a notable difference in degree: a significantly higher proportion of Democrats than Republicans generally trust their own party's leaders on the issue. Eighty-six percent of Democrats trust Obama and 81% trust the Democrats in Congress; by contrast, 61% of Republicans trust the Republicans in Congress.

Fewer than 4 in 10 political independents have much faith in either political party in Congress on healthcare reform; however, the majority of independents do trust Obama.

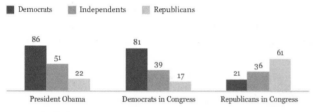

Trust in Washington Leaders on Healthcare Reform -- by Party ID

% Great deal/Fair amount

■ Democrats ▨ Independents ▨ Republicans

	Democrats	Independents	Republicans
President Obama	86	51	22
Democrats in Congress	81	39	17
Republicans in Congress	21	36	61

USA Today/Gallup, Oct. 16-19, 2009

Bottom Line

Americans' reactions to the Republicans and Democrats in Congress for handling healthcare reform are sharply partisan, and independents show little faith in either side. As a result, neither party's congressional leadership can boast that a majority of Americans are behind them on this issue.

While Republicans do not trust the president much more than they trust congressional Democrats on healthcare, political independents do see him in a more positive light. This helps lift Obama above the fray, earning him the trust of the slight majority of Americans.

Gallup's most recent reading on public support for healthcare reform finds 44% of Americans saying either that they will support the final healthcare reform bill that comes to a vote in Congress, or that they are likely to support it. Slightly more, 49%, expect to oppose the bill. With such anemic public support for reform, Sen. Reid could benefit from Obama's playing a more visible role in trying to rally public support around whatever plan the Democrats in Congress finally agree on.

Survey Methods

Results are based on telephone interviews with 1,521 national adults, aged 18 and older, conducted Oct. 16-19, 2009, including an oversample of 408 blacks, consisting of 102 interviews done as part of the random national sample and 306 interviews with blacks who had

previously participated in national Gallup Polls and agreed to be re-interviewed at a later date. The data from the national sample and re-interviews are combined and weighted to be demographically representative of the national adult population in the United States and to reflect the proper proportion of blacks in the overall population. For results based on this sample of national adults, the maximum margin of error is ±3 percentage points.

Interviews are conducted with respondents on land-line telephones (for respondents with a land-line telephone) and cellular phones (for respondents who are cell-phone only).

In addition to sampling error, question wording and practical difficulties in conducting surveys can introduce error or bias into the findings of public opinion polls.

October 29, 2009
U.S. INVESTOR OPTIMISM DOWN SLIGHTLY IN OCTOBER
Investors remain slightly optimistic overall but Index is down slightly from September

by Dennis Jacobe, Gallup Chief Economist

Although the Dow Jones average hit 10,000 earlier this month, the Gallup Index of Investor Optimism—a broad measure of investor perceptions—gave up its modest 5-point September gain, falling back to its August level of +9.

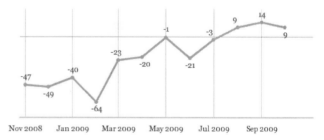

Gallup Index of Investor Optimism, November 2008-October 2009

This is the third month in a row that investors as a whole have been slightly optimistic about the investment climate. It is a sharp improvement from -47 in November a year ago as the financial crisis unfolded. The Index, which dates back to October 1996, was at its lowest ever in February of this year at -64 and peaked in January 2000 at 178.

Portfolio Optimism Down Slightly

American investors—those having $10,000 or more of investable assets—remain optimistic about the prospects for their personal investment portfolios. At 33, the Personal Dimension of the Index is down three points from its September high of 36, but it is the second best showing of the year. In this regard, investors appear to be reasonably optimistic about the future performance of their portfolios over the next 12 months. Personal portfolio optimism is up 27 points since its February low of 6, seemingly reflecting the sharp improvement in the stock and commodities markets.

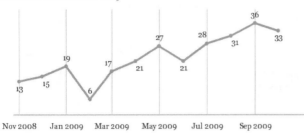

Personal Dimension, Gallup Index of Investor Optimism,
November 2008-October 2009

Economic Pessimism Continues

Investors remain pessimistic about the economic outlook as the Economic Dimension of the Index registered -24 in October, down slightly but similar to the -22 of August and September. (A negative score means investors as a whole remain pessimistic along this dimension.) Still, the level of this Dimension over the past three months represents a sharp improvement from June's -42 score and July's -31, not to mention the -70 score in February. While investors have remained neutral or positive about their own investment portfolios throughout the current recession, they have not been positive about the economy's direction at any time measured since December 2007.

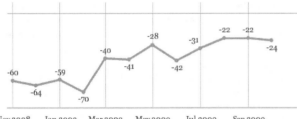

Economic Dimension, Gallup Index of Investor Optimism,
November 2008-October 2009

Commentary

While the modest decline in the Index of Investor Optimism for October does not seem to correlate with the Dow Jones Average hitting 10,000, it is fully consistent with a similar falloff in Gallup's Economic Confidence Index. In fact, consumers and investors continue to hold similarly pessimistic views of the future course of the U.S. economy. These views should be confirmed once more when the Reuters/University of Michigan Consumer Sentiment Index is released on Friday.

Further, it seems reasonable that investors show substantially more optimism about their investment portfolios than they do in the overall U.S. economy. The stock market, as well as gold, commodities, and other investments, continues to do well, but only partly in response to the improvement in the economic data. The continuing decline in the value of the dollar and the seeming substitution of commodities as an important store of value appears to be creating a sharp divergence between how investors fare on Wall Street and how the average American is doing on Main Street.

In theory, this kind of divergence should not be maintainable for too long. Still, there are all kinds of artificialities in today's global financial markets—and lots of liquidity looking for a home. As a result, investors' optimism about their investment portfolios may be warranted given the current investment climate, regardless of their perceptions concerning their outlook for the U.S. economy.

At the same time, Gallup's economic data seem consistent with the way investor and consumer perceptions of the U.S. economy have become less optimistic in October. Job creation remains anemic and consumer spending continues to be flat. It seems likely that these conditions will need to improve significantly before overall investor optimism can return to its pre-recession levels.

Author's Note: Gallup's Index of Investor Optimism—a survey of those having $10,000 or more of investable assets—peaked at 178 in January 2000, just prior to the bursting of the dot-com bubble. Last year, the Index turned negative for the first time in its history. Before last year, the low for the Index was 5 in March 2003, reflecting investor concerns at the outset of the Iraq war.

Survey Methods

Gallup Poll Daily interviewing includes no fewer than 1,000 U.S. adults nationwide each day during 2008. The Index of Investor Optimism results are based on questions asked of 1,000 or more investors over a three-day period each month, conducted Oct. 23-25, Sept. 28-30, Aug. 18-21, July 24-26, June 25-27, May 26-28, April 21-23, March 16-18, Feb. 17-19, and Jan. 16-18, 2009; and Dec. 16-18, Nov. 24-26, June 3-6, April 25-28, March 28-31, and Feb. 28-March 2, 2008. For results based on these samples, the maximum margin of sampling error is ±3 percentage points.

Results for May 2008 are based on the Gallup Panel study and are based on telephone interviews with 576 national adults, aged 18 and older, conducted May 19-21, 2008. Gallup Panel members are recruited through random selection methods. The panel is weighted so that it is demographically representative of the U.S. adult population. For results based on this sample, one can say with 95% confidence that the maximum margin of sampling error is ±5 percentage points.

For investor results prior to 2008, telephone interviews were conducted with at least 800 investors, aged 18 and older, and having at least $10,000 of investable assets. For the total sample of investors in these surveys, one can say with 95% confidence that the maximum margin of sampling error is ± 4 percentage points.

Interviews are conducted with respondents on land-line telephones (for respondents with a land-line telephone) and cellular phones (for respondents who are cell-phone only).

In addition to sampling error, question wording and practical difficulties in conducting surveys can introduce error or bias into the findings of public opinion polls.

October 29, 2009
LITTLE "OBAMA EFFECT" ON VIEWS ABOUT RACE RELATIONS
Attitudes toward race not significantly improved from previous years

by Frank Newport, Gallup Poll Editor in Chief

A majority of Americans, 56%, believe that a solution to America's race-relations problem will eventually be worked out—a figure that is roughly the same as those Gallup found in the years prior to last fall's historic election of Barack Obama as president.

Do you think that relations between blacks and whites will always be a problem for the United States, or that a solution will eventually be worked out?

National adults

■ % Always a problem   ▦ % Solution eventually worked out

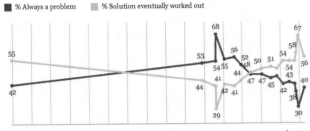

Responses to this long-standing trend today are almost exactly where they were in December 1963, when Gallup first asked this question. Fifty-five percent of Americans in 1963 were hopeful that a solution to the race-relations problem would eventually be worked out. Now, some 46 years later, the "hopeful" percentage is an almost identical 56%. In short, despite all that has happened in the intervening decades, there is scarcely more hope now than there was those many years ago that the nation's race-relations situation will be solved.

Still, the similarity between attitudes in 1963 and 2009 masks a good deal of movement on this measure in the intervening years.

The all-time low point for the "hopeful" alternative—29%—came in October 1995, shortly after a Los Angeles jury acquitted O.J. Simpson of murder. By 1998, views that a solution to race problems would eventually be worked out had improved slightly, to 41%, and they increased still more, to 50%, by 2002. By last summer, when there was general recognition that a black man, Barack Obama, would receive the Democratic nomination for president, the percentage of Americans believing in an eventual solution to the race problem had risen to 58%.

Gallup conducted a one-night poll on Nov. 5 of last year, the day after Obama's electoral victory over John McCain. The percentage of Americans giving the positive alternative to the race-relations question in that survey jumped to 67%.

Now, about a year after Obama's election, optimism that a solution to the country's race problem will eventually be worked out has settled back down to 56%. This certainly remains higher than in a number of previous years, particularly at points in the 1990s. But the current reading is not significantly improved from the sentiment that prevailed in more recent years prior to Obama's election.

Blacks continue to give much more negative responses to this question than do whites. The majority of whites are optimistic that a solution will eventually be worked out; the majority of blacks disagree.

Do you think that relations between blacks and whites will always be a problem for the United States, or that a solution will eventually be worked out?

% Solution eventually worked out, by race

■ Blacks   ▦ Whites (including Hispanics)

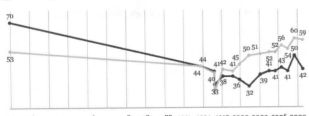

Among blacks, optimism about an eventual solution to race-relations problems has decreased since last summer, from 50% to 42%. In fact, the current 42% is essentially the same percentage that Gallup measured among blacks on several previous occasions.

Equal Job Opportunities?

A second Gallup trend question asks if blacks have as good a chance as whites "in your community" to get any kind of job for which they are qualified.

In general, do you think that blacks have as good a chance as whites in your community to get any kind of job for which they are qualified, or don't you think they have as good a chance?

National adults

■ % Have as good a chance   ▦ % Don't have as good a chance

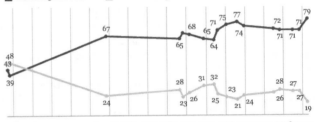

In the current poll, 79% of Americans say blacks have equal employment opportunities. This is technically the highest positive response measured to date, albeit just two points higher than what Gallup measured in the 1998 survey. Compared to last summer, the current figure represents an increase of eight percentage points.

There has been significant change on this measure over the last four and a half decades. In March 1963, when Gallup first asked this question, less than half of Americans (43%) said blacks had equal opportunities in terms of jobs. In the summer of that year, the percentage of Americans who perceived that there was equal opportunity for blacks dropped to the all-time low of 39%.

There was a sea change in attitudes by the time Gallup next asked the question, in 1978, with 67% of Americans in the summer of that year agreeing that blacks had equal opportunities. Sentiment remained at roughly this level through the mid-1990s, and then rose to 75% in 1997 and 77% in 1998.

Here again, as was the case for the broad question about eventual solutions to the race-relations problem, Americans' attitudes today are positive, but not dramatically or significantly higher than at various points prior to Obama's election.

Blacks are decidedly more pessimistic about equal job opportunities for blacks than are whites.

A large majority of whites say blacks have as good a chance as whites to get any type of job for which they are qualified. Blacks, on the other hand, are divided in their views. The current perceptions among blacks of the job situation for blacks represents an improvement from recent years, although at one point in 1995—after O.J. Simpson's acquittal—blacks were slightly more optimistic than they are now.

Racism

A third Gallup trend asks Americans about racism against blacks in the U.S. At the beginning of last summer—after Obama had essentially clinched the Democratic nomination—56% of Americans

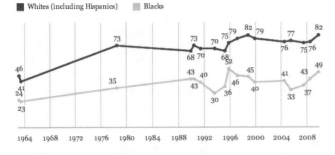

In general, do you think that blacks have as good a chance as whites in your community to get any kind of job for which they are qualified, or don't you think they have as good a chance?

% Have as good a chance

■ Whites (including Hispanics)   ▨ Blacks

agreed that there was widespread racism against blacks in the U.S. That percentage has now dropped to 51%. The slight drop over the last 20 months has occurred to some degree among both blacks and whites.

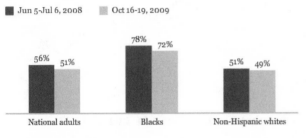

Do you think racism against blacks is or is not widespread in the U.S.?

% Yes, it is widespread

■ Jun 5-Jul 6, 2008   ▨ Oct 16-19, 2009

There has been a slight uptick (from 41% to 44%) in the percentage of Americans who perceive widespread racism *against whites* in the U.S. Again, the overall increase reflects increases among both blacks and whites.

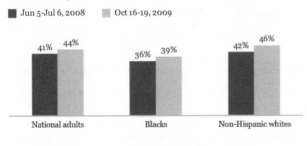

Do you think racism against whites is or is not widespread in the U.S.?

% Yes, it is widespread

■ Jun 5-Jul 6, 2008   ▨ Oct 16-19, 2009

Bottom Line

Despite the election of the first black president in U.S. history, Americans' optimism about a solution to the race problem in the U.S. and their views about the prevalence of racism against blacks are not substantially more positive now than they have been in previous years. In fact, optimism about race relations is now almost identical to where it was 46 years ago, when Gallup first asked the question.

Blacks remain significantly more negative than whites about their status in society and about the potential for an eventual solution to the race problem. The data do not suggest that blacks have become disproportionately more positive than whites as a result of Obama's election as president.

Survey Methods

Results are based on telephone interviews with 1,521 national adults, aged 18 and older, conducted Oct. 16-19, 2009, including an over-sample of 408 blacks, consisting of 102 interviews done as part of the random national sample and 306 interviews with blacks who had previously participated in national Gallup polls and agreed to be re-interviewed at a later date. The data from the national sample and re-interviews are combined and weighted to be demographically representative of the national adult population in the United States and to reflect the proper proportion of blacks in the overall population. For results based on this sample of national adults, the maximum margin of error is ±3 percentage points.

For results based on the sample of 408 blacks, the maximum margin of error is ±6 percentage points.

For results based on the sample of 933 non-Hispanic whites, the maximum margin of error is ±4 percentage points.

Interviews are conducted with respondents on land-line telephones (for respondents with a land-line telephone) and cellular phones (for respondents who are cell-phone only).

In addition to sampling error, question wording and practical difficulties in conducting surveys can introduce error or bias into the findings of public opinion polls.

October 30, 2009
DESPITE POSITIVE SIGNS, AMERICANS STILL NEGATIVE ON JOB MARKET
In August, 41% saw short-term benefits of economic stimulus

by Frank Newport, Gallup Poll Editor in Chief

The White House announced today that President Barack Obama's stimulus plan saved or created 640,000 jobs and further, that jobs linked to this year's tax cuts put the total number of jobs created this year by government actions at over one million. A review of Gallup data does, in fact, show that American workers have been reporting a slightly more positive hiring situation at their companies since July, but that there has been no change in the percentage of Americans who say it is a good time to find a quality job. When Gallup last asked directly about the stimulus in August, 41% felt that the stimulus plan had produced a positive short-term effect on the economy.

Job Creation

Gallup's Job Creation Index has been, for the most part, in positive territory since mid-September, with employees at least slightly more likely to say their companies are hiring new employees rather than to say their companies are reducing the size of their workforce. This marks an improvement from earlier this year when the index was consistently in negative territory. Although the changes involved are not large, they do suggest at least a modest improvement in the job situation in America in the latter half of this year.

Gallup Daily: Job Market

Weekly averages

■ % Hiring   ▨ % Letting Go

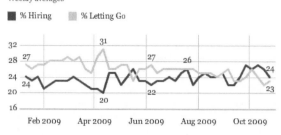

Good Time to Find a Job?

Despite these slightly more positive reports on company hiring activity from workers, Gallup's tracking of the views of all Americans on the job market have not changed this year and remain very negative. Only 1 out of 10 Americans in early October said that it is a good time to find a quality job, representing a continuation of the pattern seen all year.

Finding a Quality Job Nationwide

Thinking about the job situation in America today, would you say that it is now a good time or a bad time to find a quality job?

■ % "Good time"

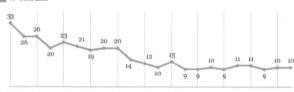

Jan '08 Mar '08 May '08 Jul '08 Sep '08 Nov'08 Jan '09 Mar '09 May '09 Jul '09 Sep '09

Taking a look at this trend over time, these views on the job market underwent a general month after month slide throughout 2008. This year, despite the stimulus money, the upward movement in the stock market, and other economic news, these perceptions have hardly budged from the negative levels at which they began the year.

Effect of the Stimulus

Americans had mixed views on the effect of the stimulus on the economy in early August. About 4 out of 10 said that the stimulus had made the economy better in the short-term and about 4 in 10 said the stimulus would make the economy better in the long term. The rest either said that the stimulus had no effect, or that it made the economy worse. More specifically, about as many Americans felt the stimulus would make the economy worse in the long term as would make it better.

Do you think the economic stimulus plan will make the economy better than if the plan had not passed, has it not had an effect, or has it made the economy worse than if the plan had not passed?

Short-term and long-term effects

■ Economy better   ▨ No effect   ▨ Economy worse

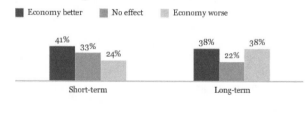

The White House announcement Friday that there have been up to 1,000,000 jobs created by government actions relating to the economy (and the news coverage that follows) may in and of itself increase Americans' positive perceptions of the impact of the stimulus on the economy, and perhaps help boost economic confidence more generally. The long-term impact of the White House tally of jobs created will, in turn, be affected by reports on jobs and unemployment that come out in the weeks ahead. Gallup's daily monitoring of the economy will continue to help gauge the way in which these factors affect the lives and attitudes of average Americans.

Survey Methods

Gallup surveys 1,000 national adults, aged 18 and older, every day and also conducts additional surveys. In most cases, the maximum margin of sampling error is ±2-3 percentage points.

Interviews are conducted with respondents on land-line telephones (for respondents with a land-line telephone) and cellular phones (for respondents who are cell-phone only).

In addition to sampling error, question wording and practical difficulties in conducting surveys can introduce error or bias into the findings of public opinion polls.

October 30, 2009
AMERICANS ON HEALTHCARE REFORM: FIVE KEY REALITIES
Gallup editors review patterns in data collected throughout the debate

by Frank Newport, Jeffrey M. Jones, and Lydia Saad, Gallup Poll Editors

Americans are closely divided on the issue of passing comprehensive healthcare reform, meaning that public opinion offers no real political advantage to either champions or opponents of the idea. That said, a review of Gallup polls conducted throughout the debate reveals five realities crucial to understanding public opinion on this issue.

1. Public Opinion on Healthcare Reform Is Divided, Yet Stable

Thus far, basic U.S. public opinion about healthcare reform has been little changed by the political debate that erupted in town halls this summer or the contentious arguments that have become a staple of television news. Despite this heated discourse and ever-changing estimates of the expected cost and other details of healthcare reform, Americans have remained about evenly divided on the issue of voting new healthcare reform legislation into law.

In early October, Gallup found 40% of Americans saying they would advise their member of Congress to vote for a healthcare bill this year and 36% saying they would advise voting against the bill. That result was little different from an early August reading. A separate and more recent Gallup question—phrased differently—also found a roughly equal divide in sentiment once those who were initially unsure were asked which way they leaned.

A number of other polling organizations show the same pattern of split sentiment on the basic question of passing a new healthcare law.

Why such stability? Partisanship is part of the answer. It appears that Republicans and Democrats dug in early on either side of the issue and have held their ground. Independents have also been remarkably fixed in their reaction, with perhaps a slight increase in support in recent weeks.

This year's relative stability contrasts with the pattern in 1994, when public opinion about President Clinton's healthcare reform initiative shifted from a solid majority in favor in January to a solid majority opposed by July.

There is an additional explanation for the current stability in healthcare attitudes. Data suggest that Americans may be more focused on the ideological underpinnings of healthcare reform than on the minutiae or specific elements that are the primary focus of ongoing debate and discussion. Gallup research has shown that supporters generally favor a new law because they want to expand coverage to the uninsured. Opponents are most likely to say they are against a new law because of worries about increased government involvement in healthcare. Both types of explanations are fundamental concerns, rather than quibbles with specific features of proposed legislation.

Reinforcing the concept of relative stability in Americans' attitudes toward the healthcare system, Gallup finds that Americans are not dramatically more likely today than they have been for much of the decade—or as far back as 1994—to believe the U.S. healthcare system is in a crisis or has major problems.

Bottom Line: Americans' positions on healthcare reform appear to be fairly entrenched. It does not seem likely that the continuing debate as a bill makes its way toward the president's desk is going to change those attitudes dramatically. If and when a new bill is passed into law, it is likely that not much more than half of the American adult population will support it.

2. Americans Do Not Have a Strong Sense of Urgency About Passing Healthcare Reform

Americans have become somewhat more likely to mention healthcare as the nation's most important problem this year, and a recent *USA Today*/Gallup poll found more Americans saying healthcare should be President Obama's top priority than did so last November. However, in both of these instances, the economy continues to dominate healthcare and all other concerns. In particular, Americans are about as likely to select the situations in Iraq and Afghanistan or the federal budget deficit as Obama's top priority as they are to select healthcare. And all three issues rank well below the economy.

Given a choice in one recent Gallup survey, less than half of Americans say Congress should pass reform this year rather than at some point in the future.

And when asked whether it would be better to enact comprehensive reform this year or reform the system more gradually, the majority of Americans opt for gradual reform.

All of these findings, coupled with the fact that Americans are not convinced that a new healthcare law would benefit them personally (to be discussed below), underscore the conclusion that the average American is not suffused with a pressing sense of urgency to see wide-ranging healthcare reform legislation passed immediately.

Bottom Line: The apparent lack of urgency on Americans' part to fix healthcare stands in contrast to the continuing sense of urgency evinced by the president and other reform advocates. Proponents may argue that this is an area in which elected leaders need to lead, not follow, public opinion. Opponents may argue, on the other hand, that passing a major new healthcare reform bill over the objections of close to half of Americans is overreaching.

3. Self-Interest Is Only Part of the Story

The substantial majority of adult Americans have health insurance, meaning that on a relative basis, few Americans are likely to support healthcare reform specifically because they personally are in direct and immediate need of obtaining health insurance. Additionally, the majority of Americans who have health insurance appear to be satisfied with it.

Gallup research shows that even among the relatively small group of adults without health insurance, fewer than half would advise their member of Congress to vote for new healthcare legislation, while the rest either would advise their member to vote against it or are unsure. Thus, even among the uninsured—those who in theory would be most likely to believe they would personally benefit from healthcare reform—self-interest is not necessarily the driving force behind their political views on healthcare.

Eight in 10 Americans say they are satisfied with the quality of their own medical care. Fairly small percentages of Americans who currently have health insurance say they have experienced major problems with reductions in what their insurance plans cover or with insurance paperwork. Healthcare costs emerge as a greater concern for Americans, but mainly on a relative basis. Forty-six percent of Americans say the cost of medical care is a major problem for them, and 38% are dissatisfied with their own healthcare costs.

Similarly, and importantly, relatively few Americans believe various aspects of their own healthcare coverage or medical care will improve under healthcare reform. Most believe their healthcare either will not change or will in fact worsen, with close to half expecting their costs to increase. Fewer than half of reform supporters believe that if a new healthcare bill passes this year, it would benefit them in terms of cost, quality, coverage, or insurance company requirements. In other words, at least half of Americans who support a bill are doing so for reasons other than the belief that it will benefit them personally. By contrast, large majorities of Americans who oppose healthcare reform believe the bill would negatively affect all four aspects of their own health insurance coverage.

These findings on the perceived impact of healthcare reform on Americans' personal situations are robust, and have been replicated across a number of different surveys conducted by different organizations.

When healthcare reform supporters are asked to provide their reasons for favoring legislation, nearly half of the reasons they give have to do with providing access for those who don't have it. Another 16% cite needing to fix the system, generally, or control costs. Only 7% say they personally or a family member needs healthcare coverage. Additionally, 8% say healthcare reform would help control costs, something that could have a personal benefit.

Finally, Gallup polling in recent years has consistently shown that a majority of Americans believe it is the government's responsibility to make sure all Americans have healthcare coverage.

Bottom Line: It may be surprising to some that even close to half of Americans support the concept of new healthcare legislation when far fewer than half appear to believe that such a new bill will benefit them personally. Others may argue from a positive perspective that Americans are willing to support the idea of legislation that, while it doesn't help them, may help others.

4. Specific Elements of Healthcare Reform Have Strong Appeal; a Few Do Not

President Obama has remarked that there is widespread agreement in Washington on certain aspects of reform, such as requiring insurance companies to cover those with pre-existing medical conditions, prohibiting insurance companies from dropping those who get sick, and providing assistance to lower-income Americans to help them obtain insurance. Despite lukewarm support for a new healthcare bill in general, existing polling from Gallup and other firms finds Americans expressing strong support for provisions such as these, or saying these are highly important to include in healthcare legislation.

The public also seems to favor requiring employers to provide health insurance to their employees, or to pay fines for not doing so.

But the fate of the healthcare legislation may ride on some of the more controversial provisions, the most notable being whether Americans would be able to purchase a government-sponsored insurance plan that would compete with private insurance plans. Gallup recently found the public essentially divided on this, with 50% in favor of including a government plan and 46% opposed. Other polls have shown slightly higher support for the "public option," results that no doubt partly reflect some confusion among Americans about such a plan.

Gallup has tested various proposals that have been suggested as ways to pay for healthcare reform. The most popular appears to be the imposition of income-tax surcharges on upper-income Americans (Gallup polling has usually found majority support for raising taxes on upper-income Americans to pay for government programs, such as Social Security reform, for example). Americans have shown consistent opposition to reducing Medicare payments, and also to taxing insurance plans that offer the most generous benefits.

Bottom Line: Emphasizing the most popular aspects of healthcare reform—of which there are several—could potentially help reform proponents expand public support for the plan more generally. This assumes Americans are not already fully cognizant that healthcare reform would achieve these objectives. Alternatively, Americans may already well appreciate these benefits, but have overriding reservations about other aspects of the bill, such as the cost.

Additionally, Americans may harbor doubts about how well government and healthcare bureaucracies can implement a highly complex new set of laws encompassing a large segment of the U.S. economy. This "practical" doubt is reinforced by recent data showing that Americans give Congress a low job approval rating, have relatively low levels of trust in the federal government, and believe that about half of all federal tax dollars are wasted.

5. Obama Retains the Upper Hand

Although passage of healthcare legislation is far from assured, President Obama has helped move healthcare reform far down the legislative track. Americans say they trust the president more than the Democrats or Republicans in Congress on the issue, and he is the only one of these three major political actors whom a majority of Americans trust. These findings are underscored by the fact that the president's job approval ratings have been running more than 20 points higher than job approval ratings for Congress.

However, at 55%, trust even for Obama is not overwhelming. And as of mid-September, a majority of Americans said they disapproved of the way Obama was handling the healthcare issue (43% approved, similar to what Gallup found in prior readings).

Americans have more confidence in President Obama than in the insurance and pharmaceutical companies that are lobbying so hard in Washington. They have roughly the same confidence in Obama as in hospitals and healthcare professors or researchers. Only doctors generate significantly more confidence on healthcare than does Obama.

Bottom Line: One major advantage held by the proponents of healthcare reform is political—healthcare reform has a more popular communicator in President Obama than the opponents of healthcare reform have in congressional Republicans. And of course, from a practical perspective, if the Democratic Party can hold together its majorities in both houses of Congress, it would be assured of passing healthcare legislation.

More broadly, six months of polling on healthcare reform has left even some seasoned political analysts scratching their heads about what Americans really want Washington to do on the issue. As reviewed above, most Americans say the healthcare system has major problems or worse, and they believe fixing healthcare needs to be a priority. Still, Americans are closely divided in their preferences for passing a healthcare reform bill, are skeptical of Obama's promise to make reform revenue neutral, and would prefer to pass healthcare reform gradually, rather than this year.

November 02, 2009

GENERIC BALLOT PROVIDES CLUES FOR 2010 VOTE

Republicans could have good year, but may not be enough for control of House

by Jeffrey M. Jones, Gallup Poll Managing Editor

One year from today, U.S. voters will head to the polls to elect all 435 members of the U.S. House of Representatives. Gallup measures voting intentions in midterm elections using the generic congressional ballot, which has proven an accurate predictor of the eventual vote in midterm elections.

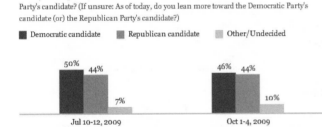

2010 Generic Congressional Ballot -- Preferences of Registered Voters

If the elections for Congress were being held today, which party's candidate would you vote for in your congressional district -- the Democratic Party's candidate (or) the Republican Party's candidate? (If unsure: As of today, do you lean more toward the Democratic Party's candidate (or) the Republican Party's candidate?)

Gallup's most recent test of the 2010 elections, from an Oct. 1-4 poll, showed 46% of registered voters saying they would support the Democratic candidate in their local district if the election were held today, compared to 44% who would vote for the Republican candidate. That was a slightly better showing for Republicans than Gallup's prior test in July, which had Democrats up by 50% to 44%.

In terms of analyzing the generic ballot for clues as to which party has the advantage well before an election, the size of the lead among registered voters offers arguably more insight than the simple fact of which party is ahead. Given the usual Democratic advantages in party identification among the general public, it is rare for Republicans to lead on the generic ballot among registered voters. This was the case even when Republicans were the majority congressional party from the mid-1990s to the mid-2000s.

But the reason the Republican Party is competitive in congressional elections is that Republicans generally turn out to vote at higher rates than Democrats. Turnout is crucial in midterm elections, and with at least 80% of Americans registered to vote but only about half that number likely to vote in the midterm elections, registered voter and actual voter preferences can differ by a lot.

As a starting point, if Democrats have close to a double-digit lead among registered voters, they are virtually ensured of also hav-

ing a lead among actual voters—whatever turnout happens to be on Election Day.

From that point, things become a little less clear-cut. Smaller Democratic leads do not necessarily mean the party is losing, but rather that the eventual election outcome will be more dependent on turnout. In general, the closer the registered-voter results get to an even split, the better Republicans can expect to do, given usual turnout patterns.

Gallup analyzes turnout patterns in a given election by applying its "likely voter" model to midterm results. However, since it is unclear how reliable likely voter models are in identifying likely voters in a low-turnout election long before Election Day, Gallup usually does not begin to estimate likely voter preferences until September or October of a midterm election year.

But early generic-ballot results based on the sample of registered voters do still give reliable—if not highly precise—indications of how the election might go.

For example, through much of 1974, 1982, and 2006—highly successful years for the Democratic Party—the generic ballot showed consistent, huge Democratic advantages among registered voters.

1974 Generic Congressional Ballot -- Preferences of Registered Voters

■ Democratic candidate　　■ Republican candidate

53%　50%　　55%　52%　51%　52%　56%

27%　25%　　23%　24%　26%　24%　30%

Jun '74　Jul '74　Aug '74　Sep '74　Oct '74

1982 Generic Congressional Ballot -- Preferences of Registered Voters

■ Democratic candidate　　■ Republican candidate

50%　47%　51%　　50%　56%　54%　　55%　51%　52%　54%

42%　34%　31%　38%　36%　37%　37%　34%　37%　36%

Feb '82　Mar '82　Apr '82　May '82　Jun '82　Jul '82　Aug '82　Sep '82　Oct '82

2006 Generic Congressional Ballot -- Preferences of Registered Voters

■ Democratic candidate　　■ Republican candidate

49%　50%　55%　54%　51%　54%　51%　50%　53%　58%　51%

43%　43%　39%　39%　42%　38%　41%　41%　41%　35%　40%

Feb '06　Apr '06　Jun '06　Aug '06　Oct '06

In 1994, leading up to a Republican landslide, the generic ballot suggested it could be a very promising year for Republicans, as the party actually enjoyed a slight lead among registered voters in several polls. When the likely voter models were applied in the final months of the campaign, Republicans held solid leads among this group of voters.

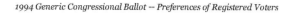

1994 Generic Congressional Ballot -- Preferences of Registered Voters

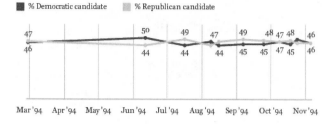

In years such as 1998 and 2002, the early reads on the generic ballot suggested the elections would be competitive, and the eventual outcome would largely depend on turnout. Those two elections were unique from the standpoint that the president's party (Democratic in 1998 and Republican in 2002) gained U.S. House seats in the midterm elections, bucking the historical trend. Turnout proved to be pivotal in 2002 as the Democrats' five-point lead among registered voters turned into a six-point deficit once likely voter preferences were measured (the actual vote on Election Day showed a five-point Republican advantage).

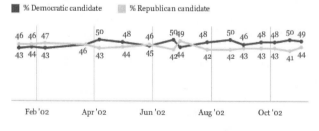

Translating Votes to Seats

The aggregated national vote in and of itself does not directly determine the election outcome since that vote is spread out over 435 districts, some of which are highly competitive while others are not competitive at all. The focus of House election results is the tally of the number of seats won by each party. Still, the national vote has proven to be highly correlated with the eventual seat distribution by party in the House of Representatives. This allows Gallup to use the generic ballot to make predictions about the eventual Democratic-Republican seat distribution and the likelihood of either party's having control after the election.

Gallup has developed a statistical model to attempt to estimate the House seat distribution based on the national vote. This model takes into account historical voting patterns in midterm elections from 1946 to 2006 and structural factors such as the president's party and the majority party in Congress at the time of the election. In

2006, Democrats enjoyed a seven-point lead among likely voters in the final pre-election voting estimate, suggesting a range of seat gains (given the model's prediction error) of 11 to 58 seats, with a 35-seat pickup the most likely outcome.

The Democrats needed only 15 seats to regain majority control from the Republicans that year, which seemed almost assured given the poll estimates, and the Democrats ended up gaining 31 seats in that election.

Given the Democrats' current majority status (they now hold 257 seats), it is unlikely that Republicans in the next election will win the number of seats necessary for them to become the majority party. Although Gallup will not be able to predict each party's share of the congressional vote with a great deal of precision until it applies likely voter models next fall, the statistical model used to predict seat distribution by party can use historical data to present a number of scenarios in terms of seat distribution, based on the ultimate vote by party.

Gallup's model shows that Democrats could lose the overall 2010 congressional vote and still retain majority-party status. With as little as 51% of the two-party vote, Democrats could expect to hold almost all of their current seats (the model would predict 251 Democratic seats held after the election, with a range of 240 to 262). And with as little as 48% of the vote, Democrats could still reasonably be expected to retain the majority of 218 seats (although they could conceivably still lose the majority at this level, given the model's error range).

Predictions of Democratic House Seats, Based on Ultimate Democratic Share of Vote

Gallup midterm election seat-prediction model

Democratic Share of two-party vote	Best prediction for Democratic share of seats	Low-end prediction for Democratic share of seats	High-end prediction for Democratic share of seats
60%	348	337	359
59%	337	326	348
58%	326	315	337
57%	316	305	327
56%	305	294	316
55%	294	283	305
54%	283	272	294
53%	272	261	283
52%	262	251	273
51%	251	240	262
50%	240	229	251
49%	229	218	240
48%	218	207	229
47%	208	197	219
46%	197	186	208
45%	186	175	197

Note: 218 seats needed for majority control

Bottom Line

Throughout the 2010 campaign, Gallup will measure voter preferences for the U.S. House, using the generic congressional ballot. A review of past midterm election-year data suggests that even early predictions can give insight into how next year's elections might go. The size of the Democratic lead among registered voters in the months ahead will be a key indicator of whether the election will be competitive. If Republicans are close to being tied or are ahead, it will suggest the possibility of a strong Republican year unless Democrats have an unusually strong and disproportionate turnout advantage.

In Gallup's most recent update, the Republicans are within two points of the Democrats among registered voters. The closeness of these results suggests that voter turnout, which Gallup will begin to assess next fall with its likely voter model, will be an important factor in the ultimate 2010 election outcome. Once probable voter turnout is known, Gallup can provide greater insight into possibilities for changes in party division in the next House of Representatives.

The possibility of a strong Republican year would be consistent with history. The president's party usually loses seats in a midterm election year. The popularity of the president is a factor in the size of those losses.

November 02, 2009

BLACKS FAR MORE SATISFIED WITH U.S. UNDER OBAMA

Blacks' satisfaction tracks closely with Democrats'; black Democrats' satisfaction up the most

by Lydia Saad, Gallup Poll Senior Editor

Blacks' satisfaction with the direction of the country has surged since Barack Obama became president in January, while satisfaction among whites has increased by far less. Today close to half of black adults nationwide, 47%, say they are satisfied with the way things are going in the country. In mid-2008, the figure was 10%.

*Percentage Satisfied With Direction of the Country -- by Race^*

In general, are you satisfied or dissatisfied with the way things are going in the United States at this time?

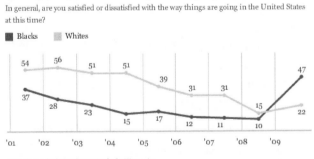

^ Blacks and whites do not include Hispanics

Increased satisfaction among blacks since 2008 is not surprising given the fact that the great majority of blacks—82% in the latest poll—identify themselves as Democrats or as leaning to the Democratic Party. Partisans typically show greater satisfaction with the direction of the country when the sitting president is a member of their political party. This is evident in Gallup's U.S. Satisfaction trend since 2001.

Across this period, the pattern of satisfaction among Democrats is very similar to that seen among blacks, with declining satisfaction

through much of George W. Bush's presidency, and the rebound in 2009. Satisfaction also fell among Republicans during Bush's second term, although it remained substantially higher than that among Democrats or independents. Now, with Obama in the White House, Republican satisfaction is at 10%, well below the other two groups' satisfaction.

Percentage Satisfied With Direction of the Country, by Party ID

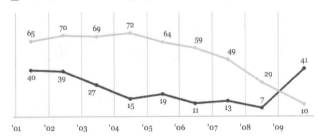

Despite the strong influence of party affiliation, it seems that more than just partisanship explains the current level of U.S. satisfaction among blacks, as black Democrats have shown a greater increase in satisfaction over the past year than white Democrats. Today, 38% of white Democrats say they are satisfied with the direction of the country, up from 5% in June/July 2008—a 33-point gain. By contrast, 51% of black Democrats today are satisfied, up from 7%—a 44-point gain. (There are too few black Republicans to enable the same trend analysis by race for Republicans.)

2008-2009 Trend in U.S. Satisfaction Among Democrats, by Race

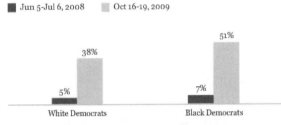

The latest results are from an Oct. 16-19 *USA Today*/Gallup poll, which included an oversample of blacks, thus providing a reliable basis for estimating the views of this segment of Americans. The historical comparisons are to Gallup's annual Minority Rights and Relations surveys from 2001 through 2008, which also included black oversamples.

Bottom Line

Close to half of all blacks today (47%) say they are satisfied with the way things are going in the country, as are 51% of black Democrats. These figures compare with 10% of Republicans, 22% of non-Hispanic whites, 38% of white Democrats, and 41% of all Democrats. Thus, of the leading racial and political groupings, blacks are the most satisfied with the direction of the United States today.

Survey Methods

Results are based on telephone interviews with 1,521 national adults, aged 18 and older, conducted Oct. 16-19, 2009, including an oversample of 408 blacks, consisting of 102 interviews done as part of the random national sample and 306 interviews with blacks who had previously participated in national Gallup polls and agreed to be re-interviewed at a later date. The data from the national sample and re-interviews are combined and weighted to be demographically representative of the national adult population in the United States and to reflect the proper proportion of blacks in the overall population. For results based on this sample of national adults, the maximum margin of error is ±3 percentage points.

Interviews are conducted with respondents on land-line telephones (for respondents with a land-line telephone) and cellular phones (for respondents who are cell-phone only).

In addition to sampling error, question wording and practical difficulties in conducting surveys can introduce error or bias into the findings of public opinion polls.

November 03, 2009
ONE YEAR AFTER ELECTION, AMERICANS LESS SURE ABOUT OBAMA
Far fewer say he will be able to control federal spending or heal political divisions

by Frank Newport, Gallup Poll Editor in Chief

Americans are much less positive than they were a year ago that President Barack Obama will be able to accomplish a number of challenges facing his administration. In particular, far fewer Americans believe he will be able to heal political divisions and control federal spending.

Will the Obama Administration Be Able to Do Each of the Following?
% Yes, it will

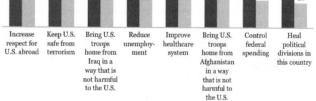

Gallup asked Americans about eight specific administration goals shortly after Obama's election last November, and updated these attitudes in mid-October 2009.

Given Obama's decline in overall job approval this year, it may not be surprising to find that Americans have become at least somewhat less optimistic about Obama's ability to accomplish these goals. The drop since last November in the percentage saying Obama would be able to accomplish them ranges from 5 percentage points for "keeping the U.S. safe from terrorism" to a 26-point drop on "healing political divisions in this country."

In spite of the declines, more than half of Americans remain confident that Obama will be able to achieve four important goals:
- Increase respect for the U.S. abroad
- Keep the U.S. safe from terrorism
- Bring U.S. troops home from Iraq in a way that is not harmful to the U.S.
- Reduce unemployment

Less than half are confident that Obama will be able to achieve success on four other goals:
- Bring U.S. troops home from Afghanistan in a way that is not harmful to the U.S.
- Improve the healthcare system
- Control federal spending
- Heal political divisions in this country

Americans are least confident that Obama will be able to heal political divisions in this country. This perception is underscored by the results of a separate question that asked about the degree of political division in the country. Two-thirds of Americans now say the country is more deeply divided on the major issues facing the country than it has been in the past several years, an increase of 11 points from the record-low reading on this last November.

Do you think the country is -- or is not -- more deeply divided this year on the major issues facing the country than it has been in the past several years?

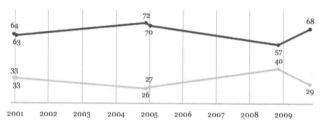

The "more deeply divided" response had been as high (and as negative) as 72% in a November 2004 survey conducted just after George W. Bush's re-election to his second term as president. The current 68% reading is just slightly below this level, but higher than was seen immediately after the Supreme Court settled the outcome of the 2000 presidential election.

Some had hoped that Obama's election would bring the nation closer together. The significant drop in views that Obama will be able to heal political divisions and the increase in views that the U.S. is more deeply divided than in previous years suggest that the American people are not convinced this has occurred.

Obama's Job Approval Ratings One Year After His Election

One year after his election, President Obama has a 53% job approval rating, putting him near the bottom of the list of elected presidents since World War II, rank-ordered on the basis of their approval ratings one year after their initial election.

Obama's current 53% job approval rating (for the week of Oct.26-Nov. 1) is ahead of Bill Clinton's rating one year after his election, and essentially tied with Reagan's in 1981 and Carter's in 1977. The other five presidents—George W. Bush, John F. Kennedy, George H.W. Bush, Richard Nixon, and Dwight Eisenhower—all had significantly higher ratings a year after their election.

Each president faced a unique set of circumstances at a similar point in his presidency. For example, George W. Bush's extremely

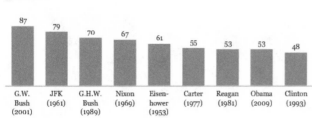

high ratings a year after his election reflected the rally effect that resulted from the Sept. 11, 2001, terrorist attacks in New York City and Washington, D.C. There is little doubt that the current bad economy and the highly partisan debate over healthcare are pulling down Obama's overall rating. Regardless of the causes, however, the data show that Obama at this point is performing below the average for other presidents a year after their election.

Obama can take some solace, however, in the fact that two of the three presidents who had about the same, or lower, ratings at this juncture in their first year in office went on to be re-elected. And George H.W. Bush lost his re-election bid, despite his lofty ratings a year after his 1988 election.

Obama's job approval ratings were at the 60% level or higher through mid-June of this year. They dropped through the summer months, but have stabilized in a fairly tight range between 50% and 54% since mid-August. The drop in Obama's ratings from his second quarter to his third quarter was the highest such drop in Gallup's history of tracking first-term presidents.

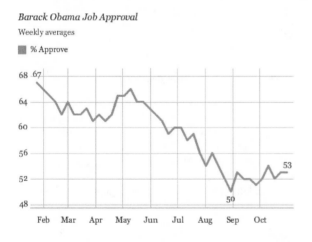

Barack Obama Job Approval

Weekly averages

■ % Approve

Bottom Line

The public's view of a president's first year in office is far from being an effective predictor of how well he will ultimately be judged as president, nor is it a good predictor of his probability of being re-elected. Still, for the moment, the data show that President Obama is performing below average in the context of other presidents a year after their election, and that Americans have become less sure that he will be able to accomplish a number of his administration's goals.

Survey Methods

Results are based on telephone interviews with 1,521 national adults, aged 18 and older, conducted Oct. 16-19, 2009, including

an oversample of 408 blacks, consisting of 102 interviews done as part of the random national sample and 306 interviews with blacks who had previously participated in national Gallup Polls and agreed to be re-interviewed at a later date. The data from the national sample and re-interviews are combined and weighted to be demographically representative of the national adult population in the United States and to reflect the proper proportion of blacks in the overall population. For results based on this sample of national adults, the maximum margin of error is ±3 percentage points.

Interviews are conducted with respondents on land-line telephones (for respondents with a land-line telephone) and cellular phones (for respondents who are cell-phone only).

In addition to sampling error, question wording and practical difficulties in conducting surveys can introduce error or bias into the findings of public opinion polls.

November 03, 2009
EXERCISE AND WELL-BEING: A LITTLE GOES A LONG WAY
Those who exercise even 1-2 days a week better off than those who do not exercise

by Brett W. Pelham, Gallup Poll Staff Writer

The Gallup-Healthways Well-Being Index reveals the extent to which even a little bit of exercise can go a long way. Compared with those who say they did not exercise at all in a given week, those who say they exercised for at least 30 minutes on 1 or 2 days are less likely to be obese. For those who say they exercised five or six days, the likelihood of obesity is cut nearly in half.

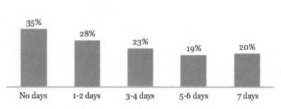

Number of Days of Exercise in the Past Week and Obesity

■ Percentage obese

Obesity is assessed on the basis of respondents' self-reports of their height and weight, which are then used to calculate standard Body Mass Index scores. Individual BMI values of 30 or above are classified as "obese."

Gallup-Healthways Well-Being Index

The results are from more than 250,000 interviews conducted in 2009 as part of the Gallup-Healthways Well-Being Index. Interestingly those who say they exercised every day last week are slightly *more* likely to be obese than those who say they exercised five or six days. The difference in not exercising at all and exercising one to two days is clearly greater than the difference between exercising three to four days and exercising five to six days.

Exercise and Life Evaluation

These Gallup-Healthways data also reveal a strong connection between exercise and how a person rates his or her own life, now and in the future, on a ladder scale where 0 is the worst possible life and 10 is the best possible life. Based on their responses to this Cantril Self-Anchoring Striving Scale, respondents are classified as "thriving," "struggling," or "suffering." Net thriving is the difference between the percentage of people "thriving" and the percentage of people "suffering." There is a 12 percentage point gap in net thriving between those who exercised 1 to 2 times in the past week and those who say they did not exercise. Simply put, even one or two days of exercise per week may pay off in higher life evaluation.

Net thriving increases further for those who exercise more frequently, but it levels off at five to six days of exercise and then drops substantially—to 43%—for those who say they exercised every day. These data cannot tell us whether exercise leads to high well-being or whether high well-being leads to exercise, but they do suggest that getting the maximum amount of exercise may not promote further gains in well-being.

Number of Days of Exercise in Past Week and Net Thriving
(Thriving Minus Suffering)

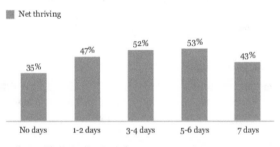

Gallup-Healthways Well-Being Index

Exercise and Emotional Health

Those who report more days of exercise also report higher scores on the Gallup-Healthways Emotional Health Index. This sub-index of the Well-Being Index is based on 10 daily experiences such as smiling or laughing a lot or being treated with respect the day before the interview. The same rule of "diminishing returns" that applies to life evaluation also seems to apply to emotional health. The gap between non-exercisers and those who report having exercised one to two days is greater, for example, than the gap between those who exercised three to four days versus five to six days. Further, those who report having exercised every day report slightly *lower* Emotional Health Index scores than those who say they exercised five to six days.

Exercise and Depression

Exercise is also related to reports of having ever been diagnosed with depression. Those who report not having exercised at all in the past week are almost twice as likely to report having been diagnosed with depression as those who report having exercised five to six days. Further, those who reported that they exercised daily were more likely, rather than less likely, to report having been diagnosed with depression in comparison with those who reported having exercised three to four or five to six days in the past week. Based on these data, one cannot say whether regular exercise reduces depression or whether

Number of Days of Exercise in Past Week and Emotional Health Index Scores

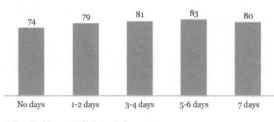

Gallup-Healthways Well-Being Index

depression reduces exercise. However, in the past decade, researchers have conducted experimental and prospective studies that follow depressed people over time. Such studies show exercise can ease feelings of depression and improve mood. The representative survey data suggest that the results of these clinical experiments may apply well to the general population.

Number of Days of Exercise in Past Week and Depression
Have you ever been told by a physician or nurse that you have any of the following: depression?

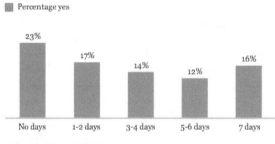

Gallup-Healthways Well-Being Index

Is Too Much Exercise Really a Bad Thing?

The finding that those who report having exercised every day have lower well-being than those who report exercising less frequently has several possible explanations. First, an intense everyday exercise regime could be physiologically and psychologically taxing. Exercise can take up a lot of time and energy. Consistent with these findings, a previous Gallup analysis found that those who exercise feel more well-rested than those who don't—except for those who exercise every day. Exercising without ever giving one's body time to rest may be less ideal than exercising five to six days per week.

A second reason why those who exercise the most days may not have the highest well-being is that some people cope with chronic illnesses by exercising daily *once they have been diagnosed*. For instance, despite the well-establish connection between inactivity and type 2 diabetes, people who report being diagnosed with diabetes are as likely as people without diabetes to report exercising every day (14% of both groups say so). Likewise, some obese people may also attempt to reduce their weight by exercising daily. These data show that obese respondents are slightly more likely to report having exercised every day (11%) than to report having exercised 5 to 6 days (9%). In other words, there is a sense in which illness may sometimes cause daily exercise.

A third reason is based on occupation and well-being. Although some people who are employed in physically demanding jobs may report exercising daily, they may still have moderate to low well-being. According to these data, for example, construction workers are more likely than professional workers to say they exercise daily (23% versus 9%, respectively), but construction workers have much lower overall well-being than professional workers.

Finally, it is possible that a few inactive people are generous in their definition of "exercising every day." Even if such people are a small minority, they might report "exercising" every day, despite a sedentary lifestyle. All this being said, there is evidence from the scientific literature on exercise for a "diminishing returns" principle. In a position paper published in 2009 in *Medicine and Science in Sports and Exercise*, a multidisciplinary team of exercise scientists concluded that "The largest increment in mortality benefit is seen when comparing sedentary adults with those in the next highest physical activity level." That same basic pattern clearly appears in these data.

Bottom Line

Gallup-Healthways Well-Being Index data reveal a robust but non-linear connection between exercise and well-being. One encouraging aspect of these findings is that they show a boost in well-being that may come from as little as one to two days of weekly exercise. That is, the well-being gap between a sedentary lifestyle and lifestyle of occasional exercise is much greater than the well-being gap between moderate and heavy exercisers. The findings not only support the notion that exercise may boost well-being, but they also suggest that it is not necessary to exercise every day of the week to reap meaningful physical and psychological benefits of exercise.

Survey Methods

Results are based on telephone interviews with 287,755 national adults, aged 18 and older, conducted Jan. 2-Oct. 21, 2009. Sample sizes for the main exercise groups range from a high of 88,419 respondents who reported exercising for no days to a low of 36,475 respondents who report having exercised for five to six days. Margins of error are less than one percentage point for all groups.

Interviews are conducted with respondents on land-line telephones (for respondents with a land-line telephone) and cellular phones (for respondents who are cell-phone only).

In addition to sampling error, question wording and practical difficulties in conducting surveys can introduce error or bias into the findings of public opinion polls.

November 04, 2009
POLITICAL CLIMATE FOR 2010 NOT AS FAVORABLE TO DEMOCRATS
Maintain edge in party strength measures, but public dissatisfied with nation's course

by Jeffrey M. Jones, Gallup Poll Managing Editor

The 2010 election cycle begins in a political climate that is shaping up to be not as favorable to the Democratic Party as the 2006 and 2008 elections were. Having capitalized on broad public discontent with the course of the nation in general and the Republican Party in particular to win control of the White House and both houses of Con-

gress, the party faces the 2010 midterm elections trying to preserve its recent gains.

Gallup's generic congressional ballot provides a summary measure of current voting intentions for Congress. This currently suggests the 2010 midterm elections could be highly competitive, and possibly a strong Republican year if usual turnout patterns prevail.

Gallup regularly tracks several measures that give an indication of the political climate and can provide insight into the reasons for Americans' current congressional voting intentions. Although Democrats retain a significant advantage in party affiliation, that advantage has dwindled over the course of this year. Also, there are ominous signs for the majority party in terms of near-record-low congressional job approval and continuing low national satisfaction ratings.

Presidential Job Approval

It is well-documented that the president's party is usually vulnerable to losing congressional seats in midterm elections, though there have been exceptions such as in the 1998 and 2002 elections. Unpopular presidents tend to suffer greater losses, and popular presidents are able to minimize these or even help achieve gains. George W. Bush experienced both outcomes, with Republican gains in 2002 when he was popular and heavy Republican losses in 2006 when he was not.

The Democrats will contest the 2010 elections with their fellow partisan, Barack Obama, in the White House. Right now, Obama's approval ratings are middling, in the low 50s, suggesting he would not be able to minimize Democratic losses to a great degree if the elections were held today. Further erosion of Obama's popularity between now and next November could prove damaging to the Democratic Party. First-term presidents who had sub-50% approval ratings at the midterms—including Harry Truman, Lyndon Johnson, Jimmy Carter, Ronald Reagan, and Bill Clinton—saw their parties suffer large congressional seat losses. In contrast, a recovery in Obama's approval rating—particularly to above 60%—could limit Democratic losses.

Presidential Job Approval and U.S. House Seat Change, Recent Midterm Elections

Year	President/Political party	% Approval	Seat gain/loss in U.S. House for president's party
2006	G.W. Bush/Republican	38	-30
2002	G.W. Bush/Republican	63	+6
1998	Clinton/Democrat	66	+5
1994	Clinton/Democrat	46	-53
1990	G.H.W. Bush/Republican	58	-8
1986	Reagan/Republican	63	-5
1982	Reagan/Republican	42	-28
1978	Carter/Democrat	49	-11
1974	Ford/Republican*	54	-43
1970	Nixon/Republican	58	-12
1966	Johnson/Democrat	44	-47
1962	Kennedy/Democrat	61	-4
1958	Eisenhower/Republican	57	-47
1954	Eisenhower/Republican	61	-18
1950	Truman/Democrat	39	-29
1946	Truman/Democrat	33	-55

* Ford took office less than three months before the midterm elections, replacing Richard Nixon, who had 24% approval when he resigned

Outlook: After a strong start, Obama's approval ratings have slumped, though they remain at or above 50%. Other recent presidents who took office during difficult economic times—Carter, Reagan, and Clinton—were below 50% at the time of the midterms, and saw their parties perform poorly in the elections. Obama hopes to avoid a similar fate.

Satisfaction With the Way Things Are Going in the Country/Ratings of the Economy

These ratings are less overtly political than presidential job approval, but have a similar relationship to election outcomes. Lower satisfaction levels and poorer ratings of the economy are associated with poorer performances for the president's party in midterm elections. Gallup has a slightly longer history of asking about satisfaction than about the economy in election years.

U.S. Satisfaction and Economy Ratings and President's Party Seat Changes, Recent Midterm Elections

Year	% Satisfied	% Rate economy positively	Seat gain/loss in U.S. House for president's party
2006	35	44	-30
2002	48	28	+6
1998	60	66	+5
1994	30	30	-53
1990	32	N/A	-8
1986	58	N/A	-5
1982	24	N/A	-28

At times, presidential approval ratings and satisfaction or economic ratings have been out of step. For example, in 1990 and 2002, the Republican Party was able to overcome either a low satisfaction rating (1990) or downbeat economic perceptions (2002) to achieve a relatively strong election showing, likely due to the popularity of the presidents at those times. Thus, presidential approval is probably the most consequential of the three measures.

In Gallup's most recent update, 26% of Americans said they were satisfied with the way things are going in the country. And recent Gallup Daily economic tracking has found only about 11% of Americans rating the economy as either excellent or good. Both measures are down significantly from what Gallup measured just before the 2006 elections and, with Democrats now in power, neither measure appears promising for the party looking ahead to 2010.

Outlook: Unless the economy turns around dramatically over the next year, the Democrats are likely to face an electorate that is very unhappy with the course of the nation and the state of the economy. But they may be able to overcome these factors to some degree if Obama can maintain or increase his popularity.

Congressional Job Approval

Often in recent decades, one party has occupied the White House and the other has controlled Congress, somewhat blurring the degree to which either party can be held accountable for the state of the nation in midterm elections. Generally, it appears the president's party is more important to voters, with that party losing seats in seven of the last nine midterm elections. By contrast, the majority party in Congress has lost seats in four of the last nine midterms.

But Congress' performance is hardly irrelevant to voters. Low congressional approval ratings have been associated with greater congressional seat turnover in midterm elections and higher approval ratings with less change, regardless of which party controls the legislative branch. The magic number appears to be a 40% approval rating for Congress, with seat losses minimized when approval exceeds that level and seat losses generally large when approval is below that figure.

Congressional Approval Ratings and President's Party Seat Changes, Recent Midterm Elections

Year	President's party	Majority party in House	% Approve of Congress	Seat gain/loss in U.S. House for president's party
2006	Republican	Republican	26	-30
2002	Republican	Republican	50	+6
1998	Democrat	Republican	44	+5
1994	Democrat	Democrat	23	-53
1990	Republican	Democrat	26	-8
1986	Republican	Democrat	42	-5
1982	Republican	Democrat	29	-28
1978	Democrat	Democrat	29	-11
1974	Republican*	Democrat	35	-43

* The president (Ford) took office less than three months before the midterm elections

Congressional approval is currently well below that mark, at 21%, and is near the 23% approval found during the 1994 elections, which saw Democrats lose their legislative majority.

Outlook: Americans' ratings of Congress hit new lows last year. After rebounding in the early part of 2009, they are back down to 21%—just seven points above the all-time low, which would usually suggest higher seat turnover. With Democrats in control of both the presidency and Congress, they are clearly vulnerable in this respect. If there is added sentiment to "throw the bums out"—which Gallup will measure next year by asking whether members of Congress deserve re-election—that would only make the situation worse.

Party ID

Shifts in national party support, as measured by the proportion of Americans who identify with or lean to either of the major political parties, can portend a better or a worse year for a party in midterm election years. It obviously is better for a party to go into an election with more supporters than the opposing party. That is certainly not a guarantee of victory, but if both parties' supporters turn out at the same rate, the party with more supporters will win.

Gallup has regularly measured leaned party identification since 1993. Since then, Democrats have gained seats in the two midterm election years when they had a substantial advantage in party support over Republicans in the third quarter (1998 and 2006), and lost seats in the two years (1994 and 2002) when that advantage was not significant. This suggests Democrats need a fairly large cushion in party support to counteract the Republicans' usual advantage in voter turnout.

Currently, Democrats enjoy a significant advantage in support over Republicans, with 48% of Americans in the third quarter of 2009 identifying as or leaning Democratic and 42% identifying as or leaning Republican. However, the Democrats' advantage has shrunk over the course of this year.

It is not unusual for the party advantage in affiliation to change in the year leading up to the midterm elections, so it is far from certain that Democrats will maintain the six-point advantage they averaged in the third quarter of this year. In fact, the Democratic advantage in party affiliation shrank in the year leading up to the

Party Identification and Leaning, Third Quarter,
Recent Midterm Election Years

Year	% Democrat/Lean Democratic	% Republican/Lean Republican	Democratic advantage
2006	50%	40%	+10
2002	46%	44%	+2
1998	48%	41%	+7
1994	46%	45%	+1

midterm elections in 1994, 1998, and 2002. In 2006, the opposite was the case, as the Democratic advantage grew.

Outlook: Democratic supporters continue to outnumber Republican supporters—clearly a benefit to the Democratic Party. A key will be whether that advantage continues to shrink, or whether Democrats can hold, if not increase, their current edge.

Turnout

Party support as measured by party affiliation, and voter preferences as measured by the generic ballot are only part of the equation in determining an election's outcome. The other component is voter turnout. If Republicans are more successful in getting their voters out to the polls—as is typical—they can overcome a Democratic advantage in support.

Gallup assesses turnout using its "likely voter" model, but does not usually do this until the fall of the election year.

For example, in the final 2002 pre-election poll, the Democrats led the Republicans by five points on the generic ballot among all registered voters, but trailed the Republicans by six points among likely voters. The Republicans won the national party vote for the House by five points that year.

Since 1970, Gallup has seen shifts to the Republicans in each midterm election year (after taking into account probable turnout when applying its likely voter model), with the change in the Democratic-Republican gap as little as 1 point (1978) to as many as 11 points (2002). In nine midterm elections since 1970 (Gallup did not make a final estimate in 1986), the average shift in the gap in the Republicans' favor has been about 5 points.

Bottom Line

Since 2006, not much has changed for the better in terms of Americans' satisfaction with the way things are going in the country, perceptions of the economy, or approval of the job Congress is doing. What has changed is that Democrats are now in control of both houses of Congress and the presidency after voter dissatisfaction led to steep Republican losses in 2006 and 2008. If national conditions do not improve considerably between now and next November, Democrats appear vulnerable to suffering heavy seat losses of their own. Two factors that are likely to be crucial in determining voter preferences for Congress in 2010 will be President Obama's job approval rating, and whether Democrats' advantage in party support continues to shrink.

November 04, 2009
IN U.S., MAJORITY NOW SAY OBAMA'S POLICIES "MOSTLY LIBERAL"
Fewer than half believe he has kept his election promises

by Lydia Saad, Gallup Poll Senior Editor

A majority of Americans now see President Barack Obama as governing from the left. Specifically, 54% say his policies as president have been mostly liberal while 34% call them mostly moderate. This contrasts with public expectations right after Obama's election a year ago, when as many expected him to be moderate as to be liberal.

Perceptions of Barack Obama's Policies

Do you think the policies that Barack Obama has pursued as president have been mostly liberal, mostly moderate, or mostly conservative?^

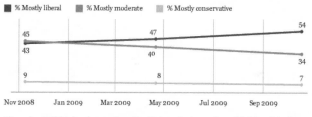

^November 2008 data based on question asking "Just your best guess, do you think the policies that Barack Obama will pursue as president will be mostly liberal, mostly moderate, or mostly conservative?"

This finding comes from a *USA Today*/Gallup survey, conducted Oct. 16-19, which offers several indications that Obama's public image has changed since his election last November. Much of that change is inauspicious for Obama.

Perhaps related to the re-evaluation of Obama's ideological orientation, fewer Americans today than in April say Obama is keeping the promises he made during the campaign.

While most Americans say it is important to them that President Obama keep the promises he made during the campaign (82%), far fewer, 48%, currently believe he has done so. This represents a slide in support for the president on this measure since April, when nearly two-thirds of Americans (65%) said he was keeping his promises.

President Obama Keeping His Promises

Generally speaking, do you think Barack Obama has or has not been keeping the promises he made during his presidential campaign?

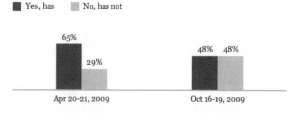

The decline in the percentage saying Obama has kept his promises is seen among all three major parties, dropping from 92% to 77% among Democrats, from 54% to 41% among independents, and from 45% to 22% among Republicans. To some degree, of course, the longer a president serves, the more opportunities there are for people to see him as breaking promises, which may account for some of this shift since the early months of Obama's presidency.

A majority of Americans (56%) say it is very important to them that Obama keep his promises and another 26% call this somewhat important. A much smaller 16% say that keeping his word is either not that important to them or not important at all.

Dampened Favorable Rating a Key Indicator

Obama's favorable rating, now 55%, is a more fundamental indicator of the post-election change in his image. Immediately after the election, 68% of Americans viewed Obama favorably. The figure rose to 78% around the time of his inauguration and registered in the mid- to high 60s from March through July. However, an early October Gallup survey showed the figure dropping to 56%, similar to the latest finding.

Barack Obama Favorable Rating

Next, we'd like to get your overall opinion of some people in the news. As I read each name, please say if you have a favorable or unfavorable opinion of these people -- or if you have never heard of them. How about -- Barack Obama?

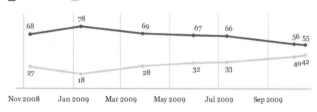

A comparison of the July and October ratings shows that Obama's image has fallen the most among Republicans and independents. While Gallup sees less change among Democrats, the finding that fewer than 90% now view Obama favorably (and 11% view him unfavorably) is noteworthy.

Trend in Favorable Views of Barack Obama, by Party ID

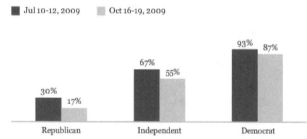

Among Democrats by ideology, Obama's favorability rating has fallen mostly among moderate Democrats, from 97% to 84%, with a smaller dip among conservative Democrats, 78% to 72%. It has held steady at 97% among liberal Democrats.

This erosion of support for Obama among moderate Democrats (as well as among Republicans and independents) may correspond with the increasing percentage of Americans perceiving that Obama is governing from the left.

Bottom Line

President Obama is not enjoying the same broad appeal and centrist image that he did in the afterglow of his election last November. Although a majority of Americans continue to view him favorably, this percentage has declined. The common perception that he would govern as a moderate has given way to a heightened belief that Obama's policies are mostly liberal. (Interpreted in the light of Amer-

icans' generally conservative leanings, this could be a problem for Obama politically.) And whereas in April most Americans believed he was sticking to the promises he made during the campaign, fewer than half now say that's the case.

These findings are reinforced by Obama's subdued job approval rating, which has been consistently tracking in the low 50s over the last several months. They also conform with Gallup findings reported earlier this week indicating that, compared to a year ago, Americans have generally lost hope that Obama can heal political divisions in the country or control federal spending, and are less optimistic about his ability to accomplish a number of other important goals.

As long as Obama's overall job approval rating remains above 50%, these setbacks would seem to be tolerable in a political sense— perhaps indicating nothing more than the cost of bold leadership at a difficult time for the country. But should he fall well below that important threshold in public support over a sustained period, the findings may point to weaknesses Obama may need to address.

Survey Methods

Results are based on telephone interviews with 1,521 national adults, aged 18 and older, conducted Oct. 16-19, 2009, including an oversample of 408 blacks, consisting of 102 interviews done as part of the random national sample and 306 interviews with blacks who had previously participated in national Gallup polls and agreed to be reinterviewed at a later date. The data from the national sample and reinterviews are combined and weighted to be demographically representative of the national adult population in the United States and to reflect the proper proportion of blacks in the overall population. For results based on this sample of national adults, the maximum margin of error is ±3 percentage points.

Interviews are conducted with respondents on land-line telephones (for respondents with a land-line telephone) and cellular phones (for respondents who are cell-phone only).

In addition to sampling error, question wording and practical difficulties in conducting surveys can introduce error or bias into the findings of public opinion polls.

November 05, 2009
HUCKABEE, ROMNEY, PALIN SEE MOST REPUBLICAN SUPPORT FOR '12
Huckabee, Romney viewed as most qualified of possible Republican presidential candidates

by Jeffrey M. Jones, Gallup Poll Managing Editor

Looking ahead to the 2012 presidential election, 71% of Republicans say they would seriously consider voting for Mike Huckabee. This gives Huckabee a slight edge over Mitt Romney (65%) and Sarah Palin (65%) in this early test of the strength of several potential Republican contenders. A majority of Republicans also say they would seriously consider voting for Newt Gingrich, but far fewer say they are currently ready to support the lesser-known Tim Pawlenty or Haley Barbour.

These results are based on a *USA Today*/Gallup poll conducted Oct. 31-Nov. 1. While this question allows respondents to express their level of support for each of the potential candidates, the three front-

Next, I'm going to read you a list of possible Republican candidates in the 2012 presidential election. Please tell me whether you would, or would not, seriously consider supporting each for president.

Based on Republicans

■ % Yes, would   ░ % No, would not

[Bar chart:]
Mike Huckabee: 71, 25
Mitt Romney: 65, 31
Sarah Palin: 65, 33
Newt Gingrich: 60, 35
Tim Pawlenty: 32, 48
Haley Barbour: 26, 52

USA Today/Gallup, Oct. 31-Nov. 1, 2009

runners that emerge are the same as when Gallup in July asked respondents which potential candidate they were *most likely* to support.

The poll suggests that the appeal of these potential challengers to Barack Obama in 2012 at this point is primarily limited to the Republican faithful. Among all Americans, Huckabee and Romney perform better than the other Republicans tested, but only about 4 in 10 Americans say they would consider voting for either.

Next, I'm going to read you a list of possible Republican candidates in the 2012 presidential election. Please tell me whether you would, or would not, seriously consider supporting each for president.

Based on national adults

■ % Yes, would   ░ % No, would not

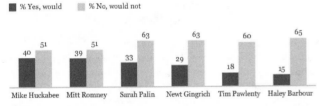
[Bar chart:]
Mike Huckabee: 40, 51
Mitt Romney: 39, 51
Sarah Palin: 33, 63
Newt Gingrich: 29, 63
Tim Pawlenty: 18, 60
Haley Barbour: 15, 65

USA Today/Gallup, Oct. 31-Nov. 1, 2009

The overall numbers are depressed in part because no more than 20% of Democrats say they would consider voting for any of the candidates (Romney 20%, Huckabee 18%, Pawlenty 11%, and Palin 10%). Those low figures are understandable given that typically about 10% of party identifiers wind up voting for the opposition's candidate in presidential elections.

Additionally, no more than 40% of independents support any of the Republicans. Huckabee (40%) and Romney (40%) tie for the lead in potential support among independents, followed by Palin (32%) and Gingrich (28%).

In addition to gauging potential support for each candidate, the poll also asked Americans to say whether they think each is qualified to be president. Huckabee and Romney are the leaders in this respect, with about half of the public saying each is qualified.

Thus, more Americans believe Huckabee (50%) and Romney (49%) are qualified to be president than say they would seriously consider voting for them (40% and 39%, respectively). The same is true for Gingrich, although there is a wider gap between the percentage who believe he is qualified (44%) and the percentage who would seriously consider supporting him (29%).

That is not the case for Palin, however. Thirty-three percent of Americans would seriously consider voting for her, but about the same number—31%—believe she is qualified to be president. In fact, Republicans are more likely to say they would seriously consider voting for Palin for president (65%) than to say she is qualified for the job (58%).

Please tell me whether you think each of the following people is or is not qualified to be president.

Based on national adults

■ % Yes, qualified   ░ % No, not qualified

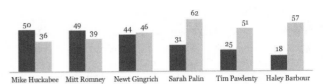
[Bar chart:]
Mike Huckabee: 50, 36
Mitt Romney: 49, 39
Newt Gingrich: 44, 46
Sarah Palin: 31, 62
Tim Pawlenty: 25, 51
Haley Barbour: 18, 57

USA Today/Gallup, Oct. 31-Nov. 1, 2009

A majority of Republicans believe each of the four higher-profile candidates is qualified to be president, including 7 in 10 who say this about Huckabee, Romney, and Gingrich. But independents and Democrats are not convinced, as less than half of both party groups believe any of the Republican candidates has the proper credentials to be president.

Views of Possible 2012 Republican Presidential Candidates as Qualified to Be President
Results by party

	% Republicans	% Independents	% Democrats
Mike Huckabee	72	48	38
Mitt Romney	71	45	37
Newt Gingrich	68	39	32
Sarah Palin	58	28	14
Tim Pawlenty	33	23	21
Haley Barbour	27	15	12

USA Today/Gallup, Oct. 31-Nov. 1, 2009

Bottom Line

Huckabee and Romney lost their 2008 bids for the Republican presidential nomination to John McCain, but each can now, along with Palin, be considered one of the early front-runners for the 2012 GOP nomination.

Although most Republicans currently regard Romney, Huckabee, and even Gingrich as more qualified than Palin, the former Alaska governor maintains a strong appeal among Republicans. Her popularity among the party's base—Palin's 72% favorable rating in July well exceeded those for Romney (56%) and Huckabee (59%) among Republicans—to a large degree seems to offset any deficit she has in perceived experience.

Survey Methods

Results are based on telephone interviews with 1,021 national adults, aged 18 and older, conducted Oct. 31-Nov. 1, 2009. For results based on the total sample of national adults, one can say with 95% confidence that the maximum margin of sampling error is ±4 percentage points.

For results based on the sample of 301 Republicans, the maximum margin of error is ±7 percentage points.

For results based on the sample of 347 independents, the maximum margin of error is ±7 percentage points.

For results based on the sample of 339 Democrats, the maximum margin of error is ±7 percentage points.

Interviews are conducted with respondents on land-line telephones and cellular phones.

In addition to sampling error, question wording and practical difficulties in conducting surveys can introduce error or bias into the findings of public opinion polls.

November 06, 2009

AMERICANS MOSTLY FAVORABLE ON DEFENSE SECRETARY GATES

Democrats view him more positively than Republicans

by Jeffrey M. Jones, Gallup Poll Managing Editor

As President Obama nears an important decision on U.S. troop levels in Afghanistan, Americans rate one of his key military advisers, Defense Secretary Robert Gates, much more positively than negatively. Forty-nine percent of Americans have a favorable opinion of Gates while 19% view him unfavorably. One in three Americans are not familiar enough with Gates to rate him.

Next, we'd like to get your overall opinion of some people in the news. As I read each name, please say if you have a favorable or unfavorable opinion of these people -- or if you have never heard of them. How about -- Secretary of Defense, Robert Gates?

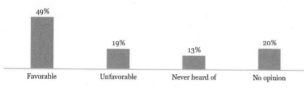

Oct. 16-19, 2009, USA Today/Gallup poll

These results are based on the Oct. 16-19 *USA Today/*Gallup poll. This is the first Gallup reading on public opinion of Gates, who served as George W. Bush's defense secretary in the latter part of his administration and whom Obama asked to remain in that role in his new administration.

Compared with other members of Obama's cabinet for whom Gallup has data, Gates is rated more positively than Vice President Joe Biden but less positively than Secretary of State Hillary Clinton. Clinton's unfavorable ratings are much higher than Gates', while Gates is the least well known of the three.

Americans' Opinions of Obama Administration Cabinet Members

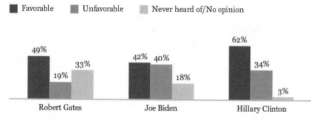

Note: Gates, Biden ratings from Oct. 16-19 poll; Clinton rating from Oct. 1-4 poll

Gallup does not have much data on prior defense secretaries, though it did take several measurements of Gates' immediate predecessor, Donald Rumsfeld. Rumsfeld averaged 49% favorable and 37% unfavorable ratings while he was secretary of defense, but had just a 27% favorable rating (and a 57% unfavorable rating) immediately after Bush replaced him with Gates in late 2006.

Gates himself is a Republican who not only served under George W. Bush but was deputy national security adviser and then CIA director under George H.W. Bush.

Despite his long service to Republican presidents, Gates receives a more positive review from Democrats than from Republicans.

This suggests that Gates' status as an Obama administration official is more influential than his political affiliation or prior service

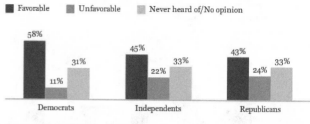

Americans' Opinions of Robert Gates, by Party Identification

Oct. 16-19, 2009, USA Today/Gallup poll

in how people view him. Federal Reserve Chairman Ben Bernanke has also served under both Bush and Obama, and Gallup observed an abrupt shift in how confident Republicans and Democrats were in his economic leadership after the change in administrations. Republicans expressed more confidence in Bernanke to recommend the right thing for the economy from 2006 to 2008 while Bush was in office, but after the change in administrations, that pattern reversed and now Democrats are much more confident in Bernanke. Whether this indicates that Americans are unaware of the political background of these officials, or merely put greater emphasis on their current service to one party or the other is unclear.

Since Gallup does not have a Bush-era rating on Gates, it is not possible to document whether a similar shift occurred in his ratings, though, as noted, such a shift would not be unprecedented.

Survey Methods

Results are based on telephone interviews with 1,521 national adults, aged 18 and older, conducted Oct. 16-19, 2009, including an oversample of 408 blacks, consisting of 102 interviews done as part of the random national sample and 306 interviews with blacks who had previously participated in national Gallup polls and agreed to be re-interviewed at a later date. The data from the national sample and re-interviews are combined and weighted to be demographically representative of the national adult population in the United States and to reflect the proper proportion of blacks in the overall population. For results based on this sample of national adults, the maximum margin of error is ±3 percentage points.

Interviews are conducted with respondents on land-line telephones (for respondents with a land-line telephone) and cellular phones (for respondents who are cell-phone only).

In addition to sampling error, question wording and practical difficulties in conducting surveys can introduce error or bias into the findings of public opinion polls.

November 09, 2009

U.S. WAITING FOR RACE RELATIONS TO IMPROVE UNDER OBAMA

Hope for long-term improvement still abounds

by Lydia Saad, Gallup Poll Senior Editor

A year out from the 2008 presidential election, the high hopes Americans had for race relations right after Barack Obama's victory at the polls have yet to be fully realized. Currently, 41% of Americans believe race relations have gotten better since Obama's win; another 35% think they have not changed, while 22% say they have gotten worse. Last November, 70% thought race relations would improve as a result of the landmark outcome.

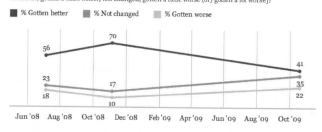

Perceived Impact of Barack Obama Presidency on Race Relations

As a result of Barack Obama's election, do you think race relations in this country have -- [gotten a lot better, gotten a little better, not changed, gotten a little worse (or) gotten a lot worse]?

Fifty-three percent of blacks and 39% of whites think relations have improved overall, but only 11% of blacks and 7% of whites think they have improved a lot.

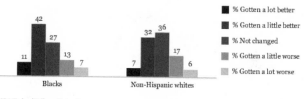

Perceived Impact of Obama on Race Relations -- by Race

USA Today/Gallup, Oct. 16-19, 2009

Still Holding Out Hope for the Long Term

Nonetheless, Obama has more than three years left in his first term in which to ease long-standing racial tensions in the country, and his very election establishes a lasting milestone for blacks that could continue to yield benefits for race relations long after he leaves office.

Americans' outlook on the Obama presidency's ultimate impact on relations remains quite bright. Sixty-one percent, nearly as high as the 70% seen in November 2008, believe race relations will improve "in the years ahead" because of Obama's presidency.

Black Americans are particularly optimistic about Obama's long-term impact, with 79% expecting relations to get better. This compares with 58% of non-Hispanic whites.

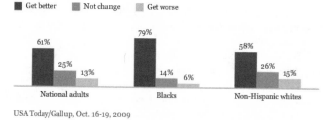

Current Outlook for Impact of Barack Obama Presidency on Race Relations

In the years ahead, as a result of Barack Obama's presidency, do you think race relations in this country will -- [get a lot better, get a little better, not change, get a little worse (or) get a lot worse] in the long term?

USA Today/Gallup, Oct. 16-19, 2009

A Milestone and Then Some

Not only was Obama's election an important "first" for black Americans, but the majority of all Americans say it represents one of the top advances for blacks—if not the singularly most important one—of the past hundred years.

Close to half of blacks themselves (44%) say it is the most important advance that has taken place for blacks during that time, and another 27% call it one of the most important. Far fewer whites, 16%, consider Obama's election the most important advance for blacks of the past century, but 40% call it one of the most important.

The 58% of Americans overall who rate Obama's election as a major milestone is a bit lower than the 71% Gallup found immediately after the 2008 election. (See tables for full trend.)

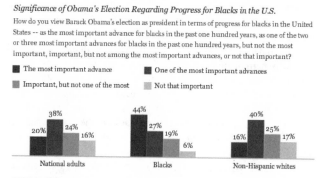

Significance of Obama's Election Regarding Progress for Blacks in the U.S.

How do you view Barack Obama's election as president in terms of progress for blacks in the United States -- as the most important advance for blacks in the past one hundred years, as one of the two or three most important advances for blacks in the past one hundred years, important, but not among the most important advances, or not that important?

USA Today/Gallup, Oct. 16-19, 2009

Few See Risk of a Backlash

In all of this polling, from June 2008 through today, relatively few Americans have believed Obama's election could hurt U.S. race relations. Less than 20% of respondents polled in June and November 2008 believed race relations would get worse to any degree as a result of an Obama presidency. Today, 22% believe race relations have already worsened because of Obama, still a fairly small minority.

Along the same lines, a different question in the latest poll finds 24% of Americans believing Obama will go too far in promoting efforts to aid the black community, identical to the percentage who last November predicted his policies would go too far. About half of Americans say his policies in this regard will be about right.

In fact, a slightly higher percentage today than last year—18%, up from 8% right after the election and 9% in May and June 2008—say Obama's policies to aid blacks will not go far enough. Among blacks, 32% now hold this view, an increase from 20% in May and June 2008.

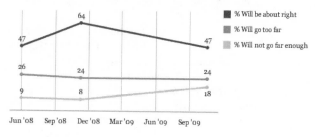

Expectations for Obama's Policies to Aid the Black Community

Next we have a question about a president's policies to help improve the standard of living of blacks in the United States. Do you think the policies of Barack Obama will go too far, will be about right, or will not go far enough in promoting efforts to aid the black community?

Bottom Line

Recent Gallup polling documents that large percentages of black Americans (72%) believe racism against blacks in the United States is widespread; also, half (49%) doubt that blacks enjoy the same job opportunities that whites have. While whites offer significantly more optimistic assessments on both of these issues, the gaps point to a perceptual gulf between the races that may contribute to ongoing racial tensions. Although some might hope that the very election of the nation's first black president would ease or eliminate these tensions, fewer than half of Americans believe such strides are already apparent. Nevertheless, widespread hope endures that long-term, Obama's election will make a positive difference.

Survey Methods

Results are based on telephone interviews with 1,521 national adults, aged 18 and older, conducted Oct. 16-19, 2009, including an oversample of 408 blacks, consisting of 102 interviews done as part of the random national sample and 306 interviews with blacks who had previously participated in national Gallup polls and agreed to be re-interviewed at a later date. The data from the national sample and re-interviews are combined and weighted to be demographically representative of the national adult population in the United States and to reflect the proper proportion of blacks in the overall population. For results based on this sample of national adults, the maximum margin of error is ±3 percentage points.

For results based on the sample of 408 blacks, the maximum margin of error is ±6 percentage points.

For results based on the sample of 933 non-Hispanic whites, the maximum margin of error is ±4 percentage points.

Interviews are conducted with respondents on land-line telephones (for respondents with a land-line telephone) and cellular phones (for respondents who are cell-phone only).

In addition to sampling error, question wording and practical difficulties in conducting surveys can introduce error or bias into the findings of public opinion polls.

November 09, 2009
NO CLEAR MANDATE FROM AMERICANS ON HEALTHCARE REFORM
Evenly split on long-term impact on healthcare system; one in four expect personal benefit

by Frank Newport, Gallup Poll Editor in Chief

Americans are evenly split on the potential impact of new healthcare legislation, should it ultimately be passed into law. Forty-one percent say a new healthcare bill would make the U.S. healthcare system better in the long run, while 40% say it would make things worse.

These new data on the impact of healthcare reform are based on a Gallup poll conducted Thursday through Sunday. Late Saturday night, a sweeping new healthcare bill passed the House, and now awaits action by the Senate. (The majority of interviews included in the current poll were completed before the House vote.) President Obama hopes the two chambers will reach agreement on a new bill by the end of the year, although some consider that timetable doubtful.

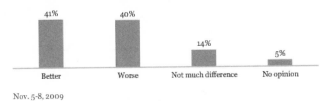

Taking everything into account, if a new healthcare bill becomes law, do you think in the long run it will make the U.S. healthcare system -- [ROTATED: better, would it not make much difference, (or make it) worse] -- than it is now?
Asked of a half sample

Nov. 5-8, 2009

Americans are more negative about the impact of a new healthcare bill on their personal situations than they are about its impact on the nation as a whole. By a 10-point margin, Americans are more likely to say a new bill would make their personal healthcare situations worse (36%), rather than better (26%). Almost 4 out of 10 say a bill would make no difference, or have no opinion on the topic.

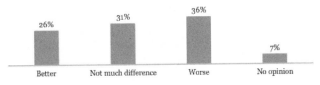

Taking everything into account, if a new healthcare bill becomes law, do you think in the long run it will make your own healthcare situation -- [ROTATED: better, would it not make much difference, (or make it) worse] -- than it is now?
Asked of a half sample

Nov. 5-8, 2009

All in all, the data reinforce previous research showing some skepticism about the long-term benefits of healthcare legislation, particularly at the personal level. Less than half of the public at this juncture perceives that if a new healthcare bill is passed into law, it would improve either the broad U.S. healthcare system or their own healthcare situations.

Should Congress Vote for or Against a New Bill?

Americans have moved in a more negative direction on the basic issue of whether a new bill should be passed into law. Thirty-eight percent now say they would advise their member of Congress to vote against a new healthcare bill this year, while 29% would advise their member to vote for it, and about a third have no opinion. When those with no opinion are asked which way they lean, the verdict becomes 48% "against," and 43% "for." Both of these results are more negative than those from early October.

Views on Healthcare Reform Remain Highly Partisan

The vote in the House on Saturday was partisan, although 39 Democrats defected from their party's leadership and voted against the bill. Only one Republican House member voted for the bill.

The views of rank-and-file Americans generally follow this pattern. The significant majority of Republicans would want their member of Congress to vote against a new healthcare bill, while a smaller majority of Democrats would want their member to vote for a bill. Independents are more negative than positive by a 2-to-1 mar-

Would you advise your member of Congress to vote for or against a healthcare bill this year, or do you not have an opinion?

As of today, would you say you lean more toward advising your member of Congress to vote for a healthcare bill, or lean more toward advising your member of Congress to vote against a healthcare bill? [COMBINED RESPONSES]

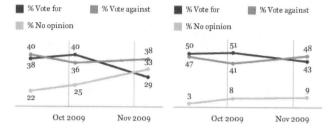

gin. Notably, Democrats are the most likely to be undecided on the issue.

Would you advise your member of Congress to vote for or against a healthcare bill this year, or do you not have an opinion?

	% Vote for	% Vote against	% No opinion
Republicans	8	68	23
Independents	22	44	33
Democrats	55	8	37

Nov. 5-8, 2009

When "leans" are taken into account, most Democrats at least lean toward the positive position and most Republicans lean toward the negative. Seventy-nine percent of Republicans either initially or after being probed to say which way they lean would want their member to vote against a new bill. Seventy-one percent of Democrats would want their member to vote for a new bill. Importantly, independents come down more against (53%) than in favor (37%).

As of today, would you say you lean more toward advising your member of Congress to vote for a healthcare bill, or lean more toward advising your member of Congress to vote against a healthcare bill?
Combined responses, including "leaners," by party ID

	% Vote for	% Vote against
Republicans	18	79
Independents	37	53
Democrats	71	18

Nov. 5-8, 2009

Bottom Line

The debate over new healthcare legislation now shifts to the Senate, at a time when the majority of Americans are not convinced that a new law would benefit either the national healthcare system or their own personal healthcare situations in the long term. The overall advice from the average American to his or her member of Congress at this point tilts negative, although about a third of Americans initially say they have no opinion on the legislation.

Survey Methods

Results are based on telephone interviews with 1,008 national adults, aged 18 and older, conducted Nov. 5-8, 2009. For results based on

the total sample of national adults, one can say with 95% confidence that the maximum margin of sampling error is ±4 percentage points.

Interviews are conducted with respondents on land-line telephones (for respondents with a land-line telephone) and cellular phones (for respondents who are cell-phone only).

In addition to sampling error, question wording and practical difficulties in conducting surveys can introduce error or bias into the findings of public opinion polls.

November 11, 2009
REPUBLICANS EDGE AHEAD OF DEMOCRATS IN 2010 VOTE
Registered voters prefer Republicans for the House, 48% to 44%

by Jeffrey M. Jones , Gallup Poll Managing Editor

Republicans have moved ahead of Democrats by 48% to 44% among registered voters in the latest update on Gallup's generic congressional ballot for the 2010 House elections, after trailing by six points in July and two points last month.

2010 Generic Congressional Ballot -- Preferences of Registered Voters

If the elections for Congress were being held today, which party's candidate would you vote for in your congressional district -- the Democratic Party's candidate (or) the Republican Party's candidate? (If unsure: As of today, do you lean more toward the Democratic Party's candidate (or) the Republican Party's candidate?)

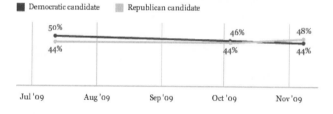

The Nov. 5-8 update comes just after Republican victories in the New Jersey and Virginia gubernatorial elections, which saw Republicans replace Democrats as governors of those states.

As was the case in last Tuesday's gubernatorial elections, independents are helping the Republicans' cause. In the latest poll, independent registered voters favor the Republican candidate by 52% to 30%. Both parties maintain similar loyalty from their bases, with 91% of Democratic registered voters preferring the Democratic candidate and 93% of Republican voters preferring the Republican.

2010 Generic Congressional Ballot Vote Preference, by Political Party
Based on registered voters

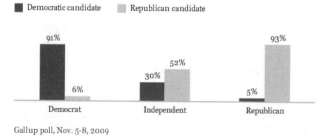

Gallup poll, Nov. 5-8, 2009

Over the course of the year, independents' preference for the Republican candidate in their districts has grown, from a 1-point advantage in July to the current 22-point gap.

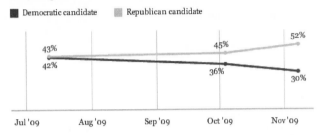

2010 Generic Congressional Ballot Vote Preference, Among Independents
Based on registered voters

■ Democratic candidate   ■ Republican candidate

The overall results would predict a likely strong Republican showing if the House elections were held today. Though the registered-voter results reported here speak to the preferences of all eligible voters, voter turnout is crucial in determining the final outcome of midterm elections. Gallup will not begin to model likely turnout until much closer to the 2010 elections, but given that Republicans usually have a turnout advantage, if normal turnout patterns prevail in the coming election, prospects for a good Democratic showing appear slim. Of course, the elections are still nearly 12 months away and conditions could shift back in the Democrats' favor over this time.

Since Gallup regularly began using the generic ballot to measure registered voters' preferences for the House of Representatives in 1950, it has been rare for Republicans to have an advantage over Democrats. This is likely because more Americans usually identify as Democrats than as Republicans, but Republicans can offset this typical Democratic advantage in preferences with greater turnout on Election Day. Most of the prior Republican registered-voter leads on the generic ballot in Gallup polling occurred in 1994 and 2002, two strong years for the GOP.

Bottom Line

Roughly a year before the 2010 midterm elections, Republicans seem well-positioned to win back some of their congressional losses in 2006 and 2008. Independents are increasingly coming to prefer the Republican candidate for Congress, and now favor the GOP by 22 points. Political conditions could still shift between now and Election Day to create a more favorable environment for Democratic candidates, but a Republican lead on the generic ballot among registered voters has been a sign of a strong Republican showing at the polls in the coming election.

Survey Methods

Results are based on telephone interviews with 894 registered voters, aged 18 and older, conducted Nov. 5-8, 2009. For results based on the total sample of national adults, one can say with 95% confidence that the maximum margin of sampling error is ±4 percentage points.

Interviews are conducted with respondents on land-line telephones (for respondents with a land-line telephone) and cellular phones (for respondents who are cell-phone only).

In addition to sampling error, question wording and practical difficulties in conducting surveys can introduce error or bias into the findings of public opinion polls.

November 11, 2009
NEW LOW IN U.S. JOB OPTIMISM
Only 8% of Americans say now is a good time to find a quality job

by Dennis Jacobe, Gallup Chief Economist

U.S. job-market optimism has reached a new low, with only 8% of Americans saying now is a good time to find a quality job—the lowest level since Gallup began tracking this measure in August 2001. Americans' optimism about this had begun to diminish even before the recession began to unfold two years ago, when 38% in November 2007 were optimistic, and there has been essentially no improvement since February of this year, when 9% held this view.

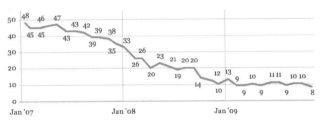

Thinking about the job situation in America today, would you say that it is now a good time or a bad time to find a quality job?

■ % "Good time"

Little Difference in Optimism by Gender, Region, Income, Education

There are only slight differences in optimism about finding a quality job between men (11%) and women (6%); differences by region range from 4% in the East to 11% in the South.

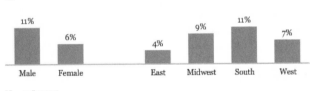

Thinking about the job situation in America today, would you say that it is now a good time or a bad time to find a quality job?

By gender and region

■ % "Good time"

Nov. 5-8, 2009

While 13% of those making less than $30,000 a year are optimistic, 6% of those making between $30,000 and $75,000 hold the same view, along with 9% of those making $75,000 or more.

Finally, 11% of those with a high school education or less are optimistic about finding a quality job, compared to 7% of those with a postgraduate education.

Commentary

Given today's double-digit unemployment rate, it is not surprising that most Americans are less than optimistic about finding a quality job. Still, the low amount of job-market optimism across genders, regions, incomes, and education levels shows that the current job situation is affecting all Americans. And it helps explain why there is increasing recognition that the combination of underemployed and

Thinking about the job situation in America today, would you say that it is now a good time or a bad time to find a quality job?

By annual income

■ % "Good time"

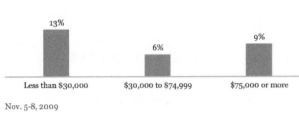

Nov. 5-8, 2009

Thinking about the job situation in America today, would you say that it is now a good time or a bad time to find a quality job?

By education

■ % "Good time"

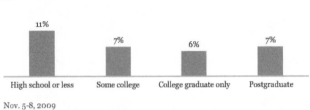

Nov. 5-8, 2009

unemployed represents a much higher percentage of the U.S. population—one in six Americans, according to government reports, and even more, according to Gallup's estimates.

Although Gallup's Job Creation Index indicates that job-market conditions across the U.S. are a little better than they were six months ago, they remain far worse than they were during the first year of the recession. It is hard to see how consumers will increase their spending or the economy will experience any real recovery on Main Street until there is not only an improvement in job creation, but also a significant increase in the availability of quality jobs.

Survey Methods

Results are based on telephone interviews with 1,008 national adults, aged 18 and older, conducted Nov. 5-8, 2009. For results based on the total sample of national adults, one can say with 95% confidence that the margin of error is ±3 percentage points.

Interviews are conducted with respondents on land-line telephones (for respondents with a land-line telephone) and cellular phones (for respondents who are cell-phone only).

In addition to sampling error, question wording and practical difficulties in conducting surveys can introduce error or bias into the findings of public opinion polls.

November 12, 2009
AMERICANS SPLIT ON AFGHANISTAN TROOP INCREASE VS. DECREASE
Thirty-five percent support Gen. McChrystal's recommendation for 40,000 additional troops

by Jeffrey M. Jones, Gallup Poll Managing Editor

As President Barack Obama prepares to make a decision on U.S. military policy in Afghanistan, 35% of Americans say he should follow the recommendation of the commanding U.S. general in Afghanistan and increase troop levels by about 40,000. Another 7% support a smaller troop increase, meaning a total of 42% of Americans support a troop increase of some size. However, nearly the same percentage, 44%, would like to see the number of U.S. troops in Afghanistan reduced.

Which of the following would you like to see President Obama do -- [ROTATED: increase the number of U.S. troops in Afghanistan by the roughly 40,000 the U.S. commanding general there has recommended, increase the number of U.S. troops in Afghanistan but by a smaller amount than the 40,000 the U.S. commanding general there has recommended, keep the number of U.S. troops in Afghanistan the same as now, (or) begin to reduce the number of U.S. troops in Afghanistan]?

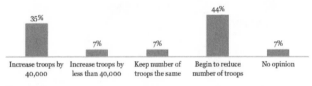

Nov. 5-8, 2009

Obama met with his national security team on Wednesday to further discuss the future U.S. strategy in Afghanistan and what resources the U.S. will need to accomplish its goals. Earlier this year, Gen. Stanley McChrystal, the U.S. commander in Afghanistan, recommended an increase of roughly 40,000 U.S. troops. Media reports suggest the Obama administration is leaning toward an increase in U.S. troops, but by a smaller amount than McChrystal has recommended.

With 44% of Americans in the Nov. 5-8 poll favoring a troop reduction and 7% wanting to keep troop levels where they are, a slim majority appears to oppose a troop increase. Last month, using a different question wording, Gallup also found the public largely divided on sending more troops to Afghanistan.

If Obama decides to increase U.S. troop levels in Afghanistan, he will be going against the wishes of the vast majority of rank-and-file Democrats. In fact, 60% of Democrats would like the president to begin to reduce troop levels in Afghanistan, while 26% support a troop increase of about 40,000 (18%) or less than that number (8%).

On the other hand, the majority of Republicans side with Gen. McChrystal's recommendation and support an increase of about 40,000 U.S. troops, with an additional 6% of Republicans favoring a smaller troop increase.

Independents are evenly divided between favoring a troop increase of any size (36% would like Obama to follow McChrystal's recommended increase and 7% favor a smaller increase) and supporting a reduction in U.S. troops (43%).

Men are much more likely than women to favor expanding the U.S. military operation in Afghanistan. A majority of men favor a troop increase (including 45% who believe Obama should follow McChrystal's recommendation) while only 32% of women agree. A

Preference for U.S. Troops in Afghanistan, by Political Party

■ Increase by 40,000   ■ Increase by less than 40,000   Keep number the same

Begin to reduce number

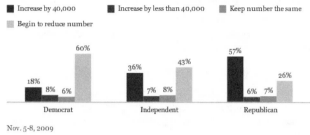

Nov. 5-8, 2009

majority of women would like to see the U.S. reduce its troop presence in Afghanistan.

Preference for U.S. Troops in Afghanistan, by Gender

■ Increase by 40,000   ■ Increase by less than 40,000

Keep number the same   Begin to reduce number

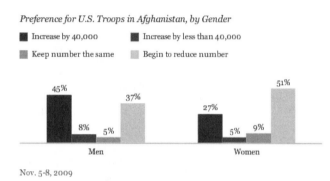

Nov. 5-8, 2009

This is not merely because women are more likely to identify as Democrats and men as Republicans, since the gender difference is apparent even when party affiliation is controlled for. Gallup has commonly found men more likely than women to favor military action.

Bottom Line

President Obama's decision on U.S. military policy in Afghanistan is arguably one of the most important of his first year in office. The decision has taken on added political drama as Obama does not appear inclined to go along with the commanding general's recommendation or the wishes of his party's supporters.

At this point, Obama would not appear to have the public's backing if he, as rumored, increases the number of U.S. troops in Afghanistan, since a slim majority would prefer that the president begin to draw down the U.S. presence in Afghanistan or keep the status quo. Such a decision would likely meet the approval of Republicans, who favor a troop increase, but not of his fellow Democrats, who are solidly opposed.

Survey Methods

Results are based on telephone interviews with 1,008 national adults, aged 18 and older, conducted Nov. 5-8, 2009. For results based on the total sample of national adults, one can say with 95% confidence that the maximum margin of sampling error is ±4 percentage points.

Interviews are conducted with respondents on land-line telephones (for respondents with a land-line telephone) and cellular phones (for respondents who are cell-phone only).

In addition to sampling error, question wording and practical difficulties in conducting surveys can introduce error or bias into the findings of public opinion polls.

November 12, 2009

MORE AMERICANS RATE LIVES WELL, BUT MORE HURTING AT WORK

Overall well-being in October down slightly; still matching pre-recession levels

by Dan Witters , Gallup Poll Staff Writer

More Americans are rating their lives better than at any time since the recession began, according to the October update of the Gallup-Healthways Well-Being Index. The Life Evaluation Index reached the 50.0 threshold for the first time, adding to gains seen since the metric hit its low point of 33.1 in November 2008.

Gallup-Healthways Life Evaluation Index

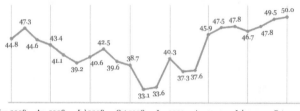

Gallup-Healthways Well-Being Index

The Life Evaluation Index is one of six sub-indexes that when combined together comprise the Gallup-Healthways Well-Being Index, which provides a comprehensive measure of Americans' emotional, physical, and fiscal health. The Gallup-Healthways Well-Being Index and each of the six sub-indexes are calculated on a scale from 0 to 100, where 100 represents fully realized well-being.

The Life Evaluation sub-index is based on the Cantril Self-Anchoring Striving Scale, which asks people to evaluate their present and future lives on a scale with steps numbered from 0 to 10, where 0 is the worst possible life and 10 is the best possible life. Those who rate today a "7" or higher and the future an "8" or higher are considered to be "thriving." Those who rate today and the future a "4" or lower on the scale are considered to be "suffering."

In October, 53.2% of American adults were classified as "thriving," a new high mark and substantially improved over the 37.4% measured last November. The percentage of "suffering" American adults also reached a new low of 3.2%. (The overall Life Evaluation Index score of 50.0 is calculated as the percentage of Americans that are "thriving" minus the percentage that are "struggling.") Most of the improvement in the Life Evaluation Index over the course of the past 12 months has been via the self-evaluation of the respondents' current state, although there has also been a more modest improvement in the self-evaluation of the future state.

Work Environment Slips to New Low

At the same time that Americans' life evaluation reached new highs, working Americans reported their most negative responses yet in their work environments. The Work Environment Index declined to 48.1 in October, its lowest level since measurement began in January 2008. The Work Environment Index has dropped more than five points since spiking to the high of 53.3 in October 2008, at the onset of the global economic collapse.

The Work Environment Index asks respondents if they are satisfied with their jobs, if they get to use their strengths at work, if their supervisor treats them more like a boss or a partner, and if their

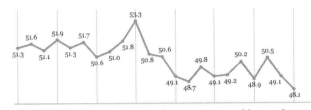

Gallup-Healthways Work Environment Index

51.3 51.6 51.9 51.1 51.3 51.7 50.6 51.0 51.8 53.3 50.8 50.6 49.1 48.7 49.8 49.1 49.2 50.2 48.9 50.5 49.1 48.1

Jan 2008   Apr 2008   Jul 2008   Oct 2008   Jan 2009   Apr 2009   Jul 2009   Oct 2009

Gallup-Healthways Well-Being Index

supervisor creates an environment that is open and trusting. Gallup only asks these questions of respondents that are currently employed by others—about 40% of the total sample, or approximately 12,000 U.S. adults per month—and, therefore, are not directly influenced by those who are currently without a job.

Overall Well-Being Index Composite Score Down Slightly

The drop in the Work Environment Index is the primary cause, despite the improved Life Evaluation Index score, of the slight decline in the overall Well-Being Index composite score. The overall Gallup-Healthways Well-Being Index slipped slightly again in October to 66.5, down now half a point from its recorded high of 67.0 in August. October marks the sixth consecutive month of scores of 66.0 or higher on the Well-Being Index, similar to levels recorded in the first half of 2008.

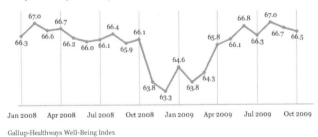

Gallup-Healthways Well-Being Index Composite Score

66.3 67.0 66.6 66.7 66.2 66.0 66.1 66.4 65.9 66.1 63.8 63.3 64.6 63.8 64.3 65.8 66.1 66.8 66.3 67.0 66.7 66.5

Jan 2008   Apr 2008   Jul 2008   Oct 2008   Jan 2009   Apr 2009   Jul 2009   Oct 2009

Gallup-Healthways Well-Being Index

Survey Methods

Results are based on telephone interviews with more than 650,000 national adults, aged 18 and older, conducted Jan. 2, 2008 through Oct.31, 2009. For monthly results based on the total sample of national adults, one can say with 95% confidence that the maximum margin of sampling error is ±0.6 percentage point.

The Work Environment Index questions are only asked of respondents that are currently employed by others or self-employed, about 40% of the total sample or approximately 12,000 adults per month.

Interviews are conducted with respondents on land-line telephones (for respondents with a land-line telephone) and cellular phones (for respondents who are cell-phone only).

In addition to sampling error, question wording and practical difficulties in conducting surveys can introduce error or bias into the findings of public opinion polls.

November 13, 2009

MORE IN U.S. SAY HEALTH COVERAGE IS NOT GOV'T. RESPONSIBILITY

Marks significant shift from the attitudes of the past decade

by Frank Newport, Gallup Poll Editor in Chief

More Americans now say it is not the federal government's responsibility to make sure all Americans have healthcare coverage (50%) than say it is (47%). This is a first since Gallup began tracking this question, and a significant shift from as recently as three years ago, when two-thirds said ensuring healthcare coverage was the government's responsibility.

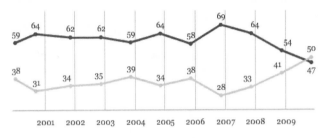

Do you think it is the responsibility of the federal government to make sure all Americans have healthcare coverage, or is that not the responsibility of the federal government?

■ % Yes, government's responsibility   ▪ % No, not government's responsibility

59 64 62 62 59 64 58 69 64 54 50
38 31 34 35 39 34 38 28 33 41 47

2001   2002   2003   2004   2005   2006   2007   2008   2009

Gallup has asked this question each November since 2001 as part of the Gallup Poll Social Series, and most recently in its Nov. 5-8 Health and Healthcare survey. There have been some fluctuations from year to year, but this year marks the first time in the history of this trend that less than half of Americans say ensuring healthcare coverage for all is the federal government's responsibility.

The high point for the "government responsibility" viewpoint occurred in 2006, when 69% of Americans agreed. In 2008, this percentage fell to 54%, its previous low reading. This year, in the midst of robust debate on a potentially imminent healthcare reform law, the percentage of Americans agreeing that it is the government's responsibility to make sure everyone has health insurance has fallen even further, by seven points, to 47%. Half of Americans now say this is *not* the government's responsibility.

The reason behind this shift is unknown. Certainly the federal government's role in the nation's healthcare system has been widely and vigorously debated over the last several months, including much focus on the "public option." These data suggest that one result of the debate has been a net decrease in Americans' agreement that ensuring all Americans have healthcare coverage is an appropriate role for the federal government.

There are major differences in views on this issue by partisanship, as would be expected given the major partisan differences on most issues relating to the role of government in the U.S. today. The views of Republicans and independents who lean Republican about the government's healthcare role are almost a precise mirror image of the views of Democrats and independents who lean Democratic.

More than 7 out of 10 Republicans say it is not the responsibility of government to see that all Americans have healthcare coverage, while more than 7 out of 10 Democrats say it is.

A look at the trends on this question shows that both Republicans and Democrats since 2006 have become less likely to choose

Do you think it is the responsibility of the federal government to make sure all Americans have healthcare coverage, or is that not the responsibility of the federal government?

By party ID

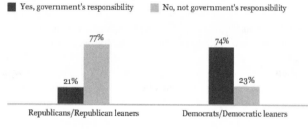

Nov. 5-8, 2009

Which of the following approaches for providing healthcare in the United States would you prefer -- [ROTATED: replacing the current healthcare system with a new government-run healthcare system, (or) maintaining the current system based mostly on private health insurance]?

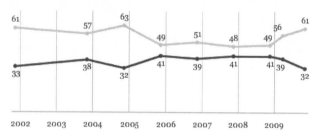

the "government responsibility" option, though Democrats' views have remained steady over the past year while Republicans' support has declined further.

Do you think it is the responsibility of the federal government to make sure all Americans have healthcare coverage, or is that not the responsibility of the federal government?

% Yes, government's responsibility

The percentage of Republicans choosing the "government responsibility" option fell 20 percentage points between 2006 and the current survey, compared to a 13-point drop among Democrats. From a longer-range perspective, however, Democrats' views today reflect essentially a return to the sentiment seen early in the decade, while Republicans now express significantly lower support.

Replace the Current System?

A second question Gallup tracks each November asks Americans directly about "replacing the current healthcare system with a new government-run health care system."

Throughout this decade, a plurality of Americans have consistently favored maintaining the current system, although support has fluctuated. In November 2007, the edge for the private system over the government-run system was just 7 points, vs. a 31-point gap in 2004. The current 29-point gap is thus at the high end of the historical range.

Almost 9 out of 10 Republicans and Republican leaders favor maintaining the current healthcare system based mostly on private health insurance. Democrats and Democratic leaders favor the concept of replacing the current system with a government-run system, but Democratic opinion is less monolithic than Republican opinion; more than a third of Democrats would favor maintaining the current system.

Which of the following approaches for providing healthcare in the United States would you prefer -- [ROTATED: replacing the current healthcare system with a new government-run healthcare system, (or) maintaining the current system based mostly on private health insurance]?

By party ID

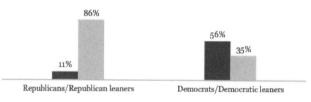

Nov. 5-8, 2009

The alternatives outlined in this question are not directly a part of the current debate; there has been no serious discussion on the part of those advocating healthcare reform of the possibility of dismantling the current system and turning it into one run completely by the government. Still, the trend line gives a good perspective on the larger issue of shifting to a more European-style healthcare system, something that the majority of Americans at this point would clearly oppose.

Bottom Line

The wording of the healthcare bill the House passed last Saturday explicitly states that one of the bill's purposes is to provide "affordable, quality healthcare for all Americans."

The current poll results indicate that, with the renewed healthcare debate since President Obama took office, Americans have become less convinced that it is an appropriate goal for the federal government to take on the responsibility of ensuring that all Americans have healthcare coverage. It is possible that the current debate has increased the average American's awareness as to the nuances of the various roles the government could play in the healthcare system, helping make the generic "make sure all Americans have healthcare coverage" sound less appealing. Plus, the current debate may have produced more skepticism among Americans that the government's role in healthcare could or should be this broad.

Most polling shows that Americans tend to favor a "public option" in which the government would provide a healthcare plan that would not be mandatory but one of several options for those seeking healthcare insurance. Americans apparently do not equate this with government's guaranteeing that all Americans have health-care coverage.

Finally, the current data confirm the basic premise that all in all, Americans do not support the idea of a government-run system as a full replacement for the current system based on private insurance.

Survey Methods

Results are based on telephone interviews with 1,008 national adults, aged 18 and older, conducted Nov. 5-8, 2009. For results based on the total sample of national adults, one can say with 95% confidence that the maximum margin of sampling error is ±3 percentage points.

Interviews are conducted with respondents on land-line telephones (for respondents with a land-line telephone) and cellular phones (for respondents who are cell-phone only).

In addition to sampling error, question wording and practical difficulties in conducting surveys can introduce error or bias into the findings of public opinion polls.

November 13, 2009

CONGRESS' APPROVAL RECOVERS SOME; INDEPENDENTS BUCK TREND

At 26%, approval remains low compared to this summer and most of the year

by Lymari Morales, Gallup Poll Staff Writer

Americans express slightly greater approval of Congress this month after last month's decline. The current 26% rating is up from 21% in October but down from 31% in August and September. Still, more than two-thirds of Americans (68%) disapprove of the way Congress is handling its job.

Do you approve or disapprove of the way Congress is handling its job?
2009 trend

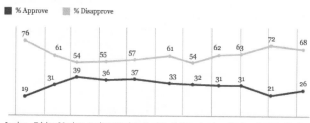

The results are from a Gallup poll conducted Nov. 5-8, as the U.S. House of Representatives labored through the weekend on healthcare reform, ultimately passing a $1 trillion bill intended to expand coverage to millions more Americans. The same survey found Americans still divided on the potential benefits of healthcare reform and more likely to oppose such a bill than to favor it.

This month's improvement in congressional approval is bipartisan, with approval among Democrats climbing from 36% to 47% and among Republicans edging up from 9% to 17%. Independents, however, buck that trend: moving from 16% to 14%, the percentage approving is the lowest it has been all year.

Do you approve or disapprove of the way Congress is handling its job?
2009 trend, by party ID
% Approve

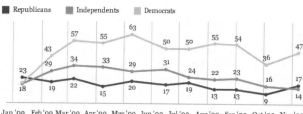

While Democrats remain nearly three times more likely than Republicans to approve of Congress, it is worth noting that general trends among the two groups have moved in tandem since mid-August.

The new 2009 low in approval from independents comes at a time when a majority of registered independents say they would likely vote Republican rather than Democratic, 52% to 30%, if elections for Congress were held today. With Republicans and Democrats exhibiting the same degree of loyalty to their parties' candidates, independents' preference for Republicans gives that party a 48% to 44% edge over Democrats among registered voters overall.

Approval of Congress is one of several key indicators to watch leading up to the 2010 midterm elections, with lower approval ratings generally relating to greater turnover in seats from one party to the other. Congress' job approval rating now precisely matches the 26% recorded in November 2006, just before control of Congress shifted from Republicans to Democrats, and is not too dissimilar from the 23% recorded in October 1994, just before control shifted from Democrats to Republicans. It is also well below its 36% average of the past two decades.

Do you approve or disapprove of the way Congress is handling its job?

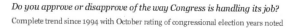

Complete trend since 1994 with October rating of congressional election years noted

Bottom Line

Despite giving Congress slightly higher marks than they did last month, Americans remain less approving of Congress than they were this summer and most of this year. The percentage of independents approving is now even lower than the percentage of Republicans approving, and less than half of Democrats approve of the Congress their party controls. Approval of Congress now matches the level Gallup found just before control of Congress changed hands in 2006, and is close to the level found before control changed hands in 1994. This will remain a key measure to watch over the next year as Democrats seek to maintain power while Republicans work to seize it.

Survey Methods

Results are based on telephone interviews with 1,008 national adults, aged 18 and older, conducted Nov. 5-8, 2009. For results based on the total sample of national adults, one can say with 95% confidence that the maximum margin of sampling error is ±4 percentage points.

Interviews are conducted with respondents on land-line telephones (for respondents with a land-line telephone) and cellular phones (for respondents who are cell-phone only).

In addition to sampling error, question wording and practical difficulties in conducting surveys can introduce error or bias into the findings of public opinion polls.

November 16, 2009
ECONOMY PICKS UP AGAIN AS MOST IMPORTANT PROBLEM IN U.S.
Healthcare remains near the top of the list

by Jeffrey M. Jones , Gallup Poll Managing Editor

Gallup finds an increase after eight consecutive monthly declines in the percentage naming the economy as the most important problem. Now, 31% of Americans mention the economy in general terms as the top problem, up from 26% last month. Even with the modest increase, only about half as many Americans mention the economy as the nation's top problem now as at the beginning of the year.

What do you think is the most important problem facing this country today?
2009 trend

▓ % Mentioning the economy in general

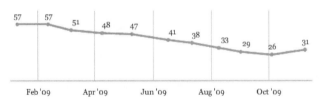

Likewise, the percentage naming any economic issue (including the economy in general terms but also specific concerns such as unemployment or inflation) also increased in November, to 58%. This figure had also declined for eight consecutive months from its peak of 86% in February, before increasing this month.

Percentage of Americans Mentioning Any Economic Issue as Most Important Problem Facing the Country Today
2009 trend

Americans' increased economic concern this month may be due to the higher October unemployment figures, which reached the 10%

level and were reported about the time the poll was being conducted (Nov. 5-8).

Unemployment itself is mentioned specifically by 20% of Americans as the most important problem, roughly the same percentage as mention healthcare (22%). Eight percent say "war" in general terms is the top problem, not including the 4% who specifically mention the war in Afghanistan and the 3% who mention the Iraq war. Eight percent also say dissatisfaction with the government is the top issue facing the country.

Top Specific Issues Mentioned as Most Important Problem, Nov. 5-8, 2009, Gallup Poll

	% Mentioning
Economy in general	31
Healthcare	22
Unemployment/Jobs	20
Wars/War in general	8
Dissatisfaction wtih government	8
Federal budget deficit	6
Situation in Afghanistan	4
Lack of money	4
Ethics/Morals	3
Education	3
Situation in Iraq	3

The 20% mentioning unemployment ties for the highest Gallup has measured since it began asking the "most important problem" question on a monthly basis in 2001. Mentions of unemployment as the nation's most important problem have been higher prior to 2001 (when Gallup asked the question on an occasional basis), including the early 1990s, early 1980s, and late 1970s.

Republicans, Democrats, and independents show a good deal of consensus on the top problems facing the country—the economy in general, unemployment, and healthcare—and there is little notable variation in the percentage of each group naming these problems.

Bottom Line

Throughout 2009, the economy has remained the dominant concern for Americans, though that concern had been easing since February. But in November, amid double-digit unemployment, Americans' economic anxiety is on the rise again, though still far below the levels of early 2009.

Survey Methods

Results are based on telephone interviews with 1,008 national adults, aged 18 and older, conducted Nov. 5-8, 2009. For results based on the total sample of national adults, one can say with 95% confidence that the maximum margin of sampling error is ±4 percentage points.

Interviews are conducted with respondents on land-line telephones (for respondents with a land-line telephone) and cellular phones (for respondents who are cell-phone only).

In addition to sampling error, question wording and practical difficulties in conducting surveys can introduce error or bias into the findings of public opinion polls.

November 16, 2009

CHRISTMAS SPENDING FORECAST REVERTS TO RECORD 2008 LOWS

Still, fewer now than last year say they will be spending less than a year ago

by Lydia Saad, Gallup Poll Senior Editor

Americans' estimate of the total amount they will spend on Christmas gifts this year has fallen precipitously over the past month, sending the figure back to last year's record lows. Americans' average Christmas spending prediction is now $638. This nearly matches the $616 recorded in November 2008, amid one of the worst holiday retail seasons in recent memory.

Projected Spending on Christmas Gifts, 1999-2009

Roughly how much money do you think you personally will spend on Christmas gifts this year?

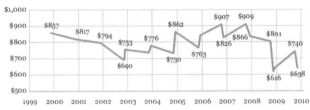

The latest result is Gallup's second holiday spending forecast for 2009, based on a Nov. 5-8 national survey. Last month, Americans predicted they would spend $740 on gifts, a figure that offered more hope for holiday retailers.

Americans' current spending prediction is roughly the same as it was last year at this time (and is nearly identical to the $639 recorded in December 2008), and, indeed, the majority (57%) now say they will spend the same amount on gifts as they did last Christmas. Further indicating that last year's stunning 3.4% drop in holiday retail spending is not likely to be repeated, fewer Americans explicitly say they will be spending less on gifts this year—now 34%, down from 46% in 2008.

*Comparative Chistmas Spending, 1999-2009^*

Is that [amount you will spend] more, less, or about the same amount as you spent last Christmas?

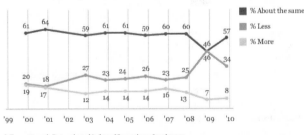

^ Recent trend. Date selected is from November of each year.

Still, the 34% who today say they will spend less is higher than at any other time in the recent past, prior to 2008. Also, as in 2008, few Americans today (now 8%) say they will be spending more than they did a year ago.

Today's measure of Americans' Christmas spending intentions is very similar to the November and December 2008 readings. However, there are some slight differences this year in the demographic patterns.

Projected Spending on Christmas Gifts -- Recent Trend by Demographic Groups

	November 2008	December 2008	November 2009
	Mean $^	Mean $^	Mean $^
National adults	616	639	638
Men	675	672	699
Women	563	608	580
18 to 34 years	552	499	657
35 to 54 years	744	694	619
55 and older	537	678	637
$75,000 or more	916	954	948
$30,000 to $74,999	562	625	634
Less than $30,000	311	331	308
East	644	685	697
Midwest	555	649	630
South	605	630	675
West	664	599	538
Have children under 18	787	761	694
No children under 18	543	585	625

^ Mean includes zero.

Most notably, young adults (those 18 to 34 years of age) are planning to spend more on gifts this year than they were in either of the final 2008 pre-Christmas polls. Middle-aged adults are planning to spend less, while—going by the midpoint of last year's readings—older adults (those 55 and older) are planning to spend about the same amount.

Intended spending appears to be holding up at last year's levels in the East, Midwest, and South, but is lower in the West. The data suggest that parents of minor children may be paring back a bit, while those without children may spend more.

Interpreting Spending Forecasts

Gallup's Christmas spending forecasts can be especially helpful in gauging whether the holiday retail season will be a boom or a bust, but small year-to-year changes—as represented by the current result—can be difficult to interpret.

Prior to 2008, Gallup found that in years when Americans' anticipated Christmas gift-spending figure equaled or exceeded that of the previous year (as in 2003 and 2004), retail sales showed fairly robust annual increases, in the 5% to 6% range. In years when Americans' anticipated gift outlays fell well below the previous year's estimate (as in 2000, 2001, and 2002), year-to-year growth in holiday season retail sales was relatively anemic, generally falling below 5%.

Last year's dip into the low $600 range, after spending predictions registered $866 in November 2007, offered a clear signal that Americans were reining in their spending to a perhaps unprecedented degree. That was borne out in actual retail sales data. According to historical patterns, the fact that Gallup's November 2009 spending projection is very similar to (and not lower than) those recorded in November and December 2008 should mean spending this year will not be as deflated as last year. Whether that means holiday spending will be flat or actually improve compared with 2008, or only decline by a smaller percentage, is unclear. However, it is unlikely to decline by as much as occurred in 2008.

Bottom Line

Americans, on average, currently plan to spend $638 on Christmas gifts this year, very close to the figure they reported last November. Also, the majority of Americans now *say* they will spend "the same amount" on gifts as they did the prior Christmas, marking a return to the pre-2008 consumer mentality. Although the still-inflated percentage saying they will "spend less" suggests retailers are not yet out of the woods, when considered with the other findings, it appears the 2009 holiday retail season will not be as depressed as last year's.

Same-store sales reports released earlier this month offered some encouraging signs about a possible uptick in spending in September and October; however, given the fragility in the economy and consumer psychology, there is no guarantee these trends will hold through December. Thus, even the flat holiday sales suggested by Gallup's latest Christmas spending intentions data may be a welcome relief to retailers at the end of a year when monthly department store-type spending through August fell roughly 4% behind 2008 levels. Gallup will publish its final Christmas spending forecast in early December.

Survey Methods

Results are based on telephone interviews with 1,008 national adults, aged 18 and older, conducted Nov. 5-8, 2009. For results based on the total sample of national adults, one can say with 95% confidence that the maximum margin of sampling error is ±4 percentage points.

Interviews are conducted with respondents on land-line telephones (for respondents with a land-line telephone) and cellular phones (for respondents who are cell-phone only).

In addition to sampling error, question wording and practical difficulties in conducting surveys can introduce error or bias into the findings of public opinion polls.

November 18, 2009
COSTS, GOVERNMENT INVOLVEMENT TOP HEALTHCARE REFORM CONCERNS
Bill's impact on personal healthcare situations, expansion of access also mentioned

by Frank Newport, Gallup Poll Editor in Chief

Asked to name their concerns if a new healthcare bill is eventually passed into law, Americans say they would be worried about the potential costs of new healthcare legislation, the increased government involvement a new law would mandate, the possibly negative impact on current healthcare delivery, and concerns that the bill won't go far enough in expanding access to healthcare.

This open-ended question was included in Gallup's Nov. 5-8 Health and Healthcare survey, and the responses were coded into categories, as displayed in the accompanying table.

Americans' worries can be grouped into four broad areas:

- Concerns about the *costs* of a new healthcare bill, including worries about personal costs and costs to businesses, costs to the overall system or to the government, and worries about increased taxes.
- Concerns about *increased government involvement* in healthcare. These include worries about the development of a new government bureaucracy, socialized medicine, and concerns about the "public option" that has been the subject of much debate in recent months.

Regardless of whether you favor or oppose healthcare legislation, what are some of the concerns you would have if a new healthcare measure is passed into law? [OPEN-ENDED]

National adults

	% Mentioning
COSTS	
Net: Costs	24
— Costs to individuals, businesses; affordability/higher premiums	13
— Costs (nonspecific)	6
— Overall costs to government, taxpayers	5
— Increased taxes	3
— How it will be paid for	2
GOVERNMENT INVOLVEMENT	
Government-run healthcare/Bureaucracy/Government takeover/Socialized medicine	18
Government plan/Public option	6
EFFECT ON HEALTHCARE	
Effect on quality of care	7
Ability to get needed treatments/Rationing care/Wait times for care	5
Effect on senior citizens/Medicare	4
Being able to see current doctors	2
Being able to keep current plan, benefits	2
EFFECT ON HEALTHCARE COVERAGE/ACCESS	
Making sure everyone is covered/has access	12
UNCERTAINTY OVER HOW PLAN WILL WORK	
Unclear how plan would work	5
OTHER CONCERNS	
Would provide coverage to illegal immigrants	3
Forcing people to have insurance/Fines for not having	2
Would pay for abortions	2
Coverage for prescriptions	1
OTHER	2
NONE/NOTHING (vol.)	9
NO OPINION	8

(vol.) = Volunteered response

Nov. 5-8, 2009

- Concerns about the possibly *negative impact* of a new healthcare bill on various aspects of healthcare delivery, including having to wait for procedures, possible healthcare rationing, the quality of seniors' healthcare, and the ability to keep one's current doctors and current healthcare plan under a new system.
- Concerns that the new bill would not go far enough in expanding healthcare access.

A small percentage of Americans mention coverage of illegal immigrants as a top concern about new healthcare legislation. Two percent mention abortion, although the majority of interviews in this survey were completed before the controversial "Stupak" amendment included in the House bill became a major focus of news coverage. Seventeen percent do not mention any concerns about a new healthcare bill.

Differences Between Those Who Support and Those Who Oppose a New Bill

In a separate question included in the survey, respondents were asked if they would advise or lean toward advising their member of Congress to vote for or against the legislation.

The accompanying table displays the concerns about new health-care legislation among the resulting two groups.

Regardless of whether you favor or oppose healthcare legislation, what are some of the concerns you would have if a new healthcare measure is passed into law?
[OPEN-ENDED]
By position on legislation

	Favor legislation	Oppose legislation
	%	%
COSTS		
Net: Costs	22	25
– Costs to individuals, businesses; affordability/higher premiums	16	10
– Costs (nonspecific)	3	9
– Overall costs to government, taxpayers	3	7
– Increased taxes	1	5
– How it will be paid for	1	3
GOVERNMENT INVOLVEMENT		
Government-run healthcare/Bureaucracy/Government takeover/ Socialized medicine	9	28
Government plan/Public option	6	7
EFFECT ON HEALTHCARE		
Effect on quality of care	6	8
Ability to get needed treatments/Rationing care/Wait times for care	6	4
Effect on senior citizens/Medicare	3	5
Being able to see current doctors	2	3
Being able to keep current plan, benefits	1	3
EFFECT ON HEALTHCARE COVERAGE/ACCESS		
Making sure everyone is covered/has access	19	4
UNCERTAINTY OVER HOW PLAN WILL WORK		
Unclear how plan would work	4	6
OTHER CONCERNS		
Would provide coverage to illegal immigrants	2	4
Forcing people to have insurance/Fines for not having	1	3
Would pay for abortions	1	3
Coverage for prescriptions	2	1
OTHER	2	2
NONE/NOTHING (VOL.)	11	5
NO OPINION	10	4

(vol.) = Volunteered response

Nov. 5-8, 2009

There is relatively little difference between those who favor and those who oppose new healthcare legislation in terms of concerns about costs, although each group may have different takes on the aspects of costs they are worried about.

The biggest differences between those who support and those who oppose a new healthcare bill relate to government involvement and access to healthcare. Those who oppose a new healthcare plan are much more likely to be concerned about government involvement than are those who favor it. On the other hand, those who favor the plan are much more likely to be concerned about the plan's not going far enough in increasing access to healthcare. A much higher percentage of reform proponents than detractors (21% vs. 9%) do not indicate anything about the potential healthcare legislation that concerns them.

Discussion

The debate over new healthcare reform legislation has moved to the Senate, where lawmakers will continue to wrestle with what could become one of the most far-reaching pieces of domestic legislation in decades. Americans remain split on the potential impact of such new legislation on the U.S. healthcare system and there is a generally even public divide between those who say they would advise or lean toward advising their representative in Congress to vote for a new healthcare bill and those who would advise their representative to vote against it.

The current findings help illuminate the specific concerns Americans would have if such a new bill is passed into law. Although House lawmakers put the word "affordable" in the title of their bill, Americans nevertheless remain worried about the cost implications of healthcare reform—to them personally, to businesses, and to the government and system as a whole.

Lawmakers are working on a new bill with the obvious conviction that it will improve the healthcare situation in the country, but many Americans appear to be worried about the possible negative effects of healthcare reform on their own situations, or simply are not clear what its impact will be.

Some Americans, particularly those who oppose a new bill, remain worried about the burgeoning role of government in healthcare that would result from the passage of a new bill. And Americans who support a new bill are worried that it may not go far enough in expanding access to healthcare to those who currently don't have it.

Survey Methods

Results are based on telephone interviews with 1,008 national adults, aged 18 and older, conducted Nov. 5-8, 2009. For results based on the total sample of national adults, one can say with 95% confidence that the maximum margin of sampling error is ±4 percentage points.

Interviews are conducted with respondents on land-line telephones (for respondents with a land-line telephone) and cellular phones (for respondents who are cell-phone only).

In addition to sampling error, question wording and practical difficulties in conducting surveys can introduce error or bias into the findings of public opinion polls.

November 18, 2009
NONSMOKERS TOP SMOKERS IN WELL-BEING ACROSS ALL INCOMES
Smokers worse off in life evaluation, mood, depression, basic access

by Brett W. Pelham, Gallup Poll Staff Writer

Smokers trail nonsmokers in well-being, regardless of income bracket, according to Gallup-Healthways Well-Being Index data collected in 2008 and 2009. In every income group, smokers are less likely than nonsmokers to be "thriving" by at least 12 percentage points.

Holding income constant is important because wealthier people are less likely to smoke and typically enjoy higher well-being. These findings thus suggest that the link between smoking and well-being goes beyond simple economics. In fact, for those making less than $60,000 per year, not smoking appears to be the equivalent of moving up one income category in evaluative well-being. What's more, nonsmokers making between $60,000 and $90,000 per year have *higher* well-being than smokers in the top income bracket.

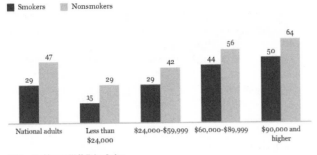

Net Thriving by Smoking Status in Four Income Groups

■ Smokers   ■ Nonsmokers

Gallup-Healthways Well-Being Index

The Gallup-Healthways Life Evaluation Index is based on the Cantril Self-Anchoring Striving Scale, which asks people to evaluate their present and future lives on a scale with steps numbered from 0 to 10, where 0 is the worst possible life and 10 is the best possible life. Those who rate today a "7" or higher and the future an "8" or higher are considered to be "thriving." Those who rate today and the future a "4" or lower on the scale are considered to be "suffering." Net thriving is the difference between people who are "thriving" and "suffering" in a given group. Compared with nonsmokers, smokers are less likely to be "thriving" in every income category.

Smoking and Emotional Health

Smokers also score lower than nonsmokers in emotional health, as defined by the Emotional Health Index. This sub-index is one of six that when combined together comprise the Gallup-Healthways Well-Being Index. The Emotional Health Index is based on 10 different items such as smiling or laughing a lot, learning or doing something interesting, or experiencing sadness or worry. In the case of emotional health, the connection between smoking and low well-being is especially pronounced for low-income respondents. While the emotional health gap between smokers and nonsmokers is 4 points for the highest income group, the gap for the lowest income group is 10 points.

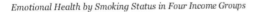

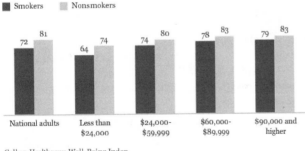

Emotional Health by Smoking Status in Four Income Groups

■ Smokers   ■ Nonsmokers

Gallup-Healthways Well-Being Index

The differences in the size of the smoking gap across income groups could mean that the emotional consequences of smoking are less pronounced for people in the higher income group. Another possibility is that people in different income groups smoke for different emotional reasons.

Smoking and Depression

One of the 10 items in the Emotional Health Index asks whether the respondent has ever been diagnosed with depression. Self-reported

smoking status is, in fact, strongly linked to depression. In all four income groups, smokers are more likely than nonsmokers to report having been depressed at some point in their lives.

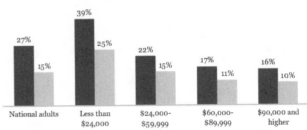

Reported Diagnosis With Depression by Smoking Status in Four Income Groups

■ Smokers   ■ Nonsmokers

Gallup-Healthways Well-Being Index

As is the case for emotional health, the connection between smoking and depression is also stronger for low-income people than for any of the other income groups. Of course, these data cannot reveal whether smoking leads to depression, whether depression leads to smoking, or whether a third variable causes both. However, these findings do reveal that the connection between these two health-related variables is particularly strong for people in the lower income bracket.

Smoking and Basic Access to Food, Shelter, and Healthcare

Compared with nonsmokers, smokers in every income group also report lower scores on the Gallup-Healthways Basic Access Index. This sub-index is based on 13 items that gauge access to things such as enough money for food, shelter, and healthcare; clean water, medicine, a safe place to exercise; and includes whether people have a doctor and whether they have health insurance. In all income groups, smokers score five to eight points lower than nonsmokers.

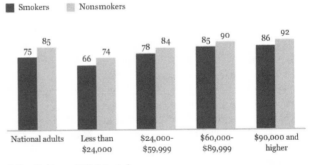

Basic Access Index Scores by Smoking Status in Four Income Groups

■ Smokers   ■ Nonsmokers

Gallup-Healthways Well-Being Index

This difference between smokers and nonsmokers is apparent for 12 of the 13 indicators in the Basic Access Index. The gap between smokers and non-smokers is largest on the items that ask about having enough money for food and enough money for healthcare. In the lowest income bracket, 54% of smokers versus 34% of nonsmokers reported not having enough money for food. The comparable values for not having enough money for healthcare are 46% and 33%. Even among the highest income group, 12% of smokers reported not having enough money for food versus 4% of nonsmokers. The equivalent comparisons for not having enough money for healthcare are 15% versus 6%. These findings are particularly distressing because they suggest that any extra health risks of smoking may be magnified by the relative lack of access to food or healthcare smokers are likely to experience. The one item that smokers and nonsmokers did not significantly differ on was in their reports of feeling safe walking alone at night.

Smoking and Physical Health

Across all income groups, smokers also fare worse than nonsmokers in physical health as reflected in lower scores on the Physical Health Index. Consistent with medical research connecting smoking to premature mortality, people who are 85 years old or older are *unlikely* to be smokers. While 26% of those aged 18 to 29 report smoking, 3% of those aged 85 and older report smoking. Of course these findings do not establish that low smoking rates are the *reason* some people live to an advanced age. Seniors may be more likely than young people, for example, to quit smoking as part of a healthier lifestyle. Nonetheless, these age differences serve as a reminder that smokers who live to a ripe old age seem to be the exception rather than the rule.

Bottom Line

Gallup-Healthways Well-Being Index data from more than 650,000 Americans interviewed in 2008 and 2009 reveal a strong connection between smoking and well-being, even when holding income constant. The Centers for Disease Control indicate that each day about 1,200 Americans die prematurely from smoking-related illnesses. According to these Gallup-Healthways data, Americans of all economic stripes, especially the poor, endure the daily toll of smoking on their health.

Survey Methods

Results are based on telephone interviews with more than 650,000 national adults, aged 18 and older, conducted Jan. 2, 2008 through Oct.31, 2009. For monthly results based on the total sample of national adults, one can say with 95% confidence that the maximum margin of sampling error for all groups is ±1 percentage point.

Sample sizes for these groups range from a high of 542,867 nonsmokers who answered the depression question to a low of 12,282 smokers in the $60,000 to $89,999 yearly income range who answered the Emotional Health Index questions.

Interviews are conducted with respondents on land-line telephones (for respondents with a land-line telephone) and cellular phones (for respondents who are cell-phone only).

In addition to sampling error, question wording and practical difficulties in conducting surveys can introduce error or bias into the findings of public opinion polls.

November 19, 2009
GREATER OPTIMISM ABOUT U.S. HEALTH SYSTEM COVERAGE, COSTS
Americans remain highly satisfied with own care

by Jeffrey M. Jones , Gallup Poll Managing Editor

As Congress debates a possible major expansion of health insurance in the United States, Gallup finds 38% of Americans rating healthcare coverage in this country as excellent or good, the highest (by eight percentage points) in the nine-year history of this question, and 12 points above last year's level.

Overall, how would you rate -- healthcare coverage in this country -- as excellent, good, only fair, or poor?

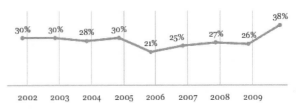

Most of the change since last year involves a shift in Americans' ratings of healthcare coverage from "only fair" to "excellent" or "good." Since last year, the percentage rating healthcare coverage as only fair has declined by 10 points, while the percentage rating it poor has changed little.

Overall, how would you rate -- healthcare coverage in this country -- as excellent, good, only fair, or poor?

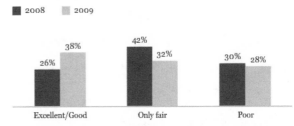

It is unclear based on the overall data whether this shift could be due to a greater appreciation for the current system among those who think it is threatened by the proposed changes, or perhaps an anticipation of better days ahead from those who support the changes. The results by party do not provide any clues as to which is the more plausible explanation, as all party groups rate U.S. health coverage more positively this year than last year.

Americans' more positive sentiments are not limited to health coverage in this country. Though there continues to be widespread dissatisfaction with the total costs of healthcare in the U.S., there has been an increase in satisfaction since last year, from 19% to 26%. This is the most positive rating since 28% said they were satisfied in 2001.

Again, the higher satisfaction scores are evident among the partisan groups—with each showing a six- to eight-point increase—but also among most demographic groups more generally.

One aspect of the healthcare system for which Americans' attitudes have not changed involves quality. The poll finds 58% rating the quality of healthcare in the U.S. as excellent or good, compared

Changes in Ratings of U.S. Healthcare Coverage as Excellent or Good, 2008-2009, by Political Party Affiliation

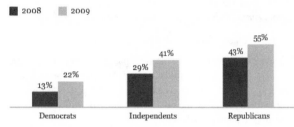

Are you generally satisfied or dissatisfied with the total cost of healthcare in this country?

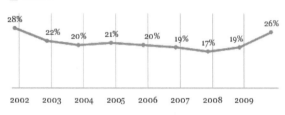

with 57% who did so last year. Gallup has always found a majority of Americans rating U.S. healthcare quality positively, but the current reading does rank on the high end of what Gallup has measured since 2001.

Overall, how would you rate -- the quality of healthcare in this country -- as excellent, good, only fair, or poor?

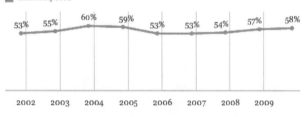

Ratings of Own Care Continue to Be Positive

Even with their improved assessments of certain aspects of the U.S. healthcare system, Americans continue to give much more positive reviews of their own healthcare in those same respects. For example, 81% rate the quality of their own care as excellent or good, and 69% rate their coverage this positively. These ratings are little changed from last year, and have not moved substantially since 2001.

These consistent, high ratings underscore the importance of allowing Americans to keep their current coverage even as the government attempts to provide health insurance to those who lack it.

Americans appear to be somewhat less positive about what they have to pay for their healthcare, but the latest poll shows these evaluations have improved somewhat in the last year. Currently, 62% of Americans say they are satisfied with the total cost they pay for healthcare, up slightly from last year's 58% and the highest level since the initial reading of 64% in 2001.

Americans who rely on Medicare or Medicaid for health coverage are somewhat more satisfied with their costs (73%) than are those who have private medical insurance (63%).

Overall, how would you rate -- [the quality of healthcare you receive/your healthcare coverage] -- as excellent, good, only fair, or poor?

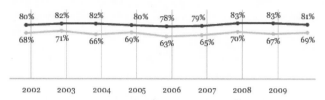

Are you generally satisfied or dissatisfied with the total cost you pay for your healthcare?

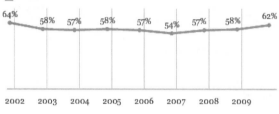

Bottom Line

As the intensity of the healthcare debate has increased over the past year, Americans' evaluations of healthcare coverage and the cost of healthcare in the U.S. have grown more positive. Still, even with the improved ratings, much less than a majority of Americans are positive in their overall evaluations of each. This fact would seem to provide sufficient justification to reform the system, though Gallup finds support for healthcare legislation lagging.

Americans continue to rate the overall quality of U.S. healthcare very highly, and give even higher marks to the quality of their own care as well as their own personal health coverage.

Survey Methods

Results are based on telephone interviews with 1,008 national adults, aged 18 and older, conducted Nov. 5-8, 2009. For results based on the total sample of national adults, one can say with 95% confidence that the maximum margin of sampling error is ±4 percentage points.

Interviews are conducted with respondents on land-line telephones (for respondents with a land-line telephone) and cellular phones (for respondents who are cell-phone only).

In addition to sampling error, question wording and practical difficulties in conducting surveys can introduce error or bias into the findings of public opinion polls.

November 19, 2009

LACK OF MONEY/WAGES TOP FAMILY FINANCIAL PROBLEM IN U.S.

Mentions exceed those for healthcare, unemployment, other financial issues

by Dennis Jacobe, Gallup Chief Economist and Jeffrey M. Jones, Managing Editor

When asked in an open-ended question to name the most important financial problem facing their families today, one in six Americans (17%) say low wages and a lack of money. Healthcare costs are next, at 14%. While the mentions of healthcare might be attributed to its prominence in the news, the issue of low wages may reflect another aspect of the job crisis in America today.

What is the most important financial problem facing your family today? [OPEN-ENDED]

	% Mentioning
Lack of money/Low wages	17
Healthcare costs	14
Too much debt/Not enough money to pay debts	10
Cost of owning/renting a home	9
Unemployment/Loss of job	7
College expenses	7
Retirement savings	5
Taxes	5
High cost of living/Inflation	4
Stock market/Investments	3

Nov. 5-8, 2009

Too much debt ranks third, at 10%, followed by the cost of renting or owning a home at 9%. Unemployment is tied for fifth with college costs at 7%.

The percentage of Americans who name lack of money/low wages now matches the high on this measure since Gallup began asking the question in January 2005. It has been the most commonly mentioned issue each of the last three times Gallup has asked this question (April, June, and November 2009), and tied with too much debt as the top issue in February 2009.

What is the most important financial problem facing your family today? [OPEN-ENDED]

% Who say "lack of money/low wages" -- trend since July 2008

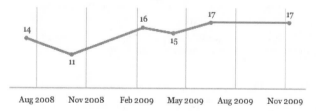

| Aug 2008 | Nov 2008 | Feb 2009 | May 2009 | Aug 2009 | Nov 2009 |

Americans' concern about lack of money/low wages may explain why Gallup has seen evidence of a "paycheck effect" in its recent weekly updates on Americans' reported spending habits, with spending increasing in and around the most common paydays (the 1st and 15th of each month) and declining in other weeks. Americans have clearly dialed back their spending this year compared to last, and, given the apparent paycheck effect, may be wait-ing for that next check before opening their wallets at their local stores.

Commentary

Federal Reserve Board Chairman Ben Bernanke noted in a speech on Monday that many employers were cutting their workers' hours and reducing their pay. In a sense, this is a natural result of a double-digit unemployment rate and nearly one in five Americans' being unemployed or underemployed. U.S. companies have done a terrific job of cutting costs and increasing productivity to maintain profitability even as top-line revenues decline. With Americans fearing for their jobs and companies operating in survival mode, wages and incomes are likely to decline.

However, this low-wage aspect of today's global surplus of available labor is often lost during the discussion of job losses and the need for job creation. Low-wage and temporary jobs may help cushion some of the worst aspects of a double-digit unemployment rate, but only the creation of high-paying, quality jobs is going to get the U.S. economy back on the path to real economic health. As long as such jobs are not being created, a lack of money will not only inhibit consumer spending but also make it increasingly difficult for many Americans to pay their bills and manage their credit.

Right now, arguments continue to flourish over how many jobs were created by the emergency stimulus program passed earlier this year. But as interesting as that debate may be politically, the focus on the numbers illustrates the complexity of the current job crisis. Pay and the longer-term viability of the jobs created may be more important than the mere number of jobs in addressing not only the unemployment problem but also the low wages hurting many American families this holiday season.

Survey Methods

Results are based on telephone interviews with 1,008 national adults, aged 18 and older, conducted Nov. 5-8, 2009. For results based on the total sample of national adults, one can say with 95% confidence that the margin of error is ±3 percentage points.

Interviews are conducted with respondents on land-line telephones (for respondents with a land-line telephone) and cellular phones (for respondents who are cell-phone only).

In addition to sampling error, question wording and practical difficulties in conducting surveys can introduce error or bias into the findings of public opinion polls.

November 20, 2009

OBAMA JOB APPROVAL DOWN TO 49%

President becomes fourth fastest to slip below the majority approval level

by Jeffrey M. Jones, Gallup Poll Managing Editor

The latest Gallup Daily tracking results show 49% of Americans approving of the job Barack Obama is doing as president, putting him below the majority approval level for the first time in his presidency.

Although the current decline below 50% has symbolic significance, most of the recent decline in support for Obama occurred in July and August. He began July at 60% approval. The ongoing,

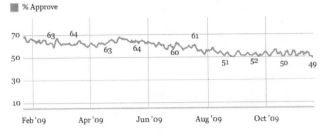

Do you approve or disapprove of the job Barack Obama is doing as president?

% Approve

contentious debate over national healthcare reform has likely served as a drag on his public support, as have continuing economic problems. Americans are also concerned about the Obama administration's reliance on government spending to solve the nation's problems and the growing federal budget deficit. Since September, Obama's approval rating had been holding in the low 50s and, although it has reached 50% numerous times, it had never dropped below 50% until now.

Of the post-World War II presidents, Obama now is the fourth fastest to drop below the majority approval level, doing so in his 10th month on the job. Gerald Ford dropped below 50% approval during his third month in office, and Bill Clinton did so in his fourth month. Ronald Reagan, like Obama, also dropped below 50% in his 10th month in office, though Reagan's drop occurred a few days sooner in that month (Nov. 13-16, 1981) than did Obama's (Nov. 17-19, 2009).

But all presidents except John Kennedy dropped below the majority approval level at some point in their presidencies, and all recovered after the first time below this mark to go back above 50% approval.

Time Between Presidents' First Sub-50% Job Approval Rating and Next Job Approval Rating Above 50%

President	Month of first sub-50% rating	Month of next rating above 50%	Full months elapsed
Truman	Feb/Mar 1946	Mar/Apr 1946	<1
Eisenhower	Mar/Apr 1958	Apr 1958	<1
Kennedy	N/A	N/A	N/A
Johnson	May 1966	Jul 1966	1
Nixon	Feb 1971	Oct 1971	7
Ford	Nov 1974	May/Jun 1975	6
Carter	Feb 1978	Nov 1978	8
Reagan	Nov 1981	Nov 1981	<1
G.H.W. Bush	Jan 1992	Jan 1993	12
Clinton	May 1993	Sep 1993	4
G.W. Bush	Jan/Feb 2004	Feb 2004	<1

Note: Kennedy never had an approval rating below 50%

Half recovered quickly—Harry Truman, Dwight Eisenhower, Ronald Reagan, and George W. Bush were back above 50% approval the same month they dipped below that mark, and Lyndon Johnson returned to majority approval in his second month after his initial sub-50% rating. The remainder continued to sink further below 50% and remained there for many months, but eventually recovered, with Ford's effort boosted by the Mayaguez incident.

George H.W. Bush took the longest time to recover, going more than a year before his approval rating was restored to the majority level. Unfortunately for him, the 1992 election at which voters denied him a second term in office occurred during this time, and his rating did not go back above 50% until just before he left office in January 1993.

Notably, most of the presidents who fell below 50% during their first term recovered in plenty of time to be re-elected. This list includes Truman, Nixon, Reagan, Clinton, and George W. Bush. Ford and Jimmy Carter recovered in the short term but could not sustain improvement long enough to convince voters they deserved a second term, and, as noted, the elder Bush recovered after he was voted out of office. Johnson may well have joined that list had he decided to seek a second term. And Eisenhower did not go below majority approval until after he had been re-elected.

Thus, Obama's descent below 50% is an important symbolic milestone in his presidency, but history suggests the odds of his regaining majority approval are high, and he could do so relatively soon, particularly since the individual nightly numbers for him in recent days have been right around the 50% mark. History would suggest his current loss of majority approval bears little relation to his chances of being elected to a second term in 2012.

Survey Methods

Results are based on telephone interviews with 1,533 national adults, aged 18 and older, conducted Nov. 17-19, 2009, as part of Gallup Daily tracking. For results based on the total sample of national adults, one can say with 95% confidence that the maximum margin of sampling error is ±4 percentage points.

Interviews are conducted with respondents on land-line telephones and cellular phones.

In addition to sampling error, question wording and practical difficulties in conducting surveys can introduce error or bias into the findings of public opinion polls.

November 20, 2009

IN U.S., MORE WOULD LIKE TO LOSE WEIGHT THAN ARE TRYING TO

Six in 10 Americans are above their ideal weight

by Jeffrey M. Jones, Gallup Poll Managing Editor

A solid majority of Americans report being heavier than their ideal weight or say they would like to lose weight, but less than half that number (27%) are seriously trying to lose weight at this time. The gap between these percentages has existed for several years.

Americans' Attitudes and Behaviors Regarding Their Weight, 2002-2009 Gallup Health Polls

■ % Over ideal weight   ■ % Would like to lose weight   ■ % Seriously trying to lose weight

A report conducted by an Emory University healthcare economist and released this week projects that as many as 40% of Americans could be classified as obese by the year 2018 and that spending on healthcare related to obesity could quadruple during that time. Gallup also publishes regular updates on obesity rates among the American public as part of its daily Gallup-Healthways Well-Being Index.

Gallup's annual Health and Healthcare poll also includes several questions about weight. The poll does not attempt to compute obesity rates but rather measures Americans' attitudes toward their weight and assesses their weight-loss behaviors. These questions have been asked each November since 2002, with some dating back further than that.

This year's poll, conducted Nov. 5-8, finds 36% of Americans currently describing themselves as "overweight," which is actually one of the lower measurements Gallup has found since 1990. The majority, 58%, say their weight is "about right," while 6% describe themselves as being "underweight."

How would you describe your own personal weight situation right now -- very overweight, somewhat overweight, about right, somewhat underweight, or very underweight?

Selected trend

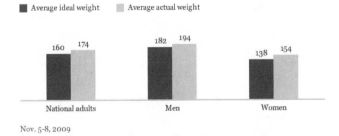

Nov. 5-8, 2009

However, when Gallup compares Americans' self-reports of their current weight to their reported ideal weight, many more, 62%, can be considered overweight.

According to the poll, the average U.S. adult weights 14 pounds more than his or her stated ideal weight (174 average actual weight versus 160 average ideal weight), with the average adult male 12 pounds heavier and the average female 16 pounds heavier than their ideal.

Difference Between Self-Reported Weight and Ideal Weight, in Pounds

Gallup has computed the average difference between Americans' self-reported actual and ideal weights 11 times since 1990, and actual weights have exceeded ideal weights by no less than 11 pounds. The gap has been about 16 pounds this decade.

Therefore, it is not surprising that most Americans, 55%, tell Gallup they would like to lose weight. Most of the rest, 37%, would like to stay at their current weight, with 7% hoping to put on weight. Losing weight has been the most common response on this question since the 1990s, with no fewer than 52% of Americans expressing a desire to lose weight across this time period.

Would you like to [ROTATED: lose weight, stay at your present weight, or put on weight]?

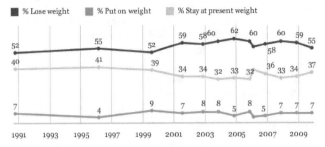

Gallup asked the same question several times in the 1950s, and during that decade, Americans were more likely to want to stay at their present weight (an average of 49% across five polls) than to lose weight (an average of 35%). (Gallup did not ask the question from 1958 to 1989.)

But wanting to lose weight and making a serious attempt at doing so are not the same thing, and Gallup finds about half as many Americans saying they are seriously trying to lose weight (27%) as saying they would like to do so (55%).

This in part may reflect a lack of will but also may reflect a lack of perceived necessity. About 24% of Americans (or roughly 4 in 10 of those whose actual weight exceeds their ideal) weigh 1 to 10 pounds more than they think they should, and these people may not see shedding the few extra pounds as worth the effort.

Comparison of Actual and Ideal Weight

	National adults	Men	Women
More than 50 lbs. over ideal weight	6%	6%	6%
21-50 lbs. over ideal weight	17%	15%	19%
11-20 lbs. over ideal weight	15%	14%	16%
1-10 lbs. over ideal weight	24%	27%	21%
At ideal weight	18%	19%	18%
1-10 lbs. under ideal weight	7%	8%	6%
11-20 lbs. under ideal weight	3%	4%	2%
More than 20 lbs. under ideal weight	1%	2%	<1%
Undesignated	9%	6%	12%

Nov. 5-8, 2009

But motivation or willpower cannot be dismissed as an explanation—even among those who are 20 pounds or more above their ideal weight, less than half (49%) say they are seriously trying to lose weight at this time.

Bottom Line

Gallup recently found obesity rates now above 30% in several states and documented a continuing rise in the percentage of Americans diagnosed with diabetes, one of the most common health problems associated with obesity.

Diet and exercise are the primary ways for Americans to lose weight and reduce the incidence of obesity in the U.S. Though many Americans express the desire to shed pounds, about half of those with that desire are following through at this time.

Survey Methods

Results are based on telephone interviews with 1,008 national adults, aged 18 and older, conducted Nov. 5-8, 2009. For results based on the total sample of national adults, one can say with 95% confidence that the maximum margin of sampling error is ±4 percentage points.

Interviews are conducted with respondents on land-line telephones (for respondents with a land-line telephone) and cellular phones (for respondents who are cell-phone only).

In addition to sampling error, question wording and practical difficulties in conducting surveys can introduce error or bias into the findings of public opinion polls.

November 23, 2009
"MOST URGENT U.S. HEALTH PROBLEM" STILL ACCESS TO HEALTHCARE
Sixteen percent now cite the flu, roughly tying with costs for second-ranked concern

by Lydia Saad, Gallup Poll Senior Editor

For the third straight year, access to healthcare leads the list of issues Americans name as the "most urgent health problem" facing the U.S., now cited by 32%. At 18%, the cost of healthcare is also widely mentioned, but to a lesser degree than it was a year ago. As a result, after many years when healthcare costs ranked as the bigger top-of-mind health problem, access now leads costs by 14 points, its widest margin.

Access and Costs -- Full Trend in Mentions as Most Urgent U.S. Health Problem
What would you say is the most urgent health problem facing this country at the present time?

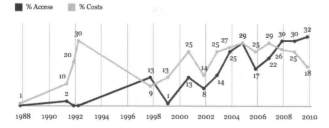

Gallup first asked Americans to name the "most urgent health problem facing this country at the present time" in 1987, and has repeated the question annually since 1999. The latest findings come from Gallup's 2009 installment of its annual Health and Healthcare poll, conducted Nov. 5-8.

Amid the worldwide H1N1 flu pandemic, Americans' mentions of flu as the nation's most urgent health problem have zoomed to 16%, up from minimal percentages citing it each of the last several years. The flu thus roughly ties healthcare costs for second on the list this year, followed by cancer and obesity. No other issue is named by more than 2% of Americans.

Top Five "Most Urgent" U.S. Health Problems -- 2008-2009
What would you say is the most urgent health problem facing this country at the present time?

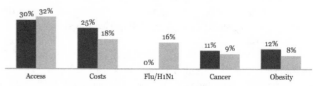

Several previous health scares—such as the bird flu in 2005 and bioterrorism in 2001—resulted in those specific issues' appearing prominently one year on the list of "most urgent health problems," only to nearly disappear the next. On the other hand, AIDS received widespread mentions for a sustained period. A striking 68% of Americans perceived AIDS as the most urgent problem in 1987. While mentions of the disease tapered off in subsequent years, they remained high through 2000, dropping below 10% in 2001. Today's 1% is the lowest on record.

This year's increased focus on flu may be displacing public concern about cancer and obesity—both of which show slight declines since 2009. However, at 9% and 8%, respectively, today's mentions of cancer and obesity still outnumber mentions of other leading public health problems, including heart disease (2%), diabetes (1%), and smoking (named by less than 0.5% of Americans).

Specific Ailments -- Full Trend in Mentions as Most Urgent U.S. Health Problem

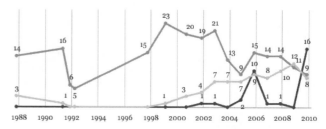

AIDS -- Full Trend in Mentions as Most Urgent U.S. Health Problem

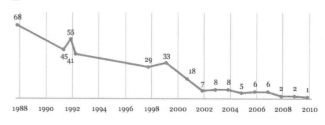

Bottom Line

Media reporting on healthcare issues in 2009 has focused heavily on two very different types of concerns: the policy issues around healthcare reform, and the medical issues around the H1N1 or swine flu. Both sets of concerns are evident in Americans' top-of-mind responses to the "most urgent health problem" facing the country today. Healthcare access and costs are perennial public concerns that have dominated the Gallup "most urgent health problem" list since concern about AIDS dropped off in the early 1990s. More recently, mentions of healthcare costs have ebbed—a finding consistent with separate Gallup research showing increased public satisfaction with the cost of healthcare—while concern about access has remained high.

Survey Methods

Results are based on telephone interviews with 1,008 national adults, aged 18 and older, conducted Nov. 5-8, 2009. For results based on the total sample of national adults, one can say with 95% confidence that the maximum margin of sampling error is ±4 percentage points.

Interviews are conducted with respondents on land-line telephones (for respondents with a land-line telephone) and cellular phones (for respondents who are cell-phone only).

In addition to sampling error, question wording and practical difficulties in conducting surveys can introduce error or bias into the findings of public opinion polls.

November 23, 2009

AMERICANS' PERSONAL BURDEN FOR HEALTHCARE COSTS STABLE

Most Americans pay at least some of the cost of their private health insurance

by Frank Newport, Gallup Poll Editor in Chief

More than 8 out of 10 Americans with private health insurance say they pay at least some of the cost themselves, and 72% of those say the amount they pay has gone up at least a little over the previous year. These percentages are little changed from previous years, suggesting that the proportion of Americans facing rising out-of-pocket health insurance costs has stabilized.

Over the past year, has the amount YOU paid for your family's health insurance -- [ROTATED: gone up a lot, gone up a little, not changed, gone down a little, (or) gone down a lot]?

Asked of those who pay all or part of their health insurance premiums

■ % Gone up a lot/Gone up a little   ■ % Not changed
▨ % Gone down a little/Gone down a lot

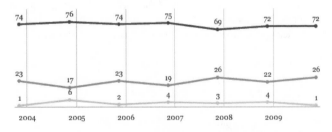

These results are from Gallup's Nov. 5-8 Healthcare update. The question about out-of-pocket costs for health insurance was asked of Americans who have private health insurance and say they pay all or part of the cost, a group constituting 48% of the adult population. The rest don't have health insurance of any kind, have health insurance through a government plan such as Medicare or Medicaid, or have private health insurance in which the employer pays all of the costs.

Among those with private insurance who pay at least some of the cost personally, the percentage since 2003 reporting cost increases has been fairly consistent. This in turn suggests a continu-

ing pattern of health insurance "price creep" over the years—at least according to the perceptions of Americans who have private health insurance.

At the same time, the proportion of Americans perceiving an increase has apparently not changed over the last year. Despite the economic crisis and the high-intensity focus on rising healthcare costs, Americans, on average, remain no more likely this year than last to say they are paying more for their families' health insurance. If anything, the percentage saying such costs have risen has been slightly lower over the last three years (2007 to 2009) than in the four previous years (2003 to 2006).

Other findings from the November Gallup health update underscore the conclusion that Americans' perceptions of healthcare this year are no more negative, and in some instances are slightly more positive, than in years past.

Health Insurance Basics

More than 8 out of 10 Americans with private health insurance say they are required to pay at least a portion of the cost themselves, and one out of four pays the entire cost personally.

Who pays the cost of premiums on your health insurance? Do you or someone in your household pay the total cost, does an employer pay the total cost, or is the cost shared between the employer and you or someone in your household?

Among adults with private health insurance

■ % Self/Household pays all   ■ % Employer pays all   ▨ % Costs are shared

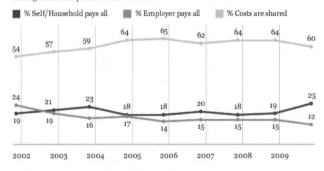

Having one's employer pay the entire tab for health insurance has become largely a thing of the past. The current 12% who continue to enjoy this state of affairs is a few points lower than last year, and well below the 24% and 19% who reported this situation in 2001 and 2002, respectively. Concomitantly, the 25% of Americans with private health insurance who say they pay the entire tab themselves is the highest of the decade. The trend on this measure has fluctuated; the previous high point—23%—was in 2003.

Survey Methods

Results are based on telephone interviews with 1,008 national adults, aged 18 and older, conducted Nov. 5-8, 2009. For results based on the total sample of national adults, one can say with 95% confidence that the maximum margin of sampling error is ±4 percentage points.

The results for those who have private health insurance and pay all or part of their health premiums are based on a sample of 456 national adults, with a maximum margin of sampling error of ±5 percentage points.

Interviews are conducted with respondents on land-line telephones (for respondents with a land-line telephone) and cellular phones (for respondents who are cell-phone only).

In addition to sampling error, question wording and practical difficulties in conducting surveys can introduce error or bias into the findings of public opinion polls.

November 24, 2009

WOMEN DISAGREE WITH NEW MAMMOGRAM ADVICE

Most women under 50 plan to buck recommendation to wait for next mammogram

by Lydia Saad, Gallup Poll Senior Editor

A new *USA Today*/Gallup poll finds three-quarters of U.S. women aged 35 to 75 disagreeing with the more relaxed medical recommendations on mammograms that were announced by a government advisory panel last week, including 47% saying they "strongly disagree" with them.

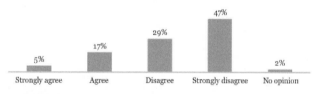

Views of New Mammogram Guidelines Among Women Aged 35 to 75

As you may know, medical guidelines have called for most women to have their first mammogram at age 40 and then to have follow-up mammograms every year. The advisory panel now recommends increasing the age for a first mammogram to age 50, and changing the frequency to every two years. What is your opinion of the new recommendations, do you -- [strongly agree, agree, disagree, (or) strongly disagree] -- with them?

USA Today/Gallup, Nov. 20-22, 2009

The poll was conducted Nov. 20-22 and includes interviews with 1,136 women aged 35 to 75 nationwide.

Most women surveyed are also skeptical about the reasoning behind the panel's recommendations that women should delay getting their first mammogram until the age of 50 (rather than the long-standing recommendation of 40 years old) and that the interval between routine mammograms should be every two years (rather than every one year). A majority of women surveyed believe the panel made its decisions based primarily on the potential cost savings (76%) involved, rather than on a fair assessment of the true risks and benefits (16%) of mammograms for women in their 40s.

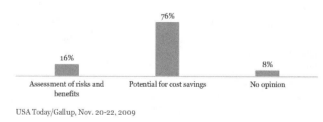

Perceived Basis for Panel's Mammogram Guidelines Among Women Aged 35 to 75

Just your best guess, do you think the panel's recommendations were mainly based on -- [a fair assessment of the true medical risks and benefits of mammograms for women in their 40s, (or mainly based on) the potential for cost savings in the healthcare system]?

USA Today/Gallup, Nov. 20-22, 2009

Not only do women disagree with the panel's recommendation to delay starting mammograms until the age of 50, but most of those in the key age group targeted by the decision—those aged 35 to 49—plan to ignore them. Specifically, 84% say they will not wait until they are 50 to get their next mammogram, but they will get one sooner than that. The finding is the same for women aged 35 to 39 as for those aged 40 to 49.

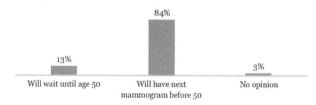

Plans for Timing of Next Mammogram Among Women Aged 35 to 49

Do you think you will, personally, wait until age 50 to get your next mammogram, or will you get one sooner than that?

USA Today/Gallup, Nov. 20-22, 2009

News Has Spread Quickly

The U.S. Preventive Services Task Force—a panel of medical experts commissioned by the federal government to review the scientific evidence regarding preventive medical services and develop practice guidelines—made its announcement about changes to mammogram screening last week.

Already, 85% of women in the 35- to 75-year-old age bracket say they have heard about the new recommendations.

Among women 35- to 75-years-old who have heard of the recommendation, the slight majority (57%) correctly state that the panel advises most women to receive their first mammogram at the age of 50. About half as many (29%) incorrectly believe the recommended age is younger than 50, while 14% are unsure.

The Stress Factor Is Real

The task force cites the stress that some women experience from false-positive mammogram results as a significant factor in arriving at its new breast cancer screening recommendations. The report states that the health risks of stress combined with the medical risks of unnecessary biopsies and other follow-up tests led the task force to conclude that the benefits of routine mammograms do not outweigh the risks for women in their 40s.

The new poll verifies that such mammogram-induced anxiety is not uncommon. Among women aged 35 to 75 who have had a mammogram (but not been diagnosed with breast cancer), 15% report that at least one mammogram experience was very stressful for them. Another 29% say that at least one mammogram experience was somewhat stressful.

The new *USA Today*/Gallup findings suggest women who have had very stressful mammogram experiences may be more inclined to agree with the task force's reasoning than those who have not had such scares. However, the vast majority of women in all stress groups disagree with the new guidelines.

Sixty-six percent of women who have had at least one very stressful mammogram experience say they disagree with the new mammogram guidelines. This compares with 81% of those who have had a somewhat stressful experience and 78% of those who have never had any kind of stressful mammogram experience.

History of Stress Due to Mammograms Among Women Aged 35-75 Who Have
Had a Mammogram (But Not Diagnosed With Breast Cancer)

We'd like to know how stressful the experiences you have had with mammograms have been for you, both in terms of the actual procedure and also any concerns raised by the test results. Which of the following applies to you —having mammograms has never been stressful for you, on at least one occasion having a mammogram was somewhat stressful for you, or on at least one occasion having a mammogram was very stressful for you?

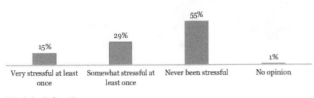

USA Today/Gallup, Nov. 20-22, 2009

Reaction to New Mammogram Guidelines Based on Personal Experience
of Stress With Mammograms

Based on women aged 35-75 who have had a mammogram (but not diagnosed with cancer)

■ Agree with new guidelines   ▨ Disagree

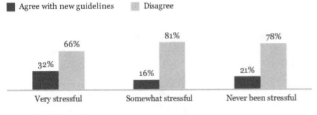

USA Today/Gallup, Nov. 20-22, 2009

Bottom Line

Women have been told for years that their best protection against breast cancer is early detection, starting with getting their first mammogram at the age of 40 and faithfully scheduling yearly updates. Their reaction to the news that this may not have been the best advice after all is one of disbelief, perhaps fueled by skepticism about the motive. For now, most women under the age of 50 believe it is in their best interests to have their next mammogram before they reach the new recommended age threshold, and they intend to do just that.

Survey Methods

Results are based on telephone interviews with a random sample of 1,136 women, aged 35-75, conducted Nov. 20-22, 2009. For results based on the total sample of women, one can say with 95% confidence that the margin of error is ±4 percentage points.

For results based on the 981 women aged 35-75 who have had a mammogram, the margin of sampling error is ±4 percentage points. For results based on the 284 women aged 35-49 who have not been diagnosed with breast cancer, the margin of sampling error is ±7 percentage points.

Interviews are conducted with respondents on land-line telephones (for respondents with a land-line telephone) and cellular phones (for respondents who are cell-phone only).

In addition to sampling error, question wording and practical difficulties in conducting surveys can introduce error or bias into the findings of public opinion polls.

November 24, 2009
OBAMA'S APPROVAL SLIDE FINDS WHITES DOWN TO 39%
Support has declined much more among whites than among nonwhites

by Jeffrey M. Jones, Gallup Poll Managing Editor

Since the start of his presidency, U.S. President Barack Obama's approval rating has declined more among non-Hispanic whites than among nonwhites, and now, fewer than 4 in 10 whites approve of the job Obama is doing as president.

Barack Obama Job Approval Rating, by Racial Group

Gallup Daily tracking, aggregated weekly

■ Whites   ▨ Nonwhites

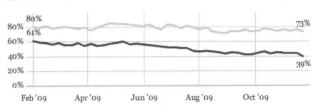

Obama last week fell below 50% approval in Gallup Daily tracking for the first time in his presidency, both in daily three-day rolling averages and in Gallup Daily tracking results aggregated weekly.

In his first full week in office (Jan. 26-Feb. 1), an average of 66% of Americans approved of the job Obama was doing, including 61% of non-Hispanic whites and 80% of nonwhites. In the most recent week, spanning Nov. 16-22 interviewing, his approval rating averaged 49% overall, 39% among whites, and 73% among nonwhites. Thus, since the beginning of his presidency, his support has dropped 22 points among whites, compared with a 7-point loss among nonwhites.

Given the 17-point drop in his approval rating among all U.S. adults, it follows that Obama's support has declined among all major demographic and attitudinal subgroups, with one notable exception— blacks.

Blacks' support for Obama has averaged 93% during his time in office, and has been at or above 90% nearly every week during his presidency. Thus, part of the reason Obama's support among nonwhites has not dropped as much as his support among other groups is because of his consistent support from blacks. (With Hispanics' approval rating down five points, greater declines among Asians, Native Americans, and those of mixed races account for his total seven-point drop among nonwhites.)

The accompanying table shows how Obama's approval rating has changed by subgroup from his first full week in office to the most recent week. The only subgroup showing a greater change than whites is Republicans, down 24 points during this time. Independents' approval of Obama has declined nearly as much (down 18 points), whereas support among Democrats is down only 6 points.

Obama's strongest support comes from blacks, Democrats, and liberals—all of whom give him approval ratings above 80%. He maintains solid support of more than 60% from nonwhites, Hispanics, and young adults.

A Closer Look at Race and Party

One reason Obama may have maintained support among blacks is their overwhelming affiliation with the Democratic Party. This is not

Barack Obama Job Approval Rating, by Demographic Group, First Full Week
in Office vs. Week of Nov. 16-22

Gallup Daily tracking, aggregated weekly

	% Approval, Jan 26-Feb 1, 2009	% Approval, Nov 16-22, 2009	Change (pct. pts.)
All adults	66	49	-17
Male	61	46	-15
Female	70	51	-19
Age 18 to 29	74	61	-13
Age 30 to 49	67	48	-19
Age 50 to 64	63	46	-17
Age 65+	61	42	-19
White	61	39	-22
Nonwhite	80	73	-7
Black	90	91	1
Hispanic	75	70	-5
East	70	51	-19
Midwest	67	50	-17
South	61	43	-18
West	68	54	-14
High school diploma or less	64	50	-14
Some college	65	46	-19
College graduate only	66	47	-19
Postgraduate	73	57	-16
Democrat	88	82	-6
Independent	62	44	-18
Republican	38	14	-24
Liberal	87	82	-5
Moderate	73	55	-18
Conservative	46	27	-19
Married	60	42	-18
Not married	72	58	-14

Barack Obama Job Approval Rating, Among Democrats, by Race

Gallup Daily tracking, aggregated weekly

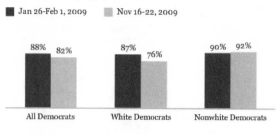

a sufficient explanation, though, because Obama's approval rating has dropped among Democrats even as it has held steady among blacks.

In fact, it appears as though Obama's relatively small loss in support among Democrats has come exclusively from white Democrats. In late January/early February, Obama averaged 87% approval among white Democrats and 90% approval among nonwhite Democrats. Now, his approval rating among white Democrats is 76%, down 11 points, but is essentially the same (if not a little higher) at 92% among nonwhite Democrats.

Bottom Line

Obama won the Democratic nomination and the presidency with strong support from blacks and other racial minorities. In fact, according to exit polls and Gallup's final pre-election estimates, he won the election despite losing by double digits to John McCain among white voters.

Those patterns of support seem to have persisted into his presidency, with his support among whites starting out lower and dropping faster than his support among nonwhites. And though he maintains widespread loyalty among Democrats, the small loss in

support he has seen from his fellow partisans seems to be exclusively from white Democrats.

It is important to note that this pattern is not unique to Obama. For example, Bill Clinton averaged 55% job approval during his presidency, including 52% among whites but a much higher 76% among nonwhites and 82% among blacks.

Survey Methods

Results are based on telephone interviews with 3,611 national adults, aged 18 and older, conducted Nov. 16-22, 2009, as part of Gallup Daily tracking. For results based on the total sample of national adults, one can say with 95% confidence that the maximum margin of error is ±2 percentage points.

For results based on the sample of 2,879 non-Hispanic whites, the maximum margin of error is ±2 percentage points.

For results based on the sample of 732 nonwhites, the maximum margin of error is ±5 percentage points.

Interviews are conducted with respondents on land-line telephones and cellular phones.

In addition to sampling error, question wording and practical difficulties in conducting surveys can introduce error or bias into the findings of public opinion polls.

November 24, 2009
AMERICANS KEEP VOLUNTEERING DURING TOUGH ECONOMIC TIMES
Well-being higher for those who volunteer versus those who do not

by Shane Lopez , Gallup Poll Staff Writer

During the economic downturn of late 2008 and the first half of 2009, Americans continued to volunteer their time to others. According to a recent Gallup survey, more than one-third of Americans reported volunteering recently in each month from September 2008 to July 2009.

Service through volunteering increased slightly during the early months of the recession, October and November of 2008, decreasing through December 2008 and January 2009 and stabilizing over the course of 2009. The findings extend the stable volunteering trend from 2002 through 2008 reported by the Corporation for National and Community Service.

Volunteering varies by age, with Americans aged 30 to 44 consistently the most active, or tied as the most active. Seniors (aged 65

Have you done any of the following in the past month? How about volunteered your time to an organization?

% Yes, have volunteered

▮ U.S. monthly average

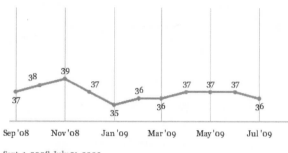

Sept. 1, 2008–July 31, 2009

and older) and young adults (18- to 29-year-olds) tend to be the least active.

Have you done any of the following in the past month? How about volunteered your time to an organization?

% Yes, have volunteered

▮ 18-29 ▮ 30-44 ▮ 45-64 ▮ 65+

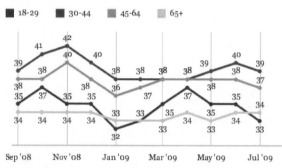

Sept.1, 2008–July 31, 2009

Volunteering and Well-Being

Generally, people who say they volunteered in the last month also experienced higher personal well-being, garnering higher scores on all six Gallup-Healthways Well-Being sub-indexes than those who did not say they volunteered. The well-being gap between those who say they volunteer and those who do not was largest on the Life Evaluation Index, at 12 points. The Life Evaluation Index is based on the Cantril Self-Anchoring Striving Scale, which asks people to evaluate their present and future lives on a scale with steps numbered from 0 to 10, where 0 is the worst possible life and 10 is the best possible life. Those who rate today a "7" or higher and the future an "8" or higher are considered to be "thriving." Those who rate today and the future a "4" or lower on the scale are considered to be "suffering." The relationship between well-being and volunteering holds across all age groups.

Bottom Line

According to the Center for Civil Society Studies, nonprofit organizations reported a greater need for volunteers during the recent economic recession. During this time, Americans continued to offer their time to organizations. More than one-third of Americans nationwide reported volunteering recently, with more 30- to 44-year-olds report-

Well-Being and Volunteering

▮ % Volunteered in the past month ▮ % Did not volunteer in the past month

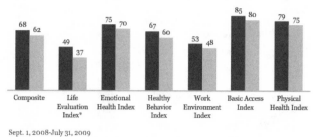

Sept. 1, 2008–July 31, 2009
*Life Evaluation Index = % thriving minus % suffering

ing volunteering than people in other age groups. People who report volunteering also report high well-being, yet it is unclear whether volunteering leads to high well-being or if high well-being facilitates volunteering behavior.

Survey Methods

Results are based on telephone interviews with 139,954 national adults, aged 18 and older, conducted from September 2008-July 2009. For results based on the total sample of national adults, one can say with 95% confidence that the maximum margin of sampling error is ±0.3 percentage points.

Interviews are conducted with respondents on land-line telephones (for respondents with a land-line telephone) and cellular phones (for respondents who are cell-phone only).

In addition to sampling error, question wording and practical difficulties in conducting surveys can introduce error or bias into the findings of public opinion polls.

November 25, 2009
IN U.S., MORE SUPPORT FOR INCREASING TROOPS IN AFGHANISTAN
Americans now tilt slightly toward sending in new troops as opposed to reducing number

by Frank Newport, Gallup Poll Editor in Chief

Americans over the last two weeks have become slightly more likely to favor sending more U.S. troops to Afghanistan, and slightly less likely to favor a reduction in forces. At this point, 47% of Americans would advise President Obama to increase the number of U.S. troops—either by the roughly 40,000 recommended by the commanding general in Afghanistan or by a smaller amount—while 39% would advise Obama to reduce the number of troops. Another 9% would opt to leave troop levels as they are, while 5% have no opinion.

President Obama on Tuesday announced that he will present his new "comprehensive strategy" on Afghanistan to the American people early next week. Obama gave no indication of exactly what he will recommend. Media reports suggest that Obama's strategy will probably include the addition of at least some new U.S. troops. It is not known whether that number will approach the 40,000 new troops the U.S. commander in Afghanistan, Gen. Stanley McChrystal, has recommended.

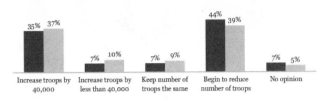

Which of the following would you like to see President Obama do -- [ROTATED: increase the number of U.S. troops in Afghanistan by the roughly 40,000 the U.S. commanding general there has recommended, increase the number of U.S. troops in Afghanistan but by a smaller amount than the 40,000 the U.S. commanding general there has recommended, keep the number of U.S. troops in Afghanistan the same as now, (or) begin to reduce the number of U.S. troops in Afghanistan]?

The question in the Nov. 20-22 *USA Today*/Gallup poll gives respondents four choices and asks them to indicate which action they would most like to see President Obama take.

Asked the same question earlier in November, Americans tilted toward the troop-reduction option over the troop-increase option, 44% to 42%. Now, the data tilt in the other direction. Those who want a troop increase outnumber those who want a reduction, 47% to 39%.

Despite these modest shifts, the data continue to show that less than half of Americans would support an Obama decision to increase troops. Similarly, slightly less than half would support a decision to leave things unchanged (9%) or to begin to withdraw troops (39%). In short, Americans remain split on the volatile subject of what to do in Afghanistan.

Republicans have historically been more supportive than Democrats of American involvement in Afghanistan. That partisan distinction continues. The majority of Democrats currently favor a reduction of troops; the majority of Republicans favor a troop increase. Independents tilt more toward the Republican position.

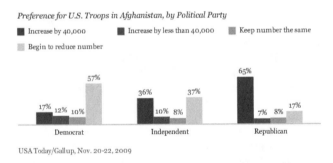

Preference for U.S. Troops in Afghanistan, by Political Party

USA Today/Gallup, Nov. 20-22, 2009

Views on Afghanistan More Broadly

President Obama is making decisions on Afghanistan at a time when Americans' perceptions that the war there is going badly for the U.S. have reached a new high. A record 66% of Americans now say things are going badly for the U.S. in Afghanistan, up from 61% in early September. At the same time, 36% say U.S. involvement was a mistake, unchanged from views over the summer.

Support for U.S. involvement in Afghanistan was very high in November 2001, shortly after then-President George W. Bush first sent U.S. troops there in the immediate aftermath of the 9/11 terrorist attacks. Nine percent said sending troops was a mistake, a percentage that fell to 6% in January 2002. Perceptions that U.S. involvement was a mistake rose thereafter, albeit modestly. Since

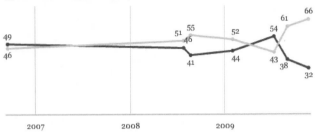

In general, how would you say things are going for the U.S. in Afghanistan -- [ROTATED: very well, moderately well, moderately badly, (or) very badly]?

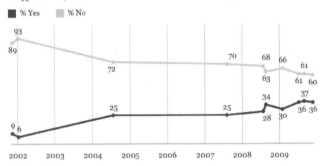

Thinking now about U.S. military action in Afghanistan that began in October 2001, do you think the United States made a mistake in sending military forces to Afghanistan, or not?

August 2008, between 30% and 37% of Americans have said it was a mistake to send troops to Afghanistan. Sixty percent in the current poll say U.S. involvement was not a mistake.

Gallup first asked Americans to assess the way things were going in Afghanistan in 2006, at which time slightly less than half said the war was going badly for the U.S. Perceptions that the war was going badly increased to above 50% in three polls in 2008 and early 2009, only to fall to a new low of 43% in July of this year. Views on the war became sharply more negative near the end of the summer—by early September, 61% said the war was going badly. Now, 66% of Americans share a negative view of the way the war is going for the U.S.

President Obama is making his decision on Afghanistan in the context of a split opinion on the war among those who identify with his own party. Fifty percent of Democrats say the war in Afghanistan has been a mistake, while 47% say it has not. Republicans overwhelmingly reject the idea that the war was a mistake. Independents echo the Republican view that it was not a mistake, though their views are more evenly divided.

Implications

President Obama's decision on U.S. military policy in Afghanistan will be one of the most important of his first year—if not his first term—as president. If, as expected, the president decides to "stay the course" in Afghanistan, he will be doing so with the understanding that most Americans agree that U.S. involvement there is warranted. At the same time, the majority of Americans now perceive that the situation there is going badly for the U.S., perhaps helping explain Americans' increased willingness to sanction sending additional troops to Afghanistan. Still, Obama will have less-than-majority support if he increases the number of U.S. troops in that country. This

Thinking now about U.S. military action in Afghanistan that began in October 2001, do you think the United States made a mistake in sending military forces to Afghanistan, or not?

By party ID

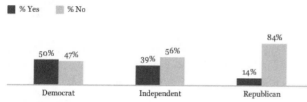

USA Today/Gallup, Nov. 20-22, 2009

underscores the political sensitivity of any decision he makes on Afghanistan, particularly given that those who identify with his own party are solidly against sending in new troops.

Survey Methods

Results are based on telephone interviews with 1,017 national adults, aged 18 and older, conducted Nov. 20-22, 2009. For results based on the total sample of national adults, one can say with 95% confidence that the maximum margin of sampling error is ±4 percentage points.

Interviews are conducted with respondents on land-line telephones (for respondents with a land-line telephone) and cellular phones (for respondents who are cell-phone only).

In addition to sampling error, question wording and practical difficulties in conducting surveys can introduce error or bias into the findings of public opinion polls.

November 27, 2009

AMERICANS AT ODDS WITH RECENT TERROR TRIAL DECISIONS

Majorities would prefer trying 9/11 kingpin in a military court, away from New York

by Lydia Saad, Gallup Poll Senior Editor

By 59% to 36%, more Americans believe accused Sept. 11 mastermind Khalid Sheikh Mohammed should be tried in a military court, rather than in a civilian criminal court. Most Republicans and independents favor holding the trial in a military court, while the slight majority of Democrats disagree.

Preferred Jurisdiction for Khalid Sheikh Mohammed Trial

Do you think it would be better to hold Khalid Sheikh Mohammed's trial in a civilian criminal court or a military court?

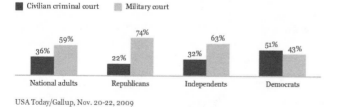

USA Today/Gallup, Nov. 20-22, 2009

These findings come from a Nov. 20-22 *USA Today*/Gallup poll conducted a week after U.S. Attorney General Eric Holder announced that Mohammed's case would move from a military tribunal in Guantanamo Bay, where the admitted terrorist was originally charged, to a federal court in New York City.

Public opinion is a bit less contrary to Holder's decision regarding the venue for the trial. Although the majority of Americans (51%) say Mohammed should face trial somewhere other than New York City, 42%—slightly higher than the percentage favoring a civilian trial—support holding the trial in the city where the vast majority of Americans lost their lives on Sept. 11.

Preferred Venue for Khalid Sheikh Mohammed Trial

As you may know, Khalid Sheikh Mohammed has described himself as the mastermind of the Sept. 11 terror attacks. He is scheduled to face trial in New York City. Just your opinion, do you think it would be better to have his trial in New York City or better to have it somewhere else?

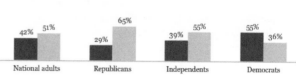

USA Today/Gallup, Nov. 20-22, 2009

The legal framework of Mohammed's case has clearly shifted along with the new jurisdiction, as he will now be granted certain constitutional rights and protections that would not have been afforded him in a military tribunal. Nevertheless, 7 in 10 Americans—including a high proportion of all party groups—believe it is very likely Mohammed will be found guilty. Only 6% think a guilty verdict is unlikely.

How likely do you think it is that Khalid Sheikh Mohammed will be found guilty -- very likely, somewhat likely, not too likely, or not at all likely?

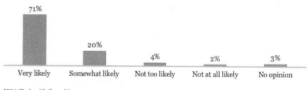

USA Today/Gallup, Nov. 20-22, 2009

The possibility that the federal trial would give Mohammed and the four others to be tried in New York a platform for airing their political views was raised last week, after a lawyer for one of the accused announced that the five defendants intend to plead not guilty for the express purpose of being able to "get their message out" in the trial.

Overall, 59% of Americans are at least somewhat concerned that a trial will give Mohammed such an opportunity; however, significantly fewer—34%—are "very concerned." Among partisans, most of the differentiation in views on this question is seen in the percentages very concerned, ranging from 50% of Republicans to 34% of independents and 21% of Democrats.

Little Disagreement Over Pursuing Death Penalty

Holder announced last week that the Justice Department will seek the death penalty for Mohammed and four other men accused of plot-

How concerned are you that a trial will give Khalid Sheikh Mohammed publicity to further his cause -- very concerned, somewhat concerned, not too concerned, or not concerned at all?

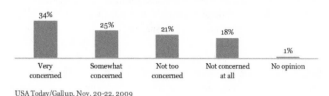

USA Today/Gallup, Nov. 20-22, 2009

ting 9/11, and Americans broadly agree with this. Three-quarters (77%) say Mohammed should get the death penalty if he is found guilty, slightly higher than the percentage telling Gallup in October (65%) that they favor the death penalty for persons convicted of murder, in general.

Despite their sharp differences over how to bring Mohammed to justice, Republicans and Democrats largely agree that, if found guilty, he should pay the ultimate price.

If Khalid Sheikh Mohammed is found guilty, do you think he should or should not get the death penalty?

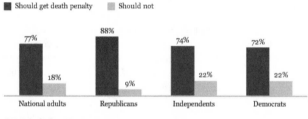

USA Today/Gallup, Nov. 20-22, 2009

Bottom Line

Two weeks after Attorney General Holder announced his decision to try the five leading 9/11 terrorism suspects in federal court in New York City, controversy about those decisions abounds.

A slight majority of Americans disagree with Holder's decision to hold the Mohammed trial in New York (51% say it should be held elsewhere) and a larger proportion disagree with his decision to move the case to a civilian court (59% would prefer to have it held in a military court). Democrats are generally supportive of the Obama administration's changes in these respects, while Republicans and independents take opposing views. At the same time, relatively few Americans (particularly Democrats and independents) are very concerned that the trial will give Mohammed a publicity platform, and most Americans are confident he will be found guilty.

Survey Methods

Results are based on telephone interviews with 1,017 national adults, aged 18 and older, conducted Nov. 20-22, 2009. For results based on the total sample of national adults, one can say with 95% confidence that the maximum margin of sampling error is ±4 percentage points.

Interviews are conducted with respondents on land-line telephones (for respondents with a land-line telephone) and cellular phones (for respondents who are cell-phone only).

In addition to sampling error, question wording and practical difficulties in conducting surveys can introduce error or bias into the findings of public opinion polls.

November 30, 2009

AMERICANS STILL LEANING AGAINST HEALTHCARE LEGISLATION

Majority disapprove of Obama's handling of the issue

by Jeffrey M. Jones, Gallup Poll Managing Editor

Americans currently tilt against Congress' passing healthcare legislation, with 49% saying they would advise their member to vote against a bill (or they lean that way) and 44% saying they would advocate a vote in favor of the bill (or lean toward advising a yes vote).

Would you advise your member of Congress to vote for or against a healthcare bill this year, or do you not have an opinion?

[IF NO OPINION]: As of today, would you say you lean more toward advising your member of Congress to vote for a healthcare bill, or lean more toward advising your member of Congress to vote against a healthcare bill?

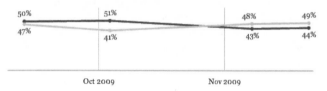

These results are based on a Nov. 20-22 *USA Today*/Gallup poll, and are essentially unchanged from a poll conducted earlier this month. Within the last month, the House has passed a version of healthcare legislation, and the Senate voted on Nov. 21 to allow debate on its healthcare bill. That debate is scheduled to begin Monday.

Since Gallup began tracking Americans' preferences for healthcare legislation earlier this year, there has never been a strong public mandate in favor of passing a law this year. The high point in support was 51% in early October. But since that time, opinion has shifted from a slightly positive position to a slightly negative one.

However, opinion on the issue is far from settled. When initially asked about their preferred course of action on healthcare legislation, 22% of Americans say they do not yet have an opinion on the matter (although 15% subsequently provide an opinion when asked if they lean one way or the other). The percentage with no opinion on the initial question has fluctuated since August, but has never been lower than the current 22% figure.

Because those who initially express no opinion divide fairly evenly between support and opposition when probed for their leaning, the trend on the initial question has been similar to the trend shown at the beginning of the article that combines initial preferences and leanings.

Support for Healthcare Legislation by Political Party

Republicans are overwhelmingly opposed to new healthcare legislation—86% would advise their member of Congress to vote against it, while 12% would want their member to support it. Democrats, on the other hand, favor it by a 76% to 17% margin. Independents oppose passage of a bill by 53% to 37%.

Support among all three party groups has declined since the early October high—falling by 6 points among Democrats, 8 among independents, and 12 among Republicans. However, Democratic

Would you advise your member of Congress to vote for or against a healthcare bill this year, or do you not have an opinion?

Initial opinion, not including leanings

■ Vote for ■ Vote against ▨ No opinion

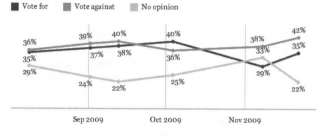

Sep 2009   Oct 2009   Nov 2009

support recovered somewhat from early November (71%) to late November (76%).

Trend in Support for Healthcare Legislation, by Political Party Affiliation

% Vote for/Lean "vote for"

■ Democrat ▨ Independent ▨ Republican

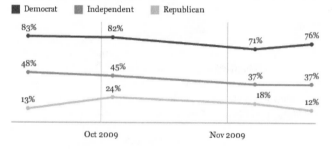

Oct 2009   Nov 2009

Obama Gets Poor Marks on Healthcare

The poll also finds 40% of Americans approving of President Obama's handling of healthcare policy, while 53% disapprove. This is slightly more negative than what Gallup found from July through September, and represents his worst review to date on this issue.

Do you approve or disapprove of the way Barack Obama is handling healthcare policy?

■ Approve ▨ Disapprove

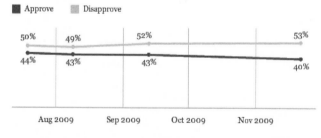

Aug 2009   Sep 2009   Oct 2009   Nov 2009

Seventy-four percent of Democrats approve of Obama's handling of the issue, but this is below the better-than 80% of Democrats who approve of the job Obama is doing as president overall.

Republicans are nearly unanimous in their views of Obama's work on healthcare, with 89% disapproving and 6% approving. Independents are nearly twice as likely to disapprove (58%) as to approve (33%).

Bottom Line

Despite the considerable efforts of Congress and the president to pass health insurance reform, the public remains reluctant to endorse that

goal. Over the past month, Gallup has found more Americans opposed to than in favor of healthcare legislation, though at least one in five say they have not made up their minds. Proportionately more independents (27%) and Democrats (24%) than Republicans (14%) are undecided, which at least improves the odds that legislation could wind up getting majority public backing. But the recent trend has been in the opposite direction, with opposition growing.

Survey Methods

Results are based on telephone interviews with 1,017 national adults, aged 18 and older, conducted Nov. 20-22, 2009. For results based on the total sample of national adults, one can say with 95% confidence that the maximum margin of sampling error is ±4 percentage points.

Interviews are conducted with respondents on land-line telephones (for respondents with a land-line telephone) and cellular phones (for respondents who are cell-phone only).

In addition to sampling error, question wording and practical difficulties in conducting surveys can introduce error or bias into the findings of public opinion polls.

November 30, 2009
AMERICANS' SPENDING ON FRI. AND SAT. DOWN 8.6% FROM '08
Americans spent an average of $106 each day on the two days after Thanksgiving

by Frank Newport , Gallup Poll Editor in Chief

Americans report spending an average of $106 each day on the Friday and Saturday after Thanksgiving this year, down 8.6% from the $116 average reported on those same days last year.

Next, we'd like you to think about your spending yesterday, not counting the purchase of a home, motor vehicle, or your normal household bills. How much money did you spend or charge yesterday on all other types of purchases you may have made, such as at a store, restaurant, gas station, online, or elsewhere?

■ Average spending, each day, Friday and Saturday after Thanksgiving

Gallup Daily tracking

Gallup analysis has suggested that spending for Christmas gifts this year will be roughly the same as last year, a weak forecast given last year's dismal overall holiday spending. Gallup's current day-to-day assessment of overall spending on the critically important days after Thanksgiving appears consistent with this earlier forecast.

Gallup's Daily consumer spending measure is based on a question asking Americans to report how much money they spent "yesterday" on all types of purchases such as "at a store, restaurant, gas station, online, or elsewhere" (excluding the purchase of a home, motor vehicle, or normal household bills). All references in this report are to the day for which the respondent is asked to estimate spending.

Estimated daily spending for the two days after Thanksgiving this year is an average of $106, compared to a daily average of $116 last year. This is an 8.6% drop, similar to what the National Retail Federation has reported. Precise estimates for spending on specific days are based on smaller sample sizes, have larger margins of error, and Gallup does not usually report them. It can be said, however, that the estimate for Thanksgiving Day itself was very low in both 2008 and 2009—as would be expected. But the daily spending trends on Friday and Saturday after Thanksgiving this year appear to be reversed in comparison to 2008. Last year, Americans reported spending more on Black Friday than on Saturday; this year, Saturday was the bigger day.

The percentage of Americans who report spending any amount of money on these two days this year is comparable to the percentage for the same days last year. On Black Friday and on Saturday, Gallup estimated that about 70% of Americans spent at least some money on each day.

By way of comparison, about half of Americans spent nothing on Thanksgiving in both years—much higher than usual, as would be expected.

Gallup's daily spending estimate is a general measure of overall spending, and is not specific to spending for holiday gifts. This spending measure has in general been lower this year compared to the same points in time last year.

Next, we'd like you to think about your spending yesterday, not counting the purchase of a home, motor vehicle, or your normal household bills. How much money did you spend or charge yesterday on all other types of purchases you may have made, such as at a store, restaurant, gas station, online, or elsewhere?

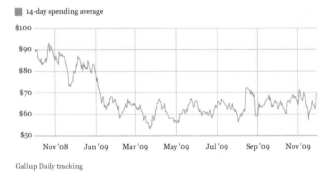

14-day spending average

Gallup Daily tracking

Thus, everything else being equal, one would expect spending on any comparable day this year—including the days after Thanksgiving—to be lower than it was last year.

It is not possible to determine the degree to which the slightly depressed spending level on Friday and Saturday this year is a result of the overall "new normal" of a more frugal lifestyle, or a specific decision to spend less on holiday presents. It is possible, although not likely, that the holiday spending component of overall spending could be increasing this year at the same time that the non-holiday portion is decreasing.

Gallup analysis last year suggested that the sharp drop-off in spending from Black Friday to Saturday could mean a lack of momentum in retail spending, which certainly turned out to be the case. (Note that spending estimates as reported in November 2008 were calculated using a different procedure for handling high-dollar estimates; all comparisons in this report are based on standardized mean values in use since January 2009 that are retrospectively comparable across both 2008 and 2009.) It is possible that the increase from Friday to Saturday this year could suggest a building momentum, which would be good news for retailers.

Some analysts point to the Monday after Thanksgiving as a critical day for online sales and/or that spending this year may be more spread out in the weeks leading to Christmas Day. Thus, it will be important to monitor Gallup's Daily spending measure in the days to come for a better read on the developing pattern of consumer spending at this crucial time for the nation's economy.

Survey Methods

Results are based on telephone interviews with 984 national adults, aged 18 and older, conducted Nov. 28-29, 2009, as part of Gallup Daily tracking. For results based on this sample of national adults, one can say with 95% confidence that the maximum margin of sampling error is ±4 percentage points.

Interviews are conducted with respondents on land-line telephones and cellular phones.

In addition to sampling error, question wording and practical difficulties in conducting surveys can introduce error or bias into the findings of public opinion polls.

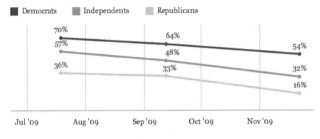

Approval Ratings of Barack Obama's Handling of the Situation in Afghanistan, by Political Party

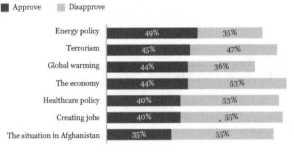

■ Democrats   ■ Independents   ■ Republicans

70%
57%
36%
64%
48%
33%
54%
32%
16%

Jul '09   Aug '09   Sep '09   Oct '09   Nov '09

December 01, 2009

OBAMA APPROVAL ON AFGHANISTAN, AT 35%, TRAILS OTHER ISSUES

Decline from 49% in September far exceeds that for other issues and for approval more broadly

by Jeffrey M. Jones, Gallup Poll Managing Editor

Americans are far less approving of President Obama's handling of the situation in Afghanistan than they have been in recent months, with 35% currently approving, down from 49% in September and 56% in July.

Do you approve or disapprove of the way Barack Obama is handling the situation in Afghanistan?

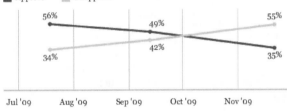

■ Approve   ■ Disapprove

56%
49%
34%
42%
55%
35%

Jul '09   Aug '09   Sep '09   Oct '09   Nov '09

Tuesday, Obama outlines his new strategy for the war in Afghanistan in a nationally televised address. The policy has been months in the making as Obama held numerous meetings with his military and foreign policy advisers, drawing some criticism for the delay in formulating a new strategy. The commanding U.S. general in Afghanistan, Gen. Stanley McChrystal, has recommended that the United States increase the number of troops it has in that country by about 40,000. Obama is expected to announce a slightly smaller increase.

The decline in Obama's approval rating on Afghanistan is evident among all party groups, with double-digit decreases since September among Republicans (17 points), independents (16 points), and Democrats (10 points).

While a slim majority of Obama's fellow Democrats approve of his handling of the issue, his new policy may not be well-received by Democrats, who have indicated opposition to troop-level increases in Afghanistan. The details of the policy will likely be more appealing to Republicans, who are supportive of putting more U.S. troops in Afghanistan.

The question about Afghanistan comes from a Nov. 20-22 *USA Today*/Gallup poll that also asked Americans to rate Obama's handling of six other issues. The president registers less than majority approval for his performance on all seven issues, with Afghanistan his worst rating. His best rating is on energy policy, with 49% approval.

Approval Ratings of Barack Obama on Issues

■ Approve   ■ Disapprove

	Approve	Disapprove
Energy policy	49%	35%
Terrorism	45%	47%
Global warming	44%	36%
The economy	44%	53%
Healthcare policy	40%	53%
Creating jobs	40%	55%
The situation in Afghanistan	35%	55%

USA Today/Gallup, Nov. 20-22, 2009

Obama's overall job approval rating has also been below the majority level for most of the time since Nov. 20 in Gallup Daily tracking, though it has inched back above the 50% mark in recent days.

The 14-point decline in Obama's approval rating on Afghanistan stands in contrast to the trend lines on other issues, including the economy, healthcare, and energy. While his current ratings on these issues are down since September, the declines have been fairly minimal.

Trend in Approval Ratings of Barack Obama on Issues

	Sep 11-13, 2009	Nov 20-22, 2009	Change
	%	%	Pct. pts.
The situation in Afghanistan	49	35	-14
The economy	46	44	-2
Healthcare policy	43	40	-3
Energy policy	50	49	-1

Note: Issues asked in Sept. 11-13 and Nov. 20-22 USA Today/Gallup polls

Bottom Line

The president's decisions on U.S. military action in Afghanistan are arguably among the most important and difficult of his presidency. He met several times with his advisers in recent weeks before outlining his new policy to the American public Tuesday night. The speech gives the president a chance to regain the confidence of Americans on the issue, after a sharp drop in his ratings over the past two months.

But the decline in Americans' evaluations of Obama on Afghanistan does not appear to have greatly affected their more general views of him, as his overall job approval rating—though down slightly since September—has not declined to nearly the same degree as his rating on Afghanistan.

Results are based on telephone interviews with 1,017 national adults, aged 18 and older, conducted Nov. 20-22, 2009. For results based on the total sample of national adults, one can say with 95% confidence that the maximum margin of sampling error is ±4 percentage points.

Interviews are conducted with respondents on land-line telephones (for respondents with a land-line telephone) and cellular phones (for respondents who are cell-phone only).

In addition to sampling error, question wording and practical difficulties in conducting surveys can introduce error or bias into the findings of public opinion polls.

December 02, 2009
MAJORITY OF AMERICANS THINK NEAR-TERM TERRORISM UNLIKELY
Thirty-nine percent say it is likely, nearing low since 2001

by Lydia Saad, Gallup Poll Senior Editor

By 57% to 39%, more Americans think a terrorist attack on the United States is unlikely to happen in the next few weeks than say an attack is likely. This is based on Gallup polling conducted Nov. 20-22, prior to President Obama's address to the nation on Afghanistan in which he said the need to fight terrorism is the primary reason he is committing more U.S. troops to the conflict there.

Perceived Likelihood of Terrorist Attack -- September 2001-November 2009

How likely is it that there will be acts of terrorism in the United States over the next several weeks -- very likely, somewhat likely, not too likely, or not at all likely?

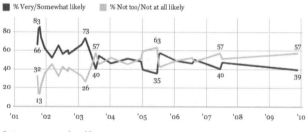

Sept. 2001 survey conducted Sept. 21-22, 2001

More specifically, 10% of Americans believe it is very likely that terrorist acts will occur in the U.S. over the next several weeks while 29% say this is somewhat likely, 36% say not too likely, and 21% say not at all likely.

How likely is it that there will be acts of terrorism in the United States over the next several weeks -- very likely, somewhat likely, not too likely, or not at all likely?

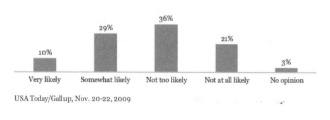

USA Today/Gallup, Nov. 20-22, 2009

Despite the recent mass killing at Ft. Hood in Texas, which some have referred to as a terrorist attack, public anxiety about the likelihood of terrorism today is on the low end of the range Gallup has recorded since establishing the question right after 9/11. In fact, the only lower reading occurred in June 2005, when 35% said terrorism was likely. That result came just weeks before suicide bombings carried out on the London transit system took 52 lives and injured hundreds of others. The bombings helped push concern about a near-term U.S. attack up to 57% in the first month after they occurred.

Today's finding is nearly identical to the reading from June 2007, when 40% said an attack was likely. However, there are significant differences by party ID between those two measurements. Republicans have grown more concerned about the chances of a terrorist attack (spanning the transition from President Bush to President Obama). Democrats have become less concerned, while the views of political independents have not changed.

Perceived Likelihood of Terrorist Attack -- 2007 vs. 2009, by Party ID
Percent very/somewhat likely

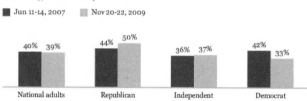

The November 2009 poll finds relatively small differences between men and women, and among various age groups, in their perceptions about the likelihood of a near-term terrorist event. However, Americans with higher levels of education are less likely to say a terrorist attack is likely than are those with no college degree.

Perceived Likelihood of Terrorist Attack, by Education

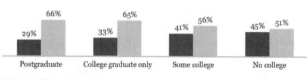

USA Today/Gallup, Nov. 20-22, 2009

Bottom Line

Since 9/11, U.S. public officials have relayed the United States' success in foiling numerous terrorist plots against the country. President Obama did the same Tuesday night, saying, "In the last few months alone, we have apprehended extremists within our borders who were sent here from the border region of Afghanistan and Pakistan to commit new acts of terror." Yet the Gallup trend shows that without the occurrence of a clear terrorist attack in the U.S. or abroad, or an obvious event—such as the beginning of military action in Iraq or Afghanistan—that might heighten the perceived risk of terrorism, Americans have been inclined to downplay the chances of terrorism in recent years. The latest finding is consistent with Gallup polling earlier this year that showed Americans' fear of becoming a victim of terrorism was near the five-year low.

Whether this relative complacency among Americans about terrorism continues, and how it affects public support for Obama's troop surge in Afghanistan, remains to be seen.

Survey Methods

Results are based on telephone interviews with 1,017 national adults, aged 18 and older, conducted Nov. 20-22, 2009. For results based on the total sample of national adults, one can say with 95% confidence that the maximum margin of sampling error is ±4 percentage points.

Interviews are conducted with respondents on land-line telephones (for respondents with a land-line telephone) and cellular phones (for respondents who are cell-phone only).

In addition to sampling error, question wording and practical difficulties in conducting surveys can introduce error or bias into the findings of public opinion polls.

December 02, 2009

AMERICANS SEE PROTECTIONISM, TAX CUTS AS WAYS TO CREATE JOBS
Offer a mixed forecast for U.S. jobs climate over the next year

by Lydia Saad, Gallup Poll Senior Editor

As President Obama holds a jobs summit Thursday to discuss ways to address the problem of growing unemployment in the United States, Americans' top prescriptions for creating more jobs are to keep manufacturing jobs in the U.S. (18%), lower taxes (14%), provide more help to small businesses (12%), and create more infrastructure work (10%).

Americans' Prescription for Increasing U.S. Jobs*

In your opinion, what would be the best way to create more jobs in the United States? (open-ended)

	National adults	Republicans	Independents	Democrats
	%	%	%	%
Keep manufacturing jobs in the U.S.	18	15	18	20
Lower taxes	14	29	14	2
Help small businesses	12	13	14	9
Create more infrastructure work	10	7	9	13
Reduce government regulation	7	8	7	3
Create more "green" jobs	6	2	6	7
Provide more "stimulus" funding	4	2	5	5
Buy American/Raise taxes on imports	4	4	4	4

* Responses named by at least 4% of Americans shown.

USA Today/Gallup, Nov. 20-22, 2009

The results are from an open-ended question asked in a *USA Today*/Gallup poll conducted Nov. 20-22, 2009. Additional tactics cited by at least 4% of Americans include reducing government regulations on business (7%), creating more green jobs (6%), providing more federal stimulus funding (4%), and implementing more pro-"buy American" policies (4%).

These ideas are strongly related to partisanship. Democrats are somewhat more likely than Republicans to focus on keeping manufacturing jobs in the U.S. and creating certain types of jobs (infrastructure work and green jobs). Republicans are significantly more

likely than Democrats to favor lowering taxes and reducing government regulation.

The Jobs Outlook Over the Next Year

Americans offer mixed forecasts for what will happen to the U.S. job market over the next year. Twenty-eight percent predict it will get worse while slightly more, 35%, say it will get better, and 36% think it will stay the same. At the extremes of this spectrum, however, more than twice as many Americans foresee the job market getting "a lot worse" as say it will get "a lot better"—14% vs. 6%, respectively.

One-Year Outlook for U.S. Job Market

Just your best guess, over the next 12 months, do you think the job market in the United States will get better, stay about the same, or get worse? (If better/worse:) Do you think it will get a lot [better/worse], or only a little [better/worse]?

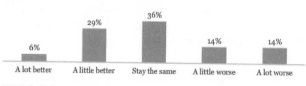

USA Today/Gallup, Nov. 20-22, 2009

These perceptions overlay Americans' fundamentally bad views of where the job market currently stands. In mid-November, Gallup found a record-low percentage of Americans—8%—saying now is a good time to find a quality job. In this context, maintaining the current jobs climate could be perceived as a negative forecast.

The main factor in public perceptions of a jobs recovery also appears to be politics—a finding that suggests Americans consider their jobs outlook to be a referendum on the Obama administration's economic policies. Republicans and independents are more likely to believe the job market will get worse, rather than better, over the next year, while an outright majority of Democrats say it will get better.

One-Year Outlook for U.S. Job Market -- Summary Forecast, by Party ID

■ Get better ■ Stay the same ▪ Get worse

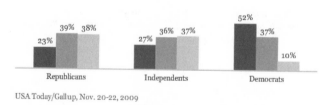

USA Today/Gallup, Nov. 20-22, 2009

Bottom Line

With the official unemployment figure now topping 10% nationwide, a lack of jobs threatens to send the American economy into a deeper recession at a time when other aspects of the economy are struggling to recover. Americans' top prescriptions for creating more jobs are instituting greater protections for U.S. manufacturing, lowering taxes, helping out small businesses, and creating more infrastructure work. Democrats largely favor more government involvement in terms of protectionism, stimulus spending, and shovel-ready jobs. Republicans tend to favor a free-enterprise approach, exemplified by lowering taxes and reducing government regulation.

Just over a third of Americans predict the job market won't change much in the next year—not a particularly positive sentiment given the current climate. Of the remainder who believe the job market will change, most—43% of all Americans—foresee fairly small changes (either improvement or decline). However, a combined 20% believe it will change a lot, with most of these saying the problems will deepen rather than improve.

Survey Methods

Results are based on telephone interviews with 1,017 national adults, aged 18 and older, conducted Nov. 20-22, 2009. For results based on the total sample of national adults, one can say with 95% confidence that the maximum margin of sampling error is ±4 percentage points.

Interviews are conducted with respondents on land-line telephones (for respondents with a land-line telephone) and cellular phones (for respondents who are cell-phone only).

In addition to sampling error, question wording and practical difficulties in conducting surveys can introduce error or bias into the findings of public opinion polls.

December 03, 2009

OBAMA'S PLAN FOR AFGHANISTAN FINDS BIPARTISAN SUPPORT

Overall, 51% of Americans support the new policy, while 40% are opposed

by Frank Newport , Gallup Poll Editor in Chief

President Obama has managed to thread the needle with his newly announced Afghanistan strategy, with his approach winning the approval of a majority of both Democrats (58%) and Republicans (55%) in a *USA Today*/Gallup poll conducted Wednesday night. At the same time, less than a majority of independents approve (45%). Among Americans overall, 51% approve of the strategy while 40% disapprove.

As you may know, President Obama has decided to increase the number of U.S. troops in Afghanistan by 30,000 while also setting a timetable that calls for the U.S. to begin withdrawing troops from that country in 2011. In general, do you favor or oppose this plan?

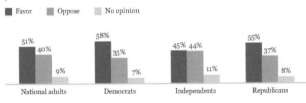

USA Today/Gallup, Dec. 2, 2009

The question used in Wednesday's poll explicitly associated the policy with President Obama, and included a reference to both the increase of 30,000 U.S. troops and the setting of a timetable that calls for the U.S. to begin withdrawing troops from Afghanistan in 2011.

The overall 51% positive reaction to the new policy is slightly higher than the 47% who in a November poll (before Obama's new

policy was announced) supported the basic concept of increasing troops in Afghanistan.

The rough similarity between the responses to two questions on Afghanistan masks a significant difference in partisan sentiment. When asked earlier about just sending troops, Democrats were much less likely than Republicans to be in favor. Now, in response to the new question asking specifically about Obama's multipart strategy, including references to increasing troops and to the timetable, Democrats and Republicans show similar levels of support. (Independents' attitudes are roughly the same in both polls.)

More generally, Obama's new policy has managed to bridge the pre-existing partisan gap on this issue to some degree, bringing the support levels of Democrats and Republicans closer together. This is an unusual situation. Most major policy initiatives that a president promulgates find support among the president's own party and opposition among the other party. In the current situation, Obama has, at least in the short term, generated majority support among Democrats—who previously had been opposed to a troop increase in Afghanistan—while holding on to majority support among Republicans. Obama's continuing problem appears to be independents, less than half of whom support the new policy.

The survey included questions asking Americans to evaluate two key components of Obama's new policy: the level of new U.S. troops being sent to Afghanistan, and the setting of a specific timetable for beginning to withdraw troops.

Overall, Americans are split on the troop-level component. Most believe that the number of new troops being sent as part of the new strategy is either too high (36%) or about right (38%). Relatively few Americans believe the number of additional troops is "too low" (18%).

What is your view of sending 30,000 more U.S. troops to Afghanistan -- do you think that number is too high, about right, or too low?

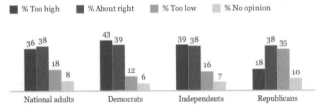

USA Today/Gallup, Dec. 2, 2009

Roughly the same percentage of Republicans and Democrats (38% to 39%) say the announced troop increase is "about right." But Democrats who disagree with the increase are much more likely to say that the troop levels are too high than too low, while Republicans who disagree tilt in the other direction. Independents have much the same pattern of sentiments as Democrats.

Regarding the timetable component of Obama's new policy, the plurality of Americans, 46%, say it is too soon to set a timetable for beginning to withdraw troops. The rest are split between the belief that the U.S. should begin withdrawing troops earlier and agreement with the timetable.

Republicans' reactions to the idea of a timetable are strongly negative: 72% say it is too soon to set one. Democrats are much more evenly split on the issue. Thirty-five percent agree with the timetable as announced, while 34% say it is too soon to set a timetable and 27% say the troops should be withdrawn sooner. Independents' views fall in between those of the two groups.

Which comes closest to your view about setting a timetable for beginning to withdraw U.S. troops from Afghanistan in 2011?

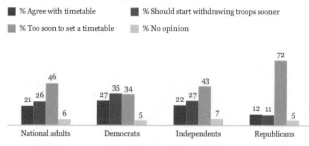

USA Today/Gallup, Dec. 2, 2009

Implications

All in all, slightly more than half of Americans support Obama's new policy in Afghanistan, while 4 out of 10 oppose it. The president at the moment enjoys an unusual situation in which a majority of both Democrats and Republicans favor his newly announced strategy. This level of bipartisan support is counterbalanced to a degree, however, by the fact that less than half of independents support the plan.

Well less than half of Democrats agree either with the level of new troops the U.S. is sending or with the specifics of the new timetable. Similarly, less than half of Republicans agree with either of these two components, and almost three out of four Republicans disagree with the concept of setting a timetable at this point.

Thus, partisan reactions to the *specific* components of the new plan do not explain the majority support for the plan among both Republicans and Democrats.

It may be that while Democrats disagree with the specifics of the timetable as announced, they approve of the idea of having *any* timetable included. And it may be that while Republicans strongly disagree with having any timetable included, they approve of the general idea of an increase of troop levels.

Whatever the explanations, the bottom line at the moment is that Obama has managed to generate a slim majority support among all Americans for his new policy. Obama faces the highest level of skepticism among independents, but has knit together a coalition of support that includes a majority of both Democrats and Republicans. Given that in large part, political and pundit voices that are solidly partisan are debating Afghanistan, this majority approval level among Democrats and Republicans may be the most politically significant short-term reaction to the new policy.

Survey Methods

Results are based on telephone interviews with 1,005 national adults, aged 18 and older, conducted Dec. 2, 2009. For results based on the total sample of national adults, one can say with 95% confidence that the maximum margin of sampling error is ±4 percentage points.

Interviews are conducted with respondents on land-line telephones and cellular phones.

In addition to sampling error, question wording and practical difficulties in conducting surveys can introduce error or bias into the findings of public opinion polls.

Polls conducted entirely in one day, such as this one, are subject to additional error or bias not found in polls conducted over several days.

December 04, 2009

IN U.S., TRUST VARIES WITH INCOME, EDUCATION, RACE, AND AGE

Money, schooling, race, age all related to trust in one's neighbors

by Brett Pelham and Steve Crabtree, Gallup Poll Staff Writers

Is community trust a luxury in America? Gallup data offer some support for that idea—82% of those making $90,000 per year or more say they would expect a neighbor who found a lost wallet or purse containing $200 to return it. In contrast, 50% of those making less than $24,000 per year expressed this kind of trust in their neighbors.

Trust in One's Neighbors by Income

If you lost a wallet or purse that contained $200, and it was found by a neighbor, do you think it would be returned with the money in it, or not?

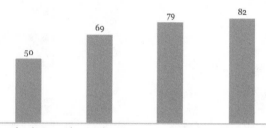

These findings are consistent with previous state-level findings showing that states with higher per-capita income levels also tend to have higher proportions of residents who express trust in their neighbors.

More Education, More Trust

More highly educated people are also more likely to express trust in their neighbors. Whereas 81% of those with an advanced degree say they believe their neighbor would return their lost wallet, 48% of those without a high school diploma express the same sentiment.

Trust in One's Neighbors by Education Level

If you lost a wallet or purse that contained $200, and it was found by a neighbor, do you think it would be returned with the money in it, or not?

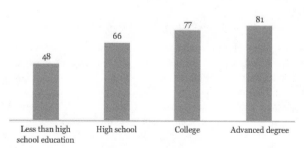

Although education is closely related to income, more analysis clearly shows that education is related to expressions of trust regardless of income. In every income category, those who are more highly educated are more likely to say their neighbor would return a lost wallet. In the lowest income category, for example, the "trust gap" between the least educated group and the most highly educated group was 27 percentage points. In the highest income category, the gap was 20 points.

How Race Is Related to Trust

Race is also strongly related to trust in one's neighbors. On average, non-Hispanic blacks and Hispanics are less likely to say they would trust a neighbor to return their wallet with the money in it than are whites and Asians.

Trust in One's Neighbors by Race

If you lost a wallet or purse that contained $200, and it was found by a neighbor, do you think it would be returned with the money in it, or not?

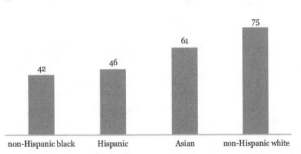

Again, the gaps don't just reflect the differences in average income among the groups. In high- and low-income categories, the "trust gap" between blacks and whites is at least 20 points. In fact, in the two lowest income groups, the gap is at least 30 points. Hispanics are also less likely to express trust than whites, with gaps of 13 to 29 points across all income groups. Finally, the gap between whites and Asians is at least 10 points in every income group.

Trust Comes With Time and Age

Averaging across all ethnic groups, older people are more likely than their younger counterparts to say they would trust a neighbor to return their wallet with the money in it. A slight majority (55%) of those aged 29 and younger say so, and this figure increases steadily among higher age groups. Among those aged 65 and older, 3 in 4 (75%) express confidence that their neighbor would return the wallet complete with its contents.

Women and Men About Equally Trusting

The only demographic variable examined here that is unrelated to trust is gender. Sixty-eight percent of women and men expressed confidence that their neighbor would return their money. The only hint of a meaningful gender difference in these data showed up among the youngest respondents. Among those aged 29 and younger, 57% of men and 53% of women expressed trust in their neighbor.

It All Adds Up

We can get an idea of the total effect of income, education, race, and age on Americans' likelihood of trusting their neighbors by looking at people whose characteristics all predict whether they will express

Trust in One's Neighbors by Age

If you lost a wallet or purse that contained $200, and it was found by a neighbor, do you think it would be returned with the money in it, or not?

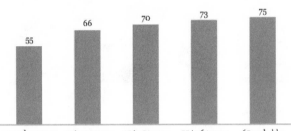

such trust. At one extreme are young, black respondents who do not have a high school education and who fall into the lowest income category; among this group, 17% say a neighbor would return their wallet with the money in it. At the other demographic extreme, the oldest group of non-Hispanic whites who have an advanced degree and make at least $90,000 per year, 90% report that their neighbors would return a lost wallet.

The additive nature of these effects is also a reminder that trust is a two-way street. Reports of trust have to do with properties of those who ponder losing their wallets and properties of those who consider returning them. People with lower incomes, for example, are more likely to live in neighborhoods with high crime rates, which may help explain their relative lack of trust. In other words, people who say they trust their neighbors are not merely expressing trust in a social vacuum. They are also describing the actual people who live in the house or apartment next door.

Implications

The Gallup data point to considerable "trust deficits" among Americans who are less financially secure, or more likely to have faced racial biases. This information is important for two reasons.

First, a growing body of research shows that social connections are important to individuals' personal well-being, so a lack of trust may reduce opportunities to build friendships among those who need them most.

Second, low levels of trust among neighbors in a community may be a result of residents' low socioeconomic status, but they may also help perpetuate it. In other words, close neighborhood ties may give people access to resources and opportunities they wouldn't otherwise have. People may be more likely to start a business in their area, for example, if they can find trusted partners to share the risk.

For these reasons, those seeking to increase opportunities for disadvantaged Americans in at-risk communities may want to consider how many people in a given community lack trust in their neighbors.

Survey Methods

Results are based on telephone interviews with more than 238,000 national adults, aged 18 and older, surveyed between Sept. 4, 2008 and Oct. 31, 2009. Sample sizes for the main demographic groups range from a low of 3,221 Asians to a high of 123,543 respondents with a high school education. Margins of error thus range from ±2 percentage points for Asians to less than ±1 percentage point for most other demographic groups.

Interviews are conducted with respondents on land-line telephones (for respondents with a land-line telephone) and cellular phones (for respondents who are cell-phone only).

In addition to sampling error, question wording and practical difficulties in conducting surveys can introduce error or bias into the findings of public opinion polls.

December 04, 2009

AMERICANS SPLIT ON WHETHER GOALS IN AFGHANISTAN WILL BE MET

Forty-eight percent say the U.S. is certain or likely to meet its goals

by Jeffrey M. Jones, Gallup Poll Managing Editor

The unveiling of President Obama's new military strategy for Afghanistan has not left Americans overly confident that it will succeed—48% say the U.S. is certain or likely to achieve its goals in the war, while 45% say the U.S. is unlikely to do so or is certain not to achieve its aims.

Now, thinking in general about the goals for U.S. military policy in Afghanistan, do you think the United States is -- certain to achieve its goals in Afghanistan, likely to achieve its goals, not likely to achieve its goals, or certain NOT to achieve its goals in Afghanistan?

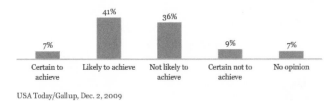

USA Today/Gallup, Dec. 2, 2009

These results are based on a one-night reaction poll of 1,000 Americans conducted Dec. 2, the night after Obama's nationally televised address to unveil the new war strategy. The poll found Americans more likely to favor (51%) than oppose (40%) the new strategy.

There are a significant number of doubters even among those who support the new war policy. Among this group, 61% believe the U.S. is likely to achieve its goals, but 35% are pessimistic. Likewise, though the majority of the new policy's opponents do not expect the U.S. to achieve its goals in Afghanistan, that is far from a unanimous position.

Perceptions of U.S. Ability to Achieve Goals in Afghanistan, by Support for New War Policy

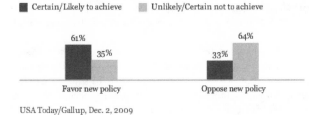

USA Today/Gallup, Dec. 2, 2009

There are modest differences in expectations for success by party, with 56% of Republicans, 47% of independents, and 45% of Democrats believing the U.S. will achieve its goals.

Cost and Security Concerns

Some opponents of escalating the United States' involvement in Afghanistan are questioning the increasing costs to the U.S. of the war effort. And many Americans share this concern, at least to some degree. The poll finds 73% saying they are worried about the war's costs making it more difficult for the U.S. to address domestic problems, including 32% who are very worried.

How worried are you that the costs of the war in Afghanistan will make it more difficult for the government to address the problems facing the United States at home -- very worried, somewhat worried, not too worried, or not worried at all?

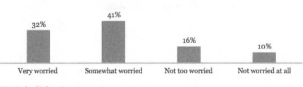

USA Today/Gallup, Dec. 2, 2009

Some Democratic members of Congress have called for a new income tax to help fund the increased cost of U.S. military operations in Afghanistan brought about by the decision to send an additional 30,000 service men and women there. However, the top two Democrats in Congress, Speaker of the House Nancy Pelosi and House Majority Leader Steny Hoyer, have come out in opposition to such a tax, making its passage highly unlikely. It would appear Pelosi and Hoyer are in tune with American public opinion; the poll shows that Americans overwhelmingly oppose a war surtax, by 68% to 24%.

While much of the Democratic criticism of the new Afghanistan policy has centered on cost, Republicans have expressed concern about setting a timetable for withdrawal. The poll finds 55% of Americans saying they are concerned that withdrawing troops from Afghanistan would make the U.S. more vulnerable to terrorist attacks, including 19% who are very concerned.

How worried are you that withdrawing U.S. troops from Afghanistan will make the United States more vulnerable to terrorist attacks -- very worried, somewhat worried, not too worried, or not worried at all?

USA Today/Gallup, Dec. 2, 2009

In line with the concerns of their party leaders, rank-and-file Democrats are more concerned about the war's costs limiting the United States' ability to address domestic problems, while rank-and-file Republicans are more concerned that withdrawing troops could affect U.S. security from terrorism.

Even if a substantial proportion of Americans doubt the United States' ability to succeed in Afghanistan or express concern about possible outcomes of the new war policy, the public generally does

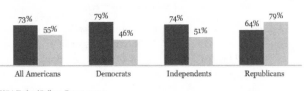

Worry About Afghanistan War Policy's Effects, by Party

■ Very/Somewhat worried about costs

▨ Very/Somewhat worried about U.S. security from terrorism

USA Today/Gallup, Dec. 2, 2009

not second-guess the initial decision to enter the war. The poll finds 62% saying that, looking back, sending troops to Afghanistan was the right thing to do, while 32% say it was the wrong thing. This is similar to what Gallup has found on its primary "mistake" trend question that measures support for the war.

Survey Methods

Results are based on telephone interviews with 1,005 national adults, aged 18 and older, conducted Dec. 2, 2009. For results based on the total sample of national adults, one can say with 95% confidence that the maximum margin of sampling error is ±4 percentage points.

Interviews are conducted with respondents on land-line telephones and cellular phones.

In addition to sampling error, question wording and practical difficulties in conducting surveys can introduce error or bias into the findings of public opinion polls.

Polls conducted entirely in one day, such as this one, are subject to additional error or bias not found in polls conducted over several days.

December 04, 2009
POST-THANKSGIVING RETAIL SPENDING TRAILS SAME WEEK IN 2008
Spending is down most sharply in the West, among men under 40

by Lydia Saad, Gallup Poll Senior Editor

The 2009 holiday retail season, which kicked off last Friday, has been marked by somewhat lower self-reported consumer spending than was seen during the comparable period a year ago. According to Gallup Daily tracking, daily consumer spending for the six-day period since Thanksgiving—spanning the Black Friday weekend and Cyber Monday—averaged $82. This is down 15% from $96 for the same six-day period in 2008.

Each day, Gallup asks Americans to say how much money they spent "yesterday" in stores, gas stations, restaurants, or online—not counting home and vehicle purchases, and their normal monthly bills. The reduced retail spending at the outset of the holiday shopping season this year compared to last is most pronounced in the West, among young adults, and more specifically among men aged 18 to 39. Only slight, and not statistically significant, changes are seen by household income and parental status.

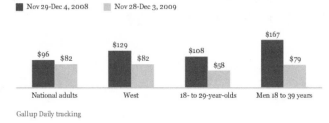

Consumer Self-Reported Average Daily Spending -- Post-Thanksgiving 2008 vs. 2009

Next, we'd like you to think about your spending yesterday, not counting the purchase of a home, motor vehicle, or your normal household bills. How much money did you spend or charge yesterday on all other types of purchases you may have made, such as at a store, restaurant, gas station, online, or elsewhere?

■ Nov 29-Dec 4, 2008   ▨ Nov 28-Dec 3, 2009

Gallup Daily tracking

Regional Spending

The year-to-year spending trend for the first week of the holiday shopping season appears to be fairly flat in all regions of the country, except for the West, where spending has dropped by more than a third, from $129 to $82. This could reflect the poorer jobs situation in the West compared to other regions, which Gallup documented earlier this week.

2008 vs. 2009 Consumer Self-Reported Average Daily Spending -- by Region

■ Nov 29-Dec 4, 2008   ▨ Nov 28-Dec 3, 2009

Gallup Daily tracking

Spending Patterns by Age

Spending levels among adults aged 30 and older are quite similar to what they were in 2008. However, spending among 18- to 29-year-olds is down sharply.

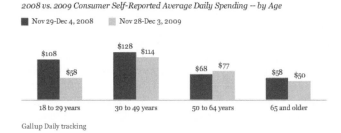

2008 vs. 2009 Consumer Self-Reported Average Daily Spending -- by Age

■ Nov 29-Dec 4, 2008   ▨ Nov 28-Dec 3, 2009

Gallup Daily tracking

The decline in spending among young adults is seen exclusively among men. Post-Thanksgiving daily retail spending among men aged 18 to 39 has averaged $79 this year, down from $167 in 2008's post-Thanksgiving week. By comparison, spending among women in that age group shows a modest but not statistically meaningful increase.

The $167 that younger men spent last year at this time was significantly higher relative to other age/gender groups than is normally seen; thus, the drop between 2008 and 2009 may be somewhat exaggerated and it will be important to monitor spending patterns by these age and gender categories as the holiday season progresses.

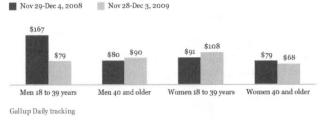

2008 vs. 2009 Consumer Self-Reported Average Daily Spending – by Gender/Age

■ Nov 29-Dec 4, 2008   ▨ Nov 28-Dec 3, 2009

Gallup Daily tracking

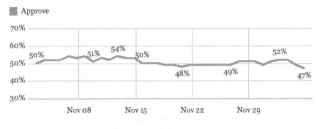

Do you approve or disapprove of the job Barack Obama is doing as president?
Recent three-day rolling averages

▨ Approve

Bottom Line

Throughout the year, Gallup has found self-reported consumer spending to be running substantially below the comparable months for 2008, and it appears that pattern is continuing as the holiday shopping season kicks off. Some segments of society—particularly younger women and residents of the Midwest and the South—are managing to spend the same as or even a little more than they did a year ago, making them potential targets of last-minute marketing efforts by holiday retailers. Other segments—particularly Westerners and men under 40 years of age—are being quite cautious at the cash register, resulting in dampened overall spending figures.

Survey Methods

For Gallup Daily tracking, Gallup interviews approximately 1,000 national adults, aged 18 and older, each day. The Gallup consumer spending results are based on random half-samples of approximately 500 national adults, aged 18 and older, each day.

The 2009 consumer spending results reported here are based on telephone interviews conducted Nov. 28 to Dec. 3, 2009, with 2,866 adults. For these results, one can say with 95% confidence that the maximum margin of sampling error is ±2 percentage points. The 2008 results are based on telephone interviews conducted Nov. 29 to Dec. 4, 2008, with 3,034 national adults. For these results, the maximum margin of sampling error is ±2 percentage points.

Interviews are conducted with respondents on land-line telephones and cellular phones.

In addition to sampling error, question wording and practical difficulties in conducting surveys can introduce error or bias into the findings of public opinion polls.

December 07, 2009
AFTER BRIEF UPTICK, OBAMA APPROVAL SLIPS TO 47%
New low follows slight increase after announcement of Afghanistan policy

by Jeffrey M. Jones, Gallup Poll Managing Editor

Barack Obama's presidential job approval rating is 47% in the latest Gallup Poll Daily tracking update, a new low for his administration to date. His approval rating has been below 50% for much of the time since mid-November, but briefly rose to 52% last week after he announced his new Afghanistan policy.

Any slight bump in support Obama received coincident with his new Afghanistan policy proved to be very short-lived, as his approval rating returned to below the majority level by the weekend, and slipped further to 47% in Dec. 4-6 polling.

Afghanistan is just one of many high-profile issues with which the president is dealing. Immediate public reaction to his new Afghanistan policy showed 51% in favor and 40% opposed, according to a Dec. 2 *USA Today*/Gallup poll.

Obama spent part of Sunday on Capitol Hill talking to lawmakers as they continue working on healthcare reform legislation. In the most recent Gallup update, more Americans said they would advise their members to vote against healthcare legislation than said they would advise them to vote for it.

Additionally, in recent days Obama has been ramping up his focus on finding ways to create jobs for out-of-work Americans, and is planning a major speech on Tuesday outlining his ideas for spurring job creation. In late November, Gallup found slight majorities of Americans disapproving of the way Obama was handling job creation and the economy more generally.

Obama travels to Oslo, Norway, this week to receive the Nobel Peace Prize. In October, Obama got a slight bump in his approval ratings after he was announced as the winner. Obama will also travel to Copenhagen, Denmark, to attend the global climate change conference.

In the new Dec. 4-6 Gallup Daily results, Obama's approval rating is 14% among Republicans, 42% among independents, and 83% among Democrats. Compared to his ratings in early November, when he averaged 53% job approval overall, his ratings are down three points among Democrats, seven points among independents, and four points among Republicans.

Thus far in December, Obama has averaged 50% job approval. That is similar to the December averages for Ronald Reagan (49%) and Bill Clinton (53%), who also took office when the economy was struggling. All other recent presidents elected to their first terms had approval averages of 57% or above in their first December in office.

Job Approval Rating Averages for Presidents in December of First Year in Office
Presidents elected to office

	December of first year	Job approval average
Dwight Eisenhower	December 1953	69%
John Kennedy	December 1961	77%
Richard Nixon	December 1969	59%
Jimmy Carter	December 1977	57%
Ronald Reagan	December 1981	49%
George H.W. Bush	December 1989	71%
Bill Clinton	December 1993	53%
George W. Bush	December 2001	86%

Bottom Line

Obama faced significant challenges upon taking office, including arguably the worst economy since the Great Depression and two ongoing wars. Obama is actively trying to address these issues while also tackling some longer-term issues like healthcare and climate change. Over the course of the year, his approval ratings have fallen, perhaps due to lack of obvious progress on many of these fronts, but also perhaps because of the public's apparent reluctance so far to embrace the healthcare reform effort.

Obama maintains the support of more than 8 in 10 Democrats, though his approval ratings among his fellow partisans have declined over the course of the year. He has seen his approval ratings among independents and Republicans slide by at least 20 points since the beginning of his term, and now stands at a personal low of 47% approval among all Americans.

Survey Methods

Results are based on telephone interviews with 1,529 national adults, aged 18 and older, conducted Dec. 4-6, 2009, as part of Gallup Daily tracking. For results based on the total sample of national adults, one can say with 95% confidence that the maximum margin of sampling error is ±3 percentage points.

Interviews are conducted with respondents on land-line telephones and cellular phones.

In addition to sampling error, question wording and practical difficulties in conducting surveys can introduce error or bias into the findings of public opinion polls.

homeowners who make their homes more energy efficient as one of several new initiatives to help create jobs in the United States.

The poll was conducted before Obama made this announcement, and found that home improvements to increase energy efficiency are widespread: 68% of Americans say they have taken steps in the past year to improve the energy efficiency of their homes.

Solid majorities of all demographic subgroups have tried to improve the energy efficiency of their homes in 2009, with little variation across groups. Americans aged 65 and older are slightly less likely than other groups (58%) to say they have taken measures to make their homes more efficient.

Across the board, cost savings is the primary motivating factor for Americans who have made their homes more energy efficient. There are differences by ideology in the relative emphasis given to cost savings versus the environment—with liberals more likely to give the environment a greater priority and conservatives far less likely to, but a majority of liberals still citing cost savings as their primary reason for taking those actions.

Main Reason for Taking Steps to Improve Energy Efficiency of Homes, by Political Ideology

Based on those who took steps to make their home more energy efficient in the past year

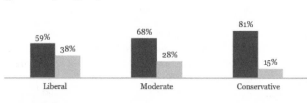

USA Today/Gallup, Nov. 20-22, 2009

December 08, 2009
SAVINGS TRUMPS ENVIRONMENT FOR MAKING HOMES GREENER
More than two-thirds of Americans say they have taken steps toward efficiency this year

by Jeffrey M. Jones, Gallup Poll Managing Editor

When it comes to making their homes more energy efficient, Americans appear to be motivated much more by finances than by environmental concerns. The vast majority of Americans who have taken steps this year to make their homes more energy efficient, 71%, say they did so mostly to save money rather than to improve the environment.

Did you take steps to make your home more energy efficient -- [ROTATED: mostly to save money (or) mostly to improve the environment]?

Based on those who took steps to make their home more energy efficient in the past year

USA Today/Gallup, Nov. 20-22, 2009

These results are based on a Nov. 20-22 *USA Today*/Gallup poll. This week, President Obama announced plans to give incentives to

Bottom Line

While Gallup has found Americans willing to take environmentally friendly actions, they may be doing so more for practical financial reasons than on behalf of the environment. That is not to deny that the environment could be a motivating factor in why Americans might undertake home improvement projects; it is just not a greater factor than cost savings for the majority of Americans.

This greater emphasis on economics may not necessarily be the case under normal economic circumstances—this year, for the first time, more Americans said economic growth ought to be a higher priority than protecting the environment.

But the new energy efficiency findings are somewhat consistent with other Gallup polling showing that the environment and energy do not rank very highly when Americans are asked to name the most important problem facing the country, or in Americans' relatively low rating of these issues as priorities for the government to address, or as factors in their vote in U.S. elections.

Survey Methods

Results are based on telephone interviews with 1,017 national adults, aged 18 and older, conducted Nov. 20-22, 2009. For results based on the total sample of national adults, one can say with 95% confidence that the maximum margin of error is ±4 percentage points.

For results based on the 673 Americans who took steps to make their homes more energy efficient, the maximum margin of error is ±4 percentage points.

Interviews are conducted with respondents on land-line telephones (for respondents with a land-line telephone) and cellular phones (for respondents who are cell-phone only).

In addition to sampling error, question wording and practical difficulties in conducting surveys can introduce error or bias into the findings of public opinion polls.

December 09, 2009

HONESTY AND ETHICS POLL FINDS CONGRESS' IMAGE TARNISHED

For first time, majority of Americans say its members have low ethics

by Lydia Saad, Gallup Poll Senior Editor

For the first time in Gallup's annual Honesty and Ethics of Professions poll, a majority of Americans—55%—say the honesty and ethical standards of "members of Congress" are low or very low—slightly worse than "senators," whose ethics are rated low by 49%. By contrast, 83% of Americans say nurses have either very high or high ethical standards, positioning them at the top of Gallup's 2009 ranking of various professions.

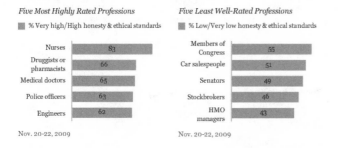

Five Most Highly Rated Professions
■ % Very high/High honesty & ethical standards

Five Least Well-Rated Professions
■ % Low/Very low honesty & ethical standards

Nov. 20-22, 2009   Nov. 20-22, 2009

The percentage of Americans now believing that members of Congress have low ethics is up from 46% in 2008 and 45% in 2007, and has more than doubled since the start of the decade—rising from 21% in November 2000 to 55% today.

A similar pattern occurred in the early 1990s, spanning a series of scandals starting with the "Keating Five" and the related savings and loan crisis, the House banking scandal, and the House post office scandal that resulted in the conviction of Rep. Dan Rostenkowski in 1996. However the percentage "low"/"very low" rating during that period topped out at 46% in 1995, lower than today's figure. For most of the past two decades, more Americans have typically said the ethical standards of members of Congress are low than have called them high. However, the spread between these two views is now the widest seen.

The deterioration in Congress' ethics rating over the past year has occurred about equally among all three party groups. The percentage rating members' honesty and ethical standards as low or very low rose by 8 points among Republicans and independents, and by 10 points among Democrats.

Pharmacists, Doctors, Police, and Engineers Also Well Regarded

Nurses are the undisputed leader in this year's list of professions—and have ranked No. 1 all but one year since they were added to the

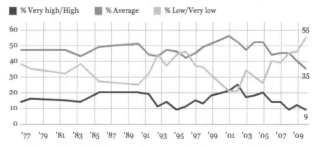

Honesty and Ethical Standards of Members of Congress

Please tell me how you would rate the honesty and ethical standards of people in these different fields -- very high, high, average, low, or very low? How about ...members of Congress?*

■ % Very high/High   ■ % Average   ■ % Low/Very low

2009 wording split sampled with "Congressmen" (trend wording); combined results shown.

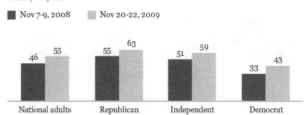

Honesty and Ethics of Members of Congress, Trend by Party ID

% Low/Very low

■ Nov 7-9, 2008   ■ Nov 20-22, 2009

list in 1999 ("firefighters" was asked as a special item in November 2001, and ranked first in the wake of the 9/11 terrorist attacks). In addition to nurses, pharmacists, medical doctors, police, and engineers are all well regarded for their honesty and ethics by more than 6 in 10 Americans. Additionally, dentists, college teachers, and members of the clergy earn high marks from at least half of Americans.

Aside from members of Congress, the only other occupational group that the majority of Americans see as having low or very low honesty and ethical standards is car salespeople. At least 40% of Americans perceive several other professions as having low integrity, including senators, stockbrokers, HMO managers, insurance salespeople, and lawyers. Still, it should be noted that two professions not included on the list this year—telemarketers and lobbyists—received even lower ratings in 2008 (60% and 64% "poor" ethics ratings, respectively) than members of Congress do today.

The full list of 22 professions included on this year's list is ranked according to the percentage of Americans rating each profession's integrity as "very high" or "high."

Bottom Line

Congress has long ranked among the worst-rated professions on Gallup's annual Honesty and Ethics of Professions list. Now, it has earned the unwelcome distinction of having a majority of Americans rate its integrity as low or very low.

Americans are deeply concerned about the nation's economy, and eager to see the nation's leaders find meaningful solutions to that and other problems. But it's not clear that Congress' perceived lack of success is entirely to blame for its poor integrity ratings. While Congress has low job approval, the 26% of Americans currently approving is higher than the 19% recorded about this time last year. However, over the same period, Americans' rating of Congress' honesty and ethics, rather than showing analogous improvement, has in fact worsened, and not just among Republicans.

Please tell me how you would rate the honesty and ethical standards of people in these different fields -- very high, high, average, low, or very low?

	Very high/ High	Average	Low/ very low	No opinion
	%	%	%	%
Nurses	83	14	2	1
Druggists or pharmacists	66	29	5	1
Medical doctors	65	28	7	1
Policemen/Police officers ^	63	26	10	*
Engineers	62	31	4	3
Dentists	57	35	7	1
College teachers	54	33	11	3
Clergy	50	36	10	4
Chiropractors	34	47	12	7
Psychiatrists	33	44	15	7
Journalists	23	45	31	1
Bankers	19	46	33	1
State governors	15	48	35	1
Lawyers	13	45	40	1
Business executives	12	48	38	2
Advertising practitioners	11	46	38	5
Senators	11	38	49	1
Insurance salesmen/Insurance salespeople^	10	47	42	1
Stockbrokers	9	40	46	5
Congressmen/Members of Congress^	9	35	55	1
HMO managers	8	40	43	8
Car salesmen/Car salespeople^	6	40	51	2

Nov. 20-22, 2009

* less than 0.5%

^ Titles for profession based on split sample: Form A respondents asked first (long-term trend) wording, Form B respondents asked second wording. Combined results of both forms shown.

Survey Methods

Results are based on telephone interviews with 1,017 national adults, aged 18 and older, conducted Nov. 20-22, 2009. For results based on the total sample of national adults, one can say with 95% confidence that the maximum margin of sampling error is ±4 percentage points.

Interviews are conducted with respondents on land-line telephones (for respondents with a land-line telephone) and cellular phones (for respondents who are cell-phone only).

In addition to sampling error, question wording and practical difficulties in conducting surveys can introduce error or bias into the findings of public opinion polls.

December 09, 2009

U.S. CLERGY, BANKERS SEE NEW LOWS IN HONESTY/ETHICS RATINGS
Police officers' image recovers

by Jeffrey M. Jones, Gallup Poll Managing Editor

The percentage of Americans rating the honesty and ethics of clergy as very high or high is down to 50% in 2009, the lowest percentage it has been in the 32 years Gallup has measured it.

Gallup conducted its annual Honesty and Ethics of professions poll Nov. 20-22 this year, with one of the major findings the deterioration in ratings of members of Congress. Nurses continue to rate as the most highly regarded profession in terms of honesty and ethics.

In last year's Honesty and Ethics update, 56% of Americans rated the clergy's honesty and ethics very high or high. The reason

Ratings of Honesty and Ethics of the Clergy

% "Very high"/"High"

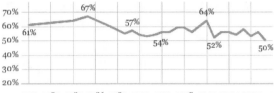

for the decline to 50% this year is unclear; but now the clergy's ratings are below where they were earlier this decade during the priest sex-abuse scandal. Ratings of the clergy dropped from their 2008 levels among both Catholics and Protestants, as well as among regular and non-regular churchgoers.

Ratings of Honesty and Ethics of the Clergy, by Religious Affiliation, 2008 and 2009

% "Very high"/"High"

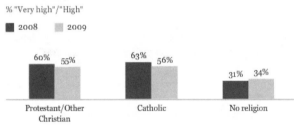

Ratings of Honesty and Ethics of the Clergy, by Church Attendance, 2008 and 2009

% "Very high"/"High"

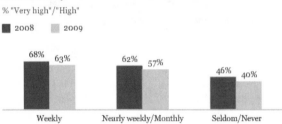

Still, ratings of the clergy remain high on a relative basis, ranking 8th of the 22 professions tested this year. The same cannot be said of bankers, whose ratings tumbled last year from 35% to 23% in the midst of the financial crisis, and fell further this year to a new low of 19%. As recently as 2005, 41% of Americans gave bankers high honesty and ethics ratings.

Ratings of Honesty and Ethics of Bankers

% "Very high"/"High"

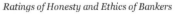
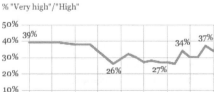

More broadly, 2009 was not a kind year in terms of how Americans rate members of various professions. In addition to the clergy and bankers, ratings of stockbrokers have hit a new low, and ratings of business executives, members of Congress, and lawyers have tied their previous lows.

Most of the 13 professions measured in both 2008 and 2009 show a decline, and only police officers' ratings improved by a meaningful amount. Ratings of clergy declined the most—six points—followed by lawyers, with a five-point drop.

Change in Honesty and Ethics Ratings of Professions, 2008 to 2009
% "Very high"/"High"

	2008	2009	Change
	%	%	Pct. pts.
Police officers	56	63	7
Medical doctors	64	65	1
Advertising practitioners	10	11	1
Business executives	12	12	0
Nurses	84	83	-1
Car salespeople	7	6	-1
Journalists	25	23	-2
Members of Congress	12	9	-3
Stockbrokers	12	9	-3
Druggists, pharmacists	70	66	-4
Bankers	23	19	-4
Lawyers	18	13	-5
Clergy	56	50	-6

The 63% very high/high ratings for police officers are their best since 2001—shortly after the Sept. 11 terrorist attacks—and the second highest in the 30+ years Gallup has asked about this profession. Over time, ratings of police officers have generally risen, though they were down below 60% the last three years.

Ratings of Honesty and Ethics of Police Officers
% "Very high"/"High"

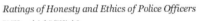

Until this year, Gallup had asked Americans to rate the honesty and ethics of "policemen," but this year conducted an experiment to see whether asking the gender-neutral phrasing "police officers" would produce the same results. A random half of respondents were asked to rate "policemen," and the other half "police officers," with both wordings producing similar results (62% and 64%, respectively).

Gallup also found deterioration in the honesty ratings of several other professions that were last measured in 2006. The most notable decline occurred for state governors, whose ratings are down seven points, from 22% in 2006 to the current 15%. This change could in part be attributed to recent sex scandals involving former New York Gov. Eliot Spitzer and current South Carolina Gov. Mark Sanford.

The new poll also documents significant decreases in the evaluated honesty of dentists and psychiatrists since 2006. Additionally,

Change in Honesty and Ethics Ratings of Professions, 2006 to 2009
% "Very high"/"High"

	2006	2009	Change
	%	%	Pct. pts.
Engineers	61	62	1
Chiropractors	36	34	-2
Insurance salespeople	13	10	-3
College teachers	58	54	-4
Senators	15	11	-4
HMO managers	12	8	-4
Dentists	62	57	-5
Psychiatrists	38	33	-5
State governors	22	15	-7

Note: Professions rated in 2006 and 2009 only

the four-point decline in ratings of senators over this time period leaves them with a new low rating, similar to the pattern Gallup reported earlier for members of Congress.

Bottom Line

Americans' ratings of the honesty and ethics of members working in several professions have established new lows in 2009, with the ratings of clergy and bankers lower now than at any other point in the last three-plus decades. And while Americans rate most professions more poorly than in their prior measurements, certain professions such as nurses, pharmacists, doctors, police officers, and engineers have maintained a high level of confidence from the American public.

Survey Methods

Results are based on telephone interviews with 1,017 national adults, aged 18 and older, conducted Nov. 20-22, 2009. For results based on the total sample of national adults, one can say with 95% confidence that the maximum margin of sampling error is ±4 percentage points.

Interviews are conducted with respondents on land-line telephones (for respondents with a land-line telephone) and cellular phones (for respondents who are cell-phone only).

In addition to sampling error, question wording and practical difficulties in conducting surveys can introduce error or bias into the findings of public opinion polls.

December 10, 2009
AMERICANS STAY POSITIVE; EMOTIONAL HEALTH AT 17-MONTH HIGH
Overall well-being in November ties second highest recorded score, just shy of recorded high

by Dan Witters, Research Director of the Gallup-Healthways Well-Being Index

Americans continue to rate their lives as well as at any time since measurement began in January 2008, according to the November update of the Gallup-Healthways Well-Being Index. The Life Evaluation Index, which reached the 50.0 threshold for the first time in October, finished November at 49.5, up more than 16 points since its low point of 33.1 last November.

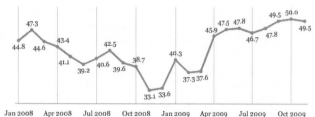

Gallup-Healthways Life Evaluation Index

Gallup-Healthways Well-Being Index

The Life Evaluation Index is one of six sub-indexes that when combined together comprise the Gallup-Healthways Well-Being Index, which provides a comprehensive measure of Americans' emotional, physical, and fiscal health. The Gallup-Healthways Well-Being Index and each of the six sub-indexes are calculated on a scale from 0 to 100, where 100 represents fully realized well-being.

The Life Evaluation sub-index is based on the Cantril Self-Anchoring Striving Scale, which asks people to evaluate their present and future lives on a scale with steps numbered from 0 to 10, where 0 is the worst possible life and 10 is the best possible life. Those who rate today a "7" or higher and the future an "8" or higher are considered to be "thriving." Those who rate today and the future a "4" or lower on the scale are considered to be "suffering."

In November, 52.9% of American adults were classified as "thriving," just shy of the recorded high from last month and substantially improved over the 37.4% measured in November of last year. The percentage of "suffering" American adults was also near its lowest point of 3.2%, measuring slightly higher at 3.4%. (The overall Life Evaluation Index score of 49.5 is calculated as the percentage of Americans that are "thriving" minus the percentage that are "struggling.")

While demography typically is related to life evaluation (and well-being generally), the upward trend in the Life Evaluation Index is evident across all demographic groups, regardless of income, education, gender, race/ethnicity, region, and job type. All four income brackets have shown remarkably consistent gains over the past 12 months.

Life Evaluation Rising for All Income Groups

■ Less than $24,000   ■ $24,000 to less than $48,000   ■ $48,000 to less than $90,000
▨ $90,000 and above

Gallup-Healthways Well-Being Index

Most of the decline—and subsequent improvement—in the Life Evaluation Index over the course of the past 12 months has been via respondents' self-evaluation of their current state, while their anticipated position on the "ladder" scale five years from now has

remained fairly steady. These data suggest a resiliency in the optimism of the American public for better days ahead even during hard times, while simultaneously demonstrating a more pliable evaluation of the current state.

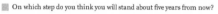

Gallup-Healthways Life Evaluation Metrics: Life Today vs. Life Five Years From Now

■ On which step of the ladder would you say you personally feel you stand at this time?
▨ On which step do you think you will stand about five years from now?

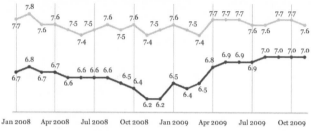

Gallup-Healthways Well-Being Index

Emotional Health Index Improves to Highest Level Since June 2008

In addition to gains in overall life evaluation, Americans' emotional health also seems to be improving. Since bottoming out at 77.5 in December 2008, the Emotional Health Index has continued to recover, reaching pre-recession levels this month for the first time this year at 79.5—the highest Emotional Health Index score since June of 2008.

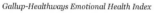

Gallup-Healthways Emotional Health Index

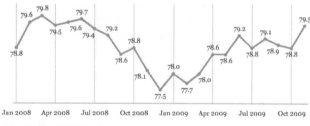

Gallup-Healthways Well-Being Index

The Emotional Health Index is another one of six sub-components of the Gallup-Healthways Well-Being Index, and it includes 10 items: smiling or laughter, learning or doing something interesting, being treated with respect, enjoyment, happiness, worry, sadness, anger, stress, and diagnosis of depression. The Emotional Health Index is primarily a composite of daily experiences. Other than the depression diagnosis metric, all remaining items ask respondents to think only about yesterday—from the morning until the end of the day—and consider with whom they spent it, what they did, and how they felt.

The percentage of American adults that experienced enjoyment yesterday was a key driving force behind the improved Emotional Health Index score in November, as this metric reached its highest recorded level this month at 84.9%, up 2.4 percentage points since the low of 82.5% in December 2008 and February 2009. Thanksgiving, which is established as one of the best days of the year in terms of net emotional health, may have contributed to this outcome.

The Emotional Health Index also improved in part because of increases in the percentages of Americans who did not experience a

Daily Experience of Enjoyment Reaches Highest Recorded Mark

Gallup-Healthways Well-Being Index

Results are based on telephone interviews with more than 683,000 national adults, aged 18 and older, conducted Jan. 2, 2008 through Nov. 30, 2009. For monthly results based on the total sample of national adults, one can say with 95% confidence that the maximum margin of sampling error is ±0.6 percentage point.

Interviews are conducted with respondents on land-line telephones (for respondents with a land-line telephone) and cellular phones (for respondents who are cell-phone only).

In addition to sampling error, question wording and practical difficulties in conducting surveys can introduce error or bias into the findings of public opinion polls.

lot of worry (68.4%) and stress (61.3%) the day before the survey. Both measures are now the highest they have been since August 2008 and much higher than the 65.3% and 59.9% measured one year ago.

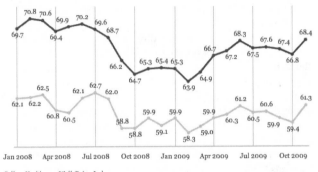

Daily Worry, Stress Improve Since One Year Ago, but Remain Below Pre-Recession Levels

■ % Did not experience a lot worry yesterday   ■ % Did not experience a lot stress yesterday

Gallup-Healthways Well-Being Index

December 10, 2009
UPPER-INCOME SPENDING REVERTS TO NEW NORMAL
Down 14% in November, while middle- and lower-income spending was up 7%

by Dennis Jacobe, Gallup Chief Economist

In a sign that the new normal in consumer spending continues unabated, upper-income Americans' self-reported average daily spending in stores, restaurants, gas stations, and online fell 14% in November, reverting to its relatively tight ($107 to $121) pre-October 2009 average monthly range. Middle- and lower-income consumer discretionary spending increased by 7% last month but remained in its tight 2009 average monthly range of $52 to $61. Still, consumer spending by both income groups continues to trail year-ago levels by 20%, even as those comparables have gotten easier to match—possibly dashing hopes that upscale retailers and big-ticket-item sales will do better this year.

Overall Well-Being Remains Near Recorded High

Thanks largely to the improving Emotional Health Index, the Overall Well-Being Index composite score inched up in November to 66.7, just shy of its recorded high of 67.0 found in August 2009 and February 2008.

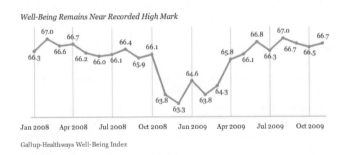

Well-Being Remains Near Recorded High Mark

Gallup-Healthways Well-Being Index

Bottom Line

Since hitting bottom in late 2008, well-being among American adults has steadily recovered over the course of this year, and it now matches pre-recession levels on most metrics. The results suggest that in terms of their everyday lives, emotions, and behaviors, Americans are remarkably close to where they were before the economic turmoil of the past 12 months. One question that continues to linger is how high can the Well-Being Index climb? So far in 23 months of measurement, 67.0 remains the highest recorded Well-Being Index score, reached twice.

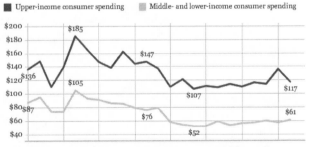

Consumer Spending by Income, 2008-2009

In U.S. dollars

■ Upper-income consumer spending   ■ Middle- and lower-income consumer spending

Self-Reported Spending Down Across Age Groups

Consumers in the child-rearing ages of 30 to 49 showed the smallest November-over-November discretionary spending decline at 15%—possibly because they have the least ability to downshift their spending as the holidays approach. Younger consumers aged 18 to 29 experienced a larger decline of 23%. Those 50 to 64 years of age reduced their year-over-year spending by 29%, while those 65 or older had a decline of 32%. Overall, those in the 30 to 49 age group had the highest average daily spending level in November ($81), while those 65 or older spent the least per day ($52).

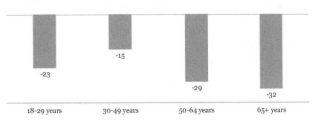

Year-Over-Year Changes in Consumer Spending, by Age,
November 2008-November 2009

■ % Change in consumer spending

Self-Reported Spending Down Across Regions

Year-over-year consumer spending declined the least on the two coasts, with the East cutting average daily spending by 13% and the West cutting spending by 17%. The declines were largest in the Midwest—down 38%—while the South was in between, at 24%. Overall, consumer discretionary spending was highest in the East and West ($71 and $75 average per day, respectively) and lowest in the Midwest ($56).

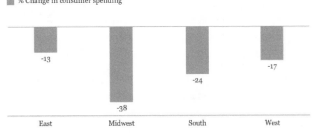

Year-Over-Year Changes in Consumer Spending, by Region,
November 2008-November 2009

■ % Change in consumer spending

Self-Reported Spending Down Across Genders

Overall, men claim greater average daily spending than women, possibly as a result of having higher average incomes and perhaps tending to more aggressively report joint spending. Men also report a larger decline in discretionary spending, at 27%, compared to the 17% self-reported by women.

Year-Over-Year Changes in Consumer Spending, by Gender,
November 2008-November 2009

■ % Change in consumer spending

Spending New Normal

Overall self-reported consumer discretionary spending has been essentially flat on a monthly basis throughout 2009 even when bro-

ken out by age, income, region, and gender. It has also been down significantly compared to the same months in 2008. The year-over-year differences have declined somewhat during recent months, but much of this closure in the 2008-2009 spending gap is a result of the easier spending comparables from last year's financial crisis.

Gallup's analysis of the relationship between job creation and consumer spending suggests that these lower spending levels are attributable, at least in part, to today's dismal job-market conditions. Further findings show that the current lack of job creation has its greatest impact on middle- and lower-income consumer spending.

In this regard, October upper-income spending provided new hope that the surge in the stock market and the increased stability of housing prices might be encouraging these consumers to break out of their year-long and relatively tight spending range. Instead, November's results show that upper-income spending reverted back to its new normal range. Given the greater discretionary spending flexibility of upper-income Americans, this reversion to the pre-October spending range tends to give added face-validity to the argument that a consumer spending new normal exists—independent of the job situation—as 2010 approaches.

On a national level, the spending new normal suggests slower economic growth than otherwise might be expected in the years ahead. In turn, reduced consumer spending will complicate the job-creation problem, not to mention fiscal and monetary policies. For example, one might argue that the federal government and monetary authorities (the Fed) need to take emergency actions to offset a temporary spending shortfall due to job losses, but the same arguments do not necessarily hold true when the spending reduction results from a new normal spending pattern—generally speaking, the private sector needs to adjust to such changes in consumer behaviors.

For retailers, small businesses, and the companies that supply and support them, a new normal spending pattern can mean complex changes involving downscaling, up-selling (people taking advantage to buy upscale for less), inventory management, and people-related adjustments. The U.S. economy is designed to allow the private sector to make such adjustments in order to optimize performance when faced with such a rapidly changing business environment. Of course, the same does not apply to maintaining the social safety net, particularly in the face of double-digit unemployment and even higher underemployment.

While the spending "new normal" may not be good for the larger economy in the short-term, it may be seen as a strong positive for individual consumer households. Consumers, like their business and banking counterparts, would be well-served to de-leverage by spending less, saving more, reducing their use of credit, and thereby strengthening their personal balance sheets. While this may not provide the immediate-term returns to the economy of the over-leveraging of recent years, a financially stronger U.S. consumer implies only good things for the longer-term well being of both the U.S. and global economies.

Survey Methods

For Gallup Daily tracking, Gallup interviews approximately 1,000 national adults, aged 18 and older, each day. The Gallup consumer spending results are based on random half-samples of approximately 500 national adults, aged 18 and older, each day. Results for November are based on telephone interviews with more than 14,000 adults. For these results, one can say with 95% confidence that the maximum margin of sampling error is ±1 percentage point. Results for the various breakouts reported here are based on interviews with more than 1,000 respondents with a maximum margin of error of ±3 percentage points.

Interviews are conducted with respondents on land-line telephones and cellular phones.

In addition to sampling error, question wording and practical difficulties in conducting surveys can introduce error or bias into the findings of public opinion polls.

December 11, 2009
RELIGIOUS INTENSITY REMAINS POWERFUL PREDICTOR OF POLITICS
Relationship is most evident among non-Hispanic whites

by Frank Newport, Gallup Poll Editor in Chief

Americans' religious intensity continues to be a major predictor of party identification. A new analysis of more than 29,000 interviews Gallup conducted in November finds that Republicans outnumber Democrats by 12 percentage points among Americans who are classified as highly religious, while Democrats outnumber Republicans by 30 points among those who are not religious.

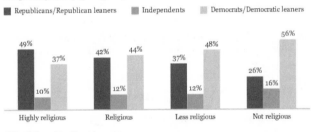

Party Identification, by Religiosity

Gallup Daily tracking, November 2009

The current analysis is based on 29,192 interviews conducted as part of Gallup Daily tracking during the month of November. Party identifiers include those who initially identify with one of the two major parties plus independents who, in a follow-up question, say they lean toward one party or the other.

Gallup has developed the religious segments based on responses to questions measuring the personal importance of religion and church attendance. Details on the classification process are available at the end of this story.

The basic relationship between religiosity and party identification is quite strong and quite straightforward. The percentage of Americans who identify with or lean toward the Republican Party drops from 49% among the highly religious to 26% among those who are not religious. The percentage who identify with or lean toward the Democratic Party rises from 37% among the highly religious to 56% among those who are not religious. For comparison, the party figures for November among all adults in these data are 40% Republicans/Republican leaners and 45% Democrats/Democratic leaners.

Thus, Republicans are in the plurality among highly religious Americans. For each of the other three groups, Democrats are equal with or higher in number than Republicans. The Democratic edge expands as religiosity decreases. Among the not-religious group, Democrats have a 30-point edge over Republicans.

Differences by Race and Ethnicity

There are significant differences in the relationship between party identification and religion within racial and ethnic groups.

Black Americans are highly Democratic, regardless of their religiosity.

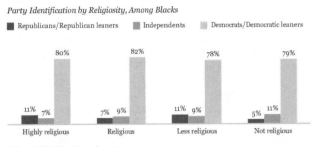

Party Identification by Religiosity, Among Blacks

Gallup Daily tracking, November 2009

Hispanics also are significantly more likely to identify as Democrats than as Republicans across religious groups, although not as much so as is the case with blacks.

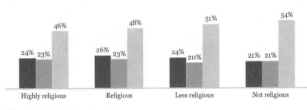

Party Identification by Religiosity, Among Hispanics of Any Race

Gallup Daily tracking, November 2009

There is a modest tendency for Hispanic identification with the Democratic Party to increase as religiosity decreases. Democratic identification rises from 46% among highly religious Hispanics to 54% among not-religious Hispanics. The percentage of Hispanics who identify as Republicans or who are independents falls slightly as religious intensity decreases. (These data are based on all Americans who identify as Hispanic, regardless of their race.)

The relationship between religiosity and party identification is most pronounced among non-Hispanic white Americans.

Party Identification by Religiosity, Among Non-Hispanic Whites

Gallup Daily tracking, November 2009

Identification as Republican drops from 62% among highly religious white Americans to 28% among whites who are not religious. On the other hand, white identification with the Democratic Party rises from 28% among the highly religious to 56% among those who are not religious.

Looked at differently, the data make it evident that Republicans are in the clear majority among non-Hispanic white Americans who are either highly religious or religious. Republican and Democratic identification are at rough parity among those classified as less religious. Democrats are clearly in the majority among whites who are not religious.

Although the country in general has become less Democratic over the last 12 months, a comparative analysis shows that almost exactly the same relationship between intensity of religion and party identification among non-Hispanic whites existed last November as exists now.

Obama Approval

Given the strong relationship between party identification and presidential job approval, it is not surprising to find that religious intensity is also highly related to Obama job approval. Previous analysis has shown that Obama has higher disapproval than approval among whites in general.

Obama Job Approval by Religiosity, Among Non-Hispanic Whites

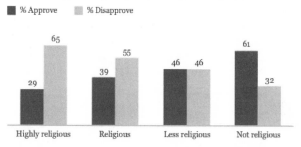

Gallup Daily tracking, November 2009

As was the case with party identification, whites who are highly religious are more than twice as likely as those who are not religious to disapprove of Obama's job performance, 65% to 32%, respectively. Those who are not religious are, in contrast, about twice as likely as those who are highly religious to approve of Obama, 61% to 29%.

Implications

The current analysis underscores the degree to which religion and politics continue to be highly intertwined in today's America, a state of affairs that has substantial implications for elections and policy issues.

The religious connection is most apparent among non-Hispanic white Americans. Blacks are strongly Democratic in their orientation, regardless of their religiosity. Hispanics also skew significantly Democratic, and while there is a tendency for less religious Hispanics to be more Democratic in orientation than more religious Hispanics, it does not alter Hispanics' basic skew in the Democratic direction.

The pattern is quite different among whites. Identification with the Republican Party overwhelms identification with the Democratic Party by more than a 2-to-1 margin among highly religious whites, and by a still-substantial margin among those who are religious. Exactly the opposite pattern obtains among whites who are

not religious, with a 2-to-1 margin in favor of Democratic versus Republican identification.

About 33% of whites are highly religious, and another 16% are religious. Thus, about half of the white population in the U.S. is both highly religious and significantly oriented toward the Republican Party.

The degree to which religion causes or drives political attitudes and voting behavior among whites is unknown. For some white Americans, religion and political orientation may be accidental bedfellows. These individuals could be Republican for a variety of reasons (e.g., agreement with the GOP's economic policy, or their state of residence) that are not at all directly related to their being highly religious. For other whites, however, there may be a direct relationship. For these individuals, religious convictions form the basis for their political and ideological positions, as would be the case for those highly sensitive to social issues such as abortion and gay marriage. Highly religious people can bring an emotion and certitude and intensity of conviction to the political marketplace that can make them a formidable force well beyond their basic numbers.

Appendix: Religious Classification

The highly religious group (34% of adult Americans) includes those who attend church at least once a week and for whom religion is important in their daily lives. The religious group (18%) attends church almost every week or once a month and say religion is important, or attend church at least once a week or almost every week and say religion is not important. The less religious group (32%) attends church seldom or never but says religion is important or attends once monthly or seldom and says religion is important. The not-religious group (16%) is those who say religion is not important and never attend church.

Survey Methods

Results are based on telephone interviews with 29,192 national adults, aged 18 and older, conducted in November 2009, as part of Gallup Daily tracking. For results based on the total sample of national adults, one can say with 95% confidence that the maximum margin of sampling error is ±1 percentage point.

Interviews are conducted with respondents on land-line telephones and cellular phones.

In addition to sampling error, question wording and practical difficulties in conducting surveys can introduce error or bias into the findings of public opinion polls.

December 14, 2009

DON'T WORRY, BE 80: WORRY AND STRESS DECLINE WITH AGE

Worry, stress lowest for those in their 80s, 90s

by Frank Newport, Gallup Poll Editor in Chief and Brett Pelham, Staff Writer

A new analysis of more than 650,000 Gallup-Healthways Well-Being Index interviews conducted in 2008 and 2009 shows that "worry" is a much more common emotion among young and middle-aged Americans than among seniors. Well over a third (37%) of those in their 40s report having experienced worry "a lot of the day yesterday." This figure drops to about 23% among those in their late 60s and drops further to 15% among those aged 91 and older.

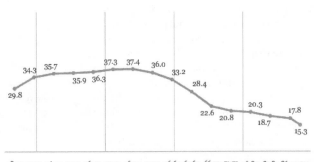

Gallup-Healthways Well-Being Index

Similar Pattern for Stress

A similar age-related pattern occurs for reports of stress. Almost half of those in their early 20s (48%) report having experienced stress a lot of the day prior to the interview. Stress begins to drop off significantly as Americans reach their mid- to late 50s, and drops to 13% among those aged 91 or older.

Percentage of All Americans Who Say They Experienced Stress During a Lot of the Day "Yesterday," January 2008-October 2009
By age

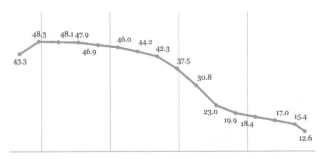

Gallup-Healthways Well-Being Index

An analysis of a number of correlates of worry and stress does not provide a direct explanation for the drop-off in these emotions as age increases.

Women More Likely Than Men to Worry at All Ages

The American population becomes proportionately more female as it ages. In these data, 52% of those aged 21 to 25 are male. This figure drops to 47% among those aged 61 to 65 and to 34% of those aged 91 and older. If men were more likely than women to worry or be stressed, then some of the explanation for the age-to-worry (and age-to-stress) relationship could be the female skew in the older age ranges.

However, men are *not* more likely than women to worry or be stressed. Just the opposite is true. There is a significant gender gap in terms of both worry and stress. At every age, women are at least slightly more likely than men to report having experienced worry or stress the day before the interview. The pattern is fairly uniform, with a 5- to 10-point gap across the age spectrum until Americans reach their 80s, when the gap narrows.

Percentage Who Say They Experienced Worry During a Lot of the Day "Yesterday," January 2008-October 2009
By age and gender

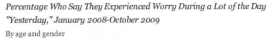

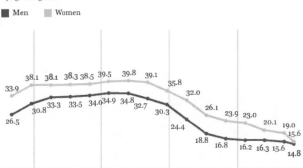

Gallup-Healthways Well-Being Index

Percentage Who Say They Experienced Stress During a Lot of the Day "Yesterday," January 2008-October 2009
By age and gender

■ Men   ■ Women

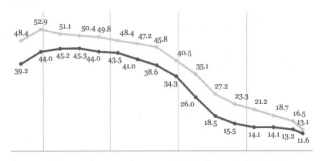

Gallup-Healthways Well-Being Index

It thus does not appear that gender is part of the explanation for the age-worry/stress relationship.

Children in the Home Not a Major Source of Worry

A demographic fact that theoretically might help explain the drop-off in worry/stress by age is whether one has children. The percentage of individuals who report having a child under 18 in the household drops precipitously by the time Americans are in their 50s (and many of the small percentage of Americans aged 60 and up who report having children in the home may well be reporting grandchildren).

There is a basic relationship between having children in the home and experiencing worry or stress. Americans with a child in the home are more likely to report worry and stress than are those who don't have a child in the home, with even greater differences in terms of reported stress.

In general, then, younger Americans are the most likely to have children in the home, and having a child in the home is related to more worry and stress. These relationships of course do not prove that it is children per se that cause worry and stress, only that there is an interrelationship among younger age and children and worry/stress.

To help disentangle these patterns, the accompanying graphs display worry and stress by age among those with children in the home and among those without.

Percentage Who Say They Experienced Worry During a Lot of the Day "Yesterday," January 2008-October 2009

By age and whether household has children younger than 18

■ Households with children   ▨ Households without children

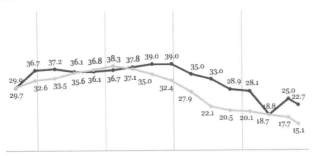

Gallup-Healthways Well-Being Index

Percentage Who Say They Experienced Stress During a Lot of the Day "Yesterday," January 2008-October 2009

By age and whether household has children younger than 18

■ Households with children   ▨ Households without children

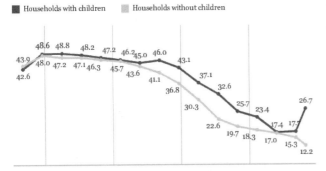

Gallup-Healthways Well-Being Index

The data show the same basic relational pattern between worry/stress and age among Americans who do not have a child in the home and among those who do. Younger Americans without children worry more and have more stress than older Americans without children. In fact, even young adults *without* children worry more and report more stress than older adults *with* children in the home. Younger Americans with children in the home worry more and have more stress than older Americans with children in the home.

Also, the gap in worry and stress between those with children in the home and those without is very small among younger Americans. Overall, the average worry percentage is 36% among those aged 50 and younger with children in the home and 35% among those aged 50 and younger without children in the home. For stress, the difference is also only one percentage point, 47% versus 46%, respec-

tively. It is apparent that the higher levels of worry among younger Americans occur regardless of whether they have children in the home. It appears that the age-worry or age-stress relationship is not simply owing to the fact that younger people generally have children in the home and older people generally do not.

Even Among Employed, Worry and Stress Drop Off With Age

Taken as a whole, Americans of all ages who are employed worry less and have less stress than Americans who are not employed.

Any analysis of the correlates of not being employed is complex, since there are many reasons people are unemployed. For some, unemployment is by choice—homemakers, those who are retired—while for others it is negatively forced on them, particularly those who are unemployed and looking for work. Still, for whatever reasons, in America today there is a significant association between being employed and *less* worry and stress. So it does not appear that the fact that older Americans are less likely to be employed is a valid explanation for their decrease in worry.

The accompanying graphs show the degree of worry and stress just among employed Americans. The basic pattern of a drop-off in the percentage of Americans exhibiting these two traits as age increases is clearly evident even among this employed group.

Percentage of Those Currently Working Who Say They Experienced Worry During a Lot of the Day "Yesterday," January 2008-October 2009

By age

■ Percent yes

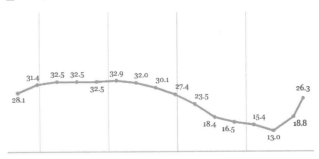

Gallup-Healthways Well-Being Index

Percentage of Those Currently Working Who Say They Experienced Stress During a Lot of the Day "Yesterday," January 2008-October 2009

By age

■ Percent yes

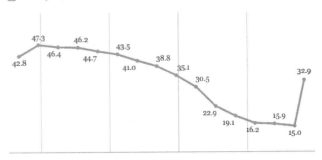

Gallup-Healthways Well-Being Index

No Impact of Religion on Worry and Stress

Older Americans are more religious than younger Americans. Could the relatively low levels of worry among those who are older be due to the calming effect of their relatively higher religiosity?

This does not appear to be the case. Thirty-two percent of more religious Americans (those for whom religion is important in their daily lives) and 33% of nonreligious Americans report having worried yesterday. The comparable values for stress are 38% and 42%, respectively. These differences are too small to explain the age effect.

Cohort vs. Generational Effect

The data reported here reflect a cross-section of the American adult population at a particular point in time—January 2008 to October 2009—and thus do not allow strong inferences to be made about the "normal" course of life events. The worry levels of the respondents included in this analysis are a combination of the life circumstances into which they were born and through which they have lived, as well as generational circumstances that affect individuals at their current ages. Thus, it is not possible with these data to determine the degree to which lack of stress and worry is a result of an individual's life history and experiences versus the individual's current circumstances (including health, family situation, and economic situation).

Given the cross-sectional nature of these data, it is not possible to determine whether these same stress- and worry-by-age patterns will persist in the years ahead. It is possible, for example, that specific life circumstances of the core baby-boom group now in their 50s will stay with them throughout their lives, and that they will not in the years ahead enjoy the decreased stress and worry levels now apparent among those who are in their 60s and older today.

Summary

Americans report a significantly lower incidence of worry and stress as they get older, particularly as they move into and beyond their mid-60s. This finding runs counter to the hypothesis that those who are older would be more apt to worry about deteriorating health, fixed incomes, or impending death. On the other hand, many seniors are beyond the point where they have to worry about varying income, and previous research has shown that seniors are the only age group satisfied with the amount of time they have to enjoy life.

These cross-sectional data do not allow for a determination of whether the worry-age phenomenon reflects a cohort effect (reflecting the particular history and life experiences of those who are older today) or a generational effect (such that past and future generations of Americans would be found to exhibit the same patterns of worry and stress). The analysis does suggest, however, that several logical reasons for older Americans' worrying less—including that they are much less likely to have children in the home or to be employed, or that they are more religious and more likely to be female—do not appear to be explanations.

Whatever the reasons, the data would appear to present good news for relatively younger Americans—particularly the very large population segment of baby boomers. Approaching on the horizon for these Americans is the distinct possibility that day-to-day worry and stress may well subside rather than increase as time goes on.

Survey Methods

Results are based on telephone interviews with more than 650,000 national adults, aged 18 and older, conducted Jan. 2, 2008-Oct. 31,

2009. For results based on the total sample of national adults, one can say with 95% confidence that the maximum margin of sampling error is less than ±1 percentage point. Sample sizes in the groups based on age range from a maximum of 72,238 respondents aged 56 to 60 to a minimum of 2,877 respondents aged 91 and older. The oldest group was thus the smallest group for all further divisions. Only 933 of the 2,877 oldest respondents are male, yielding a margin of error of ±4 percentage points for this subgroup. The largest margin of error is ±9 percentage points for the 122 respondents aged 91 and older who are currently working. Most other groups are dramatically larger than these groups. For example, there are 48,435 respondents in the 51-55 year age group who are currently working, which yields a maximum margin of error of less than ±1 percentage point.

Interviews are conducted with respondents on land-line telephones (for respondents with a land-line telephone) and cellular phones (for respondents who are cell-phone only).

In addition to sampling error, question wording and practical difficulties in conducting surveys can introduce error or bias into the findings of public opinion polls.

December 14, 2009

RACE FOR 2010 REMAINS CLOSE; DEMOCRATS RECOVER SLIGHT LEAD

Republican lead among independents narrows significantly

by Frank Newport, Gallup Poll Editor in Chief and Jeffrey M. Jones, Managing Editor

Democrats have regained the slim edge they enjoyed earlier this year over Republicans in the latest update of Gallup's generic congressional ballot for the 2010 House elections, and now have a slight 48% to 45% lead among registered voters. After having been behind in July and October, Republicans had moved ahead by four points in a Nov. 5-8 poll conducted just after the off-year elections.

2010 Generic Congressional Ballot -- Preferences of Registered Voters

If the elections for Congress were being held today, which party's candidate would you vote for in your congressional district -- the Democratic Party's candidate (or) the Republican Party's candidate? (If unsure: As of today, do you lean more toward the Democratic Party's candidate (or) the Republican Party's candidate?)

■ Democratic candidate   ■ Republican candidate

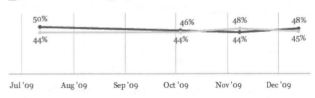

The major cause of the movement between November and the current poll is the changing preferences of independents. In the latest poll, conducted Dec. 11-13, independent registered voters tilt only slightly toward the Republican candidate, by 44% to 40%. In the November poll, independents' preference for the Republican candidate was 52% to 30%. Both parties maintain the allegiance of their bases, with 93% of Democratic registered voters preferring the

Democratic candidate and an identical 93% of Republican voters preferring the Republican.

2010 Generic Congressional Ballot Vote Preference, by Political Party
Based on registered voters

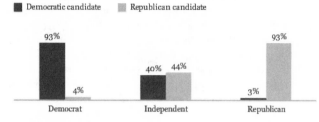

USA Today/Gallup, Dec. 11-13, 2009

The current poll reflects the narrowest margin in favor of the Republican candidate among independents since July, when the gap was one point.

2010 Generic Congressional Ballot Vote Preference, Among Independents
Based on registered voters

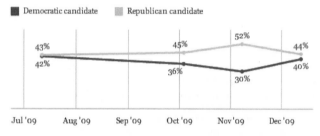

These overall results among registered voters reflect what the election outcome would be if all voters turned out to vote. Usually, turnout among registered voters in midterm elections is much lower than 100%, making the ability of each party to turn out its voters a crucial determinant of the final outcome.

It is too early in the electoral process to make any type of reliable projection of turnout for next fall's elections specifically. Republicans, however, typically enjoy a turnout advantage. Thus, even if Democrats go into the election with a slim advantage in registered voters' preferences—as is the case in the current poll—they could quite likely end up with a lower percentage of the overall congressional vote than Republicans receive.

Bottom Line

The current generic-ballot results are similar to those Gallup found in July and October of this year, and indicate that the Republican gain observed just after the Nov. 3 elections was not sustained. Shifts in candidate preference for Congress typically occur primarily among independents, whose "unanchored" status makes them much more vulnerable to short-term events in the political environment than are those who claim allegiance to either major party.

Still, despite the expected short-term fluctuations, the story over the last three months has been the relatively close standing of the two parties in Gallup's monthly trial-heat election ballots. If this continues to be the case next November, Republicans' normal turnout advantage could propel them on Election Day 2010 to a positive margin of the congressional vote over Democrats, with a resulting pickup

in House seats. Gallup is tracking the generic House ballot monthly between now and the November 2010 elections; the next update will be in early January.

Survey Methods

Results are based on telephone interviews with 898 registered voters, aged 18 and older, conducted Dec. 11-13, 2009. For results based on the total sample of national adults, one can say with 95% confidence that the maximum margin of sampling error is ±4 percentage points.

Interviews are conducted with respondents on land-line telephones (for respondents with a land-line telephone) and cellular phones (for respondents who are cell-phone only).

In addition to sampling error, question wording and practical difficulties in conducting surveys can introduce error or bias into the findings of public opinion polls.

December 15, 2009
AMERICANS FAVOR U.S. SIGNATURE ON COPENHAGEN TREATY
However, most say U.S. economy should be the higher priority at this time

by Lydia Saad, Gallup Poll Senior Editor

Just over half of Americans, 55%, favor the United States' signing a binding treaty in Copenhagen that would commit the U.S. to significantly reducing greenhouse gas emissions, while 38% oppose it. Democratic endorsement of a treaty (79% are in favor) is somewhat higher than Republican resistance (65% are opposed), while independents' views are identical to the national average.

U.S. Public Support for Signing Copenhagen Climate Change Treaty
As you may know, representatives from around the world are gathering for a United Nations conference on global climate change in Copenhagen. Do you favor or oppose the U.S. signing a binding global treaty at the Copenhagen meeting that would require the U.S. to significantly reduce greenhouse gas emissions?

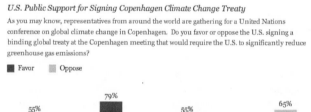

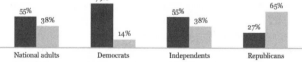

USA Today/Gallup, Dec. 11-13, 2009

The new findings come from a *USA Today*/Gallup poll conducted Dec. 11-13.

Despite this general support for the U.S.' putting pen to paper in Copenhagen, President Obama faces challenges in agreeing to some of the financial and environmental demands being placed on the U.S. at the conference, given U.S. public concerns about the potential economic impact of climate-change policy.

First and foremost, Americans clearly prefer taking major steps to improve the economy over taking major steps to reduce global warming at this time. Eighty-five percent of national adults choose improving the economy in this trade-off, including 93% of Republicans, 85% of independents, and 78% of Democrats.

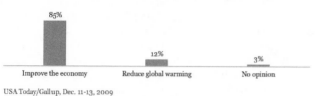

Preferred Priority: Improving the U.S. Economy vs. Reducing Global Warming

Which do you think should be a higher priority for the Obama administration right now -- [taking major steps to improve the U.S. economy (or) taking major steps to reduce global warming]?

USA Today/Gallup, Dec. 11-13, 2009
Based on 498 national adults in Form A half sample.

Americans also show more concern for the economy than for the environment in a question designed to test the alarmist arguments on both sides of the issue, but by a much smaller margin than is seen with the priority question. By 46% to 38%, more Americans say the greater risk in developing climate-change policy is the negative economic impact of taking actions to reduce global warming, rather than the negative environmental consequences of not taking those actions, with another 16% unsure.

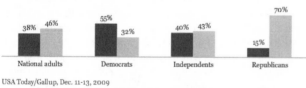

Relative Risk Assessment -- Global Warming vs. the Economy

Which worries you more -- [that the U.S. will not take the actions necessary to prevent the catastrophic effects of global warming because of fears those actions would harm the economy (or) that the U.S. will take actions to protect against global warming and those actions will cripple the U.S. economy]?

■ Not take actions to prevent catastrophic effects of global warming
▨ Will take actions that will cripple the U.S. economy

USA Today/Gallup, Dec. 11-13, 2009
Based on 527 national adults in Form B half sample.

Another question reveals that Obama could have a hard time selling the idea that laws requiring the United States to cap greenhouse gas emissions will ultimately be good for American workers. Specifically, fewer than 4 in 10 Americans (36%) believe that laws designed to reduce global warming will help the economy, while 42% believe those laws will hurt the economy. However, with an additional 17% saying the laws will have no effect on the economy, the majority view is that the economic impact will be no worse than neutral.

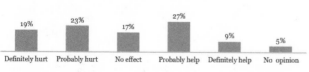

Perceived Impact of Global Warming Legislation on the Economy

Do you believe that new environmental and energy laws designed to reduce global warming will -- [definitely hurt the economy, probably hurt the economy, have no effect either way on the economy, probably help the economy, (or) definitely help the economy]?

USA Today/Gallup, Dec. 11-13, 2009

On this question, Republicans are more uniform in their criticism of global warming policies (65% say the new laws would hurt

the economy) than Democrats are in those policies' defense (54% say such laws will help).

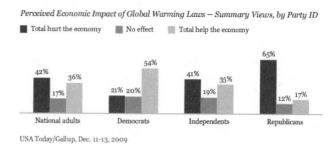

Perceived Economic Impact of Global Warming Laws -- Summary Views, by Party ID

■ Total hurt the economy   ▨ No effect   ▨ Total help the economy

USA Today/Gallup, Dec. 11-13, 2009

Bottom Line

President Obama has a fine line to walk in Copenhagen—living up to his long-standing commitment to be a global leader in reducing greenhouse gas emissions while staying mindful of the pitchforks that could be raised at home if he is perceived to be spending too much time on the issue, or selling the U.S. economy down the nearby Gulf Stream.

Americans' general reaction to U.S. participation in a global warming treaty is positive, but their greater relative concern for the economy may help to explain why Obama has yet to agree to the bigger U.S. emissions cuts and funding that much of the world is looking to him for.

Survey Methods

Results are based on telephone interviews with 1,025 national adults, aged 18 and older, conducted Dec. 11-13, 2009. For results based on the total sample of national adults, one can say with 95% confidence that the maximum margin of sampling error is ±4 percentage points.

For results based on the 498 national adults in the Form A half-sample and 527 national adults in the Form B half-sample, the maximum margins of sampling error are ±5 percentage points.

Interviews are conducted with respondents on land-line telephones (for respondents with a land-line telephone) and cellular phones (for respondents who are cell-phone only).

In addition to sampling error, question wording and practical difficulties in conducting surveys can introduce error or bias into the findings of public opinion polls.

December 16, 2009
MAJORITY OF AMERICANS STILL NOT BACKING HEALTHCARE BILL
Forty-six percent would advise their member to vote for it, or lean in that direction

by Jeffrey M. Jones, Gallup Poll Managing Editor

As the U.S. Senate continues working to craft a filibuster-proof healthcare reform bill, a new *USA Today/*Gallup poll finds public support for such efforts still below the majority level. Forty-six percent of Americans say they would advise their member of Congress to vote for healthcare legislation (or lean toward doing so), while 48% would advise a no vote (or lean in that direction).

Would you advise your member of Congress to vote for or against a healthcare bill this year, or do you not have an opinion?

(Asked of those with no opinion on healthcare bill) As of today, would you say you lean more toward advising your member of Congress to vote for a healthcare bill, or lean more toward advising your member of Congress to vote against a healthcare bill?

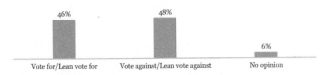

USA Today/Gallup, Dec. 11-13, 2009

Support had been at or above 50% in September and early October, but slumped to 43% by early November. It has recovered somewhat since then but remains below the earlier levels.

Combined Support for/Opposition to Healthcare Legislation This Year

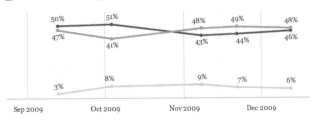

Bottom Line

As the year draws to a close, the debate over healthcare legislation is far from over. While Senate Majority Leader Harry Reid has expressed a desire to pass a bill before the end of the year, the Senate Democratic caucus still has some negotiating to do to bring a bill up for a vote that can withstand a filibuster attempt. Even if a bill passes, the House of Representatives and Senate must reconcile their two versions, which could reopen some of the more contentious debates concerning a public-option insurance plan and coverage for abortions.

The poll finds that 21% of Americans remain undecided on the bill (they currently lean in one direction or the other, or have no leaning at all), so it is possible the public will still climb on board. But as the debate has unfolded in recent months, the legislation has struggled to get even bare majority support.

Survey Methods

Results are based on telephone interviews with 1,025 national adults, aged 18 and older, conducted Dec. 11-13, 2009. For results based on the total sample of national adults, one can say with 95% confidence that the maximum margin of sampling error is ±4 percentage points.

Interviews are conducted with respondents on land-line telephones (for respondents with a land-line telephone) and cellular phones (for respondents who are cell-phone only).

In addition to sampling error, question wording and practical difficulties in conducting surveys can introduce error or bias into the findings of public opinion polls.

December 16, 2009
AMERICANS OPPOSE CLOSING GITMO, MOVING PRISONERS TO U.S.
Support is 8% among Republicans, 28% among independents, and 50% among Democrats

by Frank Newport, Gallup Poll Editor in Chief

Americans remain opposed to closing the Guantanamo Bay prison in Cuba and moving some of the terrorist suspects being held there to U.S. prisons: 30% favor such actions, while 64% do not. These attitudes could present a significant roadblock for President Obama at a time when he seeks congressional approval to move terrorist suspects from Guantanamo to a converted state prison in northwestern Illinois.

As you may know, since 2001, the United States has held people from other countries who are suspected of being terrorists in a prison at Guantanamo Bay in Cuba. Do you think the United States should -- or should not -- close this prison and move some of the prisoners to U.S. prisons?

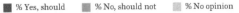

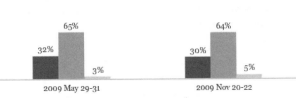

President Obama signed an executive order after his inauguration that called for the closing of Guantanamo, and he recently reiterated his commitment to doing this in his West Point speech on Afghanistan. The plans announced this week represent the first concrete effort to follow through on his promise, but occur in the context of continuing opposition from the American public. About two-thirds of Americans in the Nov. 20-22 poll oppose such a move, virtually the same as measured last May.

Republicans on Capitol Hill this week have been highly vocal in their negative responses to the proposed move. Republican Sen. Mitch McConnell of Kentucky, for example, was quoted as saying, "The administration has failed to explain how transferring terrorists to Gitmo North will make Americans safer than keeping terrorists off of our shores in the secure facility in Cuba."

McConnell and the other GOP lawmakers who have spoken out against the move are clearly representing the sentiments of rank-and-file Republicans across the country, only 8% of whom favor closing the prison and moving prisoners to the U.S.

Views on Closing Guantanamo Prison and Moving Some Prisoners to the United States, by Party ID

% Should close prison, move some prisoners to U.S.

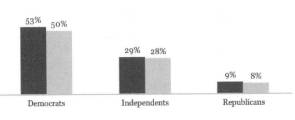

An additional political challenge for Obama is the fact that he lacks strong support among rank-and-file Democrats as well. Half of Democrats agree that the Guantanamo Bay prison should be closed and some prisoners moved to the U.S., while 45% disagree. Twenty-eight percent of independents favor the prison closure. These partisan breaks are similar to what Gallup found in May.

The prison the Obama administration has proposed taking over and converting to a home for Guantanamo terrorist suspects is in northwestern Illinois, across the Mississippi River from Iowa. Local leaders in that area have applauded the decision, which would reportedly bring hundreds of millions in new revenue to the region, along with many new jobs.

The area potentially affected by the moves is a small part of the larger Midwestern region of the country, where there is slightly higher acceptance of the decision on Guantanamo prisoners than occurs elsewhere in the country. Support is slightly lower in the South. These differences are not substantial.

Views on Closing Guantanamo Prison and Moving Some Prisoners to the United States, by Region

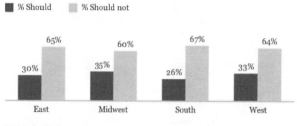

USA Today/Gallup, Nov. 20-22, 2009

Implications

President Obama's announcement this week that he plans to move terrorist suspects to Illinois from the U.S. prison at Guantanamo Bay represents a follow-through on his stated intention to ultimately close the Guantanamo prison.

The implementation of his plan will require congressional approval, since current law prohibits bringing Guantanamo prisoners into U.S. territory unless they are being put on trial. Congressional lawmakers voting on the plan to bring terrorist suspects now housed at Guantanamo to the U.S. will generally be doing so in the context of significant opposition from their constituents, thus potentially reducing the chances that the president will be able to get quick House and Senate approval for his proposal.

Survey Methods

Results are based on telephone interviews with 1,017 national adults, aged 18 and older, conducted Nov. 20-22, 2009. For results based on the total sample of national adults, one can say with 95% confidence that the maximum margin of sampling error is ±4 percentage points.

Interviews are conducted with respondents on land-line telephones (for respondents with a land-line telephone) and cellular phones (for respondents who are cell-phone only).

In addition to sampling error, question wording and practical difficulties in conducting surveys can introduce error or bias into the findings of public opinion polls.

December 17, 2009
APPROVAL OF U.S. CONGRESS ESSENTIALLY FLAT, AT 25%
Approval steady from November; majorities for—as well as against—healthcare bill disapprove

by Lymari Morales, Gallup Poll Staff Writer

With the U.S. Congress battling until the brink of Christmas to try to pass a healthcare reform bill, Americans are growing neither more positive nor more negative about their elected representatives in Washington. More than two-thirds of Americans (69%) continue to disapprove of the job Congress is doing, while 25% approve—essentially unchanged from last month.

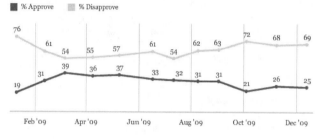

Do you approve or disapprove of the way Congress is handling its job?
2009 trend

The results are from a *USA Today/*Gallup poll conducted Dec. 11-13, 2009, as congressional leaders continued to work toward a compromise that would put a healthcare reform bill on President Barack Obama's desk—either by the end of the year or by the president's State of the Union address in January.

The lack of change from last month among Americans overall masks slight shifts by party. Approval among Democrats edged downward five percentage points, from 47% to 42%—while approval among independents edged upward by the same amount, from 14% to 19%. Republicans' approval is statistically steady this month, at 15%.

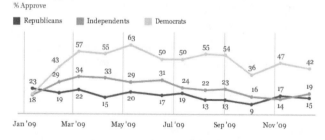

Do you approve or disapprove of the way Congress is handling its job?
2009 trend, by party ID
% Approve

The extent to which Congress is failing to win fans for its healthcare efforts is underscored by looking at how Americans' approval of Congress relates to their views on healthcare reform. Majorities of those who favor and of those who oppose a healthcare bill disapprove of the way Congress is handling its job—at 53% and 86%, respectively.

Both Obama and members of Congress have often acknowledged that passing comprehensive healthcare reform would be difficult and potentially unpopular. Congress has taken most of its

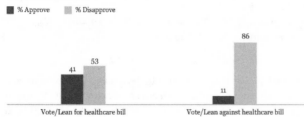

Approval of Congress, by How Americans Would Advise Their Member of Congress to Vote on Healthcare Bill

■ % Approve   ■ % Disapprove

approval hit from July to October, during the most contentious parts of the debate, but ratings appear to have hit a plateau over the past several months of more nuanced negotiations. The results—or lack thereof—of many months of time and energy spent on healthcare will be clearer by the time Gallup updates congressional approval again in January. With the vote for Congress in 2010 already looking extremely tight, congressional Democrats in particular should be resolving in the new year to find ways to move approval higher.

Survey Methods

Results are based on telephone interviews with 1,025 national adults, aged 18 and older, conducted Dec. 11-13, 2009. For results based on the total sample of national adults, one can say with 95% confidence that the maximum margin of sampling error is ±4 percentage points.

Interviews are conducted with respondents on land-line telephones (for respondents with a land-line telephone) and cellular phones (for respondents who are cell-phone only).

In addition to sampling error, question wording and practical difficulties in conducting surveys can introduce error or bias into the findings of public opinion polls.

December 18, 2009

11TH-HOUR SURGE IN AMERICANS' CHRISTMAS SPENDING INTENTIONS

December Christmas spending intentions suggest a 1% increase in holiday spending

by Lydia Saad, Gallup Poll Senior Editor

The average amount of money Americans predict they will spend on Christmas gifts this season is now $743, up from last month's estimate and a healthy increase over Americans' Christmas spending forecast at this time a year ago.

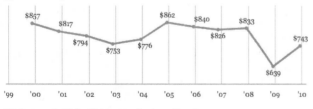

Estimated Christmas Spending, 1999-2009

Roughly how much money do you think you personally will spend on Christmas gifts this year?

■ Mean including zero

Data shown are final Gallup Christmas spending forecast for each year.

The latest data are from a *USA Today*/Gallup poll conducted Dec. 11-13.

Based on the latest Christmas spending estimate, Gallup forecasts that holiday sales this year have the potential to show a modest increase of 1%—marking a shift from last year, when Christmas spending was down 3.4% from the previous year. Gallup's Christmas spending model is based on a comparison of annual changes in consumers' Christmas spending intentions since 1999 and actual yearly changes in holiday spending for the same years.

Importantly, while Americans' current holiday spending intentions exceed the $639 recorded in December 2008, they fall well short of the levels seen in each of the previous four years. As such, spending continues to reflect a recessionary rather than economic growth mentality. Only a month ago, holiday spending intentions registered $638—indicating just how fragile the consumer mentality remains this season.

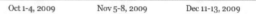

Gallup 2009 Christmas Spending Forecast

■ Mean including zero

Additionally, Christmas spending represents only a portion of total consumer spending. The rebound in Americans' 2009 Christmas spending intentions is happening in an environment in which consumers' reported daily spending still trails last year's levels by a significant amount. To some degree, Americans may be shifting their discretionary spending dollars into Christmas shopping, rather than increasing their total spending. Also, the increase between November and December in planned holiday spending may point to a late surge in Christmas shopping, particularly heading into the crucial final shopping weekend before Christmas.

Nearly 3 in 10 Will Spend $1,000 or More

Comparing Gallup's final Christmas spending forecasts for 2008 and 2009—based on surveys conducted in the first half of December for both years—the biggest shift in consumer intentions by spending category is a seven percentage-point increase, from 22% to 29%, in those planning to spend $1,000 or more. (However, this still falls below the 33% spending $1,000 or more in 2007.) Slight declines this year are seen in lower spending categories.

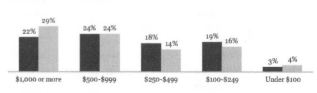

Projected Amount Will Spend on Christmas Gifts

■ Dec 4-7, 2008   ■ Dec 11-13, 2009

In line with these spending trends, Gallup's latest survey also finds that the increased spending this year compared with 2008 is primarily occurring among upper- and middle-income Americans. The spending intentions of lower-income Americans (those earning less than $30,000 per year) are holding steady at the dampened level seen in each of the past two years.

Estimated Christmas Spending by Income, 2001-2009
Mean dollar amount, including zero

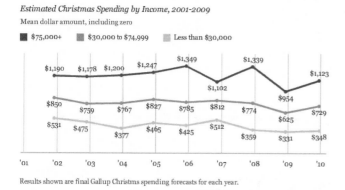

Results shown are final Gallup Christms spending forecasts for each year.

Gallup can estimate what the actual percentage change in holiday spending will be in 2009 by comparing its final spending forecast for prior years to the actual percentage changes in holiday spending that have been calculated by the National Retail Federation for those same years. The Gallup data used in this model extend back to 1999. The results of the model this year point to a 1% increase in 2009 holiday sales compared to 2008, based on the latest $743 average spending figure. This would be a welcome rebound from last year's real decline in year-over-year holiday sales of 3.4% as reported by the National Retail Federation, although still weak compared to the average 4.1% increase seen between 1999 and 2007.

Gallup Christmas Spending Forecast vs. Actual Holiday Sales Trends*
■ Gallup Final Christmas Spending Forecast ■ Actual Holiday Sales Trends (Year/Year % Change)*

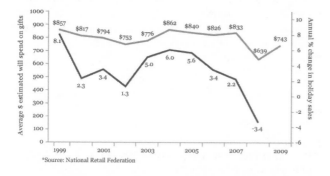

*Source: National Retail Federation

One cautionary note in the new poll comes from Americans' own assessments of whether their 2009 Christmas budget is greater or smaller than last year's. Forty-two percent now say they will spend less than what they did last Christmas, similar to the 45% saying this a year ago, but about double the norm on this measure seen earlier in the decade.

Bottom Line

The $743 Americans now predict they will spend on gifts this season is a substantial increase over the $639 they reported a year ago, and also higher than what they predicted in November of this year. Based on Gallup's model, this should translate into a significant swing in

*Comparative Christmas Spending, 1999-2009^*
Is that [amount you will spend] more, less, or about the same amount as you spent last Christmas?

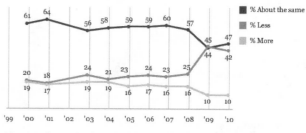

^ Recent trend. Dates selected are those closest to December for each year.

actual holiday retail sales. Instead of the 3.4% decline holiday retailers saw in 2008, they can likely expect a slight improvement in sales this year, on the order of 1%. However, given the volatility Gallup has seen on this measure since October, such an improvement clearly depends on consumers' maintaining their renewed spending momentum right through the after-Christmas sales.

Survey Methods

Results are based on telephone interviews with 1,025 national adults, aged 18 and older, conducted Dec. 11-13, 2009. For results based on the total sample of national adults, one can say with 95% confidence that the maximum margin of sampling error is ±4 percentage points.

Interviews are conducted with respondents on land-line telephones (for respondents with a land-line telephone) and cellular phones (for respondents who are cell-phone only).

In addition to sampling error, question wording and practical difficulties in conducting surveys can introduce error or bias into the findings of public opinion polls.

December 21, 2009
ECONOMY FORCING MANY IN U.S. TO CUT BACK ON HOLIDAY TRAVEL
Majority of would-be travelers say they are cutting costs or not traveling at all

by Jeffrey M. Jones, Gallup Poll Managing Editor

The economy is affecting the holiday travel plans of one in five Americans, including 8% who are still traveling more than 100 miles from home but are cutting back significantly on the cost of the trip, and 12% who are staying near home but say they would have traveled if the economy were better. The remainder are traveling but not cutting costs (15%), or are not traveling and say the economy did not influence their decision (63%).

These results are based on a Dec. 11-13 *USA Today*/Gallup poll, and indicate that 23% of Americans will be spending at least part of this holiday season away from home. The poll estimates that figure could have been 35% if the economy were in better shape.

The specific impact of the economic downturn on holiday travel is more apparent when one looks at just the 35% of Americans who can be considered "would-be travelers," including those who are traveling this year plus those who are forgoing travel because of the economy. Among this group, the majority are scaling back their

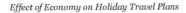

Effect of Economy on Holiday Travel Plans

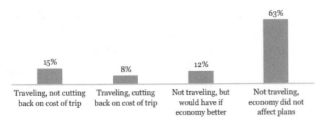

15%
Traveling, not cutting back on cost of trip

8%
Traveling, cutting back on cost of trip

12%
Not traveling, but would have if economy better

63%
Not traveling, economy did not affect plans

USA Today/Gallup, Dec. 11-13, 2009

travel plans by cutting down the cost of the trip (23%) or canceling it outright (34%).

Effect of Economy on Holiday Travel Plans

Based on those who are traveling or would have traveled if the economy were better

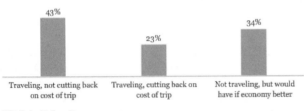

43%
Traveling, not cutting back on cost of trip

23%
Traveling, cutting back on cost of trip

34%
Not traveling, but would have if economy better

USA Today/Gallup, Dec. 11-13, 2009

Holiday travel is more common among wealthier Americans. Americans living in upper-income households (whose annual incomes are $75,000 or more) are twice as likely as lower-income Americans (whose annual incomes are under $30,000) to say they will travel during the holidays this year.

Do you, personally, plan to travel more than 100 miles from home during the holidays this year, or not?

By annual household income

17%
Less than $30,000

20%
$30,000-less than $75,000

34%
$75,000 or more

USA Today/Gallup, Dec. 11-13, 2009

And, not surprisingly, lower-income Americans are more likely to report altering their travel plans because of the economy, especially in terms of forgoing a trip altogether. This group is twice as likely as upper-income Americans to have canceled holiday travel this year.

In addition to income, holiday travel varies by age, with younger Americans much more likely than older Americans to say they plan to travel.

Bottom Line

While the majority of Americans will stay close to home for the holidays this year, a substantial proportion will be traveling a considerable distance. However, the poor economy is limiting holiday travel

Effect of the Economy on Holiday Travel Plans, by Annual Household Income

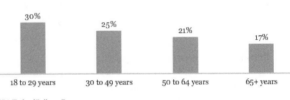

	Less than $30,000	$30,000-less than $75,000	$75,000 or more
Traveling, not cutting back on cost	8%	12%	25%
Traveling, cutting back on cost	9%	9%	9%
Not traveling, but would if economy better	18%	13%	9%
Not traveling, economy did not affect decision	62%	66%	56%

USA Today/Gallup, Dec. 11-13, 2009

Do you, personally, plan to travel more than 100 miles from home during the holidays this year, or not?

By age

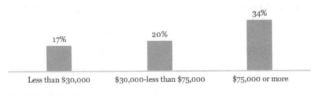

30%
18 to 29 years

25%
30 to 49 years

21%
50 to 64 years

17%
65+ years

USA Today/Gallup, Dec. 11-13, 2009

this year, with 12% of Americans saying they are forgoing travel because of the economy, and another 8% cutting the costs of their trip.

Survey Methods

Results are based on telephone interviews with 1,025 national adults, aged 18 and older, conducted Dec. 11-13, 2009. For results based on the total sample of national adults, one can say with 95% confidence that the maximum margin of sampling error is ±4 percentage points.

Interviews are conducted with respondents on land-line telephones (for respondents with a land-line telephone) and cellular phones (for respondents who are cell-phone only).

In addition to sampling error, question wording and practical difficulties in conducting surveys can introduce error or bias into the findings of public opinion polls.

December 23, 2009
TEACHERS SCORE HIGHER THAN OTHER PROFESSIONALS IN WELL-BEING
Teachers rate their lives higher in four of six well-being indexes

by Shane Lopez and Sangeeta Agrawal, Staff Writers

A career in teaching might be good for your well-being. While the Gallup-Healthways Well-Being Index previously revealed that business owners were richer in well-being than other job types, further research isolating teachers from other professionals finds teachers fare as well as or better than business owners in overall well-being.

Gallup typically includes teachers in the "professional worker" occupation category, but asks an additional question —"Are you currently a teacher in a public or private school (at any level, secondary, elementary, college, pre-school)?"—to distinguish teachers from non-teaching professionals.

Rankings by Occupation on the Gallup-Healthways Well-Being Index

Occupation	Composite Score
Teacher	71.7
Business owner	71.5
Manager/executive/official	69.3
Professional worker	69.1
Farming/fishing/forestry worker	66.5
Sales worker	65.8
Clerical or office worker	64.4
Construction or mining worker	63.7
Installation or repair worker	63.1
Service worker	62.6
Transportation worker	60.9
Manufacturing or production worker	60.6

Gallup-Healthways Well-Being Index

An analysis of data collected between July 2008 and June 2009 finds that teachers score highest (or tied for highest) among all 12 job types on how they evaluate their lives, access to resources needed to lead a healthy life, emotional health, and their likelihood of engaging in healthy behaviors. Overall, the findings reveal numerous benefits and some drawbacks related to the teaching profession.

Teachers View Their Lives in Positive Terms

The Life Evaluation Index, which is based on the Cantril Self-Anchoring Striving Scale, is one of four sub-indexes on which teachers rank first. People are asked to evaluate their present and future lives on a scale with steps numbered from 0 to 10, where 0 is the worst possible life and 10 is the best possible life. Based on their scores, teachers are at the top of the list, expressing far more optimism than all other professions.

Rankings by Occupation on the Gallup-Healthways Life Evaluation Index

Occupation	Life Evaluation Index Score
Teacher	60.4
Professional worker	53.6
Manager/executive/official	51.9
Business owner	50.4
Sales worker	47.2
Clerical or office worker	42.8
Service worker	39.7
Farming/fishing/forestry worker	37.2
Construction or mining worker	35.9
Installation or repair worker	34.4
Transportation worker	33.2
Manufacturing or production worker	31.4

Data reflect net thriving, which is the percentage thriving minus the percentage suffering.
Gallup-Healthways Well-Being Index

Next on the list, non-teaching professionals were nearly seven percentage points lower on this index than their fellow professionals in the education ranks. Business owners lagged 10 points behind teachers. Workers in many other job types had scores more than 15 points below teachers, suggesting that they tend to see their lives much less positively.

Teachers Have What They Need for a Healthy Life

Teachers are also in the top spot, tied with managers/executives/officials and non-teaching professionals, on the Gallup-Healthways Basic Access Index. The Basic Access Index measures access to resources and services needed to lead a healthy life (based on 13 indicators gauging access to food, shelter, healthcare, and a safe and satisfying place to live, among other things).

Rankings by Occupation on the Gallup-Healthways Basic Access Index

Occupation	Basic Access Index Score
Teacher	89.4
Manager/executive/official	88.8
Professional worker	88.2
Clerical or office worker	86.1
Business owner	86.0
Sales worker	85.2
Transportation worker	82.5
Installation or repair worker	82.3
Manufacturing or production worker	81.4
Service worker	79.2
Farming/fishing/forestry worker	78.5
Construction or mining worker	78.1

Gallup-Healthways Well-Being Index

Clerical/office workers, business owners, and sales workers also report a high degree of access to basic resources. Workers in the farming/fishing/forestry and construction/mining industries rank lowest on this sub-index.

Teachers Share the Top Ranking in Emotional Health

In terms of emotional health, teachers share the top spot with numerous job types including farming/fishing/ forestry workers (who topped the list in a previous analysis), non-teaching professionals, business owners, and managers/executives/officials, all of which have index scores within two points or less of teachers. A high level of emotional health involves positive daily experiences (e.g., smiling or laughter, learning or doing something interesting, being treated with respect), more positive than negative emotions, and no history of depression.

Rankings by Occupation on the Gallup-Healthways Emotional Health Index

Occupation	Emotional Health Index Score
Teacher	75.0
Farming/fishing/forestry worker	74.4
Professional worker	73.7
Business owner	73.5
Manager/executive/official	73.3
Installation or repair worker	72.9
Sales worker	72.4
Construction or mining worker	72.4
Clerical or office worker	71.9
Transportation worker	71.6
Service worker	71.5
Manufacturing or production worker	70.6

Gallup-Healthways Well-Being Index

Underscoring the level of positive emotion teachers experience on a daily basis, when surveyed, 87% of teachers said they smiled or laughed a lot yesterday. Sales workers were next in line with 86% reporting smiling or laughing a lot the day before the survey. Manufacturing/production and transportation workers smiled and laughed least often with 82% reporting that they did so a lot yesterday.

Teachers Make Healthy Choices

Teachers also rank near the top on the Healthy Behavior Index, again sharing a comparable score with farm/fishing/forestry workers and business owners; non-teaching professionals follow. The Healthy Behavior Index measures four behaviors strongly linked to health: eating healthy, smoking (scored in reverse), weekly consumption of fruits and vegetables, and weekly exercise frequency. Manufacturing/production, transportation, installation/repair, and sales workers rank lowest on the Healthy Behavior Index.

Rankings by Occupation on the Gallup-Healthways Healthy Behavior Index

Occupation	Healthy Behavior Index Score
Farming/fishing/forestry worker	67.8
Teacher	67.4
Business owner	65.9
Professional worker	63.3
Manager/executive/official	61.7
Service worker	60.3
Clerical or office worker	59.5
Construction or mining worker	59.4
Sales worker	59.0
Installation or repair worker	58.1
Transportation worker	57.9
Manufacturing or production worker	57.2

Gallup-Healthways Well-Being Index

Teachers Do Not Report the Best Work Environments

Teachers and fellow professionals lag far behind business owners, who hold the top spot on the Work Environment Index. The Work Environment Index asks people if they are satisfied with their jobs, if they get to use their strengths at work, if their supervisor treats them more like a boss or a partner, and if their work environment is open and trusting. Given that conditions in an employee's work environment are directly related to his or her engagement level, the finding may have implications for students and administrators. Teachers who are given the opportunity to do what they do best at work (91% say they get to use their strengths at work) may be more likely to engage students in the learning process.

Business owners, despite working longer hours than people in other job types, report having the best work environments—likely buoyed by the fact that many business owners are their own supervisors. Farming/fishing/forestry workers have a higher score on the index than teachers, but teachers score higher than people in construction/mining, sales, installation/repair, clerical/office work, service, manufacturing/production, and transportation.

Teachers Are as Physically Healthy as Most Workers in Other Professions

Construction/mining workers, managers/executives/officials, professionals, and business owners lead the way on the Physical Health

Rankings by Occupation on the Gallup-Healthways Work Environment Index

Occupation	Work Environment Index Score
Business owner	70.9
Farming/fishing/forestry worker	59.7
Manager/executive/official	57.3
Teacher	55.9
Professional worker	53.8
Construction or mining worker	53.3
Sales worker	49.3
Installation or repair worker	48.9
Clerical or office worker	46.7
Service worker	45.9
Manufacturing or production worker	41.9
Transportation worker	40.2

Gallup-Healthways Well-Being Index

Index, and teachers along with sales workers and installation/repair workers are close behind. This index includes nine items addressing chronic or daily illnesses, including colds and flu. When asked if they were sick with the flu yesterday, 1.2% of teachers (and business owners) said "yes," whereas the percentage of flu sufferers was as high as 2.9% for individuals in the farming/fishing/forestry industry. Teachers were more likely to report having a cold yesterday (7.0% said "yes" to this item). Service workers were most likely to report having a cold (7.4%), and business owners were the least likely (4.6%).

Rankings by Occupation on the Gallup-Healthways Physical Health Index

Occupation	Physical Health Index Score
Construction or mining worker	83.0
Manager/executive/official	82.6
Professional worker	82.2
Business owner	82.2
Sales worker	81.9
Teacher	81.8
Installation or repair worker	81.8
Farming/fishing/forestry worker	81.2
Manufacturing or production worker	80.9
Transportation worker	79.7
Clerical or office worker	79.3
Service worker	79.1

Gallup-Healthways Well-Being Index

Bottom Line

Teachers score highly on many aspects of well-being, even when compared with non-teaching professionals and business owners. It is unclear whether the relatively higher scores of teachers on several measures of well-being are because working in that profession enhances one's well-being, or if people who have higher well-being in general seek out teaching professions.

While teachers reap the personal benefits of high well-being, this level of well-being may also prove beneficial to their students and the broader community. At the same time, community leaders and administrators would do well to improve teacher's work environments not only to help boost teacher well-being, but also to boost student and community well-being even higher.

Results are based on telephone interviews with adults, aged 18 and older, who are employed in one of the 11 job categories Gallup typically uses to assess occupation. A total of 409,261 interviews were conducted July 1, 2008-June 30, 2009, as part of the Gallup-Healthways Well-Being Index. However, because many Americans are not in the workforce and because some Americans work in jobs that do not fit any of these job classifications, the final sample was 179,007.

Each occupational group has at least 3,336 respondents, which means that for most occupations and most indexes the margin of sampling error is always less than ±2 percentage points. However, because farmers and small business owners often could not answer questions about their supervisors, sample sizes for these two groups on the Work Environment Index drop as low as 1,327. The margin of error for this smallest sample size (incorporating the design effect) is ±3 percentage points. Rankings, and ties within rankings, were determined using margins of error.

Interviews are conducted with respondents on land-line telephones (for respondents with a land-line telephone) and cellular phones (for respondents who are cell-phone only).

In addition to sampling error, question wording and practical difficulties in conducting surveys can introduce error or bias into the findings of public opinion polls.

December 23, 2009

THE DECADE IN REVIEW: FOUR KEY TRENDS

Changes in approval of Congress, president; satisfaction with the U.S.; perceived top problems

by Jeffrey M. Jones, Frank Newport, and Lydia Saad, Gallup Poll Editors

As 2009 draws down, Gallup reviews four of the key trends that reveal how Americans reacted to the twists and turns experienced in public affairs and the economy over the past decade.

U.S. Satisfaction -- Trend Since January 2000

In general, are you satisfied or dissatisfied with the way things are going in the United States at this time?

■ % Satisfied

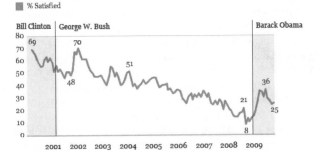

Satisfaction With the Way Things Are Going

At the start of this decade, Americans' satisfaction with the direction of the country stood at 69%, near the record-high 71% established in early 1999 that was fueled by a booming economy. Satisfaction levels quickly descended in 2001 as economic concerns mounted, and

fell below 50% in mid-August of that year (48%). However, in the first few months after the 2001 terrorist attacks, public satisfaction quickly rebounded—part of a broader "rally around the flag" effect triggered by 9/11—reaching 70% in December.

The 9/11 effect on U.S. satisfaction dissipated in less than a year, with satisfaction returning to 49% by July 2002. Americans' satisfaction with the direction of the country generally remained between 40% and 50% in 2003 (averaging 46%), but fell to an average 43% in 2004, 38% in 2005, 31% in 2006, and 28% in 2007. Satisfaction sank further—along with a faltering U.S. stock market—at the start of 2008, dropping well below 20% for the first time since 1992.

U.S. satisfaction nearly collapsed in late 2008, falling from 21% in September to 8% in October in the midst of the emerging Wall Street financial crisis. Satisfaction recovered only slightly over the next few months, then rose more sharply in April and May 2009—driven largely by increased satisfaction among Democrats under the new Obama administration. Satisfaction in 2009 peaked at 36% in August. However in the last few months of the year, it settled back into the mid-20s, finishing the decade at 25% in December—still below the decade average.

Most Important Problem

What do you think is the most important problem facing this country today?

Trend since January 2000

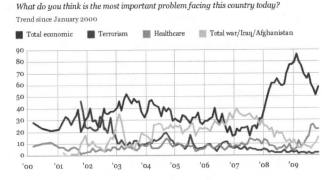

As might be imagined, Americans have identified a wide variety of issues as being "the most important problem facing this country" when asked this question throughout the decade. In Gallup's last reading of the decade—in December 2009—29 different problems were mentioned by at least 1% of Americans.

The accompanying graph tracks the decade-long trends in Americans' mentions of four of these problems: 1) the economy (a category that includes all mentions of economic issues); 2) terrorism; 3) wars (a category including either general mentions of wars or mentions of wars in Iraq and Afghanistan specifically); and 4) healthcare.

Two of these four issues—terrorism and wars—were basically not on Americans' radar in the first year and a half of the decade. That changed after the Sept. 11, 2001, terrorist attacks.

Mentions of terrorism as the nation's most important problem went from zero in early September 2001 to 46% in October of that year. Concerns over terrorism began to decline from that point on, and by decade's end, only 1% to 2% of Americans were mentioning terrorism as the country's top problem.

Americans' mentions of war as the nation's most important problem (including general mentions of war as well as specific mentions of the situations in Iraq and Afghanistan) also increased after Sept. 11, and began to rise substantially in the final months of 2002 and into 2003 as the Bush administration made it clear that the U.S. was going to become militarily involved in Iraq. By May 2003, after

Bush's "Mission Accomplished" speech on the aircraft carrier Abraham Lincoln, mentions of war as the nation's top problem fell and remained low through the summer of that year. Then, as it became evident that the Iraq war was by no means over—and as U.S. casualties mounted, hitting 1,000 in September 2004—mentions of Iraq as the nation's top problem began to increase, and basically stayed relatively high through the summer of 2008, before falling to the single digits as the decade ended. Mentions of Afghanistan as the nation's top problem were at a low 4% at decade's end.

Americans' designation of economic-related issues as the nation's top problems waxed and waned during the decade. Over 20% of Americans were mentioning some aspect of the economy as the nation's top problem in early 2000. Those concerns rose to over 50% by May 2003, but fell into the teens by late 2006 and into 2007. Then, beginning in the late fall of 2007, Americans increasingly began to mention aspects of the economy as the top problem, with a sharp rise in concerns by the winter and spring of 2008. By the summer of 2008, 60% or more of Americans were mentioning some aspect of the economy as the nation's top problem. Concern spiked even higher in the fall of 2008 and winter of 2009, reaching the decade's highest point in February of this year, when 86% of Americans spontaneously mentioned economic issues as the nation's top problem. As the decade ended, economic concerns had abated somewhat, dropping to 55% in December 2009.

The perception that healthcare is the nation's top problem was fairly scarce during most of the decade, reaching a low point of 1% in October 2001 (as terrorism overrode other concerns). By the summer of 2009, as President Obama and congressional leaders began to focus intently on new healthcare reform legislation, the public's mentioning of healthcare as the country's top problem began to rise again, reaching 26% by late August/early September. At decade's end, concerns over healthcare had drifted back to 16%.

Presidential Job Approval

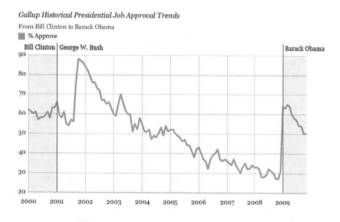

Gallup Historical Presidential Job Approval Trends
From Bill Clinton to Barack Obama

The decade has spanned the administrations of three presidents: Bill Clinton, George W. Bush, and Barack Obama.

Clinton's final year in office was fairly uneventful. Clinton had solid ratings in the high 50% and low 60% range for most of 2000, finishing his presidency on a high note with a 66% job approval rating.

Bush began his term in early 2001 with ratings also in the high 50% and low 60% range, but his job approval ratings began to settle down, and by Gallup's Sept. 7-10, 2001, survey, Bush's job approval was at 51%. Then, after the Sept. 11 terrorist attacks, Bush was the recipient of the largest rally effect in Gallup history, with his approval rating rising 39 percentage points to 90% in the space of two weeks. The 90% rating is the highest in Gallup history. Bush's approval rating—perhaps inevitably—generally sloped downward after that, but remained well above average in 2002 and for most of 2003. By the time he sought re-election in 2004, his approval rating hovered near 50%.

Bush's second term was characterized by below-average ratings, which sank to the 30% range in his final two years in office—including frequent drops into the 20s in his last year. The lowest presidential job approval rating of the decade was 25%, and Bush reached it three times in the fall of 2008, including at the time of the 2008 election to choose his successor. Bush's last approval rating, just before he left office, was 34%.

Obama took office with job approval ratings in the 60% range, beginning the honeymoon phase of his presidency, which lasted well into the summer months. By late summer, however, his approval ratings were in the low 50% range; they dipped below the majority approval level in November, and have been at or near 50% in December.

Congressional Job Approval

Do you approve or disapprove of the way Congress is handling its job?
Trend since January 2000

The decade of the 2000s saw both a new high and a new low in congressional job approval. The rally in support for government institutions after the 9/11 terror attacks extended to Congress, as 84% of Americans in October 2001 said they approved of the job Congress was doing, shattering the previous high of 57% from February 1998.

But that era of goodwill did not last, as approval ratings of Congress gradually descended—following the same general pattern seen for George W. Bush's presidential job approval ratings. By October 2005, congressional job approval fell below 30%; it was 26% in the fall of 2006 when Americans transferred party control of both houses of Congress to the Democrats in that year's midterm elections.

The change in party control only had a very short-lived positive impact on Congress' ratings, which improved 16 points from December 2006 (21%) to February 2007 (37%) after the transfer of power. By August 2007, approval had dipped to a record-tying low of 18%, and the following year, Congress' ratings established a new historical low of 14%.

The new Obama administration helped to boost ratings of Congress again in 2009; congressional approval went from 19% in January to 39% in March. But again, those higher ratings did not persist, and at the end of the decade, Congress' job rating stands at 25%.

December 24, 2009

THIS CHRISTMAS, 78% OF AMERICANS IDENTIFY AS CHRISTIAN

Over time, fewer Americans identify as Christian; more have no religious identity

by Frank Newport, Gallup Poll Editor in Chief

This Christmas season, 78% of Americans identify with some form of Christian religion, a proportion that has been declining in recent decades. The major reason for this decline has been an increase in the percentage of Americans claiming no religious identity, now at 13% of all adults.

What is your religious preference?

■ % Protestant/Other non-Catholic Christian ■ % Catholic ■ % None ■ % Other

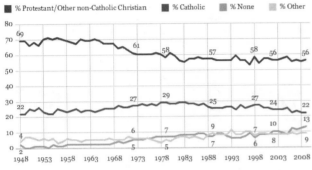

The trend results are based on annual averages of Gallup's religious identity data in America that stretch back over 60 years. One of the most significant trends documented during this period is the substantial increase in the percentage of American adults who don't identify with any specific religion. In 1948, only 2% of Americans did not identify with a religion. That percentage began to rise in the late 1960s and early 1970s. Eleven years ago, in 1998, 6% of Americans did not identify with a religion, a number that rose to 10% by 2002. This year's average of 13% of Americans who claim no religious identity is the highest in Gallup records.

The percentage of Americans who identify as Catholic, Protestant, or some other non-Catholic Christian faith has been concomitantly decreasing over the years. This suggests that one of the major patterns of religious transition in America in recent decades has been the shift from identification as Christian to the status of having no specific religious identification.

In 1948, 91% of Americans identified with a Christian faith. Twenty years ago, in 1989, 82% of Americans identified as Christian. Ten years ago, it was 84%. This year, as noted, 78% of all American adults identify with a Christian faith.

There has also been a slight increase in the percentage of Americans who identify with a religion that is not specifically classified as Christian. Sixty years ago, for example, 4% of Americans identified with a non-Christian religion. By 1989, 9% of Americans were in this non-Christian religion category, the same percentage as today.

Personal Importance of Religion

Does the decrease in religious identity signify that religion is losing its importance for Americans? There was a substantial drop in the percentage of Americans who said religion was "very important" in their lives between the 1960s and the 1970s—from 70% in 1965 to 52% by 1978—but in recent decades, this "very important" percent-

age has remained relatively steady. The overall figure today—56%—is slightly higher than it was 31 years ago.

How important would you say religion is in your own life -- very important, fairly important, or not very important?

■ % Very important ■ % Fairly important ■ % Not very important

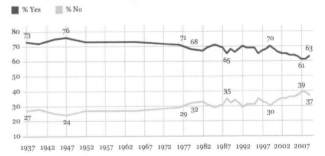

There has been a slight tendency over the years for Americans to shift from a "fairly important" category to the "not very important" category in answer to this religious importance question. The percentage saying religion is not very important in their lives was routinely in the 12% to 15% range from 1978 through the early years of this decade. In more recent years, this percentage has drifted slightly upward, and is at 19% this year.

Church Membership

As would be expected, given the drop in the percentage of Americans who have a religious identity, there has been a similar drop in the percentage of Americans who say they are a member of a church or synagogue.

Do you happen to be a member of a church or synagogue?

■ % Yes ■ % No

Gallup first asked this church membership question in 1937, at which time 73% of Americans said they were a member of a religious congregation. That percentage stayed above 70% in occasional Gallup surveys conducted through 1976, and remained in the high 60% range for the most part through the beginning of this decade. In recent years, the church membership percentage has been drifting down, reaching as low as 61% in Gallup's averages for 2007 and 2008. This year's average is 63%.

Is Religion Old-Fashioned and Out of Date?

Gallup has asked Americans over the years whether "religion can answer all or most of today's problems" or whether it "is largely old-fashioned and out of date." The majority of Americans over the last 52 years have chosen the first of these responses.

The biggest change in attitudes on this measure came between Gallup's survey in 1957—a very religious decade, based on Gallup indicators—and the data collected in more recent decades.

Do you believe that religion can answer all or most of today's problems, or that religion is largely old-fashioned and out of date?

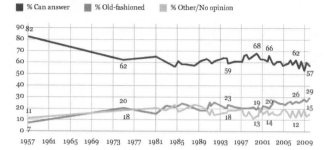

■ % Can answer ■ % Old-fashioned ▨ % Other/No opinion

The years from 1974 to the present have been marked by significant fluctuations in the answer to this question. Generally speaking, the percentage of Americans saying that religion can answer all or most of today's problems has been in a range between the mid-50s and the mid-60s. The recent decade high point was 68% in a survey conducted 10 years ago, in December 1999. The recent low point was 53% in a survey conducted last December. In two surveys conducted this year, the percentages saying that religion can answer all or most of today's problems were 60% and 57%.

A considerable percentage of Americans over the years, when confronted by the two choices offered by this question, have replied that they can't choose or have another opinion. This year, for example, 13% and 15% of Americans have given one of these answers in Gallup's two surveys that included this question.

Bottom Line

The United States remains a dominantly Christian nation. Almost 8 out of 10 Americans identify with a Christian religion. And the vast majority of those who identify with any religion identify with one that is Christian.

Yet, the percentage of Americans who in theory could celebrate Christmas this week as a specific component of their religious faith is down significantly from where it was 50 or 60 years ago. The most important reason for this shift is straightforward: there has been an increasing percentage of Americans who say they have no specific religious identity.

The fact that fewer Americans say they have a religious identity does not necessarily mean there has been a decrease in overall religiosity in America. It is possible that some proportion of those who don't identify with a specific religion are still personally or spiritually religious.

Although a little more than one out of five Americans do not identify with a Christian faith, the Christmas season has ramifications for a broader segment of society. A Gallup survey conducted last year showed that 93% of all American adults said they celebrated Christmas.

December 28, 2009
"POLITICAL WINNERS" CIRCLE FILLED BY FIGURES CLOSE TO OBAMA
Americans divided in labeling Sarah Palin as a political winner or loser

by Lydia Saad, Gallup Poll Senior Editor

In Americans' estimation, the top three political winners of 2009 are all women closely linked with the Obama administration: Michelle Obama, Hillary Clinton, and Sonia Sotomayor. Among these, Michelle Obama has the broadest support with 73% calling her a "winner" in U.S. politics this year and 21% a "loser." However, Clinton's rating is nearly as positive.

2009 Political "Winners"
Returning to politics, please tell me whether you consider each of the following to be a winner or a loser in U.S. politics this year.

■ % Winner ■ % Loser ▨ % No opinion

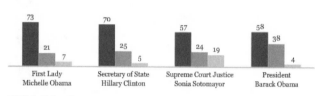

USA Today/Gallup, Dec. 11-13, 2009

President Barack Obama, himself, also falls in the political winners circle, although the percentage calling him a political loser is somewhat higher than is seen for the three women.

The picture is quite different for House Speaker Nancy Pelosi, whom half of all Americans identify as a political loser. More than half say the same of Rep. Joe Wilson (the representative who yelled "You lie!" to Obama at a joint session of Congress), as well as Gov. Mark Sanford (who is losing his wife and is under a state ethics investigation over an admitted extramarital affair), White House party crashers Tareq and Michaele Salahi, and the Republicans in Congress generally.

2009 Political "Losers"
Returning to politics, please tell me whether you consider each of the following to be a winner or a loser in U.S. politics this year.

■ % Winner ■ % Loser ▨ % No opinion

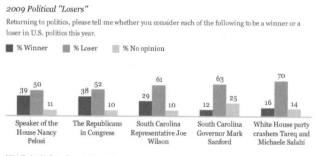

USA Today/Gallup, Dec. 11-13, 2009

In between the clear-cut political winners and losers are a number of public figures with more mixed reviews. Nearly half of Americans (46%) call Sarah Palin a winner, but slightly more (49%) call her a loser. About equal numbers of Americans call Ben Bernanke (*Time* magazine's choice for person of the year) and radio talk host Glenn Beck winners and losers, while a large segment has no opinion about either man. Senate Democratic Leader Harry Reid is more widely viewed as a loser than a winner, but not to as great a degree as Pelosi—possibly in part because of his high "no opinion" rating.

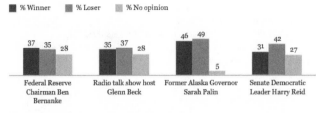

2009 Political Gray Area -- Neither "Winners" nor "Losers"

Returning to politics, please tell me whether you consider each of the following to be a winner or a loser in U.S. politics this year.

■ % Winner ■ % Loser ■ % No opinion

USA Today/Gallup, Dec. 11-13, 2009

Identifying the "winners" and "losers" emerging on Election Day is clear cut, but a far more subjective assessment in the context of the political gamesmanship that goes on in between elections. Now that the presidential election in which the McCain-Palin ticket was defeated is more than a year past, Sarah Palin is nearly as likely to be viewed as a political winner as a loser. Hillary Clinton lost a bitterly fought primary for the 2008 Democratic presidential nomination, but has been visibly filling her role as Secretary of State and has risen above the political fray in a way the president has not, with more viewing Clinton as a political winner than Barack Obama.

Survey Methods

Results are based on telephone interviews with 1,025 national adults, aged 18 and older, conducted Dec. 11-13, 2009. For results based on the total sample of national adults, one can say with 95% confidence that the maximum margin of sampling error is ±4 percentage points.

Interviews are conducted with respondents on land-line telephones (for respondents with a land-line telephone) and cellular phones (for respondents who are cell-phone only).

Returning to politics, please tell me whether you consider each of the following to be a winner or a loser in U.S. politics this year. How about -- [RANDOM ORDER]?

Ranked by net winner

	Net "winner"	"Winner"	"Loser"	No opinion
	Pct. Pts.	%	%	%
First Lady Michelle Obama	52	73	21	7
Secretary of State Hillary Clinton	45	70	25	5
Supreme Court Justice, Sonia Sotomayor	33	57	24	19
President Barack Obama	20	58	38	4
Federal Reserve Chairman Ben Bernanke	2	37	35	28
Radio talk show host Glenn Beck	-2	35	37	28
Former Alaska Governor Sarah Palin	-3	46	49	5
Speaker of the House Nancy Pelosi	-11	39	50	11
Senate Democratic Leader Harry Reid	-11	31	42	27
The Republicans in Congress	-14	38	52	10
South Carolina Representative Joe Wilson	-32	29	61	10
South Carolina Governor Mark Sanford	-51	12	63	25
White House Party crashers Tareq and Michaele Salahi	-54	16	70	14

USA Today/Gallup, Dec. 11-13, 2009

In addition to sampling error, question wording and practical difficulties in conducting surveys can introduce error or bias into the findings of public opinion polls.

December 29, 2009
PRIOR TO BOMB SCARE, WORRY ABOUT TERRORISM AT 39% IN U.S.
As of November of this year, public split on Obama's handling of terrorism

by Elizabeth Mendes, Gallup Poll Staff Writer

In a Dec. 11-13 *USA Today*/Gallup poll, conducted just two weeks before the thwarted Christmas Day bomb attempt aboard Northwest Airlines' Detroit-bound flight 253, 39% of Americans reported being very or somewhat worried that they or someone in their family will become a victim of terrorism.

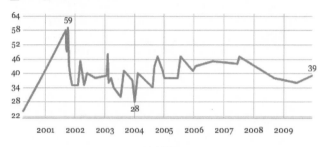

Now, thinking for a moment about terrorism, how worried are you that you or someone in your family will become a victim of terrorism -- very worried, somewhat worried, not too worried, or not worried at all?

Gallup trend since 2000

■ % Very/Somewhat worried

While similar to the 36% who said the same in June of this year, the percentage of Americans expressing worry over being a victim of terrorism is down significantly from the all-time high of 59% in October 2001, just after 9/11. After dropping to a low of 28% in January 2004, the number of Americans who are very or somewhat worried about being a victim of terrorism has fluctuated between 34% and 47% in the years since.

Friday's attempted attack thrust the Obama administration onto the media circuit, with U.S. Homeland Security Secretary Janet Napolitano stating on CNN's *State of the Union* Sunday that "the system worked," although she quickly backtracked on that language the next day. On Monday, President Obama himself took to the airwaves telling Americans to "be assured that we are doing everything in our power to keep you and your family safe and secure." It is too early to tell if the recent incident will have any long-term impact on the Americans' perceptions of the president, but the public—in a Nov. 20-22 *USA Today*/Gallup poll—appeared to be split on Obama's handling of terrorism, with 45% approving and 47% disapproving. The percentage approving of Obama's handling the terror issue had dropped 10 points from the initial 55% Gallup reading in May—mirroring the decline in Obama's overall approval rating from 61% to 49% over the same period.

In the grand scheme of issues facing the nation, Americans express relatively little concern over terrorism compared with their worries about the economy, unemployment, and healthcare. In Gallup's most recent update of its Most Important Problem trend question, 3% named terrorism as the most important problem facing the country. Twenty-six percent mentioned the economy in general terms, while unemployment and healthcare both came in at 16%.

Do you approve or disapprove of the way Barack Obama is handling terrorism?

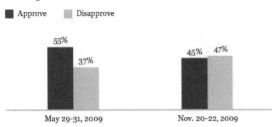

Top Specific Issues Mentioned as Most Important Problem, Dec. 11-13, 2009, USA Today/Gallup poll

	% Mentioning
Economy in general	26
Unemployment/Jobs	16
Healthcare	16
Dissatisfaction with government	9
Federal budget deficit	8
War/Wars in general	6
Lack of money	6
Ethics/Morals	5
Situation/War in Afghanistan	4
Education	3
Terrorism	3
Environment	3

Bottom Line

Americans' worries about terrorism have been at a fairly moderate level prior to the Christmas Day attempt to blow up a U.S.-bound airplane; whether or not the recent terrorism incident will affect those attitudes will become more evident in the weeks to come. Given that the incident has, apparently, sparked tightened security measures at airports and on airplanes, it will also be important to see if air travelers accept these new restrictions as warranted, or view them more as an increased burden or cost of traveling. President Obama spoke out about the incident and assured Americans that all possible precautions were being taken; Gallup tracking in the weeks ahead will also indicate whether or not there has been a possible impact on his standing in the eyes of the public.

December 29, 2009
TOURISM INDUSTRY STILL DEALING WITH CAUTIOUS CONSUMERS
More Americans say they will spend less, not more, in 2010 on vacations

by Lydia Saad, Gallup Poll Senior Editor

While half of Americans foresee no change in their travel spending in 2010 compared to 2009, a larger proportion plan to spend less in the coming year than say they will spend more. That deficit is particularly high relative to air travel and hotel stays. However, even the percentage of Americans saying they will spend less on vacations in general exceeds those saying they will spend more by a slight margin, 27% vs. 22%.

2010 Travel Spending Plans

Now I'd like to ask you about your travel plans for all of 2010 compared to all of 2009. Do you think you will spend more, less, or about the same on – [ITEM]—next year as you did this year?

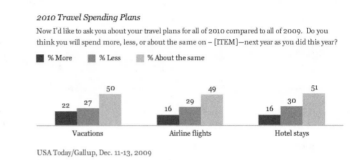

USA Today/Gallup, Dec. 11-13, 2009

In addition to broad changes in vacation spending, nearly 3 out of 10 Americans—29%—plan to spend less on airline flights specifically in 2010 than they did in 2009, while 16% say they will spend more, and about half say they will spend about the same. The same pattern is seen for hotel stays, with 30% planning to spend less and 16% planning to spend more.

According to the recent *USA Today*/Gallup poll conducted Dec. 11-13, there is little variation in Americans' 2010 travel spending intentions according to household income. All income groups—ranging from those earning $75,000 or more, to those earning less than $30,000—plan to spend less rather than more in each travel area.

Some meaningful differences are evident by age, with young adults expressing the greatest likelihood of increasing their travel expenditures. This is seen most clearly when asked about spending on vacations in general, as this is the one area where a higher percentage of those aged 18 to 34 plan to spend more rather than less (30% vs. 25%). By contrast, adults 35 to 54 and 55 and older are more likely to say they will spend less in each area, not more.

Intended Spending on Vacations in 2010 Compared to 2009 -- by Age

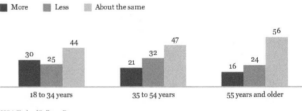

USA Today/Gallup, Dec. 11-13, 2009

The spending intentions of young adults are a bit less robust relative to airline travel and hotel stays than they are for vacations. Roughly equal percentages plan to spend more rather than less on airline travel (24% and 25% respectively), while a slightly higher percentage plan to spend less rather than more on hotel stays (29% vs. 22%). Still, the spending intentions of young adults are greater than those of older adults in all three areas.

Bottom Line

With economic gloom still pervasive across the U.S., it may be no surprise that when Americans are asked to look ahead to their vacation, airline ticket, and hotel spending next year, they are at least slightly more likely to say they will be spending less than they spent this year rather than more.

Intended Spending on Forms of Travel in 2010 Compared to 2009 -- Among Adults Aged 18 to 34

USA Today/Gallup, Dec. 11-13, 2009

These findings somewhat mirror data from the same poll showing 15% of Americans plan to travel over the holidays this year without taking steps to significantly cut back on costs, while 20% are either not travelling or reducing their holiday travel costs because of the economy.

Consumer attitudes about their overall travel spending in 2010 may differ from how they ultimately behave. Indeed, the latest government report on travel and tourism reports a significant rebound in U.S. travel spending in the third quarter of 2009 compared to the same period a year ago, reflecting increases in both business and leisure travel. This coincides with an increase in the U.S. gross domestic product more generally and is likely to extend through the fourth quarter. If so, the current data may simply, but importantly, indicate that Americans remain vigilant about their spending and therefore that airlines, hotels, and resorts must continue pushing major discounts and package deals in order to attract consumers' travel dollars.

Survey Methods

Results are based on telephone interviews with 1,025 national adults, aged 18 and older, conducted Dec. 11-13, 2009. For results based on the total sample of national adults, one can say with 95% confidence that the maximum margin of sampling error is ±4 percentage points.

Interviews are conducted with respondents on land-line telephones (for respondents with a land-line telephone) and cellular phones (for respondents who are cell-phone only).

In addition to sampling error, question wording and practical difficulties in conducting surveys can introduce error or bias into the findings of public opinion polls.

December 30, 2009
CLINTON EDGES OUT PALIN AS MOST ADMIRED WOMAN
Obama easily wins Most Admired Man title

by Jeffrey M. Jones, Gallup Poll Managing Editor

Secretary of State Hillary Clinton continues her reign as the Most Admired Woman in the eyes of Americans, but barely edges out former Alaska Gov. Sarah Palin this year, 16% to 15%. Talk show host Oprah Winfrey and first lady Michelle Obama finish third and fourth, with former Secretary of State Condoleezza Rice, Queen Elizabeth II, former British Prime Minister Margaret Thatcher, and poet Maya Angelou—all regulars on the list—joined by newcomers German Chancellor Angela Merkel and Elin Woods in the top 10.

What woman that you have heard or read about, living today in any part of the world, do you admire most? And who is your second choice?

Combined mentions shown, ranked according to total mentions

	%
1. Hillary Clinton	16
2. Sarah Palin	15
3. Oprah Winfrey	8
4. Michelle Obama	7
5. Condoleezza Rice	2
6. Queen Elizabeth II	2
7. (tie) Margaret Thatcher	1
7. (tie) Maya Angelou	1
9. (tie) Angela Merkel	1
9. (tie) Elin Nordegren Woods	1

Dec. 11-13 USA Today/Gallup poll

Hillary Clinton has now been named Most Admired Woman 14 times since 1993, spanning her career as first lady, New York senator, and now secretary of state. The three times she has not finished first during this time, she earned second place (to Laura Bush in 2001 and to Mother Teresa in 1995 and 1996).

President Barack Obama is the landslide winner among men for the second time, with 30% of Americans naming him as the Most Admired Man this year. Obama won last year with 32%, and both totals are among the highest Gallup has measured for a winner, with George W. Bush's 39% in 2001 remaining the all-time high for Most Admired Man.

Obama's similar performance to last year's is notable considering the declines in his approval and personal favorability ratings since he took office in January.

Bush finished second again this year, after winning the honor from 2001-2007. The rest of the top 10 includes former South African President Nelson Mandela, radio and TV personality Glenn Beck, Pope Benedict XVI, the Rev. Billy Graham, Microsoft founder Bill Gates, Arizona Sen. John McCain, former Presidents George H.W. Bush and Bill Clinton, and golfer Tiger Woods. Ironically, Woods—who has some of the highest personal favorability ratings in Gallup polling history—did not finish in the top 10 until this year, following a personal scandal that caused those ratings to plummet.

What man that you have heard or read about, living today in any part of the world, do you admire most? And who is your second choice?

Combined mentions, ranked according to total mentions

	%
1. Barack Obama	30
2. George W. Bush	4
3. Nelson Mandela	3
4. Glenn Beck	2
5. Pope Benedict XVI	2
6. Rev. Billy Graham	2
7. Bill Gates	2
8. John McCain	1
9. George H.W. Bush	1
10. (tie) Bill Clinton	1
10. (tie) Tiger Woods	1

Dec. 11-13 USA Today/Gallup poll

Americans' choices for Most Admired Man and Woman are influenced by their political leanings. Obama easily wins as Most Admired Man among Democrats and independents, but among Republicans George W. Bush ranks first, with Obama placing second.

Most Admired Man, by Political Party

Percent mentioning in parentheses, ranked based on number of mentions

Democrats	Independents	Republicans
1. Barack Obama (54%)	1. Barack Obama (25%)	1. George W. Bush (11%)
2. Nelson Mandela (4%)	2. Glenn Beck (3%)	2. Barack Obama (7%)
3. Bill Gates (2%)	3. George W. Bush (2%)	3. Pope Benedict XVI (4%)
4. Bill Clinton (2%)	4. Bill Gates (2%)	4. Billy Graham (4%)
5. Tiger Woods (1%)	5. Nelson Mandela (2%)	5. Glenn Beck (3%)
5. Michael Jordan (1%)	5. Pope Benedict XVI (2%)	6. John McCain (3%)

Dec. 11-13 USA Today/Gallup poll

The choices for Most Admired Woman are polarized by party, with Hillary Clinton the dominant leader among Democrats and Sarah Palin among Republicans. The two receive the same percentage of mentions from independents. Clinton still ranks among the leaders among Republicans, while Palin barely registers any mentions from Democrats.

Most Admired Woman, by Political Party

Percent mentioning in parentheses, ranked based on number of mentions

Democrats	Independents	Republicans
1. Hillary Clinton (28%)	1. Sarah Palin (14%)	1. Sarah Palin (34%)
2. Michelle Obama (14%)	2. Hillary Clinton (14%)	2. Hillary Clinton (6%)
3. Oprah Winfrey (13%)	3. Oprah Winfrey (8%)	3. Oprah Winfrey (4%)
4. Maya Angelou (2%)	4. Michelle Obama (3%)	4. Condoleezza Rice (3%)
4. Sonia Sotomayor (2%)	5. Queen Elizabeth II (3%)	5. Michelle Obama (2%)

Dec. 11-13 USA Today/Gallup poll

Graham, Queen Elizabeth II Extend Streaks

Gallup first asked Americans to name, without prompting, which living person they admire most in 1946, with Gen. Douglas MacArthur winning that year. Starting in 1948, Gallup asked separate questions to identify the Most Admired Man and Woman.

Since 1948, Billy Graham and Queen Elizabeth II have been the two individuals with the most top 10 finishes on the Most Admired Man and Woman lists, with Graham doing so a record 53 times and the British monarch achieving that distinction 42 times. Their long histories on the most admired lists are a result of their gaining notoriety at a relatively young age and living a long life.

In fact, Graham was first mentioned in the top 10 in 1955, when he was in his thirties. He has finished in the top 10 every year since 1963 (except 1976 when the question was not asked), and all but one year since 1955. Queen Elizabeth II has not been as regular a top 10 finisher as Graham—appearing five times this decade—but has a longer history of ranking among the most admired, first appearing in 1948 (as Princess Elizabeth).

In addition to Graham and Queen Elizabeth II, this year George H.W. Bush, Bill Clinton, and Nelson Mandela added another top 10 finish as Most Admired Man to their resumes, as did Margaret Thatcher, Oprah Winfrey and Hillary Clinton for Most Admired Woman. Thatcher has the longest current streak of top 10 finishes among women at 31, appearing every year since 1979.

The accompanying table shows the number of top 10 finishes for Most Admired Man and Woman historically.

Most Appearances in Top 10 for Most Admired Man		Most Appearances in Top 10 for Most Admired Woman	
Man	# of times	Woman	# of times
Billy Graham	53	Queen Elizabeth II	42
Ronald Reagan	31	Margaret Thatcher	31
Pope John Paul II	27	Jacqueline Kennedy	28
Jimmy Carter	26	Oprah Winfrey	22
Dwight Eisenhower	21	Mamie Eisenhower	21
Richard Nixon	21	Margaret Chase Smith	20
Harry Truman	20	Nancy Reagan	19
George H.W. Bush	19	Barbara Bush	19
Bill Clinton	18	Hillary Clinton	18
Nelson Mandela	18	Mother Teresa	18
Edward Kennedy	18	Clare Boothe Luce	18
Winston Churchill	17	Betty Ford	17
Colin Powell	16	Mme. Chiang Kai-Shek	17
Douglas MacArthur	15	Helen Keller	17

Survey Methods

Results are based on telephone interviews with 1,025 national adults, aged 18 and older, conducted Dec. 11-13, 2009. For results based on the total sample of national adults, one can say with 95% confidence that the maximum margin of sampling error is ±4 percentage points.

Interviews are conducted with respondents on land-line telephones (for respondents with a land-line telephone) and cellular phones (for respondents who are cell-phone only).

In addition to sampling error, question wording and practical difficulties in conducting surveys can introduce error or bias into the findings of public opinion polls.

Index

al-Maliki, Nouri, 230
American people, confidence in, 324–25
American Recovery and Reinvestment Act, 74–75
    See also stimulus package
Angelou, Maya, admiration of, 475–76
animals
    cloning of, as morally acceptable, 179, 221
    extinction of, worry about, 98, 115–16
    fur of, buying and wearing clothing made of, as morally accept-
        able, 179, 221
        trends in, 180
    medical testing on, as morally acceptable, 179, 221
approval ratings
    of Bush, George W., 3–6, 14–15
    of Congress, 5–6, 59–60, 83–84, 96, 168–69, 217, 295, 336–37,
        362–63, 417, 463–64
        largest month-to-month increases in, 60
        trends in, 470
    of Democrats in Congress, 336
    of Geithner, Timothy, 121–22
    of government agencies, 260–61
    of labor unions, 316
    of NASA, 249–50
    of Obama, Barack, 18–19, 25–26, 38–39, 68–69, 72–73, 82,
        104, 125, 132, 142–43, 191–92, 213–14, 251–52, 269,
        301–2, 334–35, 347–48, 400–401, 425–26, 447–48
        demographics of, 432
        historical context of, 26–27
        Nobel Prize and, 367–68
        quarterly averages, 380–81
        race and, 431–32
        religion and, 359
        states and, 280–81
    of Palin, Sarah, 235
    partisan gap in, historical context of, 132–33
    presidential
        Dow and, 306–9
        midterm elections and, 403–4
        trends in, 470
    of Republicans in Congress, 336
    of Supreme Court, 215, 321–22
    of United Nations, 101
Arafat, Yasser, unfavorability ratings, 374
Arizona, 270
Arkansas, 284, 290
armed forces. *See* military
athletics. *See* sports
attentiveness
    to interrogation techniques, 181, 318
    to Joe Wilson incident, 328–29
    to political news, 350–51
    to union bill, 105
automobile industry
    bailout for, 78–79, 122–23, 204–5
    "Buy American" and, 89
    fuel efficiency standards and, 38, 178
    image of, 288–89
    new-car decision and, 205
    outlook for, 79

sales personnel in, honesty and ethical standards of, 449–51
    stimulus package and, 74–75

baby boomers
    happiness and, 361
    income and, 305
    party identification of, 167
    spending and, 304–5
banks and banking
    bonuses and, 107–8
    confidence in, 150–51, 165–66, 218–19
    image of, 288–89
    language on, 73–74
    Obama, Barack, and, 71
    personnel, honesty and ethical standards of, 450–51
    primary/main bank
        confidence in, 151, 166
        intentions toward, 151
    stimulus package and, 74–75
Barbour, Haley
    qualified to be president, 407
    would support for Republican nomination, 245
    would vote for in 2012, 407
Basic Access Index
    occupations and, 467
    smoking and, 422–23
Beck, Glenn
    admiration of, 475–76
    as political winner, 472–73
beer, 225
beer summit, 269
Benedict XVI, admiration of, 475–76
Bernanke, Ben, 425
    confidence in, 138, 143–44
    as political winner, 472–73
Biden, Joe
    diplomacy and, 62
    favorability ratings, 257–58, 387–88, 408
    as main speaker for Democratic Party, 202
    opinion of, 257
    swine flu and, 161
big business. *See* corporations
bin Laden, Osama, unfavorability ratings, 374
bipartisanship, Obama, Barack, and, 337–38, 400
blacks
    healthcare reform and, 346
    health insurance and, 255
    Obama, Barack, and, 409, 431–32
    party identification of, 455
    priorities and, 389
    race relations and, 392–93
    racism and, 393
    religion and, 455
    Republican Party and, 175–76
    satisfaction with U.S. and, 399
    standard of living and, 162
    Supreme Court and, 170
    unemployment and, 118
Blair, Tony, 86

BMI (body mass index), exercise and, 186
Boehner, John
    as main speaker for Republican Party, 202
    opinion of, 248
bonds, as best investment, 168
Bork, Robert, 195
Brokaw, Tom, 167
Brown, Gordon, 85
    know who he is, 86
Buddhists, identification with, 136
budget, federal
    defense and, 117–18
    Obama, Barack, and, 84, 141, 200, 400
    waste in, as concern, 329–30
budget deficit, federal
    healthcare reform and, 268
    as most important issue, 119, 220, 242, 287, 323, 371, 418,
        474
    Obama, Barack, and, 125, 200, 253, 335
    as priority, 388–89
    stimulus package and, 75–76
    worry about, 222–23
Bush, Barbara, admiration of, 16, 476
Bush, George H. W.
    admiration of, 475–76
    approval ratings, 3–4, 14, 26, 191–92, 269, 348, 401, 426, 447
        Dow and, 307
        first month, 69
        midterm elections and, 403
        partisan gap in, 132–33
        quarterly averages for, 142–43, 252, 380–81
    expectations of, 21
    legacy of, 17
Bush, George W.
    admiration of, 475
    approval ratings, 3–6, 14–15, 26, 191–92, 269, 348, 401, 426,
        447
        Dow and, 307–8
        first month, 69
        mid-March of first year, 104
        midterm elections and, 403
        partisan gap in, 133
        quarterly averages for, 142–43, 252, 380–81
    confidence in, 21–22
    economy and, 16, 138
    education and, 292
    environment and, 148–49
    expectations of, 21
    favorability ratings, 200, 257, 374
    inauguration of, 23
    Iraq War and, 230, 233
    legacy of, 7, 17–18
    as main speaker for Republican Party, 202
    opinion of, 129
    press conference, fact-checking, 12–13
    Supreme Court and, 170
    U.S., satisfaction with, and, 164
Bush, Laura, 4
    admiration of, 15–16

Bush (G.W.) administration
    criminal investigations of, 51–52, 152–53
    Guantanamo Bay prison and, 22
    interrogation techniques and, 318
    Israel and, 10–11
business and industry
    executives
        honesty and ethical standards of, 450–51
        limits on compensation for, 210
    image of, 288–89
    owners
        Basic Access Index score, 467
        emotional health and, 467
        Healthy Behavior Index score, 468
        hours worked per week, 302
        Life Evaluation Index score, 467
        Physical Health Index score, 468
        recommend as career for young man, 279
        recommend as career for young woman, 279
        well-being and, 333, 467
        Work Environment Index score, 468
    political affiliation and, 98–100
    regulation of, 340
        ideology and, 386
    See also corporations

Cabinet (executive), opinions of, 408
California
    gay marriage ruling, 187–88
    health and, 236
Canada
    as most valuable ally, 85
    opinion of, 64
cancer
    as most urgent health problem, 428
    travel outside U.S. for treatment of, 176–77
capital punishment. See death penalty
cars. See automobile industry
Carter, Jimmy
    admiration of, 476
    approval ratings, 3–4, 14, 26, 191–92, 269, 348, 401, 426,
        447
        Dow and, 306
        first month, 69
        midterm elections and, 403
        quarterly averages for, 142–43, 252, 380–81
    legacy of, 17
Castro, Fidel, unfavorability ratings, 374
Catholics
    abortion and, 174
    church attendance and, 134–35
    clerical ethics and, 450
    identification with, 135, 471
    morality and, 120–21
    Obama, Barack, and, 159–60, 359
    party identification of, 359
    states and, 278
CDC (Centers for Disease Control and Prevention), approval rat-
    ings, 260–61

Cheney, Dick
    Bush, George W., and, 13, 17
    favorability ratings, 257, 387–88
    as main speaker for Republican Party, 202
    opinion of, 129–30
Chiang Kai-Shek, Madame, admiration of, 476
children
    extramarital, as morally acceptable, 120–21, 179, 221
    in home, swine flu worries and, 155, 161
    homosexuals and, 188
    number in classroom, 301
    worry and, 457–58
China
    death penalty and, 368
    as economic leader, 57–59
    opinion of, 64
    worry about, 131–32
chiropractors, honesty and ethical standards of, 450–51
Christianity, identification with, 135
Christmas, spending on, 419–20, 464–65
    demographics of, 419
    forecast versus actual, 465
Chrysler, 204–5
church, church attendance
    Catholicism and, 120–21, 134–35
    clerical ethics and, 450
    confidence in, 218–19
    evolution and, 50
    frequency of, 112
    homosexuals in military and, 199
    ideological trends and, 233
    membership in, 471
    Obama, Barack, and, 159
    party identification and, 113, 193
    Republican Party and, 176
Churchill, Winston, admiration of, 476
CIA (Central Intelligence Agency)
    approval ratings, 260
    interrogation techniques and, 181
cigarettes. *See* smoking
Citibank, 73
civil unions. *See* gay marriage
clergy, honesty and ethical standards of, 450–51
clerical workers
    Basic Access Index score, 467
    emotional health and, 467
    Healthy Behavior Index score, 468
    Life Evaluation Index score, 467
    Obama, Barack, and, 194
    Physical Health Index score, 468
    well-being and, 333, 467
    Work Environment Index score, 468
climate change. *See* global warming
Clinton, Bill, 188
    admiration of, 475
    approval ratings, 3–4, 14, 26, 191–92, 269, 348, 401, 426, 447
        Dow and, 307
        first month, 69
        mid-March of first year, 104
        midterm elections and, 403

partisan gap in, 133
        quarterly averages for, 142–43, 252, 380–81
    favorability ratings, 200, 257
    legacy of, 17
    U.S., satisfaction with, and, 164
Clinton, Hillary Rodham
    admiration of, 475–76
    approval ratings, 15–16
    diplomacy and, 62, 86–88, 125, 159–60
    favorability ratings, 373, 408
    image of, 13–14
    as main speaker for Democratic Party, 202
    Obama, Barack, and, 1
    as political winner, 472–73
cloning, as morally acceptable, 179, 221
college
    costs, as most important issue, 148, 425
    teachers, honesty and ethical standards of, 450–51
    See also education
Colorado
    economy and, 274
    health and, 296
    politics and, 271
    stress and, 298
community, trust in, 443–44
commuting costs, as most important issue, 148
computer industry
    image of, 288–89
    recommend as career for young man, 279–80
    recommend as career for young woman, 279–80
Congress
    AIG bonuses and, 113–14
    approval ratings, 59–60, 83–84, 96, 168–69, 217, 295, 322, 336–37, 362–63, 417, 463–64
        largest month-to-month increases in, 60
        midterm elections and, 404
        trends in, 470
        yearly averages, 169
    confidence in, 218–19, 268, 324
    economy and, 16, 31, 60, 291
    healthcare and, 261–62
    healthcare reform and, 268, 281–82, 320, 410, 436, 461–62, 464
    investigation of interrogation techniques and, 152
    labor and, 105
    members of, honesty and ethical standards of, 449–51
    as most important issue, 220, 243, 288
    Wilson, Joe, and, 328–29
    See also Democrats in Congress; Republicans in Congress
Congressional elections, generic ballot, 264, 363–64, 397–98, 411–12, 459–60
Connecticut, 236
conservatives
    abortion and, 174
    attentiveness to budget and, 84–85
    auto bailout and, 78
    Catholics and, 159
    Cuba and, 150
    energy efficiency and, 448
    gay marriage and, 187

energy
    alternative, 100–101
    Bush, George W., and, 7
    economy and, 108–9
    efficiency, motivation for, 448
    as most important issue, 323
    nuclear, support for, 110–11
    Obama, Barack, and, 335, 439
    prices, as most important issue, 148
    as priority, 19, 388–89
    See also fuel; gasoline; oil
engineers, engineering
    honesty and ethical standards of, 449–51
    recommend as career for young man, 279–80
enjoyment. *See* happiness
Ensign, John, 221
environment
    Bush, George W., and, 7
    Copenhagen treaty, 460–61
    economy and, 108–9, 461
    energy and, 101
    energy efficiency and, 448
    fuel efficiency standards and, 178
    ideological trends and, 233
    as most important issue, 243, 323, 474
    Obama, Barack, and, 148–49, 335
    outlook for, 146–47
    quality of, 147
    satisfaction with, 171
    worry about, 98, 115–16
    See also global warming
EPA (Environmental Protection Agency), approval ratings, 260
ethics
    approval ratings, 38
    as most important issue, 119, 220, 243, 288, 371, 418, 474
    Obama, Barack, and, 44
    rate honesty and ethical standards of people in different fields [list], 449–51
    See also morality; values
European Union, as economic leader, 58
euthanasia. *See* doctor-assisted suicide
evolution, 49–50
executive branch. *See* president/presidency
exercise
    amount of, 402–3
    participation in, last week, 52–53, 185–86
        depression and, 402
        emotional health and, 402
        obesity and, 401
        states and, 290
        well-being and, 402
extinction, worry about, 98, 115–16
extramarital affairs, as morally acceptable, 179, 221

family(ies), as most important issue, 220, 243, 288, 371
family values. *See* morality; values
farms, farming
    Basic Access Index score, 467
    emotional health and, 467

Healthy Behavior Index score, 468
    image of, 288–89
    Life Evaluation Index score, 467
    Obama, Barack, and, 194
    Physical Health Index score, 468
    well-being and, 333, 467
    Work Environment Index score, 468
FBI (Federal Bureau of Investigation), approval ratings, 260
FDA (Food and Drug Administration), approval ratings, 260
federal government. *See* budget, federal; government
Federal Reserve Board, approval ratings, 260–61
financial situation, personal
    able to make a major purchase, 309–10
    can buy what you need, 226, 310
    have cut back spending, 54–55, 465–66, 474–75
    healthcare costs and, 344
    as most important issue, 119
    most important issue in, 148, 425
    smoking and, 126
    stimulus package and, 256
    worry about, 41–42, 80–82, 119, 147–48
        layoffs and, 92–93
        stimulus package and, 51
    See also income; money; spending
fishers
    Basic Access Index score, 467
    emotional health and, 467
    Healthy Behavior Index score, 468
    Life Evaluation Index score, 467
    Obama, Barack, and, 194
    Physical Health Index score, 468
    well-being and, 467
    Work Environment Index score, 468
Florida, 35, 271
flu. *See* swine flu
food
    ate fruits & veggies last week, 52–53
        states and, 290
    ate healthy yesterday, 52–53
        states and, 290
Ford, Betty, admiration of, 476
Ford, Gerald
    approval ratings, 3–4, 14, 26, 426
        decline in, 380
        first to second quarter change, 143
        midterm elections and, 403
    legacy of, 17
Ford Motors, 205
foreclosure relief, 71, 75, 77–78
foreign affairs/policy
    Bush, George W., and, 7
    Cuba and, 149–50
    as most important issue, 220
    Obama, Barack, and, 62, 125, 200, 244, 253, 282–83
    worry about, 131–32
foreign aid
    as most important issue, 220, 323
    to Palestinian Authority, 87
foreign trade, approval ratings, 62–63

foresters
  Basic Access Index score, 467
  emotional health and, 467
  Healthy Behavior Index score, 468
  Life Evaluation Index score, 467
  Obama, Barack, and, 194
  Physical Health Index score, 468
  well-being and, 333, 467
  Work Environment Index score, 468
France, opinion of, 64
Franken, Al, 156
fuel, prices, as most important issue, 220, 323
fuel efficiency standards, approval ratings, 38, 178
Fuhrman, Mark, unfavorability ratings, 374

gambling, as morally acceptable, 120–21, 179, 221
  trends in, 180
Gardner, Timothy, 126
gasoline
  industry, image of, 288–89
  prices
    as most important issue, 148
    predictions for, 214
    worry about, 222–23
  See also energy; oil
Gates, Bill
  admiration of, 475–76
  favorability ratings, 408
Gates, Henry, 269
Gates, Robert, 319
gay marriage, 187–88
  factors affecting, 190–91
  ideological trends and, 233
  See also homosexuals and homosexuality
Geithner, Timothy, 54, 121–22
  AIG bonuses and, 113–14
  confidence in, 138, 143–44
gender
  abortion and, 174
  Afghanistan and, 414
  alcohol and, 225
  auto bailout and, 78
  Christmas spending and, 419
  Clinton, Hillary, and, 13
  exercise and, 186
  extramarital affairs and, 221
  foreign trade and, 63
  gun control and, 367
  healthcare reform and, 321, 346
  health habits and, 53
  health insurance and, 255
  homosexuals in military and, 199
  hours worked per week and, 303
  ideology and, 209
  Internet use and, 2–3
  job optimism and, 412
  media and, 359
  money worries and, 81, 93
  nuclear power and, 110

Obama, Barack, and, 26, 432
  party identification and, 164–65, 205–6, 314
  Republican Party and, 175–76
  Sotomayor, Sonia, and, 189, 240
  spending and, 383, 446–47, 454
  Supreme Court and, 169–70
  trust and, 444
  United Nations and, 102
  veteran status and, 184
  well-being and, 362
  worry and, 457
General Motors, 204–5
generational groups
  party identification of, 167
  spending and, 304–5
Generation X
  income and, 305
  party identification of, 167
  spending and, 305
Generation Y. See Millennials
geographic region
  alcohol and, 225
  auto bailout and, 78, 205
  "Buy American" and, 89
  Canada and, 86
  Christmas spending and, 419
  crime and, 370
  foreign trade and, 63
  Great Britain and, 86
  Guantanamo Bay prison and, 463
  gun control and, 367
  healthcare reform and, 321, 346
  health insurance and, 255
  homosexuals in military and, 199
  immigration and, 275
  job optimism and, 412
  Mexican drug violence and, 130
  money worries and, 93
  Obama, Barack, and, 432
  party identification and, 314
  Republican Party and, 175–76
  spending and, 446, 454
  state government and, 326
  swine flu worries and, 155, 161, 209
  See also states
Georgia, 271
Germany
  as most valuable ally, 85
  opinion of, 64
Gingrich, Newt
  as main speaker for Republican Party, 202
  qualified to be president, 407
  would support for Republican nomination, 245
  would vote for in 2012, 407
Ginsburg, Ruth Bader, 169, 195
Giuliani, Rudy, favorability ratings, 374
global warming
  Copenhagen treaty, 460–61
  economy and, 461

ideology and, 386
Obama, Barack, and, 439
seriousness of, 97–98
worry about, 97–98, 115–16
See also environment
Gore, Al
environment and, 98
favorability ratings, 257, 387–88
government
activity level of, 340–41
automobile industry and, 204–5
as biggest problem in healthcare, 344
business regulation and, 340
ideology and, 386
confidence in, 231, 324
education and, 301
executive compensation limits and, 210
healthcare and, 268, 415–16
healthcare reform and, 331, 420–21
health insurance and, 265
hours worked per week, 302
idealism in, Obama, Barack, and, 276–77
ideological trends and, 233
image of, 288–89
insurance sponsored by, 396
mechanisms of, Obama, Barack, and, 276–77
as most important issue, 119, 220, 243, 288, 323, 371, 418, 474
Obama, Barack, and, 44, 258
political affiliation and, 98–100
power of, 99–100, 140, 253–54, 341
as biggest threat, 144–45
projects funded by, in stimulus package, 46–47, 74–75
role of, 99, 140, 340
spending by, 141, 253–54
swine flu and, 311
tobacco regulation and, 216
tone of, 40–41, 276–77
values and, 352
waste in spending, perceptions of, 329–30
worry about, 222–23
governors, state
honesty and ethical standards of, 450–51
waste in spending perceptions and, 330
Graham, Billy, admiration of, 475–76
Great Britain. *See* United Kingdom
Greatest Generation. *See* seniors
greed, as biggest problem in healthcare, 344
greenhouse effect. *See* global warming
Greenspan, Alan, 143
grocery industry, image of, 288–89
Guantanamo Bay prison, 22–23
approval ratings, 38
closure of, support for, 196–97, 462–63
as priority, 19
gun(s)
ideological trends and, 233
ownership of, 366–67, 377
gun control
demographics of, 367
handgun ban, 366

ideology and, 386
laws should be more/less strict, 366–67
Obama, Barack, and, 377–78

Hamas, 10
happiness, 298–99, 453
age and, 361
exercise and, 186
Harter, Jim, 52, 172
hate-crime laws, 188
Hawaii
health and, 95, 236, 284, 290, 296, 298
politics and, 270, 280
health, well-being, 235–36
definition of, 96
habits, 52–53
income and, 126
most urgent problem in, 428–29
occupations and, 468
satisfaction with, 172
smoking and, 421–23
state rankings, 95–96, 290
swine flu, 155–56, 161
trends in, 236
healthcare
access to
as biggest problem in healthcare, 344, 428
reform and, 263, 266, 420–21
biggest problem in, 344
Bush, George W., and, 7
confidence in, 211, 218–19
costs
as biggest problem in healthcare, 344, 428
as most important issue, 148, 243, 288, 371, 425
reform and, 263, 266–67, 331, 333, 344, 381–82
satisfaction with, 343–44, 424
worry about, 222–23
coverage
ideological trends and, 233
rated, 423–24
reform and, 241, 344, 381–82
responsibility for, 353–54, 415–16
current status of, 267
industry, image of, 288–89
as major problem, 344
mammogram guidelines, views of, 430–31
as most important issue, 119, 220, 243, 287–88, 322–23, 371, 418, 474
Obama, Barack, and, 252–53, 282–83, 335, 400, 437, 439
as priority, 19, 388–89
quality of
insurance type and, 313
rated, 424
reform and, 266, 333, 344, 381–82
satisfaction with, 343–44
recommend as career for young man, 279–80
recommend as career for young woman, 279–80
satisfaction with, 267
travel outside U.S. for, 176–77
waste in, as biggest problem in healthcare, 344

Cuba and, 150
energy efficiency and, 448
foreign trade and, 63
gay marriage and, 187
Guantanamo Bay prison and, 22
gun control and, 367
homosexuality and, 190
homosexuals in military and, 199
identification with, 208–9
Iran and, 56
Israel and, 10
Jews and, 160
media and, 358–59
morality and, 171
Obama, Barack, and, 1, 26, 69, 432
party identification and, 193, 314–15
Republican Party and, 176
states and, 286–87
stem cell research and, 94
Supreme Court and, 322
trends in, 232–34, 385–86
values and, 352
See also political affiliation
immigrants, immigration
Bush, George W., and, 7
religion and, 136
as most important issue, 220, 288, 323
ideological trends and, 233
levels of, 275–76
as good/bad thing for country, 275
healthcare reform and, 331, 420
remittances and, 342–43
as biggest problem in healthcare, 344
ideology and, 386
income
ability to make major purchase and, 310
"Buy American" and, 89
Christmas spending and, 419
consumer confidence and, 8
economy and, 41, 110
executive compensation limits and, 210
foreign trade and, 63
generation and, 305
healthcare reform and, 321, 346–47
health habits and, 53
health insurance and, 255
hours worked per week and, 303
identity theft and, 376
Internet use and, 2–3
job optimism and, 413
media and, 359
money worries and, 81, 92
nuclear power and, 110–11
Obama, Barack, and, 69
party identification and, 314
quality of life and, 452
Republican Party and, 176
saving versus spending and, 154
smoking and, 126, 422

spending and, 55, 103, 181–82, 226–27, 250–51, 309–10, 338–39, 453, 465
stimulus package and, 256
taxes and, 137, 297
travel plans and, 183, 466
trust and, 443
See also financial situation, personal; money; wages
income tax
fairness of, 137
healthcare reform and, 241
lower-income people pay their fair share, 139
middle-income people pay their fair share, 139
Obama, Barack, and, 297–98
opinion of, 136–37
upper-income people pay their fair share, 139–40
worry about, 222–23
See also tax cuts; taxes
independents
Afghanistan and, 71, 107, 247, 319–20, 349, 414, 434–35, 439, 442–43, 446
age and, 166
AIG bonuses and, 108
attentiveness to budget and, 84–85
attentiveness to political news and, 351
auto bailout and, 78, 123
banks and, 73–74
Bernanke, Ben, and, 143–44
Biden, Joe, and, 387
bipartisanship and, 338
Boehner, John, and, 248
Bush, George W., and, 6, 14, 129
Bush, Laura, and, 15
business regulation and, 340
Canada and, 85
Cheney, Dick, and, 129–30
church attendance and, 113
Clinton, Hillary, and, 373
composition of, 193, 354–55
Congress and, 5, 60, 83, 96, 169, 217, 295, 362, 417, 449, 463
criminal investigation of Bush administration and, 52
Cuba and, 150
death penalty and, 369
defense spending and, 117–18
Democratic Party and, 227–28
Democrats in Congress and, 336
economy and, 58, 76, 110, 138, 327–28, 350
election of 2010 and, 264, 363, 411–12, 460
environment and, 97, 147, 149, 460–61
executive branch and, 324–25
executive compensation limits and, 210
extramarital affairs and, 221
foreign trade and, 63
fuel efficiency standards and, 178
Gates, Robert, and, 408
Geithner, Timothy, and, 122
gender and, 164–65
government and, 341
Great Britain and, 85
greatest president and, 49

Guantanamo Bay prison and, 22, 197, 462
gun control and, 367
healthcare confidence and, 211, 390
healthcare reform and, 259–60, 262–63, 321, 378–79, 410–11,
    436–37
health insurance responsibility and, 353, 416
homosexuals in military and, 199
ideology and, 208–9, 232, 386
image of parties and, 345
immigration and, 275
international affairs and, 131
interrogation techniques and, 181, 318
Iraq and, 107, 230, 247
Israel and, 10
job creation and, 47
job loss and, 48
job outlook and, 441
judicial branch and, 324–25
labor and, 105, 316
legislative branch and, 324–25
Limbaugh, Rush, and, 43–44
media and, 43, 358
Middle East and, 198
Mohammed trial and, 435–36
most admired man and, 476
most admired woman and, 476
Nobel Peace Prize and, 384
No Child Left Behind and, 293
nuclear power and, 110–11
Obama, Barack, and, 6, 20–21, 24, 26, 38, 43, 69, 72–73, 80,
    82, 104, 125, 127, 132, 149, 214, 253–54, 259,
    276–77, 283, 298, 350, 368, 373, 384, 406, 432, 439
Obama, Michelle, and, 127
Palestinian state and, 198
Palin, Sarah, and, 234, 375
party identification of, 314–15
party inclination of, 25
    states and, 29–31
Pelosi, Nancy, and, 248
priorities and, 19, 388–89
religion and, 113
Republican Party and, 227–28
Republicans in Congress and, 336
satisfaction of, 37, 91
satisfaction with U.S. and, 133, 164, 201, 372
Sotomayor, Sonia, and, 189, 196, 239
stem cell research and, 94
stimulus package and, 9, 31, 46, 51, 60, 256, 291
Supreme Court and, 215, 322
TARP funds and, 16
taxes and, 137, 298
terrorism and, 327, 440
threatening countries and, 213
threats to country and, 144
tobacco regulation and, 216
tone of D.C. and, 40, 276
unemployment and, 118
United Nations and, 102
values and, 352

waste in spending and, 329–30
Wilson, Joe, and, 329
India, opinion of, 64
Indiana, 271
industry. *See* business and industry
inflation
    as most important issue, 119, 148, 323, 425
    stimulus package and, 76
influenza. *See* swine flu
infrastructure, as priority, 19
installation personnel
    Basic Access Index score, 467
    emotional health and, 467
    Healthy Behavior Index score, 468
    Life Evaluation Index score, 467
    Obama, Barack, and, 194
    Physical Health Index score, 468
    well-being and, 333, 467
    Work Environment Index score, 468
insurance salespeople, honesty and ethical standards of, 450–51
interest rates, as most important issue, 148
international issues. *See* foreign affairs/policy
Internet
    industry, image of, 288–89
    shopping, swine flu and, 155, 161
    time spent on, 2–3
interrogation techniques
    approval ratings, 38, 181
    investigation of, 152–53, 318
    as not/justified, 152
investments
    as most important issue, 148, 425
    retirement, 145–46
    stocks as, 90
    which type is best, 168
investors, optimism of, 27–28, 70, 111–12, 157–58, 207, 229,
    308–9, 390–91
Iowa, 298
Iran
    death penalty and, 368
    direct diplomacy with, 55–56
    opinion of, 64, 212
    protests in, 214
    as threat, 212
    worry about, 131–32
Iraq
    opinion of, 64–65, 212
    security situation in, 230
    as threat, 212
Iraq War
    Bush, George W., and, 4, 12
    how things are going, 246–47
    ideological trends and, 233–34
    as mistake, 106, 246
    as most important issue, 119, 220, 243, 288, 323, 371, 418
    Obama, Barack, and, 72, 253, 335, 400
    opinion of, 106
    as priority, 19, 388–89
    timeframe of, 230

withdrawal from, 400
worry about, 131–32
IRS (Internal Revenue Service), approval ratings, 260
Islam. *See* Muslims
Israel
as most valuable ally, 85
Obama, Barack, and, 360
opinion of, 64, 86–88, 213
as threat, 212
U.S. role in, 10–11
worry about, 131–32
See also Middle East

Jackson, Jesse, favorability ratings, 374
Japan
as economic leader, 58
as most valuable ally, 85
opinion of, 64
Jews
identification with, 135
Obama, Barack, and, 159–60, 359–60
party identification of, 359
states and, 278
jobs
best way to create new jobs, 441
companies are hiring/letting go, 243, 372, 394
good or bad time to find a quality job, 115, 372, 394, 412–13
how many hours worked per week, 302–3
know anyone who has lost job in last six months, 48
money worries and, 92–93
Obama, Barack, and, 71, 439
outlook, 28–29, 39–40, 67–68, 88, 441
in retirement, 146
satisfaction with, 285–304
security
satisfaction with, 303
worry about, 285
states and, 35–36
stimulus package and, 9, 74, 393, 441
worry about, 47–48, 458
trends in, 286
See also employment; unemployment
John Paul II, pope
admiration of, 476
favorability ratings, 374
Johnson, Lyndon B., approval ratings, 3–4, 14, 26, 426
first to second quarter change, 143
midterm elections and, 403
joint replacement, travel outside U.S. for treatment of, 176–77
Jones, Jeff, 15
Jordan, Michael, admiration of, 476
journalists
honesty and ethical standards of, 450–51
See also media
Judaism. *See* Jews
judicial branch
confidence in, 324
as most important issue, 323
See also criminal justice system; Supreme Court

Justice Department, as investigator of interrogation techniques, 152

Kansas, 270
Keller, Helen, admiration of, 476
Kennedy, Edward, admiration of, 476
Kennedy, Jacqueline, admiration of, 476
Kennedy, John F.
approval ratings, 3–4, 26, 191, 348, 401, 426, 447
midterm elections and, 403
quarterly averages for, 142–43, 252, 380–81
as greatest president, 48–49
Kentucky, health and, 95, 236, 284, 290, 298
Kerry, John, 179
Killefer, Nancy, 42, 44
Kim, Seokho, 136

labor (organized; unions)
approval ratings, 316
as biggest threat, 144–45
card check and, 105
confidence in, 218–19
education and, 301
ideological trends and, 233
ideology and, 386
influence of, 317
members, benefits to, 317
Obama, Barack, and, 194–95
outlook for, 317
as priority, 19
Latinos/as. *See* Hispanics
Latter-Day Saints. *See* Mormons
law enforcement. *See* police and police officers
lawyer(s)
honesty and ethical standards of, 450–51
image of, 288–89
leadership
as most important issue, 220, 243, 288
Obama, Barack, and, 244, 258, 341–42
Leahy, Patrick, 51–52
legislative branch, confidence in, 324
Lewinsky, Monica, unfavorability ratings, 374
liberals
abortion and, 174
attentiveness to budget and, 84–85
auto bailout and, 78
Catholics and, 159
Cuba and, 150
energy efficiency and, 448
gay marriage and, 187
Guantanamo Bay prison and, 22
gun control and, 367
homosexuality and, 190
homosexuals in military and, 199
identification with, 208–9
Israel and, 10
Jews and, 160
media and, 359

Republican Party and, 175–76
Sotomayor, Sonia, and, 189, 240
trust and, 444
United Nations and, 102
veteran status and, 185
well-being and, 362
mental health
exercise and, 402
smoking and, 422
Merkel, Angela, admiration of, 475
Mexico
drug violence in, as concern, 130–31
opinion of, 64
as threat, 212
worry about, 131–32
Michigan
economy and, 33, 35, 273–74
health and, 236
Middle East
as most important issue, 323
Obama, Barack, and, 200
outlook for, 197–98
worry about, 131–32
See also Iraq War
Miers, Harriet, 189, 195
military
commanders should advise publicly/privately, 365
confidence in, 218–19
homosexuals and, 188, 199
as most important issue, 323
Millennials
income and, 305
party identification of, 167
spending and, 305
miners
emotional health and, 467
Healthy Behavior Index score, 468
Life Evaluation Index score, 467
Obama, Barack, and, 194
Physical Health Index score, 468
well-being and, 467
Work Environment Index score, 468
Minnesota, 95, 293
minorities, racial. See blacks; Hispanics; nonwhites; race
Mississippi
economy and, 274
health and, 95, 236, 293, 296
politics and, 270, 286
religion and, 32, 278
moderates
abortion and, 174
attentiveness to budget and, 84–85
auto bailout and, 78
Catholics and, 159
Cuba and, 150
energy efficiency and, 448
gay marriage and, 187
Guantanamo Bay prison and, 22
gun control and, 367
homosexuality and, 190

homosexuals in military and, 199
identification with, 208–9
Israel and, 10
Jews and, 160
media and, 359
morality and, 171
Obama, Barack, and, 26, 69, 432
party identification of, 208–9
Republican Party and, 176
states and, 286–87
stem cell research and, 94
trends in, 232, 385–86
values and, 352
Mohammed, Khalid Sheikh, 435–36
money
able to make a major purchase, 309–10
energy efficiency and, 448
as most important issue, 148, 220, 242, 287, 323, 371, 418, 425, 474
worry about, 226, 310
See also financial situation, personal; income; wages
Montana
health and, 284, 290, 299
politics and, 270
morality
Catholics and, 120–21
healthcare reform and, 331
as most important issue, 119, 220, 243, 288, 323, 371, 418, 474
Republican Party and, 179–80
satisfaction with, 171
stem cell research and, 94
See also ethics; values
Mormons
Obama, Barack, and, 159–60, 359
party identification of, 359
states and, 278–79
mortgage aid, 77–78
movies, industry, overall view of, 288–89
Muslims
identification with, 136
Obama, Barack, and, 159–60
mutual funds. See stocks

Napolitano, Janet, 231
NASA (National Aeronautics and Space Administration), approval ratings, 249–50, 260
national security
as most important issue, 220, 243, 323
See also defense
Nebraska, 270–71, 274
Neftzger, Amy, 53
neighbors, trust in, 443–44
Netanyahu, Benjamin, 198
Nevada, 271, 274
New Hampshire, 32
New Jersey, 299
New Mexico
economy and, 273
health and, 95, 236, 293
news, political, following, 350–51

spending and, 253–54
stem cell research and, 93
stimulus package and, 50, 393
Supreme Court and, 169–70, 195
taxes and, 137
terrorism and, 439
tone of D.C. and, 40–41, 276–77
understands problems Americans face in daily lives, 258, 342
U.S., satisfaction with, and, 37–38, 133, 163
Wilson, Joe, and, 328–29
Obama, Michelle
admiration of, 475–76
favorability ratings, 127, 387
as political winner, 472–73
Obama administration
automobile industry and, 178
economy and, 148, 256
energy and, 100
outlook for accomplishments, 400
obesity, 296–97
exercise and, 401
as most urgent health problem, 428
See also weight
occupations
emotional health and, 467–68
honesty and ethical standards of, 449–51
how many hours worked per week, 302–3
well-being and, 333–34, 466–68
O'Connor, Sandra Day, 169
office workers, Obama, Barack, and, 194
Ohio, 236
oil
industry, image of, 288–89
prices, as most important issue, 148, 220
See also energy; fuel; gasoline
Olmert, Ehud, 10
Oregon, 274

Pakistan
death penalty and, 368
opinion of, 64, 213
as threat, 212
Palestinian Arabs, worry about, 131–32
Palestinian Authority, opinion of, 64, 86–88
Palestinian state, support for, 198
Palestinian territories
opinion of, 213
as threat, 212
Palin, Sarah
admiration of, 475–76
approval ratings, 235
favorability ratings, 245, 374–75
qualified to be president, 407
would support for Republican nomination, 245
would vote for in 2012, 234–35, 407
parents
Christmas spending and, 419
No Child Left Behind and, 292–93
satisfaction with schools, 299–300

school improvement and, 301
worry and, 457–58
parochial schools, attendance at, 300
partisan gap
age and, 167, 184
gender and, 205–6
generational group and, 167
U.S., satisfaction with, and, 163–64
veteran status and, 184
party identification, 236–37, 315, 354–55
age and, 166–67
Democratic Party and, 24–25, 156–57
gender and, 164–65, 205–6
ideology and, 314–15
marital status and, 237–38
midterm elections and, 404–5
Obama, Barack, and, 1
religion and, 455–56
Republican Party and, 175–76
states and, 270–71
veteran status and, 184
See also political affiliation
Pawlenty, Tim
qualified to be president, 407
would support for Republican nomination, 245
would vote for in 2012, 407
Pelosi, Nancy, 295, 445
interrogation techniques and, 181
as main speaker for Democratic Party, 202
opinion of, 248
as political loser, 472–73
Perot, Ross, favorability ratings, 374
pharmaceutical industry
as biggest problem in healthcare, 344
confidence in, 211
image of, 288–89
pharmacists, honesty and ethical standards of, 449–51
plant species, extinction of, worry about, 98, 115–16
plastic surgery, travel outside U.S. for treatment of, 176–77
police and police officers
confidence in, 218–19
honesty and ethical standards of, 449–51
political affiliation
Afghanistan and, 70–71, 107, 247, 319–20, 349, 414, 434–35, 439, 442–43, 446
AIG bonuses and, 108
attentiveness to budget and, 84–85
attentiveness to political news and, 351
auto bailout and, 78, 123
banks and, 73–74
Bernanke, Ben, and, 143–44
Biden, Joe, and, 387
bipartisanship and, 338
Boehner, John, and, 248
Bush, George W., and, 14, 129
business regulation and, 340
Canada and, 85
Cheney, Dick, and, 129–30
Clinton, Hillary, and, 373
Congress and, 5, 60, 83, 96, 169, 217, 295, 362, 417, 449, 463

criminal investigation of Bush administration and, 52
Cuba and, 150
death penalty and, 369
defense spending and, 117–18
Democrats in Congress and, 336
economy and, 58, 76–77, 98–100, 110, 138, 222, 350
election of 2010 and, 264
environment and, 97, 147, 149, 460–61
executive branch and, 324–25
executive compensation limits and, 210
extramarital affairs and, 221
foreign trade and, 63
fuel efficiency standards and, 178
Gates, Robert, and, 408
Geithner, Timothy, and, 122
government and, 341
Great Britain and, 85
greatest president and, 49
Guantanamo Bay prison and, 22, 197, 462
gun control and, 367
healthcare confidence and, 211
healthcare reform and, 259–60, 262–63, 282, 321, 378–79, 410–11, 416, 436–37
health insurance responsibility and, 353, 416
homosexuals in military and, 199
ideology and, 386
image of parties and, 203, 345
immigration and, 275
international affairs and, 131
interrogation techniques and, 181, 318
Iran and, 56
Iraq and, 107, 230, 247
Israel and, 10
job creation and, 47
job loss and, 48
job outlook and, 441
judicial branch and, 324–25
labor and, 105, 316
legislative branch and, 324–25
Limbaugh, Rush, and, 43–44
media and, 43, 358
Middle East and, 198
Mohammed trial and, 435–36
morality and, 171
most admired man and, 476
most admired woman and, 476
Nobel Peace Prize and, 384
No Child Left Behind and, 293
nuclear power and, 110–11
Obama, Barack, and, 20–21, 24, 26, 38, 43, 69, 72–73, 80, 82, 104, 125, 127, 132, 149, 214, 253–54, 259, 276–77, 283, 298, 350, 368, 373, 384, 406, 432, 439
Obama, Michelle, and, 127
Palestinian state and, 198
Palin, Sarah, and, 234, 375
Pelosi, Nancy, and, 248
postal services and, 57
priorities and, 19, 388–89
religion and, 113, 359

Republicans in Congress and, 336
satisfaction by, 37, 91
satisfaction with U.S. and, 133, 164, 201, 372, 399
Sotomayor, Sonia, and, 189, 196, 239
states and, 29–31
stem cell research and, 94
stimulus package and, 9, 31, 46, 51, 60, 256, 291
Supreme Court and, 215, 322
TARP funds and, 16
taxes and, 137, 298
terrorism worries and, 440
threatening countries and, 213
threats to country and, 144
tobacco regulation and, 216
tone of D.C. and, 40, 276
unemployment and, 118
United Nations and, 102
values and, 352
waste in spending and, 329–30
Wilson, Joe, and, 329
See also party identification; *specific party*
politicians
confidence in, 324–25
as most important issue, 220, 243, 288
winners/losers of 2009, 472–73
pollution. *See* environment
polygamy, as morally acceptable, 179, 221
poor people. *See* poverty
Postal Service, reducing services, 56–57, 223–24
Potter, John E., 223
poverty
healthcare reform and, 331
as most important issue, 323
Powell, Colin, admiration of, 476
pre-existing condition barriers, as biggest problem in healthcare, 344
president/presidency
approval ratings
Dow and, 306–9
midterm elections and, 403–4
trends in, 470
confidence in, 218–19, 324
greatest, 48–49
honeymoon period with, 142–43, 192
presidential candidates, fuel efficiency standards and, 178
prisoners, from Guantanamo Bay
move to U.S., 462–63
in your state, 196–97
private schools, attendance at, 300
production. *See* manufacturing workers
professionals
Basic Access Index score, 467
emotional health and, 467
Healthy Behavior Index score, 468
Life Evaluation Index score, 467
Obama, Barack, and, 194
Physical Health Index score, 468
well-being and, 333, 467
Work Environment Index score, 468
prosperity. *See* economic conditions

Protestants, Protestantism
abortion and, 174
church attendance and, 134–35
clerical ethics and, 450
identification with, 135, 471
Obama, Barack, and, 159–60, 359
party identification of, 359
states and, 278
psychiatrists, honesty and ethical standards of, 450–51
public option, in healthcare reform, 331, 379, 396
public schools
attendance at, 300
confidence in, 218–19
See also education
publishing industry, image of, 288–89

quality of life. *See* Life Evaluation Index

race
foreign trade and, 63
healthcare reform and, 346
health insurance and, 255
marital status and, 238
Obama, Barack, and, 26, 409, 431–32
optimism on race relations and, 392
party identification and, 193, 455
postal services and, 57
priorities and, 389
religion and, 455
Republican Party and, 175–76
satisfaction with U.S. and, 399
standard of living and, 162
Supreme Court and, 169
trust and, 444
race relations, 391–93
Bush, George W., and, 7
as most important issue, 323
Obama, Barack, and, 408–9
racism, 392–93
radio
industry, image of, 288–89
See also media
rain forests, loss of, worry about, 98, 115–16
Reagan, Nancy, admiration of, 476
Reagan, Ronald
admiration of, 476
approval ratings, 3–5, 14, 26, 191, 269, 348, 401, 426, 447
Dow and, 306–7
first month, 69
midterm elections and, 403
quarterly averages for, 142–43, 252, 380–81
as greatest president, 48–49
legacy of, 17
real estate
as best investment, 168
industry, image of, 288–89
recession
current, 349
as most important issue, 220, 242, 323
stimulus package, 9–10

TARP funds, 16–17
travel and, 182–83
recreation, travel plans, recession and, 182–83, 465–66
region. *See* geographic region
Rehnquist, William, 169
Reid, Harry, 295
as main speaker for Democratic Party, 202
as political winner, 472–73
religion
abortion and, 174
can answer today's problems, 471–72
classification of, 456
confidence in, 218–19
identification with, 135–36, 471–72
ideological trends and, 233
importance of, 112–13, 471
morality and, 120–21
as most important issue, 220, 243, 288, 371
Obama, Barack, and, 159–60, 456
party identification and, 113, 193, 314, 455–56
remittances and, 342–43
states and, 32–33, 277–79
stress and, 459
Warren's inaugural prayer, 20
repair personnel
Basic Access Index score, 467
emotional health and, 467
Healthy Behavior Index score, 468
Life Evaluation Index score, 467
Obama, Barack, and, 194
Physical Health Index score, 468
well-being and, 467
Work Environment Index score, 468
Republican Party
abortion and, 174, 272
Afghanistan and, 71, 107, 247, 319–20, 349, 414, 434–35, 439, 442–43, 446
age and, 166, 206
AIG bonuses and, 108
attentiveness to budget and, 84–85
attentiveness to political news and, 350–51
auto bailout and, 78, 123
banks and, 73–74
Bernanke, Ben, and, 143–44
Biden, Joe, and, 387
bipartisanship and, 338
Boehner, John, and, 248
Bush, George W., and, 6, 14, 23–24, 129
Bush, Laura, and, 15
business regulation and, 340
Canada and, 85
Cheney, Dick, and, 129–30
church attendance and, 113
Clinton, Hillary, and, 373
composition of, 193–94
Congress and, 5, 60, 83, 96, 169, 217, 295, 362, 417, 449, 463
criminal investigation of Bush administration and, 52
Cuba and, 150
death penalty and, 369
defense spending and, 117–18

Democrats in Congress and, 336
economy and, 58, 76, 98–100, 110, 138, 144, 222, 327–28, 350
election of 2010 and, 264, 363, 397–98, 411–12, 459–60
election of 2012 and, 407
environment and, 97, 147, 149, 460–61
executive branch and, 324–25
executive compensation limits and, 210
extramarital affairs and, 221
foreign trade and, 63
fuel efficiency standards and, 178
Gates, Robert, and, 408
Geithner, Timothy, and, 122
gender and, 164–65, 205–6
government and, 141, 341
Great Britain and, 85
greatest president and, 49
Guantanamo Bay prison and, 22, 197, 462
gun control and, 367
healthcare confidence and, 211, 390
healthcare reform and, 259–60, 262–63, 282, 321, 378–79, 410–11, 416, 436–37
health insurance responsibility and, 353, 416
homosexuals in military and, 199
identification with, 24–25, 156, 236–37, 315, 354–55
ideology and, 208–9, 232, 386
image of, 203–4, 227–28, 345
image of parties and, 203, 345
immigration and, 275
independents and, 227–28
international affairs and, 131
interrogation techniques and, 181, 318
Iran and, 56
Iraq and, 107, 230, 247
Israel and, 10
job creation and, 47
job loss and, 48
job outlook and, 441
judicial branch and, 324–25
labor and, 105, 316
legislative branch and, 324–25
Limbaugh, Rush, and, 43–44
main person who speaks for, 202
marital status and, 237–38
media and, 43, 358
Middle East and, 198
Mohammed trial and, 435–36
morality and, 171, 179–80
most admired man and, 476
most admired woman and, 476
Nobel Peace Prize and, 384
No Child Left Behind and, 293
nuclear power and, 110–11
Obama, Barack, and, 1, 6, 20–21, 24, 26, 38, 43, 69, 72–73, 80, 82, 104, 125, 127, 132, 149, 214, 253–54, 259, 276–77, 283, 298, 350, 368, 373, 384, 406, 432, 439
Obama, Michelle, and, 127
opinion of, 203
Palestinian state and, 198
Palin, Sarah, and, 234, 375
Pelosi, Nancy, and, 248

priorities and, 19, 388–89
religion and, 113, 359
Republicans in Congress and, 336
satisfaction of, 37, 91
satisfaction with U.S. and, 133, 164, 201, 372, 399
Sotomayor, Sonia, and, 189, 196, 239
states and, 29–31, 270–71
stem cell research and, 94
stimulus package and, 9, 31, 46, 51, 60, 256, 291
Supreme Court and, 215, 322
TARP funds and, 16
taxes and, 137, 298
terrorism and, 327, 440
threatening countries and, 213
threats to country and, 144
tobacco regulation and, 216
tone of D.C. and, 40, 276
unemployment and, 118
United Nations and, 102
values and, 352
veterans and, 184
waste in spending and, 329–30
Wilson, Joe, and, 329
Republicans in Congress
approval ratings, 5, 45, 83, 336
bipartisanship and, 337–38
confidence in, 211, 389–90
economy and, 138
healthcare and, 241, 389–90
interrogation techniques and, 181
as political losers, 472–73
tone of D.C. and, 40–41
respect, as most important issue, 220, 288, 323
rest, exercise and, 186
restaurants, image of, 288–89
retail industry, image of, 288–89
retirement
income, 145–46
savings, as most important issue, 148, 425
worry about, 145–46
Rhode Island
economy and, 33, 35
happiness and, 299
politics and, 29
religion and, 278
Rice, Condoleezza, 10
admiration of, 475–76
Richardson, Bill, 18
rivers, pollution of, worry about, 115–16
Roberts, John, 170, 234, 239
initial reactions to, 189
support for, 195
Roe v. Wade. See abortion
Roman Catholic Church. *See* Catholics
Romney, Mitt
favorability ratings, 245
as main speaker for Republican Party, 202
qualified to be president, 407
would support for Republican nomination, 245
would vote for in 2012, 407

Roosevelt, Franklin, as greatest president, 48–49
Russia
    opinion of, 64
    as threat, 212
    worry about, 131–32

Salahi, Tareq and Michaele, as political losers, 472–73
sales personnel
    Basic Access Index score, 467
    emotional health and, 467
    Healthy Behavior Index score, 468
    Life Evaluation Index score, 467
    Obama, Barack, and, 194
    Physical Health Index score, 468
    recommend as career for young man, 279
    recommend as career for young woman, 279
    well-being and, 333, 467
    Work Environment Index score, 468
Sanford, Mark, 221
    as political loser, 472–73
satisfaction
    with economic conditions, 171
    with education, 299–300
    with employee-based health insurance, 304
    with environment, 171
    with health, 172
    with healthcare, 267
    with healthcare costs, 343–44, 424
    with healthcare quality, 343–44
    with health insurance coverage, 344
    with jobs, 285–304
    with job security, 303
    with morality, 171
    with standard of living, 172
    with United States, 37–38, 91, 133, 163–64, 201, 371–72, 399, 404, 469
    See also approval ratings
Saudi Arabia
    death penalty and, 368
    opinion of, 64, 87–88
savings
    patterns of, 153–54
    retirement, as most important issue, 148, 425
savings accounts, as best investment, 168
school(s)
    funding for, 301
    No Child Left Behind Act, 292–93
    vouchers and, 301
    See also education
Schwarzenegger, Arnold, favorability ratings, 374
self-employment
    hours worked per week, 302
    Obama, Barack, and, 194
    recommend as career for young man, 279
    recommend as career for young woman, 279
Senate. *See* Congress
seniors
    healthcare reform and, 331
    party identification of, 167
    spending and, 305

September 11, 2001
    and Bush, George W., approval ratings, 3–4
    and security measures, 231
service workers
    Basic Access Index score, 467
    emotional health and, 467
    Healthy Behavior Index score, 468
    Life Evaluation Index score, 467
    Obama, Barack, and, 194
    Physical Health Index score, 468
    well-being and, 333, 467
    Work Environment Index score, 468
sex, sexual activity
    between unmarried man/woman as morally acceptable, 120–21, 179, 221
    See also homosexuals and homosexuality; marriage
Silent Generation
    happiness and, 361
    spending and, 305
small business
    confidence in, 218–19
    jobs and, 441
Smith, Margaret Chase, admiration of, 476
Smith, Tom W., 136
smoking, smokers
    income and, 126
    prevalence of, 216
    rates of, 52–53
    regulation of, 216
    should be made illegal, 216
    states and, 290
    trends in, 217
    well-being and, 421–23
socialism, healthcare reform and, 331
Social Security
    as most important issue, 148, 323
    worry about, 146
soft drink tax, healthcare reform and, 241
soil, contamination of, worry about, 115–16
Sosa, Sammy, favorability ratings, 374
Sotomayor, Sonia
    admiration of, 476
    favor confirmation of, 195–96, 239
    initial reactions to, 188–89
    opinion of, 240
    as political winner, 472–73
South Carolina, 32, 270
South Dakota, 35, 271, 273–74
space program, costs
    as justified, 249
    level of, 249
special envoys, approval ratings, 38
Specter, Arlen, 156
spending
    able to make a major purchase, 309–10
    attitudes toward, 226–27, 309–10
    Christmas and, 419–20, 464–65
        demographics of, 419
        forecast versus actual, 465

telephone industry, image of, 288–89
television
    industry, image of, 288–89
    news, confidence in, 218–19
    See also media
Teresa, Mother, admiration of, 476
terrorism
    Afghanistan and, 365, 445
    Bush, George W., and, 7
    confidence in government to protect you from, 231
    Democratic Party and, 327
    Mohammed trial, 435–36
    as most important issue, 243, 323, 474
    Obama, Barack, and, 200, 400, 439
    Republican Party and, 327
    security measures still necessary, 231
    worry about, 131–32, 231, 375–76, 440, 473–74
Texas, 33, 270, 293
Thatcher, Margaret, admiration of, 475–76
Thomas, Clarence, 170, 195
Tiller, George, 201
tobacco
    companies, regulation of, 216
    See also smoking
tourism. *See* travel
town hall meetings, 283
trade deficit, as most important issue, 323
trades, recommend as career for young man, 279
traditional values. *See* values
transportation
    costs, as most important issue, 148
    mass, swine flu and, 155, 161
    workers
        Basic Access Index score, 467
        emotional health and, 467
        Healthy Behavior Index score, 468
        Life Evaluation Index score, 467
        Obama, Barack, and, 194
        well-being and, 333, 467
        Work Environment Index score, 468
travel
    to Cuba, 150
    cutting back spending on, 474–75
    healthcare and, 176–77
    holiday, cutting back on, 465–66
    industry, image of, 288–89
    recession and, 182–83
    swine flu and, 155, 161
tropical rain forests, loss of, worry about, 98, 115–16
Troubled Asset Relief Program (TARP), 16–17, 29
Truman, Harry S.
    admiration of, 476
    approval ratings, 3–4, 14, 26, 426
        decline in, 380
        first to second quarter change, 143
        midterm elections and, 403
trust, neighbors and, 443–44
turnout, midterm elections and, 405

unemployment
    money worries and, 92–93
    as most important issue, 68, 118–19, 148, 220, 242, 287, 323, 371, 418, 425, 474
    Obama, Barack, and, 400
    outlook, 28–29, 39–40, 67–68, 88, 115, 128
    race and, 118
    worry about, 47–48, 222–23
    See also employment; jobs
uninsured, 364
    as biggest problem in healthcare, 344
    demographics of, 255
    healthcare reform and, 331
    satisfaction with healthcare and, 344
    states and, 294
    travel outside U.S. for healthcare and, 177
    worry about, political affiliation and, 222–23
United Kingdom
    as most valuable ally, 85–86
    opinion of, 64, 86
United Nations
    opinion of, 101–2
    role of in world affairs today, 102
United States
    better or worse four years from now, 21
    division in, Obama, Barack, and, 400
    as economic leader, 57–59
    image of
        Bush, George W., and, 7, 12–13
        Obama, Barack, and, 61–62, 400
    Israel and, 9–10
    most important problem facing, trends in, 469–70
    satisfaction with, 37–38, 91, 133, 163–64, 201, 371–72, 399
        midterm elections and, 404
        trends in, 469
Utah
    economy and, 33
    health and, 95, 236, 284, 296
    politics and, 29, 270, 286
    religion and, 278–79

vaccines, swine flu, likely to get, 311
values
    government and, 352
    ideological trends and, 233
    ideology and, 386
    Obama, Barack, and, 258, 342
    See also morality
Vermont
    health and, 290, 293
    politics and, 280, 286
    religion and, 32, 279
veterans, Republican Party and, 184
violence. *See* crime
Virginia, 271
Volcker, Paul, 143
volunteering, 432–33